t h o m s o n . c o m

changing the way the world learns

To get extra value from this book for no additional cost, go to:

http://www.duxbury.com

thomson.com is the World Wide Web site for Brooks/Cole and ITP and is your direct source to dozens of on-line resources. *thomson.com* helps you find out about supplements, experiment with demonstration software, search for a job, and send e-mail to many of our authors. You can even preview new publications and exciting new technologies.

thomson.com: *It's where you'll find us in the future.*

Duxbury Titles of Related Interest

For more information, contact Duxbury Press at 10 Davis Drive, Belmont, CA, 94002 or go to: www.duxbury.com. To order copies, contact your local bookstore or call 1-800-354-9706.

STATISTICS

FOR MANAGEMENT AND ECONOMICS

ABBREVIATED FOURTH EDITION

Gerald Keller
Wilfrid Laurier University

Brian Warrack
Wilfrid Laurier University

Duxbury Press
An Imprint of Brooks/Cole Publishing Company

I(T)P® An International Thomson Publishing Company

Pacific Grove • Albany • Belmont • Bonn • Boston • Cincinnati • Detroit • Johannesburg • London • Madrid
Melbourne • Mexico City • New York • Paris • Singapore • Tokyo • Toronto • Washington

Sponsoring Editor: Curt Hinrichs
Editorial Assistant: Rita Jaramillo
Marketing Team: Marcy Perman, Michele Mootz
Project Developmental Editor: Cynthia Mazow
Advertising Communications: Christine Davis
Permissions Editor: May Clark
Production, Text Illustrations, Composition:
    GTS Graphics, Inc.

Production Coordinator: Mary Anne Shahidi
Interior Design: Gary Head, Janet Wood
Cover Design: Jeanne Calabrese, Vernon Boes
Cover Illustration: Cary Henrie
Text Photographs: All photos by PhotoDisc
    except page 671 © Gary Head
Manuscript Editor: Heather Stratton
Printer and Binding: Von Hoffmann Press

For more information, contact:

BROOKS/COLE PUBLISHING COMPANY
511 Forest Lodge Road
Pacific Grove, CA 93950
USA

International Thomson Editores
Seneca 53
Col. Polanco
11560 México D.F., México

International Thomson Publishing Europe
Berkshire House 168-173
High Holborn
London, WC1V 7AA
England

International Thomson Publishing GmbH
Königswinterer Strasse 418
53227 Bonn
Germany

Thomas Nelson Australia
102 Dodds Street
South Melbourne, 3205
Victoria, Australia

International Thomson Publishing Asia
60 Albert Street
#15-01 Albert Complex
Singapore 189969

Nelson Canada
1120 Birchmount Road
Scarborough, Ontario
Canada M1K 5G4

International Thomson Publishing Japan
Hirakawacho Kyowa Building, 3F
2-2-1 Hirakawacho
Chiyoda-ku, Tokyo 102, Japan

Printed in the United States of America
 2 3 4 5 6 7 8 9 10

Library of Congress Cataloging-in-Publication Data
Keller, Gerald.
    Statistics for management and economics / Gerald Keller, Brian Warrack. — Abbreviated 4th ed.
        p. cm.
    Includes bibliographical references and index.
    ISBN 0-534-35818-7 (pbk.)
    1. Management—Statistical methods. 2. Economics—Statistical methods. I. Title.
HD30.215.K45 1998
658.4'033—dc21   98-17447
                                                                                             CIP

 This book is printed on acid-free recycled paper.

The cover illustrator, Cary Henrie, has translated our sense of the power of statistics into unique visual images. Like prisms converting light into a color spectrum, statistical techniques can shape apparently unconnected numbers into a lightning bolt—a statistical summary or chart—of useful information that can be applied to make timely decisions in the worlds of business and economics.

—G.K. AND B.W

Editor's Note: Mr. Henrie's work has appeared in such publications as *Time, Sports Illustrated, Business Week,* and *Esquire.* He works exclusively on a Macintosh computer but strives for a warm, natural look, as if each piece were a painting.

Brief Contents

Contents

5

Data Collection and Sampling 156

6

Probability and Discrete Probability Distributions 174

11

Inference about the Description of a Single Population 368

12

Inference about the Comparison of Two Populations 426

Visual Preface to Statistics for Management and Economics

ABBREVIATED FOURTH EDITION

Statistics for Management and Economics, Abbreviated Fourth Edition, is about using statistical techniques and converting data into information. We emphasize real problems and data, the use of computers, Microsoft Excel and Minitab software, and the correct interpretation of statistical printouts.

Why We Wrote This Book

The first edition of this book (1988) attempted to remedy a problem in the way applied statistics was taught: The existing literature stressed the arithmetic of statistical procedures. However, we feel students need more than the ability to compute statistics—they also need the skill to select the appropriate method from the dozens of techniques taught in most introductory courses. And this skill must be taught if students are to eventually apply statistics to real problems.

Our approach teaches students how to recognize the correct procedure. As each technique is introduced, we demonstrate how to recognize when its use is appropriate and when it is not. Review chapters (13 and 19) that allow students to hone their technique-selection skills are also a feature of this approach. In each review chapter a flowchart develops the logical process for choosing the correct technique.

Our approach emphasizes three steps to the solution of statistical problems: (1) identify the technique, (2) compute the required statistics, and (3) interpret the results.

Before beginning work on this edition, we consulted business and economics statistics professors across North America. We also noted the findings of academic conferences where the subject of improving the teaching of statistics was on the agenda, such as "Making Statistics More Effective in Schools of Business" annual conferences. This book covers what may be termed "traditional statistics"—estimation, hypothesis testing, and all the techniques that are based on them—as well as modern data analysis methods.

Most teachers of business and economic statistics now use the computer with statistical software or spreadsheets. This edition makes it convenient to use the computer. We continue to use Minitab because of its simplicity and coverage and because it is used extensively in colleges and universities. Since an increasing number of business schools and industries use spreadsheets, we use the popular spreadsheet Microsoft Excel for Windows.

The Evolution of _Statistics for Management and Economics_

Rationale for the Abbreviated Fourth Edition

Differences Between the Abbreviated Fourth Edition and the Fourth Edition

While we are very gratified with the success of the fourth edition of this book, we recognize that success in any endeavor requires attention to customer needs. We have received suggestions that we provide a shorter version, which could be more easily covered in one semester. Moreover, adopters have requested that we offer additional Excel add-in macros.

The fourth edition of *Statistics for Management and Economics*, on which this abbreviated edition is based, made several significant pedagogical advances. It was the first text to integrate Microsoft Excel output, instructions and data sets. It integrated computer solving methods with their "by-hand," or manual calculation, counterparts, and it included 475 data sets and computer-based exercises. While these features have been widely accepted, there are several refinements that are included in this abbreviated edition.

This abbreviated fourth edition omits the two chapters on nonparametric statistics (nonparametric techniques are briefly described in two chapter appendixes), one review chapter, the chapter on model building (some of that material was moved to the chapter on multiple regression), and the time series and forecasting chapter.

By emphasizing the use of one of the software packages and omitting most manual calculations, instructors can easily cover the material in this edition in one semester.

This abbreviated fourth edition, like the edition on which it is based, includes Data Analysis Plus™ 2.0, a suite of Excel add-ins that greatly extends the menu capabilities of Excel. Data Analysis Plus™ 2.0 now includes add-ins for stepwise regression and prediction intervals in regression.

A Practical Approach

Our approach emphasizes the complete process of data analysis, including the skills needed before any calculations are performed, the skills needed to perform the calculations, and the knowledge to properly interpret the statistical results. All appropriate examples throughout the text contain the following pedagogical features. We find that students gain a greater appreciation for methods and a clearer understanding of their application with the following three-step problem-solving approach.

Before the Calculations: Technique Identification

Before performing any calculations on real applications, professionals must determine which method to employ, likely the most daunting challenge facing students. Most introductory courses introduce 30 to 40 statistical procedures. Ironically, technique-identification skills are seldom taught. And yet, without the ability to choose the right procedure, all else is meaningless.

When a technique is first introduced we show how statisticians decide when its use is warranted and how that decision is made. Further, students are provided the opportunity to practice identifying techniques with two review chapters, each containing examples, exercises, and cases requiring the use of techniques presented in the previous chapters. Additionally, each review chapter contains a flowchart asking the questions whose answers guide the student to the appropriate statistical method.

EXAMPLE 11.2

In most cities a municipal agency regulates the amounts charged by taxis. As you're probably aware, total taxi fares are determined by distance traveled as well as the amount of time taken for the trip. In preparing to apply for a rate increase, the general manager of a fleet of taxis wanted to know the distance customers travel by taxis on the average trip. She organized a survey wherein she asked taxi drivers to record the number of miles (to the nearest tenth) traveled by randomly selected customers. A sample of 41 customers was produced. The results appear below (and are stored in file XM11-02). The general manager wants to estimate the mean distance traveled with 95% confidence.

IDENTIFYING THE TECHNIQUE

The problem objective is to describe a single population, the distance traveled by taxi customers. The data are quantitative (miles traveled). The parameter to be estimated is the population mean μ. The confidence interval estimator is

$$\bar{x} \pm t_{\alpha/2}\frac{s}{\sqrt{n}}$$

SOLVING BY HAND

From the sample of 41 observations, we find

$$\sum x_i = 315.6 \quad \text{and} \quad \sum x_i^2 = 2,772.0$$

$$\bar{x} = \frac{\sum x_i}{n} = \frac{315.6}{41} = 7.70$$

$$s^2 = \frac{\sum x_i^2 - \frac{\left(\sum x_i\right)^2}{n}}{n-1}$$

$$= \frac{2,772.0 - \frac{(315.6)^2}{41}}{40}$$

$$= 8.57$$

$$s = \sqrt{s^2} = \sqrt{8.57} = 2.93$$

Because we want a 95% confidence interval estimate,

$$1 - \alpha = .95$$

Thus,

$$\alpha = .05 \quad \text{and} \quad \alpha/2 = .025$$

$$t_{\alpha/2, n-1} = t_{.025, 40} = 2.021$$

The 95% confidence interval estimate of μ is

$$\bar{x} \pm t_{\alpha/2}\frac{s}{\sqrt{n}} = 7.70 \pm 2.021\frac{2.93}{\sqrt{41}} = 7.70 \pm .92$$

or

$$\text{LCL} = 6.78 \quad \text{and} \quad \text{UCL} = 8.62$$

The Calculations

We offer three ways to solve most problems, *by hand, using Minitab,* and using *Microsoft Excel.*

Solving by Hand. All but the most complicated techniques are solved manually. We offer this approach for those instructors who want to teach their students how the techniques and concepts work. Instructors who so choose may completely omit this mode of solution.

Using Minitab. Throughout the book, we use Minitab (Release 11 for Windows). We provide the actual output as well as step-by-step instructions. We chose Minitab because it continues to be one of the simplest and least expensive statistical software packages. A student version of the software is available from the publisher at a discount when packaged with this text.

Using Microsoft Excel. As we do with Minitab we offer Excel output and instruction. We chose Excel because it is now, and is likely to remain, the most popular spreadsheet software. We believe that the use of spreadsheets for statistics is an excellent choice because most business and economics students already know how to use them and may already have them on their computer. And if they don't, they might as well learn how because they will ultimately have to learn about them in their jobs.

Each approach is color-coded, making it easy to focus on the mode of calculation that is preferred.

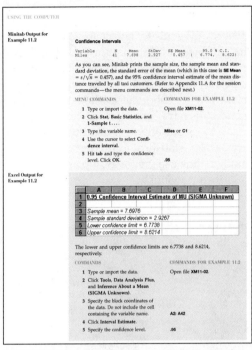

Self-contained software instructions appear following most examples and at the end of most chapters. Beige is Minitab, blue is Excel.

After the Calculations: Interpreting Results

Statistical analyses are conducted because the manager needs the information. A critical part of the process is to correctly interpret the calculations or the computer printout. In addition to showing how to identify the correct technique and calculate, we also interpret the meaning of the statistics and show how managers use this information to make decisions. Further integrating the results relates the statistical results to the objectives of the study. We develop this competence by presenting the concepts that underlie statistics.

INTERPRETING THE RESULTS	We estimate that the mean distance traveled by taxi lies between 6.77 and 8.62 miles. The general manager can use the estimate to determine the effect on her company of different pricing policies. With the interval estimate she could determine upper and lower bounds on revenues generated from the new rates. She also may be able to use the results to judge the performance and honesty of individual drivers. We remind you that the accuracy of the interval estimate is dependent upon the validity of the sampling process and the distribution of the distances (they are required to be normal). If the distribution is extremely nonnormal, the inference may be invalid.

Key Features of Our Approach

We believe that the success of this book is based on three factors.

Relevance

Historically, statistics books and courses focused on the arithmetic of statistical procedures. They devoted much time and effort to showing students how to perform the calculations manually (often teaching a variety of shortcut methods). However, arithmetic skills have little relevance to applied statistics.

We focus our attention on how statisticians actually employ statistical techniques. In one form or another, they use the three-step approach that we described previously.

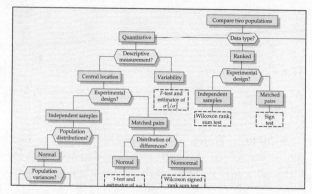

- **Teaches technique-identification skills.** Guides (see inside front cover), flowcharts, and review chapters develop this critical skill.

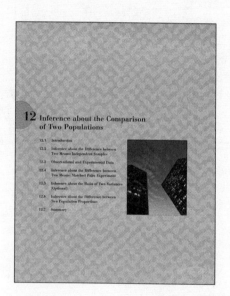

Exercises and cases that appear at the ends of chapters naturally require the use of the techniques introduced in those chapters. And, of course, choosing the correct techniques is not challenging. To help further develop technique-identification skills, two review chapters (12 and 19) contain exercises and cases that require the use of techniques previously introduced. Each review chapter features a flowchart that guides students in determining the correct problem-solving technique.

- **Uses real data in examples and exercises.** Using actual problems solved by statisticians demonstrates how statistics is practical and applies to every business and economics discipline.

> 13.9 Does caffeine consumption adversely affect heart rates? In an article in *Men's Health* (October 1992), scientists reported the results of an experiment involving caffeine consumption. The experiment used 64 men and women who drank two cups of coffee per day. For eight weeks, 32 subjects abstained from all caffeine-containing beverages, while the other 32 subjects drank six cups of coffee per day. The heart rates of the 64 volunteers were measured before and after the experiment. These data are stored in file XR13-09 using the following format.
>
> Column 1: heart rate of caffeine-abstainers before experiment
> Column 2: heart rate of caffeine-abstainers after experiment
> Column 3: heart rate of caffeine-consumers before experiment
> Column 4: heart rate of caffeine-consumers after experiment
>
> a Can we conclude that abstaining from caffeine lowers the heart rate?
> b Can we conclude from these data that increasing caffeine consumption increases the heart rate?

Textbooks that emphasize manual calculations by necessity must feature impractical examples and exercises. Typically, the problems provide summarized statistics (e.g., means and variances) and students are required to complete the calculations manually. Alternatively, examples and exercises list raw data, but the sample sizes must be small. Both approaches are unrealistic. We feature data sets, some of which are quite large. The data are stored on the CD-ROM that accompanies the book. Many of the examples, exercises, and cases are based on real studies drawn from journals, magazines, and newspapers.

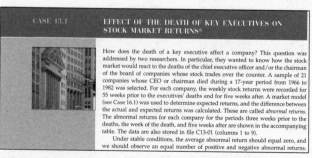

- **Provides case studies.** More extended applications based on real data suggest the wide variety of problems that require statistical solutions. Over 34 case studies are included throughout the text.

Focus on the Big Picture

In using and learning how to use statistics, organization of the material is vital. By focusing on the manual calculations, most books do not show students the power and applicability of statistics. And, in this information age, statistical techniques are more important than ever.

Today most courses use the computer and statistical software or spreadsheets. Since most instructors do not want to teach how to use the software, we provide step-by-step instructions in the use of Minitab for Windows and Microsoft Excel. These instructions appear in the book with the printouts. Therefore, it is not necessary for students to purchase separate software manuals. Additionally, most examples, exercises, and cases feature raw data stored on the disk that accompanies this book, so students do not have to spend time inputting data.

For students without access to a computer and statistical software (and to help learn concepts), we continue to teach how to calculate statistics manually (with the exception of the most complicated procedures), and most exercises can be solved in this way.

- **Includes a CD-ROM.** Raw data (in several formats, including Minitab, Excel, SAS, ASCII) rather than summary statistics for most examples, exercises, and cases increases student involvement and promotes active learning.

Confidence Intervals

```
Variable      N     Mean    StDev   SE Mean      95.0 % C.I.
Miles        41    7.698    2.927    0.457  (  6.774,   8.622)
```

As you can see, Minitab prints the sample size, the sample mean and standard deviation, the standard error of the mean (which in this case is **SE Mean** $= s/\sqrt{n} = 0.457$), and the 95% confidence interval estimate of the mean distance traveled by all taxi customers. (Refer to Appendix 11.A for the session commands—the menu commands are described next.)

MENU COMMANDS	COMMANDS FOR EXAMPLE 11.2
1 Type or import the data.	Open file **XM11-02**.
2 Click **Stat**, **Basic Statistics**, and **1-Sample t . . . .**	
3 Type the variable name.	**Miles** or **C1**
4 Use the cursor to select **Confidence interval**.	
5 Hit **tab** and type the confidence level. Click **OK**.	**.95**

Self-contained software instructions appear following most examples and at the end of most chapters. Minitab is beige; Excel is blue.

	A	B	C	D	E	F
1	0.95 Confidence Interval Estimate of MU (SIGMA Unknown)					
2						
3	Sample mean = 7.6976					
4	Sample standard deviation = 2.9267					
5	Lower confidence limit = 6.7738					
6	Upper confidence limit = 8.6214					

The lower and upper confidence limits are 6.7738 and 8.6214, respectively.

COMMANDS	COMMANDS FOR EXAMPLE 11.2
1 Type or import the data.	Open file **XM11-02**.
2 Click **Tools**, **Data Analysis Plus**, and **Inference About a Mean (SIGMA Unknown)**.	
3 Specify the block coordinates of the data. Do not include the cell containing the variable name.	**A2: A42**
4 Click **Interval Estimate**.	
5 Specify the confidence level.	**.95**

Use of Tools Used By Managers

We are all aware that statistics courses that employ computers are more useful and interesting to our students. What has inhibited us from using the computer more fully until recently has been the lack of access to hardware and software. Fortunately, most colleges and universities now have computer facilities for students. Moreover, many students have their own computers. Software is also a problem. It is difficult to justify requiring students to learn how to use statistical software packages, such as SPSS or SAS, which are used by many statisticians, but are not widely employed by managers. Many students of business and economics learn Microsoft Excel, which is the foremost analytical software used in business. However, Excel has a serious drawback. Although it features several statistical functions, it is not as complete as a statistical software package. Excel does not perform many of the techniques that are taught in an introductory statistics course and some of its output is limited. As a result, we offer Data Analysis Plus™.

Since the Fourth Edition of This Text Was Published

Other statistics textbooks have appeared that feature Excel. To date, these texts have addressed the problem of Excel's statistical limitations by describing how Excel can be programmed to perform the missing techniques. Using this approach requires students to use the computer as if it were a calculator. The emphasis shifts back to the "how" of statistics rather than the "when" and the "why." In addition, we have found this approach requires considerable time to learn Excel procedures at the expense of learning statistics.

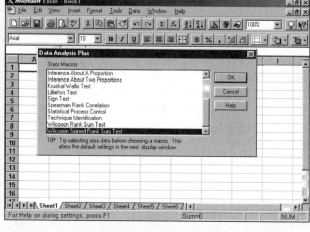

We provide an alternate approach by including Excel software add-ins that greatly expand Excel's statistical capacity. When installed, the add-ins appear in the Tools menu under Data Analyis Plus™ and can be employed in exactly the same way as the techniques that Excel offers (Analysis ToolPak). Here is a list of the macros that are stored on the CD-ROM that accompanies this book.

Box plot
Chi-squared test of a contingency table
Durbin-Watson test
Friedman test
Inference about a mean with population variance known
Inference about a mean with population variance unknown
Inference about a proportion
Inference about the difference between two proportions
Kruskal-Wallis test
Prediction interval for regression (new in this edition)
Sign test
Spearman rank correlation

Statistical process control
 chart (using R)
 chart (using S)
S chart
R chart
p chart
Stepwise regression (new in this edition)
Wilcoxon rank sum test
Wilcoxon signed rank sum test

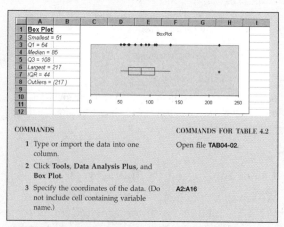

COMMANDS

1 Type or import the data into one column.

2 Click **Tools, Data Analysis Plus,** and **Box Plot.**

3 Specify the coordinates of the data. (Do not include cell containing variable name.)   A2:A16

COMMANDS FOR TABLE 4.2

Open file **TAB04-02.**

Excel Output for Example 16.2

	A	B	C	D	E	F
1	SUMMARY OUTPUT					
2						
3	Regression Statistics					
4	Multiple R	0.806307604				
5	R Square	0.650131952				
6	Adjusted R Square	0.64666187				
7	Standard Error	151.5687515				
8	Observations	100				
9						
10	ANOVA					
11		df	SS	MS	F	Significance F
12	Regression	1	4189527.721	4189527.721	182.1056015	4.44346E-24
13	Residual	98	2251362.469	22973.08642		
14	Total	99	6434890.19			
15						
16		Coefficients	Standard Error	t Stat	P-value	
17	Intercept	6533.383035	84.51232199	77.30686936	1.22253E-89	
18	Odometer	-0.031157739	0.002308896	-13.49465085	4.44346E-24	

EXCEL 97

Excel 97 Users:
If you click **Line Fits,** the predicted values of y and the residuals will automatically be printed.

COMMANDS

1 Type or import the data into two columns.

2 Click **Tools, Data Analysis . . . ,** and **Regression.**

3 Specify Input Y Range.   **B1:B101**

4 Specify Input X Range. Click OK. Click Labels (if necessary).   **A1:A101**

5 To draw the scatter diagram click **Line Fit Plots** before clicking OK.

(You can also draw the scatter diagram using the commands described in Chapter 2.)

COMMANDS FOR EXAMPLE 16.2

Open file **XM16-02.**

- **Excel 97 (in addition to previous release, 5.0 & 7.0) instructions are included.** Excel 97 instructions, when different, appear in the margins alongside their older counterparts.

- **Provides Data Analysis Plus™ 2.0.** Excel spreadsheet macros work as a statistical add-in to make the spreadsheet capable of using all of the techniques and solving the problems in the book.

- **Presents computer instructions.** Detailed instructions for both Minitab and Microsoft Excel packages make it easy for both instructors and students to employ the computer. Most chapters contain appendices of detailed instructions for Minitab and Excel.

Additional Features

Developing an Understanding of the Statistical Concepts

In Chapters 9 and 10, we introduced the procedures used to estimate and test parameters. The examples we chose to illustrate the process were unrealistic, requiring that the population variance is known when the population mean is not. We chose those examples because of their linkage to Chapter 8 (sampling distribution of the mean) and Chapter 7 (normal distribution). The concept developed in this section is that to expand the application to more realistic situations, we must use another sampling distribution. The Student t distribution was derived by W. S. Gosset for this purpose.

Another important development in this section is the use of the term "degrees of freedom." We will encounter this term many times in this book, so a brief discussion of its meaning is warranted.

The Student t distribution is based on using the sample variance to estimate the unknown population variance. The sample variance is defined as

$$s^2 = \frac{\sum (x_i - \bar{x})^2}{n - 1}$$

To compute s^2, we must first determine $\bar{x}$. Recall that sampling distributions are derived by repeated sampling of size n from the same population. In order to repeatedly take samples to compute s^2, we can choose any numbers for the first $n - 1$ observations in the sample. However, we have no choice on the nth value because the sample mean must be calculated first. To illustrate, suppose that $n = 3$ and we find $\bar{x} = 10$. We can have x_1 and x_2 assume any values without restriction. However, x_3 must be such that $\bar{x} = 10$. For example, if $x_1 = 6$ and $x_2 = 8$, then x_3 must equal 16. Therefore, there are only two degrees of freedom in our selection of the sample. We say that we lose one degree of freedom because we had to calculate $\bar{x}$.

Notice that the denominator in the calculation of s^2 is equal to the number of degrees of freedom. This is not a coincidence and will be repeated throughout this book.

Let's complete this section with a review of how we identify this technique.

- **Conceptual development.** In most cases, when a new technique is introduced, we also describe how the new tool contributes to an understanding of statistical concepts.

- **Graphical excellence.** We have added a new Chapter 3 that discusses the best way of applying graphical techniques, based on the work of Edward Tufte. This has become especially important in this age of computer graphics. Good and bad uses of statistical graphics are discussed.

- **Data collection.** A new Chapter 5 describes sources and techniques of data collection, including questionnaire design.

- **Regression diagnostics.** Three sections present methods to diagnose and remedy violations of required conditions in regression analysis. Coverage of transformations, including examples and exercises, has been expanded.

- **Covariance, correlation, and scatter diagrams.** The graphical and numerical methods that describe the association between two variables are presented in the introductory chapters.

- **Capstone chapter.** The last chapter of the book provides exercises and cases that summarize all the techniques covered in the book. We also leave students with a list of the twelve most important things to remember from their statistics course.

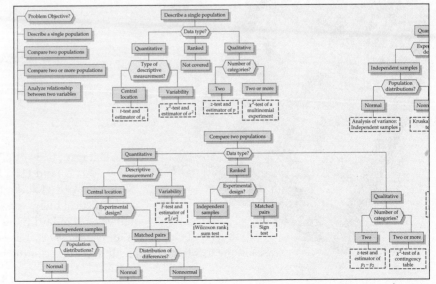

Teaching Aids

The following teaching aids are available from Duxbury Press.

Instructor's Resource Manual. Includes suggestions about teaching from the book, transparency masters, teaching notes for each case, and supplementary topics that do not appear in the textbook but that some instructors may wish to cover (formatted for easy reproduction and distribution to students). Adopters of the text may freely copy these materials.

Complete Solutions Manual. Supplies complete solutions for every exercise and case study in the book.

Test Bank. Contains test items grouped by chapter and difficulty. Computerized testing is also available in a Windows platform.

World Wide Web Teaching and Learning Center. Offers simulation experiments, additional exercises and case studies, updated information on software and the book, plus technical support. Keller and Warrack's *Statistics for Management and Economics* home page can be accessed from http://www.duxbury.com. Go to: "Online Book Companions."

Powerpoint Slides. Figures from the text and concept outlines that can be customized for lecture presentations.

Data Analysis Plus™ 2.0 and Data Disk. Provides Excel add-ins with statistical menu capability not contained in standard Excel, plus over 400 data sets for examples, exercises, and cases in the text (included in all new copies of the book).

JMP IN 3 for Windows (or Mac). Powerful statistical software (by SAS Institute) for sale to students.

StataQuest 4 for Windows. Low-cost, professionally developed statistical software that covers the breadth of techniques in this book, available at a nominal cost when purchased with this book (also available in DOS and Macintosh versions).

Learning Aids

The following learning aids are also available.

Student Solutions Manual. Furnishes detailed solutions for the textbook's even-numbered exercises. For sale to students.

Study Guide. Contains overviews of each text chapter, examples illustrating specific techniques, and exercises and their solutions. For sale to students.

SAS Instructions. Booklet that demonstrates how to use SAS with *Statistics for Management and Economics*. Available at no cost when packaged with a new copy of the book.

Just the Basics Please: A Quick Review of Math for Introductory Statistics. Reviews only those basic arithmetic and algebra skills needed with this book (by Ronald E. Shiffler and Arthur J. Adams).

Acknowledgments

This book evolved from a combined fifty years of teaching experience. We are most grateful to our colleagues and students, whose helpful suggestions, comments, and criticisms have benefited this text. We are also grateful to Jeffery Keller, who created the Excel macros; to Jonathan Buckheit, of Stanford University, and Andrew G. Roe for testing and checking the Excel macros; also to Jonathan Buckheit for creating the CD-ROM; and to Laurel Technical Services, for accuracy checking the proofs.

Each edition of this book has been greatly improved by the thoughtful and timely suggestions from the reviewers. We appreciate the excellent suggestions of the reviewers for this edition: Edgardo Buscaglia, Georgetown University; J. Lloyd Blackwell III, University of North Dakota; Siddhartha Chib, Washington University; Renato Clavijo, Robert Morris College; Sally Deloughy, Western Connecticut State University; Dan Fitzgerald, Kansas Newman College; Joel Goldsmith, Western Connecticut State University; Carolyn Hargrave, Louisiana State University; Jane Lea Harvill, Bowling Green State University; Igal Hendel, Princeton University; William J. Herald, Bowling Green State University; Carla Inclan, Georgetown University; S. Rao Jammalamadaka, University of California, Santa Barbara; Henry Loehr, Belmont Abbey College; Thomas M. Margavio, Southwest Missouri State University; Glenn Milligan, Ohio State University; Alan Olinsky, Bryant College; Marc Pak, Binghamton University; J. Wayne Patterson, Clemson University; Debra Rawlins, Illinois State University; David Rocke, University of California, Davis; Lois Schufeldt, Southwest Missouri State University; William E. Stein, Texas A&M University; William R. Stewart, College of William and Mary; Penelope R. Verhoeven, Kennesaw State College; and Reginald G. Worthley, University of Hawaii.

We also thank the reviewers of previous editions: Kelly Black, California State University, Fresno; Bruce Bowerman, Miami University; Maggie Capen, East Carolina University; Ronald L. Coccari, Cleveland State University; Henry Crouch, Pittsburg State University (Kansas); Robert D. Curley, Central State University; Phyllis Curtiss, Bowling Green State University; Tim Daciuk, Ryerson Polytechnic Institute; Joaquin Diaz-Saiz, University of Houston; Paul Eaton, Northern Illinois University; David Eldredge, Murray State University; James Ford, University of Southern California; Damodar Golhar, Western Michigan University; Myron Golin, Widener University; Laura Grover, California State University, Fullerton; Bhisham Gupta, University of Southern Maine; Paul Guy, California State University, Chico; Robert C. Hannum, University of Denver; David Heinze, California State University, Chico; Iris B. Ibrahim, Clemson University; J. Morgan Jones, University of North Carolina; Howard Kaplon, Towson State University (Maryland); John Knox, California State Polytechnic University, Pomona; John Lawrence, California State University, Fullerton; Charles Lienert, Metropolitan State College (Denver); Yih-Wu Liu, Youngstown State University; Brenda Masters, Oklahoma State University; Kevin Murphy, Oakland University; Alan Neebe, University of North Carolina at Chapel Hill; Dennis Oberhelman, University of South Carolina; J. Wayne Patterson, Clemson University; Nancy V. Phillips, University of Texas at Austin; Leonard Presby, Fairleigh Dickinson University; Carl Quitmeyer, George Mason University; Farhad Raiszadeh, University of Tennessee at Chattanooga; Donald Richter, New York University; Andrew Russakoff, St. John's University;

Lillian Russell, University of Delaware; Mike Ryan, University of South Carolina; Sunil Sapra, State University of New York, Buffalo; Dale G. Sauers, York College; Al Schainblatt, San Francisco State University; Stanley Schultz, Cleveland State University; Edwin Sexton, Wichita State University; Dale Shafer, Indiana University of Pennsylvania; Bala Shetty, Texas A&M University; Michael Sklar, Emory University; Craig Slinkman, University of Texas at Arlington; Jae H. Song, St. Cloud State University; Verne Stanton, California State University, Fullerton; William Stein, Texas A&M University; Jeffrey Strieter, State University of New York, Brockport; Will Terpening, Gonzaga University; Chipei P. Tseng, Northern Illinois University; Martin T. Wells, Cornell University; James E. Willis, Louisiana State University; Marvin Wolfmeyer, Winona State University; William Woodard, University of Hawaii; Chin Yang, Clarion University; and Ben Zirkle, Virginia Western Community College.

STATISTICS

1 What Is Statistics?

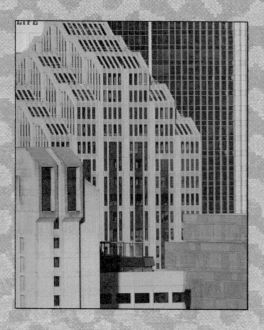

1.1 Introduction to Statistics

Statistics is a way to get information from data. That's it! Most of this textbook is devoted to describing how, when, and why managers conduct statistical procedures. You may ask, "If that's all there is to statistics, why is this book (and most other statistics books) so large?" The answer is that there are different kinds of information and data to which students of applied statistics should be exposed. We demonstrate some of these with four cases that are featured later in this book.

Case 11.2: National Patent Development Corporation*

The National Patent Development Corporation (NPD) is a company that takes newly patented products from the design stage through to sales to the consumer. NPD recently acquired a new product that can be used to replace the dentist's drill. The product, called Caridex, is a solution that dissolves decayed matter in dental cavities without requiring drilling. After some research, it was discovered that Caridex works well only on cavities on the top surface of teeth, where a small fraction of cavities occur.

It is known that 100,000 dentists in the United States treat cavities. A preliminary analysis revealed that only 10% of all dentists would use Caridex in the first year after its introduction.

The dispensing unit costs NPD $200, and it intends to sell the unit at cost. The solution costs NPD $0.50 per cavity and will be sold to dentists at a price of $2.50 per cavity. Fixed annual costs are expected to be $4 million.

NPD would like an estimate of the profit it can expect in the first year of operation. Because NPD's profits will depend completely on the number of cavities treated with Caridex during the year, NPD commissioned a survey of 400 dentists who planned to use Caridex. Each dentist was asked how many cavities he or she

---

*Based on a report by Ladenburg Thalman, a large New York–based investment firm.

anticipates treating with Caridex during an average week. The results are stored on the data disk that accompanies this book. (Some of these data are shown below.)

```
7 4 4 5 4 4 8 4 6 4 3 4 3
3 4 2 6 5 4 6 4 2 6 2 7 3
8 3 4 6 4 4 1 3 3 3
```

The data in this case are the numbers of cavities to be treated with Caridex by each of the 400 dentists who are part of this survey. The information we would ultimately like to acquire is an estimate of the first-year profits that NPD should expect from Caridex. The question we need to address is how to extract the required information from the data. One of the first things we need to be able to do is summarize the numbers. This is the function of **descriptive statistics**.

Descriptive statistics deals with methods of organizing, summarizing, and presenting data in a convenient and informative way. One form of descriptive statistics uses graphical techniques, which allow us to draw a picture that presents the data in such a way that we can easily see what numbers the dentists are reporting. We would also like to know whether most dentists anticipate treating the same approximate number of patients with Caridex or whether large differences exist among them. Chapter 2 presents a variety of graphical methods used by statisticians to present data in ways that allow the reader to extract useful information.

Another form of descriptive statistics uses numerical techniques to summarize data. One such method that you have already used frequently is the average or mean. In the same way that you calculate the average age of the employees of a company, we can compute the mean number of cavities to be treated weekly with Caridex by the 400 dentists in our survey. Chapter 4 introduces several numerical statistical measures that describe different features of the data. In Case 11.2, however, we are not so much interested in what the 400 dentists are reporting as we are in knowing the mean number of cavities to be treated with Caridex by all the country's dentists (approximately 10% of 100,000, or 10,000). To accomplish this goal we need another branch of statistics—**inferential statistics**.

Inferential statistics is a body of methods used to draw conclusions or inferences about characteristics of populations based on sample data. The population in question in Case 11.2 is the country's 10,000 dentists who will use Caridex. The cost of interviewing each would be prohibitive and extremely time-consuming. Statistical techniques make such endeavors unnecessary. Instead, we can sample a much smaller number of dentists (in this case the sample size is 400) and infer from the data in the sample the mean number of cavities to be treated with Caridex by all 10,000 dentists in the population. We can then estimate first-year profits for NPD.

Case 13.3: Quebec Separation? *Oui ou non*

Since the 1960s there has been an ongoing campaign among Quebecers to separate from Canada and form an independent nation. Should Quebec separate, the ramifications for the rest of Canada, American states that border Quebec, the North American Free Trade Agreement, and numerous multinational corporations would be enormous. In the 1993 federal election, the prosovereigntist Bloc Quebecois won 54 of Quebec's 75 seats in the House of Commons. In 1994, the separatist Parti Quebecois formed the provincial government in Quebec and promised to hold a referendum on separation. Like most political issues, polling plays an important role in trying to influence voters and to predict the outcome of the referendum vote. Shortly after the 1993 federal election, *The Financial Post Magazine*, in cooperation with several polling companies, conducted a survey of Quebecers.

A total of 641 adult Quebecers were interviewed. They were asked the following questions and provided with the accompanying response choices. (Francophones were asked the questions in French.)

1 Would you, personally, tend to favor: Quebec's staying in Canada, that is, remaining a Canadian province; or, Quebec's separating from Canada, that is, becoming an independent country?

    1 Strongly favor remaining in Canada
    2 Moderately favor remaining in Canada
    3 Moderately favor Quebec separation
    4 Strongly favor Quebec separation

2 If a referendum were held today on Quebec's sovereignty with the following question, "Do you want Quebec to separate from Canada and become an independent country?" would you vote *yes* or *no*?

    1 Yes
    0 No

The responses are stored on the data disk accompanying this book.

What conclusions can you draw from these results?

This case exemplifies one of the most common applications of statistical inference. The population we want to make inferences about is the approximately 7 million potential voters in the Province of Quebec. The sample consists of the 641 Quebecers randomly selected by the polling company. The characteristic of the population that we would like to know is the proportion of the total electorate that supports separation. Specifically, we would like to know whether more than 50% of voters will vote for separation. It must be made clear that, because we will not ask every one of the 7 million potential voters how he or she will vote, we cannot predict the outcome with 100% certainty. This is a fact that statisticians and even students of statistics must understand. A sample that is only a small fraction of the size of the population can lead to correct inferences only a certain percentage of the time. You will find that statisticians can control that fraction and usually set it between 90 and 99%.

Case 13.2: Host Selling and Announcer Commercials*

A study was undertaken to compare the effects of host selling commercials and announcer commercials on children. Announcer commercials are straightforward commercials in which the announcer describes to viewers why they should buy a particular product. Host selling commercials feature a children's show personality or television character who extols the virtues of the product. In 1975, the National

*Adapted from J. H. Miller, "An Empirical Evaluation of the Host Selling Commercial and the Announcer Commercial When Used on Children," *Developments in Marketing Science* 9 (1985): 276–78.

Association of Broadcasters prohibited using show characters to advertise products during the same program in which the characters appear. However, this prohibition was overturned in 1982 by a judge's decree.

The objective of the study was to determine whether the two types of advertisements have different effects on children watching them. Specifically, the researchers wanted to know whether children watching host selling commercials would remember more details about the commercial and would be more likely to buy the advertised product than children watching announcer commercials. The experiment consisted of two groups of children ranging in age from 6 to 10. One group of 121 children watched a program in which two host selling commercials appeared. The commercials tried to sell Canary Crunch, a breakfast cereal. A second group of 121 children watched the same program but was exposed to two announcer commercials for the same product. Immediately after the show, the children were given a questionnaire that tested their memory concerning the commercials they had watched.

Each child was rated (on a scale of 10) on his or her ability to remember details of the commercial. In addition, each child was offered a free box of cereal. The children were shown four different brands of cereal—Froot Loops (FL), Boo Berries (BB), Kangaroo Hops (KH), and Canary Crunch (CC; the advertised cereal)—and asked to pick the one they wanted. The results are stored on the data disk provided with this book. (Some of the data are shown in Table 1.1.) What conclusions can be drawn from these data?

Table 1.1		Memory Test Scores and Cereal Choices	
CHILDREN WHO WATCHED HOST SELLING COMMERCIALS		CHILDREN WHO WATCHED ANNOUNCER COMMERCIALS	
MEMORY TEST SCORES	CEREAL CHOICES	MEMORY TEST SCORES	CEREAL CHOICES
6	FL	8	BB
9	CC	6	FL
7	KH	10	CC
7	CC	8	FL
.	.	.	.
.	.	.	.
.	.	.	.
8	BB	9	CC

In this case, we want to compare the population of children who watch host commercials with the population of children who watch announcer commercials. The experiment consists of drawing samples of 121 children from each population. For each child, researchers recorded two observations. The first was the score out of 10 the child received on a test to measure his or her memory about the commercial. The second was the brand the child chose from among the four brands of breakfast cereals. Notice that, contrary to what you probably believed, data are not necessarily numbers. The test scores, of course, are numbers; however, the cereal choices are not. In Chapter 2, we will discuss the different types of data you will encounter in statistical applications and how to deal with them. The information sought by the researchers is whether there are differences in the test scores and the cereal selections between the two populations of children. By applying the appropriate statistical techniques, the researchers may be able to infer which type of commercial is more effective.

Case 16.2: Duxbury Press

The academic book business is different from most other businesses because of the way the purchasing decision is made. The customer, who is usually a student taking a university or college course, buys a specific book because the instructor of the course adopts (chooses to use) that book. Sales representatives of publishers sell their products by persuading instructors to adopt their books. Unfortunately, judging the quality of textbooks is not easy. To help with the decision process, sales representatives give free examination copies to instructors so they can review the book and decide whether or not to adopt it. In many universities, there are several sections of the same course, and book adoption committees meet to make the adoption decision.

Curt Hinrichs, an editor at Duxbury Press, was examining the latest data on the sales of the three recently published statistics textbooks. He noted that the number of examination copies was quite large, which can be a serious problem given the high cost of producing books. Duxbury distributes review copies only of the books or editions that came out in the current year. He wondered whether his sales representatives were giving away too many free books or perhaps not enough. The data set contains a code that identifies the sales region, the name of the representative, the number of free copies given to professors by that representative, and the gross revenues generated by the salesperson from the three new statistics books. These data are stored on the data disk. Curt would like to know whether there is a direct link between the number of free copies distributed and the gross revenues from new editions.

This case illustrates another statistical objective. Case 11.2 addressed the problem of describing the population of the number of cavities to be filled by Caridex. The objective of the problem described in Case 13.2 was to compare two populations, the responses of children who watch two different types of television commercials. In this case, we need to analyze the relationship between two variables, the number of examination copies distributed and revenues from sales of these books. By applying the appropriate statistical technique, Curt will be able to determine whether the two variables are related, and if so, whether distributing more examination copies produces higher sales. As you will discover, the technique also permits statisticians to include other variables to determine whether they affect revenues.

1.2 Key Statistical Concepts

As the above cases illustrate, statistical inference problems involve three key concepts: the population, the sample, and the statistical inference. We now discuss each of these concepts in more detail.

Population

A **population** is the set of all items of interest in a statistical problem. It is frequently very large and may, in fact, be infinitely large. Unlike its meaning in everyday usage, the word *population* in statistics does not necessarily refer to a group of people. It may, for example, refer to the population of diameters of ball bearings produced at a large plant. Even in situations involving a population of people, the term *population* will generally refer to the population of data. For example, in Case 11.2, the population of interest is the population of the number of cavities each dentist will treat weekly with Caridex. Thus, our population consists not of 10,000 dentists but instead of the 10,000 numbers of cavities to be treated with Caridex. Just imagine a giant container holding 10,000 slips of paper, each marked with a number equal to the number of cavities to be treated with Caridex by one particular dentist. This container is our population of interest.

A descriptive measure of a population is called a **parameter**. The parameter of interest in Case 11.2 is the mean number of cavities to be treated with Caridex by all the dentists in the population. The parameters in Case 13.3 are the proportions of all of Quebec's voters who will vote for separation. In Case 13.2, the parameters are the differences in the mean scores on the memory test and the differences in the proportions of breakfast cereals selected by each population.

Sample

A **sample** is a set of data drawn from the population. A descriptive measure of a sample is called a **statistic**. We use statistics to make inferences about parameters. In Case 11.2, the statistic we would compute is the mean number of cavities to be treated with Caridex by the 400 dentists in the sample. We would then use the sample mean to infer the value of the population mean, which is the parameter of interest in this problem. In Case 13.3, we compute the proportion of the sample of 641 Quebecers who will vote for separation. The sample statistics are then used to make inferences about the population of Quebec's voters. That is, we predict the result of the referendum.

Statistical Inference

Statistical inference is the process of making an estimate, prediction, or decision about a population based on sample data. Because populations are almost always very large, investigating each member of the population would be impractical and expensive. It is far easier and cheaper to take a sample from the population of interest and draw conclusions or make estimates about the population on the basis of information provided by the sample. However, such conclusions and estimates are not always going to be correct. For this reason, we build into the statistical inference a measure of reliability. There are two such measures, the **confidence level** and the **significance level**. The confidence level is the proportion of times that an estimating procedure will be correct. For example, in Case 11.2, we will produce an estimate of the average number of cavities to be treated with Caridex by all 10,000 dentists that has a confidence level of 95%. That means that, in the long run, estimates based on this form of statistical inference will be correct 95% of the time. When the purpose of the statistical inference is to draw a conclusion about a population, the significance level measures how frequently the conclusion will be wrong. For example, if the results of the analysis in Case 13.3 lead us to conclude that *less* than 50% of the electorate will vote yes on the referendum, a significance level of 5% means that there is a 5% chance that, in fact, *more* than 50% of the electorate support separation.

1.3 How Managers Use Statistics

As we've already pointed out, statistics is about acquiring and using information. However, the statistical result is not the end product. Managers use statistical techniques to help them make decisions. In general, statistical applications are driven by the managerial problem. The problem creates the need to acquire information. This in turn drives the data-gathering process. When the manager acquires data, he or she must convert the data into information by means of one or more statistical techniques. The information then becomes part of the decision process. We can think of the entire process as a management information system (MIS). Unfortunately, this term is often used incorrectly to describe methods of acquiring information through the use of a computer. However, MIS actually refers to the techniques of acquiring and using information, no matter how it is processed. Here is an example of how statistical methods play a critical role in the information system that ultimately produces a manager's course of action.

Many business students will take or have already taken a course in marketing. In the introductory marketing course, students are taught about market segmentation. Markets are segmented to develop products and services for specific groups of consumers. For example, the Coca-Cola Company produces several different cola products. There is Coca-Cola Classic, Coke, Diet Coke, and Caffeine-Free Diet Coke. Each product is aimed at a different market segment. Coca-Cola Classic is aimed at people who are older than 30, Coke is aimed at the teen market, Diet Coke is bought by individuals concerned about their weight or sugar intake, and Caffeine-Free Diet Coke is for people who are health-conscious. In order to segment the cola market, Coca-Cola had to determine that all consumers were not identical in their wants and needs. The company then had to determine the different parts of the market and ultimately design products that were profitable for each part of the market. As you might guess, statistics plays a critical but not exclusive role in this process.

Because there is no single way to segment a market, managers must try different segmentation variables. Segmentation variables include geographic (e.g., states, provinces, counties), demographic (e.g., age, sex, occupation, income, religion), psychographic (e.g., social class, lifestyle, personality), and behavioristic (e.g., brand loyalty, usage, benefits sought). Consumer surveys are generally used by marketing researchers to determine which segmentation variables to use. Thus, for example, Coca-Cola used age and lifestyle. The age of consumers determines generally whether they buy Coca-Cola Classic or Coke. Lifestyle determines whether they purchase regular, diet, or caffeine-free. Surveys and statistical techniques would tell the marketing manager that the "average" Coca-Cola Classic drinker is older than 30, whereas the "average" Coke drinker is a teenager. Census data and surveys are used to measure the size of the two segments. Surveys would also inform about the number of cola drinkers who are concerned about calories and/or caffeine. The conversion of the raw data in the survey into statistics is only one part of the process. The marketing manager must then make decisions about which segments to pursue (not all segments are profitable), how to sell, and how to advertise.

In this book, we will address the part of the process that collects the raw data and produces the statistical result. By necessity, we must leave the remaining elements of the decision process to the other courses that constitute business programs. We will demonstrate, however, that all areas of management can and do use statistical techniques as part of the information system.

1.4 Statistics and the Computer

In almost all practical applications of statistics, the statistician must deal with large amounts of data. For example, Case 11.2 involves 400 observations. In order to estimate first-year profits, the statistician would have to perform various computations on the data; although the calculations do not require any great mathematical skill, the sheer amount of arithmetic makes this aspect of the statistical method time-consuming and tedious. Fortunately, numerous commercially prepared computer programs are available to perform the arithmetic. In most of the examples used to illustrate statistical techniques in this book, we will provide three methods for answering the question.

1 **Solving by hand**. Except where doing so is prohibitively time-consuming, we will show how to answer the question by using hand calculations (with only the aid of a calculator). It is useful for you to produce some solutions in this way, because by doing so you will gain some insights into statistical concepts.

2 **Using Minitab**. The Minitab software package is one of the easiest packages to use. It is used by universities and businesses around the world. We will show the Minitab output for most examples and provide detailed instructions in its use. In addition, we created macros to augment Minitab's list of techniques. We use Release 11 for Windows.

3 **Using Microsoft Excel**. Many business students own a spreadsheet package, and university and college courses incorporate a spreadsheet into their curriculum. We have chosen to use Microsoft Excel because we believe that it is and will continue to be the most popular spreadsheet package. One of its drawbacks is that it offers relatively few of the statistical techniques we introduce in this book. Consequently, we created macros that can be loaded onto your computer to enable you to use Excel for almost all procedures. We provide detailed instructions for all techniques. We use version 5.0.

All three solutions are color-coded and enclosed in boxes. We anticipate that most instructors will choose some combination (but not all three) of the methods described above. For example, many instructors prefer to have students solve small-sample problems involving few calculations manually but turn to the computer for large-sample problems or more complicated techniques.

To allow as much flexibility as possible, most examples, exercises, and cases are accompanied by a set of data stored on the diskette that came with this book. You can solve these problems using a software package. In addition, we have made it possible for students without access to a computer to solve these problems.

Ideally, students will solve the small-sample, relatively simple problems by hand and use the computer to solve the others. The approach we prefer to take is to minimize the time spent on manual computations and to focus instead on selecting the appropriate method for dealing with a problem and on interpreting the output after the computer has performed the necessary computations. In this way, we hope to demonstrate that statistics can be as interesting and practical as any other subject in your curriculum.

1.5 World Wide Web and Learning Center

To assist students in the various aspects of using the computer to learn statistics, we have created a web page. It offers useful information including additional exercises and cases, corrections to the different printings and supplements, and updates on the data sets and macros (including the latest version for Excel 97). Additionally, you can e-mail the authors to make comments and ask questions about the installation of the files stored on the diskettes. The home page can be reached at *http://www.globalserve.net/~gkeller*. The site can also be accessed from the publisher's home page: *http://www.thomson.com/duxbury.html*.

IMPORTANT TERMS

Descriptive statistics	Parameter	Statistical inference
Inferential statistics	Sample	Confidence level
Population	Statistic	Significance level

Exercises

1.1 In your own words, define and give an example of each of the following statistical terms.

    a population   **b** sample   **c** parameter

    d statistic   **e** statistical inference

1.2 Briefly describe the difference between descriptive statistics and inferential statistics.

1.3 A politician who is running for the office of mayor of a city with 25,000 registered voters commissions a survey. In the survey, 48% of the 200 registered voters interviewed say they planned to vote for her.

    a What is the population of interest?   **b** What is the sample?

    c Is the value 48% a parameter or a statistic?

1.4 A manufacturer of computer chips claims that less than 10% of his products are defective. When 1,000 chips were drawn from a large production run, 7.5% were found to be defective.

    a What is the population of interest?   **b** What is the sample?

    c What is the parameter?   **d** What is the statistic?

    e Does the value 10% refer to the parameter or to the statistic?

    f Is the value 7.5% a parameter or a statistic?

    g Explain briefly how the statistic can be used to make inferences about the parameter to test the claim.

1.5 Suppose you believe that, in general, graduates of business programs are offered higher salaries upon graduating than are graduates of arts and science programs. Describe a statistical experiment that could help test your belief.

1.6 You are shown a coin that its owner says is fair in the sense that it will produce the same number of heads and tails when flipped repeatedly.

    a Describe an experiment to test this claim.

    b What is the population in your experiment?

    c What is the sample?

    d What is the parameter?

    e What is the statistic?

    f Describe briefly how statistical inference can be used to test the claim.

1.7 Suppose that in Exercise 1.6 you decide to flip the coin 100 times.

    a What conclusion would you be likely to draw if you observed 95 heads?

    b What conclusion would you be likely to draw if you observed 55 heads?

    c Do you believe that, if you flip a perfectly fair coin 100 times, you will always observe exactly 50 heads? If you answered no, what numbers do you think are possible? If you answered yes, how many heads would you observe if you flipped the coin twice? Try it several times, and report the results.

1.8 The owner of a large fleet of taxis is trying to estimate his costs for next year's operations. One major cost is fuel purchases. To estimate fuel purchases, the owner needs to know the total distance his taxis will travel next year, the cost of a gallon of fuel, and the fuel mileage of his taxis. The owner has been provided with the first two figures (distance estimate and cost). However, because of the high cost of gasoline, the owner has recently converted his taxis to operate on propane. He measures the propane mileage (in miles per gallon) for 50 taxis. The results are stored in file XR01-08.

    a What is the population of interest?

    b What is the parameter the owner needs?

    c What is the sample?

    d What is the statistic?

    e Describe briefly how the statistic will produce the kind of information the owner wants.

To help you organize the material that you are about to learn, we have divided the rest of the book into three parts. Part 1 covers descriptive statistics and probability. These topics constitute the foundation of statistical inference. As we pointed out in Chapter 1, statistical inference is the process of drawing conclusions about

1 Descriptive Techniques and Probability

populations on the basis of sample statistics. In Chapter 4, we introduce some of the statistics that will be used to make inferences about parameters. In Chapters 6 and 7, we present probability and probability distributions that will provide the link between sample statistics and population parameters. Everything that we do in this book is built upon these three chapters. However, Part 1 does much more than just lay the foundation. Both descriptive statistics and probability are subjects that are worth learning for their own intrinsic values.

We all make decisions on a daily basis, most of which are made under uncertainty. Consider an investor who must decide which investment to make, how much money to invest, and how long that investment should be held. There are a large number of events over which the investor has no control. All that the investor can do is attempt to assess the risks and returns associated with each investment. As you will discover, probability plays a central role in this assessment.

We believe that all business and economics graduates will have many opportunities to apply statistical inference techniques and concepts. Not all of them will do so, because of a lack of knowledge (despite the best efforts of statistics professors) or confidence. Descriptive techniques, however, are so common that it is virtually impossible to ignore them. Newspapers, magazines, company annual reports, and presentations are filled with applications of descriptive statistics. Knowing how to use and interpret them is a critical skill for managers and economists. Chapter 2 introduces graphical techniques, and Chapter 3 discusses how they should be used. Chapter 4 presents numerical methods, while Chapter 5 introduces the methods used to gather data.

2 Graphical Descriptive Techniques

2.1 Introduction

In Chapter 1, we pointed out that statistics is divided into two basic areas: descriptive statistics and inferential statistics. The purpose of this chapter, together with the next two, is to present the principal methods that fall under the heading of descriptive statistics. In this chapter, we introduce graphical statistical methods that allow managers visually to summarize data to extract useful information. Chapter 3 presents a discussion on how to make interesting and informative use of these techniques. Another class of descriptive techniques, numerical methods, is introduced in Chapter 4.

Managers frequently have access to large masses of potentially useful data. But before the data can be used to support a decision, they must be organized and summarized. Consider, for example, the problems faced by managers who have access to the data bases created by the use of debit cards. (Debit cards are like credit cards except that when purchases are made, the amount is immediately deducted from the customer's bank account.) The data base consists of customer information taken from the bank account application (i.e., age, income, occupation, residence, and the like), plus a history of all purchases made using the debit card. Using these data, marketing managers can determine which segments of the market are buying their products and which are not. Specialized marketing campaigns can then be developed. However, before that can be done, the data must be summarized so that the relevant information can be extracted. The use of descriptive statistical methods is often the first step in the process.

Descriptive statistics, then, involves arranging, summarizing, and presenting a set of data in such a way that the meaningful essentials of the data can be extracted and interpreted easily. Its methods make use of graphical techniques and numerical descriptive measures (such as averages) to summarize and present the data to yield useful information, allowing managers to make decisions and recommendations. Although descriptive statistical methods are quite straightforward (and far less space is devoted to them than to inferential statistical methods), their importance should not be underestimated. Most business students will encounter numerous opportunities to make valuable use of graphical and numerical descriptive statistical techniques when preparing reports and presentations in the workplace. According to a Wharton Business School study, top managers reach a consensus 25% more quickly when responding to a presentation in which graphics are used.

Recall from Chapter 1 that a **population** is the entire set of observations or measurements under study, whereas a **sample** is a set of observations selected from the population and is therefore only a part of the entire population. The descriptive methods presented in this chapter and in Chapter 3 apply equally well to data consisting of an entire population and to data consisting of a sample drawn from a population.

Before we present descriptive techniques, we need to discuss the different types of data. The type of data to be analyzed plays a critical role in determining the appropriate statistical method to apply.

2.2 Types of Data

To assist in our discussion we need to define two terms, one of which we've already used. They are *variable* and *data*. A **variable** is any characteristic of a population or sample that is of interest to us. For example, in Case 11.2 (introduced in Chapter 1), the variable in which we are interested is the number of cavities to be treated by American dentists using Caridex. In Case 13.2, there were two variables: memory test scores and cereal choices.

The term **data** refers to the actual values (measurements or observations) of variables. (Incidentally, the word *data* is plural for *datum*; datum refers to one single observation, and data refers to a group of observations.) The numbers that appear on page 3 constitute some of the data in Case 11.2. Thus, *variable* is the word we use to describe the name of the characteristic of interest, and *data* is the word that describes the actual values or observations of the variable.

Data may be either **quantitative** (numerical) or **qualitative** (categorical). When you see the word *data*, you probably think of a group of numbers, such as incomes, sales, profits, and losses. The data in these examples are quantitative—they are real numbers and are said to have an *interval scale*. All types of statistical calculations are permitted on quantitative data.

> **Quantitative Data**
> **Quantitative data** are numerical observations.

If 75 managers are surveyed and asked to state their age and annual income, the numerical responses they give are quantitative data. If the managers are also asked to indicate their marital status (single, married, divorced, or widowed), their responses are nonnumerical, but each response can still be classified as falling into one of four categories. Observations that can be sorted into categories on the basis of qualitative attributes, such as marital status, race (Asian, Black, Caucasian, Hispanic, Other), sex, occupation, or type of dwelling inhabited, constitute qualitative data. The data in these examples are simply the names of possible classifications and are said to have a *nominal scale*.

Qualitative Data

Qualitative data are categorical observations.

All we can do with qualitative data is count the number of observations in each category and then calculate the proportion or percentage of all observations that fall into each category. It is important to realize that this is the case even if numbers are used to label the categories. For example, consider once again the survey questionnaire asking managers to indicate their marital status, with the possible responses being single, married, divorced, and widowed. In order to help record the responses (for example, when they are stored and processed by a computer), such data are often converted into numbers. But data produced in this way are still *qualitative*, because the numbers merely represent the name of the response; they have no real numerical meaning. As a result, any arithmetic calculations performed on qualitative data are also meaningless. For example, suppose that we recorded the responses to the marital-status question as follows:

Single	1	Divorced	3
Married	2	Widowed	4

Suppose further that the first 10 managers interviewed responded 1, 1, 3, 4, 1, 1, 2, 3, 1, 3. If we were to calculate the average of these numerical responses, we would find it to be 2. Does this mean that the average manager was married? Now suppose that four more managers were interviewed, of whom three were widowed and one divorced. After summing all 14 numerical responses and dividing by 14, we would find that the average numerical response turns out to be 2.5. Does this mean that the average manager was married but halfway toward being divorced? Obviously, the answer to both questions is no, and the reason is that arithmetic calculations, such as averages, performed on qualitative data provide meaningless results. All we can do when the data are qualitative is count the number of times each value has occurred and then calculate the proportion (in this case) of managers who fall into each marital-status category.

Knowing the type of data being measured is important, because it is one of the factors that determines which statistical technique should be used. Usually, identifying the data as being either quantitative or qualitative will be sufficient. But in a few situations (primarily in choosing the appropriate nonparametric technique in Chapters 12 and 14), it will be necessary to recognize whether or not the nonquantitative data under consideration can be ranked. If the categories for a set of nonquantitative data can be ordered or ranked, we refer to the data as being **ranked data**. The data are then said to have an **ordinal scale**.

This would be the case, for example, if each manager were asked to classify a particular hotel as excellent, good, fair, or poor, based on the quality of accommodation provided. Because the responses here are nonquantitative and categorical, the data appear to be nominal. Notice, however, that the responses are ranked in preferential order by the quality of accommodation. The first response (excellent) is the highest rating, the second response (good) is the second-highest rating, and so on. Any numerical representation of the four answers should maintain the ranked ordering of the responses. Such a numerical system would form an *ordinal scale*. The only constraint upon our choice of numbers for this scale is that they must represent the order of the responses; the actual values to be used are arbitrary. For example, we could record the responses as follows:

Excellent	4	Fair	2
Good	3	Poor	1

Another, equally valid representation of the ratings would be the following:

Excellent	9	Fair	2
Good	5	Poor	1

And we could simply reverse our original 4-3-2-1 ratings so that excellent = 1 and poor = 4, with no effect on the statistical technique to be used.

The only information provided by ranked data that is not provided by qualitative data is the ranked order of the responses. We still cannot interpret the difference between values for ranked data, because the actual numbers used are arbitrary. For example, the 4-3-2-1 rating implies that the difference between excellent and good (4 − 3 = 1) is equal to the difference between fair and poor (2 − 1 = 1), whereas the 9-5-2-1 rating implies that the difference between excellent and good (9 − 5 = 4) is four times as large as the difference between fair and poor (2 − 1 = 1). Since both numbering systems are valid (though arbitrary), no inferences can be drawn as to the differences between values of ranked variables. Thus, statistics such as averages are often misleading. To illustrate this point, suppose that of 10 people interviewed, 4 rated their hotel accommodation excellent, 3 good, and 3 poor. The average using the 4-3-2-1 system is 2.8, which suggests that the average hotel is between fair and good. Using the 9-5-2-1 system, the average is 5.4, which implies that the average hotel is between good and excellent.

It should be understood that the mean of ranked data does provide *some* useful information and certainly more than that provided by the mean of qualitative data (which provides *no* useful information). However, because of the arbitrary nature of ranked data, the most appropriate statistical techniques are ones that put the data in order. (In Chapter 4 we present the *median*, which is calculated by placing the numbers in order and selecting the observation that falls in the middle.) You will find that an ordering process is used throughout this book whenever the data are ranked.

The types of data can be ranked according to the valid calculations they permit. Qualitative data have the lowest rank, since no calculations (other than counting the number of observations) are permitted. Ranked data come next, since we may calculate statistics using an ordering procedure (as well as counting the number of times each value is observed). Then comes quantitative data, for which all calculations are valid. It is important to understand that we can treat higher-ranked data as if they were lower-ranked. We can treat quantitative data as ranked—or even qualitative, if it suits our purposes. For example, suppose that our data consist of the times taken for athletes to run a 100-meter race. These data, of course, are quantitative. If we wish, we can calculate the mean time for a particular runner. This statistic provides us with information that summarizes how fast he or she can run. Suppose that instead of measuring time, we record position in the race. These data are ranked. Calculating the mean would give us some information, but you can see how little information is provided by determining that the average finish of a runner is (say) 2.63. What does this number tell you about the athlete's ability? On the other hand, if you know that the runner's average time is 10.03 seconds (and the world record is around 9.85 seconds), you have much more information about the runner.

The type of data being analyzed plays a critical role in determining which statistical technique to use. Section 2.3 presents graphical methods to describe a set of quantitative data. Section 2.5 introduces techniques to describe qualitative and ranked data. In the rest of this book, we will stress the importance of the data type (as well as other factors) in determining the most appropriate statistical technique to use. We conclude our discussion of data types with the following summary.

Types of Data

Quantitative Data (Interval)

Values are real numbers.
Arithmetic calculations are valid.

Qualitative Data (Nominal)

Categorical data
Values are the (arbitrary) names of possible categories.
Valid computation: count of the number of observations in each category.

Ranked Data (Ordinal)

Categorical data
Values must represent the ranked order of responses.
Valid computations: those based on an ordering process.

Cross-Sectional and Time-Series Data

Data can also be classified according to whether the observations are measured at the same time (**cross-sectional data**) or whether they represent measurements at successive points in time (**time-series data**). Marketing surveys and political opinion polls are familiar methods of collecting cross-sectional data. The data from a marketing survey might include, for example, the preferences and demographic characteristics of a sample of 1,000 consumers at the same point in time. Statistical techniques could be applied to the data, such as testing for differences in preferences between men and women.

To give another example, consider a real estate consultant who feels that the selling price of a house is a function of its size, age, and lot size. In order to estimate the specific form of the function, she collects the sample data shown in the table below. The values in the table represent cross-sectional data, being as they all are observations at the same point in time. (You will learn how to estimate such a function from these data in Chapter 17.)

The real estate consultant is also working on a separate project to forecast the monthly housing starts in the northeastern United States over the next year. To do so, she collects the monthly housing starts in this region for each of the past five years. These 60 values (housing starts) represent time-series data, being observations taken over time.

HOUSE	SELLING PRICE ($1,000s) y	HOUSE SIZE (100 FT^2) x_1	AGE (YEARS) x_2	LOT SIZE (1,000 FT^2) x_3
1	89.5	20.0	5	4.1
2	79.9	14.8	10	6.8
3	83.1	20.5	8	6.3
4	56.9	12.5	7	5.1
5	66.6	18.0	8	4.2
6	82.5	14.3	12	8.6
7	126.3	27.5	1	4.9
8	79.3	16.5	10	6.2
9	119.9	24.3	2	7.5
10	87.6	20.2	8	5.1
11	112.6	22.0	7	6.3
12	120.8	19.0	11	12.9
13	78.5	12.3	16	9.6
14	74.3	14.0	12	5.7
15	74.8	16.7	13	4.8

Generally speaking, cross-sectional data represent measurements at the micro level, such as preferences of individual consumers or prices of individual houses. Time-series data, on the other hand, frequently represent aggregated data such as housing starts, unemployment rates, or the values of the stock market index over time. Consequently, time-series data are often readily available from secondary sources, reducing the cost of their collection compared with cross-sectional data.

Although most of the data that we'll be working with in this book will be cross-sectional, time-series data will be used somewhat in the regression chapters (Chapters 16 and 17).

Exercises

2.1 Provide two examples each of qualitative, ranked, and quantitative data.

2.2 For each of the following examples of data, determine the type.

a the starting salaries of graduates from an M.B.A. program

b the months in which a firm's employees take their vacations

c the final letter grades received by students in a statistics course

d the number of miles driven annually by employees in company cars

2.3 For each of the following examples of data, determine the type.

a the month of highest sales for each firm in a sample

b the weekly closing price of gold throughout the year

c the size of soft drink (small, medium, or large) ordered by a sample of Burger King customers

d the amount of crude oil imported monthly by the United States for the past 10 years

e the marks achieved by the students in a statistics course final exam in which there are ten questions each worth 10 marks

2.4 Information concerning a magazine's readership is of interest both to the publisher and to the magazine's advertisers. A survey of 500 subscribers included the following questions. For each, determine the type of data.

    a What is your age?

    b What is your sex?

    c What is your marital status?

    d Is your annual income less than $20,000, between $20,000 and $40,000, or over $40,000?

    e How many other magazine subscriptions do you have?

2.5 A random sample of 400 university professors was taken. Each was asked the following questions. Identify the type of data.

    a What is your rank (lecturer, assistant professor, associate professor, full professor)?

    b What is your annual salary?

    c For which faculty (Arts and Science, Business, Engineering, etc.) in the university are you employed?

    d How many years have you been a professor?

2.6 Baseball fans are regularly quizzed concerning their opinions about various aspects of the sport. A sample of 300 baseball fans was asked the following questions. Identify the data type for each.

    a How many games do you attend annually?

    b Would you rate the entertainment excellent, good, fair, or poor?

    c Do you have season tickets?

    d How much money on average do you spend at the food concession at each game?

    e Rate the food: edible, barely edible, or abominable.

2.3 Graphical Techniques for Quantitative Data

In this section, we introduce several graphical methods that are used when the data are quantitative. Often, the first step taken toward summarizing a mass of numbers is to form what is known as a *frequency distribution*. This is a simple, effective method of organizing and presenting quantitative data so that one can get an overall picture of where the data are concentrated and how spread out they are. Consider the following example.

EXAMPLE 2.1

In the last decade, a number of companies have been created to compete in the long-distance telephone business. Suppose, as part of a much larger study, one such company wanted to get some information concerning the monthly bills of new subscribers in the first month after signing on with the company. A survey of 200 new residential subscribers was undertaken, and the first month's bills were recorded. These data appear in Table 2.1 and are stored in file XM02-01. As a first step, a statistician wanted to summarize the data in preparation for a presentation to the president of the company.

| Table 2.1 | Long-Distance Telephone Bills (in dollars) |

42.19	15.30	49.24	9.44	2.67	4.69	41.38	45.77
38.45	29.23	89.35	118.04	110.46	0.00	72.88	83.05
95.73	103.15	94.52	26.84	93.93	90.26	72.78	101.38
104.80	74.01	56.01	39.21	48.54	93.31	104.88	30.61
22.57	63.70	104.84	6.45	16.47	89.50	13.36	44.16
92.97	99.56	92.62	78.89	87.71	93.57	0.00	75.71
88.62	99.50	85.00	0.00	8.41	70.48	92.88	3.20
115.50	2.42	1.08	76.69	13.62	88.51	55.99	12.24
119.63	23.31	11.05	8.37	7.18	11.07	1.47	26.40
13.26	21.13	95.03	29.04	5.42	77.21	72.47	0.00
5.64	6.48	6.95	19.60	8.11	9.01	84.77	1.62
91.10	10.88	30.62	100.05	26.97	15.43	29.25	1.88
16.44	109.08	2.45	21.97	17.12	19.70	6.93	10.05
99.03	29.24	15.21	28.77	9.12	118.75	0.00	13.95
14.34	79.52	2.72	9.63	21.34	104.40	2.88	65.90
20.55	3.43	10.44	21.36	24.42	95.52	6.72	35.32
117.69	106.84	8.40	90.04	3.85	91.56	10.13	5.72
33.69	115.78	0.98	19.45	0.00	27.21	89.27	14.49
92.17	21.00	106.59	13.90	9.22	109.94	10.70	0.00
11.27	72.02	7.74	5.04	33.40	6.95	6.48	11.64
83.26	15.42	24.49	89.13	111.14	92.64	53.90	114.67
27.57	64.78	45.81	56.04	20.39	31.77	94.67	44.32
3.69	19.34	13.54	18.89	1.57	0.00	5.20	2.80
5.10	3.03	9.16	15.30	75.49	68.69	35.00	9.12
18.49	84.12	13.68	20.84	100.04	112.94	20.12	53.21

SOLUTION

Very little knowledge about the monthly bills is acquired by casually reading through Table 2.1. You probably see that most of the bills are less than $100, but that is likely to be the extent of the information garnered by browsing through the data. If you examine the data more carefully, you'll discover that the smallest bill is $0 and the largest is $119.63. This simple exercise provides you with *some* information. However, the company president will not be impressed with your statistical skills if you do not reap additional information from the data. For example, how are the numbers distributed between $0 and $119.63? Are there many small bills and some large bills, or are most of the bills in the center of the range with very few extreme values?

To acquire more information, we construct a **frequency distribution**—an arrangement or table that groups data into nonoverlapping intervals called **classes** and records the number of observations in each class. Table 2.2 provides an illustration of how this is accomplished.

Table 2.2

Frequency Distribution of Long-Distance Telephone Bills

CLASS LIMITS	FREQUENCY
0 up to 15*	71
15 up to 30	37
30 up to 45	13
45 up to 60	9
60 up to 75	10
75 up to 90	18
90 up to 105	28
105 up to 120	14
Total	200

*Class contains observations up to but not including 15.
The other classes are defined similarly.

Table 2.2 was created by more or less arbitrarily deciding that we will use eight classes. (We will shortly discuss how to decide on the number of classes to be used to build a frequency distribution.) The class width is computed by taking the difference between the largest and smallest observations and then dividing by the number of classes. Thus,

$$\text{Approximate class width} = \frac{\text{Largest value} - \text{Smallest value}}{\text{Number of classes}}$$

$$= \frac{119.63 - 0}{8} = 14.95$$

For convenience, we round this number to 15, an acceptable action because there is no fixed rule about the number of class intervals, which ultimately determines the class width. The classes are the intervals 0 up to but not including 15, 15 up to but not including 30, and so on. Notice that the class intervals were created so that there was no overlap. For example, the value 15 was included in the second class but not in the first. We then count the number of observations that fall into each class interval (or more precisely, we let the computer count the observations). The counts, or frequencies, of observations are then listed next to their respective classes. The frequency distribution is then complete, as shown in Table 2.2. The next step in the information-mining process is to draw a picture of the data by constructing a histogram.

HISTOGRAMS

The information in a frequency distribution is often grasped more easily—and the presentation is made more visually appealing—if the distribution is graphed. One very common graphical presentation is the **histogram**, which is created by drawing rectangles. The bases of the rectangles correspond to the class intervals, and the height of each rectangle equals the number of observations in that class. Figure 2.1 depicts the histogram created from the frequency distribution in Table 2.2. We call this diagram a **frequency histogram** because the numbers on the vertical axis represent the frequencies.

Figure 2.1

Histogram of Long-Distance Telephone Bills

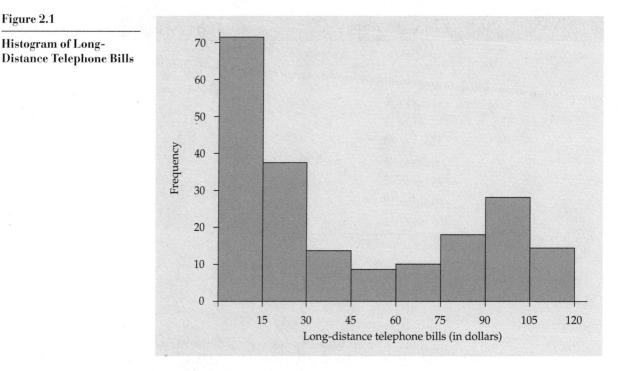

INTERPRETING THE
RESULTS

The histogram gives us quite a clear view of the way the bills are distributed. About half of the monthly bills are small (between $0 and $30), there are few bills in the middle of the range ($30 to $75), and there are a relatively large number of long-distance bills at the high end of the range. It would appear from this sample of first-month long-distance bills that the company's customers are split unevenly between light and heavy users of long-distance telephone service. At this point, it is not clear what this means to the company. Further analysis might reveal more information about our customers.

Figure 2.1 was drawn by hand to show how histograms are created and interpreted. We now show how histograms are actually drawn in practice. We employ Minitab and Excel software to do the work for us.

USING THE COMPUTER

As we promised in Chapter 1 (and the Preface), we will solve all examples in this book using three approaches (where feasible). We have already constructed the histogram by hand. We will now use Minitab and Excel to output the histogram for Example 2.1.

Appendix 2.A introduces Minitab, provides some background information, and gives instructions for inputting data and printing results. Appendix 2.B provides a similar service for the Excel package.

For each example, we present not only the output, but also the commands to produce it. For each of our software packages, we provide general instructions as well as instructions for the specific example. The Minitab instructions assume that you will be using the menu commands. However, we have also provided the session commands in Appendix 2.A. We will continue this practice throughout the book.

Minitab Output for Example 2.1

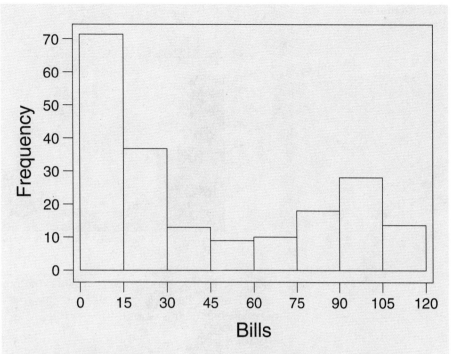

MENU COMMANDS

1 Type or import the data into a column. (See Appendix 2.A.)

2 Click **Graph** and **Histogram . . .**.

3 Type the variable name in Box 1 of **Graph variables**.

4 Use the cursor to choose the following under **Data display**: **Bar** (under **Display**) and **Graph** (under **For each**). Click **OK**.

COMMANDS FOR EXAMPLE 2.1

Open file **XM02-01**.

Bills or **C1**

Minitab will produce a histogram using its own rules to select the classes. To choose your own classes, proceed with the following steps.

5 Before clicking **OK** click **Options . . .**.

6 Use the cursor to specify **Frequency** or **Percent** (relative frequency).

7 To specify midpoints, use the cursor to select **Midpoint**. Specify **Midpoint/cutpoint positions:**, hit **tab**, and type the midpoints you want. (If the number of midpoints is too large, you will have to create the histogram using the session commands described in Appendix 2.A.)

8 To specify cutpoints, use the cursor to select **Cutpoint**. Specify the **Midpoint/cutpoint positions:**, hit **tab**, and type the cutpoints you want. (If the number of cutpoints is too large, you will have to create the histogram using the session commands.) Click **OK** twice.

Excel Output for Example 2.1

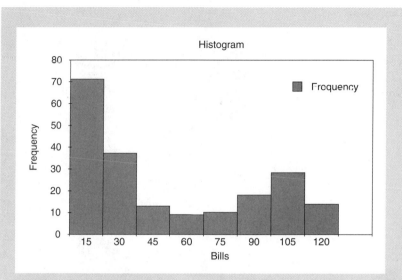

Note that the numbers that appear along the horizontal axis represent the upper limits of the class intervals even though they appear in the center of the classes on the histogram.

EXCEL 97

Excel 97 Users:
Steps 1–7 are valid. However, it is not necessary to specify the bins. If you don't list the bins, Excel will automatically construct its own set of bins from which the histogram will be drawn.

COMMANDS	COMMANDS FOR EXAMPLE 2.1
1 Type or import the data into Column A. (See Appendix 2.B.)	Open file **XM02-01**.
2 Type **Bin** in Cell B1.	
3 In B2 type the upper limit of the first interval. In B3 type the upper limit of the second interval. Drag B2 and B3 to complete the listing of bins.	**15** **30** . . **120**
4 Click **Tools**, **Data Analysis . . .** , and **Histogram**.	
5 Type the location of the data (including cell containing name, if necessary).	**A1:A201**
6 If a variable name has been included with the data, use the cursor to specify **Labels**. (That is, click the box.)	
7 Hit **tab** and type the location of the bins. If a variable name for the data has been included and you indicated that there are labels in the first row, include the cell where **Bins** is typed.	**B1:B9**

Step 8. A check mark replaces **x**.

8 Move cursor to **Chart Output** and click. (That is, mark an **x** in the box.) Click **OK**. This will produce a histogram with spaces between the rectangles. To correct, proceed as follows.

Steps 9–12. To remove the gaps between the class intervals, use the left button on the mouse and click one

9 Activate the chart by double-clicking anywhere within the boundaries of the box.

10 Move the cursor to **Format** (at the top of the screen) and click.

of the bars. Click the right button. Click (with the left button) **Format Data Series . . . .** Click **Options** and move the pointer to **Gap Width:** and change the number to 0. Click **OK.**

Step 13 is valid.

11 Click **Chart type . . . , Entire Chart, 2-D, Column,** and **Options . . . .**

12 Click **Options.** Move pointer to **Gap Width:** and change number to 0. Click **OK.**

13 To improve the appearance of the histogram, you may wish to type a new caption to replace **Bin.** If so, move pointer to the word **Bin** on the histogram and click. Type a new caption (e.g., **Bills** for Example 2.1).

CHOOSING THE NUMBER
OF CLASSES

Using the computer to draw histograms means that there is only one "job" for the statistician to perform (besides interpreting the results)—to choose the number of classes. As a general rule, we want to have a small number of classes when the number of observations is small and a large number of classes when the number of observations is large. Table 2.3 provides a rough guide for this decision.

Table 2.3	Approximate Number of Classes in Frequency Distribution		
NUMBER OF OBSERVATIONS	NUMBER OF CLASSES	NUMBER OF OBSERVATIONS	NUMBER OF CLASSES
Less than 50	5–7	1,000–5,000	11–13
50–200	7–9	5,000–50,000	13–17
200–500	9–10	More than 50,000	17–20
500–1,000	10–11		

To illustrate what happens when we have too few classes, we used both Minitab and Excel to create histograms for Example 2.1 with only five classes. Note that the smaller number of classes results in the loss of useful detail. It now appears that most of the bills are less than $25 and the rest of the bills are more or less evenly distributed between $25 and $125.

Minitab Output for Example 2.1 (Five Classes)

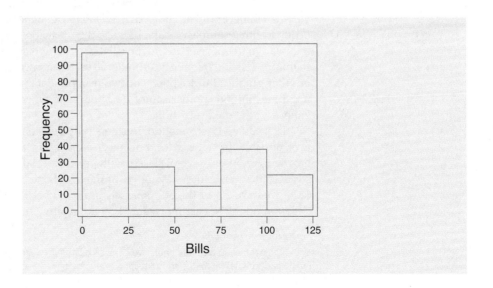

If, on the other hand, there is a small number of observations and a *large* number of classes, each class will contain few observations, which results in a histogram that yields little useful information. In Example 2.1, the number of classes would have to be quite large for that to happen.

Excel Output for Example 2.1 (Five Classes)

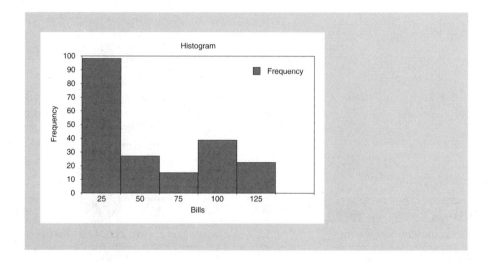

RELATIVE FREQUENCY HISTOGRAMS

Instead of showing the absolute frequency of observations in each class, it is often preferable to show the proportion (or percentage*) of observations falling into the various classes. To do this, we replace the class frequency by the **class relative frequency**.

$$\text{Class relative frequency} = \frac{\text{Class frequency}}{\text{Total number of observations}}$$

We can then talk about a **relative frequency distribution** (see Table 2.4) and a **relative frequency histogram** (see Figure 2.2). Notice that, in Figure 2.2, the area of any rectangle is proportional to the relative frequency, or proportion, of observations falling into that class. These relative frequencies are useful when you are dealing with a sample of data, because they provide insights into the corresponding relative frequencies for the population from which the sample was taken. Furthermore, relative frequencies should be used when you are comparing histograms or other graphical descriptions of two or more data sets. Relative frequencies permit a meaningful comparison of data sets even when the total numbers of observations in the data sets differ.

To facilitate interpretation, it is generally best to use equal class widths whenever possible. In some cases, however, *unequal class widths* are called for to avoid having to represent several classes with very low relative frequencies. For example, suppose that, instead of having 7% of the telephone bills falling between $105 and $120, we have 7% of the bills sparsely scattered between $105 and $165. This new situation might be best represented by the relative frequency histogram shown in

---

*Over the course of this book, we express relative frequencies (and later probabilities) variously as decimals, fractions, and percentages.

Figure 2.3, where the uppermost four classes have been combined. It is important, however, that the height of the corresponding rectangle be adjusted (from .07 to .07/4) so that the area of the rectangle remains proportional to the relative frequency of all observations falling between $105 and $165.

Table 2.4	Relative Frequency Distribution of Long-Distance Telephone Bills	
	CLASS LIMITS	**RELATIVE FREQUENCY**
	0 up to 15*	71/200 = .355
	15 up to 30	37/200 = .185
	30 up to 45	13/200 = .065
	45 up to 60	9/200 = .045
	60 up to 75	10/200 = .050
	75 up to 90	18/200 = .090
	90 up to 105	28/200 = .140
	105 up to 120	14/200 = .070
	Total	200/200 = 1.000

*Class contains observations up to but not including 15.
The other classes are defined similarly.

Figure 2.2

**Relative Frequency
Histogram of Telephone Bills**

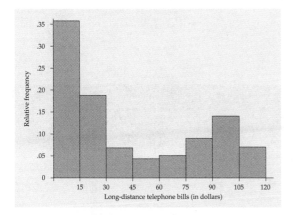

Figure 2.3

**Relative Frequency
Histogram with Unequal Class Widths**

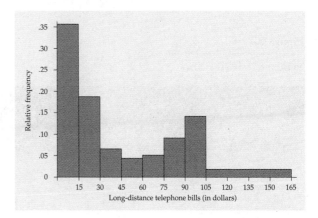

The observations in the preceding example all fall within a fairly compact range. In some cases, however, observations may be sparsely scattered over a large range of values at either end of the distribution. If this situation arises, it may be necessary to use an **open-ended class** to account for the observations, as shown in the relative frequency distribution in Table 2.5. Because incomes ranging from $75,000 to millions of dollars are scattered fairly sparsely over a wide range of values, we use a single class with no specified upper limit to capture these incomes. Notice also that Table 2.5 makes use of unequal class widths, which were discussed in the preceding paragraph.

Table 2.5	Percentage Distribution of American Family Income for 1992		
CLASS LIMITS (THOUSANDS OF DOLLARS)	PERCENTAGE	CLASS LIMITS (THOUSANDS OF DOLLARS)	PERCENTAGE
Under 5	3.7%	25 up to 35	15.0
5 up to 10	5.8	35 up to 50	19.2
10 up to 15	7.3	50 up to 75	19.6
15 up to 25	15.5	75 and over	13.9

SOURCE: *Statistical Abstract of the United States: 1994.*

Shapes of Histograms

We often wish to describe the shape of histograms. We usually do so on the basis of the following four characteristics.

Symmetry

A histogram is said to be **symmetric** if, when we draw a line down the center of the histogram, the two sides have identical shapes. Figure 2.4 depicts three symmetric histograms.

Figure 2.4

Symmetric Histograms

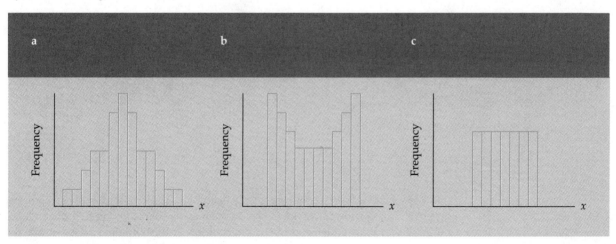

Skewness

A skewed histogram is one that features a long tail extending either to the right or to the left. The former is called **positively skewed**, and the latter is called **negatively skewed**. Figure 2.5 depicts examples of both. Incomes of individuals working for large companies are usually positively skewed, since there is a large number of relatively low-paid workers and a small number of well-paid executives. The time taken by students to write exams is frequently negatively skewed; few students turn in their papers early, preferring to wait until the formal end of the test period.

Number of Modal Classes

We will provide a definition of the mode in Chapter 4. However, we can explain here that a **modal class** is the one with the largest number of observations. Thus, a **unimodal** histogram is one with a single peak. The histograms in Figure 2.4 are unimodal. A **bimodal** histogram is one with two peaks, not necessarily equal in

Figure 2.5

Skewed Histograms

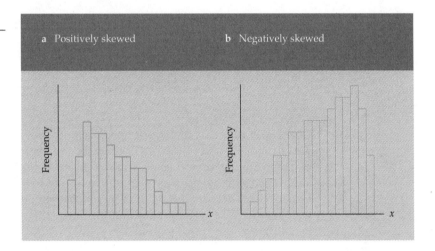

height. The histogram produced with eight classes in Figure 2.1 is bimodal. The final marks in the authors' statistics courses often appear to be bimodal. Figure 2.6 depicts one such histogram. We leave it to you to interpret the implications of this information. A **multimodal** histogram is one with two or more peaks.

Figure 2.6

Bimodal Histogram

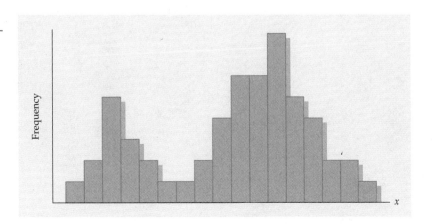

Bell-Shaped

You will discover later in this book the importance of the normal distribution, which appears bell-shaped when drawn. Figure 2.7 illustrates a bell-shaped histogram. Many statistical techniques require that the population be bell-shaped, and we often draw the histogram to check that this requirement is satisfied.

Figure 2.7

Bell-Shaped Histogram

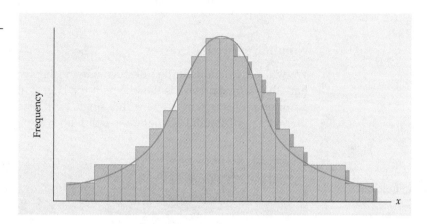

Ogives

Given a set of observations that have been grouped into classes, we've seen that the relative frequency distribution identifies the proportion of observations falling into each class. In some instances, however, our needs are better served by a cumulative relative frequency distribution. The **cumulative relative frequency** of a particular class is the proportion of observations that are less than the upper limit of that class. Table 2.6 displays the cumulative relative frequency distribution of the long-distance bills in Example 2.1.

Table 2.6	Cumulative Relative Frequencies for Example 2.1		
CLASSES	FREQUENCY	CUMULATIVE FREQUENCY	CUMULATIVE RELATIVE FREQUENCY
0 up to 15	71	71	71/200 = .355
15 up to 30	37	108	108/200 = .540
30 up to 45	13	121	121/200 = .605
45 up to 60	9	130	130/200 = .650
60 up to 75	10	140	140/200 = .700
75 up to 90	18	158	158/200 = .790
90 up to 105	28	186	186/200 = .930
105 up to 120	14	200	200/200 = 1.000

From the cumulative relative frequency distribution, we can state, for example, that 54% of the bills were less than $30 and 70% were less than $75. Another way of presenting this information is the **ogive**, which is a graphical representation of the cumulative relative frequency distribution (see Figure 2.8).

The cumulative relative frequency of each class is plotted above the *upper limit* of the corresponding class, and the points representing the cumulative relative frequencies are then joined by straight lines. The ogive is closed at the lower end by extending a straight line to the lower limit of the first class. Once an ogive like the one shown in Figure 2.8 has been constructed, the approximate proportion of observations that are less than any given value on the horizontal axis can be read from the graph. Thus, for example, we can estimate from Figure 2.8 that the proportion of long-distance bills that are less than $25 is approximately 48%. The proportion of bills less than $50 is about 62%.

Figure 2.8

Ogive for Telephone Bills

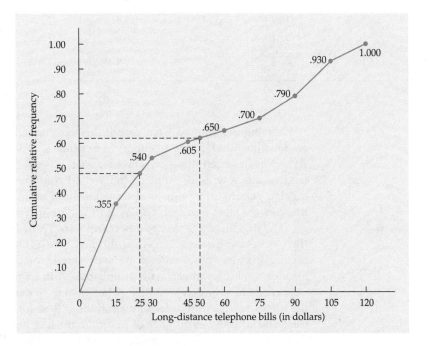

Excel can be used to produce a cumulative frequency distribution and ogive as follows. Proceed through the first seven steps in constructing a histogram (see page 29). Then use the cursor to click **Cumulative Percentage**, **Chart Output**, and **OK**. Minitab does not produce an ogive.

Stem and Leaf Displays

A statistician named John Tukey introduced a method of organizing interval-scaled data called the **stem and leaf display**. This display, which may be viewed as an alternative to the histogram, is most useful in preliminary analysis. In particular, it provides a useful first step in constructing a frequency distribution and histogram. The stem and leaf display is quite similar to the histogram. The main difference is that a stem and leaf display shows the values of the original observations, whereas the histogram "loses" them by classifying the observations. To illustrate, suppose that we had collected the 30 observations listed in Table 2.7 (and stored in file TAB02-07).

The first step in developing the display is to split each observation into two parts: a stem and a leaf. There are usually several alternatives. For example, the number 19.1 can be split so that its stem is 19 and its leaf is 1. Thus, using this definition, the **stem** consists of the digits to the left of the decimal and the **leaf** is the digit to the right of the decimal.

Table 2.7		Sample of 30 Observations					
19.1	19.8	18.0	19.2	19.5	17.3	20.0	20.3
19.6	18.5	18.1	19.7	18.4	17.6	21.2	20.6
22.2	19.1	21.1	19.3	20.8	21.2	21.0	18.7
19.9	18.7	22.1	17.2	18.4	21.4		

Having determined what constitutes the stem and the leaf of an observation, we next list the stems in a column from smallest to largest, as shown in Table 2.8. After this has been done, we consider each observation in turn and place its leaf in the same row as its stem, in the second column. The resulting stem and leaf display presents the original observations in a more organized fashion. Table 2.8 presents the stem and leaf display for the data in Table 2.7.

The first line in Table 2.8, describing stem 17, has three leaves: 6, 2, and 3. The three observations represented in the first row are therefore 17.6, 17.2, and 17.3. Similarly, seven observations are represented in the second row. Whether to arrange the leaves in each row from smallest to largest or to keep them in order of occurrence is largely a matter of personal preference. The advantage of having the leaves arranged in order of magnitude is that, for example, you can then more easily determine the number of observations less than 19.5. The disadvantage is that it's more troublesome to do the arranging. Minitab constructs stem and leaf displays with the leaves in order. Excel does not produce stem and leaf displays. Minitab's stem and leaf display is shown on page 37.

Table 2.8		Stem and Leaf Display for Data in Table 2.7		
	STEM	LEAF	STEM	LEAF
	17	623	20	038
	18	4705147	21	12204
	19	1983627571	22	12

From the stem and leaf display in Table 2.8, we can quickly determine that the observations range from 17.2 to 22.2, that most observations fall between 18.0

and 20.0, and that the shape of the distribution is not symmetrical. A stem and leaf display is similar to a histogram turned on its side, but the display has the advantage of retaining the original observations. Moreover, because the stems are listed in order of size, the middle observation(s) can be determined fairly easily. In this example, the two middle observations are 19.5 and 19.6; splitting the difference, we can assert that half the observations are below 19.5 and half are above it. On the other hand, a histogram can readily accommodate a large number of observations, can display relative frequencies, and can be adapted more easily to changes in the classes used.

USING THE COMPUTER

Minitab Stem and Leaf Display for Table 2.7

```
Stem-and-leaf of C1        N  = 30
Leaf Unit = 0.10

     3    17 236
    10    18 0144577
   (10)   19 1123567789
    10    20 038
     7    21 01224
     2    22 12
```

The numbers in the left column are called *depths*. Each depth counts the number of observations that are on its line or beyond. For example, the fifth depth, 7, reports that there are seven observations that are greater than or equal to 21, which is the lower limit of the fifth class. The sixth depth, 2, tells us that there are two observations that are greater than or equal to 22. Notice that the third depth, 10, is in parentheses. The parentheses indicate that the third class contains the observation that falls in the middle of the data, a statistic we call the *median* (which is discussed in Chapter 4). Its depth provides only the number of observations in that class. For classes below the median, the depth reports the number of observations that are less than the upper limit of that class. For example, there are 10 observations whose stems are 18 or less.

The appropriate definitions of the stem and the leaf depend, in part, on the range of the observations. Suppose that the observations in Table 2.7 had ranged from 17.2 to 55.5. In such a case, it would be reasonable to define the stem as the first digit and the leaf as the remaining two digits. The number 19.1 would then have a stem 1 and leaf 9.1, and there would be five stems in all: 1, 2, 3, 4, and 5. Because each leaf would consist of more than a single digit, the leaves in any row should be separated by commas for clarity.

MENU COMMANDS	COMMANDS FOR TABLE 2.7
1 Type or import the data into one column.	Open file **TAB02-07**.
2 Click **Graph**, **Character Graphs**, and **Stem-and-Leaf . . ..**	
3 Type the variable name.	**Observe** or **C1**

The output below shows Minitab's stem and leaf display for the data in Example 2.1.

Minitab Stem and Leaf Display for Example 2.1

Character Stem-and-Leaf Display

```
Stem-and-leaf of Bills    N = 200
Leaf Unit = 1.0

   52    0 0000000001111122222233333455555566666667788889999999
   85    1 000001111233333334455555667889999
  (23)   2 00001111123446667789999
   92    3 001335589
   83    4 12445589
   75    5 33566
   70    6 3458
   66    7 022224556789
   54    8 334457889999
   42    9 0011222233344555999
   22   10 001344446699
   10   11 0124557889
```

The stem here is the "tens" digit, and the leaf is the "ones" digit. Hence, the first row represents bills that are less than $10. The second row represents bills that are between $10 and $19.99. The last row represents the bill that is $119.63. The stem is 11, and the leaf is 9. Notice that in this display we do not show the part that is to the right of the decimal point (which is the cents part of the bill).

As you can see, the information we get from the stem and leaf display is similar to that obtained from the histogram.

Dot Plots

A dot plot is a graph that is similar to a histogram. One difference is that the horizontal axis is divided into more classes. In fact, ideally each observation would have its own position on the axis. The second difference is that the observations are represented by dots. Minitab's dot plot of the data in Example 2.1 is shown below. (Excel does not draw a dot plot.)

Minitab Dot Plot for Example 2.1

Character Dotplot

```
   : .:
   : :: .
  :: :: . :
  :::::::: :     .
  :::::::: :. .:                          .:
  :::::::::::: ::.    :  :      :.    ..:::  :  : :  .
  ::::::::::::::::::..::...:  .:..:::::::::: :::::.:::
  +---------+---------+---------+---------+---------+---------+--------Bills
  0        25        50        75       100       125
```

Notice that each $25 interval has 10 spaces on the *x*-axis. As a result, each space represents an interval that is $2.50 wide. The point representing 25 actually counts the number of bills between $25 - 1.25$ (= 23.75) and $25 + 1.25$ (= 26.25). Counting the dots at 25, we see that there were two bills that fell between $23.75 and $26.25. (See page 83 in Appendix 2.A for instructions.)

MENU COMMANDS	COMMANDS FOR EXAMPLE 2.1
1 Type or import the data into a column.	Open file **XM02-01**.
2 Click **Graph**, **Character Graphs**, and **Dotplot . . .**.	
3 Type the variable name. Click **OK**.	**Bills** or **C1**

You can see that the dot plot, histogram, and stem and leaf display all yield very similar information. The choice of which to use is mostly a matter of personal preference. Generally, dot plots and stem and leaf displays are used with smaller data sets, and histograms are used for larger ones.

Box Plots

Box plots are yet another method of graphing quantitative data. However, we will have to present this useful technique in Chapter 4, after we've discussed various statistics that are represented on the box plot.

We'll now summarize the techniques presented in this section with another example.

EXAMPLE 2.2

In 1994 and 1995, the Barnes Exhibit toured major cities all over the world, with millions of people flocking to see it. Dr. Albert Barnes was a wealthy art collector who accumulated a large number of impressionist masterpieces; the total exceeds 800 paintings. When Dr. Barnes died in 1951, he willed that his collection not be allowed to tour. However, because of the deterioration of the exhibit's home near Philadelphia, a judge ruled that the collection could go on tour to raise enough money to renovate the building. Because of the size and value of the collection, it was predicted (correctly) that in each city a large number of people would come to view the paintings. Because space was limited, most galleries had to sell tickets that were valid at only one time (much like a play). In this way, they were able to control the number of visitors at any one time. To judge how many people to let in at any time, it was necessary to know the length of time people would spend at the exhibit; longer times would dictate smaller audiences, shorter times would allow for sale of more tickets. Suppose that in one city the amount of time (rounded to the nearest minute) taken to view the complete exhibit (which consisted of only 83 paintings) by each of 400 people was measured and recorded in file XM02-02. Draw the histogram, stem and leaf display, and dot plot of these data, and interpret the results.

SOLUTION

USING THE COMPUTER

We begin by producing the stem and leaf display.

Minitab Stem and Leaf Display for Example 2.2

```
Character Stem-and-Leaf Display


Stem-and-leaf of Time      N  = 400
Leaf Unit = 1.0


    24     2  3456777788888888889999999
    98     3  000000011111122222222233333333333344444455555555566666677788888888+
  (115)    4  00000000000111111111111111122222222222222233333333333344444444444444+
   187     5  00000000011111222222233333333444444444444455555666777777777888888899+
   120     6  000000011111222222223333333333444444444555666667778889
    69     7  0000000000011111223344457888899
    38     8  01222345558889
    24     9  000111234888
    12    10  246779
     6    11  23
     4    12  15
     2    13  4
     1    14
     1    15  1
```

The stems are the "tens" digit and the leaves are the "ones." Notice that the number of leaves for stems 3, 4, and 5 have been truncated; there are too many leaves for Minitab to handle.

We draw the histogram using the stem and leaf display as our guide. We note that the smallest time was 23 minutes (stem 2 and leaf 3 on the first line), the largest time was 151 minutes, and there were 400 observations. We decided (for comparison purposes) to produce two different histograms, each having about 12 class intervals, using class widths of 10 for Minitab and 15 for Excel.

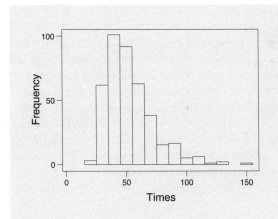

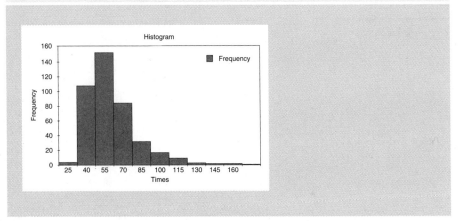

Finally, we drew the dot plot letting Minitab choose its own format.

Minitab Dot Plot for
Example 2.2

Character Dotplot

```
Each dot represents 2 points
             : :
             : :
             :.:
        .   :::  .
       ::: ::::: :        .
      .::: :::::::.:: :
    . ::::::::::::::::: :
      :::::::::::::::::.:   .      :
     .::::::::::::::::::::::::::.:  .....   . .   .       .
   ---+---------+---------+---------+---------+---------+---------+---Time
      25        50        75       100       125       150
```

INTERPRETING
THE RESULTS

All three graphical procedures tell us that the times are quite variable and the distribution is positively skewed. It appears that most visitors to the exhibit will leave within one hour, but there are many who will take an additional 30 minutes. Very few visitors stay longer than one and one-half hours. If we were to admit 400 people per hour, within a short time there would be far more people than the gallery could accommodate. Perhaps the admission of between 150 and 200 every 45 minutes would be a satisfactory plan.

Sample or Population?

Before proceeding, we should note that the descriptive methods in this chapter apply equally well to samples and to populations of data. If, for some reason, you are interested only in the long-distance telephone bills of 200 specific customers for some particular month, then the 200 observations in Table 2.1 can be considered a population, and your task simply is to summarize those 200 bills. On the other hand, if your primary interest is to obtain information concerning the distribution of the population of first-month long-distance bills of all new subscribers, the 200 bills represented in Table 2.1 may be treated as a sample, and you will want to make sure that the sample has been properly selected so that it can be used as a basis for statistical inference about the population.

Exercises

2.7　The number of items rejected daily by a manufacturer because of defects was recorded for the last 25 days. The results are as follows:

```
21   8  17  22  19  18  19  14  17  11   6  21  25
19   9  12  16  16  10  29  24   6  21  20  25
```

a　Construct a frequency distribution for these data. Use five class intervals, with the lower boundary of the first class being five items.

b　Construct a relative frequency histogram for these data.

c　What is the relationship between the areas under the histogram you have constructed and the relative frequencies of observations?

2.8　The grades on a statistics exam are as follows:

```
75  66  77  66  64  73  91  65  59  86  61  86  61  58  70
77  80  58  94  78  62  79  83  54  52  45  82  48  67  55
```

a　Construct a stem and leaf display for these data.

b　Construct a dot plot.

c　Construct a frequency distribution for these data, using six class intervals.

d　Construct a relative frequency histogram for these data.

e　Briefly describe what the histogram and the stem and leaf display tell you about the data.

f　Construct a cumulative relative frequency distribution for the grades.

g　What proportion of the grades is less than 70? Greater than 70?

2.9　A large investment firm on Wall Street wants to review the distribution of the ages of its stockbrokers. The firm feels that this information will be useful in developing plans relating to recruitment and retirement options. The ages of a sample of 25 brokers are as follows:

```
50  64  32  55  41  44  24  46  58  47  36  52  54
44  66  47  59  51  61  57  49  28  42  38  45
```

a　Construct a stem and leaf display for the ages.

b　Construct a frequency distribution for the data, using five class intervals and the value 20 as the lower limit of the first class.

c　Construct a relative frequency histogram for the data, using five class intervals and the value 20 as the lower limit of the first class.

d　Construct an ogive for the data.

e　What proportion of the total area under the histogram constructed in part (c) falls between 20 and 40?

2.10 The number of weekly sales calls by a sample of 25 salespersons for a dress manufacturer is shown below. Manually draw each of the following graphs.

    a   a histogram with five classes

    b   a histogram with 10 classes

    c   a stem and leaf display

    d   a dot plot

    e   an ogive

       24 56 43 35 37 27 29 44 34 28 33 28 46 31 38 41 48 38 27
       29 37 33 31 40 50

2.11 The amount of time (in seconds) needed for assembly-line workers to complete a weld was recorded for 40 workers. Manually draw the following graphs.

    a   a histogram with six classes

    b   a histogram with 12 classes

    c   a stem and leaf display

    d   a dot plot

    e   an ogive

       69 60 75 74 68 66 73 76 63 67 69 73 65 61 73 72 72 65 69 70
       64 61 74 76 72 74 65 63 69 73 75 70 60 62 68 74 71 73 68 67

The following exercises require the use of a computer and statistical software.

2.12 The annual income in thousands of dollars for a sample of 200 first-year accountants was recorded and stored in file XR02-12. Use a computer and software to perform the following techniques.

    a   stem and leaf display (if your software allows it)

    b   histogram

    c   dot plot

2.13 Construct an ogive for the data in Exercise 2.12. Estimate the proportion of accountants who earn

    a   less than $20,000

    b   more than $35,000

    c   between $25,000 and $40,000

2.14 Use any or all of the graphs drawn in Exercise 2.12 to describe the shape of the distribution of first-year incomes of accountants. Discuss what you have learned.

2.15 The final marks on a mathematics exam are stored in file XR02-15.

    a   Construct a stem and leaf display (if your software allows it).

    b   Construct a histogram.

    c   Briefly describe what the histogram and stem and leaf display tell you about the data.

2.16 Construct a cumulative relative frequency distribution, and draw the ogive for the marks in Exercise 2.15.

    a   Estimate the proportion of grades that are less than 70.

    b   Estimate the proportion of grades that are less than 75.

2.17 The real-estate board in a wealthy suburb wants to investigate the distribution of prices of homes sold during the past year. The prices are stored in file XR02-17.

    a   Construct a histogram (and a stem and leaf display if your software allows it).

    b   What does the histogram (and stem and leaf display) tell you about the prices?

2.18 Refer to Exercise 2.17.

    a Construct an ogive for the house prices.

    b Estimate the proportion of prices that are less than $350,000.

    c Estimate the proportion of prices that are less than $325,000.

2.19 The president of a local consumer advocacy group is concerned about reports that similar generic drugs are being sold at widely differing prices at local drug stores. A survey of 100 stores produced the selling price of one popular generic drug. These data are stored in file XR02-19.

    a Construct a histogram.

    b What does the histogram tell you about the price?

2.20 The number of customers entering a bank during each hour of operation (10:00 A.M. to 3:00 P.M.) for each of the last 100 days was recorded and stored in file XR02-20 in the following way.

Column 1: number of arrivals between 10:00 A.M. and 11:00 A.M.

Column 2: number of arrivals between 11:00 A.M. and 12:00 P.M.

Column 3: number of arrivals between 12:00 P.M. and 1:00 P.M.

Column 4: number of arrivals between 1:00 P.M. and 2:00 P.M.

Column 5: number of arrivals between 2:00 P.M. and 3:00 P.M.

    a Use whatever graphical techniques you think necessary to describe each set (column) of data.

    b Describe the shape of each time period's number of arrivals.

    c Discuss similarities and differences between time periods.

    d What are the implications of your findings?

2.4 Scatter Diagrams

Statisticians frequently need to determine how two *quantitative* variables are related to one another. For example, economists are interested in the relationship between inflation rates and unemployment rates. Financial analysts need to understand how the returns of individual stocks are related to the behavior of the entire stock market. Company executives often try to determine the effect of a price increase on the demand for their firm's products. The graphical technique used to depict relationships is the **scatter diagram**.

To draw a scatter diagram we need a set of data for two variables. We'll label one variable x and the other y. Each pair of values of x and y constitutes a point on the graph. To illustrate, consider the following example.

EXAMPLE 2.3

A small business owner has experienced fairly uniform sales levels from month to month in previous years. This year, he decided to vary his advertising expenditures from month to month to see if that would have a significant impact on the sales level. To help assess the effect of advertising on sales level, he collected the data shown in the accompanying table. Construct a scatter diagram for these data, and describe the relationship between advertising expenditure and sales level.

MONTH	ADVERTISING EXPENDITURE x (1,000S OF DOLLARS)	SALES LEVEL y (1,000S OF DOLLARS)
1	1	30
2	3	40
3	5	40
4	4	50
5	2	35
6	5	50
7	3	35
8	2	25

SOLUTION

In some cases we may feel that the value of one variable depends (to some degree) on the value of the other variable. When that is the case, the first variable is called the **dependent variable** and is plotted on the vertical axis. (Much more will be said about this in Chapter 16.) If we are concerned only with the relationship between two variables, and not whether the values of one depend on the values of the other, then the choice of variable to be plotted on the vertical axis is arbitrary. In this example, the monthly sales level is the dependent variable, labeled y.

The eight pairs of values for advertising expenditure (x) and monthly sales level (y) are plotted in Figure 2.9. The pattern of the resulting scatter diagram provides us with two pieces of information about the relationship between these two variables. We first observe that, generally speaking, sales level (y) tends to increase as advertising expenditure (x) increases. Whenever two variables such as these move together—that is, their values tend to increase together and decrease together—we say that there is a **positive relationship** between the two variables. The second observation is that the relationship between sales level and advertising expenditure appears to be *linear*. Although the eight points don't all lie on a straight line, we can imagine drawing a straight line through the scatter diagram that approximates the positive relationship between the two variables. Finding the straight line that "best fits" the scatter diagram will be addressed in Chapter 16.

Figure 2.9

Scatter Diagram for Example 2.3

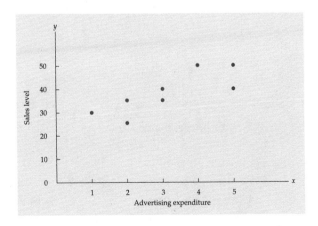

The pattern of the scatter diagram provides us with information about the relationship between the two variables. Figure 2.9 depicts a relationship that is called **linear**. A **linear relationship** is one that can be graphed with a straight line. If the two variables generally move in unison—they both increase or both decrease together—we say that there is a *positive* linear relationship. If they move in opposite directions, and the scatter diagram is a straight line, we say that there is a *negative* linear relationship (see Figure 2.10). We can have **nonlinear relationships** (see Figures 2.11 and 2.12), as well as cases where the two variables are unrelated (see Figure 2.13). We will have more to say about this subject in Section 4.5 and Chapters 16 and 17.

Figure 2.10	**Figure 2.11**	**Figure 2.12**	**Figure 2.13**
Negative Linear Relationship	**Nonlinear Relationship**	**Nonlinear Relationship**	**No Relationship**

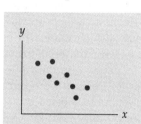 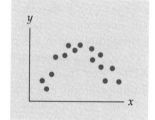 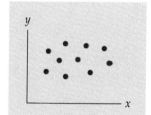

USING THE COMPUTER

Minitab Output for Example 2.3

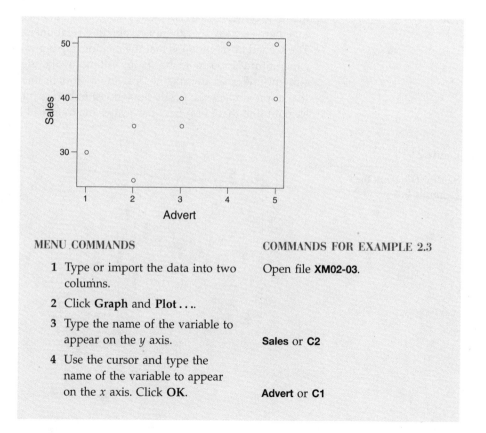

MENU COMMANDS	COMMANDS FOR EXAMPLE 2.3
1 Type or import the data into two columns.	Open file **XM02-03**.
2 Click **Graph** and **Plot**	
3 Type the name of the variable to appear on the *y* axis.	**Sales** or **C2**
4 Use the cursor and type the name of the variable to appear on the *x* axis. Click **OK**.	**Advert** or **C1**

Excel Output for Example 2.3

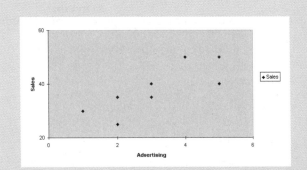

EXCEL 97

Excel 97 Users:
Step 1 is valid.
Step 2. Click the Chart Wizard icon, select **XY (Scatter)** from **Chart type,** click on the first **Chart sub-type,** and click **Next>.**
Step 3. Click **Data Range** (if necessary), and type the block coordinates in the **Data range** box. Click **Next>.**
Step 4. If you wish, you can click **Titles** (if necessary) and fill in the boxes. For Example 2.3, type **Example 2.3** in the **Chart title** box, **Advertising** in the **Value (X) Axis** box, and **Sales** in the **Value (Y) Axis** box.
Step 5. To eliminate the horizontal lines that will automatically appear on the scatter diagram, click **Gridlines** and remove the check mark. Click **Finish.**
Step 6. To change the scale, double-click the Y-axis, click **Scale,** remove the check mark under **Auto,** and change the **Minimum, Maximum,** and/or **Major** and **Minor Units.** Click **OK.** Repeat for the X-axis.
Step 7. To draw a straight line through the points, click **Chart** and **Add Trendline.** Specify **Linear** and click **OK.**

COMMANDS

1 Type or import the data into two adjacent columns. The variable to appear on the vertical axis must be in the second column.

2 Click the **ChartWizard**, move the cursor to anywhere in the spreadsheet that you wish the graph to appear, and click.

3 Type the block coordinates of the data (including cells containing the variable names) and click **Next>.**

4 Click **XY(Scatter).** Click **Next>.**

5 Select a format for the scatter diagram; click **1.**

6 To label the axes, click **Next>** and **Next>** again. Type axis titles. Click **Finish.**

COMMANDS FOR EXAMPLE 2.3

Open file **XM02-03.**

A1:B9

Category (X): **Advertising**
Category (Y): **Sales**

The scatter diagram will be drawn in the designated area. If you wish to change the scale proceed as follows.

7 Activate the chart by double-clicking anywhere within the boundaries of the box.

8 Double-click the Y-axis, click **Scale** (if necessary) and change the **Minimum, Maximum,** and/or **Major** and **Minor** Units. Click **OK.**

9 Repeat for the X-axis.

Exercises

2.21 A real estate board has collected data to help determine how the number of house sales in its region is related to interest rate levels. The numbers of houses sold in the region and the average monthly mortgage rates for 12 randomly selected months are shown in the following table.

a Draw a scatter diagram for these data with the number of houses sold on the vertical axis.

b Describe the relationship between mortgage rate and number of homes sold.

MORTGAGE RATE (%)	NUMBER OF HOUSES SOLD	MORTGAGE RATE (%)	NUMBER OF HOUSES SOLD
8.0	188	10.5	140
9.5	145	7.0	203
7.5	181	7.5	188
11.0	137	11.0	144
8.5	157	9.0	150
10.0	148	8.0	166

2.22 A firm's operating costs can be classified as fixed, variable, or mixed. Costs for items such as telephone, electrical power, and maintenance are often *mixed costs,* meaning they have both a fixed cost and a variable cost component. A manufacturing firm has recorded its electrical power costs and the total number of hours of machine time for each of 12 months in the following table.

a Draw a scatter diagram for these data with the cost of electrical power on the vertical axis.

b Describe the relationship between electrical power cost and hours of machine usage.

c Draw a straight line that approximates reasonably well the relationship between power cost and machine usage.

d Use the line drawn in part (c) to estimate the monthly fixed cost of power and the variable cost of power per thousand hours of machine time.

MACHINE TIME (THOUSANDS OF HOURS)	COST OF POWER (DOLLARS)	MACHINE TIME (THOUSANDS OF HOURS)	COST OF POWER (DOLLARS)
6	760	5	700
9	1,000	7	910
8	890	6	745
7	880	9	950
10	1,070	8	870
10	1,030	11	1,040

2.23 Because inflation reduces the purchasing power of the dollar, investors seek investments that will provide protection against inflation; that is, investments that will provide higher returns when inflation is higher. It is frequently stated that common stocks provide just such a hedge against inflation. The annual percentage rates of return on common stock* and the annual inflation rates (as measured by percentage changes in the Consumer Price Index) from 1985 through 1994 are shown in the accompanying table. (The data are also stored in file XR02-23. Column 1 stores the stock returns, and column 2 stores the inflation rates.)

---

*To understand the meaning of these rates of return, consider the 25.07% return that was realized on common stock in 1985. This means that $100 invested in common stocks at the beginning of 1985 would have yielded a profit (capital gain plus dividend) of $25.07 over the year.

YEAR	COMMON STOCK RETURN (%)	INFLATION RATE (%)
1985	25.07	4.38
1986	8.95	4.19
1987	5.88	4.12
1988	11.08	3.96
1989	21.37	5.17
1990	−14.80	5.00
1991	12.02	3.78
1992	− 1.43	2.14
1993	32.55	1.70
1994	− .18	.23

SOURCE: *Report on Canadian Economic Statistics: 1924–1994* (Canadian Institute of Actuaries, 1995)

a Construct a scatter diagram for these data with the stock returns on the vertical axis.

b Describe the relationship between common stock returns and inflation rates over the period 1985 through 1994.

c Does it appear that common stocks provide a good hedge against inflation?

The next two exercises require the use of a computer and statistical software.

2.24 Refer to Exercise 2.23. The annual percentage rates of return on common stock and the annual inflation rates (as measured by percentage changes in the Consumer Price Index) from 1960 through 1994 are stored in file XR02-24. (Column 1 stores the stock returns, and column 2 stores the inflation rates.)

a Construct a scatter diagram for these data with the stock returns on the vertical axis.

b Describe the relationship between common stock returns and inflation rates over the period 1960 through 1994. How does your answer compare with part (b) of Exercise 2.23?

c Does it appear that common stocks provide a good hedge against inflation?

2.25 Investment managers are often interested in the relationship between the monthly rate of return on an individual stock (R) and the monthly rate of return on the overall stock market (R_m). For practical purposes, R_m is taken to be the monthly rate of return on some major stock market index, such as the Dow Jones Industrial Average or the Toronto Stock Exchange 300 Index. The monthly rates of return on American Barrick Resources (North America's largest gold producer) and on the overall stock market (as measured by the TSE 300 Index) over a five-year period are stored in file XR02-25. (Column 1 stores the monthly percentage return on American Barrick Resources, and column 2 stores the monthly percentage return on the TSE 300 Index.)

a Construct a scatter diagram for these data with the returns for American Barrick Resources on the vertical axis.

b Describe the relationship between the returns on the individual stock and the returns on the overall stock market.

2.5 Pie Charts, Bar Charts, and Line Charts

Several types of commonly used graphical presentations are available besides those introduced in Sections 2.3 and 2.4. The graphical presentations considered in this section are used primarily for *qualitative data*. The increasing availability of desktop computers with color graphics enables managers quickly to summon a bar chart showing sales in various regions, a pie chart displaying major causes of accidents within their firm, or a line chart depicting the trend in productivity over time. Although types of graphical presentations are numerous, only a few of the more popular ones will be discussed here.

If the raw data to be summarized are quantitative and come from a single population, as was the case with the Barnes Exhibit data in Example 2.2, the descriptive methods presented in Section 2.3 (frequency distributions, histograms, stem and leaf displays, and dot plots) are useful and appropriate. These methods basically group the raw data into categories, which we call *classes*, and record the number of measurements that fall into each category. The categories are defined in a rather arbitrary manner, with the objective of conveying some idea of how the data are distributed. We now consider a situation in which the raw data can be naturally categorized in a more meaningful and less arbitrary manner.

Pie Charts

As we pointed out in Section 2.2, when the data are qualitative, all that statisticians can do to summarize samples and populations is count the number of times and compute the proportion of times each value occurs. The most popular graphical method for nominal data is the pie chart. To illustrate its application, consider the following example.

EXAMPLE 2.4

The student placement office at a university conducted a survey of last year's business school graduates to determine the general areas in which the graduates found jobs. The placement office intended to use the data to help decide where to concentrate its efforts in attracting companies to campus to conduct job interviews. Each graduate was asked in which area he or she found a job. The areas of employment are Accounting (1), Finance (2), General Management (3), Marketing (4), and Other (5). The data are stored in file XM02-04 using the codes 1, 2, 3, 4, and 5. Create a pie chart of the data to summarize the data.

SOLUTION

The data are qualitative because the "values" of the variable, area of employment, are the five categories. The numbers (1, 2, 3, 4, and 5) used to record the data in the file were assigned completely arbitrarily. The only legitimate statistical technique is to count the number of occurrences of each value and then to convert these counts into proportions. The results are shown on the next page.

AREA	NUMBER OF GRADUATES	PROPORTION OF GRADUATES
Accounting	73	28.9%
Finance	52	20.6
General Management	36	14.2
Marketing	64	25.3
Other	28	11.1
Total	253	100

The graphical technique we choose to use, the pie chart, exhibits the proportion of each area. A **pie chart** is simply a circle subdivided into a number of slices that represent the various categories. It should be drawn so that the size of each slice is proportional to the percentage corresponding to that category. Because the entire circle corresponds to 360°, every 1% of the observations should correspond to $.01 \times 360 = 3.6°$. The angle between the lines demarcating the Accounting sector is therefore $28.9 \times 3.6 = 104°$. The angles of the pie chart for the other four categories are calculated similarly. They are as follows.

Finance	$20.6 \times 3.6 = 74.2°$
General Management	$14.2 \times 3.6 = 51.1°$
Marketing	$25.3 \times 3.6 = 91.1°$
Other	$11.1 \times 3.6 = 40.0°$

Figure 2.14 was drawn using these angles.

Figure 2.14

Pie Chart of Employment Areas

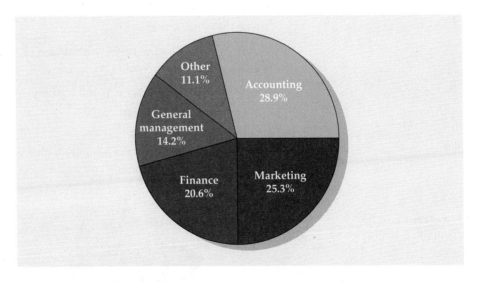

Now that you know how to construct a pie chart by hand, let's see how we actually draw such diagrams in practice.

**Minitab Pie Chart for
Example 2.4**

Pie Chart of Area

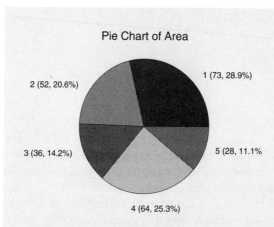

Minitab draws the first category starting at 3:00 and continues counterclock-wise. Each pie segment is denoted by its code (1, 2, 3, 4, or 5), its frequency, and its relative frequency. (See page 83 in Appendix 2.A for instructions.)

MENU COMMANDS

COMMANDS FOR EXAMPLE 2.4

1 If we have the raw data (as the data are in file **XM02-04**), type or import the observations into one column.

Open file **XM02-04**.

2 Click **Graph** and **Pie Chart . . .**.

3 Click **Chart data in:**, hit **tab**, and type the variable name.

Area or **C1**

If we already know the frequency with which each value occurs, the results should be recorded in two columns.

1 Store the codes in one column and the frequencies in a second column.

2 Click **Graph** and **Pie Chart . . .**

3 Click **Chart table**.

4 Use the cursor and type the column number where the categories are stored (**Categories in:**) and where the frequencies are stored (**Frequencies in:**). Click **OK**.

**Excel Pie Chart for
Example 2.4**

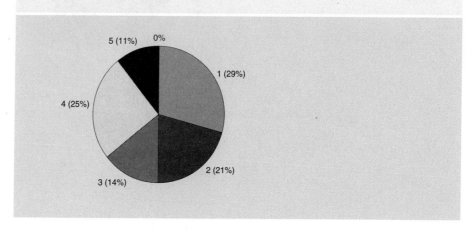

Each pie segment is denoted by its code (1, 2, 3, 4, or 5) and its relative frequency. Note that the 0% refers to the relative frequency of categories not specifically listed. Because we show all the categories, this number is zero.

EXCEL 97

Excel 97 Users:
Step 1 is valid.
Step 2. Click once inside the boundaries of the histogram. Then click **Chart, Chart type . . . , Pie** and your choice of **Chart subtype** (the first one shown is recommended). Click **OK.**
Step 3. If you wish to add a title, click **Chart** and **Chart Options . . . .** Click **Titles** and fill in the **Chart title** box. Click **Finish.**

EXCEL 97

Excel 97 Users:
Step 1 is valid.

Step 2. Click the Chart Wizard icon, **Pie,** and **Next>.** Type the block coordinates of the data and click **Next>.**
Step 3. If you wish to add a title, click **Titles** and fill in the **Chart title** box. Click **Finish.**

COMMANDS	COMMANDS FOR EXAMPLE 2.4
1 If you have access only to the raw data, (e.g., as the data are in file XM02-04), proceed through the first ten steps in constructing a histogram (see page 28.) (Use the codes representing the categories as the upper limits of the histogram intervals.)	Open file **XM02-04.**
	Bin 1 2 3 4 5 (in cells B1 to B6)
2 Click **AutoFormat . . . .**	
3 Use the cursor to choose **Pie** in the **Galleries** list.	**Pie**
4 Use the cursor to choose one of the **Formats.** We recommend number **7.** (You may wish to experiment with different Formats to determine which you prefer.)	

If you already know the number of occurrences of each value, proceed as follows.

1 Type the number of occurrences of each value in a column (column A).	**73 52 36 64 28**
2 Click the **ChartWizard,** move the cursor to anywhere in the spreadsheet that you wish the graph to appear, and click again.	
3 Type the block coordinates of the data and click **Next>.**	**A1:A5**
4 Click **Pie** to select the type of chart. Click **Next>.**	
5 Select a format for the chart. We recommend number 7. Click **Finish.**	

Other Applications of Pie Charts

Pie charts are effective whenever the objective is to display the components of a whole entity in a manner that indicates their relative sizes. In Example 2.4, we used a pie chart in a study involving qualitative data to present the number of graduates in each area of employment. Pie charts can be used in numerous other applications, often being used to simply present numbers associated with categories. Because of their eye-catching appearance, they are used extensively by newspapers and magazines—especially to show the breakdown of a budget. Similarly, treasurers might use pie charts to show the breakdown of a firm's revenues by department, or business students might use pie charts to show the amount of time devoted to daily activities (e.g., eat: 10%, sleep: 30%, and study statistics: 60%).

Pie charts also can be used to compare two breakdowns. Figure 2.15 shows the sources of revenue for the conglomerate Gulf + Western Industries before and after it sold off a large portion of its operations.

Figure 2.15

Pie Charts of Gulf + Western's Sources of Revenue

SOURCE: *New York Times*, 23 February 1986, p. 8F.

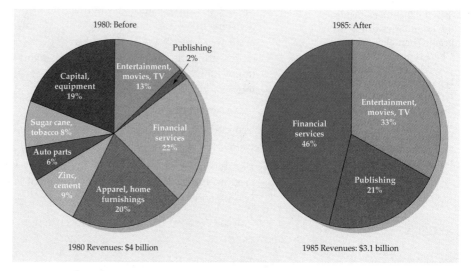

We can represent yet another bit of information by varying the sizes of the pie charts. Gulf + Western's revenues before and after the sale were $4 billion and $3.1 billion, respectively. The pie charts in Figure 2.16 reflect the different levels of revenues. The charts were drawn so that the area in the "after sale" chart was 3.1/4 = 77.5% of the area in the "before sale" chart. (This was accomplished by letting the radius of the "after sale" circle equal .88 (which is $\sqrt{.775}$) of the radius of the "before sale" circle). Pie charts with different radii must be hand-drawn; our computer software programs are not capable of this feat.

Figure 2.16

Pie Chart of Gulf + Western's Sources of Revenue

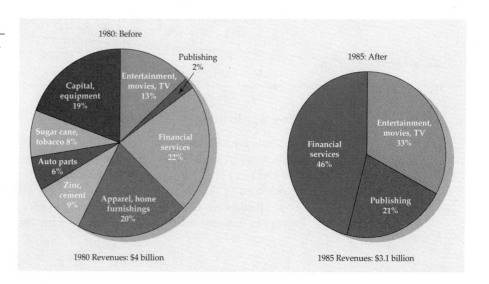

Bar Charts

Bar charts provide an alternative to pie charts. They graphically represent the frequency (or relative frequency) of each category as a bar rising vertically from the horizontal axis; the height of each bar is proportional to the frequency (or relative frequency) of the corresponding category. Because the bars correspond to categories or points, rather than to class intervals (as the rectangles of a histogram do), the widths assigned to the bars are arbitrary, although all must be equal. (The distorted impression that can be created by using unequal bar widths will be addressed in Chapter 3.) To improve clarity, a space is usually left between bars. Minitab and Excel were used to produce the bar chart for the employment data in Example 2.4.

Minitab Bar Chart for Example 2.4

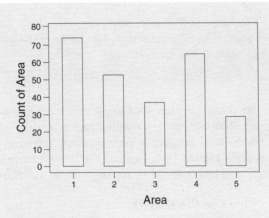

MENU COMMANDS

1 If you hve the raw data, type or import the data into a column.

2 Click **Graph** and **Chart . . ..**

3 Using the cursor specify **Function** and **Count**.

4 Use the cursor and type **C1** under Y and **C1** under X.

5 Using the cursor specify **Display** and **Bar**.

6 Click **OK**.

If we already know the frequency with which each value occurs, the results should be recorded in two columns. Column 1 contains the codes representing the categories, and column 2 contains the frequencies.

1 Click **Graph** and **Chart . . ..**

2 Use the cursor to specify **Function** and **Sum**.

3 Use the cursor and type **C2** under Y and **C1** under X.

4 Using the cursor specify **Display** and **Bar**. Click **OK**.

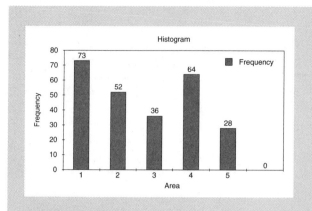

Proceed as you did to create the pie chart (page 53) with the following change. Select **Column** from the **Galleries** list instead of **Pie** to obtain vertical bars. (Select **Bar** for horizontal bars.)

Bar charts are also used to present the frequencies of qualitative data, or categories, that should be presented in a particular order. For example, Figure 2.17 shows the total number of new products introduced in North America in the six years from 1989 to 1994. Because the horizontal axis implies an order (years 1989, 1990, . . . , 1994), bar charts are superior to pie charts for such applications.

Bar Chart or Pie Chart?

Since either a bar chart or a pie chart can be used to represent qualitative data graphically, which representation should be used? The answer depends on what you want to emphasize. For example, consider the data in Table 2.9, which lists the average daily turnover (in U.S. dollars) on four currency exchange markets. The table shows the breakdown for specific currency exchanges. For example, on the London market, a total of $57 billion is traded exchanging U.S. dollars for British pounds and vice versa. If the objective is to exhibit the breakdown for each market, the pie charts in Figure 2.18 are drawn. (Minitab was used to draw the pie charts; Excel's pie charts would be almost identical.) These charts allow the reader to see how the four markets differ with respect to the proportion of the six pairs of currencies traded. Readers can easily see that on the London and New York exchanges, US$/¥, US$/DM, and US$/£ total more than half the trading volume. However, on the Tokyo exchange, US$/¥ dominates as does US$/CDN$ on the Toronto exchange.

Figure 2.17

**Number of New Products
Introduced Annually**

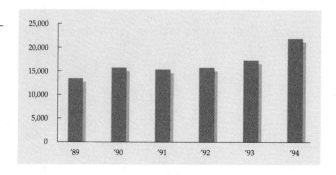

Table 2.9	Volume of Average Daily Trading on Four Currency Markets: 1992 (billions of U.S. dollars)			
CURRENCIES*	LONDON EXCHANGE MARKET	NEW YORK EXCHANGE MARKET	TOKYO EXCHANGE MARKET	TORONTO EXCHANGE MARKET
US$/¥	$39	$44	$84	$1
US$/DM	69	65	18	3
US$/£	57	17	5	1
US$/CDN$	0	6	0	16
US$/Other	69	37	3	2
Other/Other	66	23	16	0
Total	300	192	126	23

*U.S. dollars, DM = German Deutsche Marks, £ = British pounds, CDN$ = Canadian dollars, ¥ = Japanese yen

SOURCES: Bank of England, Federal Reserve Bank of New York, Bank of Japan, Bank of Canada

Figure 2.18

Pie Charts of Currency Markets

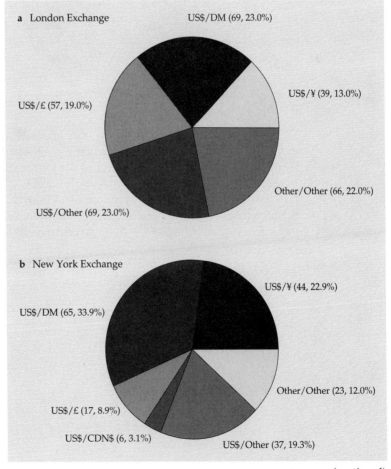

a London Exchange

US$/DM (69, 23.0%)

US$/¥ (39, 13.0%)

US$/£ (57, 19.0%)

Other/Other (66, 22.0%)

US$/Other (69, 23.0%)

b New York Exchange

US$/¥ (44, 22.9%)

US$/DM (65, 33.9%)

Other/Other (23, 12.0%)

US$/£ (17, 8.9%)

US$/CDN$ (6, 3.1%)

US$/Other (37, 19.3%)

(continued)

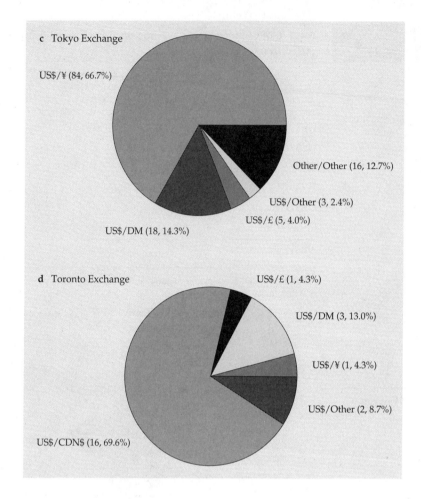

c Tokyo Exchange

US$/¥ (84, 66.7%)

Other/Other (16, 12.7%)

US$/Other (3, 2.4%)

US$/£ (5, 4.0%)

US$/DM (18, 14.3%)

d Toronto Exchange

US$/£ (1, 4.3%)

US$/DM (3, 13.0%)

US$/¥ (1, 4.3%)

US$/Other (2, 8.7%)

US$/CDN$ (16, 69.6%)

If the objective is to compare the absolute dollars traded on the four exchanges, a bar chart would be better. Figure 2.19 allows the reader to see the relative sizes, as well as breakdowns, of the four markets. Readers can easily compare the sizes of the exchange markets, an action that was impossible using the pie charts. (We used the same minimum and maximum values on the vertical axis to make this comparison legitimate.) For example, the total dollar amount of trading is much greater on the London market than on the Toronto market.

Figure 2.19

Bar Charts of Currency Markets

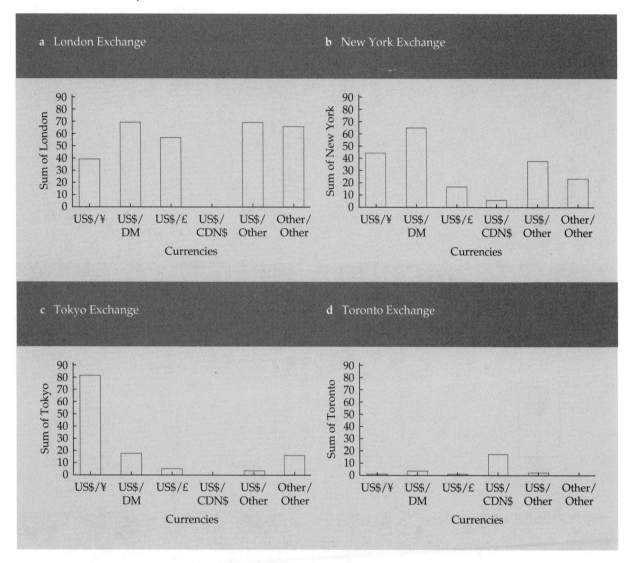

Finally, if the goal is to compare, for each pair of currencies, the volume on the four currency exchange markets, Figure 2.20 is best. It shows, for example, that the largest daily trades in U.S. dollars and Japanese yen occur on the Tokyo market, whereas the largest trades in U.S. dollars and German Deutsche Marks occur on the London and New York markets.

Figure 2.20

Trading Volume Bar Chart

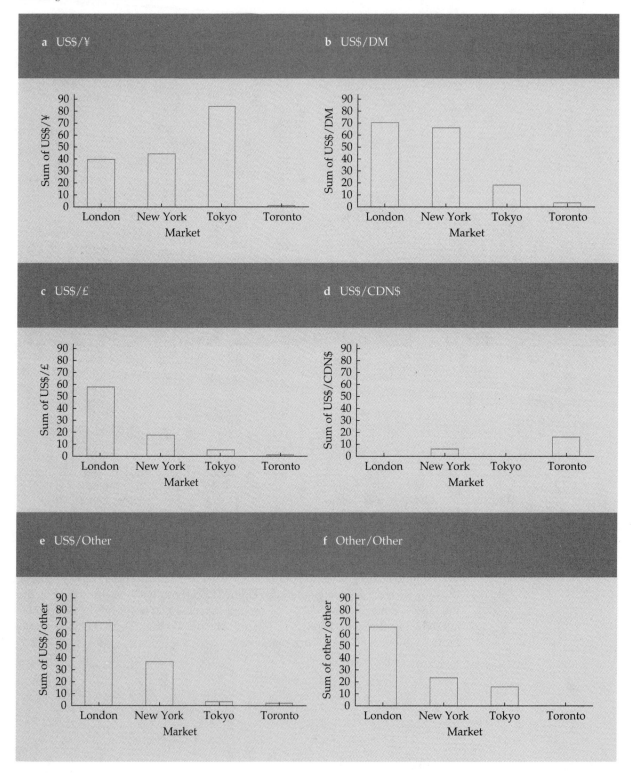

Although market shares are usually displayed graphically with a pie chart, professional chartists sometimes opt for the bar chart, as did a newspaper when it published the bar chart shown in Figure 2.21. This figure shows the share of U.S. prime-time television viewing enjoyed by each of the major television networks between September 1993 and April 1994. Figure 2.22 displays the conventional pie chart of the networks' market shares. But Figure 2.21, which omits the very sizable "Other" category, is preferable if the objective is to emphasize CBS's leadership over the other networks.

Figure 2.21

Share of U.S. Prime-Time Television Viewing (September 1993–April 1994)

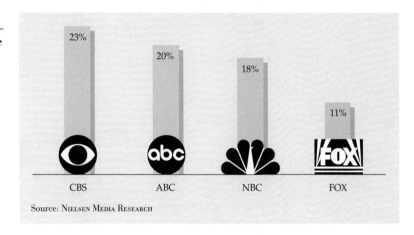

Source: NIELSEN MEDIA RESEARCH

Figure 2.22

Pie Chart of Share of U.S. Prime-Time Television Viewing (September 1993–April 1994)

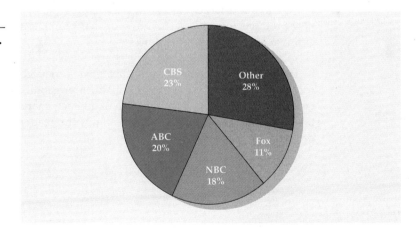

Line Charts

The last graphical technique to be considered here is the line chart. A **line chart** is obtained by plotting the frequency of a category above the point on the horizontal axis representing that category and then joining the points with straight lines. A line chart is often used when the categories are points in time; such a chart is known alternatively as a **time-series chart**. An excellent example is the graph that plots the last few weeks or months of the daily values of the Dow Jones Industrial Average (DJIA), like the one shown in Figure 2.23. See Appendix 2.A for Minitab commands to produce a line chart.

Figure 2.23

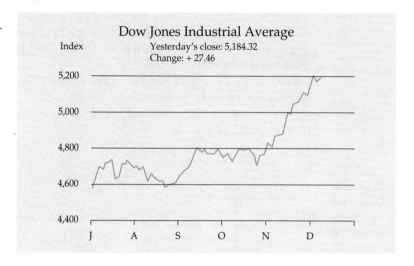

Line Charts or Bar Charts?

We can use either a line chart or a bar chart to present time-series data. In Figure 2.17, we displayed the number of new products introduced annually for 1989–1994 with a bar chart. Figure 2.24 exhibits the same data using a line chart. Which one is better? The answer depends on two factors: the objective of the graph and the number of periods. If the objective of the graph is to focus on the *trend* in the value over the year, a line chart is superior. If the goal is to emphasize the *relative sizes* of the total amounts in different years, a bar chart is recommended.

If there is a large number of periods (for example, a graph of the number of new products introduced monthly for five years), a line chart looks less cluttered and makes a clearer impression.

Pie charts, bar charts, and line charts are used extensively in reports compiled by businesses, governments, and the media. Variations on these and other pictorial representations of data abound, and their possibilities are limited only by their creators' imaginations. The objective of all such charts is to present a summary of the data clearly and in a form that allows the reader to grasp the relevant comparisons or trends quickly.

Figure 2.24

Line Chart for the Number of New Products Introduced Annually

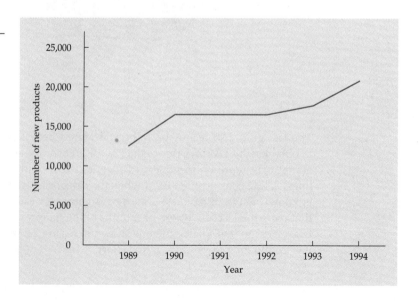

2.26 Given the following four categories and the number of times each occurs, draw a pie chart by hand.

Category	Frequency	Category	Frequency
1	14	3	27
2	43	4	16

2.27 In a taste test, 250 people were asked which of five light beers they preferred. The beers were labeled 1, 2, 3, 4, and 5. The data are stored in file XR02-27. Use your software to create the pie chart of these data.

2.28 Repeat Exercise 2.26 using a bar chart instead.

2.29 Repeat Exercise 2.27 using a bar chart instead.

2.30 A breakdown of Hewlett-Packard's sales for the six-month period November 1992 to April 1993 is as follows. (Source: Company reports.)

Computers and printers	$7,401,000,000
Test and measurement equipment	1,135,000,000
Medical equipment	553,000,000
Analytical instruments	349,000,000
Electronic components	262,000,000

Use a pie chart to describe Hewlett-Packard's sales during the six-month period.

2.31 Retirement savings plans are very popular in the United States and Canada because they are used to defer income tax. A survey conducted by the Caledon Institute of Social Policy (reported in the *Globe and Mail*, 5 February 1994) determined the percentage of different income groups that used retirement savings plans as a tax deduction in 1990. These statistics are listed below.

INCOME GROUP	PERCENTAGE USING RETIREMENT SAVINGS PLANS	INCOME GROUP	PERCENTAGE USING RETIREMENT SAVINGS PLANS
Less than $10,000	3%	50,000–79,999	51
10,000–19,999	13	80,000–99,999	57
20,000–29,999	28	100,000–250,999	63
30,000–39,999	40	Over 250,000	68
40,000–49,999	49		

Use a graphical technique to present these figures.

2.32 A variety store's monthly sales (in thousands of dollars) for the last year were as follows:

MONTH	SALES	MONTH	SALES	MONTH	SALES
January	65	May	72	September	91
February	61	June	80	October	78
March	70	July	88	November	68
April	74	August	93	December	84

a Construct a relative frequency bar chart for these data.

b Construct a line chart.

2.33 The city of North York is one of five boroughs which, together with the city of Toronto, comprise Metropolitan Toronto. Like Toronto and the other boroughs, it collects property tax to pay for local government activities as well as administrative costs. In its 1993 annual report, North York reported the administrative costs per person for each of the five boroughs and Toronto. It also described the percentage of its tax dollars that went to each of its activities. These statistics are shown in the tables below.

Table 1

Administrative Spending (Cost per Person)	CITY	ADMINISTRATIVE COST PER PERSON	CITY	ADMINISTRATIVE COST PER PERSON
	Toronto	$292.00	East York	96.67
	York	104.63	Scarborough	80.77
	Etobicoke	96.71	North York	74.21

Table 2

Percent of Total Budget Spent on Government Activities	ACTIVITY	PERCENT OF BUDGET	ACTIVITY	PERCENT OF BUDGET
	Public works	22.8%	Library	11.5
	Fire	16.9	Corporate	8.2
	Parks and recreation	16.3	Public health	6.6
	Administration	14.9	Transportation	2.8

Use graphical techniques to present the results shown in Tables 1 and 2.

2.34 The ranks of the elderly are growing. This phenomenon has enormous implications for society because elderly people require more medical care than do younger people. The following table describes the percentages of the North American and European population that were over 65, over 75, and over 80 in 1990. Also listed are forecasts for 2010 and 2025.

	PERCENTAGE OVER 65		PERCENTAGE OVER 75		PERCENTAGE OVER 80	
YEAR	NORTH AMERICA	EUROPE	NORTH AMERICA	EUROPE	NORTH AMERICA	EUROPE
1990	12.4%	13.2%	5.2%	5.8%	3.2%	3.2%
2010	14.1	17.7	7.0	8.2	4.5	4.8
2025	20.3	22.1	8.2	8.1	4.9	7.2

a Use a bar chart to present these statistics.

b Use a component bar chart to present these statistics.

2.35 For the past few years, the U.S. government has been quite concerned with its trade imbalance with the rest of the world. To develop an understanding of the problem, a statistician determined the annual American trade deficit (the difference between what the United States sells to other countries and what the United States buys from others). These data are listed below.

YEAR	TRADE DEFICIT (BILLIONS OF DOLLARS)	YEAR	TRADE DEFICIT (BILLIONS OF DOLLARS)
1983	52	1989	109
1984	107	1990	102
1985	118	1991	68
1986	138	1992	85
1987	151	1993	116
1988	119		

a Draw a line chart of the annual trade deficits.

b Draw a bar chart of the annual trade deficits.

2.36 In an article about Chinese birth rates, *Newsweek* (November 1994) presented the following statistics.

YEAR	POPULATION (BILLIONS)	FERTILITY RATE (NUMBER OF BIRTHS PER WOMAN)
1950	.55	6.2
1960	.68	5.9
1970	.79	4.8
1980	.99	2.5
1990	1.17	2.2

YEAR	POPULATION (BILLIONS)	FERTILITY RATE (NUMBER OF BIRTHS PER WOMAN)
1994	1.22	1.8
2000	1.26 (est.)	1.8 (est.)
2010	1.32 (est.)	1.8 (est.)
2020	1.45 (est.)	1.8 (est.)

Use any graphical technique you think appropriate to present these numbers.

2.37 In 1994, a spate of small aircraft crashes made the safety of turboprop airplanes an issue. As part of an analysis of different types of accidents, Airjet Ltd. determined where accidents occurred for both turboprop airplanes and jets in the period 1984–1993. The data are stored in file XR02-37 using the following format.

WHEN ACCIDENTS HAPPEN	CODE	WHEN ACCIDENTS HAPPEN	CODE
Ground	1	Cruise	5
Takeoff	2	Descent	6
Initial climb	3	Approach	7
Climb	4	Landing	8

The results for turboprops are stored in column 1, and the results for jets are stored in column 2.

a Use graphical techniques to summarize these data.

b Does it appear that turboprop airplanes and jets have similar accident patterns?

2.38 Women own about 40% of Canadian small businesses, but there are large variations in the types of businesses owned by men and women. Suppose that a survey of female-owned and male-owned small businesses was conducted and the type of business each operated was recorded in the following format.

BUSINESS	CODE	BUSINESS	CODE
Services	1	Construction	5
Retail/Wholesale/Trade	2	Manufacturing	6
Finance/Insurance/Real Estate	3	Agriculture and primary	7
Transportation/Communication	4		

The responses of women and men are stored in columns 1 and 2, respectively, in file XR02-38. Use an appropriate graphical technique to summarize and present these data.

2.39 According to recent statistics, less than 1% of all personal income tax returns are audited by the IRS. Among those audited, about 75% are required to pay more tax. However, the possibility of being audited varies greatly by state. The tables below list the ten most "dangerous" states and the ten "safest" states, and the ratio of audited returns to the total number of returns in those states. Use a graphical technique to visually present these results.

Table 1

Ten Most Dangerous States (Proportion of Audited Returns)				
Utah	1 in 21	Texas	1 in 80
Nevada	1 in 60	Massachusetts	1 in 85
California	1 in 67	Alaska	1 in 89
Georgia	1 in 73	Montana	1 in 91
Missouri	1 in 76	Wyoming	1 in 91

Table 2

Ten Safest States (Proportion of Audited Returns)				
Maine	1 in 227	Oregon	1 in 189
Wisconsin	1 in 227	South Carolina	1 in 185
Hawaii	1 in 222	Virginia	1 in 175
North Carolina	1 in 208	Michigan	1 in 175
New Jersey	1 in 204	West Virginia	1 in 169

SOURCE: National Institute of Business Management and IRS

2.6 Summary

Descriptive statistics is concerned with methods of summarizing and presenting the essential information contained in a set of data. This chapter focused on graphical methods of summarizing and presenting data.

A collection of **quantitative data** can be usefully summarized by grouping the observations to form a **frequency distribution**. Constructing a **stem and leaf display** is often helpful during preliminary analysis of the data. Either a **histogram** or a **relative frequency histogram** can be used to convey the shape of the distribution. **Scatter diagrams** describe the relationship between two quantitative variables. Other graphical techniques include **pie charts**, **bar charts**, and **line charts**.

IMPORTANT TERMS

Descriptive statistics	Bimodal
Variable	Multimodal
Data	Cumulative relative frequency
Quantitative (numerical) data	Ogive
Qualitative (categorical) data	Stem and leaf display
Ranked data	Stem
Frequency distribution	Leaf
Classes	Scatter diagram
Histogram	Linear relationship
Relative frequency distribution	Positive relationship
Relative frequency histogram	Negative relationship
Open-ended class	Nonlinear relationship
Positively skewed	Pie chart
Negatively skewed	Bar chart
Modal class	Line chart
Unimodal	Time-series chart

Supplementary Exercises

2.40 The data from the survey referred to in Exercise 2.4 (page 23) have been stored in file XR02-40 using the following format:

Column 1: age

Column 2: sex (1 = female; 2 = male)

Column 3: marital status (1 = single; 2 = married; 3 = divorced; 4 = widowed)

Column 4: annual income (1 = less than $20,000; 2 = between $20,000 and $40,000; 3 = over $40,000)

Column 5: number of other magazine subscriptions

Use whatever techniques you think necessary to describe these data.

2.41 The data from the survey in Exercise 2.5 (page 23) were stored in file XR02-41 in the following way:

Column 1: rank (1 = lecturer; 2 = assistant professor; 3 = associate professor; 4 = full professor)

Column 2: annual salary

Column 3: university faculty (1 = Arts and Sciences; 2 = Engineering; 3 = Business; 4 = other)

Column 4: years of experience

Use whatever techniques you think necessary to describe the data.

2.42 The data from the survey in Exercise 2.6 (page 23) were stored in file XR02-42 in the following way:

Column 1: number of games attended annually

Column 2: entertainment rating (4 = excellent; 3 = good; 2 = fair; 1 = poor)

Column 3: season tickets (1 = yes; 2 = no)

Column 4: average amount of money spent at the food concession at each game

Column 5: food rating (12 = edible; 7 = barely edible; 1 = abominable)

Use whatever techniques you think necessary to describe the data.

2.43 A growing concern at universities and colleges across North America is the number of professors who will retire in the next 5, 10, and 15 years. To examine the problem, a statistics professor took a random sample of 1,000 professors and recorded their ages. These data are stored in file XR02-43. Assuming that professors will retire at age 65, use graphical methods to discuss the retirement problem facing universities over the next 15 years.

2.44 In an effort to track the increasing prices of homes in a large city, a statistician took a random sample of homes sold this year and another sample of homes sold five years ago. The data are stored in columns 1 (sale prices five years ago) and 2 (sale prices this year) in file XR02-44.

a Use graphical techniques to describe the two sets of data.

b Discuss similarities and differences between the two sets of data.

2.45 The head coach of an NFL football team is trying to decide among three candidates for the position of punter. The coach knows that longer punts are desirable, but so is consistency. As an avid student of statistics, the coach often uses his knowledge in that subject to help him make decisions. He has recorded the distance of the last 100 punts for each of the three candidates and stored them in columns 1 to 3 of file XR02-45. Describe the data and provide the head coach with your recommendation.

2.46 In the last few years, regional airlines have come under scrutiny because of safety concerns. In response, the Regional Airline Association produced the results listed below (and stored in file XR02-46).

a Use graphical techniques to help make the Association's argument.

b What do the graphs tell you about regional airline safety?

YEAR	FATAL ACCIDENTS (PER 100,000 DEPARTURES)	NUMBER OF PASSENGERS (MILLIONS)
1983	.10	21
1984	.23	27
1985	.24	28
1986	.02	29
1987	.31	32
1988	.04	36
1989	.12	38
1990	.04	42

YEAR	FATAL ACCIDENTS (PER 100,000 DEPARTURES)	NUMBER OF PASSENGERS (MILLIONS)
1991	.24	42
1992	.15	48
1993	.10	53
1994	.04 (est.)	58 (est.)

2.47 Mutual funds are becoming an increasingly popular investment alternative among small investors. To help investors decide on the particular fund to invest in, various publications regularly report the average annual rate of return achieved by each of more than 100 mutual funds over the past ten years. (The annual rate of return of a mutual fund is given by $(P_1 - P_0)/P_0$, where P_0 and P_1 are the prices of the fund's shares at the beginning and end of the year, respectively. This definition assumes that no dividends are paid by the fund during the year.) Some publications also indicate each fund's level of risk by classifying the historical variability of each fund's rate of return as high, intermediate, or low. Suppose that the annual (percentage) rates of return over the past ten years for five mutual funds are stored in columns 1 through 5 of file XR02-47. Use whatever techniques you deem necessary to describe the five sets of data.

2.48 Airlines are rated on a number of dimensions, but for many passengers one of the most important is the frequency and magnitude of late arrivals and departures. Suppose that the amount of time that each departure was behind schedule was recorded for the last 250 departures for each of five airlines and was stored in columns 1 through 5 of file XR02-48.

a Present a chart that depicts the comparison of the percentage of late departures (defined as any time greater than five minutes behind schedule) for the five airlines.

b Which airline is best at adhering to its departure schedule?

2.49 Many economic analysts have predicted that North American pulp and paper mills are likely to continue to decline in the face of stiffer worldwide competition and rising costs. An analysis of the competitiveness of plants in different parts of North America reveals a wide divergence in terms of manufacturing costs. The following table lists the number of pulp mills in each of nine geographic regions that are above the average cost and below the average cost. Use a graphical technique to present these figures.

GEOGRAPHIC REGION	NUMBER OF MILLS ABOVE AVERAGE MANUFACTURING COST	NUMBER OF MILLS BELOW AVERAGE MANUFACTURING COST
U.S. South	5	37
U.S. Northeast	4	0
U.S. Central	0	1
U.S. Northwest	1	3
U.S. West	3	0
Ontario	9	2
Quebec	7	0
Western Canada	12	8
Atlantic Canada	3	1

2.50 Refer to Exercise 2.49. The following table lists the number of newsprint mills that are above and below average cost by region. Use another graphical method (different from the one used in Exercise 2.49) to describe these figures.

GEOGRAPHIC REGION	NUMBER OF MILLS ABOVE AVERAGE MANUFACTURING COST	NUMBER OF MILLS BELOW AVERAGE MANUFACTURING COST
U.S. South	1	10
U.S. Northeast	3	4

U.S. Central	0	2
U.S. Northwest	1	1
U.S. West	0	2
Ontario	4	3
Quebec	15	1
Western Canada	3	6
Atlantic Canada	3	4

2.51 A hotly debated subject in the United States is universal health coverage for all Americans. Many people in the United States are urging Congress and the President to adopt a plan similar to the Canadian plan. However, critics point out that there are a variety of shortcomings in the Canadian plan. Foremost among them is the amount of time Canadians must wait for treatment. Table 1 provides the waiting time in each of the ten provinces of Canada to see four types of specialists after a referral from a general practitioner. Table 2 lists the waiting time in each province for seven different treatments after an appointment with a specialist (source: Fraser Institute). (The data are also stored in file XR02-51, with Table 1 in cols. 1–4, and Table 2 in cols. 5–11.) Use graphical methods to present the waiting times.

Table 1

Average 1992 Wait (in Weeks) to See a Specialist After Referral from a General Practitioner		SPECIALISTS			
	PROVINCE	NEUROSURGERY	ORTHOPEDICS	CARDIOVASCULAR SURGERY	INTERNAL MEDICINE
	British Columbia	7.5	11.6	6.7	5.5
	Alberta	15.0	7.8	5.2	3.9
	Saskatchewan	4.5	11.1	6.7	2.4
	Manitoba	12.0	11.1	3.3	4.7
	Ontario	11.2	9.9	3.9	7.0
	Quebec	4.6	8.4	3.2	3.3
	New Brunswick	4.0	7.1	3.0	2.2
	Newfoundland	4.3	13.9	1.0	3.0
	Nova Scotia	3.5	8.8	3.8	4.5
	Prince Edward Island	4.2	6.0	2.8	4.5

Table 2

Average 1992 Patient Wait (in Weeks) for Treatment After Appointment with Specialist

	TREATMENT						
PROVINCE	HYSTERECTOMY	CATARACT REMOVAL	HERNIA REPAIR	BREAST BIOPSY	DISC SURGERY	PIN REMOVAL	HIP ARTHOPLASTY
British Columbia	10.4	15.4	8.0	2.5	8.1	12.2	25.1
Alberta	8.7	8.8	4.9	1.6	7.8	6.5	19.9
Saskatchewan	10.7	26.9	9.8	1.9	4.0	9.0	18.8
Manitoba	13.0	21.6	7.9	1.9	8.0	17.3	58.6
Ontario	5.8	13.2	4.6	2.0	7.5	9.7	17.0
Quebec	5.4	15.7	7.1	2.6	25.1	11.2	15.4
New Brunswick	26.6	21.1	6.0	1.8	1.0	26.0	19.5
Newfoundland	5.1	3.7	12.7	1.6	4.2	15.3	16.7
Nova Scotia	11.0	20.6	7.6	2.1	9.0	6.8	32.0
Prince Edward Island	31.0	27.0	13.7	2.3	5.1	8.0	35.0

2.52 Much progress has been made in the economic and political battles to create a more equitable society in the United States. Just how much can be measured using the statistics below? Use graphical methods to present the figures.

Education: Persons 25 years and older, with four years of college or more, by percentage of their racial group

YEAR	BLACKS	WHITES
1940	1%	5%
1971	5	12
1991	12	22

SOURCE: U.S. Bureau of the Census

Occupation: Employed civilians, 1992, by percentage of their racial group in specific jobs

	BLACKS	WHITES
Professional/managerial	17%	28%
Technical/sales/administrative	29	34
Service occupations	24	12
Construction/repairs	8	12
Laborers/operators	22	14

SOURCE: U.S. Bureau of Labor Statistics

Family Income: Percentage of racial group by total income using 1992 dollars

		BLACKS	WHITES
$50,000 to 74,999	1982	9%	19%
	1992	11	21
$75,000 to 99,999	1982	2%	7%
	1992	3	8
$100,000 and over	1982	1%	5%
	1992	2	7

SOURCE: U.S. Bureau of the Census

2.53 Perceptions of how well or poorly the economy will perform can sometimes result in self-fulfilling prophecies. As a result, executives, economists, and government officials are interested in the public's perceptions about the economy. Every year, 1,000 adults are surveyed in late December and asked "Compared with last year, do you think this coming year will be a year of economic prosperity, economic difficulty, or about the same as last year?" The responses are as follows:

1 = Prosperity

2 = Difficulty

3 = About the same

The responses (coded as 1, 2, and 3) for the years 1995, 1992, 1989, 1986, 1983, and 1980 are stored in columns 1 through 6 of file XR02-53. Use graphical methods to summarize the data and briefly describe what the graphs tell you.

2.54 Credit scoring is a statistical technique used by banks to decide whether to approve applications for loans, credit cards, and other forms of credit. The technique works by assigning a weight to the responses in an application for credit. The total weight is then used to make decisions. Higher scores represent more desirable applicants, ones whose applications will likely be accepted. To judge the effectiveness of one such scoring method, a bank recorded the scores from a random sample of 200 applicants, all of whom were given a $1,000 loan. The scorecard recommended that only the top 125 applicants be given loans. After two years, the status of each loan was determined (there were two categories: loan paid in full and defaulted on loan or is behind in payments). The scores are stored in file XR02-54; the loans paid in full are stored in column 1; column 2 contains the scores of the defaulted or late-payment loans. Use whatever graphical techniques you deem useful to present a report to the bank's board of directors, who asked you to discuss how well the scorecard works.

2.55 The 1993 annual report for the Thomson Corporation, which owns newspapers, travel agencies, and publishing companies (including Wadsworth Publishing Company, which in turn owns Duxbury Press, the publisher of this book) presented the following information.

Business Segment	SALES BY BUSINESS SEGMENT		OPERATING PROFIT BY BUSINESS SEGMENT		ASSETS BY BUSINESS SEGMENT	
	1993	1992	1993	1992	1993	1992
Thomson Information/Publishing	46%	44%	60%	57%	56%	56%
Thomson Newspapers	19	19	24	28	24	26
Thomson Travel	35	37	16	15	20	18
Total (millions of U.S. dollars)	5,849	5,980	731	688	8,213	7,907

Geographic Area	SALES BY GEOGRAPHIC AREA		OPERATING PROFIT BY GEOGRAPHIC AREA	
	1993	1992	1993	1992
United States	42%	38%	59%	61%
United Kingdom	47	50	30	25
Canada	8	9	8	11
Other Countries	3	3	3	3
Total (millions of U.S. dollars)	5,849	5,980	731	688

Use graphical techniques of your choice to describe the numbers in the tables.

2.56 United Grain Growers is one of the largest agribusiness companies in Canada. UGG has four related operations: grain handling and marketing, crop production services (which provides fertilizers, agricultural chemicals, seed, and crop management services), livestock services (which includes manufacturing and marketing of feed), and communications and information services (including grain market information and analysis). The following tables were provided in UGG's 1994 annual report. All figures are in millions of dollars.

	1990	1991	1992	1993	1994
Gross profit and revenue from services	124.9	145.7	147.8	152.8	170.6
Earnings from continuing operations (before tax)	5.3	12.9	13.7	10.0	14.3
Earnings	0.7	2.8	7.3	7.5	7.0
Working capital	30.1	49.7	53.4	49.4	91.4
Capital expenditures	16.5	4.7	6.3	24.8	27.7

	GROSS PROFIT AND REVENUE FROM SERVICES, 1994	OPERATING INCOME BEFORE INTEREST AND CORPORATE COSTS, 1994
Grain handling and marketing	107.6	11.9
Crop production services	35.5	9.2
Livestock services	15.2	1.3
Communications and information services	12.3	.0
Total	170.6	22.4

Use whatever graphical techniques you deem necessary to present the numbers above.

2.57 How does the level of an individual's education affect his or her income? An economist decided to examine this question. She took a random sample of 1,000 40- to 45-year-old people and recorded the highest education level each person achieved. The categories are

1 = did not complete primary education

2 = completed primary school

3 = completed high school

4 = received a bachelor's (or equivalent) degree

5 = received a master's or doctoral degree

The economist also recorded the annual income. These are stored in file XR02-57 using the following format.

Column 1: annual incomes of category 1

Column 2: annual incomes of category 2

Column 3: annual incomes of category 3

Column 4: annual incomes of category 4

Column 5: annual incomes of category 5

Perform whatever graphical analyses you deem necessary and report your findings (bearing in mind the purpose of collecting the data).

2.58 Exercises 2.23 and 2.24 addressed the issue of whether common stocks are a good hedge against inflation. In order to investigate the same issue for long-term bonds, the annual percentage rates of return on bonds and the annual inflation rates from 1985 through 1994 are shown in the accompanying table. (The data are also stored in file XR02-58. Column 1 stores the bond returns, and column 2 stores the inflation rates.)

YEAR	BOND RETURN (%)	INFLATION RATE (%)
1985	25.26	4.38
1986	17.54	4.19
1987	.45	4.12
1988	10.45	3.96
1989	16.29	5.17
1990	3.34	5.00
1991	24.43	3.78
1992	13.07	2.14
1993	22.88	1.70
1994	−10.46	.23

SOURCE: *Report on Canadian Economic Statistics: 1924–1994* (Canadian Institute of Actuaries, 1995)

a Construct a scatter diagram for these data, with the bond returns on the vertical axis.

b Describe the relationship between bond returns and inflation rates from 1985 to 1994.

c Does it appear that bonds provide a good hedge against inflation?

2.59 Refer to Exercise 2.58. The annual percentage rates of return on bonds and the annual inflation rates from 1960 to 1994 are stored in file XR02-59. (Column 1 stores the bond returns, and column 2 stores the inflation rates.)

a Construct a scatter diagram for these data with the bond returns on the vertical axis.

b Describe the relationship between bond returns and inflation rates from 1960 to 1994. How does your answer compare with part (b) of Exercise 2.58?

c Does it appear that bonds provide a good hedge against inflation?

CASE 2.1   PACIFIC SALMON CATCHES*

A national publication has presented a detailed study about commercial salmon fishing in the United States, Canada, Japan, and the former U.S.S.R. These four nations account for the bulk of the total annual Pacific Rim catch of salmon, which can be worth as much as $5 billion. The total size of the salmon catch in 1987 for each of these countries is shown in the following table, together with a breakdown of their catches by species.

Develop an interesting and informative graphical descriptive method to exhibit the data. Your graphical presentation should emphasize the relative sizes of the total catches for the four countries, as well as the relative importance (according to size) of the species caught for each country.

1987 Salmon Catches (in Metric Tons)

SPECIES	UNITED STATES	CANADA	JAPAN	FORMER U.S.S.R.
Sockeye	102,165	14,650	945	11,521
Pink	75,914	26,045	17,000	96,390
Chum	40,440	10,490	145,440	23,810
Coho	18,450	8,320	3,300	4,224
Chinook	18,444	5,607	—	2,304
Cherry	—	—	3,310	—
Total	255,413	65,112	169,995	138,249

*Adapted from Jere Van Dyk, "Long Journey of the Pacific Salmon," *National Geographic* 178 (July 1990): 3–37.

CASE 2.2   BOMBARDIER INC.

Bombardier Inc. is an international manufacturer and distributor of transportation equipment (such as railcars for the English Channel Tunnel), motorized consumer products (such as Ski-Doo snowmobiles and Sea-Doo watercraft), and various types of aircraft. According to Bombardier's 1995 Annual Report, "Completion of the major Eurotunnel contract led to a reduction in the level of Bombardier Eurorail's production during the year, but this was offset by higher volume in our North American facilities," as a result of "a return of consumer confidence in the economy, combined with heightened interest for personal watercraft and snowmobiles." The increase in deliveries of aircraft in 1995 also contributed to the outstanding growth in Bombardier's revenues in 1995.

It is January 1996, and you have been asked to summarize the financial data in the accompanying table, using graphical techniques, for presentation to the shareholders at Bombardier's upcoming annual meeting. Be prepared to explain your choice of graphs. In addition, prepare a sentence to accompany each graph that describes an important point being conveyed by that graph.

Bombardier's Financial Statistics

	1995	1994	1993	1992	1991
Revenues	$5,943*	$4,769	$4,448	$3,059	$2,892
By Product					
Transportation Equipment	1,310	1,312	1,238	726	697
Aerospace	2,981	2,243	2,228	1,519	1,383
Motorized Consumer Products	1,111	791	556	392	398
Other	541	423	426	422	414
By Market					
North America	3,266	2,524	2,131	1,233	1,247
Europe	2,034	1,946	2,119	1,652	1,383
Other	643	299	198	174	262
Net Income	242	176	133	108	100
Before Tax Income	346	207	151	121	121
By Product					
Transportation Equipment	66	(24)	(73)	4	20
Aerospace	141	137	181	137	113
Motorized Consumer Products	117	76	29	(9)	(30)
Other	21	18	14	(10)	17
Share Price					
High	25.00	22.00	17.38	17.60	10.31
Low	18.00	9.63	10.63	8.38	7.25

SOURCE: Bombardier Inc., Annual Reports, 1991–1995.

*All figures are rounded to the nearest million dollars, except for share price.

CASE 2.3 — THE NORTH AMERICAN FREE TRADE AGREEMENT (NAFTA)

The North American Free Trade Agreement (NAFTA) recently was enacted by the governments of the United States, Canada, and Mexico. Its effect will be to increase trade among the three countries. It is informative to compare various aspects of the countries involved. Tables 1, 2, and 3 present several statistical comparisons for 1992. Table 1 lists economic figures, Table 2 describes the magnitude of current trade, and Table 3 describes household ownership of luxury items in the three countries (sources: OECD, IMF, Statistics Canada). Use graphical techniques to present the information contained in the tables.

Table 1

Economics

	UNITED STATES	CANADA	MEXICO
Population (millions)	256	28.8	89.5
GDP (millions of U.S. dollars)	$8,000	$840	$488
Economic growth	2.6%	0.7%	2.7%
Inflation	2.6	1.5	14.5
Share of world exports	13.0	4.0	1.0

Table 2

	EXPORTS (BILLIONS OF DOLLARS)	PERCENT OF TOTAL EXPORTS
U.S. to Canada	$ 96.4	20%
Canada to U.S.	118.4	77
U.S. to Mexico	48.7	9
Mexico to U.S.	39.1	76
Canada to Mexico	0.8	0.5
Mexico to Canada	2.8	5

Table 3

What People Have

ITEM	PERCENTAGE OF HOUSEHOLDS WITH EACH ITEM		
	UNITED STATES	CANADA	MEXICO
Domestic help	7%	10%	11%
Cable television	61	71	15
Videocassette recorder	61	74	63
Color television	93	97	83
Telephone	92	98	50
Compact disc player	30	25	23
Car	88	76	54
Auto insurance	79	76	26

Minitab Instructions

Introduction to Minitab

Minitab is a statistical software package that provides a variety of techniques ideally suited for teaching a course in applied statistics. In this book, we will describe how to use *Release 11 for Windows* to generate the output of the statistical techniques described in this book. There are two ways to output results. The first is by typing commands directly into the session window. Most of these commands are the same used in earlier versions of the software. These are called *session commands* to distinguish them from the commands used by the second method, *menu commands*. Menu commands will be described in the chapters; session commands will be listed in chapter appendixes.

There are several different versions of Minitab that students may be using, based on DOS, Windows, or Macintosh. There are older versions available, as well as the latest release. There are also downsized student versions. In general, most of the session commands presented in the appendixes will work for versions other than *Release 11*. However, users of such versions should consult their manuals for instructions.

Our goal is to provide simple, direct instructions that will allow you to perform the statistical techniques described in the book. We assume that you are familiar with your computer system but that you know little, if anything, about Minitab. Students who wish to be more adept in employing Minitab are urged to refer to a Minitab manual.

Minitab consists of a worksheet and about 200 commands. When you first access Minitab, you will be either in the session window or in the data screen. You can go from one to the other. To go from the data screen to the session window, hold down the CONTROL key and hit **m**. (We call this **Ctrl-m**.) To go from the session window to the data screen, hit **Ctrl-d**. (Hold down the CONTROL key and hit **d**.) When you are in the session window, Minitab will prompt you with

MTB>

When such a prompt appears, you may type Minitab commands. This manual will show you how to use about 40 commands needed to apply the statistical techniques introduced in the textbook. We usually start a problem by either importing data (that you or someone else created) or by typing in a new set of data.

Data Input

In order for the Minitab program to perform statistical computations, data must first be input. A data set is stored in a column. The following command can be used

READ C1

Here **C1** represents *column 1*. After typing this line, press the RETURN or

ENTER key on your keyboard. Then type the data, one number per line (followed by ENTER). The computer will prompt you after each entered line with

DATA>

When all the data have been input, type

END

For example, suppose you have the following five observations: 12, 15, 8, 16, and 9. These data would be input as follows.

MTB> READ C1
DATA> 12
DATA> 15
DATA> 8
DATA> 16
DATA> 9
DATA> END

In all further illustrations of the instructions, we will not show the computer prompts.

If two or more groups of data are to be read, you could type

READ C1 C2
READ C1 C2 C3

or

READ C1 - C3

If you specify three columns of data **(C1 - C3)**, Minitab will expect you to type three numbers on each line.

Another way of inputting data is by using the SET command. This command allows you to type numbers consecutively on one or more lines. For example,

SET C1
12 15 8 16 9
END
SET C2
17 25 13 15 32
26 20 5 3
END

You can also enter data directly through the data screen. When the data screen appears, simply start typing your data. Make certain that you start at row 1. The space immediately under the column number is reserved for the name of the column. We'll discuss naming columns later. After each number, hit the **DOWN** cursor to continue in the same column. Use the cursor to move to other columns if necessary. When you've completed typing the data, hit **Ctrl-m** to go back to the session window. (You can also move the cursor to the menu across the top of the screen and select **Window** and **1 Session** or **2 Data** to toggle between the session window and the data screen.)

Subcommands

A number of Minitab commands allow subcommands. We will describe the needed subcommands as we proceed. To use a subcommand, the command must end with a semicolon and the subcommand must end with a period. The format is

COMMAND;
SUBCOMMAND.

If there are several subcommands, all but the last one must end with a semicolon and the last subcommand must end with a period. The format is

COMMAND;
SUBCOMMAND;
SUBCOMMAND.

If you end a command with a semicolon anticipating the use of a subcommand, you can change your mind by typing a period on the next line.

Corrections

Corrections can be made directly on the data screen. Use the cursor (or mouse) to go to a cell containing the number you wish to correct, and type in your new number.

Screen Output

To check to see if entered data have been input correctly, type

PRINT C1

or

PRINT C1 C2 C3

or

PRINT C1 - C3

Using the Printer

To send output to your printer (assuming that you are operating from a personal computer), hit **Ctrl-p**. Alternatively, click **File** and **Print Window . . . .** A dialog box will appear on the screen. You can use a mouse or the tab key and the cursor keys to move around this box. If you want to print everything you've generated in the session window, select **All** and **OK**. If you want to print only some of the output, make your selection *before* hitting **Ctrl-p** in the following way.

USING A MOUSE

1 Move the cursor to the starting point of your output.
2 Hold down the left button and drag to the last line and release.

3 Click **File** and **Print Window**....

4 Click **OK**.

USING THE CURSOR KEYS

1 Use the cursor keys to move to the starting point of your output.

2 Hit the SHIFT key while holding the down cursor until you move to the last line. Release the keys.

3 Click **File** and **Print Window**....

4 Click **OK**.

Saving and Retrieving Data

If you intend to use a set of data another time in the future, you can save (and later retrieve) it. To save a data set, type

SAVE 'FILENAME'

This command will store the data in such a way that only Minitab can read it. Once the data set has been saved, you can retrieve it at any time with the following command:

RETRIEVE 'FILENAME'

To save on a diskette in drive A, type

SAVE 'A:FILENAME'

Retrieve in the same way.

The data can also be stored in ASCII format. To save and retrieve the data, however, the commands must specify the columns where the data are stored. For example, if data are stored in columns 1, 2, and 3, to save on a diskette in drive A type

WRITE 'A:FILENAME' C1 - C3

To retrieve type

READ 'A:FILENAME' C1 - C3

The data associated with examples, exercises, and cases described in the book have been stored on the CD or disk that accompanies this book using the SAVE command. There are a total of 345 files occupying .824 MB. Instructions for copying the files to your computer are provided in a README file.

Other Commands

To create new variables from existing ones, use the LET command. For example,

LET C3 = C1 + C2

creates a variable that is the sum of the first two and stores the values of this variable in column 3. Some useful arithmetic operations, identified by their Minitab symbols, are:

+ addition

− subtraction

* multiplication

/ division

** exponentiation (raise to a power)

You can also use the following menu commands:

1 Click **Calc** and **Mathematical Expressions**.

2 Specify the column number of the new variable (e.g., **C2**).

3 Move the cursor to the **Expression** box and type the expression (e.g., **C1**2**). Click **OK**. This will create a new variable, which is equal to the values in column 1 squared. The squared values will be stored in column 2.

In some situations it is useful to name the variables. To do so, type

NAME C1 'INCOME'

The output will display the variable names. If you don't name the variables, the output will display the column numbers where the data are stored (e.g., **C1**, **C2**). Commands such as PRINT and DELETE can then use the variable name instead of the column number. For example, after the command

NAME C1 'INCOME' C2 'AGE'

has been entered, the command

PRINT C1 C2

is equivalent to the command

PRINT 'INCOME' 'AGE'

Variable names may be up to eight characters in length, may not begin or end with a blank, and cannot contain a single quote (') or an octothorpe (#) as part of the name. You can also place the name of the variable in the space under C1 (for data in column 2) in the data window.

To erase columns, type

ERASE C1

or

ERASE C1 - C4

When you have completed your work in Minitab, type

STOP

This restores you to the computer operating system, from which you can sign off. Alternatively, click **File** and **Exit**.

At any time, you may receive help by typing

HELP

in order to get help regarding that command. For example,

HELP READ

will produce a brief explanation of READ. Typing

HELP HELP

will give you a summary of other help that you can get from Minitab.

To issue Minitab commands (in the session window), you need only type the first four letters of that command. In fact, Minitab does not "see" any other letters. For example, all of the following commands would print the data in column 1.

PRINT C1
PRIN C1
PRINCESS C1

However, in our instructions we will provide the complete command.

Macros

Minitab does not list in its menu all of the techniques covered in this book. To overcome this problem, we have created a number of macros, which are sets of commands that can be executed all at once. The macros are designed to perform all the techniques that were not built into Minitab. Users of Minitab with our macros will not need to perform any computations manually. The macros are stored on the disk accompanying this book and will be described later.

Computer Output

To improve readability, for some examples we have deleted a portion of our computer output because it is not needed.

The instructions that follow will allow you to perform some of the techniques described in Chapter 2.

Histogram

To create a histogram when the data are stored in column 1, type

HISTOGRAM C1

Minitab will choose the midpoints and the width of the interval. However, if you wish, you may choose the midpoints yourself. Simply type

HISTOGRAM C1;
MIDPOINTS K1 K2 . . . KK.

The second line is called a *subcommand*. To use a subcommand, the preceding command must end in a semicolon and the subcommand must end with a period.

The subcommand above specifies the midpoints (**K1, K2, . . . , KK** are values to be input). Note that the midpoints must be equally spaced (e.g., **0, 2, 4, 6**, etc.). You can also specify **cutpoints**. A cutpoint is the upper limit of an interval. For example, the command and subcommand

HISTOGRAM C1;
CUTPOINTS 10 20 30 40 50.

would create a histogram whose intervals are $X < 10$, $10 \leq X < 20$, $20 \leq X < 30$, $30 \leq X < 40$, and $40 \leq X < 50$.

To create the histogram for Example 2.1, we retrieved the data stored in file XM02-01. Next we typed the command and subcommand:

HISTOGRAM C1;
CUTPOINT 15 30 45 60 75 90 105 120.

Alternatively, we could have used the subcommand:

MIDPOINT 7.5 22.5 37.5 52.5 67.5 82.5 97.5 112.5.

The output would be identical.

Stem and Leaf Display

To create a stem and leaf display when the data are stored in column 1, type

> **STEM C1;**
> **INCREMENT 1.**

where **INCREMENT** indicates that the stem values are to increase in increments of 1. For example, to create a stem and leaf display of the data in Table 2.7, use the following commands:

> **SET C1**
> **19.1 20.0 18.4 21.1 19.9 19.8 20.3 17.6 19.3 18.7**
> **18.0 19.6 21.2 20.8 22.1 19.2 18.5 19.7 21.2 17.2**
> **19.5 18.1 22.2 21.0 18.4 17.3 19.7 19.1 18.7 21.4**
> **END**
> **STEM C1;**
> **INCREMENT 1.**

Dot Plots

Type

> **DOTPLOT C1**

Minitab will produce a dot plot of the data in column 1.

Scatter Diagrams

To create a scatter diagram with the data in column 1 on the vertical axis and the data in column 2 on the horizontal axis, type

> **PLOT C1*C2**

Pie Charts

If the raw data are stored (say in column 1) we type the command

> **%PIE C1**

The raw data for Example 2.4 are stored in column 1 of file XM02-04. Retrieve the file (using instructions provided with the disk) and type

> **RETRIEVE 'A:\XM02-04'**
> **%PIE C1**

(Be prepared to wait a while; Minitab draws pie charts slowly.)

If we already know the frequency with which each value occurs, the results should be recorded in two columns. Column 1 contains the codes representing the categories, and column 2 contains the frequencies. We would then issue the following command and subcommand.

> **%PIE C1;**
> **COUNT C2.**

For Example 2.4 we input the codes and frequencies and commanded Minitab as follows.

```
READ C1 C2
1 73
2 52
3 36
4 64
5 28
END
%PIE C1;
COUNT C2.
```

Bar Charts

If the raw data are stored in column 1, type the following command and subcommand.

```
CHART COUNT(C1)*C1;
BAR.
```

If we already know the frequency with which each value occurs, the results should be recorded in two columns. Column 1 contains the codes representing the categories, and column 2 contains the frequencies. We would then issue the following command and subcommand.

```
CHART C2*C1;
BAR.
```

Line Charts

The command and subcommand

```
TSPLOT C1;
CONNECT.
```

creates a time-series plot of the data in column 1 with all the points connected.

MENU COMMANDS

1 Click **Graph** and **Time-Series Plot . . . .**
2 Specify the column number of the variable to be plotted.
3 Use the cursor to select **Index**, **Calendar**, or **Clock**. If you choose **Calendar** or **Clock**, use the cursor to select the specific format (e.g., **Day**, **Month**, **Quarter**, etc.).
4 Under **Data display:** specify **Connect**. Under **For Each** specify **Graph**.
5 Click **OK**.

Introduction

We have chosen to use Excel in addition to Minitab to produce statistical output because most students are familiar with this software. We provide simple step-by-step instructions for using Excel. We assume that students are already familiar with their computers and with Excel in general. Our instructions deal specifically with statistical components of Excel.

Data Analysis

To access the statistical tools that analyze data, click **Tools** and **Data Analysis...** If **Data Analysis** is not in the **Tools** menu, install the **Analysis ToolPak**. To do so, click **Tools** and **Add-Ins**. Then click the **Analysis ToolPak** check box.

If **Analysis ToolPak** is not listed in the **Add-ins** dialog box, click **Browse** and find the folder name and file name for the **Analysis ToolPak** add-in. It is probably in the Library/Analysis folder. If not found, the **Analysis ToolPak** was probably not included when Excel was installed. Run the setup program again.

Using the Analysis ToolPak

Click **Tools**, **Data Analysis...**, and the statistical technique you want. In the dialog box, enter the information requested. Include the input range (the data's block coordinates), specify whether the range includes variable names (Labels), and select any options you need.

Macros

Excel's menu does not include all the techniques covered in this book. So we have created several macros—sets of commands that are executed all at once—that are designed to perform many of the "missing" techniques. This will allow Excel users to avoid manual calculations. Instructions for their use are described throughout this book. The macros are stored on the CD that accompanies the book. Instructions for copying them to your computer are in the README file. After copying the macros to your computer, access them through the **Tools** menu. To use the macros, click **Tools**, **Data Analysis Plus**, and the technique you wish to use.

Data Retrieval

The CD that accompanies this book contains 345 data files occupying 7.12 MB. The instructions that copy the macros will also copy the data files to your computer. Instructions for opening these files appear throughout the book.

Different Versions of Excel

The instructions in this book are valid for Excel 5.0 and Microsoft Office 95. We include the instructions for Microsoft Office 97 where necessary. The macros and data sets are not compatible with earlier versions of Excel.

Computer Output

To improve the readability of computer printouts for most of the examples used in this book, we have deleted a portion of the output.

3 Art and Science of Graphical Presentations

3.1 Introduction

In Chapter 2, we introduced a number of graphical techniques. The emphasis was on how to construct each one manually and how to command the computer to draw them. In Chapter 3, we will discuss how to use graphical techniques effectively. We introduce the concept of **graphical excellence**, which is a term we apply to techniques that are informative and concise and that impart the information clearly to their viewers. Section 3.2 will discuss how to achieve excellence in the presentation of graphical methods. In Section 3.3, we will discuss an equally important concept, graphical integrity. In that section, we discuss how charts are often used to mislead readers.

3.2 Graphical Excellence

Graphical excellence is achieved when the following characteristics apply.

1 *The graph presents large data sets concisely and coherently.* Graphical techniques were created to summarize and describe large data sets. Small data sets are easily summarized with a table. One or two numbers can best be presented in a sentence.

2 *The ideas and concepts the statistician wants to deliver are clearly understood by the viewer.* The chart is designed to describe what would otherwise be described in words. An excellent chart is one that can replace a thousand words and still be clearly comprehended by its readers.

3 *The graph encourages the viewer to compare two or more variables.* Graphs displaying only one variable provide very little information. Graphs are often best used to depict relationships between two or more variables or to explain how and why the observed results occurred.

4 *The display induces the viewer to address the substance of the data and not the form of the graph.* The form of the graph is supposed to help present

the substance. If the form replaces the substance, the chart is not performing its function.

5 **_There is no distortion of what the data reveal_**. You _cannot_ make statistical techniques say whatever you like. A knowledgeable reader will easily see through distortions and deception. This is such an important topic that we devote Section 3.3 to its discussion.

Edward Tufte, Professor of Statistics at Yale University, summarized graphical excellence this way:

Graphical excellence is the well-designed presentation of interesting data—a matter of substance, of statistics, and of design.

Graphical excellence is that which gives the viewer the greatest number of ideas in the shortest time with the least ink in the smallest space.

Graphical excellence is nearly always multivariate.

And graphical excellence requires telling the truth about the data.

In attempting to demonstrate what constitutes excellence, we searched through newspapers, magazines, and financial reports. Unfortunately, we found far more examples of bad statistical applications than excellent ones. Fortunately, we can learn just as much about proper use of graphs by examining bad ones. Here are good and bad examples.

Examples

Graphical techniques should be used when there is a large amount of data. In general, small data sets can be presented in tabular form. Examine Figure 3.1, which is a bar chart depicting the number of visitors in 1994 to Disney theme parks around the world. Does the chart provide the reader with any more information than Table 3.1 does? From both you can see that Tokyo Disneyland drew the most visitors—about 16 million—while the others drew between 8 and 11.2 million. The bar chart is completely unnecessary for two reasons. First, there are only six numbers represented; a data set this small does not need a graphical display. Second, there is no analysis associated with the attendance figures to explain why Tokyo Disneyland outdrew the others or how these figures are related to other variables, such as profits or sales. This chart also fails to address why the reader would be interested in this "information." What concept is being imparted to the reader? None that we could see.

Figure 3.1

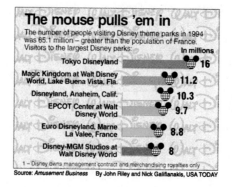

Table 3.1	Number of People Visiting Disney Theme Parks in 1994

PARK	NUMBER OF VISITORS (IN MILLIONS)
Tokyo Disneyland	16.0
Walt Disney World, Florida	11.2
Disneyland, California	10.3
EPCOT Center, Florida	9.7
Euro Disneyland, France	8.8
Disney-MGM Studios, Florida	8.0

Figure 3.2

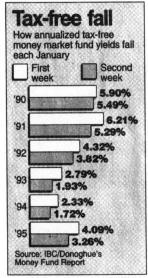

Tax-free fall

How annualized tax-free money market fund yields fall each January

☐ First week   ■ Second week

'90	5.90% / 5.49%
'91	6.21% / 5.29%
'92	4.32% / 3.82%
'93	2.79% / 1.93%
'94	2.33% / 1.72%
'95	4.09% / 3.26%

Source: IBC/Donoghue's Money Fund Report

By Marty Baumann, USA TODAY

Compare the amount of information contained in Figure 3.1 with that of Figure 3.2, which describes the January effect on tax-free money funds. The January effect is a phenomenon that results in a drop in the yield of money funds during the second week of January. It is caused by investors paying their Christmas shopping bills by taking money out of their tax-free funds, which causes the yield to drop. In Figure 3.2, the concept the author wishes to describe is clear. For each of the years 1990 to 1995, the yield during the second week of January was less than the yield during the first week. However, because of the small amount of data (there are only 12 numbers shown), a table would provide at least as much information. In fact, by adding an extra column for the difference between the first-week yield and the second-week yield, Table 3.2 provides *more* information. We clearly can see the magnitude of the difference between the yields in weeks 1 and 2.

In an article about the uneven work distribution in Canada, Figure 3.3 was drawn. A large amount of data is summarized concisely. The number of hours specified in many collective agreements had to be collected, recorded, and tabulated. The main point is clear: there is great variation in the work hours across different industries. Moreover, the reader is coaxed into analyzing the relationship between two variables: working hours and type of industry. On the negative side, a larger number of categories of working hours (e.g., 35–37.5, 37.5–40, 40–42.5, 42.5 and over) would be more useful. And, why don't the three percentages for "All Industries" add up to 100%?

Table 3.2	Yields of Tax-Free Funds for First and Second Weeks in January

YEAR	YIELD: FIRST WEEK	YIELD: SECOND WEEK	DIFFERENCE BETWEEN FIRST AND SECOND WEEKS
1990	5.90%	5.49%	0.41%
1991	6.21	5.29	0.92
1992	4.32	3.82	0.50
1993	2.79	1.93	0.86
1994	2.33	1.72	0.61
1995	4.09	3.26	0.83

Figure 3.3

Number of Working Hours by Industry (in major collective agreements)

SOURCE: Creative Statistics Company

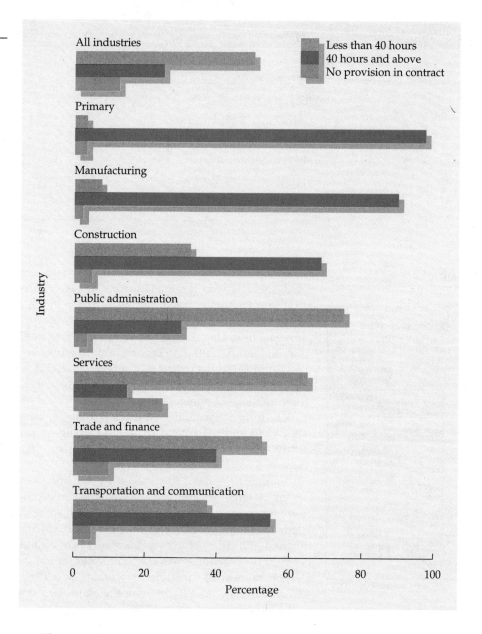

The overwhelming majority of poorly executed charts can be attributed to the contempt most people have for statistics. It is generally believed that statistics can be manipulated to prove anything that the statistician wishes to prove. It would follow that statistics and graphs mean nothing and that there are no rules governing how they should be used. This is absolute nonsense! You cannot lie to a knowledgeable viewer. It is usually easy to detect deception in the application of statistical techniques.

It is also generally accepted that statistics are boring, and authors must resort to desperate measures to attract readers. This attitude is exemplified in Figure 3.4, which is a pie chart of the percentages of the uses of sports apparel. This is one of the worst examples of graphical techniques that we have encountered. It fails on every characteristic. It contains very little data, and hence a table would suffice.

The idea that the author wants to deliver is not clear. Perhaps the creator of the chart had no ideas to impart. There is no analysis associated with the chart that would entail examining why these results were observed. Finally, because of the other shortcomings of the graph, the author was forced to enhance it by making the pie chart part of an illustration of a runner. Consequently, the viewer addresses the design rather than the substance. Statisticians refer to this type of graphical display as **chartjunk**. We make one request of our readers: if you ever create a chart like Figure 3.4, please don't tell anyone you learned statistics from this book.

Figure 3.4

SOURCE: *USA Today* (11 January, 1995)

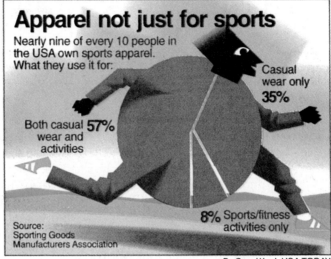

Apparel not just for sports

Nearly nine of every 10 people in the USA own sports apparel. What they use it for:

Casual wear only **35%**

Both casual **57%** wear and activities

8% Sports/fitness activities only

Source: Sporting Goods Manufacturers Association

By Sam Ward, USA TODAY

Time lines representing time-series data are often seen in the financial sections of newspapers. However, they are often devoid of substance. For example, Figure 3.5 is a time line of the number of basis points by which Quebec 10-year bonds exceed 10-year Canadian bonds. Since the late 1960s, the province of Quebec has threatened to secede from Canada, which has made many investors nervous about investing in Quebec. The chart depicts the degree of concern among investors—the greater the concern, the greater the premium that must be offered by the Quebec government. In its present form, the graph tells us very little. It could be improved by adding the time line of one or more related variables. Examples of related variables include Quebec's budget deficits, unemployment rates, and survey results showing support for separation. The authors could also indicate the dates of Quebec's provincial elections. They could also attempt to explain the spikes in 1975, 1977, and 1982 and the steady increase since 1984.

Contrast Figure 3.5 with Figure 3.6, which plots a consumer sentiment index in the United States from 1950 to 1994. The index measures how people feel about their financial prospects. The score in 1966 was arbitrarily set equal to 100. In addition to the scores, we also see the periods during which the U.S. economy underwent recessions. The years in which a new president was inaugurated as well as other key events also appear on the chart. Examining the chart provides rich details about the factors that affect Americans' perceptions of their financial circumstances. For example, recessionary periods mostly coincide with downturns in the index. From the early 1960s to 1980, there was a general downward drift. Historians would agree that this was a troubled time in the United States. The period

Figure 3.5

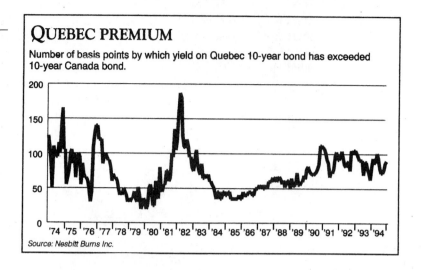

started with the assassination of President John Kennedy, followed by the Vietnam War, the rapid increase in the price of oil, gasoline shortages, the Watergate scandal, and the Iranian hostage crisis. The inauguration of Ronald Reagan as president in 1980 marked the end of the decline, and the sharpest increase in the index took place during his eight-year stint in office, during which the greatest boom in U.S. history occurred. This graph is more than just a graph; it's a short story.

Figure 3.6

SOURCE: *Newsweek*
(30 January, 1995).

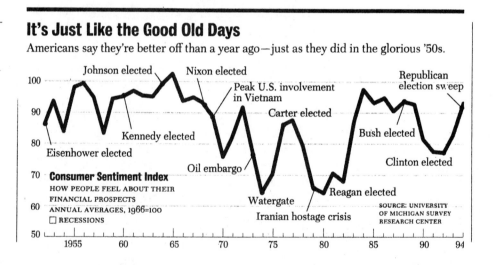

In January 1995, a financial crisis in Mexico caused many foreign investors to sell their Mexican holdings. As a result, the Mexican stock market (as measured by the *Bolsa* Index) fell by 6.6% on one day (January 9). In a story about the widespread effect of this event, *Time* magazine published the graphs shown in Figure 3.7, which are time lines for the stock market indexes in Mexico, Argentina, Brazil, and Chile. The story is summarized concisely and clearly by the graphs. The shock to the Mexican stock market reverberated across South America with equally disastrous consequences.

Figure 3.7

SOURCE: *Time*
(23 January, 1995). ©1995
Time Inc. Reprinted by
permission.

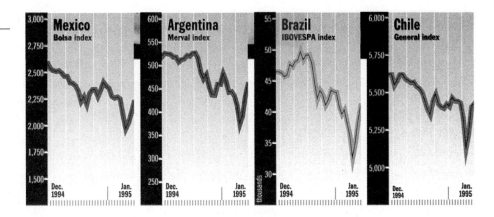

In the same section, *Time* also published an article about the fall of the Canadian dollar. Figure 3.8 depicts the time line showing the value of the Canadian dollar in U.S. dollars. It shows that in 1990 the Canadian dollar was worth about $0.86 U.S. but had dropped to about $0.71 in 1994. The article discussed several reasons for this decrease in value but pointed to Canada's rapidly increasing debt as the chief cause. The chart also included Canada's debt as a percentage of gross domestic product (GDP). As you can easily see, the debt/GDP ratio was constant between 1986 and 1989, but started a sharp increase in 1990. The argument is clear: the increasing debt produced a much lower value for the dollar.

Figure 3.8

SOURCE: *Time* (23 January, 1995). ©1995 Time Inc. Reprinted by permission.

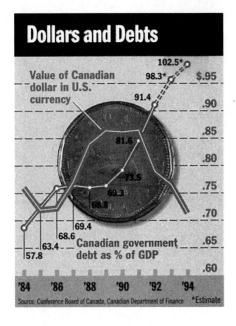

Figures 3.6, 3.7, and 3.8 illustrate one of the determinants of graphical excellence. The graphs are well designed, presenting interesting data although the Canadian dollar is extraneous. It imparts ideas concisely because it presents several variables at the same time. And finally, it does not distort the data in any way.

Exercises

3.1 Geac is a computer company that has diversified its operations into financial services, construction, manufacturing, and hotels. In its 1994 annual report, the following tables were provided.

| | SALES (MILLIONS OF DOLLARS) BY REGION | |
REGION	1994	1993
United States	67.3	40.4
Canada	20.9	18.9
Europe	37.9	35.5
Australasia	26.2	10.3
Total	152.2	105.1

| | SALES (MILLIONS OF DOLLARS) BY DIVISION | |
DIVISION	1994	1993
Customer service	54.6	43.8
Library systems	49.3	30.5
Construction and property management	17.5	7.7
Manufacturing and distribution	15.4	8.9
Financial systems	9.4	10.9
Hotels and clubs	5.9	3.4

Create charts to present these data so that the differences between 1994 and 1993 are clear.

3.2 The following chart appeared in *USA Today* (11 January, 1995). Grade it A, B, C, D, or F. Explain why you graded it the way you did.

Exercise 3.2

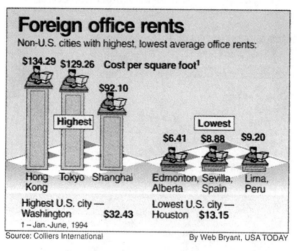

3.3 The line chart showing the value of the Canadian dollar in terms of the U.S. dollar from 1984 to 1994 is provided below.

Exercise 3.3

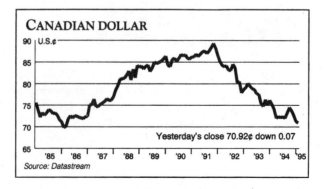

Exercise 3.4

SOURCE: *Globe and Mail*
(16 January, 1995).

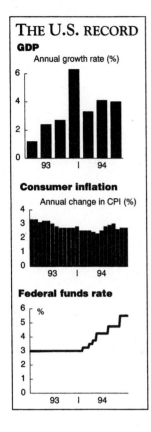

THE U.S. RECORD

GDP
Annual growth rate (%)

Consumer inflation
Annual change in CPI (%)

Federal funds rate

Exercise 3.5

a   Write as many sentences as you need to describe the chart.

b   How would you judge the amount of information that can be extracted from the chart?

c   Describe how the chart could be made more informative.

3.4   The U.S. Federal Reserve Board raises interest rates during economic booms to help control inflation and produce the so-called "soft landing" when the boom eventually ends. Signs that usually indicate that the economy is overheating and likely to result in inflation are the changes in the consumer price index and annual growth rates. In an article (*Globe and Mail*, 16 January, 1995) about increases in interest rates, the following three charts appeared. Discuss the information that is imparted by the charts. Do the charts justify increases in the interest rate?

3.5   The accompanying line chart graphs the number of hardcover books that appeared on the top-50 bestseller list each week during 1994. Grade it A, B, C, D, or F, and justify your grade. What have you learned from the chart?

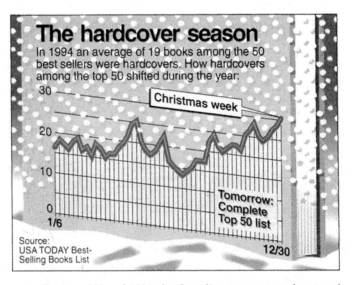

The hardcover season

In 1994 an average of 19 books among the 50 best sellers were hardcovers. How hardcovers among the top 50 shifted during the year:

Christmas week

Tomorrow: Complete Top 50 list

Source: USA TODAY Best-Selling Books List

3.6   During 1993 and 1994, the Canadian government threatened cutbacks in university funding. Students and educators protested, arguing that higher education is critical not only to the nation but to individual students as well. The following chart was produced (*Globe and Mail*, 6 October, 1994), showing the percent changes in the number of jobs for four groups with different educational attainment levels. Grade it A, B, C, D, or F, and explain your reasons for your grade assignment.

Exercise 3.6

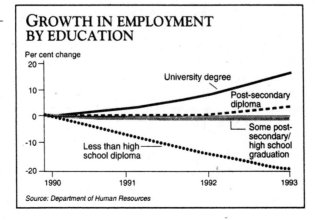

GROWTH IN EMPLOYMENT BY EDUCATION

Per cent change

University degree

Post-secondary diploma

Some post-secondary/high school graduation

Less than high school diploma

Source: Department of Human Resources

3.7 In 1987, the U.S. government established Sematech, a federally financed consortium to boost sales of semiconductors, a critical component of computers. Before 1987, the U.S. market share of semiconductors was decreasing while that of Japanese companies was increasing. The market shares of companies in the United States, Japan, and all other countries for the years 1981 to 1994 are listed below. Draw a time line of these data. Show the point at which Sematech was formed. How well does the graph describe the effect of Sematech? Grade the graph A, B, C, D, or F, and justify your grade.

Percent of Semiconductors Sold by American, Japanese, and Other Countries' Companies	YEAR	U.S.	JAPAN	ALL OTHERS
	1981	73	19	8
	1982	70	24	6
	1983	68	28	4
	1984	65	30	5
	1985	61	34	5
	1986	59	37	4
	1987	56	39	5
	1988	50	42	8
	1989	48	45	7
	1990	43	48	9
	1991	46	45	9
	1992	50	41	9
	1993	52	40	8
	1994	53	39	8

SOURCE: Creative Statistics Company

3.3 Graphical Deception

The use of graphs and charts is pervasive in newspapers, magazines, business and economic reports, and seminars, in large part due to the increasing availability of computers and software that allow the storage, retrieval, manipulation, and summary of large masses of raw data. It is therefore more important than ever to be able to evaluate critically the information presented by means of graphical techniques. In the final analysis, graphical techniques merely create a visual impression, which is easy to distort. In fact, distortion is so easy and commonplace that in 1992 the Canadian Institute of Chartered Accountants found it necessary to begin setting guidelines for financial graphics, after a study of hundreds of the annual reports of major corporations found that 8% contained at least one misleading graph that covered up bad results. Although the heading for this section mentions deception, it is quite possible for an inexperienced person inadvertently to create distorted impressions with graphs. In any event, you should be aware of possible methods of **graphical deception**. This section illustrates a few of them.

The first thing to watch for is a graph without a scale on one axis. The time-series graph of a firm's sales in Figure 3.9 might represent a growth rate of 100% or 1% over the five years depicted, depending on the vertical scale. It is best simply to ignore such graphs.

Figure 3.9

Graph Without a Vertical Scale

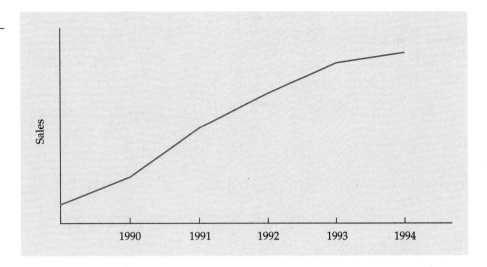

A second trap to avoid is being influenced by a graph's caption. Your impression of the trend in interest rates might be different depending on whether you read a newspaper carrying caption (a) or caption (b) in Figure 3.10.

Figure 3.10

Different Captions for the Same Graph

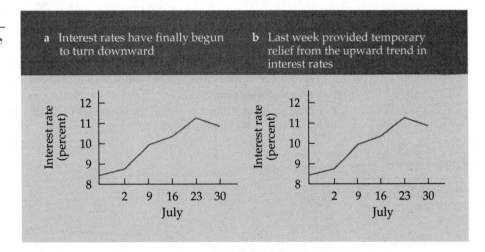

Perspective is often distorted if only absolute changes in value, rather than percentage changes, are reported. A $1 drop in the price of your $2 stock is relatively more distressing than a $1 drop in the price of your $100 stock. On January 9, 1986, newspapers throughout North America displayed graphs similar to the one shown in Figure 3.11 and reported that the stock market, as measured by the Dow Jones Industrial Average (DJIA), had suffered its worst one-day loss ever on the previous day. The loss was 39 points, exceeding even the loss of Black Tuesday—October 28, 1929. While the loss was indeed a large one, many news reports failed to mention that the 1986 level of the DJIA was much higher than the 1929 level. A better perspective on the situation could be gained by noticing that the loss on January 8, 1986, represented a 2.5% decline, while the decline in 1929 was 12.8%. As a point of interest, we note that the stock market was 12% higher within two months of this historic drop and 40% higher one year later. The worst one-day loss ever, 22%, occurred on October 19, 1987.

Figure 3.11

**Historic Drop in the
DJIA, 1986**

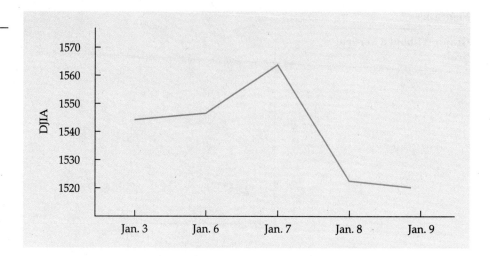

We now turn to some rather subtle methods of creating distorted impressions with graphs. Consider the graph in Figure 3.12, which depicts the growth in a firm's quarterly sales over the past year, from $100 million to $110 million. This 10% growth in quarterly sales can be made to appear more dramatic by stretching the vertical axis—a technique that involves changing the scale on the vertical axis so that a given dollar amount is represented by a greater height than before. As a result, the rise in sales appears to be greater, because the slope of the graph is visually (but not numerically) steeper. The expanded scale is usually accommodated by employing a break in the vertical axis, as in Figure 3.13(a), or by truncating the vertical axis, as in Figure 3.13(b), so that the vertical scale begins at a point greater than zero. The effect of making slopes appear steeper can also be created by shrinking the horizontal axis, in which case points on the horizontal axis are moved closer together.

Figure 3.12

**Quarterly Sales for the
Past Year**

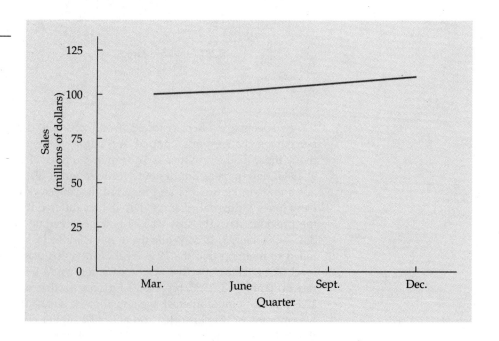

Figure 3.13

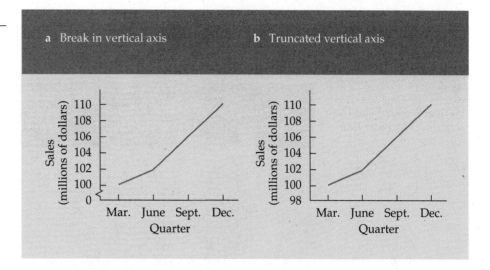

Just the opposite effect is obtained by stretching the horizontal axis; that is, spreading out the points on the horizontal axis to increase the distance between them so that slopes and trends will appear to be less steep. The graph of a firm's profits presented in Figure 3.14(a) shows considerable swings, both upward and downward, in the profits from one quarter to the next. However, the firm could convey the impression of reasonable stability in profits from quarter to quarter by stretching the horizontal axis, as shown in Figure 3.14(b).

Figure 3.14

Quarterly Profits over
Two Years

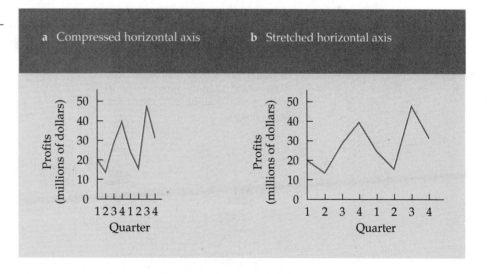

Similar illusions can be created with bar charts by stretching or shrinking the vertical or horizontal axis. Another popular method of creating distorted impressions with bar charts is to construct the bars so that their widths are proportional to their heights. The bar chart in Figure 3.15(a) correctly depicts the average weekly amount spent on food by Canadian families during three particular years. This chart correctly uses bars of equal width so that both the height and the area of each bar are proportional to the expenditures they represent. The growth in food expenditures is exaggerated in Figure 3.15(b), in which the widths of the bars increase with their heights. A quick glance at this bar chart might leave the viewer with the mistaken impression that food expenditures increased fourfold over the decade, since the 1990 bar is four times the size of the 1980 bar.

Figure 3.15

Average Weekly Food Expenditures by Canadian Families

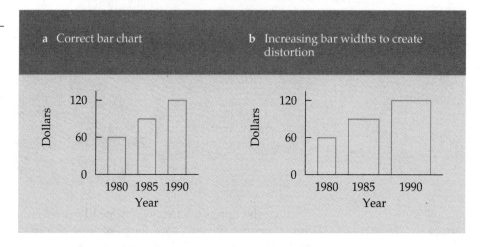

Size distortions should be watched for particularly in pictograms, which replace the bars with pictures of objects (such as bags of money, people, or animals) to enhance the visual appeal. Figure 3.16 displays the misuse of a pictogram—the snowman grows in width as well as height. The proper use of a pictogram is shown in Figure 3.17, which effectively uses pictures of Coca-Cola bottles.

Figure 3.16

Incorrect Pictogram

SOURCE: Environment Canada, Metro Toronto Branch.

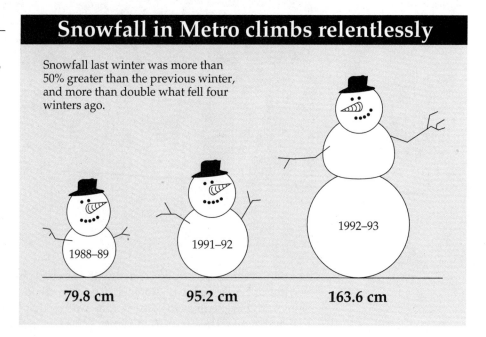

Figure 3.17

Correct Pictogram

SOURCE: *Value Line Investment Survey*, 21 May 1993.

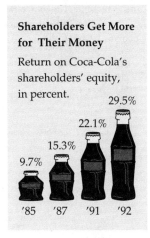

Shareholders Get More for Their Money

Return on Coca-Cola's shareholders' equity, in percent.

29.5%

22.1%

15.3%

9.7%

'85   '87   '91   '92

The preceding examples of creating a distorted impression using graphs are not exhaustive, but they include some of the more popular methods. They should also serve to make the point that graphical techniques are used to create a visual impression, and the impression you obtain may be a distorted one unless you examine the graph with care. You are less likely to be misled if you focus your attention on the numerical values that the graph represents. Begin by carefully noting the scales on both axes; graphs with unmarked axes should be ignored completely.

Exercises

3.8 The U.S. seasonally adjusted unemployment rate from July 1993 to July 1994 is listed below.

   a Draw a bar chart of these data with 6.0% as the lowest point on the vertical axis.

   b Draw a bar chart of these data with 0.0% as the lowest point on the vertical axis.

   c Discuss the impression given by the two charts.

   d Which chart would you use? Explain.

	MONTH	SEASONALLY ADJUSTED UNEMPLOYMENT RATE
1993	July	7.6%
	August	7.6
	September	7.5
	October	7.3
	November	7.3
	December	7.2
1994	January	7.0
	February	6.7
	March	6.4
	April	6.4
	May	6.3
	June	6.0
	July	6.1

SOURCE: U.S. Department of Labor

3.9 The following table lists family incomes (in thousands of 1991 dollars) and family size between 1971 and 1991. Draw time lines that describe how both variables have changed and how they appear to be related.

YEAR	FAMILY INCOME (IN THOUSANDS OF 1991 DOLLARS)	AVERAGE FAMILY SIZE
1971	39.8	3.68
1972	42.1	3.62
1973	43.5	3.60
1974	47.1	3.54
1975	48.3	3.47
1976	48.6	3.42
1977	48.2	3.40
1978	50.2	3.38
1979	50.4	3.34
1980	50.9	3.30
1981	49.2	3.27
1982	49.0	3.24
1983	48.4	3.21
1984	48.9	3.18
1985	50.2	3.17
1986	50.9	3.18
1987	52.2	3.16
1988	52.8	3.12
1989	54.2	3.10
1990	51.7	3.09
1991	51.1	3.08

SOURCE: Creative Statistics Company

3.10 Enerflex Systems, Inc., provides a full range of natural gas compression equipment by way of manufacturing and leasing services. In its 1993 annual report the following data were presented.

	1993	1992	1991	1990	1989
Sales (millions of dollars)	199	69	85	88	82
Net income (millions of dollars)	7.7	3.0	4.7	4.8	1.8
Return on equity (%)	32.9	13.6	24.4	31.7	12.0
Net income per common share ($)	1.02	0.36	0.57	0.56	0.15

a Use bar charts to present these data.

b Assume that you are an unscrupulous statistician and want to make the data appear more positive than they really are. Draw the bar charts accordingly.

3.4 Summary

This chapter completes our discussion of graphical techniques, which began in Chapter 2. In Chapter 2, we showed how and when to construct the graphs. In this chapter, we provided guidelines for the application of graphical methods. We illustrated graphical excellence and graphical deception, and in so doing, we showed you what to do and what not to do.

IMPORTANT TERMS

Graphical excellence   Chartjunk   Graphical deception

The 1994–1995 Federal budget estimates, showing where revenues are generated and where tax dollars are spent, are listed below.

REVENUES (BILLIONS OF DOLLARS)

Personal income tax		59.5
Deficit		30.2
Insurance premiums		19.3
Goods and services tax		16.5
Corporate income tax		10.3
Excise taxes and duties		10.1
Other revenues		8.2
Interest on the debt		41.0
Transfers to other levels of government		26.3
Health	6.7	
Postsecondary education	2.1	
Canada assistance plan	7.4	
Equalization	8.5	
Territories and municipalities	1.6	
Pensions		20.6
Old-age security	15.8	
Guaranteed income supplement	4.4	
Spouses allowance	0.4	
Government operations		20.5
Unemployment insurance benefits		18.3
Regular benefits	14.4	
Other	3.9	
Subsidies and other transfer payments		17.2
Grants to business	3.3	
Grants to farmers	2.3	
Grants to natives	3.8	
International assistance	2.6	
Infrastructure	0.7	
Other	4.5	
Defense		10.8
Crown corporations		4.6
Canada Mortgage and housing	2.1	
CBC	1.1	
Other	1.4	
Reserves		2.4
Veterans		1.9

Use any graphical techniques you deem necessary to present the figures above.

4 Numerical Descriptive Measures

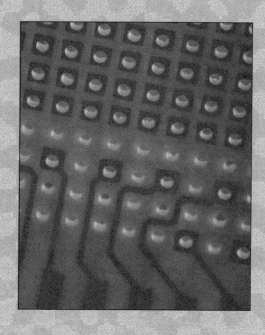

4.1 Introduction

In this chapter, we continue to examine how to summarize a large set of raw data so that the meaningful essentials can be extracted from it. Thus far, we have looked at how to group the data set into a more manageable form and how to construct various graphical representations of it. Faced with a set of measurements like the telephone data in Table 2.1, we began by finding the smallest and largest values, and then we formed a frequency distribution and histogram. These revealed the approximate shape of the distribution and indicated where the measurements were concentrated.

Although a frequency distribution is certainly useful in providing a general idea about how the data are distributed between the two extreme values, it is usually desirable to summarize the data even further by computing a few numerical descriptive measures. Numerical descriptive measures provide precise, objectively determined values that can easily be manipulated, interpreted, and compared with one another. In short, they permit a more careful analysis of the data than do the general impressions conveyed by tabular and graphical summaries. This is especially important when the data represent a sample from which inferences must be made concerning the entire population.

There are a variety of different types of descriptive measures. In Section 4.2, we introduce measures of central location, and Section 4.3 presents measures of variability. In Section 4.6, we present measures of association, which gauge the relationship between two variables. We conclude our presentation of graphical and numerical techniques for extracting information from data by discussing some general guidelines on their use.

4.2 Measures of Central Location

In computing numerical descriptive measures of the data, interest usually focuses on two measures: a measure of the central, or average, value of the data and a measure of the degree to which the observations are spread out about this average value. Measures of central location (averages) are discussed in this section, and measures of dispersion are discussed in Section 4.3. Of the various types of measures of central location, we will consider only three: the arithmetic mean, the median, and the mode.

Arithmetic Mean

By far the most popular and useful measure of central location is the **arithmetic mean**, which we will refer to simply as the *mean*. Widely known in everyday usage as the *average*, the mean of a set of measurements is defined as follows:

$$\text{Mean} = \frac{\text{Sum of the measurements}}{\text{Number of measurements}}$$

Before expressing this definition algebraically, we should introduce some notation.* If we are dealing with a population of measurements, the total number of measurements is denoted by N, and the mean is represented by μ (the lowercase Greek letter mu). If the set of measurements is a sample, the total number of measurements is denoted by n, and the sample mean is represented by $\bar{x}$ (referred to as *x*-**bar**). (If the measurements under consideration are represented by a letter other than x, such as y, the sample mean is denoted by $\bar{y}$.) Because the measurements in a sample are a subset of the measurements in the parent population, $n \leq N$ if the parent population consists of N measurements. In actual practice, you won't normally have access to all the measurements in a population, so you will most often calculate the sample mean. As we'll see in Chapter 9, the sample mean $\bar{x}$ is used to make inferences about μ (the mean of the population from which the sample was taken). In particular, the value of $\bar{x}$ is frequently used as an estimate of μ.

> **Sample Mean**
> The **mean of a sample** of n measurements $x_1, x_2, \ldots, x_n$ is defined as
> $$\bar{x} = \frac{\sum_{i=1}^{n} x_i}{n}$$

EXAMPLE 4.1

The mean of the sample of six measurements 7, 3, 9, −2, 4, and 6 is given by

$$\bar{x} = \frac{\sum_{i=1}^{n} x_i}{n} = \frac{7 + 3 + 9 - 2 + 4 + 6}{6} = 4.5$$

---

*Students unfamiliar with summation notation should read Appendix 4.B for further background.

The formula for calculating the mean of a population is the same as the formula for calculating the mean of a sample, differing only in the notation of the variables.

Population Mean

The **mean of a population** of N measurements $x_1, x_2, \ldots, x_N$ is defined as

$$\mu = \frac{\sum_{i=1}^{N} x_i}{N}$$

EXAMPLE 4.2

Suppose that the telephone bills in Table 2.1 (see page 24) represent a population of measurements. Then the population mean is

$$\mu = \frac{\sum_{i=1}^{N} x_i}{N} = \frac{42.19 + 15.30 + \cdots + 53.21}{200} = 43.59$$

Referring to the histogram of telephone bills in Figure 2.1 (page 26), we see that the value 43.59 is located at *approximately* the center of the distribution. The reason for this mean value being somewhat to the left of center is that, rather than having a symmetrical distribution of telephone bills, there is a disproportionate number of small telephone bills.

EXAMPLE 4.3

When many of the measurements in a sample (or population) have the same value, the measurements are often summarized in a frequency table. Suppose that the numbers of children in a sample of 16 employees' families were recorded as follows.

NUMBER OF CHILDREN	0	1	2	3
NUMBER OF EMPLOYEES	3	4	7	2

Notice that we are dealing with a total of $n = 16$ measurements here—one for each employee. To find the sample mean $\bar{x}$ of the number of children per employee, we divide the total number of children by the total number of employees. That is,

$$\bar{x} = \frac{\sum_{i=1}^{16} x_i}{n} = \frac{0 + 0 + 0 + 1 + \cdots + 2 + 3 + 3}{16}$$

$$= \frac{3(0) + 4(1) + 7(2) + 2(3)}{16}$$

$$= \frac{24}{16} = 1.5$$

Notice that we could find $\bar{x}$ by skipping directly to the next to the last line in this computation, where each distinct value of the measurement (number of children) is multiplied by the frequency with which it occurs and the total is then divided by the total number of measurements.

The sum of deviations of individual measurements from the mean is zero, or

$$\sum_{i=1}^{n} (x_i - \bar{x}) = 0$$

This property has an interesting physical interpretation. Imagine that the individual measurements are marked off along a weightless bar and that a 1-lb weight is placed at each such mark, as depicted in the accompanying diagram (based on measurements from Example 4.1). The bar will be in perfect balance if a support is placed at the mean; therefore, the arithmetic mean can be interpreted as the center of gravity, or the balance point.

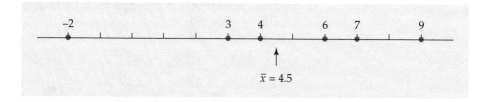

The mean is a popular measure because it is simple to compute and interpret and because it lends itself to mathematical manipulation. More important for decision makers, it is generally the best measure of central location for purposes of statistical inference. *Its one serious drawback is that it is unduly influenced by extreme observations.* For example, if the sample of six measurements in Example 4.1 is enlarged to include a seventh measurement that has a value of 22, the mean of the resulting sample of seven measurements is $49/7 = 7$. Adding a single, relatively large value to the original sample of measurements substantially increases the value of the mean. This is one reason why we sometimes resort to another measure of central location, the median.

The Median

Median

The **median** of a set of measurements is the value that falls in the middle when the measurements are arranged in order of magnitude.

When an even number of measurements is involved, any number between the two middle values would satisfy the preceding definition of *median*. In such a case, however, it is conventional to take the midpoint between the two middle values as the median.

Calculating the Median

Given n measurements arranged in order of magnitude,

$$\text{Median} = \begin{cases} \text{Middle value, if } n \text{ is odd} \\ \text{Mean of the two middle values, if } n \text{ is even} \end{cases}$$

In the examples that follow, we have arbitrarily chosen to arrange the measurements in ascending order (from smallest to largest) as a preliminary step in locating the median. Arranging them in descending order would, of course, yield identical results. The median has intuitive appeal as a measure of central location: at most half the measurements fall below the median, and at most half fall above. Because of the distorting effect of extreme observations on the mean, the median is often the preferred measure in such situations as salary negotiations.

EXAMPLE 4.4

The annual salaries (in thousands of dollars) of the seven employees of a small government department are as follows.

28, 60, 26, 32, 30, 26, 29

To find the median salary, first arrange the salaries in ascending order: 26, 26, 28, 29, 30, 32, 60. The median salary is therefore $29,000, which is clearly more representative of a typical salary than is the mean value ($33,000).

EXAMPLE 4.5

Suppose we want to find the median of the following values.

28, 60, 26, 32, 30, 26, 29, 31

Arranging the values in ascending order, we have 26, 26, 28, 29, 30, 31, 32, 60. For an even number of measurements, the convention is to locate the median at the midpoint between the two middle values. Therefore, the median in this case is 29.5—the midpoint between 29 and 30.

The median is the most appropriate measure of central location to use when the data under consideration are ranked qualitative data, rather than quantitative data. Such a situation arises whenever items are simply ranked—perhaps according to preference, degree of ability, or degree of difficulty. For example, if 11 statistical problems are ranked from 1 to 11 according to their degree of difficulty, problem 6 is the problem of median difficulty.

Mode

A third measure of central location is the mode, which indicates the most frequently occurring value in a series. The mode doesn't necessarily lie in the middle of the set of measurements, although it often does; its claim to be a measure of central location is based on the fact that it indicates the location of greatest clustering or concentration of values (just as a population center describes a location of concentrated population).

Mode

The **mode** of a set of measurements is the value that occurs most frequently.

When the data have been organized into a histogram, we are often interested in knowing which class has the largest number of observations. We refer to that class as the *modal class*. In Chapter 2, we discussed modal classes in the context of describing the shape of a histogram.

EXAMPLE 4.6

The manager of a men's store observes that the 10 pairs of trousers sold yesterday had the following waist sizes (in inches).

31, 34, 36, 33, 28, 34, 30, 34, 32, 40

The mode of these waist sizes is 34 in., and this fact is undoubtedly of more interest to the manager than are the facts that the mean waist size is 33.2 in. and the median waist size is 33.5 in.

We now look at another example, for which we'll compute all three measures of central location—first manually and then using the computer.

EXAMPLE 4.7

The ages of a sample of 10 people in a shopping mall video arcade were determined as shown below. Calculate the three measures of central location.

7, 10, 17, 8, 14, 11, 6, 17, 8, 12

SOLUTION

SOLVING BY HAND

The mean is

$$\bar{x} = \frac{\sum_{i=1}^{n} x_i}{n} = \frac{(7 + 10 + 17 + 8 + 14 + 11 + 6 + 17 + 8 + 12)}{10} = \frac{110}{10} = 11.0$$

The median is determined by placing the observations in order as follows.

6, 7, 8, 8, 10, 11, 12, 14, 17, 17

Because there is an even number of observations, the median is the average of the *two* middle numbers, which are 10 and 11. Thus, the median is 10.5. If the number of observations is an odd number, the median is the observation that falls in the middle.

The mode is the observation that occurs most frequently. The observations 8 and 17 both occur twice. All other observations occur only once. Consequently, there are two modes, 8 and 17.

The measures of location of *small* data sets can easily be calculated manually. However, the computer is used in almost all realistic problems. Here are the Minitab and Excel outputs for Example 4.7.

USING THE COMPUTER

Minitab Output for Example 4.7

Variable	N	Mean	Median	TrMean	StDev	SEMean
Ages	10	11.00	10.50	10.88	3.97	1.26

Variable	Min	Max	Q1	Q3
Ages	6.00	17.00	7.75	14.75

Minitab prints the mean and the median (as well as other statistics that we'll explain later), but not the mode.

MENU COMMANDS	COMMANDS FOR EXAMPLE 4.7
1 Type or import the data into a column.	Open file **XM04-07**.
2 Click **Stat, Basic Statistics,** and **Descriptive Statistics**	
3 Type the variable name and click **OK**.	**Ages** or **C1**

	A	B
1	*Ages*	
2		
3	Mean	11
4	Standard Error	1.256096245
5	Median	10.5
6	Mode	17
7	Standard Deviation	3.972125096
8	Sample Variance	15.77777778
9	Kurtosis	-1.079568963
10	Skewness	0.478687958
11	Range	11
12	Minimum	6
13	Maximum	17
14	Sum	110
15	Count	10
16	Confidence Level(95.000%)	2.461899757

Excel outputs all three measures of central location, as well as a variety of other statistics that we'll explain later. Notice that Excel recognizes only one mode: 17. Obviously, Excel is mistaken.

EXCEL 97

Excel 97 Users:
The instructions are unchanged. However, the way in which Excel computes the **Confidence Level** has changed. It now uses the Student *t* distribution instead of the standard normal distribution.

COMMANDS

1 Type or import the data

2 Click **Tools**, **Data Analysis . . .** , and **Descriptive Statistics**.

3 Type input range. (Include the cell containing the variable name and click **Labels in First Row**.)

4 Click **Summary Statistics** and click **OK**. To improve the appearance of the output, widen the columns (by clicking **Format**, **Column**, and **AutoFit Selection**).

COMMANDS FOR EXAMPLE 4.7

Open file **XM04-07**.

A1:A11

Mean, Median, Mode: Which Is Best?

As we've already pointed out, this textbook will emphasize the "when" of statistical analysis. This means that, for any given technique, we plan to outline the circumstances under which that technique should be employed. However, it is not always a clear-cut choice when there are several different methods available. A perfect case in point is the choice among the three measures of central location. The question arises: which measure should we use? The mean is generally the measure of central location to be used unless there are valid reasons to use some other measure. However, one disadvantage of using the mean is that it is sensitive to extreme values; a large proportion of extremely large numbers, for example, would unduly influence the mean. In such cases, the median is considered to be a better measure of central location. The mode is most useful when an important aspect of describing the data involves determining the number of times each value occurs. In that case, we're interested in knowing which value occurs most frequently.

If the data are qualitative, such as the employment areas in Example 2.4 (page 50), using the mean or the median is senseless; the mode must be used. The modal value (or employment area) in that example is accounting, because that category contains the most students. On the other hand, if the measurement data are quantitative, all three measures of central tendency are meaningful. Because the mean is the best measure of central location for the purpose of statistical inference, it will be used extensively from Chapter 9 onward. But for descriptive purposes, it is usually best to report the values of all three measures, because each conveys somewhat different information. Moreover, the relative positions of the mean and the median provide some information about the shape of the distribution of the measurements.

EXAMPLE 4.8

A professor of statistics wants to report the results of a midterm exam taken by his class of 100 students. The marks are shown below (and stored in file XM04-08). Find the mean, median, and mode of these data and describe what information they provide.

MIDTERM TEST MARKS FOR CLASS OF 100 STUDENTS

81	92	30	79	90	69	96	39	94	88	65	73	84	83	95	38	97	72	83	
87	94	93	73	78	86	57	98	93	83	99	42	99	51	84	90	88	59	74	
94	90	95	70	81	91	75	82	83	65	34	89	43	85	75	64	64	93	86	
84	95	90	84	48	81	96	91	96	83	41	100	25	48	71	89	61	77	76	
18	73	99	85	53	69	66	94	80	55	84	66	34	98	72	11	38	85	77	
96	50	71	37	16															

SOLUTION

USING THE COMPUTER

We will use our statistical software to calculate the three measures of central location using the instructions provided in Example 4.7.

Minitab Output for Example 4.8

Variable	N	Mean	Median	TrMean	StDev	SEMean
Marks	100	73.98	81.00	75.59	21.50	2.15

Variable	Min	Max	Q1	Q3		
Marks	11.00	100.00	64.25	90.00		

The mean and median are 73.98 and 81, respectively. The rest of the output will be explained later.

**Excel Output for
Example 4.8**

	A	B
1	Marks	
2		
3	Mean	73.98
4	Standard Error	2.150216339
5	Median	81
6	Mode	84
7	Standard Deviation	21.50216339
8	Sample Variance	462.3430303
9	Kurtosis	0.393660576
10	Skewness	-1.073097509
11	Range	89
12	Minimum	11
13	Maximum	100
14	Sum	7398
15	Count	100
16	Largest(25)	90
17	Smallest(25)	64
18	Confidence Level(95.000%)	4.214340342

The mean and median are 73.98 and 81, respectively. As was the case in Example 4.7, Excel identifies only one mode, 84. In fact there are two, 83 and 84, both of which occur five times. The rest of the output will be discussed later.

INTERPRETING THE
RESULTS

Most students want to know the mean, which is generally interpreted as measuring the "average" student's performance. The median tells us that half the class received a grade greater than 81% and the other half had grades below 81%. Which is the better measure? The answer depends on what we want to measure.

If we want an overall measure of how well the class performed, the mean should be used. Because the mean is computed by adding all the marks and dividing by the number of students, the mean provides a number based on the total marks of the class and thus provides a measure of the class performance. For example, the mean should be used to compare two or more sections of the same course. The median, on the other hand, gives us a mark that truly represents the center of the data. Half the class was above the median and half the class was below it.

If the marks are classified by letter grade, where A = 80 to 100, B = 70 to 79, C = 60 to 69, D = 50 to 59, and F = 0 to 49, we can count the frequency of each grade. Because we're now interested in the number of each type of grade, the mode becomes a logical measure to compute. As we pointed out in Chapter 2, we designate the category or class with the largest number of observations as the modal class. As you can see, the modal class is A.

Marks Converted to Letter Grades

GRADE	FREQUENCY
A	53
B	16
C	9
D	6
F	16

Minitab Histogram for Example 4.8

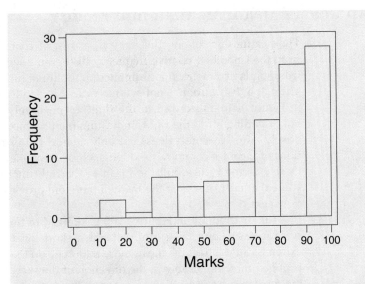

We remind you to be careful when interpreting histograms with unequal intervals. Only the heights of the rectangles are meaningful and not the areas when such histograms are produced by the computer.

Excel Histogram for Example 4.8

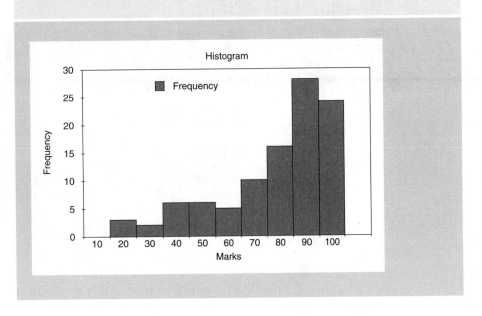

Recall that the numbers along the horizontal axis represent the upper limits of the intervals they represent. Note that, unlike Minitab and the authors, Excel counts observations equal to the upper limit of an interval as belonging to that interval. This explains the slight difference between the Minitab and Excel histograms.

Relationship among Mean, Median, and Mode

The relationship among the three measures of central location can be observed from the smoothed relative frequency histograms shown in Figure 4.1.* If the distribution is symmetrical and unimodal, the three measures coincide, as in Figure 4.1(a). If a distribution is not symmetrical, it is said to be **skewed**. The distribution in Figure 4.1(b) is **skewed to the right**, or **positively skewed**, since it has a long tail extending off to the right (indicating the presence of a small proportion of relatively large extreme values) but only a short tail extending to the left. Distributions of incomes commonly exhibit such positive skewness. As mentioned earlier, these extreme values pull the mean to the right more than the median. A mean value that is greater than the median therefore provides some evidence of positive skewness.

The distribution in Figure 4.1(c) is **skewed to the left**, or **negatively skewed**, since it has a long tail to the left but a short tail to the right. Once again, the extreme values affect the mean more than they do the median, and the mean value is pulled more noticeably in the direction of the skewness. A mean value less than the median is an indication of negative skewness.

Figure 4.1

Relationships among Mean, Median, and Mode

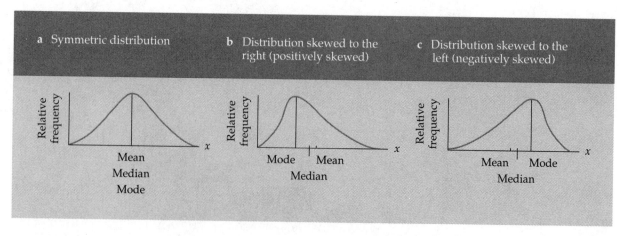

*The upper boundary of relative frequency histograms tends to look more and more like a smooth curve as the underlying data set gets larger and the class width is decreased.

Exercises

4.1 Manually calculate the mean, median, and mode or modes for the following sample.

7, 4, 6, 2, 6, 7, 3, 5

4.2 Manually calculate the three measures of central location for the following sample.

0, −3, 5, −2, −6, 4, 7, 9, 4, −3, 0, 2

4.3 What are the characteristics of a set of data for which the mean, median, and mode are identical?

4.4 Given a set of qualitative (categorical) data, what measure of central location is always appropriate?

4.5 The ages of the employees of a fast-food outlet are as follows.

19, 19, 65, 20, 21, 18, 20

a Compute the mean, the median, and the mode of the ages.

b How would these three measures of central location be affected if the oldest employee retired?

4.6 When a certain professor left one university to teach at another, a student was heard to remark, "That move will surely raise the average IQ at both universities." Explain the meaning of the remark.

4.7 Twenty families were asked how many cars they owned. Their responses are summarized in the following table.

NUMBER OF CARS	NUMBER OF FAMILIES
0	3
1	10
2	4
3	2
4	1

Determine the mean, the median, and the mode of the number of cars owned per family.

The next eight exercises require the use of a computer and statistical software.

4.8 The amount of time needed to complete a telephone survey by 100 respondents is stored in file XR04-08. (Times are rounded to the nearest whole minute.)

a Use a software package to produce the mean, median, and mode.

b Describe briefly what each measure tells you about the data.

4.9 A sample of 40 people was asked how much change they had in their pockets and wallets. Their responses (in cents) are stored in column 1 of file XR04-09.

a What are the mean, median, and mode of the data?

b Describe briefly what these measures tell you about the data.

4.10 Example 2.1 dealt with the problem of graphically summarizing the 200 long-distance bills. Recall that the data were stored in file XM02-01. Use your software to compute the mean, median, and mode of these data and interpret their values.

4.11 The summer incomes of a sample of 125 second-year business students are stored in file XR04-11.

a Calculate the mean and median of these data.

b What do the two measures of central location tell you about second-year business students' summer incomes?

c Which measure would you use to summarize the data? Explain.

4.12 Refer to Exercise 2.12, where the annual incomes of 200 first-year accountants were stored in file XR02-12.

a Determine the mean and median of the sample.

b Briefly describe what each statistic tells you.

4.13 Refer to Exercise 2.17, where the prices (in thousands of dollars) of homes in a wealthy suburb are stored in file XR02-17.

a Determine the mean and median of this sample.

b What information about the prices have you learned from the statistics in part (a)?

4.14 The owner of a hardware store that sells electrical wire by the meter is considering selling the wire in precut lengths to save on labor costs. A sample of wire sold over the course of one week was recorded and stored in file XR04-14.

a Compute the mean, median, and mode.

b For each measure of central location calculated in part (a), discuss the weaknesses in providing useful information to the owner.

c How might the owner decide upon the lengths to precut?

4.15 The amount of time (in seconds) to perform a spot weld on a car under production was recorded for 50 workers. These times are stored in file XR04-15.

a Compute the mean, median, and mode of these data.

b Discuss what information you have discovered from the statistics computed in part (a).

4.3 Measures of Variability

We are now able to compute three measures of central location, but these measures fail to tell the whole story about a distribution of measurements. For example, if you were told only that the average maximum temperature is 83.2°F in Honolulu and 79.4°F in Las Vegas, you might ask why Honolulu attracts significantly more sunseekers in the winter months than does Las Vegas. A contributing factor might be that Honolulu's climate is much more temperate year-round. Honolulu's monthly average maximum temperatures vary only from 79°F to 87°F, while those of Las Vegas vary from 56°F to 104°F. Clearly, the average maximum temperature of 83.2°F for Honolulu is far closer to the maximum monthly temperatures likely to be encountered than is Las Vegas's average maximum temperature.

Once we know the average value of a set of measurements, our next question should be: how typical is the average value of all measurements in the data set? In other words, how spread out are the measurements about their average value? Are the measurements highly variable and widely dispersed about the average value, as depicted by the smoothed relative frequency histogram in Figure 4.2(a), or do they exhibit low variability and cluster about the average value, as in Figure 4.2(b)?

The importance of looking beyond the average value is borne out by the fact that many individuals make use of the concept of variability in everyday decision making, whether or not they compute a numerical measure of the dispersion. Consider the case of Tuffy Rocknee, a college football coach, who is agonizing over which player should be assigned punting duties in Saturday's big game. Tuffy has decided to base his decision on the results of 10 practice kicks by each player. The recorded yardages are as follows.

A: 41, 55, 30, 38, 50, 42, 39, 25, 28, 52
B: 39, 42, 38, 42, 44, 40, 41, 38, 36, 40

The mean number of yards punted by each player is 40 (which you should verify), but if Tuffy is looking for consistency, he will select player B. Without actually computing a measure of dispersion (and probably not caring to know how to), Tuffy will choose the player whose punts exhibit the least variability.

Figure 4.2

**Smoothed Relative
Frequency Histograms**

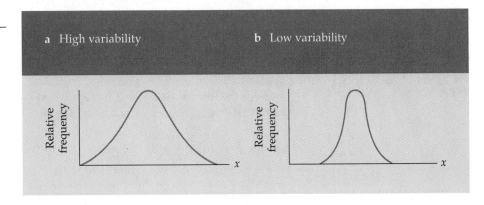

The concept of variability is of fundamental importance in statistical inference. It is therefore important that we, unlike Tuffy, be able to measure the degree of variability in a set of measurements.

Range

The first and simplest measure of variability is the range, which we already encountered when forming frequency distributions.

> **Range**
>
> The **range** of a set of measurements is the numerical difference between the largest and smallest measurements.

The usefulness of the range stems from the ease with which it can be computed and interpreted. The first observation we made concerning the telephone data in Table 2.1 was that the smallest and largest telephone bills were $0 and $119.63 respectively, which established that the range was $119.63 - 0 = 119.63$ dollars. We later computed the mean amount of the telephone bills as $43.59.

A major shortcoming of the range is that it provides us with no information on the dispersion of the values that fall between the smallest and largest observations. These intermediate values might all be clustered very closely about the mean value of $43.59, they might be dispersed fairly evenly across the range between the two extreme values, or they might be clumped in two groups near each extreme (resulting in a barbell-shaped distribution). A popular measure of the dispersion of these intermediate values is variance.

Variance

Variance is one of the two most widely accepted measures of the variability of a set of quantitative data (the other is standard deviation). Closely related to one another, variance and standard deviation take into account all the data in a set and (as we will see in Chapter 7) are of fundamental importance in statistical inference.

Consider two very small populations, each consisting of five measurements.

A: 8, 9, 10, 11, 12
B: 4, 7, 10, 13, 16

The mean of both population A and population B is 10, as you can easily verify. The population values are plotted along the horizontal x-axis in Figure 4.3. Visual inspection of these graphs indicates that the measurements in population B are more widely dispersed than those in A. We are searching for a measure of a dispersion that confirms this notion and takes into account each measurement in the population.

Consider the five measurements in population A. To obtain a measure of their dispersion, we might begin by calculating the deviation of each value from the mean.

$$(8 - 10), (9 - 10), (10 - 10), (11 - 10), (12 - 10)$$

The four nonzero deviations are represented by the double-pointed arrows above the x-axis in Figure 4.3. It might at first seem reasonable to take the sum of these deviations as a measure of dispersion, but the sum of deviations from the mean is always zero. While this difficulty could be overcome by summing the absolute values of the deviations from the mean, absolute values are somewhat difficult to work with mathematically. More mathematically tractable and more useful in statistical inference are the squares of the deviations from the mean. Thus, we might consider

$$(8 - 10)^2 + (9 - 10)^2 + (10 - 10)^2 + (11 - 10)^2 + (12 - 10)^2 = 10$$

Figure 4.3

Deviations of Measurements from the Mean

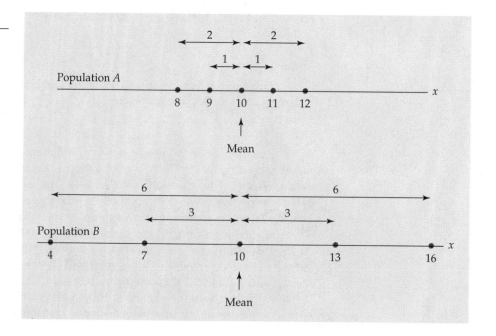

as a measure of the variability of our measurements in population A. The corresponding expression for a population of measurements $x_1, x_2, \ldots, x_N$ would be

$$\sum_{i=1}^{N} (x_i - \mu)^2$$

Unfortunately, although this sum of squared deviations has the desirable property of being larger for sets of measurements that have greater dispersion, it also increases in magnitude simply from an increase in the number of measurements in the data set—even though the larger data set may have less dispersion than a smaller one. This is remedied by taking the *average* of the *squared* deviations as the required measure of dispersion. This measure of the dispersion, or variability, of a population of measurements is called the **variance**; it is denoted by σ^2, where σ is the lowercase Greek letter *sigma*.

Letting σ_A^2 denote the variance of population A, we obtain

$$\sigma_A^2 = \frac{(8 - 10)^2 + (9 - 10)^2 + (10 - 10)^2 + (11 - 10)^2 + (12 - 10)^2}{5}$$

$$= \frac{(-2)^2 + (-1)^2 + 0^2 + 1^2 + 2^2}{5} = \frac{10}{5} = 2$$

Proceeding in an analogous manner for population B, we obtain

$$\sigma_B^2 = \frac{(4 - 10)^2 + (7 - 10)^2 + (10 - 10)^2 + (13 - 10)^2 + (16 - 10)^2}{5} = 18$$

The variance of B therefore exceeds the variance of A, consistent with our initial visual impression that the values in population B are more dispersed than those in population A.

Variance of a Population

The **variance of a population** of N measurements $x_1, x_2, \ldots, x_N$ having mean μ is defined as

$$\sigma^2 = \frac{\sum_{i=1}^{N} (x_i - \mu)^2}{N}$$

We suggest that, rather than blindly memorizing this formula, you think of the variance as being the *mean squared deviation*—the mean of the squared deviations of the measurements from their mean μ. This should help you both to remember and to interpret the formula for the variance.

Now suppose that you are working with a sample, rather than with a population. If you are given a sample of n measurements, your interest in computing the variance of the sample (denoted by s^2) lies in obtaining a good estimate of the population variance (σ^2). While it would seem reasonable to define the sample variance s^2 as the average of the squared deviations of the sample measurements from their mean $\bar{x}$, doing so tends to underestimate the population variance σ^2. This problem can be rectified, however, by defining the sample variance s^2 as the sum of the squared deviations divided by $n - 1$, rather than by n. Further discussion of this point is provided in Chapter 9.

Variance of a Sample

The **variance of a sample** of n measurements $x_1, x_2, \ldots, x_n$ having mean $\bar{x}$ is defined as

$$s^2 = \frac{\sum_{i=1}^{n} (x_i - \bar{x})^2}{n - 1}$$

Computing the variance of a large sample can be made less tedious by use of a shortcut formula derivable through simple algebraic manipulation of the formula just presented. The sample mean is usually calculated before the sample variance, in which case the value of the second summation in the shortcut formula is already known.

Shortcut Formula

The **shortcut formula** for the sample variance is

$$s^2 = \frac{1}{n - 1} \left[\sum_{i=1}^{n} x_i^2 - \frac{\left(\sum_{i=1}^{n} x_i \right)^2}{n} \right]$$

EXAMPLE 4.9

Find the mean and the variance of the following sample of measurements (in years).

3.4, 2.5, 4.1, 1.2, 2.8, 3.7

SOLUTION

The mean of this sample of six measurements is

$$\bar{x} = \frac{\sum_{i=1}^{6} x_i}{6} = \frac{3.4 + 2.5 + 4.1 + 1.2 + 2.8 + 3.7}{6} = \frac{17.7}{6} = 2.95 \text{ years}$$

To find the sample variance by means of the shortcut formula, we first compute

$$\sum_{i=1}^{6} x_i^2 = (3.4)^2 + (2.5)^2 + (4.1)^2 + (1.2)^2 + (2.8)^2 + (3.7)^2 = 57.59$$

From the computation of the mean, we already know that

$$\sum_{i=1}^{6} x_i = 17.7$$

Therefore,

$$s^2 = \frac{1}{5} \left[\sum_{i=1}^{6} x_i^2 - \frac{\left(\sum_{i=1}^{6} x_i \right)^2}{6} \right] = \frac{1}{5} \left[57.59 - \frac{(17.7)^2}{6} \right] = 1.075 \text{ (years)}^2$$

Alternatively, we could compute s^2 directly, using the definition of sample variance.

$$s^2 = \frac{(3.4 - 2.95)^2 + (2.5 - 2.95)^2 + (4.1 - 2.95)^2 + (1.2 - 2.95)^2 + (2.8 - 2.95)^2 + (3.7 - 2.95)^2}{5}$$

$$= 1.075 \text{ (years)}^2$$

Standard Deviation

Because calculating variance involves squaring the original measurements, the unit attached to a variance is the square of the unit attached to the original measurements. For example, if our original measurements are expressed in minutes, the variance is expressed in minutes squared. While variance is a useful measure of the relative variability of two sets of measurements, statisticians often want a measure of variability that is expressed in the same units as the original measurements, as is the mean. Such a measure can be obtained simply by taking the square root of the variance.

> **Standard Deviation**
>
> The **standard deviation** of a set of measurements is the positive square root of the variance of the measurements.
>
> Sample standard deviation: $s = \sqrt{s^2}$
> Population standard deviation: $\sigma = \sqrt{\sigma^2}$

For example, the standard deviation of the sample of measurements in Example 4.9 is

$$s = \sqrt{s^2} = \sqrt{1.075} = 1.037 \text{ years}$$

One important application of variance (or, alternatively, of standard deviation) arises in finance, where variance is the most popular numerical measure of risk. For example, we might be concerned with the variance of a firm's sales, profits, or return on investment. In all cases, the underlying assumption is that a larger variance corresponds to a higher level of risk. The next example illustrates this important application of variance.

EXAMPLE 4.10

Mutual funds are becoming an increasingly popular investment alternative among small investors. To help investors decide on the particular fund to invest in, various publications regularly report the average annual rate of return achieved by each of more than 100 mutual funds over the past 10 years.* Some publications also indicate each fund's level of risk by classifying the historical variability of each fund's rate of return as high, intermediate, or low.

If the annual (percentage) rates of return over the past 10 years for two mutual funds are as follows, which fund would you classify as having the higher level of risk?

Fund A: 8.3, −6.2, 20.9, −2.7, 33.6, 42.9, 24.4, 5.2, 3.1, 30.5
Fund B: 12.1, −2.8, 6.4, 12.2, 27.8, 25.3, 18.2, 10.7, −1.3, 11.4

SOLUTION

SOLVING BY HAND

For each fund, we must find the variance of the sample of rates of return. To avoid having to compute several squared deviations of returns from their mean, we'll use the shortcut formula for calculating a sample variance. For Fund A, we have

$$\sum_{i=1}^{10} x_i = 8.3 - 6.2 + \cdots + 30.5 = 160.0$$

$$\sum_{i=1}^{10} x_i^2 = (8.3)^2 + (-6.2)^2 + \cdots + (30.5)^2 = 5,083.06$$

The variance for Fund A is therefore

$$s_A^2 = \frac{1}{9}\left[\sum_{i=1}^{10} x_i^2 - \frac{\left(\sum_{i=1}^{10} x_i\right)^2}{10}\right] = \frac{1}{9}\left[5,083.06 - \frac{(160.0)^2}{10}\right] = 280.34 \ (\%)^2$$

For Fund B, we have

$$\sum_{i=1}^{10} x_i = 12.1 - 2.8 + \cdots + 11.4 = 120.0$$

$$\sum_{i=1}^{10} x_i^2 = (12.1)^2 + (-2.8)^2 + \cdots + (11.4)^2 = 2,334.36$$

The variance for Fund B is therefore

$$s_B^2 = \frac{1}{9}\left[\sum_{i=1}^{10} x_i^2 - \frac{\left(\sum_{i=1}^{10} x_i\right)^2}{10}\right] = \frac{1}{9}\left[2,334.36 - \frac{(120.0)^2}{10}\right] = 99.37 \ (\%)^2$$

Notice that, because the calculation of s^2 involves squaring the original measurements, the sample variance is expressed in $(\%)^2$, which is the square of the unit (percent) used to express the original measurements of rate of return.

---

*The annual rate of return of a mutual fund is given by $(P_1 - P_0)/P_0$, where P_0 and P_1 are the prices of the fund's shares at the beginning and end of the year, respectively. This definition assumes that no dividends are paid by the fund during the year.

Minitab Output for Example 4.10

Descriptive Statistics

Variable	N	Mean	Median	TrMean	StDev	SEMean
Fund A	10	16.00	14.60	15.41	16.74	5.29
Fund B	10	12.00	11.75	11.87	9.97	3.15

Variable	Min	Max	Q1	Q3
Fund A	−6.20	42.90	1.65	31.27
Fund B	−2.80	27.80	4.47	19.98

Use the commands described in Example 4.7 to produce descriptive statistics for the data. Minitab outputs the sample standard deviation, the minimum and maximum observations (allowing you to compute the range), quartiles, as well as the measures of central location and other statistics that we'll eventually discuss.

Excel Output for Example 4.10

	A	B	C	D
1	Fund A		Fund B	
2				
3	Mean	16	Mean	12
4	Standard Error	5.294714345	Standard Error	3.152353618
5	Median	14.6	Median	11.75
6	Mode	#N/A	Mode	#N/A
7	Standard Deviation	16.74335689	Standard Deviation	9.968617423
8	Sample Variance	280.34	Sample Variance	99.37333333
9	Kurtosis	-1.341931101	Kurtosis	-0.463939264
10	Skewness	0.216971412	Skewness	0.106952106
11	Range	49.1	Range	30.6
12	Minimum	-6.2	Minimum	-2.8
13	Maximum	42.9	Maximum	27.8
14	Sum	160	Sum	120
15	Count	10	Count	10
16	Confidence Level(95.000%)	10.37743406	Confidence Level(95.000%)	6.178490409

Use the commands described in Example 4.7 to produce descriptive statistics for the data. Excel prints the range, sample standard deviation, and sample variance, as well as a variety of other statistics, some of which we'll present in this book.

INTERPRETING THE RESULTS

From the sample data, we conclude that Fund A has the higher level of risk as measured by variance, because the variance of its rates of return exceeds that of Fund B's rates of return. Notice that Fund A has also enjoyed a higher average rate of return over the past 10 years. Specifically, the mean rates of return for Funds A and B were

$$\bar{x}_A = \frac{160.0}{10} = 16\% \quad \text{and} \quad \bar{x}_B = \frac{120.0}{10} = 12\%$$

This result is in keeping with our intuitive notion that an investment that involves a higher level of risk should produce a higher average rate of return.*

---

*Students of finance will realize that, strictly speaking, the mutual funds must be well diversified for this statement to hold when variance is used as the measure of risk.

Notice that, alternatively, we could have used standard deviation as our measure of variability. For instance, the standard deviations of the samples of rates of return for Funds A and B are

$$s_A = \sqrt{s_A^2} = \sqrt{280.34} = 16.74\%$$

and

$$s_B = \sqrt{s_B^2} = \sqrt{99.37} = 9.97\%$$

As you can see, the measurements in sample A are more variable than those in sample B, whether we use variance or standard deviation as our measure of variability. But standard deviation is the more useful measure of variability in situations where the measure is to be used in conjunction with the mean to make a statement about a single population, as we will see in the next section.

Coefficient of Variation

Would you worry more about losing $5 if you had invested $100 or $500? You probably answered "if I had invested $100," because the $5 loss then represents a greater *proportionate* change in the value of your investment. In a similar manner, we sometimes adjust the standard deviation (our measure of variability) of a data set by dividing it by the data set's mean to obtain a *proportionate* measure of variability. This measure, called the coefficient of variation, allows us to compare the *relative* variabilities of the two data sets, because it adjusts for differences in the magnitudes of the means of the data sets.

> **Coefficient of Variation**
>
> The **coefficient of variation** of a set of measurements is the standard deviation of the measurements divided by their mean.
>
> Sample coefficient of variation: $cv = \dfrac{s}{\bar{x}}$
>
> Population coefficient of variation: $CV = \dfrac{\sigma}{\mu}$

For instance, the coefficients of variation of the sample rates of return for Funds A and B in Example 4.10 are

$$cv_A = \frac{s_A}{\bar{x}_A} = \frac{16.74}{16} = 1.05 \quad \text{and} \quad cv_B = \frac{s_B}{\bar{x}_B} = \frac{9.97}{12} = .83$$

In this particular case, comparing coefficients of variation and comparing standard deviations lead to the same conclusion: the measurements in sample A are more variable. But if the mean return for Fund A in Example 4.10 was 21% with the same standard deviation of $s_A = 16.74\%$, the coefficient of variation of the returns for Fund A would then be

$$cv_A = \frac{16.74}{21} = .80$$

In this case, Fund A would have relatively less variability than Fund B (9.97/12 = .83).

The coefficient of variation is sometimes multiplied by 100 and reported as a percentage, which effectively expresses the standard deviation as a percentage of the mean. Thus, for the Fund A returns in Example 4.10, the coefficient of variation is 105%.

Exercises

4.16 Is it possible for a standard deviation to be negative? Explain.

4.17 Is it possible for the standard deviation of a data set to be larger than its variance? Explain.

4.18 Compute the mean, range, variance, and standard deviation for the following sample of data.

5, 7, 12, 14, 15, 15, 17, 20, 21, 24

4.19 Refer to the sample of data in Exercise 4.18. Try to answer each of the following questions without performing any calculations. Then verify your answers by performing the necessary calculations.

a If we drop the largest value from the sample, what will happen to the mean and variance?

b If each value is increased by 2, what will happen to the mean and variance?

c If each value is multiplied by 3, what will happen to the mean and variance?

4.20 Calculate $\bar{x}$, s^2, and s for the following sample of data.

3, −2, −4, 1, 0, −1, 2

4.21 Calculate $\bar{x}$, s^2, and s for each of the following samples of data.

a 14, 7, 8, 11, 5

b −3, −2, −1, 0, 1, 2, 3

c 4, 4, 8, 8

d 5, 5, 5, 5

4.22 Treating each of the four sets of data in Exercise 4.21 as populations, calculate μ, σ^2, and σ for each of the four populations.

4.23 Examine the three samples shown below. Without performing any calculations, indicate which sample has the largest amount of variability and which sample has the least amount of variability. Explain why.

a 27, 39, 22, 36, 31

b 32, 28, 33, 30, 27

c 34, 47, 16, 49, 39

4.24 Calculate the variance and standard deviation of the three samples listed in Exercise 4.23.

4.25 Calculate $\sum(x_i - \bar{x})$ for the three samples in Exercise 4.23. What can you infer about this calculation in general?

4.26 Create a sample of size 4 whose mean is 10 and whose variance is zero.

4.27 The number of hours a student spent studying over the past seven days was recorded as follows.

2, 5, 6, 1, 4, 0, 3

Compute the range, $\bar{x}$, s, and s^2 for these data. Express each answer in appropriate units.

4.28 Given a set of quantitative data, what is the most popular measure of central location? What is the best measure of variability? Explain both answers.

4.29 The 15 stocks in your portfolio had the following percentage changes in value over the past year.

$$3 \quad 0 \quad 6 \quad -5 \quad -2 \quad 5 \quad -18 \quad 20 \quad 14 \quad 18 \quad -10 \quad 10 \quad 50 \quad -20 \quad 14$$

a Compute μ, σ^2, and σ for this population of data. Express each answer in appropriate units.

b Compute the range and median for these data.

4.30 Consider once again the two mutual funds A and B in Example 4.10. For convenience, their annual percentage rates of return over the past 10 years are repeated here. For *each* of the 10 years, consider the portfolio obtained by investing equal amounts of money in each of the two funds. The rate of return you would have earned on the portfolio over the first year would then have been 0.5(8.3) + 0.5(12.1) = 10.2%.

Fund A: 8.3, −6.2, 20.9, −2.7, 33.6, 42.9, 24.4, 5.2, 3.1, 30.5
Fund B: 12.1, −2.8, 6.4, 12.2, 27.8, 25.3, 18.2, 10.7, −1.3, 11.4

a Compute the rate of return earned on the portfolio for each of the 10 years.

b Find the mean return on the portfolio over the past 10 years.

c Find the standard deviation of the portfolio returns over the past 10 years.

d Rank the three possible investments (Fund A, Fund B, and the portfolio) according to their average returns and according to their riskiness (as measured by standard deviation) over the past 10 years.

The next five questions require the use of a computer and statistical software.

4.31 The annual total rates of return on Canadian common stocks and long-term government bonds, for each of 30 years, are shown in Table E4.31. (The data are also stored in file XR04-31. Column 1 stores the stock returns, and column 2 stores the bond returns.) To understand the meaning of these returns, consider the 15.56% return that was realized on common stocks in 1963. This means that $100 invested in common stocks at the beginning of 1963 would have yielded a profit of $15.56 over the year, leaving a total of $115.56 at year's end.

Table E4.31

Annual Total Rates of Return (in %)

YEARS	COMMON STOCKS					LONG-TERM GOVERNMENT BONDS				
1960–64	1.66	32.54	−7.52	15.56	25.30	7.10	9.78	3.05	4.60	6.59
1965–69	6.54	−7.10	18.00	22.36	−0.96	0.96	1.55	−2.20	−0.52	−2.31
1970–74	−3.60	8.07	27.31	−0.42	−26.61	−21.98	11.55	1.11	1.71	−1.69
1975–79	19.70	10.94	9.93	29.22	44.38	2.82	19.02	5.97	1.29	−2.62
1980–84	29.93	−10.29	5.51	34.84	−2.44	2.06	−3.02	42.98	9.60	15.09
1985–89	25.07	8.95	5.88	11.08	21.37	25.26	17.54	0.45	10.45	16.29

SOURCE: *Report on Canadian Economic Statistics: 1924–1991* (Canadian Institute of Actuaries, April 1992), p. 18.

a Find the mean, the median, the range, and the standard deviation of this sample of common-stock returns.

b Repeat part (a) for the bond returns.

    c   Which type of investment (common stocks or bonds) appears to have the higher level of risk? The higher average return?

    d   Compute the mean stock return for each of the six five-year periods.

    e   Compute the mean and the standard deviation of the six mean returns in part (d). Compare these values with the mean and the standard deviation calculated in part (a), and explain any differences observed.

4.32 Refer to Exercise 4.8, where the amount of time needed to complete a telephone survey by 100 respondents is stored in column 1 of file XR04-08.

    a   Use a software package to calculate the variance and the standard deviation.

    b   Use a software package to draw the histogram.

4.33 Example 2.1 dealt with the problem of graphically summarizing the 200 long-distance bills. Recall that the data were stored in XM02-01. Use your software to compute several measures of dispersion.

4.34 Refer to Example 2.2, where a sample of 400 Barnes Exhibit visitors was timed to determine how long each took to view the exhibit. Suppose that, in fact, three samples of size 400 were taken: one in the morning, the second in the afternoon, and the third in the evening. These data are stored in columns 1, 2, and 3, respectively, of file XR04-34. (Column 2 contains the same data as in XM02-02.)

    a   Determine the mean and the median of each sample.

    b   Determine the range, variance, and standard deviation of each sample.

    c   Discuss the similarities and differences among the three samples.

    d   What are the implications of your findings?

4.35 Refer to Exercise 2.20. Recall that the number of customers entering a bank during each hour of operation for the last 100 days was recorded in columns 1 through 5 of file XR02-20.

    a   For each hour of operation, determine the mean and standard deviation.

    b   Briefly describe what the statistics in part (a) tell you.

4.4 Interpreting Standard Deviation

By now, you probably understand how variance and standard deviation can be used as relative measures of variability. If you are comparing two sets of data, the one with the larger standard deviation has the greater amount of variability. Given the standard deviation of a single set of measurements, however, you would likely have difficulty interpreting that value intuitively. The standard deviation would be more useful if it could be used to make a statement about the proportion of measurements that fall into various intervals of values.

For example, suppose you are told that the average (mean) of the final marks in an accounting course is 70, with a standard deviation of 6. The professor could convey useful information regarding the dispersion of the marks about the mean of 70 by announcing the percentage of marks that fall, for example, within 1 standard deviation of the mean; that is, within the interval

$$(x - s, x + s) = (70 - 6, 70 + 6) = (64, 76)$$

Similarly, the professor could count and announce the percentage of marks that fall within 2 standard deviations of the mean: within the interval (58, 82).

In many real-world applications, the sample of data is so large that determining the percentage of measurements lying within a particular interval by counting them would be impractical. A very good estimate of this percentage is available, however, if the distribution of the data is mound-shaped (or bell-shaped). An example of a mound-shaped distribution is shown in Figure 4.4, which displays a relative frequency histogram of the 30 telephone call durations in Table 4.1. (A smoothed outline of the histogram would resemble a mound.)

Figure 4.4

Mound-Shaped Histogram

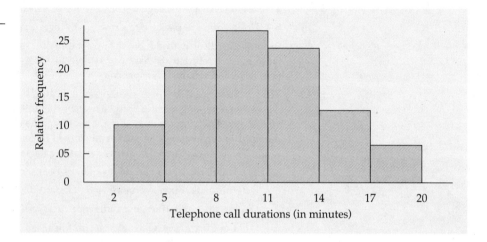

A rule of thumb, called the *Empirical Rule,* has evolved from empirical studies that have produced samples possessing mound-shaped distributions. For a sample of measurements with a mound-shaped distribution, the Empirical Rule gives the approximate percentage of the measurements that fall within 1, 2, or 3 standard deviations of the mean.

Empirical Rule

If a sample of measurements has a mound-shaped distribution, the interval

$(\bar{x} - s, \bar{x} + s)$ contains approximately 68% of the measurements
$(\bar{x} - 2s, \bar{x} + 2s)$ contains approximately 95% of the measurements
$(\bar{x} - 3s, \bar{x} + 3s)$ contains virtually all of the measurements

EXAMPLE 4.11

The durations of a sample of 30 long-distance telephone calls placed by a firm in a given week are recorded in Table 4.1.* It can be shown that this sample of 30 durations has a mean of $\bar{x} = 10.26$ and a standard deviation of $s = 4.29$. Moreover,

---

*We use a small sample size of 30 here to enable us to easily count the number of observations in various intervals for illustrative purposes.

the durations have an approximately mound-shaped distribution (see Figure 4.4). Consequently, according to the Empirical Rule, approximately 68% of the 30 durations lie in the interval

$$(\bar{x} - s, \bar{x} + s) = (10.26 - 4.29, 10.26 + 4.29)$$
$$= (5.97, 14.55)$$

You can check this result by counting the actual contents of the specified interval. In fact, this interval contains 70% (21 out of 30) of the durations—a percentage that comes very close to the Empirical Rule's approximation.

Similarly, the Empirical Rule states that approximately 95% of the durations lie in the interval

$$(\bar{x} - 2s, \bar{x} + 2s) = (10.26 - 2[4.29], 10.26 + 2[4.29])$$
$$= (1.68, 18.84)$$

In fact, all but the largest of the 30 durations fall within this interval; that is, the interval actually contains 96.7% of the telephone call durations—a percentage that comes very close to the Empirical Rule's approximation.

Table 4.1

Duration of Long-Distance Calls (in minutes)					
11.8	3.6	16.6	13.5	4.8	8.3
8.9	9.1	7.7	2.3	12.1	6.1
10.2	8.0	11.4	6.8	9.6	19.5
15.3	12.3	8.5	15.9	18.7	11.7
6.2	11.2	10.4	7.2	5.5	14.5

Example 4.11 may also be used to anticipate an idea that will be expanded upon in Chapter 7, when we deal with a particular mound-shaped distribution called the *normal distribution*. We noted in Section 2.2 that the area of any rectangle erected as part of a histogram is proportional to the percentage of the measurements that fall into the class it describes. As we've just observed, the Empirical Rule states that about 95% of the telephone call durations fall in the interval between 1.68 and 18.84 minutes. Therefore, approximately 95% of the area under the mound-shaped histogram in Figure 4.4 lies between 1.68 and 18.84. More generally, approximately 95% of the area under any mound-shaped histogram lies between $\bar{x} - 2s$ and $\bar{x} + 2s$.

As a final point, we note that the Empirical Rule forms the basis for a crude method of approximating the standard deviation of a sample of measurements that has a mound-shaped distribution. Because most of the sample measurements (about 95%) fall within 2 standard deviations of the mean, the range of the measurements is approximately equal to $4s$. After we have found the range of the measurements, we can approximate the sample standard deviation by

$$s \simeq \text{Range}/4$$

This **range approximation of s** is useful as a quick check to ensure that our computed value of s is reasonable, or "in the ballpark." For example, the range of the telephone call durations is 17.2, so $17.2/4 = 4.3$ is an approximation of s. In this case, the range approximation is very close to 4.29, our computed value of s. Such accuracy isn't generally to be expected. More will be said about this approximation in Chapter 9.

Exercises

4.36 The mean and the standard deviation of the grades of 500 students who took an economics exam were 69 and 7, respectively.

   a What are the numerical values of the endpoints of the intervals $(\bar{x} - s, \bar{x} + s)$, $(\bar{x} - 2s, \bar{x} + 2s)$, and $(\bar{x} - 3s, \bar{x} + 3s)$?

   b If the grades have a mound-shaped distribution, approximately how many students received a grade in each of the three intervals specified in part (a)?

4.37 The mean and standard deviation of the wages of 1,000 factory workers are $25,600 and $2,200, respectively. If the wages have a mound-shaped distribution, how many workers receive wages of between $23,400 and $27,800? Between $21,200 and $30,000? Between $19,000 and $32,200?

4.38 The following 20 values represent the number of seconds required to complete one spot weld by a sample of 20 automated welders on a company's production line.

     2.1, 2.7, 2.6, 2.8, 2.3, 2.5, 2.6, 2.4, 2.6, 2.7
     2.4, 2.6, 2.8, 2.5, 2.6, 2.4, 2.9, 2.4, 2.7, 2.3

   a Calculate the variance and the standard deviation for this sample of 20 measurements.

   b Use the range approximation of s to check your calculations in part (a). What assumption must you make in order to use this approximation?

4.39 A bookstore has determined that weekly sales of *Newsweek* have an approximately mound-shaped distribution, with a mean of 85 and a standard deviation of 6.

   a For what percentage of the time can we expect weekly sales to fall in the intervals $\bar{x} \pm s$ and $\bar{x} \pm 3s$?

   b For what percentage of the time can we expect weekly sales to have a value that is more than 2 standard deviations from the mean?

   c If the bookstore stocks 97 copies of *Newsweek* each week, for what percentage of weeks will there be an insufficient number of copies to meet the demand? (HINT: A mound-shaped distribution is symmetrical.)

4.40 Last year, the rates of return on the common stocks in a large portfolio had an approximately mound-shaped distribution, with a mean of 20% and a standard deviation of 10%.

   a What proportion of the stocks had a return of between 10% and 30%? Between −10% and 50%?

   b What proportion of the stocks had a return that was either less than 10% or more than 30%?

   c What proportion of the stocks had a positive return? (HINT: A mound-shaped distribution is symmetrical.)

4.41 Refer to Exercise 4.31, which deals with stock and bond returns.

   a Compute the standard deviation of both the common-stock returns and the bond returns.

   b Use the range approximation of s to check your answers to part (a).

4.42 Consider the following sample of house prices (in thousands of dollars).

```
274  429  229  435  260  222  292  419  242  202  235  215  390  359  409
375  209  265  440  365  319  338  414  249  279
```

a Calculate the variance and the standard deviation of this sample of prices.

b Compare the range approximation of s to the true value of s. Explain why you would or would not expect the approximation to be a good one for this sample.

4.5 Measures of Relative Standing and Box Plots

The measures of central location (Section 4.2) and measures of variability (Section 4.3) provide the statistician with useful information about the location and dispersion of a set of observations. The measures in this section describe another aspect of the shape of the distribution of data, as well as providing information about the relative standing of particular observations. For example, a high score on the Graduate Management Admission Test (GMAT) is one of the requirements to enter an M.B.A. program. The scores range from 200 to 800 with a mean of about 460. Suppose that you have just been told that your GMAT exam score is 600. Because entry into most programs is highly competitive, you need to know how well you did relative to the other people who have taken the test. To extract this information we need to compute percentiles.

> **Percentile**
>
> The pth **percentile** of a set of measurements is the value for which *at most* p% of the measurements are less than that value and *at most* $(100 - p)$% of the measurements are greater than that value.

For example, if the 78th percentile of GMAT scores is 600, this means that 78% of the population that took the test scored below 600; 22% scored 600 or better.

The pth percentile is defined in much the same manner as is the median, which divides a series of measurements in such a way that at most 50% of the measurements are smaller than the median and at most 50% of the measurements are greater. In fact, the median is simply the 50th percentile. Just as we have a special name for the percentile that divides the ordered set of measurements in half, we have special names for percentiles that divide the ordered set of measurements into quarters and into tenths: **quartiles*** and **deciles**. The following list identifies some of the more commonly used percentiles, together with notation for the quartiles.

---

*Quartiles are dividers—values that divide the entire range of measurements into four equal quarters. In practice, however, the word *quartile* is sometimes used to refer to one of these quarters. A measurement "in the first quartile" is in the bottom 25% of the measurements, whereas a measurement "in the upper quartile" is among the top 25%.

$$\text{First (lower) decile} = \text{10th percentile}$$
$$Q_1 = \text{First (lower) quartile} = \text{25th percentile}$$
$$Q_2 = \text{Second (middle) quartile} = \text{Median (50th percentile)}$$
$$Q_3 = \text{Third (upper) quartile} = \text{75th percentile}$$
$$\text{Ninth (upper) decile} = \text{90th percentile}$$

EXAMPLE 4.12

To find the quartiles for the set of measurements

7, 18, 12, 17, 29, 18, 4, 27, 30, 2, 4, 10, 21, 5, 8

we must first arrange the measurements in ascending order.

2, 4, 4, 5, 7, 8, 10, 12, 17, 18, 18, 21, 27, 29, 30
     ↑   ↑   ↑
   lower   median   upper
  quartile   quartile

The lower quartile is the value for which at most $.25 \times 15 = 3.75$ of the measurements are smaller and at most $.75 \times 15 = 11.25$ of the measurements are larger. The only measurement satisfying these criteria is 5, so 5 is the first quartile. The median is 12—the middle value. The upper quartile is the value for which at most $.75 \times 15 = 11.25$ of the measurements are smaller and at most $.25 \times 15 = 3.75$ of the measurements are larger. The only measurement satisfying these criteria is 21, so 21 is the third quartile.

Occasionally, you will find that the percentile you are seeking falls between two of the measurements in the data set. When this happens, to avoid becoming unnecessarily pedantic, simply choose the midpoint between the two measurements involved. This value will usually provide an adequate approximation of the required percentile. To illustrate this convention, suppose we want to find the 20th percentile of the measurements in Example 4.12. The 20th percentile would be the value for which at most 3 of the measurements are smaller and at most 12 of the measurements are larger. Because any number between the measurements 4 and 5 (inclusive) satisfies this criterion, we choose 4.5—the midpoint between 4 and 5—as the 20th percentile.

Measures of relative standing can be used in several ways to describe the shape of the distribution. For example, if the tenth decile is close to the median whereas the ninth decile is relatively far from the median, we may infer that the histogram is positively skewed. If the first and third quartiles are about the same distance from the median, it is quite probable that the histogram is approximately symmetric. Of course, we can *know* the shape by drawing the histogram, stem and leaf display, or dot plot.

We can also use quartiles to produce yet another measure of dispersion. It is called the **interquartile range** (IQR), defined as the difference between the third and first quartile. That is,

$$IQR = Q_3 - Q_1$$

This measure is most useful when the data are ranked. It is also used on quantitative data to produce a measure of dispersion that is not sensitive to extreme values.

Box Plots

When you are faced with the problem of summarizing the essential characteristics of a set of quantitative data, we have suggested that you begin by noting the smallest and largest values and then construct a histogram or stem and leaf display. We have also discussed the importance of numerical measures to describe the central location and dispersion of the data.

A **box plot**, alternatively called a **box-and-whisker plot**, is a clever pictorial display that indicates what the two extreme values of a data set are, where the data are centered, and how spread out the data are.* It does this by providing a graphic, five-number summary of the data. The five values plotted are the following.

Largest	(L)	Lower quartile	(Q_1)
Upper quartile	(Q_3)	Smallest	(S)
Median	(Q_2)		

Consider the data in Table 4.2, which lists the assets of the 15 largest North American banks, rounded off to the nearest hundred million dollars. The first step in creating a box plot is to rank the data and note the smallest and largest values. (The assets in Table 4.2 are already ranked from largest to smallest.)

The next step is to identify the other three values to be displayed. The bank with the median level of assets (85) is Security Pacific, because its rank (8) is the middle rank. The upper quartile (Q_3) is the asset value 108, because at most 75% of the asset values are smaller and at most 25% of the values are larger. Similarly, the lower quartile (Q_1) is the asset value 64, because at most 25% of the asset values are smaller and at most 75% of the values are larger.

The five values of interest are plotted in Figure 4.5. In this plot, a box with endpoints Q_1 and Q_3 is used to represent the middle half of the data. Notice that about a quarter of the data fall along the line (or **whisker**) to the left of the box, and about a quarter of the data fall along the whisker to the right of the box. The location of the median is indicated by the vertical line inside the box. The banks corresponding to some of the plotted values are also identified. The length of the box is given by the **interquartile range**.

$$IQR = Q_3 - Q_1$$
$$= 108 - 64.0 = 44.0$$

---

*The idea of a box plot was developed fairly recently by John Tukey.

Table 4.2

Largest North American Banks

BANK	ASSETS (IN 100 MILLIONS OF U.S. DOLLARS)		RANK
Citicorp, New York	$217	← largest	1
(New) Chemical Banking Corp., New York*	135		2
BankAmerica Corp., San Francisco	111		3
Royal Bank of Canada, Montreal	108	← Q_3	4
Chase Manhattan Corp., New York	98		5
CIBC, Toronto	98		6
J. P. Morgan & Co. Inc., New York	93		7
Security Pacific Corp., Los Angeles	85	← median	8
Bank of Montreal, Montreal	75		9
Bank of Nova Scotia, Toronto	75		10
NCNB Corp., Charlotte, N.C.	65		11
Bankers Trust New York Corp., New York	64	← Q_1	12
Toronto-Dominion Bank, Toronto	57		13
Wells Fargo & Co., San Francisco	56		14
First Interstate Bancorp., Los Angeles	51	← smallest	15

*This table was constructed after Chemical Banking Corp. and Manufacturers Hanover Corp. announced a proposed merger that would create the second-largest bank in the United States, but before BankAmerica bought Security Pacific, and before Wells Fargo acquired First Interstate Bancorp.

SOURCE: *Globe & Mail*, 16 July 1991, p. 82.

Strictly speaking, Figure 4.5 is *not* a box plot, although it is close to being one. One small adjustment to the whiskers is needed, which involves the concept of an *outlier*, the name given to unusually large or small values in a data set. For our purposes here, we will define an **outlier** to be a value located at a distance of more than 1.5(IQR) from the box. In our bank example, 1.5(IQR) = 1.5(44.0) = 66.0.

Figure 4.5

Display of Five Summary Values for Banks

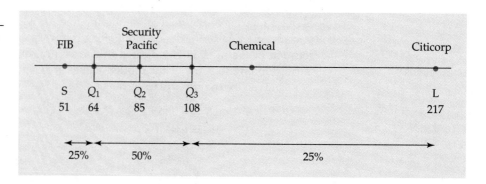

Therefore, an outlier is any value outside the interval $(64.0 - 66.0, 108 + 66.0) = (-2.0, 174.0).$* That is, the only outlier in this example is the asset value of Citicorp.

The lines, or whiskers, emanating from each end of the box in a box plot should extend to the most extreme value that is not an outlier; in this case, to the asset values of First Interstate Bancorp (FIB) and Chemical Banking. The resulting box plot is shown in Figure 4.6.

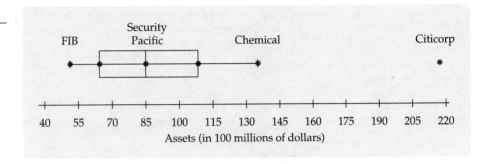

Using the Computer

Although the statistics in a box plot can be calculated manually and the box plot can also be drawn by hand, it is far easier to let the computer do the work. To show how the computer outputs box plots, we've used Minitab to print the box plot for the data in Table 4.2.

Incidentally, you can instruct Excel to include the quartiles in the list of descriptive statistics for a data set. Begin by clicking **Tools**, **Data Analysis . . .** , and **Descriptive Statistics**. To produce the quartiles (calculated for relatively large sample sizes), use the cursor to put an **x** in the boxes indicating **Kth largest** and **Kth smallest**. Specify a number equal to the sample size divided by 4. (Round to nearest integer if necessary.)

Minitab Box Plot for Table 4.2

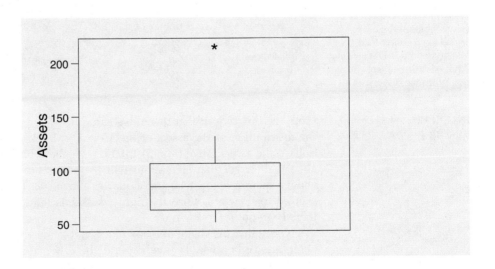

---

*The endpoints of this interval are called *fences*, outside of which all values are outliers. We will not need this terminology, however.

1 Type or import the data into a column.

Open file **TAB04-02**.

2 Click **Graph** and **Box Plot** . . . .

3 Type the name of the variable and click **OK**.

Assets or **C1**

Minitab will print the box plot lying on its side (as shown here). To put it rightside up, proceed as follows.

4 Before clicking **OK**, click **Options** . . . and click **Transpose X and Y**. Click **OK**.

Excel Box Plot for Table 4.2

EXCEL 97

Excel 97 Users:
This macro is the only **Data Analysis Plus** technique that does not work in Excel 97. Go to our web page (www.globalserve.net/ ~gkeller) to download the latest version of **Data Analysis Plus** where the box plot macro works.

COMMANDS

COMMANDS FOR TABLE 4.2

1 Type or import the data into one column.

Open file **TAB04-02**.

2 Click **Tools**, **Data Analysis Plus**, and **Box Plot**.

3 Specify the coordinates of the data. (Do not include cell containing variable name.)

A2:A16

INTERPRETING THE RESULTS

From the box plot in Figure 4.6, we can quickly grasp several points concerning the distribution of the assets of the 15 largest banks. In hundreds of millions of dollars, the assets range from 51 to 217, with about half being smaller than 85 and about half larger than 85. About half the assets lie between 64.0 and 108, with about a quarter below 64.0 and a quarter above 108. The distribution is somewhat skewed to the right, since the right whisker is longer than the left whisker and there is an outlier to the right.

Notice that the shape of a box plot is not heavily influenced by a few extreme observations, because the median and the other quartiles are not unduly influenced by extreme observations, in contrast to the situation with means and variances.

Outliers

In our discussion of box plots, we introduced the notion of an outlier: an unusually large or small value in a sample. Because an outlier is considerably removed from the main body of a sample, its validity is suspect and some investigation is needed to check that it is not the result of an error in measuring, recording, or transcribing the value. As well as providing a graphical summary of a data set, a box plot is useful for identifying outliers before performing further statistical analysis on a data set.

Exercises

4.43 What are the special names for the 25th, 50th, and 75th percentiles?

4.44 Refer to Exercise 4.29, which gives the percentage changes in value for 15 stocks. Compute the 20th percentile and 60th percentile for these data.

4.45 Refer to Exercise 4.31.

    a Find the upper and lower quartiles of the common-stock returns.

    b Find the upper and lower quartiles of the bond returns.

4.46 Consider a set of data with

$$Q_1 = 50$$
$$Q_2 = 90$$
$$Q_3 = 110$$

    a What do these statistics tell you about the shape of the distribution?

    b What can you say about the relative position of each of these observations?

        i   40

        ii   92

        iii   109

    c Calculate the interquartile range.

    d What does the interquartile range tell you about the sample?

4.47 Suppose that an analysis of incomes in a large company reveals the following.

$$Q_1 = \$23,000$$
$$Q_2 = \$31,000$$
$$Q_3 = \$46,000$$

    a What do these statistics reveal about the distribution of incomes?

    b Suppose that your income is $48,000. What can you say about your income relative to the incomes of others in the company?

    c Calculate the interquartile range.

    d Interpret the value of the interquartile range.

4.48 A box plot can be described as a five-number summary of a data set in the form of a graph. What five numbers are plotted?

4.49 Define what is meant by the terms *interquartile range* and *outlier*.

4.50 Refer to Example 4.10.

    a Draw the box plot for each sample (fund).

    b Discuss the similarities and differences between the returns for Fund *A* and Fund *B*.

4.51 A sample of 100 observations is stored in column 1 of file XR04-51.

    a Use a software package to draw the box plot.

    b What are the values of the quartiles?

    c What information can you extract from the box plot?

4.52 Refer to Example 4.8, for which the 100 test marks are stored in file XM04-08.

    a Draw the box plot.

    b What are the quartiles?

    c Are there any outliers?

    d What does the box plot tell you about the marks on the statistics exam?

4.53 Refer to Exercise 2.20, where the number of customers entering a bank during each hour of operation for the last 100 days was stored in columns 1 through 5 of file XR02-20.

    a Draw the box plot for each hour of operation.

    b What are the quartiles, and what do they tell you about the number of customers arriving each hour?

4.54 Refer to Exercise 4.31, for which the common-stock and bond returns are stored in file XR04-31.

    a Construct box plots for both the common-stock returns and the bond returns.

    b Compare the locations and shapes of the distributions of the two sets of returns based on your box plots.

    c Which type of investment (common stocks or bonds) appears to have the higher level of risk? The higher average return?

4.6 Measures of Association

In Chapter 2, we presented scatter diagrams, which graphically depict how two variables are related. In this section, we present two numerical measures of the **linear** relationship depicted in a scatter diagram. The two measures are the **covariance** and the **coefficient of correlation**.

Covariance

If we have all the observations that constitute a population, we can compute the population covariance. It is defined as follows.

$$\textbf{Population covariance} = COV(X, Y) = \frac{\sum(x_i - \mu_x)(y_i - \mu_y)}{N}$$

where μ_x is the population mean of the first variable, X; μ_y is the population mean of the second variable, Y; and N is the size of the population. The sample covariance is defined similarly, where n is the number of pairs of observations in the sample.

$$\textbf{Sample covariance} = cov(X, Y) = \frac{\sum(x_i - \bar{x})(y_i - \bar{y})}{n - 1}$$

For convenience, we label the population covariance $COV(X, Y)$ and the sample covariance $cov(X, Y)$. To illustrate how covariance measures association, consider the following three sets of sample data.

	x	y	$(x_i - \bar{x})$	$(y_i - \bar{y})$	$(x_i - \bar{x})(y_i - \bar{y})$
	2	13	-3	-7	21
Set 1	6	20	1	0	0
	7	27	2	7	14
	$\bar{x} = 5$	$\bar{y} = 20$			$17.5 = cov(X, Y)$

	x	y	$(x_i - \bar{x})$	$(y_i - \bar{y})$	$(x_i - \bar{x})(y_i - \bar{y})$
	2	27	-3	7	-21
Set 2	6	20	1	0	0
	7	13	2	-7	-14
	$\bar{x} = 5$	$\bar{y} = 20$			$-17.5 = cov(X, Y)$

	x	y	$(x_i - \bar{x})$	$(y_i - \bar{y})$	$(x_i - \bar{x})(y_i - \bar{y})$
	2	20	-3	0	0
Set 3	6	27	1	7	7
	7	13	2	-7	-14
	$\bar{x} = 5$	$\bar{y} = 20$			$-3.5 = cov(X, Y)$

In set 1, as x increases, so does y. In this case, when x is larger than its mean, y is at least as large as its mean. Thus $(x_i - \bar{x})$ and $(y_i - \bar{y})$ have the same sign or zero, which means that the product is either positive or zero. Consequently, the covariance is a positive number. In general, if two variables move in the same direction (both increase or both decrease), the covariance will be a large positive number. Figure 4.7(a) depicts a scatter diagram of one such case.

Next, consider set 2. As x increases, y decreases. Thus, the signs of $(x_i - \bar{x})$ and $(y_i - \bar{y})$ are opposite. As a result, the covariance is a negative number. If, as one variable increases, the other generally decreases, the covariance will be a large negative number. See Figure 4.7(b) for an illustrative scatter diagram.

Now consider set 3. As x increases, y exhibits no particular pattern. One product is positive, one is negative, and the third is zero. Consequently, the covariance is a small number. Generally speaking, if the two variables are unrelated (as one increases, the other shows no pattern), the covariance will be close to zero (either positive or negative). Figure 4.7(c) describes the movement of two unrelated variables.

As a measure of association, covariance suffers from a major drawback. It is usually difficult to judge the strength of the relationship from the covariance. For example, suppose that you have been told that the covariance of two variables is 250. What does this tell you about the relationship between the two variables? The sign, which is positive, tells you that as one increases, the other also generally increases. However, the degree to which the two variables move together is difficult to ascertain because we don't know whether 250 is a large number. To overcome this shortcoming, statisticians have produced another measure of association, which is based on the covariance. It is called the coefficient of correlation.

Figure 4.7

Covariance and Correlation for Various Scatter Diagrams

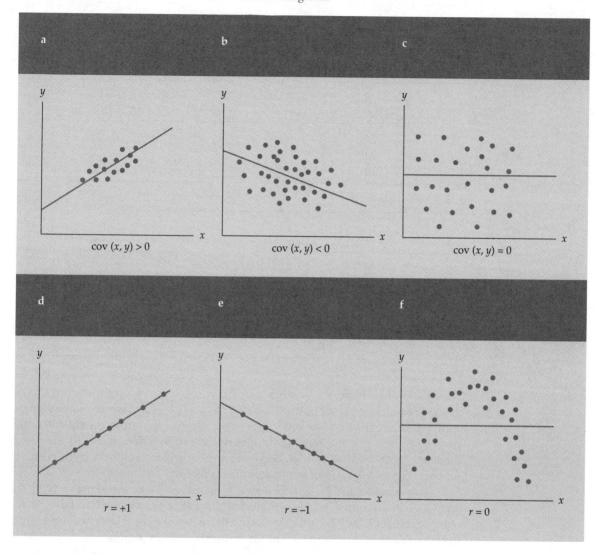

Coefficient of Correlation

The **coefficient of correlation** is the covariance divided by the standard deviations of X and Y. The **population** coefficient of **correlation** is labeled ρ (Greek letter rho) and is defined as

$$\rho = \frac{COV(X, Y)}{\sigma_x \sigma_y}$$

where σ_x and σ_y are the standard deviations of X and Y, respectively.

We label the **sample** coefficient of **correlation** r, which we define as

$$r = \frac{cov(X, Y)}{s_x s_y}$$

where s_x and s_y are the sample standard deviations of X and Y, respectively.

The coefficient of correlation will always lie between -1 and $+1$. The sign will be the same as the sign of the covariance and is interpreted in the same way. The degree of association is gauged by the value of ρ or r. For example, a correlation close to $+1$ indicates two variables that are very strongly positively related. The closer the correlation is to 1, the closer the relationship is to being described by a straight line sloping upward from left to right. Figure 4.7(d) exhibits the behavior of two variables whose correlation coefficient is $+1$.

A correlation close to -1 tells us that there is a strong negative relationship—as one variable increases, the other decreases. A perfect straight line sloping downward would produce a correlation of -1. Figure 4.7(e) describes a scatter diagram of two perfectly negatively correlated variables.

A correlation close to zero indicates that no straight line relationship exists. It may mean no pattern, such as the scatter diagram depicted in Figure 4.7(c), or a relationship that is not a straight line (Figure 4.7(f)).

All other values of the coefficient of correlation are interpreted in relation to $+1$, 0, and -1. For example, a correlation of $+.3$ means that there is weak positive association between the two variables. A correlation of $-.9$ means that there is a strong negative relationship.

EXAMPLE 4.13

A real estate agent wanted to know to what extent the selling price of a house is related to the number of square feet in the house. He took a sample of 15 homes that had recently sold, recording the price and size. These data are listed below and stored in file XM04-13. Compute the covariance and coefficient of correlation to measure how the two variables are related.

HOUSE SIZE (100 ft²)	SELLING PRICE (IN THOUSANDS OF DOLLARS)
20.0	219
14.8	190
20.5	199
12.5	121
18.0	150
14.3	198
24.9	334
16.5	188
24.3	310
20.2	213
22.0	288
19.0	312
12.3	186
14.0	173
16.7	174

SOLUTION

We begin by calculating the sample means and standard deviations. They are

$$\bar{x} = 18.0$$
$$s_x = 4.02$$
$$\bar{y} = 217.0$$
$$s_y = 63.9$$

We then compute the deviations from the mean for both x and y, and compute their products. The following table describes these calculations.

x	y	$x - \bar{x}$	$y - \bar{y}$	$(x - \bar{x})(y - \bar{y})$
20.0	219	2.0	2.0	4.0
14.8	190	−3.2	−27.0	86.4
20.5	199	2.5	−18.0	−45.0
12.5	121	−5.5	−96.0	528.0
18.0	150	0.0	−67.0	0.0
14.3	198	−3.7	−19.0	70.3
24.9	334	6.9	117.0	807.3
16.5	188	−1.5	−29.0	43.5
24.3	310	6.3	93.0	585.9
20.2	213	2.2	−4.0	−8.8
22.0	288	4.0	71.0	284.0
19.0	312	1.0	95.0	95.0
12.3	186	−5.7	−31.0	176.7
14.0	173	−4.0	−44.0	176.0
16.7	174	−1.3	−43.0	55.9

Total = 2,859.2

Thus

$$cov(X, Y) = \frac{\sum(x_i - \bar{x})(y_i - \bar{y})}{n - 1} = \frac{2,859.2}{14} = 204.2$$

The coefficient of correlation is

$$r = \frac{cov(X, Y)}{s_x s_y} = \frac{204.2}{4.02 \times 63.9} = .796$$

Minitab Output for Example 4.13

Covariances

	Size	Price
Size	16.1429	
Price	204.2286	4080.7144

Correlations (Pearson)

```
Correlation of Size and Price = 0.796
```

Minitab prints the covariance and variances. Thus $cov(X, Y) = 204.2286$, $s_x^2 = 16.1429$, and $s_y^2 = 4{,}080.7144$. The correlation between X and Y is .796.

MENU COMMANDS	COMMANDS FOR EXAMPLE 4.13
1 Type or import the data into 2 columns.	Open file **XM04-13**.
2 Click **Stat**, **Basic Statistics**, and **Covariance**	
3 Type the variable names. Click **OK**.	**Size** and **Price** or **C1** and **C2**
4 Repeat steps 2 and 3 using **Correlation** . . . instead of **Covariance**	

Excel Output for Example 4.13

	A	B	C
1		Size	Price
2	Size	15.0667	
3	Price	190.6133	3808.667

Excel prints the population covariance and variances. Thus, $Cov(X, Y) = 109.6133$, $\sigma_x^2 = 15.06667$, and $\sigma_y^2 = 3{,}808.667$. To compute the corresponding sample statistics, multiply each by $n/(n-1)$. Therefore, the sample covariance is $cov(X, Y) = 190.6133 \times (15/14) = 204.2286$.

EXCEL 97

Excel 97 Users: The commands are unchanged. However, this version of Excel calculates the *sample* covariance and variances.

COMMANDS	COMMANDS FOR EXAMPLE 4.13
1 Type or import the data into two columns.	Open file **XM04-13**.
2 Click **Tools**, **Data Analysis** . . ., and **Covariance**.	
3 Specify the coordinates of the data.	**A1:B16**

	A	B	C
1		Size	Price
2	Size	1	
3	Price	0.795716	1

From the output, we observe that $r = .795716$.

COMMANDS

Repeat the steps above, except click **Correlation** instead of **Covariance**.

The covariance provides very little useful information other than telling us that the two variables are positively related. The coefficient of correlation informs us that there is a strong positive relationship. This information can be extremely useful to real estate agents, insurance brokers, and all potential home purchasers.

Exercises

4.55 For the following sample, manually calculate the covariance and the coefficient of correlation.

x	3	6	5	9	4
y	9	12	13	16	11

4.56 Refer to Exercise 2.22, which considered the relationship between a manufacturing firm's cost of electrical power (Y) and hours of machine time (X). Data for X and Y were recorded for each of 12 months and are repeated below.

  a Compute $cov(X, Y)$ and r.

  b What do these statistics tell you about the relationship between X and Y?

MACHINE TIME (X) (1000S OF HOURS)	COST OF POWER (Y) (DOLLARS)
6	760
9	1,000
8	890
7	880
10	1,070
10	1,030
5	700
7	910
6	745
9	950
8	870
11	1,040

The next four exercises require the use of a computer and statistical software.

4.57 The data for 50 observations of variables X and Y are stored in columns 1 and 2, respectively, in file XR04-57. Determine the covariance and the correlation coefficient between X and Y, and interpret their meaning.

4.58 Refer to Exercise 2.23, which considers the relationship between common-stock returns (Y) and inflation (X). The annual common-stock returns and the annual inflation rates from 1985 to 1994 were stored in columns 1 and 2, respectively, in file XR02-23.

  a Compute $cov(X, Y)$ and r.

  b What do these statistics tell you about the relationship between common-stock returns and inflation?

4.59 Refer to Exercise 2.24, where the annual common-stock returns (Y) and the annual inflation rates (X) from 1960 to 1994 were stored in columns 1 and 2, respectively, in file XR02-24.

a Compute $cov(X, Y)$ and r.

b What do these statistics tell you about the relationship between common-stock returns and inflation over this long period?

c Does it appear that common stocks provide a good hedge against inflation?

4.60 Refer to Exercise 2.25, which considered the relationship between the monthly returns on an individual stock (R) and the monthly returns on the overall stock market (R_m). The monthly returns on American Barrick Resources and on the overall stock market were stored in columns 1 and 2, respectively, in file XR02-25.

a Compute $cov(R, R_m)$ and r.

b What do these statistics tell you about the relationship between returns on American Barrick Resources and returns on the overall stock market?

4.7 General Guidelines on the Exploration of Data

The purpose of applying graphical and numerical techniques is to describe and summarize data. Statisticians usually apply graphical techniques as a first step because we need to know the shape of the distribution. The shape of the distribution helps answer the following questions.

1 Where is the approximate center of the distribution?

2 Are the observations close to one another, or are they widely dispersed?

3 Is the distribution unimodal, bimodal, or multimodal? If there is more than one mode, where are the peaks, and where are the valleys?

4 Is the distribution symmetric? If not, is it skewed? If symmetric, is it bell-shaped?

Histograms, stem and leaf displays, dot plots, and box plots provide most of the answers. We can frequently make several inferences about the nature of the data from the shape. For example, we can assess the relative risk of investments by noting their spreads. We can attempt to improve the teaching of a course by examining whether the distribution of final grades is bimodal or skewed.

The shape can also provide some guidance on which numerical techniques to use. As we noted in this chapter, the central location of highly skewed data may be more appropriately measured by the median. We may also choose to use the interquartile range instead of the standard deviation to describe the spread of skewed data.

When we have an understanding of the structure of the data, we may proceed to further analysis. For example, we often want to determine how one variable, or several variables, affects another. Scatter diagrams, covariance, and the coefficient of correlation are useful techniques for detecting relationships between variables. A number of techniques to be introduced later in this book will help uncover the nature of these associations.

4.8 Summary

This chapter extended our discussion of **descriptive statistics**, which deals with methods of summarizing and presenting the essential information contained in a set of data. After constructing a frequency distribution to obtain a general idea about the distribution of a data set, we can use numerical measures to describe the central location and the dispersion of the data. Three popular measures of central location, or averages, are the **mean**, the **median**, and the **mode**. Taken by themselves, these measures provide an inadequate description of the data because they say nothing about the extent to which the data are dispersed about their central value. Information regarding the dispersion, or variability, of the data is conveyed by such numerical measures as the **range**, the **interquartile range**, **variance**, **standard deviation**, and **coefficient of variation**.

For the special case in which a sample of measurements has a mound-shaped distribution, the **Empirical Rule** provides a good approximation of the percentages of measurements that fall within 1, 2, or 3 standard deviations of the mean. Beginning in Chapter 9, you will learn how these two important descriptive measures (mean and standard deviation), computed for a sample of measurements, can be combined to support inferences about the mean and the standard deviation of the population from which the sample was taken.

This chapter also included an introduction to **box plots**, as well as to **covariance** and the **coefficient of correlation**, which are used to measure the relationship between two variables.

IMPORTANT TERMS

Measures of central location	Coefficient of variation
Mean	Percentiles
Median	Quartiles
Mode	Interquartile range
Bimodal	Empirical Rule
Skewed	Box plots
Measures of variability	Measures of association
Range	Covariance
Variance	Coefficient of correlation
Standard deviation	

Formulas

Population mean: $\mu = \dfrac{\sum_{i=1}^{N} x_i}{N}$

Sample mean: $\bar{x} = \dfrac{\sum_{i=1}^{n} x_i}{n}$

Population variance: $\sigma^2 = \dfrac{\sum_{i=1}^{N} (x_i - \mu)^2}{N}$

(continued)

Sample variance: $s^2 = \dfrac{\sum_{i=1}^{n} (x_i - \bar{x})^2}{n - 1}$

Population standard deviation: $\sigma = \sqrt{\sigma^2}$

Sample standard deviation: $s = \sqrt{s^2}$

Population coefficient of variation: $CV = \dfrac{\sigma}{\mu}$

Sample coefficient of variation: $cv = \dfrac{s}{\bar{x}}$

Population covariance: $COV(X, Y) = \dfrac{\sum (x_i - \mu_x)(y_i - \mu_y)}{N}$

Sample covariance: $cov(X, Y) = \dfrac{\sum (x_i - \bar{x})(y_i - \bar{y})}{n - 1}$

Population coefficient of correlation: $\rho = \dfrac{COV(X, Y)}{\sigma_x \sigma_y}$

Sample coefficient of correlation: $r = \dfrac{cov(X, Y)}{s_x s_y}$

Supplementary Exercises

4.61 Determine the mean, the median, and the standard deviation of the following sample of data.

43 46 44 55 59 48 44 50 40 54 52 42

4.62 Consider the following population of measurements.

11 −1 5 2 8 7 12 4 −6 −10 1 5

a   Find the mean, the median, and the standard deviation of this population of measurements.

b   Find the upper and lower quartiles of these measurements.

4.63 The number of items rejected daily by a manufacturer because of defects was recorded for the last 25 days. The results are as follows.

21 8 17 22 19 18 19 14 17 11 6 21 25 19 9 12 16 16 10 29
24 6 21 20 25

Find the median, the mode, $\bar{x}$, s^2, and s for these data.

4.64 Refer to Exercise 4.63.

a   Construct a frequency distribution for these data. Use five class intervals, with the lower boundary of the first class being 5 items.

b   What proportion of items falls into the interval $\bar{x} \pm 2s$?

c   Does it appear that the population from which this sample was taken has a mound-shaped distribution?

d   Compare the actual proportions of items falling into the intervals $(\bar{x} - s, \bar{x} + s)$ and $(\bar{x} - 2s, \bar{x} + 2s)$ with the proportions suggested by the Empirical Rule.

4.65 The ages of a sample of 25 brokers were recorded as follows.

50 64 32 55 41 44 24 46 58 47 36 52 54 44 66 47 59 51 61
57 49 28 42 38 45

a Construct a stem and leaf display for the ages.

b Find the median age.

c Find the lower quartile of the ages.

d Find the upper quartile of the ages.

e Find the 80th percentile of the ages.

f Does this firm have reason to be concerned about the distribution of ages of its brokers?

4.66 Refer to Exercise 4.65.

a Compute the mean of the sample of data.

b Compute the variance of the sample of data.

c Compute the standard deviation of the sample of data.

4.67 Refer to Exercise 4.65.

a Compute the range of the data.

b Compute the range approximation to the standard deviation of the data.

4.68 Refer to Exercise 4.65.

a Construct a relative frequency histogram for the data, using five class intervals and the value 20 as the lower limit of the first class.

b Locate the interval $\bar{x} \pm s$ on the histogram, and find the proportion of ages that fall in this interval. How does this proportion compare with the Empirical Rule approximation?

4.69 Refer to Exercise 4.65.

a Construct a box plot for the brokers' ages.

b Does the distribution of the ages appear to be symmetric or skewed? Explain.

4.70 In the last few years, North American car makers have significantly improved the quality of their products. To determine the degree of improvement, a survey of 200 new cars was undertaken. The number of minor flaws (e.g., slightly misaligned doors, improperly directed headlights) was recorded. These data and the data from a similar survey five years ago were stored in column 1 and column 2, respectively, in file XR04-70.

a Use a graphical technique of your choosing to compare the two sets of data.

b Use numerical techniques of your choosing to compare the two sets of data.

c Briefly describe what you've learned from your statistical analysis.

4.71 Refer to Exercise 2.45, where the head coach of an NFL football team was trying to decide between three candidates for the position of punter. He has recorded the distances of the last 100 punts for each of the three candidates and stored them in columns 1 to 3 of file XR02-45.

a Use numerical statistical techniques to describe each sample.

b Using the statistics produced in part (a), provide the head coach with your recommendation.

4.72 Refer to Exercise 2.47, which dealt with the returns on five mutual funds stored in file XR02-47.

a Use numerical statistical techniques to describe the five samples.

b Briefly discuss the ways in which you would judge the "best" fund.

4.73 Slow play on golf courses frustrates most golfers and costs owners thousands of dollars annually. To find ways to speed up the game, the manager of one course undertook a study. The amount of time to complete a round of golf taken by samples of four different groups of golf foursomes was observed and recorded in file XR04-73 using the following format.

Column 1: time taken by four men without electric carts

Column 2: time taken by four men with electric carts

Column 3: time taken by four women without electric carts

Column 4: time taken by four women with electric carts

    a   For each sample, perform the following analyses.

        i   Draw the histogram.

        ii   Calculate the mean and median.

        iii   Calculate the standard deviation.

        iv   Draw the box plot.

    b   Interpret your findings, and describe the similarities and differences among the four groups.

4.74   A growing concern for educators in the United States is the number of teenagers who have part-time jobs while they attend high school. It is generally believed that the amount of time teenagers spend working is deducted from the amount of time devoted to schoolwork. To investigate this problem, a school guidance counselor took a random sample of 200 15-year-old high school students and asked how many hours per week each worked at a part-time job. The results were recorded and stored in file XR04-74.

    a   Calculate whatever statistics you think necessary to describe the data in the sample.

    b   Interpret each statistic produced.

4.75   Refer to Exercise 2.48, where the amount of time behind schedule was recorded for the last 250 departures for each of five airlines and stored in columns 1 through 5 of file XR02-48.

    a   Use numerical statistical techniques to describe the behind-schedule times for each airline.

    b   Briefly discuss what each statistic tells you.

    c   Which airline is best at adhering to its schedule? Explain.

4.76   Refer to Exercise 2.54, where the credit scores for good and bad loans were recorded in file XR02-54. Use whatever statistical techniques you deem useful to present a report to the bank's board of directors who asked you to discuss how well the scorecard works.

4.77   Refer to Exercise 2.57, where the annual incomes of five groups were stored in file XR02-57. Perform whatever statistical analyses you care to, and report your findings (bearing in mind the purpose of collecting the data).

4.78   Refer to Exercise 2.21, which considered the relationship between the number of houses sold (Y) and the mortgage rate (X). The values of Y and X for each of 12 months (as shown in Exercise 2.21) are stored in columns 1 and 2, respectively, in file XR04-78.

    a   Compute $cov(X, Y)$ and r.

    b   What do these statistics tell you about the relationship between the level of house sales and mortgage rates based on these data?

Descriptive Statistics

The command

> **DESCRIBE C1**

instructs Minitab to print a number of useful statistics, including the mean, median, and standard deviation.

Box Plots

The command

> **BOXPLOT C1**

produces the box plot of the data in column 1.

Covariance and Coefficient of Correlation

> **COVARIANCE C1 C2**

and

> **CORRELATION C1 C2**

compute and print the *sample* covariance and coefficient of correlation for the variables stored in columns 1 and 2.

APPENDIX 4.B **Summation Notation**

This appendix offers an introduction to the use of summation notation. Because summation notation is used extensively throughout statistics, you should review this appendix even if you've had previous exposure to summation notation. Our coverage of the topic begins with an introduction to the necessary terminology and notation, follows with some examples, and concludes with four rules that are useful in applying summation notation.

Consider n numbers $x_1, x_2, \ldots, x_n$. A concise way of representing their sum is

$$\sum_{i=1}^{n} x_i$$

That is,

$$\sum_{i=1}^{n} x_i = x_1 + x_2 + \cdots + x_n$$

Notation and Terminology

1 The symbol $\sum$ is the capital Greek letter sigma and means "the sum of."

2 The letter i is called the *index of summation*. The letter chosen to represent the index of summation is arbitrary.

3 The expression $\sum_{i=1}^{n} x_i$ is read "the sum of the terms x_i, where i assumes the values from 1 to n inclusive."

4 The numbers 1 and n are called the *lower* and the *upper limits of summation*, respectively.

Summation notation is best illustrated by means of examples.

EXAMPLES

1 Suppose $x_1 = 5$, $x_2 = 6$, $x_3 = 8$, and $x_4 = 10$.

a $\displaystyle\sum_{i=1}^{4} x_i = x_1 + x_2 + x_3 + x_4 = 5 + 6 + 8 + 10 = 29$

b $\displaystyle\sum_{i=3}^{4} x_i = x_3 + x_4 = 8 + 10 = 18$

c $\displaystyle\sum_{i=1}^{2} x_i(x_i - 1) = x_1(x_1 - 1) + x_2(x_2 - 1)$
$$= 5(5 - 1) + 6(6 - 1)$$
$$= 50$$

d $\displaystyle\sum_{i=1}^{3} f(x_i) = f(x_1) + f(x_2) + f(x_3)$
$$= f(5) + f(6) + f(8)$$

2 Suppose $x_1 = 2$, $x_2 = 3$, $x_3 = 4$, $y_1 = 8$, $y_2 = 9$, and $y_3 = 13$.

a $\displaystyle\sum_{i=1}^{3} x_i y_i = x_1 y_1 + x_2 y_2 + x_3 y_3$
$$= 2(8) + 3(9) + 4(13)$$
$$= 95$$

b $\displaystyle\sum_{i=2}^{3} x_i y_i^2 = x_2 y_2^2 + x_3 y_3^2$
$$= 3(9^2) + 4(13^2)$$
$$= 919$$

c $\displaystyle\sum_{i=1}^{2} (x_i - y_i) = (x_1 - y_1) + (x_2 - y_2)$
$$= (2 - 8) + (3 - 9)$$
$$= -12$$

It is not necessary that the index of summation be a subscript, as the following examples demonstrate.

1 $\displaystyle\sum_{x=0}^{4} x = 0 + 1 + 2 + 3 + 4 = 10$

2 $\displaystyle\sum_{x=1}^{3} (x^2 - x) = (1^2 - 1) + (2^2 - 2) + (3^2 - 3) = 8$

3 $\displaystyle\sum_{x=1}^{2} 5x = 5(1) + 5(2) = 15$

4 $\displaystyle\sum_{x=0}^{3} f(x) = f(0) + f(1) + f(2) + f(3)$

5 $\displaystyle\sum_{x=1}^{2} f(x, y) = f(1, y) + f(2, y)$

6 $\displaystyle\sum_{y=3}^{5} f(x, y^2) = f(x, 3^2) + f(x, 4^2) + f(x, 5^2)$

Rules of Summation Notation

1 If c is a constant, then

$$\sum_{i=1}^{n} cx_i = c \sum_{i=1}^{n} x_i$$

2 If c is a constant, then

$$\sum_{x=1}^{n} c = nc$$

3 If a and b are constants, then

$$\sum_{i=1}^{n} (ax_i + by_i) = a \sum_{i=1}^{n} x_i + b \sum_{i=1}^{n} y_i$$

4 If c is a constant, then

$$\sum_{i=1}^{n} (x_i + c) = \sum_{i=1}^{n} x_i + nc$$

Notice that

$$\sum_{i=1}^{n} x_i^2 \neq \left(\sum_{i=1}^{n} x_i \right)^2$$

To verify this, observe that

$$\sum_{i=1}^{n} x_i^2 = x_1^2 + x_2^2 + \cdots + x_n^2$$

while

$$\left(\sum_{i=1}^{n} x_i\right)^2 = (x_1 + x_2 + \cdots + x_n)^2$$

Exercises

1 Evaluate $\sum_{i=1}^{5} (i^2 + 2i)$.

2 Evaluate $\sum_{x=0}^{2} (x^3 + 2x)$.

3 Using the accompanying set of measurements, evaluate the following sums.

a $\sum_{i=1}^{13} x_i$

b $\sum_{i=1}^{13} (2x_i + 5)$

c $\sum_{i=1}^{6} (x_i - 5)^2$

i	1	2	3	4	5	6	7	8	9	10	11	12	13
x_i	3	12	10	−6	0	11	2	−9	−5	8	−7	4	−5

5 Data Collection and Sampling

5.1 Introduction

In Chapter 1, we briefly introduced the concept of statistical inference—the process of inferring information about a population from a sample. Because information about populations can usually be described by parameters, the statistical technique used generally deals with drawing inferences about population parameters from sample statistics. (Recall that a parameter is a measurement about a population, and a statistic is a measurement about a sample.)

Working within the covers of a statistics textbook, we can assume that population parameters are known. In real life, however, calculating parameters becomes prohibitive because populations tend to be quite large. As a result, most population parameters are unknown. For example, in order to determine the mean annual income of North American blue-collar workers, we would have to ask each North American blue-collar worker what his or her income is and then calculate the mean of all the responses. Because this population consists of several million people, the task is both expensive and impractical. If we are willing to accept less than 100% accuracy, we can use statistical inference to obtain an estimate.

Rather than investigating the entire population, we select a sample of workers, determine the annual income of the workers in this group, and calculate the sample mean. While there is very little chance that the sample mean and the population mean are identical, we would expect them to be quite close. However, for the purposes of statistical inference, we need to be able to measure how close the sample mean is likely to be to the population mean. We postpone our discussion about how to do that until Chapters 8 and 9, after we have covered probability. In this chapter, however, we will discuss the basic concepts and techniques of sampling itself. But first we will take a look at various sources for collecting data.

5.2 Sources of Data

The validity of the results of a statistical analysis clearly depends on the reliability and accuracy of the data used. Whether you are actually involved in collecting the data, performing a statistical analysis on the data, or simply reviewing the results of such an analysis, it is important to realize that the reliability and accuracy of the data depend on the method of collection. Three of the most popular sources of statistical data are published data, data collected from observational studies, and data collected from experimental studies.

Published Data

The use of published data is often preferred due to its convenience, relatively low cost, and reliability (assuming that it has been collected by a reputable organization). There is an enormous amount of published data produced by government agencies and private organizations, available in printed form, on data tapes and disks, and increasingly on the Internet. Data published by the same organization that collected them are called **primary data**. An example of primary data would be the data published by the United States Bureau of the Census, which collects data on numerous industries as well as conducts the census of the population every ten years. Statistics Canada is the central statistical agency in Canada, collecting data on almost every aspect of social and economic life in the country. These primary sources of information are invaluable to decision makers in both the government and private sectors.

Secondary data refers to data that are published by an organization different from the one that originally collected and published the data. A popular source of secondary data is *The Statistical Abstract of the United States*, which compiles data from several primary government sources and is updated annually. Another example of a secondary data source is Compustat, which sells a variety of financial data tapes that contain data compiled from such primary sources as the New York Stock Exchange. Care should be taken when using secondary data, as errors may have been introduced as a result of the transcription or due to misinterpretation of the original terminology and definitions employed.

An interesting example of the importance of knowing how data collection agencies define their terms appeared in an article in *The Globe and Mail* (February 12, 1996). The United States and Canada had similar unemployment rates up until the 1980s, at which time Canada's rate started to edge higher than the U.S. rate. By February 1996, the gap had grown to almost four percentage points (9.6% in Canada compared with 5.8% in the United States). Economists from the United States and Canada met for two days to compare research results and discuss possible reasons for this puzzling gap in jobless rates. The conference organizer explained that solving this mystery matters because "we have to understand the nature of unemployment to design policies to combat it." An Ohio State University economist was the first to notice a difference in how officials from the two countries define unemployment. "If jobless people say they are searching for work, but do nothing more than read job advertisements in the newspaper, Canada counts them as unemployed. U.S. officials dismiss such 'passive' job hunters and count them as being out of the labour force altogether, so they are not counted among the jobless." Statistics Canada reported that this difference in definitions accounted for almost one-fifth of the difference between the Canadian and U.S. unemployment rates.

Observational and Experimental Studies

If relevant data are not available from published sources, it may be necessary to generate the data by conducting a study. This will especially be the case when data are needed concerning a specific company or situation. The difference between two important types of studies—observational and experimental—is best illustrated by means of an example.

EXAMPLE 5.1

Six months ago, the director of human resources for a large mutual fund company announced that the company had arranged for its salespeople to use a nearby fitness center free of charge. The director believes that fitter salespeople have more energy and an improved appearance, resulting in higher productivity. Interest and participation in the fitness initiative were high initially, but after a few months had passed, several employees stopped participating. Those who continued to exercise were committed to maintaining a good level of fitness, using the fitness center about three times per week on average.

The director recently conducted an **observational study** and determined that the average sales level achieved by those who regularly used the fitness center exceeded that of those who did not use the center. The director was tempted to use the difference in productivity levels to justify the cost to the company of making the fitness center available to employees. But the vice-president of finance pointed out that the fitness initiative was not necessarily the *cause* of the difference in productivity levels. Because the salespeople who exercised were self-selected—they determined themselves whether or not to make use of the fitness center—it is quite likely that the salespeople who used the center were those who were more ambitious and disciplined. These people would probably have had higher levels of fitness and productivity even without the fitness initiative. We therefore cannot necessarily conclude that fitness center usage led to higher productivity. It may be that other factors, such as ambition and discipline, were responsible both for higher fitness center usage and higher productivity.

The director and vice-president then discussed the possibility of conducting an **experimental study**, designed to control which salespeople made regular use of the fitness center. The director would randomly select 60 salespeople to participate in the study. Thirty of these would be randomly selected and persuaded to use the fitness center on a regular basis for six months. The other 30 salespeople selected would not be approached, but simply would have their sales performances monitored along with those using the fitness center regularly. Because these two groups were selected at random, we would expect them to be fairly similar in terms of original average fitness level, ambition, discipline, age, and other factors that might affect performance. From this experimental study, we would be more confident that any significantly higher level of productivity by the group using the fitness center regularly would be due to the fitness initiative rather than other factors.

The point of the preceding example is to illustrate the difference between an observational study and an experimental (or controlled) study. In the observational study, a survey simply was conducted to observe and record the average sales level for each group, without attempting to control any of the factors that might influence the sales levels. In the experimental study, the director controlled one factor (regular use of the fitness center) by randomly selecting who would be persuaded to use the center regularly, thereby reducing the influence of other factors on the difference between the sales levels of the two groups.

Although experimental studies make it easier to establish a cause-and-effect relationship between two variables, observational studies are used predominantly in business and economics. More often than not, surveys are conducted to collect business and economic data (such as consumer preferences or unemployment statistics), with no attempt to control any factors that might affect the variable of interest.

More will be said about observational and experimental data in Chapter 11. The design and analysis of various experimental studies will be considered in Chapters 12 through 15.

Surveys

One of the most familiar methods of collecting primary data is the survey, which solicits information from people concerning such things as their income, family size, and opinions on various issues. We're all familiar, for example, with opinion polls that accompany each political election. The Gallup poll and the Harris Survey are two well-known surveys of public opinion whose results are often reported by the media. But the majority of surveys are conducted for private use. Private surveys are used extensively by market researchers to determine the preferences and attitudes of consumers and voters. The results can be used for a variety of purposes, from helping to determine the target market for an advertising campaign to modifying a candidate's platform in an election campaign. As an illustration, consider a television network that has hired a market research firm to provide the network with a profile of owners of luxury automobiles, including what they watch on television and at what times. The network could then use this information to develop a package of recommended time slots for Cadillac commercials, including costs, that it would present to General Motors. It is quite likely that many students reading this book will one day be marketing executives who will "live and die" by such market research data.

Many researchers feel that the best way to survey people is by means of a **personal interview**, which involves an interviewer soliciting information from a respondent by asking prepared questions. A personal interview has the advantage of having a higher expected response rate than other methods of data collection. In addition, there will probably be fewer incorrect responses resulting from respondents misunderstanding some questions, because the interviewer can clarify misunderstandings when asked to. But the interviewer must also be careful not to say too much, for fear of biasing the response. To avoid introducing such biases, as well as to reap the potential benefits of a personal interview, the interviewer must be well trained in proper interviewing techniques and well informed on the purpose of the study. The main disadvantage of personal interviews is that they are expensive, especially when travel is involved. A **telephone interview** is usually less expensive, but it is also less personal and has a lower expected response rate.

A third popular method of data collection is the **self-administered questionnaire**, which is usually mailed to a sample of people selected to be surveyed. This is a relatively inexpensive method of conducting a survey and is therefore attractive when the number of people to be surveyed is large. But self-administered questionnaires usually have a low response rate and may have a relatively high number of incorrect responses due to respondents misunderstanding some questions.

Whether a questionnaire is self-administered or completed by an interviewer, it must be well designed. Proper questionnaire design takes knowledge, experience, time, and money. Some basic points to consider regarding **questionnaire design** follow.

1 First and foremost, the questionnaire should be kept as short as possible to encourage respondents to complete it. Most people are unwilling to spend much time filling out a questionnaire.

2 The questions themselves should also be short, as well as simply and clearly worded, to enable respondents to answer quickly, correctly, and without ambiguity. Even familiar terms, such as "unemployed" and "family," must be defined carefully because several interpretations are possible.

3 Questionnaires often begin with simple demographic questions to help respondents get started and become comfortable quickly.

4 Dichotomous questions (questions with only two possible responses, such as "yes" and "no") and multiple-choice questions are useful and popular because of their simplicity, but they, too, have possible shortcomings. For example, a respondent's choice of *yes* or *no* to a question may depend on certain assumptions not stated in the question. In the case of a multiple-choice question, a respondent may feel that none of the choices offered is suitable.

5 Open-ended questions provide an opportunity for respondents to express opinions more fully, but they are time-consuming and more difficult to tabulate and analyze.

6 Avoid using leading questions, such as "Wouldn't you agree that the statistics exam was too difficult?" These types of questions tend to lead the respondent to a particular answer.

7 Time permitting, it is useful to pretest a questionnaire on a small number of people in order to uncover potential problems, such as ambiguous wording.

8 Finally, when preparing the questions, think about how you intend to tabulate and analyze the responses. First determine whether you are soliciting values (i.e., responses) for a quantitative variable or a qualitative variable. Then consider which type of statistical techniques—descriptive or inferential—you intend to apply to the data to be collected, and note the requirements of the specific techniques to be used. Thinking about these questions will help to assure that the questionnaire is designed to collect the data you need.

Whatever method is used to collect primary data, we need to know something about sampling, the subject of the next section.

Exercises

5.1 Briefly describe the difference between primary data and secondary data.

5.2a **American Version**: For each of the following data sources, determine the frequency of publication and write down two specific pieces of information contained in the latest issue.

    a *The Statistical Abstract of the United States*

    b *Survey of Current Business*

    c *Federal Reserve Bulletin*

5.2b **Canadian Version**: For each of the following data sources, determine the frequency of publication and write down two specific pieces of information contained in the latest issue.

    a *Canadian Economic Observer, Statistical Summary, Statistics Canada*

    b *Bank of Canada Review*

    c *Toronto Stock Exchange Review*

5.3 Describe the difference between an observational study and an experimental study.

5.4 A soft-drink manufacturer has been supplying its cola drink in bottles to grocery stores and in cans to small convenience stores. The company is analyzing sales of this cola drink to determine which type of packaging is preferred by consumers.

    a Is this study observational or experimental? Explain your answer.

    b Outline a better method for determining whether a store will be supplied with cola in bottles or in cans, so that future sales data will be more helpful in assessing the preferred type of packaging.

5.5 **a** Briefly describe how you might design a study to investigate the relationship between smoking and lung cancer.

    b Is your study in part (a) observational or experimental? Explain why.

5.6 **a** List three methods of conducting a survey of people.

    b Give an important advantage and disadvantage of each of the methods listed in part (a).

5.7 List five important points to consider when designing a questionnaire.

5.3 Sampling

The chief motive for examining a sample rather than a population is cost. Statistical inference permits us to draw conclusions about a population parameter based on a sample that is quite small in comparison to the size of the population. For example, television executives want to know the proportion of television viewers who watch a network's programs. Because 100 million people may be watching television in the United States on a given evening, determining the actual proportion of the population that is watching certain programs is impractical and prohibitively expensive. The Nielsen ratings provide approximations of the desired information by observing what is watched by a sample of 1,000 television viewers. The proportion of households watching a particular program can be calculated for the households in the Nielsen sample. This sample proportion is then used as an **estimate** of the proportion of *all* households (the population proportion) that watched the program.

Another illustration of sampling can be taken from the field of quality control. In order to ensure that a production process is operating properly, the operations manager needs to know what proportion of items being produced is defective. If the quality-control technician must destroy the item in order to determine whether it is defective, then there is no alternative to sampling: a complete inspection of the product population would destroy the entire output of the production process.

We know that the sample proportion of television viewers or of defective items is probably not exactly equal to the population proportion we want to estimate. Nonetheless, the sample statistic can come quite close to the parameter it is designed to estimate if the **target population** (the population about which we want to draw inferences) and the **sampled population** (the actual population from which the sample has been taken) are the same. In practice, these may not be the same, as the following example illustrates.

The Nielsen Ratings

The Nielsen ratings are supposed to provide information about the television shows that all Americans are watching. Hence, the target population is the television viewers of the United States. If the sample of 1,000 viewers was drawn exclusively from the state of New York, however, the sampled population would be the television viewers of New York. In this case, the target population and the sampled population are not the same, and no valid inferences about the target population can be drawn. To allow proper estimation of the proportion of all American television viewers watching a specific program, the sample should contain men and women of varying ages, incomes, occupations, and residences in a pattern similar to that of the target population. The importance of sampling from the target population cannot be overestimated; the consequences of drawing conclusions from improperly selected samples can be costly. One of the most spectacular examples of how *not* to conduct a survey was the *Literary Digest* poll of 1936.

The *Literary Digest* Poll

The *Literary Digest* was a popular magazine of the 1920s and 1930s that had correctly predicted the outcomes of several presidential elections. In 1936, the *Digest* predicted that the Republican candidate, Alfred Landon, would defeat the Democratic incumbent, Franklin D. Roosevelt, by a 3 to 2 margin. But in that election, Roosevelt defeated Landon in a landslide victory, garnering the support of 62% of the electorate. The source of this blunder was the sampling procedure, and there were two distinct mistakes. First, the *Digest* sent out 10 million sample ballots to prospective voters. However, most of the names of these people were taken from the *Digest*'s subscription list and from telephone directories. Subscribers to the magazine and people who owned telephones tended to be wealthier than average, and such people then, as today, tended to vote Republican. Additionally, only 2.3 million ballots were returned, resulting in a self-selected sample.

Self-selected samples are almost always biased, because the individuals who participate in them are more keenly interested in the issue than are the other members of the population. You often find similar surveys conducted today when radio and television stations ask people to call and give their opinion on an issue of interest. Again, only listeners who are concerned about the topic and have enough patience to get through to the station will be included in the sample. Hence, the sampled population is comprised entirely of people who are interested in the issue, whereas the target population is made up of all the people within the listening radius of the radio station. As a result, the conclusions drawn from such surveys are frequently wrong.

An excellent example of this phenomenon occurred on ABC's "Nightline" in 1984. Viewers were given a 900 number (cost: 50 cents) and asked to phone in their responses to the question of whether the United Nations should continue to be located in the United States. More than 186,000 people called, with 67% responding no. At the same time, a (more scientific) market research poll of 500 people revealed that 72% wanted the United Nations to remain in the United States. In general, because the true value of the parameter being estimated is never known, these surveys give the impression of providing useful information. In fact, the results of such surveys are likely to be no more accurate than the results of the 1936 *Literary Digest* poll* or "Nightline's" phone-in show. Statisticians have coined two terms to describe these polls: SLOP (self-selected opinion poll) and "oy vey" (from the Yiddish lament), both of which convey the contempt that statisticians have for such data-gathering processes.

Exercises

5.8 For each of the following sampling plans, indicate why the target population and the sampled population are not the same.

a In order to determine the opinions and attitudes of customers who regularly shop at a particular mall, a surveyor stands outside a large department store in the mall and randomly selects people to participate in the survey.

b A library wants to estimate the proportion of its books that has been damaged. The librarians decide to select one book per shelf as a sample by measuring 12 inches from the left edge of each shelf and selecting the book in that location.

c Political surveyors visit 200 residences during one afternoon to ask eligible voters present in the house at the time whom they intend to vote for.

5.9 a Describe why the *Literary Digest* poll of 1936 has become infamous.

b What caused this poll to be so wrong?

5.10 a What is meant by a self-selected sample?

b Give an example of a recent poll that involved a self-selected sample.

c Why are self-selected samples not desirable?

5.4 Sampling Plans

Our objective in this section is to introduce three different sampling plans: simple random sampling, stratified random sampling, and cluster sampling. We begin our presentation with the most basic design.

Simple Random Sampling

> **Simple Random Sample**
>
> A **simple random sample** is a sample selected in such a way that every possible sample with the same number of observations is equally likely to be chosen.

---

*Many statisticians ascribe the *Literary Digest*'s statistical debacle to the wrong causes. For a better understanding of what really happened, read Maurice C. Bryson, "The *Literary Digest* Poll: Making of a Statistical Myth," *American Statistician* 30(4)(November 1976): 184–85.

One way to conduct a simple random sample is to assign a number to each element in the population, write these numbers on individual slips of paper, toss them into a hat, and draw the required number of slips (the sample size, n) from the hat. This is the kind of procedure that occurs in raffles, when all the ticket stubs go into a large, rotating drum from which the winners are selected.

Sometimes the elements of the population are already numbered. For example, virtually all adults have Social Security numbers (in the United States) or Social Insurance numbers (in Canada); all employees of large corporations have employee numbers; many people have driver's license numbers, medical plan numbers, student numbers, and so on. In such cases, choosing which sampling procedure to use is simply a matter of deciding how to select from among these numbers.

In other cases, the existing form of numbering has built-in flaws that make it inappropriate as a source of samples. Not everyone has a phone number, for example, so the telephone book does not list all the people in a given area. Many households have two (or more) adults, but only one phone listing. Couples often list the phone number under the man's name, so telephone listings are likely to be disproportionately male. Some people do not have phones, some have unlisted phone numbers, and some have more than one phone; these differences mean that each element of the population does not have an equal probability of being selected.

After each element of the chosen population has been assigned a unique number, sample numbers can be selected at random. A random-number table can be used to select these sample numbers. (See, for example, *CRC Standard Management Tables*, W. H. Beyer, Ed., Boca Raton: CRC Press.) Alternatively, we can employ a software package to generate random numbers. Both Minitab and Excel have this capability.

EXAMPLE 5.2

A government income-tax auditor has been given responsibility for 1,000 tax returns. A computer is used to check the arithmetic of each return. However, to determine if the returns have been completed honestly, the auditor must check each entry and confirm its veracity. Because it takes, on average, one hour to completely audit a return and she has only one week to complete the task, the auditor has decided to randomly select 40 returns. The returns are numbered from 1 to 1,000. Use a computer random-number generator to select the sample for the auditor.

SOLUTION

There are several software packages that can produce the random numbers we need. Minitab and Excel are two of these.

Minitab Output for Example 5.2

173	184	953	896	82	388	232	962	391	95
259	544	588	754	870	700	893	690	320	28
312	183	271	587	922	759	929	526	112	43
811	480	984	991	100	367	655	877	59	642
654	859	478	633	157	470	615	32	258	887

We generated 50 numbers between 1 and 1,000 and stored them in column 1. Although we needed only 40 random numbers, we generated 50 numbers because it is likely that some of them will be duplicates. We will use the first 40 unique random numbers to select our sample.

MENU COMMANDS	COMMANDS FOR EXAMPLE 5.2
1 Click **Calc**, **Random Data**, and **Integer**	
2 Type the number of random numbers to be generated.	**50**
3 Hit **tab** and type the column where the numbers are to be stored.	**C1**
4 Hit **tab** and type the **Minimum value**.	**1**
5 Hit **tab** and type the **Maximum value**. Click **OK**. Print the column of stored numbers.	**1000**

SESSION COMMANDS

```
RANDOM 50 C1;
INTEGERS 1 1000.
PRINT C1
```

These commands generate 50 random numbers that lie between 1 and 1,000. Each number has the same probability ($1/1,000 = .001$) of being selected. Thus, each member of the population is equally likely to be included in the sample.

Excel Output for Example 5.2

165	78	120	987	705	827	725	466	759	361
504	545	578	820	147	276	237	764	85	528
160	357	44	971	269	517	711	721	192	926
832	661	426	173	909	973	856	813	152	915
544	622	830	382	198	830	700	256	210	621

We generated 50 numbers between 1 and 1,000 and stored them in column 1. Although we needed only 40 random numbers, we generated 50 numbers because it is likely that some of them will be duplicates. We will use the first 40 unique random numbers to select our sample.

COMMANDS	COMMANDS FOR EXAMPLE 5.2
1 Click **Tools, Data Analysis . . .** , and **Random Number Generation**.	
2 Type the **Number of Variables**.	**1**
3 Hit **tab** and type the **Number of Random Numbers**.	**50**
4 Use the cursor to select the **Uniform Distribution**.	
5 Use the cursor to specify the range of the uniform distribution (**Parameters**). Click **OK**. Column A will fill with 50 numbers that range between 0 and 1.	**0 and 1**
6 Multiply column A by 1,000 and store the products in column B.	
7 Make cell C1 active, click **f_x**, **Math & Trig**, **ROUNDUP**, and **Next>**.	
8 Specify the first number to be rounded.	**B1**
9 Hit **tab** and type the **number of digits** (decimal places). Click **Finish**. Complete column C.	**0**

Excel 97 Users:
Steps 7 and 9. Change **Next>** and **Finish** to **OK**.

The first five steps command Excel to generate 50 uniformly distributed random numbers between 0 and 1 to be stored in column A. Steps 6 through 9 convert these random numbers to integers between 1 and 1,000. Each number has the same probability $(1/1,000 = .001)$ of being selected. Thus, each member of the population is equally likely to be included in the sample.

INTERPRETING THE RESULTS

The auditor would examine the tax returns selected by the computer. Using the Minitab output, she would pick returns numbered 173, 184, 953, . . . , 877, 59, and 642 (the first 40 unique numbers). Each of these would be audited to determine if they were fraudulent. If the objective is to audit these 40 returns, no statistical procedure would be employed. However, if the objective is to estimate the proportion of *all* 1,000 returns that were dishonest, she would use one of the inferential techniques that are presented later in this book.

Stratified Random Sampling

In making inferences about a population, we attempt to extract as much information as possible from a sample. The basic sampling plan, simple random sampling, often accomplishes this goal at low cost. Other methods, however, can be used to increase the amount of information about the population. One such procedure is stratified random sampling.

> **Stratified Random Sample**
>
> A **stratified random sample** is obtained by separating the population into mutually exclusive sets, or strata, and then drawing simple random samples from each stratum.

Examples of criteria for separating a population into strata (and of the strata themselves) follow.

1 Sex

     male

     female

2 Age

     under 20

     20–30

     31–40

     41–50

     51–60

     over 60

3 Occupation

     professional

     clerical

     blue-collar

     other

4 Household income

     under $15,000

     $15,000–$29,999

     $30,000–$50,000

     over $50,000

To illustrate, suppose a public opinion survey is to be conducted in order to determine how many people favor a tax increase. A stratified random sample could be obtained by selecting a random sample of people from each of the four income groups described above. We usually stratify in a way that enables us to obtain particular kinds of information. In this example, we would like to know if people in the different income categories differ in their opinions about the proposed tax increase, since the tax increase will affect the strata differently. We avoid stratifying when there is no connection between the survey and the strata. For example, little purpose is served in trying to determine if people within religious strata have divergent opinions about the tax increase.

One advantage of stratification is that, besides acquiring information about the entire population, we can also make inferences within each stratum or compare strata. For instance, we can estimate what proportion of the lowest income group favors the tax increase, or we can compare the highest and lowest income groups to determine if they differ in their support of the tax increase.

Any stratification must be done in such a way that the strata are mutually exclusive: each member of the population must be assigned to exactly one stratum.

After the population has been stratified in this way, we can employ simple random sampling to generate the complete sample. There are several ways to do this. For example, we can draw random samples from each of the four income groups according to their proportions in the population. Thus, if in the population the relative frequencies of the four groups are as listed below, our sample will be stratified in the same proportions. If a total sample of 1,000 is to be drawn, we will randomly select 250 from stratum 1, 400 from stratum 2, 300 from stratum 3, and 50 from stratum 4.

STRATUM	INCOME CATEGORIES	POPULATION PROPORTIONS
1	under $15,000	25%
2	15,000–29,999	40
3	30,000–50,000	30
4	over 50,000	5

The problem with this approach, however, is that if we want to make inferences about the last stratum, a sample of 50 may be too small to produce useful information. In such cases, we usually increase the sample size of the smallest stratum (or strata) to ensure that the sample data provide enough information for our purposes. An adjustment must then be made before we attempt to draw inferences about the entire population. This procedure is beyond the level of this book. We recommend that anyone planning such a survey consult an expert statistician or a reference book on the subject. Better still, become an expert statistician yourself by taking additional statistics courses.

Cluster Sampling

Cluster Sample

A **cluster sample** is a simple random sample of groups or clusters of elements.

Cluster sampling is particularly useful when it is difficult or costly to develop a complete list of the population members (making it difficult and costly to generate a simple random sample). It is also useful whenever the population elements are widely dispersed geographically. For example, suppose we wanted to estimate the average annual household income in a large city. To use simple random sampling, we would need a complete list of households in the city from which to sample. To use stratified random sampling, we would need the list of households, and we would also need to have each household categorized by some other variable (such as age of household head) in order to develop the strata. A less expensive alternative would be to let each block within the city represent a cluster. A sample of clusters could then be randomly selected, and every household within these clusters could be questioned to determine income. By reducing the distances the surveyor must cover to gather data, cluster sampling reduces the cost.

But cluster sampling also increases sampling error (see Section 5.5), because households belonging to the same cluster are likely to be similar in many respects, including household income. This can be partially offset by using some of the cost savings to choose a larger sample than would be used for a simple random sample.

Sample Size

Whichever type of sampling plan you select, you still have to decide what size of sample to use. Determining the appropriate sample size will be addressed in detail in Chapter 9. Until then, we can rely on our intuition, which tells us that the larger the sample size is, the more accurate we can expect the sample estimates to be.

Exercises

5.11 A statistician would like to conduct a survey to ask people their views on a proposed new shopping mall in their community. According to the latest census, there are 800 households in the community. The statistician has numbered each household (from 1 to 800), and she would like to randomly select 25 of these households to participate in the study. Use a software package to generate the sample.

5.12 A safety expert wants to determine the proportion of cars in his state with worn tire treads. The state license plate contains six digits. Use a software package to generate a sample of 20 cars to be examined.

5.13 The operations manager of a large plant with four departments wants to estimate the person-hours lost per month due to accidents. Describe a sampling plan that would be suitable for estimating the plant-wide loss and for comparing departments.

5.14 A statistician wants to estimate the mean age of children in his city. Unfortunately, he does not have a complete list of households. Describe a sampling plan that would be suitable for his purposes.

5.5 Errors Involved in Sampling

Two major types of errors can arise when a sample of observations is taken from a population: sampling error and nonsampling error. Managers reviewing the results of sample surveys and studies, as well as researchers who conduct the surveys and studies, should understand the sources of these errors.

Sampling Error

Sampling error refers to differences between the sample and the population that exist only because of the observations that happened to be selected for the sample. Sampling error is an error that we *expect* to occur when we make a statement about a population that is based only on the observations contained in a sample taken from the population. To illustrate, consider again the example described in Section 5.1 in which we wish to determine the mean annual income of North American blue-collar workers. As was stated there, we can use statistical inference to estimate the mean income (μ) of the population if we are willing to accept less than 100% accuracy. If we record the incomes of a sample of the workers and find the mean ($\bar{x}$) of this sample of incomes, this sample mean is an estimate of the desired population mean. But the value of $\bar{x}$ will deviate from the population mean (μ)

simply by chance, because the value of the sample mean depends on which incomes just happened to be selected for the sample. The difference between the true (unknown) value of the population mean (μ) and its sample estimate ($\bar{x}$) is the sampling error. The size of this deviation may be large simply due to bad luck—bad luck that a particularly unrepresentative sample happened to be selected. The only way we can reduce the expected size of this error is to take a larger sample.

Given a fixed sample size, the best we can do is to state the probability that the sampling error is less than a certain amount (as we will discuss in Chapter 8). It is common today for such a statement to accompany the results of an opinion poll. If an opinion poll states that, based on sample results, Candidate Kreem has the support of 54% of eligible voters in an upcoming election, that statement may be accompanied by the following explanatory note: This percentage is correct to within three percentage points, 19 times out of 20. This statement means that we have a certain level of confidence (95%) that the actual level of support for Candidate Kreem is between 51% and 57%.

Nonsampling Error

Nonsampling error is more serious than sampling error, because taking a larger sample won't diminish the size, or the possibility of occurrence, of this error. Even a census can (and probably will) contain nonsampling errors. **Nonsampling errors** are due to mistakes made in the acquisition of data or due to the sample observations being selected improperly.

THREE TYPES OF NONSAMPLING ERRORS

1 *Errors in Data Acquisition.* These types of errors arise from the recording of incorrect responses. This may be the result of incorrect measurements being taken because of faulty equipment, mistakes made during transcription from primary sources, inaccurate recording of data due to misinterpretation of terms, or inaccurate responses to questions concerning sensitive issues such as sexual activity or possible tax evasion.

2 *Nonresponse Error.* **Nonresponse error** refers to error (or **bias**) introduced when responses are not obtained from some members of the sample. When this happens, the sample observations that are collected may not be representative of the target population, resulting in biased results (as was discussed in Section 5.3). Nonresponse can occur for a number of reasons. An interviewer may be unable to contact a person listed in the sample, or the sampled person may refuse to respond for some reason. In either case, responses are not obtained from a sampled person, and bias is introduced. The problem of nonresponse is even greater when self-administered questionnaires are used rather than an interviewer, who can attempt to reduce the nonresponse rate by means of callbacks. As noted earlier, the *Literary Digest* fiasco was largely due to a high nonresponse rate, resulting in a biased, self-selected sample.

3 *Selection Bias.* **Selection bias** occurs when the sampling plan is such that some members of the target population cannot possibly be selected for inclusion in the sample. Together with nonreponse error, selection bias

played a role in the *Literary Digest* poll being so wrong, as voters without telephones or without a subscription to *Literary Digest* were excluded from possible inclusion in the sample taken.

Exercises

5.15 **a** Explain the difference between sampling error and nonsampling error.

b Which type of error in part (a) is more serious? Why?

5.16 Briefly describe three types of nonsampling errors.

5.17 Is it possible for a sample to yield better results than a census? Explain.

5.6 Use of Sampling in Auditing (Optional*)

The accounting profession in its role as external auditor of financial statements may be one of the principal users of a probability distribution called the Poisson distribution (covered in Chapter 6). Auditors make statistical inferences about the existence of errors and/or fraud in the accounting records in order to express an opinion on the fairness of published financial statements. The audit is divided into two phases. Phase one looks at the adequacy of the control environment. Here, *attribute sampling* is employed to estimate the **rate** of errors in the population. On the basis of these sample results, phase two of the audit employs *variable sampling* to estimate the magnitude of errors and/or defalcation caused by inadequacies in the control environment.

Historically, *classical variable sampling* (mean per unit, difference, and ratio estimation), requiring an estimate of the population standard deviation, was employed. Classical variable sampling turned out to be unsuitable, especially in the detection of fraud, because frequency of occurrence is so small (often less than one occurrence per million). Required sample sizes were often so large that the statistical inference was economically unviable, and auditors turned back to heuristic methods using nonstatistical inference.

Fortunately, the Poisson distribution (which we will soon study) allowed auditors to escape from this dilemma. When auditors noticed that the Poisson distribution was ideally suited for populations where the occurrence rate was extremely low, they developed a specialized statistical approach called PPS (Probability Proportionate to Size) or sometimes referred to as DUS (Dollar Unit Sampling), which is based on the Poisson distribution. In PPS, the individual dollar, rather than the account balance or an invoice, is defined as the sampling unit. Each dollar in the population has an equal chance of being selected, and, once selected, acts as a hook to draw in the invoice, account, etc., of which it is a part. The result is that the probability of selection into the sample becomes proportionate to size; for example, a one-million-dollar invoice is one million times more likely to be drawn for examination than a one-dollar invoice. By starting with an assumption that the underlying rate of error in the population is zero, PPS results in sample sizes that are far smaller than those suggested by classical variable sampling. Accordingly, PPS has become almost universally adopted in auditing.

The mean of the Poisson distribution is given by the expression $\mu = np$, where μ is the mean, n is the sample size (number of trials), and p is the probability of occurrence for one trial. The Poisson distribution allows the auditor to state, with

---

*This section can be omitted without loss of continuity. In any case, the reader may wish to read (or reread) this section after the Poisson distribution has been covered in Chapter 6. The authors are grateful to Professor Brian Gaber, York University, for his assistance in preparing this section.

a specified risk, the tolerable error per sample size n of the population when the sample contains x errors. The procedure is too lengthy to describe here and requires the use of specialized tables derived from the Poisson distribution. A detailed discussion of the theory can be found in the *Audit Sampling Guide*, by the Statistical Sampling Subcommittee of the American Institute of Certified Public Accountants, AICPA, New York, 1983, and the procedures for PPS are described in most auditing textbooks.

5.7 Summary

Because most populations are very large, it is extremely costly and impractical to investigate each member of the population to determine the values of the parameters. As a practical alternative, we take a sample from the population and use the sample statistics to draw inferences about the parameters. Care must be taken to ensure that the sampled population is the same as the target population.

We can choose from among several different sampling plans, including simple random sampling, stratified random sampling, and cluster sampling. Whatever sampling plan is used, it is important to realize that both sampling error and nonsampling error will occur, and to understand what the sources of these errors are.

IMPORTANT TERMS

Primary data

Secondary data

Observational study

Experimental study

Self-administered questionnaire

Questionnaire design

Target population

Sampled population

Self-selected sample

Simple random sample

Stratified random sample

Cluster sample

Sampling error

Nonsampling errors

Nonresponse error (bias)

Selection bias

6 Probability and Discrete Probability Distributions

6.1 Introduction

Probability theory is an integral part of all statistics; in particular, it is essential to the theory of statistical inference. Statistical inference provides the decision maker—perhaps a businessperson or an economist—with a body of methods that aid in decision making under uncertainty. The uncertainty arises because, in real-life situations, we rarely have perfect information regarding various inputs to a decision. Whether our uncertainty relates to the future demand for our product, the future level of interest rates, the possibility of a labor strike, or the proportion of defective widgets in the next production run, probability theory can be used to measure the degree of uncertainty involved. Probability theory allows us to go beyond ignoring uncertainty or considering it in a haphazard fashion by giving us a foundation for dealing with uncertainty in a consistent, rational manner.

In the next two sections, we provide a fairly brief introduction to the basics of probability. We then introduce the concept of a random variable, which allows us to summarize the results of an experiment in terms of numerical-valued outcomes. For example, if the experiment consists of selecting five items from a production run and observing how many are defective, the appropriate random variable is defined as "the number of defective items." This random variable enables us to focus solely on the number of defective items observed rather than having to concern ourselves with exactly which of the items selected are defective, the nature of the defects, and other such nonessential details.

After introducing random variables, we consider probability distributions, which summarize the probabilities of observing the various numerical observations. Two descriptive measures of a random variable and its probability distribution—expected value and variance—are covered next. Having considered the probability distribution of a single random variable, we next introduce the bivariate (or joint) probability distribution, which is needed to analyze the relationship between *two* random variables. We first considered the relationship between two variables back in Chapter 2, where we introduced the scatter diagram to graphically depict a bivariate relationship. The remainder of this chapter looks in detail at two specific, commonly used probability distributions: the binomial and Poisson distributions.

6.2 Assigning Probabilities to Events

Random Experiment

A logical development of probability begins with considering a random experiment, because this process generates the uncertain outcomes to which we will assign probabilities. Random experiments are of interest because they provide the raw data for statistical analysis.

> **Random Experiment**
>
> A **random experiment** is a process or course of action that results in one of a number of possible outcomes. The outcome that occurs cannot be predicted with certainty.

Following is a list of some random experiments, together with their possible outcomes:

1 Experiment: Flip a coin.
   Outcomes: heads, tails

2 Experiment: Roll a die.
   Outcomes: 1, 2, 3, 4, 5, 6

3 Experiment: Roll a die.
   Outcomes: even number, odd number

4 Experiment: Observe the unit sales of a product for one day.
   Outcomes: 0, 1, 2, 3, ...

5 Experiment: Solicit a consumer's preference between product A and product B.
   Outcomes: prefer A, prefer B, indifferent

6 Experiment: Observe change in IBM share price over one week.
   Outcomes: increase, decrease, no change

An important feature of a random experiment is that the actual outcome cannot be determined in advance. That is, the outcome of a random experiment may change if the experiment is repeated. The best we can do is talk about the probability that a particular outcome will occur.

In order to determine, in advance of an experiment, the probabilities that various outcomes will occur, we first have to know what outcomes are possible. The first step in finding the probabilities, then, is to list the possible outcomes, as we did for the foregoing six examples of random experiments. For any such listing to suit our needs, the listed outcomes must be **exhaustive**; that is, each trial of the random experiment must result in some outcome on the list. Furthermore, the listed outcomes must be **mutually exclusive**; that is, no two outcomes on the list can both occur on any one trial of the experiment. Such a listing of the possible outcomes is called a *sample space*, denoted by S.

> **Sample Space**
>
> A **sample space** of a random experiment is a list of all possible outcomes of the experiment. The outcomes listed must be mutually exclusive and exhaustive.

Stated another way, the set of possible outcomes constituting a sample space must be defined in such a way that each trial of the experiment results in exactly one outcome in the sample space. In each of the foregoing six examples of random experiments, the accompanying list of possible outcomes is a sample space for that experiment.

The individual outcomes in a sample space are called **simple events**. In assigning probabilities, you should *define simple events in such a way that they cannot be broken down, or decomposed, into two or more constituent outcomes*. For example, in the foregoing die-tossing experiment, the outcome "an even number is observed" should not be used as a simple event in a sample space, because it can be further decomposed into three outcomes: 2, 4, and 6. An outcome such as "an even number is observed," which comprises a collection of simple events, is called an *event*.

> **Event**
>
> An **event** is any collection of one or more simple events.

Events are denoted by capital letters and can be defined either in words or by a list of their component simple events. For example, the event "an even number is observed" can be described alternatively as $A = \{2, 4, 6\}$, where { } is read "the set consisting of." It is conventional, when using letters to list the simple events that form a sample space, to use E_i to denote the ith simple event in the list.

Ultimately, we want to find the probability that an event A will occur, which is denoted $P(A)$. You undoubtedly have some idea of what is meant by the word *probability*, but now let's look more closely at its meaning.

Three Approaches to Assigning Probabilities

Beginning students of probability are usually disconcerted when they learn that the word *probability* has no precise definition. Any attempt to define it leads you around a circular series of statements consisting of such synonymous terms as *likelihood*, *chance*, and *odds*. There are, however, three distinct interpretations of probability that offer three approaches to determining the probability that a particular outcome will occur.

The **classical approach** attempts to deduce the probability of an outcome logically from the symmetric nature of the experiment. If a perfectly balanced coin is flipped, for example, it is logical to expect that the outcome heads and the outcome tails are equally likely. Hence, we assert that the probability of observing an occurrence of heads is $\frac{1}{2}$. More generally, if an experiment has n possible outcomes, each of which is equally likely, the probability of any particular outcome's occurrence is $1/n$. The classical approach can often be used effectively in games of chance.

Our development of probability frequently uses examples from this area to illustrate a point, because these examples are easy to relate to. More practical situations, however, do not lend themselves to the classical, deductive approach. A businessperson will usually use either the relative frequency approach or the subjective approach.

The **relative frequency approach** expresses an outcome's probability as its long-run relative frequency of occurrence. Suppose a random experiment is repeated n times, where n is a large number. If x represents the number of times a particular outcome occurred in those n trials, the proportion x/n provides an estimate of the probability that that particular outcome will occur. For example, if 600 out of the last 1,000 customers entering a store have made purchases, the probability that any given customer entering the store will make a purchase is approximately .6. The larger n is, the better will be the estimate of the desired probability, which may be thought of as the limiting value of x/n as n becomes infinitely large. Using the relative frequency approach, then, means determining empirically the probability that a particular outcome will occur.

In many practical situations, the experimental outcomes are not equally likely, and there is no history of repetitions of the experiment. Such might be the case, for example, if you wanted to estimate the probability of striking oil at a new offshore drilling site or the likelihood of your firm's sales reaching $1 million this year. In such situations, we resort to the **subjective approach**, under which the probability assigned to an outcome simply reflects the degree to which we believe that the outcome will occur. The probability assigned to a particular outcome thus reflects a personal evaluation of the situation and may be based simply on intuition.

In many cases, however, a businessperson's intuition or subjective evaluation has probably been influenced by outcomes in similar situations, so the relative frequency approach often plays a role in the formation of the subjective probabilities. Consider, for example, a producer about to launch a new Broadway musical. The producer's subjective estimate of the probability that the show will return a profit to investors will be based on several factors, such as the reputation of the musical's principals, the quality of other Broadway shows currently running, and the state of the economy; but the producer will also be mindful of the fact that only about 25% of all Broadway musicals are profitable—a fact based on the relative frequency approach.

Assigning Probabilities

Having reviewed much of the necessary terminology, we now turn to the matter of assigning probabilities to outcomes and events. To each simple event E_i in a sample space, we want to attach a number $P(E_i)$—called the *probability of E_i*—representing the likelihood that that particular outcome will occur. Whichever of the three ways of assigning probabilities (classical, relative frequency, or subjective) is used, the probabilities assigned to simple events must satisfy the two conditions specified in the following box. Keep in mind, too, that the simple events E_i that form a sample space must be mutually exclusive and exhaustive.

Requirements of Probabilities

Given a sample space $S = \{E_1, E_2, \ldots, E_n\}$, the probabilities assigned to the simple events E_i must satisfy two basic requirements:

1 $0 \leq P(E_i) \leq 1$ for each i

2 $\sum_{i=1}^{n} P(E_i) = 1$

Suppose that probabilities have been assigned to all the simple events. We still need a method for finding the probabilities of an event that is not a simple one. Recall that an event A is just a collection of simple events; therefore, its probability can be determined in the manner described in the following box.

Probability of an Event

The probability of an event A is equal to the sum of the probabilities assigned to the simple events contained in A.

It follows from the two basic requirements that the probability of an event that is certain to occur is 1, because such an event must contain all the simple events in the sample space and the sum of all simple event probabilities must be 1. On the other hand, the probability of an event that cannot possibly occur is 0.

The two basic requirements tell us nothing about how to assign probabilities; they simply state conditions that must be met by probabilities once they have been assigned. In practice, a business manager or economist will usually resort to either the relative frequency approach or the subjective approach in assigning probabilities to events. For example, a promoter choosing a week during which to hold a two-day, outdoor rock concert might consult meteorological records. If a particular week has been rain-free for 35 of the past 50 years, then $\frac{35}{50} = .7$ would be a relative frequency estimate of the probability of that week being rain-free this year. In many decision-making situations, however, a history of comparable circumstances is not available, and a businessperson must rely on an educated guess (that is, on the subjective approach). Such is the case with a bank manager who must estimate the probability of loan default by a country whose repayment ability has been impaired by declining oil prices.

Despite the prevalence of the relative frequency approach and the subjective approach, the examples that follow illustrate the assignment of probabilities to events using the classical approach. Not only will this be helpful in situations that do call for the classical approach, but it will also help clarify basic principles underlying the formulation of a sample space and the assignment of probabilities using any approach.

Probability Trees

One very useful method of calculating probabilities is to use a **probability tree**, in which the various possible events of an experiment are represented by lines or branches of the tree. When you want to construct a sample space for an experiment, a probability tree is a useful device for ensuring that you have identified all simple events and have assigned the associated probabilities.

The mechanics of using a probability tree can be illustrated by reference to the random experiment consisting of flipping a coin twice. A sample space for this experiment is

$$S = \{HH, HT, TH, TT\}$$

where the first letter of each pair denotes the result of the first flip. A probability tree for this experiment is shown in Figure 6.1.

Whenever you can break down the process of observing the result of an experiment into stages, with a different aspect of the results observed at each stage, you can represent the various possible sequences of observations with a probability tree. In the coin example, stage 1 involves the outcome of the first flip, while stage 2 involves the outcome of the second flip. The heavy dots in Figure 6.1 are called **nodes**, and the branches emerging from a particular node represent the alternative outcomes that can occur at that point.

The initial (unlabelled) node is called the **origin**. Any path through the tree from the origin to a terminal node corresponds to one possible simple event. For example, if we follow along the top branches of the tree, we observe the simple event HH. Altogether, then, we have four simple events, each of which is equally likely. Hence,

$$P(HH) = P(HT) = P(TH) = P(TT) = .25$$

Figure 6.1

Probability Tree for Coin Example

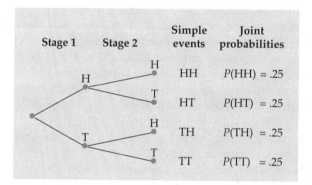

Having established the probabilities of the four simple events, we are now in a position to find the probabilities of other events we might want to consider. For example, suppose that A denotes the event of getting at least one outcome of heads, and we want to find $P(A)$. Event A occurs if we arrive at the end of any one of the top three paths in Figure 6.1. Summing the probabilities assigned to the simple events contained in A, we obtain

$$P(A) = P(HH) + P(HT) + P(TH) = .75$$

Probabilities of Combinations of Events

After determining the probabilities of some of the basic outcomes and events, we often want to compute the probabilities of more complex, related events. The notation for the probabilities of these compound events is as follows, where A and B are any two events.

$$P(A \text{ or } B) = P(A \text{ occurs } or \text{ } B \text{ occurs } or \text{ both occur})$$
$$P(A \text{ and } B) = P(A \text{ } and \text{ } B \text{ both occur})$$
$$P(\bar{A}) = P(A \text{ does } not \text{ occur})$$
$$P(A|B) = P(A \text{ occurs } given \text{ } that \text{ } B \text{ has occurred})$$

This last probability is called the **conditional** probability that A will occur, given that B has occurred. The event $\bar{A}$, called the **complement** of A, is the set of all outcomes that do not belong to A.

EXAMPLE 6.1

The number of spots turning up when a six-sided die is tossed is observed. Consider the following events.

A: The number observed is at most 2.

B: The number observed is an even number.

C: The number 4 turns up.

a Define a sample space for this random experiment and assign probabilities to the simple events.

b Find $P(A)$.

c Find $P(\bar{A})$.

d Are events A and C mutually exclusive?

e Find $P(A \text{ or } C)$.

f Find $P(A \text{ and } B)$.

g Find $P(A \text{ or } B)$.

h Find $P(C|B)$.

SOLUTION

a A sample space is $S = \{1, 2, 3, 4, 5, 6\}$. Because each of the six simple events is equally likely to occur,

$$P(1) = P(2) = P(3) = P(4) = P(5) = P(6) = \frac{1}{6}$$

A useful geometrical representation of this sample space, called a **Venn diagram**, is presented in Figure 6.2. In a Venn diagram, the entire sample space S is represented by a rectangle; points inside the rectangle represent the individual outcomes, or simple events, in S.

b The event $A = \{1, 2\}$ is represented in a Venn diagram by a closed region containing the simple events that belong to A, as shown in Figure 6.3. Because the probability of an event A is equal to the sum of the probabilities assigned to the simple events contained in A,

$$P(A) = P(1) + P(2) = \frac{1}{6} + \frac{1}{6} = \frac{2}{6}$$

c The complement of event A is $\bar{A} = \{3, 4, 5, 6\}$. Therefore,

$$P(\bar{A}) = P(3) + P(4) + P(5) + P(6) = \frac{4}{6}$$

The four simple events in $\bar{A}$ are represented in Figure 6.3 by the points lying outside the region describing event A.

d Two events A and C are mutually exclusive if the occurrence of one precludes the occurrence of the other—that is, if the event (A and C) contains no outcomes. The events A and C defined in this example are mutually exclusive because they cannot both occur. (The regions representing A and C in Figure 6.3 do not overlap.) If the number observed is 4, it is not 1 or 2.

e Because $A = \{1, 2\}$ and $C = \{4\}$, either A or C occurs if the number observed is 1, 2, or 4. The event (A or C) = $\{1, 2, 4\}$ is depicted by the total shaded area in Figure 6.3, and

$$P(A \text{ or } C) = P(1) + P(2) + P(4) = \frac{3}{6}$$

Because A and C are mutually exclusive, we could also write

$$P(A \text{ or } C) = P(A) + P(C) = \frac{2}{6} + \frac{1}{6} = \frac{3}{6}$$

But the above equality only holds for mutually exclusive events, as is evident from part (g) below.

f Both A and B occur only if the number observed is 2. Therefore,

$$P(A \text{ and } B) = P(2) = \frac{1}{6}$$

The event (A and B) is depicted by the shaded area in Figure 6.4.

g Because $A = \{1, 2\}$ and $B = \{2, 4, 6\}$, either A or B occurs if the number observed is 1, 2, 4, or 6. The event (A or B) = $\{1, 2, 4, 6\}$ is depicted by the shaded area in Figure 6.5, and

$$P(A \text{ or } B) = P(1) + P(2) + P(4) + P(6) = \frac{4}{6}$$

Note that in this case we can't find $P(A \text{ or } B)$ by simply adding together $P(A)$ and $P(B)$, for we would then get $\frac{5}{6}$. This is incorrect because we have double counted the outcome 2, as can be seen from Figure 6.5. To correct for this, we must subtract $P(A \text{ and } B)$.

Figure 6.2

Venn Diagram for Example 6.1

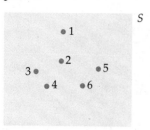

Figure 6.3

Venn Diagram Depicting Events A and C

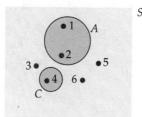

Figure 6.4

Venn Diagram Depicting (A and B)

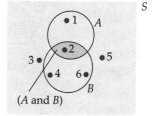

Figure 6.5

Venn Diagram Depicting (A or B)

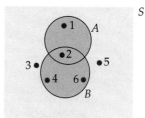

$$P(A \text{ or } B) = P(A) + P(B) - P(A \text{ and } B) = \frac{2}{6} + \frac{3}{6} - \frac{1}{6} = \frac{4}{6}$$

h We wish to find the probability that the number 4 turns up, given that the number turning up is even. If an even number turns up, we know the number is 2, 4, or 6. The information that the observed number is even has reduced our attention to these three numbers belonging to B. Of the three numbers comprising event B, only one is in $C = \{4\}$, so the required conditional probability is

$$P(C|B) = P(\text{number is 4}|\text{number is even}) = \frac{1}{3}$$

Conditional Probability

When finding the probability of an event, we can sometimes make use of partial knowledge about the outcome of the experiment. Consider, for example, the probability that a new product developed by our research department will be a success. Given no information about consumers' interest in the product, we might subjectively estimate the probability of success to be only .20. However, if we subsequently hear that the product has been test marketed and the results are positive, we would likely revise upwards our estimate of the probability of success. In light of the new information, we can talk about the *conditional probability* that the new product will be successful, given that the test-market results were positive.

We saw an illustration of the computation of a conditional probability in part (h) of Example 6.1. In that example, we are informed that, when a single die is tossed, an even number turns up (event B). We then want to find the probability that the number 4 turns up (event C), making use of our knowledge that the number is even. In other words, we are seeking the **conditional probability** that C will occur, given that B has occurred; this is written $P(C|B)$. (The vertical stroke | is read "given that"; it is followed by the event that has occurred.) To find this probability, we first note that knowing the information that an even number turned up restricts our inquiry to event B. That is, the new information has reduced the size of the relevant sample space to three possible outcomes. Of these three outcomes in the **reduced sample space**, only one belongs to event C. Hence, the desired conditional probability is

$$P(C|B) = \frac{1}{3}$$

which differs from the **unconditional probability** $P(C) = \frac{1}{6}$.

Notice that we computed the conditional probability $P(C|B)$ by dividing the number of outcomes belonging to both C and B by the number of outcomes in B. Alternatively, we can compute $P(C|B)$ as the ratio of the two probabilities $P(C \text{ and } B)$ and $P(B)$.

$$P(C|B) = \frac{1}{3} = \frac{1/6}{3/6} = \frac{P(C \text{ and } B)}{P(B)}$$

Having worked through the calculation of a particular conditional probability, we now present the general formula for a conditional probability.

Conditional Probability

Let A and B be two events such that $P(B) > 0$. The **conditional probability** that A occurs, given that B has occurred, is

$$P(A|B) = \frac{P(A \text{ and } B)}{P(B)}$$

In the preceding example, we saw that $P(C) = \frac{1}{6}$ and $P(C|B) = \frac{1}{3}$, so $P(C) \neq P(C|B)$. That is, the fact that event B occurred changes the probability that C will occur. Such events C and B are called **dependent events**.

On the other hand, if the occurrence of one event does not change the probability of occurrence of the other event, the two events are said to be **independent events**. Such is the case with events $A = \{1, 2\}$ and $B = \{2, 4, 6\}$ in Example 6.1. These events A and B are independent, because it can be shown that

$$P(A|B) = \frac{1}{3} = P(A) \qquad \text{and} \qquad P(B|A) = \frac{1}{2} = P(B)$$

Try to compute these probabilities on your own (see also Exercise 6.7). Just as important, ensure that you understand the difference in meaning between $P(A|B)$ and $P(B|A)$ for this example.

Independent and Dependent Events

Two events A and B are said to be **independent** if

$$P(A|B) = P(A) \qquad \text{or} \qquad P(B|A) = P(B)$$

Otherwise, the events are **dependent**.

If one equality in the preceding definition holds, so does the other. The concept of independence is illustrated in the following example.

EXAMPLE 6.2

A group of female managers working for an insurance company has lodged a complaint with the personnel department. While the women agree that the company has increased the number of female managers, they assert that women tend to remain in lower-level management positions when promotions are handed out. They have supported their argument by noting that, over the past three years, only 8 of the 54 promotions awarded went to women. The personnel department has responded by claiming that these numbers are misleading on two counts: first, there are far fewer female managers than male managers; second, many of the female managers have been hired during the past year, and employees are virtually never promoted during their first year at the managerial level. The personnel department has compiled the data shown in Table 6.1, in which managers who have been employed for at least one year are classified according to gender and to promotion record. The department claims that the decision to promote a manager (or not) is independent of the manager's gender. Would you agree?

SOLUTION   The events of interest are as follows.

M: A manager is male.

$\bar{M}$: A manager is female.

A: A manager is promoted.

$\bar{A}$: A manager is not promoted.

In order to show that the decision about whether or not to promote a manager is independent of the manager's gender, we must verify that

$$P(A|M) = P(A)$$

Table 6.1	Classification of Managers			
MANAGER	PROMOTED		NOT PROMOTED	TOTAL
Male	46 (0.85)		184 (0.85)	230 85
Female	8 (1.48		32 (0.148)	400 148
Total	54		216	270

If this equality holds, the probability that a man is promoted is no different from the probability that any manager is promoted. Given no information other than the data in Table 6.1, the probability that a manager is promoted is

$$P(A) = \frac{54}{270} = .20$$

If we now consider only male managers, we restrict our attention to the first row of Table 6.1. Given that a manager is male, the probability that he is promoted is

$$P(A|M) = \frac{46}{230} = .20$$

Note the distinction between this conditional probability and the **joint probability** that a manager is both male and promoted, which is $P(A \text{ and } M) = 46/270 = .17$. In any case, we have verified that $P(A) = P(A|M)$, so the events A and M are independent. From the data in Table 6.1, we must conclude that there is no discrimination in awarding promotions.

As indicated in the definition of independent events, an alternative way of showing that A and M are independent events is to verify that $P(M|A) = P(M)$. The probability that a manager is male is $P(M) = 230/270 = 46/54$, which equals $P(M|A)$, the probability that a manager who is promoted is male. Thus, we again conclude that events A and M are independent.

Before concluding this section, we draw your attention to a common misconception. Students often think that independent events and mutually exclusive events are the same thing. They are not. For example, events A and M in the preceding example are independent events, but they are not mutually exclusive, since the event (A and M) contains 46 simple events. In fact, it can be shown that *any two independent events A and B that occur with nonzero probabilities cannot be mutually exclusive*. If A and B were mutually exclusive, we would have $P(A$ and $B) = 0$ and $P(A|B) = 0$; but since A occurs with nonzero probability, $P(A) \neq P(A|B)$, so A and B cannot be independent events.

Exercises

6.1 Explain what is meant by the statement "The simple events that constitute a sample space are mutually exclusive and exhaustive."

6.2 Specify a sample space S for each of the following random experiments by listing the simple events in S.

    a The results of three flips of a coin are observed.

    b The time required to complete an assembly is recorded to the nearest minute.

    c The marital status of a loan applicant is solicited.

    d Two six-sided dice are tossed, and the sum of the spots turning up is noted.

    e The number of customers served by a restaurant on a particular day is recorded.

    f After 20 shoppers are asked if they are satisfied with parking accessibility, the number of positive responses is recorded.

6.3 A contractor has submitted a bid on each of three separate contracts. The probability of winning each contract is .5, independent of whether the other two contracts are won or lost. Find the probability of the following.

    a The contractor will win all three contracts.

    b The contractor will win exactly one contract.

    c The contractor will win at least two contracts.

6.4 A store that sells personal computers and related supplies is concerned that it may be overstocking surge suppressors. The store has tabulated the number of surge suppressors sold weekly for each of the last 80 weeks. The results are summarized in the following table.

NUMBER OF SUPPRESSORS SOLD	NUMBER OF WEEKS
0	36
1	28
2	12
3	2
4	2

The store intends to use the tabulated data as a basis for forecasting surge suppressor sales in any given week.

    a Define the random experiment of interest to the store.

    b List the simple events in the sample space.

    c Assign probabilities to the simple events.

d What approach have you used in determining the probabilities in part (c)?

e Find the probability of selling at least three surge suppressors in any given week.

6.5 The trustee of a company's pension plan has solicited the employees' feelings toward a proposed revision in the plan. A breakdown of the responses is shown in the accompanying table. Suppose that an employee is selected at random.

DECISION	BLUE-COLLAR WORKERS	WHITE-COLLAR WORKERS	MANAGERS
For	67	32	11
Against	63	18	9

Find the probability that the employee selected is

a a blue-collar worker.

b against the proposed revision.

c not a manager.

6.6 During a recent promotion, a bank offered mortgages with terms of one, two, and three years at a reduced interest rate. Customers could also choose between open and closed mortgages. Suppose that 300 mortgage applications were approved and that the numbers of mortgages of each type were as shown in the following table. The manager selects one mortgage application at random, and the relevant events are defined as follows.

L: The application selected is for a one-year mortgage.

M: The application selected is for a two-year mortgage.

N: The application selected is for a three-year mortgage.

C: The application selected is for a closed mortgage.

TYPE OF MORTGAGE	TERM OF MORTGAGE (IN YEARS)		
	1	2	3
Open	32	36	60
Closed	80	48	44

a Find $P(L)$, $P(M)$, $P(N)$, $P(C)$, and $P(\bar{C})$.

b Find the probability that the term of the mortgage selected is longer than one year.

6.7 The random experiment in Example 6.1 was to observe the number of spots turning up when a six-sided die is tossed. The events $A = \{1, 2\}$ and $B = \{2, 4, 6\}$ were considered there.

a Find $P(A|B)$.

b Find $P(B|A)$.

c Are A and B independent events? Explain.

6.8 An ordinary deck of playing cards has 13 cards of each suit. Suppose a card is selected at random from the deck.

a What is the probability that the card selected is an ace?

b Given that the card selected is a spade, what is the probability that the card is an ace?

c Are "an ace is selected" and "a spade is selected" independent events?

6.9 Suppose A and B are two mutually exclusive events. Do A and B represent independent events? Explain.

6.10 Of a company's employees, 30% are women and 6% are married women. Suppose an employee is selected at random. If the employee selected is a woman, what is the probability that she is married?

6.11 A firm classifies its customers' accounts in two ways: according to the balance outstanding and according to whether or not the account is overdue. The accompanying table gives the proportion of accounts falling into various categories. One account is selected at random.

ACCOUNT BALANCE	OVERDUE	NOT OVERDUE
Under $100	.08	.42
$100–$500	.08	.22
Over $500	.04	.16

a If the account selected is overdue, what is the probability that its balance is under $100?

b If the balance of the account selected is over $500, what is the probability that it is overdue?

c If the balance of the account selected is $500 or less, what is the probability that it is overdue?

6.12 A department store manager wants to investigate whether the method of payment chosen by customers is related to the size of the purchases. The manager has cross-classified a sample of 250 customer purchases, as shown in the following table. One of these 250 customers is selected at random.

SIZE OF PURCHASE	METHOD OF PAYMENT	
	CASH	CREDIT CARD
Under $20	51	31
$20 or more	65	103

a What is the probability that the customer selected paid by credit card?

b What is the probability that the customer selected made a purchase of under $20?

c Are the events "payment by cash" and "purchase of under $20" mutually exclusive? Explain.

d Are the events "payment by cash" and "purchase of under $20" independent? Explain.

6.13 A personnel manager has cross-classified the 400 employees of a firm according to their record of absenteeism last year and according to whether or not they were smokers, as shown in the accompanying table. One of these employees is selected at random.

NUMBER OF DAYS ABSENT	SMOKER	NONSMOKER
Less than 10	34	260
10 or more	78	28

    a   What is the probability that the employee selected was a nonsmoker?

    b   What is the probability that the employee selected was absent for 10 or more days?

    c   Are the events "nonsmoker" and "absent less than 10 days" mutually exclusive? Explain.

    d   Determine whether an employee's being absent for 10 or more days last year was independent of the employee's being a smoker.

6.14   Refer to Exercise 6.4. Find the probability that the store sells exactly two surge suppressors in a week, given that it sells at least one that week.

6.15   Insurance companies rely heavily on probability theory when they compute the premiums to be charged for various life insurance and annuity products. Probabilities are often computed on the basis of life tables like the accompanying table, which tabulates the average number of American males per 100,000 who will die during various age intervals. For example, out of 100,000 male babies born alive, 1,527 will die before their first birthday, and 29,721 will live to the age of 80. Answer the following questions based on this life table.

    a   What is the probability that a newborn male will reach the age of 50? The age of 70?

    b   What is the probability that an American male will reach the age of 70, given that he has just turned 50?

    c   What is the probability that an American male will reach the age of 70, given that he has just turned 60?

Number of Deaths at Various Ages out of 100,000 American Males Born Alive

AGE INTERVAL*	NUMBER OF DEATHS
0–1	1,527
1–10	495
10–20	927
20–30	1,901
30–40	2,105
40–50	4,502
50–60	10,330
60–70	19,954
70–80	28,538
80 and over	29,721
Total	100,000

*Interval contains all ages from lower limit up to but not including upper limit.

SOURCE: *Life Tables, Vital Statistics of the United States* (1978). U.S. Department of Health and Human Services.

6.3 Probability Rules and Trees

After determining some of the simpler probabilities of experimental outcomes and events, we can use various rules of probability to compute the probabilities of more complex, related events. Consider, for example, an aerospace company that has submitted bids on two separate federal defense contracts, A and B. Suppose the company has estimated $P(A)$ and $P(B)$, the probabilities of winning each of the contracts, as well as $P(A|B)$, the probability of winning contract A given that it wins contract B. Using the rules of probability, the company can then readily calculate various related probabilities such as $P(\bar{A})$, the probability of failing to win contract A; $P(A \text{ and } B)$, the probability of winning both contracts; and $P(A \text{ or } B)$, the probability of winning at least one of the two contracts.

Following is a summary of the rules of probability, many of which were anticipated in the solution to Example 6.1.

Complement Rule

The first rule of probability follows easily from the basic requirement that the sum of the probabilities assigned to the simple events in a sample space must be 1. Given any event A and its complement $\bar{A}$, each simple event must belong to either A or $\bar{A}$. We therefore must have

$$P(A) + P(\bar{A}) = 1$$

The complement rule is obtained by subtracting $P(\bar{A})$ from each side of the equality.

> **Complement Rule**
>
> $$P(A) = 1 - P(\bar{A})$$
>
> for any event A.

Despite its simplicity, the complement rule can be very useful. The task of finding the probability that an event will not occur and then subtracting this probability from 1 is often easier than the task of directly computing the probability that it will occur.

Addition Rule

The second rule of probability enables us to find the probability of the union of two events from the probabilities of other events.

> **Addition Rule**
>
> $$P(A \text{ or } B) = P(A) + P(B) - P(A \text{ and } B)$$
>
> where A and B are any two events.

If A and B are mutually exclusive, we have $P(A \text{ and } B) = 0$, and the addition rule simplifies to $P(A \text{ or } B) = P(A) + P(B)$. You will probably find that, more often than not, the two events of interest in practical situations will be mutually exclusive, and you will use this special form of the addition rule.

Figure 6.6

Entire Shaded Area Is Event (A or B)

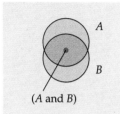

$(A \text{ and } B)$

Addition Rule for Mutually Exclusive Events

$$P(A \text{ or } B) = P(A) + P(B)$$

for any two mutually exclusive events A and B.

In general, however, we must subtract the joint probability $P(A \text{ and } B)$ in order to avoid double-counting a simple event that belongs to both A and B. This is apparent from the Venn diagram in Figure 6.6, in which (A or B) is represented by the entire shaded area. When finding the probability $P(A \text{ or } B)$ by summing $P(A)$ and $P(B)$, we must subtract $P(A \text{ and } B)$ to avoid double-counting the probability of event (A and B), which belongs to both A and B.

Multiplication Rule

The third rule of probability, which is used to find the probability of a joint event, is simply a rearrangement of the definition of conditional probability. Because

$$P(A|B) = \frac{P(A \text{ and } B)}{P(B)} \qquad \text{and} \qquad P(B|A) = \frac{P(A \text{ and } B)}{P(A)}$$

we obtain the following rule for computing the joint probability $P(A \text{ and } B)$.

Multiplication Rule

$$P(A \text{ and } B) = P(A) \cdot P(B|A)$$
$$= P(B) \cdot P(A|B)$$

for any two events A and B.

Notice that the two expressions for using the multiplication rule to find a joint probability are equivalent. Which expression to use in a particular situation depends on the information given.

For the special case in which A and B are independent events, we have $P(B|A) = P(B)$, so we can simply write $P(A \text{ and } B) = P(A) \cdot P(B)$.

Multiplication Rule for Independent Events

$$P(A \text{ and } B) = P(A) \cdot P(B)$$

for any two independent events A and B.

EXAMPLE 6.3

A computer software supplier has developed a new record-keeping package for use by hospitals. The company feels that the probability that the new package will show a profit in its first year is .6. The probability of first-year profitability drops to .3 if a competitor introduces a product of comparable quality this year, but will exceed .6 if no competing product is introduced. The supplier suggests that there is a 50–50 chance that a comparable product will be introduced this year. Define the following events.

A: A competitor introduces a comparable product.

B: The record-keeping package is profitable in its first year.

a What is the probability that both A and B will occur?

b What is the probability that either A or B will occur?

SOLUTION

Summarizing the given information, we know that

$$P(A) = .5$$
$$P(B) = .6$$
$$P(B|A) = .3$$

a Applying the multiplication rule, we conclude that the probability that a competitor will introduce a comparable product and that the first year will be profitable is

$$P(A \text{ and } B) = P(A) \cdot P(B|A) = (.5)(.3) = .15$$

b Notice that $P(A \text{ or } B)$ can be determined only after $P(A \text{ and } B)$ has been calculated. The probability that either a competitor will introduce a comparable product or that the record-keeping package will be profitable in its first year is

$$P(A \text{ or } B) = P(A) + P(B) - P(A \text{ and } B) = .5 + .6 - .15 = .95$$

Probability Trees Revisited

Having explored the meaning of conditional probability and various rules of probability, we can become a bit more precise about the notation used for probabilities on a probability tree. Consider once again the random experiment consisting of flipping a coin twice. Earlier, we expressed the sample space for this experiment as follows.

$$S = \{HH, HT, TH, TT\}$$

where the first letter of each pair denotes the result of the first flip. An alternative representation of S, differing only in the notation used, is

$$S = \{H_1 \text{ and } H_2, H_1 \text{ and } T_2, T_1 \text{ and } H_2, T_1 \text{ and } T_2\}$$

where the events are defined as follows.

H_1: Heads is observed on the first flip.

H_2: Heads is observed on the second flip.

T_1: Tails is observed on the first flip.

T_2: Tails is observed on the second flip.

The probability tree for this experiment is repeated in Figure 6.7, using new notation.

Figure 6.7

Probability Tree for Coin Example

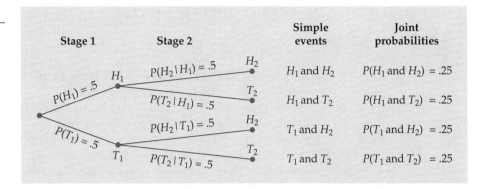

Recall that the branches emerging from a particular node represent the alternative outcomes that may occur at that point. The probability attached to each branch is the conditional probability that that branch outcome will occur, given that the outcomes represented by preceding branches have all occurred. For example, the probability attached to the top branch at stage 2 is $P(H_2|H_1) = .5$—the probability of obtaining a result of heads on the second flip, given that a result of heads was obtained on the first flip. Because the branches emerging from any particular node represent all possible outcomes that may occur at that point, the sum of the probabilities on those branches must equal 1.

Since any path through the tree from the origin to a terminal node corresponds to one possible simple event, the probability of that event is the product of the probabilities attached to the branches forming the path. For example, if we follow along the top branches of the tree, we observe the simple event (H_1 and H_2), which (according to the multiplication rule) has the probability

$$P(H_1 \text{ and } H_2) = P(H_1) \cdot P(H_2|H_1) = (.5) \cdot (.5) = .25$$

You might be wondering why we went to all the trouble of using a probability tree to determine that each of the four possible simple events occurs with a probability of $\frac{1}{4}$, because this may have been obvious to you from the beginning. The main point of this example was to introduce the mechanics of probability trees; the next example illustrates the advantages of using probability trees. In Example 6.4, the probability tree helps sort out the given information and clarifies what has to be calculated to reach a solution. In other situations, you may find a probability tree to be useful in identifying the possible simple events and their associated probabilities.

EXAMPLE 6.4

Suppose we are interested in the condition of a machine that produces a particular item. Let A designate the event "the machine is in good operating condition"; then $\bar{A}$ represents "the machine is not in good operating condition." We might know from experience that the machine is in good condition 90% of the time. That is, the initial or **prior probabilities** regarding the machine's condition are $P(A) = .9$ and $P(\bar{A}) = .1$. Given the machine's condition, we might also know the probability that a defective item will be produced (event B). Suppose that, when the machine is in good condition, only 1% of the items produced are defective, while 10% are defective when the machine is in poor condition. We therefore have the following conditional probabilities.

$$P(B|A) = .01$$
$$P(B|\bar{A}) = .10$$

The situation just described can be treated as a two-stage experiment and represented by a probability tree, as in Figure 6.8.

We are primarily concerned with the machine's condition, and we know from historical information that there is a 90% chance of its being in good condition. We can get a better idea of the likelihood that the machine is in good condition right now, however, by obtaining more information. Suppose that, without knowing the condition of the machine, we select an item from the current production run and observe that it is defective. It is then possible to revise the prior probability that the machine is in good condition (event A) in light of the new information that event B has occurred. That is, we can find the revised or **posterior probability**.

$$P(A|B) = \frac{P(A \text{ and } B)}{P(B)}$$

The value of the numerator is obtained easily from the probability tree.

$$
\begin{aligned}
P(A \text{ and } B) &= P(A) \cdot P(B|A) \\
&= (.9)(.01) \\
&= .009
\end{aligned}
$$

Figure 6.8

Probability Tree for Machine Producing Items

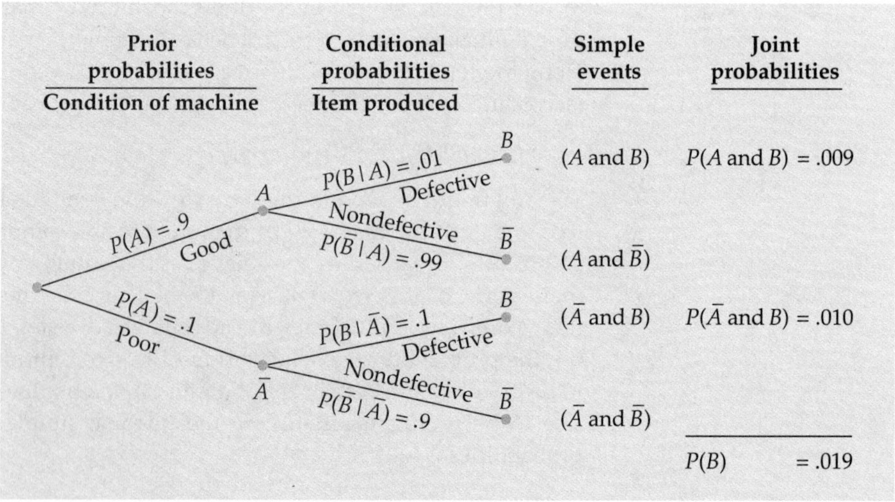

Prior probabilities Condition of machine	Conditional probabilities Item produced	Simple events	Joint probabilities
	$P(B\,|\,A) = .01$ — B Defective	$(A \text{ and } B)$	$P(A \text{ and } B) = .009$
$P(A) = .9$ Good	$P(\bar{B}\,|\,A) = .99$ Nondefective — $\bar{B}$	$(A \text{ and } \bar{B})$	
$P(\bar{A}) = .1$ Poor	$P(B\,|\,\bar{A}) = .1$ — B Defective	$(\bar{A} \text{ and } B)$	$P(\bar{A} \text{ and } B) = .010$
	$P(\bar{B}\,|\,\bar{A}) = .9$ Nondefective — $\bar{B}$	$(\bar{A} \text{ and } \bar{B})$	
		$P(B)$	$= .019$

We next note that event B occurs only if one of two simple events, $(A \text{ and } B)$ or $(\bar{A} \text{ and } B)$, occurs. The denominator is therefore

$$
\begin{aligned}
P(B) &= P(A \text{ and } B) + P(\bar{A} \text{ and } B) \\
&= .009 + .010 \\
&= .019
\end{aligned}
$$

By using the rules of probability or simply by reading from the probability tree, we obtain

$$P(A|B) = \frac{P(A \text{ and } B)}{P(B)}$$

$$= \frac{P(A \text{ and } B)}{P(A \text{ and } B) + P(\bar{A} \text{ and } B)}$$

$$= \frac{.009}{.019} = .47$$

In light of the sample information, we have revised drastically downward—from .9 to .47—the probability that the machine is currently in good condition. Based on this posterior (after sampling) probability of .47, it is likely worth paying a mechanic to check and repair the machine.

Take a moment to notice what we have done in the previous example. We were given $P(A)$ and the two conditional probabilities $P(B|A)$ and $P(B|\bar{A})$. Using the probability tree, we were able to find the related "reverse" conditional probability: $P(A|B)$. (Here we use "reverse" in the sense that the event given to have occurred is reversed.) This would not be nearly as easy to accomplish without the clarity provided by the probability tree.*

Exercises

6.16 A fair coin is flipped three times. Use a probability tree to find the probability of observing the following.

  a no heads   **b** exactly one heads

  c exactly two heads   **d** at least one tails

6.17 An aerospace company has submitted bids on two separate federal government defense contracts, A and B. The company feels that it has a 50% chance of winning contract A and a 40% chance of winning contract B. Furthermore, it believes that winning contract A is independent of winning contract B.

  a What is the probability that the company will win both contracts?

  b What is the probability that the company will win at least one of the two contracts?

6.18 Suppose the aerospace company in Exercise 6.17 feels that it has a 60% chance of winning contract A and a 30% chance of winning contract B. Given that it wins contract B, the company believes it has an 80% chance of winning contract A.

  a What is the probability that the company will win both contracts?

  b What is the probability that the company will win at least one of the two contracts?

  c If the company wins contract B, what is the probability that it will not win contract A?

---

*Some readers may recognize that we have essentially applied the formula provided by Bayes' theorem, which we do not discuss here.

6.19 A sporting goods store estimates that 20% of the students at a nearby university ski downhill and 15% ski cross-country. Of those who ski downhill, 40% also ski cross-country.

  a What percentage of these students ski both downhill and cross-country?

  b What percentage of the students do not ski at all?

6.20 A union's executive conducted a survey of its members to determine what the members felt were the important issues to be discussed during upcoming negotiations with management. Results showed that 74% felt that job security was an important issue, while 65% felt that pension benefits were an important issue. Of those who felt that pension benefits were an important issue, 60% also felt that job security was an important issue.

  a What percentage of the members felt that both job security and pension benefits were important?

  b What percentage of the members felt that at least one of these two issues was important?

6.21 Two six-sided dice are rolled, and the number of spots turning up on each is observed. Determine the probability of observing four spots on at least one of the dice. (HINT: Use the complement rule.)

6.22 A certain city has one morning newspaper and one evening newspaper. It is estimated that 20% of the city's households subscribe to the morning paper and 60% subscribe to the evening paper. Of those who subscribe to the morning paper, 80% also subscribe to the evening paper. What proportion of households does the following?

  a subscribes to both papers

  b subscribes to at most one of the papers

  c subscribes to neither paper

6.23 Individuals who want to pursue a career in investment analysis are often encouraged to obtain the professional designation of Chartered Financial Analyst (CFA). A candidate must pass three exams to obtain this designation and can take only one exam in a given year. The results of the exams held in 1993, reported by the Institute of Chartered Financial Analysis in *The CFA Study Guide (1994)*, are summarized in the accompanying table. One candidate is selected at random from those who took a CFA exam in 1993.

EXAM	NUMBER OF CANDIDATES WRITING	PERCENTAGE WHO PASSED
I	6,588	55%
II	3,679	56
III	2,542	76

  a What is the probability that the selected candidate passed?

  b What is the probability that the selected candidate took Exam I and passed?

  c If the selected candidate passed, what is the probability that the candidate took Exam III?

6.24 An assembler has been supplied with 10 electronic components, of which 3 are defective. If 2 components are selected at random, what is the probability that neither component is defective?

6.25 Approximately three out of every four Americans who filed a 1995 tax return received a refund. If three individuals are chosen at random from among those who filed a 1995 tax return, find the probabilities of the following events.

a All three received a refund.

b None of the three received a refund.

c Exactly one received a refund.

6.26 A door-to-door saleswoman sells rug shampoo in three tube sizes: small, large, and giant. The probability of finding a person at home is .6. If the saleswoman does find someone at home, the probabilities are .5 that she will make no sale, .2 that she will sell a small tube, .2 that she will sell a large tube, and .1 that she will sell a giant tube. The probability of selling more than one tube of rug shampoo at a house is 0.

    a Find the probability that, in one call, she will not sell any shampoo.

    b Find the probability that, in one call, she will sell either a large tube or a giant tube.

6.27 To determine who pays for coffee, three students each toss a coin and the odd person pays. If all coins show heads or all show tails, the students toss again. What is the probability that a decision will be reached in five or fewer tosses?

6.28 Of 20,000 small businesses surveyed, "about 82% said they employed women in some capacity." Of those that employed women, 19.5% employed no female supervisors, 50% employed only one female supervisor, and the remainder employed more than one female supervisor (*Globe and Mail*, October 1995).

    a How many of the businesses surveyed employed no women?

    b What proportion of businesses surveyed employed exactly one female supervisor?

    c What proportion of businesses surveyed employed no female supervisors?

    d Given that a firm employed women, what is the probability that it employed at least one female supervisor?

6.29 All printed circuit boards (PCBs) that are manufactured at a certain plant are inspected for flaws. Experience has shown that 50% of the PCBs produced are flawed in some way. Of the flawed PCBs, 60% are repairable, while the remainder are seriously flawed and must be discarded. A newly manufactured PCB is selected before undergoing inspection. What is the probability that it will not have to be discarded?

6.30 A foreman for an injection molding firm admits that, on 10% of his shifts, he forgets to shut off the injection machine on his line. This causes the machine to overheat and increases the chance that a defective molding will be produced during the early morning run from .5% to 5%. If the plant manager randomly selects a molding from the morning run and finds it to be defective, what is the probability that the foreman forgot to shut off the machine the previous night?

6.31 When a test is conducted to determine whether or not someone is infected with a particular virus, an incorrect test result can occur in two ways: an infected person may test negative, or a noninfected person may test positive. The latter is called a *false positive* test. It has been pointed out that the social consequences of false positive tests for the AIDS virus are particularly serious.* Such a false positive test will unnecessarily "stigmatize and frighten many healthy people," because "most people consider a positive AIDS test to be a sentence to ghastly suffering and death." Meyer and Pauker therefore assert that it is important that a patient who tests positive for the AIDS virus have a high probability of really being infected. In order to focus on the false positive rate of the test, assume throughout this question that we are dealing with a test that properly identifies all persons who really are infected with the AIDS virus.

---

*Klemens Meyer and Stephen Pauker, "Screening for HIV: Can We Afford the False Positive Rate?" *New England Journal of Medicine* (1987): 238–41.

a Assume that 5% of a population to be tested for the AIDS virus really is infected and that the test has a false positive rate of .5%. Find the probability that a person who tests positive really is infected.

b Would your answer to part (a) be higher or lower if more than 5% of the population to be tested were actually infected? Answer the question by referring to the formula for conditional probability without performing any calculations.

c Assume now that a low-risk population is to be tested. Specifically, assume that .01% of the population to be tested is actually infected with the AIDS virus and that the test has a false positive rate of .005% (which is unusually low). Find the probability that a person who tests positive really is infected.

d What would your answer to part (c) be if you assumed a false positive rate of .5%?

e Summarize the implications of your findings in parts (a) through (d).

6.4 Random Variables and Probability Distributions

In most random experiments, we're interested only in a certain aspect of the experimental outcomes. The instrument we use to focus our attention on this particular aspect of an outcome (and to assign a numerical value to the outcome accordingly) is called a random variable. Consider once again the experiment consisting of flipping a coin twice. Recall that a sample space for this experiment is $S = \{HH, HT, TH, TT\}$. Suppose that we're interested in the total number of heads that turn up. If X denotes the total number of heads turning up, the value that X takes on will vary randomly from one trial of the experiment to the next, and X is called a **random variable**. In fact, X is a function that assigns a numerical value to each simple event in the sample space S, with the possible values of X being 0, 1, and 2, as shown in Figure 6.9.

Figure 6.9

Random Variable X Assigning Values to Simple Events

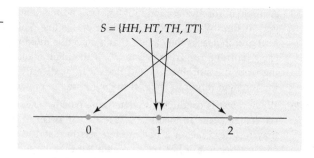

A formal definition of a random variable might read as follows.

Random Variable

A **random variable** is a function that assigns a numerical value to each simple event in a sample space.

Less formally, we might simply state that **a random variable is a variable whose numerical value is determined by the outcome of a random experiment**. Throughout this chapter, we will stress the distinction between a random variable and the values it can assume by following the convention of using capital letters such as X and Y to denote random variables and using lowercase letters such as x and y to denote their values. Although many people consider this distinction in notation unnecessary, we believe it is a useful one to maintain while you are becoming familiar with the notion of a random variable. The notational distinction is dropped in subsequent chapters, however, because the interpretation of x is usually clear from the context in which it is used.

There are two types of random variables—discrete and continuous—distinguished from one another by the number of possible values that they can assume. A **discrete** random variable has a *countable* number of possible values. Put simply, this means that a variable is discrete if we can identify the first value, the second value, and all subsequent values of the random variable. In most practical situations, a discrete random variable counts the number of times a particular attribute is observed. Examples of discrete random variables include the number of defective items in a production batch, the number of telephone calls received in a given hour, and the number of shoppers surveyed who prefer a particular product. If X denotes the number of respondents, in a survey of 400 shoppers, who state a preference for a particular product, then X can take any one of the values $x = 0, 1, 2, \ldots, 400$.

It should be noted that countable does not necessarily mean finite. It is possible to count the values of a random variable with no upper limit. One such variable is the one defined as the number of flips of a balanced coin until the first heads is observed. This random variable could equal 1 (first flip produces heads), 2 (first flip is tails and the second flip is heads), and so on. It is extremely unlikely that the value of this random variable is large (for example, we calculated the probability that 100 flips [$x = 100$] are required to produce the first heads to be 7.89×10^{-31}, which is a decimal point followed by 30 zeros and 789); nevertheless there is no upper limit on its value. Because it is countable (we can identify all possible values), it is discrete.

Discrete and Continuous Random Variables

A random variable is **discrete** if it can assume only a countable number of possible values. A random variable that can assume an uncountable number of values is **continuous**.

A continuous random variable has an uncountably infinite number of possible values; that is, it can take on any value in one or more intervals of values. Continuous random variables typically record the value of a measurement such as time, weight, or length. For example, suppose that we measure the amount of time workers on an assembly line take to complete a particular task. Suppose further that the fastest time possible is 60 seconds. What is the next possible value? Is it 61 seconds, or 60.1 seconds, or 60.01 seconds? It is impossible to specify the next value because there is an infinite number of values starting with 60. Because we cannot specify the second value or the third, or fourth, we cannot count the number of values this random variable can equal. Hence, it is a continuous random variable. We will discuss this type of random variable later.

For the time being, we will restrict our attention to discrete random variables. Having considered the values of a random variable, we now turn to the probabilities associated with those values. When we know the possible values of a random variable and the probabilities associated with those values, we have the **probability distribution** of the random variable—our main object of interest.

Discrete Probability Distribution

A table, formula, or graph that lists all possible values a discrete random variable can assume, together with their associated probabilities, is called a **discrete probability distribution**.

The probability associated with a particular value of a random variable is determined in a manner you can probably anticipate. If x is a value of a random variable X, then the probability that X assumes the value x, denoted either by $P(X = x)$ or by $p(x)$, is the sum of the probabilities associated with the simple events for which X assumes the value x.

Let's apply this rule to the experiment involving two flips of a coin. If the random variable X represents the number of heads turning up, then X can assume any one of the values 0, 1, or 2. Probabilities can be assigned to the values of X with the help of Table 6.2, which records each simple event, its probability, and the corresponding value of X. (Recall that the simple event probabilities shown in Table 6.2 were calculated in Figure 6.1 with the help of a probability tree.) For example, X takes the value 1 if either simple event HT or TH occurs, so

$$P(X = 1) = P(HT) + P(TH) = \frac{1}{4} + \frac{1}{4} = \frac{1}{2}$$

Table 6.2	Values of X Corresponding to Simple Events		
SIMPLE EVENT	x	PROBABILITY	
HH	2	1/4	
HT	1	1/4	
TH	1	1/4	
TT	0	1/4	

The distinct values of X and their associated probabilities are summarized in Table 6.3, which gives the probability distribution of X. The probability distribution of X can be presented in the tabular form shown in Table 6.3, in the graphical form of Figure 6.10, or in terms of the following formula.

$$p(x) = \begin{cases} \dfrac{1}{4} & \text{if } x = 0 \text{ or } 2 \\ \dfrac{1}{2} & \text{if } x = 1 \end{cases}$$

Table 6.3	Probability Distribution of X

x	$p(x)$
0	1/4
1	1/2
2	1/4

Figure 6.10

Graphical Presentation of Probability Distribution

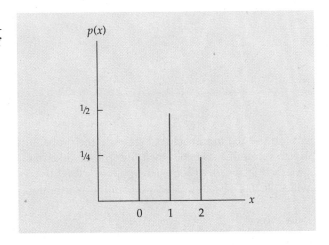

In an example such as this one, where the formula is rather cumbersome, the tabular representation of the probability distribution of X is most convenient. Whichever representation is used, a discrete probability distribution must satisfy two conditions, which follow from the basic requirements for probabilities outlined in Section 6.2.

Requirements of Discrete Probability Distribution

If a random variable X can take values x_i, then the following must be true:

1 $0 \leq p(x_i) \leq 1$ for all x_i

2 $\sum_{\text{all } x_i} p(x_i) = 1$

After a probability distribution has been defined for a random variable X, we can talk about the probability that X takes a value in some range of values. The probability that X takes a value between a and b, inclusive, denoted by $P(a \leq X \leq b)$, is obtained by summing the probabilities $p(x)$ for all values of x such that $a \leq x \leq b$. In the preceding example, we would have

$$P(1 \leq X \leq 2) = p(1) + p(2) = \frac{1}{2} + \frac{1}{4} = \frac{3}{4}$$

In other words, the probability that the total number of heads turning up is either 1 or 2 is $\frac{3}{4}$, or .75.

Probabilities as Relative Frequencies

The probabilities in the coin-tossing example were assigned using the classical approach. In practice, probabilities assigned to values of a random variable are often estimated from relative frequencies. For example, suppose that we're interested in the number of cars a dealer sells daily. The sales manager observes the results of the last 100 days, which are displayed below.

DAILY SALES (X)	FREQUENCY
0	5
1	15
2	35
3	25
4	20
	100

We can use the frequencies to estimate the probability of occurrence of each value of the random variable. Since the probabilities must sum to 1, we estimate the probabilities by dividing each frequency by the total number of days observed, which is 100. The estimated probability distribution is shown below.

DAILY SALES (X)	PROBABILITY
0	5/100 = .05
1	15/100 = .15
2	35/100 = .35
3	25/100 = .25
4	20/100 = .20
	100/100 = 1.00

If we assume that the relative frequencies calculated above are accurate estimates of the true probabilities, we can say for example that, in the long run, on 5% of the days the dealer will sell no cars and on 35% of the days the dealer will sell 2 cars. We can also state that the probability of selling more than 2 cars on any single day is the sum of the probabilities of the values of X that are greater than 2. Hence $P(X > 2) = p(3) + p(4) = .25 + .20 = .45$, which means that in the long run 45% of the days will result in sales of more than 2 cars.

Exercises

6.32 The number of accidents that occur annually on a busy stretch of highway is a random variable.

    a What are the possible values of this random variable?

    b Are the values countable? Explain.

c Is there a finite number of values? Explain.

d Is the random variable discrete or continuous? Explain.

6.33 The distance a car travels on one tank of gasoline is a random variable.

a What are the possible values of this random variable?

b Are the values countable? Explain.

c Is there a finite number of values? Explain.

d Is the random variable discrete or continuous? Explain.

6.34 The average mark (out of 100) on a statistics test is a random variable.

a What are the possible values of this random variable?

b Are the values countable? Explain.

c Is there a finite number of values? Explain.

d Is the random variable discrete or continuous? Explain.

6.35 Consider a random variable X with the following probability distribution.

x	-4	0	1	2
$p(x)$	.2	.3	.4	.1

Find the following probabilities.

a $P(X > 0)$ **b** $P(X \geq 0)$ **c** $P(0 \leq X \leq 1)$

d $P(X = -4)$ **e** $P(X = -2)$ **f** $P(X < 2)$

6.36 Consider a random variable X with the following probability distribution.

$$p(x) = .1x \qquad x = 1, 2, 3, \text{ or } 4$$

Express the probability distribution in tabular form, and use it to find the following probabilities.

a $P(X \geq 1)$ **b** $P(X > 1)$ **c** $P(2 \leq X \leq 3)$

d $P(X = 4)$ **e** $P(X = 3.5)$

6.37 Determine which of the following are not valid probability distributions, and explain why not.

a

x	1	2	3	4
$p(x)$	.2	.2	.3	.4

b

x	0	2	4	5
$p(x)$	$-.1$	.2	.3	.4

c

x	-2	-1	1	2
$p(x)$	.1	.1	.1	.7

6.38 Let X be the number of spots that turn up when a six-sided die is tossed.

a Express the probability distribution of X in tabular form.

b Express the probability distribution of X in graphical form.

6.39 Let X be the number of heads that are observed when a fair coin is flipped three times.

a Express the probability distribution of X in tabular form.

b Express the probability distribution of X in graphical form.

6.40 Let X represent the number of children under 18 years old in an American family. According to the *Statistical Abstract of the United States: 1993*, the probability distribution of X is as follows.

x	0	1	2	3	4	5
$p(x)$	.49	.21	.19	.08	.02	.01

a What proportion of American households have 2 or fewer children under 18?

b What proportion of American households have more than 3 children under 18?

c What proportion of American households have between 1 and 3 (inclusive) children under 18?

6.41 Let X represent the number of people in an American household. According to the *Statistical Abstract of the United States: 1993*, the probability distribution of X is as follows (rounded to two decimal places).

x	1	2	3	4	5	6	7
$p(x)$	.24	.31	.17	.16	.07	.03	.02

a What is the probability of a randomly selected household having fewer than 4 people?

b What is the probability of a randomly selected household having between 2 and 5 (inclusive) people?

c What is the probability of a randomly selected household having more than 6 people?

6.42 Using historical data, the personnel manager of a plant has determined that the probability distribution of X, the number of employees absent on any given day, is as follows.

x	0	1	2	3	4	5	6	7
$p(x)$	.005	.025	.310	.340	.220	.080	.019	.001

Find the following.

a $P(2 \leq X \leq 4)$

b $P(X > 5)$

c $P(X \leq 6)$

6.43 A mutual fund saleswoman has arranged to call upon three households tomorrow. Based on past experience, she feels that there is a 20% chance of closing a sale on each call and that the outcome of each call is independent of the others. Let X represent the number of sales she closes tomorrow.

a Find the probability distribution of X.

b Express the probability distribution of X graphically.

c What is the probability that more than one sale will be closed tomorrow?

6.44 Second-year business students at a certain university are required to take 10 one-semester courses. Suppose that the number of courses in which a student will receive a grade of A has a **discrete uniform distribution** (that is, each possible number has the same probability of occurrence).

a What are the possible values of the random variable and their probabilities?

b What is the probability that a second-year business student receives an A in exactly three courses?

c What is the probability that a second-year business student receives an A in more than 10 courses?

d What is the probability that a second-year business student's highest grade is a B?

6.5 Expected Value and Variance

As stated previously, probability is the link between a sample and the population from which it is taken. This is so because a probability distribution is the distribution of a population. Consider, for example, the probability distribution shown in Table 6.4, where the random variable X represents the payoff (in dollars) from a proposed investment of $25.

We can conceive of the underlying population in the following way: Imagine a barrel containing infinitely many chips, of which one-half are labeled 20, one-quarter are labeled 40, and one-quarter are labeled 60. If X denotes the label on a chip that is randomly selected from the population of chips, the probability distribution of X is as shown in Table 6.4.

Table 6.4	Probability Distribution of X	
x	$p(x)$	
20	1/2	
40	1/4	
60	1/4	

Now consider the population of labels on all chips. We might want to find the mean of this population, just as we did with the populations encountered back in Chapter 4, where we defined the *mean of a population* of N values of x to be

$$\mu = \frac{\sum_{i=1}^{N} x_i}{N} = \sum_{i=1}^{N} x_i \cdot \frac{1}{N}$$

For the infinitely large population of labels, however, we must replace $1/N$ with the probability, or relative frequency, with which x_i occurs. The mean of such a population, called the **mean value** of X, is therefore given by

$$\mu = \sum x \cdot p(x)$$

where the sum is taken over all values of X. This value is also referred to as the **expected value** of X, written $E(X)$. Hence, the expected value of the payoff from the $25 investment is

$$E(X) = \mu$$
$$= 20\left(\frac{1}{2}\right) + 40\left(\frac{1}{4}\right) + 60\left(\frac{1}{4}\right) = \$35$$

In general, we have the following definition.

Expected Value

Given a discrete random variable X with values x_i that occur with probabilities $p(x_i)$, the expected value of X is

$$E(X) = \sum_{\text{all } x_i} x_i \cdot p(x_i)$$

The expected value of a random variable X is the weighted average of the possible values it can assume, where the weights are the probabilities of occurrence of those values. The expected value of X should be interpreted simply as a weighted average of the possible values of X, rather than as a value that X is expected to assume. In fact, as the preceding example illustrates, $E(X)$ might not even be a possible value of X.

An alternative interpretation of the expected value of X employs the long-run relative frequency approach to probability described in Section 6.2. If the investment in the foregoing example were undertaken repeatedly a large number of times, the expected value of X, \$35, would be a good approximation to the average payoff resulting from the many investments.

Laws of Expected Value

Various algebraic identities or laws are available to help simplify the calculation of an expected value. Although the proofs are not difficult, the laws are stated here without proof. Exercises 6.56 and 6.57 provide you with opportunities to verify these laws.

If X and Y are random variables and c is any constant, the following identities hold.

1 $E(c) = c$

2 $E(cX) = cE(X)$

3 $E(X + Y) = E(X) + E(Y)$
   $E(X - Y) = E(X) - E(Y)$

4 $E(XY) = E(X)E(Y)$, if X and Y are independent random variables*

The utility of these laws derives from the fact that, given a function of one or more random variables, the expected value of the terms the function comprises may already be known or may be easier to compute than the expected value of the function itself. For example, if the random variable X is the number of units of an item that are produced daily, a is the variable cost of production per unit, and b is the daily fixed cost of production, the total daily production cost is $Y = aX + b$. The expected daily production cost is $E(Y) = aE(X) + b$. Calculating $E(X)$ and then using the formula is normally easier than finding $E(Y)$ directly.

---

*Although beginning students of statistics will not normally find occasion to use this law, it is included for completeness. Two random variables X and Y are said to be *independent* if the value assumed by one variable in no way affects the probability of a particular value's being assumed by the other. That is, X and Y are independent if $P(X = x | Y = y_0) = P(X = x)$ or, equivalently, if $P(Y = y | X = x_0) = P(Y = y)$, for all x_0 and y_0.

Variance

The expected value of a random variable X is a weighted average of the values of X; it therefore provides us with a measure of the central location of the distribution of X. It does not tell us, however, whether the values of X are clustered closely about the expected value or are widely scattered. That is, the mean, or expected value, of a random variable does not by itself adequately describe the random variable. Just as in Chapter 4, we need a measure of dispersion.

Recall that a popular measure of the dispersion of a population of N measurements $x_1, \ldots, x_N$ is the variance, given by

$$\sigma^2 = \frac{\sum_{i=1}^{N}(x_i - \mu)^2}{N} = \sum_{i=1}^{N}(x_i - \mu)^2 \cdot \frac{1}{N}$$

The variance of a random variable X is defined in a similar manner, with $1/N$ being replaced by $p(x_i)$. We can then describe the variance of a random variable X as the weighted average of the squared deviations of the values of X from their mean μ, with the weight attached to $(x_i - \mu)^2$ being $p(x_i)$—the probability with which that squared deviation occurs. In other words, the variance of X is the expected value of the random variable $(X - \mu)^2$.

> **Variance**
>
> Let X be a discrete random variable with possible values x_i that occur with probabilities $p(x_i)$, and let $E(X) = \mu$. The variance of X is defined to be
>
> $$\sigma^2 = E[(X - \mu)^2] = \sum_{\text{all } x_i} (x_i - \mu)^2 \, p(x_i)$$

Notice that a variance is always nonnegative, since each item in the summation is nonnegative. Alternative notations for the variance of X are σ_X^2 and $V(X)$, both of which are useful ways to indicate the random variable in question.

To illustrate the computation of variance, we consider once again the probability distribution (Table 6.4) for X, the payoff from an investment of $25. The variance of the payoff is

$$\sigma_X^2 = (20 - 35)^2\left(\frac{1}{2}\right) + (40 - 35)^2\left(\frac{1}{4}\right) + (60 - 35)^2\left(\frac{1}{4}\right) = 275 \text{ (dollars)}^2$$

A variance, considered by itself, is somewhat difficult to interpret. The notion of variance is therefore chiefly used to compare the variabilities of different distributions, which might, for example, represent the possible outcomes of alternative courses of action under consideration. One important application arises in finance, where variance is the most popular numerical measure of risk; the underlying assumption is that a larger variance corresponds to a higher level of risk.

Let Y represent the payoff from a second proposed investment of $25. The possible payoffs in this case are $10, $40, and $80, occurring with probabilities $\frac{1}{2}$, $\frac{1}{4}$, and $\frac{1}{4}$, respectively. The expected value of Y can be shown to be $35—the same as the expected value of X—but the variance of Y is 825 (dollars)^2, as you can verify. If the riskiness of the investments is measured by the variance of their payoffs, the second proposed investment is riskier than the first, since $\sigma_Y^2 > \sigma_X^2$. This risk assessment is probably consistent with the intuitive impression you would obtain from a casual comparison of the distributions of X and Y.

The variance of X is defined to be $E[(X - \mu)^2]$. By expanding $(X - \mu)^2$ and applying the laws of expected value, we can identify an alternative formulation of the variance of X.

$$\sigma_X^2 = E(X^2) - \mu^2$$

This **shortcut for computing the variance** is useful because the calculation of $E(X^2)$ is often simpler than the direct computation of σ_X^2, which involves squared deviations. Like that of any other random variable, the expected value of X^2 is obtained by taking the weighted average of its possible values.

$$E(X^2) = \sum_{i=1}^{n} x_i^2 p(x_i)$$

As was the case in Chapter 4 with a set of measurement data, we might want to express the variability of X in terms of a measure having the same units as X. Once again, this is accomplished by taking the positive square root of the variance.

> **Standard Deviation**
>
> The **standard deviation** of a random variable X, denoted σ, is the positive square root of the variance of X.

For instance, the standard deviation of X, the payoff from the first proposed investment, is

$$\sigma_X = \sqrt{275} = \$16.58$$

EXAMPLE 6.5

Now that the new models are available, a car dealership has lowered the prices on last year's models in order to clear its holdover inventory. With prices slashed, a young and aggressive salesman estimates the following probability distribution of X, the total number of cars that he'll sell next week.

x	0	1	2	3	4
$p(x)$	.05	.15	.35	.25	.20

Determine the expected value and the standard deviation of X.

SOLUTION

The expected value, variance, and standard deviation of X can be calculated directly from their definitions.

$$E(X) = \mu = \sum_{i=1}^{5} x_i p(x_i)$$
$$= 0(.05) + 1(.15) + 2(.35) + 3(.25) + 4(.20)$$
$$= 2.40$$

$$V(X) = \sigma^2 = \sum_{i=1}^{5} (x_i - 2.4)^2 p(x_i)$$
$$= (0 - 2.4)^2(.05) + (1 - 2.4)^2(.15) + (2 - 2.4)^2(.35)$$
$$+ (3 - 2.4)^2(.25) + (4 - 2.4)^2(.20)$$
$$= 1.24$$
$$\sigma = \sqrt{1.24}$$
$$= 1.11$$

The expected number of cars that the salesman will sell next week is 2.4, with a standard deviation of 1.11.

A convenient alternative for computational purposes is to record the probability distribution of X (and subsequent computations) in a table such as Table 6.5. Rather than having a column for $(x - \mu)^2$, we have chosen to use the shortcut formula for variance, which entails finding the expected value of X^2. Therefore, from Table 6.5,

$$E(X) = \mu = 2.4$$
$$V(X) = E(X^2) - \mu^2 = 7 - (2.4)^2 = 1.24$$
$$\sigma = \sqrt{1.24} = 1.11$$

Table 6.5	Computations for $E(X)$ and $E(X^2)$				
	x	$p(x)$	$xp(x)$	x^2	$x^2 p(x)$
	0	.05	0	0	0
	1	.15	.15	1	.15
	2	.35	.70	4	1.40
	3	.25	.75	9	2.25
	4	.20	.80	16	3.20
	Total		$2.40 = E(X)$		$7.00 = E(X^2)$

Laws of Variance

Just as with the calculation of expected value, various laws help simplify the calculation of variance; they are stated here without proof.

If X and Y are random variables and c is a constant, the following identities hold.

1 $V(c) = 0$

2 $V(cX) = c^2 V(X)$

3 $V(X + c) = V(X)$

4 $V(X + Y) = V(X) + V(Y)$, and

$V(X - Y) = V(X) + V(Y)$, if X and Y are independent

EXAMPLE 6.6

In Example 6.5, the young salesman estimated the probability distribution of X (the total number of cars he would sell next week) to be as follows.

x	0	1	2	3	4
$p(x)$	.05	.15	.35	.25	.20

Subsequent calculations revealed that $E(X) = 2.4$ and $V(X) = 1.24$. Now suppose that this salesman earns a fixed weekly wage of $150 plus a $200 commission for each car sold. His weekly wage is therefore $Y = 200X + 150$. What is his expected wage for next week? What is the variance of Y?

SOLUTION

The probability distribution of Y and the computations for $E(Y)$ and $E(Y^2)$ are shown in Table 6.6. From the table, we know that $E(Y) = 630$ and that $V(Y) = E(Y^2) - \mu^2 = 446{,}500 - (630)^2 = 49{,}600$. Rather than performing the mind-numbing calculations in Table 6.6, we could simply use the laws of expected value and variance.

$$
\begin{aligned}
E(Y) &= E(200X + 150) & V(Y) &= V(200X + 150) \\
&= 200E(X) + 150 & &= (200)^2 V(X) \\
&= 200(2.4) + 150 & &= (200)^2(1.24) \\
&= 630 & &= 49{,}600
\end{aligned}
$$

The young salesman's expected wage for next week is therefore $630, with a variance of 49,600 (dollars)^2.

Table 6.6	Computations for $E(Y)$ and $E(Y^2)$				
y	$p(y)$	$yp(y)$		y^2	$y^2p(y)$
150	.05	7.5		22,500	1,125
350	.15	52.5		122,500	18,375
550	.35	192.5		302,500	105,875
750	.25	187.5		562,500	140,625
950	.20	190.0		902,500	180,500
Total		$630.0 = E(Y)$			$446{,}500 = E(Y^2)$

Exercises

6.45 Let X be a random variable with the following probability distribution.

x	1	2	3	4
$p(x)$	.4	.3	.2	.1

a Find $E(X)$ and $V(X)$.

b Is $E(X)$ a possible value of X?

6.46 Let X be a random variable with the following probability distribution.

x	−4	0	1	2
$p(x)$	.2	.3	.4	.1

a Find μ and σ.

b Is μ a possible value of X?

c Find $E(X^2)$ and $E(3X^2 + 2)$.

6.47 Let X be a random variable with the following probability distribution.

x	5	10	15	20	25
$p(x)$	.05	.30	.25	.25	.15

a Find the expected value and variance of X.

b Find the expected value and variance of $Y = 4X - 3$.

6.48 Let X be a random variable with the following probability distribution.

x	−10	−5	0	5	10
$p(x)$	.10	.20	.20	.20	.30

a Find the mean and standard deviation of X.

b Find the mean and standard deviation of 2X.

c Find the mean and standard deviation of 2X + 5.

6.49 Let X be a random variable with the following probability distribution.

x	0	5	10	20
$p(x)$	.2	.3	.3	.2

a Find the mean and standard deviation of X.

b Find $E(X^2)$.

c Find $E(5X^2)$.

6.50 Let X represent the number of times a student visits a nearby pizza parlor in a 1-month period. Assume that the following table is the probability distribution of X.

x	0	1	2	3
$p(x)$	.1	.3	.4	.2

a Find the mean (μ) and the standard deviation (σ) of this distribution.

b What is the probability that the student visits the pizza parlor at least twice in a month?

c   Find $P(X \geq 1.5)$.

d   Construct a graph of the probability distribution, and locate μ and the interval $\mu \pm \sigma$ on the graph.

6.51   The owner of a small firm has just purchased a personal computer, which she expects will serve her for the next two years. The owner has been told that she "must" buy a surge suppressor to provide protection for her new hardware against possible surges or variations in the electrical current. Her son David, a recent university graduate, advises that an inexpensive suppressor could be purchased that would provide protection against one surge only. He notes that the amount of damage without a suppressor would depend on the extent of the surge. David conservatively estimates that, over the next two years, there is a 1% chance of incurring $400 damage and a 2% chance of incurring $200 damage. But the probability of incurring $100 damage is .1.

a   How much should the owner be willing to pay for a surge suppressor?

b   Determine the standard deviation of the possible amount of damage.

6.52   In Exercise 6.15, it was noted that insurance companies rely heavily on probability theory when they compute the premiums to charge for various life insurance and annuity products. Suppose a 40-year-old male purchases a $100,000 10-year term life policy from an insurance company, meaning that the insurance company must pay out $100,000 if the insured male dies within the next 10 years.

a   Use the accompanying life table to determine the insurance company's expected payout on this policy.

b   What would the expected payout be if the same policy were taken out by a 50-year-old male?

Number of Deaths at Various Ages out of 100,000 American Males Born Alive

AGE INTERVAL*	NUMBER OF DEATHS
0–1	1,527
1–10	495
10–20	927
20–30	1,901
30–40	2,105
40–50	4,502
50–60	10,330
60–70	19,954
70–80	28,538
80 and over	29,721
Total	100,000

*Interval contains all ages from lower limit up to but not including upper limit.

SOURCE: *Life Tables, Vital Statistics of the United States* (1978). U.S. Department of Health and Human Services.

6.53   Suppose you have the choice of receiving $500 in cash or receiving a gold coin that has a face value of $100. The actual value of the gold coin depends on its gold content. You are told that the coin has a 40% chance of being worth $400, a 30% chance of being worth $900, and a 30% chance of being worth its face value. If you base your decision on expected value, which should you choose?

6.54 In order to examine the effectiveness of its four annual advertising promotions, a mail-order company has sent a questionnaire to each of its customers, asking how many of the previous year's promotions prompted orders that otherwise would not have been made. The following table summarizes the data received, where the random variable X is the number of promotions indicated in the customers' responses.

x	0	1	2	3	4
$p(x)$	.10	.25	.40	.20	.05

a Assuming that the responses received were accurate evaluations of individual effectiveness and that customer behavior in the coming year will not change, what is the expected number of promotions that each customer will take advantage of next year by ordering goods that otherwise would not be purchased?

b What is the variance of X?

c A previous analysis of historical data found that the mean value of orders for promotional goods is $12.50, with the company earning a gross profit of 20% on each order. The fixed cost of conducting the four promotions next year is estimated to be $15,000, with a variable cost of $3.00 per customer for mailing and handling costs. Assuming that the survey results can be used as an accurate predictor of behavior for existing and potential customers, how large a customer base must the company have in order to cover the cost of promotions?

6.55 Let X be a random variable with mean μ and standard deviation σ. Consider a new random variable Z, obtained by subtracting the constant μ from X and dividing the result by the constant σ: $Z = (X - \mu)/\sigma$. The variable Z is called a **standardized random variable**. Use the laws of expected value and variance to show the following.

a $E(Z) = 0$ b $V(Z) = 1$

6.56 Let X and Y be two independent random variables with the following probability distributions.

x	$p(x)$	y	$p(y)$
2	.3	0	.2
4	.5	1	.6
6	.2	2	.2

To illustrate the laws of expected value and variance, verify the following equalities by separately evaluating the two sides of each.

a $E(3X) = 3E(X)$
   $V(3X) = 9V(X)$

b $E(Y + 4) = E(Y) + 4$
   $V(Y + 4) = V(Y)$

c $E(X + Y) = E(X) + E(Y)$
   $V(X + Y) = V(X) + V(Y)$

d $E(X - Y) = E(X) - E(Y)$
   $V(X - Y) = V(X) + V(Y)$

6.57 Refer to Exercise 6.56. Since X and Y are independent random variables, the probability $p(xy)$ is given by $P(X = x \text{ and } Y = y) = p(x)p(y)$.

a Verify that the probability distribution of the random variable XY is given by the following table.

xy	0	2	4	6	8	12
$p(xy)$	.20	.18	.36	.12	.10	.04

b Verify that $E(XY) = E(X)E(Y)$ by separately evaluating each side of the equality.

6.58a **Canadian Version:** You are planning a December break trip to Miami Beach. You are told that the mean daytime temperature at that time of year is 74°F with a standard deviation of 5°F. Being a Canadian, you are familiar only with the centigrade temperature scale. The relationship between the two temperature scales is represented by the formula

$$C = \left(\frac{5}{9}\right) \times (F - 32)$$

Find the mean and standard deviation of the daytime temperatures using the centigrade scale.

6.58b **American Version:** You are planning a December ski trip to Quebec City. You are told that the mean daytime temperature at that time of year is −10°C (centigrade) with a standard deviation of 3°C. Being an American, you are familiar only with the Fahrenheit temperature scale. The relationship between the two temperature scales is represented by the formula

$$F = \left(\frac{9}{5}\right)C + 32$$

Find the mean and standard deviation of the daytime temperatures using the Fahrenheit scale.

6.59 Suppose that you and a friend have contributed equally to a portfolio of $10,000 invested in a risky venture. The income (X) that will be earned on this portfolio over the next year has the following probability distribution.

x	$500	1,000	2,000
$p(x)$	.5	.3	.2

a Determine the expected value and the variance of the income earned on this portfolio.

b Determine the expected value and the variance of your share (one-half) of the income. Answer the question first by computing the expected value and the variance directly from the probability distribution of the income you will receive. Then check your answer using the laws of expected value and variance.

6.6 Bivariate Distributions (Optional*)

Thus far, we have considered the distribution of a *single* variable. The frequency distribution of a single variable was discussed in Chapter 2, and the probability distribution of a single variable was introduced earlier in this chapter. When we want to consider the relationship between two variables, however, the **bivariate (or joint) distribution** of the variables is needed.

Bivariate Frequency Distributions

Consider once again the sample of real estate data from Example 4.13, which is reproduced in Table 6.7.[†] From the data in Table 6.7, we can form the frequency distributions for X and for Y, as shown in Tables 6.8 and 6.9.

Table 6.7	
HOUSE SIZE (IN 100s OF SQUARE FEET)	**SELLING PRICE (IN 1,000s OF DOLLARS)**
X	Y
20.0	219
14.8	190
20.5	199
12.5	121
18.0	150
14.3	198
24.9	334
16.5	188
24.3	310
20.2	213
22.0	288
19.0	312
12.3	186
14.0	173
16.7	174

---

*This section may be omitted without loss of continuity.

†We have purposely chosen a small set of data to simplify the manual calculations.

Table 6.8	Frequency Distribution of House Size (X)	
HOUSE SIZE (IN 100 FT^2)	**FREQUENCY**	
12 up to 15	5	
15 up to 18	2	
18 up to 21	5	
21 up to 24	1	
24 up to 27	2	
Total	15	

Table 6.9	Frequency Distribution of Selling Price (Y)	
SELLING PRICE (1,000S OF DOLLARS)	**FREQUENCY**	
$100 up to $150	1	
150 up to 200	8	
200 up to 250	2	
250 up to 300	1	
300 up to 350	3	
Total	15	

Even more detail is contained in the **bivariate frequency distribution** of X and Y, shown in Table 6.10. From this bivariate distribution we can observe, for example, that there were 5 homes that were both 1,200 to 1,500 ft^2 in size and selling for $150,000 to $200,000. Summing the frequencies in the first row, we observe that 8 homes sold for between $150,000 and $200,000. Similarly, adding the frequencies in each of the rows, we obtain the (*marginal*) *frequencies* of variable Y, as shown in the right-hand margin of the table. Likewise, the (marginal) frequencies of X are shown in the bottom margin of the table.

Table 6.10	Bivariate Frequency Distribution of X and Y					
	X = HOUSE SIZE (IN 100 FT^2)					
SELLING PRICE (IN 1,000S OF DOLLARS)	**12 TO 15**	**15 TO 18**	**18 TO 21**	**21 TO 24**	**24 TO 27**	**$f(Y)$**
$100 to $150	1					1
150 to 200	4	2	2			8
200 to 250			2			2
250 to 300				1		1
300 to 350			1		2	3
$f(X)$	5	2	5	1	2	15

If we plot the raw (ungrouped) data in Table 6.7, we obtain the scatter diagram shown in Figure 6.11. A plot of the bivariate frequency distribution (Table 6.10) requires a three-dimensional graph, as shown in Figure 6.12.

Figure 6.11

Scatter Diagram of Real Estate Data (Table 6.7)

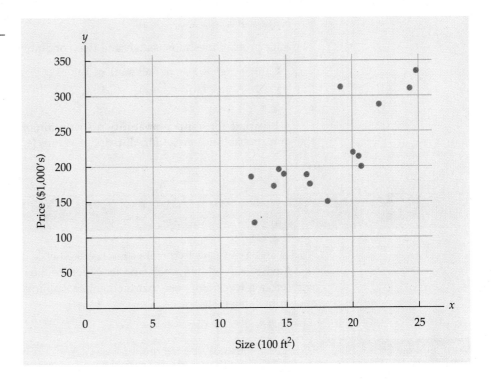

Figure 6.12

Graph of Bivariate Frequency Distribution (Table 6.10)

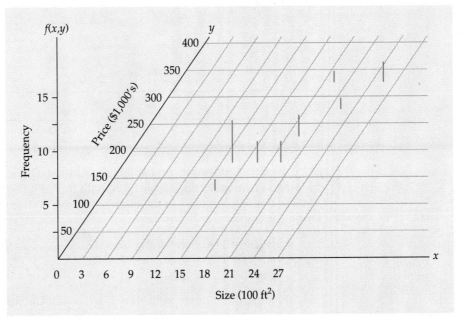

Having looked briefly at a bivariate frequency distribution for a sample of data, we next consider the bivariate probability distribution of two random variables X and Y. To simplify matters, we will restrict our discussion to *discrete* bivariate distributions.

Bivariate Probability Distributions

If X and Y are discrete random variables, the **joint probability** that X will assume the value x and Y will assume the value y is denoted $p(x,y)$.

$$p(x,y) = P(X = x \text{ and } Y = y)$$

The joint probabilities must satisfy the two conditions:

1 $0 \leq p(x,y) \leq 1$ for all pairs of values (x,y)

2 $\displaystyle\sum_{\text{all } x} \sum_{\text{all } y} p(x,y) = 1$

A **bivariate** (or **joint**) **probability distribution** of X and Y is a table that gives the joint probabilities $p(x,y)$ for all pairs of values (x,y).

EXAMPLE 6.7

Xavier and Yvette are two real estate agents. Let X denote the number of houses that Xavier will sell in a week, and let Y denote the number of houses that Yvette will sell in a week. Suppose that the joint probability distribution of X and Y is as shown in Table 6.11.

Table 6.11   **Bivariate Probability Distribution of X and Y**

Y	X			$p(y)$
	0	1	2	
0	.12	.42	.06	.60
1	.21	.06	.03	.30
2	.07	.02	.01	.10
$p(x)$	.40	.50	.10	1.00

Notice that a bivariate probability distribution (Table 6.11) is similar to a bivariate frequency distribution (Table 6.10), with probabilities having replaced frequencies. The nine probabilities in the interior of Table 6.11 are the joint probabilities $p(x,y)$. For example,

$$p(0, 0) = P(X = 0 \text{ and } Y = 0) = .12$$
$$p(0, 1) = P(X = 0 \text{ and } Y = 1) = .21$$
$$p(0, 2) = P(X = 0 \text{ and } Y = 2) = .07$$

Summing these three probabilities, we obtain the **marginal probability** $P(X = 0) = .40$ (so named because it appears in the margin of the table). Summing the probabilities in each of the other columns and rows, we obtain the other marginal probabilities.

$$p(x) = \sum_y p(x,y)$$

$$p(y) = \sum_x p(x,y)$$

Thus, the marginal probability distributions of X and Y are

x	$p(x)$		y	$p(y)$
0	.4		0	.6
1	.5		1	.3
2	.1		2	.1

These represent the probability distributions of X and Y with no consideration given to the value being assumed by the other random variable. It can be shown that $E(X) = .7$, $V(X) = .41$, $E(Y) = .5$, and $V(Y) = .45$. We will make use of these values later.

Conditional Probability

Conditional probabilities are also defined and computed just as they were earlier in this chapter. The **conditional probability** that X will assume the value x given that Y assumes the value y is

$$P(X = x | Y = y) = \frac{P(X = x \text{ and } Y = y)}{P(Y = y)}$$

For example, the probability that Xavier will sell no houses given that Yvette sells one house is

$$P(X = 0 | Y = 1) = \frac{P(X = 0 \text{ and } Y = 1)}{P(Y = 1)} = \frac{.21}{.30} = .7$$

Similarly,

$$P(X = 1 | Y = 1) = \frac{P(X = 1 \text{ and } Y = 1)}{P(Y = 1)} = \frac{.06}{.30} = .2$$

$$P(X = 2 | Y = 1) = \frac{P(X = 2 \text{ and } Y = 1)}{P(Y = 1)} = \frac{.03}{.30} = .1$$

Notice that the sum of the three conditional probabilities of X given $Y = 1$ is 1.0. This will always be the case. The sum of all the conditional probabilities of one variable given a specific value of the other variable will always be 1.0.

Notice that the conditional probability $P(X = 0 | Y = 1) = .7$ differs from the (unconditional or marginal) probability $P(X = 0) = .4$. This implies that X and Y are dependent random variables.

Two random variables X and Y are said to be *independent* if the value assumed by one variable in no way affects the probability of a particular value being assumed by the other. That is, X and Y are **independent random variables** if

$$P(X = x | Y = y) = P(X = x) \qquad \text{for all pairs of values } (x,y)$$

Recall that if A and B are independent events, their joint probability is given by $P(A \text{ and } B) = P(A) \cdot P(B)$. Similarly, if X and Y are independent random variables, their joint probabilities are given by

$$P(X = x \text{ and } Y = y) = P(X = x) \cdot P(Y = y)$$

The Sum of Two Random Variables

Many applied situations require that we consider the sum of two random variables. Referring back to Example 6.7, the random variable $X + Y$ represents the total number of houses that the two real estate agents will sell next week. The possible values that $X + Y$ can assume are 0, 1, 2, 3, and 4. The probability that $X + Y$ will assume the value 2, for example, is obtained by summing the joint probabilities of all pairs of values (x,y) for which $x + y = 2$.

$$
\begin{aligned}
P(X + Y = 2) &= p(0,2) + p(1,1) + p(2,0) \\
&= .07 + .06 + .06 \\
&= .19
\end{aligned}
$$

After computing the probabilities corresponding to the other four possible values in a similar manner, we obtain the probability distribution of $X + Y$.

$x + y$	0	1	2	3	4
$p(x + y)$	.12	.63	.19	.05	.01

Using the formulas for expected value and variance, it can be shown that $E(X + Y) = 1.2$ and $V(X + Y) = .56$.

We were able to construct the foregoing distribution of $X + Y$ since we knew the joint distribution of X and Y. In practice, the precise form of this distribution may be unknown. Frequently, however, we know (or have good estimates of) the expected values and variances of X and Y. If that is the case, we can still determine the expected value and variance of a linear combination $aX + bY$, where a and b are constants and X and Y are independent. From the laws of expected value and variance, we can write

$$E(aX + bY) = aE(X) + bE(Y)$$
$$V(aX + bY) = a^2V(X) + b^2V(Y) \qquad \text{if } X \text{ and } Y \text{ are independent}$$

To enable us to find the variance of a linear combination of X and Y when X and Y are not independent, we need to reconsider the concept of covariance (discussed in Chapter 4) in the context of random variables.

Covariance

Covariance is a statistical measure of the strength of the *linear* relationship between two random variables; it measures the degree to which the two variables tend to move together. If μ_X and μ_Y are the respective means (or expected values) of two random variables X and Y, the **covariance** of X and Y is given by

$$
\begin{aligned}
COV(X, Y) &= \sum_{\text{all } (x,y)} (x - \mu_x)(y - \mu_y) \cdot P(X = x \text{ and } Y = y) \\
&= E[(X - \mu_X)(Y - \mu_Y)] \\
&= E(XY) - \mu_X\mu_Y
\end{aligned}
$$

The last expression for covariance is often preferable for computational purposes. Recall (from Chapter 4) that the **coefficient of correlation** can now be found by dividing the covariance by the product of the standard deviations of X and Y.

$$\rho = \frac{COV(X,Y)}{\sigma_x \, \sigma_y}$$

As a numerical illustration, we will compute the covariance of the random variables X and Y in Example 6.7. The means of X and Y are

$$\mu_x = \sum x_i p(x_i) = 0(.4) + 1(.5) + 2(.1) = .7$$
$$\mu_y = \sum y_i p(y_i) = 0(.6) + 1(.3) + 2(.1) = .5$$

Hence

$$
\begin{aligned}
COV(X,Y) &= \sum_{\text{all } (x,y)} (x - \mu_x)(y - \mu_y) \cdot P(X = x \text{ and } Y = y) \\
&= (0 - .7)(0 - .5)(.12) + (0 - .7)(1 - .5)(.21) + (0 - .7)(2 - .5)(.07) \\
&\quad + (1 - .7)(0 - .5)(.42) + (1 - .7)(1 - .5)(.06) + (1 - .7)(2 - .5)(.02) \\
&\quad + (2 - .7)(0 - .5)(.06) + (2 - .7)(1 - .5)(.03) + (2 - .7)(2 - .5)(.01) \\
&= -.15
\end{aligned}
$$

This value simply tells us that there is a negative relationship between X and Y. To get an idea of the strength of that relationship, we compute the coefficient of correlation.

To compute the correlation we must first find the standard deviations of X and Y, which are calculated from the marginal probability distributions.

$$
\begin{aligned}
V(X) &= \sum (x_i - \mu_x)^2 p(x_i) \\
&= (0 - .7)^2(.4) + (1 - .7)^2(.5) + (2 - .7)^2(.1) = .41 \\
\sigma_x &= \sqrt{.41} = .64 \\
V(Y) &= \sum (y_i - \mu_y)^2 p(y_i) \\
&= (0 - .5)^2(.6) + (1 - .5)^2(.3) + (2 - .5)^2(.1) = .45 \\
\sigma_y &= \sqrt{.45} = .67
\end{aligned}
$$

Therefore,

$$\rho = \frac{COV(X,Y)}{\sigma_x \, \sigma_y} = \frac{-.15}{(.64)(.67)} = -.35$$

The value of this correlation indicates a relatively weak negative relationship between X and Y.

Loosely speaking, if X tends to assume large values when Y assumes large values and X tends to assume small values when Y assumes small values, then $COV(X,Y)$ is positive. The greater is this tendency, the larger will be the covariance. On the other hand, if X tends to assume large values when Y assumes small values, and vice versa, then $COV(X,Y)$ is negative. The covariance of X and Y will be close to zero if X and Y have little tendency to move together. In particular, if X and Y are independent random variables, $COV(X,Y) = 0$. This follows from the definition of covariance, together with the law of expected value (from the preceding section) that states

$$E(XY) = E(X)E(Y) \qquad \text{if } X \text{ and } Y \text{ are independent}$$

An expression for computing the variance of a linear combination $aX + bY$ must take into account the tendency of X and Y to move together. The measure that takes this tendency into account is $COV(X,Y)$. We now state, without proof, expressions for computing the expected value and variance of $aX + bY$ as functions of the expected value and variance of X and Y, and their covariance.

$$E(aX + bY) = aE(X) + bE(Y)$$
$$V(aX + bY) = a^2V(X) + b^2V(Y) + 2abCOV(X,Y)$$
$$= a^2V(X) + b^2V(Y) + 2ab\rho\sigma_x\sigma_y$$

This last equality makes use of the fact that

$$COV(X,Y) = \rho\sigma_x\sigma_y$$

One of the most important applications of these formulas is in the field of financial analysis. When we introduced variance and standard deviation, we pointed out that these measures are often used to assess the risk associated with investments. Financial analysts have shown that risk can be reduced by diversifying investments. Diversification is achieved by combining investments whose correlation is small. The following example illustrates this principle.

EXAMPLE 6.8

Suppose that an investor has decided to form a portfolio by putting $100,000 into each of two investments. Both investments are quite risky because the possible returns are highly variable. Investment 1 has a mean return of $15,000 (15%) with a standard deviation of $25,000. Investment 2 is expected to return $27,000, and its standard deviation is $40,000.

a Find the expected return of the portfolio.

b If the two investments' returns are perfectly positively correlated (that is, $\rho = 1$), find the standard deviation of the return on the portfolio.

c What is the portfolio's standard deviation if $\rho = .5$?

d What is the portfolio's standard deviation if $\rho = 0$?

SOLUTION

a The expected return is

$$E(X + Y) = E(X) + E(Y) = 15,000 + 27,000 = 42,000$$

The analyst expects a return of 21% (42,000/200,000).

b The variance of the portfolio's return is

$$V(X + Y) = \sigma_x^2 + \sigma_y^2 + 2\rho\sigma_x\sigma_y$$
$$= (25,000)^2 + (40,000)^2 + 2(1)(25,000)(40,000)$$
$$= 4,225,000,000$$

The standard deviation is

$$\sigma_{x+y} = 65,000$$

Notice that the standard deviation of $(X + Y)$ is the sum of the individual standard deviations of X and of Y (when $\rho = 1$).

c If $\rho = .5$

$$V(X + Y) = \sigma_x^2 + \sigma_y^2 + 2\rho\sigma_x \sigma_y$$
$$= (25{,}000)^2 + (40{,}000)^2 + 2(.5)(25{,}000)(40{,}000)$$
$$= 3{,}225{,}000{,}000$$

The standard deviation is

$$\sigma_{x+y} = 56{,}789$$

d If $\rho = 0$

$$V(X + Y) = \sigma_x^2 + \sigma_y^2 + 2\rho\sigma_x \sigma_y$$
$$= (25{,}000)^2 + (40{,}000)^2 + 2(0)(25{,}000)(40{,}000)$$
$$= 2{,}225{,}000{,}000$$

The standard deviation is

$$\sigma_{x+y} = 47{,}170$$

Notice that the expected value is not affected by the correlation and that the variance and standard deviation of the portfolio's returns decrease as the correlation coefficient decreases. This means that investors can reduce their risk without reducing their expected return by finding investments whose returns are independent, or at least weakly correlated.

Exercises

6.60 The table below lists the joint probabilities of X and Y.

	x	
y	1	2
1	.5	.1
2	.1	.3

a Find the marginal probabilities.

b Determine the mean, variance, and standard deviation for X and for Y.

c Calculate the conditional probabilities.

d Compute the covariance and the coefficient of correlation.

e Are X and Y independent? Explain.

6.61 Show that X and Y are independent given the following bivariate distribution.

	x	
y	1	2
1	.28	.42
2	.12	.18

6.62 A statistics professor developed the bivariate distribution (shown below) of the grades achieved by business students in accounting and statistics. (The corresponding grade points are shown in parentheses.)

a Find the marginal probabilities.

b Determine the mean and variance of the grade points in accounting and in statistics.

c Calculate the covariance and the coefficient of correlation.

d Are the grades in accounting and statistics independent?

	STATISTICS GRADES				
ACCOUNTING GRADES	A	B	C	D	F
A (= 4)	.05	.07	.08	.02	.00
B (= 3)	.02	.05	.09	.04	.01
C (= 2)	.02	.03	.08	.09	.03
D (= 1)	.01	.02	.06	.04	.05
F (= 0)	.00	.00	.04	.04	.06

6.63 The joint probability distribution of X and Y is shown in the accompanying table.

		x	
y	0	1	2
0	.42	.12	.06
1	.21	.06	.03
2	.07	.02	.01

a Determine the (marginal) probability distributions of X and Y.

b Are X and Y independent? Explain.

c Find $P(Y = 1 | X = 2)$.

d Find the probability distribution of $X + Y$.

e Find $E(XY)$.

f Find $COV(X,Y)$.

6.64 The concept of covariance has important applications in modern portfolio theory. Suppose we wish to form a portfolio consisting of two investments. Let X_1 and X_2 be the percentage rates of return that will be realized over the coming year on the two investments, respectively. Suppose that $E(X_1) = 20\%$, $\sigma_1 = 8\%$, $E(X_2) = 15\%$, $\sigma_2 = 5\%$, and $COV(X_1,X_2) = 4(\%)^2$. If we invest 40% of our money in the first investment and the remainder in the second investment, the rate of return on our portfolio will be $.4X_1 + .6X_2$.

a Find the expected value and variance of the rates of return on our portfolio.

b Which investment has the lowest risk as measured by the variance of its return: the first investment, the second investment, or the portfolio?

6.65 An analysis of the stock market produces the following information about the returns of two stocks.

	STOCKS	
	1	2
Expected Returns	12%	17%
Standard Deviations	25	38

a Assuming that the returns are perfectly positively correlated, find the mean and standard deviation of the return on a portfolio consisting of an equal investment in each of the two stocks.

b Repeat part (a), assuming that $\rho = .7$.

c Repeat part (a), assuming that the returns are uncorrelated.

6.66 Suppose that you wish to invest $1 million. After careful consideration of investment opportunities, you reduce the number of choices to two. The means and standard deviations of the two investments are listed below. The returns are highly correlated with $\rho = .8$. Discuss whether you should put all your money in investment 1, investment 2, or a portfolio composed of an equal amount of investments 1 and 2.

	INVESTMENTS	
	1	2
Expected Returns	12%	17%
Standard Deviations	25	38

6.67 Repeat Exercise 6.66, assuming that $\rho = 0$.

6.7 Binomial Distribution

Having considered the basic properties of probability distributions in general, we now consider in detail the binomial distribution—the first of four important specific probability distributions we will consider. The binomial distribution is probably the single most important discrete distribution. An important characteristic of the underlying binomial random experiment is that there are only two possible outcomes. Experiments with such a dichotomy of outcomes are numerous: a coin flip results in heads or tails, an election candidate is favored or not, a product is defective or nondefective, an employee is male or female, and an invoice being audited is correct or incorrect. It is conventional to apply the generic labels **success** and **failure** to the two possible outcomes. Binomial experiments of interest usually involve several repetitions or trials of the basic experiment; these trials must satisfy the conditions outlined below in the definition of a binomial experiment.

Binomial Experiment

A **binomial experiment** possesses the following properties.

1 The experiment consists of a fixed number n of trials.

2 The result of each trial can be classified into one of two categories: success or failure.

3 The probability p of a success remains constant for each trial.

4 Each trial of the experiment is independent of the other trials.

An example of a binomial experiment is to flip a coin 10 times and observe the result of each flip. Which of the two possible outcomes of each trial (flip) is designated a success is arbitrary. We will designate the appearance of heads as a success. Assuming the coin is fair, the probability of a success is $p = .5$ for each of the 10 trials. Clearly, each trial is independent of the others. Our main interest in a binomial experiment such as this is the number of successes (heads) observed in the 10 trials. The random variable that records the number of successes (heads) observed in the $n = 10$ trials is called the **binomial random variable**.

Here are two more examples of a binomial experiment.

1 Test 500 randomly selected computer chips produced at a manufacturing facility and determine whether each is defective. The number of trials is 500. There are two outcomes per trial: the product is either defective or nondefective. Assuming the defective rate is 1% and labeling the occurrence of a defective to be a success, then $p = .01$ and $q = (1 - p) = .99$. If the computer chips are selected at random for testing, the trials are independent.

2 Ask 1,500 people whether they prefer the taste of Coca-Cola over that of other colas. The number of trials is 1,500. There are two possible outcomes per trial: the respondent prefers Coca-Cola or does not. If we assume that 20% of the population prefers Coca-Cola, $p = .2$ and $q = .8$. The trials are independent.

Notice that in each example we made an assumption that allowed us to assign a value to p. Also note that we need to define what we mean by a success. In general, a success is defined arbitrarily and is not necessarily something we want to happen. When selecting computer chips, we defined success as finding a defective. The random variable of interest in these experiments is the number of successes, and is called the binomial random variable.

Binomial Random Variable

The **binomial random variable** indicates the number of successes in n trials of a binomial experiment.

A binomial random variable is therefore a discrete random variable that can take on any one of the values 0, 1, 2, . . . , n. The probability distribution of this random variable, called the **binomial probability distribution**, gives us the probability that a success will occur x times in the n trials, for $x = 0, 1, 2, . . . , n$. Rather than working out binomial probabilities from scratch each time, we would do better to have a general formula for calculating the probabilities associated with any binomial experiment. As a first step toward developing this formula, let's look at another binomial experiment.

Consider a binomial experiment consisting of $n = 3$ trials, with the two possible outcomes of each trial designated S (success) and F (failure). The binomial random variable X indicates the number of successes in the three trials. Let p denote the probability of a success in any trial, and let q denote the probability of a failure, where $q = (1 - p)$. The possible outcomes of any binomial experiment can be represented by a probability tree, with the stages corresponding to the trials of the experiment. The probability tree for this experiment is shown in Figure 6.13.

Recall from Section 6.3 that the probability attached to a branch of the tree is the conditional probability of that branch's outcome occurring. But because the trials of a binomial experiment are independent, the conditional probability that any branch outcome will occur is the same as the unconditional probability that it will occur. The simple event probabilities are obtained by applying the multiplication rule for independent events. As an example, the probability that SSF will occur is $p \cdot p \cdot q = p^2 q$.

Once all the simple event probabilities are found, the binomial probabilities appearing in Table 6.12 can be determined by summing the (simple event) probabilities associated with a given value x. For example, there is only one simple

Figure 6.13

Probability Tree for
Three Trials of a Bino-
mial Experiment

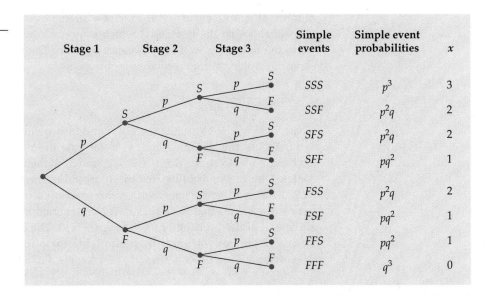

event (*FFF*) for which $x = 0$, and its probability is q^3. Hence, $p(0) = q^3$. But there are three simple events with exactly $x = 1$ success: *SFF*, *FSF*, and *FFS*. Because each of these simple events occurs with probability pq^2, the probability of exactly one success is $p(1) = 3pq^2$. The probabilities $p(2)$ and $p(3)$ are obtained in a similar manner. The complete probability distribution of X is shown in Table 6.12.

Table 6.12	Binomial Distribution for $n = 3$

x	$p(x)$
0	q^3
1	$3pq^2$
2	$3p^2q$
3	p^3

It is impractical to resort to a probability tree each time we want to find a binomial probability distribution. Instead, we need a general formula for the probability $p(x)$ of obtaining x successes in the n trials, when the probability of a success is p. To this end, notice that we will observe exactly x successes in the n trials whenever we observe a simple event with a total of x *S*'s and $(n - x)$ *F*'s. One such simple event is

$$\underbrace{SS \quad \ldots \quad S}_{x \text{ times}} \underbrace{FF \quad \ldots \quad F}_{(n - x) \text{ times}}$$

Applying the multiplication rule for independent events, we see that the probability that any such simple event will occur is $p^x q^{n-x}$, since p is the probability of a success and $q = (1 - p)$ is the probability of failure. We must now multiply this probability by the number of simple events having exactly x successes. But the number of simple events with exactly x successes is the same as the number of ways of choosing the x stages at which a success occurs. This number is found by using the following well-known **counting rule**: The number of different ways of choosing x objects from a total of n objects is

$$C_x^n = \frac{n!}{x!(n - x)!}$$

where $n! = n(n - 1)(n - 2) \cdots (2)(1)$ and $0!$ is defined to be 1.

Let's use this counting rule to determine the number of simple events that have exactly x successes (for $x = 0, 1, 2$, and 3) in the $n = 3$ trials of the experiment depicted by the probability tree in Figure 6.13. The four values to be calculated (called binomial coefficients, with values recorded in Table 6.13) can be checked against the values that were previously determined by counting the simple events at the end of the probability tree in Figure 6.13. The binomial probabilities $p(x)$ in Table 6.12 are now obtained by multiplying these four (binomial) coefficients by the corresponding probabilities $p^x q^{n-x}$, for $x = 0, 1, 2$, and 3.

Table 6.13	Binomial Coefficients ($n = 3$)
x	C_x^3
0	$C_0^3 = \dfrac{3!}{0!(3 - 0)!} = \dfrac{3!}{0!3!} = \dfrac{3 \cdot 2 \cdot 1}{(1)(3 \cdot 2 \cdot 1)} = 1$
1	$C_1^3 = \dfrac{3!}{1!(3 - 1)!} = \dfrac{3!}{1!2!} = \dfrac{3 \cdot 2 \cdot 1}{(1)(2 \cdot 1)} = 3$
2	$C_2^3 = \dfrac{3!}{2!(3 - 2)!} = \dfrac{3!}{2!1!} = \dfrac{3 \cdot 2 \cdot 1}{(2 \cdot 1)(1)} = 3$
3	$C_3^3 = \dfrac{3!}{3!(3 - 3)!} = \dfrac{3!}{3!0!} = \dfrac{3 \cdot 2 \cdot 1}{(3 \cdot 2 \cdot 1)(1)} = 1$

We are now in a position to give the general formulation of the binomial probability distribution.

> **Probability Distribution of a Binomial Experiment**
>
> If the random variable X is the number of successes in the n trials of a binomial experiment that has probability p of a success on any given trial, the probability distribution of X is given by
>
> $$P(X = x) = p(x) = C_x^n p^x q^{n-x}$$
> $$= \left(\frac{n!}{x!(n - x)!} \right) p^x q^{n-x} \qquad x = 0, 1, \ldots, n$$

Each pair of values (n, p) determines a distinct binomial distribution. Graphical representations of three binomial distributions are shown in Figure 6.14. Each of the $(n + 1)$ possible values of a binomial random variable X has a positive probability of occurring. The fact that some possible values of X do not have a vertical line above them in Figure 6.14 simply means that the probability that those values will occur is too small to be displayed on the graph. A binomial distribution is symmetrical whenever $p = .5$, and it is asymmetrical otherwise.

Figure 6.14

Graphs of Three Binomial Distributions

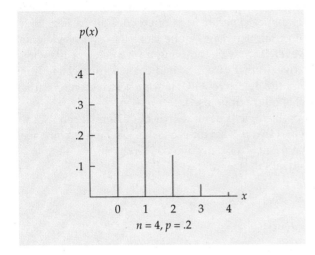

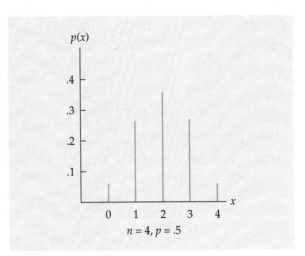

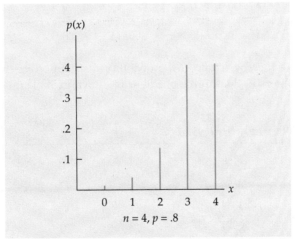

EXAMPLE 6.9

The quality-control department of a manufacturer tested the most recent batch of 1,000 catalytic converters produced and found 50 of them to be defective. Subsequently, an employee unwittingly mixed the defective converters in with the non-defective ones. If a sample of 3 converters is randomly selected from the mixed batch, what is the probability distribution of the number of defective converters in the sample?

SOLUTION
The first thing to do is to make sure that the conditions for a binomial experiment are satisfied. The experiment consists of a fixed number of $n = 3$ trials, with each trial resulting in one of two possible outcomes: a defective converter (success) or a nondefective converter (failure). The probability p of selecting a defective converter does not remain constant for each trial, however, because the probability of selecting a defective converter on a given trial depends on the results of the previous trials. In other words, the trials are not independent. The probability of selecting a defective converter on the first trial is $50/1,000 = .05$. But if a defective converter is selected on the first trial, the probability of selecting a defective converter on the second trial is $49/999 = .049$. In practical situations, this slight violation of the conditions of a binomial experiment is often considered negligible. While p does vary from trial to trial, it remains quite close to .05. The violation would become important, however, if we were sampling from a batch of 100 widgets of which only 5 were defective. In that case, p would change appreciably from trial to trial—especially if one of the defective widgets were selected on an earlier trial—and the binomial model should not be used.

Returning to the original problem, let's assume that the binomial model adequately describes the situation and that $p = .05$ for each trial. Let X be the binomial random variable indicating the number of defective converters in the sample of three. We can then compute probabilities as follows:

$$P(X = 0) = p(0) = \frac{3!}{0!3!} (.05)^0(.95)^3 = .8574$$

$$P(X = 1) = p(1) = \frac{3!}{1!2!} (.05)^1(.95)^2 = .1354$$

$$P(X = 2) = p(2) = \frac{3!}{2!1!} (.05)^2(.95)^1 = .0071$$

$$P(X = 3) = p(3) = \frac{3!}{3!0!} (.05)^3(.95)^0 = .0001$$

We thereby obtain the probability distribution of the number of defective converters in the sample of three, as shown in Table 6.14.

Table 6.14	Binomial Distribution ($n = 3$, $p = .05$)
x	$p(x)$
0	.8574
1	.1354
2	.0071
3	.0001

Using the Binomial Tables

An alternative way of presenting the binomial distribution ($n = 3$, $p = .05$) in Table 6.14 is depicted in Table 6.15. The difference here is that the probabilities in Table 6.15 are **cumulative probabilities** that represent the sum of binomial probabilities from $x = 0$ to $x = k$. If $k = 1$, for example, we have

$$P(X \leq 1) = \sum_{x=0}^{1} p(x) = p(0) + p(1)$$
$$= .8574 + .1354$$
$$= .9928$$

Table 6.15	Cumulative Binomial Distribution ($n = 3$, $p = .05$)

k	$\sum_{x=0}^{k} p(x)$
0	.8574
1	.9928
2	.9999
3	1.0000

The advantage of working with a table of cumulative binomial probabilities is that it enables us to find more quickly the probability that X will assume some value within a range of values.

Individual binomial probabilities are obtained from Table 6.15 by subtraction. For example, the probability of exactly two successes is

$$p(2) = P(X \leq 2) - P(X \leq 1)$$
$$= \sum_{x=0}^{2} p(x) - \sum_{x=0}^{1} p(x)$$
$$= .9999 - .9928$$
$$= .0071$$

Calculating binomial probabilities by means of the formula, as in Example 6.9, is time-consuming and tiresome when n is large. Fortunately, tables identifying these probabilities are available. One such table is Table 1 in Appendix B at the back of this book, which presents cumulative binomial distributions for various values of n and p. (Although the probabilities in the preceding example were computed to four decimal places, the binomial probabilities provided by Table 1 are rounded to three decimal places.) A partial reproduction of this table, for $n = 5$, is shown in Table 6.16. The 15 columns in Table 6.16, corresponding to 15 different values of p, represent 15 distinct binomial distributions. Individual tabulated values are of the form

$$P(X \leq k) = \sum_{x=0}^{k} p(x)$$

To find the probability of at most three successes in $n = 5$ trials of a binomial experiment with $p = .2$, we locate the entry corresponding to $k = 3$ and $p = .2$.

$$P(X \leq 3) = \sum_{x=0}^{3} p(x)$$
$$= p(0) + p(1) + p(2) + p(3)$$
$$= .993$$

Table 6.16

Partial Reproduction of Table 1: Binomial Probabilities for $n = 5$*

k	.01	.05	.10	p .20	.25	.30	.40	.50
0	.951	.774	.590	.328	.237	.168	.078	.031
1	.999	.977	.919	.737	.633	.528	.337	.187
2	1.000	.999	.991	.942	.896	.837	.683	.500
3	1.000	1.000	1.000	.993	.984	.969	.913	.812
4	1.000	1.000	1.000	1.000	.999	.998	.990	.969

k	.60	.70	.75	.80	.90	.95	.99
0	.010	.002	.001	.000	.000	.000	.000
1	.087	.031	.016	.007	.000	.000	.000
2	.317	.163	.104	.058	.009	.001	.000
3	.663	.472	.367	.263	.081	.023	.001
4	.922	.832	.763	.672	.410	.226	.049

*Tabulated values are $P(X \le k) = \sum_{x=0}^{k} p(x)$. (Entries are rounded to three decimal places.)

Notice that the final probability in each column (distribution) of the table—reading horizontally, the row corresponding to $k = n$—has been omitted. This probability will always be equal to 1, since, for $k = n$,

$$P(X \le k) = P(X \le n) = 1$$

We have just seen how to use Table 1 in Appendix B to save time in finding binomial probabilities. There is also a time-saving procedure for finding the mean and the variance of a binomial random variable. While these two parameters could be calculated in the usual time-consuming way—using the definitional formulas involving summations—it can be shown that the mean and the variance of a binomial random variable are given by the following pair of formulas.

Mean and Variance of Binomial Random Variables

If X is a binomial random variable, the mean and the variance of X are

$$E(X) = \mu = np$$
$$V(X) = \sigma^2 = npq$$

where n is the number of trials, p is the probability of success on any trial, and $q = (1 - p)$ is the probability of failure on any trial.

EXAMPLE 6.10

A shoe store's records show that 30% of customers making a purchase use a credit card to make payment. This morning, 20 customers purchased shoes from the store.

a Using Table 1 of Appendix B, find the probability that at least 12 of the customers used a credit card.

b What is the probability that at least 3 customers, but not more than 6, used a credit card?

c What is the expected number of customers who used a credit card?

d Find the probability that exactly 14 customers did not use a credit card.

e Find the probability that at least 9 customers did not use a credit card.

SOLUTION

If making a payment with a credit card is designated a success, we have a binomial experiment with $n = 20$ and $p = .3$. Let X denote the number of customers who used a credit card.

a We must first express the probability we seek in the form $P(X \leq k)$, since this is the form in which probabilities are tabulated in Table 1.

$$P(X \geq 12) = P(X = 12) + P(X = 13) + \cdots + P(X = 20)$$
$$= P(X \leq 20) - P(X \leq 11)$$

Because the probabilities in a binomial distribution must sum to 1, $P(X \leq 20) = 1$. From Table 1, $P(X \leq 11) = .995$. Therefore,

$$P(X \geq 12) = 1 - .995 = .005$$

The probability that at least 12 customers used a credit card is .005.

b Expressing the probability we seek in the form used for the probabilities tabulated in Table 1, we have

$$P(3 \leq X \leq 6) = P(X = 3) + P(X = 4) + P(X = 5) + P(X = 6)$$
$$= P(X \leq 6) - P(X \leq 2)$$
$$= .608 - .035 = .573$$

The probability that between 3 and 6 customers used a credit card is .573.

c The expected number of customers who used a credit card is

$$E(X) = np = 20(.3) = 6$$

d Let Y denote the number of customers who did not use a credit card. The probability that a customer did not use a credit card is $(1 - .3) = .7$. This part of the example can be solved in either of two ways.

i You can interchange the designations of success and failure and work with $p = .7$.

ii You can express the required probability in terms of the number of customers who did not use a credit card, and proceed with $p = .3$.

Method (i) is probably easier to use with the tables in the text. In many cases, however, binomial tables with p values above .5 are not available, and method (ii) must be used.

Using method (i), we begin by recognizing that, since the original assignment of the designations *success* and *failure* was arbitrary, we can interchange them. If not using a credit card is designated as a success, then $p = .7$. From Table 1, we find that

$$P(Y = 14) = P(Y \leq 14) - P(Y \leq 13)$$
$$= .584 - .392$$
$$= .192$$

In method (ii), we retain the original designation, according to which using a credit card is a success and $p = .3$. If 14 customers did not use a credit card, the number of customers who did use one is $(20 - 14) = 6$. Hence,

$$P(Y = 14) = P(X = 6)$$
$$= P(X \leq 6) - P(X \leq 5)$$
$$= .608 - .416$$
$$= .192$$

Using either method, we find that the probability that exactly 14 customers did not use a credit card is .192.

e Again, let Y denote the number of customers who did not use a credit card. If not using a credit card is designated a success, then $p = .7$. Expressing the required probability in terms of values tabulated in Table 1, we have

$$P(Y \geq 9) = 1 - P(Y \leq 8)$$
$$= 1 - .005$$
$$= .995$$

The probability that at least 9 customers did not use a credit card is .995.

Using the Computer to Find Binomial Probabilities

There are a few software packages that compute probabilities in addition to their more traditional duties involving statistical procedures. Minitab and Excel are two of these, allowing us to easily produce the probability distributions for various random variables. In Appendixes 6.A and 6.B we describe the Minitab and Excel commands that output $p(x)$ and $P(X \leq x)$ for any value of x, where X is a binomial random variable.

Exercises

6.68 Evaluate the following binomial coefficients.

   a C_2^5 b C_2^6 c C_4^6

   d C_0^7 e C_7^7

6.69 Consider a binomial random variable X with $n = 4$ and $p = .6$.

   a Find the probability distribution of X, and graph it.

   b Find $P(X \leq 2)$.

   c Find the mean and the variance of X.

6.70 Let X be a binomial random variable. Use the formula to compute the following probabilities.

a $P(X = 2)$, if $n = 8$ and $p = .1$

b $P(X = 5)$, if $n = 9$ and $p = .5$

c $P(X = 9)$, if $n = 10$ and $p = .95$

6.71 Use Table 1 in Appendix B to check your answers to Exercise 6.70.

6.72 Let X be a binomial random variable. Use the formula to compute the following probabilities.

a $P(X = 3)$, if $n = 5$ and $p = .2$

b $P(X = 2)$, if $n = 6$ and $p = .3$

c $P(X = 5)$, if $n = 7$ and $p = .75$

6.73 Use Table 1 in Appendix B to check your answers to Exercise 6.72.

6.74 Given a binomial random variable X with $n = 15$ and $p = .3$, find the following probabilities, using Table 1 in Appendix B.

a $P(X \leq 2)$ **b** $P(X \geq 7)$ **c** $P(X = 6)$

d $P(4 \leq X \leq 8)$ **e** $P(X \geq 12)$ **f** $P(7 < X < 10)$

6.75 Given a binomial random variable X with $n = 25$ and $p = .6$, find the following probabilities, using Table 1 in Appendix B.

a $P(X \leq 10)$ **b** $P(X \geq 12)$ **c** $P(X = 15)$

d $P(18 \leq X \leq 21)$ **e** $P(18 < X < 21)$

6.76 A sign on the gas pumps of a certain chain of gasoline stations encourages customers to have their oil checked, claiming that one out of every four cars should have its oil topped up.

a What is the probability that exactly 3 of the next 10 cars entering a station should have their oil topped up?

b What is the probability that at least half of the next 10 cars entering a station should have their oil topped up? At least half of the next 20 cars?

6.77 A multiple-choice quiz has 15 questions. Each question has five possible answers, of which only one is correct.

a What is the probability that sheer guesswork will yield at least seven correct answers?

b What is the expected number of correct answers by sheer guesswork?

6.78 A student majoring in accounting is trying to decide upon the number of firms to which she should apply. Given her work experience, grades, and extracurricular activities, she has been told by a placement counselor that she can expect to receive a job offer from 80% of the firms to which she applies. Wanting to save time, the student applies to only five firms. Assuming the counselor's estimate is correct, find the probability that the student receives the following.

a no offers

b at most two offers

c between two and four offers (inclusive)

d five offers

6.79 An auditor is preparing for a physical count of inventory as a means of verifying its value. Items counted are reconciled with a list prepared by the storeroom supervisor. Normally, 20% of the items counted cannot be reconciled without reviewing invoices. The auditor selects 10 items.

a Find the probability of each of the following

    i Up to 4 items cannot be reconciled.

    ii At least 6 items cannot be reconciled.

    iii Between 4 and 6 items (inclusive) cannot be reconciled.

b If it normally takes 20 minutes to review the invoice for an item that cannot be reconciled and 1 hour for the balance of the count, how long should the auditor expect the physical count to take?

6.80 Flight delays at major American airports are an increasing source of exasperation to executives, who may miss important appointments as a result. About 190,000 flights were delayed by more than 15 minutes during the first six months of 1984, with many of the delays lasting hours (*Fortune*, 1 October 1984). During this period, 13% of all arrivals and departures at New York's LaGuardia Airport experienced delays of at least 15 minutes. The corresponding level of delays at Denver's Stapleton Airport was about 5%. Suppose an executive made three round trips from Denver and New York during this period.

a Find the probability that the executive experienced at least four delays of 15 minutes or more at Stapleton Airport during arrival or departure.

b Find the probability that the executive experienced no delays of 15 minutes or more upon arrival at or departure from LaGuardia Airport during the three trips.

c Find the probability that the executive experienced no delays of 15 minutes or more during the three round trips.

d What assumptions have you made in solving the first three parts of this exercise?

6.8 Poisson Distribution

A second important discrete distribution is the Poisson distribution. While a binomial random variable counts the number of successes that occur in a fixed number of trials, a Poisson random variable counts the number of rare events (successes) that occur in a specified time interval or a specified region. Activities to which the Poisson distribution can be successfully applied include counting the number of telephone calls received by a switchboard in a specified time period, counting the number of arrivals at a service location (such as a service station, tollbooth, or grocery checkout counter) in a given time period, and counting the number of bacteria in a specified culture. In order for the Poisson distribution to be appropriately applied to situations such as these, three conditions must be satisfied, as enumerated in the accompanying box. In the following description of a Poisson experiment, *success* refers to the occurrence of the event of interest, and *interval* refers to either an interval of time or an interval of space (such as an area or region).

Poisson Experiment

A Poisson experiment possesses the following properties.

1 The number of successes that occur in any interval is independent of the number of successes that occur in any other interval.

2 The probability that a success will occur in an interval is the same for all intervals of equal size and is proportional to the size of the interval.

3 The probability that two or more successes will occur in an interval approaches zero as the interval becomes smaller.

The Poisson model thus is applicable when the events of interest occur *randomly*, *independently* of one another, and *rarely*, as specified by the preceding conditions. In particular, condition 3 specifies what is meant by *rarely*. The arrival of individual diners at a restaurant, for example, would not fit the Poisson model because diners usually arrive with companions, violating the independence condition.

Poisson Random Variable

The **Poisson random variable** indicates the number of successes that occur during a given time interval or in a specified region in a Poisson experiment.

Probability Distribution of Poisson Random Variables

If X is a Poisson random variable, the probability distribution of X is given by

$$P(X = x) = p(x) = \frac{e^{-\mu}\mu^x}{x!} \qquad x = 0, 1, 2, \ldots$$

where μ is the average number of successes occurring in the given time interval or region, and $e = 2.71828 \ldots$ is the base of the natural logarithms.

Notice that, since μ (the average number of successes occurring in a specified interval) appears in the formula for the Poisson probability $p(x)$, we must obtain an estimate of μ—usually from historical data—before we can apply the Poisson distribution. Care must be taken to ensure that the intervals specified in the definitions of X and μ are the same size and that the same units are used for each.

Although the formula can be used to compute a Poisson probability, it requires us to calculate $e^{-\mu}$. If your calculator will not perform this calculation, you must resort to tabulated values of $e^{-\mu}$, but this becomes impractical when you want to find the probability that a Poisson random variable will assume any one of a large number of specified values. Fortunately, there is an easier method. To ease the computation of Poisson probabilities, we have included tabulated values of cumulative Poisson probabilities in Table 2 of Appendix B.

There is no limit to the number of values a Poisson random variable can assume. The Poisson random variable is a discrete random variable with infinitely many possible values—unlike the binomial random variable, which has only a finite number of possible values. If X is a Poisson random variable for which μ is the average number of successes that occur in a specified interval, the expected value and the variance of X have the same value.

$$E(X) = V(X) = \mu$$

The graphs of three specific Poisson distributions are shown in Figure 6.15.

Figure 6.15

**Graphs of Three Poisson
Distributions**

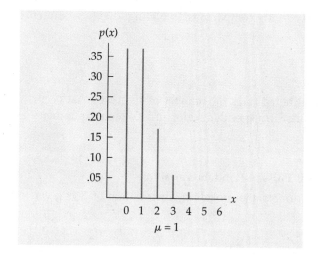

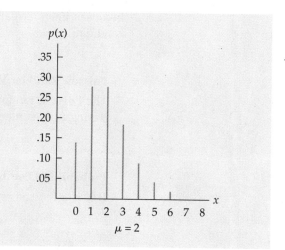

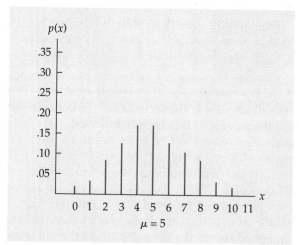

EXAMPLE 6.11

A tollbooth operator has observed that cars arrive randomly at an average rate of
360 cars per hour.

a Using the formula, calculate the probability that only two cars will arrive
during a specified one-minute period.

b Using Table 2 of Appendix B, find the probability that only two cars will
arrive during a specified one-minute period.

c Using Table 2, find the probability that at least four cars will arrive during a
specified one-minute period.

SOLUTION

Let X denote the number of arrivals during the one-minute period. Then the mean
value of X is $\mu = 360/60 = 6$ cars per minute. Notice that we have defined both
X and μ in terms of the same time interval, one minute.

a According to the formula for a Poisson probability, the probability of exactly two arrivals is

$$P(X = 2) = \frac{(e^{-6})(6^2)}{2!}$$
$$= \frac{(.00248)(36)}{2 \cdot 1}$$
$$= .0446$$

The value of e^{-6} was obtained by using a calculator.

b According to the cumulative Poisson probabilities in Table 2, the probability of exactly two arrivals is

$$P(X = 2) = P(X \leq 2) - P(X \leq 1)$$
$$= .062 - .017$$
$$= .045$$

c The probability of at least four arrivals is

$$P(X \geq 4) = 1 - P(X \leq 3)$$
$$= 1 - .151$$
$$= .849$$

Using the Computer to Find Poisson Probabilities

Minitab and Excel can be used to calculate Poisson probabilities. In Appendixes 6.A and 6.B, we describe the commands that will output $p(x)$ and $P(X \leq x)$ for any values of x from any Poisson distribution.

Poisson Approximation of the Binomial

Although binomial and Poisson random variables have distinct distributions, the two distributions are related. If we imagine a Poisson random variable whose interval has been subdivided into n (where n is large) very small subintervals, the probability of a success in any subinterval is approximately $p = \mu/n$, and we have an approximate binomial random variable. Similarly, a binomial distribution for which the number of trials n is large and the probability p of a success is very small can be approximated by a Poisson distribution. This approximation is useful because for large values of n, binomial probability tables are often unavailable.

The appropriate Poisson distribution to use for the approximation will have $\mu = np$, the mean for the binomial distribution. In order for the approximation to be a good one, p should be very small. It is conventional to suggest that at the least, we should have $p < .05$.

EXAMPLE 6.12

A warehouse engages in **acceptance sampling** to determine if it will accept or reject incoming lots of designer sunglasses, some of which invariably are defective. Specifically, the warehouse has a policy of examining a sample of 50 sunglasses from each lot and accepting the lot only if the sample contains no more than two defective pairs. What is the probability of a lot's being accepted if, in fact, 2% of the sunglasses in the lot are defective?

SOLUTION

We are dealing with a binomial experiment for which $n = 50$ and $p = .02$. The required probability cannot be found by using the binomial tables in this text because n is too large. But since $p < .05$ and the expected number of defective sunglasses in the sample is $np = 50(.02) = 1$, the required probability can be approximated by using the Poisson distribution with $\mu = 1$. From Table 2 of Appendix B, we find that the probability that a sample contains at most two defective pairs of sunglasses is .920.

For purposes of illustrating how well the Poisson distribution approximates the binomial distribution in this example, we have reproduced the two distributions in Table 6.17. Probabilities corresponding to values of x greater than 7 are omitted because they consist entirely of zeros to four decimal places. Summing the first three probabilities in the table, we see that the true (binomial) probability of accepting a lot containing 2% defective sunglasses is .922, while the Poisson approximation to this probability is .920. The Poisson approximation to the binomial distribution in this example is excellent.

Table 6.17	Comparison of Binomial and Poisson Probabilities		
x	BINOMIAL PROBABILITY ($n = 50$, $p = .02$)	POISSON PROBABILITY ($\mu = np = 1$)	
0	.364	.368	
1	.372	.368	
2	.186	.184	
3	.061	.061	
4	.014	.015	
5	.003	.003	
6	.000	.001	

Exercises

6.81 Compute the following Poisson probabilities, using the formula.
  a $P(X = 4)$, if $\mu = 1$
  b $P(X \leq 1)$, if $\mu = 1.5$
  c $P(X \geq 2)$, if $\mu = 2$

6.82 Repeat Exercise 6.81 using Table 2 of Appendix B.

6.83 Let X be a Poisson random variable with $\mu = 5$. Use Table 2 to find the following probabilities.
  a $P(X \leq 5)$ b $P(X = 5)$ c $P(X \geq 7)$

6.84 Suppose X is a Poisson random variable whose distribution has a mean of 2.5. Use Table 2 to find the following probabilities.

a $P(X \leq 3)$ b $P(X = 6)$

c $P(X \geq 2)$ d $P(X > 2)$

6.85 Graph the probability distribution of a Poisson random variable with $\mu = .5$.

6.86 Let X be a binomial random variable with $n = 25$ and $p = .01$.

a Use Table 1 in Appendix B to find $P(X = 0)$, $P(X = 1)$, and $P(X = 2)$.

b Approximate the three probabilities in part (a) using the appropriate Poisson distribution. (You will need a calculator.) Compare your approximations with the exact probabilities found in part (a).

6.87 Let X be a binomial random variable with $n = 25$ and $p = .05$.

a Use Table 1 in Appendix B to find $P(X = 0)$, $P(X = 1)$, and $P(X = 2)$.

b Approximate the three probabilities in part (a) using the appropriate Poisson distribution. (You will need a calculator.) Compare your approximations with the exact probabilities found in part (a).

6.88 The number of calls received by a switchboard operator between 9 and 10 A.M. has a Poisson distribution with a mean of 12. Find the probability that the operator received at least five calls during the following periods.

a between 9 and 10 A.M.

b between 9 and 9:30 A.M.

c between 9 and 9:15 A.M.

6.89 The marketing manager of a company has noted that she usually receives 10 complaint calls from customers during a week (consisting of 5 working days) and that the calls occur at random. Find the probability of her receiving exactly 5 such calls in a single day.

6.90 The numbers of accidents that occur on an assembly line have a Poisson distribution, with an average of three accidents a week.

a Find the probability that a particular week will be accident-free.

b Find the probability that at least three accidents will occur in a week.

c Find the probability that exactly five accidents will occur in a week.

d If the accidents occurring in different weeks are independent of one another, find the expected number of accidents in a year.

6.91 During the summer months (June to August, inclusive), an average of 5 marriages per month take place in a small city. Assuming that these marriages occur randomly and independently of one another, find the probability of the following.

a Fewer than 4 marriages will occur in June.

b At least 14 but not more than 18 marriages will occur during the entire 3 months of summer.

c Exactly 10 marriages will occur during the 2 months of July and August.

6.92 The number of arrivals at a service counter between 1:00 and 3:00 P.M. has a Poisson distribution with a mean of 14.

a Find the probability that the number of arrivals between 1:00 and 3:00 P.M. is at least 8.

b Find the probability that the number of arrivals between 1:30 and 2:00 P.M. is at least 8.

c Find the probability of there being exactly 1 arrival between 2:00 and 3:00 P.M.

6.93 A snow-removal company bills its customers on a per-snowfall basis, rather than at a flat monthly rate. Based on the fee it charges per snowfall, the company will just break even in a month that has exactly six snowfalls. Suppose that the average number of snowfalls per month (during the winter) is eight.

    a What is the probability that the company will just break even in a given winter month?

    b What is the probability that the company will make a profit in a given winter month?

6.94 A biologist knows that about 1% of a certain breed of frogs mutate. Given a random sample of 50 developing frogs, what is the probability that the sample will contain at least 1 mutated frog?

6.95 A paper manufacturer claims that less than 1 in 100 of its reels (two-ton rolls) of paper is flawed. A customer has just received a large shipment of these reels and proceeds to check a random sample of 600 of them for flaws. Of this sample, 14 reels are found to be flawed.

    a What was the probability of finding at least 14 flawed reels in this sample?

    b Based on your answer to part (a), what would you conclude about the manufacturer's claim?

6.9 Summary

Gamblers, businesspeople, and economists frequently find themselves in decision-making situations involving uncertain events. Probability is the basic tool they use to make rational judgments in such situations. The first step in assigning probabilities to uncertain events is to form a **sample space**—a listing of all the simple events that can result from a random experiment. A **probability** (number between 0 and 1) is then assigned to each simple event, measuring the likelihood of occurrence of that outcome. The use of a **probability tree** often facilitates both the formation of a sample space and the assignment of probabilities to its simple events. Probabilities can then be computed for more complex events in accordance with rules of probability. The notion of **conditional probability** allows us to express the probability that a particular event will occur when some partial knowledge of the experimental outcome is available.

The concept of a random variable permits us to summarize the results of an experiment in terms of numerical-valued events. Specifically, a **random variable** assigns a numerical value to each simple event of an experiment. A random variable is **discrete** if it can assume at most a countably infinite number of values; it is **continuous** if it can take any of infinitely many values within some interval of values. Once the **probability distribution** of a random variable is known, we can determine its **expected value**, its **variance**, and the probability that it will assume various values. These abilities will stand us in good stead when we reach the study of statistical inference, where we will want to determine the probability that any particular sample will be selected from a population over which the random variable is defined.

Two discrete random variables that frequently arise in real-world applications are the **binomial** and the **Poisson**. We described the characteristics of random experiments that give rise to each of these random variables and gave the formulas for their probability distributions.

IMPORTANT TERMS

Random experiment

Exhaustive

Mutually exclusive

Sample space

Simple event

Event

Probability of an event

Complement of an event

Conditional probability

Independent events

Probability tree

Joint probability

Random variable

Discrete random variable

Continuous random variable

Discrete probability distribution

Expected value of a discrete random variable

Variance of a discrete random variable

Standard deviation of a random variable

Bivariate (or joint) distribution

Marginal probability

Covariance

Binomial experiment

Binomial random variable

Binomial probability distribution

Poisson experiment

Poisson random variable

Poisson probability distribution

SUMMARY OF FORMULAS

$$P(A|B) = \frac{P(A \text{ and } B)}{P(B)}$$

$$P(A) = 1 - P(\bar{A})$$

$$P(A \text{ or } B) = P(A) + P(B) - P(A \text{ and } B)$$

$$P(A \text{ and } B) = P(A) \cdot P(B|A)$$
$$= P(B) \cdot P(A|B)$$

$$\mu = E(X) = \sum_{i=1}^{N} x_i \cdot p(x_i)$$

$$\sigma^2 = \sum_{i=1}^{N} (x_i - \mu)^2 \cdot p(x_i)$$

Bivariate

$$p(x,y) = P(X = x \text{ and } Y = y)$$

$$P(X = x | Y = y) = \frac{P(X = x \text{ and } Y = y)}{P(Y = y)}$$

$$COV(X,Y) = \sum_{\text{all } (x,y)} (x - \mu_x)(y - \mu_y) \cdot P(X = x \text{ and } Y = y)$$

$$\rho = \frac{COV(X, Y)}{\sigma_x \sigma_y}$$

Binomial

$$P(X = x) = p(x) = C_x^n \cdot p^x \cdot q^{n-x}, \quad \text{where } q = 1 - p$$

$$= \left(\frac{n!}{x!(n - x)!} \right) p^x \cdot q^{n-x}, \quad x = 0, 1, \ldots, n$$

$$E(X) = \mu = np$$

$$V(X) = \sigma^2 = npq$$

Poisson

$$P(X = x) = p(x) = \frac{e^{-\mu} \cdot \mu^x}{x!}, \qquad x = 0, 1, 2, \ldots$$
$$E(X) = V(X) = \mu$$

Supplementary Exercises

6.96 There are three approaches to determining the probability that an outcome will occur: classical, relative frequency, and subjective. Which approach is appropriate in determining each of the following probabilities?

a It will rain tomorrow.

b A coin toss will result in heads.

c A Michelin tire will last more than 40,000 miles.

d When a single card is selected from a well-shuffled deck, it will be a diamond.

e An automobile will pass quality-control inspection.

f A firm's sales will grow by at least 10% next year.

6.97 Two six-sided dice are rolled, and the number of spots turning up on each is observed. Find the probability of each of the following.

a observing three spots on one die and five spots on the other

b observing exactly one die that has two spots showing

c observing that the sum of the spots showing is 7

d observing that the sum of the spots showing is 8

e observing that the sum of the spots showing is an even number

f observing that the sum of the spots showing is 8, given that the sum is an even number

6.98 Referring to Exercise 6.97, define the following events.

A: The sum of the spots showing is 2, 3, or 12.

B: The sum of the spots showing is an even number.

Are *A* and *B* independent events? Explain.

6.99 Exactly 100 employees of a firm have each purchased one ticket in a lottery, with the draw to be held at the firm's annual party. Of the 80 men who purchased tickets, 25 are single. Only 4 of the women who purchased tickets are single.

a Find the probability that the lottery winner is married.

b Find the probability that the lottery winner is a married woman.

c If the winner is a man, what is the probability that he is married?

6.100 A customer service supervisor regularly conducts a survey of customer satisfaction as part of a management control system. The results of his latest survey show that 5% of those surveyed are not satisfied with the service they receive. While only 30% of those surveyed are in arrears, 80% of the dissatisfied customers are in arrears. If the report on one customer surveyed is selected at random, find the probability that this customer has the following characteristics.

a in arrears and dissatisfied

b either in arrears or dissatisfied or both

6.101 As input into his pricing policy, the owner of an appliance store is interested in the relationship between the price at which an item is sold (regular or sale price) and the customer's decision on whether or not to purchase an extended warranty. The owner has constructed the accompanying table of probabilities, based on a study of 2,000 sales invoices. Suppose one sales invoice is selected at random, with the relevant events being defined as follows.

A: Item is purchased at regular price.

B: Item is purchased at sale price.

C: Extended warranty is purchased.

D: Extended warranty is not purchased.

	EXTENDED WARRANTY	
	PURCHASED	NOT PURCHASED
Regular Price	.21	.57
Sale Price	.14	.08

Express each of the following probabilities in words, and find its value.

a $P(A)$ **b** $P(\bar{A})$ **c** $P(C)$ **d** $P(C|A)$

e $P(C|B)$ **f** $P(D|B)$ **g** $P(B|D)$ **h** $P(C|D)$

i $P(A \text{ or } B)$ **j** $P(A \text{ and } D)$

6.102 The director of an insurance company's computing center estimates that the company's computer has a 20% chance of "catching" a computer virus. However, she feels that there is only a 6% chance of the computer's "catching" a virus that will completely disable its operating system. If the company's computer should "catch" a virus, what is the probability that the operating system will be completely disabled?

6.103 It is known that 3% of the tickets in a certain scratch-and-win game are winners, in the sense that the purchaser of such a ticket will receive a prize. If three tickets are purchased at random, what is the probability of each of the following?

a All three tickets are winners.

b Exactly one of the tickets is a winner.

c At least one of the tickets is a winner.

6.104 A financial analyst estimates that a certain mutual fund has a 60% chance of rising in value by more than 15% over the coming year. She also predicts that the stock market in general, as measured by the S & P 500 Index, has only a 20% chance of rising more than 15%. But if the Index does so, she feels that the mutual fund has a 95% chance of rising by more than 15%.

a Find the probability that both the S & P 500 Index and the mutual fund will rise in value by more than 15%.

b Find the probability that either the Index or the mutual fund, or both, will rise by more than 15%.

6.105 Because the likelihood of an event's occurring is sometimes expressed in terms of betting *odds* rather than probability, it is useful to be able to convert odds into probabilities, and vice versa. If the odds of an event's occurring are a to b, then the probability that the event will occur is $a/(a + b)$. The probability that the event will not occur is therefore $b/(a + b)$. Find the probability that an event A will occur, if the odds that A will occur are as follows.

a 4 to 1   **b** 3 to 2   **c** 3 to 5

6.106 Many authors have developed models, based on financial ratios, that predict whether or not a company will go bankrupt in the next year. In a test of one such model, the model correctly predicted the bankruptcy of 85% of firms that in fact did fail, and it correctly predicted nonbankruptcy for 82% of firms that did not fail.* Suppose the model maintains the same reliability when applied to a new group of

---

*Edward Altman and Mario Lavallee, "Business Failure Classification in Canada," *Journal of Business Administration* 12 (1980): 147–64.

100 firms, of which 4 fail in the year following the time at which the model makes its predictions.

   a Determine the number of firms for which the model's prediction will prove to be correct.

   b Find the probability that one of these firms will go bankrupt, given that the model has predicted it will do so.

6.107 A gas plant in Texas is equipped with a standby generator that automatically starts up if the main power fails. It is estimated that, on any given day, there is a 1.5% chance that the main power supply will fail. The standby generator is 95% reliable; should it fail, there is also a battery-driven utility power system (UPS) available. The UPS consists of six batteries connected in parallel so that power is supplied by the UPS if any one of the six batteries is properly charged. The UPS can supply sufficient power for *n* hours, where *n* is the number of batteries properly charged. For each of the six batteries, there is a probability of .1 that it is not properly charged.

   a Find the probability that all three power sources will fail at the same time.

   b Find the probability that the UPS can supply power for at least two hours.

6.108 A novelty shop sells coins that come up heads two-thirds of the time. The result of flipping two of these coins is observed.

   a Define a sample space for this experiment.

   b Assign probabilities to the simple events.

   c Find the probability of observing exactly one heads.

6.109 A modern version of Russian roulette was invented recently on a small southern Ontario campus by three students (Able, Baker, and Carter): line up six identical cars, two of which have had the master brake cylinder secretly removed by participating sweethearts. Each player then randomly selects one car, and one by one (in alphabetical order) they drive at high speed toward the edge of the cliff. At the cliff, they slam on the brakes in time to stop. The first player over the cliff loses, and the game stops. Before they will agree to play the game, however, the students want to understand the odds better, so they have posed the following two questions.

   a What is each player's probability of losing?

   b What is the probability that there will be no loser?

   If it were your job to advise them, how would you answer each of these probing questions?

6.110 Rachel has reached the finals of her tennis club's annual tournament, but she must await the outcome of a match between Linda and Tina before knowing who her opponent will be. Observers feel that Rachel has a 50% chance of winning if she plays Linda and a 75% chance of winning if she plays Tina. They also believe that the probability that Linda will reach the finals is .8. After the final match is played, you are told that Rachel won. What is the probability that she played Linda?

6.111 Consider a roulette wheel that is divided into 36 equal segments, numbered from 1 to 36. The wheel has stopped at an even number on each of the last 16 spins. On the next spin of the wheel, would you bet on an even number or an odd number? Explain your answer.

6.112 Bill and Irma are planning to take a two-week vacation in Hawaii, but they can't decide whether to spend one week on each of the islands of Maui and Oahu, two weeks on Maui, or two weeks on Oahu. Agreeing to leave the decision to chance, Bill places two Maui brochures in one envelope, two Oahu brochures in a second

envelope, and a brochure from each of the two islands in a third env
to select one envelope, and they will spend two weeks on Maui if t
Maui brochures, and so on. After selecting one envelope at rando
one brochure from the envelope and notes that it is a Maui broc
probability that the other brochure in the envelope is a Maui brochu
ceed with caution!)

6.113 Let X be a random variable with the following probability distribution.

x	0	2	4	6	8
$p(x)$	.10	.20	.25	.30	.15

   a   Find the expected value and the standard deviation of X.

   b   Find $E(X^2)$.

   c   Find $E(4X^2 - 5)$.

   d   Find the expected value and the standard deviation of $3X + 7$.

6.114 Two coins are selected from a box containing four coins: a nickel, two dimes, and a quarter. Let X be the number of dimes selected.

   a   Express the probability distribution of X in tabular form.

   b   Express the probability distribution of X in graphical form.

6.115 A large manufacturer has purchased an insurance policy for \$500,000 per year to insure itself against four specific types of losses. The cost associated with each type of loss and its probability are listed in the following table.

COST	PROBABILITY	COST	PROBABILITY
\$100,000	.15	\$1,500,000	.08
800,000	.10	2,500,000	.04

Of the total cost of the policy, 20% goes to cover administrative expenses.

   a   What is the expected *profit* to the insurance company on this policy?

   b   What is the standard deviation of the profits to the insurance company?

6.116 Let X, Y, and W be the three random variables with the following probability distribution.

x	$p(x)$	y	$p(y)$	w	$p(w)$
2	1/4	2	1/8	1	1/4
4	1/4	4	3/8	4	1/4
6	1/4	6	3/8	6	1/4
8	1/4	8	1/8	9	1/4

   a   Determine the means of X, Y, and W simply by inspection.

   b   Verify your answers to part (a) by calculating the means.

   c   Without performing any calculations, determine which of the three distributions has the smallest variance and which has the largest. Explain your reasoning. (HINT: Compare X with Y and X with W.)

   d   Verify your answer to part (c) by computing the variances.

6.117 An investor intends to place one-quarter of his funds in a real estate venture and the remaining three-quarters in a portfolio of common stocks. The real estate venture has an expected return of 28% with a standard deviation of 20%, while the stock portfolio has an expected return of 12% with a standard deviation of 6%. Assume that the returns on these two investments are independent.

  a What are the expected value and the standard deviation of the return on the total amount of funds invested? (HINT: Let X be the return on the real estate venture, let Y be the return on the stock portfolio, and express the return on the total funds invested as a function of X and Y.)

  b Using the variance of the possible returns on an investment as a measure of its relative riskiness, rank the real estate venture, the stock portfolio, and the combination of the two in order of increasing riskiness.

6.118 Exercise 6.40 gave the probability distribution of the number of children in American families. Use the data in that exercise to find the probability distribution of the number of children in families having at least one child. (This is called a **conditional probability distribution**.)

6.119 Let X be a binomial random variable with $n = 20$ and $p = .4$. Use Table 1 of Appendix B to find the following probabilities.

  a $P(X \le 3)$ **b** $P(X = 3)$ **c** $P(X \ge 6)$
  d $P(X > 9)$ **e** $P(4 < X \le 8)$ **f** $P(7 \le X \le 9)$

6.120 The BDW car dealership sells one sports model, the FX500. Of the customers who buy this model, 50% choose fire-engine red as the color, 30% choose snow white, and 20% choose jet black.

  a What is the probability that at least 6 of the next 10 customers who buy an FX500 model will choose red cars?

  b On average, a customer who buys a red FX500 orders options worth $3,000. Customers who buy white FX500 models buy only $2,000 worth of options, and those who buy black FX500 models buy $1,500 worth of options. What is the expected value of the options bought by the next 10 customers who buy an FX500?

6.121 Financing acquisitions often takes the form of putting together a leveraged buyout (LBO), in which a substantial portion of the purchase price is financed by debt. Bankers look at a number of factors when evaluating an LBO proposal. In the United States, an estimated 70% of all LBO proposals are not accepted by bankers (*Canadian Business*, August 1985). If 25 LBO proposals are randomly selected for consideration by a bank, find the probability that each of the following occurs.

  a Not more than 8 are accepted.
  b Exactly 8 are accepted.
  c More than 8 are accepted.
  d At least 5 but fewer than 12 are accepted.

6.122 What assumptions did you make in answering Exercise 6.121?

6.123 ACME Plumbing Supply has just received a shipment of 5,000 stainless steel valves that are designed to be used in chemical plants producing acidic chemicals that corrode regular steel valves. Minutes after receiving the valves, the supplier calls to inform ACME that one of its employees inadvertently included 100 regular steel valves in the shipment. Unfortunately, there is no way to distinguish the regular valves from the stainless ones without extensive testing. At about the same time, ACME receives an emergency order for 5 of the stainless steel valves from one of its largest customers.

  a If ACME decides to fill the order for 5 stainless steel valves, what is the probability that 1 or more will be regular steel valves?

b If ACME explains its predicament to the customer and ships 6 v
the customer is to test prior to use, what is the probability that
them will be stainless steel?

6.124 Suppose a machine breaks down occasionally as a result of a part
wears out, and suppose these breakdowns occur randomly and indepen
average number of breakdowns per 8-hour day is four, and the distribution o
breakdowns is stable within the 8-hour day.

   a Find the probability that no breakdowns will occur during a given day.

   b Find the probability that at most two breakdowns will occur during the first
hour of the day.

   c What is the minimum number of spare parts that management should have on
hand on a given day if it wants to be at least 90% sure that the machine will
not be idle at any time during the day because of a lack of parts?

6.125 The MacTell Toy Company produces toy fire trucks. Suppose that records kept on
the imperfections per fire truck show that the imperfections observed arise independently of one another and are unpredictable in nature. That is, the distribution of
the number of imperfections approximates a Poisson distribution. The records also
indicate that the fire trucks are produced with a mean imperfection rate of .5 per
truck.

   An order for 1,000 toy fire trucks has been received. The cost department must
estimate the total cost of repairing the trucks before the work begins. Past experience indicates that the first imperfection on each fire truck costs 20¢ to repair, while
each subsequent imperfection on a fire truck costs 10¢ to repair. (Thus, a truck with
three imperfections costs 40¢ to repair.) Find the total expected repair cost involved
in supplying the order for 1,000 fire trucks.

6.126 In 1986, the Bank of Canada made some changes in the design and coloring of its
$5 bills. Users of banks' automated teller machines soon discovered that the
machines would sometimes make a mistake, due to the coloring, and would issue
two $5 bills when only one was called for. The manufacturer of the machines claims
that remedying the problem isn't worth the cost, because the chance that a mistake
will be made on any one transaction is only 1 in 500. If one of these machines han-
dles 250 transactions on a given day, what is the probability that the machine will
make more than two mistakes that day?

6.127 The sales manager for a national women's apparel distributor claims that 20% of
the company's orders are for a low-end line of apparel, 70% are for a medium line,
and 10% are for a high-end line.

   a If the next 5 orders are independent of one another, what is the probability that
at least 3 of them will be for a medium line of apparel?

   b If the next 15 orders are independent of one another, what is the probability
that at most 8 of them will be for a low-end line of apparel?

   c Suppose that 30% of orders for a low-end line of apparel include an order for
some accessories (such as hats or jewelry), 50% of orders for a medium line
include an order for accessories, and 40% of orders for a high-end line include
an order for accessories. What is the probability that an order for accessories
will be included in the next order for an apparel line?

6.128 A boat broker in Florida receives an average of 26 orders per year for an exotic
model of cruiser. Assuming that the demand for this model is uniform throughout
the year, what is the probability that the boat broker will receive the following?

   a exactly 1 order for this model in a given week

   b exactly 2 orders for this model over a given two-week period

   c exactly 4 orders for this model over a given four-week period

6.129 A maintenance worker in a large paper-manufacturing plant knows that, on average, the main pulper (which beats solid materials to a pulp) breaks down six times per 30-day month. Find the probability that, on a given day, she will have to repair the pulper the following number of times.

a exactly once

b at least once

c at least once but not more than twice

6.130 The scheduling manager for a certain hydro-power utility company knows that there are an average of 12 emergency calls regarding power failures per month. Assume that a month consists of 30 days.

a Find the probability that the company will receive at least 12 emergency calls during a specified month.

b Suppose the utility company can handle a maximum of 3 emergency calls per day. What is the probability that there will be more emergency calls than the company can handle on a given day?

CASE 6.1 **LET'S MAKE A DEAL**

A number of years ago, there was a popular television game show called "Let's Make a Deal." The host, Monty Hall, would randomly select contestants from the audience and, as the title suggests, he would make deals for prizes. Contestants would be given relatively modest prizes and then would be offered the opportunity to risk that prize to win better ones.

Suppose you are a contestant on this show. Monty has just given you a free trip worth $500 to a locale that is of little interest to you. He now offers you a trade: give up the trip in exchange for a gamble. On the stage are three curtains, A, B, and C. Behind one of them is a brand new car worth $20,000. Behind the other two curtains, the stage is empty. You decide to gamble and you select Curtain A. In an attempt to make things more interesting, Monty then exposes an empty stage by opening Curtain C (he knows that there is nothing behind Curtain C). He then offers you the free trip again if you now quit or, if you like, propose another deal. What do you do?

CASE 6.2 **GAINS FROM MARKET TIMING**

Many investment managers employ a strategy called *market timing*, which involves forecasting the direction of the overall stock market and adjusting one's investment holdings accordingly. A study conducted by Sharpe* provides insight into how accurate a manager's forecasts must be in order to make a market-timing strategy worthwhile.

---

*William F. Sharpe, "Likely Gains from Market Timing," *Financial Analysts' Journal* 31 (1975): 60–69.

Sharpe considers the case of a manager who, at the beginning of each year, either invests all funds in stocks for the entire year (if a good year is forecast) or places all funds in cash equivalents for the entire year (if a bad year is forecast). A good year is defined as one in which the rate of return on stocks (as represented by the Standard and Poor's Composite Index) is higher than the rate of return on cash equivalents (as represented by U.S. Treasury bills). A bad year is one that is not good. The average annual returns for the period from 1934 to 1972 on stocks and on cash equivalents, both for good years and for bad years, are shown in the accompanying table. Two-thirds of the years from 1934 to 1972 were good years.

a Suppose a manager decides to remain fully invested in the stock market at all times rather than employing market timing. What annual rate of return can this manager expect?

b Suppose a market timer accurately predicts a good year 80% of the time and accurately predicts a bad year 80% of the time. What is the probability that this manager will predict a good year? What annual rate of return can this manager expect?

c What is the expected rate of return for a manager who has perfect foresight?

d Consider a market timer who has no predictive ability whatsoever, but who recognizes that a good year will occur two-thirds of the time. Following Sharpe's description, imagine this manager "throwing a die every year, then predicting a good year if numbers 1 through 4 turn up, and a bad year if number 5 or 6 turns up." What is the probability that this manager will make a correct prediction in any given year? What annual rate of return can this manager expect?

| | AVERAGE ANNUAL RETURNS | |
TYPE OF YEAR	STOCKS	CASH EQUIVALENTS
Good year	22.99%	2.27%
Bad year	−7.70	2.68

CALCULATING PROBABILITIES ASSOCIATED WITH THE STOCK MARKET

The Value Line Investment Survey is a stock market advisory service that is well known for its fine performance record. Value Line follows 1,700 stocks. Every week it assigns each stock a ranking of from 1 (best) to 5 (worst) indicating the stock's timeliness for purchase. There are always 100 stocks in the (top) Rank 1 group.

Suppose that, at the beginning of a calendar year, a portfolio (called the passive Rank 1 portfolio) consisting of the 100 Rank 1 stocks is formed and is held, unchanged, for one year. At the end of the year, the rate of return on this passive Rank 1 portfolio is compared to the return on the market portfolio, which consists of all 1,700 stocks. Holloway observed that the passive Rank 1 portfolio outperformed the market portfolio in each of the 14 years from 1965 to 1978, with the exception of 1970.* The probability that this would occur by chance is .00085. After noting that the performances of the two portfolios were almost identical in two of the years (1975 and 1976), Holloway stated: "Even if we count these two years as failures, the probability of obtaining the Value Line results by *chance* is only .0286." Subsequently, Gregory took exception to this statement and wrote: "That observation is a misuse of statistics."[†] He pointed out that, while the probability of .0286 would be correct if applied to an advisory service selected at random, Value Line was selected *because of* its fine performance record. Gregory then noted that "out of a population of, say, 20 investment advisory services, the probability of finding at least one with 3 [or fewer] bad years out of 14 is .44." In other words, it isn't all that surprising to find one advisory service with such a good performance record.

Holloway also examined an active portfolio strategy, in which the Rank 1 portfolio was "updated weekly to consist always of the 100 Rank 1 stocks." This strategy "outperformed the market in each of the 14 consecutive years" from 1965 to 1978, neglecting the brokerage commission incurred whenever a stock was bought or sold. Although the probability of achieving this performance by chance is only .000061, analysis of results that included brokerage commissions indicated that performance under this active strategy was not significantly superior to the performance of the passive Rank 1 portfolio.

In another phase of Holloway's study, the 100 Rank 1 stocks were partitioned into 5 subportfolios. Holloway monitored the performance of each of the 5 subportfolios over the 4 years from 1974 to 1977, thereby observing 20 returns. These were compared with the 20 corresponding returns from a passive (buy-and-hold) strategy. The active strategy performed better than the passive strategy in 17 of these 20 cases when brokerage commissions were not considered, but it was superior in only 12 of these cases when brokerage costs were included. Are either of these two results significantly different from what could be expected to happen simply by chance?

Verify the values of the four different probabilities mentioned in this case.

*Clark Holloway, "A Note on Testing an Aggressive Investment Strategy Using Value Line Ranks," *Journal of Finance* 36(3) (1981): 711–19.

†N. A. Gregory, "Testing an Aggressive Investment Strategy Using Value Line Ranks: A Comment," *Journal of Finance* 38(1) (1983): 257–70.

Calculating Binomial and Poisson Probabilities

Menu Commands

To calculate binomial probabilities, proceed as follows.

1 Click **Calc**, **Probability Distributions**, and **Binomial . . . .**
2 Use the cursor to specifiy either **Probability** [to compute $p(x)$] or **Cumulative probability** [to compute $P(X \le x)$].
3 Hit **tab** and type the value of n (**Number of trials:**).
4 Hit **tab** and type the value of p (**Probability of success:**).
5 Click **Input column**, hit **tab**, and type the value of x. Click **OK**.

If you have several values of x, store them in a column (say, column 1) and proceed as above, except at step 5, click **Input column**, hit **tab**, and type the column number (**C1**). Click **OK**.

To compute Poisson probabilities click **Poisson . . .** instead of **Binomial . . .** in step 1.

Session Commands

Use the **PDF** command with an appropriate subcommand to compute binomial probabilities. For example, to determine the probability that a binomial random variable with $n = 10$ and $p = .3$ is equal to 4, type the following command and subcommand

> **PDF 4;**
> **BINOMIAL 10 .3.**

To compute cumulative probabilities use the **CDF** command. For example, to find $P(X \le 4)$ where X is binomial distributed with $n = 10$ and $p = .3$, type

> **CDF 4;**
> **BINOMIAL 10 .3.**

If you have several values of x, store them in a column (say, column 1) and type

> **PDF C1; (or CDF C1;)**
> **BINOMIAL 10 .3.**

To compute Poisson probabilities use the **POISSON** subcommand and specify the value of μ. For example,

> **PDF 4;**
> **POISSON 6.**

will produce $P(X = 4)$ given that X is Poisson distributed with $\mu = 6$. We can also use the **CDF** command, and we can calculate the probabilities of the a column of values of x.

EXCEL 97

Calculating Binomial and Poisson Probabilities

Excel 97 Users:
Click **OK** instead of **Next>** and **Finish.**

To calculate binomial probabilities, proceed as follows.

1 Click f$_x$, **Function Category: Statistical**, and **Function Name: BINOMDIST**. Click **Next >**.

2 Use the cursor and type the value of x (**number_s**), the number of n (**trials**), the probability of success p (**probability**), and true (**cumulative**). Click **Finish**. This will produce $P(X \le x)$. If you type false (**cumulative**), Excel will compute $P(X = x)$.

To compute Poisson probabilities click **POISSON** instead of **BINOMDIST** in step 1.

7 Continuous Probability Distributions

7.1 Introduction

This chapter continues our discussion of probability distributions. We begin by describing continuous probability distributions in general, and then we take a detailed look at the normal distribution, which is the most important specific continuous distribution. The normal distribution will be used extensively when we cover statistical inference. We conclude with a discussion of yet another important specific continuous distribution: the exponential distribution.

7.2 Continuous Probability Distributions

Up to this point, we have focused our attention on discrete distributions—distributions of random variables that have either a finite number of possible values (for example, $x = 0, 1, 2, \ldots, n$) or a countably infinite number of values ($x = 0, 1, 2, \ldots$). In contrast, a continuous random variable has an uncountably infinite number of possible values and can assume any value in the interval between two points a and b ($a < x < b$). Whereas discrete random variables typically involve counting, continuous random variables typically involve measurement attributes such as length, weight, time, and temperature.

One major distinction between a continuous and a discrete random variable relates to the numerical events of interest. We can list all possible values of a discrete random variable, and it is meaningful to consider the probability that a particular individual value will be assumed. On the other hand, we cannot list all the values of a continuous random variable—because there is always another possible value between any two of its values—so the only meaningful events for a continuous random variable are intervals. *The probability that a continuous random variable X will assume any particular value is zero.* While this may appear strange at first, it becomes reasonable when you consider that you could not possibly assign a positive probability to each of the (uncountably) infinitely many values of X and still have the probabilities sum to 1. This situation is analogous to the fact that, while a line segment has a positive length, no single point on the line segment does. For a continuous random variable X, then, it is meaningful only to talk only about the probability that the value assumed by X will fall within some interval of values.

We first encountered continuous data in Chapter 2, when we considered the distribution of long-distance telephone bills. We encountered continuous distributions again in Chapter 4, when we discussed the Empirical Rule. In particular, we illustrated the application of the Empirical Rule using the distribution of a sample of telephone call durations. The relative frequency histogram for these telephone call durations (Figure 4.5) is reproduced in Figure 7.1, with one slight alteration: the heights of the rectangles have been scaled down so that the total area under the histogram is equal to 1. The area under a rectangle now represents the proportion of measurements falling into that class. For example, the area under the first rectangle is $3(3/90) = 3/30$, which is the proportion of telephone call durations falling between 2 and 5 minutes. If we had taken a very large sample of measurements, the resulting relative frequency distribution would closely approximate the relative frequency distribution of the entire population of telephone call durations, and the proportion represented by the area of a rectangle would be a very good approximation of the true probability of obtaining a measurement in the class interval corresponding to that rectangle. Experience has shown that, as the size of the sample of measurements becomes larger and as the class width is reduced, the outline of the relative frequency distribution tends toward a smooth curve. That is, the shape of the relative frequency polygon (adjusted to have a total area equal to 1) for the entire population of measurements progressively approaches a smooth curve.

Figure 7.1

Relative Frequency Histogram

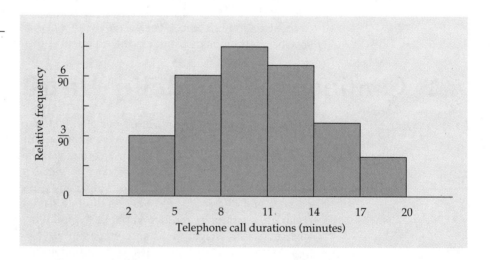

When dealing with continuous data, we attempt to find a function $f(x)$, called a **probability density function**, whose graph approximates the relative frequency polygon for the population. A probability density function $f(x)$ must satisfy two conditions:

1 $f(x)$ is nonnegative.

2 The total area under the curve representing $f(x)$ equals 1.

It is important to note that $f(x)$ is not a probability. That is, $f(x) \neq P(X = x)$. As previously mentioned, the probability that X will take any specific value is zero: $P(X = x) = 0$. Given a probability density function $f(x)$, the area under the graph of $f(x)$ between the two values a and b is the probability that X will take a value between a and b.* This area is the shaded area in Figure 7.2.

Figure 7.2

Probability Density Function $f(x)$ [Shaded Area Is $P(a < X < b)$]

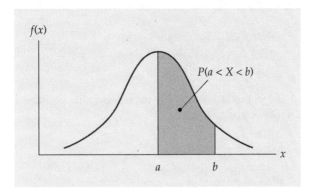

A continuous random variable X has an expected value and a variance, just as a discrete variable does. Earlier in this chapter, we saw how to compute the expected value and the variance of any discrete random variable; we also saw that when dealing with a well-known discrete distribution such as the binomial or Poisson, we need not calculate the expected value and the variance from their definitions, because these parameters are well known. Similarly, most continuous distributions used in practice are well-known distributions with expected values and variances that are also well known and therefore need not be computed.†

Uniform Distribution

A continuous distribution that possesses appealing descriptive simplicity but unfortunately has limited practical application (except as a theoretical tool) is the **uniform distribution**. The domain of a uniform random variable X consists of all values within some interval $a \leq x \leq b$.

---

*Students who have taken calculus will recognize that

$$P(a < X < b) = \int_a^b f(x)\, dx$$

The two conditions to be satisfied by a probability density function $f(x)$ are $f(x) \geq 0$ and

$$\int_{-\infty}^{\infty} f(x)\, dx = 1$$

†For students who are interested and know calculus, the expected value and the variance of a continuous random variable X with probability density function $f(x)$ are given by

$$E(X) = \mu = \int_{-\infty}^{\infty} x f(x)\, dx$$

$$V(X) = \sigma^2 = \int_{-\infty}^{\infty} (x - \mu)^2 f(x)\, dx$$

These expressions are the same as those for the discrete case, except that summation is replaced by integration.

Uniform Distribution

A random variable X, defined over an interval $a \le x \le b$, is uniformly distributed if its probability density function is given by

$$f(x) = \frac{1}{b - a} \qquad a \le x \le b$$

It can be shown that the expected value and the variance of a uniform random variable X are as follows.

$$E(X) = \frac{a + b}{2}$$

$$V(X) = \frac{(b - a)^2}{12}$$

Note that the expected value of X is simply the midpoint of the domain of X, which should appeal to your intuition, given the symmetrical shape of the probability density function of X. As is evident from Figure 7.3, the values of a uniform random variable X are distributed evenly, or uniformly, across the domain of X. In other words, intervals of equal size within the domain of X are equally likely to contain the value that the variable X will assume.

Figure 7.3

Uniform Distribution

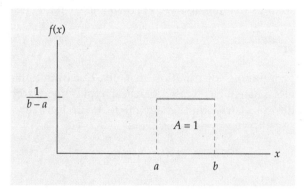

Notice that the total area A under the uniform density function $f(x)$ equals 1, as is required for any probability function. The area A of the rectangle under $f(x)$ is the height of the rectangle, $1/(b - a)$, times its base.

$$A = \left(\frac{1}{b - a} \right) \cdot (b - a) = 1$$

The probability that X will take a value within any given interval is found in a similar manner by multiplying $1/(b - a)$ by the width of the interval in question.

EXAMPLE 7.1

A manufacturer has observed that the time that elapses between the placement of an order with a just-in-time supplier and the delivery of the parts is uniformly distributed between 100 and 180 minutes.

a Define and graph the density function.

b What proportion of orders takes between 2 and 2.5 hours to be delivered?

SOLUTION

a If X denotes the number of minutes that elapse between the placement and delivery of the order, then X can take any value in the interval $100 \leq x \leq 180$. Because the width of the interval is 80, the height of the density function must be 1/80, in order for the total area under the density function to equal 1. That is, the density function is

$$f(x) = 1/80, \qquad 100 \leq x \leq 180$$

The graph of this function is shown in Figure 7.4.

Figure 7.4

Shaded Area Is
$P(120 \leq X \leq 150)$

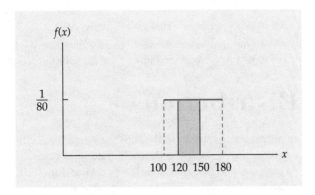

b The required probability, which is represented by the shaded area in Figure 7.4, is

$$P(120 \leq X \leq 150) = (\text{Base})(\text{Height}) = (150 - 120)(1/80) = .375$$

Exercises

7.1 Consider a random variable X with a probability density function described by

$$f(x) = -.5x + 1, \qquad 0 \leq x \leq 2$$

a Graph the density function $f(x)$.

b Verify that $f(x)$ is a probability density function.

c Find $P(X \geq 1)$.

d Find $P(X \leq .5)$.

e Find $P(X = 1.5)$.

7.2 Consider a random variable X having the uniform density function $f(x)$, with $a = 20$ and $b = 30$.

a Define and graph the density function $f(x)$.

b Verify that $f(x)$ is a probability density function.

c Find $P(22 \leq X \leq 30)$.

d Find $P(X = 25)$.

e Find $P(X \leq 25)$.

7.3   Consider a random variable X with probability density function described by

$$f(x) = \begin{cases} .2 + .04x, & -5 \le x \le 0 \\ .2 - .04x, & 0 \le x \le 5 \end{cases}$$

    a   Graph the density function $f(x)$.

    b   Verify that $f(x)$ is a probability density function.

    c   Find $P(X \ge -2)$.

    d   Find $P(X \le 3)$.

    e   Find $P(3 \le X \le 5)$.

7.4   A hospital receives a pharmaceutical delivery each morning at a time that varies uniformly between 7:00 and 8:00 A.M.

    a   Find the probability that the delivery on a given morning will occur between 7:15 and 7:30 A.M.

    b   What is the expected time of delivery?

    c   Find the probability that the time of delivery will be within 1 standard deviation of the expected time—that is, within the interval $\mu - \sigma \le x \le \mu + \sigma$.

7.3 Normal Distribution

The normal distribution is the most important specific continuous distribution that we will consider in some detail. Other important continuous distributions (most of which we will encounter in later chapters) include the exponential distribution, the Student t distribution, the chi-squared distribution, and the F distribution. The graph of the normal distribution is the familiar symmetrical, bell-shaped curve shown in Figure 7.5. One reason for the importance of the normal distribution is that it usefully models or describes the distributions of numerous random variables that arise in practice, such as the heights or weights of a group of people, the total annual sales of a firm, the grades of a class of students, and the measurement errors that arise in the performance of an experiment. In examples such as these, the observed measurements tend to cluster in a symmetrical fashion about the central value, giving rise to a bell-shaped distribution curve.

Figure 7.5

Symmetrical, Bell-Shaped Normal Distribution

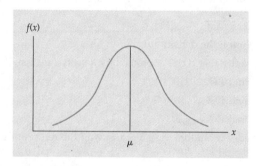

A second reason for the normal distribution's importance is that this distribution provides a useful approximation to many other distributions, including discrete ones such as the binomial distribution. Finally, as we will see in Chapter 9, the normal distribution is the cornerstone distribution of statistical inference, representing the distribution of the possible estimates of a population parameter that may arise from different samples. This last point, in fact, is the main reason for the importance of the normal distribution.

Normal Distribution

A random variable X with mean μ and variance σ^2 is normally distributed if its probability density function is given by

$$f(x) = \left(\frac{1}{\sigma\sqrt{2\pi}}\right)e^{-(1/2)[(x-\mu)/\sigma]^2}, \quad -\infty < x < \infty$$

where $\pi = 3.14159\ldots$ and $e = 2.71828\ldots$.

A random variable that is normally distributed is called a **normal random variable**. A normal random variable can take on any real value from $-\infty$ to $+\infty$, and the normal probability density function $f(x)$ is continuous and has a positive value for all values of x. As is the case with any other probability density function, the value of $f(x)$ here is not the probability that X assumes the value x, but an expression of the height of the curve at the value x. Moreover, the entire area under the curve depicting $f(x)$ must equal 1.

It is apparent from the formula for the probability density function that a normal distribution is completely determined once the parameters μ and σ^2 are specified. That is, a whole family of different normal distributions exists, but one differs from another only in the location of its mean μ and in the variance σ^2 of its values; all normal distributions have the same symmetrical, bell-shaped appearance. Figure 7.6 depicts three normal distributions with the same variance but different means, while Figure 7.7 shows three normal distributions with the same mean but different variances. Notice that the shape of the distribution becomes flatter and more spread out as the variance becomes larger.

Figure 7.6

Normal Distributions with the Same Variance but Different Means

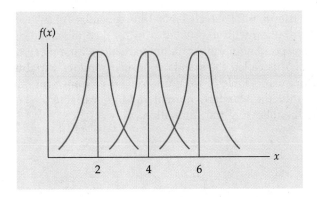

Figure 7.7

Normal Distributions with the Same Mean but Different Variances

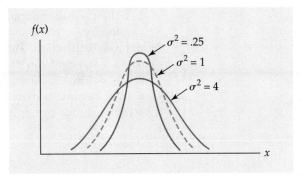

Finding Normal Probabilities

After we determine that a situation can be modeled appropriately by using a normal distribution, we'll want to find various normal probabilities, which are represented by areas under the normal curve. The procedure for finding normal probabilities is illustrated in the following example.

Suppose that the length of time students take in writing a standard entrance examination is known to be normally distributed, with a mean of 60 minutes and a standard deviation of 8 minutes. If we observe the time taken by a particular student, what is the probability that the student's time will be between 60 and 70 minutes?

Given that X denotes the time taken to write the entrance examination, the probability we are seeking is written $P(60 < X < 70)$.* This probability is given by the area under the normal curve between 60 and 70, depicted by the shaded region in Figure 7.8(a). The actual calculation of such an area (probability) is difficult, however, so we will resort to the tabulated areas provided by Table 3 in Appendix B.†

Because each pair of values for the parameters μ and σ^2 gives rise to a different normal distribution, there are infinitely many possible normal distributions, making it impossible to provide a table of areas for each one. Fortunately, we can make do with just one table.

Figure 7.8

Shaded Area Is
$P(60 < X < 70)$
$= P(0 < Z < 1.25)$

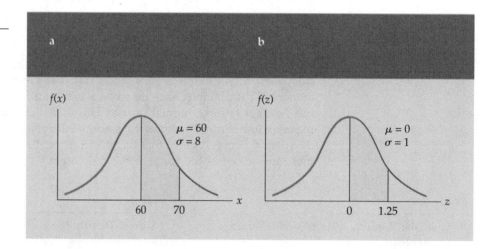

The particular normal distribution for which Table 3 in Appendix B has been constructed is the normal distribution with $\mu = 0$ and $\sigma = 1$, called the **standard normal distribution**. The corresponding normal random variable, with a mean of 0 and a standard deviation of 1, is called the **standard normal random variable** and is denoted Z. Thus, before using Table 3, we must convert or transform our normal random variable X into the standard normal random variable Z. We accomplish this by applying the following transformation.

---

*Recall that the probability that a continuous random variable X will assume any particular value is zero. Hence, $P(60 \leq X \leq 70) = P(60 < X < 70)$. These two forms for expressing a normal probability will therefore be used interchangeably.

†For students familiar with calculus, the probability that X takes a value between a and b is given by

$$P(a < X < b) = \int_a^b \left(\frac{1}{\sigma\sqrt{2\pi}} \right) e^{-(1/2)[(x - \mu)/\sigma]^2} \, dx$$

Standard Normal Random Variable

$$Z = \frac{X - \mu_x}{\sigma_x}$$

For our example, we obtain

$$Z = \frac{X - 60}{8}$$

We can easily verify, using the laws of expected value and of variance, that we have created a random variable Z with a mean of 0 and a standard deviation of 1 (see Exercise 6.55). Moreover, it can be shown that Z is normally distributed. The interpretation of Z is most important. A value of Z equals the distance from the corresponding value of X to μ, measured in standard deviations of X.

In order to find the desired probability, $P(60 < X < 70)$, we must first determine the interval of z-values corresponding to the interval of x-values of interest: $60 < x < 70$. Using elementary algebra, we know that $60 < x < 70$ holds whenever

$$\frac{60 - 60}{8} < \frac{x - 60}{8} < \frac{70 - 60}{8}$$

or

$$0 < z < 1.25$$

We therefore obtain

$$P(60 < X < 70) = P(0 < Z < 1.25)$$

Thus, we can find the required area (probability) by finding the corresponding area under the standard normal curve, which is depicted by the shaded area in Figure 7.8(b). Areas like this that correspond to probabilities of the form $P(0 < Z < z_0)$ are tabulated in Table 3 in Appendix B. Table 3 is reproduced here as Table 7.1.

In Table 3 (and in Table 7.1), a value of z that is correct to the first decimal place is found in the left-hand column; the second decimal place is located across the top row. We need to find $P(0 < Z < 1.25)$, which is represented by the area over the interval from 0 to 1.25. To find this area corresponding to $z = 1.25$, first locate 1.2 in the left-hand column and then move across the row until you reach the column with .05 at the top. The area corresponding to $z = 1.25$ is .3944, so

$$P(60 < X < 70) = P(0 < Z < 1.25)$$
$$= .3944$$

The probability that a particular student will take between 60 and 70 minutes to write the entrance exam is therefore .3944.

We repeat that the z-value corresponding to a given value x_0 has an important interpretation. Because $(x_0 - \mu)$ expresses how far x_0 is from the mean, the corresponding z-value

$$z_0 = \frac{x_0 - \mu}{\sigma}$$

tells us how many standard deviations x_0 is from the mean. Moreover, if z_0 is positive, then x_0 lies to the right of the mean; conversely, if z_0 is negative, then x_0 lies to the left of the mean. Thus, in the preceding example, the value 70 lies 1.25 standard deviations to the right of the mean value of 60; that is, $70 = 60 + 1.25(8)$.

Table 7.1 Reproduction of Table 3: Standard Normal Curve Areas

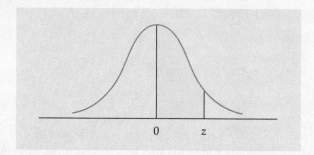

z	.00	.01	.02	.03	.04	.05	.06	.07	.08	.09
0.0	.0000	.0040	.0080	.0120	.0160	.0199	.0239	.0279	.0319	.0359
0.1	.0398	.0438	.0478	.0517	.0557	.0596	.0636	.0675	.0714	.0753
0.2	.0793	.0832	.0871	.0910	.0948	.0987	.1026	.1064	.1103	.1141
0.3	.1179	.1217	.1255	.1293	.1331	.1368	.1406	.1443	.1480	.1517
0.4	.1554	.1591	.1628	.1664	.1700	.1736	.1772	.1808	.1844	.1879
0.5	.1915	.1950	.1985	.2019	.2054	.2088	.2123	.2157	.2190	.2224
0.6	.2257	.2291	.2324	.2357	.2389	.2422	.2454	.2486	.2517	.2549
0.7	.2580	.2611	.2642	.2673	.2704	.2734	.2764	.2794	.2823	.2852
0.8	.2881	.2910	.2939	.2967	.2995	.3023	.3051	.3078	.3106	.3133
0.9	.3159	.3186	.3212	.3238	.3264	.3289	.3315	.3340	.3365	.3389
1.0	.3413	.3438	.3461	.3485	.3508	.3531	.3554	.3577	.3599	.3621
1.1	.3643	.3665	.3686	.3708	.3729	.3749	.3770	.3790	.3810	.3830
1.2	.3849	.3869	.3888	.3907	.3925	.3944	.3962	.3980	.3997	.4015
1.3	.4032	.4049	.4066	.4082	.4099	.4115	.4131	.4147	.4162	.4177
1.4	.4192	.4207	.4222	.4236	.4251	.4265	.4279	.4292	.4306	.4319
1.5	.4332	.4345	.4357	.4370	.4382	.4394	.4406	.4418	.4429	.4441
1.6	.4452	.4463	.4474	.4484	.4495	.4505	.4515	.4525	.4535	.4545
1.7	.4554	.4564	.4573	.4582	.4591	.4599	.4608	.4616	.4625	.4633
1.8	.4641	.4649	.4656	.4664	.4671	.4678	.4686	.4693	.4699	.4706
1.9	.4713	.4719	.4726	.4732	.4738	.4744	.4750	.4756	.4761	.4767
2.0	.4772	.4778	.4783	.4788	.4793	.4798	.4803	.4808	.4812	.4817
2.1	.4821	.4826	.4830	.4834	.4838	.4842	.4846	.4850	.4854	.4857
2.2	.4861	.4864	.4868	.4871	.4875	.4878	.4881	.4884	.4887	.4890
2.3	.4893	.4896	.4898	.4901	.4904	.4906	.4909	.4911	.4913	.4916
2.4	.4918	.4920	.4922	.4925	.4927	.4929	.4931	.4932	.4934	.4936
2.5	.4938	.4940	.4941	.4943	.4945	.4946	.4948	.4949	.4951	.4952
2.6	.4953	.4955	.4956	.4957	.4959	.4960	.4961	.4962	.4963	.4964
2.7	.4965	.4966	.4967	.4968	.4969	.4970	.4971	.4972	.4973	.4974
2.8	.4974	.4975	.4976	.4977	.4977	.4978	.4979	.4979	.4980	.4981
2.9	.4981	.4982	.4982	.4983	.4984	.4984	.4985	.4985	.4986	.4986
3.0	.4987	.4987	.4987	.4988	.4988	.4989	.4989	.4989	.4990	.4990

SOURCE: Abridged from Table 1 of A. Hald, *Statistical Tables and Formulas* (New York: John Wiley & Sons), 1952. Reproduced by permission.

As we have just seen, we can obtain desired probabilities for any normal distribution from probabilities tabulated for the standard normal distribution. A table of probabilities for just one normal distribution supplies us with all the information we need, because normal distributions differ from one another only in their means and variances. The probability that the variable will assume a value within z_0 standard deviations of the mean remains constant from one normal random variable to the next. In other words, if X is any normal random variable with mean μ and standard deviation σ, then

$$P(\mu - z_0\sigma < X < \mu + z_0\sigma) = P(-z_0 < Z < z_0)$$

We first caught a glimpse of this concept when we took up the Empirical Rule in Chapter 4. According to this rule, about 68% of the values from a mound-shaped distribution (such as the normal distribution) lie within 1 standard deviation of the mean, about 95% of the values lie within 2 standard deviations of the mean, and almost 100% of the values lie within 3 standard deviations.*

Therefore, probabilities of the form $P(-z_0 < Z < z_0)$ need only be tabulated for one normal distribution, because they are the same for all others. In fact, because a normal distribution is symmetrical, it suffices to tabulate probabilities of the form $P(0 \leq Z \leq z_0)$. The probabilities found in Table 3 in Appendix B, then, are of the form $P(0 \leq Z \leq z_0)$, for values of z_0 from .00 to 3.09. Given that the total area under the normal curve equals 1, any desired probability can be obtained by adding and subtracting probabilities of this form.

EXAMPLE 7.2

Determine the following probabilities.

   a $P(Z \geq 1.47)$

   b $P(-2.25 \leq Z \leq 1.85)$

   c $P(.65 \leq Z \leq 1.36)$

SOLUTION

   a It is always advisable to begin by sketching a diagram and indicating the area of interest under the normal curve, as shown in Figure 7.9. Area A_1 corresponds to the required probability, and area A_2 is the area between $z = 0$ and $z = 1.47$. Because the entire area under the normal curve equals 1, and because the curve is symmetrical about $z = 0$, the entire area to the right of $z = 0$ is .5. Therefore,

$$A_1 + A_2 = .5$$

---

*For the special mound-shaped distribution called the *normal distribution*, Table 3 in Appendix B identifies the precise percentages as 68.26, 95.44, and 99.74, respectively.

Figure 7.9

Shaded Areas Are
$P(0 < Z < 1.47)$ **and**
$P(Z \geq 1.47)$ **in Example**
7.2(a)

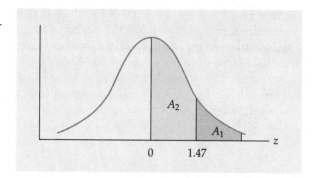

Area A_2 is of the form that can be found in Table 3. Locating $z = 1.47$ in Table 3, we find that area A_2 is .4292, so $P(0 \leq Z \leq 1.47) = .4292$. The required probability is therefore

$$P(Z \geq 1.47) = A_1$$
$$= .5 - A_2$$
$$= .5 - .4292$$
$$= .0708$$

b Whenever the area of interest straddles the mean, as in this situation, we must express it as the sum of the portions to the left and to the right of the mean. The required probability $P(-2.25 \leq Z \leq 1.85)$ corresponds to the sum of the areas A_1 and A_2 in Figure 7.10. That is,

$$P(-2.25 \leq Z \leq 1.85) = A_1 + A_2$$

Figure 7.10

Shaded Area Is
$P(-2.25 \leq Z \leq 1.85)$
in Example 7.2(b)

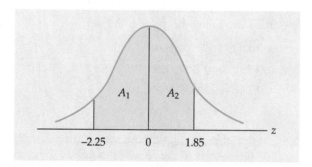

From Table 3, we find that $A_2 = .4678$. Because the normal distribution is symmetrical, we can write

$$A_1 = P(-2.25 \leq Z \leq 0) = P(0 \leq Z \leq 2.25)$$

Locating $z = 2.25$ in Table 3, we find that $A_1 = .4878$. Therefore, the required probability is

$$P(-2.25 \leq Z \leq 1.85) = A_1 + A_2$$
$$= .4878 + .4678$$
$$= .9556$$

c $P(.65 \leq Z \leq 1.36)$ corresponds to the shaded area A in Figure 7.11. Since Table 3 only provides areas from zero up to some positive value of Z, we must express A as the difference between two such areas. If A_1 is the area between $z = 0$ and $z = 1.36$, then $A_1 = .4131$ (from Table 3). Similarly, if A_2 is the area between $z = 0$ and $z = .65$, then $A_2 = .2422$. Therefore,

$$
\begin{aligned}
P(.65 \le Z \le 1.36) &= A \\
&= A_1 - A_2 \\
&= P(0 \le Z \le 1.36) - P(0 \le Z \le .65) \\
&= .4131 - .2422 \\
&= .1709
\end{aligned}
$$

Figure 7.11

Shaded Area Is
$P(0.65 \le Z \le 1.36)$ **in**
Example 7.2(c)

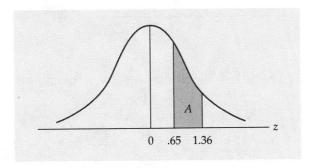

EXAMPLE 7.3

A venture capital company feels that the rate of return (X) on a proposed investment is approximately normally distributed, with a mean of 30% and a standard deviation of 10%.

a Find the probability that the return will exceed 55%.

b Find the probability that the return will be less than 22%.

SOLUTION

a Figure 7.12 shows the required area A_1, together with values of Z corresponding to selected values of X. The value of Z corresponding to $x = 55$ is

$$
z = \frac{x - \mu}{\sigma} = \frac{55 - 30}{10} = 2.5
$$

Therefore,

$$
\begin{aligned}
P(X > 55) &= A_1 \\
&= P(Z > 2.5) \\
&= .5 - P(0 \le Z \le 2.5) \\
&= .5 - .4938 \\
&= .0062
\end{aligned}
$$

The probability that the return will exceed 55% is .0062.

Figure 7.12

Corresponding Values of
X and Z for Example 7.3

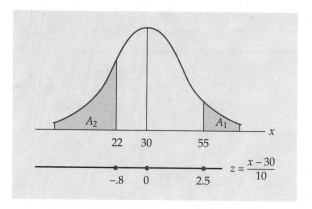

b Figure 7.12 shows the required area A_2. By the same logic as that used in part (a),

$$P(X < 22) = A_2$$

$$= P\left(Z < \frac{22 - 30}{10}\right)$$

$$= P(Z < -.8) = P(Z > .8)$$

$$= .5 - P(0 \le Z \le .8)$$

$$= .5 - .2881$$

$$= .2119$$

The probability that the return will be less than 22% is .2119.

In Appendix 7.A, we describe how Minitab and Excel can be employed to solve these problems.

As we progress throughout this book, we will have need to use the normal table "backwards." That is, we will have a probability, and we will have to find the z-value associated with that probability. Here is an example.

EXAMPLE 7.4

If Z is a standard normal variable, determine the value z for which $P(Z \le z) = .6331$.

SOLUTION

Because the area to the left of 0 is .5 in Figure 7.13, z must be a positive number. Since the area between 0 and z is $P(0 \le Z \le z)$,

$$.6331 = .5 + P(0 \le Z \le z)$$

Therefore,

$$P(0 \leq Z \leq z) = .6331 - .5 = .1331$$

Locating the area .1331 in the body of Table 3, we find that the corresponding value of z is .34. Therefore,

$$P(Z \leq .34) = .6331$$

Figure 7.13

Shaded Area Is
$P(0 \leq Z \leq z)$ **in**
Example 7.4

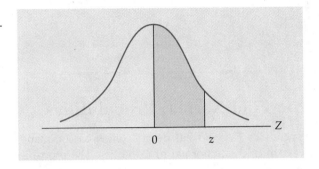

EXAMPLE 7.5

This example introduces some notation that you will use frequently in statistical inference, beginning in Chapter 9. If Z is a standard normal random variable and A is any probability, then z_A represents that value for which the area under the standard normal curve to the right of z_A is A. In other words,

$$P(Z > z_A) = A$$

Thus, because the normal distribution is symmetrical, $-z_A$ represents that value for which the area under the standard normal curve to the left of $-z_A$ is A. Determine $z_{.025}$.

SOLUTION

Since the area in Figure 7.14 between $z = 0$ and $z = z_{.025}$ is given by $P(0 \leq Z \leq z_{.025})$, the desired value $z_{.025}$ is the z-value in Table 3 corresponding to the area $P(0 \leq Z \leq z_{.025})$. But the area under the curve to the right of $z_{.025}$ is .025, so

$$P(0 \leq Z \leq z_{.025}) = .5 - .025 = .475$$

From Table 3, the z-value corresponding to the area .475 is

$$z_{.025} = 1.96$$

so

$$P(Z > 1.96) = .025$$

From symmetry, the area to the left of $z = -1.96$ is also .025. That is,

$$P(Z < -1.96) = .025$$

Figure 7.14

Locating $z_{.025}$ in
Example 7.5

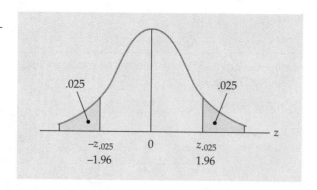

Using the Computer to Find Normal Probabilities

Appendixes 7.A and 7.B describe how to command Minitab and Excel, respectively, to calculate normal probabilities. The probability that is produced is of the form $P(X < x)$, which means that the output is the probability that a normal random variable with a given mean and standard deviation falls between $-\infty$ and x. That is, the computer will print $P(-\infty < X < x)$ for any value of x. Note that the normal table (Table 3 in Appendix B) lists the probabilities of the form $P(0 < Z < z)$.

Normal Approximation to the Binomial

The normal distribution can be used to approximate a number of other probability distributions, including the binomial distribution. The normal approximation to the binomial is useful whenever the number of trials n is so large that the binomial tables cannot be used. Because the normal distribution is symmetrical, it best approximates binomial distributions that are reasonably symmetrical. Therefore, since a binomial distribution is symmetrical when the probability p of a success equals .5, the best approximation is obtained when p is reasonably close to .5. The farther p is from .5, the larger n must be in order for a good approximation to result.

The normal approximation to the binomial distribution works best when only a very small probability exists that the approximating normal random variable will assume a value that falls outside the binomial range ($0 \leq X \leq n$). Generally, this is satisfied if $np \geq 5$ and $nq \geq 5$, so a conventional rule of thumb is that the normal distribution will provide an adequate approximation of a binomial distribution if $np \geq 5$ and $nq \geq 5$. Recall that the Poisson distribution can be used to approximate binomial probabilities when p is small, say $p < .05$.

Given a binomial distribution with n trials and probability p of a success on any trial, the mean of the binomial distribution is $\mu = np$, and the variance is $\sigma^2 = npq$. We therefore choose the normal distribution with $\mu = np$ and $\sigma^2 = npq$ to be the approximating distribution.

To see how the approximation works, consider the binomial distribution with $n = 20$ and $p = .5$, the graph of which is shown in Figure 7.15. Although it is not necessary to use the normal approximation in this case, we have purposely chosen n to be small enough that the binomial tables can be used as a check against the normal approximation. We will approximate the binomial probabilities by using the normal distribution with mean $\mu = (20)(.5) = 10$ and variance $\sigma^2 = 20(.5)(.5) = 5$ (or standard deviation $\sigma = 2.24$). Let X denote the binomial random variable, and let Y denote the normal random variable. The binomial probability $P(X = 10)$, represented by the height of the line above $x = 10$ in Figure 7.15, is equal to the area of the rectangle erected above the interval from 9.5 to 10.5. This area (or probability) is approximated by the area under the normal curve between 9.5 and 10.5. That is,

$$P(X = 10) \cong P(9.5 \leq Y \leq 10.5)$$

The .5 that is added to and subtracted from 10 is called the *continuity correction factor*; it corrects for the fact that we are using a continuous distribution to approximate a discrete distribution. To check the accuracy of this particular approximation, we can use the binomial tables to obtain

$$P(X = 10) = .176$$

Figure 7.15

Normal Approximation to Binomial Distribution

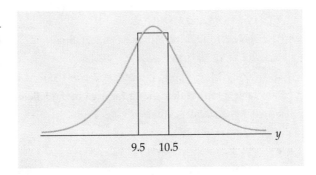

From Table 3, the normal approximation is

$$P(9.5 \leq Y \leq 10.5) = P\left(\frac{9.5 - 10}{2.24} \leq Z \leq \frac{10.5 - 10}{2.24}\right)$$
$$= P(-.22 \leq Z \leq .22)$$
$$= 2(.0871)$$
$$= .1742$$

The approximation for any other value of X would proceed in the same manner. In general, the binomial probability $P(X = x_0)$ is approximated by the area under the normal curve between $(x_0 - .5)$ and $(x_0 + .5)$.

Suppose, in the present example, that we want to approximate the binomial probability $P(5 \leq X \leq 12)$. This probability would be approximated by the area under the normal curve between 4.5 and 12.5. That is,

$$P(5 \leq X \leq 12) \cong P(4.5 \leq Y \leq 12.5)$$
$$= P\left(\frac{4.5 - 10}{2.24} \leq Z \leq \frac{12.5 - 10}{2.24}\right)$$
$$= P(-2.46 \leq Z \leq 1.12)$$
$$= P(0 \leq Z \leq 2.46) + P(0 \leq Z \leq 1.12)$$
$$= .4931 + .3686$$
$$= .8617$$

As a check, the binomial tables yield

$$P(5 \leq X \leq 12) = .862$$

As a final note, we point out that including the continuity correction factor when finding the probability associated with an interval becomes less important as n becomes larger. In subsequent chapters, we will ignore the continuity correction factor when n exceeds 25.

Exercises

7.5 Use Table 3 of Appendix B to find the area under the standard normal curve between the following values.

a $z = 0$ and $z = 2.3$

b $z = 0$ and $z = 1.68$

c $z = .24$ and $z = .33$

d $z = -2.575$ and $z = 0$

e $z = -2.81$ and $z = -1.35$

f $z = -1.73$ and $z = .49$

7.6 Use Table 3 to find the following probabilities.

a $P(Z \geq 1.7)$ b $P(Z \geq -.95)$ c $P(Z \leq -1.96)$

d $P(Z \leq 2.43)$ e $P(-2.97 \leq Z \leq -1.38)$ f $P(-1.14 \leq Z \leq 1.55)$

7.7 Use Table 3 to find the value z for each of the following.

a $P(0 \leq Z \leq z) = .41$

b $P(Z \geq z) = 0.25$

c $P(Z \geq z) = .9$

d $P(Z \leq z) = .95$

e $P(Z \leq z) = .2$

f $P(-z \leq Z \leq z) = .88$

7.8 Determine z_A and locate its value on a graph of the standard normal distribution for each of the following values of A.

a .005   b .01   c .05

7.9 Let X be a normal random variable with a mean of 50 and a standard deviation of 8. Find the following probabilities.

a $P(X \geq 52)$ b $P(X < 40)$ c $P(X = 40)$

d $P(X > 40)$ e $P(35 < X \leq 64)$ f $P(32 \leq X \leq 37)$

7.10 If X is a normal random variable with a mean of 50 and a standard deviation of 8, how many standard deviations away from the mean is each of the following values of X?

a $x = 52$ b $x = 40$ c $x = 35$

d $x = 64$ e $x = 32$ f $x = 37$

7.11 Let X be a binomial random variable with $n = 100$ and $p = .6$. Approximate the following probabilities, using the normal distribution.

a $P(X = 65)$ b $P(X \leq 70)$ c $P(X > 50)$

7.12 The time required to assemble an electronic component is normally distributed, with a mean of 12 minutes and a standard deviation of $1\frac{1}{2}$ minutes. Find the probability that a particular assembly takes the following length of time.

a more than 14 minutes

b more than 8 minutes

c less than 14 minutes

d less than 10 minutes

e between 10 and 15 minutes

7.13 The lifetime of a certain brand of tires is approximately normally distributed, with a mean of 45,000 miles and a standard deviation of 2,500 miles. The tires carry a warranty for 40,000 miles.

    a What proportion of the tires will fail before the warranty expires?

    b What proportion of the tires will fail after the warranty expires but before they have lasted for 41,000 miles?

7.14 A firm's marketing manager believes that total sales for the firm next year can be modeled by using a normal distribution, with a mean of $2.5 million and a standard deviation of $300,000.

    a What is the probability that the firm's sales will exceed $3 million?

    b What is the probability that the firm's sales will fall within $150,000 of the expected level of sales?

    c In order to cover fixed costs, the firm's sales must exceed the break-even level of $1.8 million. What is the probability that sales will exceed the break-even level?

    d Determine the sales level that has only a 9% chance of being exceeded next year.

7.15 Empirical studies have provided support for the belief that a common stock's annual rate of return is approximately normally distributed. Suppose you have invested in the stock of a company for which the annual return has an expected value of 16% and a standard deviation of 10%.

    a Find the probability that your one-year return will exceed 30%.

    b Find the probability that your one-year return will be negative.

    c Suppose this company embarks on a new high-risk, but potentially highly profitable venture. As a result, the return on the stock now has an expected value of 25% and a standard deviation of 20%. Answer parts (a) and (b) in light of the revised estimates regarding the stock's return.

    d As an investor, would you approve of the company's decision to embark on the new venture?

7.16 A steel fabricator produces pipes with a diameter that is approximately normally distributed, with a mean of 10 cm and a variance of .01 cm^2.

    a Suppose the tolerance limit for these pipes is .2 cm, so pipes with a diameter falling within the interval $10 \pm .2$ cm are acceptable. What proportion of the pipes produced will be acceptable?

    b Suppose that pipes with too small a diameter can be reworked, but that pipes with too large a diameter must be scrapped. Suppose also that the tolerance has been reduced to .1 cm. What proportion of the pipes must be scrapped?

7.17 Mensa is an organization whose members possess IQs in the top 2% of the population.

    a If IQs are normally distributed, with a mean of 100 and a standard deviation of 16, what is the minimum IQ necessary for admission?

    b If three individuals are chosen at random from the general population, what is the probability that all three satisfy the minimum requirement for admission to Mensa?

c If two individuals are chosen at random from the general population, what is the probability that at least one of them exceeds the minimum requirement for admission to Mensa?

7.18 Universities throughout the United States and Canada are concerned about the aging of their faculty members, as the average age of professors is at a historic high. A very large number of faculty members will retire within the next decade, making it difficult to find adequate replacements to fill all the positions that will become available. Suppose that North American professors have a median age of 46.4 years, and 36% of them are at least 50 years of age. Assume that the ages of these professors are normally distributed.

a Determine the standard deviation of the ages.

b Assume that there are currently 40,000 professors at North American universities and that the mandatory retirement age is 65. What is the minimum number of professors who will retire during the next decade?

7.19 The maintenance department of a city's electric power company finds that it is cost-efficient to replace all streetlight bulbs at once, rather than replacing the bulbs individually as they burn out. Assume that the lifetime of a bulb is normally distributed, with a mean of 3,000 hours and a standard deviation of 200 hours.

a If the department wants no more than 1% of the bulbs to burn out before they are replaced, after how many hours should all the bulbs be replaced?

b If two bulbs are selected at random from among those that have been replaced, what is the probability that at least one of them has burned out?

7.20 Companies are interested in the demographics of those who listen to the radio programs they sponsor. A radio station has determined that only 20% of listeners phoning in to a morning talk program are male. During a particular week, 200 calls are received by this program.

a What is the probability that at least 50 of these 200 callers are male?

b What is the probability that more than half of these 200 callers are female?

c There is a 30% chance that the number of male callers among the 200 total callers does not exceed what?

7.21 Due to an increasing number of nonperforming loans, a Texas bank now insists that several stringent conditions be met before a customer is granted a consumer loan. As a result, 60% of all customers applying for a loan are rejected. If 40 new loan applications are selected at random, what is the probability of the following?

a At least 12 are accepted.

b At least half of them are accepted.

c No more than 16 are accepted.

d The number of applications rejected is between 20 and 30, inclusive.

7.22 Historical data collected at a paper mill reveal that 40% of sheet breaks are due to water drops, which result from the condensation of steam. Suppose that the causes of the next 50 sheet breaks are monitored and that the sheet breaks are independent of one another.

a Find the expected value and the standard deviation of the number of sheet breaks that will be caused by water drops.

b What is the probability that at least 25 of the breaks will be due to water drops?

c What is the probability that the number of breaks due to water drops will be between 10 and 25, inclusive?

7.4 Exponential Distribution

Another important continuous distribution, the **exponential distribution**, is closely related to the Poisson distribution, even though the latter distribution is discrete. Recall that a Poisson random variable counts the number of occurrences of an event during a given time interval. In contrast, an exponential random variable, X, can be used to measure the time that elapses before the first occurrence of an event, where occurrences of the event follow a Poisson distribution. Equivalently, an exponential random variable can be used to measure the time that elapses between occurrences of an event. For example, the exponential distribution can be used to model the length of time before the first telephone call is received by a switchboard or the length of time between arrivals at a service location (such as a service station, tollbooth, or grocery checkout counter). It has been used with considerable success in applications involving waiting times, and it can also be used to model the length of life of various electronic components, such as tubes and transistors.

> **Exponential Distribution**
>
> A random variable X is exponentially distributed if its probability density function is given by
>
> $$f(x) = \lambda e^{-\lambda x}, \qquad x \geq 0$$
>
> where $e = 2.71828\ldots$ and λ is the parameter of the distribution ($\lambda > 0$).

It can be shown that the mean and the standard deviation of an exponential probability distribution are equal to each other.

$$\mu = \sigma = 1/\lambda$$

Recall that the normal distribution is a two-parameter distribution: the distribution is completely specified once the values of the two parameters μ and σ are known. In contrast, the exponential distribution is a one-parameter distribution: the distribution is completely specified once the value of the parameter λ is known. If X is an exponential random variable that measures the time that elapses before the first occurrence of an event, where occurrences of the event follow a Poisson distribution, then λ is the average number of occurrences of the event per unit of time.

The graphs of three exponential distributions, corresponding to three different values of λ, are shown in Figure 7.16. Notice that, for any exponential density function $f(x)$, $f(0) = \lambda$ and $f(x)$ approaches zero as x approaches infinity.

Recall that, for a continuous random variable, probabilities are represented by areas under the graph of the probability density function $f(x)$. In the case of an exponential random variable X, it can be shown that the probability that X will take a value greater than a specified nonnegative number a is $e^{-\lambda a}$.*

---

*For students familiar with calculus,

$$P(X \geq a) = \int_a^\infty \lambda e^{-\lambda x}\, dx = -e^{-\lambda x}\big|_a^\infty = e^{-\lambda a}$$

Figure 7.16

Graphs of Three Exponential Distributions

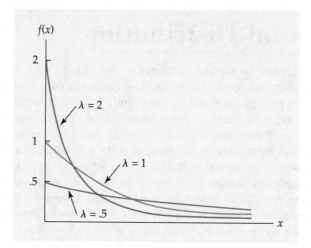

Probability That an Exponential Variable Exceeds the Number a

If X is an exponential variable,

$$P(X \geq a) = e^{-\lambda a}$$

The value of $e^{-\lambda a}$ can be obtained with the aid of a calculator. Since the total area under the graph of $f(x)$ must equal 1,

$$P(X \leq a) = 1 - e^{-\lambda a}$$

for any nonnegative number a.

The probability that X will take a value between two numbers a and b can now be obtained by subtraction.

$$P(a \leq X \leq b) = P(X \leq b) - P(X \leq a)$$
$$= e^{-\lambda a} - e^{-\lambda b}$$

As an illustration of the relationship between the exponential and Poisson distributions, let us consider once again the situation described in Example 6.11.

EXAMPLE 7.6

A tollbooth operator has observed that cars arrive randomly and independently at an average rate of 360 cars per hour.

a Use the exponential distribution to find the probability that the next car will *not* arrive within half a minute.

b Use the Poisson distribution to find the probability required in part (a).

SOLUTION

a Let X denote the time *in minutes* that will elapse before the next car arrives. It is important that X and λ be defined in terms of the same units. Thus, λ is the average number of cars arriving per minute: $\lambda = 360/60 = 6$. According to the formula for exponential probabilities, the probability that at least half a minute will elapse before the next car arrives is

$$P(X \geq .5) = e^{-6(.5)} = e^{-3}$$
$$= .0498$$

This probability is represented by the shaded area in Figure 7.17.

Figure 7.17

Shaded Area Is $P(X \geq .5)$ in Example 7.6

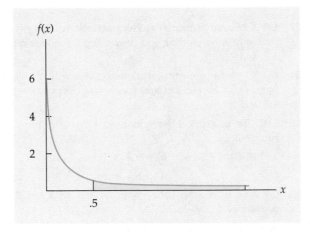

b Let Y be the number of cars that will arrive in the next half minute. Then Y is a Poisson random variable, with $\mu = .5(\lambda) = 3$ cars per half minute. We want to find the probability that no cars will arrive within the next half minute. Using the formula for a Poisson probability, we find

$$P(Y = 0 | \mu = 3) = \frac{(e^{-3})(3^0)}{0!}$$
$$= .0498$$

EXAMPLE 7.7

The lifetime of a transistor is exponentially distributed, with a mean of 1,000 hours. Find the probability that such a transistor will last between 1,000 and 1,500 hours.

SOLUTION

Let X denote the lifetime (in hours) of a transistor. Since the mean lifetime is 1,000 hours, $\lambda = 1/\mu = 1/1,000 = .001$. The required probability is therefore

$$P(1,000 \leq X \leq 1,500) = e^{-.001(1000)} - e^{-.001(1500)}$$
$$= e^{-1} - e^{-1.5}$$
$$= .3679 - .2231$$
$$= .1448$$

Using the Computer to Find Exponential Probabilities

In Appendixes 7.A and 7.B, we provide Minitab and Excel instructions, respectively, to allow you to calculate exponential probabilities. The output is the probability that an exponential random variable with a given mean is less than x. That is, the computer prints $P(X < x)$.

Exercises

7.23 Let X be an exponential random variable with $\lambda = 1$. Sketch the graph of the distribution of X by plotting and connecting the points representing $f(x)$ for $x = 0, .5, 1, 1.5$, and 2.

7.24 Let X be an exponential random variable with $\lambda = 3$. Sketch the graph of the distribution of X by plotting and connecting the points representing $f(x)$ for $x = 0, .5, 1, 1.5$, and 2.

7.25 Let X be an exponential random variable with $\lambda = 1.5$. Find the following probabilities.

   a $P(X \geq 1)$ **b** $P(X \leq 3)$

   c $P(2 \leq X \leq 4)$ **d** $P(X \geq .5)$

7.26 Let X be an exponential random variable with $\lambda = 3$. Find the following probabilities.

   a $P(X \geq 2)$ **b** $P(X \leq 4)$

   c $P(1 \leq X \leq 3)$ **d** $P(X = 2)$

7.27 Let X be an exponential random variable with $\lambda = 2$. Find the probability that X will take a value within 1.5 standard deviations of its mean.

7.28 Let X be an exponential random variable with $\lambda = 4$. Find the probability that X will take a value within 1.2 standard deviations of its mean.

7.29 The expected value of an exponential random variable, X, is $1/\lambda$. Find the probability that X will take a value that is less than its expected value.

7.30 Suppose that customers arrive at a checkout counter at an average rate of two customers per minute and that their arrivals follow the Poisson model.

   a   Sketch a graph of the (exponential) distribution of the time that will elapse before the next customer arrives by plotting and joining the points representing $f(t)$ for $t = 0, .5, 1, 1.5$, and 2.

   b   Use the appropriate exponential distribution to find the probability that the next customer will arrive within 1 minute; within 2 minutes.

   c   Use the exponential distribution to find the probability that the next customer will not arrive within the next 1.5 minutes.

   d   Use the appropriate Poisson distribution to answer part (c).

7.31 The length of life of a certain type of electronic tube is exponentially distributed, with a mean of 400 hours.

   a   Find the probability that a tube will last more than 1,000 hours.

   b   Find the probability that a tube will fail within the first 300 hours.

   c   Find the probability that the length of life of a tube will be between 600 and 800 hours.

7.32 A firm has monitored the duration of long-distance telephone calls placed by its employees to help it decide which long-distance package to purchase. The duration of calls was found to be exponentially distributed, with a mean of 5 minutes.

a   What proportion of calls last more than 2 minutes?

b   What proportion of calls last more than 5 minutes?

c   What proportion of calls are shorter than 10 minutes?

7.33   Airplanes arrive at an airport according to the Poisson model, with a mean time between arrivals of 5 minutes.

a   Find the probability that a plane will arrive within the next 5 minutes.

b   Find the probability that no planes will arrive during a given 30-minute period.

c   Find the probability that no more than one plane will arrive during a given 30-minute period.

7.5 Summary

This chapter was devoted to a discussion of continuous random variables and their probability distributions. A random variable is **continuous** if it can take any of infinitely many values within some interval of values.

The **normal probability distribution** is the most important continuous distribution. Besides approximating the distribution of numerous random variables that arise in practice, the normal distribution is the cornerstone distribution of statistical inference. Finally, we considered the **exponential distribution**, a continuous distribution that is especially useful in applications involving waiting lines, or queuing.

IMPORTANT TERMS

Uniform distribution	Standard normal random variable
Normal probability distribution	Exponential random variable
Normal random variable	Exponential probability distribution

SUMMARY OF FORMULAS

Standard Normal Random Variable

$$Z = \frac{X - \mu}{\sigma}$$

Exponential Probability

$$P(X \geq a) = e^{-\lambda a}$$

Supplementary Exercises

7.34   Use Table 3 of Appendix B to find the following probabilities.

a $P(Z > 1.64)$

b $P(1.23 \leq Z \leq 2.71)$

c $P(Z < .52)$

d $P(-.68 < Z \leq 2.42)$

7.35 Use Table 3 of Appendix B to find the following probabilities, where X has a normal distribution with $\mu = 24$ and $\sigma = 4$.

  a $P(X > 30)$ **b** $P(25 < X < 27)$

  c $P(X \leq 26)$ **d** $P(18 \leq X \leq 23)$

7.36 Suppose that the actual amount of instant coffee a filling machine puts into 6-ounce cans varies from can to can and that the actual fill may be considered a random variable having a normal distribution, with a standard deviation of .04 ounces. If only 2 out of every 100 cans contain less than 6 ounces of coffee, what must be the mean fill of these cans?

7.37 A soft-drink bottling plant uses a machine that fills bottles with drink mixture. The contents of the bottles filled are normally distributed, with a mean of 16 ounces and a variance of 4 (ounces)^2.

  a   Determine the weight exceeded by only the heaviest 10% of the filled bottles.

  b   Determine the probability that the combined weight of two of these bottles is less than 30 ounces. (HINT: If X_1 and X_2 are normally distributed variables, then $Y = X_1 + X_2$ is also normally distributed.)

7.38 Consumer advocates frequently complain about the large variation in the prices charged by different pharmacies for the same prescription. A survey of pharmacies in Chicago by one such advocate revealed that the prices charged for 100 tablets of Tylenol 3 were normally distributed, with about 90% of the prices ranging between $8.25 and $11.25. The mean price charged was $9.75. What proportion of the pharmacies charged over $10.25 for the prescription?

7.39 Suppose that men's heights are normally distributed, with a mean of 5 feet 9 inches and a standard deviation of 2 inches. Find the minimum ceiling height of an airplane in which at most 2% of the men walking down the aisle will have to duck their heads.

7.40 Suppose X is a binomial random variable with $n = 100$ and $p = .20$. Use the normal approximation to find the probability that X takes a value between 22 and 25 (inclusive).

7.41 Venture-capital firms provide financing for small, high-risk enterprises that have the potential to become highly profitable. A successful venture-capital firm notes that it provides financing for only 10% of the proposals it reviews. Of the 200 proposals submitted this year, what is the probability that more than 30 will receive financing?

Calculating Normal and Exponential Probabilities

Menu Commands

To calculate $P(X < x)$ when X is normally distributed, follow the procedure below.

1 Click **Calc**, **Probability Distributions**, and **Normal . . . .**

2 Use the cursor to specify **Cumulative probability**. (If you specify **Probability density**, you will compute the value of the normal function at x, a value that has little meaning for you.)

3 Hit **tab** and type the value of the **Mean**.

4 Hit **tab** and type the value of the **Standard deviation**.

5 Click **Input column**, hit **tab**, and type the value of x. Click **OK**.

If you have several values of x, store them in a column (say, column 1) and proceed as above, except at step 5, click **Input column**, hit **tab**, and type the value of x. Click **OK**.

To compute exponential probabilities click **Exponential . . .** instead of **Normal . . .** in step 1.

Session Commands

To find the probability that a normally distributed random variable is less than a given value, type

CDF K1;

NORMAL K2 K3.

where **K1** is the value of x, **K2** is the mean μ, and **K3** is the standard deviation σ.

If you have several values of x, store them in a column (say, column 1) and type

CDF C1;

NORMAL K2 K3.

To compute exponential probabilities use the **EXPONENTIAL** subcommand instead of the **NORMAL**.

EXCEL 97

Calculating Normal and Exponential Probabilities

Excel 97 Users:
Click **OK** instead of **Next>**
and **Finish.**

To calculate $P(X < x)$ when X is normally distributed, follow the procedure described below.

Commands

1 Click **f$_x$, Function Category: Statistical**, and **Function Name: NORMDIST.** Click **Next>**.

2 Use the cursor and type the value of x (**x**), the mean of the distribution (**mean**), the standard deviation of the distribution (**standard_dev**), and true (**cumulative**). Click **Finish.** (Typing false will produce $f(x)$, which is merely the value of the normal function at x, a value that has little meaning for you.)

To compute exponential probabilities click **EXPONDIST** instead of **NORMDIST** in step 1. Type the value of x, λ (lambda), and true (cumulative) at step 2.

2 Statistical Inference

of statistical methods that involve some form of inference. These techniques deal with different types of data and different kinds of information that we wish to extract from the data. All of these techniques have been proven to be useful to managers, economists, and decision makers.

While these techniques differ widely in the arithmetic needed to produce the results, they are very similar conceptually. In fact, they are so similar that students often encounter difficulty in deciding which technique to use. We will spend a considerable amount of time attempting to ease this difficulty. A major emphasis in this book is in developing technique-recognition skills. Three review chapters are provided to assist you in this development.

2

8 Sampling Distributions

8.1 Introduction

In Chapter 1, we briefly introduced the concept of statistical inference—the process of inferring information about a population from a sample. Because information about populations can usually be described by parameters, the statistical technique used generally deals with drawing inferences about population parameters from sample statistics. Recall that a parameter is a measurement about a population, and a statistic is a measurement about a sample.

Working within the covers of a statistics textbook, we can assume that population parameters are known. In real life, however, calculating parameters becomes prohibitive because populations tend to be quite large. As a result, most population parameters are unknown. For example, in order to determine the mean annual income of North American blue-collar workers, we would have to ask each North American blue-collar worker what his or her income is and then calculate the mean of all the responses. Because this population consists of several million people, the task is both expensive and impractical. If we are willing to accept less than 100% accuracy, we can use statistical inference to obtain an estimate.

Rather than investigating the entire population, we take a sample, determine the annual income of the workers in this group, and calculate the sample mean. While there is very little chance that the sample mean and the population mean are identical, we would expect them to be quite close. However, for the purposes of statistical inference, we need to be able to measure how close the sample mean is likely to be to the population mean. The **sampling distribution** provides this service. It plays a critical role in statistics, because the measure of proximity it provides is the key to statistical inference. In this chapter, we will discuss the sampling distribution of the sample mean. Other sampling distributions will be introduced as they are needed throughout this book.

8.2 Sampling Distribution of the Mean

The following problem illustrates the importance of the sampling distribution in statistical inference. The management of a large oil company is trying to assess the effectiveness of its periodic sales campaigns. During a campaign, customers who buy at least 5 gallons of gasoline are given free coupons that can be used to get discounts in local restaurants. Because of the advertising, printing, and other costs involved, management is willing to continue to schedule the campaigns only if it is satisfied that mean daily sales of gasoline during the sales push are at least 18,000 gallons per station. In a random sample of 100 stations during the last campaign, mean daily sales were 18,200 gallons. On the basis of this statistic, should the oil company continue the coupon giveaways?

Before we attempt to answer the question, let's make sure that the issues are clear. The parameter of interest is μ, the mean daily sales during the campaign (the population mean) by all the stations owned by the company. If management were satisfied that mean daily sales exceed 18,000 gallons, it would approve of the campaign. The only statistic available, however, is the sample mean, $\bar{x}$, of 100 stations. Our initial reaction is that, since the sample mean (which equals 18,200) exceeds 18,000, the population mean exceeds 18,000; however, this is not necessarily correct. The conclusion that can be drawn about the population mean very much depends on how close $\bar{x}$ is expected to be to μ. If management believes that $\bar{x}$ is close to μ, it will be confident that the population mean is greater than 18,000. Conversely, if $\bar{x}$ can be quite different from μ, the population mean actually may be less than 18,000. Unfortunately, from the information provided, we cannot determine the expected proximity of $\bar{x}$ and μ. That is the function of the sampling distribution, which we discuss next. When we have completed our discussion of the sampling distribution, we will return to this problem and answer the question.

To grasp the idea of a sampling distribution, consider the population created by throwing a fair die infinitely many times, with the random variable x indicating the number of spots showing on any one throw. The probability distribution of the random variable x is as follows.

x	1	2	3	4	5	6
$p(x)$	$\frac{1}{6}$	$\frac{1}{6}$	$\frac{1}{6}$	$\frac{1}{6}$	$\frac{1}{6}$	$\frac{1}{6}$

The population is infinitely large, since we can throw the die infinitely many times (or at least imagine doing so). From the definitions of expectation and variance, we calculate the population mean to be

$$
\begin{aligned}
\mu &= E(x) \\
&= \sum x \cdot p(x) \\
&= 1\left(\frac{1}{6}\right) + 2\left(\frac{1}{6}\right) + \cdots + 6\left(\frac{1}{6}\right) \\
&= 3.5
\end{aligned}
$$

and the population variance to be

$$
\begin{aligned}
\sigma^2 &= V(x) \\
&= \sum (x - \mu)^2 \cdot p(x) \\
&= (1 - 3.5)^2 \left(\frac{1}{6}\right) + (2 - 3.5)^2 \left(\frac{1}{6}\right) + \cdots + (6 - 3.5)^2 \left(\frac{1}{6}\right) \\
&= 2.92
\end{aligned}
$$

Now suppose that μ is unknown and that we want to estimate its value by using the sample mean $\bar{x}$, calculated from a sample of size $n = 2$. In actual practice, only one sample would be drawn, and hence there would be only one value of $\bar{x}$; but in order to assess how closely $\bar{x}$ estimates the value of μ, we will develop the sampling distribution of $\bar{x}$ by evaluating every possible sample of size 2.

Consider all the possible different samples of size 2 that could be drawn from the parent population. Figure 8.1 depicts this process. For each sample, we compute the mean as shown in Table 8.1. Because the value of the sample mean varies randomly from sample to sample, we can regard $\bar{x}$ as a new random variable created by sampling. Table 8.1 lists all the possible samples and their corresponding values of $\bar{x}$.

Figure 8.1

Drawing Samples of Size 2 from a Population

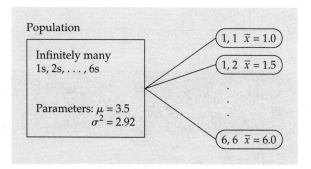

Table 8.1	All Samples of Size 2 and Their Means				
SAMPLE	**$\bar{x}$**	**SAMPLE**	**$\bar{x}$**	**SAMPLE**	**$\bar{x}$**
1, 1	1.0	3, 1	2.0	5, 1	3.0
1, 2	1.5	3, 2	2.5	5, 2	3.5
1, 3	2.0	3, 3	3.0	5, 3	4.0
1, 4	2.5	3, 4	3.5	5, 4	4.5
1, 5	3.0	3, 5	4.0	5, 5	5.0
1, 6	3.5	3, 6	4.5	5, 6	5.5
2, 1	1.5	4, 1	2.5	6, 1	3.5
2, 2	2.0	4, 2	3.0	6, 2	4.0
2, 3	2.5	4, 3	3.5	6, 3	4.5
2, 4	3.0	4, 4	4.0	6, 4	5.0
2, 5	3.5	4, 5	4.5	6, 5	5.5
2, 6	4.0	4, 6	5.0	6, 6	6.0

There are 36 different possible samples of size 2; since each sample is equally likely, the probability of any one sample's being selected is $\frac{1}{36}$. However, $\bar{x}$ can assume only 11 different possible values: 1.0, 1.5, 2.0, . . . , 6.0, with certain values of $\bar{x}$ occurring more frequently than others. The value $\bar{x} = 1.0$ occurs only once, so its probability is $\frac{1}{36}$. The value $\bar{x} = 1.5$ can occur in two ways; hence, $p(1.5) = \frac{2}{36}$. The probabilities of the other values of $\bar{x}$ are determined in similar fashion, and the sampling distribution of $\bar{x}$ that results is shown in Table 8.2.

The most interesting aspect of the sampling distribution of $\bar{x}$ is how different it is from the distribution of x, as can be seen in Figure 8.2.

Table 8.2	Sampling Distribution of $\bar{x}$						
	$\bar{x}$	$p(\bar{x})$		$\bar{x}$	$p(\bar{x})$	$\bar{x}$	$p(\bar{x})$
	1.0	$\frac{1}{36}$		3.0	$\frac{5}{36}$	5.0	$\frac{3}{36}$
	1.5	$\frac{2}{36}$		3.5	$\frac{6}{36}$	5.5	$\frac{2}{36}$
	2.0	$\frac{3}{36}$		4.0	$\frac{5}{36}$	6.0	$\frac{1}{36}$
	2.5	$\frac{4}{36}$		4.5	$\frac{4}{36}$		

Figure 8.2

Distributions of x and $\bar{x}$

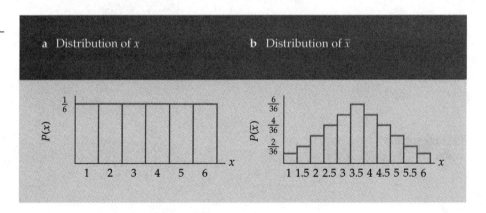

a Distribution of x

b Distribution of $\bar{x}$

We can also compare the mean and variance of the two distributions. Using our definition of expectation and variance, we determine the mean of $\bar{x}$,

$$
\begin{aligned}
\mu_{\bar{x}} &= E(\bar{x}) \\
&= \sum \bar{x} \cdot p(x) \\
&= 1.0\left(\frac{1}{36}\right) + 1.5\left(\frac{2}{36}\right) + \cdots + 6.0\left(\frac{1}{36}\right) \\
&= 3.5
\end{aligned}
$$

and the variance of $\bar{x}$,

$$
\begin{aligned}
\sigma_{\bar{x}}^2 &= V(\bar{x}) \\
&= \sum (\bar{x} - \mu_{\bar{x}})^2 \cdot p(\bar{x}) \\
&= (1.0 - 3.5)^2\left(\frac{1}{36}\right) + (1.5 - 3.5)^2\left(\frac{2}{36}\right) + \cdots + (6.0 - 3.5)^2\left(\frac{1}{36}\right) \\
&= 1.46
\end{aligned}
$$

It is important to recognize that the distribution of $\bar{x}$ is different from the distribution of x. Figure 8.2 shows that the shapes of the two distributions differ. From our previous calculations, we know that the mean of the sampling distribution of $\bar{x}$ is equal to the mean of the distribution of x; that is, $\mu_{\bar{x}} = \mu$. However, the variance of $\bar{x}$ is not equal to the variance of x; we calculated $\sigma^2 = 2.92$, while $\sigma_{\bar{x}}^2 = 1.46$. It is no coincidence that the variance of $\bar{x}$ is exactly half the variance of x, as we will see shortly.

Don't get lost in the terminology and notation. Remember that μ and σ^2 are the parameters of the population of x. In order to create the sampling distribution of $\bar{x}$, we repeatedly drew samples of size 2 from the population and calculated $\bar{x}$ for each sample. Thus, we treat $\bar{x}$ as a brand-new random variable, with its own distribution, mean, and variance. The mean is denoted $\mu_{\bar{x}}$, and the variance is denoted $\sigma_{\bar{x}}^2$.

If we now repeat the sampling process with the same population but with other values of n, we produce somewhat different sampling distributions of $\bar{x}$. Figure 8.3 shows the sampling distributions of $\bar{x}$ when $n = 5, 10,$ and 25. As n grows larger, the number of possible values of $\bar{x}$ also grows larger; consequently, the histograms depicted in Figure 8.3 have been smoothed (to avoid drawing a large number of rectangles). Observe that in each case $\mu_{\bar{x}} = \mu$ and $\sigma_{\bar{x}}^2 = \sigma^2/n$.

Figure 8.3

Sampling Distributions of $\bar{x}$ When $n = 5, 10,$ and 25

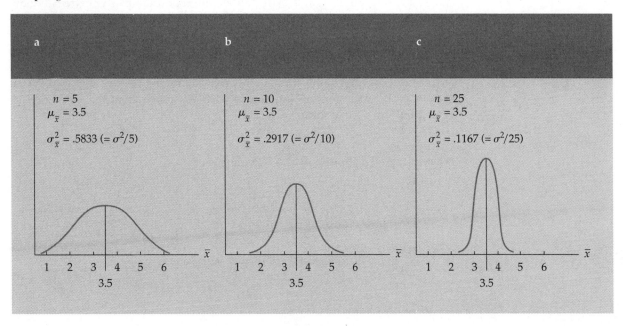

Notice that in each case the variance of the sampling distribution is less than that of the parent population; that is, $\sigma_{\bar{x}}^2 < \sigma^2$. Given that $\sigma_{\bar{x}}^2 < \sigma^2$, a randomly selected value of $\bar{x}$ (the mean of the number of spots observed in, say, five throws of the die) is likely to be closer to the mean value of 3.5 than is a randomly selected value of x (the number of spots observed in one throw). Indeed, this is what you would expect, because in five throws of the die you are likely to get some 5s and 6s and some 1s and 2s, which will tend to offset one another in the averaging process and produce a sample mean reasonably close to 3.5. As the number of throws of the die increases, the likelihood that the sample mean will be close to 3.5 also increases. Thus, we observe in Figure 8.3 that the sampling distribution of $\bar{x}$ becomes narrower (or more concentrated about the mean) as n increases.

Another thing that happens as n gets larger is that the sampling distribution of $\bar{x}$ becomes increasingly bell-shaped. This phenomenon is summarized in the **central limit theorem**.

Central Limit Theorem

If a random sample is drawn from any population, the sampling distribution of the sample mean is approximately normal for a sufficiently large sample size. The larger the sample size, the more closely the sampling distribution of $\bar{x}$ will resemble a normal distribution.

The accuracy of the approximation alluded to in the central limit theorem depends on the probability distribution of the parent population and on the sample size. If the population is normal, then $\bar{x}$ is normally distributed for all values of n. If the population is nonnormal, then $\bar{x}$ is approximately normal only for larger values of n. In many practical situations, a sample size of $n > 30$ may be sufficiently large to allow us to use the normal distribution as an approximation for the sampling distribution of $\bar{x}$. We urge you, however, to be cautious about the sample size. If a population is extremely nonnormal (examples of extremely nonnormal populations include bimodal and highly skewed distributions), the sampling distribution will also be nonnormal—even for moderately large values of n.

In our previous discussion, we demonstrated that the mean of $\bar{x}$ is equal to the mean of the original population. That is, $\mu_{\bar{x}} = \mu$. We also showed that the variance of $\bar{x}$ is equal to the population variance divided by the sample size. That is, $\sigma_{\bar{x}}^2 = \sigma^2/n$.* We can now summarize what we know about the sampling distribution of the sample mean.

Sampling Distribution of the Sample Mean

1 $\mu_{\bar{x}} = \mu$

2 $\sigma_{\bar{x}}^2 = \sigma^2/n$, or $\sigma_{\bar{x}} = \sigma/\sqrt{n}$ (The standard deviation of $\bar{x}$ is called the **standard error** of the mean.)

3 If x is normal, $\bar{x}$ is normal. If x is nonnormal, $\bar{x}$ is approximately normally distributed for sufficiently large sample sizes.

---

*The variance of $\bar{x}$ is σ^2/n if the population from which we are sampling is infinitely large. If the population is finite, the variance of $\bar{x}$ is

$$\sigma_{\bar{x}}^2 = \left(\frac{\sigma^2}{n}\right)\left(\frac{N-n}{N-1}\right)$$

where N is the population size and $(N - n)/(N - 1)$ is the finite population correction factor. In most practical situations (including all examples and exercises in this book), the target population is finite but very large relative to the sample size (e.g., the population of television viewers in North America). In such cases, the finite population correction factor is so close to one that we can ignore it. As a general rule, include the finite population correction factor only if the sample size is greater than 1% of the population size.

Creating The Sampling Distribution Empirically

In the analysis above, we created the sampling distribution of the mean theoretically. We did so by listing *all* of the possible samples of size 2 and their probabilities. (They were all equally likely with probability $\frac{1}{36}$.) From this distribution, we produced the sampling distribution. We could also create the distribution empirically by actually tossing two fair dice repeatedly, calculating the sample mean for each sample, counting the number of times each value of $\bar{x}$ occurs, and computing the relative frequencies to estimate the theoretical probabilities. If we toss the two dice a large enough number of times, the relative frequencies and theoretical probabilities (computed above) will be similar. Try it yourself. Toss two dice 500 times, count the number of times each sample mean occurs, and construct the sampling distribution. Obviously, this approach is far from ideal because of the excessive amount of time required to toss the dice enough times to make the relative frequencies good approximations for the theoretical probabilities. However, we can use the computer to quickly "simulate" tossing dice many times.

In the Study Guide, we introduce simulation experiments, which will enable students to create sampling distributions. We show how to use Minitab and Excel to generate a large number of samples to construct sampling distributions empirically. The experiments will deal with the effect of the population distribution and the sample size on the sampling distribution of the mean. Other simulation experiments will let students discover for themselves some of the key statistical concepts that we discuss in this textbook.

EXAMPLE 8.1

The foreman of a bottling plant has observed that the amount of soda pop in each "32-ounce" bottle is actually a normally distributed random variable, with a mean of 32.2 ounces and a standard deviation of .3 ounces.

a Find the probability that if a customer buys one bottle, that bottle will contain more than 32 ounces.

b Find the probability that if a customer buys a carton of four bottles the mean of the four will be greater than 32 ounces.

SOLUTION

a Because the random variable is the amount of soda in one bottle, we want to find $P(x > 32)$, where x is normally distributed, $\mu = 32.2$, and $\sigma = .3$. Hence,

$$P(x > 32) = P\left(\frac{x - \mu}{\sigma} > \frac{32 - 32.2}{.3}\right)$$
$$= P(z > -.67)$$
$$= .7486$$

b Now we want to find the probability that the mean of four filled bottles exceeds 32 ounces. That is, we want $P(\bar{x} > 32)$. From our previous analysis and from the central limit theorem, we know the following.

1 $\bar{x}$ is normally distributed.

2 $\mu_{\bar{x}} = \mu = 32.2$

3 $\sigma_{\bar{x}} = \sigma/\sqrt{n} = .3/\sqrt{4} = .15$

Hence,

$$P(\bar{x} > 32) = P\left(\frac{\bar{x} - \mu}{\sigma_{\bar{x}}} > \frac{32 - 32.2}{.15}\right)$$
$$= P(z > -1.33)$$
$$= .9082$$

Figure 8.4 illustrates the distributions used in this example.

Figure 8.4

Distribution of x and Sampling Distribution of $\bar{x}$ in Example 8.1

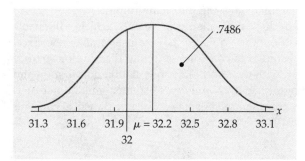
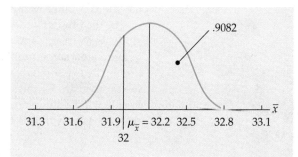

In Example 8.1(b), we began with the assumption that both μ and σ were known. Then, using the sampling distribution, we made a probability statement about $\bar{x}$. Unfortunately, the values of μ and σ are not usually known, so an analysis such as that in Example 8.1 cannot usually be conducted. However, we can use the sampling distribution to infer something about an unknown value of μ on the basis of a sample mean.

EXAMPLE 8.2

The dean of a business school claims that the average weekly income of graduates of his school one year after graduation is $600.

a If the dean's claim is correct, and if the distribution of weekly incomes has a standard deviation of $100, what is the probability that 25 randomly selected graduates have an average weekly income of less than $550?

b If a random sample of 25 graduates had an average weekly income of $550, what would you conclude about the validity of the dean's claim?

SOLUTION

a We want to find $P(\bar{x} < 550)$. The distribution of x, the weekly income, is likely positively skewed, but not sufficiently so to make the distribution of $\bar{x}$ extremely nonnormal. As a result, the central limit theorem tells us that $\bar{x}$ is approximately normally distributed. We also know that $\mu_{\bar{x}} = 600$ and $\sigma_{\bar{x}} = 100/\sqrt{25} = 20$. Thus,

$$P(\bar{x} < 550) = P\left(\frac{\bar{x} - \mu}{\sigma_{\bar{x}}} < \frac{550 - 600}{20}\right)$$
$$= P(z < -2.5)$$
$$= .0062$$

b The probability of observing a sample mean as low as $550 when the population mean is $600 is extremely small, as Figure 8.5 indicates. Because this event is quite rare and thus quite unlikely, we would have to conclude that the dean's claim is probably unjustified.

Figure 8.5

Sampling Distribution of $\bar{x}$ for Example 8.2

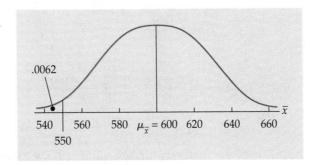

Our conclusion in part (b) of Example 8.2 illustrates a form of statistical inference called **hypothesis testing**. Another form of inference is **estimation**, which we will now use to answer part (b) in a different way. We know that about 95% of the values of $\bar{x}$ will fall within two standard errors of μ. (In this example, the standard error is $\sigma_{\bar{x}} = 20$.) Thus, 95% of the values of $\bar{x}$ will fall within $40 of μ. As a result, we would infer that μ lies somewhere between $510 and $590. Since the dean claimed that $\mu = 600$, which does not fall into this interval, we would conclude that the claim is not supported by the statistical result. Both forms of statistical inference will be explained in Chapters 9 and 10.

Let's now return to the problem introduced at the beginning of this section and see how the sampling distribution allows us to answer the question. Recall the issue: does a sample of 100 gas stations showing a mean daily sale of 18,200 gallons give management a basis for confidently concluding that the mean sale of all gas stations exceeds 18,000 gallons?

Suppose the population standard deviation of daily sales is known to be 8,000 gallons. From the discussion in this section, we know the following.

1 $\bar{x}$ is approximately normally distributed.

2 $\mu_{\bar{x}} = \mu$

3 $\sigma_{\bar{x}} = \dfrac{\sigma}{\sqrt{n}} = \dfrac{8,000}{\sqrt{100}} = 800$

If we assume that the mean daily sale of all gas stations during the campaign is only 18,000, then

$$\mu_{\bar{x}} = \mu = 18{,}000$$

We can then calculate

$$P(\bar{x} > 18{,}200) = P\left(\frac{\bar{x} - \mu}{\sigma_{\bar{x}}} > \frac{18{,}200 - 18{,}000}{800}\right)$$
$$= P(z > .25)$$
$$= .4013$$

This means that there is a fairly large probability that $\bar{x}$ can be 18,200 or more when, in fact, μ is equal to 18,000. As a result, management would not have reason to be very confident that the coupons are effective.

To put this result in perspective, suppose the population standard deviation is 1,000 gallons, instead of 8,000 gallons. Now,

$$\sigma_{\bar{x}} = \frac{\sigma}{\sqrt{n}} = \frac{1{,}000}{\sqrt{100}} = 100$$

and

$$P(\bar{x} > 18{,}200) = P\left(\frac{\bar{x} - \mu}{\sigma_{\bar{x}}} > \frac{18{,}200 - 18{,}000}{100}\right)$$
$$= P(z > 2.0)$$
$$= .0228$$

This indicates that we would be quite unlikely to observe a value of $\bar{x}$ as large as 18,200 from a population whose mean is only 18,000. Hence, in this case, management would be justified in concluding that μ is actually larger than 18,000 and that the campaigns are successful.

As we've just seen, the sampling distribution allows us to draw inferences about population parameters. In the rest of this book, we will use various sampling distributions to test and estimate several different parameters. In each application, the sampling distribution is a critical component of the technique that is used.

Developing an Understanding of Statistical Concepts

Understanding how the sampling distribution is created and used may be the most important factor in learning about statistics. There are several critical concepts that were developed in this section. First, the sampling distribution is the distribution of a sample statistic, which is created by repeated sampling from a given population. Second, the parameters (mean and standard deviation) of the sampling distribution are related to the parameters of the original population. Third, the connection between the sampling distribution and the original population is at the heart of statistical inference. Understanding the contents of this section will go a long way toward developing an understanding of statistics.

Exercises

8.1   A normally distributed population has a mean of $\mu = 40$ and a standard deviation of 12. What does the central limit theorem say about the sampling distribution of the mean if samples of size 100 are drawn from this population?

8.2   Refer to Exercise 8.1. Suppose that the population is not normally distributed. Does this change your answer? Explain.

8.3 A sample of $n = 100$ observations is drawn from a normal population, with $\mu = 1,000$ and $\sigma = 200$. Find the following.

    a $P(\bar{x} > 1,050)$ **b** $P(\bar{x} < 960)$ **c** $P(\bar{x} > 1,100)$

8.4 Suppose the sample size in Exercise 8.3 was 16. Find the following.

    a $P(\bar{x} > 1,050)$ **b** $P(\bar{x} < 960)$ **c** $P(\bar{x} > 1,100)$

8.5 Given a large population whose mean is 50 and whose standard deviation is 5,

    a   find the probability that a random sample of 4 has a mean between 49 and 52.

    b   find the probability that a random sample of 16 has a mean between 49 and 52.

    c   find the probability that a random sample of 25 has a mean between 49 and 52.

8.6 Repeat Exercise 8.5 where the standard deviation is 10.

8.7 The heights of North American women are normally distributed with a mean of 64 inches and a standard deviation of 2 inches.

    a   What is the probability that a randomly selected woman is taller than 66 inches?

    b   A random sample of four women is selected. What is the probability that the sample mean is greater than 66 inches?

    c   What is the probability that the mean height of a random sample of 100 women is greater than 66 inches?

8.8 Refer to Exercise 8.7. If the population of women's heights is *not* normally distributed, which, if any, of the questions can you answer? Explain.

8.9 An automatic machine in a manufacturing process is operating properly if the lengths of an important subcomponent are normally distributed, with mean $\mu = 117$ cm and standard deviation $\sigma = 5.2$ cm.

    a   Find the probability that one randomly selected unit has a length greater than 120 cm.

    b   Find the probability that, if four units are randomly selected, their mean length exceeds 120 cm.

    c   Find the probability that, if four units are randomly selected, all four have lengths that exceed 120 cm.

8.10 The mean and standard deviation of the number of customers who enter a supermarket each hour are 600 and 200, respectively. The supermarket is open 16 hours per day. What is the probability that the total number of customers who enter the store in one day is greater than 10,000? (HINT: Calculate the average hourly number of customers to achieve 10,000 in one 16-hour day.)

8.11 The marks on a statistics midterm test are normally distributed with a mean of 75 and a standard deviation of 6.

    a   What proportion of the class has a midterm test mark that is less than 70?

    b   What is the probability that a class of 50 has an average midterm test mark that is less than 70?

8.12 The amount of time spent by North American adults watching television per day is normally distributed with a mean of 6 hours and a standard deviation of 1.5 hours.

    a   What proportion of the population watches television for more than 7 hours per day?

    b   What is the probability that the average number of hours spent watching television by a random sample of five adults is more than 7 hours?

    c   What is the probability that in a random sample of five adults all watch television for more than 7 hours per day?

8.13 The manufacturer of cans of salmon that are supposed to have a net weight of 6 ounces tells you that the net weight is actually a random variable with a mean of 6.05 ounces and a standard deviation of .18 ounce. Suppose you take a random sample of 36 cans.

a Find the probability that the mean weight of the sample is less than 5.97 ounces.

b Suppose your random sample of 36 cans of salmon produces a mean weight that is less than 5.97 ounces. Comment on the statement made by the manufacturer.

8.14 The sign on the elevator in the Peters Building, which houses the School of Business and Economics at Wilfrid Laurier University, states, "Maximum Capacity 1,140 Kilograms (2,500 pounds) or 16 Persons." A professor of business statistics wonders what the probability is that 16 people would weigh more than 1,140 kilograms. Discuss what the professor needs (besides the ability to calculate probabilities) in order to satisfy his curiosity.

8.15 Refer to Exercise 8.14. Suppose that the professor discovers that people who use the elevator weigh on average 75 kilograms with a standard deviation of 10 kilograms. Calculate the probability that the professor seeks.

8.3 Summary

The central limit theorem states that the sampling distribution of the mean is approximately normal (for large n or for approximately normally distributed populations), with mean μ and variance σ^2/n.

In this chapter, we used the sampling distribution to calculate probabilities associated with $\bar{x}$. In Chapters 9 and 10, we will use the sampling distribution for statistical inference.

IMPORTANT TERMS

Sampling distribution

Sampling distribution of the sample mean

Standard error of the mean

Central limit theorem

Table 8.3

Summary of Formulas	
	$\mu_{\bar{x}} = \mu$
	$\sigma_{\bar{x}}^2 = \dfrac{\sigma^2}{n}$
	$\sigma_{\bar{x}} = \dfrac{\sigma}{\sqrt{n}}$

9 Introduction to Estimation

9.1 Introduction

Having discussed descriptive statistics (Chapter 4), probability distributions (Chapters 6 and 7), and sampling distributions (Chapter 8), we are ready to tackle statistical inference. As we explained in Chapter 1, statistical inference is the process by which we acquire information and draw conclusions about populations from samples. There are two general procedures for making inferences about populations: estimation and hypothesis testing. In this chapter, we introduce the concepts and foundations of estimation and demonstrate them with simple examples. In Chapter 10, we describe the fundamentals of hypothesis testing. Because most of what we do in the remainder of this book applies the concepts of estimation and hypothesis testing, understanding Chapters 9 and 10 are vital to your development as a statistician.

9.2 Concepts of Estimation

As its name suggests, the objective of *estimation* is to determine the approximate value of a population parameter on the basis of a sample statistic. For example, the sample mean is employed to estimate the population mean. We refer to the sample mean as the *estimator* of the population mean. Once the sample mean has been computed, its value is called the *estimate*.

Point and Interval Estimators

We can use sample data to estimate a population parameter in two ways. First, we can compute the value of the estimator and consider that value as the estimate of the parameter. Such an estimator is called a *point estimator*.

Point Estimator

A **point estimator** draws inferences about a population by estimating the value of an unknown parameter using a single value or point.

In drawing inferences about a population, it is intuitively reasonable to expect that a large sample will produce more accurate results, because it contains more information than a smaller sample does. But point estimators don't have the capacity to reflect the effects of larger sample sizes. The second way of estimating a population parameter is to use an **interval estimator**.

Interval Estimator

An **interval estimator** draws inferences about a population by estimating the value of an unknown parameter using an interval.

As you will see, the interval estimator is affected by the sample size; because it possesses this feature, we will deal mostly with interval estimators in this text.

To illustrate the difference between point and interval estimators, suppose that a statistics professor wants to estimate the mean summer income of his second-year business students. Selecting 25 students at random, he calculates the sample mean weekly income to be $400. The point estimate is the sample mean. That is, he estimates the mean weekly summer income of *all* second-year business students to be $400. Using the technique described below, he may instead use an interval estimate; he estimates that the average second-year business student earns between $350 and $450 each week during the summer.

Numerous applications of estimation occur in the real world. For example, television network executives want to know the proportion of television viewers who are tuned in to their networks; an economist wants to know the mean income of university graduates. In each of these cases, in order to accomplish the objective exactly, the interested party would have to examine each member of the population and then calculate the parameter of interest. For instance, network executives would have to ask each person in the country what he or she is watching to determine the proportion of people who are watching their shows. Since there are millions of television viewers, the task is both impractical and prohibitively expensive. An alternative would be to take a random sample from this population, calculate the sample mean, and use that as an estimator of the population proportion. The use of the sample proportion to estimate the population proportion seems logical. The selection of the sample statistic to be used as an estimator, however, depends on the characteristics of that statistic. Naturally, we want to use the statistic with the most desirable qualities for our purposes.

One desirable quality of an estimator is *unbiasedness*.

Unbiased Estimator

An **unbiased estimator** of a population parameter is an estimator whose expected value is equal to that parameter.

This means that, if you were to take an infinite number of samples, calculate the value of the estimator in each sample, then average these values, the average value would equal the parameter. This amounts to saying that, on average, the sample statistic is equal to the parameter.

As an illustration, $\bar{x}$ is an unbiased estimator of μ, because $E(\bar{x}) = \mu$, which we demonstrated in Chapter 8.

Figure 9.1 depicts the sampling distribution of $\bar{x}$ when samples are drawn from a population whose mean is 0. As you can see, the mean value of $\bar{x}$ is 0. Figure 9.2 describes the sampling distribution of a biased estimator of the population mean from the same population. The mean of this distribution is not equal to 0.

Figure 9.1

Sampling Distribution of $\bar{x}$ and x

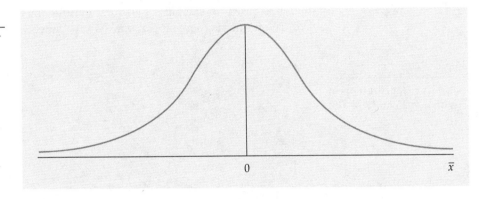

Figure 9.2

Sampling Distribution of a Biased Estimator of μ

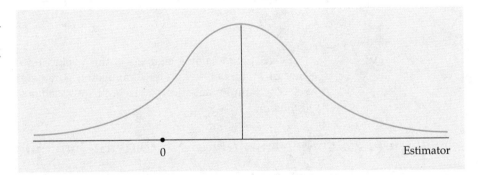

As a second illustration, recall that in Chapter 4 we defined the sample variance s^2 to be $\sum(x_i - \bar{x})^2/(n - 1)$. At the time, it seemed odd that we divided by $n - 1$ rather than by n. The reason for choosing $n - 1$ was to make $E(s^2) = \sigma^2$, so that the definition of s^2 produces an unbiased estimator of σ^2. Defining s^2 as $\sum(x_i - \bar{x})^2/n$ would result in a biased estimator of σ^2, specifically one that produced an average s^2 smaller than the true value of σ^2.

Knowing that an estimator is unbiased only assures us that its expected value equals the parameter; it does not tell us how close the estimator is to the parameter. Another desirable quality is that the estimator be as close to its parameter as possible, and certainly, as the sample size grows larger, the sample statistic should come closer to the population parameter. This quality is called **consistency**.

Consistency

An unbiased estimator is said to be consistent if the difference between the estimator and the parameter grows smaller as the sample size grows larger.

The measure we use to gauge closeness is the variance (or the standard deviation). Thus, $\bar{x}$ is a consistent estimator of μ, because the variance of $\bar{x}$ is σ^2/n. This implies that as n grows larger, the variance σ^2/n grows smaller. As a consequence, an increasing proportion of sample means falls close to μ. Figure 9.3 depicts two sampling distributions of $\bar{x}$ when samples are drawn from a population whose mean is 0 and whose standard deviation is 10. One sampling distribution is based on samples of size 25, and the other is based on samples of size 100. The former is more spread out than the latter.

Figure 9.3

Sampling Distributions of $\bar{x}$ with $n = 25$ and $n = 100$

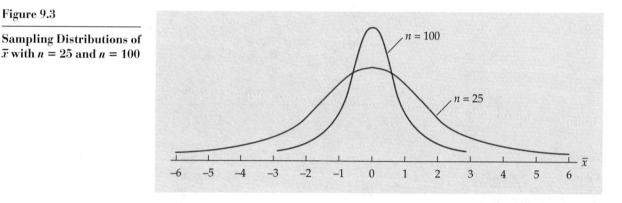

Over the remaining chapters of this book, we will present the statistical inference of a number of different population parameters, and in each case, we will select a sample statistic that is both unbiased and consistent to serve as the estimator.

Developing an Understanding of Statistical Concepts

In this section, we described two desirable characteristics of estimators, unbiasedness and consistency. An understanding of statistics requires that you know that there are several potential estimators for each parameter, but that we choose the estimators used in this book because they are unbiased and consistent.

9.3 Estimating the Population Mean When the Population Variance Is Known

We now describe how an interval estimator is produced from a sampling distribution. We choose to demonstrate estimation with an example that in general is unrealistic. However, this liability is offset by the example's simplicity. When you understand more about estimation, you will be able to apply the technique to more realistic situations.

Suppose we have a population with mean μ and variance σ^2. The population mean μ is assumed to be unknown, and our task is to estimate its value. As we just discussed, the technique of estimation involves drawing a random sample of size n and calculating the sample mean $\bar{x}$.

In Chapter 8, we saw that $\bar{x}$ is normally distributed (if x is normally distributed) or approximately normally distributed (if x is nonnormal and n is sufficiently large*). This means that the variable

$$z = \frac{\bar{x} - \mu}{\sigma/\sqrt{n}}$$

is standard normally distributed (or approximately so). As we did in Chapter 8, we can make probability statements about this variable. For example,

$$P(-1.96 < \frac{\bar{x} - \mu}{\sigma/\sqrt{n}} < 1.96) = .95$$

If you're wondering where the figure 1.96 (and -1.96) came from, recall the normal distribution we presented in Chapter 7. We showed that $z_{.025} = 1.96$, where $z_{.025}$ is the value of the standard normal random variable such that the area to its right under the standard normal curve is .025. Figure 9.4 depicts the probability statement. Notice that since the area to the right of 1.96 is .025, and the area to the left of -1.96 is also .025, the area between -1.96 and 1.96 is .95. (Remember, the entire area under any curve is 1.)

Figure 9.4

Distribution of

$$z = \frac{\bar{x} - \mu}{\sigma/\sqrt{n}}$$

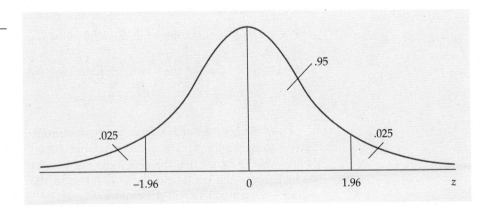

With some algebraic manipulation, we can express the probability statement in a different but equivalent form. That is,

$$.95 = P\left(\frac{-1.96\sigma}{\sqrt{n}} < \bar{x} - \mu < \frac{1.96\sigma}{\sqrt{n}}\right)$$

$$= P\left(\bar{x} - 1.96\frac{\sigma}{\sqrt{n}} < \mu < \bar{x} + 1.96\frac{\sigma}{\sqrt{n}}\right)$$

---

*The value of n required to make the approximation valid depends on the extent of non-normality in the population.

This equation says that, with repeated sampling from this population, the proportion of values of $\bar{x}$ for which the interval $\bar{x} - 1.96\sigma/\sqrt{n}$ to $\bar{x} + 1.96\sigma/\sqrt{n}$ captures μ is equal to .95. This interval is called the **95% confidence interval estimator** of μ. A shortcut method of representing it is

$$\bar{x} \pm 1.96\frac{\sigma}{\sqrt{n}}$$

We will also use interval notation

$$\left(\bar{x} - 1.96\frac{\sigma}{\sqrt{n}}, \bar{x} + 1.96\frac{\sigma}{\sqrt{n}} \right)$$

We can use probabilities other than 95%. For instance, if we want 90% probability, the interval becomes

$$\bar{x} \pm 1.645\frac{\sigma}{\sqrt{n}}$$

This is called the 90% confidence interval estimator of μ.

We can also represent the interval estimator of μ for any probability. We will let $1 - \alpha$ (Greek letter *alpha*) equal the probability.

Confidence Interval Estimator of μ

$$\bar{x} \pm z_{\alpha/2}\frac{\sigma}{\sqrt{n}}$$

The probability $1 - \alpha$ is called the *confidence level*.

$\bar{x} - z_{\alpha/2}\dfrac{\sigma}{\sqrt{n}}$ is called the *lower confidence limit* (LCL).

$\bar{x} + z_{\alpha/2}\dfrac{\sigma}{\sqrt{n}}$ is called the *upper confidence limit* (UCL).

From the confidence level $1 - \alpha$, we determine α, $\alpha/2$, and finally $z_{\alpha/2}$ from Table 3 in Appendix B. (The notation we developed in Chapter 7 means that $z_{\alpha/2}$ is the value of z such that the area to its right under the standard normal curve is $\alpha/2$.) Because the confidence level is equal to the probability that the interval includes the actual value of μ, we generally set $1 - \alpha$ relatively close to 1 (usually between .90 and .99).

In Table 9.1, we list four commonly used confidence levels and their associated values of $z_{\alpha/2}$. Make sure that you know how to use Table 3 to determine these and other values of $z_{\alpha/2}$.

Table 9.1

	Four Commonly Used Confidence Levels and $z_{\alpha/2}$			
CONFIDENCE LEVEL $1 - \alpha$		α	$\alpha/2$	$z_{\alpha/2}$
.90		.10	.05	$z_{.05} = 1.645$
.95		.05	.025	$z_{.025} = 1.96$
.98		.02	.01	$z_{.01} = 2.33$
.99		.01	.005	$z_{.005} = 2.575$

As an illustration, suppose we want to estimate the mean value of the distribution resulting from the throw of a fair die. Because we know the distribution, we also know that $\mu = 3.5$ and $\sigma = 1.71$. Pretend now that we know only that $\sigma = 1.71$, that μ is unknown, and that we want to estimate its value. In order to estimate μ, we draw a sample of size $n = 100$ and calculate $\bar{x}$. The confidence interval estimator of μ is

$$\bar{x} \pm z_{\alpha/2}\frac{\sigma}{\sqrt{n}}$$

The 90% confidence interval estimator is

$$\bar{x} \pm z_{\alpha/2}\frac{\sigma}{\sqrt{n}} = \bar{x} \pm 1.645\ \frac{1.71}{\sqrt{100}} = \bar{x} \pm .28$$

This notation means that, if we repeatedly draw samples of size 100 from this population, 90% of the values of $\bar{x}$ will be such that μ would lie somewhere between $\bar{x} - .28$ and $\bar{x} + .28$, and 10% of the values of $\bar{x}$ will produce intervals that would not include μ. To illustrate this point, imagine that we draw 40 samples of 100 observations each. The values of $\bar{x}$ and the resulting confidence interval estimates of μ are shown in Table 9.2. Notice that not all the intervals include the true value of the parameter. Samples 5, 16, 22, and 34 produce values of $\bar{x}$ that in turn produce confidence intervals that exclude μ.

Students often react to this situation by asking, "What went wrong with samples 5, 16, 22, and 34?" The answer is *nothing*. Statistics does not promise 100% certainty. In fact, in this illustration, we expected 90% of the intervals to include μ and 10% to exclude μ. Since we produced 40 confidence intervals, we expected that 4.0 (10% of 40) intervals would not contain $\mu = 3.5$.* It is important to understand that, even when the statistician performs experiments properly, a certain proportion (in this example, 10%) of the experiments will produce incorrect estimates by random chance.

---

*In this illustration, exactly 10% of the 40 sample means produced interval estimates that excluded the value of μ, but this will not always be the case. Remember, we expect 10% of the sample means in the long run to result in intervals excluding μ. This group of 40 sample means does not constitute "the long run."

Table 9.2

90% Confidence Interval Estimates of μ

SAMPLE	$\bar{x}$	LCL = $\bar{x}$ − .28	UCL = $\bar{x}$ + .28	DOES INTERVAL INCLUDE μ = 3.5?
1	3.55	3.27	3.83	Yes
2	3.61	3.33	3.89	Yes
3	3.47	3.19	3.75	Yes
4	3.48	3.20	3.76	Yes
5	3.80	3.52	4.08	No
6	3.37	3.09	3.65	Yes
7	3.48	3.20	3.76	Yes
8	3.52	3.24	3.80	Yes
9	3.74	3.46	4.02	Yes
10	3.51	3.23	3.79	Yes
11	3.23	2.95	3.51	Yes
12	3.45	3.17	3.73	Yes
13	3.57	3.29	3.85	Yes
14	3.77	3.49	4.05	Yes
15	3.31	3.03	3.59	Yes
16	3.10	2.82	3.38	No
17	3.50	3.22	3.78	Yes
18	3.55	3.27	3.83	Yes
19	3.65	3.37	3.93	Yes
20	3.28	3.00	3.56	Yes
21	3.40	3.12	3.68	Yes
22	3.88	3.60	4.16	No
23	3.76	3.48	4.04	Yes
24	3.40	3.12	3.68	Yes
25	3.34	3.06	3.62	Yes
26	3.65	3.37	3.93	Yes
27	3.45	3.17	3.73	Yes
28	3.47	3.19	3.75	Yes
29	3.58	3.30	3.86	Yes
30	3.36	3.08	3.64	Yes
31	3.71	3.43	3.99	Yes
32	3.51	3.23	3.79	Yes
33	3.42	3.14	3.70	Yes
34	3.11	2.83	3.39	No
35	3.29	3.01	3.57	Yes
36	3.64	3.36	3.92	Yes
37	3.39	3.11	3.67	Yes
38	3.75	3.47	4.03	Yes
39	3.26	2.98	3.54	Yes
40	3.54	3.26	3.82	Yes

We can improve the confidence associated with the interval estimate. If we let the confidence level $1 - \alpha$ equal .95, the confidence interval estimator is

$$\bar{x} \pm z_{\alpha/2}\frac{\sigma}{\sqrt{n}} = \bar{x} \pm 1.96\frac{1.71}{\sqrt{100}} = \bar{x} \pm .34$$

Because this interval is wider, it is more likely to include the value of μ. If you redo Table 9.2, this time using a 95% confidence interval estimator, only samples 16, 22, and 34 will produce intervals that do not include μ. (Notice that we expected 5% of the intervals to exclude μ and that we actually observed $3/40 = 7.5\%$.) The 99% confidence interval estimate is

$$\bar{x} \pm z_{\alpha/2}\frac{\sigma}{\sqrt{n}} = \bar{x} \pm 2.575\frac{1.71}{\sqrt{100}} = \bar{x} \pm .44$$

Applying this confidence interval to the sample means listed in Table 9.2 would result in having all 40 interval estimates include the population mean $\mu = 3.5$. (We expected 1% of the intervals to exclude μ; we observed $0/40 = 0\%$.)

In actual practice, only one sample will be drawn, and thus only one value of $\bar{x}$ will be calculated. The resulting confidence interval estimate will either correctly include the parameter or incorrectly exclude it. Unfortunately, statisticians do not know whether in each case they are correct; they know only that, in the long run, they will incorrectly estimate the parameter some of the time. Statisticians accept that as a fact of life, as should the people who use statistical results.

The following example illustrates how estimation techniques are applied. It will also be used to illustrate how we intend to solve problems in the rest of this book. The solution process that we advocate and use throughout this book is by and large the same one that statisticians use to apply their trade in the real world. The process is divided into three stages. The first step is to identify the correct statistical technique. Of course, for this example you will have no difficulty identifying the technique, since at this point you only know one.

The second step is to perform the calculations. We will do this in three ways. To illustrate how the computations are completed, we will do the arithmetic manually with the assistance of a calculator. Solving problems by hand often provides insights into the statistical inference technique. We will also use Minitab and Excel. The choice of which one to use is left to the instructor and student.

In the third and last step of the solution, we intend to interpret the results and deal with the question that began the problem. This may be more difficult than it appears, because to be capable of properly interpreting statistical results one needs to have an understanding of the fundamental principles underlying statistical inference. This last step will emphasize this understanding.

EXAMPLE 9.1

The sponsors of television shows targeted at the children's market wanted to know the amount of time children spend watching television, since the types and number of programs and commercials are greatly influenced by this information. As a result, it was decided to survey 100 North American children and ask them to keep track of the number of hours of television they watch each week. The data were recorded and appear below. (They are also stored on the data disk in file XM09-01.) From past experience, it is known that the population standard deviation of the weekly amount of television watched is $\sigma = 8.0$ hours. The television sponsors want an estimate of the amount of television watched by the average North American child. A confidence level of 95% is judged to be appropriate.

AMOUNT OF TIME SPENT WATCHING TELEVISION EACH WEEK

39.7	21.5	40.6	15.5	43.9	33.0	21.0	15.8	27.1	23.8	18.3	23.4	20.6
28.4	29.8	41.3	36.8	35.5	27.2	21.0	19.7	22.8	30.0	22.1	30.8	34.7
15.0	23.6	38.9	29.1	28.7	29.3	20.3	36.1	21.6	15.1	43.8	29.0	30.2
26.5	20.5	24.1	29.3	14.7	13.9	37.1	32.5	24.4	22.9	24.5	19.5	29.9
46.4	31.6	20.6	38.0	21.8	23.2	22.0	35.3	17.0	24.4	34.9	24.0	32.9
15.1	23.4	19.5	26.5	42.4	38.6	23.4	37.8	26.5	22.7	27.0	16.4	39.4
38.7	9.5	20.6	21.3	33.5	23.0	35.7	23.4	30.8	27.7	25.2	50.3	31.3
28.9	31.2	15.6	32.8	17.0	11.3	26.9	26.9	21.9				

SOLUTION

IDENTIFYING THE TECHNIQUE

The parameter to be estimated is μ, the mean amount of television watched by all North American children. At this point, we have described only one estimator. Thus, the interval estimator that we intend to employ is

$$\bar{x} \pm z_{\alpha/2}\frac{\sigma}{\sqrt{n}}$$

The next step is to perform the computations. As we discussed above, we will perform the calculations in three ways: manually, using Minitab, and using Excel.

SOLVING BY HAND

We need four values to construct the interval estimate of μ. These are

$$\bar{x}, z_{\alpha/2}, \sigma, \text{ and } n$$

Using our calculator, we determine the summation $\Sigma x_i = 2{,}719.1$. From this, we find

$$\bar{x} = \frac{\Sigma x_i}{n} = \frac{2{,}719.1}{100} = 27.191$$

The confidence level is represented by $1 - \alpha$. For this problem, we want a 95% confidence level, which means that $1 - \alpha = .95$. Thus, $\alpha = .05$ and $\alpha/2 = .025$. Using Table 3 in Appendix B, or more simply, Table 9.1, we find

$$z_{\alpha/2} = z_{.025} = 1.96$$

We are told that the population standard deviation is $\sigma = 8.0$. And finally, the sample size is $n = 100$. Substituting $\bar{x}$, $z_{\alpha/2}$, σ, and n into the confidence interval estimator described above, we produce

$$\bar{x} \pm z_{\alpha/2}\frac{\sigma}{\sqrt{n}} = 27.191 \pm z_{.025}\frac{8.0}{\sqrt{100}} = 27.191 \pm 1.96\frac{8.0}{\sqrt{100}} = 27.191 \pm 1.57$$

Thus, the lower confidence limit is 25.621 and the upper confidence limit is 28.761.

USING THE COMPUTER

Minitab Computer Output for Example 9.1

Confidence Intervals

```
The assumed sigma = 8.00

Variable      N      Mean     StDev   SE Mean        95.0 % C.I.
Time        100    27.191     8.373    0.800   (   25.622.   28.760)
```

The output includes the value of σ, the sample size, the mean, and the sample standard deviation (StDev = 8.373, which is not needed for this interval estimate). Also printed is the standard error SE Mean = $\sigma/\sqrt{n} = 0.800$) and last, but not least, the 95% confidence interval estimate of the population mean. To produce this output, see the menu commands below or refer to Appendix 9.A for the session commands.

MENU COMMANDS	COMMANDS FOR EXAMPLE 9.1
1 Type or import the data into one column.	Open file **XM09-01**.
2 Click **Stat**, **Basic Statistics**, and **1-Sample z . . . .**	
3 Type the variable name.	**Time** or **C1**
4 Use the cursor to select **Confidence interval**.	
5 Hit **tab** and type the confidence level.	**95.0**
6 Hit **tab** and type the value of the population standard deviation σ (**Sigma:**). Click **OK**.	**8.0**

Excel Output for Example 9.1

	A	B	C	D	E	F
1	0.95 Confidence Interval Estimate of MU (SIGMA Known)					
2						
3	Sample mean = 27.191					
4	SIGMA = 8					
5	Lower confidence limit = 25.623					
6	Upper confidence limit = 28.759					

The statistics are $\bar{x} = 27.191$, LCL = 25.623, and UCL = 28.759. We created a macro to address this problem. To execute it, see the commands below or refer to Appendix 9.B for an alternative method.

COMMANDS	COMMANDS FOR EXAMPLE 9.1
1 Type or import the data into one column.	Open file **XM09-01**.
2 Click **Tools**, **Data Analysis Plus**, and **Inference About a Mean (SIGMA Known)**.	
3 Specify the block coordinates of the data. (Either highlight the data before clicking **Tools** or type the block coordinates when Excel asks you to do so.) Do not include cell containing the variable name.	**A2: A101**

continued

INTERPRETING THE RESULTS

We estimate that the average number of hours children spend watching television each week lies somewhere between

LCL = 25.622 hours　　　and　　　UCL = 28.760 hours.

From this estimate, a network executive may decide (for example) that since the average child watches at least 25.622 hours of television per week, the number of commercials children see is sufficiently high to satisfy the program's sponsors. A number of other decisions may follow from that one.

Of course, the point estimate ($\bar{x} = 27.191$ hours per week) alone would not provide enough information to the executive. He would also need to know how low the population mean is likely to be; and for other decisions, he might need to know how high the population mean is likely to be. A confidence interval estimate gives him that information.

Interpreting the Confidence Interval Estimate

In Example 9.1, we found the 95% confidence interval estimate of the mean number of hours that children watch television per week to be LCL = 25.622 and UCL = 28.760. Some people erroneously interpret this interval to mean that there is a 95% probability that the population mean lies between 25.622 and 28.760. This interpretation is wrong because it implies that the population mean is a variable about which we can make probability statements. In fact, the population mean is a fixed but unknown quantity. Consequently, we cannot interpret the confidence interval estimate of μ as a probability statement about μ.

To translate the interval estimate properly, we must remember that the interval estimator was derived from the sampling distribution of the mean. In Chapter 8, we showed that the sample mean is a random variable with mean μ and standard deviation $\sigma/\sqrt{n}$. It follows that the lower confidence limit and the upper confidence limit are themselves random variables. That is,

$$LCL = \bar{x} - z_{\alpha/2}\frac{\sigma}{\sqrt{n}}$$

is approximately normally distributed with mean $\mu - z_{\alpha/2}\sigma/\sqrt{n}$ and standard deviation $\sigma/\sqrt{n}$, and

$$UCL = \bar{x} + z_{\alpha/2}\frac{\sigma}{\sqrt{n}}$$

is approximately normally distributed with mean $\mu + z_{\alpha/2}\sigma/\sqrt{n}$ and standard deviation $\sigma/\sqrt{n}$. Figure 9.5 depicts the sampling distributions of LCL and UCL.

Figure 9.5

Sampling Distributions of
LCL and UCL

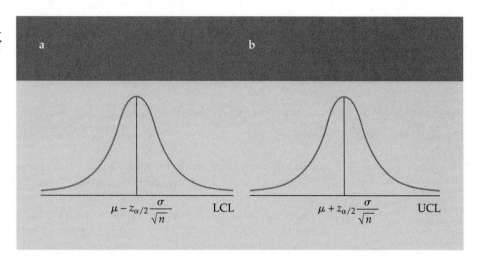

To elaborate further, let's return to the die-tossing illustration we used above. The mean and standard deviation of the population of die tosses is $\mu = 3.5$ and $\sigma = 1.71$, respectively. With $n = 100$ and $1 - \alpha = .90$, the following statements are equivalent.

1 $\bar{x}$ is approximately normally distributed with mean $\mu = 3.5$ and standard deviation $\sigma/\sqrt{n} = 1.71/\sqrt{100} = .171$.

2 LCL $= \bar{x} - z_{\alpha/2}\sigma/\sqrt{n} = \bar{x} - 1.645 \times 1.71/\sqrt{100} = \bar{x} - .28$, which is approximately normally distributed with mean $3.5 - .28 = 3.22$ and standard deviation $\sigma/\sqrt{100} = .171$.

3 UCL $= \bar{x} + z_{\alpha/2}\sigma/\sqrt{n} = \bar{x} + 1.645 \times 1.71/\sqrt{100} = \bar{x} + .28$, which is approximately normally distributed with mean $3.5 + .28 = 3.78$ and standard deviation $\sigma/\sqrt{100} = .171$.

Figure 9.6 describes the sampling distributions of the confidence limits.

Figure 9.6

Sampling Distribution of
LCL and UCL (Die
Tossing)

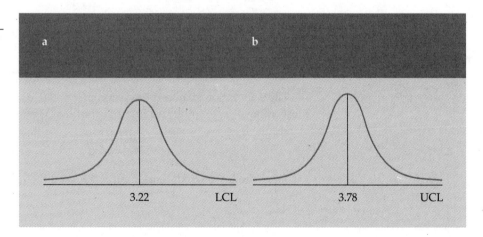

It must be understood that LCL and UCL are related since both are based on the value of the sample mean. Thus, if LCL lies between 2.94 (3.22 − .28) and 3.5, UCL will lie between 3.5 and 4.06 (3.78 + .28). In that case, the interval estimate is correct. This will occur for 90% of the sample means. That is, 90% of the sample means will produce an LCL that is less than 3.5 and a UCL that is greater than 3.5. Another example should solidify your understanding of the technique.

EXAMPLE 9.2

To help make a decision about expansion plans, the president of a music company needs to know how many compact discs teenagers buy annually. Accordingly, she commissions you, a recent hiree, to conduct a survey. Suppose that you randomly selected 250 teenagers and asked each to report the number of CDs purchased in the previous 12 months. The responses are stored in file XM09-02. Some of the data are listed below. Estimate with 99% confidence the mean number of CDs purchased annually by all teenagers. (Assume that the population standard deviation is known to be $\sigma = 3.0$ CDs.)

NUMBER OF COMPACT DISCS PURCHASED BY SAMPLE OF 250 TEENAGERS

14 4 10 4 0 9 4 1 5 3 4 2 1 2 1 5 7 4 4 . . . 7 11 4

SOLUTION

IDENTIFYING THE TECHNIQUE

The first step in the process is to estimate the mean number of CDs purchased. Thus, the parameter to be estimated is μ and its interval estimator is

$$\bar{x} \pm z_{\alpha/2}\frac{\sigma}{\sqrt{n}}$$

SOLVING BY HAND

Using our calculator, we determine the summation $\Sigma x_i = 1{,}065$. From this, we find

$$\bar{x} = \frac{\Sigma x_i}{n} = \frac{1{,}065}{250} = 4.26$$

The confidence level is set at 99%; thus $1 - \alpha = .99$, $\alpha = .01$, and $\alpha/2 = .005$. Using Table 3 in Appendix B, or Table 9.1, we find

$$z_{\alpha/2} = z_{.005} = 2.575$$

The population standard deviation is $\sigma = 3.0$, and the sample size is $n = 250$. Substituting $\bar{x}$, $z_{\alpha/2}$, σ, and n into the confidence interval estimator, we find

$$\bar{x} \pm z_{\alpha/2}\frac{\sigma}{\sqrt{n}} = 4.26 \pm z_{.005}\frac{3.0}{\sqrt{250}} = 4.26 \pm 2.575\frac{3.0}{\sqrt{250}} = 4.26 \pm .49$$

Thus, the lower confidence limit is 3.77 and the upper confidence limit is 4.75.

Minitab Output for
Example 9.2

Confidence Intervals

The assumed sigma = 3.00

```
Variable      N      Mean    StDev  SE Mean      99.0 % C.I.
CDs          250     4.260   3.328   0.190   (   3.771.   4.749)
```

Excel Output for
Example 9.2

	A	B	C	D	E	F
1	0.99 Confidence Interval Estimate of MU (SIGMA Known)					
2						
3	Sample mean = 4.26					
4	SIGMA = 3					
5	Lower confidence limit = 3.7713					
6	Upper confidence limit = 4.7487					

INTERPRETING THE
RESULTS

From the output, we estimate that the mean annual purchases of CDs by teenagers falls between 3.77 and 4.75. In a report to the president we would state that we're quite confident that the average teenager buys at least 3.77 but no more than 4.75 CDs annually. We express our confidence by noting that this statistical procedure is correct 99% of the time.

Developing an Understanding of Statistical Concepts

The interval estimator is derived directly from the sampling distribution, an algebraic manipulation that will be repeated throughout this book. In Chapter 8, we used the sampling distribution to make probability statements about the sample mean. Although the form has changed, the interval estimator is also a probability statement about the sample mean. It states that there is $1 - \alpha$ probability that the sample mean will be equal to a value such that the interval $\bar{x} - z_{\alpha/2}\,\sigma/\sqrt{n}$ to $\bar{x} + z_{\alpha/2}\,\sigma/\sqrt{n}$ will include the population mean. Once the sample mean is computed, the interval acts as the lower and upper limits of the interval estimate of the population mean.

Exercises

9.1 In a random sample of 400 observations from a population whose standard deviation is 10, a statistician calculated the sample mean as $\bar{x} = 75$. Find the 95% confidence interval estimate of the population mean. Interpret what the interval estimate tells you.

9.2 Describe what happens to the width of a confidence interval of a mean when each of the following happens.

a The confidence level increases.

b The sample size decreases.

c The value of the population standard deviation increases.

d The value of $\bar{x}$ increases.

9.3 The following data represent a random sample of 10 observations taken from a normal population whose standard deviation is 2. Estimate the population mean with 90% confidence.

7, 3, 9, 11, 5, 4, 8, 3, 10, 9

9.4 The following observations were drawn from a normal population whose standard deviation is known to be 12. Determine the 90% confidence interval estimate of the population mean. Interpret what the interval estimate tells you.

12, 8, 22, 15, 30, 6, 39, 48

9.5 A random sample of 400 observations was drawn from a population whose standard deviation is 90. The data are stored in file XR09-05 with some of the observations shown below. Estimate the population mean with 95% confidence.

SAMPLE OF 400 OBSERVATIONS

895 961 1,007 1,015 952 1,099 1,028 1,131 978 . . . 871 1,132 906

Use a software package to solve this problem.	OR	The mean of the data is $\bar{x} = 1,010$ Complete your answer manually.

9.6 In a survey conducted to determine, among other things, the cost of vacations, 64 individuals were randomly sampled. Each person was asked to compute the cost of her or his most recent vacation. Some of the observations are exhibited below, and all the data are stored in file XR09-06. Assuming that the standard deviation is $400, estimate with 95% confidence the average cost of all vacations.

COST OF VACATIONS OF 64 RESPONDENTS

798 1,268 1,595 1,819 1,495 1,282 1,582 . . . 1,444 1,502 950

Use a software package to solve this problem.	OR	The mean of the data is $\bar{x} = 1,350$ Complete your answer manually.

9.7 In an article about disinflation, various investments were examined. The investments included stocks, bonds, and real estate. Suppose that a random sample of 200 rates of return on real estate investments were computed and stored in file XR09-07. Some of these data are shown below. Assuming that the standard deviation of all rates of return on real estate investments is 2.1%, estimate the mean rate of return on all real estate investments with 90% confidence. Interpret the estimate.

RATES OF RETURN FOR 200 REAL ESTATE INVESTMENTS

11.63 10.43 14.92 12.93 11.12 10.41 9.01 12.33 . . . 9.27 10.58 12.79

<table>
<tr><td>Use a software package to solve this problem.</td><td>OR</td><td>The mean of the data is $\bar{x} = 12.1$
Complete your answer manually.</td></tr>
</table>

9.8 A statistics professor is in the process of investigating how many classes university students miss each semester. To help answer this question, she took a random sample of 100 university students and asked each to report how many classes he or she had missed in the previous semester. These data are stored in file XR09-08. (Some of these data are listed below.) Estimate the mean number of classes missed by all students at the university. Use a 99% confidence level and assume that the population standard deviation is known to be 2.2 classes.

NUMBER OF CLASSES MISSED

4 0 1 6 1 2 1 4 5 1 6 5 6 2 0 . . . 3 5 4

<table>
<tr><td>Use a software package to solve this problem.</td><td>OR</td><td>The mean of the data is $\bar{x} = 3.88$
Complete your answer manually.</td></tr>
</table>

9.9 As part of a project to develop better lawn fertilizers, a research chemist wanted to determine the mean weekly growth rate of Kentucky Bluegrass, a common type of grass. A sample of 250 blades of grass was measured, and the amount of growth in one week was recorded. These data are stored in file XR09-09. A partial listing of the data appears below. Assuming that weekly growth is normally distributed with a standard deviation of .10 inches, estimate with 99% confidence the mean weekly growth of Kentucky Bluegrass. Briefly interpret what the interval estimate tells you about the growth of Kentucky Bluegrass.

LENGTHS OF SAMPLE OF BLADES OF GRASS

.86 .88 .97 .93 .82 .87 .81 .99 .94 .94 .95 . . . .92 .85 .92

<table>
<tr><td>Use a software package to solve this problem.</td><td>OR</td><td>The mean of the data is $\bar{x} = .89$
Complete your answer manually.</td></tr>
</table>

9.10 A time study of a large production facility was undertaken to determine the mean time required to assemble a widget. A random sample of the times to assemble 50 widgets was recorded and stored in file XR09-10. Some of the observations are exhibited below. An analysis of the assembly times reveals that they are normally distributed with a standard deviation of 1.3 minutes. Estimate with 95% confidence the mean assembly time for all widgets. What do your results tell you about the assembly times?

ASSEMBLY TIMES (IN MINUTES)

12.84   15.58   15.61   14.75   12.62   15.54   15.24   13.56   . . .   16.05   16.36   13.13

Use a software package to solve this problem.	OR	The mean of the data is $\bar{x} = 14.74$ Complete your answer manually.

9.4 Selecting the Sample Size

As you saw in Section 9.3, interval estimates can often provide useful information about the value of a parameter. If the interval is too wide, however, its use is quite limited. For example, estimating that the mean income of university students during the summer break falls between $300 and $10,000 provides very little useful information. One way for statisticians to control the width of the interval is by determining the sample size necessary to produce narrow intervals. To do this, we must specify two factors.

1 the desired confidence level of the interval estimator

2 the bound of the error of estimation, where error of estimation is the absolute difference between the point estimate and the parameter

We denote the bound on the error of estimation by B. Thus, the confidence interval estimator of a population mean can be expressed as

$$\bar{x} \pm B$$

Since the interval estimator of a population mean is

$$\bar{x} \pm z_{\alpha/2}\frac{\sigma}{\sqrt{n}}$$

it follows that

$$z_{\alpha/2}\frac{\sigma}{\sqrt{n}} = B$$

Simplifying this equation, we get the following result.

Sample Size Necessary to Estimate μ

$$n = \left(\frac{z_{\alpha/2}\sigma}{B}\right)^2$$

To solve for n, we have to use some value for σ. This value may be approximated from previous experiments or from prior knowledge about the population. A popular method of approximating the population standard deviation in normal or near-normal populations is to begin by approximating the range of the random variable. A conservative estimate of σ is then

$\sigma \simeq \text{Range}/4.$

This formula is based on the normal distribution. About 95% of a population falls within two standard deviations of the mean. (See Figure 9.7.) The interval $\mu - 2\sigma$ to $\mu + 2\sigma$ represents a range of 4 standard deviations. Thus,

$$\text{Range} \simeq 4\sigma$$

or

$$\sigma \simeq \text{Range}/4.$$

Figure 9.7
_____

Normal Distribution

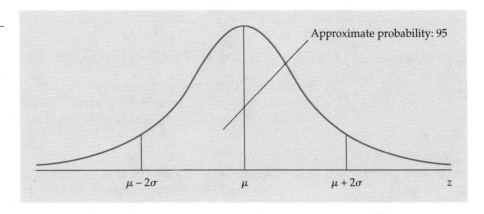

This method is quite effective because approximating the range is often easy. It should be noted, however, that the estimate is valid only for approximately normal populations.

EXAMPLE 9.3

The operations manager of a large production plant would like to estimate the average amount of time a worker takes to assemble a new electronic component. After observing a number of workers assembling similar devices, she noted that the shortest time taken was 10 minutes, while the longest time taken was 22 minutes. How large a sample of workers should she take if she wishes to estimate the mean assembly time to within 20 seconds? Assume that the confidence level is to be 99%.

SOLUTION

The confidence level is $1 - \alpha = .99$. Thus,

$$z_{\alpha/2} = z_{.005} = 2.575$$

The error bound is

$$B = 20 \text{ seconds}$$

and the range is

$$\text{Range} = 22 - 10 = 12 \text{ minutes} = 720 \text{ seconds}.$$

As a result, we approximate σ as

$$\sigma \approx \text{Range}/4 = 720/4 = 180 \text{ seconds.}$$

We can now solve for n.

$$n = \left(\frac{z_{\alpha/2}\sigma}{B}\right)^2 = \left(\frac{(2.575)(180)}{20}\right)^2 = 537.08$$

which we round up to 538 (to produce the interval estimate we want).

The operations manager should randomly sample 538 workers in order to estimate the mean assembly time to within 20 seconds, with 99% confidence.

Developing an Understanding of Statistical Concepts

Statisticians can determine the sample size to draw that allows them to produce interval estimates whose widths are planned. This is often necessary to achieve the accuracy and confidence required to make decisions and recommendations.

Exercises

9.11 Determine the sample size that is required to estimate a population mean to within 0.2 units with 90% confidence when the standard deviation is 1.0.

9.12 Find n, given that we want to estimate μ to within 10 units, with 95% confidence, and assuming that $\sigma = 100$.

9.13 Determine the sample size necessary to estimate a population mean to within five units, with 99% confidence. We know that the range of the population is 200 units.

9.14 A medical statistician wants to estimate the average weight loss of people who are on a new diet plan. In a preliminary study, he found that the smallest weight loss was three pounds and the largest weight loss was 39 pounds. How large a sample should he take to estimate the mean weight loss to within two pounds, with 90% confidence?

9.15 Suppose that a sample of the size you determined in Exercise 9.14 was drawn with $\bar{x} = 20$ pounds.

    a Determine the 90% confidence interval estimate of the mean weight loss.

    b You should have answered part (a) in less than five seconds. Why?

9.16 A forester would like to estimate the mean tree diameter of a large tract of trees. He wants to estimate μ to within 0.5 inch, with 99% confidence. A quick survey reveals that the smallest tree has a diameter of two inches, while the largest tree has a diameter of 27 inches.

    a How large a sample should he take?

    b Suppose that a random sample of the size determined in part (a) produced $\bar{x} = 18$ inches. Find the 99% confidence interval estimate of the mean diameter of all the trees in the tract.

9.5 Summary

This chapter introduced the concepts of estimation and the estimator of a population mean when the population variance is known. It also presented a formula to calculate the sample size necessary to estimate a population mean. Both formulas are shown in Table 9.3.

IMPORTANT TERMS

Estimator

Point estimator

Interval estimator

Unbiased estimator

Consistency

Confidence interval estimator

Sample size necessary to estimate μ

Confidence level

Lower confidence limit (LCL)

Upper confidence limit (UCL)

Bound on the error of estimation

Table 9.3	Confidence Interval Estimator of μ and the Formula to Determine the Sample Size Necessary to Estimate μ

Confidence interval estimator of μ: $\bar{x} \pm z_{\alpha/2}\dfrac{\sigma}{\sqrt{n}}$

Sample size necessary to estimate μ: $n = \left(\dfrac{z_{\alpha/2}\sigma}{B}\right)^2$

Supplementary Exercises

9.17 The image of the Japanese manager is that of a workaholic with little or no leisure time. In a survey, a random sample of 250 Japanese middle managers was asked how many hours per week they spent in leisure activities (e.g., sports, movies, television). The results of the survey are stored in file XR09-17. (Some of the observations are listed below.) Assuming that the population standard deviation is six hours, estimate with 90% confidence the mean leisure time per week for all Japanese middle managers. What do these results tell you?

NUMBER OF HOURS OF LEISURE TIME

20 28 27 27 23 11 19 15 20 16 10 13 . . . 19 22 22

Use a software package to solve this problem.	OR	The mean of the data is $\bar{x} = 19.28$ Complete your answer manually.

9.18 One measure of physical fitness is the amount of time it takes for the pulse rate to return to normal after exercise. A random sample of 100 women aged 40–50 exercised on stationary bicycles for 30 minutes. The amount of time it took for their pulse rates to return to pre-exercise levels was measured and recorded. Some of the data are shown below, and all the data are stored in file XR09-18. If the times are normally distributed with a standard deviation of 2.3 minutes, estimate with 99% confidence the true mean pulse-recovery time for all 40–50-year-old women. Interpret the results.

RECOVERY TIMES (MINUTES)

17 17 13 12 15 14 19 13 14 19 17 18 . . . 14 16 14

Use a software package to solve this problem.	OR	The mean of the data is $\bar{x} = 15.00$ Complete your answer manually.

9.19 A survey of 20 randomly selected companies asked them to report the annual income of their presidents. These data are listed below and also stored in file XR09-19. Assuming that incomes are normally distributed with a standard deviation of $30,000, determine the 90% confidence interval estimate of the mean annual income of all company presidents. Interpret the statistical results.

SALARIES OF COMPANY PRESIDENTS (IN THOUSANDS OF DOLLARS)

283 264 265 278 229 281 258 293 301 318 230 260 256 248 213 271
261 221 290 200

Use a software package to solve this problem.	OR	The mean of the data is $\bar{x} = 261.0$ Complete your answer manually.

9.20 The operations manager of a plant making cellular telephones has proposed rearranging the production process to be more efficient. She wants to estimate the time to assemble the telephone using the new arrangement. She believes that the fastest assembly time is 380 seconds and the slowest time is 440 seconds. How large a sample of workers should she take to estimate the mean assembly time to within two seconds with 95% confidence?

9.21 A random sample of 300 business executives was asked how many vacation days they take annually. The results are stored in file XR09-21. Some of these numbers are listed below. Estimate with 95% confidence the mean number of vacation days all business executives take annually if the population standard deviation is known to be five days. What do the statistics tell you about the population in question?

VACATION DAYS

18 24 17 26 25 22 28 40 32 20 28 26 29 . . . 17 23 25

Use a software package to solve this problem.	OR	The mean of the data is $\bar{x} = 22.84$ Complete your answer manually.

Estimating a Population Mean When the Population Variance Is Known

To produce a 90% confidence interval estimate of μ, type

ZINTERVAL 90 K C1

which specifies that $\sigma = $ **K** and that the data are stored in column 1. If you omit "**90**," Minitab will output a 95% confidence interval estimate. To produce the 95% confidence interval estimate of the mean in Example 9.1, we would type

ZINTERVAL 8 C1

APPENDIX 9.B **Excel Instructions**

Instead of using the macro we created, you can use one of Excel's built-in functions.

1 Click f_x, **Statistical**, **CONFIDENCE**, and **Next>**.

2 Specify alpha, standard deviation, and (sample) size, and click **Finish**. The active cell will contain the value $z_{\alpha/2}\sigma/\sqrt{n}$, from which you can produce LCL and UCL.

10 Introduction to Hypothesis Testing

10.1 Introduction

In Chapter 9, we introduced estimation and showed how it is used. Now we're going to present the second general procedure of making inferences about a population—hypothesis testing. The purpose of this type of inference is to determine whether enough statistical evidence exists to enable us to conclude that a belief or hypothesis about a parameter is reasonable. Examples of hypothesis testing include the following.

Example 1 Thousands of new products are developed every year. For a variety of reasons, most never reach the market. Products that reach the final stages are evaluated by marketing managers who attempt to predict how well the product will sell. Statistics in general, and hypothesis testing specifically, often help in this assessment. Suppose that a company has developed a new product that it hopes will be very successful. After a complete financial analysis, the company's directors have determined that if more than 10% of potential customers buy the product, the company will make a profit. A random sample of potential customers is asked whether they would buy the product. The sampling procedure and data collection would be as described in Chapter 5. Statistical techniques would convert the raw data into information that would permit the marketing manager to decide whether to proceed. The parameter is the proportion of customers who would buy the product. The hypothesis to test is that the proportion is greater than 10%. In Chapter 11, we present the technique that would be used in this example.

Example 2 Scientific and medical discoveries are tested to determine whether they are improvements over current technology. When a new drug is developed, it is usually tested to determine whether it is effective. The test is conducted by selecting a random sample of patients suffering from the disease that the drug is intended to cure. Half the sample is given the new drug and the other half is given a placebo, which looks like a drug but contains no medication. The experiment is called "double-blind" because neither the patients nor the doctors know whether each patient is taking the drug or the placebo. The effectiveness of each is then measured. We can measure the degree of improvement and compute means or we can count the number of patients cured and determine proportions. In either case, we compare the two samples, and using methods presented in Chapter 12, we can infer whether the new drug works.

Example 3 Forecasting is one of the most important topics in statistics. Managers often need forecasts of product demand, commodity prices, and general economic activity to help make decisions. Economists and statisticians create equations called mathematical models that are designed to forecast. Hypothesis testing is used extensively in evaluating how well the model is likely to perform. Suppose that a stock analyst wants to predict the return on a particular investment. The analyst would collect data for a variety of variables that she thinks are related to return on investment. Using techniques introduced in Chapters 19, 20, and 21, she would develop the model. She would conduct various tests of hypotheses to determine whether the model is likely to produce accurate forecasts.

In the next section, we will introduce the concepts of hypothesis testing, and in Section 10.3 we will develop the method employed to test a hypothesis about a population mean when the population variance is known. The rest of the chapter deals with related topics.

10.2 Concepts of Hypothesis Testing

There are four major components of a test of hypothesis. They are

1 Null hypothesis

2 Alternative hypothesis

3 Test statistic

4 Rejection region

Null Hypothesis

The null hypothesis, which is denoted H_0 (H-naught), always specifies a single value for the population parameter. For example, if we wanted to test whether the mean weight loss of people who have participated in a new weight program is 10 pounds, we would test

H_0: $\mu = 10$

Alternative Hypothesis

This hypothesis, denoted H_A, is the more important one, because it is the hypothesis that answers our question. The alternative hypothesis can assume three possible forms.

1 If a tire company wanted to know whether the average life of its new radial tire exceeds its advertised value of 50,000 miles, the company would specify the alternative hypothesis as

H_A: $\mu > 50,000$

2 If the company wanted to know whether the average life of the tire is less than 50,000 miles, it would test

$$H_A: \mu < 50,000$$

3 If the company wanted to determine whether the average life of the tire differs from the advertised value, its alternative hypothesis would be

$$H_A: \mu \neq 50,000$$

In all three cases, the null hypothesis would be

$$H_0: \mu = 50,000$$

The crucial things to remember about the two hypotheses are summarized as follows.

Null Hypothesis

The null hypothesis H_0 must specify that the parameter is equal to a single value.

Alternative Hypothesis

The alternative hypothesis H_A answers the question by specifying that the parameter is one of the following.

    1 Greater than the value shown in the null hypothesis

    2 Less than the value shown in the null hypothesis

    3 Different from the value shown in the null hypothesis

Test Statistic

The purpose of the test is to determine whether it is appropriate to reject or not reject the null hypothesis. (As we will explain later, we use the term *not reject* instead of *accept* because the latter can lead to an erroneous conclusion.)

Test Statistic

The test statistic is the sample statistic upon which we base our decision to either reject or not reject the null hypothesis.

For most tests of hypothesis, the test statistic is derived from the point estimator of the parameter being tested. For example, because the sample mean $\bar{x}$ is the point estimator of the population mean μ, it will be used as the basis for the test statistic in tests of hypotheses about the population mean.

Rejection Region

> **Rejection Region**
>
> The rejection region is a range of values such that, if the test statistic falls into that range, we decide to reject the null hypothesis.

To illustrate, suppose we want to test

H_0: $\mu = 1,000$

If we find that the sample mean (which is the test statistic) is quite different from 1,000, we say that $\bar{x}$ falls into the rejection region, and we reject the null hypothesis. On the other hand, if $\bar{x}$ is close to 1,000, we cannot reject the null hypothesis. The key question answered by the rejection region is when is the value of the test statistic sufficiently different from the hypothesized value of the parameter to enable us to reject the null hypothesis. The process we use in answering this question depends on the probability of our making a mistake when testing the hypothesis.

Because the conclusion we draw is based on sample data, the chance of our making one of two possible errors will always exist. As indicated in Figure 10.1, the null hypothesis is either true or false, and we must decide either to reject it or not to reject it. Therefore, two correct decisions are possible: rejecting H_0 when it is false and not rejecting H_0 when it is true. Conversely, two incorrect decisions are possible: rejecting H_0 when it is true (this is called a **Type I error**, and the probability of committing it is α) and not rejecting H_0 when it is false (this is called a **Type II error**, and the probability of committing it is β). The probability α is called the **significance level**.

We would like both α and β to be as small as possible, but unfortunately there is an inverse relationship between α and β. Thus, for a given sample size, any decrease in α results in an increase in β. (See Section 10.5.) The value of α is selected by the decision maker and is usually between 1% and 10%.

Figure 10.1

Results of a Test of Hypothesis

	H_0 is true	H_0 is false
Reject H_0	Type I error $P(\text{Type I error}) = \alpha$	Correct decision
Do not reject H_0	Correct decision	Type II error $P(\text{Type II error}) = \beta$

As we illustrated how confidence interval estimates are produced and interpreted, we will illustrate how tests of hypotheses are conducted by testing the population mean when the population variance is known. As you will discover, almost all tests are conducted in the same way. We begin by identifying the technique, which usually involves recognizing the parameter to be tested. This is followed by specifying the null and alternative hypotheses. Next comes the test statistic and the rejection region. Finally, we calculate (or let the computer calculate) the value of the test statistic, make a decision, and answer the question posed in the problem.

10.3 Testing the Population Mean When the Population Variance Is Known

Consider the following example.

The supervisor of a production line that assembles computer keyboards has been experiencing problems since a new process was instituted. He notes that there has been an increase in defective units and occasional backlogs when one station's productivity is not matched by the other stations'. Upon reviewing the process, the supervisor discovered that the management scientists who developed the production process assumed that the amount of time to complete a critical part of the process is normally distributed with a mean of 130 seconds and a standard deviation of 15 seconds. He is satisfied that the process time is normally distributed with a standard deviation of 15 seconds, but he is unsure about the mean time. In order to examine the problem, he measures the times for 100 assemblies. The mean of these times was calculated to be 126.8. Can the supervisor conclude at the 5% significance level that the assumption that the mean assembly time is 130 seconds is incorrect?

SOLUTION

In this problem we want to know if the average assembly time is different from 130 seconds. Thus, the parameter of interest is the population mean and the hypotheses to be tested are

H_0: $\mu = 130$

H_A: $\mu \neq 130$

As we discussed in Section 10.2, the test statistic is the best estimator of the parameter. In Chapter 9, we pointed out that the best estimator of a population mean is the sample mean. In this example, a sample of 100 assemblies produced a sample mean of $\bar{x} = 126.8$ seconds. To answer the question posed in this example, we need to answer the question "Is a sample mean of 126.8 sufficiently different from 130 to allow us to infer that the population mean is not equal to 130?" To answer this question, we need to specify the fourth component of the test, the rejection region.

It seems reasonable to reject the null hypothesis if the value of the sample mean is either large or small relative to 130. If we had calculated the sample mean to be, say, 1,300 or 1.3, it would be quite apparent that the null hypothesis is false and we would reject it. On the other hand, values of $\bar{x}$ close to 130 (such as 131) do not allow us to reject the null hypothesis because it is entirely possible to observe a sample mean of 131 from a population whose mean is 130. Unfortunately, the decision is not always so obvious. In this example, the sample mean was calculated to be 126.8, a value neither very far away from nor close to 130. In order to make a decision about this sample mean, we need to set up the rejection region. Suppose we define the value of the sample mean that is just small enough to reject the null hypothesis as $\bar{x}_S$ and the value of the sample mean that is just large enough to reject the null hypothesis as $\bar{x}_L$. We can now specify the rejection region as

Reject H_0 if $\bar{x} < \bar{x}_S$ or $\bar{x} > \bar{x}_L$

Since a Type I error is defined as rejecting a true null hypothesis, and the probability of committing a Type I error is α, it follows that

$$\alpha = P(\text{rejecting } H_0 \text{ given that } H_0 \text{ is true})$$
$$= P(\bar{x} < \bar{x}_S \text{ or } \bar{x} > \bar{x}_L \text{ given that } H_0 \text{ is true})$$

Figure 10.2 depicts the sampling distribution and the rejection region. (The central limit theorem tells us that the sampling distribution of the sample mean is either normal or approximately normal for sufficiently large sample sizes.)

If α is the probability that $\bar{x}$ falls into the rejection region, then $1 - \alpha$ is the probability that it doesn't. Thus,

$$P(\bar{x}_S < \bar{x} < \bar{x}_L \text{ given that } H_0 \text{ is true}) = 1 - \alpha$$

From Section 8.2, we know that the sampling distribution of $\bar{x}$ is normal or approximately normal, with mean μ and standard deviation $\sigma/\sqrt{n}$. As a result, we can standardize $\bar{x}$ and obtain the following conditional probability:

$$P\left(\frac{\bar{x}_S - \mu}{\sigma/\sqrt{n}} < z < \frac{\bar{x}_L - \mu}{\sigma/\sqrt{n}} \text{ given that } H_0 \text{ is true}\right) = 1 - \alpha$$

From Section 7.3, we have

$$P(-z_{\alpha/2} < z < z_{\alpha/2}) = 1 - \alpha$$

Figure 10.2

Sampling Distribution of $\bar{x}$

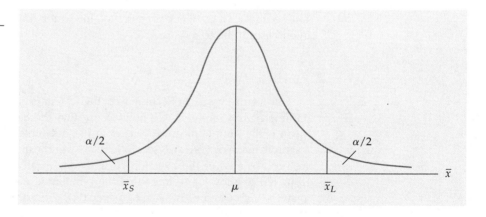

Since the last two probability statements involve the same distribution (standard normal) and the same probability $(1 - \alpha)$, it follows that the limits are identical. Thus,

$$\frac{\bar{x}_S - \mu}{\sigma/\sqrt{n}} = -z_{\alpha/2} \quad \text{and} \quad \frac{\bar{x}_L - \mu}{\sigma/\sqrt{n}} = z_{\alpha/2}$$

In this example, we know that $\sigma = 15$ and $n = 100$, and because the probabilities defined above are conditional upon the null hypothesis being true, we have $\mu = 130$. And finally, with $\alpha = .05$, $z_{\alpha/2} = z_{.025} = 1.96$. We can now solve for $\bar{x}_S$ and $\bar{x}_L$. First, we find

$$\frac{\bar{x}_S - \mu}{\sigma/\sqrt{n}} = -z_{\alpha/2}$$

$$\frac{\bar{x}_S - 130}{15/\sqrt{100}} = -1.96$$

$$\bar{x}_S = 127.06$$

Similarly, we find

$$\frac{\bar{x}_L - 130}{15/\sqrt{100}} = 1.96$$

$$\bar{x}_L = 132.94$$

Therefore, the rejection region is

$$\bar{x} < 127.06 \quad \text{or} \quad \bar{x} > 132.94$$

The sample mean was found to be $\bar{x} = 126.8$. Since the sample mean is in the rejection region, we reject the null hypothesis. Thus, there is sufficient evidence to infer that the mean assembly time is not equal to 130 seconds.

Notice that the test of hypothesis judges the size of the difference between the hypothesized value of the mean ($\mu = 130$) and the value of the test statistic, the sample mean ($\bar{x} = 126.8$). Our calculations determined that any value of $\bar{x}$ between 127.06 and 132.94 would result in what we judge to be a small difference between the statistic and the parameter. Remember that even if the null hypothesis is true, it is quite unlikely that in a sample of 100, the sample mean would exactly equal 130. On the other hand, values of $\bar{x}$ far from 130, although theoretically possible, are quite unlikely. This suggests that the assumption that the null hypothesis is true is probably incorrect, and in that case we reject the null hypothesis.

The preceding test used the test statistic $\bar{x}$; as a result, the rejection region had to be set up in terms of $\bar{x}$. An easier method to use specifies that the test statistic be the standardized value of $\bar{x}$. That is, we use the **standardized test statistic**

$$z = \frac{\bar{x} - \mu}{\sigma/\sqrt{n}}$$

and the rejection region consists of all values of z that are less than $-z_{\alpha/2}$ or greater than $z_{\alpha/2}$. Algebraically, the rejection region is

$$z < -z_{\alpha/2} \quad \text{or} \quad z > z_{\alpha/2}$$

This is more easily represented as

$$|z| > z_{\alpha/2}$$

We can redo Example 10.1 using the standardized test statistic.

H_0: $\mu = 130$

H_A: $\mu \neq 130$

Test statistic: $z = \dfrac{\bar{x} - \mu}{\sigma/\sqrt{n}}$

Rejection region: $|z| > z_{\alpha/2} = z_{.025} = 1.96$

Value of the test statistic: $z = \dfrac{\bar{x} - \mu}{\sigma/\sqrt{n}} = \dfrac{126.8 - 130}{15/\sqrt{100}} = -2.13$

Conclusion: Since $|-2.13| = 2.13$, which is greater than 1.96, reject the null hypothesis and conclude that there is enough evidence to infer that the mean time is not equal to 130 seconds.

As you can see, the conclusions we draw from using the test statistic $\bar{x}$ and the standardized test statistic z are identical. Figures 10.3 and 10.4 depict the two sampling distributions highlighting the equivalence of the two tests.

Figure 10.3

Sampling Distribution of $\bar{x}$ for Example 10.1

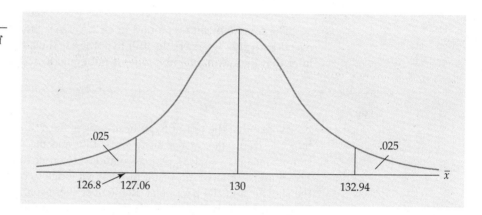

Figure 10.4

Sampling Distribution of $z = \dfrac{\bar{x} - \mu}{\sigma/\sqrt{n}}$ for Example 10.1

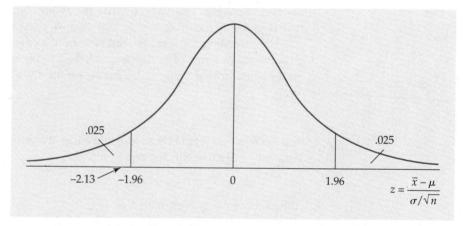

Because of its convenience and because statistical software packages use them, the standardized test statistic will be used throughout this book. Deferring to popular usage we will refer to the *standardized test statistic* simply as the *test statistic*.

Interpreting the Results of the Test

In Example 10.1, we rejected the null hypothesis. Does this *prove* that the alternative hypothesis is true? The answer is *no*: because our conclusion is based on sample data (and not on the entire population), we can never prove anything by using statistical inference. Consequently, we summarize the test by stating that *there is enough statistical evidence to infer that the null hypothesis is false and that the alternative hypothesis is true.*

Now suppose that $\bar{x}$ had equaled 128.4 instead of 126.8. We would then have calculated $z = -1.07$, which is not in the rejection region. Could we conclude on this basis that there is enough statistical evidence to infer that the null hypothesis is true and hence that $\mu = 130$? Again the answer is *no* because it is absurd to suggest that a sample mean of 128.4 provides *any* evidence to infer that the population mean is 130. Because we're testing a single value of the parameter under the null hypothesis, we can never have enough statistical evidence to establish that the null hypothesis is true (unless we sample the entire population).

Consequently, if the value of the test statistic does not fall into the rejection region, rather than say we *accept the null hypothesis* (which implies that we're stating that the null hypothesis is true) we state that we *do not reject the null hypothesis*, and we conclude that *not enough evidence exists to show that the alternative hypothesis is true*. While it may appear that we're being overly technical, such is not the case. Your ability to set up tests of hypotheses properly and to interpret their results correctly very much depends on your understanding of this point. Notice that no matter what the result of the test, the conclusion is based on the alternative hypothesis. In the final analysis, there are only two possible conclusions of a hypothesis test.

Conclusions of a Test of Hypothesis

If we *reject the null hypothesis*, we conclude that there is enough statistical evidence to infer that the alternative hypothesis is true.

If we *do not reject the null hypothesis*, we conclude that there is not enough statistical evidence to infer that the alternative hypothesis is true.

Observe that, in the end, the alternative hypothesis is the more important one. It is the alternative hypothesis that answers the question, not the null hypothesis. This point is crucial. Whatever you're trying to show statistically must be represented by the alternative hypothesis (bearing in mind that you have only three choices for the alternative hypothesis—greater than, less than, and not equal to).

When we introduced statistical inference in Chapter 9, we pointed out that the first step in the solution is to identify the technique. Part of this process when the problem involves hypothesis testing is the specification of the hypotheses. Because the alternative hypothesis answers the question, we will identify it first. The null hypothesis automatically follows because the null hypothesis must specify equality. However, by tradition, when we list the two hypotheses, the null hypothesis comes first, followed by the alternative hypothesis. All examples in this book will follow that format.

The test illustrated by Example 10.1 is called a **two-tail test**—so called because the rejection region is equally partitioned into the two tails of the sampling distribution. We now introduce the **one-tail test**, which is characterized by a rejection region located in only one tail of the sampling distribution.

One-Tail Test of Hypothesis

In Example 10.1, we wanted to determine if there was enough statistical evidence to infer that the mean was different from 130. Obviously, there are two ways for the mean to be different: the mean could be larger than or smaller than 130. For this reason, the rejection region is located in the two tails of the sampling distribution. However, as we pointed out in Section 10.2, there are three possible forms of the alternative hypothesis. That is, besides testing to see if the mean differs from some specific value, we can also test to determine if the mean is *greater than* some value, or we can test to determine if the mean is *less than* some value. For these kinds of tests we must structure the rejection region differently. As you're about to see, these tests will feature rejection regions that are located in only one tail of the sampling distribution.

EXAMPLE 10.2

There are a variety of government agencies devoted to ensuring that food producers package their products in such a way that the weight or volume of the contents listed on the label is correct. For example, bottles of catsup whose labels state that the contents have a net weight of 16 ounces, must have a net weight of at least 16 ounces. However, it is impossible to check all packages sold in the country. As a result, statistical techniques are used. A random sample of the product is selected and its contents measured. If the mean of the sample provides sufficient evidence to infer that the mean weight of all bottles is less than 16 ounces, the product label is deemed to be unacceptable. Suppose that a government inspector weighs the contents of a random sample of 25 bottles of catsup labeled "Net weight: 16 ounces" and records the measurements below. (The data are also stored on the data disk in file XM10-02.) Using a 5% significance level, can the inspector conclude that the product label is unacceptable? (Assume that the inspector knows from previous experiments that the standard deviation of the weight of all catsup bottles is 0.4 ounces.)

NET WEIGHT OF "16-OUNCE" CATSUP BOTTLES

15.8	16.0	16.2	15.7	15.4	16.1	16.2	17.3	15.0	16.8	15.6	15.9	16.0	16.2
15.6	16.0	16.8	15.7	15.6	15.3	15.7	15.8	15.6	15.5	15.7			

SOLUTION

IDENTIFYING THE
TECHNIQUE

The objective of the study is to draw a conclusion about the mean weight of all catsup bottles. Thus, the parameter to be tested is the population mean μ. We want to know if there is enough statistical evidence to show that the population mean is less than 16 ounces. Thus, the alternative hypothesis is

$$H_A: \mu < 16$$

The null hypothesis automatically follows.

$H_0: \mu = 16$

The test statistic is the only we've presented thus far. It is

$$z = \frac{\bar{x} - \mu}{\sigma/\sqrt{n}}$$

In this example, we do not divide the significance level by 2 and define the rejection region as the two tails of the sampling distribution. Instead, we locate the rejection region in the left tail of the sampling distribution. To understand why, remember that we're trying to decide if there is enough statistical evidence to infer that the mean is less than 16 (which is the alternative hypothesis). If we observe a large sample mean (and hence a large value of z), do we want to reject the null hypothesis in favor of the alternative? The answer is an emphatic no. It is absurd to conclude that if the sample mean is say, 20, there is enough evidence to conclude that the mean of all bottles is *less* than 16. Consequently, we want to reject the null hypothesis only if the sample mean (and hence the value of z) is small. How small is small enough? The answer is determined by the significance level and the rejection region. Thus, we set up the rejection region as

$$z < -z_\alpha = -z_{.05} = -1.645$$

Why do we use z_α and not $z_{\alpha/2}$? Because we want the probability of incorrectly rejecting the null hypothesis to be α. Since we reject the null hypothesis only when z is too small, it follows that the rejection region is $z < -z_\alpha$.

Note that the direction of the inequality in the rejection region ($z < -z_\alpha$) matches the direction of the inequality in the alternative hypothesis ($\mu < 16$). Also note the negative sign, since the rejection region is in the left tail (containing values of z less than zero) of the sampling distribution.

We will perform the calculations by hand as well as by computer. (The Minitab and Excel outputs are shown on the following page.)

SOLVING BY HAND

From the data, we compute the sample mean. It is

$\bar{x} = 15.90$

Since the population standard deviation is known to be $\sigma = .4$, the sample size is $n = 25$, and the value of μ is hypothesized to be 16, we compute the value of the test statistic as

$$z = \frac{\bar{x} - \mu}{\sigma/\sqrt{n}} = \frac{15.90 - 16}{.4/\sqrt{25}} = -1.25$$

Because the value of the test statistic, $z = -1.25$, is not less than -1.645, we do not reject the null hypothesis in favor of the alternative hypothesis. There is insufficient evidence to infer that the mean is less than 16 ounces.

Minitab Output for Example 10.2

Z-Test

```
Test of mu = 16.0000 vs mu < 16.0000
The assumed sigma = 0.400

Variable      N      Mean    StDev    SE Mean        Z    P-Value
Weight       25   15.9000   0.5017    0.0800    −1.25       0.11
```

Minitab summarizes the test that we're performing (**Test of mu = 16.0000 vs mu < 16.0000**) with the population standard deviation assumed to be equal to 0.4 (**The assumed sigma = 0.400**). The output includes the sample size, the mean, standard deviation, standard error of the mean (**SE Mean = $\sigma/\sqrt{n}$**), value of the test statistic, and a quantity that we will discuss in the next section, the *p*-value of the test. We describe the menu commands below. (See Appendix 10.A for the session commands.)

MENU COMMANDS	COMMANDS FOR EXAMPLE 10.2
1 Type or import the data into one column.	Open file **XM10-02**.
2 Click **Stat**, **Basic Statistics**, and **1-Sample z . . . .**	
3 Type the variable name.	**Catsup** or **C1**
4 Use the cursor to choose **Test mean.**	
5 Hit **tab**, type the value of μ under the null hypothesis.	**16**
6 Use the cursor to select **less than**, **not equal**, or **greater than**.	**less than**
7 Hit **tab** and type the value of the population standard deviation σ. Click **OK**.	**.4**

Excel Output for Example 10.2

	A	B	C	D	E
1	**Test of Hypothesis About MU (SIGMA Known)**				
2					
3	Test of MU = 16 Vs MU less than 16				
4	SIGMA = 0.4				
5	Sample mean = 15.9				
6	Test Statistic: z = -1.25				
7	P-Value = 0.1056				

This Excel macro summarizes the test we're performing. The value of the test statistic is $z = -1.25$. The p-value of the test will be discussed in the next section. The instructions for the execution of this macro are provided below. See Appendix 10.B for an alternative method.

COMMANDS	COMMANDS FOR EXAMPLE 10.2
1 Type or import the data.	Open file **XM10-02**.
2 Click **Tools**, **Data Analysis Plus**, and **Inference About a Mean (SIGMA Known)**.	
3 Specify the block coordinates of the data. Do not include cell containing the variable name.	**A2:A26**
4 Click **Test of Hypothesis**.	
5 Specify σ.	**.4**
6 Specify the value of μ under the null hypothesis.	**16**
7 Click the appropriate alternative hypothesis.	**MU less than 16**

INTERPRETING THE
RESULTS

Because we were not able to reject the null hypothesis, we say that there is not enough evidence to infer that the mean weight of all catsup bottles is less than 16 ounces. Note that there was *some* evidence to indicate that the population mean is less than 16 ounces. (We did find the sample mean to be 15.9.) However, to reject the null hypothesis we need enough statistical evidence, and in this case we simply did not have enough reason to reject the null hypothesis in favor of the alternative. In the absence of evidence to show that the mean weight of all catsup bottles is less than 16 ounces, the inspector would not find the labels to be unacceptable.

Figure 10.5 depicts the sampling distribution.

Figure 10.5

Sampling Distribution for Example 10.2

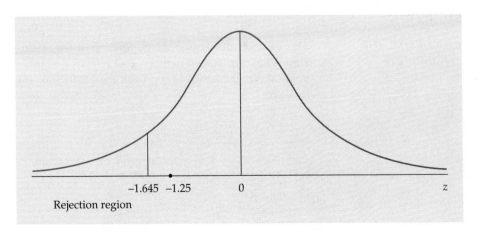

Setting Up the Hypotheses in One-Tail Tests

In our experience, we've observed that students often have difficulty in setting up one-tail tests of hypotheses. It must be understood that the whole point of the test-of-hypothesis procedure is to determine if there is enough statistical evidence to *support the alternative hypothesis*. Thus, to set up the alternative hypothesis, simply decide what the point of the exercise is. In Example 10.1, the objective was to determine if the mean of the population of assembly times was *not equal* to 130 seconds. Consequently, we set up the alternative hypothesis as $H_A: \mu \neq 130$. Because the null hypothesis must specify a single value (if it didn't, what value would we use to compute the test statistic?), the null hypothesis automatically becomes $H_0: \mu = 130$.

In Example 10.2, the purpose of the test was to determine if there was enough evidence to infer that the mean weight of the bottles was *less* than 16 ounces (and hence that the labels were unacceptable). We set up the alternative hypothesis as $H_A: \mu < 16$ and the null hypothesis as $H_0: \mu = 16$.*

You will note that even though we summarize tests by listing the null hypothesis first (by tradition), we actually determine the alternative hypothesis first; the null hypothesis is automatically defined. Let's examine one more example to solidify your understanding of hypothesis testing.

EXAMPLE 10.3

The manager of a department store is thinking about establishing a new billing system for the store's credit customers. After a thorough financial analysis, she determines that the new system will be cost-effective only if the mean monthly account is greater than $70. A random sample of 200 monthly accounts is drawn, for which the sample mean account is $74. (The data are stored in file XM10-03.) The manager knows that the accounts are normally distributed with a standard deviation of $30. Is there enough evidence at the 5% significance level to conclude that the new system will be cost-effective?

SOLUTION

IDENTIFYING THE TECHNIQUE

This example deals with the population of the credit accounts at the store. To conclude that the system will be cost-effective requires us to show that the mean account for all customers is greater than $70. Thus the null and alternative hypotheses are

---

* Some statisticians prefer to specify the null hypothesis as the opposite of the alternative hypothesis. For Example 10.2, such statisticians would state the hypotheses as

$H_0: \mu \geq 16$
$H_A: \mu < 16$

However, they would use $\mu = 16$ in calculating the value of the test statistic (just as we did) and therefore actually test the null hypothesis $H_0: \mu = 16$. Their interpretation of the test would be identical to ours.

$$H_0: \mu = 70$$
$$H_A: \mu > 70$$

The remainder of the test follows.

Test statistic: $z = \dfrac{\bar{x} - \mu}{\sigma/\sqrt{n}}$

Rejection region: $z > z_\alpha = z_{.05} = 1.645$

The sample mean is $\bar{x} = 74$ from a sample of $n = 200$. The population standard deviation is known to be $\sigma = 30$. The null hypothesis specifies $\mu = 70$. Substituting all the parts into the test statistic, we find

Value of the test statistic: $z = \dfrac{\bar{x} - \mu}{\sigma/\sqrt{n}} = \dfrac{74 - 70}{30/\sqrt{200}} = 1.89$

Conclusion: Reject H_0

USING THE COMPUTER

Minitab Output for Example 10.3

Z-Test

```
Test of mu = 70.00 vs mu > 70.00
The assumed sigma = 30.0

Variable       N       Mean      StDev    SE Mean        Z    P-Value
Accounts     200      74.00      34.53       2.12     1.89      0.030
```

Excel Output for Example 10.3

	A	B	C	D	E
1	**Test of Hypothesis About MU (SIGMA Known)**				
2					
3	Test of MU = 70 Vs MU greater than 70				
4	SIGMA = 30				
5	Sample mean = 74.005				
6	Test Statistic: z = 1.888				
7	P-Value = 0.0295				

INTERPRETING THE RESULTS

There is enough evidence for us to infer that the mean account is greater than $70. This means that the data support the belief that the new billing system will be cost-effective. However, bear in mind that the statistical inference is only as good as the data-gathering process. If the sample has not been randomly selected, the results may be meaningless. It is also worth remembering that we have not proven the cost-effectiveness of the new system, just that the data indicate potential success. If the manager is satisfied with the financial and statistical analyses, she should adopt the system.

Figure 10.6 describes the sampling distribution in this test.

Figure 10.6

Sampling Distribution for
Example 10.3

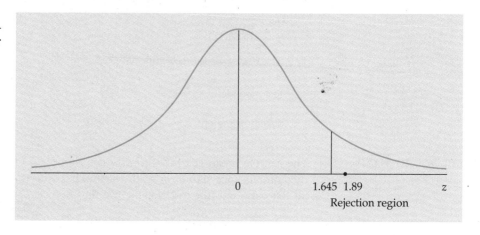

Nonstatistical Applications of Hypothesis Testing

You will find as you progress through this book that a great many statistical techniques involve hypothesis testing. Obviously, we believe that hypothesis testing is
central to the entire subject of statistics. However, we also believe that hypothesis
testing is a vital concept in fields outside statistics. In this subsection, we demonstrate the application of hypothesis testing in two such fields.

Criminal Trials

An excellent example of a nonstatistical application of the concepts of hypothesis
testing is in the conduct of our criminal justice system. When a person is accused
of a crime, he or she faces a trial. The jury must decide the verdict in the same
way that a statistician draws a conclusion about a test of hypothesis. The case
begins with the null and alternative hypotheses.

H_0: The defendant is innocent.

H_A: The defendant is guilty.

The jury does not know the truth about the hypotheses. They must, however,
make a decision based on the evidence. After the prosecution and defense make
their arguments, the jury must decide whether there is enough evidence to support
the alternative hypothesis. If so, the defendant is found guilty and sentenced. If
the jury finds that there is not enough evidence to support the alternative hypothesis, they render a verdict of not guilty. Notice that they do not conclude that the
defendant is innocent—merely not guilty. Our justice system does not allow for a
conclusion that the defendant is innocent. Just as in statistical hypothesis testing,
juries can make mistakes. A Type I error occurs when an innocent person is found
guilty and a Type II error occurs when a guilty person is acquitted. In the British
and North American justice systems, we place the burden of proof on the prosecution. In theory, this decreases the probability of Type I errors and increases Type
II errors. Our society regards the conviction of innocent people to be a greater sin
than the acquittal of guilty people. An American Supreme Court justice once said
that it is better to acquit 100 guilty men than to convict one innocent one. In statistical terms, the justice said that the probability of a Type II error should be 100
times the probability of a Type I error.

Drug Testing

Every year, dozens of new drugs are developed. It is the responsibility of the federal government to judge the safety and effectiveness of the drugs before allowing them to be sold to the public. This, too, is an example of hypothesis testing. The null and alternative hypotheses are

H_0: The drug is not safe and effective.

H_A: The drug is safe and effective.

In most cases, the regulators do not know with certainty what will happen when and if the drug is approved for sale. They must make a decision based on "sample" information. They will usually examine the experiments that were performed on laboratory animals as well as human testing before making a decision. Two types of error are possible. When the government approves a drug that turns out to be either unsafe or ineffective, a Type I error is committed. If the government disapproves a drug that is actually safe and effective, it is making a Type II error. Unfortunately, it is difficult to decide which error is more serious. Type I errors may lead to deaths through the use of unsafe and/or unnecessary drugs. But so too can Type II errors. By denying the public the use of a drug that works, regulators may be responsible for preventable deaths.

If you understand the concepts of hypothesis testing, you will likely find numerous nonstatistical applications in your own life. Just think about the kinds of decisions you commonly make. Most involve a judgment based on a limited amount of information. A misjudgment may lead to one of the two types of error.

Developing an Understanding of Statistical Concepts

As is the case with the interval estimator, the test statistic and rejection region are derived from the sampling distribution. At its core, the hypothesis testing procedure is another form of probability statement based on the sampling distribution. We assume that the value of the mean under the null hypothesis is true. We then compute the test statistic and determine whether it is likely that such a value could be calculated from a population whose mean is specified by the null hypothesis. If we deem the outcome to be unlikely, we reject the null hypothesis.

Exercises

10.1 For each of the following tests, determine the rejection region.

    a H_0: $\mu = 1{,}000$
          H_A: $\mu \neq 1{,}000$
          $\alpha = .05$

    b H_0: $\mu = 50$
          H_A: $\mu > 50$
          $\alpha = .01$

    c H_0: $\mu = 15$
          H_A: $\mu < 15$
          $\alpha = .10$

10.2 Determine if there is enough statistical evidence at the 1% significance level to infer from the following information that the population mean is less than 250.

$\bar{x} = 247$, $\sigma = 40$, $n = 400$

10.3 A random sample of 200 observations from a normal population whose standard deviation is 100 produced a mean of 150. Does this statistic provide sufficient evidence at the 5% significance level to infer that the population mean is less than 160?

10.4 Determine if there is enough statistical evidence at the 1% significance level to infer that the population mean is not equal to 50, given that $\bar{x} = 56$, $\sigma = 10$, and $n = 25$.

10.5 Suppose that the following observations were drawn from a normal population whose standard deviation is 10. Test with $\alpha = .10$ to determine whether there is enough evidence to conclude that the population mean differs from 25.

21 37 33 47 28 16 29 37 41 20

10.6 Given the following data drawn from a population whose standard deviation is known to be 1, test to determine if there is enough evidence at the 5% significance level to infer that the population mean is greater than 5.

7 3 3 9 8 4 8 7 8 5 9 5 7 4 8 5 6 3 9 4 7 4 6 3 9

10.7 A machine that produces ball bearings is set so that the average diameter is .50 inch. In a sample of 100 ball bearings, it was found that $\bar{x} = .51$ inch. Assuming that the standard deviation is .05 inch, can we conclude at the 5% significance level that the mean diameter is not .50 inch?

10.8 A manufacturer of light bulbs advertises that, on average, its long-life bulb will last for more than 5,000 hours. To test the claim, a statistician took a random sample of 100 bulbs and measured the amount of time until each bulb burned out. Some of the results are listed below and all the data are stored in file XR10-08. If we assume that the lifetime of this type of bulb has a standard deviation of 400 hours, can we conclude at the 5% significance level that the claim is true?

LENGTHS OF LIFE OF LIGHT BULBS

4,531 4,061 5,361 4,805 5,334 5,128 5,129 ... 5,235 4,943 5,820

Use a software package to solve this problem.	OR	The mean of the data is $\bar{x} = 5,065$ Complete your answer manually.

10.9 In the midst of labor–management negotiations, the president of a company argues that the company's blue-collar workers, who are paid an average of $30,000 per year, are well paid because the mean annual income of all blue-collar workers in the country is less than $30,000. That figure is disputed by the union, which does not believe that the mean blue-collar income is less than $30,000. To test the company president's belief, an arbitrator draws a random sample of 350 blue-collar workers from across the country and asks each to report his or her annual income. The results are stored in file XR10-09. (Some of these data are shown below.) If the arbitrator assumes that the blue-collar incomes are distributed with a standard deviation of $8,000, can it be inferred at the 5% significance level that the company president is correct?

ANNUAL INCOME OF SAMPLE OF BLUE-COLLAR WORKERS

29,109 21,546 30,417 10,104 19,279 27,578 ... 33,310 43,229 32,430

Use a software package to solve this problem.	OR	The mean of the data is $\bar{x} = 29{,}120$ Complete your answer manually.

10.10 A dean of a business school claims that the GMAT scores of applicants to the school's M.B.A. program have increased during the past five years. Five years ago, the mean and standard deviation of GMAT scores of M.B.A. applicants were 560 and 50, respectively. Twenty applications for this year's program were randomly selected and the GMAT scores recorded. These are listed below and are also stored in file XR10-10. If we assume that the distribution of GMAT scores of this year's applicants is the same as that of five years ago, with the possible exception of the mean, can we conclude at the 5% significance level that the dean's claim is true?

GMAT SCORES OF SAMPLE OF CURRENT M.B.A. STUDENTS

597 504 603 494 560 549 535 539 637 540 625 500 545 577
606 584 607 606 585 587

Use a software package to solve this problem.	OR	The mean of the data is $\bar{x} = 569$ Complete your answer manually.

10.11 A study in the *Academy of Management Journal* (D. R. Woods and R. L. LaForge, "The Impact of Comprehensive Planning on Financial Performance," *Academy of Management Journal* 22 [3] [1979]: 516–526) reported that the average annual return on investment for American banks was 10.2% with a standard deviation of 0.8%. The article hypothesized that banks that exercised comprehensive planning would outperform the average bank. A random sample of 26 banks that exercised comprehensive planning was drawn, and the return on investment for each was calculated and listed below. The data are also stored in file XR10-11. Assuming that the return on investment is normally distributed with a standard deviation of 0.8%, can we conclude at the 10% significance level that the article's hypothesis is correct?

RETURNS ON INVESTMENT FOR BANKS THAT EXERCISED COMPREHENSIVE PLANNING

10.00 11.90 9.90 10.09 10.20 10.31 9.96 10.34 10.30 10.50 10.23
10.72 11.54 10.81 10.15 9.04 11.55 10.81 8.69 10.74 10.31 10.76
10.92 11.26 11.21 10.76

Use a software package to solve this problem.	OR	The mean of the data is $\bar{x} = 10.50$ Complete your answer manually.

10.12 Past experience indicates that the monthly long-distance telephone bill is normally distributed with a mean of $17.85 and a standard deviation of $3.87. After an advertising campaign aimed at increasing long-distance telephone usage, a random sample of 25 household bills was taken. The results are listed below and stored in file XR10-12.

a Do the data allow us to infer at the 10% significance level that the campaign was successful?

b What assumption must you make to answer part (a)?

MONTHLY LONG-DISTANCE BILLS

19.61	20.14	19.57	19.26	14.03	19.24	15.98	24.85	26.00	19.46	18.29
16.91	26.15	19.64	16.75	20.52	25.47	18.19	12.56	28.47	14.13	19.72
17.05	13.92	12.38								

> Use a software package to solve this problem.
>
> OR
>
> The mean of the data is $\bar{x} = 19.13$ Complete your answer manually.

10.4 The *p*-Value of a Test of Hypothesis

It's important for you to realize that the result of a statistical procedure is only one of several factors considered by a manager prior to making a decision. In Example 10.3, for instance, the manager concluded that there was enough statistical evidence to show that the proposed billing system would be cost-effective. However, other issues must be evaluated, too. For example, the new system might be difficult for employees to use, causing costly mistakes. Moreover, we did not prove that the new system would be cost-effective; we merely showed that statistical evidence existed to that effect. What is really needed in this situation is a measure of how much statistical evidence exists, so that it can be weighed in relation to other factors. In this section, we present such a measure: the *p*-value of a test.

> **p-Value**
>
> The *p*-value of a test of hypothesis is the smallest value of α that would lead to rejection of the null hypothesis.

To understand this definition, review Example 10.3, where the value of the test statistic was $z = 1.89$ and where, with $\alpha = .05$, the rejection region was $z > 1.645$. In that instance, we rejected the null hypothesis. Notice that our test's conclusion very much depended on the choice of the significance level α. Had we chosen, say, $\alpha = .01$, the rejection region would have been $z > 2.33$ and we could not reject the null hypothesis. Notice, however, that we did not have to decrease α very much in order to change the decision. Values of $\alpha = .02$ or .025 or even .029 lead to the same conclusion as $\alpha = .01$, but $\alpha = .03$ produces the rejection region $z > 1.88$, which does result in rejecting the null hypothesis.

Table 10.1 summarizes the relationship between the different values of α and our test conclusion. As you can see, the smallest value of α that would lead to the rejection of the null hypothesis (that is, the p-value) must lie between .029 and .030. We can determine this value more accurately and more simply by realizing that the p-value is the probability that $z > 1.89$. From Table 3 in Appendix B, we find

$$p\text{-value} = P(z > 1.89) = .0294$$

Table 10.1	Rejection Region for a Variety of Values of α for Example 10.3	
VALUE OF α	REJECTION REGION	DECISION WITH $z = 1.89$
.01	$z > 2.33$	Do not reject H_0
.02	$z > 2.05$	Do not reject H_0
.025	$z > 1.96$	Do not reject H_0
.029	$z > 1.90$	Do not reject H_0
.030	$z > 1.88$	Reject H_0
.05	$z > 1.645$	Reject H_0

Figure 10.7 demonstrates how we determine this value.

Figure 10.7

p-Value of the Test in Example 10.3

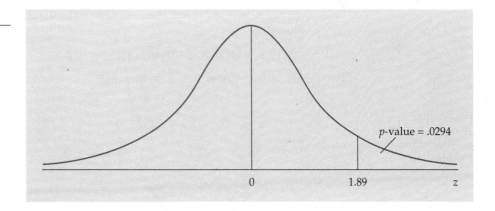

It is important to understand that the calculation of the p-value depends on, among other things, the alternative hypothesis. For Example 10.2, where the hypotheses were

H_0: $\mu = 16$

H_A: $\mu < 16$

we found $z = -1.25$. Because the rejection region is

$z < -z_\alpha$

the *p*-value is the probability that *z* is less than -1.25. That is,

$$p\text{-value} = P(z < -1.25) = .1056$$

Figure 10.8 depicts this calculation.

Figure 10.8

p-**Value of the Test in
Example 10.2**

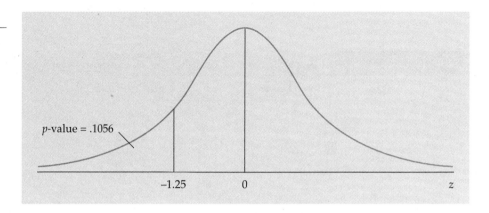

The *p*-value of a two-tail test is computed somewhat differently. As an illustration, consider Example 10.1, where we tested

$$H_0: \mu = 130$$
$$H_A: \mu \neq 130$$

and found $z = -2.13$. Because the rejection region in a two-tail test is $|z| > z_{\alpha/2}$, the probability that *z* is less than -2.13 must be doubled in order to determine the *p*-value. That is,

$$p\text{-value} = 2P(z < -2.13) = 2(.0166) = .0332$$

Figure 10.9 describes this computation.

Figure 10.9

p-**Value of the Test in
Example 10.1**

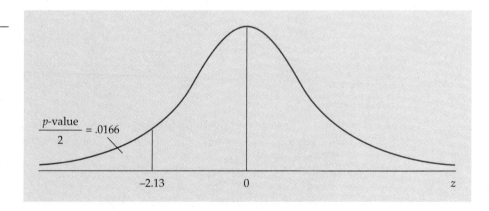

Summary of Calculation of the *p*-Value

Let z_a be the actual value of the test statistic, and let μ_0 be the value of μ specified under the null hypothesis.

If H_A: $\mu > \mu_0$, p-value = $P(z > z_a)$.

If H_A: $\mu < \mu_0$, p-value = $P(z < z_a)$.

If H_A: $\mu \neq \mu_0$, p-value = $2P(z > z_a)$ if $z_a > 0$

$\qquad\qquad\qquad\qquad\qquad = 2P(z < z_a)$ if $z_a < 0$

or, perhaps more simply, p-value = $2P(z > |z_a|)$.

Interpreting the *p*-Value

The p-value is an important number because it measures the amount of statistical evidence that supports the alternative hypothesis. To understand this interpretation fully, again refer to Example 10.3, where we tested

H_0: $\mu = 70$

H_A: $\mu > 70$

We found $\bar{x} = 74$, which yielded $z = 1.89$ and p-value = .0294. Had we observed $\bar{x} = 70$, then the test statistic would be $z = 0$ and the p-value = .5, which indicates that there is very little evidence to infer that the population mean is greater than 70. If $\bar{x}$ had equaled 77, the test statistic would equal 3.30 with a p-value of .0005, indicating that there is a great deal of evidence to infer that the mean exceeds 70.

In Table 10.2, we list several values of $\bar{x}$, the resulting test statistics, and p-values. Notice that as $\bar{x}$ increases, so does the test statistic. However, as the test statistic increases, the p-value decreases. Figure 10.10 illustrates this relationship. As $\bar{x}$ moves farther away from the value specified in the null hypothesis, 70, there is more evidence to indicate that the alternative hypothesis is true. This is reflected in the value of the test statistic and in the p-value. That is, the more evidence that exists to reject the null hypothesis in favor of the alternative hypothesis, the *greater* is the test statistic and the *smaller* is the p-value.

Table 10.2	Test Statistics and *p*-Values for Example 10.3	
SAMPLE MEAN $\bar{x}$	TEST STATISTIC $z = \dfrac{\bar{x} - \mu}{\sigma/\sqrt{n}}$	*p*-VALUE
70	0	.5000
71	.47	.3192
72	.94	.1736
73	1.41	.0793
74	1.89	.0294
75	2.36	.0091
76	2.83	.0023
77	3.30	.0005

Figure 10.10

Relationship Between z and p-Value in Example 10.3

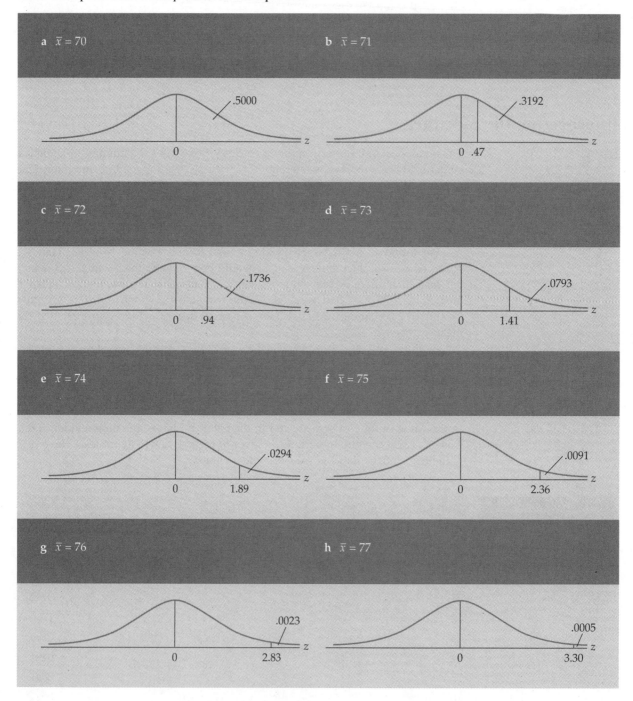

To illustrate further, consider Example 10.2, where we tested

H_0: $\mu = 16$

H_A: $\mu < 16$

In this example, smaller values of $\bar{x}$ represent stronger support of the alternative hypothesis. Smaller values of $\bar{x}$ produce smaller test statistics with smaller p-values. Table 10.3 demonstrates this point. In this example, as in Example 10.3, the greater the evidence to support the alternative hypothesis, the smaller the p-value.

Table 10.3	Test Statistics and p-Values for Example 10.2	
SAMPLE MEAN $\bar{x}$	TEST STATISTIC $z = \dfrac{\bar{x} - \mu}{\sigma/\sqrt{n}}$	p-VALUE
16.00	0	.5000
15.95	$-.63$	.2643
15.90	-1.25	.1056
15.85	-1.88	.0301
15.80	-2.50	.0062
15.75	-3.13	.0009

Interpreting the p-Value

A small p-value indicates that there is ample evidence to support the alternative hypothesis.

A large p-value indicates that there is little evidence to support the alternative hypothesis.

Because the p-value measures the statistical evidence supporting the alternative hypothesis, we can use the p-value to make the decision.

Using the p-Value to Draw Conclusions

In order to draw conclusions about the hypotheses in Section 10.3, we had to use Table 3 in Appendix B and a predetermined value of α to determine the rejection region in each case and to discover whether or not the test statistic value fell into the rejection region. We will call this approach the *rejection region method*. The p-value method is simpler. All we need to do is judge whether the p-value is small enough to justify our rejecting the null hypothesis in favor of the alternative. What is considered small enough? The answer to this question is that the manager decides. In Example 10.3, we found the p-value to be .0294. If the manager decided that, for this test (taking into account all the other factors), anything less than .01 was small enough to support the alternative hypothesis, then a p-value of .0294 would be relatively large and she would conclude that the statistical evidence did not establish that the system was cost-effective. However, if she felt that .05 or less was small enough to support the alternative hypothesis, then the p-value of .0294 would be relatively small. It follows that she would conclude from the statistical evidence that the system was cost-effective.

EXAMPLE 10.4

A major portion of waiters' and waitresses' incomes is derived from tips. This income, of course, must be reported on income tax forms. Government tax auditors assume that the average weekly total of tips is $100. A recently hired tax accountant who formerly worked as a waitress believes that this figure underestimates the true total. As a result, she has investigated the weekly tips of a randomly selected group of 150 waiters and waitresses and has found the mean to be $104. A partial listing of the data appears below and all are stored in file XM10-04. Assuming that the population standard deviation is $22, calculate the *p*-value of the test to determine whether there is enough evidence to support the tax accountant's assertion.

WEEKLY TIPS FOR WAITERS AND WAITRESSES

124.80 134.40 59.57 126.23 126.21 . . . 112.12 105.56 74.78

SOLUTION

To calculate the *p*-value, we proceed in the usual way to perform a hypothesis test, except that we do not specify a significance level and a rejection region. Because we want to determine whether there is sufficient evidence to show that the average weekly tip total exceeds $100, we set up the null and alternative hypotheses as follows.

H_0: $\mu = 100$

H_A: $\mu > 100$

SOLVING BY HAND

The test statistic and its value are

$$z = \frac{\bar{x} - \mu}{\sigma/\sqrt{n}} = \frac{104 - 100}{22/\sqrt{150}} = 2.23$$

Therefore

$$p\text{-value} = P(z > 2.23) = .0129$$

USING THE COMPUTER

Minitab Output for Example 10.4

Z-Test

```
Test of mu = 100.00 vs mu > 100.00
The assumed sigma = 22.0

Variable      N      Mean    StDev   SE Mean      Z    P-Value
Tips        150    104.00    22.47      1.80    2.23     0.013
```

Excel Output for Example 10.4

	A	B	C	D	E
1	**Test of Hypothesis About MU (SIGMA Known)**				
2					
3	Test of MU = 100 Vs MU greater than 100				
4	SIGMA = 22				
5	Sample mean = 103.9969				
6	Test Statistic: z = 2.2251				
7	P-Value = 0.013				

It is up to the accountant to judge the size of the p-value. If she decides that in conjunction with other factors this p-value is small, she will conclude that the reported weekly total of \$100 underestimates the true total. If the accountant believes that the p-value is large, she will conclude that there is not enough evidence to infer that \$100 is not an accurate estimate of the true total of tips. It is probably safe to say that most people would agree that this p-value is small, and hence, the average amount of money earned by waiters and waitresses in tips exceeds \$100. Once again, we note that the results are dubious if the sampling process is flawed or if the population standard deviation is not equal to \$22.

Figure 10.11 depicts the sampling distribution and the p-value.

Figure 10.11

---

p-Value of the Test in
Example 10.4

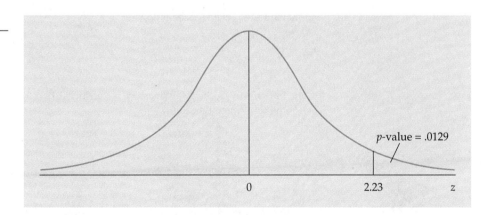

p-value = .0129

0   2.23 z

Why Do We Need the p-Value and the Rejection Region Methods to Conduct Tests?

The presentation of the p-value as another method of conducting statistical tests raises the question, why do we need two criteria for deciding whether or not to reject the null hypothesis? Ideally, all tests should be conducted using p-values because the p-value provides more information than does the rejection region method. Unfortunately, we are sometimes unable to determine a test's p-value. The test statistic presented in this chapter is the standard normal distribution for which a table (Table 3 in Appendix B) exists that allows us to calculate the p-value. However, in the rest of this book, we will be dealing with sampling distributions whose tables make calculating the p-value quite difficult (if not impossible). If you're using a computer to produce your statistics, the software packages will usually print the p-values. However, Minitab and Excel, like other software, do not print the p-value for all tests. Consequently, you will have to interpret the value of the test statistic and judge its magnitude relative to some critical value that you'll obtain from a table.

There is another reason why we need to understand both methods of testing. You will frequently encounter printed articles in reports and magazines that only print the value of the test statistic. To properly understand the article, you will have to find the rejection region and make your decision by calculating the value of the test statistic and determining whether it falls in the rejection region.

Exercises

10.13 Find the p-value of the following test.

H_0: $\mu = 200$

H_A: $\mu \neq 200$

$z = 2.63$

10.14 Find the p-value of the following test.

H_0: $\mu = 25$

H_A: $\mu \neq 25$

$\bar{x} = 29, \sigma = 15, n = 100$

10.15 Find the p-value of the following test.

H_0: $\mu = 25$

H_A: $\mu > 25$

$z = 1.86$

10.16 In performing the following test, a statistician found $z = 1.75$. Find the p-value of the test. (HINT: Be careful.)

H_0: $\mu = 600$

H_A: $\mu < 600$

10.17 Find the p-value of the following test.

H_0: $\mu = 0$

H_A: $\mu > 0$

$z = 0.0$

10.18 Find the p-value of the test conducted in Exercise 10.8.

10.19 Find the p-value of the test conducted in Exercise 10.9.

10.20 Almost everyone who regularly drives his or her car in a large North American city agrees that traffic is getting worse. A randomly selected sample of 100 cars had their speeds measured on a freeway during rush hour. The sample mean is 17.2 mph (miles per hour). Traffic engineers determined that two years ago the mean and standard deviation of speeds on the same freeway during rush hour were 18.6

and 6.2 mph, respectively. Find the p-value of the test to determine how much evidence exists to support the generally held belief that traffic is getting worse. (Assume that the standard deviation of speeds today is unchanged from that of two years ago.)

10.21 Find the p-value of the test conducted in Exercise 10.12.

10.5 Calculating the Probability of a Type II Error

As you have seen, to properly interpret the results of a test of hypothesis requires that you be able to judge the p-value of the test. However, to do so also requires that you have an understanding of the relationship between Type I and Type II errors. In this section, we describe how the probability of a Type II error is computed.

Recall Example 10.1, where we conducted the test using the sample mean as the test statistic and we computed the rejection region as

$$\bar{x} < 127.06 \quad \text{or} \quad \bar{x} > 132.94$$

A Type II error occurs when a false null hypothesis is not rejected. Thus, in Example 10.1, if $\bar{x}$ falls between 127.06 and 132.94, we will not reject the null hypothesis. If the null hypothesis is false, the probability of a Type II error is defined as

$$\beta = P(127.06 < \bar{x} < 132.94 \text{ given that } H_0 \text{ is false})$$

The condition that the null hypothesis is false only tells us that the mean is not equal to 130. If we want to compute β, we need to specify a value for μ. Suppose that we want to determine the probability of making a Type II error when, in actual fact, $\mu = 135$. That is,

$$\beta = P(127.06 < \bar{x} < 132.94 \text{ given that } \mu = 135)$$

We know that $\bar{x}$ is normally distributed with mean μ and standard deviation $\sigma/\sqrt{n}$. To proceed, we standardize $\bar{x}$ and use Table 3 in Appendix B as follows.

$$\beta = P\left(\frac{127.06 - 135}{15/\sqrt{100}} < \frac{\bar{x} - \mu}{\sigma/\sqrt{n}} < \frac{132.94 - 135}{15/\sqrt{100}}\right)$$
$$= P(-5.29 < z < -1.37) = .0853$$

This means that, if μ is actually equal to 135, the probability of incorrectly not rejecting the null hypothesis is .0853. Figure 10.12 graphically represents the calculation of β. Notice that, in order to calculate the probability of a Type II error, we had to express the rejection region in terms of the unstandardized test statistic $\bar{x}$, and we had to specify a value of μ other than the one shown in the null hypothesis. The one we used above was arbitrarily selected. In a practical setting, we would choose a value of interest to us. The following example illustrates how to choose that value and how to compute β.

Figure 10.12

Calculation of β for Example 10.1

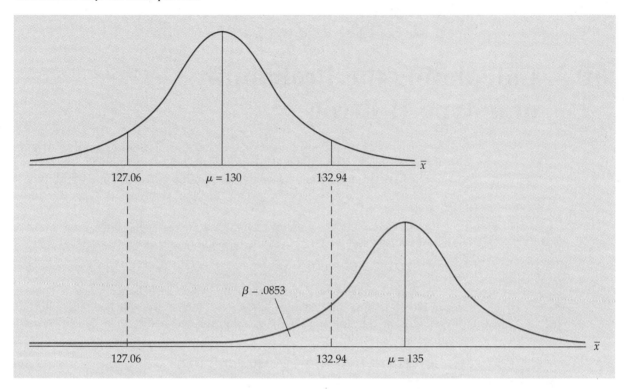

EXAMPLE 10.5

The feasibility of constructing a profitable electricity-producing windmill depends on the average velocity of the wind. For a certain type of windmill, the average wind speed would have to exceed 20 mph in order for its construction to be feasible. To test whether or not a particular site is appropriate for this windmill, 50 readings of the wind velocity are taken, and the average is calculated. The test is designed to answer the question, is the site feasible? That is, is there sufficient evidence to conclude that the average wind velocity exceeds 20 mph? We want to test the following hypotheses.

$$H_0: \mu = 20$$
$$H_A: \mu > 20$$

If, when the test is conducted, a Type I error is committed (rejecting the null hypothesis when it is true), we would conclude mistakenly that the average wind velocity exceeds 20 mph. The consequence of this decision is that the windmill would be built on an inappropriate site. Because this error is quite costly, we specify a small value for α, $\alpha = .01$. If a Type II error is committed (not rejecting the null hypothesis when it is false), we would conclude mistakenly that the average wind velocity does not exceed 20 mph. As a result, we would not build the windmill on that site, even though the site is a good one. The cost of this error is not very large, since, if the site under consideration is judged to be inappropriate, the search for a good site would simply continue. But suppose that a site where the wind velocity is greater than or equal to 25 mph is extremely profitable. To judge the effectiveness of this test (to determine if our selection of $\alpha = .01$ and $n = 50$ is appropriate), we compute the probability of committing this error. Our task is to calculate β when $\mu = 25$. (Assume that we know that $\sigma = 12$ mph.)

SOLUTION

Our first step is to set up the rejection region in terms of $\bar{x}$. The rejection region is

$$z > z_\alpha = z_{.01} = 2.33$$

so we have

$$z = \frac{\bar{x} - \mu}{\sigma/\sqrt{n}} = \frac{\bar{x} - 20}{12/\sqrt{50}} > 2.33$$

Solving the inequality, we express the rejection region as

$$\bar{x} > 23.95$$

The second step is to describe the region where the null hypothesis is not rejected as

$$\bar{x} < 23.95$$

Thus,

$$\beta = P(\bar{x} < 23.95 \text{ given that } \mu = 25) = P\left(\frac{\bar{x} - \mu}{\sigma/\sqrt{n}} < \frac{23.95 - 25}{12/\sqrt{50}}\right)$$

$$= P(z < -.62) = .2676$$

The probability of not rejecting the null hypothesis when $\mu = 25$ is .2676. (See Figure 10.13.) This means that, when the mean wind velocity is 25 mph, there is a 26.76% probability of erroneously concluding that the site is not profitable. If this probability is considered too large, we can reduce it by either increasing α or increasing n.

For example, if we increase α to .10 and leave $n = 50$, then $\beta = .0475$. With $\alpha = .10$, however, the probability of building on a site that is not profitable is too large. If we let $\alpha = .01$ but increase n to 100, then $\beta = .0329$. (We recommend that you perform these computations yourself.) Now both α and β are quite small, but the cost of sampling has increased. Nonetheless, the cost of sampling is small in comparison to the costs of making Type I and Type II errors in this situation.

Another way of judging a test is to measure its *power*—the probability of its leading us to reject the null hypothesis when it is false—rather than measuring the probability of a Type II error. Thus, the power of the test is equal to $1 - \beta$. In the present example, the power of the test with $n = 50$ and $\alpha = .01$ is $1 - .2676 = .7324$. When more than one test can be performed in a given situation, we would naturally prefer to use the test that is correct more frequently. If (given the same alternative hypothesis, sample size, and significance level) one test has a higher power than a second test, the first test is said to be more powerful.

Figure 10.13

Calculation of β for Example 10.5

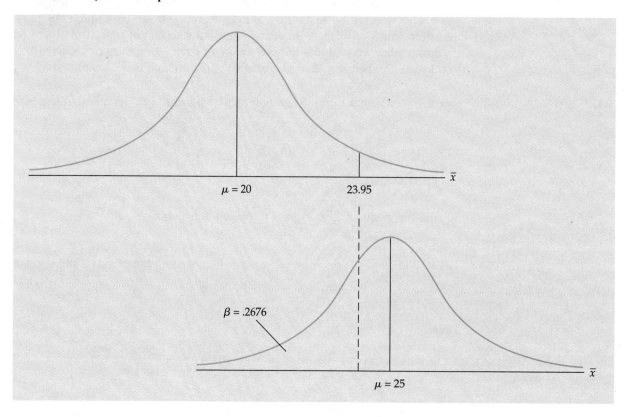

Developing an Understanding of Statistical Concepts

A critical concept in statistics is the relationship between the probabilities of Type I and Type II errors. If we attempt to lower the probability of a Type I error, we increase the probability of a Type II error (assuming that the sample size is fixed). This inverse relationship affects the way in which we decide whether a p-value is small enough to reject the null hypothesis in favor of the alternative. If we demand that the p-value be very small (say 1% or less) in order to reject the null hypothesis, we make the occurrence of a Type II error more likely than would be the case with a larger p-value standard. As a result, we must always consider the consequences of both a Type I and a Type II error. This concept extends outside the field of statistics. There are many nonstatistical applications of hypothesis testing where we must consider the costs and probabilities associated with making incorrect choices.

Exercises

10.22 Calculate the probability of a Type II error for the following test of hypothesis, given that $\mu = 203$.

H_0: $\mu = 200$

H_A: $\mu \neq 200$

$\alpha = .05$, $\sigma = 10$, $n = 100$

10.23 Find the probability of a Type II error for the test below, given that $\mu = 1,050$.

$H_0: \mu = 1,000$

$H_A: \mu > 1,000$

$\alpha = .01, \sigma = 50, n = 25$

10.24 Given the following test of hypothesis, find β if $\mu = 48$.

$H_0: \mu = 50$

$H_A: \mu < 50$

$\alpha = .05, \sigma = 10, n = 40$

10.25 For the test of hypothesis

$H_0: \mu = 1,000$

$H_A: \mu \neq 1,000$

with

$\alpha = .05, \sigma = 200, n = 100$

find β when $\mu = 900, 940, 980, 1,020, 1,060, 1,100$.

10.26 For Exercise 10.25, graph μ (on the horizontal axis) versus β (on the vertical axis). If necessary, calculate β for additional values of μ. The resulting graph is called the **operating characteristic (OC) curve**.

10.27 For Exercise 10.25, graph μ versus $1 - \beta$. Recall that $1 - \beta$ is called the *power* of the test; as a consequence, the graph is called the **power curve**.

10.28 Repeat Exercises 10.25 through 10.27 with $n = 25$.

10.29 What do you notice about the graphs in Exercises 10.27 and 10.28? What are the implications of your observations?

10.30 Refer to Exercise 10.10. Find the probability of erroneously concluding that there is not enough evidence to support the claim when, in fact, the true mean GMAT score is 600.

10.31 A school-board administrator believes that the average number of days absent per year among students is less than 10 days. From past experience, he knows that the population standard deviation is 3 days. In testing to determine whether his belief is true, he could use either of the following plans.

i $n = 100, \alpha = .05$

ii $n = 100, \alpha = .01$

iii $n = 250, \alpha = .05$

Which plan has the lower probability of a Type II error, given that the true population average is 9 days.

10.32 Suppose we want to test a null hypothesis that the mean of a population is 145 against an alternative hypothesis that the mean is less than 145. A sample of 100 measurements drawn from the population (whose standard deviation is 20) yields a mean of 140. If the probability of a Type I error is chosen to be .05, calculate the probability of a Type II error, assuming that the true population mean equals 142.

10.6 The Road Ahead

We had two principal goals to accomplish in Chapters 9 and 10. First, we wanted to present the concepts of estimation and hypothesis testing. Second, we wanted to show how to produce confidence interval estimates and conduct tests of hypotheses. The importance of both of these goals should not be underestimated. Almost everything that follows this chapter will involve either estimating a parameter or testing a set of hypotheses. Consequently, Sections 9.3 and 10.3 set the pattern for the way in which statistical techniques are applied. It is no exaggeration to state that if you understand how to produce and use interval estimates and how to conduct and interpret hypothesis tests, then you are halfway to the ultimate goal of being a competent statistician. It is fair for you to ask what more you must accomplish to achieve this goal. The answer, simply put, is much more of the same.

In the chapters that follow, we plan to present about three dozen different statistical techniques that can be (and frequently are) employed by decision makers. To calculate the value of test statistics or interval estimates requires nothing more than the ability to add, subtract, multiply, divide, and compute square roots. If you intend to use the computer, all you need to know are the commands. The key, then, to applying statistics is knowing which formula to calculate or which set of commands to issue. Thus, the real challenge of the subject lies in the problem of identifying which statistical method is the most appropriate one to use.

Most students have some difficulty in recognizing the particular kind of statistical problem they are addressing unless, of course, the problem appears among the exercises at the end of a section that just introduced the technique needed. Unfortunately, in practice, statistical problems do not appear already so coded. Consequently, we have adopted an approach to teaching statistics that is designed to help identify the statistical technique.

A number of factors determine which statistical method should be used, but two are especially important: the type of data and the purpose of the statistical inference. In Chapter 2, we pointed out that there are effectively three types of data—qualitative, ranked, and quantitative. Recall that qualitative data represent categories such as marital status, occupation, and gender. Statisticians often record qualitative data by assigning numbers to the responses (e.g., 1 = single; 2 = married; 3 = divorced; 4 = widowed). Because these numbers are assigned completely arbitrarily, any calculations performed on them are meaningless. All that we can do with qualitative data is count the number of times each category is observed. Ranked data are obtained from questions whose answers represent a rating or ranking system. For example, if students are asked to rate a university professor, the responses may be *excellent, good, fair,* or *poor.* To draw inferences about such data, we convert the responses to numbers. Any numbering system is valid as long as the order of the responses is preserved. Thus "4 = excellent; 3 = good; 2 = fair; 1 = poor" is just as valid as "10 = excellent; 5 = good; 2 = fair; 1 = poor." Because of this feature, the most appropriate statistical procedures for ranked data are ones based on a ranking process. Quantitative data are real numbers such as those representing income, age, height, weight, and volume. Computation of means and variances is permissible.

The second key factor in determining the statistical technique is the purpose of doing the work. Every statistical method has some specific objective. There are five such objectives addressed in this book.

PROBLEM OBJECTIVES

1 **Describe a single population.** Our objective here is to describe some property of a population of interest. The decision about which property to describe is generally dictated by the type of data. For example, suppose the population of interest consists of all purchasers of home computers. If we are interested in the purchasers' incomes (for which the data are quantita-

tive), we may calculate the mean or the variance to describe that aspect of the population. But if we are interested in the brand of computer that has been bought (for which the data are qualitative), all we can do is compute the proportion of the population that purchases each brand.

2 **Compare two populations.** In this case, our goal is to compare a property of one population with a corresponding property of a second population. For example, suppose the populations of interest are male and female purchasers of computers. We could compare the means of their incomes, or we could compare the proportion of each population that purchases a certain brand. Once again, the data type generally determines what kinds of properties we compare.

3 **Compare two or more populations.** We might want to compare the average income in each of several locations in order (for example) to decide where to build a new shopping center. Or we might want to compare the proportions of defective items in a number of production lines in order to determine which line is the best. In each case, the problem objective involves comparing two or more populations.

4 **Analyze the relationship between two variables.** There are numerous situations in which we want to know how one variable is related to another. Governments need to know what effect rising interest rates have on the unemployment rate. Companies want to investigate how the sizes of their advertising budgets influence sales volume. In most of the problems in this introductory text, the two variables to be analyzed will be of the same type: we will not attempt to cover the fairly large body of statistical techniques that has been developed to deal with two variables of different types.

5 **Analyze the relationship among two or more variables.** Our objective here is usually to forecast one variable (called the **dependent variable**) on the basis of several other variables (called **independent variables**). We will deal with this problem only in situations in which all variables are quantitative.

Table 10.4 lists the types of data and the five problem objectives. For each combination, the table specifies the chapter and/or section where the appropriate statistical technique is presented. For your convenience, a more detailed version of this table is reproduced inside the front cover of this book.

A Brief Comment About Derivations

Because this book is about statistical applications, we assume that our readers have little interest in the mathematical derivations of the techniques described. However, it might be helpful for you to have some understanding about the process that produces the formulas.

As described above, factors such as the problem objective and the type of data determine the parameter to be estimated and tested. For each parameter, statisticians have determined which statistic to use. That statistic has a sampling distribution that can usually be expressed as a formula. For example, in this chapter, the parameter of interest was the population mean μ, whose best estimator is the sample mean $\bar{x}$. Assuming that the population variance σ^2 is known, the sampling distribution of $\bar{x}$ is normal (or approximately so) with mean μ and standard deviation $\sigma/\sqrt{n}$. The sampling distribution can be described by the formula

$$z = \frac{\bar{x} - \mu}{\sigma/\sqrt{n}}$$

This formula also describes the test statistic for μ with σ^2 known. With a little algebra, we were able to derive (in Section 9.3) the confidence interval estimator of μ.

In future chapters, we will repeat this process, which in several cases involves the introduction of a new sampling distribution. While its shape and formula will differ from the sampling distribution used in this chapter, the pattern will be the same. In general, the formula that expresses the sampling distribution will describe the test statistic. Then some algebraic manipulation (which we will not show) produces the confidence interval estimator. Consequently, we will reverse the order of presentation of the two techniques. That is, we will present the test of hypothesis first, followed by the confidence interval estimator.

Table 10.4	Guide to the Statistical Techniques Showing Where Each Technique Is Introduced		
		DATA TYPE	
PROBLEM OBJECTIVE	QUALITATIVE	RANKED	QUANTITATIVE
Describe a single population	Sec 11.4, 15.2	Not covered	Sec 11.2, 11.3
Compare two populations	Sec 12.6	Appendix 12.C	Sec 12.2, 12.4, 12.5, Appendix 12.C
Compare two or more populations	Sec 15.3	Appendix 14.B	Chapter 14, Appendix 14.B
Analyze the relationship between two variables	Sec 15.3	Appendix 16.C	Chapter 16
Analyze the relationship among two or more variables	Not covered	Not covered	Chapter 17

10.7 Summary

In this chapter, we introduced the concepts of hypothesis testing and applied them to testing hypotheses about a population mean. We showed how to specify the null and alternative hypotheses, set up the rejection region, compute the value of the test statistic, and finally, to make a decision. Equally as important, we discussed how to interpret the test results. This chapter also demonstrated another way to make decisions—by calculating and using the p-value of the test. To help interpret test results, we showed how to calculate the probability of a Type II error. Finally, we provided a road map of how we plan to present statistical techniques. We complete this summary by listing the formulas described in this chapter.

IMPORTANT TERMS

Null hypothesis

Alternative hypothesis

Test statistic

Rejection region

Type I error

Type II error

Significance level

Two-tail test

One-tail test

p-value of a test

Problem objective

Table 10.5

Summary of Formulas

Test statistic: $z = \dfrac{\bar{x} - \mu}{\sigma/\sqrt{n}}$

p-value of the test: $P(z > z_a)$ if H_A: $\mu > \mu_0$

$P(z < z_a)$ if H_A: $\mu < \mu_0$

$2P(z > |z_a|)$ if H_A: $\mu \neq \mu_0$

Probability of a Type II error: $\beta = P(\bar{x}_S < \bar{x} < \bar{x}_L$ given that $\mu =$ other than that specified under the null hypothesis)

Supplementary Exercises

10.33 In an attempt to reduce the number of person-hours lost as a result of industrial accidents, a large production plant installed new safety equipment. In a test of the effectiveness of the equipment, a random sample of 50 departments was chosen. The number of person-hours lost in the month prior to and the month after the installation of the safety equipment was recorded. The percentage change was calculated, and the data stored in file XR10-33. (Some of these data are listed below.) Assume that the population standard deviation is $\sigma = 5$. What conclusion can you draw using a 10% significance level?

$$-9.38 \quad 6.82 \quad -5.58 \quad \ldots \ldots \quad .82 \quad .02 \quad -1.28$$

Use a software package to solve this problem.	OR	The mean of the data is $\bar{x} = -1.2$ Complete your answer manually.

10.34 A highway patrol officer believes that the average speed of cars traveling over a certain stretch of highway exceeds the posted limit of 55 mph. The speeds of a random sample of 200 cars were recorded and stored in file XR10-34. (Some of these data are listed below.) Do these data provide sufficient evidence at the 1% significance level to support the officer's belief? What is the p-value of the test? (Assume that the standard deviation is known to be 5.)

$$53 \quad 50 \quad 54 \quad \ldots \quad 56 \quad 50 \quad 63$$

Use a software package to solve this problem.	OR	The mean of the data is $\bar{x} = 55.8$ Complete your answer manually.

10.35 An automotive expert claims that the large number of self-serve gasoline stations has resulted in poor automobile maintenance, and that the average tire pressure is more than 4 psi (pounds per square inch) below its manufacturer's specification. As a quick test, 10 tires are examined, and the number of psi each tire is below specification is recorded. The resulting data are as follows.

7 9 2 0 5 6 3 5 8 9

If we assume that tire pressure is normally distributed with $\sigma = 1.5$ psi, can we infer at the 10% significance level that the expert is correct? What is the p-value?

10.36 For the past few years, the number of customers of a drive-up bank in New York has averaged 20 per hour, with a standard deviation of 3 per hour. This year, another bank one mile away opened a drive-up window. The manager of the first bank believes that this will result in a decrease in the number of customers. The number of customers who arrived during 15 randomly selected hours was recorded and listed below. Can we conclude at the 5% significance level that the manager is correct? What is the p-value?

17 23 22 15 18 16 21 15 19 20 17 15 22 16 21

10.37 A fast-food franchiser is considering building a restaurant at a certain location. Based on financial analyses, a site is acceptable only if the number of pedestrians passing the location averages more than 100 per hour. The number of pedestrians observed for each of 40 hours was recorded and stored in file XR10-37, with some of these data listed below. Assuming that the population standard deviation is known to be 12, can we conclude that the site is acceptable? (Set your own significance level.)

97 101 97 ... 116 112 123

Use a software package to solve this problem.	OR	The mean of the data is $\bar{x} = 105.7$ Complete your answer manually.

10.38 In recent years, a number of companies have been formed that offer competition to AT&T in long-distance calls. All advertise that their rates are lower than AT&T's, and as a result their bills will be lower. AT&T has responded by arguing that for the average consumer there will be no difference in billing. Suppose that a statistician working for AT&T determines that the mean and standard deviation of monthly long-distance bills for all its residential customers are $17.85 and $3.87, respectively. He then takes a random sample of 100 customers and recalculates their last month's bill using the rates quoted by a leading competitor. These data are stored in file XR10-38. A partial listing of the data appears below. Assuming that the standard deviation of this population is the same as for AT&T, can we conclude at the 5% significance level that there is a difference between AT&T's bills and those of the leading competitor?

15.60   13.45   18.85   ...   17.46   16.54   17.20

Use a software package to solve this problem.	OR	The mean of the data is $\bar{x} = 17.55$ Complete your answer manually.

To perform a two-tail test of μ, type

ZTEST K1 K2 C1

where **K1** is the value of μ under the null hypothesis, **K2** is the population standard deviation σ, and the data are stored in column 1. For example,

ZTEST 100 10 C1

tests

H_0: $\mu = 100$
H_A: $\mu \neq 100$

where $\sigma = 10$. To perform a one-tail test, use the subcommand **ALTERNATIVE**. (Remember that, when using a subcommand, you must end the preceding command with a semicolon and you must end the subcommand with a period.) The subcommand

ALTERNATIVE 1

performs a one-tail test with

H_A: $\mu > $ **K1**

The subcommand

ALTERNATIVE −1

tests the alternative hypothesis

H_A: $\mu < $ **K1**

To conduct the test in Example 10.2, type

ZTEST 16 .4 C1;
ALTERNATIVE −1.

Instead of using the macro we created, you can use Excel's built-in **ZTEST**.

1 Click f_x, **Statistical**, **ZTEST**, and **Next>**.

2 Specify the location of the data (array). E.g. **A1:A26** (for Example 10.2).

3 Specify the value of the parameter under the null hypothesis (x). E.g., **16**.

4 Specify the value of the population standard deviation (sigma). E.g., **.4**.

5 Click **Finish**.

EXCEL 97

Excel 97 Users:
Click **OK** instead of **Next>**
and **Finish**

Excel will output a value it erroneously claims to be the two-tail *p*-value. It is actually $P(z > $ calculated value of z). In Example 10.2, $z = -1.25$. Thus, Excel prints $P(z > -1.25)$, which is .8944. Since the alternative hypothesis states that $\mu < 16$, we calculate the *p*-value by subtracting .8944 from 1. Thus, *p*-value = .1056.

11 Inference about the Description of a Single Population

11.1 Introduction

In the previous two chapters, we introduced the concepts of statistical inference and showed how to estimate and test a population mean. However, the illustration we chose is unrealistic because the techniques require us to use the population standard deviation σ, which, in general, is unknown. The purpose, then, of Chapters 9 and 10 was to set the pattern for the way in which we plan to present other statistical techniques. That is, we will begin by identifying the parameter to be estimated or tested. We will then specify the parameter's estimator (each parameter has an estimator chosen because of the characteristics we discussed at the beginning of Chapter 9) and its sampling distribution. Using simple mathematics, statisticians have derived the confidence interval estimator and the test statistic. This pattern will be used repeatedly as we introduce new techniques.

In Section 10.6, we described the five problem objectives addressed in this book, and we laid out the order of presentation of the statistical methods. In this chapter, we will present techniques employed when the problem objective is to describe a single population. When the data are quantitative, the parameters of interest are the population mean μ and the population variance σ^2. In Section 11.2, we describe how to make inferences about the population mean under the more realistic assumption that the population variance is unknown. In Section 11.3, we continue to deal with quantitative data, but our parameter of interest becomes the population variance.

In Chapter 2 and in Section 10.6, we pointed out that when the data are qualitative, the only computation that makes sense is determining the proportion of times each value occurs. Section 11.4 discusses inference about the proportion p.

Here are three examples of inference about the description of a single population.

Example 1 The number of automatic teller machines (ATMs) has grown dramatically in the last several years. It has been estimated that for each transaction performed by an ATM instead of a teller, a bank saves more than one dollar. However, because of the cost of installation and maintenance, the number and placement of ATMs must be carefully planned. To help determine potential savings and thus whether a particular site should have an ATM, a bank conducted a survey to estimate the frequency with which each of several thousand potential ATM users will actually use the ATM annually. The problem objective is to describe the population of potential ATM users. The data are quantitative, because the bank intends to determine how many times per year each person will use the ATM. The parameter to be estimated is the mean frequency of use annually per person. From this statistic, the bank can estimate annual savings to decide whether to install an ATM.

Example 2 Bottlenecks in a production line can occur for a variety of reasons. For example, if the amount of time taken to complete a certain task is always greater than some others on an assembly line, several workers and/or machines will be idle while others will be overworked. In designing the way in which products will be produced, managers must consider a number of factors in order to avoid bottlenecks. Suppose that in an experiment to measure the amount of time required to complete a task on an assembly line, a random sample of workers' times is measured. The problem objective is to describe the population of workers' times—data that are quantitative. The managers would like to draw inferences about the central location of the times, in which case the parameter to be estimated or tested is the population mean. Equally important in this scenario is the variability of the times, because a great deal of variation can cause bottleneck problems even when the mean assembly times of different tasks are identical. Consequently, management will also draw inferences about the population variance. Several different production designs will be examined before a final decision is made.

Example 3 The profits of television networks depend greatly on the number of viewers who are tuned into each network. In most North American cities, viewers can choose from among the major networks and an assortment of independent stations, cable, and pay TV. Because the population of television viewers is so large (over 100 million in the United States and over 10 million in Canada), statistical techniques are used to draw inferences about it. In North America, this service is provided by several firms, including A. C. Nielsen, and the results are known as the Nielsen ratings. The problem objective is to describe the population of television viewers. Each respondent would be asked (among other things) which programs he or she watches at particular times. The data are qualitative. Consequently, the parameter of interest is the proportion of viewers who watch each program.

11.2 Inference about a Population Mean When the Population Variance Is Unknown

In Sections 9.3 and 10.3, we demonstrated how to estimate and test the population mean when the population variance is known. The confidence interval estimator and the test statistic were derived from the sampling distribution of the sample mean with σ^2 known, expressed as

$$z = \frac{\bar{x} - \mu}{\sigma/\sqrt{n}}$$

In this section, we assume that σ^2 is unknown. Consequently, the sampling distribution above cannot be used. Instead, we substitute the sample standard deviation s in place of the unknown population standard deviation σ. The result is called a **t-statistic** because that is what mathematician William S. Gosset called it. In 1908, Gosset showed that the t-statistic defined as

$$t = \frac{\bar{x} - \mu}{s/\sqrt{n}}$$

is **Student t** distributed when the sampled population is normally distributed. (Gosset published his findings under the pseudonym "Student," hence the Student t distribution.)

Student t Distribution

Figure 11.1 depicts a Student t distribution. As you can see, the Student t distribution is similar to the standard normal distribution. Like the standard normal distribution, the Student t distribution is symmetrical about zero. It is also mound-shaped, whereas the normal distribution is bell-shaped. Figure 11.2 shows both a Student t and a standard normal distribution. The former is more widely dispersed than the latter. The extent to which the Student t distribution is more spread out than the standard normal distribution is determined by a function of the sample size called the **degrees of freedom** (abbreviated d.f.), which varies by the t-statistic. (This application is only the first of several different statistics that are Student t distributed.) For this application, the number of degrees of freedom equals the sample size minus 1. That is, d.f. $= n - 1$. Figure 11.3 depicts Student t distributions with several different degrees of freedom. Notice that as the degrees of freedom grow larger, the Student t distribution's dispersion gets smaller.

Figure 11.1

Student t Distribution

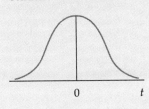

0   t

Figure 11.2

Student t and Standard Normal Distribution

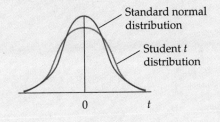

Standard normal distribution

Student t distribution

0   t

Figure 11.3

Student *t* Distributions

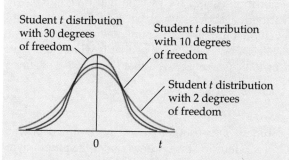

For the purpose of computing confidence interval estimates and setting up rejection regions for tests of hypothesis, we need to be able to determine critical values. Table 4 in Appendix B specifies values of t_A, where t_A equals the value of t for which the area to its right under the Student t curve is equal to A. (See Figure 11.4.) This table is reproduced as Table 11.1.

Figure 11.4

Student *t* Value Such that the Area to Its Right Under the Curve Is *A*

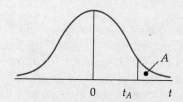

Observe that t_A is provided for degrees of freedom ranging from 1 to 200 and ∞. To read this table, simply identify the degrees of freedom and find that value or the closest number to it. Then locate the column representing the t_A value you want. We denote this value $t_{A,df}$. For example, if we want the value of t such that the area under the Student t curve is .05 and the number of degrees of freedom is 10, we locate 10 in the first column and move across this row until we locate the value under the heading $t_{.05}$. We find (see Table 11.2)

$$t_{.05,10} = 1.812$$

Table 11.1

Critical Values of the Student *t* Distribution

DEGREES OF FREEDOM	$t_{.100}$	$t_{.05}$	$t_{.025}$	$t_{.01}$	$t_{.005}$
1	3.078	6.314	12.706	31.821	63.657
2	1.886	2.920	4.303	6.965	9.925
3	1.638	2.353	3.182	4.541	5.841
4	1.533	2.132	2.776	3.747	4.604
5	1.476	2.015	2.571	3.365	4.032
6	1.440	1.943	2.447	3.143	3.707
7	1.415	1.895	2.365	2.998	3.499
8	1.397	1.860	2.306	2.896	3.355
9	1.383	1.833	2.262	2.821	3.250
10	1.372	1.812	2.228	2.764	3.169
11	1.363	1.796	2.201	2.718	3.106
12	1.356	1.782	2.179	2.681	3.055
13	1.350	1.771	2.160	2.650	3.012
14	1.345	1.761	2.145	2.624	2.977
15	1.341	1.753	2.131	2.602	2.947
16	1.337	1.746	2.120	2.583	2.921
17	1.333	1.740	2.110	2.567	2.898
18	1.330	1.734	2.101	2.552	2.878
19	1.328	1.729	2.093	2.539	2.861
20	1.325	1.725	2.086	2.528	2.845
21	1.323	1.721	2.080	2.518	2.831
22	1.321	1.717	2.074	2.508	2.819
23	1.319	1.714	2.069	2.500	2.807
24	1.318	1.711	2.064	2.492	2.797
25	1.316	1.708	2.060	2.485	2.787
26	1.315	1.706	2.056	2.479	2.779
27	1.314	1.703	2.052	2.473	2.771
28	1.313	1.701	2.048	2.467	2.763
29	1.311	1.699	2.045	2.462	2.756
30	1.310	1.697	2.042	2.457	2.750
35	1.306	1.690	2.030	2.438	2.724
40	1.303	1.684	2.021	2.423	2.705
45	1.301	1.679	2.014	2.412	2.690
50	1.299	1.676	2.009	2.403	2.678
60	1.296	1.671	2.000	2.390	2.660
70	1.294	1.667	1.994	2.381	2.648
80	1.292	1.664	1.990	2.374	2.639
90	1.291	1.662	1.987	2.369	2.632
100	1.290	1.660	1.984	2.364	2.626
120	1.289	1.658	1.980	2.358	2.617
140	1.288	1.656	1.977	2.353	2.611
160	1.287	1.654	1.975	2.350	2.607
180	1.286	1.653	1.973	2.347	2.603
200	1.286	1.653	1.972	2.345	2.601
∞	1.282	1.645	1.960	2.326	2.576

SOURCE: From M. Merrington, "Table of Percentage Points of the *t*-Distribution," *Biometrika* 32 (1941): 300. Reproduced by permission of the Biometrika trustees.

Table 11.2	Finding $t_{.05,10}$				
DEGREES OF FREEDOM	$t_{.100}$	$t_{.05}$	$t_{.025}$	$t_{.01}$	$t_{.005}$
1	3.078	6.314	12.706	31.821	63.657
2	1.886	2.920	4.303	6.965	9.925
3	1.638	2.353	3.182	4.541	5.841
4	1.533	2.132	2.776	3.747	4.604
5	1.476	2.015	2.571	3.365	4.032
6	1.440	1.943	2.447	3.143	3.707
7	1.415	1.895	2.365	2.998	3.499
8	1.397	1.860	2.306	2.896	3.355
9	1.383	1.833	2.262	2.821	3.250
10	1.372	1.812	2.228	2.764	3.169
11	1.363	1.796	2.201	2.718	3.106
12	1.356	1.782	2.179	2.681	3.055

If the number of degrees of freedom is 25, we find (see Table 11.3)

$$t_{.05,25} = 1.708$$

Table 11.3	Finding $t_{.05,25}$				
DEGREES OF FREEDOM	$t_{.100}$	$t_{.05}$	$t_{.025}$	$t_{.01}$	$t_{.005}$
1	3.078	6.314	12.706	31.821	63.657
2	1.886	2.920	4.303	6.965	9.925
3	1.638	2.353	3.182	4.541	5.841
4	1.533	2.132	2.776	3.747	4.604
5	1.476	2.015	2.571	3.365	4.032
			•		
			•		
			•		
21	1.323	1.721	2.080	2.518	2.831
22	1.321	1.717	2.074	2.508	2.819
23	1.319	1.714	2.069	2.500	2.807
24	1.318	1.711	2.064	2.492	2.797
25	1.316	1.708	2.060	2.485	2.787
26	1.315	1.706	2.056	2.479	2.779

If the number of degrees of freedom is 74, we find the number of degrees of freedom closest to 74 listed in the table, which is 70. (See Table 11.4.)

$$t_{.05,74} \approx t_{.05,70} = 1.667$$

Table 11.4		Finding $t_{.05,70}$				
DEGREES OF FREEDOM	$t_{.100}$	$t_{.05}$	$t_{.025}$	$t_{.01}$	$t_{.005}$
1	3.078	6.314	12.706	31.821	63.657
2	1.886	2.920	4.303	6.965	9.925
3	1.638	2.353	3.182	4.541	5.841
4	1.533	2.132	2.776	3.747	4.604
5	1.476	2.015	2.571	3.365	4.032
			•		
			•		
			•		
45	1.301	1.679	2.014	2.412	2.690
50	1.299	1.676	2.009	2.403	2.678
60	1.296	1.671	2.000	2.390	2.660
70	1.294	1.667	1.994	2.381	2.648
80	1.292	1.664	1.990	2.374	2.639
90	1.291	1.662	1.987	2.369	2.632
100	1.290	1.660	1.984	2.364	2.626
120	1.289	1.658	1.980	2.358	2.617
140	1.288	1.656	1.977	2.353	2.611
160	1.287	1.654	1.975	2.350	2.607
180	1.286	1.653	1.973	2.347	2.603
200	1.286	1.653	1.972	2.345	2.601
∞	1.282	1.645	1.960	2.326	2.576

In his 1908 article, Gosset showed that when the number of degrees of freedom is infinitely large, t_A is equal to z_A. (As the sample size increases, s approaches σ, and hence t approaches z.) That is, the Student t distribution is identical to the standard normal distribution. As you can see, the last row in the Student t table shows values of t_A with d.f. $= \infty$ that are equal to the z_A values we used in the previous chapter. (They do not appear equal except for $t_{.05,\infty} = z_{.05} = 1.96$ because we had only two decimal places to measure z_A, whereas the t_A values have three decimal places.) Notice the similarity between the values of t_A with 200 degrees of freedom and those with an infinite number of degrees of freedom. Consequently, when we have a Student t distribution with degrees of freedom greater than 200, we will approximate it by a Student t distribution with an infinite number of degrees of freedom (which is the same as the standard normal distribution).

It should be noted that the statistic $(\bar{x} - \mu)/(s/\sqrt{n})$ has the Student t distribution only if the sample is drawn from a normal population. However, this application of the t distribution is said to be **robust**; this means that the t distribution also provides an adequate approximate sampling distribution of the t-statistic for moderately nonnormal populations. Thus, the statistical inference techniques that follow are valid except when applied to distinctly nonnormal populations.

In actual practice, some statisticians ignore the preceding requirement or blindly assume that the population is normal or only somewhat nonnormal. We urge you not to be one of them. Because we seldom get to know the true value of the parameter in question, our only way of knowing whether the statistical technique is valid is to be certain that the requirements underlying the technique are satisfied. At the very least, you should draw the histogram of any random variable that you are assuming is normal to ensure that the assumption is not badly violated.

Testing the Population Mean When the Population Variance Is Unknown

With exactly the same logic used to develop the test statistic in Section 10.3, we derive the following test statistic.

Test Statistic for μ When σ^2 Is Unknown

When the population variance is unknown and the population is normally distributed, the test statistic for testing hypotheses about μ is

$$t = \frac{\bar{x} - \mu}{s/\sqrt{n}}$$

which has a Student t distribution with $n - 1$ degrees of freedom.

Note that we have now presented two different test statistics for testing the population mean. In Section 10.3, we tested μ under the assumption that the population variance σ^2 was known. In that case we employed the test statistic

$$z = \frac{\bar{x} - \mu}{\sigma/\sqrt{n}}$$

However, as we've already discussed, the application of this statistic is quite rare in practice. Consequently, henceforth when we test hypotheses about a population mean we will use the test statistic

$$t = \frac{\bar{x} - \mu}{s/\sqrt{n}}$$

because the population variance is unknown.

EXAMPLE 11.1

The Imaginex Corporation owns a factory that produces sulfuric acid, used primarily in automobile batteries. Because of changing conditions, the plant's output is quite variable. The company's president has observed that the output is normally distributed with a mean of 8,200 liters per hour. He recently has been informed that the government is considering a new law that would require him to alter the way in which the chemical is manufactured. Unsure about whether he should lobby against the legislation, he undertakes an experiment. He reorganizes production facilities to comply with the proposed law and observes the hourly output for two working days (16 hours). The data are shown below (and stored in file XM11-01). Do these data indicate that the new legislation will reduce output? A significance level of 5% is considered appropriate.

HOURLY OUTPUT

8,283 8,121 7,905 8,097 7,969 8,101 8,069 8,240 8,410 8,483 8,510
7,480 8,097 8,237 7,682 8,076

SOLUTION

IDENTIFYING THE TECHNIQUE

The problem objective is to describe the population of hourly sulfuric acid output from the plant using production facilities modified to comply with the proposed legislation. The data are quantitative, indicating that the parameter to be tested is the population mean. Because the president wants to know whether he can conclude that there will be a decrease in production from the current level of 8,200 liters per hour, the alternative hypothesis will specify H_A: $\mu < 8,200$. The test statistic is

$$t = \frac{\bar{x} - \mu}{s/\sqrt{n}}$$

whose number of degrees of freedom is $n - 1$. The complete test follows.

H_0: $\mu = 8,200$

H_A: $\mu < 8,200$

Test statistic: $t = \dfrac{\bar{x} - \mu}{s/\sqrt{n}}$

Rejection region:

$$t < -t_{\alpha,n-1} = -t_{.05,15} = -1.753$$

To calculate the value of the test statistic, we need to calculate the sample mean $\bar{x}$ and the sample standard deviation s. The value of μ is specified by the null hypothesis and $n = 16$. From the data we find

$$\sum x_i = 129{,}760 \quad \text{and} \quad \sum x_i^2 = 1{,}053{,}451{,}072$$

Thus

$$\bar{x} = \frac{\sum x_i}{n} = \frac{129{,}760}{16} = 8{,}110$$

and

$$s^2 = \frac{\sum x_i^2 - \dfrac{\left(\sum x_i\right)^2}{n}}{n-1} = \frac{1{,}053{,}451{,}072 - \dfrac{(129{,}760)^2}{16}}{16 - 1} = 73{,}164.8$$

Thus,

$$s = \sqrt{s^2} = \sqrt{73{,}164.8} = 270.5$$

Value of the test statistic:

$$t = \frac{\bar{x} - \mu}{s/\sqrt{n}} = \frac{8{,}110 - 8{,}200}{270.5/\sqrt{16}} = -1.33$$

Conclusion: Do not reject H_0.

Minitab Output for Example 11.1

T-Test of the Mean

```
Test of mu = 8200.0 vs. mu < 8200.0

Variable     N      Mean     StDev   SE Mean        T    P-Value
Output      16    8110.0     270.5      67.6    -1.33       0.10
```

The menu commands are shown below. Appendix 11.A describes the session commands for this procedure.

MENU COMMANDS	COMMANDS FOR EXAMPLE 11.1
1 Type or import the data.	Open file **XM11-0**.
2 Click **Stat, Basic Statistics**, and **1-Sample t . . . .**	
3 Type the variable name.	**Output** or **C1**
4 Use the cursor to choose **Test mean.**	
5 Hit **tab** and type the value of μ under the null hypothesis.	**8200**

6 Use the cursor to select **less than**, **not equal**, or **greater than**. Click **OK**.   **less than**

Excel Output for Example 11.1

	A	B	C	D	E
1	**Test of Hypothesis About MU (SIGMA Unknown)**				
2					
3	Test of MU = 8200 Vs MU less than 8200				
4	Sample standard deviation = 270.4877				
5	Sample mean = 8110				
6	Test Statistic: t = -1.3309				
7	P-Value = 0.1015				

The commands used to execute this macro are listed below.

COMMANDS	COMMANDS FOR EXAMPLE 11.1
1 Type or import the data.	Open file **XM11-01**.
2 Click **Tools**, **Data Analysis Plus**, and **Inference about a Mean (SIGMA Unknown)**.	
3 Specify the block coordinates of the data. Do not include cell containing the variable name.	**A2: A17**
4 Click **Test of Hypothesis**.	
5 Specify the value of μ under the null hypothesis.	**8200**
6 Click the appropriate alternative hypothesis.	**MU less than 8200**

INTERPRETING THE RESULTS

No manager should have to make an important decision on the basis of results such as those above. First, a p-value of .1015 provides *some* evidence that the new law would decrease production. However, the evidence is quite weak. Second, a sample of size 16 may be theoretically acceptable, but practically unreliable. (A sample of 16 observations is used here to illustrate the technique and to simplify calculations for those conducting the procedure manually.) The only conclusion a prudent statistician would reach is that an experiment with a larger sample size is warranted on the basis of this test. The cost of a larger experiment is small compared to the costs of making either a Type I or a Type II error.

Figure 11.5 depicts the sampling distribution, the value of the test statistic, and its p-value.

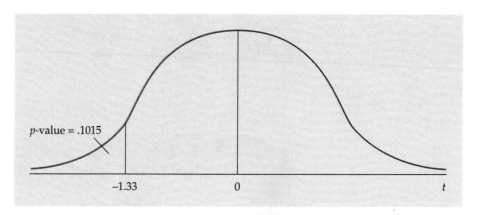

Figure 11.5

Sampling Distribution for Example 11.1

p-value = .1015

−1.33   0   *t*

Estimating the Population Mean When the Population Variance Is Unknown

Using the identical algebraic manipulation we employed to produce the confidence interval estimator of the population mean when the population variance is known (see Section 9.3), we develop the following estimator.

> **Confidence Interval Estimator of μ When σ^2 Is Unknown**
>
> $$\bar{x} \pm t_{\alpha/2}\frac{s}{\sqrt{n}} \qquad \text{d.f.} = n - 1$$

As was the case with testing a population mean, we have two different interval estimators of μ. In practice, we use the one presented here because it is almost always the case that the population variance is unknown.

EXAMPLE 11.2

In most cities a municipal agency regulates the amounts charged by taxis. As you're probably aware, total taxi fares are determined by distance traveled as well as the amount of time taken for the trip. In preparing to apply for a rate increase, the general manager of a fleet of taxis wanted to know the distance customers travel by taxis on the average trip. She organized a survey wherein she asked taxi drivers to record the number of miles (to the nearest tenth) traveled by randomly selected customers. A sample of 41 customers was produced. The results appear below (and are stored in file XM11-02). The general manager wants to estimate the mean distance traveled with 95% confidence.

DISTANCE TRAVELED BY TAXI

8.2	9.1	11.2	5.0	6.4	9.5	10.1	7.9	8.3	6.8	6.9	7.9	1.1	6.7	11.4	6.9
6.5	8.0	1.5	8.2	7.6	14.1	7.0	10.0	7.1	8.0	8.1	4.4	5.9	2.3	13.3	9.2
2.8	13.0	8.3	10.4	9.0	3.5	9.8	6.5	7.7						

SOLUTION

IDENTIFYING THE TECHNIQUE

The problem objective is to describe a single population, the distance traveled by taxi customers. The data are quantitative (miles traveled). The parameter to be estimated is the population mean μ. The confidence interval estimator is

$$\bar{x} \pm t_{\alpha/2}\frac{s}{\sqrt{n}}$$

SOLVING BY HAND

From the sample of 41 observations, we find

$$\sum x_i = 315.6 \quad \text{and} \quad \sum x_i^2 = 2{,}772.0$$

$$\bar{x} = \frac{\sum x_i}{n} = \frac{315.6}{41} = 7.70$$

$$s^2 = \frac{\sum x_i^2 - \dfrac{\left(\sum x_i\right)^2}{n}}{n-1}$$

$$= \frac{2{,}772.0 - \dfrac{(315.6)^2}{41}}{40}$$

$$= 8.57$$

$$s = \sqrt{s^2} = \sqrt{8.57} = 2.93$$

Because we want a 95% confidence interval estimate,

$$1 - \alpha = .95$$

Thus,

$$\alpha = .05 \quad \text{and} \quad \alpha/2 = .025$$

$$t_{\alpha/2,n-1} = t_{.025,40} = 2.021$$

The 95% confidence interval estimate of μ is

$$\bar{x} \pm t_{\alpha/2}\frac{s}{\sqrt{n}} = 7.70 \pm 2.021\frac{2.93}{\sqrt{41}} = 7.70 \pm .92$$

or

$$\text{LCL} = 6.78 \quad \text{and} \quad \text{UCL} = 8.62$$

**Minitab Output for
Example 11.2**

Confidence Intervals

```
Variable        N      Mean    StDev   SE Mean      95.0 % C.I.
Miles          41     7.698    2.927    0.457   (  6.774,   8.622)
```

As you can see, Minitab prints the sample size, the sample mean and standard deviation, the standard error of the mean (which in this case is **SE Mean** $= s/\sqrt{n} = 0.457$), and the 95% confidence interval estimate of the mean distance traveled by all taxi customers. (Refer to Appendix 11.A for the session commands—the menu commands are described next.)

MENU COMMANDS	COMMANDS FOR EXAMPLE 11.2
1 Type or import the data.	Open file **XM11-02**.
2 Click **Stat, Basic Statistics**, and **1-Sample t . . . .**	
3 Type the variable name.	**Miles** or **C1**
4 Use the cursor to select **Confidence interval**.	
5 Hit **tab** and type the confidence level. Click **OK**.	**.95**

**Excel Output for
Example 11.2**

	A	B	C	D	E	F
1	**0.95 Confidence Interval Estimate of MU (SIGMA Unknown)**					
2						
3	Sample mean = 7.6976					
4	Sample standard deviation = 2.9267					
5	Lower confidence limit = 6.7738					
6	Upper confidence limit = 8.6214					

The lower and upper confidence limits are 6.7738 and 8.6214, respectively.

COMMANDS	COMMANDS FOR EXAMPLE 11.2
1 Type or import the data.	Open file **XM11-02**.
2 Click **Tools, Data Analysis Plus**, and **Inference About a Mean (SIGMA Unknown)**.	
3 Specify the block coordinates of the data. Do not include the cell containing the variable name.	**A2: A42**
4 Click **Interval Estimate**.	
5 Specify the confidence level.	**.95**

We estimate that the mean distance traveled by taxi lies between 6.77 and 8.62 miles. The general manager can use the estimate to determine the effect on her company of different pricing policies. With the interval estimate she could determine upper and lower bounds on revenues generated from the new rates. She also may be able to use the results to judge the performance and honesty of individual drivers. We remind you that the accuracy of the interval estimate is dependent upon the validity of the sampling process and the distribution of the distances (they are required to be normal). If the distribution is extremely nonnormal, the inference may be invalid.

Checking the Required Conditions

When we introduced the Student t distribution, we pointed out that the t-statistic is Student t distributed only if the population from which we've sampled is normal. We also noted that the techniques introduced in this section are robust, meaning that if the population is nonnormal, the techniques are still valid provided that the population is not *extremely* nonnormal. Although there are several statistical tests that can determine if data are nonnormal, at this point we suggest drawing the histogram to see the shape of the distribution. Our two software packages can be used to draw the histograms for both Examples 11.1 and 11.2 (Figures 11.6 and 11.7). We arbitrarily chose Minitab to output the histograms shown below. (Excel's histograms are quite similar.) Both histograms suggest that the variables may be normally distributed or at least not extremely nonnormal.

Figure 11.6

Histogram for Example 11.1

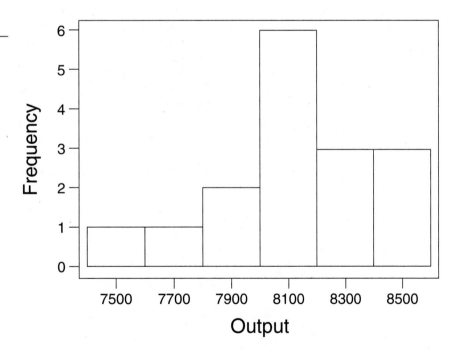

Figure 11.7

Histogram for Example 11.2

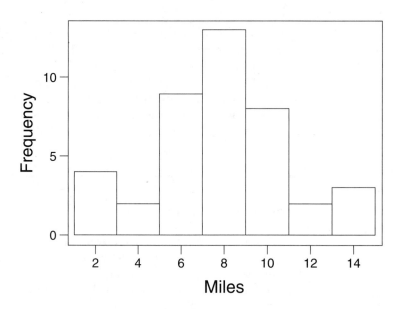

Developing an Understanding of the Statistical Concepts

In Chapters 9 and 10, we introduced the procedures used to estimate and test parameters. The examples we chose to illustrate the process were unrealistic, requiring that the population variance is known when the population mean is not. We chose those examples because of their linkage to Chapter 8 (sampling distribution of the mean) and Chapter 7 (normal distribution). The concept developed in this section is that to expand the application to more realistic situations, we must use another sampling distribution. The Student t distribution was derived by W. S. Gosset for this purpose.

Another important development in this section is the use of the term "degrees of freedom." We will encounter this term many times in this book, so a brief discussion of its meaning is warranted.

The Student t distribution is based on using the sample variance to estimate the unknown population variance. The sample variance is defined as

$$s^2 = \frac{\sum (x_i - \bar{x})^2}{n - 1}$$

To compute s^2, we must first determine $\bar{x}$. Recall that sampling distributions are derived by repeated sampling of size n from the same population. In order to repeatedly take samples to compute s^2, we can choose any numbers for the first $n - 1$ observations in the sample. However, we have no choice on the nth value because the sample mean must be calculated first. To illustrate, suppose that $n = 3$ and we find $\bar{x} = 10$. We can have x_1 and x_2 assume any values without restriction. However, x_3 must be such that $\bar{x} = 10$. For example, if $x_1 = 6$ and $x_2 = 8$, then x_3 must equal 16. Therefore, there are only two degrees of freedom in our selection of the sample. We say that we lose one degree of freedom because we had to calculate $\bar{x}$.

Notice that the denominator in the calculation of s^2 is equal to the number of degrees of freedom. This is not a coincidence and will be repeated throughout this book.

Let's complete this section with a review of how we identify this technique.

Exercises

11.1 A random sample of 10 observations was drawn from a large population. These are

7 12 8 4 9 3 4 9 5 2

  a Estimate the population mean with 90% confidence.

  b Test to determine if we can infer at the 5% significance level that the population mean is not equal to 5.

  c What is the required condition of the techniques used in parts (a) and (b)?

11.2 The following observations were drawn from a large population. (The data are also stored in file XR11-02.)

22 18 25 28 19 20 24 26 19 26 27 22 23 25 25 18 20 26
18 26 27 24 20 19 18

  a Estimate the population mean with 95% confidence.

  b Test to determine if we can infer at the 10% significance level that the population mean is greater than 20.

  c What is the required condition of the techniques used in parts (a) and (b)? Use a graphical technique to check to see if that required condition is satisfied.

Use a software package to solve this problem.	OR	The mean and standard deviation of the data are $\bar{x} = 22.6$ and $s = 3.416$ Complete your answer manually.

11.3 The following data were drawn from a normal population. Estimate the population mean with 90% confidence.

14 18 23 25 32 17 19 26 34 25

11.4 A random sample of 75 observations from a normal population is stored in file XR11-04. Test the following hypotheses, with $\alpha = .05$.

$H_0: \mu = 103$

$H_A: \mu \neq 103$

Use a software package to solve this problem.	OR	The mean and standard deviation of the data are $\bar{x} = 99.45$ and $s = 21.25$ Complete your answer manually.

11.5 Do the following data allow us to conclude, with $\alpha = .10$, that μ is greater than 7?

4 8 12 11 14 6 12 8 9 5

11.6 A growing concern for educators in the United States is the number of teenagers who have part-time jobs while they attend high school. It is generally believed that the amount of time teenagers spend working is deducted from the amount of time devoted to school work. To investigate this problem, a school guidance counselor took a random sample of 200 15-year-old high school students and asked how many hours per week each worked at a part-time job. The results were recorded and stored in file XR11-06. Some of these data are listed below. Estimate with 95% confidence the mean amount of time all 15-year-old high school students devote per week to part-time jobs.

HOURS OF WORK PER WEEK

0 6 4 7 0 6 5 0 2 3 12 5 ... 9 5 0

Use a software package to solve this problem.	OR	The mean and standard deviation of the data are $\bar{x} = 5.125$ and $s = 3.310$ Complete your answer manually.

11.7 A federal agency responsible for enforcing laws governing weights and measures routinely inspects packages to determine if the weight of the contents is at least as great as that advertised on the package. A random sample of 50 containers whose packaging states that the contents weigh 8 ounces was drawn. The contents were weighed and the results (to the nearest tenth) are stored in file XR11-07. Some of these observations are shown below. Estimate the mean weight of all the containers with 99% confidence.

WEIGHT OF CONTENTS

8.3 7.4 7.9 8.1 8.1 7.9 8.0 7.8 8.2 7.8 ... 8.8 8.4 7.8

Use a software package to solve this problem.	OR	The mean and standard deviation of the data are $\bar{x} = 8.0540$ and $s = .316$ Complete your answer manually.

11.8 A diet doctor claims that the average North American is more than 20 pounds overweight. To test his claim, a random sample of 100 North Americans were weighed, and the difference between their actual weight and their ideal weight was calculated. Some of the data are listed below, and all the data are stored in file XR11-08. Do these data allow us to infer at the 5% significance level that the doctor's claim is true?

NUMBER OF POUNDS NORTH AMERICANS ARE OVERWEIGHT

32 8 8 9 22 14 14 13 29 11 ... 17 33 34

Use a software package to solve this problem.	OR	The mean and standard deviation of the data are $\bar{x} = 24.35$ and $s = 15.8$. Complete your answer manually.

11.9 A courier service advertises that its average delivery time is less than six hours for local deliveries. A random sample of times for 50 deliveries to an address across town was stored in file XR11-09. A portion of this sample is shown below.

    a Is this sufficient evidence to support the courier's advertisement, at the 5% level of significance?

    b What assumption must be made in order to answer part (a)? Use whatever graphical technique you deem appropriate to confirm that the required condition is satisfied.

DELIVERY TIMES

    5.2 5.4 5.0 6.6 5.8 6.2 4.9 4.0 7.1 5.4 ... 7.4 4.4 4.1

Use a software package to solve this problem.	OR	The mean and standard deviation of the data are $\bar{x} = 5.87$ and $s = 1.02$. Complete your answer manually.

11.10 A manufacturer of a brand of designer jeans has pitched her advertising to develop an expensive and classy image. The suggested retail price is $75. However, she is concerned that retailers are undermining her image by offering the jeans at discount prices. To better understand what is happening, she randomly samples 15 retailers who sell her product and determines the price. The results are listed below. She would like an estimate of the mean selling price of the jeans at all retail stores.

    a Determine the 95% confidence interval estimate.

    b What assumption must be made to be sure that the estimate produced in part (a) is valid? Use a graphical technique to check the required condition.

PRICE OF JEANS (TO THE NEAREST DOLLAR)

    65 75 69 59 54 70 69 75 59 63 70 79 57 64 69

11.11 Ecologists have long advocated recycling newspapers as a way of saving trees and reducing landfills. In recent years a number of companies have gone into the business of collecting used newspapers from households and recycling them. A financial analyst for one such company has recently computed that the firm would make a profit if the mean weekly newspaper collection from each household exceeded two pounds. In a study to determine the feasibility of a recycling plant, a random sample of 100 households was drawn, and the weekly weight of newspapers discarded for recycling for each household was recorded and stored in file XR11-11 with a part of the sample data listed below. Do these data provide sufficient evidence at the 1% significance level to allow the analyst to conclude that a recycling plant would be profitable?

2.3 2.7 2.0 2.5 2.0 2.8 2.0 2.4 2.4 1.4 ... 2.5 2.0 1.7

Use a software package to solve this problem.	OR	The mean and standard deviation of the data are $\bar{x} = 2.12$ and $s = .37$ Complete your answer manually.

11.3 Inference about a Population Variance (Optional)

In Section 11.2, where we presented the inferential methods about a population mean, we were interested in acquiring information about the central location of the population. As a result, we tested and estimated the population mean. If we are interested instead in making an inference about the variability, the parameter we need to investigate is the population variance σ^2. Inference about the variance can be used to make decisions in a variety of problems. For example, quality-control engineers must ensure that their company's products meet specifications. One way of judging the consistency of a production process is to compute the variance of the size, weight, or volume of the product. That is, if the variation in product size, weight, or volume is large, it is likely that an unsatisfactorily large number of products will lie outside the specifications for that product. Another example comes from the subject area of finance. Investors use the variance of the returns on a portfolio of stocks, bonds, or other investments as a measure of the uncertainty and risk inherent in that portfolio. Investors often go to great lengths to avoid risky investments.

The task of deriving the test statistic and the interval estimator provides us with another opportunity to show how statistical techniques in general are developed. We begin by identifying the best estimator. That estimator has a sampling distribution, from which we produce the test statistic and the confidence interval estimator.

Point Estimator

The point estimator for σ^2 is the sample variance introduced in Section 4.3 and used repeatedly, most recently in the section above to test and estimate μ. The statistic s^2 has the desirable characteristics presented in Section 9.2; that is, s^2 is an unbiased, consistent estimator of σ^2.

Sampling Distribution of s^2

To create the sampling distribution of the sample variance, we repeatedly take samples of size n from a normal population whose variance is σ^2, calculate s^2 for each sample, and then draw the histogram. The result would appear similar to Figure 11.8. The actual shape would vary according to the sample size and the value of σ^2. However, no matter the sample size or the value of σ^2, the sampling distribution would be positively skewed.

Figure 11.8

Histogram of s^2

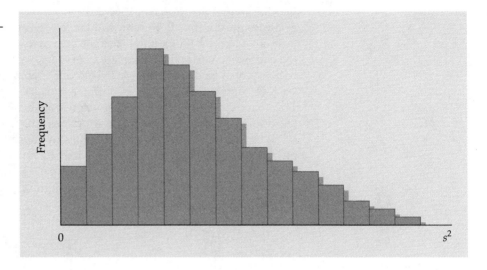

Mathematicians have shown that the sum of squared differences $\sum(x_i - \bar{x})^2$ (which is equal to $(n - 1)s^2$) divided by the population variance is distributed according to what is called the **chi-squared distribution** provided that the sampled population is normal. The statistic

$$\chi^2 = \frac{(n - 1)s^2}{\sigma^2}$$

is called the **chi-squared statistic** and is denoted by the Greek letter *chi* squared.

Chi-Squared Distribution

The chi-squared distribution is positively skewed ranging between 0 and ∞. Like that of the Student t distribution, its shape depends on its number of degrees of freedom. Figure 11.9 depicts several chi-squared distributions with different numbers of degrees of freedom.

Figure 11.9

Chi-Squared Distributions

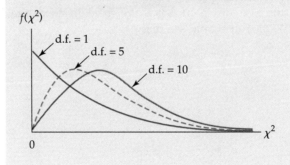

The value of χ^2 such that the area to its right under the chi-squared curve is equal to A is denoted χ_A^2. We cannot use $-\chi_A^2$ to represent the point such that the area to its *left* is A (as we did with z and t) because the χ^2-statistic is always greater than 0. To represent the left-tail critical values, we note that if the area to the left of a point is A, the area to its right must be $1 - A$ since the entire area under the chi-squared curve (as well as all continuous distributions) must equal 1. Thus, χ_{1-A}^2 denotes the point such that the area to its *left* is A. Figure 11.10 depicts a chi-squared distribution with χ_A^2 and χ_{1-A}^2. Table 5 in Appendix B, reproduced below as Table 11.5, lists the critical values of the chi-squared distribution for degrees of freedom equal to 1 to 30, 40, 50, 60, 70, 80, 90, and 100. For example, to find the point in a chi-squared distribution with eight degrees of freedom such that the area to its right is .05, locate eight degrees of freedom in the left column and $\chi_{.050}^2$ across the top row. The intersection of the row and column contains the value we seek as shown in Table 11.6. That is,

$$\chi_{.050,8}^2 = 15.5073$$

Figure 11.10

χ_A^2 and χ_{1-A}^2

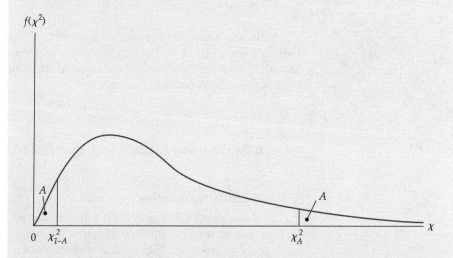

To find the point in the same distribution such that the area to its *left* is .05, find the point such that the area to its *right* is .95. Locate $\chi_{.950}^2$ across the top row and eight degrees of freedom down the side (also shown in Table 11.6). You should see that

$$\chi_{.950,8}^2 = 2.73264$$

Table 11.5	Critical Values of χ^2								

DEGREES OF FREEDOM	$\chi^2_{.995}$	$\chi^2_{.990}$	$\chi^2_{.975}$	$\chi^2_{.950}$	$\chi^2_{.900}$	$\chi^2_{.100}$	$\chi^2_{.050}$	$\chi^2_{.025}$	$\chi^2_{.010}$	$\chi^2_{.005}$
1	0.0000393	0.0001571	0.0009821	0.0039321	0.0157908	2.70554	3.84146	5.02389	6.63490	7.87944
2	0.0100251	0.0201007	0.0506356	0.102587	0.210720	4.60517	5.99147	7.37776	9.21034	10.5966
3	0.0717212	0.114832	0.215795	0.351846	0.584375	6.25139	7.81473	9.34840	11.3449	12.8381
4	0.206990	0.297110	0.484419	0.710721	1.063623	7.77944	9.48773	11.1433	13.2767	14.8602
5	0.411740	0.554300	0.831211	1.145476	1.61031	9.23635	11.0705	12.8325	15.0863	16.7496
6	0.675727	0.872085	1.237347	1.63539	2.20413	10.6446	12.5916	14.4494	16.8119	18.5476
7	0.989265	1.239043	1.68987	2.16735	2.83311	12.0170	14.0671	16.0128	18.4753	20.2777
8	1.344419	1.646482	2.17973	2.73264	3.48954	13.3616	15.5073	17.5346	20.0902	21.9550
9	1.734926	2.087912	2.70039	3.32511	4.16816	14.6837	16.9190	19.0228	21.6660	23.5893
10	2.15585	2.55821	3.24697	3.94030	4.86518	15.9871	18.3070	20.4831	23.2093	25.1882
11	2.60321	3.05347	3.81575	4.57481	5.57779	17.2750	19.6751	21.9200	24.7250	26.7569
12	3.07382	3.57056	4.40379	5.22603	6.30380	18.5494	21.0261	23.3367	26.2170	28.2995
13	3.56503	4.10691	5.00874	5.89186	7.04150	19.8119	22.3621	24.7356	27.6883	29.8194
14	4.07468	4.66043	5.62872	6.57063	7.78953	21.0642	23.6848	26.1190	29.1413	31.3193
15	4.60094	5.22935	6.26214	7.26094	8.54675	22.3072	24.9958	27.4884	30.5779	32.8013
16	5.14224	5.81221	6.90766	7.96164	9.31223	23.5418	26.2962	28.8454	31.9999	34.2672
17	5.69724	6.40776	7.56418	8.67176	10.0852	24.7690	27.5871	30.1910	33.4087	35.7185
18	6.26481	7.01491	8.23075	9.39046	10.8649	25.9894	28.8693	31.5264	34.8053	37.1564
19	6.84398	7.63273	8.90655	10.1170	11.6509	27.2036	30.1435	32.8523	36.1908	38.5822
20	7.43386	8.26040	9.59083	10.8508	12.4426	28.4120	31.4104	34.1696	37.5662	39.9968
21	8.03366	8.89720	10.28293	11.5913	13.2396	29.6151	32.6705	35.4789	38.9321	41.4010
22	8.64272	9.54249	10.9823	12.3380	14.0415	30.8133	33.9244	36.7807	40.2894	42.7956
23	9.26042	10.19567	11.6885	13.0905	14.8479	32.0069	35.1725	38.0757	41.6384	44.1813
24	9.88623	10.8564	12.4011	13.8484	15.6587	33.1963	36.4151	39.3641	42.9798	45.5585
25	10.5197	11.5240	13.1197	14.6114	16.4734	34.3816	37.6525	40.6465	44.3141	46.9278
26	11.1603	12.1981	13.8439	15.3791	17.2919	35.5631	38.8852	41.9232	45.6417	48.2899
27	11.8076	12.8786	14.5733	16.1513	18.1138	36.7412	40.1133	43.1944	46.9630	49.6449
28	12.4613	13.5648	15.3079	16.9279	18.9392	37.9159	41.3372	44.4607	48.2782	50.9933
29	13.1211	14.2565	16.0471	17.7083	19.7677	39.0875	42.5569	45.7222	49.5879	52.3356
30	13.7867	14.9535	16.7908	18.4926	20.5992	40.2560	43.7729	46.9792	50.8922	53.6720
40	20.7065	22.1643	24.4331	26.5093	29.0505	51.8050	55.7585	59.3417	63.6907	66.7659
50	27.9907	29.7067	32.3574	34.7642	37.6886	63.1671	67.5048	71.4202	76.1539	79.4900
60	35.5346	37.4848	40.4817	43.1879	46.4589	74.3970	79.0819	83.2976	88.3794	91.9517
70	43.2752	45.4418	48.7576	51.7393	55.3290	85.5271	90.5312	95.0231	100.425	104.215
80	51.1720	53.5400	57.1532	60.3915	64.2778	96.5782	101.879	106.629	112.329	116.321
90	59.1963	61.7541	65.6466	69.1260	73.2912	107.565	113.145	118.136	124.116	128.299
100	67.3276	70.0648	74.2219	77.9295	82.3581	118.498	124.342	129.561	135.807	140.169

SOURCE: From C. M. Thompson, "Tables of the Percentage Points of the χ^2-Distribution," *Biometrika* 32 (1941): 188–89. Reproduced by permission of the Biometrika Trustees.

Table 11.6   Finding $\chi^2_{.050,8}$ and $\chi^2_{.950,8}$

DEGREES OF FREEDOM	$\chi^2_{.995}$	$\chi^2_{.990}$	$\chi^2_{.975}$	$\chi^2_{.950}$	$\chi^2_{.900}$	$\chi^2_{.100}$	$\chi^2_{.050}$	$\chi^2_{.025}$	$\chi^2_{.010}$	$\chi^2_{.005}$
1	0.0000393	0.0001571	0.0009821	0.0039321	0.0157908	2.70554	3.84146	5.02389	6.63490	7.87944
2	0.0100251	0.0201007	0.0506356	0.102587	0.210720	4.60517	5.99147	7.37776	9.21034	10.5966
3	0.0717212	0.114832	0.215795	0.351846	0.584375	6.25139	7.81473	9.34840	11.3449	12.8381
4	0.206990	0.297110	0.484419	0.710721	1.063623	7.77944	9.48773	11.1433	13.2767	14.8602
5	0.411740	0.554300	0.831211	1.145476	1.61031	9.23635	11.0705	12.8325	15.0863	16.7496
6	0.675727	0.872085	1.237347	1.63539	2.20413	10.6446	12.5916	14.4494	16.8119	18.5476
7	0.989265	1.239043	1.68987	2.16735	2.83311	12.0170	14.0671	16.0128	18.4753	20.2777
8	1.344419	1.646482	2.17973	2.73264	3.48954	13.3616	15.5073	17.5346	20.0902	21.9550
9	1.734926	2.087912	2.70039	3.32511	4.16816	14.6837	16.9190	19.0228	21.6660	23.5893
10	2.15585	2.55821	3.24697	3.94030	4.86518	15.9871	18.3070	20.4831	23.2093	25.1882
11	2.60321	3.05347	3.81575	4.57481	5.57779	17.2750	19.6751	21.9200	24.7250	26.7569
12	3.07382	3.57056	4.40379	5.22603	6.30380	18.5494	21.0261	23.3367	26.2170	28.2995
13	3.56503	4.10691	5.00874	5.89186	7.04150	19.8119	22.3621	24.7356	27.6883	29.8194
14	4.07468	4.66043	5.62872	6.57063	7.78953	21.0642	23.6848	26.1190	29.1413	31.3193
15	4.60094	5.22935	6.26214	7.26094	8.54675	22.3072	24.9958	27.4884	30.5779	32.8013

Testing the Population Variance

As we discussed in Section 10.6, the formula that describes the sampling distribution is the formula of the test statistic.

> **Test Statistic for σ^2**
>
> The test statistic used to test hypotheses about σ^2 is
>
> $$\chi^2 = \frac{(n-1)s^2}{\sigma^2}$$
>
> which is chi-squared distributed with $(n-1)$ degrees of freedom when the population random variable is normally distributed with variance equal to σ^2.

EXAMPLE 11.3

Container-filling machines are used to package a variety of liquids, including milk, soft drinks, and paint. Ideally, the amount of liquid should vary only slightly, since large variations will cause some containers to be underfilled (cheating the customer) and some to be overfilled (resulting in costly waste). The president of a company that developed a new type of machine boasts that this machine can fill 1 liter (1,000 cubic centimeters) containers so consistently that the variance of the fills will be less than 1 cc. To examine the veracity of the claim, a random sample of 25 1-liter fills was taken and the results recorded. To avoid rounding problems, the results were coded by subtracting 1,000. These data are listed below and also stored in file XM11-03. Do these data allow the president to make this claim at the 5% significance level?

SAMPLE OF 25 "ONE-LITER" FILLS (IN CC MINUS 1,000)

```
.3  1.0  −.5  −.3  −.7  −.2  −1.3  .6  −.6  −.6  1.0  −.6  −.5  −1.5  1.3  −.4
−.2  0.0  −1.5  1.4  −1.9  .7  −.9  1.1  .7
```

SOLUTION

IDENTIFYING THE TECHNIQUE

The problem objective is to describe the population of 1-liter fills from this machine. The data are quantitative, and we're interested in the variability of the fills. It follows that the parameter of interest is the population variance. Because we want to determine whether there is enough evidence to support the claim, the alternative hypothesis is

$$H_A: \sigma^2 < 1$$

The null hypothesis automatically follows as

$$H_0: \sigma^2 = 1$$

The complete test is shown below.

$$H_0: \sigma^2 = 1$$
$$H_A: \sigma^2 < 1$$

Test statistic:

$$\chi^2 = \frac{(n-1)s^2}{\sigma^2}$$

Rejection region:

$$\chi^2 < \chi^2_{1-\alpha,n-1} = \chi^2_{.95,24} = 13.8484$$

SOLVING BY HAND

The test statistic is

$$\chi^2 = \frac{(n-1)s^2}{\sigma^2}$$

The numerator is $(n-1)s^2$, which is equal to $\Sigma(x_i - \bar{x})^2$, which in turn equals $\Sigma x_i^2 - [(\Sigma x_i)^2/n]$. From the data we find

$$\sum x_i = -3.6$$
$$\sum x_i^2 = 21.3$$

Thus,

$$\sum x_i^2 - \frac{\left(\sum x_i\right)^2}{n} = 21.3 - \frac{(-3.6)^2}{25} = 20.8$$

As usual, the value of the parameter is taken from the null hypothesis, $\sigma^2 = 1$. The value of the test statistic is

$$\chi^2 = \frac{(n-1)s^2}{\sigma^2} = \frac{\sum(x_i - \bar{x})^2}{\sigma^2} = \frac{20.8}{1} = 20.8$$

Conclusion: Do not reject the null hypothesis.

USING THE COMPUTER

Neither Minitab nor Excel tests the population variance. We can, however, use the computer to calculate the sample variance, from which we can compute the test statistic.

INTERPRETING THE RESULTS

There is not enough evidence to infer that the claim is true. As we discussed before, the result does not say that the variance is *greater* than 1; it merely states that we are unable to show that the variance is *less* than 1. The χ^2-test of σ^2 is somewhat more sensitive to violations of the normality requirement than the t-test of μ. Consequently, we must be more careful to ensure that the fills are normally distributed.

Figure 11.11 depicts the sampling distribution, rejection region, and test statistic.

Figure 11.11

Sampling Distribution for Example 11.3

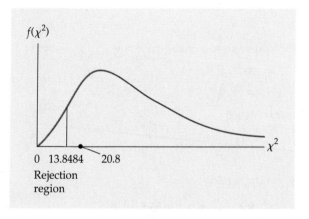

Estimating the Population Variance

Using the notation developed above, we can make the following probability statement.

$$P(\chi^2_{1-\alpha/2} < \chi^2 < \chi^2_{\alpha/2}) = 1 - \alpha$$

Substituting $\chi^2 = [(n-1)s^2/\sigma^2]$ we have

$$P\left(\chi^2_{1-\alpha/2} < \frac{(n-1)s^2}{\sigma^2} < \chi^2_{\alpha/2}\right) = 1 - \alpha$$

Using a little algebraic manipulation, we can isolate σ^2 in the center of the probability statement, which produces the following interval estimator.

Confidence Interval Estimator of σ^2

Lower confidence limit (LCL) $= \dfrac{(n-1)s^2}{\chi^2_{\alpha/2}}$

Upper confidence limit (UCL) $= \dfrac{(n-1)s^2}{\chi^2_{1-\alpha/2}}$

EXAMPLE 11.4

Estimate with 99% confidence the population variance of the fills using the data presented in Example 11.3.

SOLUTION

SOLVING BY HAND

In the solution to Example 11.3, we found $(n-1)s^2$ to be 20.8. From Table 5 in Appendix B we find

$$\chi^2_{\alpha/2,n-1} = \chi^2_{.005,24} = 45.5585$$
$$\chi^2_{1-\alpha/2,n-1} = \chi^2_{.995,24} = 9.88623$$

Thus,

$$\text{LCL} = \frac{(n-1)s^2}{\chi^2_{\alpha/2}} = \frac{20.8}{45.5585} = .46$$

$$\text{UCL} = \frac{(n-1)s^2}{\chi^2_{1-\alpha/2}} = \frac{20.8}{9.88623} = 2.10$$

We estimate that the variance of the fills is a number that lies between .46 and 2.10.

USING THE COMPUTER

As we pointed out above, we can use the computer only to compute the sample variance. The remainder of the procedure is computed manually.

INTERPRETING THE RESULTS

In Example 11.3, we saw that there was insufficient evidence to infer that the population variance is less than 1. Here we can see that σ^2 is estimated to lie between .46 and 2.10. (Part of the interval is above 1, which tells us that the variance may be larger than 1, confirming the conclusion we reached in Example 11.3.) We may be able to use this estimate to calculate the percentage of overfilled and underfilled bottles. We can use it also to choose among competing machines.

A Brief Discussion of the Derivation of
the Chi-Squared Distribution (Optional)

The chi-squared distribution is derived by squaring a standard normal random variable. Thus, z^2 is chi-squared distributed with one degree of freedom. If we add n independent chi-squared random variables each with one degree of freedom, the sum is chi-squared distributed with n degrees of freedom. Mathematicians can show that

$$\frac{(n-1)s^2}{\sigma^2}$$

is equal to

$$\sum_{i=1}^{n} \left(\frac{x_i - \mu}{\sigma} \right)^2 - \left(\frac{\bar{x} - \mu}{\sigma/\sqrt{n}} \right)^2$$

The first term is chi-squared distributed with n degrees of freedom, and the second term is chi-squared distributed with one degree of freedom. Thus,

$$\frac{(n-1)s^2}{\sigma^2}$$

is chi-squared distributed with $n - 1$ degrees of freedom. As with the Student t distribution, we "lose" one degree of freedom because we must use the sample mean to calculate s^2. Once again, the denominator in the calculation of s^2 defines the number of degrees of freedom.

Let's review how we recognize when to use the techniques introduced in this section.

Factors that Identify the Chi-Squared Test and Estimator of σ^2

1 Problem objective: describe a single population

2 Data type: quantitative

3 Descriptive measurement: variability

Exercises

11.12 Test the hypotheses below at the 5% significance level

$H_0: \sigma^2 = 100$

$H_A: \sigma^2 > 100$

given the following data.

85 59 66 81 35 57 55 63 63 66

11.13 The following data were drawn from a normal population.

92 93 54 58 74 53 63 83 64 51 103

At the 1% significance level, test to determine if there is enough evidence to conclude that the population variance is less than 500.

11.14 A random sample of 100 observations was taken from a normal population. The sample variance was computed to be $s^2 = 29.76$. Do these data provide sufficient evidence at the 10% significance level to infer that the population variance differs from 20?

11.15 Given the following sample, estimate the population variance with 95% confidence.

    4 5 6 5 5 6 5 6

11.16 The following observations were drawn from a normal population.

   497 511 498 494 479 526 510 515 515 489 489 488 491

    a   Can we infer at the 1% significance level that the population variance differs from 100?

    b   Estimate σ^2 with 90% confidence.

11.17 One important factor in inventory control is the variance of the daily demand for the product. A management scientist has developed the optimal order quantity and reorder point, assuming that the variance is equal to 250. Recently, the company has experienced some inventory problems, which induced the operations manager to doubt the assumption. To examine the problem, the manager took a sample of 25 daily demands recorded below and stored them in file XR11-17. Do these data provide sufficient evidence at the 5% significance level to infer that the management scientist's assumption about the variance is wrong?

   470 497 486 451 474 458 457 458 461 492 503 472 491 449
   498 502 488 484 460 482 487 464 470 494 467

11.18 Refer to Example 11.17. What are the smallest and largest values that σ^2 is likely to assume? (Define "likely" as 95% confidence.)

11.19 Some traffic experts believe that the major cause of highway collisions is the differing speeds of cars. That is, when some cars are driven slowly while others are driven at speeds well in excess of the speed limit, cars tend to congregate in bunches increasing the probability of accidents. Thus, the greater the variation in speeds, the greater the number of collisions that occur. Suppose that one expert believes that when the variance exceeds 50 (mph)^2, the number of accidents will be unacceptably high. A random sample of the speeds of 200 cars on a highway with one of the highest accident rates in the country is taken, and the sample variance calculated; it is $s^2 = 79.9$.

    a   Can we conclude at the 5% significance level that the variance in speeds exceeds 50 (mph)^2?

    b   Estimate the variance of all cars using the highway with 90% confidence.

11.20 One problem facing the manager of maintenance departments is when to change the bulbs in streetlamps. If bulbs are changed only when they burn out, it is quite costly to send crews out to change only one bulb at a time. This method also requires someone to report the problem, and in the meantime, the light is off. If each bulb lasts approximately the same amount of time, they can all be replaced periodically, producing significant cost savings in maintenance. Suppose that a financial analysis of the lights at Yankee Stadium has concluded that it will pay to replace all of the lightbulbs at the same time if the variance of the lives of the bulbs is less than 200 hours. The length of life of the last 100 bulbs was recorded and stored in file XR11-20. (Some of these data are listed below.) What conclusion can be drawn from these data? (Use a software package to help solve this problem, and use a 5% significance level.)

LENGTH OF LIFE OF SAMPLE OF 100 BULBS

   2,000 1,996 1,994 1,991 1,999 1,978 1,979 ... 2,005 1,984 2,018

11.4 Inference about a Population Proportion

In this section, we continue to address the problem of describing a single population, but we now deal with qualitative data. As we've already discussed, when the data are qualitative, we can only count the number of times each value of the variable occurs. From these counts we compute proportions. Thus, the parameter of interest in this section is the population proportion p.

Earlier in this book, we introduced the binomial probability distribution whose parameter is the proportion p (Chapter 6). It follows that in order to draw inferences about a population proportion we will gather data from a binomial experiment.

Sampling Distribution of the Sample Proportion

The logical statistic used in making inferences about a population proportion is the sample proportion. Thus, given a sample drawn from the population of interest, we will calculate the number of successes divided by the sample size. As we did in Chapter 6 when we discussed the binomial distribution, we label the number of successes x; hence, the sample proportion is x/n. We denote this sample proportion by $\hat{p}$ (read p-hat).

Recall that the mean of x is

$$E(x) = np$$

and that the standard deviation of x is

$$\sigma_x = \sqrt{npq}$$

where p is the population proportion of successes and $q = 1 - p$.

Using the rules of expectation and variance, we can show without difficulty that

$$E(\hat{p}) = p$$

and that the standard deviation of $\hat{p}$ is

$$\sigma_{\hat{p}} = \sqrt{\frac{pq}{n}}$$

Hence, $\hat{p}$ is an unbiased and consistent estimator of p. Because x is a binomial random variable, we can use the binomial distribution to test and estimate p. However, the binomial random variable is discrete, making it awkward to use in statistical inference. But in Chapter 7 we pointed out that the binomial distribution can be approximated by the normal distribution, provided that n is sufficiently large. As a result, we have the following definition.

Sampling Distribution of $\hat{p}$

The sample proportion $\hat{p}$ is approximately normally distributed, with mean p and the standard deviation $\sqrt{pq/n}$ provided that n is large ($np \geq 5$ and $nq \geq 5$).

Figure 11.12 depicts this distribution. Since $\hat{p}$ is approximately normal, it follows that the standardized variable

$$z = \frac{\hat{p} - p}{\sqrt{pq/n}}$$

is approximately standard normally distributed. (This requires that $np \geq 5$ and $nq \geq 5$. Some students wrongly assume that, if the sample size is too small, the sampling distribution is Student t. In fact, when n is too small for $np \geq 5$ and $nq \geq 5$, any inference about p must be based on the actual distribution of $\hat{p}$, which is based on the binomial distribution.)

This variable will be the basis for the hypothesis tests and estimation of p. We begin with the hypothesis testing technique.

Figure 11.12

Sampling Distribution of $\hat{p}$

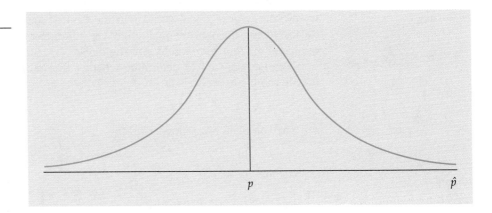

Testing a Population Proportion

The null and alternative hypotheses of tests of proportions are set up in the same way as the hypotheses of tests about means and variances. That is, the alternative hypothesis answers the question, while the null hypothesis indicates that p is equal to some specific value. The test statistic is derived from the sampling distribution of $\hat{p}$.

Test Statistic for p

$$z = \frac{\hat{p} - p}{\sqrt{pq/n}}$$

EXAMPLE 11.5*

An inventor has developed a system that allows visitors to museums, zoos, and other attractions to get information at the touch of a digital code. For example, zoo

*This example is adapted from an actual product described on "Venture," CBC Television, December 1, 1991.

patrons can listen to an announcement (recorded on a microchip) about each animal they see. It is anticipated that the devices would rent for $3.00 each. The installation cost for the complete system is expected to be about $400,000. The Milwaukee Zoo is interested in having the system installed, but management is uncertain about whether to take the risk. A financial analysis of the problem indicates that if more than 10% of the zoo's visitors rent the system, the zoo will make a profit. To help make the decision, a random sample of 400 zoo visitors is given details of the system's capabilities and cost. If 52 people say that they would rent the device, can the management of the zoo conclude that the investment would result in a profit?

SOLUTION

IDENTIFYING THE TECHNIQUE

The problem objective is to describe the population of zoo visitors. The responses to the survey are "Yes, I would rent the device" and "No, I would not rent the device." Thus, the data are qualitative. The parameter to be tested is the proportion of all zoo visitors who would rent the device.

Because we want to determine whether that proportion would exceed 10%, the alternative hypothesis is

$$H_A: p > .10$$

The complete test follows.

$$H_0: p = .10$$
$$H_A: p > .10$$

Test statistic: $z = \dfrac{\hat{p} - p}{\sqrt{pq/n}}$

SOLVING BY HAND

The sample proportion is

$$\hat{p} = \frac{52}{400} = .13$$

The value of the test statistic is

$$z = \frac{\hat{p} - p}{\sqrt{pq/n}} = \frac{.13 - .10}{\sqrt{(.10)(.90)/400}} = 2.0$$

The p-value of the test is $P(z > 2.0) = .0228$.

USING THE COMPUTER

Most statistical software packages do not perform tests of hypothesis about p. However, it is often the case that the survey responses are stored on disk. For example, suppose that in Example 11.5 the data are stored using the following codes.

0 = No, I would not rent the device.
1 = Yes, I would rent the device.

We could use the computer to count the number of each type of response. From these results, we can calculate $\hat{p}$ and the value of the test statistic (as we did above). (See Appendixes 11.A and 11.B for details.)

We can also instruct the computer to calculate the value of the test statistic from raw data. Because we frequently encounter this type of problem, we created Minitab and Excel macros to output the required statistics.

Minitab Output for Example 11.5

```
H0: p = 0.1000

HA: p  >  0.1000

p-hat =  0.13000

z =  2.00000

p-value =  0.02275
```

The data must be stored in column 1 so that 1 = success and 0 = failure. If necessary you can recode the data. (See Appendix 11.A.)

COMMANDS	COMMANDS FOR EXAMPLE 11.5
1 Type or import the data into column 1 (1 = success and 0 = failure).	Open file **XM11-05**.
2 Put the diskette in drive A and type **%A:TESTP**	**%A:TESTP**
3 At the **DATA** prompt, type the value of p specified by the null hypothesis and a code to specify the alternative hypothesis. The code is the same as is used in test procedure subcommands. That is, $-1 = (H_A:p < p_0)$, $0 = (H_A:p \neq p_0)$, and $1 = (H_A:p > p_0)$. Hit **Return**.	.1 1

Excel Output for Example 11.5

	A	B	C	D
1	**Test of Hypothesis About p**			
2				
3	Test of p = 0.1 Vs p greater than 0.1			
4	Sample Proportion = 0.13			
5	Test Statistic = 2			
6	P-Value = 0.0228			

COMMANDS	COMMANDS FOR EXAMPLE 11.5
1 Type or import the data into one column.	Open file **XM11-05**.
2 Click **Tools**, **Data Analysis Plus**, and **Inference About a Proportion**.	
3 Specify the block coordinates. (Exclude cell containing the variable name.)	**A2: A401**
4 Specify the code used to represent a success.	**1**
5 Click **Test of Hypothesis**.	
6 Specify the value of p under the null hypothesis.	**.10**
7 Click the appropriate alternative hypothesis.	**p greater than .1**

INTERPRETING THE RESULTS

A p-value of 2.28% provides strong evidence to infer that the proportion of all zoo visitors who would rent the device exceeds 10%. However, before proceeding with the project, the manager of the zoo should make certain that the experiment was properly performed. Was the sample of 400 zoo visitors randomly selected? If a substantial number of visitors who were asked to respond refused, then the sample may be partially self-selected, which may invalidate the conclusion. Did all of the respondents understand the operation of the device? If the description was unclear, some of the responses are useless. However, if the manager is satisfied with the experiment, the project should be launched.

Figure 11.13 describes the sampling distribution, the test statistic, and its p-value.

Figure 11.13

Sampling Distribution for Example 11.5

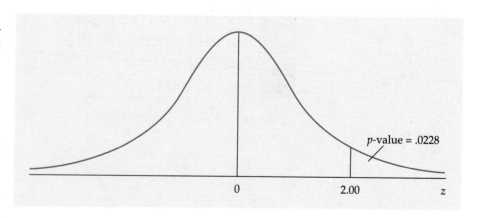

Estimating a Population Proportion

Using the same algebra employed in Sections 9.3 and 11.2, we attempt to construct the interval estimator of p from the sampling distribution of $\hat{p}$. The result is

$$\hat{p} \pm z_{\alpha/2}\sqrt{\frac{pq}{n}}$$

This formula is useless, however, because p and q are unknown. (If they were known, there would be no need to estimate p.) As a result, we estimate the standard deviation of $\hat{p}$ with $\sqrt{\hat{p}\hat{q}/n}$ to produce the following formula.

Confidence Interval Estimator of p

$$\hat{p} \pm z_{\alpha/2}\sqrt{\frac{\hat{p}\hat{q}}{n}}$$

The use of this estimator is based on the assumption that $\hat{p}$ is approximately normally distributed. As we explained above, this assumption requires that the sample size be sufficiently large—np and nq must be at least 5. However, since p and q are unknown, we will define n as sufficiently large to use the confidence interval estimator above if $n\hat{p}$ and $n\hat{q} \geq 5$.

EXAMPLE 11.6

In the autumn of 1992, Hurricane Andrew struck South Florida with near-record-level winds. Many homes were destroyed, and a subsequent investigation revealed that poor building-code rules and enforcement contributed to the loss of life and property damage. In a special report in the *Miami Herald* (20 December 1992), reporters analyzed the damage done to homes built before 1980 and to those built after 1980. One of the findings was that, in areas where the sustained winds were under 97 mph (with gusts between 85 and 127 mph), 33% of the houses built after 1980 were uninhabitable. Suppose that statistic was based on a sample of 300 houses. Estimate with 99% confidence the proportion of all houses built after 1980 that were uninhabitable after being hit by hurricane winds under 97 mph.

SOLUTION

IDENTIFYING THE
TECHNIQUE

The problem objective is to describe the population of homes in areas of South Florida where Hurricane Andrew's sustained wind velocity was less than 97 mph. Each house is categorized as being either habitable or uninhabitable. We recognize that the data are qualitative. To help you differentiate between qualitative and quantitative data, suppose that the report had analyzed the *cost* of repairing the damage. In that case, for each home analysts would have recorded the cost of repairs, and thus the data would be quantitative.

The parameter of interest is the proportion of uninhabitable homes. The interval estimator is

$$\hat{p} \pm z_{\alpha/2} \sqrt{\frac{\hat{p}\hat{q}}{n}}$$

The sample size is $n = 300$, and the sample proportion is $\hat{p} = .33$ (and $\hat{q} = 1 - \hat{p} = .67$). We set the confidence level at 99%, so $\alpha = .01$, $\alpha/2 = .005$, and $z_{\alpha/2} = z_{.005} = 2.575$. The 99% confidence interval estimate of p is

$$\hat{p} \pm z_{\alpha/2} \sqrt{\frac{\hat{p}\hat{q}}{n}} = .33 \pm 2.575 \sqrt{\frac{(.33)(.67)}{300}} = .33 \pm .070$$

The lower and upper confidence limits are

$$\text{LCL} = .26 \quad \text{and} \quad \text{UCL} = .40$$

As was the case with testing population proportions, statistical software packages are not designed to compute interval estimates. However, we have created macros to print the lower and upper confidence limits of the interval estimate of p.

Minitab Output for Example 11.6

```
Confidence level = 99%

p-hat =  0.33333

Lower confidence limit =  0.26323

Upper confidence limit =  0.40344
```

COMMANDS

1 Type or import the data into column 1 (1 = success and 0 = failure).

2 Put the diskette in drive A and type **%A:ESTP**

3 At the **DATA** prompt, type the confidence level (in percent). Hit **Return**.

COMMANDS FOR EXAMPLE 11.6

Open file **XM11-06**.

%A:ESTP

99

Excel Output for Example 11.6

	A	B	C	D
1	0.99 Confidence Interval Estimate of p			
2				
3	Sample proportion = 0.3333			
4	Lower confidence limit = 0.2632			
5	Upper confidence limit = 0.4034			

INTERPRETING THE RESULTS

We estimate that between 26 and 40% of all homes in the designated area were uninhabitable after Hurricane Andrew. We can use this estimate in a variety of ways. First, the estimate provides us with a measure of the magnitude of the damage. For example, we can say that at least 26% of the homes were uninhabitable. Second, we can compare these results with damage estimates of homes built before 1980 and with damage estimates in other areas where the wind velocity was lower or higher than 97 mph. Third, the interval estimate may allow us to estimate the cost of repairs.

Selecting the Sample Size to Estimate a Population Proportion

In Chapter 9, when we discussed how to determine the sample size to estimate a population mean, we pointed out that the value of n depends on three things: the parameter to be estimated, the confidence level, and the desired degree of accuracy. If the parameter to be estimated is a population proportion, then $z_{\alpha/2}$ reflects the desired confidence level, and $z_{\alpha/2}\sqrt{\hat{p}\hat{q}/n}$ is equal to the error bound B. To determine the required sample size, we find the following value.

Sample Size Necessary to Estimate p

$$n = \left(\frac{z_{\alpha/2}\sqrt{\hat{p}\hat{q}}}{B}\right)^2$$

Suppose that in preparing for the survey in Example 11.6, we wanted to estimate the proportion of uninhabitable homes to within .03, with 95% confidence. This means that when the sample is taken, we wish the interval estimate to be $\hat{p} \pm .03$. Hence, $B = .03$. Since $1 - \alpha = .95$, we know that $z_{\alpha/2} = 1.96$; therefore

$$n = \left(\frac{1.96\sqrt{\hat{p}\hat{q}}}{.03}\right)^2$$

To solve for n, we need to know $\hat{p}$ and $\hat{q}$. Unfortunately, these values are unknown, because the sample has not yet been taken. At this point, we can use either of two methods to solve for n.

Method 1 If we have no knowledge of even the approximate values of $\hat{p}$ and $\hat{q}$, we let $\hat{p} = \hat{q} = .5$. We choose $\hat{p} = .5$ (and thus $\hat{q} = .5$) because the product $\hat{p}\hat{q}$ equals its maximum value for this value of $\hat{p}$. (Figure 11.14 illustrates this point.) This, in turn, results in a conservative value of n, and as a result, the confidence interval will be no wider than the interval $\hat{p} \pm .03$. If, when the sample is drawn, $\hat{p}$ does not equal .5, the interval estimate will be better (that is, narrower) than planned. Thus,

$$n = \left(\frac{1.96\sqrt{(.5)(.5)}}{.03} \right)^2 = (32.67)^2 = 1,068$$

If it turns out that $\hat{p} = .5$, the interval estimate is $.5 \pm .03$. If not, the interval estimate will be narrower. For instance, if it turns out that $\hat{p} = .2$, the estimate is $.2 \pm .024$, which is better than we had planned.

Figure 11.14

$\hat{p}$ Versus $\hat{p}\hat{q}$

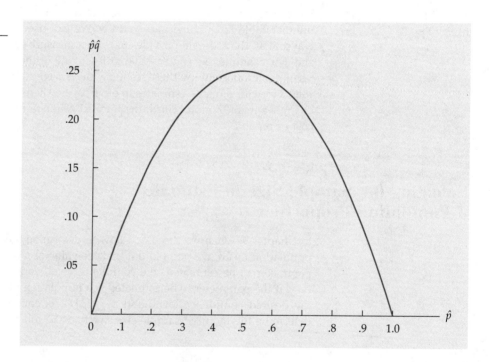

Method 2 If we have some idea about the value of $\hat{p}$, we can use that quantity to determine n. For example, if we believe that $\hat{p}$ will turn out to be approximately .2, we can solve for n as follows.

$$n = \left(\frac{1.96\sqrt{(.2)(.8)}}{.03} \right)^2 = (26.13)^2 = 683$$

Notice that this produces a smaller value of n (thus reducing sampling costs) than does method 1. If $\hat{p}$ actually lies between .2 and .8, however, the estimate will not be as good as we wanted, because the interval will be wider than desired.

Method 1 is often used to determine the sample size used in public opinion surveys reported by newspapers, magazines, television, and radio. These polls usually estimate proportions to within 3%, with 95% confidence. (The media often state the confidence level as "19 times out of 20.") If you've ever wondered why opinion polls almost always estimate proportions to within 3%, consider the sample size required to estimate a proportion to within 1%.

$$n = \left(\frac{1.96\sqrt{(.5)(.5)}}{.01} \right)^2 = (98)^2 = 9,605$$

The sample size 9,605 is 9 times the sample size needed to estimate a proportion to within 3%. Thus, to divide the width of the interval by 3 requires multiplying the sample size by 9. The cost would also increase considerably. For most applications, the increase in accuracy (created by decreasing the width of the interval estimate) does not overcome the increased cost. Interval estimates with 5% or 10% bounds (sample sizes 385 and 97, respectively) are generally considered too wide to be useful. Thus, the 3% bound is the happy compromise between cost and accuracy.

Testing Hypotheses about Proportions Using the Binomial Distribution (Optional)

As we pointed out in this section, the distribution of $\hat{p}$ is related to the binomial distribution. Because the binomial random variable is discrete, we find it awkward to use the binomial distribution to make inferences about the population proportion. As a consequence, we use the normal approximation of the binomial (introduced in Chapter 7) to test and estimate proportions. However, it should be noted that we can use the binomial distribution to test hypotheses about p. To illustrate, consider Example 11.5 where we wanted to know whether there was sufficient evidence to infer that the proportion of people who would use the new device is greater than 10%. In a sample of 400, we found $x = 52$ people who said they would use the device. We can calculate the p-value of the test. It is

$$P(x \geq 52, \text{ given that } n = 400 \text{ and } p = .10)$$

Note that the p-value is the probability that the number of successes is greater than or equal to the actual number of successes in the sample, the sample size is 400, and under the null hypothesis the probability of success is .10. For smaller values of n, tables may be used. For larger values of n, we must use the computer.

Minitab and Excel can compute the probability that x is less than 52 (by computing the probability that x is less than or equal to 51), from which the p-value may be determined. (See Appendixes 11.A and 11.B for details.)

Minitab Output for
$P(x \leq 51)$

Cumulative Distribution Function

Binomial with n = 400 and p = 0.100000

```
        x       P( X <= x)
    51.00          0.9689
```

Excel prints the value (output not shown)

0.968901

Thus

$$p\text{-value} = 1 - .9689 = .0311$$

Using the normal approximation, we found the p-value to be .0228. Recall that the normal approximation to the binomial improves as n increases. For larger sample sizes, the p-value extracted from the normal distribution will more closely approximate the exact binomial p-value.

We can use this method for all tests of p, particularly for small values of n where the normal approximation may be poor. We can also develop a confidence interval estimator of p. However, it is more complicated than a test; we will not investigate this procedure any further.

We complete this section by reviewing the factors that tell us when to test and estimate a population proportion.

Factors that Identify the z-Test and Interval Estimator of p

1 Problem objective: describe a single population

2 Data type: qualitative

Exercises

11.21 Test each of the following hypotheses.

a H_0: $p = .45$
    H_A: $p \neq .45$
    $\alpha = .05$ $n = 100$ $\hat{p} = .40$

b H_0: $p = .7$
    H_A: $p > .7$
    $\alpha = .01$ $n = 1,000$ $\hat{p} = .75$

c H_0: $p = .25$
    H_A: $p < .25$
    $\alpha = .10$ $n = 2,000$ $\hat{p} = .23$

11.22 Given that $\hat{p} = .84$ and $n = 600$, estimate p with 90% confidence.

11.23 In a random sample of 250, we found 75 successes. Estimate the population proportion of success, with 99% confidence.

11.24 If $\hat{p} = .57$ and $n = 100$, can we conclude at the 5% level of significance that the population proportion p is greater than .50?

11.25 Suppose that, in a sample of 200, we observe 140 successes. Is this sufficient evidence at the 1% significance level to indicate that the population proportion of successes is greater than 65%?

11.26 Find the p-value of the test in Exercise 11.25.

11.27 In a television commercial, the manufacturer of a toothpaste claims that more than four out of five dentists recommend the ingredients in his product. To test that claim, a consumer-protection group randomly samples 400 dentists and asks each one whether he or she would recommend a toothpaste that contained the ingredients. The responses are 0 = No and 1 = Yes. The responses are stored in file XR11-27. At the 5% significance level, can the consumer group infer that the claim is true?

11.28 A professor of business statistics recently adopted a new textbook. At the completion of the course, 100 randomly selected students were asked to assess the book. The responses are as follows.

Excellent (1), Good (2), Adequate (3), Poor (4)

The results are stored in file XR11-28 using the codes in parentheses.

a Do these results allow us to conclude at the 5% significance level that more than 50% of all business students would rate it as excellent?

b Do these results allow us to conclude at the 5% significance level that more than 90% of all business students would rate it as at least adequate?

Use a software package to solve this problem.	OR	The frequency distribution is 1 57 2 35 3 4 4 4 Complete your answer manually.

11.29 Another part of the analysis alluded to in Example 11.6 dealt with areas of South Florida where wind velocities were higher than 115 mph. Suppose that, after examining a sample of 300 homes, a statistician recorded whether the house was uninhabitable (1) or habitable (0). The results are stored in file XR11-29. With 90% confidence, estimate the proportion of all homes exposed to winds of more than 115 mph that were uninhabitable after Hurricane Andrew.

Use a software package to solve this problem.	OR	The frequency distribution is 0 158 1 142 Complete your answer manually.

11.30 The January 3, 1993, edition of the *Atlanta Journal* reported on a survey conducted in October of 1992. A random sample of 612 residents of Georgia were asked "Do you feel that things in Georgia are generally going in the right direction, or do you feel things have gotten off on the wrong track?" The possible responses are as follows.

Right track (1), Wrong track (2), No opinion (0)

The responses are stored in file XR11-30. Estimate with 99% confidence the proportion of all Georgians who had an opinion and that opinion was that things have gotten off on the wrong track.

Use a software package to solve this problem.	OR	The frequency distribution is 0 50 1 365 2 197 Complete your answer manually.

11.31 Pat Statsdud (recall that Pat is a student in the lowest quarter of an introductory statistics course) is a regular participant in a weekly poker game. After playing for a year, Pat has observed the number of games that have been won (Pat made money) and lost (Pat lost money). The results are stored in file XR11-31 in the following way.

Games won (1), Games lost (0)

If the first 52 games can be considered to be a random sample of all games, calculate the p-value of a test to measure the amount of evidence needed to infer that Pat has a less than 50% probability of winning any game.

Use a software package to solve this problem.	OR	The frequency distribution is 0 29 1 23 Complete your answer manually.

11.32 In the same survey referred to in Exercise 11.30, respondents were also asked "How would you rate the quality of public schools in your community?" The responses and their numerical codes are as follows.

Excellent (4), Good (3), Fair (2), Poor (1), No Opinion (0)

The data were stored in file XR11-32. Estimate with 95% confidence the fraction of all Georgians who believe that the quality of the public schools in their communities is excellent. (Decide for yourself how to deal with respondents who answered "no opinion".)

Use a software package to solve this problem.	OR	The frequency distribution is 0 121 1 42 2 93 3 174 4 182 Complete your answer manually.

11.5 The Myth of the Law of Averages (Optional)

Josh Billings, the U.S. humorist who provided Will Rogers with some of his best lines, once remarked that "The trouble with the world ain't ignorance, it's the stuff folks know that ain't so." There are no statistical topics that exemplify this description more than the "law of averages." Let's be clear on this: there is no law of averages. There is something called the law of large numbers, which states that, given a binomial experiment with p greater than zero, the sample proportion $\hat{p}$ approaches the theoretical probability p as n increases. This can be seen by examining the sampling distribution presented in Section 11.4. That is, $\hat{p}$ is approximately normally distributed with mean p and standard deviation $\sqrt{pq/n}$. As a result, as n increases, the standard deviation decreases, which means that the probability that $\hat{p}$ and p differ by a given amount increases as n increases.

To illustrate, suppose that our experiment consists of flipping a balanced coin. The probability that the sample proportion differs from $p = .5$ by less than .01 can be computed for any value of n. For $n = 100$, we find

$$P(.49 < \hat{p} < .51) = P\left(\frac{.49 - .5}{\sqrt{(.5)(.5)/100}} < \frac{\hat{p} - p}{\sqrt{pq/n}} < \frac{.51 - .5}{\sqrt{(.5)(.5)/100}}\right)$$
$$= P(-.2 < z < .2)$$
$$= .1586$$

With $n = 400$, $P(.49 < \hat{p} < .51) = .3108$.
With $n = 10,000$, $P(.49 < \hat{p} < .51) = .9544$.
With $n = 1,000,000$, $P(.49 < \hat{p} < .51) = 1$.

As you can see, the probability that $\hat{p}$ differs from .5 by less than .01 approaches 1 as n increases. In ordinary English, the law of large numbers means that in the long run the sample proportion will be quite close to the population proportion.

Unfortunately, among the statistically uneducated, the words *long run* are usually omitted. Thus, for these people, the law of averages means the law of *small numbers*. The usual interpretation is that after a small number of successes, the law of averages dictates that a failure is due on the next trial. Consider these examples taken from *Chance* magazine, Volume 8, No. 2, Spring 1995.

The first example refers to an announcer discussing the likelihood of basketball player Sam Parker of the Los Angeles Lakers making the seventh consecutive free throw in a game against the Golden State Warriors.

As Los Angeles Laker Sam Parker comes up for a seventh free throw, announcer Chick Hearn notes that Parker had made the last six out of six free throws and concludes that 'the law of averages starts working for Golden State' (15 December 1990).

There are several problems with Mr. Hearn's statement. First, the law of large numbers refers to *future* trials, which means that the results of the previous six free throws have nothing whatever to do with the free throws that follow. That is, if Sam Parker's long-term success percentage is, say, 90%, the probability of making the next free throw is 90%, regardless of what happened on the previous 6, 60, or

600 free throws. Mr. Hearn's comment is equivalent to saying that after six tosses of a balanced coin that resulted in heads, the probability of heads on the seventh toss is something other than 50%. Second, if we wanted to comment on the probability that Sam Parker will make all of the next seven free throws we will need to know the probability of success on each trial.

While sportscasters are among the worst offenders, there are many uninformed in all walks of life. Here is one from a person who knows that the law of averages is mythical.

> *"What I think is our best determination is it will be a colder than normal winter,"* said Pamela Naber Knox, a Wisconsin state climatologist. *"I'm basing that on a couple of different things. First, in looking at the past few winters, there has been a lack of really cold weather. Even though we are not supposed to use the law of averages, we are due,"* said Naber Knox, an instructor in meteorology at the University of Wisconsin-Madison (Associated Press, Fall 1992).

Just because we have not observed a success in several consecutive trials does not mean that the probability of success increases in subsequent trials.

Another variation of the mistakes above applies the law of averages so that if we've observed a larger than expected number of successes in the past, we should observe a larger number of failures in the future. In other words, the law of averages acts as a balancer in all aspects of our lives. Consider this example.

> *"The law of averages is what baseball is all about,"* says [Ralph] Kiner. *"It is the leveling influence of the long season. A .250-hitter may hit .200 or .300 for a given period. But he will eventually level off at .250. The same is true of pitchers. Illnesses, sore arms, good and bad clubs are all part of it. But the law is inflexible. A player will average out to his true ability."* What this means in Seaver's case is that he is now paying for his 1969 season in which he had a 25−7 record . . . (*"Baseball Law of Averages Taking Toll on Seaver."* New Haven Register, 2 June 1974. *Quoted by Gary Smith (1985) in* Statistical Reasoning, *Boston: Allyn and Bacon, p. 175).*

In this quote, Hall-of-Fame pitcher Tom Seaver was required to have a season with a larger number of losses than average because in 1969 he had a smaller number of losses than average. The problem with this "reasoning" is that we don't know an individual player's batting average or a pitcher's won−lost percentage until his career is over. The law of large numbers states that a baseball player's batting average over an increasing number of at-bats will more closely approximate his career average. Unfortunately, we don't know what that average is while the player is active.

Here is probably the worst example in the aforementioned *Chance* article. This was taken from a literary review of actor Marlon Brando's autobiography where he discussed, among other things, his very active love life.

> *Brando has had so many lovers, it would be surprising if they were all of one gender; the law of averages alone would make him bisexual* (Los Angeles Times, *18 September 1994, Book Reviews, p. 13).*

This reference to the law of averages states that when n is very large, we are certain to observe at least one success even if $p = 0$. This is equivalent to flipping a two-headed coin thousands of times and expecting eventually to observe tails.

Unfortunately, there is no shortage of egregious illustrations of the mythical law of averages. We hope that none of our readers will be so quoted in the future.

11.6 Summary

The inferential methods presented in this chapter address the problem of describing a single population. When the data are quantitative, the parameters of interest are the population mean μ and the population variance σ^2. The Student t distribution is used to test and estimate the mean when the population variance is unknown. The chi-squared distribution is used to make inferences about a population variance. When the data are qualitative, the parameter to be tested and estimated is the population proportion p. The sample proportion follows an approximate normal distribution, which produces the test statistic and the interval estimator. We also discussed how to determine the sample size required to estimate a population proportion. Table 11.7 summarizes the formulas used in this chapter. We completed this chapter by pointing out that there is no law of averages despite its ubiquitous use.

IMPORTANT TERMS

t-statistic

Student t distribution

Degrees of freedom

χ^2-statistic

Chi-squared distribution

Table 11.7	Summary of Formulas to Describe a Single Population			
PARAMETERS	TEST STATISTIC	ESTIMATOR		REQUIRED CONDITION
μ	$t = \dfrac{\bar{x} - \mu}{s/\sqrt{n}}$	$\bar{x} \pm t_{\alpha/2}\dfrac{s}{\sqrt{n}}$		x is normally distributed.
σ^2	$\chi^2 = \dfrac{(n-1)s^2}{\sigma^2}$	$(\text{LCL}) = \dfrac{(n-1)s^2}{\chi^2_{\alpha/2}}$		x is normally distributed.
		$(\text{UCL}) = \dfrac{(n-1)s^2}{\chi^2_{1-\alpha/2}}$		
p	$z = \dfrac{\hat{p} - p}{\sqrt{pq/n}}$	$\hat{p} \pm z_{\alpha/2}\sqrt{\dfrac{\hat{p}\hat{q}}{n}}$		np and $nq \geq 5$ (for test) $n\hat{p}$ and $n\hat{q} \geq 5$ (for estimation)

Supplementary Exercises

11.33 One of the issues that came up in a recent municipal election was the high cost of housing. A candidate seeking to unseat an incumbent claimed that the average family spends more than 30% of its annual income on housing. A housing expert was asked to investigate the claim. A random sample of 125 households was drawn, and each household was asked to report the percentage of household income spent on housing costs. Some of these data are listed below, and all the data are stored in file XR11-33.

a Is there enough evidence at the 5% significance level to infer that the candidate is correct?

b Using a confidence level of 95%, estimate the mean percentage spent on housing by all households.

c What is the required condition for the techniques used in parts (a) and (b)? Use a graphical technique to check whether it is satisfied.

HOUSING COSTS AS A PERCENTAGE OF TOTAL INCOME

25 28 29 28 35 36 30 27 28 16 31 36 . . . 37 39 27

Use a software package to solve this problem.	OR	The mean and standard deviation of the data are $\bar{x} = 31.95$ and $s = 7.19$ Complete your answer manually.

11.34 To help forecast the winner in a Democratic senate primary, a survey was conducted. A random sample of 681 registered Democrats was asked for whom they intended to vote in the primary to be held the following day. The results are stored in file XR11-34 using the following codes.

Barbara Gore (1), Bill Quail (2), Pat Bush (3), Undecided (4)

a Estimate with 90% confidence the proportion of all voters who will vote for Pat Bush. (Before answering, decide how to deal with the undecided responses.)

b Can we conclude at the 10% significance level that Bill Quail will receive more than 35% of the vote?

Use a software package to solve this problem.	OR	The frequency distribution is 1 246 2 260 3 121 4 54 Complete your answer manually.

11.35 The "just-in-time" policy of inventory control (developed by the Japanese) is growing in popularity. For example, General Motors recently spent $2 billion on its Oshawa, Ontario, plant so that it will be less than one hour from most suppliers. Suppose that an automobile parts supplier claims to deliver parts to any manufacturer in an average time of less than one hour. In an effort to test the claim, a manufacturer recorded the times of 24 deliveries from this supplier. These data are stored in file XR11-35 and listed below. Can we conclude at the 5% level of significance that the supplier's assertion is correct?

DELIVERY TIMES (IN MINUTES)

55 62 53 72 58 57 51 64 58 52 58 48 45 55 64 62 59 51
61 69 63 60 61 49

Use a software package to solve this problem.	OR	The mean and standard deviation of the data are $\bar{x} = 57.79$ and $s = 6.58$ Complete your answer manually.

11.36 Robots are being used with increasing frequency on production lines to perform monotonous tasks. To determine whether a robot welder should replace human welders in producing automobiles, an experiment was performed. The time for the robot to complete a series of welds was found to be 38 seconds. A random sample of 20 workers was taken, and the time for each worker to complete the welds was measured and listed below. The mean was calculated to be 38 seconds, the same as the robot's time. However, the robot's time did not vary, whereas there was variation among the workers' times. An analysis of the production line revealed that if the variance exceeds 16 seconds^2, there will be problems. Perform an analysis of the data, and determine whether problems using human welders are likely. (Use a 10% significance level.)

TIME TO COMPLETE WELDS (IN SECONDS)

35 25 30 36 37 42 34 44 39 44 40 46 38 42 33 33 39 39
43 41

11.37 The television networks often compete on the evening of an election day to be the first to identify the winner of the election correctly. One commonly used technique is the random sampling of voters as they exit the polling booths. Suppose that, in a two-candidate race, 500 voters were asked for whom they voted. The results were stored in file XR11-37 using the code 1 = Democrat and 2 = Republican. Can we conclude at the 5% level of significance that the Republican candidate will win?

Use a software package to solve this problem.	OR	The frequency distribution is 1 232 2 268 Complete your answer manually.

11.38 Suppose that, in a large state university (with numerous campuses), the marks in an introductory statistics course are normally distributed with a mean of 68%. To determine the effect of requiring students to pass a calculus test (which at present is not a prerequisite), a random sample of 50 students who have taken calculus is given a statistics course. The marks out of 100 are stored in file XR11-38. Some of these observations are listed below.

a Estimate with 95% confidence the mean statistics mark for all students who have taken calculus.

b Do these data provide evidence at the 5% significance level to infer that students with a calculus background would perform better in statistics than students with no calculus?

STATISTICS MARKS FOR STUDENTS WITH CALCULUS BACKGROUND

79 66 88 78 66 80 62 71 81 77 79 ... 61 69 72

Use a software package to solve this problem.	OR	The mean and standard deviation of the data are $\bar{x} = 71.88$ and $s = 10.03$ Complete your answer manually.

11.39 Duplicate bridge is a game in which players compete for master points. When a player receives 300 master points, he or she becomes a life master. Since that title comes with a year's free subscription to the American Contract Bridge League's (ACBL) monthly bulletin, the ACBL is interested in knowing the status of non-life masters. Suppose that a random sample of 50 non-life masters was asked how many master points they have. The results are stored in file XR11-39. (Some of the results are shown below.) The ACBL would like an estimate of the mean number of master points held by all non-life masters. A confidence level of 90% is considered adequate in this case.

NUMBER OF MASTER POINTS

112 71 248 211 133 170 84 173 153 135 ... 104 149 81

Use a software package to solve this problem.	OR	The mean and standard deviation of the data are $\bar{x} = 126.64$ and $s = 62.15$ Complete your answer manually.

11.40 A national health care system was an issue in the 1992 presidential election campaign and is likely to be a subject of debate for many years. The issue arose because of the large number of Americans who have no health insurance. Under the present system, free health care is available to poor people, while relatively well-off Americans buy their own health insurance. Those who are considered working poor and who are in the lower middle class economic stratum appear to be most unlikely to have adequate medical insurance. To investigate this problem, a statistician surveyed 250 families whose gross income last year was between $10,000 and $15,000. Family heads were asked whether they have medical insurance coverage. The answers were stored in file XR11-40 (1 = Has medical insurance and 0 = Doesn't have medical insurance). The statistician wanted an estimate of the fraction of all families whose incomes are in the range of $10,000 to $15,000 who have medical insurance. Perform the necessary calculations to produce an interval estimate with 90% confidence.

Use a software package to solve this problem	OR	The frequency distribution is 1 158 0 92 Complete your answer manually.

11.41 The routes of postal deliverers are carefully planned so that each deliverer works between 7 and 7.5 hours per shift. The planned routes assume an average walking speed of 2 miles per hour and no shortcuts across lawns. In an experiment to examine the amount of time deliverers actually spend completing their shifts, a random sample of 75 postal deliverers was secretly timed. The data from the survey are stored in file XR11-41. (Some of these data are shown below.)

a Estimate with 99% confidence the mean shift time for all postal deliverers.

b Check to determine if the required condition for this statistical inference is satisfied.

c Is there enough evidence at the 10% significance level to conclude that postal workers are on average spending less than seven hours per day doing their jobs?

SHIFT TIMES

6.9 6.9 7.3 7.0 7.0 6.8 7.0 6.8 6.6 7.0 . . . 7.1 7.0 7.0

Use a software package to solve this problem.	OR	The mean and standard deviation of the data are $\bar{x} = 6.91$ and $s = .226$ Complete your answer manually.

11.42 The manager of a branch of a major bank wants to improve service. She is thinking about giving one dollar to any customer who waits in line for a period of time that is considered excessive. (The bank ultimately decided that more than eight minutes is excessive.) However, to get a better idea about the level of current service, she undertakes a survey of customers. A student is hired to measure the time spent waiting in line by a random sample of 50 customers. Using a stop watch, the student determined the amount of time between the time the customer joined the line and the time he or she reached the teller. The times were recorded and are listed below. (The times are also stored in file XR11-42.)

a Construct a 90% confidence interval estimate of the mean waiting time for the bank's customers.

b Check to ensure that the required condition for the estimate is satisfied.

WAITING TIME IN BANK LINEUP

1.4   6.1 10.4   6.4   3.5   9.0 10.9   4.8   9.0   5.6   9.6   9.4   5.6   6.6   1.2   3.9
1.4   6.6   8.9   7.1   4.8   5.2   3.2   2.4   5.8   3.9   5.9 10.7   4.1   6.8   2.9   2.0
7.2   8.6   5.9   7.5   4.5   1.9   1.0   3.9   8.7   3.2   4.6   4.0   4.1   2.3 11.0 10.8
7.3   7.9

Use a software package to solve this problem.	OR	The mean and standard deviation of the data are $\bar{x} = 5.79$ and $s = 2.86$ Complete your answer manually.

11.43 Refer to Exercise 11.42. Estimate with 95% confidence the fraction of all customers who would wait for more than eight minutes.

11.44 In an examination of consumer loyalty in the travel business, 72 first-time visitors to a tourist attraction were asked whether they planned to return (P. K. Tat and J. R. Thompson, "An Exploratory Study of Brand Loyalty in Setting Travel Destinations," *Developments in Marketing Science* 6 (1983): 563–65.). The responses were stored in file XR11-44 where 1 = Yes and 0 = No. Estimate with 95% confidence the proportion of all first-time visitors who planned to return to the same destination.

Use a software package to solve this problem.	OR	The frequency distribution is 0 24 1 48 Complete your answer manually.

11.45 An advertisement for a major home appliance manufacturer claims that its repair personnel are the loneliest in the world because its appliances require the smallest number of service calls. To examine this claim, a researcher drew a random sample of 100 owners of five-year-old washing machines. The number of service calls made in the five-year period were recorded and stored in file XR11-45. (Some of these data are shown below.) Find the 90% confidence interval estimate of the mean number of service calls for all five-year-old washing machines.

SERVICE CALLS

1 0 1 0 1 2 2 4 1 0 5 2 2 2 . . . 0 0 0

Use a software package to solve this problem.	OR	The mean and standard deviation of the data are $\bar{x} = 1.10$ and $s = .98$ Complete your answer manually.

11.46 An oil company sends out monthly statements to its customers who purchased gasoline and other items using the company's credit card. Until now, the company has not included a preaddressed envelope for returning payments. The average and the standard deviation of the number of days before payment is received are 10.5 and 3.3, respectively. As an experiment to determine whether enclosing preaddressed envelopes speeds up payment, 100 customers selected at random were sent preaddressed envelopes with their bills. The number of days to payment was recorded and stored in file XR11-46. A portion of the sample data are listed below.

a Do the data provide sufficient evidence at the 5% level of significance to establish that enclosure of preaddressed envelopes improves the average speed of payments?

b Can we conclude at the 5% significance level that the variability in payment speeds decreases when a preaddressed envelope is sent?

NUMBER OF DAYS TO PAYMENT

9 14 8 9 9 11 9 9 4 8 9 4 . . . 12 12 11

Use a software package to solve this problem.	OR	The mean and standard deviation of the data are $\bar{x} = 9.74$ and $s = 2.88$ Complete your answer manually.

11.47 A rock promoter is in the process of deciding whether to book a new band for a rock concert. He knows that this band appeals almost exclusively to teenagers. According to the latest census, there are 400,000 teenagers in the area. The promoter decides to do a survey to try to estimate the proportion of teenagers who will attend the concert. How large a sample should be taken in order to estimate the proportion to within .02 with 99% confidence?

11.48 In Exercise 11.47, suppose that the promoter decided to draw a sample of size 600 (because of financial considerations). Each teenager was asked whether he or she would attend the concert. The answers were stored in file XR11-48 using the following codes: 2 = Yes, I will attend; 1 = No, I will not attend; 0 = Don't know. Estimate with 95% confidence the number of teenagers who will attend the concert.

Use a software package to solve this problem.	OR	The frequency distribution is
		0 33
		1 479
		2 88
		Complete your answer manually.

11.49 The owner of a downtown parking lot suspects that the person she hired to run the lot is stealing some money. The receipts as provided by the employee indicate that the average number of cars parked in the lot is 125 per day and that, on average, each car is parked for three and a half hours. In order to determine whether the employee is stealing, the owner watches the lot for five days. On those days, the number of cars parked is as follows.

120   130   124   127   128

The time spent on the lot for the 629 cars that the owner observed during the five days was stored in file XR11-49. Can the owner conclude at the 5% level of significance that the employee is stealing? (HINT: Since there are two ways to steal, two tests should be performed.)

CASE 11.1* NUMBER OF UNINSURED MOTORISTS

A number of years ago the Michigan legislature passed a law requiring insurance for all drivers. Prior to this event drivers did not have to be covered by insurance. The law was challenged on the grounds that it discriminated against poor people who would not be able legally to drive. At issue at the trial was the number of Michigan motorists who would be coerced by the law into buying insurance. To do so, it was necessary to count the number of uninsured motorists. (These would be the people who would be forced by law to buy insurance.) There were a total of 4,505,665 license plates for passenger vehicles registered in Michigan at the time. An investigation of each one of these to determine whether they had insurance

*Adapted from L. Katz, "Presentation of a Confidence Interval Estimate as Evidence in a Legal Proceeding," Department of Statistics, Michigan State University (1974).

coverage would be prohibitively expensive and time-consuming. It was decided that the state would draw a random sample of motorists and estimate the number of Michigan's driving population who were uninsured from the sample data. A random sample of 249 license plates was drawn using statistically sound sampling methods. Each was investigated to determine its insurance status. The license plates sampled were placed in one of three categories. The categories and the codes on the disk are as follows.

| Insured | 1 | Not insured | 2 | Missing | 3 |

(License plates that were drawn for the sample but where investigators were unable to find the car or its owner were classified as missing.)

The data are stored in column 1 of file C11-01.

Your job is to estimate the proportion of all Michigan passenger vehicles that are not insured. (Decide for yourself how to deal with the missing vehicles.) From this interval estimate, find upper and lower limits for the estimated number of motorists who would have been forced by law to buy insurance.

CASE 11.2*   NATIONAL PATENT DEVELOPMENT CORPORATION

The National Patent Development Corporation (NPD) is a company that takes newly patented products from the design stage through to sales to the consumer. In 1986, NPD acquired a new product that can be used to replace a dentist's drill. The product, called Caridex, is a solution that dissolves decayed matter in dental cavities without requiring drilling. After some research, it was discovered that Caridex works well only on cavities on the top surface of teeth, where a small fraction of cavities occur.

It is known that 100,000 dentists in the United States treat cavities. A preliminary analysis revealed that only 10% of all dentists would use Caridex in the first year after its introduction.

The dispensing unit costs NPD $200, and it intends to sell the unit at cost price. The solution costs NPD $0.50 per cavity and will be sold to dentists at a price of $2.50 per cavity. Fixed annual costs are expected to be $4 million.

NPD would like an estimate of the profit it can expect in the first year of operation. Because NPD profits will depend completely on the number of cavities treated with Caridex during the year, NPD commissioned a survey of 400 dentists who planned to use Caridex. Each dentist was asked how many cavities he or she anticipates treating with Caridex during an average week. The results are stored in file C11-02.

Put yourself in the position of the manager responsible for Caridex at NPD. Determine upper and lower limits on your estimate of first-year profits from Caridex. Can you conclude from the survey that Caridex will make a profit in its first year?

---

*Based on a report by Ladenburg Thalman—a large, New York-based investment firm. The survey is fictitious.

Testing a Population Mean When the Population Variance Is Unknown

The command

TTEST K1 C1

performs a two-tail test using the data stored in column 1. **K1** is the value of μ specified by the null hypothesis. The subcommand **ALTERNATIVE** allows us to perform a one-tail test. We produce the required statistics for Example 11.1 with the following commands.

TTEST 8200 C1;
ALTERNATIVE −1.

Estimating a Population Mean When the Population Variance Is Unknown

The command

TINTERVAL 90 C1

produces the 90% confidence interval estimate of μ from data in column 1. Omitting the "90" results in Minitab producing a 95% confidence interval estimate of the mean.

Inference about a Population Proportion

Minitab does not conduct tests about population proportions nor does it produce confidence interval estimates. Fortunately, there are several courses of action we can take. Assuming that we have only the raw data, we can compute the sample proportion $\hat{p}$ and complete the calculations manually. Alternatively, we can create a macro that performs the necessary work. To output the frequencies, proceed as described below. The commands

TALLY C1;
PERCENTS.

will produce the percent of each value (the values must be integers) of the data stored in column 1.

MENU COMMANDS

To compute the percentages only:

    1 Click **Stat**, **Tables**, and **Tally**.

    2 Use the cursor to select **Percents**. Click **OK**.

The value of the test statistic and the interval estimate can be calculated manually using the value of $\hat{p}$ produced by Minitab.

Minitab Macro

We can compute the value of the test statistic and the interval estimate without manual calculations by running Minitab macros. A macro is a series of commands that are stored so that they can be executed with a single command. Several Minitab macros have been stored on the disk that accompanies this book. To execute a macro, place the disk in drive A and follow the instructions described in the chapter.

Recoding the Data

If the data are not recorded so that 1 = success and 0 − failure, we use the **CODE** command to convert the data. Suppose that in a brand preference survey, responses of people who chose brands A, B, and C are stored as 1, 2, and 3, respectively, in column 1. If we want to estimate the proportion who prefer brand B, we must recode the data so that 1 = brand B and 0 = others (i.e., 1 = success and 0 = failure). The following command accomplishes the task.

    CODE (1) 0 (2) 1 (3) 0 C1 C1

The command instructs Minitab to examine the data in column 1. All 1s are converted to 0s, all 2s are converted to 1s, and all 3s are converted to 0s. We can now use our macros.

We can also use the **CODE** command to convert quantitative data to qualitative data. For example, if we've recorded the marks from a recent test in column 1 and we would like to convert them to letter grades (A = 80–100; B = 70–79; C = 60–69; D = 50–59; F = 0–49), we would type the following.

    CODE (0:49)0 (50:59)1 (60:69)2 (70:79)3 (80:100)4 C1 C2

Column 2 would contain numbers representing the letter grades (0 = F; 1 = D; 2 = C; 3 = B; 4 = A).

Recoding to Omit Data

Minitab uses an asterisk (*) to denote missing data. Suppose that in a political survey where the Democrat and Republican candidates are the only ones running for office, we ask a random sample of potential voters for whom they intend to vote. Some voters will vote for the Democratic candidate, some will vote for the Republican candidate, and others haven't decided (or refuse to say or don't know how they will vote). In estimating or testing a proportion, we wish to count only those who have said that they will vote for one of the two candidates. To instruct Minitab to omit those who haven't yet decided, refuse to say, or don't know, we represent their responses with an asterisk. It may be necessary in some cases to recode the data. For example, if we originally coded the data in the following way

1 = Democrat

2 = Republican

3 = Refuse to say

4 = Don't know

5 = Haven't decided

and stored the responses in column 1, we can test to determine if the Democratic candidate will garner more than 50% of the vote by coding the data.

CODE (2)0 (3:5)* C1 C1

Thus, 1 = success, 0 = failure, and all other responses will be omitted by Minitab. We can now use one of the macros.

Calculating the *p*-Value Directly from the Binomial Distribution (Optional)

The **CDF** (Cumulative Density Function) command is used to find the probability that a random variable is less than or equal to a given value. A subcommand specifies the distribution. For Example 11.5, we find the probability that a binomial random variable with $n = 400$ and $p = .10$ is less than or equal to 51 in the following way.

Type

CDF 51;

BINOMIAL 400 .1.

The *p*-value can be computed from this value.

MENU COMMANDS

1 Click **Calc, Probability Distributions,** and **Binomial.**

2 Use the cursor to specify that you want the **cumulative probability.**

3 Specify the **number of trials** and **probability of success.**

4 Use the cursor to select **input constant** and specify the value of x. Click **OK.**

EXCEL 97

Excel 97 Users:
Click **OK** instead of **Next>**
and **Finish**

Inference about a Population Proportion

To count the number of times a particular value (category) occurs, proceed as follows.

1 Click **f$_x$**, **Statistical**, **COUNTIF**, and **Next>**.

2 Specify the range and the criteria (code that identifies a success), and click **Finish**.

The number of successes will be printed from which you can calculate $\hat{p}$, test statistic, and interval estimate manually.

Calculating the *p*-Value Directly from the Binomial Distribution (Optional)

We can find the probability that a random variable is less than or equal to a given value.

1 Click **f$_x$**, **Statistical**, **BINOMDIST**, and **Next>**.

2 Specify the value of x (**number_s**), n (**trials**), and p (**probability_s**).

3 Indicate that you want the cumulative probability by typing **TRUE**. Click **Finish**.

For Example 11.5, we find the probability that a binomial random variable with $n = 400$ and $p = .10$ is less than or equal to 51 in the following way.

1 Click **f$_x$**, **Statistical**, **BINOMDIST**, and **Next>**.

2 Specify the value of x (**51**), n (**400**), and p (**.1**).

3 Indicate that you want the cumulative probability by typing **TRUE**. Click **Finish**.

Recoding the Data

For a test of one or two proportions **(Data Analysis Plus),** the data must be integers. If the data are not in this form, you can recode them. For example, suppose that the data in column A are real numbers and you wish to estimate the proportion of negative numbers. In cell B1 type

```
=IF((A1 < 0), 1, 0)
```

This command tells Excel to place a 1 in cell B1 if A1 is less than 0. If A1 is *not* less than 0, Excel will place a 0 in cell B1. Drag to fill in the rest of column B. You can now perform a test of hypothesis or estimate the proportion of 1s in column B.

12 Inference about the Comparison of Two Populations

12.1 Introduction

We can compare learning how to employ statistical techniques to learning how to drive a car. We began by describing what you are going to do in this course (Chapter 1), followed by a presentation of the essential background material (Chapters 2 through 8). Learning the concepts of statistical inference and applying them the way we did in Chapters 9 and 10 is akin to driving a car in an empty parking lot. You're driving, but it's not a realistic experience. Learning Chapter 11 is like driving on a quiet side street with little traffic. The experience represents real driving, but much of the difficulties have been eliminated. In this chapter, you begin to drive for real, with many of the actual problems faced by licensed drivers, and the experience prepares you to tackle the next difficulty.

In this chapter, we present a variety of techniques whose objective is to compare two populations. In Sections 12.2 and 12.4, we deal with quantitative variables; the parameter of interest is the difference between two means. The difference between these two sections introduces yet another factor that determines the correct statistical method—the design of the experiment used to gather the data. In Section 12.2, the samples are independently drawn, whereas in Section 12.4, the samples are taken from a matched pairs experiment. In Section 12.3, we discuss the difference between observational and experimental data, a distinction that is critical to the way in which we interpret statistical results.

Section 12.5 presents the procedures employed to infer whether two population variances differ. The parameter is the ratio σ_1^2/σ_2^2. (When comparing two variances, we use the ratio rather than the difference because of the nature of the sampling distribution.)

Section 12.6 addresses the problem of comparing two populations of qualitative data. The parameter to be tested and estimated is the difference between two proportions.

The following examples illustrate situations in which the problem objective is to compare two populations.

Example 1 Operations managers of production facilities are always looking for ways to improve productivity in their plants. This can be accomplished by rearranging sequences of operations, acquiring new technology, or improving the training of workers. When one or more such changes are made, their effect on the operation of the entire plant is of interest. The manager can measure the effect by comparing productivity after the innovation with productivity before the innovation. Because productivity is often measured by the mean number of units produced per hour, the parameter of interest is the difference between two means $\mu_1 - \mu_2$. We may also be interested in comparing the consistency before and after the innovation; the parameter to be tested or estimated is σ_1^2/σ_2^2.

Example 2 Market managers and advertisers are eager to know which segments of the population are buying their products. If they can determine these groups, they can target their advertising messages and tailor their products to these customers. For example, if advertisers determine that the decision to purchase a particular household product is made more frequently by men than by women, the interests and concerns of men will be the focus of most commercial messages. The advertising media also depend on whether the product is of greater interest to men or to women. The most common way of measuring this factor is to find the difference in the proportions of men and women buying the product. In these situations, the parameter to be tested or estimated is the difference between two proportions $p_1 - p_2$.

Example 3 Medical scientists are involved in various research projects. A number of projects are examining ways to reduce cholesterol levels, since high levels of cholesterol are linked to heart attacks and strokes. One method of testing the effectiveness of a new drug is to give the drug to one group of people and a placebo (a pill with no medicine) to another group of people. To judge how well the drug works, the reduction in cholesterol would be measured for each person. The mean reduction for those taking the drug could be compared with the mean reduction for those taking the placebo. The objective is to test to see if the former is greater than the latter. The parameter is the difference between two means $\mu_1 - \mu_2$.

Example 4 Politicians are constantly concerned about how the voting public perceives their actions and behaviors. Politicians are particularly concerned with the extent to which constituents approve of their behavior and the ways in which that approval changes over time. As a result, they frequently poll the public to determine the proportion of voters who support them and whether that support has changed since the previous survey. The parameter of interest to them is the difference between two proportions $p_1 - p_2$, where p_1 is the proportion of support at present and p_2 is the proportion of support at the time of the previous survey.

12.2 Inference about the Difference between Two Means: Independent Samples

In order to test and estimate the difference between two population means, the statistician draws random samples from each of two populations. In this section, we discuss independent samples. In Section 12.4, where we present the matched pairs experiment, the distinction between independent samples and matched pairs will be made clear. For now, we define independent samples as samples completely unrelated to one another.

Figure 12.1 depicts the sampling process. Observe that we draw a sample of size n_1 from population 1 and a sample of size n_2 from population 2. For each sample, we compute the sample means and sample variances.

Figure 12.1

Independent Samples from Two Populations

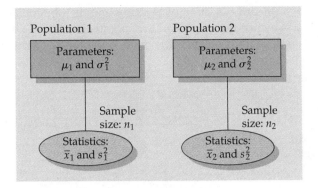

Because this is the fourth parameter that we've discussed, we can proceed to the test statistic and interval estimator directly. The best estimator of the difference between two population means $\mu_1 - \mu_2$ is the difference between two sample means $\bar{x}_1 - \bar{x}_2$. Statisticians have derived the sampling distribution of $\bar{x}_1 - \bar{x}_2$.

Sampling Distribution of $\bar{x}_1 - \bar{x}_2$

1 $\bar{x}_1 - \bar{x}_2$ is normally distributed if the populations are normal and approximately normal if the populations are nonnormal and the sample sizes are large.

2 The expected value of $\bar{x}_1 - \bar{x}_2$ is

$$E(\bar{x}_1 - \bar{x}_2) = \mu_1 - \mu_2$$

3 The variance of $\bar{x}_1 - \bar{x}_2$ is

$$V(\bar{x}_1 - \bar{x}_2) = \frac{\sigma_1^2}{n_1} + \frac{\sigma_2^2}{n_2}$$

Thus,

$$z = \frac{(\bar{x}_1 - \bar{x}_2) - (\mu_1 - \mu_2)}{\sqrt{\dfrac{\sigma_1^2}{n_1} + \dfrac{\sigma_2^2}{n_2}}}$$

is a standard normal (or approximately normal) random variable. It follows that the test statistic is

$$z = \frac{(\bar{x}_1 - \bar{x}_2) - (\mu_1 - \mu_2)}{\sqrt{\dfrac{\sigma_1^2}{n_1} + \dfrac{\sigma_2^2}{n_2}}}$$

The confidence interval estimator is

$$(\bar{x}_1 - \bar{x}_2) \pm z_{\alpha/2}\sqrt{\frac{\sigma_1^2}{n_1} + \frac{\sigma_2^2}{n_2}}$$

However, these formulas are rarely used because the population variances σ_1^2 and σ_2^2 are almost always unknown. Consequently, it is necessary to estimate the standard deviation of the sampling distribution. The way to do this depends on whether the two unknown population variances are equal. When they are equal, the test statistic and confidence interval estimator are as follows.

> **Test Statistic for $\mu_1 - \mu_2$ when $\sigma_1^2 = \sigma_2^2$**
>
> $$t = \frac{(\bar{x}_1 - \bar{x}_2) - (\mu_1 - \mu_2)}{\sqrt{s_p^2\left(\dfrac{1}{n_1} + \dfrac{1}{n_2}\right)}} \qquad \text{d.f.} = n_1 + n_2 - 2$$
>
> where
>
> $$s_p^2 = \frac{(n_1 - 1)s_1^2 + (n_2 - 1)s_2^2}{n_1 + n_2 - 2}$$

The quantity s_p^2 is called the **pooled variance estimate** of the common variance. It is the weighted average of the two sample variances. The requirement that the population variances are equal makes this calculation feasible, since we need only one estimate of the common value of σ_1^2 and σ_2^2. It makes sense for us to use the pooled variance estimate because, in combining both samples, we produce a better estimate.

The test statistic is Student t distributed, with $n_1 + n_2 - 2$ degrees of freedom, provided that the two populations are normal. The confidence interval estimator is derived by mathematics that by now has become routine.

> **Confidence Interval Estimator of $\mu_1 - \mu_2$ when $\sigma_1^2 = \sigma_2^2$**
>
> $$(\bar{x}_1 - \bar{x}_2) \pm t_{\alpha/2}\sqrt{s_p^2\left(\dfrac{1}{n_1} + \dfrac{1}{n_2}\right)}$$

We will refer to the above formulas as the *equal-variances* test statistic and confidence interval estimator, respectively.

The question naturally arises, how do we know when the population variances are equal? The answer is that since σ_1^2 and σ_2^2 are unknown, we can't know for certain whether they're equal. However, we can use the sample variances s_1^2 and s_2^2 to make inferences about the population variances. In Section 12.5, we will present a statistical technique that will allow us to test for equality. However, for now we will simply examine the sample variances and informally judge their relative values to determine whether we can assume that the population variances are equal.

When the population variances are unequal, we cannot use the pooled variance estimate. Instead, we estimate each population variance with its sample variance. Unfortunately, the sampling distribution of the resulting statistic

$$\frac{(\bar{x}_1 - \bar{x}_2) - (\mu_1 - \mu_2)}{\sqrt{\dfrac{s_1^2}{n_1} + \dfrac{s_2^2}{n_2}}}$$

is neither normal nor Student t. However, it can be approximated by a Student t distribution with degrees of freedom equal to

$$\text{d.f.} = \frac{(s_1^2/n_1 + s_2^2/n_2)^2}{\left(\dfrac{(s_1^2/n_1)^2}{n_1 - 1} + \dfrac{(s_2^2/n_2)^2}{n_2 - 1}\right)}$$

The test statistic and confidence interval estimator are easily derived from the sampling distribution.

Test Statistic for $\mu_1 - \mu_2$ when $\sigma_1^2 \neq \sigma_2^2$

$$t = \frac{(\bar{x}_1 - \bar{x}_2) - (\mu_1 - \mu_2)}{\sqrt{\dfrac{s_1^2}{n_1} + \dfrac{s_2^2}{n_2}}} \qquad \text{d.f.} = \frac{(s_1^2/n_1 + s_2^2/n_2)^2}{\left(\dfrac{(s_1^2/n_1)^2}{n_1 - 1} + \dfrac{(s_2^2/n_2)^2}{n_2 - 1}\right)}$$

Confidence Interval Estimator of $\mu_1 - \mu_2$ when $\sigma_1^2 \neq \sigma_2^2$

$$(\bar{x}_1 - \bar{x}_2) \pm t_{\alpha/2}\sqrt{\dfrac{s_1^2}{n_1} + \dfrac{s_2^2}{n_2}}$$

We will refer to the above formulas as the *unequal-variances* test statistic and confidence interval estimator, respectively.

EXAMPLE 12.1

Despite some controversy, scientists generally agree that high-fiber cereals reduce the likelihood of various forms of cancer. However, one scientist claims that people who eat high-fiber cereal for breakfast will consume, on average, fewer calories for lunch than people who don't eat high-fiber cereal for breakfast (*Toronto Star*, 2 July 1991). If this is true, high-fiber cereal manufacturers will be able to claim another advantage of eating their product—potential weight reduction for dieters. As a preliminary test of the claim, 30 people were randomly selected and asked what they regularly eat for breakfast and lunch. Each person was identified as either a consumer or a nonconsumer of high-fiber cereal, and the number of calories consumed at lunch was measured and recorded. These data are listed below and stored in columns 1 and 2 of file XM12-01. Can the scientist conclude at the 5% significance level that his belief is correct?

CALORIES CONSUMED AT LUNCH

Consumers of High-Fiber Cereal	Nonconsumers of High-Fiber Cereal
640 605 529 591 596 564	502 703 735 707 523 534 768
615 560 635 623	626 620 589 736 565 686 529
	632 951 744 632 593 847

SOLUTION

In order to assess the claim, the scientist needs to compare the population of consumers of high-fiber cereal to the population of nonconsumers. The data are quantitative (obviously, we've recorded real numbers). This problem objective–data type combination tells us that the parameter to be tested is the difference between two means $\mu_1 - \mu_2$. The claim to be tested is that the mean caloric intake of consumers (μ_1) is less than that of nonconsumers (μ_2). Hence, the alternative hypothesis is

$$H_A: (\mu_1 - \mu_2) < 0$$

To identify the test statistic, the scientist instructs the computer to output the sample standard deviations. They are

$$s_1 = 35.7 \quad \text{and} \quad s_2 = 115.7$$

There is reason to believe that the population variances are unequal. Thus, we use the unequal-variances test statistic.

$$t = \frac{(\bar{x}_1 - \bar{x}_2) - (\mu_1 - \mu_2)}{\sqrt{\dfrac{s_1^2}{n_1} + \dfrac{s_2^2}{n_2}}} \qquad \text{d.f.} = \frac{(s_1^2/n_1 + s_2^2/n_2)^2}{\left(\dfrac{(s_1^2/n_1)^2}{n_1 - 1} + \dfrac{(s_2^2/n_2)^2}{n_2 - 1}\right)}$$

The complete test follows.

$$H_0: (\mu_1 - \mu_2) = 0$$
$$H_A: (\mu_1 - \mu_2) < 0$$

Test statistic: $t = \dfrac{(\bar{x}_1 - \bar{x}_2) - (\mu_1 - \mu_2)}{\sqrt{\dfrac{s_1^2}{n_1} + \dfrac{s_2^2}{n_2}}}$

From the data we calculated the following statistics.

$$\bar{x}_1 = 595.8$$
$$\bar{x}_2 = 661.1$$
$$s_1 = 35.7$$
$$s_2 = 115.7$$

The number of degrees of freedom of the test statistic is

$$\begin{aligned}
\text{d.f.} &= \frac{(s_1^2/n_1 + s_2^2/n_2)^2}{\left(\dfrac{(s_1^2/n_1)^2}{n_1 - 1} + \dfrac{(s_2^2/n_2)^2}{n_2 - 1}\right)} \\[2mm]
&= \frac{[(35.7)^2/10 + (115.7)^2/20]^2}{\left(\dfrac{[(35.7)^2/10]^2}{10 - 1} + \dfrac{[(115.7)^2/20]^2}{20 - 1}\right)} \\[2mm]
&= 25.01
\end{aligned}$$

which we round to 25. The rejection region is

$$t < -t_{\alpha,\text{d.f.}} = -t_{.05,25} = -1.708$$

The value of the test statistic is

$$t = \frac{(\bar{x}_1 - \bar{x}_2) - (\mu_1 - \mu_2)}{\sqrt{\dfrac{s_1^2}{n_1} + \dfrac{s_2^2}{n_2}}}$$

$$= \frac{(595.8 - 661.1) - 0}{\sqrt{\dfrac{(35.7)^2}{10} + \dfrac{(115.7)^2}{20}}}$$

$$= -2.31$$

Conclusion: Reject the null hypothesis.

Minitab Ouput for Example 12.1

Two Sample T-Test and Confidence Interval

```
Twosample T for Consmers vs Noncnsmr
              N      Mean    StDev   SE Mean
Consmers     10     595.8     35.7       11
Noncnsmr     20      661      116        26

95% C.I. for mu Consmers - mu Noncnsmr: ( -123,  -7)
T-Test mu Consmers = mu Noncnsmr (vs <): T= -2.31  P=0.015  DF=  25
```

The value of the test statistic is $t = -2.31$ where the number of degrees of freedom is 25. The *p*-value is .015. Appendix 12.A describes how to generate these results using the session commands. The menu commands are listed below.

MENU COMMANDS	COMMANDS FOR EXAMPLE 12.1
1 Type or import the data.	Open file **XM12-01**.
2 Click **Stat, Basic Statistics**, and **2-Sample t . . . .**	
3 Use the cursor to select **Samples in one column** (stacked data) or **Samples in different columns** (unstacked data). (See the "Manipulating Data" subsection on page 440 for a discussion of stacked and unstacked data.)	**Samples in different columns**
4 Hit **tab**, and type each variable name.	**Consmers Noncnsmr** or **C1 C2**
5 Use the cursor to select one of **less than, not equal to**, or **greater than**.	**less than**
6 Use the cursor to indicate that the population variances are not equal. (Leave box empty.) Click **OK**.	

The output includes the 95% confidence interval estimate of $\mu_1 - \mu_2$. To alter the confidence level use the cursor and type the desired level.

	A	B	C
1	t-Test: Two-Sample Assuming Unequal Variances		
2			
3		Consumers	Nonconsumers
4	Mean	595.8	661.1
5	Variance	1273.511111	13375.25263
6	Observations	10	20
7	Hypothesized Mean Difference	0	
8	df	25	
9	t Stat	-2.31433179	
10	P(T<=t) one-tail	0.014576434	
11	t Critical one-tail	1.708140189	
12	P(T<=t) two-tail	0.029152868	
13	t Critical two-tail	2.05953711	

Excel prints sample means, variances, and sizes. It also prints the statistical results related to the test of hypothesis. The value of the test statistic **t Stat** is −2.31433179 with a one-tail *p*-value of .014576434. Excel also outputs the critical values (using a 5% significance level) for a one-tail and a two-tail test. It also provides the two-tail test *p*-value, which is not needed in this example.

COMMANDS	COMMANDS FOR EXAMPLE 12.1
1 Type or import the data into two columns.	Open file **XM12-01**.
2 Click **Tools, Data Analysis...**, and *t*-**Test: Two-Sample Assuming Unequal Variances**.	
3 Specify **Variable 1 Range**.	**A1:A11**
4 Specify **Variable 2 Range**.	**B1:B21**
5 Specify the **Hypothesized Mean Difference** and click **Labels** (if necessary). Click **OK**.	**0**

**INTERPRETING THE
RESULTS**

The *p*-value of the test is small, which leads us to conclude that these data provide enough evidence to infer that consumers of high-fiber cereal do eat fewer calories at lunch than do nonconsumers. However, there are several reasons to be cautious about concluding that high-fiber cereals constitute an effective contribution to weight loss. First, the sample sizes are small. (Larger sample sizes are more realistic, but inhibit manual calculations.) Second, the data were likely self-reported, which means that each person determined the number of calories recorded that he or she consumed. Such data are often unreliable. Ideally, a less subjective method of counting calories should be used. Finally, the way in which the experiment was performed may lead to several contradictory interpretations of the data. We will discuss this important issue in the next section.

See Figure 12.2, which depicts the sampling distribution of the test statistic.

Figure 12.2

Sampling Distribution for
Example 12.1

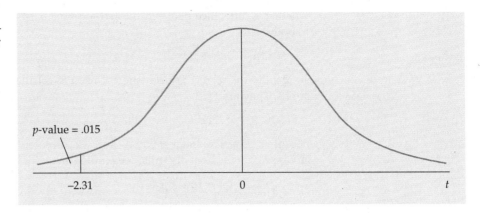

We can estimate the difference in mean caloric intake. The Minitab output includes the 95% confidence interval estimate of $\mu_1 - \mu_2$. The Excel output includes the sample means and variances, as well as the critical value of t (**t Critical two-tail** $= t_{\alpha/2}$). From these results, we can complete the computation of the confidence interval estimate. Thus, we estimate that nonconsumers of high-fiber cereal eat an average of between 7 and 123 calories more than do consumers.

EXAMPLE 12.2

The plant manager of a company that manufactures office equipment believes that worker productivity is a function of, among other things, the design of the job, which refers to the sequence of worker movements. Two designs are being considered for the production of a new type of ergonomic computer desk. To help decide which should be used, an experiment was performed. Twenty-five randomly selected workers assembled the desk using design A, and 25 workers assembled the product using design B. The assembly times in minutes were recorded and are exhibited below and stored in file XM12-02. The plant manager would like to know whether the assembly times of the two designs differ. A 5% significance level is judged to be appropriate.

ASSEMBLY TIMES

Design A	Design B
6.8 5.0 7.9 5.2 7.6 5.0 5.9	5.2 6.7 5.7 6.6 8.5 6.5 5.9
5.2 6.5 7.4 6.1 6.2 7.1 4.6	6.7 6.6 4.2 4.2 4.5 5.3 7.9
6.0 7.1 6.1 5.0 6.3 7.0 6.4	7.0 5.9 7.1 5.8 7.0 5.7 5.9
6.1 6.6 7.7 6.4	4.9 5.3 4.2 7.1

SOLUTION

IDENTIFYING THE
TECHNIQUE

The data are quantitative, and the objective of the experiment is to compare the two populations of assembly times. The parameter of interest is the difference between two population means $\mu_1 - \mu_2$. The plant manager wants to determine whether a difference between the two designs exists. As a result, the alternative hypothesis is

$$H_A: (\mu_1 - \mu_2) \neq 0$$

To identify the correct test statistic, we need to calculate the sample standard deviations. They are

$$s_1 = .921 \quad \text{and} \quad s_2 = 1.14$$

Because s_1 is approximately equal to s_2, we can infer that the population variances are approximately equal. Thus, we employ the equal-variances test statistic.

$$t = \frac{(\bar{x}_1 - \bar{x}_2) - (\mu_1 - \mu_2)}{\sqrt{s_p^2\left(\dfrac{1}{n_1} + \dfrac{1}{n_2}\right)}}$$

The complete test is shown below.

$$H_0: (\mu_1 - \mu_2) = 0$$
$$H_A: (\mu_1 - \mu_2) \neq 0$$

Test statistic: $t = \dfrac{(\bar{x}_1 - \bar{x}_2) - (\mu_1 - \mu_2)}{\sqrt{s_p^2\left(\dfrac{1}{n_1} + \dfrac{1}{n_2}\right)}}$

SOLVING BY HAND

The number of degrees of freedom is

$$\text{d.f.} = n_1 + n_2 - 2 = 25 + 25 - 2 = 48$$

The rejection region is

$$|t| > t_{\alpha/2,\text{d.f.}} = t_{.025,48} \simeq 2.009$$

We determined the following statistics.

$$\bar{x}_1 = 6.288$$
$$\bar{x}_2 = 6.016$$
$$s_1 = .921$$
$$s_2 = 1.142$$
$$s_p^2 = \frac{(n_1 - 1)s_1^2 + (n_2 - 1)s_2^2}{n_1 + n_2 - 2}$$
$$= \frac{(25 - 1)(.921)^2 + (25 - 1)(1.142)^2}{25 + 25 - 2}$$
$$= 1.075$$

The value of the test statistic is

$$t = \frac{(\bar{x}_1 - \bar{x}_2) - (\mu_1 - \mu_2)}{\sqrt{s_p^2\left(\dfrac{1}{n_1} + \dfrac{1}{n_2}\right)}}$$
$$= \frac{(6.288 - 6.016) - 0}{\sqrt{1.075\left(\dfrac{1}{25} + \dfrac{1}{25}\right)}}$$
$$= .93$$

Conclusion: Do not reject the null hypothesis.

Minitab Output for Example 12.2

Two Sample T-Test and Confidence Interval

```
Twosample T for Design A vs Design B
            N     Mean    StDev   SE Mean
Design A   25    6.288    0.921    0.18
Design B   25    6.02     1.14     0.23

95% C.I. for mu Design A - mu Design B: ( -0.32,  0.86)
T-Test mu Design A = mu Design B (vs not =): T= 0.93  P=0.36  DF=  48
Both use Pooled StDev = 1.04
```

The value of the test statistic is $t = .93$ with a p-value of .36. The 95% confidence interval estimate of $\mu_1 - \mu_2$ is $(-.32, .86)$.

MENU COMMANDS	COMMANDS FOR EXAMPLE 12.2
1 Type or import the data.	Open file **XM12-02**.
2 Click **Stat**, **Basic Statistics**, and **2-Sample t . . . .**	
3 Use the cursor to select **Samples in one column** or **Samples in different columns.**	**Samples in different columns.**
4 Hit **tab** and type each variable name.	**Design-A Design-B** or **C1 C2**
5 Use the cursor to select one of **less than**, **not equal to**, or **greater than**.	**not equal to**
6 Use the cursor to indicate that the population variances are equal. (Click the box.) Click **OK**.	

Excel Output for Example 12.2

	A	B	C
1	t-Test: Two-Sample Assuming Equal Variances		
2			
3		Design A	Design B
4	Mean	6.288	6.016
5	Variance	0.847766667	1.303066667
6	Observations	25	25
7	Pooled Variance	1.075416667	
8	Hypothesized Mean Difference	0	
9	df	48	
10	t Stat	0.927332603	
11	P(T<=t) one-tail	0.179196744	
12	t Critical one-tail	1.677224191	
13	P(T<=t) two-tail	0.358393488	
14	t Critical two-tail	2.01063358	

The value of the test statistic is .927332603. Because this is a two-tail test, the p-value is .358393488. We can use the value **t Critical two-tail** and the descriptive statistics to compute the confidence interval estimate.

COMMANDS	COMMANDS FOR EXAMPLE 12.2
1 Type or import the data into two columns.	Open file **XM12-02**.
2 Click **Tools, Data Analysis...**, and **t-Test: Two-Sample Assuming Equal Variances.**	
3 Specify **Variable 1 Range.**	**A1:A26**
4 Specify **Variable 2 Range.**	**B1:B26**
5 Specify the **Hypothesized Mean Difference** and click **Labels** (if necessary). Click **OK**.	**0**

INTERPRETING THE RESULTS

We conclude that there is little evidence to infer that the mean times differ. Once again, the manager should determine that all of the required conditions are satisfied (see the following subsection) and that there are no other factors that need to be considered. For example, is the quality of the finished product identical using the two designs? Is it possible that one design is better than another, but this experiment failed to demonstrate it because it takes longer to adapt to the new production design than this experiment allowed? If the conclusion stands, however, the manager should choose the design using some other criterion, such as worker preference. Figure 12.3 describes the sampling distribution of the test statistic.

Figure 12.3

Sampling Distribution for Example 12.2

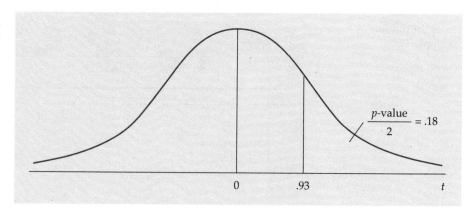

Checking the Required Condition

Both the equal-variances and unequal-variances techniques require that the populations are normally distributed. As before, we can check to see if the requirement is satisfied by drawing the histograms of the data. To illustrate, we used Minitab

(Excel histograms are almost identical) to create the histograms for Example 12.2 (Figures 12.4 and 12.5). Although the histograms are not bell-shaped, it appears that the assembly times are at least approximately normal. Because this technique is robust, we can be confident in the validity of the results.

Figure 12.4

Histogram of Assembly Times for Design A

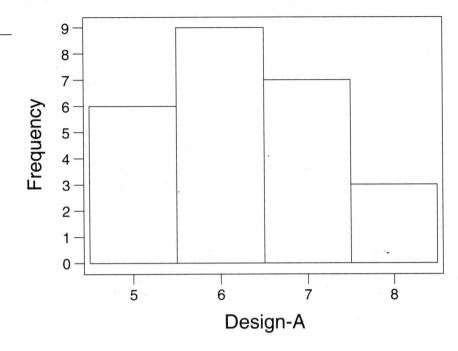

Figure 12.5

Histogram of Assembly Times for Design B

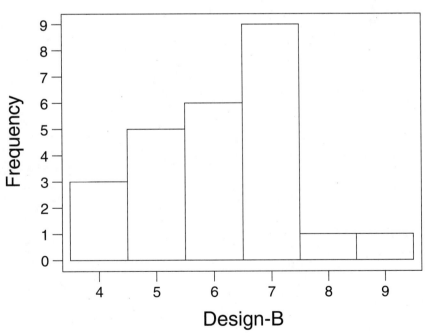

Violation of the Required Condition

When the normality requirement is unsatisfied, we can use a nonparametric technique—the Wilcoxon rank sum test for independent samples (Appendix 12.C)—to replace the equal-variances test of $\mu_1 - \mu_2$. We have no alternative to the unequal-variances test of $\mu_1 - \mu_2$ when the populations are very nonnormal.

Manipulating Data

There are two ways in which the data associated with the problems presented in this section may be stored. As we discuss in Appendixes 12.A and 12.B, we can store the observations of one sample in one column and the observations of the second sample in another column. When the data are stored in this manner, we say that the data are *unstacked*. Alternatively, we can *stack* the data by storing all the observations from both samples in one column and use a second column to store codes identifying the sample the observation is drawn from. Here is an example of unstacked data.

COLUMN 1 (SAMPLE 1)	COLUMN 2 (SAMPLE 2)
12	18
19	23
13	25

Here are the same data in stacked form.

COLUMN 1	COLUMN 2
12	1
19	1
13	1
18	2
23	2
25	2

It should be understood that the data need not be in order. Hence, they could have been stored in this way.

COLUMN 1	COLUMN 2
18	2
25	2
13	1
12	1
23	2
19	1

If there are two populations to compare and only one variable, it is probably better to record the data in unstacked form. However, it is frequently the case that we want to observe several variables and compare them. For example, suppose that we survey male and female M.B.A.s and ask each to report his or her income, number of years of education, and number of years of experience. These data are usually stored in stacked form using the following format.

Column 1: code identifying female (1) and male (2)

Column 2: income

Column 3: years of education

Column 4: years of experience

To compare incomes, we would use columns 1 and 2. Columns 1 and 3 are used to compare education and columns 1 and 4 are used to compare experience levels.

Most statistical software requires one form or the other. Some of Minitab's procedures allow either format, while others specify only one. Excel (with the exception of some of our macros) demands that the data must be unstacked. Fortunately, both of our software packages allow the statistician to alter the format. (See Appendixes 12.A and 12.B for details.) We say "fortunately" because this allowed us to store the data in either form on the data disk provided with this book. In fact, we've used both forms to allow you to practice your ability to manipulate the data as necessary. You will need this ability to perform statistical techniques in this and other chapters in this book.

Developing an Understanding of Statistical Concepts

The method we use to compute the standard deviation of the sampling distribution of $\bar{x}_1 - \bar{x}_2$ depends on whether the population variances are equal. When they are equal we calculate and use the pooled variance estimate s_p^2. An important principle is being applied here and will be again in this chapter (Section 12.6) and in later chapters. The principle can be loosely stated as: where possible, it is advantageous to pool sample data to estimate the sampling distribution standard deviation. In the application above, we are able to pool because we assume that the two samples were drawn from populations with a common variance. Combining both samples increases the accuracy of the estimate. Thus, s_p^2 is a better estimator of the common variance than either s_1^2 or s_2^2 separately.

When the two population variances are unequal, we cannot pool the data and produce a common estimator. We must compute s_1^2 and s_2^2 and use them to estimate σ_1^2 and σ_2^2, respectively.

Here is a summary of how we recognize the techniques presented in this section.

> **Factors that Identify the Equal-Variances t-Test and Estimator of $\mu_1 - \mu_2$**
>
> 1 Problem objective: compare two populations
>
> 2 Data type: quantitative
>
> 3 Descriptive measurement: central location
>
> 4 Experimental design: independent samples
>
> 5 Population variances: equal

> **Factors that Identify the Unequal-Variances *t*-Test and Estimator of $\mu_1 - \mu_2$**
>
> 1 Problem objective: compare two populations
>
> 2 Data type: quantitative
>
> 3 Descriptive measurement: central location
>
> 4 Experimental design: independent samples
>
> 5 Population variances: not equal

Exercises

12.1 The data obtained from sampling from two populations are stored in file XR12-01. (Column 1 contains the data, and column 2 specifies the sample.) Some of these data are shown below.

a Conduct a test to determine whether the population means differ. (Use $\alpha = .05$.)

b Estimate the difference in population means with 95% confidence.

c What is the required condition(s) of the techniques employed in parts (a) and (b)?

d Check to ensure that the required condition(s) is satisfied.

Observations: 25 15 38 28 20 ... 39 −3 26
Sample: 1 1 1 1 1 ... 2 2 2

Use a software package to solve this problem.	OR	The following statistics were computed from the data. $n_1 = 100$, $\bar{x}_1 = 19.07$, $s_1 = 9.57$ $n_2 = 140$, $\bar{x}_2 = 16.38$, $s_2 = 25.16$ Complete your answer manually.

12.2 Random samples were drawn from each of two populations. The data are stored in columns 1 (sample 1) and 2 (sample 2) in file XR12-02. A partial listing of the data is exhibited below. Is there sufficient evidence at the 5% significance level to infer that the mean of population 1 is greater than the mean of population 2?

Sample 1: 110 115 115 118 60 104 128 ... 105 114 . 115
Sample 2: 67 82 46 120 89 67 65 ... 108 89 73

Use a software package to solve this problem.	OR	The following statistics were computed from the data. $n_1 = 25$, $\bar{x}_1 = 101.68$, $s_1 = 19.07$ $n_2 = 25$, $\bar{x}_2 = 80.32$, $s_2 = 25.14$ Complete your answer manually.

12.3 Two samples of 40 observations from each of two populations were taken. The data are stored in columns 1 (all observations) and 2 (code specifying the sample) in file XR12-03. Do these data provide sufficient evidence at the 1% significance level to infer that the mean of population 2 is greater than the mean of population 1?

Observations: 5 5 7 4 7 ... 8 2 5
Sample: 1 1 1 1 1 ... 2 2 2

Use a software package to solve this problem.	OR	The following statistics were computed from the data. $\bar{x}_1 = 4.925$, $s_1 = 1.141$ $\bar{x}_2 = 6.200$, $s_2 = 2.090$ Complete your answer manually.

12.4 A statistician gathered data from two populations and stored them in columns 1 (sample 1) and 2 (sample 2) in file XR12-04. All of the data are listed below. Can the statistician infer at the 10% significance level that the mean of population 1 is less than the mean of population 2?

Sample 1: 18 13 12 12 20 21 22 20 18 12
Sample 2: 9 26 19 27 22 25 18 26 18 14

12.5 The president of Tastee Inc., a baby-food producer, claims that her company's product is superior to that of her leading competitor, because babies gain weight faster with her product. To test the claim a survey was undertaken. Mothers of newborn babies were asked which baby food they intended to feed their babies. Those who responded Tastee or the leading competitor were asked to keep track of their babies' weight gains over the next two months. There were 15 mothers who indicated that they would feed their babies Tastee and 25 who responded that they would feed their babies the product of the leading competitor. Each baby's weight gain (in ounces) is shown in the accompanying table. The data are stored in column 1 (Tastee) and column 2 (leading competitor) in file XR12-05.

a Can we conclude that, using weight gain as our criterion, Tastee baby food is indeed superior? (Conduct the test using a 5% significance level.)

b Estimate with 95% confidence the difference between the mean weight gains of the two products.

c Check to ensure that the required condition(s) is satisfied.

Weight Gain (in ounces)

TASTEE BABY FOOD	COMPETITOR'S BABY FOOD
30 37 36 36 39 29 31 38 37 39 42 44 41 37 38	28 32 29 33 38 33 37 36 31 30 29 26 27 32 31 33 37 33 31 29 27 26 33 31 32

Use a software package to solve this problem.	OR	The following statistics were computed from the data. $\bar{x}_1 = 36.93$, $s_1 = 4.23$ $\bar{x}_2 = 31.36$, $s_2 = 3.35$ Complete your answer manually.

12.6 Medical experts advocate the use of vitamin and mineral supplements to help fight infections. A study, undertaken by Dr. Ranjit Schneider of Memorial University (reported in the British journal *Lancet*, November 1992), recruited 96 men and women age 65 and older. Half of them received daily supplements of vitamins and minerals, while the other half received placebos. The supplements contained the daily recommended amounts of 18 vitamins and minerals. These included vitamins B-6, B-12, C, D, and E, thiamine, riboflavin, niacin, calcium, copper, iodine, iron, selenium, magnesium, and zinc. The doses of vitamins A and E were slightly less than the daily requirements. The supplements included four times the amount of beta-carotene that the average person ingests daily. The number of days of illness from infections (ranging from colds to pneumonia) were recorded for each person. The data are stored in stacked form in file XR12-06 (code 1 = supplements and code 2 = placebo). Some data are listed below. Can we infer at the 5% significance level that taking vitamin and mineral supplements daily increases the body's immune system?

Days of Illness:	59	51	45	33	...	35	33	47
Supplement/placebo:	1	1	1	1	...	2	2	2

Use a software package to solve this problem.	OR	The following statistics were computed from the data. $\bar{x}_1 = 39.46$, $s_1 = 12.96$ $\bar{x}_2 = 43.81$, $s_2 = 11.95$ Complete your answer manually.

12.7 Automobile insurance companies take many factors into consideration when setting rates. These factors include age, marital status, and miles driven per year. In order to determine the effect of gender, 100 male and 100 female drivers were surveyed. Each was asked how many miles he or she drove in the past year. The distances (in thousands of miles) are stored in stacked format (code 1 = male and code 2 = female) in file XR12-07. (A partial listing of the data is shown below.)

  a Can we conclude at the 5% significance level that male and female drivers differ in the numbers of miles driven per year?

  b Estimate with 95% confidence the difference in mean distance driven by male and female drivers.

  c Check to ensure that the required condition(s) of the techniques used in parts (a) and (b) is satisfied.

Miles driven:	11.2	9.2	6.4	14.1	...	10.3	15.1	7.1
Male/female:	1	1	1	1	...	2	2	2

Use a software package to solve this problem.	OR	The following statistics were computed from the data. $\bar{x}_1 = 10.23$, $s_1 = 2.87$ $\bar{x}_2 = 9.66$, $s_2 = 2.90$ Complete your answer manually.

12.8 The president of a company that manufactures automobile air conditioners is considering switching his supplier of condensers. Supplier A, the current producer of condensers for the manufacturer, prices its product 5% higher than supplier B does. Since the president wants to maintain his company's reputation for quality, he wants to be sure that supplier B's condensers last at least as long as supplier A's. After a careful analysis, the president decided to retain supplier A if there is sufficient statistical evidence that supplier A's condensers last longer on the average than supplier B's condensers. In an experiment, 30 midsize cars were equipped with air conditioners using type A condensers while another 30 midsize cars were equipped with type B condensers. The number of miles (in thousands) driven by each car before the condenser broke down was recorded, and the data stored in unstacked format (column 1 = supplier A and column 2 = supplier B) in file XR12-08. Some of these data are exhibited below. Should the president retain supplier A? (Use a 10% significance level.)

Supplier A: 156 146 93 152 ... 106 83 125
Supplier B: 109 86 75 131 ... 88 115 103

Use a software package to solve this problem.	OR	The following statistics were computed from the data. $\bar{x}_1 = 115.5$, $s_1 = 21.7$ $\bar{x}_2 = 109.4$, $s_2 = 22.4$ Complete your answer manually.

12.9 High blood pressure is a leading cause of strokes. Medical researchers are constantly seeking ways to treat patients suffering from this condition. A specialist in hypertension claims that regular aerobic exercise can reduce high blood pressure just as successfully as drugs, with none of the adverse side effects. To test the claim, 50 patients who suffer from high blood pressure were chosen to participate in an experiment. For 60 days, half the sample exercised three times per week for one hour; the other half took the standard medication. The percentage reduction in blood pressure was recorded for each individual, and the resulting data are stored in unstacked format (column 1 = exercise and column 2 = drug) in file XR12-09. Some of the data are shown below.

a Can we conclude at the 1% significance level that exercise is more effective than medication in reducing hypertension?

b Estimate with 95% confidence the difference in mean percentage reduction in blood pressure between drugs and exercise programs.

Exercise: 10 14 12 13 ... 17 15 15
Drug: 7   7   7 11 ... 16 12   8

Use a software package to solve this problem.	OR	The following statistics were computed from the data. $\bar{x}_1 = 13.52$, $s_1 = 2.40$ $\bar{x}_2 = 9.92$, $s_2 = 3.63$ Complete your answer manually.

12.10 In assessing the value of radio advertisements, sponsors not only measure the total number of listeners, but also record their ages. The 18-to-34 age group is considered to spend the most money. To examine the issue, the manager of an FM station commissioned a survey. One objective was to measure the difference in listening habits between the 18-to-34 and 35-to-50 age groups. The survey asked 250 people in each age category how much time they spent listening to FM radio per day. The results (in minutes) were recorded and stored in file XR12-10 (column 1 = listening times and column 2 identifies the age group: 1 = 18-to-34 and 2 = 35-to-50). Some data are shown below.

a Can we conclude at the 5% significance level that a difference exists between the two groups?

b Estimate with 95% confidence the difference in mean time listening to FM radio between the two age groups.

c Are the required conditions satisfied for the techniques you used in parts (a) and (b)?

Listening times: 75 30 50 87 ... 135 50 0
Age group: 1   1   1   1 ...   2   2 2

Use a software package to solve this problem.	OR	The following statistics were computed from the data. $\bar{x}_1 = 59.0$, $s_1 = 30.8$ $\bar{x}_2 = 53.0$, $s_2 = 43.3$ Complete your answer manually.

12.11 A statistics professor is about to select a statistical software package for her course. One of the most important features, according to the professor, is the ease with which students learn to use the software. She has narrowed the selection to two possibilities: software A, a menu-driven statistical package with some high-powered techniques, and software B, a spreadsheet that has the capability of performing most techniques. To help make her decision, she asks 40 statistics students selected at random to choose one of the two packages. She gives each student a statistics problem to solve by computer and the appropriate manual. The amount of time (in minutes) each student needs to complete the assignment was recorded and stored in unstacked format (column 1 = package A and column 2 = package B) in file XR12-11. A partial listing of the data is provided below.

a Can the professor conclude from these data that the two software packages differ in the amount of time needed to learn how to use them? (Use a 1% significance level.)

b Estimate with 95% confidence the difference in the mean amount of time needed to learn to use the two packages.

c What are the required conditions for the techniques used in parts (a) and (b)?

d Check to see if the required conditions are satisfied.

Package A: 88 83 70 81 ... 105 82 75
Package B: 55 57 67 47 ...   60 49 67

Use a software package to solve this problem.	OR	The following statistics were computed from the data. $n_1 = 24$, $\bar{x}_1 = 74.71$, $s_1 = 24.02$ $n_2 = 16$, $\bar{x}_2 = 52.50$, $s_2 = 9.04$ Complete your answer manually.

12.12 One factor in low productivity is the amount of time wasted by workers. Wasted time includes time spent cleaning up mistakes, waiting for more material and equipment, and performing any other activity not related to production. In a project designed to examine the problem, an operations management consultant took a survey of 200 workers in companies that were classified as successful (on the basis of their latest annual profits) and another 200 workers from unsuccessful companies. The amount of time (in hours) wasted during a standard 40-hour workweek was recorded for each worker. These data are stored in columns 1 (successful companies) and 2 (unsuccessful companies) in file XR12-12. Some data appear below.

a Do these data provide enough evidence at the 1% significance level to infer that the amount of time wasted in unsuccessful firms exceeds that of successful ones?

b Estimate with 95% confidence how much more time is wasted in unsuccessful firms than in successful ones.

| Successful company: | 5.8 | 2.0 | 6.5 | 5.3 | ... | 4.1 | 2.0 | 5.3 |
| Unsuccessful company: | 7.6 | 2.7 | 10.1 | 4.1 | ... | 5.8 | 8.3 | 0.8 |

Use a software package to solve this problem.	OR	The following statistics were computed from the data. $\bar{x}_1 = 5.02$, $s_1 = 1.39$ $\bar{x}_2 = 7.80$, $s_2 = 3.09$ Complete your answer manually.

12.3 Observational and Experimental Data

As we've pointed out several times, the ability to properly interpret the results of a statistical technique is a critical skill for students to develop. This ability is dependent on your understanding of Type I and Type II errors and the fundamental concepts that are part of statistical inference. However, there is another component that needs to be understood: the difference between **observational** and **experimental** data. To explain this difference, we will re-examine Examples 12.1 and 12.2 and analyze the way the data were obtained in each example.

In Example 12.1, we randomly selected 30 people and, on the basis of *their* responses, assigned them to one of two groups: high-fiber consumers and non-consumers. We then recorded the number of calories consumed at lunch for the members of each group. Such data are called *observational*. Now examine Example

12.2, where the data were gathered by randomly assigning 25 workers to assemble desks using design A and 25 workers to assemble desks using design B. Data produced in this manner are said to be *experimental* or *controlled*. The statistical technique to be applied is not affected by whether the data are observational or experimental. However, the interpretation of the results may be affected.

In Example 12.1, we found that there was evidence to infer that people who eat high-fiber cereal for breakfast consume fewer calories at lunch than do nonconsumers of high-fiber cereal. From this result, we're inclined to believe that eating a high-fiber cereal at breakfast may be a way to reduce weight. However, other interpretations are possible. For example, people who eat fewer calories are probably more health conscious, and such people are more likely to eat high-fiber cereal as part of a healthy breakfast. In this interpretation, high-fiber cereals do not necessarily lead to fewer calories at lunch. Instead another factor, general health consciousness, leads to both fewer calories at lunch *and* high-fiber cereal for breakfast. Notice that the conclusion of the statistical procedure is unchanged. On average, people who eat high-fiber cereal consume fewer calories at lunch. However, because of the way the data were gathered, we have more difficulty interpreting this result.

Suppose that we redo Example 12.1 using the experimental approach. We randomly select 30 people to participate in the experiment. We randomly assign 15 (or 10, as we had in the original experiment) to eat high-fiber cereal for breakfast and the other 15 to eat something else. We then record the number of calories each person consumes at lunch. Ideally, in this experiment both groups will be similar in all other dimensions, including health consciousness. (Larger sample sizes increase the likelihood that the two groups will be similar.) If the statistical result is about the same as in Example 12.1, we may have some valid reason to believe that high-fiber cereal leads to a decrease in caloric intake.

Experimental data are usually more expensive to obtain because of the planning required to set up the experiment; observational data usually require less work to gather. Furthermore, in many situations it is impossible to conduct a controlled experiment. For example, suppose that we want to determine if engineering students outperform arts students in M.B.A. programs. In a controlled experiment we would randomly assign some students to achieve a degree in engineering and other students to obtain an arts degree. We would then make them sign up for an M.B.A. program where we would record their grades. Unfortunately for statistical despots (and fortunately for the rest of us), we live in a democratic society, which makes the coercion necessary to perform this controlled experiment impossible.

To answer our question about the relative performance of engineering and arts students, we have no choice but to obtain our data by observational methods. We would take a random sample of engineering students and arts students who have already entered M.B.A. programs and record their grades. If we find that engineering students do better, we may tend to conclude that an engineering background better prepares students for an M.B.A. program. However, it may be true that better students tend to choose engineering as their undergraduate major, and that better students achieve higher grades in all programs, including the M.B.A. program.

Although we've discussed observational and experimental data in the context of the test of the difference between two means, you should be aware that the issue of how the data are obtained is relevant to the interpretation of all the techniques that follow.

Exercises

12.13 Examine Exercises 12.5 to 12.12. Which of the data sets were obtained by observational methods and which were obtained through controlled experiments? Explain the reasons for your choices.

12.14 Provide two interpretations of the results you produced in Exercise 12.5.

12.15 Discuss how the data in Exercise 12.5 could have been obtained through a controlled experiment.

12.16 Suppose that you are analyzing one of the hundreds of statistical studies linking smoking with lung cancer. The study analyzed thousands of randomly selected people, some of whom had lung cancer. The statistics indicate that those who have lung cancer smoked on average significantly more than those who did not have lung cancer.

  a Explain how you know that the data are observational.

  b Is there another interpretation of the statistics besides the obvious one that smoking causes lung cancer? If so, what is it? (Students who produce the best answers will be eligible for a job in the public relations department of a tobacco company.)

  c Is it possible to conduct a controlled experiment to produce data that addresses the question of the relationship between smoking and lung cancer? If so, describe the experiment.

12.4 Inference about the Difference between Two Means: Matched Pairs Experiment

We continue our presentation of statistical techniques that address the problem of comparing two populations of quantitative data. In Section 12.2, the parameter of interest was the difference between two population means, where the data were generated from independent samples. In this section, the data are gathered from a matched pairs experiment. To illustrate why matched pairs experiments are needed and how we deal with data produced in this way, consider the following example.

EXAMPLE 12.3

Tire manufacturers are constantly researching ways to produce tires that last longer. New innovations are tested by professional drivers on race tracks. However, any promising inventions are also test-driven by ordinary drivers. The latter tests are closer to what the tire companys' customers will actually experience. Suppose that to determine whether a new steel-belted radial tire lasts longer than the company's current model, two new-design tires were installed on the rear wheels of 20 randomly selected cars and two existing-design tires were installed on the rear wheels of another 20 cars. All drivers were told to drive in their usual way until the tires wore out. The number of miles driven by each driver was recorded and is shown below, as well as being stored in file XM12-03. Can the company infer that the new tire will last on average longer than the existing tire?

Distance (in thousands of miles) Until Wear-Out	NEW-DESIGN TIRE										EXISTING-DESIGN TIRE									
	70	83	78	46	74	56	74	52	99	57	47	65	59	61	75	65	73	85	97	84
	77	84	72	98	81	63	88	69	54	97	72	39	72	91	64	63	79	74	76	43

SOLUTION

The objective is to compare two populations of quantitative data. The parameter is the difference between two means $\mu_1 - \mu_2$. (μ_1 = mean distance to wear-out for the new-design tire, and μ_2 = mean distance to wear-out for the existing-design tire.) Because we want to determine whether the new tire lasts longer, the alternative hypothesis will specify that μ_1 is greater than μ_2. Calculation of the sample variances allows us to use the equal-variances test statistic.

$$H_0: (\mu_1 - \mu_2) = 0$$
$$H_A: (\mu_1 - \mu_2) > 0$$

$$\text{Test statistic: } t = \frac{(\bar{x}_1 - \bar{x}_2) - (\mu_1 - \mu_2)}{\sqrt{s_p^2 \left(\frac{1}{n_1} + \frac{1}{n_2} \right)}}$$

USING THE COMPUTER

Minitab Output for Example 12.3

Two Sample T-Test and Confidence Interval

```
Twosample T for New-Dsn vs Exst-Dsn
            N      Mean     StDev    SE Mean
New-Dsn    20      73.6      15.6       3.5
Exst-Dsn   20      69.2      15.1       3.4

95% C.I. for mu New-Dsn - mu Exst-Dsn: ( -5.4,  14.2)
T-Test mu New-Dsn = mu Exst-Dsn (vs >): T= 0.91   P=0.18   DF=  38
Both use Pooled StDev = 15.3
```

Excel Output for Example 12.3

	A	B	C
1	t-Test: Two-Sample Assuming Equal Variances		
2			
3		New Design	Existing Design
4	Mean	73.6	69.2
5	Variance	243.4105263	226.8
6	Observations	20	20
7	Pooled Variance	235.1052632	
8	Hypothesized Mean Difference	0	
9	df	38	
10	t Stat	0.907447484	
11	P(T<=t) one-tail	0.184944575	
12	t Critical one-tail	1.685953066	
13	P(T<=t) two-tail	0.36988915	
14	t Critical two-tail	2.024394234	

The value of the test statistic ($t = .91$) and its p-value (.18) indicate that there is very little evidence to support the hypothesis that the new-design tire lasts longer on average than the existing-design tire.

As was the case with some earlier examples, we have some evidence to support the alternative hypothesis, but not enough. Note that the difference in sample means is $(\bar{x}_1 - \bar{x}_2) = (73.6 - 69.2) = 4.4$. However, we judge the difference in sample means in relation to the standard deviation of the sampling distribution. As you can easily calculate,

$$s_p^2 = 235.1$$

and

$$\sqrt{s_p^2 \left(\frac{1}{n_1} + \frac{1}{n_2} \right)} = 4.85$$

Consequently, the value of the test statistic is $t = 4.4/4.85 = .91$, a value that does not allow us to reject the null hypothesis. We can see that although the difference between the sample means was quite large, the variability of the data, as measured by s_p^2, was also large, resulting in a small test statistic value.

EXAMPLE 12.4

Suppose now we redo the experiment in the following way. On 20 randomly selected cars, one of each type of tire is installed on the rear wheels and, as above, the cars are driven until the tires wear out. The number of miles until wear-out occurred is shown below and stored in file XM12-04. Can we conclude from *these* data that the new tire is superior?

Distance (in thousands of miles) Until Wear-Out

CAR	NEW-DESIGN TIRES	EXISTING-DESIGN TIRES
1	57	48
2	64	50
3	102	89
4	62	56
5	81	78
6	87	75
7	61	50
8	62	49
9	74	70
10	62	66

(continued)

Distance (in thousands of miles) Until Wear-Out (*continued*)	CAR	NEW-DESIGN TIRES	EXISTING-DESIGN TIRES
	11	100	98
	12	90	86
	13	83	78
	14	84	90
	15	86	98
	16	62	58
	17	67	58
	18	40	41
	19	71	61
	20	77	82

The experiment described in Example 12.3 is one where the samples are independent. That is, there was no relationship between the observations in one sample and the observations in the second sample. However, in this example the experiment was designed in such a way that each observation in one sample is matched with an observation in the other sample. The matching is conducted by using the same set of cars for each sample. Thus, it is logical to compare the distance until wear-out for both types of tires for *each car*. This type of experiment is called **matched pairs**. Here is how we conduct the test.

For each car, we calculate the matched pairs difference between the distances obtained with each type of tire.

Matched Pairs Differences	CAR	DIFFERENCE	CAR	DIFFERENCE
	1	9	11	2
	2	14	12	4
	3	13	13	5
	4	6	14	−6
	5	3	15	−12
	6	12	16	4
	7	11	17	9
	8	13	18	−1
	9	4	19	10
	10	−4	20	−5

The experimental design tells us that the parameter of interest is the *mean of the population of differences*, which we label μ_D. Note that $\mu_1 - \mu_2 = \mu_D$, but that we test μ_D because of the way the experiment was performed. The hypotheses to be tested are

$$H_0: \mu_D = 0$$
$$H_A: \mu_D > 0$$

We have already presented inferential techniques about a population mean. Recall that in Chapter 11 we introduced the t-test of μ. Thus, to test hypotheses about μ_D, we use the test statistic

$$t = \frac{\bar{x}_D - \mu_D}{s_D/\sqrt{n_D}}$$

which is Student t distributed with $n_D - 1$ degrees of freedom, provided that the differences are normally distributed. (Aside from the subscript D, this test statistic is identical to the one presented in Chapter 11.) We conduct the test in the usual way.

SOLVING BY HAND

Rejection region:

$$t > t_{\alpha, n_D-1} = t_{.05,19} = 1.729$$

Using the differences computed above, we found the following statistics.

$$\bar{x}_D = 4.55$$
$$s_D = 7.22$$

Value of the test statistic:

$$
\begin{aligned}
t &= \frac{\bar{x}_D - \mu_D}{s_D/\sqrt{n_D}} \\
&= \frac{4.55 - 0}{7.22/\sqrt{20}} \\
&= 2.82
\end{aligned}
$$

Conclusion: Reject the null hypothesis.

USING THE COMPUTER

Minitab Output for Example 12.4

T-Test of the Mean

Test of mu = 0.00 vs mu > 0.00

Variable	N	Mean	StDev	SE Mean	T	P-Value
Diff	20	4.55	7.22	1.61	2.82	0.0055

The value of the test statistic is $t = 2.82$, and its p-value is .0055. Thus, we reject the null hypothesis.

MENU COMMANDS	COMMANDS FOR EXAMPLE 12.4
1 Type or import the data into two columns.	Open file **XM12-04**.
2 Calculate the paired differences: click **Calc** and **Mathematical Expressions**	
3 Specify the variable name that will store the differences.	**Diff** or **C3**
4 Use the cursor and type the mathematical expression. Click **OK**.	**C1 − C2**
5 Click **Stat**, **Basic Statistics**, and **1-Sample** t	
6 Type the variable name of the paired differences.	**Diff** or **C3**
7 Use the cursor to choose **Test mean**.	
8 Hit **tab**, and type the value of μ_D under the null hypothesis.	**0**
9 Use the cursor to select one of **less than**, **not equal**, or **greater than**. Click **OK**.	**greater than**

Excel Output for Example 12.4

	A	B	C
1	t-Test: Paired Two Sample for Means		
2			
3		*New Design*	*Existing Design*
4	Mean	73.6	69.05
5	Variance	242.7789474	316.3657895
6	Observations	20	20
7	Pearson Correlation	0.914678935	
8	Hypothesized Mean Difference	0	
9	df	19	
10	t Stat	2.817586929	
11	P(T<=t) one-tail	0.005496978	
12	t Critical one-tail	1.729131327	
13	P(T<=t) two-tail	0.010993955	
14	t Critical two-tail	2.093024705	

The value of the test statistic is 2.817586929, and its *p*-value (one-tail) is .005496978. Thus, we reject the null hypothesis.

COMMANDS	COMMANDS FOR EXAMPLE 12.4
1 Type or import the data into two columns.	Open file **XM12-04**.
2 Click **Tools, Data Analysis . . .**, and *t*-**Test: Paired Two-Sample for Means**.	
3 Specify **Variable 1 Range**.	**A1:A21**
4 Specify **Variable 2 Range**.	**B1:B21**
5 Specify **Hypothesized Mean Difference** and click **Labels** (if necessary). Click **OK**.	**0**

Incidentally, data from matched pairs experiments are almost always stored in unstacked form. We sometimes include a third column identifying the matched pair.

INTERPRETING THE RESULTS

With this experimental design we have enough statistical evidence to infer that the new type of tire is superior to the existing type. As is the case with other techniques, we must check that the required conditions are satisfied, and that the sampling procedure is reliable. If the technique is valid, we can use this result to authorize a larger matched pairs experiment. If a similar conclusion is reached, we can use it to launch an effective advertising campaign. Figure 12.6 depicts the sampling distribution.

Figure 12.6

Sampling Distribution for Example 12.4

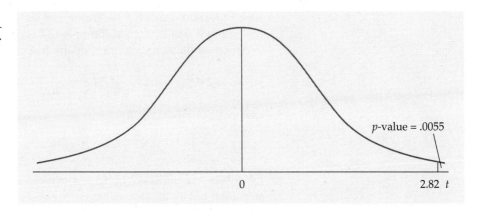

Estimating the Mean Difference

Using the usual algebra, we derive the confidence interval estimator of μ_D. It is

$$\bar{x}_D \pm t_{\alpha/2} \frac{s_D}{\sqrt{n_D}}$$

The 95% confidence interval estimate of the mean difference is

$$4.55 \pm 2.093 \frac{7.22}{\sqrt{20}} = 4.55 \pm 3.38$$

or

LCL = 1.17 and UCL = 7.93

As was the case when we discussed estimating a single population mean (Section 11.2), both Minitab and Excel can be used to produce the confidence interval estimate.

Independent Samples or Matched Pairs: Which Experimental Design Is Better?

Examples 12.3 and 12.4 demonstrated that the experimental design is an important factor in statistical inference. However, these two examples raise several questions about experimental designs. These are:

1 Why does the matched pairs experiment result in rejecting the null hypothesis, whereas the independent samples experiment could not?

2 Should we always use the matched pairs experiment? In particular, are there disadvantages to its use?

3 How do we recognize when a matched pairs experiment has been performed?

Here are our answers.

1 The matched pairs experiment worked in Example 12.4 by reducing the variation in the data. To understand this point, examine the statistics from both examples. In Example 12.3, we found $\bar{x}_1 - \bar{x}_2 = 4.4$. In Example 12.4, we computed $\bar{x}_D = 4.55$. Thus, the numerators of the two test statistics were almost identical. However, the reason that the test statistic in Example 12.3 was so much smaller than in Example 12.4 was because of the standard deviations of the sampling distributions. In Example 12.3, we calculated

$$s_p^2 = 235.1 \quad \text{and} \quad \sqrt{s_p^2 \left(\frac{1}{n_1} + \frac{1}{n_2} \right)} = 4.85$$

Example 12.4 produced

$$s_D^2 = 52.16 \quad \text{and} \quad \frac{s_D}{\sqrt{n_D}} = 1.615$$

As you see, the difference in the test statistics was caused not by the numerator but by the denominator. This raises another question. Why was the variation in the data of Example 12.3 so much greater than the variation in the data of Example 12.4? If you examine the data and statistics from Example 12.3, you will find that there was a great deal of variation *between* the cars. That is, some drivers drove in a way that extended the life of the tires, while others drove faster and braked harder, resulting in shorter tire lives. This high level of variation made the difference between the sample means appear to be small. As a result, we could not reject the null hypothesis.

Looking at the data from Example 12.4, we see that there is very little variation among the paired differences. Now the variation caused by different driving habits has been markedly decreased. The smaller variation causes the value of the test statistic to be larger. Consequently, we reject the null hypothesis.

2   Will the matched pairs experiment always produce a larger test statistic than the independent samples experiment? The answer is not necessarily. Suppose that in our example we found that most drivers drove in about the same way and that there was very little difference among drivers in the distances until tire wear-out. In such circumstances, the matched pairs experiment would result in no significant decrease in variation when compared to independent samples. It is possible that the matched pairs experiment may be *less* likely to reject the null hypothesis than the independent samples experiment. The reason can be seen by calculating the degrees of freedom. In Example 12.3, the number of degrees of freedom was 38, whereas in Example 12.4, it was 19. Even though we had the same number of observations (20 in each sample), the matched pairs experiment had half the number of degrees of freedom as the equivalent independent samples experiment. For exactly the same value of the test statistic, a smaller number of degrees of freedom in a Student t distributed test statistic yields a larger p-value. What this means is that if there is little reduction in variation to be achieved by the matched pairs experiment, the statistician should choose instead to conduct the experiment with independent samples.

3   As you've seen, in this book we deal with questions arising from experiments that have already been conducted. Thus, one of your tasks is to determine the appropriate test statistic. In the case of comparing two populations of quantitative data, you must decide whether the samples are independent (in which case the parameter is $\mu_1 - \mu_2$) or matched pairs (in which case the parameter is μ_D) in order to select the correct test statistic. To help you do so, we suggest you ask and answer the following question: does some natural relationship exist between *each pair* of observations that provides a logical reason to compare the first observation of sample 1 with the first observation of sample 2, the second observation of sample 1 with the second observation of sample 2, and so on? If so, the experiment was conducted by matched pairs. If not, it was conducted using independent samples.

Observational and Experimental Data

The points we made in Section 12.3 are also valid in this section. That is, we can design a matched pairs experiment where the data are gathered using a controlled experiment or by observation. The data in Examples 12.3 and 12.4 are experimental, which means the statistician randomly assigned the tires to the cars. As a consequence, when we established that the new-design tire lasted longer, we were able to conclude that the new tire is indeed superior. Because very few cars would be equipped with different brands of tires on their rear wheels, in this type of problem only experimental data are available.

In most applications of the matched pairs experiment, the data are experimental because of the control required to conduct such experimental designs.

Checking the Required Condition

The validity of the results of the t-test of μ_D depends on the normality of the differences. The Minitab histogram (Figure 12.7) confirms that assuming normality in this example is reasonable.

Figure 12.7

Histogram of Matched Pairs Differences in Example 12.4

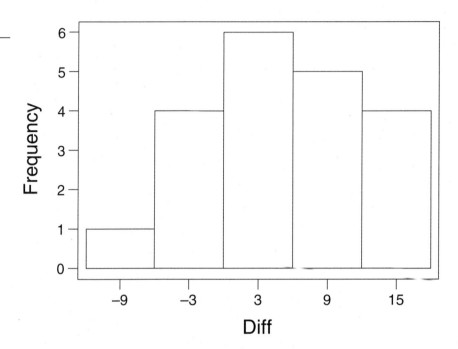

Violation of the Required Condition

If the differences are very nonnormal, we cannot use the t-test of μ_D. We can, however, employ a nonparametric technique—the Wilcoxon signed rank sum test for matched pairs, which we present in Appendix 12.C.

Developing an Understanding of Statistical Concepts

Two of the most important principles in statistics were applied in this section. The first is the concept of analyzing sources of variation. In Examples 12.3 and 12.4, we showed that by reducing the variation among drivers we were able to detect a real difference between tire brands. This was an application of the more general procedure of analyzing data and attributing some fraction of the variation to several sources. In Example 12.4, the two sources of variation were the car drivers and the tire brands. However, we were not interested in the variation among drivers because we weren't interested in determining whether drivers actually differ. Instead, we merely wanted to eliminate that source of variation, making it easier to determine if tire brand represented a real source of variation, and thus that one tire design is superior to another tire design.

In Chapter 14, we will introduce a technique called the *analysis of variance*, which does what its name suggests; it analyzes sources of variation in an attempt to detect real differences. In most applications of this procedure, we will be interested in each source of variation and not simply in reducing one source. We refer to the process as *explaining* the variation. The concept of explaining variation also will be applied in Chapters 16 and 17.

The second principle demonstrated in this section is that statisticians can design data-gathering procedures in such a way that we can analyze sources of variation. Before conducting the experiment in Example 12.4, the statistician suspected that there are large differences among drivers in the way they wear tires out. Consequently he (or she) set up the experiment so that the effects of those differences were mostly eliminated. It is also possible to design experiments that allow for easy detection of real differences and minimize the costs of data-gathering. Unfortunately, we will not present this topic. However, you should understand that the entire subject of the design of experiments is an important one, because managers often need to be able to analyze data to detect differences, and the cost is almost always a factor.

Here is a summary of the test statistic, confidence interval estimator, and how we determine when to use the inferential techniques about the matched pairs experiment.

Test Statistic for μ_D

$$t = \frac{\bar{x}_D - \mu_D}{s_D/\sqrt{n_D}} \qquad \text{d.f.} = n_D - 1$$

Confidence Interval Estimator of μ_D

$$\bar{x}_D \pm t_{\alpha/2} \frac{s_D}{\sqrt{n_D}}$$

Factors that Identify the t-Test and Estimator of μ_D

1 Problem objective: compare two populations

2 Data type: quantitative

3 Descriptive measurement: central location

4 Experimental design: matched pairs

Exercises

12.17 Given the following data generated from a matched pairs experiment, test to determine if we can infer that the mean of population 1 exceeds the mean of population 2. (Use $\alpha = .01$.)

PAIR	SAMPLE 1	SAMPLE 2
1	20	17
2	23	16
3	15	9
4	18	19
5	19	15

12.18 The data below and stored in file XR12-18 were produced from a matched pairs experiment. Determine whether these data are sufficient to infer at the 5% significance level that the two population means differ.

Pair:	1	2	3	4	5	6	7	8	9	10
Sample 1:	7	12	19	17	22	18	30	33	40	48
Sample 2:	10	13	18	21	25	19	31	31	44	47

12.19 The following data were generated from a matched pairs experiment. (The data are stored in columns 1 and 2 of file XR12-19.)

a Estimate with 90% confidence the mean difference.

b Briefly describe what the interval estimate in part (a) tells you.

Pair:	1	2	3	4	5	6	7	8	9	10
Sample 1:	3	12	15	10	17	14	10	9	16	8
Sample 2:	7	13	14	14	23	13	12	12	18	9

12.20 Samples of size 12 were drawn independently from two normal populations. These data are listed below and stored in columns 1 and 2 of file XR12-20. A matched pairs experiment was then conducted; 12 pairs of observations were drawn from the same populations. These data are also shown below and stored in columns 3 and 4 of file XR12-20.

a Using the data taken from independent samples, test to determine whether the means of the two populations differ. (Use $\alpha = .05$.)

b Using the data taken from independent samples, estimate with 95% confidence the difference between the two population means.

c Repeat part (a) using the matched pairs data.

d Repeat part (b) using the matched pairs data.

e Describe the differences between parts (a) and (c) and between (b) and (d). Discuss why these differences occurred.

INDEPENDENT SAMPLES

Sample 1:	66	19	88	72	61	32	75	61	71	54	79	40
Sample 2:	69	37	66	59	27	18	47	67	83	61	32	37

MATCHED PAIRS

Pair:	1	2	3	4	5	6	7	8	9	10	11	12
Sample 1:	55	45	52	87	78	42	62	90	23	60	67	53
Sample 2:	48	37	43	75	78	35	45	79	12	53	59	37

12.21 Repeat Exercise 12.20 using the data below, which are also stored in columns 1 through 4 of file XR12-21.

INDEPENDENT SAMPLES

Sample 1:	199	261	295	183	161	104	199	248	105	197	249	218
Sample 2:	286	211	121	134	210	68	166	157	258	184	116	203

MATCHED PAIRS

Pair:	1	2	3	4	5	6	7	8	9	10	11	12
Sample 1:	218	144	286	208	234	256	133	87	224	212	256	133
Sample 2:	154	160	239	198	211	241	136	39	192	183	215	117

12.22 Repeat Exercise 12.20 using the data below, which are also stored in columns 1 through 4 of file XR12-22.

INDEPENDENT SAMPLES

Sample 1:	103	86	101	112	111	100	95	105	119	89	104	99
Sample 2:	71	86	100	89	92	105	85	85	97	98	107	96

MATCHED PAIRS

Pair:	1	2	3	4	5	6	7	8	9	10	11	12
Sample 1:	91	120	97	94	107	107	91	118	94	101	87	102
Sample 2:	88	75	108	84	97	92	92	76	86	97	107	98

12.23 Discuss what you have discovered from Exercises 12.20 to 12.22.

12.24 In an effort to determine whether or not a new type of fertilizer is more effective than the type currently in use, researchers took 12 two-acre plots of land scattered throughout the county. Each plot was divided into two equal-sized subplots, one of which was treated with the current fertilizer and the other of which was treated with the new fertilizer. Wheat was planted, and the crop yields were measured. These data are stored in file XR12-24 and listed below.

    a   Can we conclude at the 5% significance level that the new fertilizer is more effective than the current one?

    b   Estimate with 95% confidence the difference in mean crop yields between the two fertilizers.

    c   What is the required condition(s) for the validity of the results obtained in parts (a) and (b)?

    d   Is the required condition(s) satisfied?

    e   Are these data experimental or observational? Explain.

    f   How should the experiment be conducted if the researchers believed that the land throughout the county was pretty much the same?

Plot:	1	2	3	4	5	6	7	8	9	10	11	12
Current fertilizer:	56	45	68	72	61	69	57	55	60	72	75	66
New fertilizer:	60	49	66	73	59	77	61	60	58	75	72	71

12.25 Do waiters or waitresses earn larger tips? To answer this question, a restaurant consultant undertook a preliminary study. The study involved measuring the percentage of the total bill left as a tip for one randomly selected waiter and one randomly selected waitress in each of 20 restaurants during a one-week period. Some of the results are listed below, and all are stored in columns 1 and 2 of file XR12-25. What conclusions can be drawn from these data? (Use a 5% significance level.)

Restaurant:	1	2	3	4	...	18	19	20
Waiter:	11	15	11	8	...	11	14	11
Waitress:	15	13	13	13	...	14	11	12

Use a software package to solve this problem.	OR	The following statistics were computed. $\bar{x}_D = -1.05, s_D = 2.59$ Complete your answer manually.

12.26 In order to determine the effect of advertising in the Yellow Pages, Bell Telephone took a sample of 40 retail stores that did not advertise in the Yellow Pages last year but did so this year. The annual sales (in thousands of dollars) for each store in both years were recorded and stored in file XR12-26. Some of these observations appear below.

a   Estimate with 90% confidence the improvement in sales between the two years.

b   Can we infer at the 5% significance level that advertising in the Yellow Pages improves sales?

c   Check to ensure that the required condition(s) of the techniques above is satisfied.

d   Would it be advantageous to perform this experiment with independent samples? Explain why or why not.

Store:	1	2	3	4	...	38	39	40
Sales this year:	189	225	106	146	...	137	128	159
Sales last year:	151	224	30	132	...	82	148	179

Use a software package to solve this problem.   OR   The following statistics were computed.
$\bar{x}_D = 19.75$, $s_D = 30.63$
Complete your answer manually.

12.27 The president of a large company is in the process of deciding whether to adopt a lunchtime exercise program. The purpose of such programs is to improve the health of workers and, in so doing, reduce medical expenses. To get more information she instituted an exercise program for the employees in one office. The president knows that during the winter months medical expenses are relatively high because of the incidence of colds and flu. Consequently, she decides to use a matched pairs design by recording medical expenses for the 12 months before the program and for 12 months after the program. The "before" and "after" expenses (in thousands of dollars) are compared on a month-to-month basis and shown below.

a   Do the data indicate that exercise programs reduce medical expenses? (Test with $\alpha = .05$.)

b   Estimate with 95% confidence the mean savings produced by exercise programs.

c   Was it appropriate to conduct a matched pairs experiment? Explain.

Month:	Jan	Feb	Mar	Apr	May	Jun	Jul	Aug	Sep	Oct	Nov	Dec
Before program:	68	44	30	58	35	33	52	69	23	69	48	30
After program:	59	42	20	62	25	30	56	62	25	75	40	26

12.28 Research scientists at a pharmaceutical company have recently developed a new nonprescription sleeping pill. They decide to test its effectiveness by measuring the time it takes for people to fall asleep after taking the pill. Preliminary analysis indicates that the time to fall asleep varies considerably from one person to another. Consequently, they organize the experiment in the following way. A random sample of 50 volunteers who regularly suffer from insomnia is chosen. Each person is given one pill containing the newly developed drug and one placebo. (A placebo is a pill that contains absolutely no medication.) Participants are told to take one pill one night and the second pill one night a week later. (They do not know whether the pill they are taking is the placebo or the real thing, and the order of use is random.) Each participant is fitted with a device that measures the time until sleep occurs. Some of the results are listed below, and all the data are stored in columns 1 and 2 of file XR12-28. Can we conclude that the new drug is effective? (Use a 5% significance level.)

Volunteer:	1	2	3	4	...	48	49	50
Drug:	38.4	9.8	12.0	11.6	...	21.0	15.7	10.2
Placebo:	39.2	25.0	26.2	28.6	...	27.2	24.5	27.7

Use a software package to solve this problem.	OR	The following statistics were computed. $\bar{x}_D = -3.47, s_D = 10.04$ Complete your answer manually.

12.5 Inference about the Ratio of Two Variances (Optional)

In Sections 12.2 and 12.4, we dealt with statistical inference concerning the difference between two population means. The problem objective in each case was to compare two populations of quantitative data, and our interest was in comparing measures of central location. This section discusses the statistical techniques to use when the problem objective and the data type are the same as in Sections 12.2 and 12.4, but our interest is in comparing variability. Here we will study the ratio of two population variances σ_1^2/σ_2^2. We make inferences about the *ratio* because the sampling distribution features ratios rather than differences.

In the previous chapter, we presented the procedures used to draw inferences about a single population variance. We pointed out that variance can be used to address problems where we need to know the variance in order to judge the consistency of a production process. We also use variance to measure the risk associated with a portfolio of investments. In this section we compare two variances, enabling us to compare the consistency of two production processes. We can also compare the relative risks of two sets of investments.

There is one other important use of the statistical methods to be presented in this section. One of the factors that determine the correct technique when testing or estimating the difference between two means from independent samples is whether the two unknown population variances are equal. Statisticians often test for the equality of σ_1^2 and σ_2^2 before deciding which of the two procedures introduced in Section 12.2 is to be used.

We will proceed in a manner that is probably becoming quite familiar.

Parameter

As you will see shortly, we compare two population variances by determining the ratio. Consequently, the parameter of interest is σ_1^2/σ_2^2.

Point Estimator of σ_1^2/σ_2^2

We have previously noted that the sample variance (defined in Chapter 4) is an unbiased and consistent estimator of the population variance. Not surprisingly, the estimator of the parameter σ_1^2/σ_2^2 is the ratio of the two sample variances drawn from their respective populations. The point estimator is s_1^2/s_2^2.

Sampling Distribution of s_1^2/s_2^2

The sampling distribution of s_1^2/s_2^2 is said to be **F distributed** provided that we have independently sampled from two normal populations. (The F distribution is presented below.)

Statisticians have shown that the ratio of two independent chi-squared variables divided by their degrees of freedom is F distributed. The degrees of freedom of the F distribution are identical to the degrees of freedom for the two chi-squared distributions. In Section 11.3, we pointed out that $(n - 1)s^2/\sigma^2$ is chi-squared distributed provided that the sampled population is normal. If we have independent samples drawn from two normal populations, then both $(n_1 - 1)s_1^2/\sigma_1^2$ and $(n_2 - 1)s_2^2/\sigma_2^2$ are chi-squared distributed. If we divide each by their respective numbers of degrees of freedom and take the ratio, we produce

$$\frac{\dfrac{(n_1 - 1)s_1^2/\sigma_1^2}{(n_1 - 1)}}{\dfrac{(n_2 - 1)s_2^2/\sigma_2^2}{(n_2 - 1)}}$$

which simplifies to

$$\frac{s_1^2/\sigma_1^2}{s_2^2/\sigma_2^2}$$

This statistic is F distributed with $\nu_1 = n_1 - 1$ and $\nu_2 = n_2 - 1$ degrees of freedom.

> ### F Distribution
>
> Variables that are F distributed range from 0 to ∞. The approximate shape of the distribution is depicted in Figure 12.8. The exact shape is determined by two numbers of degrees of freedom. Because the statistic is a ratio, the number of degrees of freedom is labeled as either the *numerator degrees of freedom*, denoted ν_1 (Greek letter nu), or the *denominator degrees of freedom*, denoted ν_2. Table 6 in Appendix B provides the critical values for the F distribution. It lists values of F_{A,ν_1,ν_2}, where F_{A,ν_1,ν_2} is the value of F with ν_1 and ν_2 degrees of freedom such that the area to its right under the F distribution is A. That is,
>
> $$P(F > F_{A,\nu_1,\nu_2}) = A$$

Part of Table 6 (for $A = .05$) is reproduced here as Table 12.1. To determine any critical value, find the numerator degrees of freedom ν_1 across the top row and the denominator degrees of freedom ν_2 down the first column. The intersection of that row and that column shows the critical value. To illustrate, suppose that we want to find $F_{.05,5,7}$. Table 6 in Appendix B provides the critical values for three values of A: .05, .025, and .01. (Table 12.1 lists some of the critical values for $A = .05$.) The numerator number of degrees of freedom is 5, which we find across the top row, and the denominator number of degrees of freedom is 7, which we locate in the first column. The intersection is 3.97. Thus, $F_{.05,5,7} = 3.97$. (See Table 12.2.)

Note that the order in which the degrees of freedom appear is important. To find $F_{.05,7,5}$ (numerator degrees of freedom = 7 and denominator degrees of freedom = 5), we locate 7 across the top row and 5 down the first column. The number in the intersection is $F_{.05,7,5} = 4.88$.

Table 6 provides only values of F_A, which are the values of F that are in the right tail of the F distribution. The left-tail values, which we label F_{1-A} (as we did to denote the left-tail values of the chi-squared distribution), are not listed. They are not provided because we can easily determine the values of F_{1-A} from the values of F_A. Mathematicians have derived the following formula.

$$F_{1-A,\nu_1,\nu_2} = \frac{1}{F_{A,\nu_2,\nu_1}}$$

For example,

$$F_{.95,4,8} = \frac{1}{F_{.05,8,4}} = \frac{1}{6.04} = .166$$

Figure 12.8

F **Distribution**

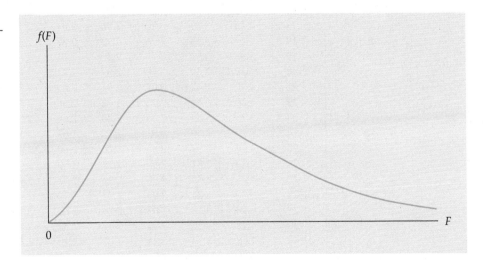

Table 12.1　　　**Percentage Points of the *F* Distribution, *A* = .05**

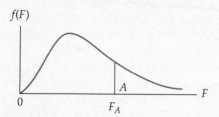

ν_2	\multicolumn{9}{c}{NUMERATOR DEGREES OF FREEDOM (ν_1)}								
	1	**2**	**3**	**4**	**5**	**6**	**7**	**8**	**9**
1	161.4	199.5	215.7	224.6	230.2	234.0	236.8	238.9	240.5
2	18.51	19.00	19.16	19.25	19.30	19.33	19.35	19.37	19.38
3	10.13	9.55	9.28	9.12	9.01	8.94	8.89	8.85	8.81
4	7.71	6.94	6.59	6.39	6.26	6.16	6.09	6.04	6.00
5	6.61	5.79	5.41	5.19	5.05	4.95	4.88	4.82	4.77
6	5.99	5.14	4.76	4.53	4.39	4.28	4.21	4.15	4.10
7	5.59	4.74	4.35	4.12	3.97	3.87	3.79	3.73	3.68
8	5.32	4.46	4.07	3.84	3.69	3.58	3.50	3.44	3.39
9	5.12	4.26	3.86	3.63	3.48	3.37	3.29	3.23	3.18
10	4.96	4.10	3.71	3.48	3.33	3.22	3.14	3.07	3.02
11	4.84	3.98	3.59	3.36	3.20	3.09	3.01	2.95	2.90
12	4.75	3.89	3.49	3.26	3.11	3.00	2.91	2.85	2.80
13	4.67	3.81	3.41	3.18	3.03	2.92	2.83	2.77	2.71
14	4.60	3.74	3.34	3.11	2.96	2.85	2.76	2.70	2.65
15	4.54	3.68	3.29	3.06	2.90	2.79	2.71	2.64	2.59
16	4.49	3.63	3.24	3.01	2.85	2.74	2.66	2.59	2.54
17	4.45	3.59	3.20	2.96	2.81	2.70	2.61	2.55	2.49
18	4.41	3.55	3.16	2.93	2.77	2.66	2.58	2.51	2.46
19	4.38	3.52	3.13	2.90	2.74	2.63	2.54	2.48	2.42
20	4.35	3.49	3.10	2.87	2.71	2.60	2.51	2.45	2.39
21	4.32	3.47	3.07	2.84	2.68	2.57	2.49	2.42	2.37
22	4.30	3.44	3.05	2.82	2.66	2.55	2.46	2.40	2.34
23	4.28	3.42	3.03	2.80	2.64	2.53	2.44	2.37	2.32
24	4.26	3.40	3.01	2.78	2.62	2.51	2.42	2.36	2.30
25	4.24	3.39	2.99	2.76	2.60	2.49	2.40	2.34	2.28
26	4.23	3.37	2.98	2.74	2.59	2.47	2.39	2.32	2.27
27	4.21	3.35	2.96	2.73	2.57	2.46	2.37	2.31	2.25
28	4.20	3.34	2.95	2.71	2.56	2.45	2.36	2.29	2.24
29	4.18	3.33	2.93	2.70	2.55	2.43	2.35	2.28	2.22
30	4.17	3.32	2.92	2.69	2.53	2.42	2.33	2.27	2.21
40	4.08	3.23	2.84	2.61	2.45	2.34	2.25	2.18	2.12
60	4.00	3.15	2.76	2.53	2.37	2.25	2.17	2.10	2.04
120	3.92	3.07	2.68	2.45	2.29	2.17	2.09	2.02	1.96
∞	3.84	3.00	2.60	2.37	2.21	2.10	2.01	1.94	1.88

Denominator Degrees of Freedom

SOURCE: From M. Merrington and C. M. Thompson, "Tables of Percentage Points of the Inverted Beta (*F*)-Distribution," *Biometrika* 33 (1943): 73–88. Reproduced by permission of the Biometrika Trustees.

Table 12.2		Finding $F_{.05,5,7}$								
	ν_1				NUMERATOR DEGREES OF FREEDOM					
ν_2		1	2	3	4	5	6	7	8	9
	1	161.4	199.5	215.7	224.6	230.2	234.0	236.8	238.9	240.5
	2	18.51	19.00	19.16	19.25	19.30	19.33	19.35	19.37	19.38
	3	10.13	9.55	9.28	9.12	9.01	8.94	8.89	8.85	8.81
	4	7.71	6.94	6.59	6.39	6.26	6.16	6.09	6.04	6.00
	5	6.61	5.79	5.41	5.19	5.05	4.95	4.88	4.82	4.77
	6	5.99	5.14	4.76	4.53	4.39	4.28	4.21	4.15	4.10
	7	5.59	4.74	4.35	4.12	3.97	3.87	3.79	3.73	3.68
Denominator Degrees	8	5.32	4.46	4.07	3.84	3.69	3.58	3.50	3.44	3.39
of Freedom	9	5.12	4.26	3.86	3.63	3.48	3.37	3.29	3.23	3.18
	10	4.96	4.10	3.71	3.48	3.33	3.22	3.14	3.07	3.02
	11	4.84	3.98	3.59	3.36	3.20	3.09	3.01	2.95	2.90
	12	4.75	3.89	3.49	3.26	3.11	3.00	2.91	2.85	2.80
	13	4.67	3.81	3.41	3.18	3.03	2.92	2.83	2.77	2.71
	14	4.60	3.74	3.34	3.11	2.96	2.85	2.76	2.70	2.65
	15	4.54	3.68	3.29	3.06	2.90	2.79	2.71	2.64	2.59

Testing σ_1^2/σ_2^2

In this book, our null hypothesis will *always* specify that the two variances are equal. As a result, the ratio will equal 1. Thus, the null hypothesis will always be expressed as

H_0: $\sigma_1^2/\sigma_2^2 = 1$

The alternative hypothesis can state that the ratio is either not equal to 1, greater than 1, or less than 1. Technically, the test statistic is

$$F = \frac{s_1^2/\sigma_1^2}{s_2^2/\sigma_2^2}$$

However, under the null hypothesis, which states that $\sigma_1^2/\sigma_2^2 = 1$, the test statistic becomes as follows.

> **Test Statistic for σ_1^2/σ_2^2**
>
> The test statistic employed to test hypotheses about σ_1^2/σ_2^2 is
>
> $F = s_1^2/s_2^2$
>
> which is F distributed with $\nu_1 = n_1 - 1$ and $\nu_2 = n_2 - 1$ degrees of freedom provided that the populations are normal.

EXAMPLE 12.5

In Example 12.1, we applied the unequal-variances t-test of $\mu_1 - \mu_2$. We chose that test statistic after computing the standard deviation of the sample of consumers of high-fiber cereal to be 35.7 and the standard deviation of the sample of nonconsumers of high-fiber cereal to be 115.7. The difference between the two sample standard deviations appears to indicate that the population standard deviations (and, of course, variances) differ. We can make this process more formal by conducting an F-test of σ_1^2/σ_2^2.

SOLUTION

The test proceeds as follows.

$$H_0: \sigma_1^2/\sigma_2^2 = 1$$
$$H_A: \sigma_1^2/\sigma_2^2 \neq 1$$

Test statistic: $F = s_1^2/s_2^2$

SOLVING BY HAND

The rejection region (assuming that $\alpha = .05$) is

$$F > F_{\alpha/2, \nu_1, \nu_2} = F_{.025, 9, 19} = 2.88$$

or

$$F < F_{1-\alpha/2, \nu_1, \nu_2} = F_{.975, 9, 19} = \frac{1}{F_{.025, 19, 9}} \approx \frac{1}{3.67} = .272$$

The value of the test statistic is

$$F = \frac{s_1^2}{s_2^2} = \frac{35.7^2}{115.7^2} = .0952$$

Conclusion: Reject the null hypothesis.

USING THE COMPUTER

Minitab does not conduct this procedure. You can, however, compute the sample variances using Minitab and complete the calculation manually.

Excel Output for Example 12.5

	A	B	C
1	F-Test Two-Sample for Variances		
2			
3		Consumers	Nonconsumers
4	Mean	595.8	661.1
5	Variance	1273.511111	13375.25263
6	Observations	10	20
7	df	9	19
8	F	10.50265876	
9	P(F<=f) one-tail	0.000530147	
10	F Critical one-tail	0.412763157	

Excel calculates the F-statistic by determining the ratio of the larger variance divided by the smaller variance. Since $s_2^2 = 13{,}375.25263$ and $s_1^2 = 1{,}273.511111$, the output is $F = s_2^2/s_1^2 = 10.50265876$. The one-tail p-value is .000530147. Thus, the p-value of the test we're conducting is $2 \times .000530147 = .00106294$.

EXCEL 97

Excel 97 Users:
Excel computes the ratio of the sample variance of **Variable Range 1** divided by the sample variance of the **Variable Range 2**.

COMMANDS	COMMANDS FOR EXAMPLE 12.5
1 Type or import the data into two columns.	Open file **XM12-01**.
2 Click **Tools, Data Analysis . . .**, and **F-Test Two-Sample for Variances**.	
3 Specify the **Variable 1 Range**.	**A1:A11**
4 Specify the **Variable 2 Range**. Click **Labels** (if necessary) and click **OK**.	**B1:B21**

INTERPRETING THE RESULTS

There is strong evidence to infer that the population variances are unequal. It follows that we were justified in testing the $\mu_1 - \mu_2$ by employing the unequal-variance t-test. Of course, the normality of the data must also be checked, not only for the validity of the test employed in Example 12.1, but also in this test.

Figure 12.9 describes the sampling distribution, rejection region, and test statistic.

Figure 12.9

Sampling Distribution for Example 12.5

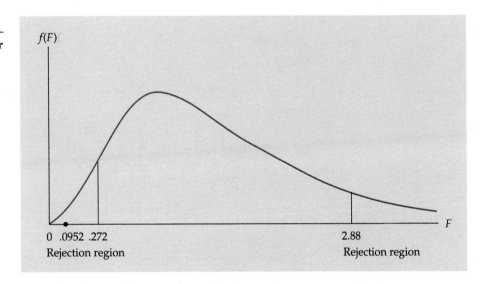

Estimating the Ratio of Two Population Variances

Another way of expressing the notation associated with the F distribution is

$$P(F_{1-\alpha/2} < F < F_{\alpha/2}) = 1 - \alpha$$

This states that the probability that an F distributed random variable falls between $F_{1-\alpha/2}$ and $F_{\alpha/2}$ is $1 - \alpha$. If we substitute the F statistic

$$F = \frac{s_1^2/\sigma_1^2}{s_2^2/\sigma_2^2}$$

into the equation, we produce

$$P\left(F_{1-\alpha/2} < \frac{s_1^2/\sigma_1^2}{s_2^2/\sigma_2^2} < F_{\alpha/2}\right) = 1 - \alpha$$

Applying algebra, we isolate σ_1^2/σ_2^2 in the center of the probability statement. Incorporating the formula

$$F_{1-\alpha/2,\nu_1,\nu_2} = \frac{1}{F_{\alpha/2,\nu_2,\nu_1}}$$

we get the following.

Confidence Interval Estimator of σ_1^2/σ_2^2

$$\text{LCL} = \left(\frac{s_1^2}{s_2^2}\right)\frac{1}{F_{\alpha/2,\nu_1,\nu_2}}$$

$$\text{UCL} = \left(\frac{s_1^2}{s_2^2}\right)F_{\alpha/2,\nu_2,\nu_1}$$

where $\nu_1 = n_1 - 1$ and $\nu_2 = n_2 - 1$

To determine the 95% confidence interval estimate of the ratio of the two population variances in Example 12.1, we find

$$F_{\alpha/2,\nu_1,\nu_2} = F_{.025,9,19} = 2.88$$

and

$$F_{\alpha/2,\nu_2,\nu_1} = F_{.025,19,9} \approx 3.67$$

Thus,

$$\text{LCL} = \left(\frac{s_1^2}{s_2^2}\right)\frac{1}{F_{\alpha/2,\nu_1,\nu_2}} = \left(\frac{35.7^2}{115.7^2}\right)\frac{1}{2.88} = .033$$

$$\text{UCL} = \left(\frac{s_1^2}{s_2^2}\right)F_{\alpha/2,\nu_2,\nu_1} = \left(\frac{35.7^2}{115.7^2}\right)3.67 = .349$$

We infer that σ_1^2/σ_2^2 lies between .033 and .349.

Factors that Identify the F-Test and Estimator of σ_1^2/σ_2^2

1 Problem objective: compare two populations

2 Data type: quantitative

3 Descriptive measurement: variability

Exercises

12.29 Given the data below, test the following hypotheses (with $\alpha = .10$).

$$H_0: \sigma_1^2/\sigma_2^2 = 1$$
$$H_A: \sigma_1^2/\sigma_2^2 \neq 1$$

Sample 1: 7 4 9 12 8 6 9 14
Sample 2: 10 7 13 18 4 8 21 20 5 8

12.30 Random samples from two normal populations produced the following results. Is there enough evidence at the 5% significance level to infer that the population variances differ?

Sample 1: 27 52 41 20 33 59 41 28 29 51
Sample 2: 18 15 19 31 49 12 48 29 45 50

12.31 Can we conclude at the 1% significance level from the data stored in columns 1 and 2 of file XR12-31 that the variance of population 1 is less than that of population 2? Some of the data are shown below.

Sample 1: 36 −6 24 24 ... 20 21 23
Sample 2: 121 123 122 102 ... 105 107 106

Use a software package to solve this problem.	OR	The variances of the two samples were computed; they are $n_1 = 50, s_1^2 = 76.56$ $n_2 = 50, s_2^2 = 129.05$ Complete your answer manually.

12.32 Refer to Exercise 12.31. Estimate the ratio of population variances with 95% confidence.

12.33 Refer to Exercise 12.5. Test to determine whether the use of the equal-variances t-test of $\mu_1 - \mu_2$ was justified. (Use $\alpha = .05$.)

12.34 The weekly returns of two portfolios were recorded for one year with the results stored in columns 1 and 2 of file XR12-34. Some of these data are exhibited below. Can we conclude at the 5% significance level that portfolio 2 is riskier than portfolio 1?

Portfolio 1: .22 .59 .11 −.05 ... .10 .15 .23
Portfolio 2: .32 .35 .48 .36 ... .32 .56 −.02

Use a software package to solve this problem.	OR	The variance of the two samples were computed; they are $s_1^2 = .0261$ and $s_2^2 = .0875$ Complete your answer manually.

12.35 An important statistical measurement in service facilities (such as restaurants and banks) is the variability in service times. As an experiment, two bank tellers were observed, and the service times for each of 100 customers were recorded and stored in columns 1 and 2 of file XR12-35. A partial listing of the results is shown below. Do these data allow us to infer at the 10% significance level that the variance in service times differs between the two tellers?

Teller 1:   7.2 5.4 3.7 6.4 ... 6.3 6.4 7.8
Teller 2: 10.9 6.0 6.7 8.3 ... .1 9.1 4.7

| Use a software package to solve this problem. | OR | The variances of the two samples were computed; they are $s_1^2 = 3.35$ and $s_2^2 = 10.95$ Complete your answer manually. |

12.6   Inference about the Difference between Two Population Proportions

In this section, we present the procedures for drawing inferences about the difference between populations whose data are qualitative. When data are qualitative, the only meaningful computation is to count the number of occurrences of each type of outcome and calculate proportions. Consequently, the parameter to be tested and estimated in this section is the difference between two population proportions, $p_1 - p_2$.

In order to draw inferences about $p_1 - p_2$, we take a sample of size n_1 from population 1 and a sample of size n_2 from population 2 (Figure 12.10 depicts the sampling process). For each sample, we count the number of successes (recall that we call anything we're looking for a success) in each sample, which we label x_1 and x_2, respectively. The sample proportions are then computed.

$$\hat{p}_1 = \frac{x_1}{n_1} \quad \text{and} \quad \hat{p}_2 = \frac{x_2}{n_2}$$

Statisticians have proved that the statistic $\hat{p}_1 - \hat{p}_2$ is an unbiased consistent estimator of the parameter $p_1 - p_2$.

Figure 12.10

Sampling from Two Populations of Qualitative Data

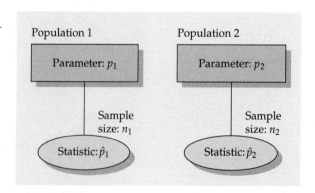

Sampling Distribution of $\hat{p}_1 - \hat{p}_2$

Using the same mathematics as in Chapter 11 to derive the sampling distribution of the sample proportion $\hat{p}$, we determine the sampling distribution of the difference between two sample proportions.

Sampling Distribution of $\hat{p}_1 - \hat{p}_2$

1 The statistic $\hat{p}_1 - \hat{p}_2$ is approximately normally distributed provided the sample sizes are large enough so that $n_1 p_1$, $n_1 q_1$, $n_2 p_2$, and $n_2 q_2$ are all greater than or equal to 5. (Since p_1, q_1, p_2, and q_2 are unknown, we express the sample size requirement as $n_1 \hat{p}_1$, $n_1 \hat{q}_1$, $n_2 \hat{p}_2$, and $n_2 \hat{q}_2 \geq 5$.)

2 The mean of $\hat{p}_1 - \hat{p}_2$ is

$$E(\hat{p}_1 - \hat{p}_2) = p_1 - p_2$$

3 The variance of $\hat{p}_1 - \hat{p}_2$ is

$$V(\hat{p}_1 - \hat{p}_2) = \frac{p_1 q_1}{n_1} + \frac{p_2 q_2}{n_2}$$

The standard deviation is

$$\sigma_{\hat{p}_1 - \hat{p}_2} = \sqrt{\frac{p_1 q_1}{n_1} + \frac{p_2 q_2}{n_2}}$$

Thus, the variable

$$z = \frac{(\hat{p}_1 - \hat{p}_2) - (p_1 - p_2)}{\sqrt{\dfrac{p_1 q_1}{n_1} + \dfrac{p_2 q_2}{n_2}}}$$

is approximately standard normally distributed.

Testing the Difference between Two Population Proportions

We would like to use the z-formula just described as our test statistic; however, the standard deviation of $\hat{p}_1 - \hat{p}_2$, which is

$$\sigma_{\hat{p}_1 - \hat{p}_2} = \sqrt{\frac{p_1 q_1}{n_1} + \frac{p_2 q_2}{n_2}}$$

is unknown, since both p_1 and p_2 (and, of course, q_1 and q_2) are unknown. As a result, the standard deviation of $\hat{p}_1 - \hat{p}_2$ must be estimated from the sample data. There are two different estimators of this quantity, and the determination of which one to use depends on the null hypothesis. If the null hypothesis states that $p_1 - p_2 = 0$, the hypothesized equality of the two population proportions allows us to pool the data from the two samples. Thus, the estimated standard deviation of $\hat{p}_1 - \hat{p}_2$ is

$$\sqrt{\hat{p}\hat{q}\left(\frac{1}{n_1} + \frac{1}{n_2}\right)}$$

where $\hat{p}$ is the **pooled proportion estimate**, defined as

$$\hat{p} = \frac{x_1 + x_2}{n_1 + n_2}$$

and where

$$\hat{q} = 1 - \hat{p}$$

The principle used in estimating the standard deviation of $\hat{p}_1 - \hat{p}_2$ is analogous to that applied in Section 12.2 to produce the pooled variance estimate s_p^2, which is used to test $\mu_1 - \mu_2$ with σ_1^2 and σ_2^2 unknown but equal. That principle roughly states that, where possible, pooling data from two samples produces a better estimator of the standard deviation. Here, pooling is made possible by hypothesizing (under the null hypothesis) that $p_1 = p_2$. (In Section 12.2, we used the pooled variance estimate because we assumed that $\sigma_1^2 = \sigma_2^2$.) We will call this application *Case 1*.

Test Statistic for $p_1 - p_2$: Case 1

If the null hypothesis specifies

$$H_0: (p_1 - p_2) = 0$$

the test statistic is

$$z = \frac{(\hat{p}_1 - \hat{p}_2) - (p_1 - p_2)}{\sqrt{\hat{p}\hat{q}\left(\dfrac{1}{n_1} + \dfrac{1}{n_2}\right)}}$$

Because we hypothesize $p_1 - p_2 = 0$, we simplify the test statistic to

$$z = \frac{(\hat{p}_1 - \hat{p}_2)}{\sqrt{\hat{p}\hat{q}\left(\dfrac{1}{n_1} + \dfrac{1}{n_2}\right)}}$$

The second case applies when, under the null hypothesis, we state that H_0: $(p_1 - p_2) = D$, where D is some value *other than zero*. Under such circumstances, we cannot pool the sample data to estimate the standard deviation of $\hat{p}_1 - \hat{p}_2$. The appropriate test statistic is described next as *Case 2*.

Test Statistic for $p_1 - p_2$: Case 2

If the null hypothesis specifies

$$H_0: (p_1 - p_2) = D \qquad (D \neq 0)$$

the test statistic is

$$z = \frac{(\hat{p}_1 - \hat{p}_2) - (p_1 - p_2)}{\sqrt{\dfrac{\hat{p}_1\hat{q}_1}{n_1} + \dfrac{\hat{p}_2\hat{q}_2}{n_2}}}$$

Notice that this test statistic is determined by simply substituting the sample statistics $\hat{p}_1$, $\hat{q}_1$, $\hat{p}_2$, and $\hat{q}_2$ in the standard deviation of the sampling distribution.

You will find that, in most practical applications (including the exercises and cases in this book), Case 1 applies—in most problems, we want to know if the two population proportions differ; that is,

$$H_A: (p_1 - p_2) \neq 0$$

or if one proportion exceeds the other; that is,

$$H_A: (p_1 - p_2) > 0 \qquad \text{or} \qquad H_A: (p_1 - p_2) < 0$$

In some problems, however, the objective is to determine if one proportion exceeds the other by a specific nonzero quantity. In such situations, Case 2 applies.

EXAMPLE 12.6

In a study that was highly publicized, doctors discovered that aspirin seems to help prevent heart attacks. The research project, which was scheduled to last for five years, employed 22,000 American physicians (all male). Half took an aspirin tablet three times per week, while the other half took a placebo on the same schedule. After three years, researchers determined that 104 of those who took aspirin and 189 of those who took the placebo had had heart attacks. Compute the p-value of a test to determine whether these results indicate that aspirin is effective in reducing the incidence of heart attacks.

SOLUTION

IDENTIFYING THE
TECHNIQUE

The problem objective is to compare two populations. The first is the population of men who take aspirin regularly, and the second is the population of men who do not regularly take aspirin. The data are qualitative because there are only two possible observations: "the man suffered a heart attack" and "the man did not suffer a heart attack." These two factors tell us that the parameter to be tested is the difference between two population proportions $p_1 - p_2$ (where p_1 = proportion of all men who regularly take aspirin who suffer a heart attack, and p_2 = proportion of all men who do not take aspirin who suffer a heart attack). Because we want to know if aspirin is effective in reducing heart attacks, the alternative hypothesis is

$$H_A: (p_1 - p_2) < 0$$

The null hypothesis must be

$$H_0: (p_1 - p_2) = 0$$

which tells us that this is an application of Case 1. Thus, the test statistic is

$$z = \frac{(\hat{p}_1 - \hat{p}_2)}{\sqrt{\hat{p}\hat{q}\left(\dfrac{1}{n_1} + \dfrac{1}{n_2}\right)}}$$

The complete test:

$H_0: (p_1 - p_2) = 0$

$H_A: (p_1 - p_2) < 0$

Test statistic: $z = \dfrac{(\hat{p}_1 - \hat{p}_2)}{\sqrt{\hat{p}\hat{q}\left(\dfrac{1}{n_1} + \dfrac{1}{n_2}\right)}}$

Solving by Hand

Value of the test statistic:

$$\hat{p}_1 = \frac{104}{11,000} = .009455$$

$$\hat{p}_2 = \frac{189}{11,000} = .01718$$

$$\hat{p} = \frac{104 + 189}{11,000 + 11,000} = \frac{293}{22,000} = .01332$$

$$z = \frac{(\hat{p}_1 - \hat{p}_2)}{\sqrt{\hat{p}\hat{q}\left(\dfrac{1}{n_1} + \dfrac{1}{n_2}\right)}} = \frac{(.009455 - .01718)}{\sqrt{(.01332)(.98668)\left(\dfrac{1}{11,000} + \dfrac{1}{11,000}\right)}} = -5.02$$

p-value $= P(z < -5.02) = 0$

Conclusion: Reject the null hypothesis.

USING THE COMPUTER   Most software packages do not conduct inferential techniques involving two proportions. However, we created macros in Minitab and Excel to compute test statistics and interval estimators for $p_1 - p_2$. We assume that the raw data consist of 1s and 0s, where 1 = suffered a heart attack and 0 = did not suffer a heart attack. Sample 1 data are stored in column 1, and sample 2 data are stored in column 2.

Minitab Output for Example 12.6

```
H0:p1-p2 = 0

HA:p1-p2   <   0

p1-hat =   0.00945

p2-hat =   0.01718

z = -4.99915

p-value =   0.00000
```

Note: we did not create a file for this example; the samples are large and disk space was limited.

1 Type or import the data into columns 1 and 2 (1 = success and 0 = failure).

2 Put the diskette in A drive and type **%A:TEST2P1**.

3 At the **DATA** prompt, type the code to specify the alternative hypothesis. The code is the same as is used in test procedure subcommands. That is, $-1 = (H_A: p_1 - p_2 < 0)$, $0 = (H_A: p_1 - p_2 \neq 0)$, and $1 = (H_A: p_1 - p_2 > 0)$.
Hit **Return**.

Excel Output for Example 12.6

	A	B	C	D
1	**Test of Hypothesis About P1-P2**			
2				
3	Test of P1-P2 = 0 Vs P1-P2 less than 0			
4	Sample 1 proportion = 0.009455			
5	Sample 2 proportion = 0.017182			
6	Test Statistic = -4.99915			
7	P-Value = 0			

Note: we did not create a file for this example; the samples are large, and disk space was limited.

COMMANDS

1 Type or import the data into columns A (sample 1) and B (sample 2). Manipulate the data if necessary. (See Appendix 12.B.)

2 Click **Tools**, **Data Analysis Plus**, and **Inference about Two Proportions**.

3 Specify the block coordinates. Do not include cells containing variable names.

4 Specify the code used to record success.

5 Click **Test of Hypothesis (Case 1)**.

6 Click the appropriate alternative hypothesis.

There is overwhelming evidence to infer that aspirin reduces the incidence of heart attacks among men. In fact, the evidence was so strong that the experiment, which was originally scheduled to run for five years, was cut short after only three years so that the results could be made public. The effect on aspirin sales around the world was quite impressive.

It should be noted that this experiment was conducted so that neither the scientists nor the subjects were aware of which pill each subject took. This type of experiment is called "double-blind" and is often used in medical research because it is considered to be more reliable. One of the flaws in the aspirin study is that all of the subjects were male physicians. Consequently, the effect of taking aspirin regularly on women is unknown. Moreover, to claim that aspirin reduces the frequency of heart attacks among *all* men is based on the assumption that male physicians are similar to all men, a contention that is easily disputed. Nevertheless, medical researchers appear to be satisfied in advising middle-aged people who are not adversely affected by aspirin to take aspirin regularly. Figure 12.11 describes the sampling distribution of the test statistic.

Figure 12.11

**Sampling Distribution for
Example 12.6**

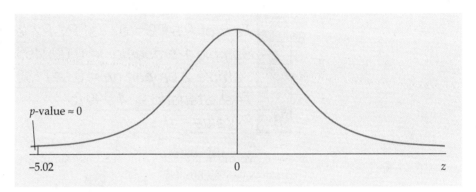

EXAMPLE 12.7

The process that is used to produce a complex component used in medical instruments typically results in defective rates in the 40% range. Recently, two innovative processes have been developed to replace the existing process. Process 1 appears to be more promising, but it is considerably more expensive to purchase and operate than process 2. After a thorough analysis of the costs, management decides that it will adopt process 1 only if the proportion of defective components it produces is more than 8% smaller than that produced by process 2. In a test to guide the decision, both processes were used to produce 300 components. Of the 300 components produced by process 1, 33 were found to be defective, while 84 out of the 300 produced by process 2 were defective. Using a significance level of 1%, conduct a test to help management make a decision.

SOLUTION

IDENTIFYING THE
TECHNIQUE

The problem objective is to compare two populations (components produced by the two processes), and the data are qualitative because we will classify each observation as either "defective" or "nondefective." It follows that the parameter to be tested is the difference between two population proportions $p_1 - p_2$, where p_1 = proportion of all components produced by process 1 that are defective, and p_2 = proportion of all components produced by process 2 that are defective. Because we want to determine if there is enough evidence for us to infer that p_1 is more than .08 less than p_2, the alternative hypothesis is

$$H_A: (p_1 - p_2) < -.08$$

If you're having trouble setting up this alternative hypothesis, try this: we want to know if p_1 is more than 8% *smaller* than p_2, which means that we want to know if p_2 is more than 8% *greater* than p_1. We can set up the alternative hypothesis as

$$H_A: (p_2 - p_1) > .08$$

Because we prefer to specify the parameter as $p_1 - p_2$ (rather than $p_2 - p_1$), we multiply the inequality in the second alternative hypothesis by -1 to yield the first alternative hypothesis.

The null hypothesis automatically follows as

$$H_0: (p_1 - p_2) = -.08$$

which tells us that this test requires the test statistic defined in Case 2. Thus, the test statistic is

$$z = \frac{(\hat{p}_1 - \hat{p}_2) - (p_1 - p_2)}{\sqrt{\dfrac{\hat{p}_1 \hat{q}_1}{n_1} + \dfrac{\hat{p}_2 \hat{q}_2}{n_2}}}$$

Here is the complete test.

$$H_0: (p_1 - p_2) = -.08$$
$$H_A: (p_1 - p_2) < -.08$$

Test statistic: $z = \dfrac{(\hat{p}_1 - \hat{p}_2) - (p_1 - p_2)}{\sqrt{\dfrac{\hat{p}_1 \hat{q}_1}{n_1} + \dfrac{\hat{p}_2 \hat{q}_2}{n_2}}}$

SOLVING BY HAND

Rejection region: $z < -z_\alpha = -z_{.01} = -2.33$

Value of the test statistic:

$$\hat{p}_1 = \frac{33}{300} = .11$$

$$\hat{p}_2 = \frac{84}{300} = .28$$

$$z = \frac{(\hat{p}_1 - \hat{p}_2) - (p_1 - p_2)}{\sqrt{\dfrac{\hat{p}_1 \hat{q}_1}{n_1} + \dfrac{\hat{p}_2 \hat{q}_2}{n_2}}} = \frac{(.11 - .28) - (-.08)}{\sqrt{\dfrac{(.11)(.89)}{300} + \dfrac{(.28)(.72)}{300}}} = -2.85$$

Conclusion: Reject the null hypothesis.

Macros were created to address this problem. The data are 1s (successes) and 0s (failures) stored in columns 1 (sample 1) and 2 (sample 2).

Minitab Output for Example 12.7

```
H0: p1 - p2 =-0.0800

HA: p1 - p2   <  -0.0800

p1-hat =  0.11000

p2-hat =  0.28000

z = -2.84842

p-value =  0.00220
```

Minitab prints the values of the sample proportions $\hat{p}_1$ and $\hat{p}_2$, test statistic ($z = -2.84842$), and the p-value (0.00220).

COMMANDS	COMMANDS FOR EXAMPLE 12.7
1 Type or import the data into columns 1 and 2 (1 = success and 0 = failure).	Open file **XM12-07**.
2 Put the diskette in drive A and type **%A:TEST2P2**.	**%A:TEST2P2**
3 At the **DATA** prompt, type the value of $p_1 - p_2$ under the null hypothesis and the code to specify the alternative hypothesis (see Example 12.6). Hit **Return**.	**−.08 −1**

Excel Output for Example 12.7

	A	B	C	D	E
1	**Test of Hypothesis About P1-P2**				
2					
3	Test of P1-P2 = -0.08 Vs P1-P2 less than -0.08				
4	Sample 1 proportion = 0.11				
5	Sample 2 proportion = 0.28				
6	Test Statistic = -2.8484				
7	P-Value = 0.0022				

The value of the test statistic is -2.8484 and its p-value is .0022.

COMMANDS	COMMANDS FOR EXAMPLE 12.7
1 Type or import the data into columns A (sample 1) and B (sample 2).	Open file **XM12-07**.
2 Click **Tools**, **Data Analysis Plus**, and **Inference about Two Proportions**.	
3 Specify the block coordinates. Do not include cells containing the variable names.	**A2:B301**
4 Specify the code used to record success.	**1**
5 Click **Test of Hypothesis (Case 2)**.	
6 Specify the value of $p_1 - p_2$ under the null hypothesis.	**−.08**
7 Click the appropriate alternative hypothesis.	**P1 − P2 less than −.08**

INTERPRETING THE RESULTS

There is sufficient evidence to conclude that the proportion of defective components produced by innovation 1 is more than 8% smaller than the proportion of defective components produced by innovation 2. Judging from the magnitude of the p-value, it appears that the evidence is overwhelming. It follows that the firm should adopt innovation 1.

Figure 12.12 depicts the sampling distribution of this test statistic.

Figure 12.12

Sampling Distribution for Example 12.7

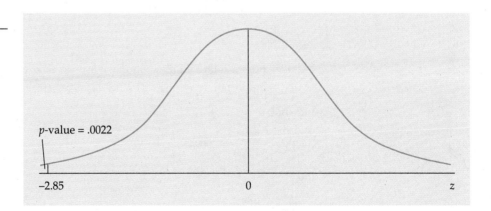

p-value = .0022

−2.85   0   z

Estimating the Difference between Two Population Proportions

The interval estimator of $p_1 - p_2$ can very easily be derived from the sampling distribution of $\hat{p}_1 - \hat{p}_2$.

Confidence Interval Estimator of $p_1 - p_2$

$$(\hat{p}_1 - \hat{p}_2) \pm z_{\alpha/2} \sqrt{\frac{\hat{p}_1 \hat{q}_1}{n_1} + \frac{\hat{p}_2 \hat{q}_2}{n_2}}$$

This formula is valid when $n_1 \hat{p}_1$, $n_1 \hat{q}_1$, $n_2 \hat{p}_2$, and $n_2 \hat{q}_2$ exceed 5. Notice that the standard deviation of $\hat{p}_1 - \hat{p}_2$ is estimated using $\hat{p}_1$, $\hat{q}_1$, $\hat{p}_2$, and $\hat{q}_2$. In this application, we cannot use the pooled proportion estimate because we cannot assume that $p_1 = p_2$.

EXAMPLE 12.8

Estimate with 95% confidence the proportion of men who would avoid a heart attack if they started taking aspirin regularly. If 100 million men adopt the practice of the regular use of aspirin, estimate the number of men who would avoid heart attacks.

SOLUTION

We already know that the parameter of interest is $p_1 - p_2$. The confidence interval estimator is

$$(\hat{p}_1 - \hat{p}_2) \pm z_{\alpha/2} \sqrt{\frac{\hat{p}_1 \hat{q}_1}{n_1} + \frac{\hat{p}_2 \hat{q}_2}{n_2}}$$

SOLVING BY HAND

Recall that

p_1 = proportion of all men who take aspirin who suffer a heart attack

p_2 = proportion of all men who do not take aspirin who suffer a heart attack

and that

$$\hat{p}_1 = \frac{104}{11,000} = .009455$$

and

$$\hat{p}_2 = \frac{189}{11,000} = .01718$$

The 95% confidence interval estimate of $p_1 - p_2$ is

$$(\hat{p}_1 - \hat{p}_2) \pm z_{\alpha/2}\sqrt{\frac{\hat{p}_1\hat{q}_1}{n_1} + \frac{\hat{p}_2\hat{q}_2}{n_2}}$$

$$= (.009455 - .01718) \pm 1.96\sqrt{\frac{(.009455)(.990545)}{11{,}000} + \frac{(.01718)(.98282)}{11{,}000}}$$

$$= -.007725 \pm .003028$$

The confidence interval estimate is $(-.010753, -.004697)$.

USING THE COMPUTER

Minitab Output for Example 12.8

```
Confidence level = 95%

p1-hat =  0.00945

p2-hat =  0.01718

Lower confidence limit = -0.01076

Upper confidence limit = -0.00470
```

Recall that no file for this example was created.

COMMANDS

1 Type or import the data into columns 1 and 2 (1 = success, and 0 = failure).

2 Put the diskette in drive A and type **%A:EST2P**.

3 At the **DATA** prompt, type the confidence level (in percent). Hit **Return**.

Excel Output for Example 12.8

	A	B	C	D	E
1	**0.95 Confidence Interval Estimate of P1-P2**				
2					
3	Sample 1 proportion = 0.009455				
4	Sample 2 proportion = 0.017182				
5	Lower confidence limit = -0.010755				
6	Upper confidence limit = -0.004699				

Recall that no file for this example was created.

INTERPRETING THE
RESULTS

We estimate that the proportion of men who suffer a heart attack is between .470% and 1.08% *less* for men who take aspirin than for those who do not. If 100 million men start taking aspirin, between 470,000 and 1,080,000 of them will avoid heart attacks. The criticism we discussed at the end of Example 12.6 applies to this example as well. The interval estimate certainly applies to all male physicians, likely to all males, and perhaps to women as well.

The test statistics, confidence interval estimator, and the critical factors that identify their use are listed below.

Test Statistics for $p_1 - p_2$

Case 1: $z = \dfrac{(\hat{p}_1 - \hat{p}_2)}{\sqrt{\hat{p}\hat{q}\left(\dfrac{1}{n_1} + \dfrac{1}{n_2}\right)}}$

Case 2: $z = \dfrac{(\hat{p}_1 - \hat{p}_2) - (p_1 - p_2)}{\sqrt{\dfrac{\hat{p}_1\hat{q}_1}{n_1} + \dfrac{\hat{p}_2\hat{q}_2}{n_2}}}$

Confidence Interval Estimator of $p_1 - p_2$

$(\hat{p}_1 - \hat{p}_2) \pm z_{\alpha/2}\sqrt{\dfrac{\hat{p}_1\hat{q}_1}{n_1} + \dfrac{\hat{p}_2\hat{q}_2}{n_2}}$

Factors that Identify the z-Test and Estimator of $p_1 - p_2$

1 Problem objective: compare two populations

2 Data type: qualitative

Exercises

12.36 Perform the following tests.

   a $H_0: p_1 - p_2 = 0$

       $H_A: p_1 - p_2 \neq 0$

       $n_1 = 100 \quad x_1 = 50 \quad n_2 = 150 \quad x_2 = 90 \quad \alpha = .05$

   b $H_0: p_1 - p_2 = .05$

       $H_A: p_1 - p_2 > .05$

       $n_1 = 500 \quad x_1 = 200 \quad n_2 = 400 \quad x_2 = 100 \quad \alpha = .05$

12.37 Calculate the p-value of each test in Exercise 12.36.

12.38 Determine the 95% confidence interval estimate of $p_1 - p_2$ given the following statistics:

$$n_1 = 93 \quad x_1 = 16 \quad n_2 = 121 \quad x_2 = 29$$

12.39 A random sample of $n_1 = 1,000$ from population 1 and a random sample of $n_2 = 600$ from population 2 produced the data in columns 1 and 2, respectively, in file XR12-39. The results are either success (1) or failure (0).

   a   Test at the 1% significance level to determine whether we can infer that the two population proportions of success differ.

   b   Estimate $p_1 - p_2$ with 99% confidence.

Use a software package to solve this problem.	OR	The frequency distributions are as follows. Column 1: number of 0s, 301; number of 1s, 699 Column 2: number of 0s, 156; number of 1s, 444 Complete your answer manually.

12.40 The data stored in columns 1 and 2 in file XR12-40 were drawn from random samples from two populations of qualitative data where 1 = success and 0 = failure.

   a   Do these data allow us to infer at the 1% significance level that p_1 is greater than p_2?

   b   Do these data allow us to infer at the 1% significance level that p_1 exceeds p_2 by more than 3%?

   c   Estimate $p_1 - p_2$ with 95% confidence.

Use a software package to solve this problem.	OR	The frequency distributions are as follows. Column 1: number of 0s, 268; number of 1s, 232 Column 2: number of 0s, 311; number of 1s, 189 Complete your answer manually.

12.41 Cold and allergy medicines have been available for a number of years. One serious side effect of these medications is that they cause drowsiness, which makes them dangerous for industrial workers. In recent years, a nondrowsy cold and allergy medicine has been developed. One such product, Hismanal, is claimed by its manufacturer to be the first, once-a-day nondrowsy allergy medicine. The nondrowsy part of the claim is based on a clinical experiment in which 1,604 patients were given Hismanal and 1,109 patients were given a placebo. Drowsiness was reported by 7.1% of the first group and 6.4% of the second group. Do these results allow us to infer at the 5% significance level that Hismanal's claim is false?

12.42 Surveys have been widely used by politicians around the world as a way of monitoring the opinions of the electorate. Six months ago, a survey was undertaken to determine the degree of support for a national party leader. Of a sample of 1,100, 56% indicated that they would vote for this politician. This month, another survey of 800 voters revealed that 46% now support the leader.

a At the 5% significance level, can we infer that the national leader's popularity has decreased?

b At the 5% significance level, can we infer that the national leader's popularity has decreased by more than 5%?

c Estimate the decrease in percentage support between now and six months ago.

12.43 Refer to Example 12.6. A not-so-widely-publicized British study attempted to replicate the American research plan; however, it used only 5,000 men (2,500 took aspirin, and 2,500 took the placebo). Suppose that the respective proportions of men who suffered heart attacks were exactly the same as in the American study. Do such results allow us to draw the same conclusion?

12.44 An insurance company is thinking about offering discounts on its life insurance policies to nonsmokers. As part of its analysis, it randomly selects 200 men who are 60 years old and asks them if they smoke at least one pack of cigarettes per day and if they have ever suffered from heart disease. The results are stored in file XR12-44 using the following format.

Column 1: sample of smokers: 1 = suffer from heart disease; 0 = do not suffer from heart disease

Column 2: sample of nonsmokers: 1 = suffer from heart disease; 0 = do not suffer from heart disease

a Can the company conclude at the 5% significance level that smokers have a higher incidence of heart disease than nonsmokers?

b Estimate with 90% confidence the difference in the fraction of men suffering from heart disease between smokers and nonsmokers.

Use a software package to solve this problem.	OR	The frequency distributions are as follows. Column 1: number of 0s, 37; number of 1s, 19 Column 2: number of 0s, 119; number of 1s, 25 Complete your answer manually.

12.45 The impact of the accumulation of carbon dioxide in the atmosphere caused by burning fossil fuels such as oil, coal, and natural gas has been hotly debated for more than a decade. Some environmentalists and scientists have predicted that the excess carbon dioxide will increase the earth's temperature over the next 50 to 100 years with disastrous consequences. This belief is often called the "greenhouse effect." Other scientists claim that we don't know what the effect will be, and yet others believe that the earth's temperature is likely to decrease. Given the debate among scientists, it is not surprising that the general population is confused. To gauge the public's opinion on the subject, two years ago a random sample of 400 people was asked if they believed in the greenhouse effect. This year, 500 people were asked the same question. The results are stored in file XR12-45 using the following format.

Column 1: results two years ago: 1= believe greenhouse effect; 0 = do not believe greenhouse effect

Column 2: results this year: 1 = believe greenhouse effect; 0 = do not believe greenhouse effect

a Can we infer at the 5% significance level that there has been a decrease in belief in the greenhouse effect?

b Estimate the real change in the public's opinion about the subject. Use a 90% confidence level.

Use a software package to solve this problem.	OR	The frequency distributions are as follows. Column 1: number of 0s, 152; number of 1s, 248 Column 2: number of 0s, 240; number of 1s, 260 Complete your answer manually.

12.46 A market researcher employed by a chain of service centers offering no-wait oil and filter changes wants to know whether men and women differ in their use of the company's services. Such information would be useful in designing advertising. A random sample of 500 people was selected, and each was asked whether they have their oil and filters changed at the no-wait service center. The responses and the sex of the respondents were stored in file XR12-46 in the following way.

Column 1: female: 1 = use no-wait service; 0 = do not use no-wait service

Column 2: male: 1 = use no-wait service; 0 = do not use no-wait service

Can we conclude at the 5% significance level that men and women differ in their use of this oil-change service?

Use a software package to solve this problem.	OR	The frequency distributions are as follows. Column 1: number of 0s, 171; number of 1s, 67 Column 2: number of 0s, 176; number of 1s, 86 Complete your answer manually.

12.7 Summary

In this chapter, we presented a variety of techniques that allow statisticians to compare two populations. When the data are quantitative and we are interested in measures of central location, we encountered two more factors that must be considered when choosing the appropriate technique. When the samples are independent, we can use either the equal-variances or unequal-variances formulas. When the samples are matched pairs, we have only one set of formulas. We introduced the F distribution, which is used to make inferences about two population variances. When the data are qualitative, the parameter of interest is the difference between two proportions. For this parameter we had two test statistics and one confidence interval estimator. All these techniques are summarized in Table 12.3. Finally, we discussed observational and experimental data, important concepts in attempting to interpret statistical findings.

Table 12.3	Summary of Inference about Comparing Two Populations		
PARAMETER	TEST STATISTIC	CONFIDENCE INTERVAL ESTIMATOR	REQUIRED CONDITIONS
$\mu_1 - \mu_2$	$t = \dfrac{(\bar{x}_1 - \bar{x}_2) - (\mu_1 - \mu_2)}{\sqrt{s_p^2\left(\dfrac{1}{n_1} + \dfrac{1}{n_2}\right)}}$ d.f. $= n_1 + n_2 - 2$	$(\bar{x}_1 - \bar{x}_2) \pm t_{\alpha/2}\sqrt{s_p^2\left(\dfrac{1}{n_1} + \dfrac{1}{n_2}\right)}$	Samples are independent; populations are normal; $\sigma_1^2 = \sigma_2^2$.
$\mu_1 - \mu_2$	$t = \dfrac{(\bar{x}_1 - \bar{x}_2) - (\mu_1 - \mu_2)}{\sqrt{\dfrac{s_1^2}{n_1} + \dfrac{s_2^2}{n_2}}}$ d.f. $= \dfrac{(s_1^2/n_1 + s_2^2/n_2)^2}{\left(\dfrac{(s_1^2/n_1)^2}{n_1 - 1} + \dfrac{(s_2^2/n_2)^2}{n_2 - 1}\right)}$	$(\bar{x}_1 - \bar{x}_2) \pm t_{\alpha/2}\sqrt{\dfrac{s_1^2}{n_1} + \dfrac{s_2^2}{n_2}}$	Samples are independent; populations are normal; $\sigma_1^2 \neq \sigma_2^2$.
μ_D	$t = \dfrac{\bar{x}_D - \mu_D}{s_D/\sqrt{n_D}}$ d.f. $= n_D - 1$	$\bar{x}_D \pm t_{\alpha/2}\dfrac{s_D}{\sqrt{n_D}}$	Samples are matched pairs; differences are normal.
σ_1^2/σ_2^2	$F = s_1^2/s_2^2$ $\nu_1 = n_1 - 1$ $\nu_2 = n_2 - 1$	$\text{LCL} = \left(\dfrac{s_1^2}{s_2^2}\right)\dfrac{1}{F_{\alpha/2,\nu_1,\nu_2}}$ $\text{UCL} = \left(\dfrac{s_1^2}{s_2^2}\right)F_{\alpha/2,\nu_2,\nu_1}$	Populations are normal.
$p_1 - p_2$	Case 1: $H_0\colon (p_1 - p_2) = 0$ $z = \dfrac{(\hat{p}_1 - \hat{p}_2)}{\sqrt{\hat{p}\hat{q}\left(\dfrac{1}{n_1} + \dfrac{1}{n_2}\right)}}$ Case 2: $H_0\colon (p_1 - p_2) = D$ $(D \neq 0)$ $z = \dfrac{(\hat{p}_1 - \hat{p}_2) - (p_1 - p_2)}{\sqrt{\dfrac{\hat{p}_1\hat{q}_1}{n_1} + \dfrac{\hat{p}_2\hat{q}_2}{n_2}}}$	$(\hat{p}_1 - \hat{p}_2) \pm z_{\alpha/2}\sqrt{\dfrac{\hat{p}_1\hat{q}_1}{n_1} + \dfrac{\hat{p}_2\hat{q}_2}{n_2}}$	$n_1\hat{p}_1,\ n_1\hat{q}_1,\ n_2\hat{p}_2,\ n_2\hat{q}_2 \geq 5$

Supplementary Exercises

12.47 Is eating oat bran an effective way to reduce cholesterol? Early studies indicated that eating oat bran daily reduces cholesterol levels by 5 to 10%. Reports of this study resulted in the introduction of many new breakfast cereals with various percentages of oat bran as an ingredient. However, a January 1990 experiment performed by medical researchers in Boston, Massachusetts, cast doubt on the effectiveness of oat bran. In that study, 20 volunteers ate oat bran for breakfast, and another 20 volunteers ate another grain cereal for breakfast. At the end of six weeks, the percentage of cholesterol reduction was computed for both groups. These data are listed below and stored in file XR12-47. What can we conclude at the 5% significance level?

Oat bran (% cholesterol reduction): 14, 18, 4, 9, 4, 0, 12, 2, 8, 12, 10, 11, 12, 6, 15, 17, 12, 4, 14
Other cereal (% cholesterol reduction): 3, 3, 8, 11, 9, 7, 12, 13, 18, 2, 7, 5, 1, 5, 3, 13, 11, 2, 19, 9

12.48 An inspector for the Atlantic City Gaming Commission suspects that a particular blackjack dealer may be cheating when he deals at expensive tables. To test her belief, she observed 500 hands each at the $100-limit table and the $3,000-limit table. For each hand, she recorded whether the dealer won (code = 1) or lost (code = 0). When a tie occurs there is no winner or loser. These data are stored in file XR12-48. (Column 1 stores the outcomes for the $100-limit table, and column 2 stores the outcomes for the $3,000-limit table.) Can the inspector conclude at the 10% significance level that the dealer is cheating at the more expensive table?

| Use a software package to solve this problem. | OR | The frequency distributions are as follows. Column 1: number of 0s, 234; number of 1s, 257; Column 2: number of 0s, 218; number of 1s, 272; Complete your answer manually. |

12.49 A restaurant located in an office building decides to adopt a new strategy for attracting customers to the restaurant. Every week it advertises in the city newspaper. To measure how well the advertising is working, the restaurant owner recorded the weekly gross sales for the 10 weeks after the campaign began and the weekly gross sales for the 10 weeks immediately prior to the campaign. These data are listed below.

a Can the restaurateur conclude at the 5% significance level that the advertising campaign is successful?

b Assume that the profit is 20% of the gross. If the ads cost $100 per week, can the restaurateur conclude that the ads are worthwhile?

c What are the required conditions for the test results to be valid in parts (a) and (b)?

d Does it appear that the required conditions are satisfied?

Gross sales during campaign ($100s): 54, 60, 57, 58, 73, 59, 54, 56, 61, 55
Gross sales before campaign ($100s): 56, 49, 48, 44, 45, 52, 54, 50, 57, 45

12.50 Because of the high cost of energy, home owners in northern climates need to find ways to cut their heating costs. A building contractor wanted to investigate the effect on heating costs of increasing the insulation. As an experiment, he located a large subdevelopment built around 1970 with minimal insulation. His plan was to insulate some of the houses and compare the heating costs in the insulated homes with those that remained uninsulated. However, it was clear to him that the size of the house was a critical factor in determining heating costs. Consequently, he found 12 pairs of identical-sized houses ranging from 1,200 to 2,800 square feet. He insulated one house in each pair (levels of R20 in the walls and R32 in the attic) and left the other house unchanged. The heating cost for the following winter season was recorded for each house. The data are listed below and stored in file XR12-50. (Column 1 = size of the house, column 2 = heating cost of uninsulated house, column 3 = heating cost of insulated house.)

a Do these data allow the contractor to infer at the 1% significance level that the heating cost for the insulated house is less than that for the uninsulated one?

b Estimate with 95% confidence the mean savings due to insulating the house.

c What is the required condition for the use of the techniques in parts (a) and (b)?

d Does it appear that the required condition is satisfied?

House size (in hundreds of square feet):   12   14   15   16   18   19   21   22   23   24   26   28
Heating cost (uninsulated house):   504   550   571   608   622   620   682   699   741   855   900   912
Heating cost (insulated house):   452   474   524   542   557   557   619   641   670   800   838   850

12.51 In recent years, a number of state governments have passed mandatory seat-belt laws. Although the use of seat belts is known to save lives and reduce serious injuries, compliance with seat-belt laws is not universal. In an effort to increase the use of seat belts, a government agency sponsored a two-year study. Among its objectives was to determine if there was enough evidence to justify the following conclusions.

a Seat-belt usage increased between last year and this year.

b This year seat belts were used more frequently by women than by men.

To test these beliefs, a random sample of female and male drivers last year and this year were sampled and asked whether they always used their seat belts. The responses were stored in file XR12-51 in the following way.

Column 1: last year's survey responses, female respondents: 1 = wear seat belt; 0 = do not wear seat belt

Column 2: last year's survey responses, male respondents: 1 = wear seat belt; 0 = do not wear seat belt

Column 3: this year's survey responses, female respondents: 1 = wear seat belt; 0 = do not wear seat belt

Column 4: this year's survey responses, male respondents: 1 = wear seat belt; 0 = do not wear seat belt

What conclusions can be drawn from the results? (Use a 5% significance level.)

Use a software package to solve this problem	OR	The frequency distributions are as follows. Column 1: number of 0s, 58; number of 1s, 146 Column 2: number of 0s, 104; number of 1s, 163 Column 3: number of 0s, 38; number of 1s, 150 Column 4: number of 0s, 72; number of 1s, 166 Complete your answer manually.

12.52 An important component of the cost of living is the amount of money spent on housing. Housing costs include rent (for tenants), mortgage payments and property tax (for home owners), heating, electricity, and water. An economist undertook a five-year study to determine how housing costs have changed. Five years ago, he took a random sample of 200 households and recorded the percentage of total income spent on housing. This year, he took another sample of 200 households. The data are stored in columns 1 (five years ago) and 2 (this year) in file XR12-52.

    a Conduct a test (with $\alpha = .10$) to determine whether the economist can infer that housing cost as a percentage of total income has increased over the last five years.

    b Use whatever statistical method you deem appropriate to check the required condition(s) of the test used in part (a).

Use a software package to solve this problem.	OR	The following statistics were computed from the data. $\bar{x}_1 = 32.42, s_1 = 6.08$ $\bar{x}_2 = 33.72, s_2 = 6.75$ Complete your answer manually.

12.53 In designing advertising campaigns to sell magazines, it is important to know how much time each of a number of demographic groups spends reading magazines. In a preliminary study, 40 people were randomly selected. Each was asked how much time per week he or she spent reading magazines; additionally, each was categorized by sex and by income level (high or low). The data are stored in file

XR12-53 in the following way: column 1 = time spent reading magazines per week in minutes for all respondents; column 2 = sex (1 = male and 2 = female); column 3 = income level (1 = low and 2 = high).

a Is there sufficient evidence at the 5% significance level to conclude that men and women differ in the amount of time spent reading magazines?

b Is there sufficient evidence at the 5% significance level to conclude that high-income individuals devote more time to reading magazines than low-income people?

c Does it appear that the required conditions for the above tests are satisfied?

Use a software package to solve this problem.	OR	The following statistics for reading times were computed. Males: $\bar{x} = 39.75$; $s = 28.35$ Females: $\bar{x} = 49.00$; $s = 27.08$ Low income: $\bar{x} = 33.10$; $s = 16.69$ High income: $\bar{x} = 56.84$; $s = 32.37$ Complete your answer manually.

12.54 In a study to determine whether sex affects salary offers for graduating M.B.A. students, 25 pairs of students were selected. Each pair consisted of a female and a male student who were matched according to their grade-point averages, courses taken, ages, and previous work experience. The highest salary offered (in thousands of dollars) to each graduate was recorded and stored in file XR12-54. (Column 1 = salary offer for females and column 2 = salary offer for males.) These data are shown below.

a Is there enough evidence at the 10% significance level to infer that sex is a factor in salary offers?

b Discuss why the experiment was organized in the way it was.

c Is the required condition for the test in part (a) satisfied?

M.B.A. pair:	1	2	3	4	5	6	7	8	9	10	11	12	13
Female salary offer:	71	55	68	61	62	54	44	49	42	55	67	69	69
Male salary offer:	72	60	70	63	61	49	48	47	40	53	69	72	71

M.B.A. pair:	14	15	16	17	18	19	20	21	22	23	24	25
Female salary offer:	71	47	68	48	49	62	42	42	47	47	57	46
Male salary offer:	71	48	72	53	50	54	46	44	50	47	58	42

12.55 Have North Americans grown to distrust television and newspaper journalists? A survey was conducted this year to compare what Americans currently thought of the press versus what they said three years ago. The survey asked respondents whether they agreed with the following statements.

1 Press reports are "often inaccurate."

2 Press "tends to favor one side" when reporting on political and social issues.

3 Press "often invades people's privacy."

The responses are stored in file XR12-55 using the following format.

Column 1: this year's survey response to Question 1: 1 = agree; 0 = disagree

Column 2: this year's survey response to Question 2: 1 = agree; 0 = disagree

Column 3: this year's survey response to Question 3: 1 = agree; 0 = disagree

Column 4: three-years-ago survey response to Question 1: 1 = agree; 0 = disagree

Column 5: three-years-ago survey response to Question 2: 1 = agree; 0 = disagree

Column 6: three-years-ago survey response to Question 3: 1 = agree; 0 = disagree

Can we conclude at the 5% significance level that Americans have become more distrustful of television and newspaper reporting this year than they were three years ago?

Use a software package to solve this problem.	OR	The frequency distributions are. Column 1: number of 0s, 227; number of 1s, 173 Column 2: number of 0s, 172; number of 1s, 228 Column 3: number of 0s, 88; number of 1s, 312 Column 4: number of 0s, 260; number of 1s, 140 Column 5: number of 0s, 195; number of 1s, 205 Column 6: number of 0s, 109; number of 1s, 291 Complete your answer manually.

12.56 Before deciding which of two types of stamping machines should be purchased, the plant manager of an automotive parts manufacturer wants to determine the number of units that each produces. The two machines differ in cost, reliability, and productivity. The firm's accountant has calculated that machine A must produce 25 more nondefective units per hour than machine B to warrant buying machine A. To help decide, both machines were operated for 24 hours. The total number of units and the number of nondefective units produced by each machine per hour were recorded. These data are stored in file XR12-56 (column 1 = total number of units produced by machine A; column 2 = number of defectives produced by machine A; column 3 = total number of units produced by machine B; column 4 = number of defectives produced by machine B) and listed as follows. Determine which machine should be purchased. (Use a 5% significance level.)

MACHINE A		MACHINE B	
TOTAL NUMBER OF UNITS PER HOUR	NUMBER OF DEFECTIVES	TOTAL NUMBER OF UNITS PER HOUR	NUMBER OF DEFECTIVES
247	10	219	12
242	13	218	4
250	3	205	12
233	10	216	17
241	11	222	23
244	11	216	14
252	11	218	15
236	14	197	4
244	19	217	18
255	14	205	15
229	11	210	6
255	16	219	11
250	12	207	14
252	16	227	18
235	8	208	4
225	8	207	14
233	7	223	10
243	11	203	7
238	22	228	24
232	4	215	17
237	5	213	22
247	11	211	16
247	10	214	17
221	8	236	18

12.57 Refer to Exercise 12.56. Can we conclude at the 5% significance level that the defective rate differs between the two machines?

12.58 The growing use of bicycles to commute to work has caused many cities to create exclusive bicycle lanes. These lanes are usually created by disallowing parking on streets that formerly allowed curbside parking. Merchants on such streets complain that the removal of parking will cause their businesses to suffer. To examine this problem, the mayor of a large city decided to launch an experiment on one busy street that had one-hour parking meters. The meters were removed and a bicycle lane was created. The mayor asked the three businesses (a dry cleaner, a doughnut shop, and a convenience store) in one block to record daily sales for two complete weeks (Sunday to Saturday) prior to the change and two complete weeks after the change. The data are stored in file XR12-58 (column 1 = day of the week, column 2 = sales before change for dry cleaner, column 3 = sales after change for dry cleaner, column 4 = sales before change for doughnut shop, column 5 = sales after change for doughnut shop, column 6 = sales before change for convenience store, and column 7 = sales after change for convenience store) and listed as follows. What conclusions can you draw from these data?

| DAY | DRY CLEANER | | DOUGHNUT SHOP | | CONVENIENCE STORE | |
---	SALES BEFORE	SALES AFTER	SALES BEFORE	SALES AFTER	SALES BEFORE	SALES AFTER
Sunday	195	173	319	317	307	287
Monday	194	204	347	331	393	390
Tuesday	146	153	306	301	407	394
Wednesday	186	184	316	306	352	314
Thursday	178	168	324	318	337	308
Friday	146	145	339	340	445	419
Saturday	161	141	272	248	440	429
Sunday	190	185	285	284	357	320
Monday	162	157	312	284	389	354
Tuesday	154	154	346	325	410	398
Wednesday	153	163	266	268	314	270
Thursday	172	175	309	282	359	339
Friday	174	170	315	268	425	380
Saturday	141	145	258	262	310	272

12.59 There may be a new health concern—too much iron in our bodies. An article in the *Wall Street Journal* (17 January 1992) reported that some scientists have implicated iron as a factor in various diseases, including cancer. Part of the problem, it is believed, is that iron builds up in the body over many years. To examine the issue, a random sample of 20-year-old men and women and 40-year-old men and women was drawn. The amount of iron in their bodies was measured and recorded. The results are stored in file XR12-59 in the following way: column 1 shows the amount of stored iron in men (in milligrams); column 2 indicates the men's ages; column 3 shows the amount of stored iron in women; column 4 lists the women's ages.

a Conduct a test to measure the amount of statistical evidence that exists to infer that 40-year-old men have more iron in their bodies than do 20-year-old men.

b Repeat part (a) for women.

c Use a graphical technique to confirm that the required condition for the tests above is satisfied.

Use a software package to solve this problem.	OR	The following statistics were computed. 20-year-old men: $\bar{x} = 125.74$; $s = 5.65$ 40-year-old men: $\bar{x} = 129.93$; $s = 5.65$ 20-year-old women: $\bar{x} = 134.5$; $s = 6.01$ 40-year-old women: $\bar{x} = 141.11$; $s = 6.28$ Complete your answer manually.

SPECIALTY ADVERTISING RECALL*

Advertisers are extremely interested not only in having customers hear about their products but also in having consumers remember the product and its name. It is generally believed that, if an advertisement is seen only once, the amount of recall diminishes over time. In an experiment to study the amount of recall in specialty advertising, 355 people were randomly selected. Each received by mail three specialty items with imprinted advertising: a ballpoint pen with the name American Airlines printed on it, a key ring with the letters TIW on it, and a note pad with the name General Electric imprinted on the cover. One week later, 164 of these people were asked if they remembered the products received and if they could also recall the products' sponsors. One month after the products were received, the remaining 191 people were asked the same questions. The numbers of those who could recall the products and the sponsors' names are shown in Tables A and B.

Do these data indicate that the level of recall about these specialty items decreases over time?

Table A

Product Recall

| PRODUCT | NUMBER WHO RECALLED PRODUCT | |
	ONE WEEK	ONE MONTH
Ballpoint pen	140	159
Key ring	141	125
Note pad	149	150

Table B

Sponsor's Name Recall

| SPONSOR'S NAME | NUMBER WHO RECALLED SPONSOR'S NAME | |
	ONE WEEK	ONE MONTH
American Airlines	74	63
TIW	45	36
General Electric	74	58

BONANZA INTERNATIONAL†

Bonanza International is one of the top 15 fast-food franchisers in the United States. Like McDonald's, Burger King, and most others, Bonanza uses a menu board to inform customers about its products. One of Bonanza's bright young executives believes that not all positions on the board are equal; specifically, that the

---

*Adapted from A. Raj, C. R. Stoner, and R. A. Schreiber, "Advertising Specialties: A Note on Recall," *Developments in Marketing Science* 8 (1985): 308–11.

†Adapted from M. G. Sobol and T. E. Barry, "Item Positioning for Profits: Menu Boards at Bonanza International," *Interfaces* (February): 55–60.

position of the menu item on the board influences sales. If this hypothesis is true, Bonanza would be well advised to place its high-profit items in the positions that produce the highest sales.

After watching the eye movements of several people, the executive determined that customers first look at the upper right-hand corner, then cross the top row toward the left-hand side, then move down to the lower left-hand corner, and finally scan across the bottom toward the right.

This analysis suggests that items listed in the upper right-hand corner may achieve higher sales than items listed in the lower left-hand corner. In order to test this hypothesis, 10 stores with similar characteristics were selected as test restaurants, and two moderately popular items were selected as test menu items. During weeks one and three (of a four-week study), item A was placed in the upper right-hand corner, and item B was placed in the lower left-hand corner. During weeks two and four, the positions were reversed. The number of sales of each item was recorded, and the results are summarized in Tables A and B. These data are also stored in columns 1 through 4 of file C12-02.

On the basis of the data, what can you conclude regarding the executive's belief?

Table A

Sales of Item A

STORE	SALES WITH ITEM A IN UPPER RIGHT-HAND CORNER	SALES WITH ITEM A IN LOWER LEFT-HAND CORNER
1	642	485
2	912	681
3	221	138
4	312	237
5	295	258
6	775	725
7	511	553
8	726	524
9	476	384
10	570	529

Table B

Sales of Item B

STORE	SALES WITH ITEM B IN UPPER RIGHT-HAND CORNER	SALES WITH ITEM B IN LOWER LEFT-HAND CORNER
1	372	351
2	334	312
3	160	136
4	285	305
5	271	189
6	464	430
7	327	310
8	642	557
9	213	215
10	493	446

One of the problems encountered in teaching accounting in a business program is the issue of what to do with students who have taken one or more accounting courses in high school. Should these students be exempted from the introductory accounting course usually offered in the first or second year of the business program? Some professors have argued that high school courses do not have the breadth or depth of university courses, and that as a consequence, high school accounting students should not be exempted. Others think that the high school accounting course coverage is sufficiently close to that of the university course, and that forcing students with high school accounting to "retake" the course is a waste of time and resources.

In order to examine the problem, students who were enrolled in the third year of the Bachelor of Commerce program at St. Mary's University were sampled. In the third year of this program, two introductory accounting half-credits are required: ACT 241 and ACT 242. Of the 638 students enrolled in ACT 241 in the fall semester, 374 were selected because of the similarities in their educational backgrounds (excluding high school accounting). Student files were examined for all 374 students, of whom 275 continued on to ACT 242 in the winter semester. For each student, researchers recorded the grade in ACT 241 and the grade in ACT 242 (if it was taken), as well as the number of high school accounting courses (either 0, 1, or 2). The results are stored in the file C12-03 on the data disk, using the following format.

Column 1: grade in ACT 241 (4 = A, 3 = B, 2 = C, 1 = D, 0 = F)

Column 2: number of high school accounting courses taken by the students registered in ACT 241

Column 3: grades in ACT 242

Column 4: number of high school accounting courses taken by the students registered in ACT 242

The researchers would like to know by how much students with one or two high school accounting courses outperform those with no high school accounting and, as a consequence of this finding, what exemption policy should be adopted.

---

*Adapted from E. Morass, G. Walsh, and N. M. Young, "Accounting for Performance: An Analysis of the Relationship Between Success in Introductory Accounting in University and Prior Study of Accounting in High School," *Proceedings of the 14th Annual Atlantic Schools of Business Conference* (1984): 13–44.

Manipulating Data

Minitab can draw inferences about $\mu_1 - \mu_2$ when the data are stacked or unstacked. However, other techniques require one format only. In this part of the appendix, we discuss how to change the format of the data.

Suppose that we have the following unstacked data.

COLUMN 1	COLUMN 2
12	18
19	23
13	25

To stack the data, we type

> **STACK C1 C2 C3;**
> **SUBSCRIPTS C4.**

which commands Minitab to take the data that are in columns 1 and 2 and stack them in column 3 and place the subscripts in column 4. The result would be

COLUMN 3	COLUMN 4
12	1
19	1
13	1
18	2
23	2
25	2

The **UNSTACK** command is employed to convert stacked data into the unstacked format. To illustrate, suppose that we have the following stacked data.

COLUMN 1	COLUMN 2
5	2
3	1
8	1
4	2
9	1

To unstack these data, we type

> **UNSTACK C1 C3 C4;**
> **SUBSCRIPTS C2.**

These commands tell Minitab to take the observations in column 1 and divide them into columns 3 and 4 according to the subscripts that are listed in column 2. Note that we need to know how many different subscripts there are in order to use the **UNSTACK** command. In this illustration we knew that there were only two samples and thus there were only two subscripts in column 2. As a result, we unstacked column 1 into two columns (columns 3 and 4). If there were five samples (subscripts 1, 2, 3 , 4, and 5) we would issue the commands

UNSTACK C1 C3 − C7;
SUBSCRIPTS C2.

Descriptive Statistics and Graphs for Stacked Data

When the data are stacked, you can unstack the data before instructing Minitab to calculate the descriptive statistics or draw various graphs. Alternatively, you can use the **BY** subcommand.

To compute descriptive statistics when the data are stacked, type the following command and subcommand. (We assume that the data are stored in column 1, and the codes are stored in column 2.)

DESCRIBE C1;
BY C2.

The descriptive statistics of the data in column 1 for each code in column 2 will be printed.

Menu Commands

1 Click **Stat**, **Basic Statistics**, and **Descriptive Statistics** . . . .
2 Type the variable name of the data.
3 Use the cursor to specify **By variable**, hit **tab** and type the variable name of the codes. Click **OK**.

To draw the stem and leaf displays, type the session command, end it with a semicolon, and type the **BY** subcommand. For example,

STEM C1;
BY C2.

would produce a stem and leaf display of the data in column 1 for each code in column 2. To create histograms and box plots, first type **GSTD** followed by the sessionn command and the **BY** subcommand. For example, type

GSTD
HISTOGRAM C1;
BY C2.

The histogram created in this way will be composed of asterisks and will be turned on its side. Box plots will also be drawn somewhat differently. Type **GPRO** after these commands to restore Minitab's histograms and box plots.

Menu Commands

    1 Click **Graph**, **Character Graphs**, and any one of **Histogram . . .** , **Box-plot . . .** , **Dotplot . . .** , or **Stem-and-Leaf . . . .** (If you select **Histogram** or **Boxplot**, the **GSTD** and **GPRO** commands will be automatically issued.)

    2 Type the variable name of the data.

    3 Use the cursor to specify **By variable**, hit **tab** and type the variable name of the codes. Click **OK**.

Inference about the Difference between Two Means: Independent Samples

To test the following hypotheses,

$$H_0: (\mu_1 - \mu_2) = 0$$
$$H_A: (\mu_1 - \mu_2) \neq 0$$

type

    TWOSAMPLE C1 C2

if the data are unstacked, where samples 1 and 2 are stored in columns 1 and 2. If the data are stacked, type

    TWOT C1 C2

where column 1 contains the data from both samples, and column 2 contains the coded values identifying the sample. If the population variances are equal, use the **POOLED** subcommand. To conduct a one-tail test add the **ALTERNATIVE** subcommand. The output will include the 95% confidence interval estimate of $\mu_1 - \mu_2$. To alter this value, type the desired confidence level after **TWOSAMPLE** or **TWOT** in the commands described above. For example,

    TWOSAMPLE 99 C1 C2

will yield the 99% confidence interval estimate of $\mu_1 - \mu_2$, as well as conduct the test of hypothesis.

    Minitab automatically tests the following null hypothesis.

$$H_0: (\mu_1 - \mu_2) = 0$$

It is possible to instruct Minitab to test for differences other than zero. To test

$$H_0: (\mu_1 - \mu_2) = D \qquad (\text{where } D \neq 0)$$

proceed as follows.

    1 Ensure that the data are unstacked in columns 1 and 2.

    2 Type

        LET C2 = C2 + D (Type hypothesized difference.)
        TWOS C1 C2

You can use the **ALTERNATIVE** subcommand to conduct a one-tail test.

Inference about the Difference between Two Means: Matched Pairs

If the paired observations are stored in columns 1 and 2, the command

LET C3 = C1 − C2

calculates the differences and stores them in column 3. The command

TTEST 0 C3

performs a two-tail test of μ_D, where the null hypothesis is

$$H_0: \mu_D = 0$$

The **ALTERNATIVE** subcommand performs a one-tail test. The command

TINTERVAL .90 C3

computes the 90% confidence interval estimate of μ_D.

APPENDIX 12.B Excel Instructions

Manipulating Data

In order to use Excel to test $\mu_1 - \mu_2$, the data must be unstacked. Suppose that the data are stacked in the following way: column A stores the observations, and column B stores the indexes. If the data are scrambled (not in order), proceed with steps 1, 2, and 3 below. Otherwise, go to step 4.

1 Highlight columns A and B.
2 Click **Data** and **Sort** . . . .
3 Specify column B and **Ascending**. Click **OK**.

The data will now be unscrambled—all the observations from the first sample will occupy the top rows of column A, and the observations from the second sample will occupy the bottom rows of column A. To unstack, issue the following commands. (The following commands assume that there are only two samples.)

4 Highlight the rows of column A that were taken from sample 2.
5 Click **Edit** and **Cut**.
6 Make cell C1 active.
7 Click **Edit** and **Paste**.
8 Delete column B.

Columns A and B will now store the unstacked data.

There are several statistical procedures to be conducted by Excel in later chapters that require the data to be stacked. If the data are presented to you in unstacked form, you will have to stack them. Suppose that there are two sets of observations now stored in columns A and B. To stack the observations of A on B proceed as follows.

1 Highlight the cells in column B.

2 Click **Edit** and **Cut**.

3 Make the first empty cell in column A active. Click **Edit** and **Paste**.

4 Type the codes in column B.

Columns A and B will now contain the stacked data—all the observations in column A and the codes identifying the sample in column B.

APPENDIX 12.C Nonparametric Statistics

In Chapter 2, we introduced the three data types: quantitative, qualitative, and ranked. Thus far in this book, we have introduced the statistical techniques that are used to make inferences about quantitative and qualitative data. In the unabridged fourth edition of the book, Chapter 13 is used to present the techniques that address ranked data, a group of methods called nonparametric statistics. In this, the abbreviated edition of that book, we have chosen to omit that chapter. However, it is useful for you to be aware of the existence of these methods and have some knowledge of how they work. In this appendix, we briefly describe when and how nonparametric statistical techniques are employed. If you wish to learn more about how these methods are applied, see the unabridged fourth edition of this book.

As we have already pointed out, when the data are ranked, the mean is not the most appropriate measure of location. As a result, when we wish to compare two populations of ranked data we will test characteristics of populations without referring to specific parameters. For this reason, these techniques are called nonparametric methods. Rather than testing to determine whether μ_1 and μ_2 differ, we test to determine whether the two population locations differ.

Although nonparametric methods are designed to test ranked data, they have another area of application. Both tests described in Sections 12.2 and 12.4 require that the populations be normally distributed. If the data are extremely nonnormal, the t-tests are invalid. Fortunately, nonparametric techniques can be used instead. For this reason, nonparametric procedures are often (perhaps more accurately) called **distribution-free statistics**. The techniques presented here can be used when the data are quantitative and the required condition of normality is unsatisfied. In such circumstances we will treat the quantitative data as if they were ranked. For this reason, even when the data are quantitative and the mean is the appropriate measure of location, we will choose instead to test population locations. That is, the null hypothesis will specify that the two population locations are the same. Figure 12.C.1 depicts the population distributions when the null hypothesis is true. Notice that, since we don't know (or care) anything about the shape of the distributions, we represent them as completely nonnormal. The alternative hypothesis can take on any one of the following three forms.

Figure 12.C.1

Population Locations Are the Same

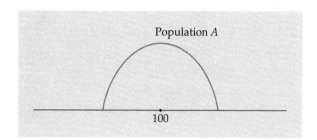 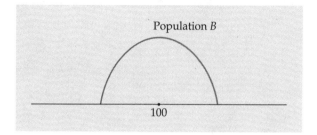

1 If we want to know whether there is sufficient evidence to infer that there is a difference between the two populations, the alternative hypothesis is

H_A: The location of population A is different from the location of population B.

2 If we want to know whether we can conclude that the random variable in population A is larger in general than the random variable in population B (see Figure 12.C.2), the alternative hypothesis is

H_A: The location of population A is to the right of the location of population B.

Figure 12.C.2

Location of Population A to the Right of the Location of Population B

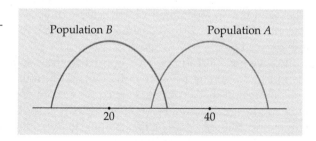

3 If we want to know whether we can conclude that the random variable in population A is smaller in general than the random variable in population B (see Figure 12.C.3), the alternative hypothesis is

H_A: The location of population A is to the left of the location of population B.

Figure 12.C.3

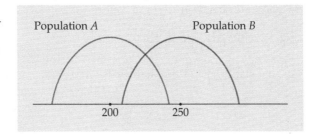

As usual, the alternative hypothesis specifies whatever we're trying to show.

Nonparametric techniques employ a ranking procedure as a critical part of the calculations. You've already dealt with such a process in this book. In Chapter 4, we introduced the median as a measure of central location. The median is computed by placing the observations in order and selecting the observation that falls in the middle. Thus, the measure of central location of ranked data is the median, a statistic that is the product of a ranking process.

There are several nonparametric procedures that can be used to test for differences between two populations. We discuss three in this book. They are the Wilcoxon rank sum test, the sign test, and the Wilcoxon signed rank sum test.

Minitab performs all three tests. Data Analysis Plus contains a macro for each procedure.

Wilcoxon Rank Sum Test

The *Wilcoxon rank sum test* is employed to solve problems with the following characteristics.

1. Problem objective: compare two populations
2. Data type: ranked or quantitative but nonnormal
3. Experimental design: independent samples

Test Statistic

1. Label the sample with the smaller number of observations A and the other sample B. If the two sample sizes are equal, arbitrarily assign the labels. Let n_1 = sample size of A and n_2 = sample size of B. The total sample size is $n = (n_1 + n_2)$.
2. Rank all observations, with 1 = smallest observation and n = largest observation. In case of ties, average the ranks of the tied observations.
3. Calculate the sum of the ranks of sample A, which is the test statistic T.

Sampling Distribution of *T*

We judge the value of T relative to its sampling distribution. For small samples (both sample sizes are less than or equal to 10), special tables are required (not available in this edition). For samples exceeding 10, the test statistic is approximately normally distributed with mean

$$E(T) = \frac{n_1(n_1 + n_2 + 1)}{2}$$

and standard deviation

$$\sigma_T = \sqrt{\frac{n_1 n_2 (n_1 + n_2 + 1)}{12}}$$

Thus, the standardized test statistic is

$$z = \frac{T - E(T)}{\sigma_T}$$

Minitab Menu Commands

1 Type or import the data in unstacked format—sample A in column 1 and sample B in column 2.

2 Click **Stat, Nonparametrics**, and **Mann-Whitney. . . .** (Minitab performs the Mann-Whitney test rather than the Wilcoxon test. However, the tests are equivalent and quite similar. The test statistic T is outputted as W. The p-value is printed.)

3 Type the variable name for the **First Sample**.

4 Hit **tab** and type the variable name of the **Second Sample**.

5 Use the cursor to select **less than, not equal too**, or **greater than**. Click **OK**.

Excel Commands

1 Type or import the data in stacked format. That is, the observations in both samples are in the first column, and the codes (1 and 2) identifying the sample are stored in an adjacent column.

2 Click **Tools, Data Analysis Plus**, and **Wilcoxon Rank Sum Test**.

3 Specify the block coordinates of the data. Do not include cells containing the variable names.

4 Click the appropriate alternative hypothesis.

Sign Test

The *sign test* is applied to solve problems with the following characteristics.

1 Problem objective: compare two populations

2 Data type: ranked

3 Experimental design: matched pairs

The null and alternative hypotheses are identical to those we test for the Wilcoxon rank sum test.

Test Statistic

1 For each matched pair, calculate the difference between the observation in sample A and the observation in sample B.

2 Count the number of positive differences and the number of negative differences.

3 The test statistic is x, the number of positive differences. The sample size n is the number of nonzero differences. That is, n = sum of the number of positive differences and the number of negative differences.

Sampling Distribution of x

The number of positive differences, denoted x, is a binomial random variable. Under the null hypothesis, $p = .5$. Thus, the sign test is none other than the z-test of p first developed in Section 11.4.

Recall from Chapter 7 that the binomial distribution can be approximated by the normal distribution provided that n is large (np and nq must be at least 5). Thus, the standardized test statistic is (with $p = q = .5$)

$$z = \frac{x - .5n}{.5\sqrt{n}}$$

Minitab Menu Commands

1. Type or import the data into two columns. (We'll assume columns 1 and 2.)
2. Create a new variable, the paired differences. Click **Calc** and **Mathematical Expressions. . . .**
3. Specify the variable name of the differences. (We usually use **Diff**.)
4. Hit **tab** twice and type the mathematical expression **(Cl − C2)**
5. Click **Stat**, **Nonparametrics**, and **1-Sample Sign. . . .**
6. Type the variable name for the paired differences.
7. Use the cursor to select **Test median**, hit **tab**, and type **0**.
8. Use the cursor to select **less than**, **not equal to**, or **greater than**. Click **OK**.

Excel Commands

1. Type or import the data into two adjacent columns.
2. Click **Tools, Data Analysis Plus**, and **Sign Test**.
3. Specify the block coordinates of the data. Do not include cells containing variable names.
4. Click the appropriate alternative hypothesis.

Wilcoxon Signed Rank Sum Test

The *Wilcoxon signed rank sum test* is used on problems with the following factors.

1. Problem objective: compare two populations
2. Data type: quantitative but nonnormal
3. Experimental design: matched pairs

Test Statistic

1. Compute the paired differences $D = A − B$.
2. Eliminate all differences where $D = 0$.
3. Rank the absolute values of D where 1 = smallest value of $|D|$ and n = largest value of $|D|$ and where n = number of nonzero differences. (Average the ranks of tied observations.)
4. Compute the sum of the ranks of the positive differences, which we label T, the test statistic.

Sampling Distribution of T

For n less than or equal to 30 we need special tables to determine the critical values. For $n > 30$, T is approximately normally distributed with mean

$$E(T) = \frac{n(n + 1)}{4}$$

and standard deviation

$$\sigma_T = \sqrt{\frac{n(n + 1)(2n + 1)}{24}}$$

Thus, the standardized test statistic is

$$z = \frac{T - E(T)}{\sigma_T}$$

The test statistic is standard normally distributed provided that the number of differences exceeds 30.

Minitab Menu Commands

1 Type or import the data. The data must be unstacked.

2 Create a new variable, the paired difference. (See the sign test above for instructions.)

3 Click **Stat, Nonparametrics**, and **1-Sample Wilcoxon**.

4 Type the variable name of the paired difference.

5 Use the cursor to select **Test median**, hit **tab**, and type **0**.

6 Use the cursor to select **less than, not equal to**, or **greater than**. Click **OK**.

Excel Commands

1 Type or import the data into two adjacent columns.

2 Click **Tools, Data Analysis Plus**, and **Wilcoxon Signed Rank Sum Test**.

3 Specify the block coordinates of the data. Do not include cells containing variable names.

4 Click the appropriate alternative hypothesis.

13 Statistical Inference: A Review of Chapters 11 and 12

13.1 Introduction

13.2 Guide to Identifying the Correct Technique: Chapters 11 and 12

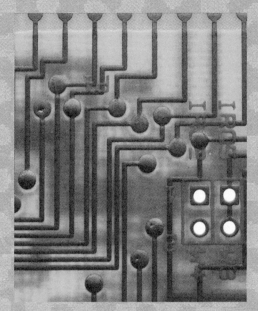

13.1 Introduction

This chapter is more than just a review of the previous two chapters. It is a critical part of your development as a statistician. When you solved problems at the end of each section in the preceding chapters (you *have* been solving problems at the end of each section covered, haven't you?), you probably had no great difficulty identifying the correct technique to use. You used the statistical technique introduced in that section. While those exercises provided practice in setting up hypotheses, calculating test statistics or interval estimates, or producing computer output and interpreting the results, you did not address a fundamental question faced by statisticians: which technique to use. If you still do not appreciate the dimension of this problem, consider the following, which lists all the inferential methods covered thus far (including the three nonparametric techniques introduced in Appendix 12.C).

t-test and estimator of μ

χ^2-test and estimator of σ^2

z-test and estimator of p

t-test and estimator of $\mu_1 - \mu_2$ (equal variances formulas)

t-test and estimator of $\mu_1 - \mu_2$ (unequal variances formulas)

t-test and estimator of μ_D

F-test and estimator of σ_1^2/σ_2^2

z-test (cases 1 and 2) and estimator of $p_1 - p_2$

Wilcoxon rank sum test for independent samples

Sign test

Wilcoxon signed rank sum test for matched pairs

Counting tests and confidence interval estimators of a parameter as two different techniques, there are a total of 20 statistical procedures presented thus far, and there is much left to be done. Faced with statistical problems that require the use of some of these techniques (such as in real-world applications or on a midterm test), most students need some assistance in identifying the appropriate method. In the next section we discuss in greater detail how to make this decision. At the end of this chapter you will have the opportunity to practice your decision skills; we've provided exercises and cases that cumulatively require all of the inferential techniques introduced in Chapters 11 and 12 (but not the nonparametric methods described in Appendix 12.C). Solving these problems will require you to do what statisticians must do. You must analyze the problem, identify the technique or techniques, calculate the test statistics or interval estimates, or employ statistical software and a computer to yield the required statistics and interpret the results.

13.2 Guide to Identifying the Correct Technique: Chapters 11 and 12

As you've probably already discovered, the two most important factors in determining the correct statistical technique are the problem objective and the data type. In some situations, once these have been recognized, the technique automatically follows. In other cases, however, several additional factors must be identified before you can proceed. For example, when the problem objective is to compare two populations and the data are quantitative, three other significant issues must be addressed: the experimental design (independent samples or matched pairs), whether the data are normally distributed, and if the samples are independently drawn from normal populations, whether the unknown population variances are equal.

The flowchart in Figure 13.1 represents the logical process that leads to the identification of the appropriate method. We've also included a more detailed guide to the statistical techniques that lists the formulas of the test statistics, the confidence interval estimators, and required conditions.

EXAMPLE 13.1

Is the antilock braking system (ABS), now available as a standard feature on many cars, really effective? The ABS works by automatically pumping brakes extremely quickly on slippery surfaces so the brakes do not lock, avoiding an uncontrollable skid. If ABS is effective, we would expect that cars equipped with ABS would have fewer accidents, and the costs of repairs for the accidents that do occur would be smaller. To investigate the effectiveness of ABS, the Highway Loss Data Institute gathered data on a random sample of 1991 General Motors cars that did not have ABS and 1992 GM cars that were equipped with ABS. For each year, the Institute recorded whether the car was involved in an accident and, if so, the cost of making repairs. Suppose that these data are stored in file XM13-01 using the following format.

   Column 1: 1991 model; 1 = accident, 0 = no accident

   Column 2: 1991 model; cost of repair (if no accident, cost = $0)

   Column 3: 1992 model; 1 = accident, 0 = no accident

   Column 4: 1992 model; cost of repair (if no accident, cost = $0)

Figure 13.1

Flowchart of Techniques: Chapters 11 and 12

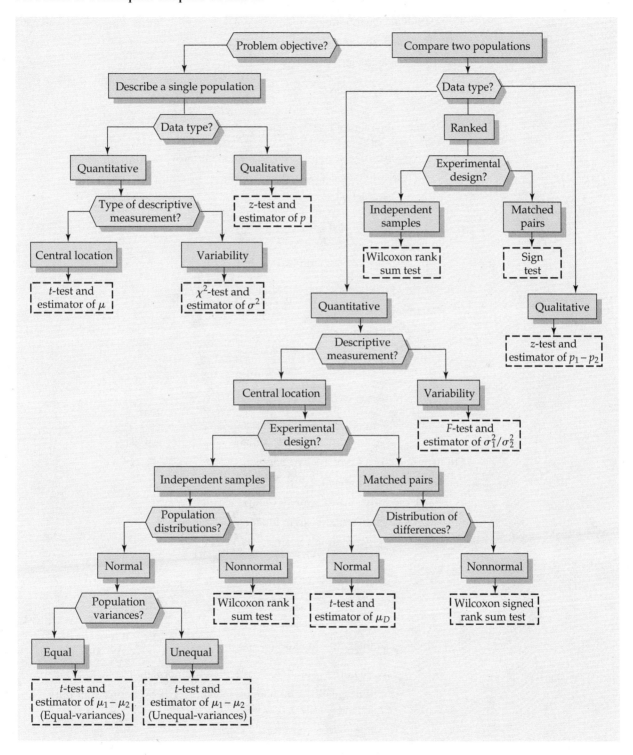

| Table 13.1 | Summary of Statistical Inference Techniques |

Problem objective: Describe a single population.

    Data type: Quantitative

        Descriptive measurement: Central location

            Parameter: μ

            Test statistic: $t = \dfrac{\bar{x} - \mu}{s/\sqrt{n}}$

            Interval estimator: $\bar{x} \pm t_{\alpha/2}\dfrac{s}{\sqrt{n}}$

            Required condition: Population is normal.

        Descriptive measurement: Variability

            Parameter: σ^2

            Test statistic: $\chi^2 = \dfrac{(n-1)s^2}{\sigma^2}$

            Interval estimator: $LCL = \dfrac{(n-1)s^2}{\chi^2_{\alpha/2}}$ $UCL = \dfrac{(n-1)s^2}{\chi^2_{1-\alpha/2}}$

            Required condition: Population is normal.

    Data type: Qualitative

        Parameter: p

        Test statistic: $z = \dfrac{\hat{p} - p}{\sqrt{pq/n}}$

        Interval estimator: $\hat{p} \pm z_{\alpha/2}\sqrt{\dfrac{\hat{p}\hat{q}}{n}}$

        Required condition: $np \geq 5$ and $nq \geq 5$ (for test)

                          $n\hat{p} \geq 5$ and $n\hat{q} \geq 5$ (for estimate)

Problem objective: Compare two populations.

    Data type: Quantitative

        Descriptive measurement: Central location

            Experimental design: Independent samples

                Population variances: $\sigma_1^2 = \sigma_2^2$

                Parameter: $\mu_1 - \mu_2$

                Test statistic: $t = \dfrac{(\bar{x}_1 - \bar{x}_2) - (\mu_1 - \mu_2)}{\sqrt{s_p^2\left(\dfrac{1}{n_1} + \dfrac{1}{n_2}\right)}}$

                Interval estimator: $(\bar{x}_1 - \bar{x}_2) \pm t_{\alpha/2}\sqrt{s_p^2\left(\dfrac{1}{n_1} + \dfrac{1}{n_2}\right)}$

                Required condition: Populations are normal.

                If populations are nonnormal, apply Wilcoxon rank sum test for independent samples.

                Population variances: $\sigma_1^2 \neq \sigma_2^2$

                Parameter: $\mu_1 - \mu_2$

Table 13.1 (continued)

Test statistic: $t = \dfrac{(\bar{x}_1 - \bar{x}_2) - (\mu_1 - \mu_2)}{\sqrt{\dfrac{s_1^2}{n_1} + \dfrac{s_2^2}{n_2}}}$

d.f. $= \dfrac{(s_1^2/n_1 + s_2^2/n_2)^2}{\left(\dfrac{(s_1^2/n_1)^2}{n_1 - 1} + \dfrac{(s_2^2/n_2)^2}{n_2 - 1} \right)}$

Interval estimator: $(\bar{x}_1 - \bar{x}_2) \pm t_{\alpha/2} \sqrt{\dfrac{s_1^2}{n_1} + \dfrac{s_2^2}{n_2}}$

Required condition: Populations are normal.

Experimental design: Matched pairs

Parameter: μ_D

Test statistic: $t = \dfrac{\bar{x}_D - \mu_D}{s_D/\sqrt{n_D}}$

Interval estimator: $\bar{x}_D \pm t_{\alpha/2} \dfrac{s_D}{\sqrt{n_D}}$

Required condition: Differences are normal.

If differences are nonnormal, apply Wilcoxon signed rank sum test for matched pairs.

Nonparametric technique: Wilcoxon signed rank sum test for matched pairs

Test statistic: $T = T^+$ or $z = \dfrac{T - E(T)}{\sigma_T}$

Required condition: Populations are identical in shape and spread.

Descriptive measurement: Variability

Parameter: σ_1^2/σ_2^2

Test statistic: $F = s_1^2/s_2^2$

Interval estimator: $\text{LCL} = \left(\dfrac{s_1^2}{s_2^2} \right) \dfrac{1}{F_{\alpha/2,\nu_1,\nu_2}}$

$\text{UCL} = \left(\dfrac{s_1^2}{s_2^2} \right) F_{\alpha/2,\nu_2,\nu_1}$

Required condition: Populations are normal.

Data type: Ranked

Experimental design: Independent samples

Nonparametric technique: Wilcoxon rank sum test for independent samples

Test statistic: $T = T_A$ or $z = \dfrac{T - E(T)}{\sigma_T}$

Required condition: Populations are identical in shape and spread.

| Table 13.1 | (continued) |

Experimental design: Matched pairs

Nonparametric technique: Sign test

Test statistic: $z = \dfrac{x - .5n}{.5\sqrt{n}}$

Required conditions: Populations are identical in shape and spread, and $n \geq 10$.

Data type: Qualitative

Parameter: $p_1 - p_2$

Test statistic:

Case 1: $H_0: (p_1 - p_2) = 0$

$$z = \frac{(\hat{p}_1 - \hat{p}_2)}{\sqrt{\hat{p}\hat{q}\left(\dfrac{1}{n_1} + \dfrac{1}{n_2}\right)}}$$

Case 2: $H_0: (p_1 - p_2) = D(D \neq 0)$

$$z = \frac{(\hat{p}_1 - \hat{p}_2) - (p_1 - p_2)}{\sqrt{\dfrac{\hat{p}_1\hat{q}_1}{n_1} + \dfrac{\hat{p}_2\hat{q}_2}{n_2}}}$$

Interval estimator: $(\hat{p}_1 - \hat{p}_2) \pm z_{\alpha/2}\sqrt{\dfrac{\hat{p}_1\hat{q}_1}{n_1} + \dfrac{\hat{p}_2\hat{q}_2}{n_2}}$

Required conditions: $n_1\hat{p}_1$, $n_1\hat{q}_1$, $n_2\hat{p}_2$, and $n_2\hat{q}_2 \geq 5$

Using frequency of accidents and cost of repairs as measures of effectiveness, can we conclude that ABS is effective? If so, estimate how much better are cars equipped with ABS compared to cars without ABS.

SOLUTION

This is a typical illustration of the work that statisticians perform and the way they do it. The Highway Loss Data Institute wants to determine whether ABS is effective. Even before the data are gathered, the statistician must decide which techniques to apply. To do so requires the statistician to frame the questions so that tests of hypotheses or interval estimators can be specified. Simply asking whether ABS works is not sufficiently well defined. Because there are several ways to measure the effectiveness of ABS, the following questions were posed.

a Is there sufficient evidence to infer that the accident rate is lower in ABS-equipped cars than in cars without ABS? (If ABS is effective, we would expect a lower accident rate in ABS-equipped cars.)

b Is there sufficient evidence to infer that the cost of repairing accident damage in ABS-equipped cars is less than that of cars without ABS? (When accidents do occur we expect the severity of accidents to be lower in ABS-equipped cars, assuming that ABS is effective.)

c Assuming that we discover that ABS-equipped cars suffer less damage in accidents, estimate how much cheaper they are to repair on average than cars without ABS.

These questions allow the statistician to select the appropriate techniques. We will proceed through the flowchart to illustrate how this is done. When the data are gathered and stored in the computer, the statistician executes the commands to output the results. The results are interpreted to answer the central question: is ABS effective?

Because we wish to emphasize technique recognition and interpretation of the results, we will answer the questions using only Minitab and Excel.

QUESTION (a): IDENTIFYING THE TECHNIQUE

The first factor to identify in the flowchart is the problem objective. In Question (a), the problem objective is to compare two populations: 1991 model results and 1992 model results. Next, we're asked to determine the data type. The data are qualitative. (The values of the random variable are "accident occurred" and "no accident occurred.") The flowchart identifies the technique as the z-test and estimator of $p_1 - p_2$. To answer this question, we conduct the z-test of $p_1 - p_2$. Let

p_1 = proportion of 1991 model cars involved in an accident
p_2 = proportion of 1992 model cars involved in an accident

Because we want to know whether ABS brakes are effective in reducing accidents, we specify the alternative hypothesis as

$H_A: (p_1 - p_2) > 0$

The complete test follows.

$H_0: (p_1 - p_2) = 0$
$H_A: (p_1 - p_2) > 0$

Test statistic: $z = \dfrac{(\hat{p}_1 - \hat{p}_2)}{\sqrt{\hat{p}\hat{q}\left(\dfrac{1}{n_1} + \dfrac{1}{n_2}\right)}}$ (Note that this test statistic is defined by case 1.)

USING THE COMPUTER

(Note: It was necessary to manipulate the data—see Appendix 13.A for details.)

Minitab Output for Example 13.1(a)

```
HO:p1-p2 = 0

HA:p1-p2   >  0

p1-hat =  0.08400

p2-hat =  0.07600

z =  0.46625

p-value =  0.32052
```

Excel Output for Example 13.1(a)

	A	B	C	D	E
1	**Test of Hypothesis About P1-P2**				
2					
3	Test of P1-P2 = 0 Vs P1-P2 greater than 0				
4	Sample 1 proportion = 0.084				
5	Sample 2 proportion = 0.076				
6	Test Statistic = 0.4663				
7	P-Value = 0.3205				

CONCLUSION

There is not enough evidence to infer that ABS-equipped cars have fewer accidents than cars without ABS.

QUESTION (b): IDENTIFYING THE TECHNIQUE

The problem objective is to compare two populations. The data are quantitative because we measure the cost of repairs, which is a real number. The flowchart now asks about the descriptive measurement, which we identify as central location. (We want to know whether one population mean is larger than another.) The next question asks us to identify the experimental design. Because there is no relationship between the two samples, we know that the samples are independent. The next factor we need to specify is whether the populations are normally distributed. The histograms of the costs for 1991 and 1992 (see Figures 13.2 and 13.3) do not appear to be bell-shaped. However, it is doubtful that they supply sufficient evidence to indicate that the costs are nonnormal (Note that the flowchart indicates that if the data are nonnormal, we should employ the nonparametric technique Wilcoxon rank sum test briefly discussed in Appendix 12.C.) The flowchart then asks whether the population variances are equal. Once again, looking at the computer printouts (page 520), we see that $s_1 = 716$ and $s_2 = 639$ (Minitab output) or $s_1^2 = 512,898.4$ and $s_2^2 = 408,221.4$ (Excel output), which gives us reason to believe that $\sigma_1^2 = \sigma_2^2$. (We performed the F-test of the ratio of two variances to make this decision. The result $F = 1.26$ indicates that there is not enough evidence to infer that the variances differ.) Thus, we need to conduct the equal-variances t-test of $\mu_1 - \mu_2$.

Let

μ_1 = mean cost of repairing 1991 model cars damaged in accidents
μ_2 = mean cost of repairing 1992 model cars damaged in accidents

Because we want to know whether μ_1 is greater than μ_2, we specify the alternative hypothesis as

$H_A: (\mu_1 - \mu_2) > 0$

The complete test follows.

$H_0: (\mu_1 - \mu_2) = 0$

$H_A: (\mu_1 - \mu_2) > 0$

Test statistic: $t = \dfrac{(\bar{x}_1 - \bar{x}_2) - (\mu_1 - \mu_2)}{\sqrt{s_p^2\left(\dfrac{1}{n_1} + \dfrac{1}{n_2}\right)}}$

USING THE COMPUTER

Figure 13.2

Histogram of Cost of Repairs of 1991 Cars

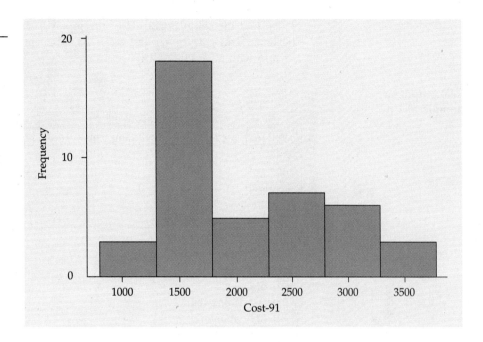

Figure 13.3

Histogram of Cost of Repairs of 1992 Cars

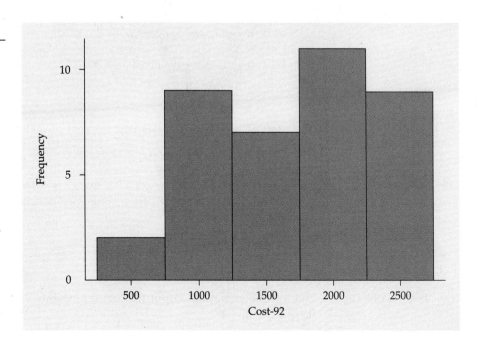

Two Sample T-Test and Confidence Interval

```
Twosample T for Cost-91 vs Cost-92
            N     Mean    StDev   SE Mean
Cost-91    42     2036      716       111
Cost-92    38     1708      639       104

95% C.I. for mu Cost-91 - mu Cost-92: ( 25, 632)
T-Test mu Cost-91 = mu Cost-92 (vs >): T= 2.15 P=0.017 DF= 78
Both use Pooled StDev = 681
```

Notice that the samples consist of the repair costs of the cars damaged in collisions. Thus, $n_1 = 42$, and $n_2 = 38$. The value of the test statistic is $t = 2.15$ with a p-value of .017.

	A	B	C
1	t-Test: Two-Sample Assuming Equal Variances		
2			
3		Cost-91	Cost-92
4	Mean	2035.905	1707.579
5	Variance	512898.4	408221.4
6	Observations	42	38
7	Pooled Variance	463243.9	
8	Hypothesized Mean Difference	0	
9	df	78	
10	t Stat	2.154625	
11	P(T<=t) one-tail	0.017139	
12	t Critical one-tail	1.664625	
13	P(T<=t) two-tail	0.034277	
14	t Critical two-tail	1.990848	

Notice that the samples consist of the repair costs of the cars damaged in collisions. Thus, $n_1 = 42$ and $n_2 = 38$. The value of the test statistic is $t = 2.154625$ with a p-value of .017139.

CONCLUSION

The t-test of $\mu_1 - \mu_2$ indicates that the cost of repairs is less for ABS-equipped cars than cars without ABS.

QUESTION (c):

To measure how much better off a car owner is with ABS, we determine the 95% confidence interval estimate of the difference between the two mean costs. The interval estimator is

$$(\bar{x}_1 - \bar{x}_2) \pm t_{\alpha/2}\sqrt{s_p^2\left(\frac{1}{n_1} + \frac{1}{n_2}\right)}$$

USING THE COMPUTER

The Minitab computer output for part (b) exhibits the interval estimate we seek. It is (25, 632).

Excel does not produce the interval estimate. However, we can easily do so given that Excel printed the sample means and the pooled variance.

Using a 95% confidence level, we have

$$t_{\alpha/2} = t_{.025,78} \approx 1.990$$

The 95% confidence interval estimate is

$$(\bar{x}_1 - \bar{x}_2) \pm t_{\alpha/2}\sqrt{s_p^2\left(\frac{1}{n_1} + \frac{1}{n_2}\right)}$$

$$= (2,035.9 - 1,707.6) \pm 1.990\sqrt{463,243.9\left(\frac{1}{42} + \frac{1}{38}\right)}$$

$$= 328.3 \pm 303.2$$

$$\text{LCL} = 25.1 \quad \text{and} \quad \text{UCL} = 631.5$$

INTERPRETING ALL OF THE STATISTICAL RESULTS

The data indicate that the accident rate in ABS-equipped cars may be no lower than that of cars without ABS. However, the cost of repairing the accident damage is less for the former group. We estimate that the average repair bill for an ABS-equipped car is between $25 and $632 less than a car not equipped with ABS. Can we now say conclusively that ABS is effective? Unfortunately, this is only one interpretation of the results.

Because the experiment uses observational data, we must be careful about the meaning of the tests. It is possible that poor drivers will buy ABS-equipped cars and better drivers will not. If so, the results would tend to indicate that ABS is either ineffective, as in part (a), or not as effective as it really is, as in parts (b) and (c). Experimental data may have been able to overcome this problem. Experimental data could be gathered by randomly selecting people to drive either ABS-equipped cars or cars without ABS for one year and recording the data. In this way the drivers in both groups should be quite similar, making the comparison more definitive.

Another problem in interpreting the results to proclaim that ABS is effective is that it is possible that driving ABS-equipped cars changes the behavior of the drivers. They may drive more dangerously in the mistaken belief that ABS will save them. It may be possible to remedy this problem by not telling the drivers which type they have been assigned to drive. However, most drivers will likely know from the feel and performance of the brakes. Another experiment can be undertaken to determine whether driving behavior is indeed altered by ABS. (See Exercise 13.22.)

Yet another difficulty arose because the experiment was performed using different model years. The ABS-equipped cars were all 1992 models, and the cars without ABS were all 1991 models. The results we observed may be due to differences either in the repair costs or the performance of the models between 1991 and 1992 cars. Undoubtedly, it would have been better to compare 1992 cars with and without ABS. (Note that we are merely reporting the way the Highway Loss Data Institute actually conducted the study; we are not endorsing their methods. We may have gathered the data in a different way.)

Besides teaching you how to identify the appropriate statistical technique, this example also highlights the issues that must be considered when interpreting the results.

Exercises

The purpose of the exercises that follow is twofold. First, the exercises provide you with practice in the critical skill of identifying the correct technique. Second, they allow you to improve your ability to determine the statistics needed to answer the question and interpret the results. We believe that the first skill is underdeveloped, because up to now you have had little practice. The exercises you've worked on have appeared at the end of sections and chapters where the correct techniques have just been presented. Determining the correct technique should not have been difficult. Because the exercises that follow were selected from the types that you have already encountered at the ends of Chapters 11 and 12, they will help you develop your technique-identification skills.

We suggest that you take a two-step approach to the exercises. The first step is to identify the parameter, set up the hypotheses and specify the test statistic (for a test of hypothesis), or specify the interval estimator. To make the problems realistic, we provide only the raw data in the same way that most statisticians encounter it. We do not provide summarized statistics (e.g., mean, variance, or frequency distributions) as we've done in previous exercises. (By doing so, we would be indirectly telling you which technique to use.) As a consequence, students who do not have access to a computer and statistical software cannot calculate the value of the test statistic or interval estimator. Such students should nevertheless perform the first step—identify the technique that should be used and specify the hypotheses or estimator. Students with a computer and statistical software should perform both steps.

Remember, knowing how to conduct tests of hypothesis and interval estimation does not in itself make you a statistician. You must be capable of identifying the correct procedure to use in addition to the capability of interpreting the results.

You will note that in the exercises that require a test of hypothesis we do not specify a significance level. We have left this decision to you. The computer will usually print the *p*-value. (If it doesn't, you can calculate it from the value of the test statistic.) After analyzing the issues raised in the exercise, use your own judgment to determine whether the *p*-value is small enough to reject the null hypothesis.

13.1 Shopping malls are more than places where we buy things. We go to malls to watch movies; buy breakfast, lunch, and dinner; exercise; meet friends; and, in general, to socialize. Thus, the financial well-being of malls concerns us all. In a study of malls, a random sample of 100 mall shoppers was asked a variety of questions concerning their shopping behavior. This survey was first conducted three years ago. The results of the following questions asked this year and three years ago are stored in file XR13-01.

  1 How many hours do you spend in malls during an average week?

  2 How many stores do you visit during an average week?

  3 How many trips to malls do you make in an average month?

  The results are stored in columns 1, 2, and 3. Column 4 contains a code indicating the year the survey was done (1 = this year and 2 = three years ago). Can we conclude that the owners of stores in the mall should be worried?

13.2 It is often useful for retailers to determine why their potential customers chose to visit their store. Possible reasons include advertising, advice from a friend, or previous experience. To determine the effect of full-page advertisements in the local newspaper, the owner of an electronic-equipment store asked 200 randomly selected people who visited the store whether they had seen the ad. He also determined whether the customers had bought anything, and if so, how much they spent. The results are stored in file XR13-02 in the following way.

  Column 1 = amount spent at store

  Column 2 = 0 (did not purchase anything) or 1 (made a purchase)

  Column 3 = 0 (did not see advertisement) or 1 (saw advertisement)

a   Can the owner conclude that customers who see the ad are more likely to make a purchase than those who do not see the ad?

b   Can the owner conclude that customers who see the ad spend more than those who do not see the ad?

c   Estimate with 95% confidence the proportion of all customers who see the ad who then make a purchase.

d   Estimate with 95% confidence the mean amount spent by customers who see the ad.

13.3   In an attempt to reduce the number of person-hours lost as a result of industrial accidents, a large multiplant corporation installed new safety equipment in all departments and all plants. To test the effectiveness of the equipment, a random sample of 25 plants was drawn. The number of person-hours lost in the month prior to installation of the safety equipment and in the month after installation were recorded. The results are stored in columns 1 (number of person-hours lost before installation) and 2 (number of person-hours lost after installation) of file XR13-03. Can we conclude that the equipment is effective?

13.4   The United States Postal Service (USPS) offers a service called Priority Mail that promises two-day delivery. It costs about $3.00 to send a letter by Priority Mail within the United States. A spokesperson for the USPS claims that it has a success rate of more than 95% in delivering letters within the two-day deadline. Station WARY in Miami (as reported in their newscast of December 24, 1992) decided to conduct an experiment to determine whether the $3.00 cost is worthwhile. Letters were sent by Priority Mail and by ordinary mail (at that time, a 29¢ stamp) from New York City to Cleveland, Ohio. Letters that arrived within the deadline were recorded with a 1; letters that were late were recorded with a 0. The data are stored in file XR13-04. (Column 1 stores the results of Priority Mail, and column 2 stores the data for ordinary mail.)

a   Do these data provide sufficient evidence to support the spokesperson's claim?

b   Do these data provide sufficient evidence to infer that Priority Mail delivers letters within two days more frequently than does ordinary mail?

13.5   The electric company is considering an incentive plan to encourage its customers to pay their bills promptly. The plan is to discount the bills 1% if the customer pays within five days, as opposed to the usual 25 days. As an experiment, 50 customers are offered the discount on their September bill. The amount of time each takes to pay his or her bill is recorded. The amount of time a random sample of 50 customers not offered the discount take to pay their bills is also recorded. Both sets of data are stored in file XR13-05. (Column 1 represents the first set of customers, and column 2 represents the second set.) Do these data allow us to infer that the discount plan works?

13.6   The proliferation of self-serve pumps at gas stations has generally resulted in poorer automobile maintenance. One feature of poor maintenance is low tire pressure, which results in shorter tire life and higher gasoline consumption. To examine this problem, an automotive expert took a random sample of cars across the country and measured the tire pressure. The difference between the recommended tire pressure and the observed tire pressure was recorded and stored in file XR13-06. (A recording of 8 means that that tire is 8 pounds per square inch [psi] less than the amount recommended by the tire manufacturer.) Suppose that for each psi below recommendation, tire life decreases by 100 miles and gasoline consumption increases by 0.1 gallons per mile. Estimate with 95% confidence the effect on tire life and gasoline consumption.

13.7   To examine the effect that a tough midterm test has on student evaluations of professors, a statistics professor had her class evaluate her teaching effectiveness before the midterm test. The questionnaire asked for opinions on a number of dimensions, but the last question is considered the most important. It is "How would you rate the overall performance of the instructor?" The possible responses range from 1 (poor) to 10 (excellent). After a difficult test, the evaluation was redone. The evaluation scores before and after the test for each of the 40 students in the class are stored in file XR13-07 as follows.

Column 1: student number (1 to 40)

Column 2: evaluation score before the test

Column 3: evaluation score after the test

Do the data allow the professor to conclude that the results of the midterm negatively influence student opinion?

13.8 The town of Stratford, Ontario, is very much dependent upon the Shakespearean Festival it holds every summer for its financial well-being. Thousands of people visit Stratford to attend one or more Shakespearean plays and spend money in hotels, restaurants, and gift shops. As a consequence, any sign that the number of visitors will decrease in the future is cause for concern. Two years ago, a survey of 100 visitors asked how likely it was that they would return within the next two years. This year the survey was repeated with another 100 visitors. The likelihood of returning within two years was measured as a probability ranging from 0 to 100%

The data are stored in column 1 (survey results from two years ago) and column 2 (survey results from this year) in file XR13-08. Conduct whichever statistical procedures you deem necessary to determine whether the citizens of Stratford should be concerned about the results of the two surveys.

13.9 Does caffeine consumption adversely affect heart rates? In an article in *Men's Health* (October 1992), scientists reported the results of an experiment involving caffeine consumption. The experiment used 64 men and women who drank two cups of coffee per day. For eight weeks, 32 subjects abstained from all caffeine-containing beverages, while the other 32 subjects drank six cups of coffee per day. The heart rates of the 64 volunteers were measured before and after the experiment. These data are stored in file XR13-09 using the following format.

Column 1: heart rate of caffeine-abstainers before experiment

Column 2: heart rate of caffeine-abstainers after experiment

Column 3: heart rate of caffeine-consumers before experiment

Column 4: heart rate of caffeine-consumers after experiment

a   Can we conclude that abstaining from caffeine lowers the heart rate?

b   Can we conclude from these data that increasing caffeine consumption increases the heart rate?

13.10 A fast-food franchiser is considering building a restaurant at a downtown location. Based on a financial analysis, a site is acceptable only if the number of pedestrians passing the location during the work day averages more than 200 per hour. To help decide whether to build on the site, a statistician observes the number of pedestrians that pass the site each hour over a 40-hour work week. These data are stored in file XR13-10. Should the franchiser build on this site?

13.11 There has been much debate about the effects of secondhand smoke. A recent U.S. government study (*Globe and Mail*, 20 June 1991) observed samples of households with children living with at least one smoker and households with children living with no smokers. Each child's health was measured. The data from this study are stored in file XR13-11 in the following way.

Column 1: children living with at least one smoker; 1 = child is in fair to poor health; 0 = child is healthy

Column 2: children living with no smokers; 1 = child is in fair to poor health; 0 = child is healthy

a   Can we infer that children in smoke-free households are less likely to be in fair to poor health?

b   Assuming that there are 10 million children living in homes with at least one smoker, estimate with 95% confidence the number of children who are in fair to poor health.

13.12 An actual U.S. government-funded study surveyed people to determine how they eat spaghetti. The study recorded whether respondents consume spaghetti by winding it on a fork or cutting the noodles into small pieces. Not included in the study, evidently, are those who slurp the noodles directly from their plates without using dining implements at all. The responses are stored in file XR13-12 (1 = wind the strands, and 2 = cut the strands). Can we conclude that more Americans eat their spaghetti by winding on a fork than by cutting the strands?

13.13 In most offices, the copier is the most frequently used and abused machine. Consequently, office machine manufacturers attempt to engineer greater reliability into the copying machines they make. The production manager of an office equipment manufacturer claims that less than 25% of all its copying machines require maintenance within the first year of operation. Prior to making a major purchase, the president of a large company asks 150 recent buyers of this copier if they required maintenance in the first year and, if so, how frequently. The number of repair calls is stored in file XR13-13.

a   Do these data support the claim that less than 25% of all machines require maintenance in the first year?

b   If the president plans to buy 100 copiers, estimate with 95% confidence the number of service calls he can expect in the first year.

13.14 Most people who quit smoking cigarettes do so for health reasons. However, some quitters find that they gain weight after quitting, and scientists estimate that the health risks of smoking two packs of cigarettes per day and of carrying 65 extra pounds of weight are about equivalent. In an attempt to learn more about the effects of quitting smoking, the U.S. Centers for Disease Control conducted a study (reported in *Time*, 25 March 1991). A sample of 1,885 smokers was taken. During the course of the experiment, some of the smokers quit their habit. The amount of weight gained by all of the subjects was recorded and stored in file XR13-14. The file is organized in the following way.

Column 1: weight gain of females in the study

Column 2: code indicating whether female was a continuing smoker (1) or a quitter (0)

Column 3: weight gain of males in the study

Column 4: code indicating whether male was a continuing smoker (1) or a quitter (0)

a   Do these data allow us to conclude that quitting smoking results in weight gains among females?

b   Do these data allow us to conclude that quitting smoking results in weight gains among males?

13.15 Golf-equipment manufacturers compete against one another by offering a bewildering array of new products and innovations. Oversized clubs, square grooves, and graphite shafts are examples of such innovations. The effect of these new products on the average golfer is, however, much in doubt. One product, a perimeter-weighted iron, was designed to increase the consistency of distance and accuracy. The most important aspect of irons is consistency, which means that ideally there should be no variation in distance from shot to shot. To examine the relative merits of two brands of perimeter-weighted irons, an average golfer used the 7-iron, hitting 100 shots using each of two brands. The distance in yards was recorded and stored in columns 1 (Brand A) and 2 (Brand B) in file XR13-15. Can the golfer conclude that Brand B is superior to Brand A?

13.16 No one disputes the value of physical exercise. Regular exercise has been proven to prolong life and decrease the incidence of certain diseases. But what about exercise of the mind? Are there ways in which one can exercise one's intellect without resorting to the mental equivalent of boring calisthenics? The answer may lie in the game of bridge. In a study undertaken at Scripps College in California, researchers tested 50 bridge players and 50 nonplayers aged between 55 and 91 (as reported in the *ACBL Bulletin*, July 1992). The test measured working memory, reasoning, reaction time, and vocabulary. The results of the tests are stored in file XR13-16 (column 1 = working memory; column 2 = reasoning; column 3 = reaction time; column 4 = vocabulary; column 5 = code, where 1 = bridge player and 2 = nonplayer). Bearing in mind that the game of bridge places demands on memory and reasoning, but requires only 15 words and can be played quite slowly, what do these data tell you about the effects of playing bridge?

13.17 Advertising is critical in the residential real estate industry. Agents are always seeking ways to increase sales through improved advertising methods. A particular agent believes that he can increase the number of inquiries (and thus the probability of making a sale) by describing the house for sale without indicating its asking price. To support his belief, he conducted an experiment in which 100 houses for sale were advertised in two ways—with and without the asking price. The number of inquiries for each house was recorded as well as whether the customer saw the ad with or without the asking price shown. The number of inquiries for each house is stored in file XR13-17 in the following way.

Column 1: house number (1 to 100)

Column 2: number of inquiries from customers who saw ad with the asking price shown

Column 3: number of inquiries from customers who saw ad without the asking price shown

Do these data allow the real estate agent to infer that ads with no price shown are more effective in generating interest in a house?

13.18 In a study to determine the effectiveness of a new cavity-fighting toothpaste, 200 10-year-old children were randomly selected. Half were told to use the new product, while the other half continued to use one of the leading brands. The experiment began with all the children visiting a dentist and having all cavities filled. After two years, the children visited their dentist again and the number of cavities was counted. The number of cavities for children using the new toothpaste and the number of cavities for children using one of the leading brands are stored in columns 1 and 2, respectively, in file XR13-18. Can we conclude that the new toothpaste is more effective than the leading brands?

13.19 Suppose that the experiment described in Exercise 13.18 was redone in the following way: 50 10-year-old children were told to use the leading brand for one year and then switch to the new toothpaste for a second year (with any cavities that occurred in the first year to be filled before the start of the second year). Another 50 children use the new toothpaste in the first year and the leading brand in the second year. The number of cavities occurring in each year are stored in file XR13-19 using the following format.

Column 1: first group of 50 children; number of cavities after year 1

Column 2: first group of 50 children; number of cavities after year 2

Column 3: second group of 50 children; number of cavities after year 1

Column 4: second group of 50 children; number of cavities after year 2

a Assuming that the order of toothpaste use is irrelevant, can we conclude that the new toothpaste is more effective than the leading brands?

b Is there any way to determine whether the order is actually irrelevant? If so, do it.

13.20 Periodically, coupons that can be used to purchase products at discount prices appear in newspapers. The goal is to persuade shoppers to take advantage of the coupon to visit the store and buy other products. The manager of a supermarket chain wonders whether the coupons actually work. As part of her analysis, she places 25-cent coupons for bread in the newspaper. Over the next two days, she randomly samples 500 shoppers and determines whether they used the coupon and how much they spent on groceries, not including bread. These data are stored in file XR13-20 (column 1: 1 = used coupon, 2 = did not use coupon; column 2: amount spent). Can the manager conclude that coupon users spend more money on groceries than do non-coupon-users?

13.21 According to the latest census, the number of households in a large metropolitan area is 425,000. The home-delivery department of the local newspaper reports that there are 104,320 households that receive daily home delivery. To increase home delivery sales, the marketing department launches an expensive advertising campaign. A financial analyst tells the publisher that for the campaign to be successful, home delivery sales must increase to more than 110,000 households. Anxious to see if the campaign is working, the publisher authorizes a telephone survey of 400 households within one week of the beginning of the campaign and asks each household head whether or not he or she has the newspaper delivered. The responses are stored in file XR13-21 (1 = yes; 0 = no).

a Do these data indicate that the campaign will increase home delivery sales?

b Do these data allow the publisher to conclude that the campaign will be successful?

13.22 Does driving an ABS-equipped car change the behavior of drivers? To help answer this question the following experiment was undertaken. A random sample of 200 drivers who currently operate cars without ABS was selected. Each person was given an identical car to drive for one year. Half the sample were given cars that had ABS, and the other half were given cars with standard-equipment brakes. Computers on the cars recorded the average speed (in miles per hour) during the year. These data are stored in file XR13-22. Column 1 contains the average speeds of the drivers who were given ABS-equipped cars, and column 2 stores the speeds of the drivers who were given cars with standard brakes. Can we infer that operating an ABS-equipped car changes the behavior of the driver?

EFFECT OF THE DEATH OF KEY EXECUTIVES ON STOCK MARKET RETURNS*

How does the death of a key executive affect a company? This question was addressed by two researchers. In particular, they wanted to know how the stock market would react to the deaths of the chief executive officer and/or the chairman of the board of companies whose stock trades over the counter. A sample of 21 companies whose CEO or chairman died during a 17-year period from 1966 to 1982 was selected. For each company, the weekly stock returns were recorded for 55 weeks prior to the executives' deaths and for five weeks after. A market model (see Case 16.1) was used to determine expected returns, and the difference between the actual and expected returns was calculated. These are called *abnormal returns*. The abnormal returns for each company for the periods three weeks prior to the deaths, the week of the death, and five weeks after are shown in the accompanying table. The data are also stored in file C13-01 (columns 1 to 9).

Under stable conditions, the average abnormal return should equal zero, and we should observe an equal number of positive and negative abnormal returns. The researchers believed that in the weeks before the deaths ($t = -3, -2, -1$), the abnormal returns would indicate stable conditions. However, after the deaths ($t = 0, 1, 2, 3, 4, 5$), they would exhibit the effects of bad news—the abnormal returns would be negative. What conclusions can you draw from the data?

Abnormal Returns (in %) for Weeks $t = -3, -2, \ldots, 5$

COMPANY	$t = -3$	-2	-1	0	1	2	3	4	5
1	−2.73%	−6.03%	6.67%	2.50%	−11.63%	5.59%	−4.53%	−2.09%	−2.65%
2	−1.01	−3.30	−0.69	7.97	−4.37	1.63	−0.98	4.14	2.31
3	−2.53	6.89	−2.03	−7.17	−1.01	−1.51	−4.97	−1.48	0.27
4	−3.87	−2.53	−2.60	−0.45	−0.32	6.91	−2.19	3.12	−1.62
5	7.22	−1.21	2.19	−0.02	−1.52	−2.36	−5.16	−8.31	1.45
6	9.88	6.51	−1.17	−5.04	−1.26	0.03	3.05	−4.10	4.01
7	2.20	−6.26	9.93	−5.32	−4.14	−4.45	−5.97	11.54	3.67
8	−1.72	3.40	−2.68	−0.59	−0.11	−4.93	2.12	−1.59	1.89
9	3.68	−6.36	10.41	−0.22	5.71	−3.63	−1.01	0.65	−4.54
10	−5.90	2.58	−1.34	−1.90	−0.83	8.51	−1.80	0.73	−1.75
11	0.15	6.09	−0.16	−0.73	−3.10	−3.31	6.05	−3.89	−0.27
12	−1.19	−0.87	−0.26	−2.48	3.42	4.54	4.33	−0.44	3.66
13	−2.06	4.32	1.67	−0.62	−0.66	0.08	3.57	6.79	1.91
14	1.60	1.22	−4.04	−1.33	−0.85	0.66	−4.72	−2.49	0.84
15	6.82	5.94	6.46	3.08	−0.68	−2.71	9.19	0.14	0.98
16	2.40	−1.39	2.94	−3.19	−10.91	8.11	3.99	4.27	−0.68
17	3.51	−3.49	7.32	−5.53	−2.13	−0.49	0.55	1.49	−3.80
18	−5.03	0.32	−2.49	−7.46	−0.66	0.14	1.35	1.44	−2.35
19	−6.02	1.68	−1.26	−7.51	1.19	−2.67	−0.67	−0.13	−1.85
20	−0.54	0.68	−0.17	−5.33	−2.38	−7.56	1.10	1.21	0.26
21	−8.65	1.22	7.06	−0.75	1.77	−1.96	5.99	−1.64	−2.32

*Adapted from D. L. Warnell and W. N. Davidson, III, "The Death of Key Executives in Small Firms: Effects on Investor Wealth." *Journal of Small Business Management* 27(2)(April 1989): 10–16.

HOST SELLING AND ANNOUNCER COMMERCIALS*

A study was undertaken to compare the effects of host selling commercials and commercials in which the announcer describes to viewers why they should buy a particular product. Host selling commercials feature a children's show personality or television character who extols the virtues of the product. In 1975, the National Association of Broadcasters prohibited using show characters to advertise products during the same program in which the characters appear. However, this prohibition was overturned in 1982 by a judge's decree.

The objective of the study was to determine whether the two types of advertisements have different effects on children watching them. The experiment utilized two groups of children ranging in age from 6 to 10. One group of 121 children watched a program in which two host selling commercials appeared. The commercials tried to sell Canary Crunch, a breakfast cereal. A second group of 121 children watched the same program but was exposed to two announcer commercials for the same product. Immediately after the show, the children were given a questionnaire that tested their memory concerning the commercials they had watched. Each child was graded (on a scale of 10) on his or her ability to remember details of the commercial. In addition, each child was offered a free box of cereal. The children were shown four different brands of cereal—Froot Loops, Boo Berries, Kangaroo Hops, and Canary Crunch (the advertised cereal)—and asked to pick the one they wanted. The results are stored in file C13-02 in the following way.

Column 1: score of all 242 children on the recall test

Column 2: children's choice of cereal, where 1 = Froot Loops, 2 = Boo Berries, 3 = Kangaroo Hops, and 4 = Canary Crunch

Column 3: 1 = children who watched host commercials, and 2 = children who watched announcer commercials

What conclusions can be drawn from these data?

QUEBEC SEPARATION: *OUI OU NON?*

Since the 1960s, there has been an ongoing campaign among Quebecers to separate from Canada and form an independent nation. Should Quebec separate, the ramifications for the rest of Canada, American states that border Quebec, the North American Free Trade Agreement, and numerous multinational corporations would be enormous. In the 1993 federal election, the prosovereigntist Bloc Quebecois won 54 of Quebec's 75 seats in the House of Commons. In 1994, the separatist Parti Quebecois formed the provincial government in Quebec and promised to hold a referendum on separation. Like most political issues, polling plays an important

---

*Adapted from J. H. Miller, "An Empirical Evaluation of the Host Selling Commercial and the Announcer Commercial When Used on Children," *Development in Marketing Science* 8 (1985): 276–78.

role in trying to influence voters and to predict the outcome of the referendum vote. Shortly after the 1993 federal election, *The Financial Post Magazine*, in cooperation with several polling companies, conducted a survey of Quebecers.

A total of 641 adult Quebecers were interviewed. They were asked the following questions and provided with the accompanying responses. (Francophones were asked the questions in French.)

1 Would you, personally, tend to favor: Quebec's staying in Canada, that is, remaining a Canadian province; or Quebec's separating from Canada, that is, becoming an independent country?

    1 strongly favor remaining in Canada
    2 moderately favor staying in Canada
    3 moderately favor Quebec's separation
    4 strongly favor Quebec's separation

2 If a referendum were held today on Quebec's sovereignty with the following question, "Do you want Quebec to separate from Canada and become an independent country?" would you vote yes or no?

    1 yes
    0 no

The responses are stored in columns 1 and 2 in file C13-03.

    a If the vote were held on the day the survey was taken, would the majority vote no?
    b Do more Quebecers favor staying in Canada?
    c Is there a difference between Quebecers who moderately favor staying in Canada and Quebecers who moderately favor Quebec separation in terms of how they would vote on the referendum?

CASE 13.4   **TEXACO'S SEASONAL PROMOTIONS**

At one time, brand loyalty in the gasoline market was quite strong. Consumers tended to buy their gasoline from one particular company, seldom straying to another. However, drivers now shop for low prices or convenience. Consequently, an important part of a service station chain's marketing strategy is the sales promotion in which customers receive free gifts with their purchases. Most companies plan to make money on the promotion because the increase in sales offsets the cost of the gifts. Additionally, they hope to increase sales immediately after the end of the promotion because customers tend to buy where they've shopped before.

The managers of a Texaco division are considering a Christmas promotional campaign (October 15 to December 31) in which customers who buy at least five gallons (25 liters in Canada) will receive a package of Christmas wrapping paper. The cost per package is $0.21. Currently, the mean retail price is $1.20 per gallon. The costs, including delivery, are $0.92 per gallon. An integral part of the campaign is the additional advertising, which is estimated to cost $40,000.

Before launching the campaign, Texaco wants to be quite confident that the program will be profitable. The decision is usually based on sales experience with previous similar promotions. In the previous year, a similar promotional campaign was undertaken. Each of 32 stations that participated (not all stations are required to participate in any campaign) kept track of the monthly gasoline volume before, during, and after the campaign, as well as the number of gifts given away during the month the campaign lasted. These data are stored in file C13-04 using the following format.

Column 1: monthly volume (in thousands of gallons) before the campaign

Column 2: monthly volume during the campaign

Column 3: monthly volume after the campaign

Column 4: number of free gifts

Assuming that 100 stations will participate in the promotion, can the executives confidently conclude that the campaign will be profitable? What are the prospects for additional profits after the campaign?

APPENDIX 13.A Manipulating the Data

In realistic problems where several techniques must be applied, it is frequently necessary to manipulate the data in preparation for using a software package. In this appendix, we describe how the data in file XM13-01 were manipulated.

Question 13.1(a)

To use the Minitab and Excel macros to test $p_1 - p_2$, we must store the successes (1) and failures (0) in the first two columns. In Minitab, we type

> **LET C2 = C3**

In Excel, we simply delete column 2 (column B).

Question 13.1(b)

To test $\mu_1 - \mu_2$, we need to unstack the data in columns 2 and 4 so that only the nonzero values are included.

Minitab Commands

> **UNSTACK C2 C5 C6;**
> **SUBSCRIPT C1.**
> **UNSTACK C4 C7 C8;**
> **SUBSCRIPT C3.**

Columns 6 and 8 now store the costs of repairing the damage incurred in the accidents for the 1991 and 1992 models, respectively. We can now apply the t-test of $\mu_1 - \mu_2$ on columns 6 and 8.

Excel Instructions

To test $\mu_1 - \mu_2$, we need to unstack the data in columns B and D so that only the nonzero values are included.

    1 Highlight columns A and B.

    2 Click **Data** and **Sort. . . .**

    3 Specify column A and **Descending**. Click **OK**.

    4 Highlight the rows of column B where column A = 1.

    5 Click **Edit** and **Cut**.

    6 Make cell **E1** active.

    7 Click **Edit** and **Paste**.

Column E will now contain the cost of repairing the damage to the 42 1991 model cars involved in collisions.

Repeat for columns C and D. The cost of repairs for the 1992 model cars should be stored in column F. If you wish, you can name the variables (as we did). Now conduct the t-test of $\mu_1 - \mu_2$.

14 Analysis of Variance

14.1 Introduction

The technique presented in this chapter allows statisticians to compare two or more populations of quantitative data. The technique is called the **analysis of variance** and it is an extremely powerful and commonly used procedure. The analysis of variance allows statisticians to determine whether differences exist among population means. Ironically, the procedure works by analyzing the sample variance, hence the name. We will examine several different forms of the technique. Examples of problems where the statistical methods introduced in this chapter would be applied follow.

Example 1 A supermarket chain store executive needs to determine whether or not the sales of a new product are affected by the aisle in which the product is stored. If there are ten aisles in the store, the experiment would consist of locating the product in a different aisle in each of ten weeks and recording the daily sales. The executive would conduct an analysis of variance, which tests to determine if differences exist among mean daily sales. The parameters are $\mu_1, \mu_2, \ldots, \mu_{10}$ (mean daily sales for each aisle).

Example 2 A farm products manufacturer wants to determine if the yields of a crop differ when the soil is treated with various fertilizers. Similar plots of land are planted with the same type of seed but are fertilized differently. At the end of the growing season, the crop yields from the different plots are recorded. The analysis of variance procedure is applied, and the mean yields for each fertilizer are computed. Historically, this type of experiment was one of the first to employ the analysis of variance, and the terminology of the original experiment is still used. No matter what the experiment, the test is designed to determine whether there are significant differences among the **treatment means**.

Example 3 Golf equipment manufacturers are constantly researching new designs and materials in the goal of producing golf clubs that are capable of hitting longer distances. When new products are produced, they are tested in several ways. In one experiment, average golfers hit golf balls with the new clubs and with their older clubs. Suppose that 100 golfers are asked to use their own drivers and two newly designed ones. The distances that the balls travel are recorded. The analysis of variance technique is applied to determine whether there are differences among the mean distances for each of the three drivers. If differences exist, further research is conducted to determine which designs and/or materials are best.

In each of the examples above we are able to classify the populations using only one criterion or **factor**. Each population is called a factor **level**. In Example 1, the factor that defines the populations is the aisle where the product is stored, and there are 10 levels. The type of fertilizer is the factor in Example 2. In Example 3, the factor is the design of the golf club, and there are three levels of this factor.

To illustrate a problem where there are two factors that describe the populations, suppose that in Example 1 we could place the product on one of three shelves (bottom, middle, or top) in each aisle. In this case, there are two factors. Factor 1 is the aisle, which has 10 levels, and factor 2 is the shelf, which has 3 levels. In all there are 30 populations.

In Section 14.2, we introduce the **single-factor analysis of variance**, which is also called the **one-way analysis of variance**. In Section 14.3, we briefly describe some of the other analysis of variance techniques that are available to the statistician. In Section 14.4, we introduce one of these.

14.2 Single-Factor (One-Way) Analysis of Variance: Independent Samples

The analysis of variance is a procedure that tests to determine whether differences exist among two or more population means. The name of the technique derives from the way in which the calculations are performed. That is, the technique analyzes the variance of the data to determine whether we can infer that the population means differ. As in Chapter 12, the experimental design is a determinant in identifying the proper method to use. In this section, we describe the procedure to apply when the samples are independently drawn. In Section 14.4, we introduce the single-factor model when the experiment is designed so that the samples are matched.

Figure 14.1 depicts the sampling process for drawing independent samples. The mean and variance of population j ($j = 1, 2, \ldots, k$) are labeled μ_j and σ_j^2, respectively. Both parameters are unknown. For each population, we draw independent random samples. For each sample, we can compute the mean $\bar{x}_j$ and the variance s_j^2.

Figure 14.1

Sampling Scheme for Independent Samples

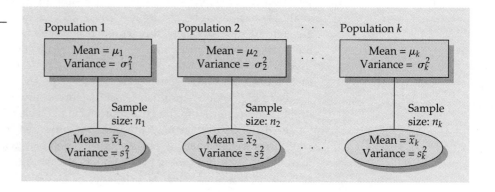

EXAMPLE 14.1

An apple juice manufacturer has developed a new product—a liquid concentrate that, when mixed with water, produces 1 liter of apple juice. The product has several attractive features. First, it is more convenient than canned apple juice, which is the way apple juice is currently sold. Second, because the apple juice that is sold in cans is actually made from concentrate, the quality of the new product is at least as high as canned apple juice. Third, the cost of the new product is slightly lower than canned apple juice. The marketing manager has to decide how to market the new product. She can create advertising that emphasizes convenience, quality, or price. In order to facilitate a decision, she conducts an experiment. In three different small cities, she launches the product with advertising stressing the convenience of the liquid concentrate (e.g., easy to carry from store to home and takes up less room in the freezer) in one city. In the second city, the advertisements emphasize the quality of the product ("average" shoppers are depicted discussing how good the apple juice tastes). Advertising that highlighted the relatively low cost of the liquid concentrate is used in the third city. The number of packages sold weekly is recorded for the twenty weeks following the beginning of the campaign. These data are stored in file XM14-01 and are listed in the accompanying table. The marketing manager wants to know if differences in sales exist among the three cities.

Weekly Sales in the Three Cities	CITY 1 (CONVENIENCE)	CITY 2 (QUALITY)	CITY 3 (PRICE)
	529	804	672
	658	630	531
	793	774	443
	514	717	596
	663	679	602
	719	604	502
	711	620	659
	606	697	689
	461	706	675
	529	615	512
	498	492	691
	663	719	733
	604	787	698
	495	699	776
	485	572	561
	557	523	572
	353	584	469
	557	634	581
	542	580	679
	614	624	532

SOLUTION   You should confirm that the data are quantitative and that the problem objective is to compare three populations (sales of the liquid concentrate in the three cities).

Following the pattern that we have used repeatedly in this book, we introduce the statistical technique by specifying the null and alternative hypotheses. The null hypothesis will state that there are no differences among the population means. Hence,

$$H_0: \mu_1 = \mu_2 = \mu_3$$

The analysis of variance determines whether there is enough statistical evidence to show that the null hypothesis is false. Consequently, the alternative hypothesis will always specify the following.

H_A: At least two means differ.

The next step is to determine the test statistic, which is somewhat more involved than the test statistics we have introduced thus far. The process of performing the analysis of variance is facilitated by the notation in Table 14.1.

Table 14.1	Notation for the Single-Factor Analysis of Variance: Independent Samples

INDEPENDENT SAMPLES FROM k POPULATIONS (TREATMENTS)

	TREATMENT		
1	**2**		**k**
x_{11}	x_{12}	$\ldots$	x_{1k}
x_{21}	x_{22}	$\ldots$	x_{2k}
.	.	$\ldots$	.
.	.	$\ldots$	.
.	.	$\ldots$	.
$x_{n_1 1}$	$x_{n_2 2}$	$\ldots$	$x_{n_k k}$

For Each Treatment (Column)				
Sample Size	n_1	n_2	$\ldots$	n_k
Sample Mean	$\bar{x}_1$	$\bar{x}_2$	$\ldots$	$\bar{x}_k$

x_{ij} = ith observation of the jth sample

n_j = number of observations in the sample taken from the jth population

$$\bar{x}_j = \text{mean of the } j\text{th sample} = \frac{\sum_{i=1}^{n_j} x_{ij}}{n_j}$$

$$\bar{\bar{x}} = \text{grand mean of all the observations} = \frac{\sum_{j=1}^{k}\sum_{i=1}^{n_j} x_{ij}}{n}$$

where $n = n_1 + n_2 + \ldots + n_k$ and k is the number of populations. Notice that we allow the sample sizes to be different.

The variable x is called the **response variable**, and its values are called **responses**. The unit that we measure is called an **experimental unit**. In this example, the response variable is weekly sales, and the experimental units are the weeks in the three cities when we record sales figures. The sales figures are the responses.

As you can see, there is only one factor, advertising approach, that defines the populations, and there are three levels of this factor. They are advertising that emphasizes convenience, advertising that emphasizes quality, and advertising that emphasizes price.

The test statistic is computed in accordance with the following rationale. If the null hypothesis is true, the population means would all be equal. We would then expect that the sample means would be close to one another. If the alternative hypothesis is true, however, there would be large differences between some of the sample means. The statistic that measures the proximity of the sample means to each other is called the **between-treatments variation**, denoted SST, which stands for **sum of squares for treatments**.

Sum of Squares for Treatments

$$SST = \sum_{j=1}^{k} n_j (\bar{x}_j - \bar{\bar{x}})^2$$

As you can deduce from this formula, if the sample means are close to each other, all of the sample means would be close to the grand mean, and as a result, SST would be small. In fact, SST achieves its smallest value (zero) when all the sample means are equal. That is, if

$$\bar{x}_1 = \bar{x}_2 = \ldots = \bar{x}_k$$

then

$$SST = 0$$

It follows that a small value of SST supports the null hypothesis.

In this example, we compute the sample means and the grand mean as

$$\bar{x}_1 = 577.55$$

$$\bar{x}_2 = 653.00$$

$$\bar{x}_3 = 608.65$$

$$\bar{\bar{x}} = 613.07$$

Then

$$SST = \sum_{j=1}^{k} n_j (\bar{x}_j - \bar{\bar{x}})^2$$
$$= 20(577.55 - 613.07)^2 + 20(653.00 - 613.07)^2 + 20(608.65 - 613.07)^2$$
$$= 57,512.23$$

If large differences exist among the sample means, at least some sample means differ considerably from the grand mean, producing a large value of SST. It is then reasonable to reject the null hypothesis in favor of the alternative hypothesis. The key question to be answered in this test (as in all other statistical tests) is, "How large does the statistic have to be for us to justify rejecting the null hypothesis?" In our example, SST = 57,512.23. Is this value large enough to indicate that the population means differ? To answer this question, we need to know how much variation exists in the weekly sales, which is measured by the **within-treatments variation**, which is denoted by SSE (**sum of squares for error**). The within-treatments variation provides a measure of the amount of variation we can expect from the random variable we've observed.

> **Sum of Squares for Error**
>
> $$SSE = \sum_{j=1}^{k}\sum_{i=1}^{n_j}(x_{ij} - \bar{x}_j)^2$$

To understand this concept, examine Tables 14.2 and 14.3 and Figures 14.2 and 14.3. Table 14.2 and Figure 14.2 describe an example in which, because the variation within each sample is quite small, SST is judged to be a large number. That is, this random variable displays very little variation. Consequently, the differences among the sample means appear to be caused by real differences among the population means. Contrast this example with the one depicted in Table 14.3. The value of SST in Table 14.3 is equal to that in Table 14.2. However, the variation within the samples is large, which tells us that this random variable features a great deal of variation. By comparison, SST is small, and we would conclude that the differences among the sample means do not allow us to infer that the population means differ.

Table 14.2	Relatively Large Variation between Samples		

	TREATMENT		
1	**2**	**3**
10	15	20
10	16	20
11	14	20
10	16	20
9	14	20
$\bar{x}_1 = 10$	$\bar{x}_2 = 15$	$\bar{x}_3 = 20$

Table 14.3	Relatively Small Variation between Samples		

	TREATMENT		
1	**2**	**3**
1	19	5
12	31	33
20	4	20
10	9	12
7	12	30
$\bar{x}_1 = 10$	$\bar{x}_2 = 15$	$\bar{x}_3 = 20$

Figure 14.2

Figure 14.3

Relatively Large Variation between Samples

Relatively Small Variation between Samples

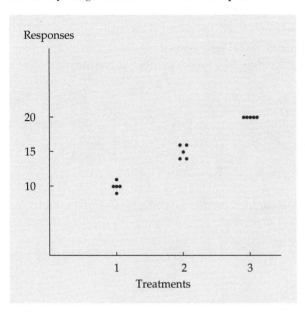

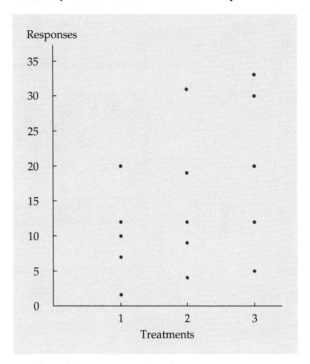

When SSE is partially expanded, we get

$$SSE = \sum_{i=1}^{n_1}(x_{i1} - \bar{x}_1)^2 + \sum_{i=1}^{n_2}(x_{i2} - \bar{x}_2)^2 + \ldots + \sum_{i=1}^{n_k}(x_{ik} - \bar{x}_k)^2$$

If you examine each of the k components of SSE, you'll see that each is a measure of the variability of that sample. If we divide each component by $n_j - 1$, we compute the sample variances. We can express this by rewriting SSE as

$$SSE = (n_1 - 1)s_1^2 + (n_2 - 1)s_2^2 + \ldots + (n_k - 1)s_k^2 = \sum_{j=1}^{k}(n_j - 1)s_j^2$$

where s_j^2 is the sample variance of sample j. SSE is thus the combined or *pooled* variation of the k samples. This is an extension of a calculation we made in Section 12.2, where we tested and estimated the difference between two means using the pooled estimate of the common population variance (denoted s_p^2). One of the required conditions for that statistical technique is that the population variances are equal. That same condition is now necessary for us to use SSE. That is, we require that

$$\sigma_1^2 = \sigma_2^2 = \ldots = \sigma_k^2$$

Returning to our example, we calculate the sample variances as follows.

$s_1^2 = 10,774.44$

$s_2^2 = 7,238.61$

$s_3^2 = 8,669.47$

Thus,

$$SSE = (n_1 - 1)s_1^2 + (n_2 - 1)s_2^2 + (n_3 - 1)s_3^2$$
$$= 19(10,774.44) + 19(7,238.61) + 19(8,669.47)$$
$$= 506,967.88$$

The next step is to compute quantities called the **mean squares**. The **mean square for treatments** is computed by dividing SST by the number of treatments minus 1.

Mean Square for Treatments

$$MST = \frac{SST}{k - 1}$$

The **mean square for error** is determined by dividing SSE by the total sample size (labeled n) minus the number of treatments.

Mean Square for Error

$$MSE = \frac{SSE}{n - k}$$

Finally, the test statistic is defined as the ratio of the two mean squares.

Test Statistic

$$F = \frac{MST}{MSE}$$

SAMPLING DISTRIBUTION OF THE TEST STATISTIC

The test statistic is F-distributed with $k - 1$ and $n - k$ degrees of freedom provided that the response variable is normally distributed. In Section 12.5, we introduced the F distribution and used it to test and estimate the ratio of two population variances. (If you did not cover Section 12.5 [or if you did, but need a review] turn to pages 464 to 467 for an introduction to the F distribution.) The test statistic in that application was the ratio of two sample variances s_1^2 and s_2^2.

If you examine the definitions of SST and SSE, you will see that both measure variation similar to the numerator in the formula used to calculate the sample variance s^2 used throughout this book. When we divide SST by $k - 1$ and SSE by $n - k$ to calculate MST and MSE, respectively, we're actually computing variance estimators. Thus, the ratio $F = MST/MSE$ is the ratio of two sample variances. The degrees of freedom for this application are the denominators in the mean squares. That is, $\nu_1 = k - 1$, and $\nu_2 = n - k$. For Example 14.1, the degrees of freedom are

$$\nu_1 = k - 1 = 3 - 1 = 2$$

and

$$\nu_2 = n - k = 60 - 3 = 57$$

In our example, we found

$$MST = \frac{SST}{k-1} = \frac{57,512.23}{2} = 28,756.12$$

$$MSE = \frac{SSE}{n-k} = \frac{506,967.88}{57} = 8,894.17$$

$$F = \frac{MST}{MSE} = \frac{28,756.12}{8,894.17} = 3.23$$

The purpose of calculating the F-statistic is to determine whether or not the value of SST is large enough to reject the null hypothesis. As you can see, if SST is large, F will be large. Hence, we reject the null hypothesis only if

$$F > F_{\alpha,k-1,n-k}$$

If we let $\alpha = .05$, the rejection region for Example 14.1 is

$$F > F_{\alpha,k-1,n-k} = F_{.05,2,57} \approx 3.15$$

(Because the table does not show the critical value when the denominator degrees of freedom equal 57, we use the closest value, which is 60.) Figure 14.4 depicts the F distribution and the rejection region.

Figure 14.4

F Distribution and Rejection Region

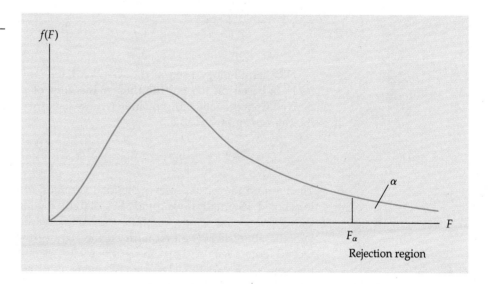

We found the value of the test statistic to be $F = 3.23$. Thus, we conclude that there is enough evidence to infer that the mean weekly sales differ among the three cities.

The results of the analysis of variance are usually reported in an analysis of variance (ANOVA) table. Table 14.4 shows the general organization of the ANOVA table, while Table 14.5 shows the ANOVA table for Example 14.1.

Table 14.4 — ANOVA Table for the Single-Factor Analysis of Variance: Independent Samples

SOURCE OF VARIATION	DEGREES OF FREEDOM	SUMS OF SQUARES	MEAN SQUARES	F-STATISTIC
Treatments	$k - 1$	SST	$MST = \dfrac{SST}{(k-1)}$	$F = \dfrac{MST}{MSE}$
Error	$n - k$	SSE	$MSE = \dfrac{SSE}{(n-k)}$	
TOTAL	$n - 1$	SS(Total)		

Table 14.5 — ANOVA Table for Example 14.1

SOURCE OF VARIATION	DEGREES OF FREEDOM	SUMS OF SQUARES	MEAN SQUARES	F-STATISTIC
Treatments	2	57,512.23	28,756.12	$F = 3.23$
Error	57	506,967.88	8,894.17	
TOTAL	59	564,480.11		

The terminology used in the ANOVA table (and, for that matter, in the test itself) is based on the **partitioning of the sum of squares**. Such partitioning is derived from the following equation (whose validity can be demonstrated by using the rules of summation).

$$\sum_{j=1}^{k}\sum_{i=1}^{n_j}(x_{ij} - \bar{\bar{x}})^2 = \sum_{j=1}^{k} n_j(\bar{x}_j - \bar{\bar{x}})^2 + \sum_{j=1}^{k}\sum_{i=1}^{n_j}(x_{ij} - \bar{x}_j)^2$$

The term on the left represents the total variation of all the data. This expression is denoted **SS(Total)**. If we divide SS(Total) by the total sample size minus 1 (that is, by $n - 1$), we would compute the sample variance (assuming that the null hypothesis is true). The first term on the right of the equal sign is SST, and the second term is SSE. As you can see, the total variation SS(Total) is partitioned into two sources of variation. The sum of squares for treatments (SST) is the variation attributed to the differences among the treatment means, while the sum of squares for error (SSE) measures the amount of variation within the samples. The preceding equation can be restated as

SS(Total) = SST + SSE

The test is then based on the comparison of SST and SSE.

Recall that in discussing the advantages and disadvantages of the matched pairs experiment in Section 12.4, we pointed out that statisticians frequently seek ways to reduce or explain the variation in a random variable. In the analysis of variance introduced in this section, the sum of squares for treatments explains some of the variation. The sum of squares for error measures the amount of variation that is unexplained. If SST explains a significant portion of total variation, we conclude that the population means differ. In Section 14.4, we will introduce another experimental design of the analysis of variance, one that attempts to reduce or explain even more of the variation.

If you've felt some appreciation for the computer and statistical software sparing you from the need to manually perform the statistical techniques in earlier chapters, your appreciation should now grow, because the computer will allow you to avoid the incredibly time-consuming and boring task of performing the analysis of variance by hand. As usual, we've solved Example 14.1 using Minitab and Excel, whose outputs are shown below.

USING THE COMPUTER

Minitab Output for Example 14.1

One-Way Analysis of Variance

```
Analysis of Variance
Source      DF        SS        MS        F        p
Factor       2     57512     28756     3.23    0.047
Error       57    506984      8894
Total       59    564496

                                    Individual 95% CIs For Mean
                                    Based on Pooled StDev
 Level      N      Mean    StDev   ---+---------+---------+---------+---
Convnce     20    577.55   103.80  (--------*-------)
Quality     20    653.00    85.08                    (--------*-------)
Price       20    608.65    93.11        (--------*-------)
                                    ---+---------+---------+---------+---
Pooled StDev =   94.31            550       600       650       700
```

The first half of the printout gives us the ANOVA table, including the p-value, which is equal to .047. The second half lists the sample sizes, sample means, and sample standard deviations. It also graphically depicts the confidence interval estimates of the population means, using a technique not covered in this book. The graphs provide some information about whether the means differ, and if so, how. You can see that the interval of the second mean is almost completely to the right of the interval representing the first mean. This confirms what the test statistic told us. That is, that there is evidence to infer that the population means differ. (Appendix 14.A lists the session commands.)

MENU COMMANDS

1 Type or import the data.

If the data are unstacked,

  2 Click **Stat, ANOVA,** and **Oneway (Unstacked)** . . . .

  3 Type the variable names of the treatments. Click **OK**.

If the data are stacked,

  2 Click **Stat, ANOVA,** and **Oneway** . . . .

  3 Type the variable name of the response variable and the variable name of the factor. Click **OK**.

COMMANDS FOR EXAMPLE 14.1

Open file **XM14-01**.

Convnce, Quality, and **Price** or **C1**, **C2**, and **C3**.

Excel Output for Example 14.1

	A	B	C	D	E	F	G
1	Anova: Single Factor						
2							
3	SUMMARY						
4	Groups	Count	Sum	Average	Variance		
5	Convnce	20	11551	577.55	10774.99737		
6	Quality	20	13060	653	7238.105263		
7	Price	20	12173	608.65	8670.239474		
8							
9							
10	ANOVA						
11	Source of Variation	SS	df	MS	F	P-value	F crit
12	Between Groups	57512.23333	2	28756.11667	3.233041411	0.046772987	3.15884563
13	Within Groups	506983.5	57	8894.447368			
14							
15	Total	564495.7333	59				

Excel prints the sizes, sums of observations, means, and variances for each sample. It also outputs the analysis of variance table from which we learn that the value of the test statistic is $F = 3.233041411$, and its p-value is .046772987.

COMMANDS   **COMMANDS FOR EXAMPLE 14.1**

1 Type or import the data. They   Open file **XM14-01**.
  must be in unstacked form. That
  is, the observations in each sample
  must occupy a different column.
  The columns must be adjacent.

2 Click **Tools, Data Analysis . . . ,**
  and **Anova: Single Factor.**

3 Type the input range. Click **Labels**   **A1:C21**
  in First Row (if necessary).

4 Specify **Grouped by Columns**.
  Click **OK**.

INTERPRETING THE RESULTS

The p-value is .047, which means there is evidence to infer that mean weekly sales of the apple juice concentrate are different in at least two of the cities. Can we conclude that the effect of the advertising approaches differ? Recall that it is easier to answer this type of question when the data are obtained through a controlled experiment. In this example, the marketing manager randomly assigned an advertising approach to each city. Thus, the data are experimental. As a result, we are quite confident that the approach used to advertise the product will produce different sales figures.

Figure 14.5 depicts the sampling distribution of the test statistic.

Incidentally, when the data are obtained through a controlled experiment in the single-factor analysis of variance, we call the experimental design the **completely randomized design of the analysis of variance**.

Figure 14.5

Sampling Distribution for Example 14.1

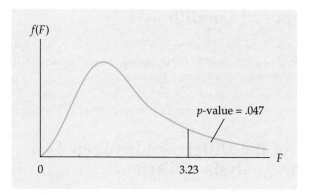

Checking the Required Conditions

The *F*-test of the analysis of variance requires that the random variable is normally distributed and that the population variances are equal. The normality requirement is easily checked by producing the histograms for each sample. From the Minitab histograms below (Figures 14.6, 14.7, and 14.8), we can see that there is no reason to believe that the requirement is not satisfied. The equality of variances requirement is examined by printing the sample standard deviations or variances. Minitab output includes the standard deviations while Excel calculates the variances. The similarity of sample variances allows us to assume that the population variances are equal.

Figure 14.6

Histogram of Weekly Sales in City 1

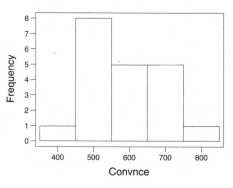

Figure 14.7

Histogram of Weekly Sales in City 2

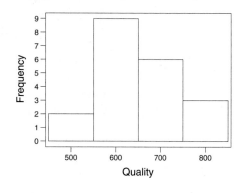

Figure 14.8

Histogram of Weekly Sales in City 3

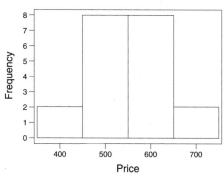

Violation of the Required Conditions

If the data are not normally distributed, we can replace the independent samples single-factor model of the analysis of variance with its nonparametric counterpart, which is the Kruskal–Wallis test. (See Appendix 14.B) If the population variances are unequal, we can use several methods to correct the problem. However, these corrective measures are beyond the level of this book.

Can We Use *t*-Tests of the Difference between Two Means Instead of the Analysis of Variance?

The analysis of variance tests to determine whether there are differences among two or more population means. The *t*-test of $\mu_1 - \mu_2$ determines whether there is a difference between two population means. The question arises: can we use *t*-tests instead of the analysis of variance? That is, instead of testing all the means in one test as in the analysis of variance, why not test each pair of means? In Example 14.1, we would test $\mu_1 - \mu_2$, $\mu_1 - \mu_3$, and $\mu_2 - \mu_3$. If we found no evidence of a difference in each test, we would conclude that none of the means differ. If there was evidence of a difference in at least one test, we would conclude that some of the means differ.

There are two reasons why we don't use multiple *t*-tests instead of one *F*-test. First, we would have to perform many more calculations. Even with a computer, this extra work is tedious. Second, and more importantly, conducting multiple tests increases the probability of making Type I errors. To understand why, consider a problem where we want to compare six populations, all of which are identical. If we conduct an analysis of variance where we set the significance level at 5%, there is a 5% chance that we would reject the true null hypothesis. That is, there is a 5% chance that we would conclude that differences exist when in fact they don't.

To replace the *F*-test, we would perform 15 *t*-tests. (This number is derived from the number of combinations of pairs of means to test, which is $C_2^6 = 6 \times \frac{5}{2}$ = 15.) These are tests of $\mu_1 - \mu_2$, $\mu_1 - \mu_3$, $\mu_1 - \mu_4, \ldots, \mu_5 - \mu_6$. Each test would have a 5% probability of erroneously rejecting the null hypothesis. The probability of committing one or more Type I errors is about 54%.*

One remedy for this problem is to decrease the significance level. In this illustration, we would perform the *t*-tests with $\alpha = .05/15$, which is equal to .0033. Unfortunately, this would increase the probability of a Type II error. No matter the significance level, performing multiple *t*-tests increases the likelihood of making mistakes. Consequently, when we want to compare more than two populations of quantitative data, we use the analysis of variance.

Now that we've argued that the *t*-tests cannot replace the analysis of variance, we need to argue that the analysis of variance cannot replace the *t*-test.

---

*The probability of committing at least one Type I error is computed from a binomial distribution with $n = 15$ and $p = .05$. Thus

$$P(X \geq 1) = 1 - P(X = 0) = 1 - .463 = .537$$

Can We Use the Analysis of Variance Instead of the *t*-Test of $\mu_1 - \mu_2$?

The analysis of variance is the first of several techniques that allow us to compare two or more populations. Most of the examples and exercises deal with more than two populations. However, it should be noted that like all other techniques whose objective is to compare two or more populations, we can use the analysis of variance to compare only two populations. If that's the case, why do we need techniques to compare exactly two populations? Specifically, why do we need the *t*-test of $\mu_1 - \mu_2$ when the analysis of variance can be used to test two population means?

To understand why we still need the *t*-test to make inferences about $\mu_1 - \mu_2$, suppose that we plan to use the analysis of variance to test two population means. The null and alternative hypotheses are

H_0: $\mu_1 = \mu_2$
H_A: At least two means differ.

Of course, the alternative hypothesis specifies that $\mu_1 \neq \mu_2$. However, if we want to determine whether μ_1 is greater than μ_2 (or *vice versa*), we cannot use the analysis of variance since this technique only allows us to test for a difference. Thus, if we want to test to determine if one population mean exceeds the other, we must use the *t*-test of $\mu_1 - \mu_2$ (with $\sigma_1^2 = \sigma_2^2$). Moreover, the analysis of variance requires that the population variances are equal. If they are not, we must use the unequal variances test statistic.

Relationship between the *F*-Statistic and the *t*-Statistic (Optional)

It is probably useful for you to understand the relationship between the *t*-statistic and the *F*-statistic. The test statistic for testing hypotheses about $\mu_1 - \mu_2$ with equal variances is

$$t = \frac{(\bar{x}_1 - \bar{x}_2) - (\mu_1 - \mu_2)}{\sqrt{s_p^2 \left(\frac{1}{n_1} + \frac{1}{n_2} \right)}}$$

If we square this quantity, the result is the *F*-statistic. That is, $F = t^2$. To illustrate this point, we'll redo Example 12.2 using the analysis of variance. If you reexamine Example 12.2, you'll see that the null and alternative hypotheses were

H_0: $\mu_1 = \mu_2$
H_A: $\mu_1 \neq \mu_2$

Because we were able to assume that the population variances were equal, the test statistic was as follows.

$$t = \frac{(\bar{x}_1 - \bar{x}_2) - (\mu_1 - \mu_2)}{\sqrt{s_p^2 \left(\frac{1}{n_1} + \frac{1}{n_2} \right)}}$$

The value of the test statistic was $t = .93$ with a *p*-value of .36. Using the analysis of variance (the Minitab output is shown below; Excel's is similar), we find that the value of the test statistic is $F = .86$, which is $(.93)^2$, and that the *p*-value is .358.

Thus, we draw exactly the same conclusion using the analysis of variance as we did when we applied the t-test of $\mu_1 - \mu_2$.

Minitab Analysis of Variance for Example 12.2

One-Way Analysis of Variance

```
Analysis of Variance
Source    DF      SS      MS       F        p
Factor     1    0.92    0.92     0.86    0.358
Error     48   51.62    1.08
Total     49   52.54
                                Individual 95% CIs For Mean
                                Based on Pooled StDev
 Level    N    Mean    StDev  ----+---------+---------+---------+--
Design-A  25   6.288   0.921            (-------------*-------------)
Design-B  25   6.016   1.142  (-------------*------------)
                              ----+---------+---------+---------+--
Pooled StDev = 1.037          5.70      6.00      6.30      6.60
```

Developing an Understanding of Statistical Concepts

Conceptually and mathematically, the F-test of the independent samples single-factor analysis of variance is an extension of the t-test of $\mu_1 - \mu_2$. Moreover, as we discussed above, if we simply want to determine if a difference between two means exists, we can use the analysis of variance. The advantage of using the analysis of variance is that we can partition the total sum of squares, which enables us to measure how much variation is attributable to differences *among* populations and how much variation is attributable to differences *within* populations. As we pointed out in Section 12.4, explaining the variation is an extremely important topic, one that will be seen again in another model of the analysis of variance and in regression analysis (Chapters 16 and 17).

Let's review how we recognize the need to use this model of the analysis of variance.

Factors that Identify the Independent Samples Single-Factor Analysis of Variance

1 Problem objective: compare two or more populations

2 Data type: quantitative

3 Experimental design: independent samples

4 Population distributions: normal

Exercises

14.1 Provide an example with $k = 4$ where SST = 0.

14.2 Provide an example with $k = 4$ where SSE = 0.

14.3 The completely randomized design of the analysis of variance experiment produced the statistics below. Determine the ANOVA table.

STATISTIC	TREATMENT			
	1	2	3	4
n	16	16	16	16
$\bar{x}$	158.6	149.2	151.3	157.6
s^2	95.3	102.1	96.8	99.1

14.4 Using the following statistics, test to determine whether differences exist among the population means. (Use $\alpha = .01$.)

$n_1 = 49$ $\quad$ $n_2 = 45$ $\quad$ $n_3 = 29$

$\bar{x}_1 = 8.36$ $\quad$ $\bar{x}_2 = 7.91$ $\quad$ $\bar{x}_3 = 9.02$

$s_1 = 2.98$ $\quad$ $s_2 = 3.15$ $\quad$ $s_3 = 3.62$

14.5 Random samples of 25 were taken from each of three populations. The data are stored in columns 1 to 3, respectively, in file XR14-05. Some of these data are listed below.

a Can we conclude at the 5% significance level that there are differences among the population means?

b What are the required conditions for the test applied in part (a)?

c Use whatever techniques you deem necessary to check the required conditions.

Sample 1: 24, 23, 29, . . ., 24
Sample 2: 32, 8, 20, . . ., 35
Sample 3: 18, 16, 23, . . ., 23

Use a software package to solve this problem.	OR	The sample means and standard deviations were computed as follows. Sample 1: $\bar{x}_1 = 19.64$; $s_1 = 6.80$ Sample 2: $\bar{x}_2 = 23.32$; $s_2 = 6.44$ Sample 3: $\bar{x}_3 = 19.40$; $s_3 = 5.99$ Complete your answer manually.

14.6 The data in file XR14-06 were generated by drawing random samples from five populations. (Columns 1 through 5 are used.) Some of these data appear below.

a Is there sufficient evidence at the 5% significance level to infer that differences exist among the population means?

b What are the required conditions for the test in part (a)?

c Are the required conditions satisfied?

Sample 1: 48, 44, 60, . . ., 52
Sample 2: 80, 32, 59, . . ., 62
Sample 3: 33, 38, 58, . . ., 1
Sample 4: 48, 25, 83, . . ., 66
Sample 5: 38, 45, 37, . . ., 52

14.7 Because there are no national or regional standards, it is difficult for university admission committees to compare graduates of different high schools. University administrators have noted that an 80% average at a high school with low standards may be equivalent to a 70% average at another school with higher standards of grading. In an effort to more equitably compare applications, a pilot study was initiated. Random samples of students who were admitted the previous year were drawn. All of the students entered the business program with averages between 74% and 76% from a random sample of four local high schools. Their average grades in the first year at the university were computed and stored in columns 1 through 4 of file XR14-07. Some of the grades are listed below.

a Can the university admissions officer conclude at the 5% significance level that there are differences in grading standards among the four high schools?

b What are the required conditions for the test conducted in part (a)?

c Does it appear that the required conditions of the test in part (a) are satisfied?

HIGH SCHOOL A	HIGH SCHOOL B	HIGH SCHOOL C	HIGH SCHOOL D
81.5	64.6	56.5	53.1
61.8	67.0	61.7	64.8
61.0	61.1	53.3	65.3
.	.	.	.
.	.	.	.
.	.	.	.
61.8	55.6	58.5	62.6

14.8 The friendly folks at the Internal Revenue Service (IRS) are always looking for ways to improve the wording and format of its tax return forms. Three new forms have been developed recently. To determine which, if any, are superior to the current form, 120 individuals were asked to participate in an experiment. Each of the three new forms and the currently used form were filled out by 30 different people. The amount of time (in minutes) taken by each person to complete the task was recorded and stored in columns 1 through 4 (forms 1 through 4, respectively) in file XR14-08.

a What conclusions can be drawn from these data? (Use $\alpha = .05$.)

b What are the required conditions for the test conducted in part (a)?

c Does it appear that the required conditions of the test in part (a) are satisfied?

FORM 1	FORM 2	FORM 3	FORM 4
23	88	116	103
59	114	123	122
68	81	64	105
.	.	.	.
.	.	.	.
.	.	.	.
56	104	61	161

Use a software package to solve this problem.	OR	The sample means and standard deviations were computed as follows. Form 1: $\bar{x}_1 = 90.17$; $s_1 = 31.49$ Form 2: $\bar{x}_2 = 95.77$; $s_2 = 30.01$ Form 3: $\bar{x}_3 = 106.83$; $s_3 = 30.47$ Form 4: $\bar{x}_4 = 111.17$; $s_4 = 31.99$ Complete your answer manually.

14.9 A manufacturer of outdoor brass lamps and mailboxes has received numerous complaints about premature corrosion. The manufacturer has identified the cause of the problem as being the low-quality lacquer used to coat the brass. He decides to replace his current lacquer supplier with one of five possible alternatives. In order to judge which is best, he uses each of the five lacquers to coat 25 brass mailboxes and puts all 125 mailboxes outside. He records, for each, the number of days until the first sign of corrosion is observed. The results are stored in columns 1 through 5 of file XR14-09, with some of the observations listed below.

a Is there sufficient evidence at the 5% significance level to allow the manufacturer to conclude that differences exist among the five lacquers?

b What are the required conditions for the test conducted in part (a)?

c Does it appear that the required conditions of the test in part (a) are satisfied?

LACQUER 1	LACQUER 2	LACQUER 3	LACQUER 4	LACQUER 5
133	173	161	160	154
171	182	115	221	180
142	214	137	208	222
.	.	.	.	.
.	.	.	.	.
.	.	.	.	.
165	185	185	138	181

Use a software package to solve this problem.	OR	The sample means and standard deviations were computed as follows. Lacquer 1: $\bar{x}_1 = 162.40$; $s_1 = 34.87$ Lacquer 2: $\bar{x}_2 = 185.64$; $s_2 = 41.47$ Lacquer 3: $\bar{x}_3 = 155.80$; $s_3 = 34.13$ Lacquer 4: $\bar{x}_4 = 182.60$; $s_4 = 40.72$ Lacquer 5: $\bar{x}_5 = 178.80$; $s_5 = 34.00$ Complete your answer manually.

14.10 A study performed by a Columbia University professor (described in *Report on Business*, August 1991) counted the number of times per minute professors from three different departments said "uh" or "ah" during lectures to fill gaps between words. The data derived from observing 100 minutes from each of the three departments are stored in file XR14-10 of the data disk. (Column 1 contains all the data for the English department, column 2 stores the data for the mathematics department, and column 3 stores the data for the political science department.) A partial listing of the data appears below. If we assume that the more frequent use of "uh" and "ah" results in more boring lectures, can we conclude at the 5% significance level that some departments' professors are more boring than others?

ENGLISH	MATHEMATICS	POLITICAL SCIENCE
4	1	5
9	8	4
8	4	9
.	.	.
.	.	.
.	.	.
2	5	8

Use a software package to solve this problem.	OR	The sample means and standard deviations were computed as follows. English department: $\bar{x}_1 = 5.81$; $s_1 = 2.49$ Mathematics department: $\bar{x}_2 = 5.30$; $s_2 = 2.01$ Political science department: $\bar{x}_3 = 5.33$; $s_3 = 1.98$ Complete your answer manually.

14.11 (A computer and a software package are required to solve this problem.) In 1994 the chief executive officers of the major tobacco companies testified before a Senate subcommittee. One of the accusations made was that tobacco firms added nicotine to their cigarettes, which made them even more addictive to smokers. Company scientists argued that the amount of nicotine in cigarettes depended completely on the size of the tobacco leaf. That is, during poor growing seasons the tobacco leaves would be smaller than in normal or good growing seasons. However, since the amount of nicotine in a leaf is a fixed quantity, smaller leaves would result in cigarettes having more nicotine (since a greater fraction of the leaf would be used to make a cigarette). To examine the issue, a university chemist took random samples of tobacco leaves that were grown in greenhouses where the amount of water was allowed to vary. Three different groups of tobacco leaves were grown. Group 1 leaves were grown with about an average season's rainfall. Group 2 leaves were given about 67% of group 1's water, and group 3 leaves were given 33% of group 1's water. The size of the leaf (in grams) and the amount of nicotine in each leaf were measured and stored in file XR14-11. Column 1 contains the leaf size, column 2 contains the amount of nicotine (in milligrams), and column 3 stores the group number. Some of these data are listed below. What conclusions can you draw from these data?

LEAF SIZE	NICOTINE CONTENT	GROUP
15.43	13.34	1
37.34	12.26	1
25.98	6.26	1
.	.	.
.	.	.
.	.	.
19.78	11.20	3

14.3 Analysis of Variance Models

Since we introduced the matched pairs experiment in Section 12.4, the experimental design has been one of the factors that determines which technique we use. As we pointed out in that section, statisticians often design experiments to help extract the information they need to assist them in making decisions. The independent samples single-factor analysis of variance is only one of many different experimental designs of the analysis of variance. For each design, we can describe the behavior of the response variable using a mathematical expression or model. Although we will not exhibit the mathematical expressions (we introduce models in Chapter 16) in this chapter, we think it is useful for you to be aware of the elements that distinguish one model or experimental design from another. In this section, we present some of these elements, and, in so doing, we introduce two of the models that will be presented later in this chapter.

Single-Factor and Multifactor Models

As we pointed out, the group of treatments or populations is called a factor. The model described in Section 14.2 is a single-factor analysis of variance, because it addresses the problem of comparing two or more populations defined on the basis of only one factor. A **multifactor** model is one where there are two or more factors that define the treatments. The technique employed to address Example 14.1 is a single-factor model because the treatments were the three advertising approaches. That is, the factor is the advertising approach, and the three levels are advertising that emphasizes convenience, advertising that emphasizes quality, and advertising that emphasizes price.

Suppose that in another study, the medium used to advertise also varied: we can advertise on television or in newspapers. We would then develop a **two-factor** analysis of variance model where the first factor, advertising approach, has three levels and the second factor, advertising medium, has two levels. We will not present any multifactor models in this edition of the book.

Independent Samples and Blocks

In Section 12.4 and Appendix 12.C, we introduced statistical techniques where the data were gathered from a matched pairs experiment. As we pointed out in Section 12.4, this type of experimental design reduces the variation within the samples, making it easier to detect differences between the two populations. When the problem objective is to compare more than two populations, the experimental design that is the counterpart of the matched pairs experiment is called the **randomized block design**. The term *block* refers to a matched group of observations from each population. Here is an example.

To determine whether incentive pay plans are effective, a statistician selected three groups of five workers who assemble electronic equipment. Each group will be offered a different incentive plan. The treatments are the incentive plans, the response variable is the number of units produced in one day, and the experimental units are the workers. If we obtain data from independent samples, we may not be able to detect differences among the pay plans because of variation among workers. If there are differences among workers, we need to identify the source of the differences. Suppose, for example, that we know that more experienced workers produce more units no matter what the pay plan. We could improve the experiment if we were to block the workers into five groups of three according to their experience. The three workers with the most experience will represent block 1, the next three will constitute block 2, and so on. As a result, the workers in each block will have approximately the same amount of experience. By designing the experiment in this way, the statistician removes the effect of different amounts of experience on the response variable. By doing so, we improve the chances of detecting real differences among pay incentives.

We can also perform a blocked experiment by using the same subject (person, plant, store) for each treatment. For example, we can determine whether sleeping pills are effective by giving three brands of pills to the same group of people to measure the effects. Such applications are called **repeated measures** design. Technically, this is a different design than the randomized block. However, the single-factor model is analyzed in the same way for both designs. Hence, we will treat repeated measures designs as randomized block designs.

In Section 14.4, we introduce the technique used to calculate the test statistic for this type of experiment.

Fixed- and Random-Effects Models

If our analysis includes *all* possible levels of a factor, the technique is called a **fixed-effects** model of the analysis of variance. If the levels included in the study represent a random sample of all the levels that exist, the technique is called a **random-effects** model. In Example 14.1, there were only three possible advertising approaches. Consequently, the study is a fixed-effects experiment. However, if there were other advertising approaches besides the three described in the example, and we wanted to know whether there were differences in sales among all the advertising approaches, the application would be a random-effects model. Here's another example.

To determine if there is a difference in the number of units produced by the machines in a large factory, four machines out of 50 in the plant are randomly selected for study. The number of units each produces per day for 10 days will be recorded. This experiment is a random-effects experiment because the statistical results will allow us to determine whether there are differences among the 50 machines.

In some models, there are no differences in calculations of the test statistic between fixed and random effects. However, in others, including the two-factor model, the calculations are different.

14.4 Single-Factor Analysis of Variance: Randomized Blocks

The purpose of designing a randomized block experiment is to reduce the within-treatments variation to more easily detect differences among the treatment means. In the independent samples single-factor analysis of variance, we partitioned the total variation into the between-treatments and the within-treatments variation. That is

SS(Total) = SST + SSE

In the randomized block design of the analysis of variance, we partition the total variation into three sources of variation.

SS(Total) = SST + SSB + SSE

where **SSB**, the **sum of squares for blocks**, measures the variation among the blocks. When the variation associated with the blocks is removed, SSE is reduced, making it easier to determine if differences exist among the treatment means.

At this point in our presentation of statistical inference, we will deviate from our usual procedure of solving examples in three ways: manually, using Minitab, and using Excel. The calculations for this model and for the model presented in the next section are so time-consuming that solving them by hand is pointless. Consequently, while we will continue to present the concepts by discussing how the statistics are calculated, we will solve the problems only by computer.

To help you understand the formulas, we will use the following notation.

$\bar{x}[T]_j$ = mean of the observations in the jth treatment

$\bar{x}[B]_i$ = mean of the observations in the ith block

b = number of blocks

Table 14.6 summarizes the notation we use in this model.

Table 14.6	Notation for the Randomized Block Design of the Analysis of Variance				
	BLOCKED SAMPLES FROM k POPULATIONS (TREATMENTS)				
	TREATMENT				
BLOCK	1	2		k	BLOCK MEAN
1	x_{11}	x_{12}	...	x_{1k}	$\bar{x}[B]_1$
2	x_{21}	x_{22}	...	x_{2k}	$\bar{x}[B]_2$
.	.	.	...	.	
.	.	.	...	.	
.	.	.	...	.	
b	x_{b1}	x_{b2}	...	x_{bk}	$\bar{x}[B]_b$
Treatment mean	$\bar{x}[T]_1$	$\bar{x}[T]_2$	...	$\bar{x}[T]_k$	

The definitions of SS(Total) and SST in the randomized block design are identical to those in the independent samples design. SSE in the independent samples design is equal to the sum of SSB and SSE in the randomized block design.

Sums of Squares in the Randomized Block Design

$$\text{SS(Total)} = \sum_{j=1}^{k}\sum_{i=1}^{b}(x_{ij} - \bar{\bar{x}})^2$$

$$\text{SST} = \sum_{j=1}^{k}b(\bar{x}[T]_j - \bar{\bar{x}})^2$$

$$\text{SSB} = \sum_{i=1}^{b}k(\bar{x}[B]_i - \bar{\bar{x}})^2$$

$$\text{SSE} = \sum_{j=1}^{k}\sum_{i=1}^{b}(x_{ij} - \bar{x}[T]_j - \bar{x}[B]_i + \bar{\bar{x}})^2$$

The total sum of squares is partitioned.

$$\text{SS(Total)} = \text{SST} + \text{SSB} + \text{SSE}$$

The test is conducted by determining the mean squares.

> **Mean Squares for the Randomized Block Design**
>
> $$MST = \frac{SST}{k - 1}$$
>
> $$MSB = \frac{SSB}{b - 1}$$
>
> $$MSE = \frac{SSE}{n - k - b + 1}$$

Finally, the test statistic is

> **Test Statistic for the Randomized Block Design**
>
> $$F = \frac{MST}{MSE}$$

which is F-distributed with $k - 1$ and $n - k - b + 1$ degrees of freedom.

An interesting, and sometimes useful, by-product of the test of the treatment means is that we can also test to determine if the block means differ. This will allow us to determine whether the experiment *should* have been conducted as a randomized block design. (If there are no differences among the blocks, the randomized block design is *less* likely to detect real differences among the treatment means.) Such a discovery could be useful in future similar experiments. The test of the block means is almost identical to that of the treatment means except the test statistic is

$$F = \frac{MSB}{MSE}$$

which is F-distributed with $b - 1$ and $n - k - b + 1$ degrees of freedom.

Like the independent samples design, the statistics generated in the randomized block design are summarized in an ANOVA table, whose general form is exhibited in Table 14.7.

Table 14.7	ANOVA Table for the Randomized Block Design			
SOURCE OF VARIATION	**DEGREES OF FREEDOM**	**SUMS OF SQUARES**	**MEAN SQUARES**	***F*-STATISTICS**
Treatments	$k - 1$	SST	$MST = \dfrac{SST}{(k - 1)}$	$F = \dfrac{MST}{MSE}$
Blocks	$b - 1$	SSB	$MSB = \dfrac{SSB}{(b - 1)}$	$F = \dfrac{MSB}{MSE}$
Error	$n - k - b + 1$	SSE	$MSE = \dfrac{SSE}{(n - k - b + 1)}$	
TOTAL	$n - 1$	SS(Total)		

EXAMPLE 14.2

The advertising revenues commanded by a radio station depend on the number of listeners it has. The manager of a station that plays mostly hard rock music wants to learn more about its listeners—mostly teenagers and young adults. In particular, he wants to know if the amount of time they spend listening to radio music varies by the day of the week. If the manager discovers that the mean time per day is about the same, he will schedule the most popular music evenly throughout the week. Otherwise, the top hits will be played mostly on the days that attract the greatest audience. An opinion survey company is hired, and it randomly selects 200 teenagers and asks them to record the amount of time spent listening to music on the radio for each day of the previous week. The data are stored in file XM14-02U (unstacked data—column 1 contains the teenagers' identification codes and columns 2 through 8 store the listening times for Sunday through Saturday), and in file XM14-02S (stacked data—column 1 contains the times, column 2 stores the codes for the days, and column 3 stores the codes for teenagers 1 to 200). Some of the data are shown below. What can the manager conclude from these data?

	TIME SPENT LISTENING TO RADIO MUSIC (IN MINUTES)						
TEENAGER	SUNDAY	MONDAY	TUESDAY	WEDNESDAY	THURSDAY	FRIDAY	SATURDAY
1	65	40	32	48	60	75	110
2	90	85	75	90	78	120	100
3	30	30	20	25	30	60	70
.	.	.	.	.	.	.	.
.	.	.	.	.	.	.	.
.	.	.	.	.	.	.	.
200	80	95	90	80	80	120	120

SOLUTION

IDENTIFYING THE
TECHNIQUE

The problem objective is to compare seven populations, and the data are quantitative. Because the survey company recorded the listening times for each day of the week for each teenager, we identify the experimental design as randomized block. The response variable is the amount of time listening to FM radio, the treatments are the days of the week, and the blocks are the 200 teenagers. The complete test is as follows.

H_0: $\mu_1 = \mu_2 = \ldots = \mu_7$

H_A: At least two means differ.

Test statistic: $F = \dfrac{\text{MST}}{\text{MSE}}$

Minitab Output for Example 14.2

```
Analysis of Variance for Times

Source      DF          SS          MS       F       P
Day          6      28673.7      4779.0   11.91   0.000
Teenager   199     209834.6      1054.4    2.63   0.000
Error     1194     479125.1       401.3
Total     1399     717633.5
```

The value of the F-statistic to determine if differences exist among days of the weeks is 11.91. Its p-value is .000. Notice that the results indicate that differences among the teenagers also exist. The value of that F-statistic is $F = 2.63$ with a p-value of .000. (Appendix 14.A features the session commands used to apply the analysis of variance for this model.)

MENU COMMANDS	COMMANDS FOR EXAMPLE 14.2
1 Type or import the data. The data must be in stacked form with column 1 containing the responses, column 2 containing the treatment levels, and column 3 containing the block levels.	Open file **XM14-02S**.
2 Click **Stat**, **ANOVA**, and **Balanced ANOVA**	
3 Type the name of the response variable.	**Times** or **C1**
4 Hit **tab** and type the variable names that constitute the model. That is, the variable name of the treatments and the variable name of the blocks. Click **OK**.	**Day Teenager** or **C2 C3**

Excel Output for Example 14.2

	A	B	C	D	E	F	G
1	Anova: Two-Factor Without Replication						
2	Source of Variation	SS	df	MS	F	P-value	F crit
3	Rows	209834.6	199	1054.445	2.627722	1.04E-23	1.187531
4	Columns	28673.73	6	4778.955	11.90936	5.14E-13	2.106162
5	Error	479125.1	1194	401.2773			
6							
7	Total	717633.5	1399				

The output includes block statistics and column statistics (not shown), and the ANOVA table. The value of the F-statistic to determine if differences exist among days of the weeks (columns) is 11.90936. Its p-value is 0 (5.14E$-$13 is very close to zero). Notice that the results indicate that differences among the teenagers (rows) also exist. The value of that F-statistic is $F = 2.627722$ with a p-value of 0.

INTERPRETING THE RESULTS

There is very strong evidence to infer that on certain days the mean listening time is greater than on other days. An examination of the results reveals that on Fridays and Saturdays, teenagers usually spend more time listening to radio music. The top hits should be played more frequently on those days.

The sampling distribution of $F = MST/MSE$ is shown in Figure 14.9.

Figure 14.9

Sampling Distribution for Example 14.2

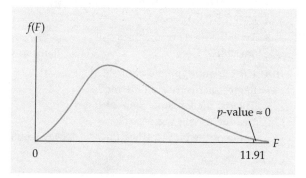

Checking the Required Conditions

The F-test of the randomized block design of the analysis of variance has the same requirements as the independent samples design. That is, the random variable must be normally distributed, and the population variances must be equal. The histograms (not shown) appear to support the validity of our results; the listening times appear to be normal. The equality of variances requirement also appears to be met.

Violation of the Required Conditions

When the random variable is not normally distributed, we can replace the randomized block model of the analysis of variance with the Friedman test, which is introduced in Appendix 14.B.

Criteria for Blocking

In Section 12.4, we listed the advantages and disadvantages of performing a matched pairs experiment. The same comments are valid when we discuss performing a blocked experiment. The purpose of blocking is to reduce the variation caused by differences among the experimental units. By grouping the experimental units into homogeneous blocks with respect to the response variable, the statistician increases the chances of detecting actual differences among the treatment means. Hence, we need to find criteria for blocking that significantly affect the response variable. For example, suppose that a statistician wants to determine which of four methods of teaching statistics is best. In an independent samples design he might take four samples of 10 students, teach each sample by a different method, grade the students at the end of the course, and perform an F-test to determine if differences exist. However, it is likely that there are very large differences among students *within* each class that may hide differences *between* classes. To reduce this variation, the statistician needs to identify variables that are linked to a student's grade in statistics. For example, overall ability of the student, completion of mathematics courses, and exposure to other statistics courses are all related to performance in a statistics course.

The experiment could be performed in the following way. The statistician selects four students at random whose average grade before statistics is 95–100. He then randomly assigns the students to one of the four classes. He repeats the process with students whose average is 90–95, 85–90, . . ., and 50–55. The final grades would be used to test for differences among the classes.

Any characteristics that are related to the experimental units are potential blocking criteria. For example, if the experimental units are people, we may block according to age, gender, income, work experience, intelligence, residence (country, county, or city), weight, or height. If the experimental unit is a factory and we're measuring number of units produced hourly, blocking criteria include workforce experience, age of the plant, and quality of suppliers.

Developing an Understanding of Statistical Concepts

As we explained above, the randomized block experiment is an extension of the matched pairs experiment discussed in Section 12.4. In the matched pairs experiment, we simply remove the effect of the variation caused by differences among the experimental units. The effect of this removal is seen in the decrease in the value of the standard error (compared to the standard error in the test statistic produced from independent samples) and the increase in the value of the t-statistic. In the randomized block design of the analysis of variance, we actually measure the variation among the blocks by computing SSB. The sum of squares for error is reduced by SSB, making it easier to detect differences among the treatments. Additionally, we can test to determine whether the blocks differ—a procedure we were unable to perform in the matched pairs experiment.

To illustrate, let's return to Examples 12.3 and 12.4, which were experiments to determine whether there was a difference between two tire designs. (In fact, we tested to determine whether the new-design tires outlast the existing-design tires. However, the analysis of variance can only test for differences.) In Example 12.3 (independent samples), there was insufficient evidence to infer a difference between the two types of tires. In Example 12.4 (matched pairs experiment), there was enough evidence to infer a difference. As we pointed out in Section 12.4, matching cars allowed us to more easily discern a difference between the two types of tires. If we repeat Examples 12.3 and 12.4 using the analysis of variance, we come to the same conclusion. The Minitab outputs are shown below. (The Excel printouts are similar.)

Analysis of Variance: Example 12.3

One-Way Analysis of Variance

```
Analysis of Variance
Source     DF      SS        MS        F         p
Factor      1     194       194      0.82     0.370
Error      38    8934       235
Total      39    9128
```

```
                                 Individual 95% CIs For Mean
                                 Based on Pooled StDev
   Level    N    Mean   StDev   ------+---------+---------+---------+
New-Dsn    20   73.60   15.60                  (-------------*-------------)
Exst-Dsn   20   69.20   15.06   (-------------*-------------)
                                 ------+---------+---------+---------+
Pooled StDev = 15.33              65.0      70.0      75.0      80.0
```

Analysis of Variance: Example 12.4

```
Analysis of Variance for Distance

Source     DF         SS        MS        F       P
Tire        1      207.02    207.02     7.94   0.011
Car        19    10128.28    533.07    20.44   0.000
Error      19      495.48     26.08
Total      39    10830.78
```

In Example 12.3, we partition the total sum of squares [SS(Total) = 9,128] into two sources of variation: SST = 194 and SSE = 8,934. In Example 12.4, the total sum of squares is SS(Total) = 10,830.78, SST (sum of squares for tires) = 207.02, SSB (sum of squares for cars) = 10,128.28, and SSE = 495.48. As you can see, the total sums of squares for both examples are about the same (9,128 and 10,830.78), and the sums of squares for treatments are also approximately equal (194 and 207.02). However, where the two calculations differ is in the sums of squares for error. SSE in Example 12.4 is much smaller than SSE in Example 12.3 because the randomized block experiment allows us to measure and remove the effect of the variation among cars. The sum of squares for blocks (sum of squares for cars) is 10,128.28, a statistic that measures how much variation exists among the cars. As a result of removing this variation, SSE is small. Thus, we conclude in Example 12.4 that the tires differ whereas there was not enough evidence in Example 12.3 to draw the same conclusion.

We'll complete this section by listing the factors that we need to recognize to use this model of the analysis of variance.

Factors that Identify the Randomized Block Design of the Analysis of Variance

1 Problem objective: compare two or more populations

2 Data type: quantitative

3 Experimental design: blocked samples

4 Population distributions: normal

Exercises

14.12 Provide an example with $k = 3$ and $b = 4$, in which SST = 0 and SSB and SSE are not equal to zero.

14.13 Provide an example with $k = 3$ and $b = 4$, in which SSB = 0 and SST and SSE are not equal to zero.

14.14 Is it possible to have a randomized block design of the analysis of variance in which SSE = 0 and SSB is not equal to zero? Explain.

14.15 The following data were generated from a randomized block design.

  a Test to determine whether the treatment means differ. (Use $\alpha = .05$.)

  b Test to determine whether the block means differ. (Use $\alpha = .05$.)

	TREATMENT		
BLOCK	1	2	3
1	7	12	8
2	10	8	9
3	12	16	13
4	9	13	6
5	12	10	11

14.16 A randomized block experiment produced the data listed below.

  a Can we infer at the 5% significance level that the treatment means differ?

  b Can we infer at the 5% significance level that the block means differ?

	TREATMENT			
BLOCK	1	2	3	4
1	6	5	4	4
2	8	5	5	6
3	7	6	5	6

14.17 Suppose that the following statistics were calculated from data gathered from a randomized block design with $k = 4$ and $b = 10$.

SS(Total) = 1,210
SST = 275
SSB = 625

  a Can we conclude from these statistics that the treatment means differ? (Use $\alpha = .01$.)

  b Can we conclude from these statistics that the block means differ? (Use $\alpha = .01$.)

14.18 Data from a randomized block experiment (three treatments and 10 blocks) are stored in file XR14-18U (unstacked data in columns 1 to 3), with some of these data shown below. The data are also stored in file XR14-18S (stacked data—responses in column 1, treatments in column 2, and blocks in column 3). Can we conclude that the treatment means differ? (Use $\alpha = .01$.)

| | TREATMENT | | |
BLOCK	1	2	3
1	56	62	59
2	65	75	70
3	74	71	73
.	.	.	.
.	.	.	.
.	.	.	.
10	27	33	30

Use a software package to solve this problem.

OR

The following sums of squares were computed.
SS(Total) = 7,743.0;
SST = 151.3;
SSB = 7,396.3
Complete your answer manually.

14.19 In recent years, lack of confidence in the Postal Service has led many companies to send all of their correspondence by private courier. A large company is in the process of selecting one of three possible couriers to act as its sole delivery method. To help in making the decision, an experiment was performed whereby letters were sent using each of the three couriers at 10 different times of the day to a delivery point across town. The number of minutes required for delivery was recorded, listed below, and stored in file XR14-19U (columns 1 through 3 list the delivery times of couriers 1, 2, and 3) and in file XR14-19S (column 1 stores the delivery times, column 2 specifies the courier, and column 3 stores the time of day code).

a Can we conclude at the 5% significance level that there are differences in delivery times among the three couriers?

b Did the statistician choose the correct design? Explain.

| | COURIER | | |
TIME OF DAY	1	2	3
9:00 A.M.	75	63	62
9:30 A.M.	82	80	67
10:00 A.M.	74	61	60
10:30 A.M.	59	55	53
11:00 A.M.	60	63	51
11:30 A.M.	63	61	57
12:00 P.M.	69	68	62

12:30 P.M.	63	69	73
1:00 P.M.	59	58	63
1:30 P.M.	64	58	65
2:00 P.M.	71	72	70
2:30 P.M.	75	70	61

Use a software package to solve this problem.	OR	The following sums of squares were computed. SS(Total) = 1,849.6; SST = 204.2; SSB = 1,150.2 Complete your answer manually.

14.20 Exercise 14.8 described an experiment that involved comparing the completion times associated with four different income tax forms. Suppose the experiment is redone in the following way. Thirty people are asked to fill out all four forms. The completion times (in minutes) are recorded and stored in columns 1 through 4 of file XR14-20U and columns 1 (completion times), 2 (forms), and 3 (taxpayer) of file XR14-20S. Some of these data are shown below.

a Is there sufficient evidence at the 1% significance level to infer that differences in the completion times exist among the four forms?

b Comment on the suitability of this experimental design in this problem.

	TAX FORM			
TAXPAYER	A	B	C	D
1	109	115	126	120
2	98	103	107	108
3	29	27	53	38
.	.	.	.	.
.	.	.	.	.
.	.	.	.	.
30	100	112	107	120

Use a software package to solve this problem.	OR	The following sums of squares were computed. SS(Total) = 136,812.3; SST = 4,206.1; SSB = 126,842.6 Complete your answer manually.

14.21 A recruiter for a computer company would like to determine whether there are differences in sales ability among business, arts, and science graduates. She takes a random sample of 20 business graduates who have been working for the company for the past two years. Each is then matched with an arts graduate and a science graduate with similar educational and working experience. The commission earned by each (in thousands of dollars) in the last year was recorded and stored in columns 1, 2, and 3, respectively, of file XR14-21U. The data are also stored in columns 1 (commission), 2 (undergraduate program), and 3 (block) of file XR14-21S. A partial listing of the data appears below. Is there sufficient evidence at the 5% significance level to allow the recruiter to conclude that there are differences in sales ability among the holders of the three types of degrees?

	UNDERGRADUATE PROGRAM		
BLOCK	BUSINESS	ARTS	SCIENCE
1	42.8	42.4	44.4
2	25.9	28.0	31.0
3	33.1	34.9	30.0
.	.	.	.
.	.	.	.
.	.	.	.
20	38.1	34.9	41.0

Use a software package to solve this problem.

OR

The following sums of squares were computed.
SS(Total) = 3,257.27;
SST = 10.26;
SSB = 3,020.30
Complete your answer manually.

14.22 Many North Americans suffer from high levels of cholesterol, which can lead to heart attacks. For those with very high levels (over 280), doctors prescribe drugs to reduce cholesterol levels. A pharmaceutical company has recently developed three such drugs. To determine if any differences exist in their benefits, an experiment was organized. The company selected 25 groups of three men, each of whom had levels in excess of 280. In each group, the men were matched according to age and weight. The drugs were administered over a two-month period, and the reduction in cholesterol was recorded. The data are stored in the first three columns of file XR14-22U, with some of the results listed below. The data are also stored in columns 1 (cholesterol reduction), 2 (drug), and 3 (age/weight group). Do these results allow the company to conclude at the 5% significance level that differences exist among the three new drugs?

	DRUG		
AGE/WEIGHT GROUP	A	B	C
1	6.6	12.6	2.7
2	7.1	3.5	2.4
3	7.5	4.4	6.5
.	.	.	.
.	.	.	.
.	.	.	.
25	28.4	31.2	26.1

14.5 Summary

The analysis of variance allows us to test for differences among the populations when the data are quantitative. Two different models were introduced in this chapter. The first model is the independent samples single-factor model. In this model, the treatments are defined as the levels of one factor, and the experimental design specifies independent samples. The second model also defines the treatments on the basis of one factor. However, the randomized block design uses data gathered by observing the results of a matched or blocked experiment. Both models of the analysis of variance are based on partitioning the total sum of squares into sources of variation from which the mean squares and F-statistics are computed.

IMPORTANT TERMS

Analysis of variance	ANOVA table
Treatment means	Total sum of squares SS(Total)
Between-treatments variation	One-way analysis of variance
Sum of squares for treatments (SST)	Completely randomized design
Response variable	Single factor
Responses	Two-factor
Experimental units	Repeated measures
Factor	Fixed effects
Level	Random effects
Within-treatments variation	Block means
Sum of squares for error (SSE)	Between-blocks variation
Mean squares	Sum of squares for blocks (SSB)

Supplementary Exercises

The purpose of the next nine exercises is to provide you with an opportunity to practice your technique-recognition skills. The exercises feature data generated from either an independent samples design or a randomized block design. Your job is to identify which procedure to apply. If you have a computer and software, you should also produce the statistical results and interpret them.

14.23 The possible imposition of a residential property tax has been a sensitive political issue in a large city that consists of five boroughs. Currently, property tax is based on an assessment system that dates back to 1950. This system has produced numerous inequities whereby newer homes tend to be assessed at higher values than older homes. A new system based on the market value of the house has been proposed. Opponents of the plan argue that residents of some boroughs would have to pay considerably more on the average, while residents of other boroughs would pay less. As part of a study examining this issue, several homes in each borough were assessed under both plans. The percentage increase (a decrease is represented by a negative increase) in each case was recorded and stored in columns 1 through 5 of file XR14-23. A partial listing of these data appears below.

a Can we conclude at the 1% significance level that there are differences in the effect the new assessment system would have on the five boroughs?

b What are the required conditions for your conclusions to be valid?

c Discuss how these required conditions would be checked.

BOROUGH A	BOROUGH B	BOROUGH C	BOROUGH D	BOROUGH E
11	9	18	16	12
8	0	14	13	1
15	21	−3	23	12
.	.	.	.	.
.	.	.	.	.
.	.	.	.	.
4	11	32	22	1

14.24 The editor of the student newspaper was in the process of making some major changes in the newspaper's layout. He was also contemplating changing the typeface of the print used. To help himself make a decision, he set up an experiment in which 20 individuals were asked to read four newspaper pages, with each page printed in a different typeface. If the reading speed differed, then the typeface that was read fastest would be used. However, if there was not enough evidence to allow the editor to conclude that such differences existed, the current typeface would be continued. The times (in seconds) to completely read one page were stored in columns 1 to 4 of file XR14-24, with some of the data listed below. What should the editor do?

INDIVIDUAL	TYPEFACE 1	TYPEFACE 2	TYPEFACE 3	TYPEFACE 4
1	110	123	115	115
2	118	119	110	134
3	148	184	139	143
.	.	.	.	.
.	.	.	.	.
.	.	.	.	.
20	129	147	110	137

14.25 Each year billions of dollars are lost because of worker injuries on the job. Costs can be decreased if injured workers can be rehabilitated quickly. As part of an analysis of the amount of time taken for workers to return to work, a sample of male blue-collar workers aged 35 to 45 who suffered a common wrist fracture was taken. The researchers believed that the physical condition of the individual affects recovery time. Each man's physical condition was evaluated and categorized as very physically fit, average, or in poor condition. The number of days until the wrist returned to full function was measured for each individual. These data are stored in file XR14-25 in the following way.

Column 1: time to recover for very fit workers

Column 2: time to recover for average workers

Column 3: time to recover for workers in poor physical condition.

Some of the data are shown below.

Can we conclude at the 5% significance level that physical condition affects recovery times?

VERY FIT	AVERAGE	POOR
26	34	48
30	18	43
37	39	32
.	.	.
.	.	.
.	.	.
39	30	41

14.26 The marketing manager of a large ski resort wants to advertise that his ski resort has the shortest lift lines of any resort in the area. To avoid the possibility of a false advertising liability suit, he collects data on the average wait in line at his resort and at each of two competing resorts on each of 15 days. These results are stored in columns 2 through 4 of file XR14-26. (Column 1 indicates the day, and columns 2 through 4 store the waiting times.) Some data are shown below.

    a   Can he conclude at the 5% significance level that there are differences in waiting times among the three resorts?

    b   What are the required conditions for the techniques above?

    c   How would you check to determine that the required conditions are satisfied?

DAY	RESORT 1	RESORT 2	RESORT 3
1	8	6	7
2	5	7	5
3	9	11	12
.	.	.	.
.	.	.	.
.	.	.	.
15	6	7	7

14.27 A popularly held belief about university professors is that they don't work very hard, and that the higher their rank, the less work they do. A statistics student decided to determine whether the belief is true. She took a random sample of 100 university instructors. Each professor was surveyed and asked to report confidentially the number of weekly hours of work. These data are stored in file XR14-27 in the following way. Some of the data are exhibited below.

Column 1: hours of work

Column 2: Code representing rank (1 = instructor, 2 = assistant professor, 3 = associate professor, and 4 = full professor)

Test to determine if differences exist among the ranks of university instructors. (Use $\alpha = .05$.)

INSTRUCTOR	ASSISTANT PROFESSOR	ASSOCIATE PROFESSOR	FULL PROFESSOR
43	39	48	43
39	47	44	44
45	49	33	39
.	.	.	.
.	.	.	.
.	.	.	.
39	39	34	48

14.28 In marketing children's products, it's extremely important to produce television commercials that hold the attention of the children who view them. A psychologist hired by a marketing research firm wants to determine whether differences in attention span exist among children watching advertisements for different types of products. One hundred fifty children under 10 years of age were recruited for an experiment. One third watched a 60-second commercial for a new computer game, one third watched a commercial for a breakfast cereal, and another third watched a commercial for children's clothes. Their attention spans were measured. The results (in seconds) were stored in the first three columns of file XR14-28, with some of the data listed below. Do these data provide enough evidence to conclude that there are differences in attention span among the three products advertised?

COMPUTER GAME	BREAKFAST CEREAL	CHILDREN'S CLOTHES
28	46	30
34	30	25
20	37	39
.	.	.
.	.	.
.	.	.
29	45	30

14.29 Upon reconsidering the experiment in Exercise 14.28, the psychologist decides that the age of the child may influence the attention span. Consequently, the experiment is redone in the following way. Three 10-year-olds, three 9-year-olds, three 8-year-olds, three 7-year-olds, three 6-year-olds, three 5-year-olds, and three 4-year-olds are randomly assigned to watch one of the commercials, and their attention spans are measured. The data are shown below. Do the results indicate that there are differences in the abilities of the products advertised to hold children's attention?

AGES	COMPUTER GAME	BREAKFAST CEREAL	CHILDREN'S CLOTHES
10	45	43	38
9	46	42	37
8	42	40	30
7	38	41	37
6	39	41	35
5	33	37	30
4	27	25	20

14.30 North American automobile manufacturers have become more concerned with quality because of foreign competition. One aspect of quality is the cost of repairing damage caused by accidents. A manufacturer is considering several new types of bumpers. In order to test how well they react to low-speed collisions, 40 bumpers of each of five different types were installed on mid-size cars, which were then driven into a wall at 5 miles per hour. The cost of repairing the damage in each case was assessed, and the relevant data stored in columns 1 to 5 of file XR14-30. Some of these results are shown below.

Is there sufficient evidence to infer at the 1% significance level that the bumpers differ in their reactions to low-speed collisions?

BUMPER 1	BUMPER 2	BUMPER 3	BUMPER 4	BUMPER 5
268	470	525	470	412
407	301	362	367	383
374	428	440	380	424
.	.	.	.	.
.	.	.	.	.
.	.	.	.	.
563	559	549	485	473

CASE 14.1

EFFECTS OF FINANCIAL PLANNING ON SMALL BUSINESSES*

In the United States, approximately one-half million small businesses fail annually. Many researchers have investigated small businesses in order to determine the factors distinguishing those that succeed from those that fail. One set of researchers suggested that a potential factor is the degree of planning. They identified three different levels of planning.

1 Structured strategic planning—this involves producing a formalized written description of long-term plans with a 3- to 15-year horizon.

2 Structured operational planning—this type of planning deals with short-term issues such as action plans for the current fiscal year.

3 Unstructured planning—this covers arrangements in which there is no formal or informal planning.

A random sample of 73 firms participated in the study. The mean age of the firms was 9.2 years, mean annual revenues were $4.25 million, and mean net income was $300,000. On average, 71 people were employed. These statistics suggest that the 73 participating companies are fairly representative of the population to be investigated.

The companies were analyzed over a five-year period (1979 to 1984), and the following four measures of performance were used.

---

*Adapted from J. S. Bracker, B. W. Keats, and J. N. Pearson, "Planning and Financial Performance among Small Firms in a Growth Industry," *Strategic Management Journal* 9 (1988): 591–603.

1 revenue growth—average sales growth in percent over the five years

2 net income growth—growth in percent average net income (before taxes) over the five years

3 present value growth—average book value growth in percent over the five years

4 CEO cash compensation growth—percent average growth in the cash payments to chief executive officers over the five years

The data are stored in file C14-01 using the following format.

Column 1: revenue growth for all companies

Column 2: income growth for all companies

Column 3: present value growth for all companies

Column 4: compensation growth for all companies

Column 5: index 1 = companies with structured strategic planning
2 = companies with structured operational planning
3 = companies with unstructured planning

What conclusions and recommendations can be derived from these data?

CASE 14.2 **DIVERSIFICATION STRATEGY FOR MULTINATIONAL COMPANIES***

One of the many goals of management researchers is to identify factors that differentiate between success and failure and among different levels of success in businesses. In this way, it may be possible to help more businesses become successful. Among multinational enterprises (MNEs), two factors to be examined are the degree of product diversification and the degree of internationalization. *Product diversification* refers to efforts by companies to increase the range and variety of the products they produce. The more unrelated the products are, the greater is the degree of diversification created. *Internationalization* is a term that expresses geographic diversification. Companies that sell their products to many countries are said to employ a high degree of internationalization.

Three management researchers set out to examine these issues. In particular, they wanted to test two hypotheses.

1 MNEs employing strategies that result in more product diversification outperform those with less product diversification.

2 MNEs employing strategies that result in more internationalization outperform those with less internationalization.

Company performance was measured in two ways.

1 Profit-to-sales is the ratio of profit to total sales, expressed as a percentage.

---

*Adapted from J. M. Geringer, P. W. Beamish, and R. C. da Costa, "Diversification Strategy and Internationalization: Implication for MNE Performance," *Strategic Management Journal* 10 (1989): 109–19.

2 Profit-to-assets is the ratio of profit to total assets, expressed as a percentage.

A random sample of 189 companies was selected. For each company, the profit-to-sales and profit-to-assets were measured. In addition, each company was judged to have a low (1), medium (2), or high (3) level of diversification. The degree of internationalization was measured on a five-point scale where 1 = lowest level and 5 = highest level.

The results are stored in file C14-02 on the data disk, using the following format.

Column 1: profit-to-sales ratio

Column 2: profit-to-assets ratio

Column 3: levels of diversification

Column 4: degrees of internationalism

What do these data tell you about the researchers' hypotheses?

Analysis of Variance: Independent Samples Single-Factor Model

When the data are stacked (with the observations in column 1 and the codes in column 2), type

ONEWAY C1 C2

or

ANOVA C1 = C2

The latter command only prints the ANOVA table. It does not print sample statistics.

When the data are unstacked (i.e., the observations from each sample are in different columns—say columns 1 to 4), type

AOVONEWAY C1 - C4

Analysis of Variance: Randomized Block Design

To perform the analysis of variance using the randomized block design, the data must be stacked. Column 1 contains the observations, column 2 the treatment codes, and column 3 the block codes. Type

TWOWAY C1 C2 C3

This command does not print the F-statistic or its p-value.

We recommend

ANOVA C1 = C2 C3

which tells Minitab that the observations in column 1 are affected by the treatments (column 2) and the blocks (column 3).

In Appendix 12.C, we briefly introduced nonparametric techniques and identified the factors that dictate the use of the Wilcoxon rank sum test, the sign test, and the Wilcoxon signed rank sum test. All of these techniques are used to compare two populations. In this chapter we introduced the analysis of variance, which is applied to compare two or more populations. As you've seen, one of the requirements of the analysis of variance is that the response variable is normally distributed. If the response variable is not normal or the data are ranked, we must use a nonparametric procedure. The Kruskal-Wallis test is employed when the samples are independent. The Friedman test is applied when the samples are blocked.

Kruskal-Wallis Test

The *Kruskal-Wallis test* is applied to problems with the following characteristics.

1 Problem objective: compare two or more populations
2 Data type: ranked or quantitative but nonnormal
3 Experimental design: independent samples

Test Statistic

1 Rank all observations. As before, 1 = smallest observation, and n = largest observation, where $n = n_1 + n_2 + \ldots + n_k$. In case of ties, average the ranks.
2 Calculate the sum of the ranks of each sample denoted $T_1, T_2, \ldots, T_k$ (k is the number of populations).
3 The test statistic is

$$H = \left[\frac{12}{n(n+1)} \sum \frac{T_j^2}{n_j} \right] - 3(n+1)$$

Sampling Distribution of H

If the sample sizes are at least 5, H is approximately chi-squared distributed with $k-1$ degrees of freedom.

Minitab Menu Commands

1 Type or import the data. The data must be stacked.
2 Click **Stat, Nonparametric,** and **Kruskal-Wallis. . . .**
3 Type the name of the response variable. Hit **tab** and type the name of the factor levels (code variable). Click **OK**.

Excel Commands

1 Type or import the data. The data must be stacked.
2 Click **Tools, Data Analysis Plus,** and **Kruskal-Wallis Test**.
3 Specify the block coordinates of the data. Do not include cells containing the variable names.

Friedman Test

The Friedman test is applied to problems with the following characteristics.

1 Problem objective: compare two or more populations

2 Data type: ranked or quantitative but nonnormal

3 Experimental design: blocks

Test Statistic

1 Rank all observations within each block, where 1 = smallest observation and k = largest observation. Average the ranks of ties.

2 Compute the rank sums $T_1, T_2, \ldots, T_k$.

3 Compute the test statistic

$$F_r = \left[\frac{12}{b(k)(k+1)} \sum T_j^2\right] - 3b(k+1)$$

Sampling Distribution of F_r

If either the number of populations (k) or the number of blocks (b) is at least 5 (that is $k \geq 5$ or $b \geq 5$), F_r is approximately chi-squared distributed with $k-1$ degrees of freedom.

Minitab Menu Commands

1 Type or import the data. The data must be stacked; the responses are stored in column 1, the treatment codes are stored in column 2, and the block codes are stored in column 3.

2 Click **Stat, Nonparametric**, and **Friedman. . . .**

3 Type the name of the **Response** variable.

4 Hit **tab** and type the name of the **Treatment** variable.

5 Hit **tab** and type the name of the **Blocks** variable. Click **OK**.

Excel Commands

1 Type or import the data. The data must be stored in rows and columns where the columns represent the treatments and the rows represent the blocks.

2 Click **Tools, Data Analysis Plus**, and **Friedman Test**.

3 Specify the block coordinates of the data. Do not include cells containing the variable names.

15 Additional Tests for Qualitative Data

15.1 Introduction

This chapter develops two statistical techniques that involve qualitative data. The first is a **goodness-of-fit test** applied to data produced by a multinomial experiment, a generalization of a binomial experiment. The second uses data arranged in a table (called a **contingency table**) to determine whether or not two classifications of a population of qualitative data are statistically independent; this test can also be interpreted as a comparison of two or more populations. The sampling distribution of the test statistics in both tests is the chi-squared distribution introduced in Chapter 11.

Following are two examples of situations in which chi-squared tests could be applied.

Example 1 Firms periodically estimate the proportion (or market share) of consumers who prefer their products, as well as the market shares of competitors. These market shares may change over time as a result of advertising campaigns or the introduction of new improved products. To determine whether the actual current market shares are in accord with its beliefs, a firm might sample several consumers and compute, for each of k competing companies, the proportion of consumers sampled who prefer that company's product. Such an experiment, in which each consumer is classified as preferring one of the k companies, is called a *multinomial experiment*. If only two companies were considered ($k = 2$), we would be dealing with the familiar binomial experiment. After computing the proportion of consumers preferring each of the k companies, a goodness-of-fit test could be conducted to determine whether the sample proportions (or market shares) differ significantly from those hypothesized by the firm. The problem objective is to describe the population of consumers, and the data are qualitative.

Example 2 For advertising and other purposes, it is important for a company to understand which segments of the market prefer which of its products. For example, it would be helpful for an automotive manufacturer to know if there is a relationship between the buyer preferences for its various models and the sex of the consumer. After conducting a survey to solicit consumers' preferences, the firm could classify each respondent according to two qualitative variables: model preferred and sex. A test could then be conducted to determine whether consumers' preferences are independent of their sex. Rather than interpreting this test as a test of the independence of two qualitative variables defined over a single population, we could view male and female consumers as representing two different populations. Then we could interpret the test as testing for differences in preferences between these two populations.

15.2 Chi-Squared Test of a Multinomial Experiment

This section presents another test designed to describe a single population of qualitative data. The first such test was introduced in Section 11.4, where we discussed the statistical procedure employed to test hypotheses about a population proportion. In that case, the qualitative variable could assume one of only two possible values, *success* or *failure*. Our tests dealt with hypotheses about the proportion of successes in the entire population. Recall that the experiment that produces the data is called a binomial experiment. In this section, we introduce the **multinomial experiment**, which is an extension of the binomial experiment, wherein there are two *or more* possible outcomes per trial.

> **Multinomial Experiment**
>
> A multinomial experiment is one possessing the following properties.
>
> 1 The experiment consists of a fixed number n of trials.
>
> 2 The outcome of each trial can be classified into one of k categories, called **cells**.
>
> 3 The probability p_i that the outcome will fall into cell i remains constant for each trial. Moreover, $p_1 + p_2 + \ldots + p_k = 1$.
>
> 4 Each trial of the experiment is independent of the other trials.

As you can see when $k = 2$, the multinomial experiment is identical to the binomial experiment. Just as we count the number of successes (recall that we label the number of successes x) and failures in a binomial experiment, we count the number of outcomes falling into each of the k cells in a multinomial experiment. In this way, we obtain a set of observed frequencies $o_1, o_2, \ldots, o_k$ where o_i is the **observed frequency** of outcomes falling into cell i, for $i = 1, 2, \ldots, k$. Because the experiment consists of n trials and an outcome must fall into some cell,

$$o_1 + o_2 + \ldots + o_k = n$$

Just as we used the number of successes x (by calculating the sample proportion $\hat{p}$, which is equal to x/n) to draw inferences about p, so do we use the observed frequencies to draw inferences about the cell probabilities. We'll proceed in what by now has become a standard procedure. We will set up the hypotheses and develop the test statistic and its sampling distribution. We'll demonstrate the process with the following example.

EXAMPLE 15.1

A professor of statistics occasionally engages in practical demonstrations of probability theory. (That is, he bets on horse races.) His current method of assessing probabilities and applying wagering strategy has not been particularly successful. (He usually loses.) To help improve his cash flow, he decides to learn more about the outcomes of races. In particular, he would like to know whether some post positions are more favorable than others, so that horses starting in these positions win more frequently than horses starting in other positions. If this is true, it is likely that the return on his investment will be positive often enough to overcome the more frequently occurring negative return. (He may be able to win money.) He records the post positions of the winners of 300 randomly selected races. These data are summarized in the accompanying table. Using a significance level of 5%, can the professor conclude that some post positions win more frequently than others?

Results of 300 Races

POST POSITION i	OBSERVED FREQUENCY o
1	44
2	65
3	42
4	60
5	46
6	43
	TOTAL 300

SOLUTION

The population in question is the population of winning post positions for all races. Although the data may appear at first glance to be quantitative, they are in fact qualitative. The numbers from one to six simply give unique names to each of the post positions. Thus, computing the mean winning post position, for example, would be meaningless. The experiment described in this example matches the properties of a multinomial experiment. It follows that the parameters of interest are the probabilities (or proportions) $p_1, p_2, \ldots, p_6$ that post positions 1 to 6 are the winning positions. To determine if some post positions win more frequently than others, we specify under the null hypothesis that all post positions are equally likely to win. That means that the probabilities $p_1, p_2, \ldots, p_6$ are equal, which means that they're all equal to 1/6 (since their total must equal 1). Thus,

$$H_0: p_1 = 1/6, p_2 = 1/6, p_3 = 1/6, p_4 = 1/6, p_5 = 1/6, p_6 = 1/6$$

Because the point of the experiment is to determine whether at least one post position wins more frequently than the others, we specify the alternative hypothesis as

$$H_A: \text{At least one } p_i \text{ is not equal to its specified value.}$$

TEST STATISTIC

If the null hypothesis is true, we would expect each post position to win one-sixth of the races, and since $n = 300$, we expect that each post position would win $300(1/6) = 50$ times. In general, the **expected frequency** for each post position is given by

$$e_i = np_i$$

This expression is derived from the formula for the expected value of a binomial random variable first seen in Section 6.7.

$$E(X) = np$$

If the expected frequencies, e_i, and the observed frequencies, o_i, are quite different, we would conclude that the null hypothesis is false, and we would reject it. However, if the expected and observed frequencies are similar, we would not reject the null hypothesis. The test statistic we employ to assess whether the differences between the expected and observed frequencies are large is

$$\chi^2 = \sum_{i=1}^{k} \frac{(o_i - e_i)^2}{e_i}$$

The sampling distribution of the test statistic is approximately chi-squared distributed with $k - 1$ degrees of freedom, provided that the sample size is large. We will discuss this condition later. (The chi-squared distribution was introduced in Section 11.4. See page 389 for a review or, perhaps, introduction to this distribution and Table 5 in Appendix B.)

The table below demonstrates the calculation of the χ^2-statistic. Thus, the value of the test statistic is $\chi^2 = 9.80$. As usual, we need to judge the magnitude of the test statistic to determine our conclusion. This is the function of the rejection region.

POST POSITION i	OBSERVED FREQUENCY o_i	EXPECTED FREQUENCY e_i	$(o_i - e_i)$	$\dfrac{(o_i - e_i)^2}{e_i}$
1	44	50	−6	0.72
2	65	50	15	4.50
3	42	50	−8	1.28
4	60	50	10	2.00
5	46	50	−4	0.32
6	43	50	−7	0.98
	300	300		$\chi^2 = 9.80$

REJECTION REGION

When the expected and observed values are similar, the test statistic

$$\chi^2 = \sum_{i=1}^{k} \frac{(o_i - e_i)^2}{e_i}$$

will be small. Thus, a small χ^2-statistic supports the null hypothesis. If some expected values are quite different from their respective observed values, the χ^2-statistic will be large. Consequently, we want to reject the null hypothesis in favor of the alternative hypothesis when χ^2 is greater than $\chi^2_{\alpha, k-1}$. That is, the rejection region is $\chi^2 > \chi^2_{\alpha, k-1}$.

In Example 15.1, $k = 6$; the rejection region is $\chi^2 > \chi^2_{\alpha, k-1} = \chi^2_{.05,5} = 11.0705$. We've already calculated the test statistic and found it to be

$$\chi^2 = 9.80$$

Therefore, we conclude that there is not enough statistical evidence to infer that some post positions win more frequently than others. What this means is that the professor cannot use the post position to help determine a winner. The professor would be advised to seek some other way of deciding on which horse to bet; or yet better advice would be to quit betting on the horses. Figure 15.1 depicts the sampling distribution and the rejection region.

Figure 15.1

Sampling Distribution of the Test Statistic: Example 15.1

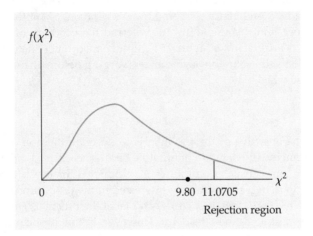

While it is common to test for no differences in the cell probabilities $p_1, p_2, \ldots, p_k$ (as we did in Example 15.1), we are not restricted to this formulation. We may hypothesize a different value for each p_i, as long as the sum of the probabilities is 1. Moreover, the test described in this section is also called a goodness-of-fit test because it can be used to test how well data fit a hypothesized distribution. In this application, we would use the hypothesized distribution to calculate a set of probabilities and employ the chi-squared test of a multinomial experiment to test the belief. We have chosen not to present this type of problem, but it is conceptually no more difficult than the type we have presented.

Before we perform this example, let's summarize the factors that allow us to recognize when to use the statistical procedure described in this section.

Factors that Identify the Chi-Squared Test of a Multinomial Experiment

1 Problem objective: describe a single population

2 Data type: qualitative

3 Number of categories: two or more

EXAMPLE 15.2

Two companies, A and B, have recently conducted aggressive advertising campaigns in order to maintain and possibly increase their respective shares of the market for fabric softener. These two companies enjoy a dominant position in the market. Before the advertising campaigns began, the market share of company A was 45%, while company B had 40% of the market. Other competitors accounted for the remaining 15%. To determine whether these market shares changed after the advertising campaigns, a marketing analyst solicited the preferences of a random sample of 200 customers of fabric softener. Of the 200 customers, 102 indicated a preference for company A's product, 82 preferred company B's fabric softener, and the remaining 16 preferred the products of one of the competitors. Can the analyst infer at the 5% significance level that customer preferences have changed from the levels they were at before the advertising campaigns were launched?

SOLUTION

IDENTIFYING THE TECHNIQUE

The objective of the problem is to describe the population of fabric softener customers. The data are qualitative because each respondent will choose one of three possible answers—product A, product B, or other. If there were only two categories, or if we were only interested in the proportion of one company's customers (which we label as *successes* and label the others as *failures*), we would identify the technique as the z-test of p. However, in this problem we're interested in the proportions of all three categories. We recognize this experiment as a multinomial experiment, and we identify the technique as the chi-squared test of a multinomial experiment.

Because we want to know if the market shares have changed, we specify those pre-campaign market shares in the null hypothesis.

H_0: $p_1 = .45$, $p_2 = .40$, $p_3 = .15$

The alternative hypothesis attempts to answer our question, "Have the proportions changed?" Thus,

H_A: At least one p_i is not equal to its specified value.

The complete test follows:

H_0: $p_1 = .45$, $p_2 = .40$, $p_3 = .15$

H_A: At least one p_i is not equal to its specified value.

Test statistic: $\chi^2 = \sum_{i=1}^{k} \frac{(o_i - e_i)^2}{e_i}$

Rejection region: $\chi^2 > \chi^2_{\alpha,k-1} = \chi^2_{.05,2} = 5.99147$

SOLVING BY HAND

The expected values are as follows.

$e_1 = np_1 = 200(.45) = 90$

$e_2 = np_2 = 200(.40) = 80$

$e_3 = np_3 = 200(.15) = 30$

The value of the test statistic is

$$\chi^2 = \sum_{i=1}^{k} \frac{(o_i - e_i)^2}{e_i} = \frac{(102 - 90)^2}{90} + \frac{(82 - 80)^2}{80} + \frac{(16 - 30)^2}{30} = 8.18$$

Conclusion: Reject the null hypothesis.

USING THE COMPUTER

If we have only raw data (codes representing the categories), we can use the computer to determine the frequency of each category. See Appendixes 11.A and 11.B for specific instructions. Minitab users can complete the calculation manually or with the assistance of their computer. Excel computes the p-value of this test. See Appendix 15.B.

INTERPRETING THE RESULTS

There is sufficient evidence to infer that the proportions have changed since the advertising campaigns. If the sampling was conducted properly, we can be quite confident in our conclusion. This technique has only one required condition, which is satisfied. (See rule of five described below.) It is probably a worthwhile exercise to determine the nature and causes of the changes. The results of this analysis will determine the design and timing of other advertising campaigns.

Rule of Five

The test statistic used to compare the relative sizes of observed and expected frequencies is

$$\chi^2 = \sum_{i=1}^{k} \frac{(o_i - e_i)^2}{e_i}$$

We previously stated that this test statistic has an approximate chi-squared distribution. In fact, the actual distribution of this test statistic is discrete, but it can be approximated conveniently by using a continuous chi-squared distribution when the sample size n is large, just as we approximated the discrete binomial distribution by using the normal distribution. This approximation may be poor, however, if the expected cell frequencies are small. For the (discrete) distribution of the test statistic to be adequately approximated by the (continuous) chi-squared distribution, the conventional (and conservative) rule—known as the **rule of five**— is to *require that the expected frequency for each cell be at least 5.* Where necessary, cells should be combined in order to satisfy this condition. The choice of cells to be combined should be made in such a way that meaningful categories result from the combination.

Consider the following modification of Example 15.2. Suppose that three companies (A, B, and C) have recently conducted aggressive advertising campaigns; the market shares prior to the campaigns were $p_1 = .45$ for company A, $p_2 = .40$ for company B, $p_3 = .13$ for company C, and $p_4 = .02$ for other competitors. In a

---

*To be on the safe side, this rule of thumb is somewhat conservative. A discussion of alternatives to the rule of five can be found in W. J. Conover, *Practical Nonparametric Statistics* (New York: John Wiley, 1971), p. 152, and in S. Siegel, *Nonparametric Statistics for the Behavioral Sciences* (New York: McGraw-Hill, 1956), p. 178.

test to see if market shares changed after the advertising campaigns, the null hypothesis would now be

$$H_0: p_1 = .45, p_2 = .40, p_3 = .13, p_4 = .02$$

Hence, if the preferences of a sample of 200 customers were solicited, the expected frequencies would be

$$e_1 = 90 \qquad e_2 = 80 \qquad e_3 = 26 \qquad e_4 = 4$$

Since the expected cell frequency e_4 is less than 5, the rule of five requires that it be combined with one of the other expected frequencies (say, e_3) to obtain a combined cell frequency of (in this case) 30. Although e_4 could have been combined with e_1 or e_2, we have chosen to combine it with e_3 so that we still have a separate category representing each of the two dominant companies (A and B). After this combination is made, the null hypothesis reads

$$H_0: p_1 = .45, p_2 = .40, p_3 = .15$$

where p_3 now represents the market share of all competitors of companies A and B. Therefore, the appropriate number of degrees of freedom for the chi-squared test statistic would be $k - 1 = 3 - 1 = 2$, where k is the number of cells after some have been combined to satisfy the rule of five.

Exercises

15.1 Consider a multinomial experiment involving $n = 300$ trials and $k = 5$ cells. The observed frequencies resulting from the experiment are shown in the accompanying table, and the null hypothesis to be tested is as follows.

$$H_0: p_1 = .1, p_2 = .2, p_3 = .3, p_4 = .2, p_5 = .2$$

Test the hypothesis at the 1% significance level.

Cell	1	2	3	4	5
Frequency	24	65	86	70	55

15.2 Consider a multinomial experiment involving $n = 150$ trials and $k = 4$ cells. The observed frequencies resulting from the experiment are shown in the accompanying table, and the null hypothesis to be tested is as follows.

$$H_0: p_1 = .3, p_2 = .3, p_3 = .2, p_4 = .2$$

Cell	1	2	3	4
Frequency	38	50	38	24

Test the hypotheses, using $\alpha = .05$.

15.3 For Exercise 15.2, retest the hypotheses, assuming that the experiment involved twice as many trials ($n = 300$) and that the observed frequencies were twice as high as before, as shown in the accompanying table.

Cell	1	2	3	4
Frequency	76	100	76	48

15.4 (A computer and statistical software are required to solve this problem.) The results of a multinomial experiment with $k = 5$ are stored in file XR15-04. Each outcome is identified by the numbers 1 through 5 stored in column 1. Test to determine if there is enough evidence to infer that the proportion of each outcome is the same. (Use $\alpha = .10$.)

15.5 To determine whether a single die is balanced, or fair, the die was rolled 600 times. The observed frequencies with which each of the six sides of the die turned up are recorded in the following table. Is there sufficient evidence at the 5% significance level to allow you to conclude that the die is not fair?

FACE	OBSERVED FREQUENCY
1	114
2	92
3	84
4	101
5	107
6	102

15.6 For Exercise 15.5, suppose that the die was rolled 1,200 times and that the observed frequencies were twice as high as before, as recorded in the accompanying table. Is there now sufficient evidence at the 5% significance level to conclude that the die is not fair?

FACE	OBSERVED FREQUENCY
1	228
2	184
3	168
4	202
5	214
6	204

15.7 Grades assigned by an economics instructor have historically followed a symmetrical distribution: 5% A's, 25% B's, 40% C's, 25% D's, and 5% F's. This year, a sample of 150 grades revealed 11 A's, 32 B's, 62 C's, 29 D's, and 16 F's. Can you conclude, at the 1% level of significance, that this year's grades are distributed differently from grades in the past?

15.8 A firm has been accused of engaging in prejudicial hiring practices. According to the most recent census, the percentages of whites, blacks, and Hispanics in the community where the firm is located are 70%, 12%, and 18%, respectively. A random sample of 200 employees of the firm revealed that 165 were white, 14 were black, and 21 were Hispanic. What can you conclude at the 5% significance level from these data?

15.9 (A computer and statistical software are required to solve this problem.) Financial managers are interested in the speed with which customers who make purchases on credit pay their bills. In addition to calculating the average number of days that unpaid bills (called accounts receivable) remain outstanding, they often prepare an aging schedule. An aging schedule classifies outstanding accounts receivable according to the time that has elapsed since billing and records the proportion of accounts receivable belonging to each classification. A large firm has determined its aging schedule for the past five years. These results are shown in the accompanying table. During the past few months, however, the economy has taken a downturn. The company would like to know if the recession has affected the aging schedule. A random sample of 250 accounts receivable was drawn and each account was classified (and stored in file XR15-09) as follows.

1 = 0–29 days outstanding

2 = 60–59 days outstanding

3 = 60–89 days outstanding

4 = 90 or more days outstanding

NUMBER OF DAYS OUTSTANDING	PROPORTION OF ACCOUNTS RECEIVABLE PAST FIVE YEARS
0–29	.72
30–59	.15
60–89	.10
90 and over	.03

Determine whether the aging schedule has changed. (Use $\alpha = .05$.)

15.3 Chi-Squared Test of a Contingency Table

In this section, we introduce another chi-squared test, this one designed to satisfy two different problem objectives. The **chi-squared test of a contingency table** is used to determine if there is enough evidence to infer that two qualitative variables are related and to infer that differences exist among two or more populations of qualitative variables. Completing both objectives entails classifying items according to two different criteria. To see how this is done, consider the following example.

One of the issues that came up in a recent national election (and is likely to arise in many future elections) is how to deal with a sluggish economy. Specifically, should governments cut spending, raise taxes, inflate the economy (by printing more money), or do none of the above and let the deficit rise? And like most issues, politicians need to know which parts of the electorate support these options. Suppose that a random sample of 1,000 people was asked which option they support and their political affiliations. The possible responses to the question about political affiliation were Democrat, Republican, and Independent (which included a variety of political persuasions). The responses were summarized in a table called a **contingency** or **cross-classification table**, shown below. Do these results allow us to conclude that political affiliation affects support for the economic options?

ECONOMIC OPTIONS	POLITICAL AFFILIATION		
	DEMOCRAT	REPUBLICAN	INDEPENDENT
Cut spending	101	282	61
Raise taxes	38	67	25
Inflate the economy	131	88	31
Let deficit increase	61	90	25

SOLUTION

One way to solve the problem is to consider that there are two variables represented by the contingency table. The variables are economic option and political affiliation. Both are qualitative. The values of economic option are "cut spending," "raise taxes," "inflate the economy," and "let deficit increase." The values of political affiliation are "Democrat," "Republican," and "Independent." The problem objective is to analyze the relationship between the two variables. Specifically, we want to know whether one variable affects the other.

Another way of addressing the problem is to determine whether differences exist among Democrats, Republicans, and Independents. In other words, we treat each political group as a separate population. Each population has four possible values, represented by the four economic options. (We can also answer the question by treating the economic options as populations and the political affiliations as the values of the random variable.) Here the problem objective is to compare three populations.

As you will shortly discover, both objectives lead to the same test. Consequently, we can address both objectives at the same time.

The null hypothesis will specify that there is no relationship between the two variables. We state this in the following way.

H_0: The two variables are independent.

The alternative hypothesis specifies that one variable affects the other, which is expressed as

H_A: The two variables are dependent.

If the null hypothesis is true, political affiliation and economic option are independent of one another. This means that whether someone is a Democrat, Republican, or Independent does not affect his economic choice. Consequently, there is no difference among Democrats, Republicans, and Independents in their support for the four economic options. If the alternative hypothesis is true, political affiliation does affect which economic option is preferred. Thus, there are differences among the three political groups.

TEST STATISTIC

The test statistic is the same as the one employed to test proportions in the multinomial experiment. That is, the test statistic is

$$\chi^2 = \sum_{i=1}^{k} \frac{(o_i - e_i)^2}{e_i}$$

where k is the number of cells in the contingency table. If you examine the null hypotheses described in the chi-squared test of a multinomial experiment and in the one specified above, you will discover a major difference. In the chi-squared test of a multinomial experiment, the null hypothesis specifies values for the probabilities p_i. The null hypothesis for the chi-squared test of a contingency table only states that the two variables are independent. However, we need the probabilities in order to compute the expected values (e_i), which in turn permit us to calculate the value of the test statistic. (The entries in the contingency table are the observed values, o_i.) The question immediately arises: from where do we get the probabilities? The answer is that they will come from the data after we assume that the null hypothesis is true.

If we consider each political affiliation to be a separate population, each column of the contingency table represents a multinomial experiment with four cells. If the null hypothesis is true, the three multinomial experiments should produce similar proportions in each cell. We can estimate the cell probabilities by calculating the total in each row and dividing by the sample size. Thus,

$$P(\text{cut spending}) \simeq \frac{444}{1,000}$$

$$P(\text{raise taxes}) \approx \frac{130}{1,000}$$

$$P(\text{inflate the economy}) \approx \frac{250}{1,000}$$

$$P(\text{let deficit increase}) \approx \frac{176}{1,000}$$

We can calculate the expected values for each cell in the three multinomial experiments by multiplying these probabilities by the total number of people in each political group. By adding down each column, we find that there were 331 respondents who identified themselves as Democrats, 527 as Republicans, and 142 as Independents.

Expected Values of the Economic Options of Democrats

ECONOMIC OPTION	EXPECTED VALUE
Cut spending	$331 \times \dfrac{444}{1,000} = 146.96$
Raise taxes	$331 \times \dfrac{130}{1,000} = 43.03$
Inflate economy	$331 \times \dfrac{250}{1,000} = 82.75$
Let deficit increase	$331 \times \dfrac{176}{1,000} = 58.26$

Expected Values of the Economic Options of Republicans

ECONOMIC OPTION	EXPECTED VALUE
Cut spending	$527 \times \dfrac{444}{1,000} = 233.99$
Raise taxes	$527 \times \dfrac{130}{1,000} = 68.51$
Inflate economy	$527 \times \dfrac{250}{1,000} = 131.75$
Let deficit increase	$527 \times \dfrac{176}{1,000} = 92.75$

Expected Values of the Economic Options of Independents

ECONOMIC OPTION	EXPECTED VALUE
Cut spending	$142 \times \dfrac{444}{1,000} = 63.05$
Raise taxes	$142 \times \dfrac{130}{1,000} = 18.46$
Inflate economy	$142 \times \dfrac{250}{1,000} = 35.50$
Let deficit increase	$142 \times \dfrac{176}{1,000} = 24.99$

Notice that the expected values are computed by multiplying the column total by the row total and dividing by the sample size.

> **Expected Frequencies for a Contingency Table**
> The expected frequency of the cell in column j and row i is
> $$e_{ij} = \frac{(\text{Column } j \text{ total})(\text{Row } i \text{ total})}{\text{Sample size}}$$

The expected cell frequencies are shown in parentheses in the table below. As in the case of the chi-squared test of the multinomial experiment, the expected cell frequencies should satisfy the rule of five.

Contingency Table for Example 15.3

	POLITICAL AFFILIATION		
ECONOMIC OPTIONS	DEMOCRAT	REPUBLICAN	INDEPENDENT
Cut spending	101 (146.96)	282 (233.99)	61 (63.05)
Raise taxes	38 (43.03)	67 (68.51)	25 (18.46)
Inflate the economy	131 (82.75)	88 (131.75)	31 (35.50)
Let deficit increase	61 (58.26)	90 (92.75)	25 (24.99)

We can now calculate the value of the test statistic. It is

$$\chi^2 = \sum_{i=1}^{12} \frac{(o_i - e_i)^2}{e_i}$$

$$= \frac{(101 - 146.96)^2}{146.96} + \frac{(38 - 43.03)^2}{43.03} + \frac{(131 - 82.75)^2}{82.75} + \frac{(61 - 58.26)^2}{58.26}$$

$$+ \frac{(282 - 233.99)^2}{233.99} + \frac{(67 - 68.51)^2}{68.51} + \frac{(88 - 131.75)^2}{131.75} + \frac{(90 - 92.75)^2}{92.75}$$

$$+ \frac{(61 - 63.05)^2}{63.05} + \frac{(25 - 18.46)^2}{18.46} + \frac{(31 - 35.50)^2}{35.50} + \frac{(25 - 24.99)^2}{24.99}$$

$$= 70.675$$

Notice that we continue to use a single subscript in the formula of the test statistic when we should use two subscripts, one for the rows and one for the columns. We feel that it is clear that for each cell, we need to calculate the squared difference between the observed and expected frequencies divided by the expected frequency. We don't believe that the satisfaction of using the mathematically correct notation would overcome the unnecessary complication.

REJECTION REGION

To determine the rejection region, we need to know the number of degrees of freedom associated with this χ^2-statistic. The number of degrees of freedom for a contingency table with r rows and c columns is

d.f. $= (r - 1)(c - 1)$

For Example 15.3, the number of degrees of freedom is

$$\text{d.f.} = (r - 1)(c - 1) = (4 - 1)(3 - 1) = 6$$

If we use a 5% significance level, the rejection region is $\chi^2 > \chi^2_{\alpha,(r-1)(c-1)} = \chi^2_{.05,6} = 12.5916$.

Because $\chi^2 = 70.675$, we reject the null hypothesis and conclude that there is evidence of a relationship between political affiliation and support for the economic options. It follows that the three political affiliations differ in their support for the four economic options. We can see from the data that Republicans generally favor cutting spending, whereas Democrats prefer to inflate the economy.

USING THE COMPUTER

Minitab and Excel (using one of our macros) can produce the χ^2-statistic from either a contingency table that is already tabulated or raw data. To illustrate, we created two files for Example 15.3. File XM15-03T contains the complete contingency table; file XM15-03R contains the raw data using the following codes.

COLUMN 1 (ECONOMIC OPTIONS)   COLUMN 2 (PARTY AFFILIATION)

1 = Cut spending   1 = Democrat

2 = Raise taxes   2 = Republican

3 = Inflate economy   3 = Independent

4 = Increase deficit

Here are the outputs and instructions.

Minitab Output for Example 15.3

```
Chi-Square Test

Expected counts are printed below observed counts

        Democrat  Rpublcn Indpndnt    Total
    1        101      282       61      444
         146.96   233.99    63.05

    2         38       67       25      130
          43.03    68.51    18.46

    3        131       88       31      250
          82.75   131.75    35.50

    4         61       90       25      176
          58.26    92.75    24.99

Total        331      527      142     1000

ChiSq = 14.376 +   9.852 +   0.067 +
         0.588 +   0.033 +   2.317 +
        28.134 +  14.528 +   0.570 +
         0.129 +   0.082 +   0.000 = 70.675
df = 6,  p = 0.000
```

The output includes the observed and expected frequencies and the χ^2-statistic. The outputs vary slightly, depending on the format of the inputs. The output above was produced from the completed table (file XM15-03T). The p-value is printed. When the raw data are input, the p-value is not printed.

MENU COMMANDS (COMPLETED TABLE)

1 Type or import the data. The columns are the columns of the table.

2 Click **Stat**, **Tables**, and **Chisquare Test** . . . .

3 Type the names of the variables representing the columns. Click **OK**.

MENU COMMANDS (RAW DATA)

1 Type or import the data. Column 1 represents the codes for one qualitative variable, and column 2 represents the codes for the other qualitative variable.

2 Click **Stat**, **Tables**, and **Cross Tabulation** . . . .

3 Type the names of the variables.

4 Use the cursor to specify **Chisquare analysis**, and **Above and Expected Count**. Click **OK**.

COMMANDS FOR EXAMPLE 15.3

Open file **XM15-03T**.

Democrat, Rpublcn, Indpndnt
or **C1, C2, C3**

COMMANDS FOR EXAMPLE 15.3

Open file **XM15-03R**.

Option Party or **C1 C2**

Excel Output for Example 15.3

	A	B	C	D	E
1	Contingency Table				
2					TOTAL
3		101	282	61	444
4		38	67	25	130
5		131	88	31	250
6		61	90	25	176
7	TOTAL	331	527	142	1000
8	Test Statistic CHI-Squared = 70.6749				
9	P-Value = 0				

COMMANDS (COMPLETED TABLE)

1 Type or import the data. The columns are the columns of the table.

2 Click **Tools**, **Data Analysis Plus**, and **CHI-Square Test of a Contingency Table**.

COMMANDS FOR EXAMPLE 15.3

Open file **XM15-03T**.

EXAMPLE 15.4

The operations manager of a company that manufactures shirts wants to determine whether there are differences in the quality of workmanship among the three daily shifts. She randomly selects 600 recently made shirts and carefully inspects them. Each shirt is classified as either perfect or flawed, and the shift that produced it is also recorded. The accompanying table summarizes the number of shirts that fell into each cell. Do these data provide sufficient evidence at the 5% significance level to infer that there are differences in quality among the three shifts?

Contingency Table Classifying Shirts

	SHIFT		
SHIRT CONDITION	1	2	3
Perfect	240	191	139
Flawed	10	9	11

SOLUTION

IDENTIFYING THE TECHNIQUE

The problem objective is to compare three populations (the shirts produced by the three shifts). The data are qualitative because each shirt will be classified as either *perfect* or *flawed*. This problem-objective/data-type combination indicates that the statistical procedure to be employed is the chi-squared test of a contingency table. The null and alternative hypotheses are as follows.

H_0: The two variables are independent.

H_A: The two variables are dependent.

Test statistic: $\chi^2 = \sum_{i=1}^{k} \frac{(o_i - e_i)^2}{e_i}$ d.f. $= (r - 1)(c - 1)$

SOLVING BY HAND

We calculated the row and column totals and used them to determine the expected values. For example, the expected number of perfect shirts produced in shift 1 is

$$e_1 = \frac{250 \times 570}{600} = 237.5$$

The remaining expected values are computed in a like manner. The original table and expected values are shown in the table below.

| | SHIFT | | | |
SHIRT CONDITION	1	2	3	TOTAL
Perfect	240 (237.5)	191 (190.0)	139 (142.5)	570
Flawed	10 (12.5)	9 (10.0)	11 (7.5)	30
TOTAL	250	200	150	600

The value of the test statistic is

$$\chi^2 = \sum_{i=1}^{6} = \frac{(o_i - e_i)^2}{e_i}$$
$$= \frac{(240 - 237.5)^2}{237.5} + \frac{(10 - 12.5)^2}{12.5} + \frac{(191 - 190.0)^2}{190.0} + \frac{(9 - 10.0)^2}{10.0} + \frac{(139 - 142.5)^2}{142.5} + \frac{(11 - 7.5)^2}{7.5}$$
$$= 2.36$$

Conclusion: Do not reject the null hypothesis.

USING THE COMPUTER

Minitab Output for Example 15.4

Chi-Square Test

Expected counts are printed below observed counts

```
        Shift-1  Shift-2  Shift-3   Total
    1       240      191      139     570
         237.50   190.00   142.50

    2        10        9       11      30
          12.50    10.00     7.50

Total      250      200      150     600

ChiSq =   0.026 +  0.005 +  0.086 +
          0.500 +  0.100 +  1.633 = 2.351
df = 2, p = 0.309
```

	A	B	C	D	E
1	Contingency Table				
2					TOTAL
3		240	191	139	570
4		10	9	11	30
5	TOTAL	250	200	150	600
6	Test Statistic CHI-Squared = 2.3509				
7	P-Value = 0.3087				

There is not enough evidence to allow us to conclude that there are differences in quality among the three shifts. Had we discovered differences, we would attempt to determine why the shifts differ in quality. Possible explanations include workers on one shift using a different operating procedure or incompetent supervisors. In this case, since no significant differences were detected, any improvements in quality must be accomplished over all three shifts. These could include, for example, acquiring newer machines, training the employees, or instituting statistical process control. (See Chapter 18.).

Rule of Five

In the previous section, we pointed out that the expected values should be at least five to ensure that the chi-squared distribution provides an adequate approximation of the sampling distribution. In a contingency table where one or more cells have expected values of less than 5, we need to combine rows or columns to satisfy the rule of five. To illustrate, suppose that we want to test for dependence in the following contingency table.

			TOTAL
10	14	4	28
12	16	7	35
8	8	4	20
TOTAL 30	38	15	83

The expected values are as follows.

10.1	12.8	5.1
12.7	16.0	6.3
7.2	9.2	3.6

The expected value of the cell in row 3 and column 3 is less than 5. To eliminate the problem, we can add column 3 to one of columns 1 and 2 or add row 3 to either row 1 or row 2. The combining of rows or columns should be done so that the combination forms a logical unit, if possible. For example, if the columns represent the age groups, young (under 40), middle-aged (40–65), and senior (over 65), it is logical to combine columns 2 and 3. The observed and expected values are combined to produce the following table (expected values in parentheses).

		TOTAL
10 (10.1)	18 (17.9)	28
12 (12.6)	23 (22.3)	35
8 (7.2)	12 (12.8)	20
TOTAL 30	53	83

The degrees of freedom must be changed as well. The number of degrees of freedom of the original contingency table is $(3 - 1) \times (3 - 1) = 4$. The number of degrees of freedom of the combined table is $(3 - 1) \times (2 - 1) = 2$. The rest of the procedure is unchanged.

Here is a summary of the factors that tell us when to apply the chi-squared test of a contingency table. Note that there are two problem objectives satisfied by this statistical procedure.

Factors that Identify the Chi-Squared Test of a Contingency Table

1 Problem objectives: analyze the relationship between two variables; compare two or more populations

2 Data type: qualitative

Exercises

15.10 Conduct a test to determine whether the two classifications L and M are independent, using the data in the accompanying contingency table. (Use $\alpha = .01$.)

	M_1	M_2
L_1	29	67
L_2	56	38

15.11 Conduct a test to determine whether the two classifications R and C are independent, using the data in the accompanying contingency table and $\alpha = .10$.

	C_1	C_2	C_3
R_1	40	32	48
R_2	30	48	52

15.12 The trustee of a company's pension plan has solicited the opinions of a sample of the company's employees about a proposed revision of the plan. A breakdown of the responses is shown in the accompanying table. Is there evidence at the 10% significance level to infer that the responses differ among the three groups of employees?

RESPONSES	BLUE-COLLAR WORKERS	WHITE-COLLAR WORKERS	MANAGERS
For	67	32	11
Against	63	18	9

15.13 To determine if commercials viewed during happy television programs are more effective than those viewed during sad television programs, a study was conducted in which a random sample of students viewed an upbeat segment from "Real People" with commercials, while another random sample of students viewed a very sad segment from "Sixty Minutes" with commercials. The students were then asked what they were thinking during the final commercial. From their responses, they were categorized as thinking primarily about the commercial (1), thinking primarily about the program (2), or thinking about both (3). The results were stored in file XR15-13. (Column 1 lists the program, 1 = "Real People" and 2 = "Sixty Minutes," and column 2 lists the responses.) Do commercials viewed during happy television programs appear to have a different effect than those viewed during sad television programs? (Source: Marvin E. Goldberg and Gerald J. Gorn, "Happy and Sad TV Programs: How They Affect Reactions to Commercials," *Journal of Consumer Research* 14 (1987): 387–403.) (Use $\alpha = .05$.)

Use a software package to solve this problem.	OR	The numbers of combinations of responses and programs are as follows. (1,1): 50, (1,2): 15, (1,3): 8 (2,1): 11, (2,2): 42, (2,3): 25 Complete your answer manually.

15.14 Acute otitis media, an infection of the middle ear, is a very common childhood illness. Although it is normally treated with amoxicillin, emerging resistance to the antibiotic has promoted the search for an alternative. A recent article discussed the efficacy of one such alternative: trimethoprim-sulfamethoxazole. In this study, 203 "patients were randomly assigned to receive either amoxicillin (1) or trimethoprim-sulfamethoxazole (2) by means of a computer-generated table of random numbers." Each patient was judged to be cured (1), improved (2), or to have no improvement (3). The data are stored in columns 1 (drug) and 2 (outcome) of file XR15-14. Can we conclude from these data that there are differences in outcomes for children treated with amoxicillin and for children treated with trimethoprim-sulfamethoxazole? (Use $\alpha = .10$.) (Source: William Feldman, Joanne Momy, and Corinne Dulberg, "Trimethoprim-Sulfamethoxazole v. Amoxicillin in the Treatment of Acute Otitis Media," *Canadian Medical Association Journal* 139 (1988): 961–64.)

Use a software package to solve this problem.	OR	The numbers of combinations of drugs and outcomes are as follows. (1,1): 60, (1,2): 31, (1,3): 12 (2,1): 65, (2,2): 22, (2,3): 13 Complete your answer manually.

15.15 An antismoking group recently had a large advertisement published in local newspapers throughout Florida. Several statistical facts and medical details were included, in the hope that the ad would have meaningful impact on smokers. The antismoking group is concerned, however, that smokers might have read less of the advertisement than did nonsmokers. This concern is based on the belief that a reader tends to spend more time reading articles that agree with his or her predisposition. The antismoking group has conducted a survey asking those who saw the advertisement if they read the headline only (1), some detail (2), or most of the advertisement (3). The questionnaire also asks respondents to identify themselves as either a heavy smoker—more than two packs per day (1), a moderate smoker—between one and two packs per day (2), a light smoker—less than one pack per day (3), or a nonsmoker (4). The results are stored in file XR15-15. (Column 1: type of smoker; column 2: survey responses.) Do the data indicate that the antismoking group has reason to be concerned? (Use $\alpha = .05$.)

Use a software package to solve this problem.	OR	The numbers of combinations of smoker categories and survey responses are as follows. (1,1): 33, (1,2): 24, (1,3): 19 (2,1): 23, (2,2): 17, (2,3): 26 (3,1): 16, (3,2): 27, (3,3): 46 (4,1): 14, (4,2): 38, (4,3): 57 Complete your answer manually.

15.16 An investor who can correctly forecast the direction and size of changes in foreign currency exchange rates is able to reap huge profits in the international currency markets. A knowledgeable reader of the *Wall Street Journal* (in particular, of the currency futures market quotations) can determine the direction of change in various exchange rates that is predicted by all investors, viewed collectively. Predictions from 216 investors, together with the subsequent actual directions of change, are stored in file XR15-16. (Column 1: predicted change where 1 = positive and 2 = negative; column 2: actual change where 1 = positive and 2 = negative.)

a Test the hypothesis (with $\alpha = .10$) that a relationship exists between the predicted and actual directions of change.

b To what extent would you make use of these predictions in formulating your forecasts of future exchange rate changes?

Use a software package to solve this problem.	OR	The numbers of combinations of predicted changes and actual changes are as follows. (1,1): 65 (1,2): 64 (2,1): 39 (2,2): 48 Complete your answer manually.

15.4 Summary of Tests on Qualitative Data

At this point in the textbook, we've described four tests used when the data are qualitative. These are as follows.

1 z-test of p (Section 11.4)

2 z-test of $p_1 - p_2$ (Section 12.6)

3 Chi-squared test of a multinomial experiment (Section 15.2)

4 Chi-squared test of a contingency table (Section 15.3)

In the process of presenting these techniques, it was necessary to concentrate on one technique at a time and focus on the kinds of problems each addresses. However, this approach tends to conflict somewhat with our promised goal of emphasizing the "when" of statistical inference. In this section, we summarize the statistical tests on qualitative data to ensure that you are capable of selecting the correct method.

There are two critical factors in identifying the technique used when the data are qualitative. The first, of course, is the problem objective. The second is the number of categories that the qualitative variable can assume. Table 15.1 provides a guide to help select the correct technique.

Table 15.1	Statistical Techniques for Qualitative Data		
PROBLEM OBJECTIVE	**NUMBER OF CATEGORIES**	**STATISTICAL TECHNIQUE**
Describe a single population	2	z-test of p or the chi-squared test of a multinomial experiment
Describe a single population	2 or more	chi-squared test of a multinomial experiment
Compare two populations	2	z-test of $p_1 - p_2$ or the chi-squared test of a contingency table
Compare two populations	2 or more	chi-squared test of a contingency table
Compare two or more populations	2 or more	chi-squared test of a contingency table
Analyze the relationship between two variables	2 or more	chi-squared test of a contingency table

Notice that when we describe a single population of qualitative data with exactly two categories, we can use either of two techniques. We can employ the z-test of p or the chi-squared test of a multinomial experiment. These two tests are equivalent because if there are only two categories, the multinomial experiment is actually a binomial experiment (one of the categorical outcomes is labeled success and the other is labeled failure). Mathematical statisticians have established that if we square the value of z, the test statistic for the test of p, we produce the χ^2-statistic. That is, $z^2 = \chi^2$. Thus, if we want to conduct a two-tail test of a population proportion, we can employ either technique. However, the chi-squared test of a binomial experiment can only test to determine if the hypothesized values of p_1 (which we can label p) and p_2 (which we can call q) are not equal to their specified values. Consequently, to perform a one-tail test of a population proportion, we must use the z-test of p. (This issue was discussed in Chapter 14 when we pointed out that we can use either the t-test of $\mu_1 - \mu_2$ or the analysis of variance to conduct a test to determine if two population means differ.)

When we test for differences between two populations of qualitative data with two categories, we can also use either of two techniques: the z-test of $p_1 - p_2$ (case 1) or the chi-squared test of a contingency table. Once again, we can use either technique to perform a two-tail test about $p_1 - p_2$. (Squaring the value of the z-statistic yields the value of χ^2-statistic.) However, one-tail tests must be conducted by the z-test of $p_1 - p_2$. The rest of the table is quite straightforward. Notice that when we want to compare two populations when there are two or more categories, we use the chi-squared test of a contingency table.

Figure 15.2 offers another summary of the tests that deal with qualitative data introduced in this book. There are two groups of tests: ones that test hypotheses about single populations and ones that test either for differences or for independence. In the first set, we have the z-test of p, which can be replaced by the chi-squared test of a multinomial experiment. The latter test is employed when there are more than two catagories.

To test for differences between two proportions, we apply the z-test of $p_1 - p_2$. We can use instead the chi-squared test of a contingency table, which can be applied to a variety of other problems.

Figure 15.2

Tests on Qualitative Data

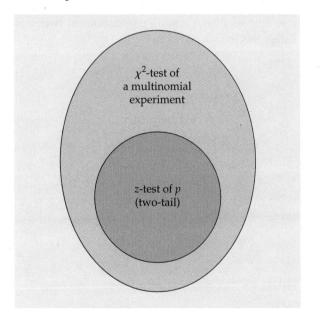

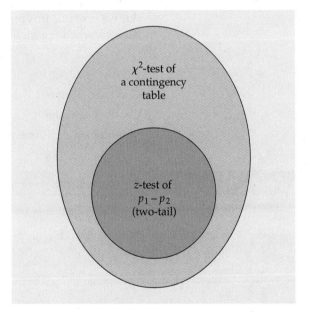

Developing an Understanding of Statistical Concepts

Table 15.1 and Figure 15.2 summarize how we deal with qualitative data. We determine the frequency of each category and use these frequencies to compute test statistics. We can then compute proportions to calculate z-statistics or use the frequencies to calculate χ^2-statistics. Because squaring a standard normal random variable produces a chi-squared variable, we can employ either statistic to test for differences. As a consequence, when you encounter qualitative data in the problems described in this book (and other introductory applied statistics books), the most logical starting point in selecting the appropriate technique will be either a z-statistic or a χ^2-statistic. However, you should know that there are other statistical procedures that can be applied to qualitative data, techniques that are not included in this book.

Exercises

15.17 Repeat Exercise 11.21(a), using the techniques presented in this chapter.

15.18 Refer to Exercise 11.31. Using a technique presented in this chapter, determine whether we can conclude that Pat's probability of winning is not equal to 50%.

15.19 Repeat Exercise 12.39(a), using a technique presented in this chapter.

15.20 Repeat Exercise 12.46, using a technique presented in this chapter.

15.5 Summary

This chapter describes two statistical techniques used to test hypotheses for qualitative data. The first is the chi-squared test of a multinomial experiment (also called a goodness-of-fit test). It is used to describe a single population when there are two or more categories. The second is the chi-squared test of a contingency table, which is employed to satisfy two different objectives. We use the chi-squared test of a contingency table to determine if two qualitative variables are dependent. But we also use this procedure to compare two or more populations or two populations when the number of categories is more than two.

IMPORTANT TERMS

Goodness-of-fit test   Observed frequency

Contingency table   Expected frequency

Multinomial experiment   Rule of five

Table 15.2	Summary of Formulas
$e_i = np_i$	
$\chi^2 = \displaystyle\sum_{i=1}^{k} \frac{(o_i - e_i)^2}{e_i}$	

Supplementary Exercises

15.21 An organization dedicated to ensuring fairness in television game shows is investigating "Wheel of Fortune." In this show, three contestants are required to solve puzzles by selecting letters. Each contestant gets to select the first letter and continues selecting until he or she chooses a letter that is not in the hidden word, phrase, or name. The order of contestants is random. However, contestant 1 gets to start game 1, contestant 2 starts game 2, and so on. The contestant who wins the most money is declared the winner, and he or she is given an opportunity to win a grand prize. Usually, more than three games are played per show, and as a result it appears that contestant 1 has an advantage: contestant 1 will start two games, whereas contestant 3 will usually start only one game. To see if this is the case, a random sample of 30 shows was taken and the starting position of the winning contestant for each show was recorded. These are shown in the following table.

STARTING POSITION	NUMBER OF WINNERS
1	14
2	10
3	6

Do the tabulated results allow us to conclude at the 10% significance level that the game is unfair?

15.22 Econetics Research Corporation, a well-known Montreal-based consulting firm, wants to test how it can influence the proportion of questionnaires returned from surveys. Believing that the inclusion of an inducement to respond may be important, it sends out 1,000 questionnaires: 200 promise to send respondents a summary of the survey results, 300 indicate that 20 respondents (selected by lottery) will be awarded gifts, and 500 are accompanied by no inducements. Of these, 80 questionnaires promising a summary, 100 questionnaires offering gifts, and 120 questionnaires offering no inducements are returned. What can you conclude from these results? (Use $\alpha = .05$.)

15.23 It has been estimated that employee absenteeism costs North American companies more than $100 billion per year. As a first step in addressing the rising cost of absenteeism, the personnel department of a large corporation recorded the weekdays during which individuals in a sample of 362 absentees were away over the past several months. Do these data suggest that absenteeism is higher on some days of the week than on others? (Use $\alpha = .05$.)

Day of the Week	Mon	Tues	Wed	Thurs	Fri
Number Absent	87	62	71	68	74

15.24 Suppose that the personnel department in Exercise 15.23 continued its investigation by categorizing absentees according to the shift on which they worked, as shown in the accompanying table. Is there sufficient evidence at the 10% significance level of a relationship between the days on which employees are absent and the shift on which the employees work?

SHIFT	MONDAY	TUESDAY	WEDNESDAY	THURSDAY	FRIDAY
Day	52	28	37	31	33
Evening	35	34	34	37	41

15.25 A management behavior analyst has been studying the relationship between male/female supervisory structures in the workplace and the level of employees' job satisfaction. The results of a recent survey are shown in the table below. Conduct a test with $\alpha = .05$ to determine whether the level of job satisfaction depends on the boss/employee gender relationship.

LEVEL OF SATISFACTION	BOSS/EMPLOYEE			
	FEMALE/MALE	FEMALE/FEMALE	MALE/MALE	MALE/FEMALE
Satisfied	21	25	54	71
Neutral	39	49	50	38
Dissatisfied	31	48	10	11

15.26 In a 1993 Coca-Cola promotion, specially marked cans were sold. On the tabs, one of the letters A, C, E, H, M, O, S, or W or one of the words "can" or "shirt" was imprinted. Customers who sent in tabs with the letters that spelled "cash" were given $1,500. Tabs that spelled the word "awesome" earned one of several trips. Customers with tabs spelling the word "can" received a free can of Coke, and people with a tab with the word "shirt" received a T-shirt. The Coca-Cola company announced that there were a total of 35 million cans with imprinted tabs. A further breakdown revealed the following numbers.

CAN IMPRINT	NUMBER OF CANS	PROPORTION
Can	3,000,000	1/11.7
Shirt	10,000	1/3,500
A	5,331,483	1/6.6
E	5,331,483	1/6.6
C	1,000	1/35,000
H	5,331,483	1/6.6
M	5,331,483	1/6.6
O	5,331,483	1/6.6
S	5,331,483	1/6.6
W	100	1/350,000

Suppose that a Coca-Cola lover purchased 1,000 cans and counted the number of tabs with each imprint. The results are as follows.

CAN IMPRINT	NUMBER OF CANS
Can	95
Shirt	0
A	140
E	161
C	0
H	148
M	141
O	143
S	172
W	0

Because the Coca-Cola lover won only 95 free cans of Coke, he suspected that the numbers supplied by Coke were false. Conduct a test with $\alpha = .10$ to see if the Coke lover is right.

15.27 During the decade of the 1980s, professional baseball thrived in North America. Attendance rose continuously from 45 million in 1984 to 58 million in 1991. However, in 1992, attendance dropped about 2 million. In addition, the number of television viewers also decreased. In order to examine the popularity of baseball relative to other sports, surveys were performed. In 1985 and again in 1993, a Harris Poll asked a random sample of 500 people to name their favorite sport. The results, which were published in the *Wall Street Journal* (6 July 1993), are exhibited below.

a   Do these results indicate at the 5% significance level that North Americans changed their favorite sport between 1985 and 1993?

b   Do these results indicate at the 5% significance level that the popularity of baseball has changed between 1985 and 1993?

Percentage of People Citing a Given Sport as Their Favorite	SPORT	1985	1993
	Professional football	24%	24%
	Baseball	23%	18%
	Professional basketball	6%	12%
	College basketball	10%	8%
	College football	10%	7%
	Golf	3%	6%
	Auto racing	5%	6%
	Tennis	5%	4%
	Other	14%	15%

CASE 15.1 — PREDICTING THE OUTCOMES OF BASKETBALL, BASEBALL, FOOTBALL, AND HOCKEY GAMES FROM INTERMEDIATE SCORES*

Some basketball fans generally believe that it doesn't pay to watch an entire game because the outcome is determined in the last few minutes (some say the last two minutes) of the game. Is this really true, and, if so, is basketball different in this respect from other professional sports played in North America? For example, is it true that the team that leads a baseball game after seven innings almost always wins the game? To address these questions, three researchers tracked basketball, baseball, football, and hockey games. The results of games during the 1990 season (for baseball and football) and during the 1990–1991 season (for basketball and hockey) were recorded. The numbers of games won by the early-game leader and by the late-game leader were recorded. Early-game leaders are defined as the teams that are ahead after one quarter of basketball and football, one period of hockey, or three innings of baseball. Late-game leaders are defined as the teams that are ahead after three quarters of basketball and football, two periods of hockey, or seven innings of baseball.

The researchers also wanted to know how the home team fared in each sport and whether the home team–visiting team circumstance affected the outcome of the late-game leader. Tables A through D summarize the relevant results. Apply any statistical techniques you think necessary, and discuss their conclusions.

Table A

Number of Early-Game Leader Wins and Early-Game Leader Losses

SPORT	n	LEADER WINS	LEADER LOSSES
Basketball	189	132	57
Baseball	80	65	15
Football	73	40	33
Hockey	75	52	23

*Adapted from H. Cooper, K. M. DeNeve, and F. Mosteller, "Predicting Professional Sports Game Outcomes from Intermediate Game Scores," *Chance* 5, Nos. 3–4 (1992): 18–22

SPORT	n	LEADER WINS	LEADER LOSSES
Basketball	189	150	39
Baseball	92	86	6
Football	93	72	21
Hockey	80	65	15

Table C

Number of Home-Team
and Visiting-Team Wins

SPORT	n	HOME-TEAM WINS	VISITING-TEAM WINS
Basketball	198	127	71
Baseball	100	53	47
Football	99	57	42
Hockey	93	50	43

Table D

Number of Home-Team
and Visiting-Team Wins
as a Function of Which
Team Was the Late-
Game Leader

	GAME WINNER	
LATE-GAME LEADER	HOME TEAM	VISITING TEAM
Basketball ($n=189$)		
Home Team	94	11
Visiting Team	28	56
Other sports combined ($n = 265$)		
Home Team	123	16
Visiting Team	26	100

CASE 15.2   CAN EXPOSURE TO A CODE OF PROFESSIONAL ETHICS HELP MAKE MANAGERS MORE ETHICAL?*

In many North American business schools, the issue of whether a course on ethics should be compulsory has been hotly debated. The empirical evidence appears to be far from consistent on the effects of such courses. To help shed more light on the issue, two researchers organized a study in which they took a random sample of 68 accounting students and 132 nonaccounting students. As part of their curriculum, the accounting students were exposed to the American Institute of Certified Public Accountants' code of professional ethics. The nonaccounting business students did not take any course that dealt with issues of ethical behavior.

All 200 students in the study were taking a required senior-level policy course. As part of the course, they were assigned to read the article "Crisis in Conscience at Quasar" by A. Fendrock (*Harvard Business Review*, March–April 1968, 112–20). In the case, Universal, the parent company, learned that the senior managers of

---

*Adapted from W. E. Fulmer and B. R. Cargile, "Ethical Perceptions of Accounting Students: Does Exposure to a Code of Professional Ethics Help?" *Issues in Accounting Education* (Fall 1987): 207–19.

one of its subsidiaries, Quasar, deliberately lied about financial conditions in their monthly report to corporate headquarters. Quasar's president, John Kane, and its controller, Hugh Kay, were forced to resign. Universal wanted to know why no one at Quasar provided any information about the true financial conditions, whether any other executives were accomplices to the phony reports, and what could be done to avert such occurrences in the future. Universal sent a fact finder to interview other executives at Quasar—George Kessler, vice president, manufacturing; William Heller, vice president, engineering; Peter Loomis, vice president, marketing; Donald Morgan, chief accountant; and Paul Brown, vice president, industrial relations.

After studying the case, students completed the questionnaire shown below. The results are stored in file C15-02. (The responses to questions 1 to 10 for all students are stored in columns 1 to 10; column 11 indicates whether the student was an accounting student [1] or a nonaccounting business student [2].)

Does it appear that accounting students exposed to a code of ethics answer the questionnaire differently from nonaccounting business students not exposed to the same code?

QUASAR QUESTIONNAIRE

1 If you had been John Kane, president of Quasar, do you think you would have been tempted to withhold the bad news from corporate management at the parent company?

    2 Yes _____
    1 No _____

2 Do you think that under the circumstances you would have withheld the bad news?

    2 Yes _____
    1 No _____

3 If you were in the position of Loomis, Kessler, or Heller, would you have felt that your loyalty to the president of Quasar transcended your loyalty to the total company?

    2 Yes _____
    1 No _____

4 Do you think you would have gone around the president and reported the bad news to corporate headquarters at Universal?

    2 Yes _____
    1 No _____

5 Do you think corporate management was right to request the resignation of Quasar's president?

    2 Yes _____
    1 No _____

6 Do you think corporate management was right to request the resignation of Quasar's controller?

    2 Yes _____
    1 No _____

7 Do you feel that a subsidiary's executives (other than the president) should communicate directly with corporate management of the parent as a regular procedure?

    2 Yes ____

    1 No ____

8 Do you think Kane's withholding the bad news was (check one) . . .

    1 practical ____?

    2 unethical ____?

    3 poor judgment ____?

9 Do you think the blame lies with (check just one) . . .

    1 Universal's corporate management ____?

    2 Quasar's president ____?

    3 Quasar's controller ____?

    4 other____?

10 Is the problem one of (check just one) . . .

    1 poor organization ____?

    2 lack of communication ____?

    3 excessive personal loyalty ____?

    4 inadequate supervision ____?

    5 other____?

Minitab Instructions

Chi-Squared Test of a Contingency Table

If the contingency table is complete (i.e., we know the number of occurrences of each combination of the two classifications), the **CHISQUARE** command is used. For Example 15.4, we would input the counts in the following way.

```
READ C1 - C3
240 191 139
 10   9  11
END
```

The command

```
CHISQUARE C1 - C3
```

produces the χ^2-statistic.

If we have only the raw data (column 1 contains the codes for classification variable 1 and column 2 contains the codes for classification variable 2), type

```
TABLE C1 C2;
CHISQUARE 2.
```

If you omit the "2" in the subcommand, the expected values will not be printed.

Excel Instructions

Chi-Squared Test of a Multinomial Experiment

Excel can be used to compute the chi-squared statistic in the goodness-of-fit test (multinomial experiment). Type the observed values into one column, and in another column type the expected values. (If you wish, you can type the cell probabilities specified in the null hypothesis and let Excel convert these into the expected values.)

Click f_x, **Statistical**, and **CHITEST**. Specify the range of the observed values and the range of the expected values, and click **FINISH**. Only the p-value of the test will be printed.

16 Simple Linear Regression and Correlation

16.1 Introduction

This chapter is the first in a series of three in which the problem objective is to analyze the relationship among quantitative variables. **Regression analysis** is used to predict the value of one variable on the basis of other variables. This technique may be the most commonly used statistical procedure because, as you can easily appreciate, almost all companies and government institutions forecast variables such as product demand, interest rates, inflation rates, prices of raw materials, and labor costs.

The technique involves developing a mathematical equation that describes the relationship between the variable to be forecast, which is called the **dependent variable**, and variables that the statistician believes are related to the dependent variable. The dependent variable is denoted y, while the related variables are called **independent variables** and are denoted $x_1, x_2, \ldots, x_k$ (where k is the number of independent variables).

If we are interested only in determining *whether* a relationship exists, we employ correlation analysis. We have already introduced this technique. In Chapter 2, we presented the graphical method to describe the association between two quantitative variables—the scatter diagram. We introduced the coefficient of correlation and covariance in Chapter 4. We discussed correlation and covariance again in Chapter 7.

Because regression analysis involves a number of new techniques and concepts, we divided the presentation into three chapters. In this chapter, we present techniques that allow us to determine the relationship between only two variables. In Chapter 17, we expand our discussion to more than two variables.

Here are three examples of regression analysis.

Example 1 The product manager in charge of a particular brand of children's breakfast cereal would like to predict the demand for the cereal during the next year. In order to use regression analysis, she and her staff list the following variables as likely to affect sales.

Price of the product

Number of children 5 to 12 years of age (the target market)

Price of competitor's products

Effectiveness of advertising (as measured by advertising exposure)

Annual sales this year

Annual sales in previous years

Example 2 A gold speculator is considering a major purchase of gold bullion. He would like to forecast the price of gold two years from now (his planning horizon), using regression analysis. In preparation, he produces the following list of independent variables.

Interest rates

Inflation rate

Price of oil

Demand for gold jewelry

Demand for industrial and commercial gold

Dow Jones Industrial Average

Example 3 A real estate agent wants to more accurately predict the selling price of houses. She believes that the following variables affect the price of a house.

Size of the house (number of square feet)

Number of bedrooms

Frontage of the lot

Condition

Location

In each of these examples, the primary motive for using regression analysis is forecasting. Nonetheless, analyzing the relationship among variables can also be quite useful in managerial decision making. For instance, in the first application, the product manager may want to know how price is related to product demand so that a decision about a prospective change in pricing can be made.

Another application comes from the field of finance. The capital asset pricing model analyzes the relationship between the returns of a particular stock and the behavior of a stock index (such as the S&P 500 Index). Its function is not to predict the stock's price but to assess the risk of the stock versus the risk of the stock market in general. (See Case 16.1.)

Regardless of why regression analysis is performed, the next step in the technique is to develop a mathematical equation or model that accurately describes the nature of the relationship that exists between the dependent variable and the independent variables. This stage—which is only a small part of the total process—is described in the next section. In the ensuing sections of this chapter (and in Chapter 17), we will spend considerable time assessing and testing how well the model fits the actual data. Only when we're satisfied with the model do we use it to estimate and forecast.

16.2 Model

The job of developing a mathematical equation can be quite complex, because we need to have some idea about the nature of the relationship between each of the independent variables and the dependent variable. For example, the gold speculator mentioned in Example 2 needs to know how interest rates affect the price of gold. If he proposes a linear relationship, that may imply that as interest rates rise (or fall), the price of gold will rise or fall. A quadratic relationship may suggest that the price of gold will increase over a certain range of interest rates but will decrease over a different range. Perhaps certain combinations of values of interest rates and other independent variables influence the price in one way, while other combinations change it in other ways. The number of different mathematical models that could be proposed is virtually infinite.

You might have encountered various models in previous courses. For instance, the following represent relationships in the natural sciences.

$E = mc^2$, where E = Energy, m = Mass, and c = Speed of light

$F = ma$, where F = Force, m = Mass, and a = Acceleration

$S = at^2/2$, where S = Distance, t = Time, and a = Gravitational acceleration

In other business courses, you might have seen the following equations.

Profit = Revenue − Costs

Total cost = Fixed cost + (Variable cost × Number of units produced)

The above are all examples of **deterministic** models, so named because—except for small measurement errors—such equations allow us to determine the value of the dependent variable (on the left side of the equation) from the value of the independent variables. In many practical applications of interest to us, deterministic models are unrealistic. For example, is it reasonable to believe that we can determine the selling price of a house solely on the basis of its size? Unquestionably, the size of a house affects its price, but many other variables (some of which may not be measurable) also influence price. What must be included in most practical models is a method to represent the randomness that is part of a real-life process. Such a model is called **probabilistic**.

To create a probabilistic model, we start with a deterministic model that approximates the relationship we want to model. We then add a random term that measures the error of the deterministic component. Suppose that in Example 3 described above, the real estate agent knows that the cost of building a new house is about $75 per square foot and that most lots sell for about $25,000. The approximate selling price would be

$y = 25,000 + 75x$

where y = Selling price and x = Size of the house in square feet. A house of 2,000 square feet would therefore be estimated to sell for

$y = 25,000 + 75(2,000) = 175,000$

We know, however, that the selling price is not likely to be exactly $175,000. Prices may actually range from $100,000 to $250,000. In other words, the deterministic model is not really suitable. To represent this situation properly, we should use the probabilistic model

$$y = 25{,}000 + 75x + \epsilon$$

where ϵ (the Greek letter epsilon) represents the random term (also called the error variable)—the difference between the actual selling price and the estimated price based on the size of the house. The random term thus accounts for all the variables, measurable and immeasurable, that are not part of the model. The value of ϵ will vary from one sale to the next, even if x remains constant. That is, houses of exactly the same size will sell for different prices because of differences in location, selling season, decorations, and other variables.

In the three chapters devoted to regression analysis, we will present only probabilistic models. Additionally, to simplify the presentation, all models will be linear. In this chapter, we restrict the number of independent variables to one. The model to be used in this chapter is called the **first-order linear model**—sometimes called the **simple linear regression model**.

First-Order Linear Model

$$y = \beta_0 + \beta_1 x + \epsilon$$

where

y = dependent variable

x = independent variable

β_0 = y-intercept

β_1 = slope of the line (defined as the ratio rise/run or change in y/change in x)

ϵ = error variable

Figure 16.1 depicts the deterministic component of the model.

Figure 16.1

First-Order Linear Model: Deterministic Component

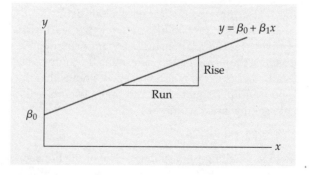

The problem objective addressed by the model is to analyze the relationship between two variables, x and y, both of which must be quantitative. To define the relationship between x and y, we need to know the value of the coefficients of the linear model β_0 and β_1. However, these coefficients are population parameters, which are almost always unknown. In the next section, we discuss how these parameters are estimated.

Exercises

16.1 Graph each of the following straight lines. Identify the intercept and the slope.

a $y = 2 + 3x$

b $y = 5 - 2x$

c $y = 2 + 4x$

d $y = x$

e $y = 4$

16.2 For each of the following data sets, plot the points on a graph and determine whether a linear model is reasonable.

a

x	2	3	5	7	9
y	6	9	4	7	8

b

x	1	3	5	4	7
y	5	7	10	9	16

c

x	7	9	2	3	6
y	4	1	6	10	5

16.3 Graph the following observations of x and y.

x	1	2	3	4	5	6
y	4	6	7	7	9	11

Draw a straight line through the data. What are the intercept and the slope of the line you drew?

16.3 Least Squares Method

We estimate the parameters β_0 and β_1 in a way similar to the methods used to estimate all the other parameters discussed in this book. We draw a random sample from the populations of interest and calculate the sample statistics we need. Because β_0 and β_1 represent the coefficients of a straight line, their estimators are based on drawing a straight line through the sample data. To see how this is done, consider the following simple example.

EXAMPLE 16.1

Given the following six observations of variables x and y, determine the straight line that fits these data.

x	2	4	8	10	13	16
y	2	7	25	26	38	50

SOLUTION

As a first step we graph the data, as shown in Figure 16.2. Recall (from Chapter 2) that this graph is called a scatter diagram. The scatter diagram usually reveals whether or not a straight-line model fits the data reasonably well. Evidently, in this case a linear model is justified. Our task is to draw the straight line that provides the *best possible fit*.

Figure 16.2

Scatter Diagram for Example 16.1

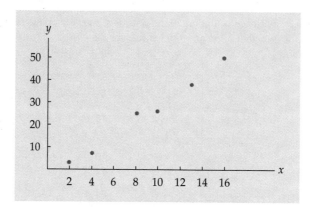

We can define what we mean by *best* in various ways. For example, we can draw the line that minimizes the sum of the differences between the line and the points. Because some of the differences will be positive (points above the line), and others will be negative (points below the line), a canceling effect might produce a straight line that does not fit the data at all. To eliminate the positive and negative differences, we will draw the line that minimizes the sum of *squared* differences. That is, we want to determine the line that minimizes

$$\sum_{i=1}^{n}(y_i - \hat{y}_i)^2$$

where y_i represents the observed value of y and $\hat{y}_i$ represents the value of y calculated from the equation of the line. That is,

$$\hat{y}_i = \hat{\beta}_0 + \hat{\beta}_1 x_i$$

The technique that produces this line is called the **least squares method**. The line itself is called the **least squares line**, the **fitted line**, or the **regression line**. The "hats" on the coefficients remind us that they are estimators of the parameters β_0 and β_1.

By using calculus, we can produce formulas for $\hat{\beta}_0$ and $\hat{\beta}_1$. Although we're sure that you are keenly interested in the calculus derivation of the formulas, we will not provide them, because we promised to keep the mathematics to a minimum. Instead, we offer the following, which were derived by calculus.

Calculation of $\hat{\beta}_0$ and $\hat{\beta}_1$

$$\hat{\beta}_1 = \frac{\text{SS}_{xy}}{\text{SS}_x}$$

where

$$SS_{xy} = \sum (x_i - \bar{x})(y_i - \bar{y})$$
$$SS_x = \sum (x_i - \bar{x})^2$$
$$\hat{\beta}_0 = \bar{y} - \hat{\beta}_1 \bar{x}$$

and where

$$\bar{y} = \frac{\sum y_i}{n} \qquad \text{and} \qquad \bar{x} = \frac{\sum x_i}{n}$$

The formula for SS_x should look familiar; it is the numerator in the calculation of sample variance s^2. We introduced the SS notation in Chapter 14; it stands for sum of squares. The statistic SS_x is the sum of squared differences between the observations of x and their mean. Strictly speaking, SS_{xy} is not a sum of squares. The formula for SS_{xy} *may* be familiar; it is the numerator in the calculation for covariance and the coefficient of correlation (introduced in Chapter 4).

As was the case with the analysis of variance procedures introduced in Chapter 14, calculating the statistics manually in any realistic example is extremely time-consuming. Naturally, we recommend the use of statistical software to produce the statistics we need. However, it may be worthwhile to manually perform the calculations for several small-sample problems. Such efforts may provide you with insights into the working of regression analysis. To that end we provide shortcut formulas for the various statistics that are computed in this chapter.

Shortcut Formulas for SS_x and SS_{xy}

$$SS_x = \sum x_i^2 - \frac{\left(\sum x_i \right)^2}{n}$$

$$SS_{xy} = \sum x_i y_i - \frac{\sum x_i \sum y_i}{n}$$

As you can see, to estimate the regression coefficients by hand, we need to determine the following summations.

Sum of x: $\sum x_i$

Sum of y: $\sum y_i$

Sum of x-squared: $\sum x_i^2$

Sum of x times y: $\sum x_i y_i$

Returning to our example we find

$$\sum x_i = 53$$
$$\sum y_i = 148$$
$$\sum x_i^2 = 609$$
$$\sum x_i y_i = 1,786$$

Using these summations in our shortcut formulas, we find

$$SS_x = \sum x_i^2 - \frac{\left(\sum x_i\right)^2}{n} = 609 - \frac{(53)^2}{6} = 140.833$$

and

$$SS_{xy} = \sum x_i y_i - \frac{\sum x_i \sum y_i}{n} = 1{,}786 - \frac{53 \times 148}{6} = 478.667$$

Finally, we calculate

$$\hat{\beta}_1 = \frac{SS_{xy}}{SS_x} = \frac{478.667}{140.833} = 3.399$$

and

$$\hat{\beta}_0 = \bar{y} - \hat{\beta}_1 \bar{x} = \frac{148}{6} - 3.399 \times \left(\frac{53}{6}\right) = -5.356$$

Thus, the least squares line is

$$\hat{y} = -5.356 + 3.399x$$

Figure 16.3 describes the regression line. As you can see, the line fits the data quite well. We can measure how well by computing the value of the minimized sum of squared differences. The differences between the points and the line are called **residuals**, denoted r_i. That is,

$$r_i = y_i - \hat{y}_i$$

Figure 16.3

Scatter Diagram with Regression Line: Example 16.1

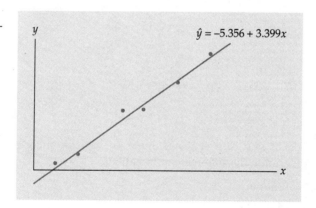

The residuals are the observed values of the error variable. Consequently, the minimized sum of squared differences is called the **sum of squares for error**, denoted SSE.

Sum of Squares for Error

$$SSE = \sum (y_i - \hat{y}_i)^2$$

The calculation of SSE in this example is shown in Figure 16.4. Notice that we compute $\hat{y}_i$ by substituting x_i into the formula for the regression line. The residuals are the differences between the observed values y_i and the computed values $\hat{y}_i$. The following table describes the calculation of SSE.

i	x_i	y_i	$\hat{y}_i = -5.356 + 3.399x_i$	RESIDUAL $y_i - \hat{y}_i$	RESIDUAL SQUARED $(y_i - \hat{y}_i)^2$
1	2	2	1.442	0.558	0.3114
2	4	7	8.240	−1.240	1.5376
3	8	25	21.836	3.164	10.0109
4	10	26	28.634	−2.634	6.9380
5	13	38	38.831	−0.831	0.6906
6	16	50	49.028	0.972	0.9448
				$\sum(y_i - \hat{y}_i)^2 =$	20.4332

Thus, SSE $= 20.4332$. No other straight line will produce a sum of squared errors as small as 20.4332. In that sense, the regression line fits the data best. The sum of squares for error is an important statistic because it is the basis for other statistics that assess how well the linear model fits the data. We will introduce these statistics later in this chapter.

Figure 16.4

Calculation of SSE: Example 16.1

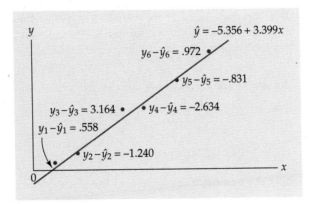

We now apply the technique to a more practical problem.

EXAMPLE 16.2

Car dealers across North America use the "Red Book" to help them determine the value of used cars that their customers trade in when purchasing new cars. The book, which is published monthly, lists the trade-in values for all basic models of cars. It provides alternative values of each car model according to its condition and optional features. The values are determined on the basis of the average paid at recent used-car auctions. (These auctions are the source of supply for many used-car dealers.) However, the Red Book does not indicate the value determined by the odometer reading, despite the fact that a critical factor for used-car buyers is how far the car has been driven. To examine this issue, a used-car dealer randomly selected 100 three-year old Ford Tauruses that were sold at auction during the past month. Each car was in top condition and equipped with automatic transmission, AM/FM cassette tape player, and air conditioning. The dealer recorded the price and the number of miles on the odometer. These data are stored in file XM16-02; some of the data are listed below. The dealer wants to find the regression line.

CAR	ODOMETER READING	AUCTION SELLING PRICE
1	37,388	$5,318
2	44,758	5,061
3	45,833	5,008
.	.	.
.	.	.
.	.	.
100	36,392	5,133

SOLUTION

Notice that the problem objective is to analyze the relationship between two quantitative variables. Because we want to know how the odometer reading affects the selling price, we identify the former as the independent variable, which we label x, and the latter as the dependent variable, which we label y.

SOLVING BY HAND

To determine the coefficient estimates, we must compute SS_x and SS_{xy}. They are

$$SS_x = \sum(x_i - \bar{x})^2 = 4{,}309{,}340{,}160$$

and

$$SS_{xy} = \sum(x_i - \bar{x})(y_i - \bar{y}) = -134{,}269{,}296$$

Using the sums of squares, we find the slope coefficient.

$$\hat{\beta}_1 = \frac{SS_{xy}}{SS_x} = \frac{-134{,}269{,}296}{4{,}309{,}340{,}160} = -.0311577$$

To determine the intercept, we need to find $\bar{x}$ and $\bar{y}$. They are

$$\bar{y} = \frac{\sum y_i}{n} = \frac{541{,}141}{100} = 5{,}411.41$$

and

$$\bar{x} = \frac{\sum x_i}{n} = \frac{3{,}600{,}945}{100} = 36{,}009.45$$

Thus,

$$\hat{\beta}_0 = \bar{y} - \hat{\beta}_1 \bar{x} = 5{,}411.41 - (-.0311577)(36{,}009.45) = 6{,}533.38$$

The sample regression line is

$$\hat{y} = 6{,}533 - 0.0312x$$

The complete printouts are shown below. The printouts include more statistics than we need right now. However, we will be discussing the rest of the printouts later. We have also included the scatter diagrams, which is often a first step in the regression analysis. Notice that there does appear to be a straight-line relationship between the two variables.

Minitab Output for Example 16.2

Regression Analysis

```
The regression equation is
Price = 6533 - 0.0312 Odometer

Predictor        Coef        Stdev      t-ratio         p
Constant      6533.38       84.51        77.31      0.000
Odometer    -0.031158     0.002309      -13.49      0.000

s = 151.6       R-sq = 65.0%     R-sq(adj) = 64.7%

Analysis of Variance

SOURCE          DF          SS          MS         F         p
Regression       1      4183528     4183528    182.11     0.000
Error           98      2251362       22973
Total           99      6434890
```

MENU COMMANDS	COMMANDS FOR EXAMPLE 16.2
1 Type or import the data into two columns.	Open file **XM16-02**.
2 Click **Stat**, **Regression**, and **Regression . . . .**	
3 Type the name of the dependent (**Response**) variable.	**Price** or **C2**
4 Hit **tab**, and type the name of the independent (**Predictors**) variable. Click **OK**.	**Odometer** or **C1**

1 Click **Stat**, **Regression**, and **Fitted Line Plot** . . . .

2 Type the name of the dependent variable (**Response [Y]**).   **Price** or **C2**

3 Use the cursor, and type the name of the independent variable (**Predictor [X]**).   **Odometer** or **C1**

Alternatively, you can draw the scatter diagram using the commands described in Chapter 2. Click **OK**.

Excel Output for Example 16.2

	A	B	C	D	E	F
1	SUMMARY OUTPUT					
2						
3	*Regression Statistics*					
4	Multiple R	0.806307604				
5	R Square	0.650131952				
6	Adjusted R Square	0.64656187				
7	Standard Error	151.5687515				
8	Observations	100				
9						
10	ANOVA					
11		*df*	*SS*	*MS*	*F*	*Significance F*
12	Regression	1	4183527.721	4183527.721	182.1056015	4.44346E-24
13	Residual	98	2251362.469	22973.08642		
14	Total	99	6434890.19			
15						
16		*Coefficients*	*Standard Error*	*t Stat*	*P-value*	
17	Intercept	6533.383035	84.51232199	77.30686935	1.22253E-89	
18	Odometer	-0.031157739	0.002308896	-13.49465085	4.44346E-24	

EXCEL 97

Excel 97 Users:
If you click **Line Fits,** the predicted values of y and the residuals will automatically be printed.

COMMANDS   **COMMANDS FOR EXAMPLE 16.2**

1 Type or import the data into two columns.   Open file **XM16-02**.

2 Click **Tools**, **Data Analysis** . . . , and **Regression**.

3 Specify **Input Y Range**.   **B1:B101**

4 Specify **Input X Range**. Click **OK**. Click **Labels** (if necessary).   **A1:A101**

5 To draw the scatter diagram click **Line Fit Plots** before clicking **OK**.

(You can also draw the scatter diagram using the commands described in Chapter 2.)

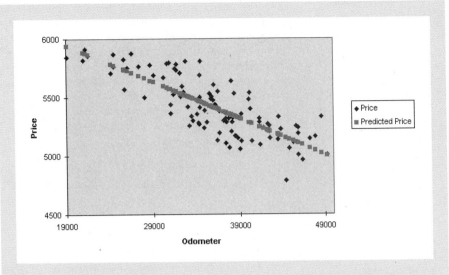

In the line fit plot (scatter diagram), the diamonds are the values of y and the squares are the predicted values of y. Use a ruler to join the squares to draw the regression line.

The scatter diagram will be drawn with the two axes starting at zero. This may cause the points to be bunched together leaving large blank spaces in the diagram. To modify the chart, proceed as follows.

EXCEL 97

Excel 97 Users:
To change the scale of the axes, double-click the Y-axis, remove the check mark under **Auto,** and change the **Minimum, Maximum,** and/or **Major and Minor Units.** Click **OK.** Repeat for the X-axis.

6 Activate the chart by double-clicking anywhere within the boundaries of the box.

7 Double-click the Y-axis, click **Scale** (if necessary) and change the **Minimum, Maximum,** and/or **Major and Minor Units.** Click **OK.**   **4500** (Minimum) **6000** (Maximum) **500** (Major Units) **100** (Minor Units)

8 Repeat for the X-axis.   **19000 50000 10000 2000**

INTERPRETING THE COEFFICIENTS

The coefficient $\hat{\beta}_1$ is -0.0312, which means that for each additional mile on the odometer, the price decreases by an average of $0.0312 (3.12 cents).

The intercept is $\hat{\beta}_0 = 6,533$. Technically, the intercept is the point at which the regression line and the y-axis intersect. This means that when $x = 0$ (i.e., the car was not driven at all) the selling price is \$6,533. We might be tempted to interpret this number as the price of cars that have not been driven. However, in this case, the intercept is probably meaningless. Because our sample did not include any cars with zero miles on the odometer, we have no basis for interpreting $\hat{\beta}_0$. As a general rule, we cannot determine the value of y for a value of x that is far outside the range of the sample values of x. In this example, the smallest and largest values of x are 19,057 and 49,223, respectively. Because $x = 0$ is not in this interval, we cannot safely interpret the value of y when $x = 0$.

In the sections that follow, we will return to this problem and the computer output to introduce other statistics associated with regression analysis.

Exercises

Most of the exercises that follow were created to allow you to see how regression analysis is used to solve realistic problems. As a result, most feature a large number of observations. We anticipate that most students will solve these problems using a computer and statistical software. However, for students without these resources, we have computed the sums of x and y, the sums of squares of x and y, and the sums of products that will permit them to complete the calculations manually. We believe that it is pointless for students to compute the sums from the raw data except for several small-sample exercises that are found below. In any case, students will have previously computed sums as part of a variety of procedures, including sample variance (Chapter 4), covariance and correlation (Chapter 4), and analysis of variance (Chapter 14).

16.4 Given the following six points,

x	-5	-2	0	3	4	7
y	15	9	7	6	4	1

   a draw the scatter diagram.

   b determine the least squares line.

16.5 The observation of two variables was recorded as shown below.

x	1	2	3	4	5	6	7	8	9
y	5	28	17	14	27	33	39	26	30

   a Draw the scatter diagram.

   b Find the least squares line.

16.6 In television's early years, most commercials were 60 seconds long. Now, however, commercials can be any length. The objective of commercials remains the same—to have as many viewers as possible remember the product in a favorable way and eventually buy it. In an experiment to determine how the length of a commercial affects people's memory of it, 60 randomly selected people were asked to watch a one-hour television program. In the middle of the show, a commercial advertising a brand of toothpaste appeared. Each viewer watched a commercial whose length varied between 20 and 60 seconds. The essential content of the commercials was the same. After the show, each person was given a test to measure how much he or she remembered about the product. The commercial times and test scores (on a 30-point test) are stored in file XR16-06. Some of the data are shown below.

   a Draw a scatter diagram of the data to determine whether a linear model appears to be appropriate.

   b Determine the least squares line.

   c Interpret the coefficients.

RESPONDENT	LENGTH OF COMMERCIAL	MEMORY TEST SCORE
1	52	24
2	40	20
3	36	16
.	.	.
.	.	.
.	.	.
60	48	21

Use a software package to solve this problem.	OR	Σ Length = 2280 Σ Test = 828 Σ Length^2 = 98,080 Σ Test^2 = 14,256 Σ (Length) (Test) = 34,524 Complete your answer manually.

16.7 After several semesters without much success, Pat Statsdud (a student in the lower quarter of a statistics course) decided to try to improve. Pat needed to know the secret of success for university and college students. After many hours of discussion with other, more successful, students, Pat postulated a rather radical theory: the longer one studied, the better one's grade. To test the theory, Pat took a random sample of 100 students in an economics course and asked each to report the average amount of time he or she studied economics and the final mark received. These data are stored in columns 1 (study time in hours) and 2 (final mark out of 100) in file XR16-07. Some of the observations are exhibited below.

a Determine the sample regression line.

b Interpret the coefficients.

c Is the sign of the slope logical? If the slope had had the opposite sign, what would that tell you?

STUDENT	STUDY TIME	FINAL MARK
1	30	71
2	5	30
3	36	82
.	.	.
.	.	.
.	.	.
100	16	52

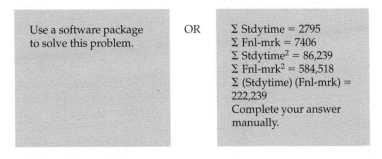

Use a software package to solve this problem.	OR	Σ Stdytime = 2795 Σ Fnl-mrk = 7406 Σ Stdytime^2 = 86,239 Σ Fnl-mrk^2 = 584,518 Σ (Stdytime) (Fnl-mrk) = 222,239 Complete your answer manually.

16.8 The term "regression" was originally used in 1885 by Sir Francis Galton in his analysis of the relationship between the heights of children and parents. He formulated the "law of universal regression," which specifies that "each peculiarity in a man is shared by his kinsmen, but on average in a less degree." (Evidently, people spoke this way in 1885.) In 1903 two statisticians, K. Pearson and A. Lee, took a random sample of 1,078 father–son pairs to examine Galton's law ("On the Laws of

Inheritance in Man, I. Inheritance of Physical Characteristics," *Biometrika* 2: 457–462). Their sample regression line was

Son's height = 33.73 + .516 × Father's height

a   Interpret the coefficients.

b   What does the regression line tell you about the heights of sons of tall fathers?

c   What does the regression line tell you about the heights of sons of short fathers?

16.9   Suppose that a statistician wanted to update the study described in Exercise 16.8. She collected data on 400 father–son pairs and stored the data in columns 1 (fathers' heights in inches) and 2 (sons' heights in inches) in file XR16-09. Some of the data appear below.

a   Determine the sample regression line.

b   What does the value of $\hat{\beta}_0$ tell you?

c   What does the value of $\hat{\beta}_1$ tell you?

FATHER–SON PAIR	FATHERS' HEIGHTS	SONS' HEIGHTS
1	59	67
2	69	75
3	73	71
.	.	.
.	.	.
.	.	.
400	64	66

Use a software package to solve this problem.	OR	Σ Fathers = 26,857 Σ Sons = 27,479 Σ Fathers^2 = 1,809,803 Σ Sons^2 = 1,893,381 Σ (Fathers) (Sons) = 1,848,149 Complete your answer manually.

16.10   The Trans-Alaska Pipeline System carries crude oil from Prudhoe Bay on Alaska's North Slope 800 miles to the port of Valdez, on the south coast of Alaska. The pipeline carries a mixture of different qualities of oil. Quality of oil is measured in API Gravity degrees—the higher the degrees API, the higher the quality. Because the pipeline mixes oils of different degrees, shippers in Valdez receive oil of different quality than they purchased. To compensate shippers, a "Quality Bank" was established. The owners of the pipeline proposed compensating shippers 15 cents per barrel for every degree below the level to which the shippers agreed. However, a refinery near Fairbanks, which receives 26-degree oil and mixes it with 20-degree oil, objected to the proposal. It suggested a 3.09 to 5.35 cent differential. Because oil carriers are required to establish "just and reasonable" rates, a hearing before an administrative law judge was held. At the hearing, an expert hired by the shippers produced the table below to show the relationship between quality and price per barrel of Mideast oil. (Data stored in file XR16-10.) Use regression analysis to determine the appropriate compensation.

MIDEAST OIL DEGREES API	PRICE/BARREL
27.0	$12.02
28.5	12.04
30.8	12.32
31.3	12.27
31.9	12.49
34.5	12.70
34.0	12.80
34.7	13.00
37.0	13.00
41.1	13.17
41.0	13.19
38.8	13.22
39.3	13.27

SOURCE: M. O. Finkelstein and B. Levin, *Statistics for Lawyers* (Springer-Verlag, 1990), 338–39.

16.11 All Canadians have government-funded health insurance, which pays for any medical care they require. However, when traveling out of the country, Canadians usually acquire supplementary health insurance to cover the difference between the costs incurred for emergency treatment and what the government program pays. In the United States this cost differential can be prohibitive. Until recently, private insurance companies (such as Blue Cross) charged everyone the same weekly rate, regardless of age. However, because of rising costs and the realization that older people frequently incur greater medical emergency expenses, insurers had to change their premium plans. They decided to offer rates that depend on the age of the customer. To help determine the new rates, one insurance company gathered data concerning the age and mean daily medical expenses of a random sample of 1,348 Canadians during the previous 12-month period. The data are stored in file XR16-11 (column 1 = age; column 2 = mean daily medical expense). A partial listing of the data appears below.

a Determine the sample regression line.

b Interpret the coefficients.

c What rate plan would you suggest?

RESPONDENT	AGE	MEAN DAILY MEDICAL EXPENSE
1	62	0.00
2	64	11.60
3	65	21.28
.	.	.
.	.	.
.	.	.
1,348	85	36.13

| Use a software package to solve this problem. | OR | Σ Age = 75,487
Σ Expense = 8,997.6
Σ Age^2 = 4,534,677
Σ Expense^2 = 302,356
Σ (Age) (Expense) = 573,262
Complete your answer manually. |

16.4 Error Variable: Required Conditions

In the previous section, we described the least squares method of estimating the coefficients of the probabilistic model. A critical part of this model is the error variable ϵ. In the next section, we present methods of assessing how well the straight line fits the data. In order for these methods to be valid, however, four requirements involving the probability distribution of the error variable must be satisfied.

Required Conditions for the Error Variable

1 The probability distribution of ϵ is normal.

2 The mean of the distribution is zero; that is, $E(\epsilon) = 0$.

3 The standard deviation of ϵ is σ_ϵ, which is a constant no matter what the value of x is.

4 The errors associated with any two values of y are independent. As a result, the value of the error variable at one point does not affect the value of the error variable at another point.

Requirements 1, 2, and 3 can be interpreted in another way: for each value of x, y is a normally distributed random variable whose mean is

$$E(y) = \beta_0 + \beta_1 x$$

and whose standard deviation is σ_ϵ. Notice that the mean depends on x. To reflect this dependence, the expected value is sometimes expressed as

$$E(y|x) = \beta_0 + \beta_1 x$$

The standard deviation, however, is not influenced by x, because it is a constant over all values of x. Figure 16.5 depicts this interpretation.

In Section 16.8, we will discuss how departures from these required conditions affect the regression analysis and how they are identified.

Experimental and Observational Data

Statisticians often design controlled experiments where regression analysis will be used. They do so by setting several different values of x and observing the corresponding values of y. For example, the data in Exercise 16.6 were gathered through a controlled experiment. To determine the effect of the length of a television commercial on its viewers' memories of the product advertised, the statistician arranged for 60 television viewers to watch a commercial of differing lengths and then tested their memories of that commercial. Each viewer was randomly assigned a commercial length. The values of x ranged from 20 to 60 and were set by the statistician as part of the experiment. For each value of x, the distribution of the memory test scores is assumed to be normally distributed with a constant variance.

Figure 16.5

Distribution of y Given x

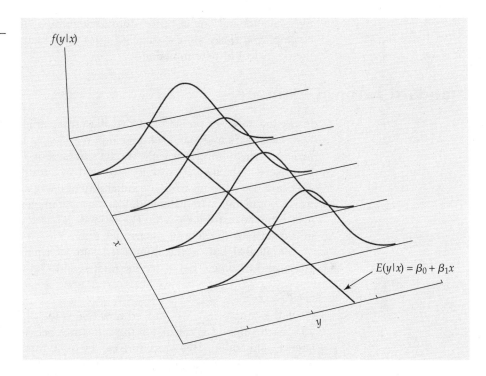

In many cases, it is difficult or impossible to design a controlled experiment. Thus, we have no alternative to gathering observational data. As was the case with other techniques, whether the data are observational or experimental does not affect the choice of statistical method. That is, we can apply regression analysis to both experimental and observational data. However, when the data are observational there are often several competing interpretations of the results. To illustrate, suppose that an analysis of observational data showed that there is a linear relationship (with a positive value of $\hat{\beta}_1$) between a professor's salary and teaching evaluations. We may interpret these results to infer that better teachers are more highly rewarded. However, it may be that a university's best researchers are also its best teachers, and, because research is rewarded, there appears to be a relationship between salary and teaching evaluations. A multiple regression analysis (Chapter 17) may be able to produce a definite conclusion.

16.5 Assessing the Model

The least squares method produces the best straight line. However, there may in fact be no relationship or perhaps a nonlinear (e.g., quadratic) relationship between the two variables. If so, the use of a linear model is pointless. Consequently, it is important for us to assess how well the linear model fits the data. If the fit is poor, we should discard the linear model and seek another one.

Several methods are used to evaluate the model. In this section, we present two statistics and one test procedure to determine whether a linear model should be employed. They are the standard error of estimate, the t-test of the slope, and the coefficient of determination.

Standard Error of Estimate

In Section 16.4, we pointed out that the error variable ϵ is normally distributed with mean zero and standard deviation σ_ϵ. If σ_ϵ is large, some of the errors will be large, which implies that the model's fit is poor. If σ_ϵ is small, the errors tend to be close to the mean (which is zero), and, as a result, the model fits well. Hence, we could use σ_ϵ to measure the suitability of using a linear model. Unfortunately, σ_ϵ is a population parameter and, like most parameters, is unknown. We can, however, estimate σ_ϵ from the data. The estimate is based on the statistic we introduced in Section 16.2, the sum of squares for error, SSE.

Recall that SSE is the minimized sum of squared differences between the points and the line. That is, for the least squares line,

$$SSE = \sum(y_i - \hat{y}_i)^2$$

For Example 16.1, we showed how SSE is found. We determined the value of $\hat{y}$ for each value of x, calculated the difference between y and $\hat{y}$, squared the difference, and added. This procedure can be quite time-consuming. Fortunately, we can also express SSE as a function of sums of squares.

Simplified Calculation for SSE

$$SSE = SS_y - \frac{SS_{xy}^2}{SS_x}$$

where

$$SS_y = \sum(y_i - \bar{y})^2$$

which can also be expressed as

$$SS_y = \sum y_i^2 - \frac{(\sum y_i)^2}{n}$$

We can estimate σ_ϵ^2 by dividing SSE by the number of observations minus 2. That is, the sample statistic

$$s_\epsilon^2 = \frac{\text{SSE}}{n-2}$$

is an unbiased estimator of σ_ϵ^2. The square root of s_ϵ^2 is called the **standard error of estimate**.

Standard Error of Estimate

$$s_\epsilon = \sqrt{\frac{\text{SSE}}{n-2}}$$

EXAMPLE 16.3

Find the standard error of estimate for Example 16.2.

SOLUTION

SOLVING BY HAND

To compute the standard error of estimate, we need to find the sum of squares for error. This requires the calculation of SS_x, SS_{xy}, and SS_y. In Example 16.2, we calculated

$$\text{SS}_x = 4{,}309{,}340{,}160 \quad \text{and} \quad \text{SS}_{xy} = -134{,}269{,}296$$

From the data we find

$$\text{SS}_y = \sum(y_i - \bar{y})^2 = 6{,}434{,}890$$

We can now determine the sum of squares for error.

$$\text{SSE} = \text{SS}_y - \frac{\text{SS}_{xy}^2}{\text{SS}_x} = 6{,}434{,}890 - \frac{(-134{,}269{,}296)^2}{4{,}309{,}340{,}160} = 2{,}251{,}363$$

Thus, the standard error of estimate is

$$s_\epsilon = \sqrt{\frac{\text{SSE}}{n-2}} = \sqrt{\frac{2{,}251{,}363}{100-2}} = 151.569$$

USING THE COMPUTER

Minitab Output for Example 16.3

Refer to page 623 to examine the Minitab printout for Example 16.2. Minitab reports the standard error of estimate simply as

$$s = 151.6$$

Refer to page 624 to examine the Excel printout for Example 16.2. Excel reports the standard error of estimate as

Standard Error 151.5687515

INTERPRETING THE
RESULTS

The smallest value that s_ϵ can assume is zero, which occurs when SSE = 0, that is, when all the points fall on the regression line. Thus, when s_ϵ is small, the fit is excellent, and the linear model is likely to be an effective analytical and forecasting tool. If s_ϵ is large, the model is a poor one, and the statistician should improve it or discard it.

We judge the value of s_ϵ by comparing it to the values of the dependent variable y, or more specifically to the sample mean $\bar{y}$. In this example, because $s_\epsilon = 151.6$ and $\bar{y} = 5,411.4$, we would have to admit that the standard error of estimate is not very small. On the other hand, it is not a large number. Because there is no predefined upper limit on s_ϵ, it is difficult to assess the model in this way (except in cases where s_ϵ is obviously a small number). In general, the standard error of estimate cannot be used as an absolute measure of the model's utility.

Nonetheless, s_ϵ is useful in comparing models. If the statistician has several models from which to choose, the one with the smallest value of s_ϵ should generally be the one used. As you'll see, s_ϵ is also an important statistic in other procedures associated with regression analysis.

Testing the Slope

To understand this method of assessing the linear model, consider the consequences of applying the regression technique to two variables that are not at all linearly related. If we could observe the entire population and draw the scatter diagram, we would observe the graph shown in Figure 16.6. The line is horizontal, which means that the value of y is unaffected by the value of x. Recall that a horizontal straight line has a slope of zero, that is, $\beta_1 = 0$.

Figure 16.6

$\beta_1 = 0$

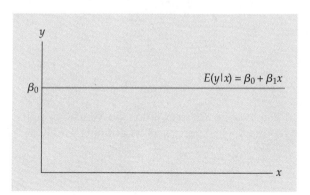

Because we rarely examine complete populations, the parameters are unknown. However, we can draw inferences about the population slope β_1 from the sample slope $\hat{\beta}_1$.

The process of testing hypotheses about β_1 is identical to the process of testing any other parameter. We begin with the hypotheses. The null hypothesis specifies that there is no linear relationship, which means that the slope is zero. Thus, we specify

$$H_0: \beta_1 = 0$$

We can conduct one- or two-tail tests of β_1. Most often, we perform a two-tail test to determine whether there is sufficient evidence to infer that a linear relationship exists. We test

$$H_A: \beta_1 \neq 0$$

The test statistic is

$$t = \frac{\hat{\beta}_1 - \beta_1}{s_{\hat{\beta}_1}}$$

where $s_{\hat{\beta}_1}$ is the standard deviation of $\hat{\beta}_1$ (also called the standard error of $\hat{\beta}_1$). It is defined as

$$s_{\hat{\beta}_1} = \frac{s_\epsilon}{\sqrt{SS_x}}$$

If the error variable is normally distributed, the test statistic is Student t-distributed with $n - 2$ degrees of freedom.

EXAMPLE 16.4

Test to determine whether there is enough evidence in Example 16.2 to infer that there is a linear relationship between the price and the odometer reading. Use a significance level of 5%.

SOLUTION

SOLVING BY HAND

We test the hypotheses

$$H_0: \beta_1 = 0$$
$$H_A: \beta_1 \neq 0$$

Rejection region: $|t| > t_{\alpha/2, n-2} = t_{.025, 98} \approx 1.984$

To compute the value of the test statistic, we need $\hat{\beta}_1$ and $s_{\hat{\beta}_1}$. In Example 16.2, we found $SS_x = 4{,}309{,}340{,}160$ and $\hat{\beta}_1 = -.0311577$. In Example 16.3, we found $s_\epsilon = 151.569$. Thus,

$$s_{\hat{\beta}_1} = \frac{s_\epsilon}{\sqrt{SS_x}} = \frac{151.569}{\sqrt{4{,}309{,}340{,}160}} = .002309$$

The value of the test statistic is

$$t = \frac{\hat{\beta}_1 - \beta_1}{s_{\hat{\beta}_1}} = \frac{-.0311577 - 0}{.002309} = -13.49$$

Conclusion: Reject the null hypothesis.

USING THE COMPUTER

Minitab Output for Example 16.4

The output below was taken from the Minitab output for Example 16.2 on page 623.

```
Predictor        Coef       Stdev    t-ratio        p
Constant      6533.38       84.51      77.31    0.000
Odometer    -0.031158    0.002309     -13.49    0.000
```

The printout includes the standard deviation of $\hat{\beta}_1$ (**Stdev**), the t-statistic (**t-ratio**), and the two-tail p-value of the test. These values are .002309, -13.49, and 0.000, respectively. Notice the printout includes a test for β_0. However, as we've pointed out before, interpreting the value of the y-intercept can lead to erroneous, if not ridiculous, conclusions. As a result, we will ignore the test of β_0.

Excel Output for Example 16.4

The output below was taken from the Excel output for Example 16.2 on page 624.

	A	B	C	D	E
16		Coefficients	Standard Error	t Stat	P-value
17	Intercept	6533.383035	84.51232199	77.30686935	1.22253E-89
18	Odometer	-0.031157739	0.002308896	-13.49465085	4.44346E-24

The printout includes the standard deviation of $\hat{\beta}_1$ (**Standard Error**), the t-statistic (**t Stat**), and the two-tail p-value of the test (**P-value**). These values are .002308896, -13.49465085, and $4.44346E - 24$ (which is practically 0), respectively. Notice the printout includes a test for β_0. However, as we've pointed out before, interpreting the value of the y-intercept can lead to erroneous, if not ridiculous, conclusions. As a result, we will ignore the test of β_0.

INTERPRETING THE RESULTS

The value of the test statistic is $t = -13.49$, with a p-value of 0.000. There is overwhelming evidence to infer that a linear relationship exists. (Figure 16.7 depicts the sampling distribution of the test statistic.) What this means is that the odometer reading does affect the auction selling price of the cars.

Figure 16.7

Sampling Distribution of
$$\frac{\hat{\beta}_1 - \beta_1}{s_{\hat{\beta}1}} \text{ for}$$
Example 16.4

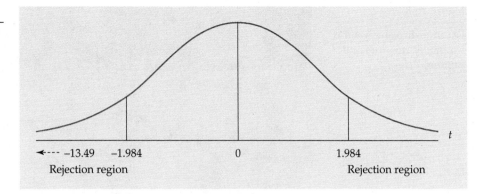

As was the case when we interpreted the y-intercept, the conclusion we draw here is valid only over the range of the values of the independent variable. That is, we can infer that there is a linear relationship between odometer reading and auction price for the three-year-old Ford Tauruses whose odometer reading lies between 19,057 and 49,223 miles (the minimum and maximum values of x in the sample). Because we have no observations outside this range, we do not know how, or even whether, the two variables are related. Figure 16.8 depicts several possible relationships over a wider range of values of x than the sample data in Example 16.2. As you can see, all three figures show a linear relationship when x lies between 20,000 and 50,000 miles. Outside this range the relationship may be linear (Figure 16.8a) or nonlinear (Figures 16.8b and 16.8c). This issue is particularly important to remember when we use the regression equation to estimate or forecast. (See Section 16.6.)

Coefficient of Determination

The test of β_1 addresses only the question of whether there is enough evidence to infer that a linear relationship exists. In many cases, however, it is also useful to measure the strength of that linear relationship, particularly when we want to compare several different models. The statistic that performs this function is the coefficient of determination.

The **coefficient of determination**, denoted R^2, is computed in the following way.

Coefficient of Determination

$$R^2 = \frac{SS_{xy}^2}{SS_x \cdot SS_y}$$

With a little algebra, mathematicians can show that

$$R^2 = 1 - \frac{SSE}{SS_y}$$

Figure 16.8

Relationships between
Odometer Reading and
Auction Price

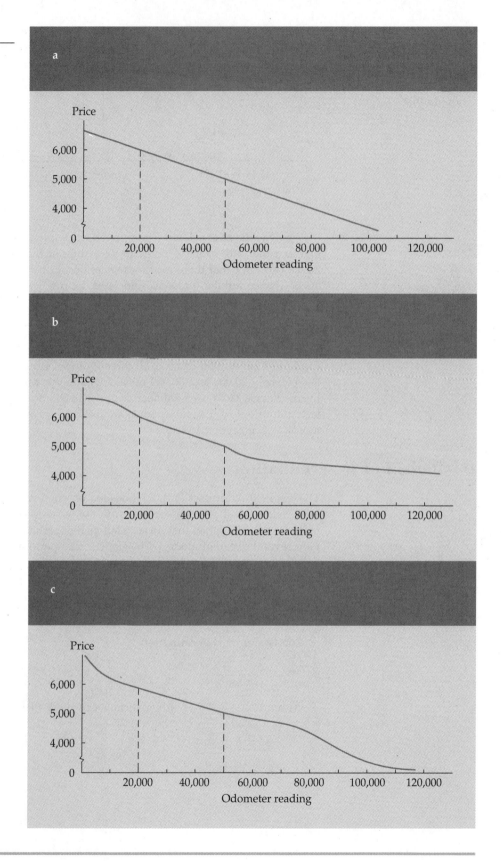

The significance of this formula is based on the analysis of variance technique. In Chapter 14, we partitioned the total sum of squares into two sources of variation. Here, we begin the discussion by observing that the deviation between y_i and $\bar{y}$ can be decomposed into two parts. That is,

$$(y_i - \bar{y}) = (y_i - \hat{y}_i) + (\hat{y}_i - \bar{y})$$

This equation is represented graphically (for $i = 1$) in Figure 16.9.

Now we ask, why are the values of y different from one another? In Example 16.2, we observe that the auction selling prices of the cars vary, and we'd like to explain why. From Figure 16.9, we see that part of the difference between y_i and $\bar{y}$ is the difference between $\hat{y}_i$ and $\bar{y}$, which is accounted for by the difference between x_i and $\bar{x}$. That is, some of the price variation is *explained* by the odometer reading. The other part of the difference between y_i and $\bar{y}$, however, is accounted for by the difference between y_i and $\hat{y}_i$. This difference is the residual, which to some degree reflects variables not otherwise represented by the model. (These variables likely include the local supply and demand for this type of used car, the color of the car, and other relatively small details.) As a result, we say that this part of the difference is *unexplained* by the odometer variation.

If we now square both sides of the equation, sum over all sample points, and perform some algebra, we produce

$$\sum(y_i - \bar{y})^2 = \sum(y_i - \hat{y}_i)^2 + \sum(\hat{y}_i - \bar{y})^2$$

The quantity on the left side of this equation is SS_y, which is a measure of the variation in the dependent variable (selling price). The first quantity on the right side of the equation is SSE, and the second term is denoted SSR, for **sum of squares for regression**. We can rewrite the equation as

$$SS_y = SSE + SSR$$

where

Figure 16.9

Analysis of the Deviation

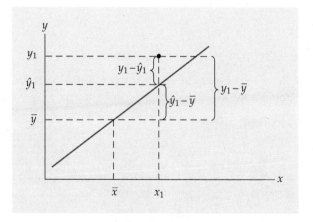

$$SS_y = \sum(y_i - \bar{y})^2$$
$$SSE = \sum(y_i - \hat{y}_i)^2$$
$$SSR = \sum(\hat{y}_i - \bar{y})^2$$

As we did in the analysis of variance, we partition the variation of y into two parts: SSE, which measures the amount of variation in y that remains unexplained;

and SSR, which measures the amount of variation in y that is explained by the variation in the independent variable (odometer reading).

Returning to our formula for R^2, we see that

$$R^2 = 1 - \frac{\text{SSE}}{\text{SS}_y} = \frac{\text{SS}_y - \text{SSE}}{\text{SS}_y} = \frac{\text{SSR}}{\text{SS}_y}$$

It follows that R^2 measures the proportion of the variation in y that is explained by the variation in x. Incidentally, the notation R^2 is derived from the fact that the coefficient of determination is the coefficient of correlation squared. Recall that we introduced the sample coefficient of correlation in Chapter 4 and labeled it r. (To be consistent with computer output, we capitalize r in the definition of the coefficient of determination.) We will discuss the coefficient of correlation in Section 16.7.

EXAMPLE 16.5

Find the coefficient of determination for the data in Example 16.2.

SOLUTION

SOLVING BY HAND

From our previous examples, we found

$$\text{SS}_y = 6,434,890 \quad \text{and} \quad \text{SSE} = 2,251,363$$

Thus,

$$R^2 = 1 - \frac{\text{SSE}}{\text{SS}_y} = 1 - \frac{2,251,363}{6,434,890} = 1 - .3499 = .6501$$

USING THE COMPUTER

Minitab Output for Example 16.5

Refer to page 623 to examine the Minitab printout for Example 16.2. Minitab reports the coefficient of determination as

R-sq   65.0%

Excel Output for Example 16.5

Refer to page 624 to examine the Excel printout for Example 16.2. Excel reports the coefficient of determination as

R Square   .650131952

Both Minitab and Excel print a second R^2 statistic called the **coefficient of determination adjusted for degrees of freedom.** We will define and describe this statistic in Chapter 17.

We found that R^2 is equal to 65%. This statistic tells us that 65% of the variation in the auction selling prices is explained by the variation in the odometer readings. The remaining 35% is unexplained. Unlike the value of a test statistic, the coefficient of determination does not have a critical value that enables us to draw conclusions. We know that the higher the value of R^2, the better the model fits the data. From the t-test of β_1 we know already that there is evidence of a linear relationship. The coefficient of determination merely supplies us with a measure of the strength of that relationship. As you will discover in the next chapter, when we improve the model, the value of R^2 increases.

Other Parts of the Computer Printout

The last part of the printout shown on pages 623 to 624 relates to our discussion of the interpretation of the value of R^2, where its meaning is derived from the partitioning of the variation in y. The values of SSR and SSE are shown in an analysis of variance table similar to the tables introduced in Chapter 14. The general format of the table is shown below. The F-test performed in the ANOVA table will be explained in Chapter 17.

General Form of the ANOVA Table in the Simple Regression Model

SOURCE	d.f.	SUMS OF SQUARES	MEAN SQUARES	F-VALUE
Regression	1	SSR	MSR = SSR/1	F = MSR/MSE
Error	$n - 2$	SSE	MSE = SSE/$(n - 2)$	
TOTAL	$n - 1$	SS_y		

Note: Excel calls the second source of variation "Residual."

Developing an Understanding of Statistical Concepts

Once again, we encounter the concept of explained variation. We first discussed this concept in Chapter 12 when we introduced the matched pairs experiment, where that experiment was designed to reduce the variation among experimental units. This concept was extended in the analysis of variance, where we partitioned the total variation into two or more sources (depending on the model). And now in regression analysis, we use the concept to measure how the dependent variable is affected by the independent variable. We partition the variation of the dependent variable into two sources: the variation explained by the variation in the independent variable and the unexplained variation. The greater the explained variation, the better the model is. We often refer to the coefficient of determination as a measure of the *explanatory power* of the model.

Cause and Effect Relationship

A common mistake is made by many students when they attempt to interpret the results of a regression analysis when there is evidence of a linear relationship. They imply that changes in the independent variable *cause* changes in the dependent variable. It must be emphasized that we cannot infer a causal relationship from statistics alone. Any inference about the cause of the changes in the dependent variable must be justified by a reasonable theoretical relationship. For example, statistical tests established that the more one smoked, the greater the probability of developing lung cancer. However, this analysis did not prove that smoking causes lung cancer. It only demonstrated that smoking and lung cancer were somehow related. Only when medical investigations established the connection were scientists able to confidently declare that smoking causes lung cancer.

As another illustration, consider Example 16.2 where we showed that the odometer reading is linearly related to the auction price. While it seems reasonable to conclude that decreasing the odometer reading would cause the auction price to rise, this conclusion may not be entirely true. It is theoretically possible that the price is determined by the overall condition of the car and that the condition generally worsens when the car is driven longer. Another analysis would be needed to establish the veracity of this conclusion.

Be cautious about the use of the terms "explained variation" and "explanatory power of the model." Do not interpret the word "explained" to mean "caused." We say that coefficient of determination measures the amount of variation in y that is explained (not caused) by the variation in x. Thus, regression analysis can only show that a statistical relationship exists. We cannot infer that one variable causes another.

Exercises

16.12 Refer to Exercise 16.6.

   a Determine the standard error of estimate, and interpret its value.

   b Can we conclude at the 5% significance level that the length of the commercial and people's memories of it are linearly related?

   c Determine the coefficient of determination. What does this statistic tell you about the regression line?

16.13 Refer to Exercise 16.7.

   a Determine the standard error of estimate, and interpret its value.

   b Test at the 10% significance level to determine whether there is evidence of a linear relationship between study time and the final mark.

   c Determine the coefficient of determination. What does this statistic tell you about the regression line?

16.14 Refer to Exercise 16.9.

   a Determine the standard error of estimate, and describe what this statistic tells you about the regression line.

   b Can we conclude at the 1% significance level that the heights of fathers and sons are linearly related?

   c Determine the coefficient of determination and discuss what its value tells you about the two variables.

16.15 Refer to Exercise 16.10. Use whatever statistics you think useful to describe the reliability of your suggested compensation plan.

16.16 Refer to Exercise 16.11. Use whatever statistics you think useful to describe the reliability of your insurance premium plan.

16.17 An economist wanted to investigate the relationship between office rents and vacancy rates. Accordingly, he took a random sample of monthly office rents and the percentage of vacant office space in 30 different cities. The results were stored in file XR16-17 (column 1 = percent of vacancy rates and column 2 = monthly rents in dollars per square foot). Some of the observations are listed below.

a   Determine the regression line.

b   Interpret the coefficients.

c   Can we conclude from these data that higher vacancy rates result in lower rents?

d   Measure how well the linear model fits the data. Discuss what this (these) measure(s) tell you.

CITY	VACANCY RATE	MONTHLY RENT
1	3	21.45
2	11	15.35
3	17	14.29
.	.	.
.	.	.
.	.	.
30	14	17.93

Use a software package to solve this problem.

OR

Σ Vacancy = 340
Σ Rent = 511.73
Σ Vacancy^2 = 4882
Σ Rent^2 = 8931.8
Σ (Vacancy) (Rent) = 5496.4
Complete your answer manually.

16.18   Physicians have been recommending more exercise for their patients, particularly those who are overweight. One benefit of regular exercise appears to be a reduction in cholesterol, a substance associated with heart disease. In order to study the relationship more carefully, a physician took a random sample of 50 patients who do not exercise. He measured their cholesterol levels. He then started them on regular exercise programs. After four months, he asked each patient how many minutes per week (on average) he or she exercised and also measured their cholesterol levels. The results are stored in file XR16-18 (column 1 = weekly exercise in minutes; column 2 = cholesterol level before exercise program; and column 3 = cholesterol level after exercise program). A partial listing of the data appears below.

a   Determine the regression line that relates exercise time with cholesterol reduction.

b   Interpret the coefficients.

c   Can we conclude at the 5% significance level that the amount of exercise is linearly related to cholesterol reduction?

d   Measure how well the linear model fits.

WEEKLY EXERCISE	"BEFORE" CHOLESTEROL LEVEL	"AFTER" CHOLESTEROL LEVEL
319	216	170
122	233	204
487	251	195
.	.	.
.	.	.
.	.	.
212	243	214

Use a software package to solve this problem.

OR

Σ Exercise = 14,157
Σ Reduction = 1390
Σ Exercise^2 = 4,676,837
Σ Reduction^2 = 49,492
Σ (Exercise) (Reduction) = 454,354
Complete your answer manually.

16.6 Using the Regression Equation

Using the techniques in Section 16.5, we can assess how well the linear model fits the data. If the model fits satisfactorily, we can use it to forecast and estimate values of the dependent variable. To illustrate, suppose that in Example 16.2, the used car dealer wanted to predict the selling price of a three-year-old Ford Taurus with 40,000 miles on the odometer. Using the regression equation, with $x = 40,000$, we get

$$\hat{y} = 6,533 - 0.0312x = 6,533 - 0.0312(40,000) = 5,285$$

Thus, the dealer would predict that the car would sell for $5,285.

By itself, however, this value does not provide any information about how closely the value will match the true selling price. To discover that information, we must use a confidence interval. In fact, we can use one of two intervals: the prediction interval (for a particular value of y) or the confidence interval estimate (for the expected value of y).

Predicting the Particular Value of y for a Given x

The first interval we present is used whenever we want to predict one particular value of the dependent variable, given a specific value of the independent variable. This confidence interval, often called the **prediction interval**, is calculated as follows.

Prediction Interval

$$\hat{y} \pm t_{\alpha/2, n-2} \, s_\epsilon \sqrt{1 + \frac{1}{n} + \frac{(x_g - \bar{x})^2}{SS_x}}$$

where x_g is the given value of x and

$$\hat{y} = \hat{\beta}_0 + \hat{\beta}_1 x_g$$

Estimating the Expected Value of y for a Given x

The conditions described in Section 16.4 imply that for a given value of x, there is a population of values of y whose mean is

$$E(y) = \beta_0 + \beta_1 x$$

To estimate its value, we would use the following interval.

Confidence Interval Estimator of the Expected Value of y

$$\hat{y} \pm t_{\alpha/2, n-2} \, s_\epsilon \sqrt{\frac{1}{n} + \frac{(x_g - \bar{x})^2}{SS_x}}$$

Unlike the formula for the prediction interval described above, this formula does not include the 1 under the square-root sign. As a result, the confidence interval estimate of the expected value of y will be narrower than the prediction interval for the same given value of x and confidence level. This is because the expected value of y is a constant that happens to be unknown, whereas a single value of y is a random variable, which is more difficult to predict accurately.

EXAMPLE 16.6

a A used-car dealer is about to bid on a three-year-old Ford Taurus equipped with automatic transmission, air conditioner, and AM/FM cassette tape player, and with 40,000 miles on the odometer. To help him decide how much to bid, he needs to predict the selling price.

b The used-car dealer alluded to above has an opportunity to bid on a lot of cars offered by a rental company. The rental company has 250 Ford Tauruses, all equipped with automatic transmission, air conditioning, and AM/FM cassette tape players. All of the cars in this lot have about 40,000 miles on the odometer. The dealer would like an estimate of the selling price of all the cars in the lot.

SOLUTION

a   The dealer would like to predict the selling price of a *single* car. Thus, he needs to employ the prediction interval

$$\hat{y} \pm t_{\alpha/2,n-2}\, s_\epsilon \sqrt{1 + \frac{1}{n} + \frac{(x_g - \bar{x})^2}{SS_x}}$$

b   The dealer wants to determine the mean price of a large lot of cars, so he needs to calculate the confidence interval estimate of the expected value.

$$\hat{y} \pm t_{\alpha/2,n-2}\, s_\epsilon \sqrt{\frac{1}{n} + \frac{(x_g - \bar{x})^2}{SS_x}}$$

Technically, this formula is used for infinitely large populations. However, we can interpret our problem as attempting to determine the average selling price of *all* Ford Tauruses equipped as described above, all with 40,000 miles on the odometer. The critical factor in part (b) is the need to estimate the mean price of a number of cars.

We arbitrarily select a 95% confidence level.

From previous calculations, we have the following.

$$\hat{y} = 6{,}533 - 0.0312x = 6{,}533 - 0.0312(40{,}000) = 5{,}285$$

$$s_\epsilon = 151.6, \quad SS_x = 4{,}309{,}340{,}160, \quad \text{and} \quad \bar{x} = 36{,}009$$

From Table 4 in Appendix B, we find

$$t_{.025,98} \approx 1.984$$

a   The 95% prediction interval is

$$\hat{y} \pm t_{\alpha/2,n-2}\, s_\epsilon \sqrt{1 + \frac{1}{n} + \frac{(x_g - \bar{x})^2}{SS_x}}$$

$$= 5{,}285 \pm 1.984 \times 151.6 \sqrt{1 + \frac{1}{100} + \frac{(40{,}000 - 36{,}009)^2}{4{,}309{,}340{,}160}}$$

$$= 5{,}285 \pm 303$$

The lower and upper limits of the prediction interval are 4,982 and 5,588, respectively.

b   The 95% confidence interval estimate of the expected selling price is

$$\hat{y} \pm t_{\alpha/2,n-2}\, s_\epsilon \sqrt{\frac{1}{n} + \frac{(x_g - \bar{x})^2}{SS_x}}$$

$$= 5{,}285 \pm 1.984 \times 151.6 \sqrt{\frac{1}{100} + \frac{(40{,}000 - 36{,}009)^2}{4{,}309{,}340{,}160}}$$

$$= 5{,}285 \pm 35$$

The lower and upper limits of the confidence interval estimate of the expected value are 5,250 and 5,320, respectively.

Minitab Output for Example 16.6

```
    Fit    Stdev.Fit       95.0% C.I.          95.0% P.I.
  5287.1        17.7   ( 5251.9,  5322.3)  ( 4984.2,  5590.0)
```

The output includes the calculated value of y (**Fit**), the standard deviation of y (**Stdev.Fit**), which is

$$s_\epsilon \sqrt{\frac{1}{n} + \frac{(x_g - \bar{x})^2}{SS_x}}$$

the 95% confidence interval estimate of the expected value of y (**95% C.I.**) and the 95% prediction interval (**95% P.I.**).

MENU COMMANDS	COMMANDS FOR EXAMPLE 16.6
1 Proceed through the first 4 steps of regression analysis described on page 623. Do not click **OK**.	
2 Click **Options**.	
3 Use the cursor and type the given value(s) of x (**Prediction intervals for new observations**).	**40000**
4 Use the cursor (if necessary) and type the confidence level. Click **OK** twice.	**95**

Excel Output for Example 16.6

0.95	**Prediction Interval**	
Predicted value =	5287.073	
Lower limit =	4984.238	
Upper limit =	5589.909	
0.95	**Confidence Interval Estimate**	
Lower limit =	5251.874	
Upper limit =	5322.273	

The output includes the calculated value of y (**Predicted value**), the 95% prediction interval and the 95% confidence interval estimate of the expected value of y.

INTERPRETING THE
RESULTS

We predict (using Minitab's results) that one car will sell for between $4,984.20 and $5,590.00. The average selling price of the population of three-year-old Ford Tauruses is estimated to lie between $5,251.90 and $5,322.30. Because predicting the selling price of one car is more difficult than estimating the mean selling price of all similar cars, the prediction interval is wider than the confidence interval estimate of the expected value. (The intervals using Excel are essentially the same.)

The Effect of the Given Value of x on the Confidence Intervals

If the two intervals were calculated for various values of x and graphed, Figure 16.10 would be produced. Notice that both intervals are represented by curved lines. This is due to the fact that the farther the given value of x is from $\bar{x}$, the greater the estimation error becomes. This factor is measured by

$$\frac{(x_g - \bar{x})^2}{SS_x}$$

which appears in both the prediction interval and the confidence interval estimate.

Figure 16.10

Confidence Intervals and Prediction Intervals

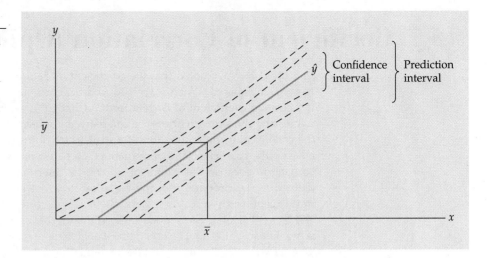

Exercises

16.19 Refer to Exercise 16.6.

    a   Predict with 95% confidence the memory test score of a viewer who watched a 36-second commercial.

    b   Estimate with 95% confidence the mean memory test score of people who watch 36-second commercials.

16.20 Refer to Exercise 16.7.

    a   Predict with 90% confidence the final mark of a student who studied for 25 hours.

    b   Estimate with 90% confidence the average mark of all students who study for 25 hours.

16.21 Refer to Exercise 16.9. A statistician wants to produce an interval estimate of the height of a man whose father is 72 inches tall. What formula should be used? Produce such an interval using a confidence level of 99%.

16.22 Refer to Exercise 16.11.

    a   Predict with 95% confidence the daily emergency medical expense of an average 65-year-old Canadian.

    b   Estimate with 95% confidence the mean daily emergency medical expense of all 65-year-old Canadians.

16.23 Refer to Exercise 16.18.

    a   Predict with 95% confidence the reduction in cholesterol level of an individual who plans to exercise for 100 minutes per week for a total of four months.

    b   Suppose that an individual whose cholesterol level is 250 is planning to exercise for 250 minutes per week. Predict with 95% confidence his cholesterol level after four months.

16.7 Coefficient of Correlation (Optional)

In Section 16.5, we noted that the coefficient of determination is the coefficient of correlation squared. When we introduced the coefficient of correlation (also called the **Pearson coefficient of correlation**) in Chapter 4, we pointed out that it is used to measure the strength of association between two variables. Why then do we use the coefficient of determination as our measure of the regression model's fit? The answer: the coefficient of determination is a better measure than the coefficient of correlation because the values of R^2 can be interpreted precisely. That is, R^2 is defined as the proportion of the variation in y that is explained by the variation in x. Except for $r = -1, 0$, and 1, the coefficient of correlation cannot be interpreted. (When $r = -1$ or 1, every point falls on the regression line, and when $r = 0$, there is no linear pattern.) However, the coefficient of correlation can be useful in another way. We can use it to test for a relationship between two variables.

In cases where we are interested in determining *how* the independent variable affects the dependent variable, we estimate and test the linear regression model. The t-test of β_1 allows us to determine whether a linear relationship actually exists. The test requires that for each value of x, y is a normally distributed random variable with mean $E(y|x) = \beta_0 + \beta_1 x$ and standard deviation σ_ϵ. (See Figure 16.5.)

There are many circumstances where we are interested only in determining *whether* a linear relationship exists and not the form of the relationship. In some cases, we cannot even identify which variable is the dependent variable and which is the independent variable. In such applications, we can calculate the coefficient of correlation and use it to test for linear association.

As we pointed out in Chapter 4, the population coefficient of correlation is denoted ρ (the Greek letter rho). Because ρ is a population parameter, we must estimate its value from the data. The sample coefficient of correlation is denoted r and is defined as follows.

Sample Coefficient of Correlation

$$r = \frac{SS_{xy}}{\sqrt{SS_x \cdot SS_y}}$$

To use the coefficient of correlation as a test of the linear association requires that the two variables are bivariate normally distributed. In Chapter 6, we introduced bivariate distributions, which provide the joint probability for two variables. The form of the bivariate normal distribution is given in Figure 16.11. As you can see, it is a three-dimensional bell curve.

Figure 16.11

Bivariate Normal
Distribution

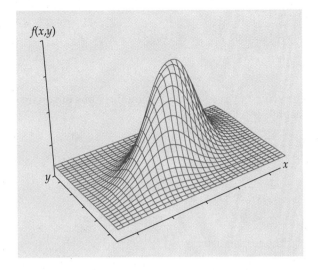

$f(x,y)$

Testing the Coefficient of Correlation

When there is no linear relationship between two variables, $\rho = 0$. To determine whether we can infer that ρ is zero, we test the following hypotheses.

$H_0: \rho = 0$

$H_A: \rho \neq 0$

The test statistic is defined as follows.*

Test Statistic for Testing $\rho = 0$

$$t = r\sqrt{\frac{n-2}{1-r^2}}$$

which is Student t-distributed with $n - 2$ degrees of freedom, provided that the variables are normally distributed.

EXAMPLE 16.7

Using the data in Example 16.2, test to determine whether we can infer that a linear relationship exists between selling price and odometer reading. Use a significance level of 5%.

---

*This test statistic is used only when testing $\rho = 0$. To test other values of ρ, another test statistic should be employed.

SOLUTION

We test

$$H_0: \rho = 0$$
$$H_A: \rho \neq 0$$

SOLVING BY HAND

The value of r is calculated using the sums of squares previously calculated in this chapter.

$$r = \frac{SS_{xy}}{\sqrt{SS_x \cdot SS_y}}$$

$$= \frac{-134{,}269{,}296}{\sqrt{4{,}309{,}340{,}160 \times 6{,}434{,}890}}$$

$$= -.8063$$

The test statistic is

$$t = r\sqrt{\frac{n-2}{1-r^2}}$$

$$= (-.8063)\sqrt{\frac{(100-2)}{1-(-.8063)^2}}$$

$$= -13.49$$

The rejection region is

$$|t| > t_{\alpha/2, n-2} = t_{.025, 98} \approx 1.984$$

We reject the null hypothesis.

USING THE COMPUTER

Minitab Output for Example 16.7

Correlations (Pearson)

```
Correlation of Price and Odometer = -0.806
```

Minitab prints the coefficient of correlation. The test can be completed manually.

MENU COMMANDS	COMMANDS FOR EXAMPLE 16.7
1 Type or import the data into two columns.	Open file **XM16-02**.
2 Click **Stat, Basic Statistics,** and **Correlation . . . .**	
3 Type the variable names. Click **OK**.	**Price Odometer** or **C1 C2**

	A	B	C
1		*Odometer*	*Price*
2	Odometer	1	
3	Price	-0.806307604	1

Excel prints the coefficient of correlation. The test can be completed manually.

COMMAND	COMMANDS FOR EXAMPLE 16.7
1 Type or import the data into two adjacent columns.	Open file **XM16-02**.
2 Click **Tools, Data Analysis . . .** , and **Correlation**.	
3 Specify the **Input Range**. Click **Labels in First Row** (if necessary). Click **OK**.	**A1:B101**

INTERPRETING THE RESULTS

There is overwhelming evidence to infer that the two variables are linearly related.

If you review Example 16.4 where we tested the slope coefficient β_1, you will find the same value of the test statistic, the same rejection region, and of course, the same conclusion as we produced above. This is not a coincidence; the two tests are identical. This should be no surprise, since data are the same and the objective is the same: to determine whether two variables are linearly related. Hence, it is necessary to perform only one test, either the t-test of β_1 or the t-test of ρ. (We performed both tests to show you that they are identical.)

Exercises

16.24 Given the following data

x	115	220	86	99	50	110
y	1.0	1.3	0.6	0.8	0.5	0.7

Calculate the Pearson correlation coefficient, and test to determine whether we can infer that a linear relationship exists between the two variables. (Use $\alpha = .05$.)

16.25 Refer to Exercise 16.6. Determine the coefficient of correlation. Conduct a test at the 5% significance level to determine whether a linear relationship exists between length of commercial and memory test score.

16.26 Refer to Exercise 16.10. Determine the correlation coefficient. Test it to determine whether the quality and price of oil are linearly related.

16.27 The weekly returns of two stocks are recorded for a 13-week period. These data are stored in file XR16-27 and listed below.

Can we infer at the 5% significance level that the stocks are correlated?

WEEK	STOCK 1	STOCK 2
1	−7	6
2	−4	6
3	−7	−4
4	−3	9
5	2	3
6	−10	−3
7	−10	7
8	5	−3
9	1	4
10	−4	7
11	2	9
12	6	5
13	−13	−7

16.28 The general manager of an engineering firm wants to know if a draftsman's experience influences the quality of his work. She selects 24 draftsmen at random and records their years of work experience and the number of promotions. These data are stored in file XR16-28 (column 1 = work experience in years, and column 2 = number of promotions) and listed below. Can we infer from these data that years of work experience is a factor in determining the number of promotions?

DRAFTSMAN	EXPERIENCE	PROMOTIONS	DRAFTSMAN	EXPERIENCE	PROMOTIONS
1	1	2	13	8	3
2	17	5	14	20	6
3	20	5	15	21	4
4	9	6	16	19	3
5	2	3	17	1	1
6	13	5	18	22	4
7	9	4	19	20	5
8	23	6	20	11	4
9	7	3	21	18	7
10	10	6	22	14	5
11	12	7	23	21	4
12	24	3	24	21	2

16.8 Regression Diagnostics—I

In Section 16.4, we described the required conditions for the validity of regression analysis. Simply put, the error variable must be normally distributed with a constant variance, and the errors must be independent of each other. In this section, we show how to diagnose violations. Additionally, we discuss how to deal with observations that are unusually large or small. Such observations must be investigated to determine if an error was made in recording them.

Residual Analysis

Most departures from required conditions can be diagnosed by examining the residuals, which we discussed in Section 16.3. Most computer packages allow you to output the values of the residuals and apply various graphical and statistical techniques to this variable.

We can also compute the standardized residuals. We standardize residuals in the same way we standardize all variables, by subtracting the mean and dividing by the standard deviation. The mean of the residuals is zero, and because the standard deviation σ_ϵ is unknown, we must estimate its value. The simplest estimate is the standard error of estimate s_ϵ. Thus

$$\text{Standardized residual} = \frac{r_i}{s_\epsilon}$$

Excel calculates and outputs this standardized residual. A partial list for Example 16.2 is shown below. (See Appendix 16.B for instructions.)

	OBSERVATION	RESIDUALS	STANDARDIZED RESIDUALS
Partial List of Residuals and Standardized Residuals from Excel for Example 16.2	1	−50.458	−.33290
	2	−77.825	−.51346
	3	−97.331	−.64215
	4	223.207	1.47265
	5	238.473	1.57336
	.	.	.
	.	.	.
	.	.	.
	97	−184.415	−1.21671
	98	−240.258	−1.58514
	99	43.875	.28948
	100	−266.491	−1.75822

We can also standardize by computing the standard deviation of each residual. Mathematicians have determined that the standard deviation of residual i is defined as follows.

Standard Deviation of the ith Residual

$$s_{r_i} = s_\epsilon \sqrt{1 - h_i}$$

where

$$h_i = \frac{1}{n} + \frac{(x_i - \bar{x})^2}{SS_x}$$

The quantity h_i should look familiar; it was used in the formula for the prediction interval and the confidence interval estimate of the expected value of y in Section 16.6. Minitab computes this version of the standardized residuals. (For details see Appendix 16.A.) Minitab's version is more generally accepted. Below we list some of the residuals and standardized residuals for Example 16.2.

Partial List of Residuals and Standardized Residuals from Minitab for Example 16.2	OBSERVATION	RESIDUALS	STANDARDIZED RESIDUALS
	1	−50.458	−.33465
	2	−77.825	−.52074
	3	−97.331	−.65282
	4	223.207	1.48468
	5	238.473	1.58474
	.	.	.
	.	.	.
	.	.	.
	97	−184.415	−1.22330
	98	−240.258	−1.59461
	99	43.875	.29128
	100	−266.491	−1.76710

An analysis of the residuals will allow us to determine if the error variable is non-normal, whether the error variance is constant, and whether the errors are independent. We begin with nonnormality.

Nonnormality

In Chapter 7, we introduced the normal probability distribution with the comment that it is the most important distribution in statistics. By now you must agree if for no other reason than the number of techniques that require normality. As we've done throughout this book, we can check for normality by producing a histogram of the residuals to see if it appears that the error variable is normally distributed. If the histogram appears to at least resemble a bell shape, it is probably safe to assume the normality requirement has been met.

**Minitab Histogram of
Residuals: Example 16.2**

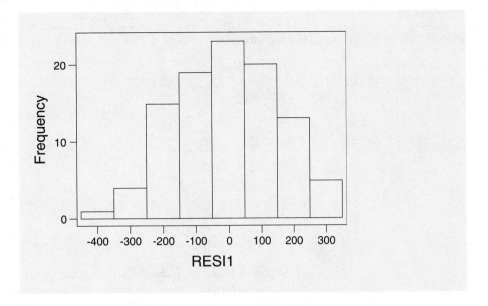

Minitab's histogram of the residuals for Example 16.2 is shown above. The histogram suggests that the error variable is approximately normally distributed. It should be noted that the tests applied in regression analysis are robust, which means that only when the error variable is quite nonnormal are the test results called into question.

Heteroscedasticity

The variance of the error variable σ_ϵ^2 is required to be constant. When this requirement is violated, the condition is called **heteroscedasticity**. (You can impress friends and relatives by using this term. If you can't pronounce it, try **homoscedasticity**, which refers to the condition where the requirement is satisfied.) One method of diagnosing heteroscedasticity is to plot the residuals against the predicted values of y. We then look for a change in the spread of variation of the plotted points. Figure 16.12 describes such a situation. Notice that, in this illustration, σ_ϵ^2 appears to be small when $\hat{y}$ is small and large when $\hat{y}$ is large. Of course, many other patterns could be used to depict this problem.

Figure 16.13 illustrates a case in which σ_ϵ^2 is constant. As a result, there is no apparent change in the variation of the residuals.

Figure 16.12

Plot of Residuals Depicting Heteroscedasticity

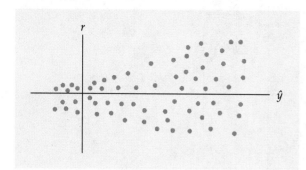

Figure 16.13

Plot of Residuals Depicting Homoscedasticity

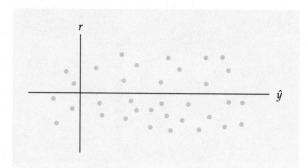

Minitab's plot of the residuals versus the predicted values of y for Example 16.2 is shown below. There does appear to be a decrease in the variance for larger values of $\hat{y}$. However, it is far from clear that there is a problem here.

Minitab Plot of Residuals Versus Predicted Values: Example 16.2

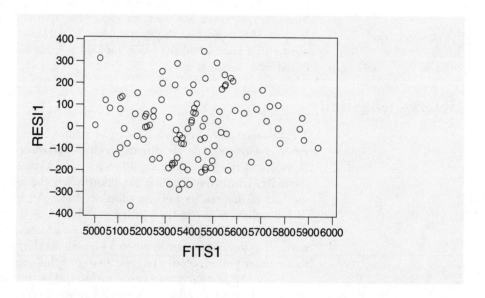

Nonindependence of the Error Variable

In Chapter 2, we briefly described the difference between cross-sectional and time series data. Cross-sectional data are observations made at approximately the same time, whereas a time series is a set of observations taken at successive points of time. The data in Example 16.2 are cross-sectional because all of the prices and odometer readings were taken at about the same time. If we were to observe the auction price of cars every week for (say) a year, that would constitute a time series.

Condition 4 states that the values of the error variable are independent. When the data are time series, the errors often are correlated. Error terms that are correlated over time are said to be **autocorrelated** or **serially correlated.** For example, suppose that, in an analysis of the relationship between annual gross profits and some independent variable, we observe the gross profits for the years 1977 to 1996. The observed values of y are denoted $y_1, y_2, \ldots, y_{20}$, where y_1 is the gross profit for 1977, y_2 is the gross profit for 1978, and so on. If we label the residuals $r_1, r_2, \ldots, r_{20}$, then—if the independence requirement is satisfied—there should be no relationship among the residuals. However, if the residuals are related, it is likely that autocorrelation exists.

We can often detect autocorrelation by graphing the residuals against the time periods. If a pattern emerges, it is likely that the independence requirement has been violated. Figures 16.14 (alternating positive and negative residuals) and 16.15 (increasing residuals) exhibit patterns indicating some form of autocorrelation. (Notice that we joined the points to make it easier to see the patterns.) Figure 16.16 shows no pattern (the residuals appear to be randomly distributed over the time periods), and thus, likely represents the occurrence of independent errors.

Figure 16.14

Plot of Residuals versus Time Indicating Autocorrelation

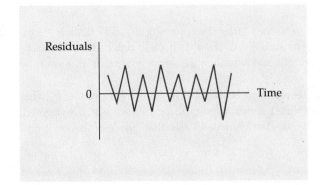

Figure 16.15

Plot of Residuals versus Time Indicating Autocorrelation

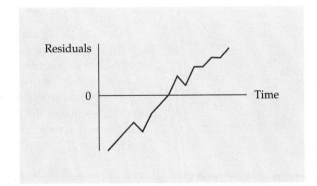

Figure 16.16

Plot of Residuals versus Time Indicating Independence

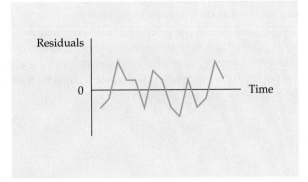

In Chapter 17, we introduce the Durbin–Watson test, which is another statistical test to determine if one form of this problem is present.

We will describe a number of remedies to violations of the required conditions in Chapter 17.

Outliers

An outlier is an observation that is unusually small or unusually large. To illustrate, consider Example 16.2, where the range of odometer readings was 19,057 to 49,223 miles. If we had observed a value of 5,000 miles, we would identify that point as an outlier. There are several possibilities that we need to investigate.

1 There was an error in recording the value.
   To detect an error we would check the point or points in question. In Example 16.2, we could check the car's odometer to determine if a mistake was made. If so, we would correct it before proceeding with the regression analysis.

2 The point should not have been included in the sample.
   Occasionally, measurements are taken from experimental units that do not belong with the sample. We can check to ensure that the car with the 5,000-mile odometer reading was actually three years old. We should also investigate the possibility that the odometer was rolled back. In either case, the outlier should be discarded.

3 The observation was simply an unusually large or small value that belongs to the sample and that was recorded properly.
   In this case we would do nothing to the outlier. It would be judged to be valid.

Outliers can be identified from the scatter diagram. Figure 16.17 depicts a scatter diagram with one outlier. The statistician should check to determine if the measurement was recorded accurately and whether the experimental unit should be included in the sample.

The standardized residuals also can be helpful in identifying outliers. Large absolute values of the standardized residuals should be thoroughly investigated. Minitab automatically reports standardized residuals that are less than -2 and greater than 2.

Figure 16.17

Scatter Diagram with One Outlier

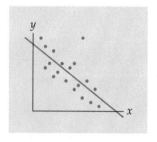

Influential Observations

Occasionally, in a regression analysis, one or more observations have a large influence on the statistics. Figure 16.18 describes such an observation and the resulting least squares line. If the point had not been included, the least squares line in Figure 16.19 would have been produced. Obviously, one point has had an enormous influence on the results. Influential points can be identified by the scatter diagram. The point may be an outlier and as such must be investigated thoroughly. Minitab also identifies influential observations.

Figure 16.18

**Scatter Diagram with One
Influential Observation**

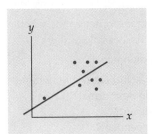

Figure 16.19

**Scatter Diagram without
the Influential Observation**

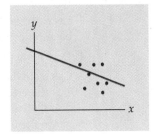

On page 623, we showed the Minitab output for Example 16.2. We omitted the last part of this output, an omission we correct below. Minitab lists unusual observations, which consist of observations with large standardized residuals (marked R) and observations whose values of x give them a large influence (marked X). These are the points to be checked for accuracy and to ensure that the observations belong to the sample.

**Minitab List of Unusual
Observations**

```
Unusual Observations
Obs. Odometer     Price      Fit  Stdev.Fit  Residual   St.Resid
   8     19057   5845.0   5939.6       42.0     -94.6    -0.65 X
  14     34470   5805.0   5459.4       15.6     345.6     2.29R
  19     48613   5333.0   5018.7       32.8     314.3     2.12R
  63     21221   5911.0   5872.2       37.4      38.8     0.26 X
  74     20962   5820.0   5880.3       37.9     -60.3     0.41 X
  78     44330   4787.0   5152.2       24.5    -365.2    -2.44R
```

R denotes an obs. with a large st. resid.
X denotes an obs. whose X value gives it large influence.

Points 14, 19, and 78 have standardized residuals that are greater than $|2|$, and so are judged to be unusual. Notice that points 8, 63, and 74 are identified as points that have a large influence. These three points are the three smallest odometer readings. Their removal would change the regression equation in a substantive way.

Procedure for Regression Diagnostics

The order of the material presented in this chapter is dictated by pedagogical requirements. Consequently, we presented the least squares method, methods of assessing the model's fit, predicting and estimating using the regression equation, coefficients of correlation, and finally, the regression diagnostics. In a practical application, the regression diagnostics would be conducted earlier in the process. It is appropriate to investigate violations of the required conditions when the model is assessed and before using the regression equation to predict and estimate. The following steps describe the entire process.

1 Develop a model that has a theoretical basis. That is, for the dependent variable in question find an independent variable that you believe is linearly related to it.

2 Gather data for the two variables. Ideally, conduct a controlled experiment. If that is not possible, collect observational data.

3 Draw the scatter diagram to determine whether a linear model appears to be appropriate. Identify possible outliers.

4 Determine the regression equation.

5 Calculate the residuals and check the required conditions.
    Is the error variable nonnormal?
    Is the variance constant?
    Are the errors independent?
    Check the outliers and influential observations.

6 Assess the model's fit.
    Compute the standard error of estimate.
    Test to determine whether there is a linear relationship. (Test β_1 or ρ.)
    Compute the coefficient of determination.

7 If the model fits the data, use the regression equation to predict a particular value of the dependent variable and/or estimate its mean.

Exercises

16.29 Refer to Exercise 16.4.

a Use the regression equation you produced to determine the predicted values of y.

b Use the predicted and actual values of y to calculate the residuals.

c Compute the standardized residuals.

d Identify possible outliers.

e Plot the residuals against the predicted values of y. Does the variance appear to be constant? Explain.

16.30 Refer to Exercise 16.5.

a Use the regression equation you produced to determine the predicted values of y.

b Use the predicted and actual values of y to calculate the residuals.

c Compute the standardized residuals.

d Identify possible outliers.

e Plot the residuals against the predicted values of y. Does the variance appear to be constant? Explain.

16.31 Each of the following pairs of values represents an actual value of y and a predicted value of y (based on a simple regression model). Graph the predicted values of y (on the horizontal axis) versus the residuals (on the vertical axis). In each case, determine from the graph whether the requirement that the variance of the error variable be constant is satisfied.

a

y	155 112 163 130 143 182 160 104 125 161 189 102 142 149 180
$\hat{y}$	143 108 180 133 146 193 140 101 126 176 200 97 145 151 158

b	y	10	22	29	15	24	13	17	23	11	27	19	26	20	14
	$\hat{y}$	7	21	29	13	25	16	19	22	14	27	17	27	22	11
c	y	46	40	53	60	56	62	44	49	52	59	45	55	47	61	42	57	50
	$\hat{y}$	48	43	54	63	54	65	46	47	49	56	41	53	44	57	45	62	51

The following exercises require a computer and statistical software.

16.32 Refer to Exercise 16.6.

   a Determine the residuals and the standardized residuals.

   b Draw the histogram of the residuals. Does it appear that the errors are normally distributed? Explain.

   c Identify possible outliers.

   d Plot the residuals versus the predicted values of y. Does it appear that heteroscedasticity is a problem? Explain.

16.33 Refer to Exercise 16.7.

   a Determine the residuals and the standardized residuals.

   b Draw the histogram of the residuals. Does it appear that the errors are normally distributed? Explain.

   c Identify possible outliers.

   d Plot the residuals versus the predicted values of y. Does it appear that heteroscedasticity is a problem? Explain.

16.34 Refer to Exercise 16.9.

   a Determine the residuals and the standardized residuals.

   b Draw the histogram of the residuals. Does it appear that the errors are normally distributed? Explain.

   c Identify possible outliers.

   d Plot the residuals versus the predicted values of y. Does it appear that heteroscedasticity is a problem? Explain.

16.35 Refer to Exercise 16.10.

   a Determine the residuals and the standardized residuals.

   b Draw the histogram of the residuals. Does it appear that the errors are normally distributed? Explain.

   c Identify possible outliers.

   d Plot the residuals versus the predicted values of y. Does it appear that heteroscedasticity is a problem? Explain.

16.36 Refer to Exercise 16.11.

   a Determine the residuals and the standardized residuals.

   b Draw the histogram of the residuals. Does it appear that the errors are normally distributed? Explain.

   c Identify possible outliers.

   d Plot the residuals versus the predicted values of y. Does it appear that heteroscedasticity is a problem? Explain.

16.9 Summary

Simple linear regression and correlation are techniques for analyzing the relationship between two quantitative variables. Regression analysis assumes that the two variables are linearly related. The least squares method produces estimates of the intercept and the slope of the regression line. Considerable effort is expended in assessing how well the linear model fits the data. We calculate the standard error of estimate, which is an estimate of the standard deviation of the error variable. We test the slope to determine whether there is sufficient evidence of a linear relationship. The strength of the linear association is measured by the coefficient of determination. When the model provides a good fit, we can use it to predict the particular value and to estimate the expected value of the dependent variable. We can also use the Pearson correlation coefficient to measure and test the relationship between two normally distributed variables. We completed this chapter with a discussion of how to diagnose violations of the required conditions.

IMPORTANT TERMS

Dependent variable

Independent variable

Deterministic model

Probabilistic model

First-order linear model

Simple linear regression model

Error variable

Scatter diagram

Least squares method

Regression line

Residuals

Sum of squares for error

Standard error of estimate

Coefficient of determination

Sum of squares for regression

Prediction interval

Pearson coefficient of correlation

Heteroscedasticity

Homoscedasticity

Autocorrelation

Supplementary Exercises

16.37 The manager of Colonial Furniture has been reviewing weekly advertising expenditures. During the past six months all advertisements for the store have appeared in the local newspaper. The number of ads per week has varied from one to seven. The store's sales staff has been tracking the number of customers who enter the store each week. The number of ads and the number of customers per week for the past 26 weeks have been stored in the file XR16-37. Some of these data are listed below.

   a   Determine the sample regression line.

   b   Interpret the coefficients.

   c   Can the manager infer at the 5% significance level that the larger the number of ads, the larger the number of customers?

   d   Find and interpret the coefficient of determination.

   e   In your opinion, is it a worthwhile exercise to use the regression equation to predict the number of customers who will enter the store, given that Colonial intends to advertise five times in the newspaper? If so, find a 95% prediction interval. If not, explain why not.

WEEK	NUMBER OF ADS	NUMBER OF CUSTOMERS
1	5	353
2	6	319
3	3	440
.	.	.
.	.	.
.	.	.
26	7	367

Use a software package to solve this problem.	OR	Σ Ads = 107 Σ Customer = 10,005 Σ Ads^2 = 527 Σ Customer^2 = 4,313,803 Σ (Ads) (Customer) = 43,025 Complete your answer manually.

16.38 The president of a company that manufactures car seats has been concerned about the number and cost of machine breakdowns. The problem is that the machines are old and becoming quite unreliable. However, the cost of replacing them is quite high, and the president is not certain that the cost can be made up in today's slow economy. To help make a decision about replacement, he gathered data about last month's costs for repairs and the ages (in months) of the plant's 20 welding machines. These data are stored in file XR16-38. A partial listing is exhibited below.

a Find the sample regression line.

b Interpret the coefficients.

c Determine the standard error of estimate, and discuss what this statistic tells you.

d Conduct a test at whatever significance level you deem suitable to determine whether the age of a machine and its monthly cost of repair are linearly related.

e Find and interpret the coefficient of determination.

f Is the fit of the simple linear model good enough to allow the president to predict the monthly repair cost of a welding machine that is 120 months old? If so, find a 95% prediction interval. If not, explain why not.

MACHINE	AGE	COST OF REPAIRS
1	110	$327.67
2	113	376.68
3	114	392.52
.	.	.
.	.	.
.	.	.
20	137	416.04

Use a software package to solve this problem.	OR	Σ Age = 2267 Σ Repairs = 7904.1 Σ Age^2 = 264,161 Σ Repairs^2 = 3,201,549 Σ (Age) (Repairs) = 913,730 Complete your answer manually.

16.39 It is doubtful that any sport collects more statistics than baseball. This surfeit of statistics allows fans to conduct a great variety of statistical analyses. For example, fans are always interested in determining which factors lead to successful teams. The table below lists the team batting average and the team winning percentage for the 14 American League teams at the end of a recent season. We will assume that these data represent a random sample of the relationship between batting average and winning percentage for all time. These data are also stored in file XR16-39.

TEAM	TEAM BATTING AVERAGE	TEAM WINNING PERCENTAGE
Baltimore	.254	.414
Boston	.269	.519
California	.255	.500
Chicago	.262	.537
Cleveland	.254	.352
Detroit	.247	.519
Kansas City	.264	.506
Milwaukee	.271	.512
Minnesota	.280	.586
New York	.256	.438
Oakland	.248	.519
Seattle	.255	.512
Texas	.270	.525
Toronto	.257	.562

SOURCE: Creative Statistics Company

a Find the sample regression line, and interpret the coefficients.

b Find the standard error of estimate, and describe what this statistic tells you.

c Do these data provide sufficient evidence at the 5% significance level to conclude that higher team batting averages lead to higher winning percentages?

d Find the coefficient of determination, and interpret its value.

e Predict with 90% confidence the winning percentage of a team whose batting average is .275.

<table>
<tr><td>Use a software package to solve this problem.</td><td>OR</td><td>Σ Team-B-A = 3.6420
Σ Winning% = 7.00
Σ Team-B-A² = .94862
Σ Winning%² = 3.5488
Σ(Team-B-A)(Winning%)
= 1.8246
Complete your answer manually.</td></tr>
</table>

16.40 In an effort to further analyze a baseball team's winning percentage, the Creative Statistics Company determined each team's earned run average (ERA). (An earned run average is the number of earned runs a baseball team gives up in an average nine-inning game.) These data, together with the team's winning percentage, are stored in file XR16-40 and listed below.

a Find the sample regression line, and interpret the coefficients.

b Find the standard error of estimate, and describe what this statistic tells you.

c Do these data provide sufficient evidence to conclude that lower earned run averages lead to higher winning percentages?

d Find the coefficient of determination, and interpret its value.

e Predict with 90% confidence the winning percentage of a team whose ERA is 4.00.

TEAM	TEAM EARNED RUN AVERAGE	TEAM WINNING PERCENTAGE
Baltimore	4.59	.414
Boston	4.01	.519
California	3.69	.500
Chicago	3.79	.537
Cleveland	4.23	.352
Detroit	4.51	.519
Kansas City	3.92	.506
Milwaukee	4.14	.512
Minnesota	3.69	.586
New York	4.42	.438
Oakland	4.57	.519
Seattle	3.79	.512
Texas	4.47	.525
Toronto	3.50	.562

SOURCE: Creative Statistics Company

16.41 In the last decade, society in general and the judicial system in particular have altered their opinions on the seriousness of drunken driving. In most jurisdictions, driving an automobile with a blood-alcohol level in excess of .08 is a felony. Because of a number of factors, it is difficult to provide guidelines on when it is safe for someone who has consumed alcohol to drive a car. In an experiment to examine the relationship between blood-alcohol level and the weight of a drinker, 16 men of varying weights were each given three beers to drink, and one hour later their blood-alcohol level was measured. These data are stored in file XR16-41 and listed below.

Can we conclude that blood-alcohol level and weight are related? (Use α = .05.)

INDIVIDUAL	WEIGHT (POUNDS)	BLOOD-ALCOHOL LEVEL
1	229	.18
2	200	.12
3	223	.19
4	217	.15
5	164	.14
6	191	.17
7	168	.16
8	218	.14
9	151	.09
10	229	.16
11	216	.10
12	214	.16
13	159	.17
14	161	.13
15	219	.15
16	166	.14

16.42 Several years ago, Coca-Cola attempted to change its 100-year-old recipe. One reason why the company's management felt this was necessary was competition from Pepsi Cola. Respondents of surveys of Pepsi drinkers indicated that they preferred Pepsi because it was sweeter than Coke. As part of the analysis that led to Coke's ill-fated move, the management of Coca-Cola performed extensive surveys wherein consumers tasted various versions of the new Coke. Suppose that a random sample of 200 cola drinkers was given versions of Coke with different amounts of sugar. After tasting the product, each drinker was asked to rate the taste quality on a 5-point scale where 1 = poor and 5 = excellent.

The responses and sugar content (percent by volume) of the version tasted were recorded in columns 1 and 2, respectively, of file XR16-42. Some of these data are shown below. Can management infer at the 5% significance level that sugar content affects drinkers' ratings of the cola?

RATING	SUGAR
1	5
1	6
4	21
.	.
.	.
.	.
2	11

16.43 An agronomist wanted to investigate the factors that determine crop yield. Accordingly, she undertook an experiment wherein a farm was divided into 30 one-acre plots. The amount of fertilizer applied to each plot was varied. Corn was then planted, and the amount of corn harvested at the end of the season was recorded. These data were stored in file XR16-43. Some of the data are shown below.

a Find the sample regression line, and interpret the coefficients.

b Find the standard error of estimate, and interpret its value.

c Can the agronomist conclude at the 5% significance level that there is a linear relationship between the amount of fertilizer and the crop yield?

d Find the coefficient of determination, and interpret its value.

e Does the simple linear model appear to be a useful tool in predicting crop yield from the amount of fertilizer applied? If so, produce a 95% prediction interval of the crop yield when 300 pounds of fertilizer are applied. If not, explain why not.

PLOT	AMOUNT OF FERTILIZER	CROP YIELD
1	210	43.5
2	220	150.2
3	230	39.5
.	.	.
.	.	.
30	500	77.5

Use a software package to solve this problem.

OR

Σ Fertilizer = 10,650
Σ Yield = 2460.8
Σ Fertilizer^2 = 4,005,500
Σ Yield^2 = 224,063
Σ (Fertilizer)(Yield) = 887,212
Complete your answer manually.

16.44 One general belief held by observers of the business world is that taller men earn more money than shorter men. In a University of Pittsburgh study (reported in the *Wall Street Journal*, 30 December 1986), 30 M.B.A. graduates, all about 30 years old, were polled and asked to report their annual incomes and their heights. These data are stored in file XR16-44, with some of them listed below.

a Determine the sample regression line, and interpret the coefficients.

b Find the standard error of estimate, and interpret its value.

c Do these data provide sufficient statistical evidence to infer at the 5% significance level that taller M.B.A.'s earn more money than shorter ones?

d Provide a measure of the strength of the linear relationship between income and height.

e Do you think that this model is good enough to be used to estimate and predict income on the basis of height? If not, explain why not. If so,

    i estimate with 95% confidence the mean income of all six-foot men with M.B.A.'s.

    ii predict with 95% confidence the income of a man 5 feet 10 inches tall with an M.B.A.

MBA	HEIGHT (IN INCHES)	INCOME
1	70	$34,330
2	67	37,410
3	69	34,630
.	.	.
.	.	.
.	.	.
30	70	40,170

Use a software package to solve this problem.

OR

Σ Height = 2088
Σ Income = 1,089,590
Σ Height^2 = 145,582
Σ Income^2 = 39,809,607,100
Σ (Height) (Income) = 75,918,550
Complete your answer manually.

MARKET MODEL OF STOCK RETURNS*

A well-known model in finance, called the *market model,* assumes that monthly rate of return on a stock (R) is linearly related to the monthly rate of return on the overall market R_m. The mathematical description of the model is

$$R = \beta_0 + \beta_1 R_m + \epsilon$$

where the error term ϵ is assumed to satisfy the requirements of the linear regression model. For practical purposes, R_m is taken to be the monthly rate of return on some major stock market index, such as the New York Stock Exchange Composite Index.

The coefficient β_1, called the stock's *beta-coefficient,* measures how sensitive the stock's rate of return is to changes in the level of the overall market. For example, if $\beta_1 > 1$ ($\beta_1 < 1$), the stock's rate of return is more (or less) sensitive to changes in the level of the overall market than is the average stock. The monthly rates of return for Northern Telecom stock and for the overall market over a five-year period are stored in file C16-01. (Column 1 stores the monthly percentage return for Northern Telecom; column 2 stores the monthly percentage return for all of the stocks on the Toronto Stock Exchange.)

a What is the sample regression line?

b Is there sufficient evidence to infer at the 5% significance level that there is a linear relationship between the return on the Northern Telecom stock and the return on the total market?

c Is there sufficient evidence to infer at the 5% significance level that Northern Telecom is less sensitive than the average stock?

d Discuss the significance of the findings.

DUXBURY PRESS

The academic book business is different from most other businesses because of the way purchasing decisions are made. The customer, who is usually a student taking a university or college course, buys a specific book because the instructor of the course adopts (chooses to use) that book. Sales representatives of publishers sell their products by persuading instructors to adopt their books. Unfortunately, judging the quality of textbooks is not easy. To help with the decision process, sales representatives give free examination copies to instructors so that they can review the book and decide whether or not to adopt it. In many universities, there are several sections of the same course, and book adoption committees meet to make the adoption decision.

Curt Hinrichs, an editor at Duxbury Press, is examining the latest sales data for 20 statistics textbooks that Duxbury publishes. He notes that the number of examination copies is quite large, which can be a serious problem, given the high cost of producing books. He wonders whether his sales representatives are giving away too many free books, or perhaps not enough. The data that he is examining

---

*Adapted from James H. Lorie, Peter Dodd, and Mary Hamilton Kimpton, *The Stock Market: Theories and Evidence,* 2d ed. (Homewood, Ill.: Richard D. Irwin, 1985).

contain a code that identifies the sales representative (there is a total of 78 sales-people), the gross revenues from the sales of the statistics books, and the number of free copies. These data are stored in columns 1 to 3, respectively, of file C16-02. Curt would like to know if there is a direct link between the number of free copies and the number of books sold or the gross revenues from the sales of the books.

Perform an analysis to provide Curt with the information he needs.

CASE 16.3

PREDICTING UNIVERSITY GRADES
FROM HIGH SCHOOL GRADES*

Ontario High school students must complete a minimum of six Ontario Academic Credits (OACs) to gain admission to a university in the province. Most students take more than six OACs because universities take the average of the best six in deciding which students to admit. Most programs at universities require high school students to select certain courses. For example, science programs require two of chemistry, biology, and physics. Students applying to engineering must complete at least two mathematics OACs as well as physics. In recent years, one business program began an examination of all aspects of their program including the criteria used to admit students. Students are required to take English and calculus OACs, and the minimum high school average is about 85%. Strangely enough, even though students are required to complete English and calculus, the marks in these subjects are not included in the average unless they are in the top six courses in a student's transcript. To examine the issue, the registrar took a random sample of students who recently graduated with the BBA (Bachelor of Business Administration) degree. He recorded the university GPA (range 0 to 12), the high school average based on the best six courses, and the high school average using English and calculus and the four next best marks. These data are stored in columns 1 to 3, respectively, in file C16-03. What conclusion can you draw from these data?

---

*The authors are grateful to Leslie Grauer for her help in this case.

Minitab Instructions

Simple Linear Regression

The command

    REGRESS C2 1 C1

computes the least squares line when the values of x and y are stored in columns 1 and 2, respectively. The term "1" refers to the use of only one independent variable—in this case, the variable stored in column 1.

    The **PREDICT** subcommand is used to produce the 95% confidence interval estimate of the expected value of y for a given x and the 95% prediction interval. To change the confidence level, use the **CONFIDENCE** subcommand. For example, we would produce the 99% confidence interval estimate of the expected value and the 99% prediction interval of the price when the odometer reads 40,000 miles in the following way.

    REGRESS C2 1 C1;
    PREDICT 40000;
    CONFIDENCE 99.

    To draw the scatter diagram, type

    PLOT C2*C1

The variable in column 2 will appear along the vertical axis.

Diagnosing Violations of Required Conditions

To calculate the residuals, standardized residuals, and predicted values, type the following command and subcommands.

    REGRESS C2 1 C1;
    RESIDUALS C3;
    SRESIDUALS C4;
    FITS C5.

The residuals will be stored in column 3, standardized residuals in column 4, and predicted values (**FITS**) in column 5. To examine the normality requirement, we draw the histogram of the residuals.

    HISTOGRAM C3

To determine if the variance is constant, we plot residuals and predicted values.

    PLOT C3*C5

1 Click **Stat**, **Regression**, and **Regression** . . . .

2 Specify the dependent (**Response**) variable and the independent (**Predictors**) variable.

3 Use the cursor to select **Residuals**, **Standard. resids**, and **Fits**. Click **OK**.

The standardized residuals will be stored in the first available empty column; the predicted values and residuals will be stored in the next two columns.

4 Click **Stat**, **Regression**, and **Residual Plots** . . . .

5 Specify the **Residuals** and **Fits**. Click **OK**.

Minitab will produce a normal probability plot (a straight line indicates normality), a plot of the residuals in the order of the observations, a histogram of the residuals, and a plot of the residuals versus the predicted values.

APPENDIX 16.B Excel Instructions

DIAGNOSING VIOLATIONS OF REQUIRED CONDITIONS

Proceed with the first four steps of regression analysis described on page 624. Before clicking **OK** (in step 4), execute the following commands.

1 Use the cursor to select **Residuals**, **Standardized Residuals**, and **Residual Plots**. Click **OK**. The predicted values of y, residuals, and standardized residuals will be printed. A plot of the residuals versus the predicted values of y will also be output. (Change the scale if necessary.)

2 Draw the histogram of the residuals (see Chapter 2 for instructions on how to draw a histogram).

APPENDIX 16.C Spearman Rank Correlation Coefficient

In this chapter we dealt only with quantitative variables and have assumed that all the conditions for the validity of the statistical inference have been met. In many situations, however, one or both variables may be ranked; or if both variables are quantitative, the normality requirement may not be satisfied. In such cases, we measure and test to determine if a relationship exists by employing a nonparametric technique, the **Spearman rank correlation coefficient**.

The Spearman rank correlation coefficient is employed in problems with the following characteristics.

1 Problem objective: analyze the relationship between two variables

2 Data type: ranked or quantitative but nonnormal

The population Spearman correlation coefficient is labeled ρ_s and the sample statistic used to estimate its value is labeled r_s.

It is calculated by ranking each variable from 1 (smallest) to n (largest). We then calculate the Pearson correlation coefficient of the ranks. That is,

$$r_s = \frac{SS_{ab}}{\sqrt{SS_a \, SS_b}}$$

where a and b are the ranks

We can test to determine if a relationship exists between the two variables. The hypotheses to be tested are

$$H_0: \rho_s = 0$$
$$H_A: \rho_s \neq 0$$

(We can also conduct one-tail tests.)

Test Statistic

For samples smaller than or equal to 30, the test statistic is r_s. To determine whether we should reject the null hypothesis, we need the Spearman rank correlation coefficient table (not shown here). For samples greater than 30, the test statistic is

$$z = r_s \sqrt{n - 1}$$

which is standard normally distributed.

Minitab Menu Commands

1 Type or import the data into two columns.

2 Click **Manip** and **Rank. . . .**

3 Type the name of the first variable (arbitrary choice).

4 Hit **tab** and specify the column where the ranks are to be stored.

5 Click **Manip** and **Rank** and repeat step 2 for the second variable. Click **OK**.

6 Click **Stat**, **Basic Statistics**, and **Correlation. . . .**

7 Type the variable names of the ranked variables. Click **OK.**

Excel Commands

1 Type or import the data into two adjacent columns.

2 Click **Tools**, **Data Analysis Plus**, and **Spearman Rank Correlation**.

3 Specify the block coordinates of the data. Do not include cells containing the variable names.

17 Multiple Regression

17.1 Introduction

In the previous chapter, we employed the simple linear regression model to analyze how one quantitative variable (the dependent variable y) is affected by another quantitative variable (the independent variable x). The restriction of using only one independent variable was motivated by the need to simplify the introduction to regression analysis. Although there are a number of applications where we purposely develop a model with only one independent variable (see Case 16.1, for example), in general we prefer to include as many independent variables as can be shown to significantly affect the dependent variable. Arbitrarily limiting the number of independent variables also limits the usefulness of the model.

In this chapter, we allow for any number of independent variables. In so doing, we expect to develop models that fit the data better than would a simple linear regression model. We will proceed in a manner similar to that in Chapter 16. We begin by describing the multiple regression model and listing the required conditions. We let the computer produce the required statistics and use them to assess the model's fit and diagnose violations of the required conditions. We will employ the model by interpreting the coefficients, predicting the particular value of the dependent variable, and estimating its expected value.

17.2 Model and Required Conditions

We now assume that k independent variables are potentially related to the dependent variable. Thus, the model is represented by the following equation.

$$y = \beta_0 + \beta_1 x_1 + \beta_2 x_2 + \cdots + \beta_k x_k + \epsilon$$

where y is the dependent variable, $x_1, x_2, \ldots, x_k$ are the independent variables, β_0, $\beta_1, \ldots, \beta_k$ are the coefficients, and ϵ is the error variable. The independent variables may actually be functions of other variables. For example, we might define some of the independent variables as follows.

$$x_2 = x_1^2$$

$$x_5 = x_3 \cdot x_4$$

$$x_7 = \log(x_6)$$

The error variable is retained because, even though we have included additional independent variables, deviations between values in the model and the actual values of y will still occur. Incidentally, when there is more than one independent variable in the regression analysis, we refer to the graphical depiction of the equation as a **response surface** rather than as a straight line. Figure 17.1 depicts a scatter diagram of a response surface with $k = 2$. (When $k = 2$, the regression equation creates a **plane**.) Of course, whenever k is greater than 2, we can only imagine the response surface; we cannot draw it.

Figure 17.1

Scatter Diagram and Response Surface with $k = 2$

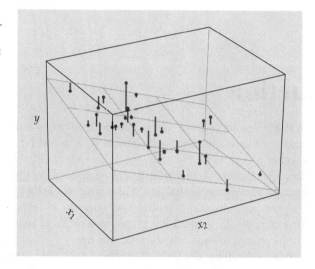

An important part of the regression analysis comprises several statistical techniques that evaluate how well the model fits the data. These techniques require the following conditions, which we introduced in the previous chapter.

Required Conditions for the Error Variable

1 The probability distribution of the error variable ϵ is normal.

2 The mean of the distribution is zero.

3 The standard deviation of ϵ is σ_ϵ, which is a constant.

4 The errors are independent.

In Section 16.8, we discussed how to recognize when the requirements are unsatisfied. Those same procedures can be used to detect violations of required conditions in the multiple regression model.

We now proceed as we did in Chapter 16; we discuss how the model's coefficients are estimated and how we assess the model's fit. However, there is one major difference between Chapters 16 and 17. In Chapter 16, we allowed for the possibility that some students will perform the calculations manually. The multiple regression model involves so many computations that it is virtually impossible to conduct the analysis without a computer. All analyses in this chapter will be performed by Minitab and Excel. Your job will be to interpret the output.

17.3 Estimating the Coefficients and Assessing the Model

The procedures introduced in Chapter 16 are extended to the multiple regression model. However, in Chapter 16, we discussed how to interpret the coefficients first, followed by a discussion of how to assess the model's fit. In practice, we reverse the process. That is, the first step is to determine how well the model fits. If the model's fit is poor, there is no point in a further analysis of the coefficients of that model. A much higher priority is assigned to the task of improving the model. In this chapter, we will show how a regression analysis is performed. The steps we will use are as follows.

1 Use a computer and software to generate the coefficients and the statistics used to assess the model.

2 Diagnose violations of required conditions. If there are problems, we attempt to remedy them.

3 Assess the model's fit. There are three statistics that perform this function: the standard error of estimate, the coefficient of determination, and the *F*-test of the analysis of variance. The first two were introduced in Chapter 16, the third will be introduced here.

4 If we're satisfied with the model's fit and that the required conditions are met, we can attempt to interpret the coefficients and test them as we did in Chapter 16. We use the model to predict or estimate the expected value of the dependent variable.

We illustrate these techniques with the following example.

EXAMPLE 17.1

Deciding where to locate a new retail store is one of the most important decisions that a manager can make. The president of a chain of video rental stores plans to use a regression model to help select a location for a new store. She decides to use annual gross revenue as a measure of success, which is the dependent variable. The president believes that determinants of success include the following variables.

Number of people living within one mile of the store (**PEOPLE**)

Mean income of households within one mile of the store (**INCOME**)

Number of competitors within one mile of the store (**COMPTORS**)

Rental price of a newly released movie (**PRICE**)

The president randomly selects 50 video stores and records the values of each of the variables listed above plus annual gross revenue (**REVENUE**). These data are stored in columns 1 to 5 in file XM17-01, some of which are shown below. She proposes the following multiple regression model.

$$\text{REVENUE} = \beta_0 + \beta_1 \text{ PEOPLE} + \beta_2 \text{ INCOME} + \beta_3 \text{ COMPTORS} + \beta_4 \text{ PRICE} + \epsilon$$

A computer is used to produce the required statistics. Analyze that output.

STORE	GROSS ANNUAL REVENUE	NUMBER OF PEOPLE	MEAN INCOME	NUMBER OF COMPETITORS	RENTAL PRICE
1	$323,581	5,556	$42,746	3	$2.49
2	343,682	5,917	43,106	2	2.99
3	375,264	5,483	46,993	5	2.99
.	.	.	.	.	.
.	.	.	.	.	.
.	.	.	.	.	.
50	314,170	5,453	35,821	3	2.49

SOLUTION

Minitab and Excel were used to produce the outputs below. From these printouts we can see that the sample regression equation is

$$\text{REVENUE} = -20{,}297 + 6.44 \text{ PEOPLE} + 7.27 \text{ INCOME} - 6{,}709 \text{ COMPTORS} + 15{,}969 \text{ PRICE}$$

Minitab Output for Example 17.1

Regression Analysis

The regression equation is
Revenue = − 20297 + 6.44 People + 7.27 Income − 6709 Comptors + 15969 Price

Predictor	Coef	Stdev	t-ratio	p
Constant	−20297	54939	−0.37	0.714
People	6.439	3.705	1.74	0.089
Income	7.2723	0.9358	7.77	0.000
Comptors	−6709	3819	−1.76	0.086
Price	15969	10219	1.56	0.125

s = 25140   R-sq = 58.8%   R-sq(adj) = 55.1%

Analysis of Variance

SOURCE	DF	SS	MS	F	p
Regression	4	40585375744	10146343936	16.05	0.000
Error	45	28440403968	632008960		
Total	49	69025775616			

MENU COMMANDS   COMMANDS FOR EXAMPLE 17.1

1 Type or import the data.   Open file **XM17-01**.

2 Click **Stat, Regression**, and
  Regression . . . .

3 Type the name of the dependent
  variable (**Response**).   **Revenue or C1**

4 Hit **tab**, and type the names of the independent variables (**Predictors**). Click **OK**.

People, Income, Comptors, Price or C2, C3, C4, C5

Excel Output for Example 17.1

	A	B	C	D	E	F	G
1	SUMMARY OUTPUT						
2							
3	Regression Statistics						
4	Multiple R	0.766795					
5	R Square	0.587974					
6	Adjusted R Square	0.55135					
7	Standard Error	25139.79					
8	Observations	50					
9							
10	ANOVA						
11		df	SS	MS	F	Significance F	
12	Regression	4	4.06E+10	1.01E+10	16.05411	3.08E-08	
13	Residual	45	2.84E+10	6.32E+08			
14	Total	49	6.90E+10				
15							
16		Coefficients	Standard Error	t Stat	P-value		
17	Intercept	-20297.2	54939.09	-0.36945	0.713526		
18	People	6.439423	3.705117	1.737981	0.089054		
19	Income	7.272305	0.935795	7.771261	7.43E-10		
20	Comptors	-6709.43	3818.543	-1.75707	0.085709		
21	Price	15968.76	10219.03	1.56265	0.125141		

COMMANDS

1 Type or import the data into adjacent columns.

2 Click **Tools**, **Data Analysis ...**, and **Regression**.

3 Specify the block coordinates of the dependent variable (**Input Y Range:**).

4 Hit **tab**, and specify the block coordinates of the independent variables (**Input X Range:**). Click **Labels** (if necessary). Click **OK**.

COMMANDS FOR EXAMPLE 17.1

Open file **XM17-01**.

A1:A51

B1:E51

We assess the model in three ways: the standard error of estimate, the coefficient of determination (both introduced in Chapter 16), and the F-test of the analysis of variance (presented below).

STANDARD ERROR OF ESTIMATE

Recall that σ_ϵ is the standard deviation of the error variable ϵ and that, because σ_ϵ is a population parameter, it is necessary to estimate its value by using s_ϵ. In multiple regression, the standard error of estimate is defined as follows.

Standard Error of Estimate

$$s_\epsilon = \sqrt{\frac{\text{SSE}}{n - k - 1}}$$

As we noted in Chapter 16, each of our software packages reports the standard error of estimate in a different way. Minitab outputs s_ϵ for Example 17.1 as

s = 25140

and Excel outputs this value as

Standard Error 25139.79

Recall that we judge the magnitude of the standard error of estimate relative to the values of the dependent variable, and particularly to the mean of y. In this example, $\bar{y} = 343{,}966$ (not shown in printouts). It appears that the standard error of estimate is not particularly small.

COEFFICIENT OF DETERMINATION

Recall from Chapter 16 that the coefficient of determination is defined as

$$R^2 = 1 - \frac{\text{SSE}}{\text{SS}_y}$$

For Example 17.1, Minitab prints

R-sq = 58.8%

and Excel outputs

R Square 0.587974

This means that 58.8% of the variation in gross revenues is explained by the four independent variables, while 41.2% remains unexplained.

Notice that Minitab and Excel print a second R^2 statistic, called the **coefficient of determination adjusted for degrees of freedom**, which has been adjusted to take into account the sample size and the number of independent variables. The rationale for this statistic is that, if the number of independent variables k is large relative to the sample size n, the unadjusted R^2 value may be unrealistically high. To understand this point, consider what would happen if the sample size is 2 in a simple linear regression model. The line will fit the data perfectly resulting in $R^2 = 1$ when, in fact, there may be no linear relationship. To avoid creating a false impression, the adjusted R^2 is often calculated. Its formula follows.

Coefficient of Determination Adjusted for Degrees of Freedom

$$\text{Adjusted } R^2 = 1 - \frac{\text{SSE}/(n - k - 1)}{\text{SS}_y/(n - 1)}$$

If n is considerably larger than k, the actual and adjusted R^2 values will be similar. But if SSE is quite different from zero and k is large compared to n, the actual and adjusted values of R^2 will differ substantially. If such differences exist, the analyst should be alerted to a potential problem in interpreting the coefficient of determination. In Example 17.1, the adjusted coefficient of determination is 55.1%, indicating that, no matter how we measure the coefficient of determination, the model's fit is moderately good.

TESTING THE UTILITY
OF THE MODEL

In the simple linear regression model, we tested the slope coefficient to determine whether sufficient evidence existed to allow us to conclude that there was a linear relationship between the independent variable and the dependent variable. However, because there is only one independent variable in that model, the t-test also tested to determine whether that model is useful. When there is more than one independent variable, we need another method to test the overall utility of the model. The technique is a version of the analysis of variance, which we introduced in Chapter 14.

To test the utility of the regression model, we specify the following hypotheses.

H_0: $\beta_1 = \beta_2 = \cdots = \beta_k = 0$

H_A: At least one β_i is not equal to zero.

If the null hypothesis is true, none of the independent variables $x_1, x_2, \ldots, x_k$ is linearly related to y, and therefore the model is useless. If at least one β_i is not equal to zero, the model does have some utility.

When we introduced the coefficient of determination in Chapter 16, we noted that the variation in the dependent variable (measured by SS_y) can be decomposed into two parts: the explained variation (measured by SSR) and the unexplained variation (measured by SSE). That is,

$SS_y = SSR + SSE$

Furthermore, we established that, if SSR is large relative to SSE, the coefficient of determination will be high—signifying a good model. On the other hand, if SSE is large, most of the variation will be unexplained, which indicates that the model provides a poor fit and consequently has little utility.

The test statistic is the same one we encountered in Section 14.2, where we tested for the equivalence of k population means. In order to judge whether SSR is large enough relative to SSE to allow us to infer that at least one coefficient is not equal to zero, we compute the ratio of the two mean squares. (Recall that the **mean square** is the sum of squares divided by its degrees of freedom; recall, too, that the ratio of two mean squares is F-distributed, as long as the underlying population is normal—a required condition for this application.) The calculation of the test statistic is summarized in an analysis of variance (ANOVA) table, which in general appears as follows.

Analysis of Variance Table for Regression Analysis

SOURCE OF VARIATION	DEGREES OF FREEDOM	SUMS OF SQUARES	MEAN SQUARES	F-STATISTIC
Regression	k	SSR	$MSR = SSR/k$	$F = MSR/MSE$
Residual	$n - k - 1$	SSE	$MSE = SSE/(n - k - 1)$	
TOTAL	$n - 1$	SS_y		

```
Analysis of Variance

SOURCE        DF            SS            MS         F        p
Regression     4 40585375744 10146343936      16.05    0.000
Error         45 28440403968     632008960
Total         49 69025775616
```

	A	B	C	D	E	F	G
1	ANOVA						
2		df	SS	MS	F	Significance F	
3	Regression	4	4.06E+10	1.01E+10	16.05411	3.08E-08	
4	Residual	45	2.84E+10	6.32E+08			
5	Total	49	6.9E+10				

A large value of F indicates that most of the variation in y is explained by the regression equation and that the model is useful. A small value of F indicates that most of the variation in y is unexplained. The rejection region allows us to determine whether F is large enough to justify rejecting the null hypothesis. For this test, the rejection region is

$$F > F_{\alpha, k, n-k-1}$$

In Example 17.1, the rejection region (assuming $\alpha = .05$) is

$$F > F_{\alpha, k, n-k-1} = F_{.05, 4, 45} \approx 2.61$$

As you can see from the printout, $F = 16.05$. The printout also includes the p-value of the test, which is 0.000. Obviously, there is a great deal of evidence to infer that the model is useful.

F-TEST, R^2, AND s_ϵ

Although each assessment measurement offers a different perspective, all agree in their assessment of how well the model fits the data, because all are based on the sum of squares for error, SSE. The standard error of estimate is

$$s_\epsilon = \sqrt{\frac{SSE}{n - k - 1}}$$

and the coefficient of determination is

$$R^2 = 1 - \frac{SSE}{SS_y}$$

When the response surface hits every single point, SSE = 0. Hence, $s_\epsilon = 0$, and $R^2 = 1$.

If the model provides a poor fit, we know that SSE will be large (its maximum value is SS_y), s_ϵ will be large, and (since SSE is close to SS_y) R^2 will be close to zero.

The F-statistic also depends on SSE. Specifically,

$$F = \frac{(SS_y - SSE)/k}{SSE/(n - k - 1)}$$

When SSE = 0,

$$F = \frac{SS_y/k}{0/(n - k - 1)}$$

which is infinitely large. When SSE is large, SSE is close to SS_y and F is quite small. The relationship among s_ϵ, R^2, and F is summarized in Table 17.1.

Table 17.1	Relationship among s_ϵ, R^2, and F				
	SSE	s_ϵ	R^2	F	ASSESSMENT OF MODEL
	0	0	1	∞	Perfect
	Small	Small	Close to 1	Large	Good
	Large	Large	Close to 0	Small	Poor
	SS_y	$\sqrt{\dfrac{SS_y}{n - k - 1}}^{*}$	0	0	Useless

*When n is large and k is small, this quantity is approximately equal to the standard deviation of y.

If we're satisfied that the model fits the data as well as possible, and that the required conditions are satisfied (see Section 17.5), we can interpret and test the individual coefficients and use the model to predict and estimate.

INTERPRETING THE COEFFICIENTS

The intercept is $\hat{\beta}_0 = -20,297$. This is the value of **REVENUE** when **PEOPLE** = **INCOME** = **COMPTORS** = **PRICE** = 0. As we observed in Chapter 16, it is often misleading to try to interpret the value of the intercept. If we did so in this case, we might state that the gross annual revenue of a video store where nobody lives within one mile, there are no competitors, and movies rent for nothing is *negative* $20,297.

The relationship between **REVENUE** and **PEOPLE** is measured by $\hat{\beta}_1 = 6.44$. This indicates that in this model, for each additional person living within one mile of the store, the gross revenue increases on average by $6.44 (assuming that the other independent variables are held constant).

The relationship between **REVENUE** and **INCOME** is measured by $\hat{\beta}_2 = 7.27$, which tells us that for each additional dollar of mean household income, the gross revenue increases by an average of $7.27 (assuming that the other independent variables in this model are held constant).

The coefficient $\hat{\beta}_3 = -6,709$ specifies that for each additional competitor within one mile of the store, the annual revenue decreases by an average of $6,709 (assuming that the other independent variables in this model are held constant).

Finally, the coefficient $\hat{\beta}_4 = 15,969$ tells us that for each additional dollar increase in the rental price of a movie, gross revenue increases on average by $15,969 (assuming that the other independent variables in this model are held constant).

TESTING THE COEFFICIENTS

In Chapter 16, we described how to test to determine whether there is sufficient evidence to infer that in the simple linear regression model x and y are linearly related. The null and alternative hypotheses were

CHAPTER 17: MULTIPLE REGRESSION | **685**

$$H_0: \beta_1 = 0$$
$$H_A: \beta_1 \neq 0$$

The test statistic was

$$t = \frac{\hat{\beta}_1 - \beta_1}{s_{\hat{\beta}_1}}$$

which is Student t distributed with $n - 2$ degrees of freedom.

In the multiple regression model, we have more than one independent variable; for each such variable, we can test to determine if there is enough evidence of a linear relationship between it and the dependent variable.

Testing the Coefficients

$$H_0: \beta_i = 0$$
$$H_A: \beta_i \neq 0$$

(for $i = 1, 2, \ldots, k$); the test statistic is

$$t = \frac{\hat{\beta}_i - \beta_i}{s_{\hat{\beta}_i}}$$

which is Student t distributed with d.f. $= n - k - 1$.

To illustrate, we test each of the coefficients in the multiple regression model in Example 17.1. The tests that follow are performed just as all other tests in this book have been performed. We set up the null and alternative hypotheses, identify the test statistic, and use the computer to calculate the value of the test statistic and its p-value. For each independent variable, we test ($i = 1, 2, 3, 4$).

$$H_0: \beta_i = 0$$
$$H_A: \beta_i \neq 0$$

Refer to page 680 (Minitab) or 681 (Excel), and examine the computer output for Example 17.1. The output includes the t-tests of β_i.

TEST OF β_1

Value of the test statistic: $t = 1.74$; p-value $= .089$.
There is some evidence to infer that the number of people living within one mile of the store and the store's gross revenue are linearly related.

TEST OF β_2

Value of the test statistic: $t = 7.77$; p-value $= .000$.
There is overwhelming evidence to indicate that the mean income of households within one mile of the store and the store's gross revenue are linearly related.

TEST OF β_3

Value of the test statistic: $t = -1.76$; p-value $= .086$.
There is some evidence to infer that the number of competitors within one mile of the store and the store's gross revenue are linearly related.

TEST OF β_4

Value of the test statistic: $t = 1.56$; p-value $= .125$.
There is little evidence to infer that the rental price of movies and the store's gross revenue are linearly related in this model.

| A CAUTIONARY NOTE ABOUT INTERPRETING THE RESULTS | We have discovered that in this model the mean household income is strongly linearly related to gross revenue. Additionally, the number of people living within one mile and the number of competitors within one mile are also linearly related to revenue but are not as strongly related as mean household income. There is no evidence to infer that the fourth variable, rental price, is linearly related to revenue. In choosing the site of a new store, the president should look for locations where the mean household income is high. The number of people living nearby and the number of other video stores should also be considered. |

Care should be taken in interpreting the results of the tests. We might find that in one model there is enough statistical evidence to show that a particular independent variable is linearly related to y, while in another model, not enough evidence exists to infer a linear relationship. As a result, whenever we do not reject the null hypothesis, we will state that there is not enough evidence to show that the independent variable and y are linearly related *in this model*. This issue will be explored further in Section 17.5.

A couple of warnings must attend any conclusions drawn from the tests. First, if one or more of the required conditions is violated, the results may be invalid. This possibility will be investigated in Section 17.5. Second, because all the independent variables were observed over a relatively narrow range, it is dangerous to extrapolate far outside this range. For example, it is likely that the effect of raising the rental price would be greater if the rental price were increased to, say, $6. Remember that we can draw valid conclusions about the model only for values within the range of the observed values of the independent variables.

t-Tests and the Analysis of Variance

The t-tests of the individual coefficients allow us to determine whether $\beta_i \neq 0$ (for $i = 1, 2, \ldots, k$), which tells us whether a linear relationship exists between x_i and y. There is a t-test for each independent variable. Consequently, the computer automatically performs k t-tests. (It actually conducts $k + 1$ t-tests, including the one for β_0, which we usually ignore.) The F-test in the analysis of variance combines these t-tests into a single test. That is, we test all the β_i at one time to determine if at least one of them is not equal to zero. The question naturally arises, why do we need the F-test if it is nothing more than the combination of the previously performed t-tests? Recall that we addressed this issue before. In Chapter 14, we pointed out that we can replace the analysis of variance by a series of t-tests of the difference between two means. However, by doing so we increase the probability of making a Type I error. That means that even when there is no linear relationship between each of the independent variables and the dependent variable, multiple t-tests will likely show some are significant. As a result, you will conclude erroneously that, since at least one β_i is not equal to zero, the model has some utility. The F-test, on the other hand, is performed only once. Because the probability that a Type I error will occur in a single trial is equal to α, the chance of erroneously concluding that the model is useful is substantially less with the F-test than with multiple t-tests.

There is another reason why the F-test is superior to multiple t-tests. Because of a commonly occurring problem called *multicollinearity*, the t-tests may indicate that some independent variables are not linearly related to the dependent variable, when in fact they are. The problem of multicollinearity does not affect the F-test, nor does it inhibit us from developing a model that fits the data well. Multicollinearity will be discussed in Section 17.5.

The *F*-Test and the *t*-Test in the Simple Linear Regression Model

It is useful for you to know that we can use the *F*-test to test the utility of the simple linear regression model. However, this test is identical to the *t*-test of β_1. The *t*-test of β_1 in the simple linear regression model tells us whether that independent variable is linearly related to the dependent variable. However, because there is only one independent variable, the *t*-test of β_1 also tells us whether the model is useful, which is the purpose of the *F*-test.

The relationship between the *t*-test of β_1 and the *F*-test can be explained mathematically. Statisticians can show that if we square a *t*-statistic with ν degrees of freedom we produce an *F*-statistic with 1 and ν degrees of freedom. (We briefly discussed this relationship in Chapter 14.) To illustrate, consider Example 16.2 on pages 621–625. We found the *t*-statistic for β_1 to be -13.49, with degrees of freedom equal to 98 (d.f. $= n - 2 = 100 - 2 = 98$). The *p*-value was 0. The output included the analysis of variance table where $F = 182.11$ and *p*-value $= 0$. The *t*-statistic squared is $t^2 = (-13.49)^2 = 181.98$, which is approximately 182.11. (The difference is due to rounding errors.) Notice that the degrees of freedom of the *F*-statistic are 1 and 98. Thus, we can use either test to test the utility of the simple linear regression model.

Using the Regression Equation

As was the case with simple linear regression, we can use the multiple regression equation in two ways: we can produce the prediction interval for a particular value of *y*, and we can produce the confidence interval estimate of the expected value of *y*. Like the other calculations associated with multiple regression, we call upon the computer to do the work.

Suppose that in Example 17.1 we want to predict the annual gross revenue of a video store that has 5,000 people living within one mile, the mean household income in that neighborhood is $40,000, there are three competitors within one mile, and the rental price of a video is $2.49. Both Minitab and Excel print the predicted value, the prediction interval, and the confidence interval estimate of the expected value.

Minitab Prediction and Confidence Interval Estimate for Example 17.1

```
  Fit   Stdev.Fit      95.0% C.I.           95.0% P.I.
322426       5875  ( 310590,  334262)  ( 270416,  374436)
```

MENU COMMANDS	COMMANDS FOR EXAMPLE 17.1
1 Click **Stat, Regression,** and **Regression . . . .**	
2 Type the name of the dependent variable (**Response**).	**Revenue** or **C1**
3 Hit **tab**, and type the name of the independent variables (**Predictors**). Click **OK**.	**C2–C5**
4 Click **Options**, and provide the given values of the independent variables. Click **OK** twice.	**5000 40000 3 2.49**

Excel Prediction Interval and Confidence Interval Estimate for Example 17.1

0.95 Prediction Interval	
Predicted value =	322426.1
Lower limit =	270427.6
Upper limit =	374424.6
0.95 Confidence Interval Estimate	
Lower limit =	310592.6
Upper limit =	334259.5

Using the Minitab results (Excel's output differs slightly), we predict that the annual gross revenue of a video store with 5,000 people and three competitors within one mile, in a neighborhood with a mean household income of $40,000 and a video rental price of $2.49, will fall between $270,416 and $374,436. The average gross revenue of all stores that fit the category is estimated to lie between $310,590 and $334,262.

Exercises

17.1 A developer who specializes in summer cottage properties is considering purchasing a large tract of land adjoining a lake. The current owner of the tract has already subdivided the land into separate building lots and has prepared the lots by removing some of the trees. The developer wants to forecast the value of each lot. From previous experience, she knows that the most important factors affecting the price of the lot are size, number of mature trees, and distance to the lake. From a nearby area, she gathers the relevant data for 60 recently sold lots. These data are stored in file XR17-01. (Column 1 = price in thousands of dollars, column 2 = lot size in thousands of square feet, column 3 = number of mature trees, and column 4 = distance to the lake in feet.) A multiple regression analysis was performed. The Minitab and Excel printouts are shown below.

a   What is the standard error of estimate? Interpret its value.

b   What is the coefficient of determination? What does this statistic tell you?

c   What is the coefficient of determination, adjusted for degrees of freedom? Why does this value differ from the coefficient of determination? What does this tell you about the model?

d   Test the overall utility of the model. What does the p-value of the test statistic tell you?

e   Interpret each of the coefficients.

f   Test to determine whether each of the independent variables is linearly related to the price of the lot.

```
The regression equation is
Price = 51.4 + 0.700 Lot-size + 0.679 Trees - 0.378 Distance

Predictor      Coef      Stdev     t-ratio       p
Constant      51.39      23.52        2.19    0.033
Lot-size     0.6999     0.5589        1.25    0.216
Trees        0.6788     0.2293        2.96    0.004
Distance    -0.3784     0.1952       -1.94    0.058

s = 40.24      R-sq = 24.2%      R-sq(adj) = 17.2%
```

```
Analysis of Variance

SOURCE        DF        SS        MS        F        p
Regression     3      29030      9677      5.97     0.001
Error         56      90694      1620
Total         59     119724
```

	A	B	C	D	E	F	G
2							
3	Regression Statistics						
4	Multiple R	0.492414					
5	R Square	0.242472					
6	Adjusted R Square	0.20189					
7	Standard Error	40.24353					
8	Observations	60					
9							
10	ANOVA						
11		df	SS	MS	F	Significance F	
12	Regression	3	29029.72	9676.572	5.974883	0.001315	
13	Residual	56	90694.33	1619.542			
14	Total	59	119724				
15							
16		Coefficients	Standard Error	t Stat	P-value		
17	Intercept	51.39122	23.5165	2.185326	0.033064		
18	Lot size	0.699904	0.558855	1.252389	0.215633		
19	Trees	0.678813	0.229306	2.960292	0.0045		
20	Distance	-0.37836	0.195237	-1.93796	0.057676		

17.2   After analyzing the results of Exercise 16.7, Pat decided that a certain amount of studying could actually improve final grades. However, too much studying would not be warranted, since Pat's ambition (if that's what one could call it) was to ultimately graduate with the absolute minimum level of work. Pat was registered in a statistics course, which had only three weeks to go before the final exam, and where the final grade was determined in the following way.

Assignment	20%
Midterm test	30%
Final exam	50%

In order to determine how much work to do for the remaining three weeks, Pat needed to be able to predict the final exam mark on the basis of the assignment mark and the midterm mark. Pat's marks on these were 12/20 and 14/30, respectively. Accordingly, Pat undertook the following analysis. The final exam mark, assignment mark, and midterm test mark for 30 students who took the statistics course last year were collected. These data are stored in columns 1 to 3, respectively, in file XR17-02. A multiple regression analysis was performed using Minitab and Excel with the results following.

a   What is the standard error of estimate? Briefly describe how you interpret this statistic.

b   What is the coefficient of determination? What does this statistic tell you?

c   What is the coefficient of determination, adjusted for degrees of freedom? What do this statistic and the one alluded to in part (b) tell you about the model?

d   Test the overall utility of the model. What does the p-value of the test statistic tell you?

e Interpret each of the coefficients.

f Can Pat infer from these results that the assignment mark is linearly related to the final grade?

g Can Pat infer from these results that the midterm mark is linearly related to the final grade?

h Which variable appears to be a better predictor of the final exam mark? Explain. Suggest several reasons for your answer.

```
The regression equation is
Final = 13.0 + 0.194 Assgnmnt + 1.11 Midterm

Predictor        Coef       Stdev      t-ratio         p
Constant       13.009       3.528         3.69     0.001
Assgnmnt       0.1940      0.2004         0.97     0.342
Midterm        1.1121      0.1219         9.12     0.000

s = 3.752        R-sq = 76.3%      R-sq(adj) = 74.5%

Analysis of Variance

SOURCE          DF           SS           MS        F          p
Regression       2      1223.18       611.59    43.43      0.000
Error           27       380.18        14.08
Total           29      1603.37
```

	A	B	C	D	E	F	G
1	SUMMARY OUTPUT						
2							
3	Regression Statistics						
4	Multiple R	0.87343264					
5	R Square	0.76288458					
6	Adjusted R Square	0.74532048					
7	Standard Error	3.75244589					
8	Observations	30					
9							
10	ANOVA						
11		df	SS	MS	F	Significance F	
12	Regression	2	1223.183712	611.5919	43.4343	3.65E-09	
13	Residual	27	380.1829546	14.08085			
14	Total	29	1603.366667				
15							
16		Coefficients	Standard Error	t Stat	P-value		
17	Intercept	13.0090831	3.52778605	3.687605	0.001005		
18	Assgnmnt	0.19398917	0.20043678	0.967832	0.341718		
19	Midterm	1.11208008	0.12194434	9.119571	9.87E-10		

17.3 The president of a company that manufactures drywall wants to analyze the factors that affect demand for his product. Drywall is used to construct walls in houses and offices. Consequently, the president decides to develop a regression model in which the dependent variable is monthly sales of drywall (in hundreds of 4×8 sheets) and the independent variables are

Number of building permits issued in the county

Five-year mortgage rates (in percentage points)

Vacancy rate in apartments (in percentage points)

Vacancy rate in office buildings (in percentage points)

To estimate a multiple regression model, he took the monthly observations from the past two years. The data are stored in columns 1 to 5, respectively, in file XR17-03. A computer was used to produce the output below.

a What is the standard error of estimate? Can you use this statistic to assess the model's fit? If so, how?

b What is the coefficient of determination, and what does it tell you about the regression model?

c What is the coefficient of determination, adjusted for degrees of freedom? What do this statistic and the statistic referred to in part (b) tell you about how well this model fits the data?

d Test the overall utility of the model. What does the p-value of the test statistic tell you?

e Interpret each of the coefficients.

f Test to determine whether each of the independent variables is linearly related to drywall demand.

g Which independent variable appears to be the best predictor of drywall demand? Explain.

```
The regression equation is
Drywall = - 112 + 4.76 Permits + 17.0 Mortgage - 10.5 A-vacncy + 1.31 O-vacncy

Predictor      Coef      Stdev     t-ratio        p
Constant      -111.8     134.3      -0.83      0.416
Permits        4.7631    0.3950     12.06      0.000
Mortgage      16.99     15.16        1.12      0.276
A-vacncy     -10.528     6.394      -1.65      0.116
O-vacncy       1.308     2.791       0.47      0.645

s = 40.13      R-sq = 89.4%     R-sq(adj) = 87.1%

Analysis of Variance

SOURCE        DF         SS          MS          F         p
Regression     4       256793       64198      39.86     0.000
Error         19        30602        1611
Total         23       287395
```

	A	B	C	D	E	F	G
1	SUMMARY OUTPUT						
2							
3	Regression Statistics						
4	Multiple R	0.94526234					
5	R Square	0.89352089					
6	Adjusted R Square	0.87110424					
7	Standard Error	40.132385					
8	Observations	24					
9							
10	ANOVA						
11		df	SS	MS	F	Significance F	
12	Regression	4	256793.4001	64198.35	39.85969	5.45E-09	
13	Residual	19	30601.55826	1610.608			
14	Total	23	287394.9583				
15							
16		Coefficients	Standard Error	t Stat	P-value		
17	Intercept	-111.82756	134.3426803	-0.83241	0.415521		
18	Permits	4.7630519	0.395047377	12.05691	2.39E-10		
19	Mortgage	16.9885383	15.15862665	1.120718	0.276374		
20	A-vacncy	-10.527775	6.394431168	-1.6464	0.116123		
21	O-vacncy	1.3079397	2.790775113	0.468665	0.644641		

17.4 Suppose that the statistician who did the analysis described in Exercise 16.9 wanted to investigate other factors that determine heights. As part of the same study, he also recorded the heights of the mothers. These values are stored in column 3 of file XR17-04. (Columns 1 and 2 contain the data from Exercise 16.9.) The multiple regression printouts are shown below.

a What is the standard error of estimate, and what does this statistic tell you?

b What is the coefficient of determination? What does this statistic tell you?

c What is the coefficient of determination, adjusted for degrees of freedom? What do this statistic and the one referred to in part (b) tell you about how well the model fits the data?

d Test the overall utility of the model. What does the test result tell you?

e Interpret each of the coefficients.

f Do these data allow the statistician to infer that the heights of the sons and the fathers are linearly related?

g Do these data allow the statistician to infer that the heights of the sons and the mothers are linearly related?

```
The regression equation is
Son = 37.6 + 0.485 Father — 0.0229 Mother

Predictor        Coef       Stdev      t-ratio        p
Constant        37.560      3.203       11.73      0.000
Father         0.48493     0.04118      11.78      0.000
Mother        -0.02292     0.03945      -0.58      0.562

s = 3.227       R-sq = 26.7%      R-sq(adj) = 26.3%

Analysis of Variance

SOURCE        DF         SS          MS         F         p
Regression     2       1507.45     753.73     72.37     0.000
Error        397       4134.94      10.42
Total        399       5642.40
```

	A	B	C	D	E	F	G
1	SUMMARY OUTPUT						
2							
3	Regression Statistics						
4	Multiple R	0.51688031					
5	R Square	0.26716526					
6	Adjusted R Square	0.2634734					
7	Standard Error	3.22730203					
8	Observations	400					
9							
10	ANOVA						
11		df	SS	MS	F	Significance F	
12	Regression	2	1507.452581	753.7263	72.36598	1.60E-27	
13	Residual	397	4134.944919	10.41548			
14	Total	399	5642.3975				
15							
16		Coefficients	Standard Error	t Stat	P-value		
17	Intercept	37.5597153	3.202867629	11.7269	1.79E-27		
18	Father	0.48493232	0.041175436	11.77722	1.15E-27		
19	Mother	-0.0229237	0.039450505	-0.58107	0.56152		

17.5 The assistant dean of the school of business wanted to find a better way of deciding which students should be accepted into the M.B.A. program. Currently, the records of the applicants are examined by the admissions committee, which looks at undergraduate GPA and the score on the Graduate Management Admissions Test (GMAT). However, decisions are made informally. In order to provide a more systematic method, the assistant dean took a random sample of 100 students who entered the program two years ago. He recorded each student's M.B.A. GPA, undergraduate GPA, and GMAT score. The data are stored in columns 1 to 3 of file XR17-OS. The assistant dean then conducted a regression analysis with the results shown below.

a Use whatever statistics you deem necessary to assess the model's fit. Is this model likely to be useful in predicting M.B.A. GPA?

b Can we infer that the GMAT score is linearly related to M.B.A. GPA?

c Predict with 95% confidence the M.B.A. GPA of a student whose undergraduate GPA is 3.2 and whose GMAT score is 620.

```
The regression equation is
MBA-GPA = - 1.87 + 0.411 UnderGPA + 0.0114 GMAT

Predictor      Coef       StDev         T        P
Constant     -1.874       1.784     -1.05    0.296
UnderGPA     0.41083     0.08553      4.80    0.000
GMAT         0.011408    0.002464     4.63    0.000

S = 0.9910      R-Sq = 28.0%      R-Sq(adj) = 26.5%

Analysis of Variance

Source       DF         SS          MS        F        P
Regression    2      37.001      18.500    18.84    0.000
Error        97      95.259       0.982
Total        99     132.260
```

SUMMARY OUTPUT

Regression Statistics	
Multiple R	0.5289
R Square	0.2798
Adjusted R Square	0.2649
Standard Error	0.9910
Observations	100

ANOVA

	df	SS	MS	F	Significance F
Regression	2	37.00	18.500	18.84	1.22E-07
Residual	97	95.26	0.982		
Total	99	132.26			

	Coefficients	Standard Error	t Stat	P-value
Intercept	-1.8743	1.7839	-1.0507	0.2960
UnderGPA	0.4108	0.0855	4.8035	5.67491E-06
GMAT	0.0114	0.0025	4.6294	1.13748E-05

17.6 The admissions officer of a university is trying to develop a formal system of deciding which students to admit to the university. She believes that determinants of success include the standard variables—high school grades and SAT scores. However, she also believes that students who have participated in extracurricular activities are more likely to succeed than those who have not. To investigate the issue, she randomly sampled 25 fourth-year students and recorded the following variables.

GPA for the first three years at the university (range: 0 to 12)

GPA from high school (range: 0 to 12)

SAT score (range: 200 to 800)

Number of hours on average spent per week in organized extracurricular activities in the last year of high school

The data are stored in columns 1 to 4 of file XR17-06.

a Develop a model that helps the admissions officer decide which students to admit, and use the computer to generate the usual statistics.

b What is the standard error of estimate? What does this statistic tell you?

c What is the coefficient of determination? Interpret its value.

d What is the coefficient of determination, adjusted for degrees of freedom? Interpret its value.

e Test the overall utility of the model. What does the *p*-value of the test statistic tell you?

f Interpret each of the coefficients.

g Test to determine whether each of the independent variables is linearly related to the dependent variable.

h Predict with 95% confidence the GPA for the first three years of university for a student whose high school GPA is 10, whose SAT score is 600, and who worked an average of two hours per week on organized extracurricular activities in the last year of high school.

i Estimate with 90% confidence the mean GPA for the first three years of university for all students whose high school GPA is 8, whose SAT score is 550, and who worked an average of 10 hours per week on organized extracurricular activities in the last year of high school.

17.7 The marketing manager for a chain of hardware stores needed more information about the effectiveness of the three types of advertising that the chain used. These are localized direct mailing (in which flyers describing sales and featured products are distributed to homes in the area surrounding a store), newspaper advertising, and local television advertisements. To determine which type is most effective, the manager collected one week's data from 100 randomly selected stores. For each store, the following variables were recorded.

Weekly gross sales

Weekly expenditures on direct mailing

Weekly expenditures on newspaper advertising

Weekly expenditures on television commercials

All variables were recorded in thousands of dollars and stored in columns 1 to 4, respectively, in file XR17-07.

a Find the regression equation.

b What are the coefficient of determination and the coefficient of determination, adjusted for degrees of freedom? What do these statistics tell you about the regression equation?

c What does the standard error of estimate tell you about the regression model?

d Test the overall utility of the model. What does the p-value of the test statistic tell you?

e Which independent variables are linearly related to weekly gross sales? Explain.

f Predict with 95% confidence next week's gross sales if a local store spent $800 on direct mailing, $1,200 on newspaper advertisements, and $2,000 on television commercials.

g Estimate with 95% confidence the mean weekly gross sales for all stores that spend $800 on direct mailing, $1,200 on newspaper advertising, and $2,000 on television commercials.

h Discuss the difference between the two intervals found in parts (f) and (g).

17.8 In an effort to explain to customers why their electricity bills have been so high lately, and how, specifically, they could save money by reducing the thermostat settings on both space heaters and water heaters, an electric utility company has collected total kilowatt consumption figures for last year's winter months, as well as thermostat settings on space and water heaters, for 100 homes. The data are stored in columns 1 (consumption), 2 (space heater thermostat setting), and 3 (water heater thermostat setting) of file XR17-08.

a Determine the regression equation.

b Determine the standard error of estimate, and comment about what it tells you.

c Determine the coefficient of determination, and comment about what it tells you.

d Test the utility of the model, and describe what this test tells you.

e Predict with 95% confidence the electricity consumption of a house whose space heater thermostat is set at 70 and whose water heater thermostat is set at 130.

f Estimate with 95% confidence the average electricity consumption for houses whose space heater thermostat is set at 70 and whose water heater thermostat is set at 130.

17.9 One of the critical factors that determine the success of a catalogue store chain is the availability of products that consumers want to buy. If a store is sold out, future sales to that customer are less likely. Because of this stores are regularly resupplied by delivery trucks operating from a central warehouse. In an analysis of a chain's operations, the general manager wanted to determine the factors that determine how long it takes to unload delivery trucks. A random sample of 50 deliveries to one store was observed. The times (in minutes) to unload the truck, the total number of boxes, and the total weight (in hundreds of pounds) of the boxes were recorded and stored in XR17-09.

a Determine the multiple regression model.

b How well does the model fit the data?

c Interpret and test the coefficients? What does this analysis tell you?

17.10 Refer to Exercise 17.1.

   a   Predict with 90% confidence the selling price of a 40,000-square-foot lot that has 50 mature trees and is 25 feet from the lake.

   b   Estimate with 90% confidence the average selling price of 50,000-square-foot lots that have 10 mature trees and are 75 feet from the lake.

17.11 Refer to Exercise 17.2.

   a   Predict Pat's final exam mark with 95% confidence.

   b   Predict Pat's final grade with 95% confidence.

17.12 Refer to Exercise 17.3. Predict next month's drywall sales with 95% confidence if the number of building permits is 50, the five-year mortgage rate is 9.0%, and the vacancy rates are 3.6% in apartments and 14.3% in office buildings.

17.4 Qualitative Independent Variables

When we introduced regression analysis, we pointed out that all the variables must be quantitative. But in many real-life cases, one or more independent variables are qualitative. For example, suppose that the used-car dealer in Example 16.2 believed that the color of a car is a factor in determining its auction price. Color is clearly a qualitative variable. If we assign numbers to each possible color, these numbers will be completely arbitrary, and using them in a regression model will usually be pointless. For example, if the dealer believes the colors that are most popular, white and silver, are likely to lead to higher prices than other colors, he may assign a code of 1 to white cars, a code of 2 to silver cars, and a code of 3 to all other colors. Columns 1 and 2 of file XM16-02A contain the auction price and the odometer reading (identical to file XM16-02). Column 3 includes codes identifying the color of the Ford Tauruses referred to in the original problem. If we now conduct a multiple regression analysis, the results below would be obtained.

Minitab Output for Example 16.2 with COLOR Variable

Regression Analysis

```
The regression equation is
Price = 6580 - 0.0313 Odometer - 21.7 Color

Predictor       Coef       Stdev     t-ratio        p
Constant     6580.18       92.96       70.79    0.000
Odometer    -0.031278    0.002306      -13.56    0.000
Color          -21.67       18.11       -1.20    0.234

s = 151.2        R-sq = 65.5%      R-sq(adj) = 64.8%

Analysis of Variance

SOURCE       DF          SS          MS         F       p
Regression    2     4216263     2108131     92.17   0.000
Error        97     2218627       22872
Total        99     6434890
```

	A	B	C	D	E	F	G
1	SUMMARY OUTPUT						
2							
3	Regression Statistics						
4	Multiple R	0.80945608					
5	R Square	0.65521914					
6	Adjusted R Square	0.64811026					
7	Standard Error	151.236382					
8	Observations	100					
9							
10	ANOVA						
11		df	SS	MS	F	Significance F	
12	Regression	2	4216263.208	2108132	92.16906	3.72E-23	
13	Residual	97	2218626.982	22872.44			
14	Total	99	6434890.19				
15							
16		Coefficients	Standard Error	t Stat	P-value		
17	Intercept	6580.18261	92.95884157	70.78598	2.64E-85		
18	Odometer	-0.0312779	0.002306019	-13.5636	3.94E-24		
19	Color	-21.67052	18.11407695	-1.19634	0.234482		

The regression equation is

PRICE = 6,580 − .0313 **ODOMETER** − 21.7 **COLOR**

Aside from the inclusion of the variable **COLOR**, this equation is very similar to the one we produced in the simple regression model (**PRICE** = 6533 − 0.0312 **ODOMETER**). An examination of the output above reveals that the variable representing color is not linearly related to price (t-statistic = −1.20, and p-value = .234). There are two possible explanations for this result. First, there is no relationship between color and price. Second, color is a factor in determining the car's price, but the way in which the dealer assigned the codes to the colors made detection of that fact impossible. That is, the dealer treated the qualitative variable, color, as a quantitative variable. To further understand why we cannot use qualitative data in regression analysis, try to interpret the coefficient of **COLOR**. Such an effort is similar to attempting to interpret the mean of a sample of qualitative data. It is futile. Even though this effort failed, it is possible to include qualitative variables in the regression model. This is accomplished through the use of indicator variables.

An **indicator variable** (also called a **dummy variable**) is a variable that can assume either of only two values (usually 0 and 1), where one value represents the existence of a certain condition and the other value indicates that the condition does not hold. In this illustration we would create two indicator variables to represent the color of the car.

I_1 = 1 (if color is white)

= 0 (if color is not white)

and

I_2 = 1 (if color is silver)

= 0 (if color is not silver)

Notice first that because both I_1 and I_2 can assume only two values (0 and 1), there is only one interval. (Remember what determines a quantitative variable; the intervals between values are consistent and constant.) Since there is only one interval (the interval between 0 and 1) for each variable, that interval is consistent and constant. Thus, the indicator variables are quantitative. (It should be mentioned that we can define the indicator variables so that they can assume values 1, 0, and −1. We won't pursue this course of action because the results are identical.) Second, we need two indicator variables to represent three colors. A white car is represented by $I_1 = 1$ and $I_2 = 0$. A silver car is indicated by $I_1 = 0$ and $I_2 = 1$. Because cars that are painted some other color are neither white nor silver, they are represented by $I_1 = 0$ and $I_2 = 0$. It should be apparent that we cannot have $I_1 = 1$ and $I_2 = 1$, if we assume that Ford Tauruses are not two-toned.

In general, to represent a qualitative variable that has m possible categories, we must create $m - 1$ indicator variables.

Interpreting and Testing the Coefficients of Indicator Variables

In columns 4 and 5 of file XM16-02A, we stored the values of I_1 and I_2. We then performed a multiple regression analysis using variables **ODOMETER**, I_1, and I_2. The printouts are shown below.

Minitab Output for Example 16.2 with Two Indicator Variables

Regression Analysis

```
The regression equation is
Price = 6350 - 0.0278 Odometer + 45.2 I-1 + 148 I-2

Predictor        Coef        Stdev      t-ratio          p
Constant      6350.32        92.17        68.90      0.000
Odometer    -0.027770     0.002369       -11.72      0.000
I-1             45.24        34.08         1.33      0.188
I-2            147.74        38.18         3.87      0.000

s = 142.3       R-sq = 69.8%      R-sq(adj) = 68.9%

Analysis of Variance

SOURCE         DF           SS            MS          F          p
Regression      3      4491749       1497250      73.97      0.000
Error          96      1943141         20241
Total          99      6434890
```

Excel Output for Example 16.2 with Two Indicator Variables

	A	B	C	D	E	F	G
1	SUMMARY OUTPUT						
2							
3	Regression Statistics						
4	Multiple R	0.83548216					
5	R Square	0.69803044					
6	Adjusted R Square	0.68859389					
7	Standard Error	142.27105					
8	Observations	100					
9							
10	ANOVA						
11		df	SS	MS	F	Significance F	
12	Regression	3	4491749.241	1497250	73.97095	7.22E-25	
13	Residual	96	1943140.949	20241.05			
14	Total	99	6434890.19				
15							
16		Coefficients	Standard Error	t Stat	P-value		
17	Intercept	6350.32311	92.16652879	68.90053	1.50E-83		
18	Odometer	-0.0277698	0.002368579	-11.7242	3.14E-20		
19	I-1	45.2409793	34.08443045	1.327321	0.187551		
20	I-2	147.738011	38.18498973	3.869007	0.000199		

The regression equation is

PRICE $= 6,350 - .0278$ **ODOMETER** $+ 45.2 I_1 + 148 I_2$

The intercept ($\hat{\beta}_0$) and the coefficient of **ODOMETER** ($\hat{\beta}_1$) are interpreted in the usual manner. When **ODOMETER** $= I_1 = I_2 = 0$, the dependent variable **PRICE** equals 6,350. For each additional mile on the odometer, the auction price decreases, on average, by 2.78 cents. Now examine the remaining two coefficients.

$$\hat{\beta}_2 = 45.2$$
$$\hat{\beta}_3 = 148$$

These tell us that, on average, a white car sells for \$45.20 more than other colors and a silver car sells for \$148 more than other colors. The reason both comparisons are made with other colors is that such cars are represented by $I_1 = I_2 = 0$. Thus, for a non-white and non-silver car, the equation becomes

$$\hat{y} = \hat{\beta}_0 + \hat{\beta}_1 x_1 + \hat{\beta}_2(0) + \hat{\beta}_3(0)$$

which is

PRICE $= \hat{\beta}_0 + \hat{\beta}_1$ **ODOMETER** $= 6,350 - .0278$ **ODOMETER**

For a white car ($I_1 = 1$ and $I_2 = 0$), the regression equation is

PRICE $= \hat{\beta}_0 + \hat{\beta}_1$ **ODOMETER** $+ \hat{\beta}_2(1) + \hat{\beta}_3(0)$

which is

PRICE $= 6,350 - .0278$ **ODOMETER** $+ 45.2 = 6,395.2 - .0278$ **ODOMETER**

Finally, for a silver car ($I_1 = 0$ and $I_2 = 1$), the regression equation is

PRICE $= \hat{\beta}_0 + \hat{\beta}_1$ **ODOMETER** $+ \hat{\beta}_2(0) + \hat{\beta}_3(1)$

which simplifies to

PRICE $= 6,350 - .0278$ **ODOMETER** $+ 148 = 6,498 - .0278$ **ODOMETER**

Figure 17.2 depicts the graph of **PRICE** versus **ODOMETER** for the three different color categories. Notice that the three lines are parallel (with slope $= \hat{\beta}_1 = -.0278$), while the intercepts differ.

Figure 17.2

Price versus Odometer for Three Colors

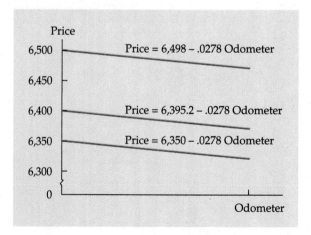

We can also perform the usual t-tests of β_2 and β_3; however, because the variables I_1 and I_2 represent different groups (the three color categories), these t-tests allow us to draw inferences about the differences in auction prices among the groups.

The test of β_2 is conducted as follows.

$H_0: \beta_2 = 0$

$H_A: \beta_2 \neq 0$

Test statistic: $t = 1.33$ (p-value $= .188$)

There is insufficient evidence to infer that white Tauruses sell for more or less than do non-white, non-silver Tauruses. To determine if silver-colored Tauruses sell for more or less than other colors, we test

$H_0: \beta_3 = 0$

$H_A: \beta_3 \neq 0$

Test statistic: $t = 3.87$ (p-value $= .000$)

We can conclude that there are differences in price between silver-colored Tauruses and the other category.

Exercises

17.13 Create and identify indicator variables to represent the following qualitative variables.

   a   religious affiliation (Catholic, Protestant, and others)

   b   working shift (8:00 A.M.–4:00 P.M., 4:00 P.M.–12:00 midnight, and 12:00 midnight–8:00 A.M.)

   c   supervisor (Jack Jones, Mary Brown, George Fosse, and Elaine Smith)

17.14 In a study of computer applications, a survey asked which microcomputer a number of companies used. The following indicator variables were created.

$I_1 = 1$ (if IBM) $I_2 = 1$ (if Macintosh)

  $= 0$ (if not) $= 0$ (if not)

What computer is being referred to by each of the following pairs of values?

   a $I_1 = 0$ $I_2 = 1$ **b** $I_1 = 1$ $I_2 = 0$ **c** $I_1 = 0$ $I_2 = 0$

17.15 Suppose that in Exercise 21.3, the assistant dean believed that the type of undergraduate degree also influenced the student's GPA as a graduate student. The most common undergraduate degrees of students attending the graduate school of business are B.B.A. (Business Administration), B.Eng., B.Sc., and B.A. Because the type of degree is a qualitative variable, the following three indicator variables were created.

$I_1 = 1$ (if degree is B.B.A.)

  $= 0$ (if not)

$I_2 = 1$ (if degree is B.Eng.)

  $= 0$ (if not)

$I_3 = 1$ (if degree is B.Sc.)

  $= 0$ (if not)

The model to be estimated is

MBA-GPA $= \beta_0 + \beta_1 \text{U-GPA} + \beta_2 \text{GMAT} + \beta_3 I_1 + \beta_4 I_2 + \beta_5 I_3 + \epsilon$

The data for the 100 students are stored in columns 1 to 6 of file XR17-15. (Columns 1 to 3 are identical to columns 1 to 3 of file XR17-05.) The Minitab and Excel printouts appear below.

a Test to determine whether each of the independent variables is linearly related to M.B.A.-GPA.

b Can we conclude that, on average, the B.B.A. graduate performs better than the B.A. graduate?

c Predict with 95% confidence the graduate school GPA of a B.Eng. whose undergraduate GPA was 3.0 and whose GMAT score was 700.

d Repeat part (c) for a B.A. student.

```
The regression equation is
MBA-GPA = - 0.44 + 0.313 UnderGPA + 0.00934 GMAT + 0.922 I-1 + 1.50 I-2
        + 0.620 I-3

Predictor       Coef        Stdev     t-ratio       p
Constant      -0.437        1.661       -0.26    0.793
UnderGPA      0.31322      0.07947       3.94    0.000
GMAT         0.009341     0.002255       4.14    0.000
I-1           0.9224       0.2274        4.06    0.000
I-2           1.5009       0.2671        5.62    0.000
I-3           0.6204       0.2649        2.34    0.021

s = 0.8605      R-sq = 47.4%     R-sq(adj) = 44.6%

Analysis of Variance

SOURCE       DF          SS          MS          F         p
Regression    5      62.664      12.533      16.93     0.000
Error        94      69.596       0.740
Total        99     132.260
```

	A	B	C	D	E	F	G
1	SUMMARY OUTPUT						
2							
3	Regression Statistics						
4	Multiple R	0.68832808					
5	R Square	0.47379555					
6	Adjusted R Square	0.44580595					
7	Standard Error	0.86045232					
8	Observations	100					
9							
10	ANOVA						
11		df	SS	MS	F	Significance F	
12	Regression	5	62.6639733	12.53279	16.92756	6.67E-12	
13	Residual	94	69.5955507	0.740378			
14	Total	99	132.259524				
15							
16		Coefficients	Standard Error	t Stat	P-value		
17	Intercept	-0.4370959	1.660724489	-0.2632	0.792976		
18	UnderGPA	0.31322243	0.079474585	3.941165	0.000156		
19	GMAT	0.00934075	0.002254705	4.142782	7.50E-05		
20	I-1	0.92242509	0.227351851	4.057258	0.000103		
21	I-2	1.50090085	0.267072094	5.619834	1.94E-07		
22	I-3	0.62038068	0.264891724	2.342016	0.021291		

17.16 The manager of an amusement park would like to be able to predict daily attendance in order to develop more accurate plans about how much food to order and how many ride operators to hire. After some consideration, he decided that the following three factors are critical.

Yesterday's attendance

Weekday or weekend

Predicted weather

He then took a random sample of 40 days. For each day, he recorded the attendance, the previous day's attendance, day of the week, and weather forecast. The first independent variable is quantitative, but the other two are qualitative. Accordingly, he created the following sets of indicator variables.

$I_1 = 1$ (if weekend)

   $= 0$ (if not)

$I_2 = 1$ (if mostly sunny is predicted)

   $= 0$ (if not)

$I_3 = 1$ (if rain is predicted)

   $= 0$ (if not)

These data are stored in file XR17-16. A multiple regression analysis was performed. The Minitab and Excel printouts are shown below.

a Is this model likely to be useful in predicting attendance? Explain.

b Can we conclude that weather is a factor in determining attendance?

c Do these results provide sufficient evidence that weekend attendance is, on average, larger than weekday attendance?

```
The regression equation is
Attndnce = 3490 + 0.369 Yest-Att + 1623 I-1 + 733 I-2 - 766 I-3

Predictor        Coef        Stdev      t-ratio          p
Constant       3490.5        469.2         7.44      0.000
Yest-Att      0.36855      0.07789         4.73      0.000
I-1           1623.1        492.5          3.30      0.002
I-2            733.5        394.4          1.86      0.071
I-3           -765.5        484.7         -1.58      0.123

s = 810.8      R-sq = 70.0%      R-sq(adj) = 66.6%

Analysis of Variance

SOURCE          DF           SS           MS          F          p
Regression       4     53729536     13432384      20.43      0.000
Error           35     23007438       657355
Total           39     76736976
```

	A	B	C	D	E	F	G
1	SUMMARY OUTPUT						
2							
3	Regression Statistics						
4	Multiple R	0.83676635					
5	R Square	0.70017793					
6	Adjusted R Square	0.66591255					
7	Standard Error	810.774553					
8	Observations	40					
9							
10	ANOVA						
11		df	SS	MS	F	Significance F	
12	Regression	4	53729534.81	13432384	20.43398	9.28E-09	
13	Residual	35	23007438.17	657355.4			
14	Total	39	76736972.98				
15							
16		Coefficients	Standard Error	t Stat	P-value		
17	Intercept	3490.4666	469.1553935	7.439894	1.04E-08		
18	Yest-Att	0.36854708	0.077894712	4.731349	3.60E-05		
19	I-1	1623.09579	492.5496774	3.295294	0.002258		
20	I-2	733.464632	394.3718224	1.85983	0.071331		
21	I-3	-765.54291	484.6620809	-1.57954	0.123209		

17.17 Refer to Exercise 17.9 where the amount of time to unload a truck was analyzed. The manager realized that another variable may affect unloading time, the time of day. He recorded the following codes: 1 = morning; 2 = early afternoon; 3 = late afternoon. These codes are stored in column 4 of file XR17-17. (Columns 1 to 3 are identical to columns 1 to 3 of file XR17-09.)

   a Run a regression using the codes for time of day.

   b Create indicator variables to represent time of day. Perform a regression analysis with these new variables.

   c Which model fits better? Explain.

   d Does time of day affect the time to unload?

17.18 Profitable banks are ones that make good decisions on loan applications. Credit scoring is the statistical technique that helps banks make that decision. However, many branches overturn credit scoring recommendations, while other banks do not use the technique. In an attempt to determine the factors that affect loan decisions, a statistician surveyed 100 banks and recorded the percentage of bad loans (any loan that is not completely repaid), the average size of the loan, and whether a scorecard is used, and if so, whether scorecard recommendations are overturned more than 10% of the time. These results are stored in columns 1 (percentage good loans); 2 (average loan); and 3 (code 1 = no scorecard; 2 = scorecard overturned more than 10% of the time; and 3 = scorecard overturned less than 10% of the time) in file XR17-18.

   a Create indicator variables to represent the codes.

   b Perform a regression analysis.

   c How well does the model fit the data?

   d Is multicollinearity a problem?

   e Interpret and test the coefficients. What does this tell you?

   f Predict with 95% confidence the percentage of bad loans for a bank whose average loan is $10,000 and which does not use a scorecard.

17.19 Refer to Exercise 16.38, where a simple linear regression model was used to analyze the relationship between welding machine breakdowns and the age of the machine. The analysis proved to be so useful to company management that they decided to expand the model to include other machines. Data were gathered for two other machines. These data as well as the original data are stored in file XR17-19 in the following way.

   Column 1: cost of repairs

   Column 2: age of machine

   Column 3: machine (1 = welding machine; 2 = lathe; 3 = stamping machine)

   a Develop a multiple regression model.

   b Interpret the coefficients.

   c Can we conclude that welding machines cost more to repair than other machines?

17.20 A baseball fan has been collecting data from a newspaper on the various American League teams. She wants to explain each team's winning percentage as a function of its batting average and its earned run average, plus an indicator variable for whether the team fired its manager within the last 12 months (code = 1 if it did and 0 if it did not). The data for 50 randomly selected teams (over the past 5 seasons) are stored in the first 4 columns respectively of file XR17-20.

   a Conduct a regression analysis of the data.

   b Interpret the coefficients.

c Are the signs of the coefficients as expected? Explain.

d Can we infer that a team that fires its manager has a lower winning percentage over the next 12 months than teams that do not?

17.21 Pay equity for men and women has been an ongoing source of conflict for a number of years in North America. Suppose that a statistician is investigating the factors that affect salary differences between female and male university professors. He believes that the following variables have some impact on a professor's salary: number of years since first degree; highest degree (code = 1 if highest degree is a Ph.D. and 0 if highest degree is not a Ph.D.); average score on teaching evaluations; number of papers in refereed journals; and sex (1 = professor is male; 0 = professor is female).

A random sample of 100 university professors was taken and the data stored in file XR17-21.

Column 1: annual salary

Column 2: number of years since first degree

Column 3: highest degree

Column 4: mean score on teaching evaluations

Column 5: number of articles published

Column 6: sex

a Can the statistician conclude that a multiple regression model is useful in analyzing salaries?

b Can the statistician conclude at the 5% significance level that there is sex discrimination?

17.5 Regression Diagnostics—II

In Section 16.8, we discussed how to determine whether the required conditions are unsatisfied. The same procedures can be used to diagnose problems in the multiple regression model. Here is a brief summary of the diagnostic procedure we described in Chapter 16.

Calculate the residuals and check the following.

1 Is the error variable nonnormal?
Draw the histogram of the residuals.

2 Is the error variance constant?
Plot the residuals versus the predicted values of y.

3 Are the errors independent (time-series data)?
Plot the residuals versus the time periods.

4 Are there observations that are inaccurate or do not belong to the target population?
Double-check the accuracy of outliers and influential observations.

If the error is nonnormal and/or the variance is not a constant, there are several remedies that can be attempted. These are described at the end of this section.

Outliers and influential observations are checked by examining the data in question to ensure accuracy.

Nonindependence of a time series can sometimes be detected by graphing the residuals and the time periods and looking for evidence of autocorrelation. In Section 17.7, we introduce the **Durbin–Watson test**, which tests for one form of autocorrelation. We will offer a corrective measure for nonindependence.

There is another problem that is applicable to multiple regression models only. Multicollinearity is a condition wherein the independent variables are highly correlated. Multicollinearity distorts the *t*-tests of the coefficients, making it difficult to determine whether any of the independent variables are linearly related to the dependent variable. It also makes interpreting the coefficients problematic. We will discuss this condition and its remedy next.

Multicollinearity

Multicollinearity (also called *collinearity* and *intercorrelation*) is a condition that exists when the independent variables are correlated with one another. The adverse effect of multicollinearity is that the estimated regression coefficients ($\hat{\beta}_1$, $\hat{\beta}_2$, etc.) tend to have large sampling variability. That is, the standard errors are large. Consequently, when the coefficients are tested, the *t*-statistics will be small, which infers that there is no linear relationship between the affected independent variables and the dependent variable. In some cases, this inference will be wrong. Fortunately, multicollinearity does not affect the *F*-test of the analysis of variance. We will illustrate the effects and remedy with the following example.

EXAMPLE 17.2

A real estate agent wanted to develop a model to predict the selling of a home. The agent believed that the most important variables in determining the price of a house are its size, number of bedrooms, and lot size. Accordingly, he took a random sample of 100 homes that were recently sold and recorded the selling price, the number of bedrooms, the size (in square feet), and the lot size (in square feet). These data are stored in columns 1 through 4 of file XM17-02. Some of the data follow. Analyze the relationship among the four variables.

PRICE (PRICE)	NUMBER OF BEDROOMS (BEDROOMS)	HOUSE SIZE (H-SIZE)	LOT SIZE (LOT-SIZE)
$124,100	3	1,290	3,900
218,300	4	2,080	6,600
117,800	3	1,250	3,750
.	.	.	.
.	.	.	.
.	.	.	.
155,900	4	1,620	4,800

SOLUTION

The proposed multiple regression model is

PRICE $= \beta_0 + \beta_1$ **BEDROOMS** $+ \beta_2$ **H-SIZE** $+ \beta_3$ **LOT-SIZE** $+ \epsilon$

The regression output (shown below) reveals that none of the independent variables is significantly related to the selling price. However, the F-test ($F = 40.73$ and p-value $= 0$) indicates that the complete model fits quite well.

Minitab Output for Example 17.2

Regression Analysis
```
The regression equation is
Price = 37718 + 2306 Bedrooms + 74.3 H-Size − 4.4 Lot-Size

Predictor       Coef        Stdev      t-ratio         p
Constant       37718        14177         2.66     0.009
Bedrooms        2306         6994         0.33     0.742
H-Size         74.30        52.98         1.40     0.164
Lot-Size       −4.36        17.02        −0.26     0.798

s = 25023        R-sq = 56.0%      R-sq(adj) = 54.6%

Analysis of Variance

SOURCE       DF            SS            MS          F         p
Regression    3   76501721088    25500573696      40.73     0.000
Error        96   60109045760      626135872
Total        99   1.36611E+11
```

Excel Output for Example 17.2

	A	B	C	D	E	F	G
1	SUMMARY OUTPUT						
2							
3	Regression Statistics						
4	Multiple R	0.74833					
5	R Square	0.559998					
6	Adjusted R Square	0.546248					
7	Standard Error	25022.71					
8	Observations	100					
9							
10	ANOVA						
11		df	SS	MS	F	Significance F	
12	Regression	3	76501718347	2.55E+10	40.7269	4.57E-17	
13	Residual	96	60109046053	6.26E+08			
14	Total	99	1.37E+11				
15							
16		Coefficients	Standard Error	t Stat	P-value		
17	Intercept	37717.59	14176.74195	2.660526	0.009145		
18	Bedrooms	2306.081	6994.19244	0.329714	0.742335		
19	H-Size	74.29681	52.97857934	1.402393	0.164023		
20	Lot-Size	-4.36378	17.0240013	-0.25633	0.798244		

If we run three simple regression models where the independent variable is (1) the number of bedrooms, (2) the house size, and (3) the lot size, the output below is produced. This result tells us that each of the independent variables is strongly related to selling price.

Regression Analysis

The regression equation is
Price = 25422 + 35439 Bedrooms

Predictor	Coef	Stdev	t-ratio	p
Constant	25422	15642	1.63	0.107
Bedrooms	35439	4237	8.36	0.000

s = 28519   R-sq = 41.7%   R-sq(adj) = 41.1%

Analysis of Variance

SOURCE	DF	SS	MS	F	p
Regression	1	56905924608	56905924608	69.97	0.000
Error	98	79704842240	813314688		
Total	99	1.36611E+11			

Regression Analysis

The regression equation is
Price = 40066 + 64.2 H-Size

Predictor	Coef	Stdev	t-ratio	p
Constant	40066	10521	3.81	0.000
H-Size	64.203	5.759	11.15	0.000

s = 24790   R-sq = 55.9%   R-sq(adj) = 55.5%

Analysis of Variance

SOURCE	DF	SS	MS	F	p
Regression	1	76385714176	76385714176	124.30	0.000
Error	98	60225052672	614541376		
Total	99	1.36611E+11			

Regression Analysis

The regression equation is
Price = 38940 + 21.0 Lot-Size

Predictor	Coef	Stdev	t-ratio	p
Constant	38940	10837	3.59	0.001
Lot-Size	20.982	1.921	10.92	0.000

s = 25077   R-sq = 54.9%   R-sq(adj) = 54.4%

Analysis of Variance

SOURCE	DF	SS	MS	F	p
Regression	1	74984898560	74984898560	119.24	0.000
Error	98	61625868288	628835392		
Total	99	1.36611E+11			

Excel Output for Example 17.2 (Simple Linear Regressions)

	A	B	C	D	E	F	G
1	SUMMARY OUTPUT						
2							
3	Regression Statistics						
4	Multiple R	0.645411					
5	R Square	0.416555					
6	Adjusted R Square	0.410602					
7	Standard Error	28518.67					
8	Observations	100					
9							
10	ANOVA						
11		df	SS	MS	F	Significance F	
12	Regression	1	5.69E+10	5.69E+10	69.9679	4.20E-13	
13	Residual	98	7.97E+10	8.13E+08			
14	Total	99	1.37E+11				
15							
16		Coefficients	Standard Error	t Stat	P-value		
17	Intercept	25422.36	15641.57	1.625308	0.107309		
18	Bedrooms	35439.02	4236.745	8.364682	4.20E-13		

	A	B	C	D	E	F	G
1	SUMMARY OUTPUT						
2							
3	Regression Statistics						
4	Multiple R	0.747762					
5	R Square	0.559149					
6	Adjusted R Square	0.55465					
7	Standard Error	24789.94					
8	Observations	100					
9							
10	ANOVA						
11		df	SS	MS	F	Significance F	
12	Regression	1	7.64E+10	7.64E+10	124.2971	3.97E-19	
13	Residual	98	6.02E+10	6.15E+08			
14	Total	99	1.37E+11				
15							
16		Coefficients	Standard Error	t Stat	P-value		
17	Intercept	40066.39	10521.44	3.808072	0.000244		
18	H-Size	64.20343	5.758743	11.14886	3.97E-19		

	A	B	C	D	E	F	G
1	SUMMARY OUTPUT						
2							
3	Regression Statistics						
4	Multiple R	0.740874					
5	R Square	0.548894					
6	Adjusted R Square	0.544291					
7	Standard Error	25076.59					
8	Observations	100					
9							
10	ANOVA						
11		df	SS	MS	F	Significance F	
12	Regression	1	7.50E+10	7.50E+10	119.2441	1.23E-18	
13	Residual	98	6.16E+10	6.29E+08			
14	Total	99	1.37E+11				
15							
16		Coefficients	Standard Error	t Stat	P-value		
17	Intercept	38940.29	10836.88	3.593312	0.000513		
18	Lot-Size	20.98154	1.921405	10.91989	1.23E-18		

The *t*-tests in the multiple regression model infer that no independent variable is a factor in determining the selling price. The three simple linear regression models contradict this conclusion. They tell us that the number of bedrooms, the house size, and the lot size are *all* linearly related to the price. How do we account for this contradiction? The answer is that the three independent variables are correlated with each other. It is reasonable to believe that larger houses have more bedrooms and are situated on larger lots, and that smaller houses have fewer bedrooms and are located on smaller lots. To confirm this belief, we computed the correlation among the three independent variables. The coefficient of correlation between number of bedrooms and house size is .846 (see Appendixes 17.A and 17.B to learn how to print correlations); the correlation between number of bedrooms and lot size is .837; the correlation between house size and lot size is .994. In the multiple regression model, multicollinearity affected the *t*-tests so that they inferred that none of the independent variables is linearly related to price when, in fact, all are.

Another problem caused by multicollinearity is the interpretation of the coefficients. We interpret the coefficients as measuring the change in the dependent variable when the corresponding independent variable increases by one unit while all the other independent variables are held constant. This interpretation may be impossible when the independent variables are highly correlated, because when the independent variable increases by one unit, some or all of the other independent variables will change. In the multiple regression model in this example, the coefficient of **BEDROOMS** is 2,306. Without multicollinearity we would interpret this coefficient to mean that for each additional bedroom the average price increases by $2,306, provided that the other variables are held constant. However, since **BEDROOMS** is correlated with **H-SIZE** and **LOT-SIZE**, it is impossible to increase **BEDROOMS** by 1 *and* hold the other variables constant.

This raises two important questions for the statistician. First, how do we recognize the problem when it occurs, and second, how do we avoid or correct it?

Multicollinearity exists in virtually all multiple regression models. In fact, finding two completely uncorrelated variables is rare. The problem becomes serious, however, only when two or more independent variables are highly correlated. Unfortunately, we do not have a critical value that indicates when the correlation between two independent variables is large enough to cause problems. To complicate the issue, multicollinearity also occurs when a combination of several independent variables is correlated with another independent variable or with a combination of other independent variables. Consequently, even with access to all of the correlation coefficients, determining when the multicollinearity problem has reached the serious stage may be extremely difficult.

Minimizing the effect of multicollinearity is often easier than recognizing it. The statistician must try to include independent variables that are independent of each other. For example, the real estate agent wanted to include house size, the number of bedrooms, and the lot size, three variables that are clearly related. Rather than developing a model that uses all such variables, the statistician may choose to include only house size, plus several other variables that measure other aspects of a house's value.

Another alternative is to use a stepwise regression package. Forward stepwise regression brings independent variables into the equation one at a time. Only if an independent variable improves the model's fit is it included. If two variables are strongly correlated, the inclusion of one of them in the model makes the second one unnecessary. Backward stepwise regression starts with all the independent variables included in the equation and removes variables if they are not strongly related to the dependent variable. Because the stepwise technique excludes redundant variables, it minimizes multicollinearity. Stepwise regression is presented in Section 17.6.

Remedying Violations of Required Conditions

The most commonly used method to remedy nonnormality or heteroscedasticity is to transform the dependent variable. There are several points to note about this procedure. First, the actual form of the transformation depends on which condition is unsatisfied and on the specific nature of the violation. Because there are many different ways to violate the required conditions of the statistical techniques, the list of transformations given here is unavoidably incomplete. Second, these transformations can be useful in improving the model. That is, if the linear model appears to be quite poor, we often can improve the model's fit by transforming y. Third, many computer software systems allow us to make transformations quite easily. You might want to experiment to see the effect these transformations have on your statistical results.

Here is a brief list of the most commonly used transformations.

1 *Log Transformation*: $y' = \log y$ (provided $y > 0$). The log transformation is used when (a) the variance of the error variable increases as y increases or (b) the distribution of the error variable is positively skewed.

2 *Square Transformation*: $y' = y^2$. Use this transformation when (a) the variance is proportional to the expected value of y or (b) the distribution of the error variable is negatively skewed.

3 *Square-Root Transformation*: $y' = \sqrt{y}$ (provided that $y > 0$). The square-root transformation is helpful when the variance is proportional to the expected value of y.

4 *Reciprocal Transformation*: $y' = 1/y$. When the variance appears to significantly increase when y increases beyond some critical value, the reciprocal transformation is recommended.

The following example will illustrate how we diagnose a violation of the required condition, its consequences, and how we remedy the problem.

EXAMPLE 17.3

A statistics professor wanted to know whether time limits on quizzes affected the marks on the quiz. Accordingly, he took a random sample of business statistics students and split them into five groups of 20 students each. All students took a quiz that involved simple manual calculations. Each group was given a different time limit. Group 1 was limited to 40 minutes; group 2, 45 minutes; group 3, 50 minutes; group 4, 55 minutes; and group 5, 60 minutes. The quizzes were marked (out of 40) and recorded in file XM17-03. (Column 1 stores the time limits, and column 2 stores the marks.) Conduct a complete regression analysis, including diagnostics.

SOLUTION   The following regression model was postulated.

MARK $= \beta_0 + \beta_1$ TIME $+ \epsilon$

The Minitab and Excel outputs are exhibited below.

Minitab Output for Example 17.3

Regression Analysis

```
The regression equation is
Mark = - 2.20 + 0.550 Time

Predictor         Coef         Stdev      t-ratio          p
Constant        -2.200         1.646        -1.34      0.184
Time            0.55000       0.03259       16.88      0.000

s = 2.305       R-sq = 74.4%      R-sq(adj) = 74.1%

Analysis of Variance

SOURCE          DF           SS           MS          F          p
Regression       1         1512.5       1512.5     284.77     0.000
Error           98          520.5          5.3
Total           99         2033.0
```

Excel Output for Example 17.3

	A	B	C	D	E	F	G
1	SUMMARY OUTPUT						
2							
3	Regression Statistics						
4	Multiple R	0.86253952					
5	R Square	0.74397442					
6	Adjusted R Square	0.74136192					
7	Standard Error	2.3046094					
8	Observations	100					
9							
10	ANOVA						
11		df	SS	MS	F	Significance F	
12	Regression	1	1512.5	1512.5	284.7743	9.42E-31	
13	Residual	98	520.5	5.311224			
14	Total	99	2033				
15							
16		Coefficients	Standard Error	t Stat	P-value		
17	Intercept	-2.2	1.645820309	-1.33672	0.184409		
18	Time	0.55	0.032592099	16.87526	9.42E-31		

The regression equation is

MARK $= -2.2 + .55$ TIME

The standard error of estimate, the coefficient of determination, and the t-test of β_1 (and the F-test) all indicate a relatively good model. The residuals and the predicted values were calculated. The histogram of the residuals and the plot of the residuals versus the predicted values of y were produced by Minitab and are exhibited next.

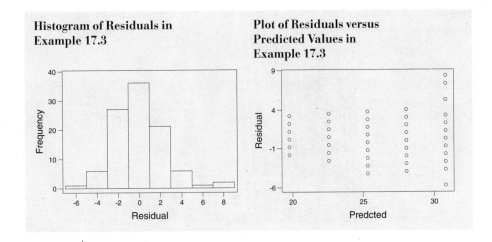

Histogram of Residuals in Example 17.3

Plot of Residuals versus Predicted Values in Example 17.3

The error variable appears to be normal. However, the variance is clearly not constant; it increases as the predicted marks increase. The remedy we will apply is to transform the dependent variable. We will attempt the following two transformations.

1 $y' = \log_e(y)$ We will label the new variable **LOGMARK**.

2 $y' = 1/y$ We will label the new variable **1/MARK**.

Once again we use our software package to estimate the regression equation. The printouts appear below.

Minitab Output for Example 17.3 (LOGMARK)

Regression Analysis
The regression equation is
Logmark = 2.13 + 0.0217 Time

Predictor	Coef	Stdev	t-ratio	p
Constant	2.12958	0.06030	35.32	0.000
Time	0.021716	0.001194	18.19	0.000

s = 0.08444   R-sq = 77.1%   R-sq(adj) = 76.9%

Analysis of Variance

SOURCE	DF	SS	MS	F	p
Regression	1	2.3579	2.3579	330.72	0.000
Error	98	0.6987	0.0071		
Total	99	3.0566			

Excel Output for Example 17.3 (LOGMARK)

	A	B	C	D	E	F	G
1	SUMMARY OUTPUT						
2							
3	Regression Statistics						
4	Multiple R	0.87830037					
5	R Square	0.77141155					
6	Adjusted R Square	0.76907901					
7	Standard Error	0.0844372					
8	Observations	100					
9							
10	ANOVA						
11		df	SS	MS	F	Significance F	
12	Regression	1	2.357901025	2.357901	330.7181	3.58E-33	
13	Residual	98	0.698704801	0.00713			
14	Total	99	3.056605826				
15							
16		Coefficients	Standard Error	t Stat	P-value		
17	Intercept	2.12958205	0.060300222	35.31632	1.51E-57		
18	Time	0.0217159	0.001194122	18.18566	3.58E-33		

Histogram of Residuals in Example 17.3 (LOGMARK)

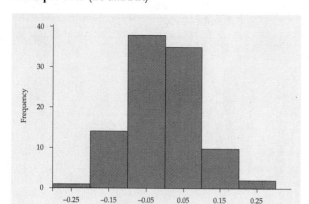

Plot of Residuals versus Predicted Values in Example 17.3 (LOGMARK)

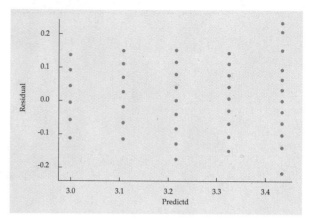

The histogram of the residuals indicates that the error variable may be normal. The plot of the residuals versus the predicted values of the dependent variable shows some change in the variance. However, the change is smaller than in the original model. Thus, the transformation has decreased the degree of heteroscedasticity.

Minitab Output for Example 17.3 (1/MARK)

Regression Analysis
```
The regression equation is
1/Mark = 0.0846 −0.000876 Time

Predictor        Coef        Stdev      t-ratio          p
Constant      0.084574     0.002389       35.40      0.000
Time        −0.00087647  0.00004731      −18.53      0.000

s = 0.003345     R-sq = 77.8%      R-sq(adj) = 77.6%

Analysis of Variance

SOURCE         DF           SS           MS           F          p
Regression      1      0.0038410    0.0038410     343.21      0.000
Error          98      0.0010968    0.0000112
Total          99      0.0049377
```

Excel Output for Example 17.3 (1/MARK)

	A	B	C	D	E	F	G
1	SUMMARY OUTPUT						
2							
3	Regression Statistics						
4	Multiple R	0.88197717					
5	R Square	0.77788373					
6	Adjusted R Square	0.77561724					
7	Standard Error	0.00334535					
8	Observations	100					
9							
10	ANOVA						
11		df	SS	MS	F	Significance F	
12	Regression	1	0.003840987	0.003841	343.2104	8.73E-34	
13	Residual	98	0.001096752	1.12E-05			
14	Total	99	0.004937739				
15							
16		Coefficients	Standard Error	t Stat	P-value		
17	Intercept	0.08457426	0.002389056	35.40071	1.22E-57		
18	Time	-0.0008765	4.73E-05	-18.5259	8.73E-34		

Histogram of Residuals in Example 17.3 (1/MARK)

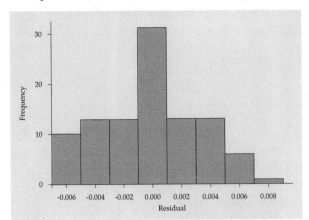

Plot of Residuals versus Predicted Values in Example 17.3 (1/MARK)

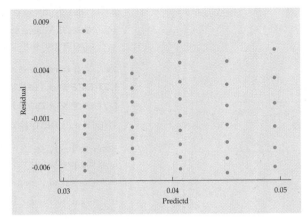

The problem of heteroscedasticity has been resolved. However, the error variable does not appear to be normal. Thus, the logarithmic transformation is judged to be superior.

By remedying a violation of the required condition, we have improved the fit. As you can see, both transformed dependent variable models have larger coefficients of determination and F-statistics. (Note that we cannot use the standard error of estimate to make the comparison because the dependent variables are different.)

In practice, statisticians often experiment with different transformations to determine which one works best. Ideally, we look for transformations where the required conditions are well satisfied and whose fit is best.

Exercises

17.22 Refer to Exercise 17.1. The residuals and predicted values for the regression equation were determined. The histogram of the residuals and the graph of the residuals versus the predicted values are shown below.

   a   Does it appear that the normality requirement is violated? Explain.

   b   Is the error variable variance constant? Explain.

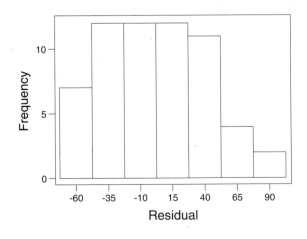

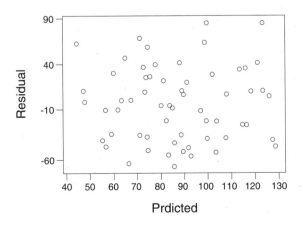

17.23 Refer to Exercise 17.1. The correlations for each pair of independent variables are shown below.

    a   What do these correlations tell you about the independent variables?

    b   What do these statistics tell you about the t-tests of the coefficients in the multiple regression model?

PAIR OF INDEPENDENT VARIABLES	CORRELATION
LOT-SIZE and **TREES**	.286
LOT-SIZE and **DISTANCE**	−.189
TREES and **DISTANCE**	.079

17.24 Refer to Exercise 17.2. The histogram of the residuals and the graph of the residuals and the predicted values are shown below.

    a   Does it appear that the normality requirement is violated? Explain.

    b   Is the error variable variance constant? Explain.

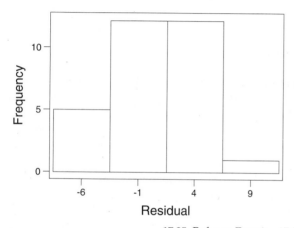

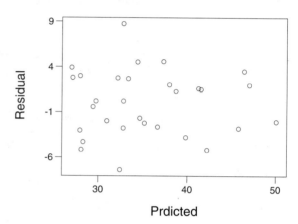

17.25 Refer to Exercise 17.2. The correlation between **ASSGNMNT** and **MIDTERM** is .104.

    a   What does this correlation tell you about the independent variables?

    b   What does it say about the t-tests of β_1 and β_2 in the multiple regression model?

17.26 Refer to Exercise 17.4. The histogram of the residuals and the graph of the residuals and the predicted values are shown below.

    a   Does it appear that the normality requirement is violated? Explain.

    b   Is the error variable variance constant? Explain.

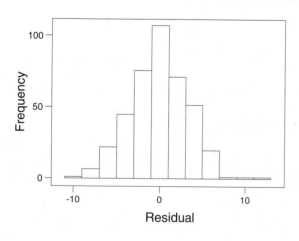

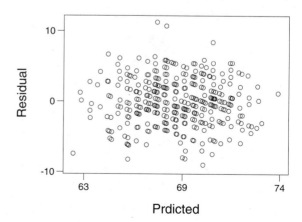

17.27 Refer to Exercise 17.4. The correlation between **FATHER** and **MOTHER** is .251.

    a What does this correlation tell you about the independent variables?

    b What does it say about the t-tests of β_1 and β_2 in the multiple regression model?

The following exercises require the use of a computer and statistical software.

17.28 The observations of variables y, x_1, and x_2 are stored in columns 1, 2, and 3, respectively, of file XR17-28.

    a Conduct a regression analysis of these data.

    b Calculate the residuals and standardized residuals. Identify any observations that should be checked.

    c Draw a histogram of the residuals. Is it likely that the normality requirement is violated?

    d Plot the residuals versus the predicted values of y. Is the variance of the error variable constant?

    e If heteroscedasticity exists, propose several possible remedies. Attempt each and report your findings.

17.29 The observations of variables y, x_1, and x_2 are stored in columns 1, 2, and 3, respectively, of file XR17-29.

    a Conduct a regression analysis of these data.

    b Calculate the residuals and standardized residuals. Identify the observations that should be checked for accuracy.

    c Draw a histogram of the residuals. Is it likely that the normality requirement is violated?

    d Plot the residuals versus the predicted values of y. Is the variance of the error variable constant?

    e If heteroscedasticity exists, propose several possible remedies. Attempt each and report your findings.

17.30 Determine whether there are violations of the required conditions in the regression model used in Exercise 16.38. Which, if any, observations should be checked to ensure that they were correctly recorded?

17.31 Refer to Exercise 16.44. Conduct an analysis of the residuals to determine whether any of the required conditions are violated. Identify any observations that should be checked for accuracy.

17.32 Refer to Exercise 17.6.

    a Is multicollinearity a problem? Explain.

    b Determine the residuals and predicted values using the regression equation.

    c Draw a histogram of the residuals. Does it appear that the error variable is normally distributed?

    d Plot the residuals (on the vertical axis) and the predicted values (on the horizontal axis). Is the variance of the error variable constant?

    e Identify observations that should be checked for accuracy.

17.33 Refer to Exercise 17.7.

    a Use whatever techniques you deem necessary to check the normality requirement and for heteroscedasticity.

    b Is multicollinearity a problem? Explain.

    c Identify all observations that should be checked.

17.34 Refer to Exercise 17.8.

    a   Use whatever techniques you deem necessary to check the normality requirement and for heteroscedasticity.

    b   Is multicollinearity a problem? Explain.

17.35 An M.B.A. program that was started two decades ago wanted to analyze the factors that affect student performance. The dean of the School of Business decided to build a multiple regression model where the dependent variable is the M.B.A. grade point average (GPA) for each of 100 randomly selected M.B.A. students who graduated in the past three years. The independent variables are the undergraduate GPA, the Graduate Management Admissions Test score (GMAT), and the number of years of work experience prior to entering the program. These data are stored in columns 1 to 4, respectively, in file XR17-35.

    a   Conduct a multiple regression analysis.

    b   Use whatever statistical techniques you deem necessary to diagnose any violations of required conditions.

    c   Are the coefficients and t-tests of the coefficients affected by multicollinearity? Explain.

    d   Briefly describe what the coefficients tell you.

    e   Test to determine which independent variables affect the dependent variable.

    f   Use whatever statistics you wish to assess the model's fit.

17.36 Supermarkets frequently price products such as bread and milk to attract customers to the store. A manager of a dairy that supplies milk to a supermarket wanted to know how sales of milk are affected by different prices. Consequently, she recorded the weekly sales of milk at one supermarket, the price of a quart of her company's brand (price A), and the price of a quart of her competitor's brand (price B). The data for the past 52 weeks are stored in columns 1 through 3, respectively, in file XR17-36.

    a   Develop a regression model, and use a software package to produce the statistics.

    b   Perform a complete diagnostic analysis to determine whether the required conditions are satisfied.

    c   If one or more conditions are unsatisfied, attempt to remedy the problem.

    d   Use whatever procedures you wish to assess how well the model fits the data.

    e   Interpret and test each of the coefficients.

    f   Is multicollinearity a problem that affects your answer in part (e)? Explain.

17.37 The general manager of the Cleveland Indians baseball team is in the process of determining which minor-league players to draft. He is aware that his team needs home-run hitters and would like to find a way to predict the number of home runs a player will hit. Being an astute statistician, he gathers a random sample of players and records the number of home runs each player hit in his first two full years as a major-league player and the number of home runs he hit in his last full year in the minor leagues. These data are stored in columns 1 and 2, respectively, in file XR17-37.

    a   Develop a regression model, and use a software package to produce the statistics.

    b   Perform a complete diagnostic analysis to determine whether the required conditions are satisfied. Which conditions, if any, are unsatisfied? Suggest a way to remedy the problem.

    c   After correcting the problem, use the computer to calculate the statistics for the new model.

d Use whatever procedures you wish to assess how well the model fits the data.

e Is the number of minor-league home runs an indicator of the number of major-league home runs?

17.6 Stepwise Regression

In the previous section we introduced multicollinearity and described the problems it causes by distorting the t-tests of the coefficients. If one of our objectives is to determine whether and how each independent variable affects the dependent variable, it is necessary to reduce the extent of multicollinearity.

As we discussed, one of the ways to reduce multicollinearity is to include independent variables that appear to be uncorrelated. In many cases this may be difficult to accomplish because there are many ways for variables to be related. For example, one variable may be a function of several other variables. Consequently, a correlation matrix may not reveal the problem. In this section, we introduce stepwise regression, a procedure that eliminates correlated independent variables.

Stepwise regression is an iterative procedure that adds and deletes one independent variable at a time. The decision to add or delete a variable is made on the basis of whether that variable improves the model. Minitab features this and related procedures. Excel does not. However, we created a macro for this purpose. It should be noted that this macro is different from the ones you have encountered thus far in this book. The instructions for its use and the format of the data are described in Appendix 17.B.

Stepwise Regression Procedure

The procedure begins by computing the simple regression model for each independent variable. The independent variable with the largest F-statistic (which in a simple regression model is the t-statistic squared) or equally, with the smallest p-value is chosen as the first entering variable. (Minitab uses the F-statistic, and the Excel macro can use either the F-statistic or the p-value.) The standard is usually set at $F = 4.0$, chosen because the significance level is about 5%. The standard may be changed in both Minitab and Excel. The standard is called the *F-to-enter*. If no independent variable exceeds the F-to-enter, the procedure ceases with no regression model produced. If at least one variable exceeds the standard, the procedure continues. It then considers whether the model would be improved by adding a second independent variable. It examines all such models to determine which is best and whether the F-statistic of the second variable (with the first variable already in the equation) is greater than the F-to-enter.

If two independent variables are highly correlated, only one of them will enter the equation. Once the first variable is included, the added explanatory power of the second variable will be minimal and its F-statistic will not be large enough to enter the model. In this way multicollinearity is reduced.

The procedure continues by deciding whether to add another independent variable at each step. The computer also checks to see if the inclusion of previously added variables is warranted. At each step the p-values of all variables are computed and compared to the *F-to-remove*. If a variable's F-statistic falls below this standard, it is removed from the equation.

These steps are repeated until no more variables are added or removed.

EXAMPLE 17.4

In Exercise 16.39, we examined the relationship between a baseball team's winning percentage and its batting average. Exercise 16.40 looked at the relationship between the winning percentage and the earned run average. In an attempt to learn more about the variables that determine winning and losing, several more variables were recorded. Variables that are believed to be related to scoring runs are batting average, home runs, stolen bases, bases on balls received, and number of strikeouts. Variables related to runs allowed are earned runs, hits, errors, bases on balls allowed, and strikeouts of opposing players. The data from the American League for a recent season are stored in file XM17-04 and are listed below.

Table A shows, for example, that the Baltimore Orioles' winning percentage was .414 (actually 67 wins and 95 losses in the 162-game season); they scored a total of 686 runs and had a team batting average of .254 (1,421 hits in 5,604 at bats) with 170 home runs, 50 stolen bases, 528 bases on balls, and 974 strikeouts. Table B exhibits defensive statistics. It shows, for example, that Orioles pitchers gave up a total of 796 runs, of which 743 were earned. (An unearned run is a run that is scored because of an error.) Pitchers allowed 1,534 hits, issued 504 bases on balls, and struck out 868 opposing batters. The defense made 91 errors.

Table A

Offensive Statistics

TEAM	WINNING %	RUNS	BATTING AVERAGE	HOME RUNS	STOLEN BASES	BASES ON BALLS	STRIKEOUTS
Baltimore	.414	686	.254	170	50	528	974
Boston	.519	731	.269	126	59	593	820
California	.500	653	.255	115	94	448	928
Chicago	.537	758	.262	139	134	610	896
Cleveland	.352	576	.254	79	84	449	888
Detroit	.519	817	.247	209	109	699	1,185
Kansas City	.506	727	.264	117	119	523	969
Milwaukee	.512	799	.271	116	106	556	802
Minnesota	.586	776	.280	140	107	526	747
New York	.438	674	.256	147	109	473	861
Oakland	.519	760	.248	159	151	642	981
Seattle	.512	702	.255	126	97	588	811
Texas	.525	829	.270	177	102	596	1,039
Toronto	.562	684	.257	133	148	499	1,043

Defensive Statistics

TEAM	RUNS	EARNED RUNS	HITS	ERRORS	BASES ON BALLS	STRIKEOUTS
Baltimore	796	743	1,534	91	504	868
Boston	712	642	1,405	116	530	999
California	649	591	1,351	102	543	990
Chicago	681	622	1,302	116	601	923
Cleveland	759	678	1,551	149	441	862
Detroit	794	726	1,570	104	593	739
Kansas City	722	639	1,473	125	529	1,004
Milwaukee	744	674	1,498	118	527	859
Minnesota	652	595	1,402	95	488	876
New York	777	709	1,510	133	506	936
Oakland	776	734	1,425	107	655	892
Seattle	674	616	1,387	110	628	1,003
Texas	814	734	1,486	134	662	1,022
Toronto	622	569	1,301	127	523	971

SOURCE: Creative Statistics Company

Perform an analysis to determine which variables affect a team's winning percentage.

SOLUTION

Here is an example where we cannot use all the recorded variables in a regression model that attempts to explain the variation in a team's winning percentage. There are two problems. First, when there are few observations relative to the number of variables, the model will almost always appear to fit well when in fact, it may not. Consider a simple regression model (one independent variable) with only 3 observations. It is likely that the regression equation will appear to fit well yet there may be no linear relationship. Thus, to enable us to assess how well each of the variables affects the winning percentage, it is necessary to reduce the number of variables.

Second, it is likely that some of the independent variables are correlated either directly with each other or correlated with a combination of independent variables. As a result, it will be impossible to determine whether each independent variable is linearly related to the winning percentage.

In fact, the multiple regression model created by using all 12 independent variables was estimated (results not shown). The coefficient of determination was 98.67% (the adjusted coefficient of determination was 82.67%) and the standard error of estimate was quite small (0.0252), but the *F*-test was not significant (*p*-value = .3057) and no *t*-test was significant. (All *p*-values were greater than .47.) These results are so contradictory that it is impossible to properly interpret the results. A large coefficient of determination and small standard error of estimate indicate a good fit. However, the large *p*-values for the *F*-test and the *t*-tests indicate that the model is not useful and that none of the independent variables affects a team's winning percentage.

We then employed Minitab's stepwise regression and our Excel macro. The results are shown below.

Minitab Output for Example 17.4

```
Stepwise Regression
F-to-Enter:      4.00      F-to-Remove:      4.00

Response is Win_Pct  on 12 predictors, with N =   14

      Step        1        2
Constant    0.07162  0.46240

Rns_Scrd  0.00059  0.00074
T-Ratio      3.21    10.90

Rns_Alw            -0.00069
T-Ratio             -9.09

S          0.0463   0.0166
R-Sq        46.13    93.67
```

MENU COMMANDS

COMMANDS FOR EXAMPLE 17.4

1 Click **Stat, Regression,** and **Stepwise. . . .**

2 Type the name of the dependent variable (**Response**).
   C1

3 Hit **tab** and type the names of the independent variables (**Predictors**).
   C2-C12

4 To change the **F to enter** and/ or **F to remove**, click **Options.**

5 Type the new values for *F* to **enter** and *F* to **remove**. Click **OK** twice.

Results of stepwise regression

Step 1 - Entering variable: Rns_Scrd

Summary measures

Multiple R	0.6792
R-Square	0.4613
Adj R-Square	0.4164
StErr of Est	0.0463

ANOVA Table

Source	df	SS	MS	F	p-value
Explained	1	0.0220	0.0220	10.2766	0.0076
Unexplained	12	0.0257	0.0021		

Regression coefficients

	Coefficient	Std Err	t-value	p-value
Constant	0.0716	0.1342	0.5336	0.6034
Rns_Scrd	0.0006	0.0002	3.2057	0.0076

Step 2 - Entering variable: Rns_Alw

Summary measures

		Change	% Change
Multiple R	0.9678	0.2886	%42.5
R-Square	0.9367	0.4754	%103.0
Adj R-Square	0.9252	0.5088	%122.2
StErr of Est	0.0166	-0.0297	-%64.2

ANOVA Table

Source	df	SS	MS	F	p-value
Explained	2	0.0448	0.0224	81.3769	0.0000
Unexplained	11	0.0030	0.0003		

Regression coefficients

	Coefficient	Std Err	t-value	p-value
Constant	0.4624	0.0645	7.1704	0.0000
Rns_Scrd	0.0007	0.0001	10.9019	0.0000
Rns_Alw	-0.0007	0.0001	-9.0884	0.0000

Instructions Stepwise Regression

Another author created this macro. Consequently, the instructions will vary from those of other macros in Data Analysis Plus.

In this macro we include the variable names. The rules governing variable names are:

1 Names must start with a letter or underscore.

2 Don't use entirely numerical names (e.g., 55).

3 Don't use names that are the same as cell addresses (e.g., A2).

4 Don't use R or C.

5 Avoid symbols other than letters, numbers, and underscores.

6 Blanks are acceptable, but this macro will change them to underscores.

COMMANDS	COMMANDS FOR EXAMPLE 17.4
1 Type or import the data. Place the cursor anywhere in the data set.	
2 Click **Tools**, **Data Analysis Plus**, and **Stepwise Regression**.	
3 Specify the dependent variable (**response variable**).	**Win_Pct**
4 Specify the independent variables	Highlight all the independent variables.
5 Select the **Significance option**. Click **OK** to choose **p-values** as the criteria. Click **OK** to accept the default values for **p-to-enter** and **p-to-leave**.	
6 Select whichever scatterplots you wish outputted. Click **OK**.	
7 Select the location of the output. Click **OK**.	

INTERPRETING THE RESULTS

All one-independent variable models are proposed, and the one that fits best is chosen. As you can see, in step 1 the variable **Rns_Scrd** was judged to be best. The model is

$$\text{Win\_Pct} = .07162 + .00059 \text{ Rns\_Scrd}$$

Its standard error of estimate is .0463, and the coefficient of determination is 46.13%.

In step two, each of the remaining independent variables is included in a two-variable model with **Rns_Scrd**. The best two-variable model is selected. Thus, **Rns_Alw** is included with **Rns_Scrd**. At the same time, the new F-statistic for **Rns_Scrd** is computed and compared to the F-to-remove. Evidently it is large enough, and **Rns_Scrd** is retained. The regression equation is

$$\text{Win\_Pct} = .4624 + .00074 \text{ Rns\_Scrd} - .00069 \text{ Rns\_Alw}$$

The standard error of estimate is .0166, and the coefficient of determination is 93.67%.

In step 3, the remaining independent variables are examined. All three-variable models (with **Rns_Scrd** and **Rns_Alw**) are tested. If the new independent variable's F-statistic is larger than the F-to-enter, that variable is added to the equation. In this example, the F-statistic of each of the remaining variables was not sufficiently large. No other variables were added to the model. This means that whatever explanatory power is provided by variables, such as the number of home runs a team hits or the number of stolen bases it allows, has already been factored into the model with the inclusion of the number of runs scored and the number of runs allowed.

For baseball fans this result is rather obvious (although it was probably not obvious until we pointed this out). The two most important variables in determining a team's winning percentage are the number of runs the team scores and the number of runs the team allows the opponents to score. We don't need sophisticated statistical methods to tell us that. However, stepwise regression could now be useful in identifying which offensive-related variables (Table A) are linearly related to the number of runs a team scores and which defensive variables (Table B) are linearly related to the number of runs a team gives up. (See Exercises 17.42 and 17.43.) In this way, a manager may be able to determine what characteristics of a team are most important in producing a winning team. This information could be most useful in deciding trades, drafts, and free agent signings.

Exercises

The following exercises require the use of a computer and statistical software.

17.38 Refer to Exercise 17.1.

    a Use a stepwise regression procedure to produce the regression equation.

    b What differences are there between this printout and the one produced in Exercise 17.1?

17.39 Refer to Exercise 17.3.

    a Use a stepwise regression procedure to produce the regression equation.

    b What differences are there between this printout and the one produced in Exercise 17.3?

17.40 Refer to Exercise 17.5.

    a Use a stepwise regression procedure to produce the regression equation.

    b What differences are there between this printout and the one produced in Exercise 17.5?

17.41 Refer to Example 17.2.

    a Use a stepwise regression procedure to produce the regression equation.

    b What differences are there between this printout and the one produced in Example 17.2?

17.42 Refer to Example 17.4. Use stepwise regression to find which offensive variables (Table A) are linearly related to the number of runs scored.

17.43 Refer to Example 17.4. Use stepwise regression to find which defensive variables (Table B) are linearly related to the number of runs allowed.

17.7 Regression Diagnostics—III (Time Series)

In Chapter 16, we pointed out that, in general, we check to see if the errors are independent when the data constitute a times series—data gathered sequentially over a series of time periods. In Section 16.8, we described the graphical procedure for determining whether the required condition that the errors are independent is violated. We plot the residuals versus the time periods and look for patterns. In this section, we augment that procedure with the **Durbin–Watson** test.

Durbin–Watson Test

The Durbin–Watson test allows the statistician to determine whether there is evidence of **first-order autocorrelation**—a condition in which a relationship exists between consecutive residuals r_i and r_{i-1}, where i is the time period. The Durbin–Watson statistic is defined as

$$d = \frac{\sum_{i=2}^{n} (r_i - r_{i-1})^2}{\sum_{i=1}^{n} r_i^2}$$

The range of the values of d is

$$0 \leq d \leq 4$$

where small values of d ($d < 2$) indicate a positive first-order autocorrelation and large values of d ($d > 2$) imply a negative first-order autocorrelation. Positive first-order autocorrelation is a common occurrence in business and economic time series. It occurs when consecutive residuals tend to be similar. In that case, $(r_i - r_{i-1})^2$ will be small, producing a small value for d. Negative first-order autocorrelation occurs when consecutive residuals differ widely. For example, if positive and negative residuals generally alternate, $(r_i - r_{i-1})^2$ will be large, and as a result, d will be greater than 2. Figures 17.3 and 17.4 depict positive autocorrelation, whereas Figure 17.5 illustrates negative autocorrelation. Notice that in Figure 17.3, residuals generally grow larger over time, while in Figure 17.4, they grow smaller. In both figures, consecutive residuals are similar. In Figure 17.5, the first residual is a positive number, which is followed by a negative residual. The remaining residuals follow this pattern (with some exceptions). Consecutive residuals are quite different.

Figure 17.3

Positive First-Order Autocorrelation

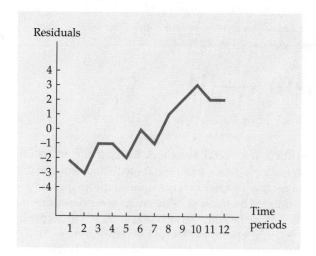

Figure 17.4

Positive First-Order Autocorrelation

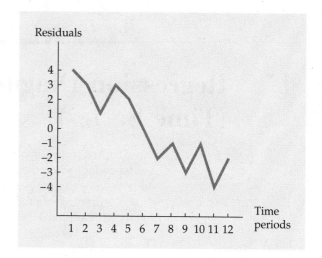

Figure 17.5

Negative First-Order Autocorrelation

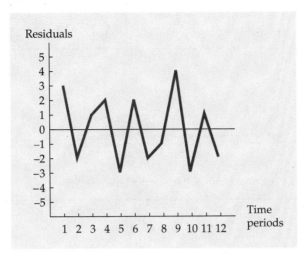

Table 7 in Appendix B is designed to test for positive first-order autocorrelation by providing values of d_L and d_U for a variety of values of n and k and for $\alpha = .01$ and $.05$.

The decision is made in the following way. If $d < d_L$, we conclude that there is enough evidence to show that positive first-order autocorrelation exists. If $d > d_U$, we conclude that there is not enough evidence to show that positive first-order autocorrelation exists. And if $d_L \leq d \leq d_U$, the test is inconclusive. The recommended course of action when the test is inconclusive is to continue testing with more data until a conclusive decision can be made.

For example, to test for positive first-order autocorrelation with $n = 20$, $k = 3$, and $\alpha = .05$, we test the following hypotheses.

H_0: There is no first-order autocorrelation.

H_A: There is positive first-order autocorrelation.

The decision is made as follows.

If $d < d_L = 1.00$, reject the null hypothesis in favor of the alternative hypothesis.

If $d > d_U = 1.68$, do not reject the null hypothesis.

If $1.00 \leq d \leq 1.68$, the test is inconclusive.

To test for negative first-order autocorrelation, we change the critical values. If $d > 4 - d_L$, we conclude that negative first-order autocorrelation exists. If $d < 4 - d_U$, we conclude that there is not enough evidence to show that negative first-order autocorrelation exists. If $4 - d_U \leq d \leq 4 - d_L$, the test is inconclusive.

We can also test simply for first-order autocorrelation by combining the two one-tail tests. If $d < d_L$ or $d > 4 - d_L$, we conclude that autocorrelation exists. If $d_U \leq d \leq 4 - d_U$, we conclude that there is no evidence of autocorrelation. If $d_L \leq d \leq d_U$ or $4 - d_U \leq d \leq 4 - d_L$, the test is inconclusive. The significance level will be 2α (where α is the one-tail significance level). Figure 17.6 describes the range of values of d and the conclusion for each interval.

Figure 17.6

Durbin–Watson Test

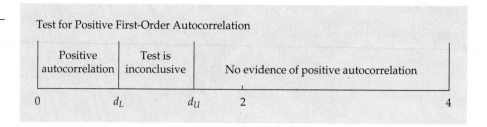

Test for Positive First-Order Autocorrelation

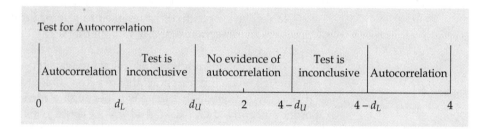

Test for Negative First-Order Autocorrelation

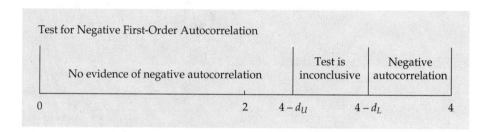

Test for Autocorrelation

For time-series data, we add the Durbin–Watson test to our list of regression diagnostics. That is, we determine whether the error variable is normally distributed with constant variance (as we did in Section 17.5), we identify outliers and (if our software allows it) influential observations that should be verified, and we conduct the Durbin–Watson test.

EXAMPLE 17.5

Christmas week is a critical period for most ski resorts. Because many students and adults are free from other obligations, they are able to spend several days indulging in their favorite pastime, skiing. A large proportion of gross revenue is earned during this period. A ski resort in Vermont wanted to determine the effect that weather had on their sales of lift tickets. The manager of the resort collected the number of lift tickets sold during Christmas week, the total snowfall (in inches), and the average temperature (in degrees Fahrenheit) for the past 20 years. These data are listed below and stored in columns 1 to 3, respectively, of file XM17-05. Develop the multiple regression model, and diagnose any violations of the required conditions.

TOTAL NUMBER OF TICKETS	TOTAL SNOWFALL	AVERAGE TEMPERATURE
(TICKETS)	(SNOWFALL)	(TEMPURE)
6,835	19	11
7,870	15	−19
6,173	7	36
7,979	11	22
7,639	19	14
7,167	2	−20
8,094	21	39
9,903	19	27
9,788	18	26
9,557	20	16
9,784	19	−1
12,075	25	−9
9,128	3	37
9,047	17	−15
10,631	0	22
12,563	24	2
11,012	22	32
10,041	7	18
9,929	21	32
11,091	11	−15

SOLUTION

We estimated the model

$$\text{TICKETS} = \beta_0 + \beta_1 \text{ SNOWFALL} + \beta_2 \text{ TEMPURE} + \epsilon$$

The Minitab and Excel printouts follow.

Minitab Output for Example 17.5

Regression Analysis

```
The regression equation is
Tickets = 8308 + 74.6 Snowfall − 8.8 Tempture

Predictor      Coef      Stdev    t-ratio       p
Constant     8308.0      903.7       9.19   0.000
Snowfall      74.59      51.57       1.45   0.166
Tempture      -8.75      19.70      -0.44   0.662

s = 1712        R-sq = 12.0%     R-sq(adj) = 1.7%

Analysis of Variance

SOURCE       DF          SS          MS       F       p
Regression    2     6793798     3396899    1.16   0.337
Error        17    49807212     2929836
Total        19    56601008
```

Excel Output for Example 17.5

	A	B	C	D	E	F	G
1	SUMMARY OUTPUT						
2							
3	Regression Statistics						
4	Multiple R	0.34645292					
5	R Square	0.12002963					
6	Adjusted R Square	0.0165037					
7	Standard Error	1711.67641					
8	Observations	20					
9							
10	ANOVA						
11		df	SS	MS	F	Significance F	
12	Regression	2	6793798.248	3396899	1.159416	0.337271	
13	Residual	17	49807213.95	2929836			
14	Total	19	56601012.2				
15							
16		Coefficients	Standard Error	t Stat	P-value		
17	Intercept	8308.01142	903.7284951	9.193039	5.24E-08		
18	Snowfall	74.5932494	51.57482923	1.446311	0.166276		
19	Tempture	-8.7537378	19.70435896	-0.44425	0.662462		

As you can see, the coefficient of determination is low ($R^2 = 12.0\%$ and adjusted $R^2 = 1.7\%$) and the p-value of the F-test is .337, which indicates that the model is a poor one. We used Minitab to determine the residuals and the predicted values. We then drew the histogram, plotted the residuals versus the predicted values of y, and plotted the residuals versus the time periods. (The observations constitute a time series because we observed the results from the past 20 years.) (Appendixes 16.A and 16.B described how to produce the residuals and predicted values. Appendixes 17.A and 17.B provide instructions for the rest of the diagnosis.)

Minitab Histogram of Residuals in Example 17.5

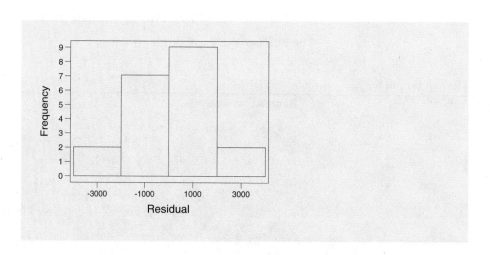

The histogram of the residuals indicates that the error variable may be normally distributed.

Minitab Plot of Residuals versus Predicted Values of y in Example 17.5

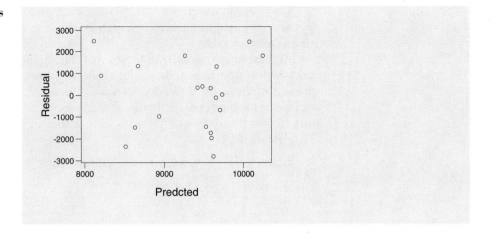

The graph of the residuals and predicted values seems to indicate that the variance of the error variable is constant.

Minitab Plot of Residuals versus Time Periods in Example 17.5

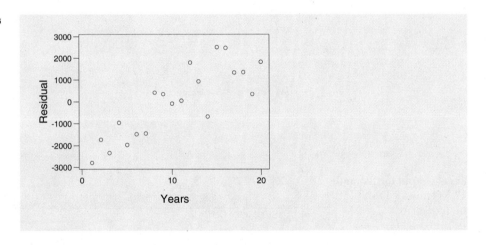

This graph reveals a serious problem. There is a strong relationship between consecutive values of the residuals, which indicates that the requirement that the errors be independent has been violated. To confirm this diagnosis, we used Minitab to calculate the Durbin–Watson statistic (see Appendix 17.B for the Excel commands that output the Durbin–Watson statistic). It is

Durbin–Watson statistic = 0.59

The critical values are determined by noting that $n = 20$ and $k = 2$ (there are two independent variables in the model). If we wish to test for positive first-order autocorrelation with $\alpha = .05$, we find in Table 7(a) in Appendix B

$$d_L = 1.10 \quad \text{and} \quad d_U = 1.54$$

The null and alternative hypotheses are

H_0: There is no first-order autocorrelation.

H_A: There is positive first-order autocorrelation.

The rejection region is $d < d_L = 1.10$. Since $d = .59$, we reject the null hypothesis and conclude that there is enough evidence to infer that positive first-order autocorrelation exists.

Autocorrelation usually indicates that the model has been misspecified. Specifically, we need to include one or more independent variables that have time-ordered effects on the dependent variable. The simplest such independent variable represents the time periods. To illustrate, we included a third independent variable that records the year since the data were gathered. Thus, **YEARS** $= 1, 2, \ldots, 20$. The new model is

$$\text{TICKETS} = \beta_0 + \beta_1 \text{ SNOWFALL} + \beta_2 \text{ TEMPTURE} + \beta_3 \text{ YEARS} + \epsilon$$

The results are shown below.

Minitab Output for Example 17.5 (Time Variable Included)

```
Regression Analysis

The regression equation is
Tickets = 5966 + 70.2 Snowfall - 9.2 Tempture + 230 Years

Predictor        Coef       Stdev     t-ratio         p
Constant        5965.6      631.3        9.45     0.000
Snowfall         70.18      28.85        2.43     0.027
Tempture         -9.23      11.02       -0.84     0.414
Years           229.97      37.13        6.19     0.000

s = 957.2         R-sq = 74.1%      R-sq(adj) = 69.2%

Analysis of Variance

SOURCE        DF         SS              MS          F         p
Regression     3    41940216        13980072      15.26     0.000
Error         16    14660795          916300
Total         19    56601012
```

Excel Output for Example 17.5 (Time Variable Included)

	A	B	C	D	E	F	G
1	SUMMARY OUTPUT						
2							
3	Regression Statistics						
4	Multiple R	0.86080195					
5	R Square	0.74097999					
6	Adjusted R Square	0.69241374					
7	Standard Error	957.235434					
8	Observations	20					
9							
10	ANOVA						
11		df	SS	MS	F	Significance F	
12	Regression	3	41940217.38	13980072	15.2571	5.93E-05	
13	Residual	16	14660794.82	916299.7			
14	Total	19	56601012.2				
15							
16		Coefficients	Standard Error	t Stat	P-value		
17	Intercept	5965.58764	631.2517853	9.450409	6.00E-08		
18	Snowfall	70.1830592	28.85142183	2.432568	0.027101		
19	Tempture	-9.2328023	11.01970866	-0.83784	0.414459		
20	Years	229.969972	37.13208681	6.193295	1.29E-05		

As we did before, we calculate the residuals and conduct regression diagnostics using Minitab. The results appear below.

Minitab Histogram of Residuals in Example 17.5 (Time Variable Included)

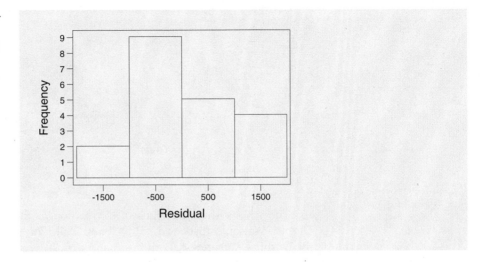

The histogram of the residuals indicates that the errors may be normally distributed.

Minitab Plot of Residuals versus Predicted Values of y in Example 17.5 (Time Variable Included)

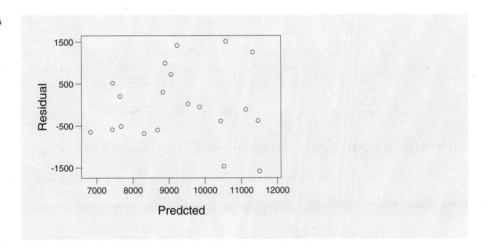

The graph of the residuals and predicted values seems to indicate that the variance of the error variable is constant.

Minitab Plot of Residuals versus Time Periods in Example 17.5 (Time Variable Included)

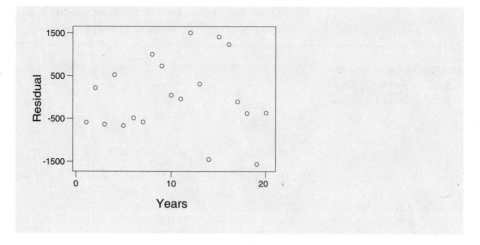

The graphs show no signs of a violation of the required conditions. The Durbin–Watson statistic is $d = 1.88$. From Table 7(a), we find the critical values of the Durbin–Watson test. With $k = 3$ and $n = 20$, we find

$d_L = 1.00$ and $d_U = 1.68$

Since $d > 1.68$, we conclude that there is not enough evidence to infer the presence of positive first-order autocorrelation.

Notice that the model is improved dramatically. The F-test tells us that the model is useful. The t-tests tell us that both the amount of snowfall and time are significantly linearly related to the number of lift tickets. This information could prove useful in advertising for the resort. For example, if there has been a recent snowfall, they could emphasize that in their advertising. If no new snow has fallen, they may emphasize their snow-making facilities.

Developing an Understanding of Statistical Concepts

Notice that the addition of the variable **YEARS** explained a large proportion of the variation in the number of lift tickets sold. That is, the resort experienced a relatively steady increase in sales over the past 20 years. Once this variable was included in the model, the variable **SNOWFALL** became significant because it was able to explain some of the remaining variation in lift ticket sales. Without **YEARS**, **SNOWFALL** and **TEMPTURE** were unable to explain a significant proportion of the variation in ticket sales. The graph of the residuals versus the time periods and the Durbin–Watson test enabled us to identify the problem and correct it. In overcoming the autocorrelation problem, we improved the model so that we identified **SNOWFALL** as an important variable in determining ticket sales. This result is quite common. Correcting a violation of a required condition will frequently improve the model.

17.44 Given the following information, perform the Durbin–Watson test to determine whether first-order autocorrelation exists.

$$n = 25 \quad k = 5 \quad \alpha = .10 \quad d = .90$$

17.45 Test the following hypotheses with $\alpha = .05$.

H_0: There is no first-order autocorrelation.

H_A: There is positive first-order autocorrelation.

$$n = 50 \quad k = 2 \quad d = 1.38$$

17.46 Test the following hypotheses with $\alpha = .02$.

H_0: There is no first-order autocorrelation.

H_A: There is first-order autocorrelation.

$$n = 90 \quad k = 5 \quad d = 1.60$$

17.47 Test the following hypotheses with $\alpha = .05$.

H_0: There is no first-order autocorrelation.

H_A: There is negative first-order autocorrelation.

$$n = 33 \quad k = 4 \quad d = 2.25$$

Exercises 17.48–17.50 and Exercises 17.54–17.56 require statistical software and a computer.

17.48 One hundred observations of variables y, x_1, and x_2 were taken over 100 consecutive time periods. The data are stored in the first three columns, respectively, of file XR17-48.

   a   Conduct a regression analysis of these data.

   b   Calculate the residuals and standardized residuals.

   c   Identify observations that should be checked.

   d   Draw the histogram of the residuals. Does it appear that the normality requirement is satisfied?

   e   Plot the residuals versus the predicted values of y. Is the error variance constant?

   f   Plot the residuals versus the time periods. Perform the Durbin–Watson test. Is there evidence of autocorrelation?

   g   If autocorrelation was detected in part (f), propose an alternative regression model to remedy the problem. Use the computer to generate the statistics associated with this model.

   h   Redo parts (a) through (f). Compare the two models.

17.49 Weekly sales of a company's product (y) and those of its main competitor (x) were recorded for one year. These data are stored in chronological order in columns 1 (company's sales) and 2 (competitor's sales) of file XR17-49.

   a   Conduct a regression analysis of these data.

   b   Calculate the residuals and standardized residuals.

   c   Identify observations that should be checked.

   d   Draw the histogram of the residuals. Does it appear that the normality requirement is satisfied?

   e   Plot the residuals versus the predicted values of y. Is the error variance constant?

   f   Plot the residuals versus the time periods. Perform the Durbin–Watson test. Is there evidence of autocorrelation?

g If autocorrelation was detected in part (f), propose an alternative regression model to remedy the problem. Use the computer to generate the statistics associated with this model.

h Redo parts (a) through (f). Compare the two models.

17.50 Observations of variables y, x_1, x_2, and x_3 were taken over 80 consecutive time periods. The data are stored in the first four columns, respectively, of file XR17-50.

a Conduct a regression analysis of these data.

b Calculate the residuals and standardized residuals.

c Identify observations that should be checked.

d Draw the histogram of the residuals. Does it appear that the normality requirement is satisfied?

e Plot the residuals versus the predicted values of y. Is the error variance constant?

f Plot the residuals versus the time periods. Perform the Durbin–Watson test. Is there evidence of autocorrelation?

g If autocorrelation was detected in part (f), propose an alternative regression model to remedy the problem. Use the computer to generate the statistics associated with this model.

h Redo parts (a) through (f). Compare the two models.

17.51 Refer to Exercise 17.3. The histogram of the residuals and the graph of the residuals and the predicted values are shown below.

a Does it appear that the normality requirement is violated? Explain.

b Is the error variable variance constant? Explain.

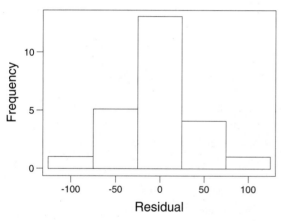

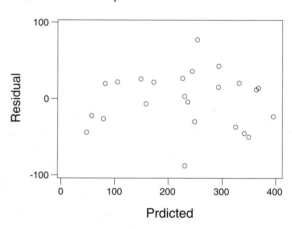

17.52 Refer to Exercise 17.3. The correlations for each pair of independent variables are shown below.

a What do these correlations tell you about the independent variables?

b Is it likely that the t-tests of the coefficients are meaningful? Explain.

PAIR OF INDEPENDENT VARIABLES	CORRELATION
PERMITS & MORTGAGE	.005
PERMITS & A-VACNCY	−.150
PERMITS & O-VACNCY	−.103
MORTGAGE & A-VACNCY	−.040
MORTGAGE & O-VACNCY	−.033
A-VACNCY & O-VACNCY	.065

17.53 Refer to Exercise 17.3. The Durbin–Watson statistic is $d = 1.75$. What does this statistic tell you about the regression model?

17.54 Refer to Exercise 16.37. Perform a complete regression diagnostic analysis of the simple regression model used in that exercise. That is, determine whether the error variable is normal with constant variance and whether the errors are independent. Identify any observations that should be checked for accuracy.

17.55 Refer to Case 16.1.

    a Compute the residuals and the standardized residuals.

    b Draw the histogram of the residuals. Does it appear that the normality requirement is satisfied?

    c Are there observations that should be checked to ensure that they were recorded properly and whether they properly belong in the sample?

    d Calculate the predicted values of the dependent variable, and plot them versus the residuals. Does it appear that the variance of the error variable is constant?

    e Plot the residuals versus the time periods. Does it appear that the errors are not independent?

    f Calculate the Durbin–Watson statistic and test to determine whether first-order autocorrelation exists.

17.56 The manager of a tire store in Minneapolis has been concerned with the high cost of inventory. The current policy is to stock all the snow tires that are predicted to sell over the entire winter at the beginning of the season (end of October). The manager can reduce inventory costs by having suppliers deliver snow tires regularly from October to February. However, he needs to be able to predict weekly sales to avoid stockouts that will ultimately lose sales. To help develop a forecasting model, he records the number of snow tires sold weekly during the last winter and the amount of snowfall (in inches) in each week. These data are stored in columns 1 and 2, respectively, in file XR17-56.

    a Develop a regression model, and use a software package to produce the statistics.

    b Perform a complete diagnostic analysis to determine whether the required conditions are satisfied.

    c If one or more conditions are unsatisfied, attempt to remedy the problem.

    d Use whatever procedures you wish to assess how well the new model fits the data.

    e Interpret and test each of the coefficients.

17.8 Summary

The multiple regression model extends the model introduced in Chapter 16. The statistical concepts and techniques are similar to those presented in simple linear regression. The coefficients are estimated using formulas derived from the least squares method. We assess the model's fit in three ways: standard error of estimate, the coefficient of determination (and the coefficient of determination adjusted for degrees of freedom), and the F-test of the analysis of variance. We employ the t-tests of the coefficients to determine whether each of the independent variables is linearly related to the dependent variable. Indicator variables allow the statistician to include independent qualitative variables. The stepwise regression method (as well as forward selection and backward elimination methods) is used to reduce the number of independent variables.

As we did in Chapter 16, we showed how to diagnose violations of required conditions. Transformations were shown to be the best way of dealing with nonnormality and heteroscedasticity. We introduced multicollinearity and demonstrated its effect and remedy. Finally we presented the Durbin-Watson test to detect first-order autocorrelation.

IMPORTANT TERMS

Response surface	Stepwise regression
Plane	Forward selection
Coefficient of determination adjusted degrees of freedom	Backward elimination
	Transformations
F-test	Durbin-Watson test
Indicator variable	First-order autocorrelation
Multicollinearity	

Supplementary Exercises

The following exercises require the use of a computer and statistical software.

17.57 When one company buys another company, it is not unusual that some workers are terminated. The severance benefits offered to the laid-off workers are often the subject of dispute. Suppose that the Laurier Company recently bought the Wilfrid Company and subsequently terminated 20 of Wilfrid's employees. As part of the buyout agreement, it was promised that the severance packages offered to the former Wilfrid employees would be equivalent to those offered to Laurier employees who had been terminated in the past year. Thirty-six-year-old Bill Smith, a Wilfrid employee for the past 10 years, earning $32,000 per year, was one of those let go. His severance package included an offer of five weeks' severance pay. Bill complained that this offer was less than that offered to Laurier's employees when they were laid off, in contravention of the buyout agreement. A statistician was called in to settle the dispute. The statistician was told that severance is determined by three factors: age, length of service with the company, and pay. To determine how generous the severance package had been, a random sample of 50 Laurier ex-employees was taken. For each, the following variables were recorded. (The data are stored in columns 1 to 4, respectively, of file XR17-57.)

Number of weeks of severance pay

Age of employee

Number of years with the company

Annual pay (in thousands of dollars)

  a Determine the regression equation. Interpret the coefficients.

  b Comment on how well the model fits the data.

  c Do all the independent variables belong in the equation? Explain.

  d Are the required conditions satisfied? Explain.

  e Perform an analysis to determine if Bill is correct in his assessment of the severance package.

17.58 The agronomist referred to in Exercise 16.43 believed that the amount of rainfall as well as the amount of fertilizer used would affect the crop yield. She redid the experiment in the following way. Thirty greenhouses were rented. In each, the amount of fertilizer and the amount of water were varied. At the end of the growing season, the amount of corn was recorded with the data stored in file XR17-58 (column 1 = crop yield in kilograms; column 2 = amount of fertilizer applied in kilograms; column 3 = amount of water in liters per week).

a Determine the sample regression line, and interpret the coefficients.

b Do these data allow us to infer at the 5% significance level that there is a linear relationship between the amount of fertilizer and the crop yield?

c Do these data allow us to infer at the 5% significance level that there is a linear relationship between the amount of water and the crop yield?

d What can you say about the multiple regression model's fit?

e Predict the crop yield when 100 kilograms of fertilizer and 1,000 liters of water are applied. Use a confidence level of 95%.

f Are the required conditions satisfied? Explain.

g Is multicollinearity a problem in this model? Explain.

17.59 Regression analysis is often used in medical research to examine the variables that affect various biological processes. A study performed by P. Wainwright, C. Pelkman, and D. Wahlsten investigated nutritional effects on preweaning mouse pups. In the experiment, the amount of nutrients was varied by rearing the pups in different litter sizes. After 32 days, the body weight and brain weight (both measured in grams) were recorded. These data are listed below and also stored in file XR17-59 (column 1 = brain weight; column 2 = litter size; column 3 = body weight).

a Conduct a multiple regression analysis where the dependent variable is the brain weight. Interpret the coefficients.

b Can we infer at the 5% significance level that there is a linear relationship between litter size and brain weight?

c Can we infer at the 5% significance level that there is a linear relationship between body weight and brain weight?

d What is the coefficient of determination, and what does it tell you about this model?

e Test the overall utility of the model. (Use $\alpha = .05$.)

f Predict with 95% confidence the brain weight of a mouse pup that came from a litter of 10 pups and whose body weight is 8 grams.

g Estimate with 95% confidence the mean weight of all mouse pups that came from litters of 6 pups and whose body weight is 7 grams.

LITTER SIZE	BODY WEIGHT	BRAIN WEIGHT
3	9.447	.444
3	9.780	.436
4	9.155	.417
4	9.613	.429
5	8.850	.425
5	9.610	.434
6	8.298	.404
6	8.543	.439
7	7.400	.409
7	8.335	.429
8	7.040	.414
8	7.253	.409

LITTER SIZE	BODY WEIGHT	BRAIN WEIGHT
9	6.600	.387
9	7.260	.433
10	6.305	.410
10	6.655	.405
11	7.183	.435
11	6.133	.407
12	5.450	.368
12	6.050	.401

SOURCE: Matthews, D. E. and Farewell, V. T., *Using and Understanding Medical Statistics* (Karger, 1988).

17.60 Refer to Exercise 17.59. Suppose that the experiment did not record the body weights of the mice.

    a Conduct a simple linear regression analysis where the dependent variable is brain weight and the independent variable is litter size. Interpret the coefficients.

    b Can we infer at the 5% significance level that there is a linear relationship between brain weight and litter size?

    c What is the coefficient of determination, and what does it tell you about this model?

    d Test the overall utility of the model with $\alpha = .05$. Compare the results of this test with the test performed in part (b).

    e Predict with 95% confidence the brain weight of a mouse pup that came from a litter of 10 pups.

    f Estimate with 95% confidence the mean weight of all mouse pups that came from litters of 6 pups.

    g Compare the results of this analysis with the analysis undertaken in Exercise 17.59.

17.61 The administrator of a school board in a large county was analyzing the average mathematics test scores in the schools under her control. She noticed that there were dramatic differences in scores among the schools. In an attempt to improve the scores of all the schools, she attempted to determine the factors that account for the differences. Accordingly, she took a random sample of 40 schools across the county and, for each, determined the mean test score last year, the percentage of teachers in each school who have at least one university degree in mathematics, the mean age, and the mean annual income of the mathematics teachers. These data are stored in columns 1 to 4, respectively, of file XR17-61.

    a Conduct a regression analysis to develop the equation.

    b Is the model useful in explaining the variation among schools? Explain.

    c Are the required conditions satisfied? Explain.

    d Is multicollinearity a problem? Explain.

    e Interpret and test the coefficients (with $\alpha = .05$).

    f Predict the test score at a school where 50% of the mathematics teachers have mathematics degrees, the mean age is 43, and the mean annual income is $48,300.

17.62 Life insurance companies are keenly interested in predicting how long their customers will live, because their premiums and profitability depend on such numbers. An actuary for one insurance company gathered data from 100 recently deceased male customers. He recorded the age at death of the customer plus the ages at death of his mother and father, the mean ages at death of his grandmothers, and the mean ages at death of his grandfathers. These data are recorded in columns 1 to 5, respectively, of file XR17-62.

   a Perform a multiple regression analysis on these data.

   b Is the model likely to be useful in predicting men's longevity?

   c Are the required conditions satisfied?

   d Is multicollinearity a problem here?

   e Interpret and test the coefficients.

   f Predict with 95% confidence the longevity of a man whose parents lived to the age of 70, whose grandmothers averaged 80 years, and whose grandfathers averaged 75.

   g Estimate with 95% confidence the mean longevity of men whose mothers lived to 75, whose fathers lived to 65, whose grandmothers averaged 85 years, and whose grandfathers averaged 75.

17.63 University students often complain that universities reward professors for research but not for teaching, and argue that professors react to this situation by devoting more time and energy to the publication of their findings and less time and energy to classroom activities. Professors counter that research and teaching go hand in hand; more research makes better teachers. A student organization at one university decided to investigate the issue. They randomly selected 50 economics professors who are employed by a multicampus university. The students recorded the salaries of the professors, their average teaching evaluations (on a 10-point scale), and the total number of journal articles published in their careers. These data are stored in columns 1 to 3, respectively, in file XR17-63. Perform a complete analysis (produce the regression equation, assess it, and diagnose it) and report your findings.

17.64 Lotteries have become important sources of revenue for governments. Many people have criticized lotteries, however, referring to them as a tax on the poor and uneducated. In an examination of the issue, a random sample of 100 adults was asked how much they spend on lottery tickets and was interviewed about various socio-economic variables. The purpose of this study is to test the following beliefs.

   1 Relatively uneducated people spend more on lotteries than do relatively educated people.

   2 Older people buy more lottery tickets than younger people.

   3 People with more children spend more on lotteries than people with fewer children.

   4 Relatively poor people spend a greater proportion of their income on lotteries than relatively rich people.

The following data were stored in columns 1 to 5, respectively, of file XR17-64.

Amount spent on lottery tickets as a percentage of total household income

Number of years of education

Age

Number of children

Personal income (in thousands of dollars)

   a Develop the multiple regression equation.

   b Is the complete model useful?

c   Are the required conditions satisfied?

d   Is multicollinearity a problem?

e   Test each of the beliefs. What conclusions can you draw?

CASE 17.1   DUXBURY PRESS REVISITED

After performing the simple regression analysis, Curt was disappointed with the results. The coefficient of determination was quite low, indicating a weak linear relationship. This suggested that the number of free copies is not an indicator of sales revenues. However, he was assured by all of the statistics authors that regression is a useful and commonly used tool. Consequently, Curt decided to improve the model by including additional variables that measure the ability of his representatives. He determined the number of years of experience and the total sales in dollars in the previous year. These data are stored in file C17-01 in the following way.

Column 1: code representing sales zone

Column 2: sales revenues from statistics books in 1993

Column 3: number of free copies

Column 4: years of experience

Column 5: sales revenues from statistics books in 1992

Include the additional variables in the model, and discuss your findings.

Minitab Instructions

Multiple Regression

The command

REGRESS C1 3 C2 – C4

will produce the regression equation

$$\hat{y} = \hat{\beta}_0 + \hat{\beta}_1 x_1 + \hat{\beta}_2 x_2 + \hat{\beta}_3 x_3$$

The "3" in the command specifies the number of independent variables in the equation. The subcommand

PREDICT K1 K2 K3

will output the 95% confidence interval estimate of the expected value of y and the 95% prediction interval when the given values of x_1, x_2, and x_3 are K_1, K_2, and K_3, respectively.

Diagnosing Violations of the Required Conditions and Other Problems

To plot the residuals against time periods, create a new variable (if necessary) representing time periods. For example, if there are 100 time periods, type

SET C10
1:100
END

These instructions will place the numbers 1, 2, . . . , 100 in column 10. You can then plot the residuals versus **C10**.

To calculate the Durbin–Watson statistic, proceed through the usual steps to conduct a regression analysis. Add the subcommand

DW

which computes and prints the Durbin–Watson statistic.

(Using the menu commands, follow steps 1 through 4 on pages 680 and 681. Before clicking **OK**, click **Options** and **Durbin–Watson statistic**. Click **OK** twice.)

Multicollinearity is investigated by computing the correlations between independent variables. If the independent variables are stored in columns 2 to 6, type

CORRELATION C2 – C6

which produces the correlation matrix listing all the correlations.

Creating Indicator Variables

If the qualitative variable has three categories represented by 1, 2, and 3, we can let Minitab create the indicator variables using the **CODE** command. For example, if the categories are stored in column 1, we would proceed as follows. Define the indicator variables

I_1 = 1 if category = 1

= 0 if not

I_2 = 1 if category = 2

= 0 if not

Type the following commands.

CODE (1) 1 (2:3) 0 C1 C2
CODE (1) 0 (2) 1 (3) 0 C1 C3

The first command instructs Minitab to store in column 2 a "1" whenever the category is 1 (C1 = 1) and a "0" whenever the category is 2 or 3. The second command stores a "0" in column 3 whenever the category is 1 (C1 = 1) or 3 (C1 = 3). It stores a "1" in column 3 whenever the category is 2 (C1 = 2). Thus, column 2 stores the values of I_1 and column 3 stores the values of I_2.

Stepwise Regression

Type

STEPWISE C1 C2 – C5

to perform a stepwise regression where the dependent variable is stored in column 1 and the independent variables are stored in columns 2 through 5. To change the F to enter value, use the **FENTER** subcommand with the new value (e.g., **FENTER 6.0**). To change the F to remove value, use the **FREMOVE** subcommand.

To conduct the forward selection procedure, change the F-to-remove to 0. That is, type

STEPWISE C1 C2 – C5;
FREMOVE 0;
FENTER 4.

To conduct backward elimination, specify 10,000 for F-to-enter, and 4.0 for F-to-remove. Use the **ENTER** subcommand to list all the independent variables. That is, type

STEPWISE C1 C2 – C5;
ENTER C2 – C5;
FENTER 10000;
FREMOVE 4.

Diagnosing Violations of Required Conditions

To plot the residuals against time periods, create a new variable (if necessary) representing time periods. For example, if there are 100 time periods, store the numbers 1 to 100 in a vacant column. You can then plot the residuals versus time periods.

To calculate the Durbin–Watson statistic, proceed through the usual steps to conduct a regression analysis and create the residuals. Highlight the list of residuals and click **Tools**, **Data Analysis Plus**, and **Durbin–Watson Statistic**.

Multicollinearity is investigated by computing the correlations between independent variables. To produce the correlations between all independent variables, proceed as follows.

1 Click **Tools**, **Data Analysis . . .** , and **Correlation**.

2 Specify the block coordinates of the independent variables.

Stepwise Regression

Before beginning place the cursor somewhere in the data set. If you don't, you will be forced to close the macro and repeat.

The macro will ask about missing values. The data sets that are stored on the diskettes do not have missing values. Simply accept the default and proceed. However, if you have created your own data set that has missing values, click the box to erase the check mark.

Instead of specifying the block coordinates of the data, you simply specify variable names for the dependent and the independent variables.

The dependent variable must be quantitative. It cannot be an indicator (dummy) variable. You may use independent indicator variables.

You will be asked to specify the significance options, which refers to the way the stepwise regression decides which variables enter and which variables leave. Until you learn more about these choices we suggest that you accept the defaults.

The macro will draw several different plots. Specify the ones you want.

The output will be placed on the same worksheet as the data or on a different worksheet. If you choose the latter, the macro will ask you to name the worksheet.

Applications

3

18 Statistical Process Control

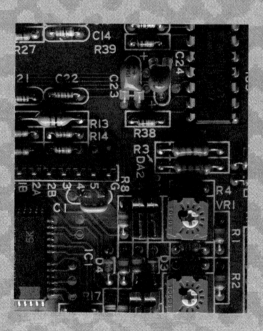

18.1 Introduction

At this point, you have seen several different applications of hypothesis testing. We now want to present another, slightly different form of hypothesis testing called **statistical process control** or **SPC** (formerly called **quality control**). Statistical process control refers to one of a variety of statistical techniques used to develop and maintain a firm's ability to produce high-quality goods and services. In the last few years, quality has become much more important to North American companies. It is easy to see why. In many industries, foreign countries have been able to produce goods that are more reliable and less costly than their North American counterparts. A critical factor in this phenomenon is the extensive use of statistical process control.

There are two general approaches to the management of quality. The first approach is to produce the product and, at the completion of the production process, inspect the unit to determine whether it conforms to specifications; if it doesn't, it is either discarded or repaired. This approach has several drawbacks. Foremost among them is that it is costly to produce substandard products regardless of whether they are later discarded or fixed. In recent years, this approach has been employed by a decreasing number of companies. Instead, many firms have adopted the **detection approach**. Using the concepts of hypothesis testing, statisticians concentrate on the production process. Rather than inspect the product, we inspect the process to determine when the process starts producing units that do not conform to specifications. This allows us to correct the production process before it creates a large number of defective products.

In the next section, we discuss the problem of process variation and why it is often the key to the management of quality. We also introduce the concept and logic of control charts and show why they work. In the rest of the chapter, we introduce four specific control charts.

18.2 Process Variation

The key to understanding SPC is understanding that all production processes result in variation; that is, no product is exactly the same as another. You can see for yourself that this is true by weighing, for example, two boxes of breakfast cereal that are each supposed to weigh 16 ounces. Not only will they not weigh exactly 16 ounces, but they will not even have equal weights. All products exhibit some degree of variation. There are two sources of variation. **Chance variation** is caused by a number of randomly occurring events that are part of the production process and that in general cannot be eliminated without changing the process. **Assignable variation** is caused by specific events or factors that are frequently temporary and that can usually be identified and eliminated. To illustrate, consider a paint company that produces and sells paint in one-gallon cans. The cans are filled by an automatic valve that regulates the amount of paint in each can. Because of a variety of factors, the actual amount of fill will vary from can to can, even when the valve is working the way it was designed to work. However, occasionally the valve will malfunction, causing the cans to be either overfilled or underfilled. Perhaps the best way to understand what is happening is to consider the volume of paint in each can as a random variable. If the only sources of variation are caused by chance, then each can's volume is drawn from identical distributions. That is, each distribution has the same shape, mean, and standard deviation as depicted in Figure 18.1. Under such circumstances the production process is said to be **under control**. In recognition of the fact that variation in output will occur even when the process is under control and operating properly, most processes are designed so that their products will fall within designated specification limits. For example, the process that fills the paint cans may be designed so that the cans contain between .98 and 1.02 gallons.

Figure 18.1

Identical Process Distributions

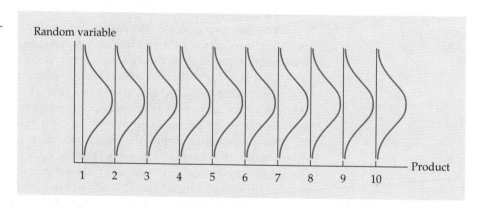

Inevitably, some event or combination of factors in a production process will cause the process distribution to change. When it does, the process is said to be **out of control**. There are several possible ways for the process to go out of control. Here is a list of the most commonly occurring possibilities and their likely assignable causes.

1. **Level shift** This is a change in the mean of the process distribution. Assignable causes include machine breakdown, new machine and/or operator, or a change in the environment. In the paint-can illustration, a temperature or humidity change may affect the density of the paint, causing less paint in each can. Figure 18.2 depicts a decrease in the process mean level of paint.

Figure 18.2

Level Shift: Change in Process Distribution Mean

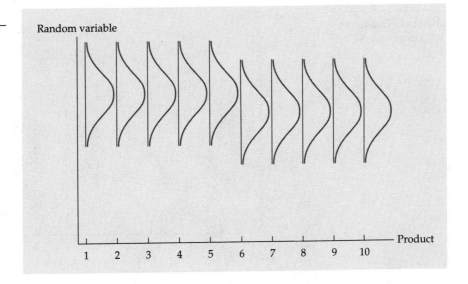

2. **Instability** This is the name we apply to the process when the standard deviation increases. (As we discuss later, a decrease in the standard deviation is desirable.) This may be caused by a machine in need of repair, defective materials, wear of tools, or an incompetent operator. Suppose, for example, that a part in the valve that controls the amount of paint wears down, causing greater variation than normal. Figure 18.3 describes the process distributions in this example.

Figure 18.3

Instability: Increase in Process Distribution Standard Deviation

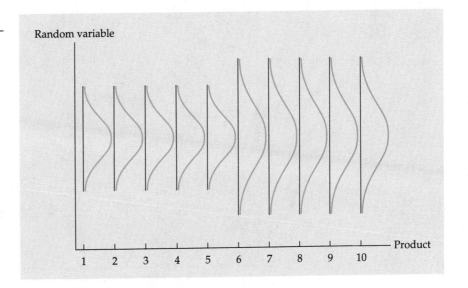

3 Trend When there is a slow, steady shift (either up or down) in the process distribution mean, the result is a trend. This is frequently the result of less-than-regular maintenance, operator fatigue, residue or dirt buildup, or gradual loss of lubricant. If the paint-control valve becomes increasingly clogged, we would expect to see a steady decrease in the amount of paint delivered. Figure 18.4 describes this effect.

Figure 18.4

Trend: Steady Change in Process Distribution Mean

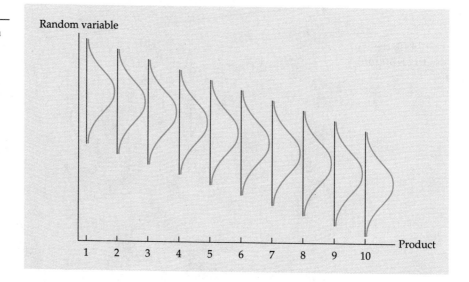

4 Cycle This is a repeated series of small observations followed by large observations. Likely assignable causes include environmental changes, worn parts, or operator fatigue. If there are changes in the voltage in the electricity that runs the machines in the paint-can example, we might see series of overfilled cans and series of underfilled cans. See Figure 18.5.

Figure 18.5

Cycle: Large and Small Observations

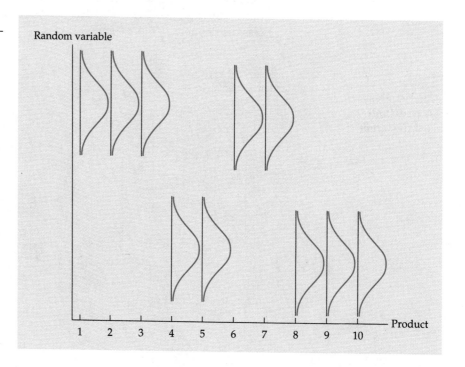

The key to quality is to detect when the process goes out of control so that we can correct the malfunction and restore control of the process. The control chart is the statistical method that we use to detect problems.

Control Charts

A *control chart* is a plot of statistics over time. For example, an $\bar{x}$ chart plots a series of sample means taken over a period of time. Each control chart contains a *centerline* and *control limits*. (See Figure 18.6.) The control limit above the centerline is called the *upper control limit* and that below the centerline is called the *lower control limit*. If, when the sample statistics are plotted, all points are randomly distributed between the control limits, we conclude that the process is under control. If the points are not randomly distributed between the control limits, we conclude that the process is out of control.

Figure 18.6

Control Chart

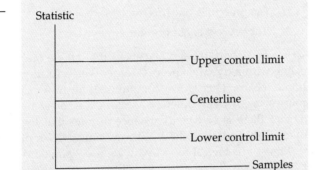

To illustrate the logic of control charts, let us suppose that in the paint-can example described above, we want to determine whether the central location of the distribution has changed from one period to another. We will draw our conclusion from an $\bar{x}$ chart. For the moment, let us assume that we know the mean μ and standard deviation σ of the process when it is under control. We can construct the $\bar{x}$ chart, as shown in Figure 18.7. The chart is drawn so that the vertical axis plots the values of $\bar{x}$ that will be calculated and the horizontal axis tracks the samples in the order in which they are drawn. The centerline is the value of μ. The control limits are set at three standard deviations from the centerline. Because the standard deviation of $\bar{x}$ (the statistic we intend to track in this chart) is $\sigma/\sqrt{n}$, we define the control limits as follows.

$$\text{Lower control limit} = \mu - 3\frac{\sigma}{\sqrt{n}}$$

$$\text{Upper control limit} = \mu + 3\frac{\sigma}{\sqrt{n}}$$

Figure 18.7

x̄ Chart: μ and σ Known

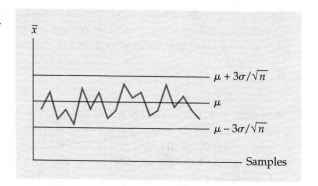

After we've constructed the control chart by drawing the centerline and control limits, we use it to plot the sample means, which are joined to make it easier to interpret. The principles underlying control charts are identical to the principles of hypothesis testing. The null and alternative hypotheses are

H_0: The process is under control.

H_A: The process is out of control.

For an x̄ chart, the test statistic is the sample mean x̄. However, because we're dealing with a dynamic process rather than a fixed population, we test a series of sample means. That is, we compute the mean for each of a continuing series of samples taken over time. For each series of samples, we want to determine whether there is sufficient evidence to infer that the process mean has changed. We reject the null hypothesis if at any time the sample mean falls outside the control limits. It is logical to ask why we use 3 standard deviations and not 2 or 1.96 or 1.645, as we did when we tested hypotheses about a population mean in Chapter 10. The answer lies in the way in which all tests are conducted. Because test conclusions are based on sample data, there are two possible errors. In SPC, a Type I error occurs if we conclude that the process is out of control when in fact it is not. The error can be quite expensive, because the production process must be stopped and the causes of the variation found and repaired. Consequently, we want the probability of a Type I error to be small. With control limits set at 3 standard deviations from the mean, the probability of a Type I error is $\alpha = P(|z| > 3)$ = .0026. A small value of α results in a relatively large value of the probability of a Type II error. This means that, for each sample, we are less likely to recognize when the process goes out of control. However, because we will be performing a series of tests (one for each sample), we will eventually discover that the process is out of control and take steps to rectify the problem.

Suppose that in order to test the production process that fills one-gallon paint cans, we choose to take a sample of size 4 every hour. Let us also assume that we know the mean and standard deviation of the process distribution of the amount of paint when the process is under control, say $\mu = 1.01$ and $\sigma = .02$. (This means that when the valve is working the way it was designed, the amount of paint put into each can is a random variable whose mean is 1.01 gallons and whose standard deviation is .02 gallons.) Thus,

$$\text{Centerline} = \mu = 1.01$$
$$\text{Lower control limit} = \mu - 3\sigma/\sqrt{n} = 1.01 - 3(.02)/\sqrt{4} = 1.01 - .03 = .98$$
$$\text{Upper control limit} = \mu + 3\sigma/\sqrt{n} = 1.01 + 3(.02)/\sqrt{4} = 1.01 + .03 = 1.04$$

Figure 18.8 depicts a situation in which the first 15 samples were taken when the process was under control. However, after the 15th sample was drawn, the process went out of control and produced sample means outside the control limits. We conclude that the process distribution has changed, because the data display variability beyond that predicted for a process with the specified mean and standard deviation. This means that the variation is assignable, and that the cause needs to be identified and corrected.

Figure 18.8

$\bar{x}$ Chart: Process Out of Control

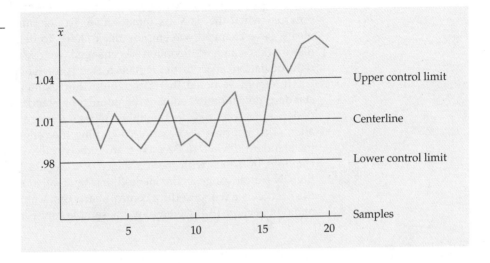

As we stated above, SPC is a slightly different form of hypothesis testing. The concept is the same but there are differences that you should be aware of. The most important difference is that when we tested means and proportions in Chapters 10 and 11, we were dealing with fixed but unknown parameters of populations. For instance, in Example 10.4 the population we dealt with was the account balances of the department store customers. The population mean balance was a constant value that we simply did not know. The purpose of the test was to determine if there was enough statistical evidence to allow us to infer that the mean balance was greater than $70. So we took one sample and based the decision on the sample mean. When dealing with a production process, it's important to realize that the process distribution itself is variable. That is, at any time, the process distribution of the amount of paint fill may change if the valve malfunctions. Consequently, we do not simply take one sample and make the decision. Instead, we plot a number of statistics over time in the control chart. Simply put, in Chapters 10 through 17, we assumed static population distributions with fixed but unknown parameters and in this chapter, we assume a dynamic process distribution with variable parameters.

In our demonstration of the logic of control charts, we resorted to traditional methods of presenting inferential methods; we assumed that the process parameters were known. When the parameters are unknown, we estimate their values from the sample data. In the next two sections, we discuss how to construct and use control charts in more realistic situations.

In Sections 18.3 and 18.4, we present control charts when the data are quantitative. In the context of statistical process control, we call these **control charts for** variables. Section 18.5 demonstrates the use of control charts that record whether a unit is defective or nondefective. These are called **control charts for attributes**.

18.3 Control Charts for Variables: $\bar{x}$ and S Charts

There are several ways to judge whether a change in the process distribution has occurred when the data are quantitative. To determine whether the distribution means have changed, we employ the $\bar{x}$ **chart**. To determine whether the process distribution standard deviation has changed, we use the S (which stands for standard deviation) chart or the R (which stands for range) chart.

It should be noted that throughout this textbook we have used the sample standard deviation to estimate the population standard deviation. However, for a variety of reasons, SPC frequently employs the range instead of the standard deviation. This is primarily because computing the range is simpler than computing the standard deviation. Because many practitioners conduct SPC performing calculations by hand (with the assistance of a calculator), they select the computationally simple range as the method to estimate the process standard deviation. In this section, we will introduce control charts that feature the sample standard deviation. In Section 18.4, we employ the sample range to construct our charts.

$\bar{x}$ Chart

As we explained above, if we know the mean and standard deviation of the process distribution, we can compute the centerline and control limits. However, it is unrealistic to believe that the mean and standard deviation of the process distribution are known. Thus, in order to construct the $\bar{x}$ chart, we need to estimate the relevant parameters from the data.

We begin by drawing samples when the process is under control. We discuss later how to determine that the process is under control. For each sample, we compute the mean and the standard deviation. The estimator of the mean of the distribution is the mean of the sample means (denoted $\bar{\bar{x}}$)

$$\bar{\bar{x}} = \frac{\sum_{j=1}^{k} \bar{x}_j}{k}$$

where $\bar{x}_j$ is the mean of the jth sample and there are k samples.

To estimate the standard deviation of the process distribution, we calculate the sample variance s_j^2 for each sample. We then compute the pooled standard deviation*, which we denote S and define as

$$S = \sqrt{\frac{\sum_{j=1}^{k} s_j^2}{k}}$$

---

*This formula requires that the sample size is the same for all samples, a condition that is satisfied throughout this chapter.

In the previous section, where we assumed that the process distribution mean and variance were known, the centerline and control limits were defined as

$$\text{Centerline} = \mu$$
$$\text{Lower control limit} = \mu - 3\sigma/\sqrt{n}$$
$$\text{Upper control limit} = \mu + 3\sigma/\sqrt{n}$$

Since the values of μ and σ are unknown, we must use the sample data to estimate them. The estimator of μ is $\bar{x}$ and the estimator of σ is S. Therefore the centerline and control limts are

Centerline and Control Limits for $\bar{x}$ Chart

$$\text{Centerline} = \bar{\bar{x}}$$
$$\text{Lower control limit} = \bar{\bar{x}} - 3S/\sqrt{n}$$
$$\text{Upper control limit} = \bar{\bar{x}} + 3S/\sqrt{n}$$

EXAMPLE 18.1*

Lear Seating of Kitchener, Ontario, manufactures seats for Chrysler, Ford, and General Motors cars. Several years ago, Lear instituted statistical process control, which has resulted in improved quality and lower costs. One of the components of a front-seat cushion is a wire spring, produced from 4 mm (millimeter) steel wire. A machine is employed to bend the wire so that the spring's length is 500 mm. If the springs are longer than 500 mm, they will loosen and eventually fall out. If they are too short, they won't easily fit into position. (In fact, in the past, when there was a relatively large number of short springs, workers incurred arm and hand injuries when attempting to install the springs.) In order to determine if the process is under control, random samples of four springs are taken every two hours. The last 25 samples are shown in Table 18.1 (and stored in file XM18-01). Construct an $\bar{x}$ chart from these data.

Table 18.1

25 Samples of Springs for Example 18.1	SAMPLE			
	1	501.02	501.65	504.34	501.10
	2	499.80	498.89	499.47	497.90
	3	497.12	498.35	500.34	499.33
	4	500.68	501.39	499.74	500.41
	5	495.87	500.92	498.00	499.44
	6	497.89	499.22	502.10	500.03
	7	497.24	501.04	498.74	503.51
	8	501.22	504.53	499.06	505.37

(continued)

*The authors are grateful to Pat Bourke, Barry Cress, Kevin Lewis, and Brial Riehl of Lear Seating Ltd. for their assistance in writing this example and several exercises.

9	499.15	501.11	497.96	502.39
10	498.90	505.99	500.05	499.33
11	497.38	497.80	497.57	500.72
12	499.70	500.99	501.35	496.48
13	501.44	500.46	502.07	500.50
14	498.26	495.54	495.21	501.27
15	497.57	497.00	500.32	501.22
16	500.95	502.07	500.60	500.44
17	499.70	500.56	501.18	502.36
18	501.57	502.09	501.18	504.98
19	504.20	500.92	500.02	501.71
20	498.61	499.63	498.68	501.84
21	499.05	501.82	500.67	497.36
22	497.85	494.08	501.79	501.95
23	501.08	503.12	503.06	503.56
24	500.75	501.18	501.09	502.88
25	502.03	501.44	502.76	503.79

SOLUTION

SOLVING BY HAND

The means and standard deviations for each sample were computed and listed in Table 18.2. We then calculated the mean of the means and the pooled standard deviation. These statistics are as follows.

$$\bar{\bar{x}} = 500.380$$
$$S = 1.956$$

Table 18.2

Means and Standard Deviations of Samples in Example 18.1

SAMPLE					$\bar{x}_j$	s_j
1	501.02	501.65	504.34	501.10	502.027	1.56689
2	499.80	498.89	499.47	497.90	499.015	0.83309
3	497.12	498.35	500.34	499.33	498.785	1.37556
4	500.68	501.39	499.74	500.41	500.555	0.68268
5	495.87	500.92	498.00	499.44	498.557	2.15204
6	497.89	499.22	502.10	500.03	499.810	1.76323
7	497.24	501.04	498.74	503.51	500.133	2.74085
8	501.22	504.53	499.06	505.37	502.545	2.93381
9	499.15	501.11	497.96	502.39	500.152	1.97782
10	498.90	505.99	500.05	499.33	501.068	3.31578
11	497.38	497.80	497.57	500.72	498.367	1.57771
12	499.70	500.99	501.35	496.48	499.630	2.21625
13	501.44	500.46	502.07	500.50	501.117	0.77994
14	498.26	495.54	495.21	501.27	497.570	2.81996
15	497.57	497.00	500.32	501.22	499.027	2.05853
16	500.95	502.07	500.60	500.44	501.015	0.73487
17	499.70	500.56	501.18	502.36	500.950	1.11886
18	501.57	502.09	501.18	504.98	502.455	1.72412
19	504.20	500.92	500.02	501.71	501.712	1.79633

20	498.61	499.63	498.68	501.84	499.690	1.50694
21	499.05	501.82	500.67	497.36	499.725	1.94345
22	497.85	494.08	501.79	501.95	498.918	3.74115
23	501.08	503.12	503.06	503.56	502.705	1.10603
24	500.75	501.18	501.09	502.88	501.475	0.95480
25	502.03	501.44	502.76	503.79	502.505	1.01261

Thus, the centerline and control limits are

$$\text{Centerline} = \bar{\bar{x}} = 500.380$$
$$\text{Lower control limit} = \bar{\bar{x}} - 3S/\sqrt{n} = 500.380 - 3(1.956)/\sqrt{4} = 497.446$$
$$\text{Upper control limit} = \bar{\bar{x}} + 3S/\sqrt{n} = 500.380 + 3(1.956)/\sqrt{4} = 503.314$$

The centerline and control limits are drawn and the sample means plotted in the order in which they occurred. To examine the chart, see the Minitab or Excel printout below.

USING THE COMPUTER

Minitab Output for Example 18.1

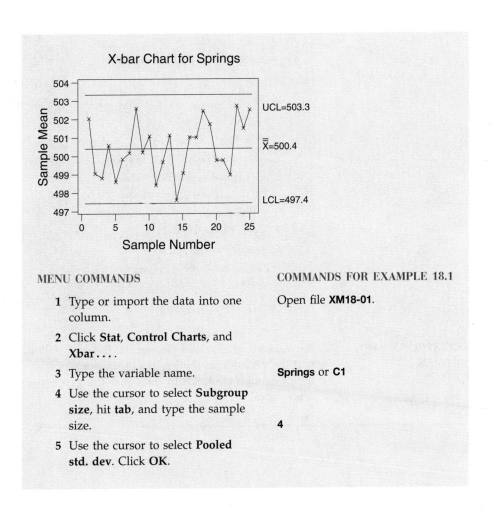

MENU COMMANDS

1 Type or import the data into one column.

2 Click **Stat**, **Control Charts**, and **Xbar . . . .**

3 Type the variable name.

4 Use the cursor to select **Subgroup size**, hit **tab**, and type the sample size.

5 Use the cursor to select **Pooled std. dev**. Click **OK**.

COMMANDS FOR EXAMPLE 18.1

Open file **XM18-01**.

Springs or **C1**

4

Excel Output for Example 18.1

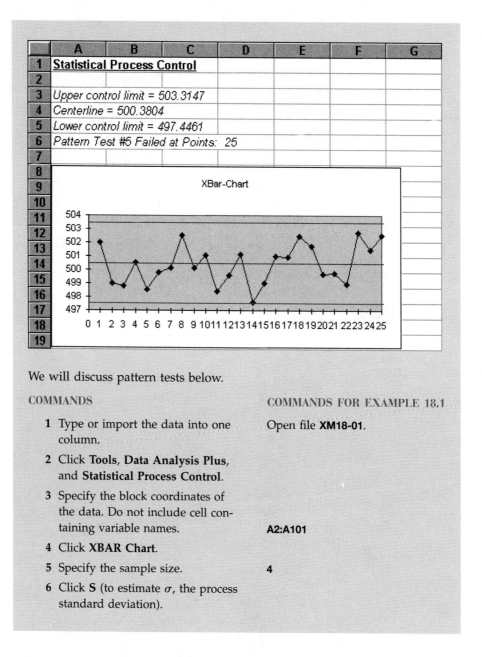

	A	B	C	D	E	F	G
1	**Statistical Process Control**						
2							
3	Upper control limit = 503.3147						
4	Centerline = 500.3804						
5	Lower control limit = 497.4461						
6	Pattern Test #5 Failed at Points: 25						
7							

XBar-Chart

We will discuss pattern tests below.

COMMANDS

1 Type or import the data into one column.

2 Click **Tools**, **Data Analysis Plus**, and **Statistical Process Control**.

3 Specify the block coordinates of the data. Do not include cell containing variable names.

4 Click **XBAR Chart**.

5 Specify the sample size.

6 Click **S** (to estimate σ, the process standard deviation).

COMMANDS FOR EXAMPLE 18.1

Open file **XM18-01**.

A2:A101

4

INTERPRETING THE RESULTS

As you can see, no point lies outside the control limits. We conclude from this fact that the variation in the lengths of the springs is caused by chance. That is, there is not enough evidence to infer that the process is out of control. No remedial action is called for.

Pattern Tests to Determine When the Process Is Out of Control

When we tested hypotheses in the other parts of this book, we used only one sample statistic to make a decision. However, in statistical process control, the decision is made from a series of sample statistics. In the $\bar{x}$ chart we make the decision after plotting at least 25 sample means. As a result, we can develop tests that are based on the pattern the sample means make when plotted. To describe them, we need to divide the $\bar{x}$ chart between the control limits into six zones, as shown in Figure 18.9. The C zones represent the area within one standard deviation of the centerline. The B zones are the regions between one and two standard deviations from the centerline. The spaces between two and three standard deviations from the centerline are defined as A zones.

Figure 18.9

Zones of $\bar{x}$ Charts

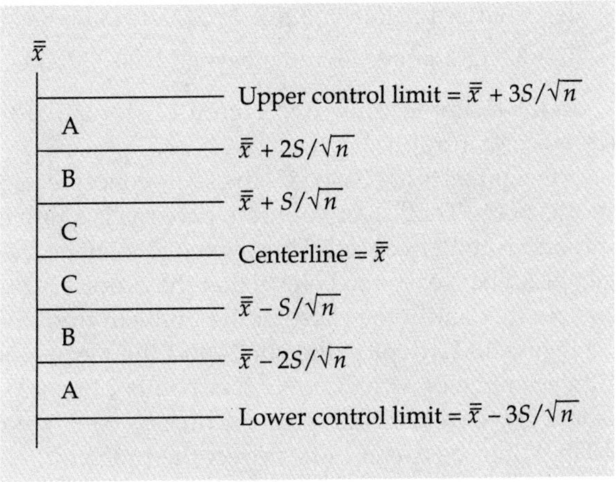

The width of the zones is 1 standard deviation of $\bar{x}$, which is estimated as $S/\sqrt{n}$. In Example 18.1, the width of each zone is $S/\sqrt{n} = 1.956/\sqrt{4} = .978$. Figure 18.10 describes the centerline, control limits, and zones for Example 18.1.

Figure 18.10

Zones for $\bar{x}$ Chart: Example 18.1

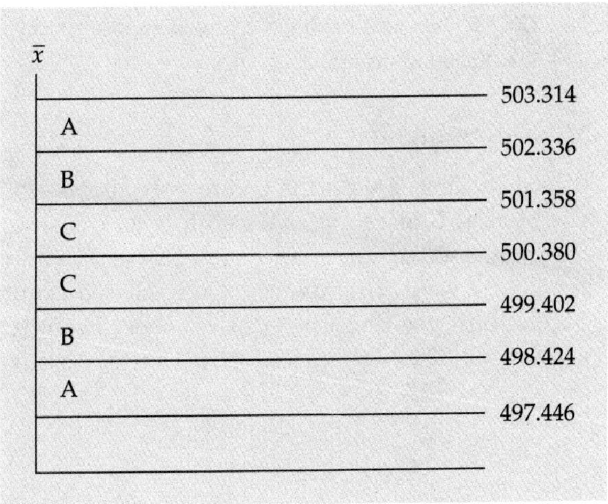

There are several pattern tests that can be applied. Below we list eight tests that are conducted by Minitab (and by the Excel macro we created).

Test 1: one point beyond zone A. This is the method discussed above, where we conclude that the process is out of control if any point is outside the control limits.

Test 2: nine points in a row in zone C or beyond (on the same side of the centerline).

Test 3: six increasing or six decreasing points in a row.

Test 4: fourteen points in a row alternating up and down.

Test 5: two out of three points in a row in zone A or beyond (on the same side of the centerline).

Test 6: four out of five points in a row in zone B or beyond (on the same side of the centerline).

Test 7: fifteen points in a row in zone C (on both sides of the centerline).

Test 8: eight points in a row beyond zone C (on both sides of the centerline).

In the examples shown in Figure 18.11, each of the eight tests indicates a process out of control.

All eight tests are based on the same concepts used to test hypotheses throughout this book. That is, any of these patterns is a rare event, unlikely to occur when a process is under control. Thus, when any one of these patterns is recognized, the statistician has reason to believe that the process is out of control. In fact, it is often possible to identify the cause of the problem from the pattern in the control chart.

Figure 18.12 depicts the zones and the means for Example 18.1. After a thorough examination, we discover that points 23 and 25 are in zone A above the centerline. Thus, we conclude that the process went out of control at point 25. A technician would be called in to correct the problem.

Minitab Pattern Test Results: Example 18.1

Minitab has the capability to conduct all eight tests and report when any of them indicate that the process is out of control. For Example 18.1, Minitab printed the following when it was commanded to conduct the pattern tests.

TEST 5. Two of 3 points in a row in zone A or beyond (on one side of CL).
Test Failed at points: 25

Menu Commands

Before clicking **OK** on the commands above, use the cursor to select **Tests For Special Causes** and **All eight**. If you wish to apply specific tests, click **Selected**, use the cursor and click **Tests . . .**, and use the cursor to select the test(s) you want. To draw the zones, click **S Limits . . .** and type **1 2 3** in the **Sigma limit positions:** box (the number of standard deviations of $\bar{x}$ from the centerline). Click **OK** twice. Switch to the session window to view the test results.

Figure 18.11

Examples of Patterns Indicating Process Out of Control

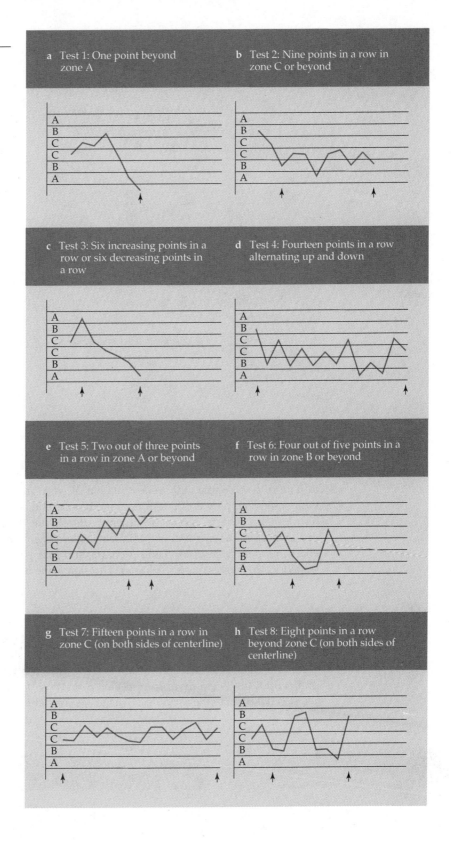

a Test 1: One point beyond zone A

b Test 2: Nine points in a row in zone C or beyond

c Test 3: Six increasing points in a row or six decreasing points in a row

d Test 4: Fourteen points in a row alternating up and down

e Test 5: Two out of three points in a row in zone A or beyond

f Test 6: Four out of five points in a row in zone B or beyond

g Test 7: Fifteen points in a row in zone C (on both sides of centerline)

h Test 8: Eight points in a row beyond zone C (on both sides of centerline)

Figure 18.12

$\bar{x}$ chart with Zones: Example 18.1

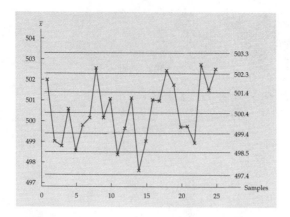

Excel Pattern Test Results: Example 18.1

Excel automatically performs all eight tests. It reported

	A	B	C	D	E	F	G	H	I
1	Pattern Test #5 Failed at Points:			25					
2									
3									
4									

Pattern Tests in Practice

There appears to be a great deal of disagreement among statisticians with regard to pattern tests. Some authors and statistical software packages apply eight tests while others employ a different number. In addition, some statisticians apply pattern tests to $\bar{x}$ charts, but not to other charts. Rather than joining the debate with our own opinions, we will use Minitab's rules. There are eight pattern tests for $\bar{x}$ charts, no pattern tests for S and R charts, and four pattern tests for the chart presented in the next section (P charts). The same rule applies to our Excel macros.

S Charts

The **S chart** graphs sample standard deviations to determine if the process distribution standard deviation has changed. The format is similar to that of the $\bar{x}$ chart: there is a centerline and control limits. However, the formulas for the centerline and control limits are more complicated than those for the $\bar{x}$ chart. Consequently, we will not display the formulas; instead we will let the computer do all the work.

EXAMPLE 18.2

Using the data provided in Example 18.1, determine whether there is evidence to indicate that the process distribution standard deviation has changed over the period when the samples were taken.

SOLUTION

Minitab Output for Example 18.2

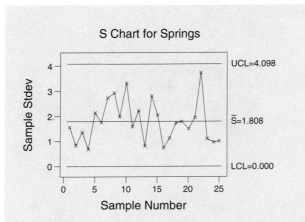

The centerline and control limits are functions of S, which we found to be 1.956 (in Example 18.1). The centerline is denoted $\bar{S}$ and is equal to 1.808.

MENU COMMANDS	COMMANDS FOR EXAMPLE 18.2
1 Type or import the data into one column.	Open file **XM18-01**.
2 Click **Stat**, **Control Charts**, and **S**	
3 Type the variable name.	**Springs** or **C1**
4 Use the cursor to select **Subgroup size**, hit **tab**, and type the sample size.	**4**
5 Use the cursor to select **Pooled std. dev**. Click **OK**.	

Excel Output for Example 18.2

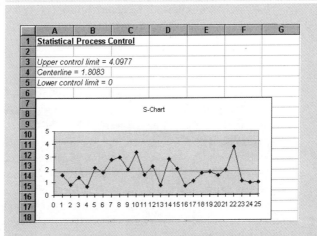

The centerline and control limits are functions of S, which we found to be 1.956 (in Example 18.1).

COMMANDS	COMMANDS FOR EXAMPLE 18.2
1 Type or import the data into one column.	Open file **XM18-01**.
2 Click **Tools, Data Analysis Plus,** and **Statistical Process Control**.	
3 Specify the block coordinates of the data. Do not include cell containing variable name.	**A2:A101**
4 Click **S Chart**.	
5 Specify the sample size.	**4**

INTERPRETING THE RESULTS

There are no points outside the control limits. Because we do not apply any of the pattern tests, we conclude that there is no evidence to believe that the standard deviation has changed over this period.

Good News and Bad News from S Charts

In analyzing the S charts, we would conclude that the process distribution has changed if we observe points outside the control limits. Obviously, points above the upper control limit indicate that the process standard deviation has increased—an undesirable situation. Points below the lower control limit also indicate that the process standard deviation has changed. However, cases in which the standard deviation has decreased are welcome occurrences because reducing the variation generally leads to improvements in quality. The operations manager should investigate cases where the sample standard deviations or ranges are small to determine the factors that produced such results. The objective is to determine if permanent improvements in the production process can be made. Care must be exercised in cases where the S chart reveals a *decrease* in the standard deviation, since this is often caused by improper sampling.

Using the $\bar{x}$ and S Charts

In this section, we have introduced $\bar{x}$ and S charts as separate procedures. In actual practice, however, the two charts must be drawn and assessed together. The reason for this is that the $\bar{x}$ chart uses S to calculate the control limits and zone boundaries. Consequently, if the S chart indicates that the process is out of control, the value of S will not lead to an accurate estimate of the standard deviation of the process distribution. The usual procedure is to draw the S chart first. If it indicates that the process is under control, we then draw the $\bar{x}$ chart. If the $\bar{x}$ chart also indicates that the process is under control, we are then in a position to use both charts to maintain control. If either chart shows that the process was out of control at some time during the creation of the charts, we can detect and fix the problem, then redraw the charts with new data.

We can often diagnose the problem from the patterns exhibited in the control charts. For example, a level shift is easily detected from the $\bar{x}$ chart shown in Figure

18.13. Figure 18.14 describes an $\bar{x}$ chart where a trend has occurred. Cycles are also detected from $\bar{x}$ charts. (See Figure 18.15.) Instability is diagnosed from the S chart as shown in Figure 18.16. A knowledgeable operations manager would be capable of determining the problem and needed repairs from these charts.

Figure 18.13

$\bar{x}$ Chart: Level Shift

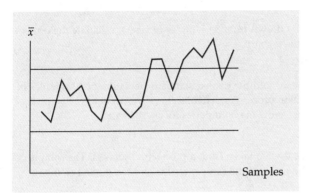

Figure 18.14

$\bar{x}$ Chart: Trend

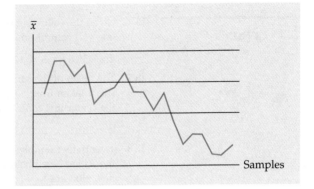

Figure 18.15

$\bar{x}$ Chart: Cycle

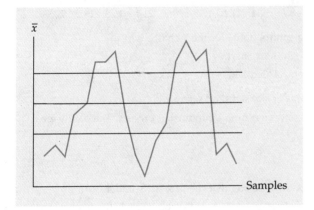

Figure 18.16

S Chart: Instability

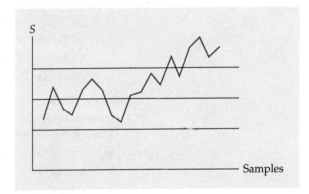

Developing an Understanding of Statistical Concepts

The concepts that underlie statistical process control are the same as the fundamental principles of hypothesis testing. That is, statistics that are not consistent with the null hypothesis lead us to reject the null hypothesis. However, there are two critical differences between SPC and hypothesis testing. First, in SPC we test processes rather than parameters of populations. That is, we test to determine whether there is evidence that the process distribution has changed. Second, in SPC we test a series of statistics taken over time. From a pedagogical point of view, there is another fundamental difference. Most students of statistics have difficulty identifying the correct hypothesis-testing procedure to employ. However, SPC applications tend to be rather uncomplicated. We use control charts for variables (as in this and the next section) to determine whether the process is under control when the product produced must be measured quantitatively. Identifying the correct technique is seldom difficult and thus does not require technique-identification skills developed throughout this book.

Exercises

18.1 Given the following statistics drawn from 30 samples of size 4, calculate the centerline and control limits for the $\bar{x}$ chart.

$$\bar{\bar{x}} = 453.6 \qquad S = 12.5$$

18.2 The mean of the sample means and the pooled standard deviation of 40 samples of size 9 taken from a production process under control are shown below. Compute the centerline, control limits, and zone boundaries for the $\bar{x}$ chart.

$$\bar{\bar{x}} = 181.1 \qquad S = 11.0$$

18.3 Twenty-five samples of size 4 were taken from a production process. The sample means are listed below. The mean of the sample means and the pooled standard deviation are

$$\bar{\bar{x}} = 13.3 \qquad S = 3.8$$

Sample	1	2	3	4	5	6	7	8	9	10	11	12	13
$\bar{x}_j$	14.5	10.3	17.0	9.4	13.2	9.3	17.1	5.5	5.3	16.3	10.5	11.5	8.8

Sample	14	15	16	17	18	19	20	21	22	23	24	25
$\bar{x}_j$	12.6	10.5	16.3	8.7	9.4	11.4	17.6	20.5	21.1	16.3	18.5	20.9

   a Find the centerline and control limits for the $\bar{x}$ chart.

   b Plot the sample means on the $\bar{x}$ chart.

   c Is the process under control? Explain.

The following exercises require a computer and statistical software.

18.4 Thirty samples of size 4 were drawn from a production process. The data were stored in file XR18-04.

   a Construct an S chart.

   b Construct an $\bar{x}$ chart.

   c Do the charts allow you to conclude that the process is under control?

   d If the process went out of control, which of the following is the likely cause: level shift, instability, trend, or cycle?

18.5 The fence of a saw is set so that it automatically cuts 2-by-4s into 96-inch lengths needed to produce prefabricated homes. To ensure that the lumber is cut properly, 3 pieces of wood are measured after each 100 cuts are made. The measurements in inches for the last 40 samples are stored in file XR18-05.

   a Do these data indicate that the process is out of control?

   b If so, when did it go out of control? What is the likely cause: level shift, instability, trend, or cycle?

   c Speculate on how the problem could be corrected.

18.6 An Arc Extinguishing Unit (A.E.U.) is used in the high-voltage electrical industry to eliminate the occurrence of electrical flash from one live 25,000-volt switch contact to another. A small but important component of an A.E.U. is a nonconductive sliding bearing called a (ST-90811) pin guide. The dimensional accuracy of this pin guide is critical to the overall operation of the A.E.U. If any one of its dimensions is "out of spec" (specification), the part will bind within the A.E.U., causing failure. This would cause the complete destruction of both the A.E.U. and the 25,000-volt switch contacts, resulting in a power blackout. A pin guide has a square shape with a circular hole in the center, as shown below with its specified dimensions and tolerance limits.

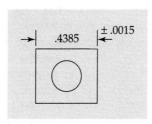

Due to the critical nature of the dimensions of the pin guide, statistical process control is used during long production runs to check that the production process is under control. Suppose that samples of five pin guides are drawn every hour. The results of the last 25 samples are stored in file XR18-06. Do these data allow the technician to conclude that the process is out of control?

18.7 KW Paints is a company that manufactures various kinds of paints and sells them in 1-liter and 4-liter cans. The cans are filled on an assembly line with an automatic valve regulating the amount of paint. If the cans are overfilled, paint and money will be wasted. If the cans are underfilled, customers will complain. To ensure that the proper amount of paint goes into each can, statistical process control is used. Every hour 5 cans are opened, and the volume of paint is measured. The results from the last 30 hours from the 1-liter production line are stored in file XR18-07. To avoid rounding errors, we recorded the volumes (in millimeters) after subtracting 1,000. Thus, the file contains the amounts of overfill and underfill. Draw the $\bar{x}$ and S charts to determine if the process is under control.

18.8 Lear Seating of Kitchener, Ontario, produces seats for Cadillacs and other GM cars and trucks. The Cadillac seat includes a part called the EK headrest. The frame of the headrest is made from steel rods. A machine is used to bend the rod into a U-shape described below. The width is critical; if it is too wide or too narrow, it will not fit into the holes drilled into the seat frame. The process is checked by drawing samples of size 3 every two hours. The last 20 samples are stored in file XR18-08.

    a   What do these data tell you about the process?

    b   If it went out of control, at what sample did this occur?

    c   What is the likely assignable cause?

EK Headrest Frame

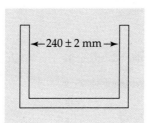

18.4 Control Charts for Variables: $\bar{x}$ and R Charts (Optional)

As you have already seen, we can use the sample variances to estimate the process distribution standard deviation. For technicians who perform the analysis by hand, the calculation of sample variances is relatively time-consuming. Moreover, the formulas that convert S to the centerline and the control limits are complicated. As a consequence, many companies prefer to estimate the process standard deviation by computing the sample ranges. This change affects the creation of the $\bar{x}$ chart and how we test to see if the process standard deviation has changed.

Recall that the range is the difference between the largest and smallest observations in a sample. As a first step in estimating the process standard deviation, we calculate the range for each sample and the mean of the sample ranges (denoted $\bar{R}$).

$$\bar{R} = \frac{\sum_{j=1}^{k} R_j}{k}$$

where R_j is the range of the jth sample.

Mathematicians have developed methods that produce estimates of the standard deviation that are based on the sample range. We estimate the process standard deviation by $\bar{R}/d_2$, where d_2 is a constant that depends on the sample size. Table 8 in Appendix B lists the values of d_2 (as well as other constants required in statistical process control) for sample sizes between 2 and 25. Thus,

$$\text{Lower control limit} = \bar{\bar{x}} - \frac{3(\bar{R}/d_2)}{\sqrt{n}}$$

$$\text{Upper control limit} = \bar{\bar{x}} + \frac{3(\bar{R}/d_2)}{\sqrt{n}}$$

We can simplify the control limits by letting

$$A_2 = \frac{3}{d_2\sqrt{n}}$$

where the values of A_2 are also listed in Table 8 in Appendix B. Using A_2, we can rewrite the control limits.

Centerline and Control Limits for the $\bar{x}$ Chart: Using the Sample Ranges

$$\text{Centerline} = \bar{\bar{x}}$$
$$\text{Lower control limit} = \bar{\bar{x}} - A_2\bar{R}$$
$$\text{Upper control limit} = \bar{\bar{x}} + A_2\bar{R}$$

EXAMPLE 18.3

Repeat Example 18.1, using the sample ranges instead of the sample standard deviations.

SOLUTION

SOLVING BY HAND

Table 18.3 lists the samples, the sample means, and the sample ranges. From these statistics, we find

$$\bar{\bar{x}} = 500.380 \quad \text{and} \quad \bar{R} = 3.934$$

The centerline is drawn at $\bar{\bar{x}} = 500.380$. From Table 8 in Appendix B, we find that with $n = 4$, $A_2 = .729$. The control limits are

Lower control limit $= \bar{\bar{x}} - A_2\bar{R} = 500.380 - .729(3.934) = 497.512$

Upper control limit $= \bar{\bar{x}} + A_2\bar{R} = 500.380 + .729(3.934) = 503.248$

To conduct the pattern tests, we need to determine the width of the zones. The simplest way to do this is to note that the difference between the upper control limit and the centerline is 3 standard deviations of $\bar{x}$. Thus,

$$\text{Width of zones} = \frac{503.248 - 500.380}{3} = .956$$

See the Minitab output below to examine this $\bar{x}$ chart. No mean lies outside the control limits. However, we can see that two out of three points (points 23, 24, and 25) lie in zone A above the centerline.

Table 18.3

Means and Ranges of Samples in Example 18.1

SAMPLE					$\bar{x}_j$	R_j
1	501.02	501.65	504.34	501.10	502.027	3.32
2	499.80	498.89	499.47	497.90	499.015	1.90
3	497.12	498.35	500.34	499.33	498.785	3.22
4	500.68	501.39	499.74	500.41	500.555	1.65
5	495.87	500.92	498.00	499.44	498.557	5.05
6	497.89	499.22	502.10	500.03	499.810	4.21
7	497.24	501.04	498.74	503.51	500.133	6.27
8	501.22	504.53	499.06	505.37	502.545	6.31
9	499.15	501.11	497.96	502.39	500.152	4.43
10	498.90	505.99	500.05	499.33	501.068	7.09
11	497.38	497.80	497.57	500.72	498.367	3.34
12	499.70	500.99	501.35	496.48	499.630	4.87
13	501.44	500.46	502.07	500.50	501.117	1.61
14	498.26	495.54	495.21	501.27	497.570	6.06
15	497.57	497.00	500.32	501.22	499.027	4.22
16	500.95	502.07	500.60	500.44	501.015	1.63
17	499.70	500.56	501.18	502.36	500.950	2.66
18	501.57	502.09	501.18	504.98	502.455	3.80
19	504.20	500.92	500.02	501.71	501.712	4.18
20	498.61	499.63	498.68	501.84	499.690	3.23
21	499.05	501.82	500.67	497.36	499.725	4.46

(continued)

22	497.85	494.08	501.79	501.95	498.918	7.87
23	501.08	503.12	503.06	503.56	502.705	2.48
24	500.75	501.18	501.09	502.88	503.475	2.13
25	502.03	501.44	502.76	503.79	502.505	2.35

Minitab Output for Example 18.3

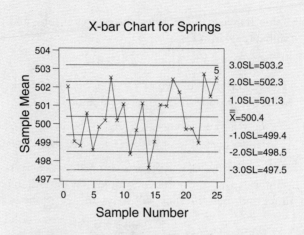

X-bar Chart for Springs

The centerline is 500.4 and the lower and upper control limits are 497.5 and 503.2, respectively. No point lies outside the control limits. Once again, the data fail test 5 at points 23, 24, and 25. Minitab announces this result by placing a "5" at sample 25 on the chart.

MENU COMMANDS

Follow the instructions provided in Example 18.1, except specify **Rbar estimate** instead of **Pooled std. dev.**

Excel Output for Example 18.3

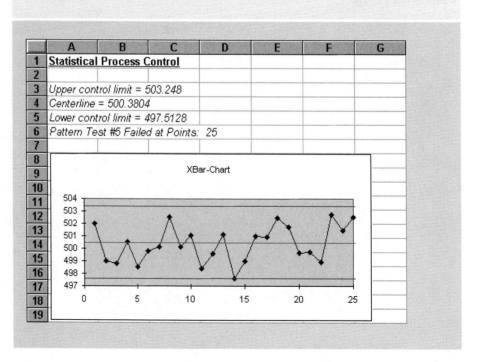

The centerline is 500.3804 and the lower and upper control limits are 497.5128 and 503.248, respectively. No point lies outside the control limits. Once again, the data fail test 5 at points 23, 24, and 25.

COMMANDS

Follow the instructions provided in Example 18.1, except click **R** instead of **S** (to estimate σ).

INTERPRETING THE
RESULTS

Because we used the sample ranges instead of the sample standard deviations, the control limits differed (only slightly) from those computed in Example 18.1. However, the results are the same. We discover that the process went out of control at point 25. The production process would be stopped and corrective action taken.

R Charts

In general, if we use the sample ranges to help create the $\bar{x}$ chart, we use the R *chart*, which graphs sample ranges, to determine when and if the process distribution standard deviation changes. The format is similar to that of the $\bar{x}$ and S charts. The centerline is the mean of the ranges $\bar{R}$. As was the case with the $\bar{x}$ chart, we need an estimate of the standard deviation of the ranges. We estimate that standard deviation with

$$d_3\frac{\bar{R}}{d_2}$$

where d_3 is another constant provided by Table 8 in Appendix B. The control limits are as follows.

$$\text{Lower control limit} = \bar{R} - 3d_3\frac{\bar{R}}{d_2} = \bar{R}\left(1 - \frac{3d_3}{d_2}\right)$$

$$\text{Upper control limit} = \bar{R} + 3d_3\frac{\bar{R}}{d_2} = \bar{R}\left(1 + \frac{3d_3}{d_2}\right)$$

We simplify these formulas by letting

$$D_3 = 1 - \frac{3d_3}{d_2}$$

$$D_4 = 1 + \frac{3d_3}{d_2}$$

Values for D_3 and D_4 are provided in Table 8 in Appendix B for $n = 2$ to 25. For n less than or equal to 6, D_3 is actually negative. However, since a negative control limit is meaningless, the values of D_3 in Table 8 for n less than or equal to 6 are reported as zero.

> **Centerline and Control Limits for R Chart**
>
> $$\text{Centerline} = \bar{R}$$
> $$\text{Lower control limit} = D_3\bar{R}$$
> $$\text{Upper control limit} = D_4\bar{R}$$

EXAMPLE 18.4

Using the data from Example 18.1, construct the R chart.

SOLUTION

SOLVING BY HAND

In Example 18.3, we found $\bar{R} = 3.934$. To calculate the control limits, we find in Table 8 in Appendix B that with $n = 4$, $D_3 = 0$ and $D_4 = 2.282$. Thus,

$$\text{Centerline} = \bar{R} = 3.934$$
$$\text{Lower control limit} = D_3\bar{R} = 0(3.934) = 0$$
$$\text{Upper control limit} = D_4\bar{R} = 2.282(3.934) = 8.977$$

See computer output below to examine the R chart. There is no apparent evidence to infer that the process standard deviation has changed.

USING THE COMPUTER

Minitab Output for Example 18.4

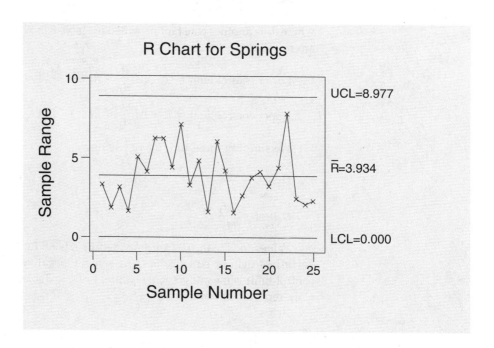

1 Type or import the data into one column.

2 Click **Stat**, **Control Charts**, and **R . . . .**

3 Type the variable name.

4 Use the cursor to select **Subgroup size**, hit **tab**, and type the sample size.

5 Use the cursor to select **Rbar estimate**. Click **OK**.

Open file **XM18-01**.

Springs or **C1**

4

Excel Output for Example 18.4

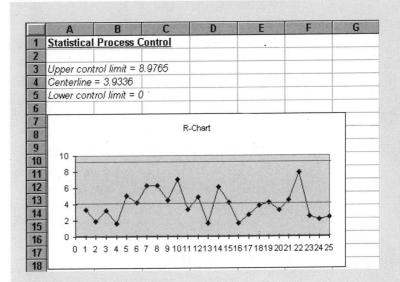

	A	B	C	D	E	F	G
1	**Statistical Process Control**						
2							
3	Upper control limit = 8.9765						
4	Centerline = 3.9336						
5	Lower control limit = 0						

R-Chart

COMMANDS

1 Type or import the data into one column.

2 Click **Tools**, **Data Analysis Plus**, and **Statistical Process Control**.

3 Specify the block coordinates of the data. Do not include cell containing the variable name.

4 Click **R Chart**.

5 Specify the sample size.

COMMANDS FOR EXAMPLE 18.4

Open file **XM18-01**.

A2:A101

4

The R chart indicates that the process distribution standard deviation is unchanged. However, we discovered that the process mean has been altered. Thus, after we've repaired the machine we start anew. We draw more samples and create the $\bar{x}$ and S (or R) charts. When both charts show that the process is under control, we then use them to maintain control.

Note the similarity between centerline and control limits of the $\bar{x}$ chart using R and the $\bar{x}$ chart using S. Obviously the two methods of estimating σ are quite similar. This is confirmed by examining the R chart and the S chart. The two charts are almost identical yielding the same conclusion.

Exercises

18.9 The following statistics were calculated from 30 samples of size 4.

$$\bar{\bar{x}} = 175.6 \qquad \bar{R} = 11.8$$

Calculate the following.

a the centerline and control limits for the $\bar{x}$ chart

b the boundaries of the zones for the $\bar{x}$ chart

c the centerline and control limits for the R chart

18.10 The means of the sample means and sample ranges of 40 samples of size 9 taken from a process under control are $\bar{\bar{x}} = 27.3$ and $\bar{R} = 6.1$.

a Calculate the centerline and control limits for the $\bar{x}$ chart.

b Calculate the zone boundaries for the $\bar{x}$ chart.

c Calculate the centerline and control limits for the R chart.

18.11 The mean of the sample ranges of 50 samples of size 10 taken from a process under control is $\bar{R} = 5.89$. Calculate the centerline and control limits for the R chart.

18.12 Twenty-five samples of size $n = 4$ were drawn. For each sample, the mean and range were computed as shown below.

a Draw the R chart.

b Draw the $\bar{x}$ chart.

c Does it appear that the process is under control?

Sample	1	2	3	4	5	6	7	8	9	10	11	12	13
$\bar{x}_j$	19	22	18	16	18	19	21	23	13	18	23	19	2
R_j	7	11	6	18	5	10	7	7	6	12	8	12	24

Sample	14	15	16	17	18	19	20	21	22	23	24	25
$\bar{x}_j$	26	12	20	22	24	17	12	26	15	24	27	13
R_j	11	13	16	7	20	11	13	10	6	14	20	18

18.13 Twenty samples of size $n = 6$ were drawn. For each sample, the mean and range were computed as shown below.

a Draw the R chart.

b Draw the $\bar{x}$ chart.

c Does it appear that the process is under control?

Sample	1	2	3	4	5	6	7	8	9	10
$\bar{x}_j$	28.6	26.4	26.8	25.9	27.5	27.9	27.0	28.3	29.1	27.9
R_j	7.3	6.2	5.9	6.3	7.3	7.9	6.0	5.8	7.1	6.8

Sample	11	12	13	14	15	16	17	18	19	20
$\bar{x}_j$	29.3	25.9	26.7	27.1	26.9	28.7	28.5	27.7	27.8	28.2
R_j	7.2	4.3	5.0	7.5	7.9	8.1	7.1	8.6	9.4	8.4

18.14 Plastic pipe is used in almost all new homes; it is used in sinks and toilets. If the pipes are too wide or too narrow, they will not connect properly with other pieces of pipe. A manufacturer of 3-inch-diameter pipes employs statistical process control to maintain the quality of its products. The sampling plan is to draw a sample of three 10-foot-long pipes every hour and measure the diameters. Twenty hours ago, the production process was shut down for repairs. The results of the 20 samples taken since then are shown in the accompanying table and stored in file XR18-14. Draw the R and $\bar{x}$ charts. Has the process gone out of control? If so, when?

SAMPLE				$\bar{x}$	R_j
1	3.059	3.002	3.006	3.02233	.057
2	2.980	3.065	3.007	3.01733	.085
3	2.916	3.065	2.959	2.98000	.149
4	2.988	3.020	3.030	3.01267	.042
5	2.986	3.037	3.007	3.01000	.051
6	2.911	2.918	2.938	2.92233	.027
7	2.947	2.977	2.986	2.97000	.039
8	3.025	2.947	2.989	2.98700	.078
9	2.939	3.040	3.040	3.00633	.101
10	2.959	3.023	3.037	3.00633	.078
11	3.002	2.910	2.999	2.97033	.092
12	2.966	2.977	2.922	2.95500	.055
13	2.948	3.008	2.934	2.96333	.074
14	3.000	2.950	2.968	2.97267	.050
15	2.964	2.989	3.070	3.00767	.106
16	3.025	3.017	2.960	3.00067	.065
17	2.996	3.015	2.963	2.99133	.052
18	2.981	2.977	3.067	3.00833	.090
19	3.037	2.935	2.990	2.98733	.102
20	3.011	3.021	2.945	2.99233	.076
				$\bar{\bar{x}} = 2.9892$	$\bar{R} = .07345$

The following exercises require the use of a computer and statistical software.

18.15 Refer to Exercise 18.5.

a Draw the R chart.

b Draw the $\bar{x}$ chart (using the sample ranges to estimate the process standard deviation).

c Is the process under control?

18.16 Refer to Exercise 18.6. Using the R and $\bar{x}$ charts, determine if the process is under control.

18.17 Refer to Exercise 18.7. Using the R and $\bar{x}$ charts, determine if the process is under control.

18.18 Refer to Exercise 18.8. Use the R and $\bar{x}$ charts to discover whether the process appears to be under control.

18.5 Control Chart for Attributes: p Chart

In this section, we introduce a control chart that is used to monitor a process whose results are categorized as either defective or nondefective. We construct a **p chart** to track the proportion of defective units in a series of samples.

p Chart

We draw the p chart in a way similar to the construction of the $\bar{x}$ chart. We draw samples of size n from the process at a minimum of 25 time periods. For each sample, we calculate the sample proportion of defective units, which we label $\hat{p}_j$. We then compute the mean of the sample proportions, which is labeled $\bar{p}$. That is

$$\bar{p} = \frac{\sum\limits_{j=1}^{k} \hat{p}_j}{k}$$

The centerline and control limits are defined as follows.

> **Centerline and Control Limits for the p Chart**
> $$\text{Centerline} = \bar{p}$$
> $$\text{Lower control limit} = \bar{p} - 3\sqrt{\frac{\bar{p}(1-\bar{p})}{n}}$$
> $$\text{Upper control limit} = \bar{p} + 3\sqrt{\frac{\bar{p}(1-\bar{p})}{n}}$$
>
> If the lower control limit is negative, set it equal to zero.

Pattern Tests

As we did in the sections above, we use Minitab's pattern tests. Minitab performs only tests 1 to 4, which are as follows.

Test 1: one point beyond zone A.

Test 2: nine points in a row in zone C or beyond (on the same side of the centerline).

Test 3: six increasing or six decreasing points in a row.

Test 4: fourteen points in a row alternating up and down.

EXAMPLE 18.5

A company that produces 3.5-inch computer disks has been receiving complaints from its customers about the large number of disks that will not store data properly. Company management has decided to institute statistical process control in order to remedy the problem. Every hour, a random sample of 200 disks is taken, and each disk is tested to determine whether it is defective. The results of the first 40 hours are shown in the accompanying table and stored in file XM18-05. Using these data, draw a p chart to monitor the production process. Was the process out of control when the sample results were generated?

SAMPLE	NUMBER OF DEFECTIVES	SAMPLE	NUMBER OF DEFECTIVES	SAMPLE	NUMBER OF DEFECTIVES
1	19	15	18	29	10
2	5	16	20	30	18
3	16	17	13	31	15
4	20	18	6	32	16
5	6	19	8	33	5
6	12	20	3	34	14
7	18	21	8	35	3
8	6	22	7	36	10
9	13	23	4	37	19
10	15	24	19	38	13
11	10	25	3	39	19
12	6	26	19	40	9
13	7	27	9		
14	10	28	10		

SOLUTION

SOLVING BY HAND

For each sample, we compute the proportion of defective disks and calculate the mean sample proportion. We find $\bar{p} = .05762$. Thus,

Centerline $= \bar{p} = .05762$

Lower control limit $= \bar{p} - 3\sqrt{\dfrac{\bar{p}(1-\bar{p})}{n}} = .05762 - 3\sqrt{\dfrac{(.05762)(1-.05762)}{200}} = .008188$

Upper control limit $= \bar{p} + 3\sqrt{\dfrac{\bar{p}(1-\bar{p})}{n}} = .05762 + 3\sqrt{\dfrac{(.05762)(1-.05762)}{200}} = .1071$

Since

$$\sqrt{\dfrac{\bar{p}(1-\bar{p})}{n}} = \sqrt{\dfrac{(.05762)(1-.05762)}{200}} = .01648$$

the boundaries of the zones are as follows.

Zone C: .05762 ± .01648 = (.04114, .0741)

Zone B: .05762 ± 2(.01648) = (.02467, .09057)

Zone A: .05762 ± 3(.01648) = (.008188, .1071)

The output below exhibits this p chart. There is no evidence to infer that the process is out of control.

Minitab Output for Example 18.5

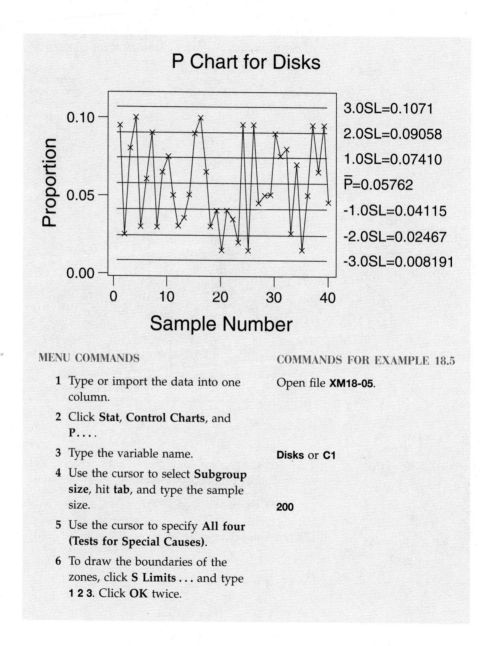

P Chart for Disks

3.0SL=0.1071

2.0SL=0.09058

1.0SL=0.07410

$\bar{P}$=0.05762

-1.0SL=0.04115

-2.0SL=0.02467

-3.0SL=0.008191

MENU COMMANDS	COMMANDS FOR EXAMPLE 18.5
1 Type or import the data into one column.	Open file **XM18-05**.
2 Click **Stat**, **Control Charts**, and **P**....	
3 Type the variable name.	**Disks** or **C1**
4 Use the cursor to select **Subgroup size**, hit **tab**, and type the sample size.	**200**
5 Use the cursor to specify **All four (Tests for Special Causes)**.	
6 To draw the boundaries of the zones, click **S Limits**... and type **1 2 3**. Click **OK** twice.	

Excel Output for Example 18.5

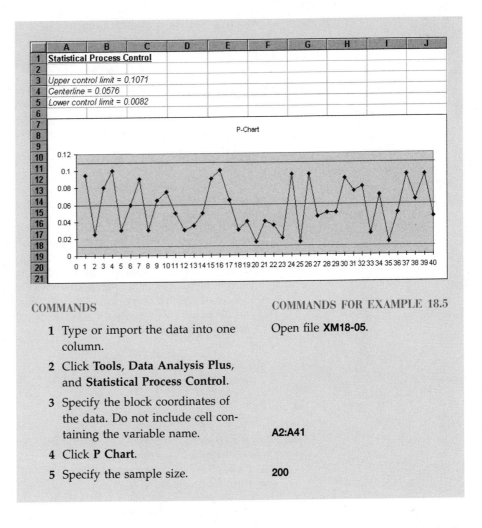

	A	B	C	D	E	F	G	H	I	J
1	Statistical Process Control									
2										
3	Upper control limit = 0.1071									
4	Centerline = 0.0576									
5	Lower control limit = 0.0082									

P-Chart

COMMANDS

1 Type or import the data into one column.

2 Click **Tools, Data Analysis Plus**, and **Statistical Process Control**.

3 Specify the block coordinates of the data. Do not include cell containing the variable name.

4 Click **P Chart**.

5 Specify the sample size.

COMMANDS FOR EXAMPLE 18.5

Open file **XM18-05**.

A2:A41

200

INTERPRETING THE RESULTS

None of the points lies outside the control limits (test 1), and the other test results are negative. There is no evidence to infer that the process is out of control.

The comment we made about R charts is also valid for p charts. That is, sample proportions that are less than the lower control limit indicate a change in the process that we would like to make permanent. We need to investigate the reasons for such a change just as vigorously as we investigate the causes of large proportions of defects.

18.19 In order to ensure that a manufacturing process is under control, 40 samples of size 1,000 were drawn and the number of defectives in each sample was counted. The mean sample proportion was 0.035. Compute the centerline and control limits for the p chart.

18.20 Random samples of 200 widgets were taken on an assembly line every hour for the past 25 hours. The number of defective widgets is shown in the accompanying table and stored in file XR18-20. Are there any points beyond the control limits? If so, what do they tell you about the production process?

Sample	1	2	3	4	5	6	7	8	9	10	11	12	13
Number of defectives	3	5	3	2	2	11	12	6	7	5	0	7	8

Sample	14	15	16	17	18	19	20	21	22	23	24	25
Number of defectives	2	10	6	4	2	10	5	4	11	10	13	14

18.21 Raytheon of Canada Limited produces printed circuit boards (PCBs), which involve a number of soldering operations. At the end of the process, the PCBs are tested to determine if they work properly. There are several causes of PCB failure. Possible causes include bad flux, improper heating, and impurities. A reject rate of less than 0.80% is considered acceptable. Statistical process control is used by Raytheon to constantly check quality. Every hour, 500 PCBs are tested. The number of defective PCBs for the past 25 hours is shown in the accompanying table and stored in file XR18-21. Draw a p chart and apply the pattern tests to determine if the process is under control.

Sample	1	2	3	4	5	6	7	8	9	10	11	12	13
Number of defectives	3	1	2	2	1	2	3	3	3	2	3	0	0

Sample	14	15	16	17	18	19	20	21	22	23	24	25
Number of defectives	0	2	0	0	2	4	1	1	1	4	1	3

18.22 A plant produces 1,000 cordless telephones daily. A random sample of 100 telephones is inspected each day. After 30 days, the following number of defectives was found. (The data are also stored in file XR18-22.) Construct a p chart to determine if the process is out of control.

Sample	1	2	3	4	5	6	7	8	9	10
Number of defectives	5	0	4	3	0	3	1	1	5	0

Sample	11	12	13	14	15	16	17	18	19	20
Number of defectives	2	1	6	0	3	0	5	5	8	5

Sample	21	22	23	24	25	26	27	28	29	30
Number of defectives	0	1	9	6	11	6	6	4	5	10

18.23 The Woodsworth Publishing Company produces millions of books containing hundreds of millions of pages each year. To ensure the quality of the printed page, Woodsworth uses statistical process control. In each production run, 1,000 pages are randomly inspected. The examiners look for print clarity and whether the material is properly centered on the page. The number of defective pages in the last 40 production runs is listed in the accompanying table and stored in file XR18-23. Draw the p chart. Using the pattern tests, can we conclude that the production process is under control?

SAMPLE	NUMBER OF DEFECTIVE PAGES	SAMPLE	NUMBER OF DEFECTIVE PAGES	SAMPLE	NUMBER OF DEFECTIVE PAGES
1	11	15	18	29	21
2	9	16	19	30	17
3	17	17	17	31	20
4	19	18	15	32	17
5	15	19	7	33	17
6	15	20	16	34	18
7	18	21	17	35	23
8	21	22	22	36	29
9	18	23	12	37	24
10	6	24	12	38	27
11	27	25	12	39	23
12	14	26	16	40	21
13	7	27	12		
14	18	28	9		

18.6 Summary

In this chapter, we introduced statistical process control and explained how it contributes to the maintenance of quality. We discussed how control charts detect changes in the process distribution and introduced the $\bar{x}$ chart, S chart, R chart, and p chart.

IMPORTANT TERMS

Statistical process control

Quality control

Under control

Out of control

Specification limits

Centerline

Upper and lower control limits

Control charts for variables

Control chart for attributes

$\bar{x}$ chart

S chart

R chart

p chart

The following exercises require the use of a computer and statistical software.

18.24 The degree to which nuts and bolts are tightened in numerous places on a car is often important. For example, in Toyota cars, a nut holds the rear signal light. If the nut is not tightened sufficiently, it will loosen and fall off; if it is too tight, the light may break. The nut is tightened with a torque wrench with a set clutch. The target torque is 8 kgf/cm (kilogram-force per centimeter) with a tolerance of 2 kgf/cm (7 to 9 kgf/cm). Statistical process control is employed to constantly check the process. Random samples of size 4 are drawn after every 200 nuts are tightened. The data from the last 25 samples are stored in file XR18-24. (The authors are grateful to Ted Couves for contributing this exercise.)

   a Determine if the process is under control.

   b If it is out of control, identify when this occurred and the likely cause.

18.25 A company that manufactures batteries employs statistical process control to ensure that its product functions properly. The sampling plan for the D-cell batteries calls for samples of 500 batteries to be taken and tested. The number of defective batteries in the last 30 samples is stored in file XR18-25. Determine whether the process is under control.

18.26 The seats for the F-150 series Ford trucks are manufactured by Lear Seating. The frames must be 1,496 mm wide with a tolerance of 3 mm. Frames that are wider than 1,497.5 mm or narrower than 1,494.5 mm result in assembly problems, because seat cushions and/or other parts won't fit. The process is tested by drawing random samples of five frames every two hours. The last 25 samples are stored in file XR18-26. What can we conclude from these data?

18.27 A courier delivery company advertises that it guarantees delivery by noon the following day. The statistical process control plan calls for sampling 2,000 deliveries each day to ensure that the advertisement is reasonable. The number of late deliveries for the last 30 days is stored in file XR18-27. What can we conclude from these data?

18.28 Long Manufacturing produces heat exchangers, primarily for the automotive industry. One such product, a transmission oil cooler, is used in the cooling of bus transmissions. It is composed of a series of copper tubes that are soldered into a header. The header must have a diameter of 4.984 inches with a tolerance of .006 inches. Oversize headers result in an inability to assemble the components. Undersize headers result in fluid mixing and possible failure of the device. For every 100 headers produced, the operations manager draws a sample of size 4. The data from the last 25 samples are stored in file XR18-28. What can we conclude from these data?

18.29 Refer to Exercise 18.28. Nuts and bolts are used in the assembly of the transmission oil coolers. They are supposed to be tightened by a torque wrench to 7 foot-pounds with a tolerance of 2 foot-pounds. To test the process, three nuts are tested every three hours. The results for the last 75 hours are stored in file XR18-29. Does it appear that the process is under control?

18.30 Optical scanners are used in all large supermarkets to speed the checkout process. Whenever the scanner fails to read the bar code on the product, the cashier is required to manually punch the code into the register. Obviously, unreadable bar codes slow the checkout process. Statistical process control is used to determine whether the scanner is working properly. Once a day at each checkout counter, a sample of 500 scans is taken and the number of times the scanner is unable to read the bar code is determined. (The sampling process is performed automatically by the cash register.) The results for one checkout counter for the past 25 days are stored in file XR18-30.

    a Draw the appropriate control chart(s).

    b Does it appear that the process went out of control? If so, identify when this happened and suggest several possible explanations for the cause.

18.31 Almost all computer hardware and software producers offer a toll-free telephone number to solve problems associated with their product. The ability to work quickly to resolve difficulties is critical. One software maker's policy is that all calls must be answered by a software consultant within 120 seconds. (All calls are initially answered by computer and the caller is put on hold until a consultant attends to the caller.) To help maintain the quality of the service, four calls per day are monitored. The amount of time before the consultant responds to the caller is recorded. The record of the last 30 days is stored in file XR18-31.

    a Draw the appropriate control chart(s).

    b Does it appear that the process went out of control? If so, when did this happen, and what are the likely causes and remedies?

18.32 Motor oil is packaged and sold in plastic bottles. The bottles are often handled quite roughly, either in delivery to the stores (bottles are packed in boxes, which are stacked to conserve truck space), in the stores themselves, or by the consumer. The bottles must be hardy enough to withstand this treatment without leaking. Before leaving the plant, the bottles undergo statistical process control procedures. Five out of every 10,000 bottles are sampled. The burst strength (the pressure required to burst the bottle) is measured in pounds per square inch (psi). The process is designed to produce bottles that can withstand up to 800 psi. The burst strengths of the last 30 samples are stored in file XR18-32.

    a Draw the appropriate control chart(s).

    b Does it appear that the process went out of control? If so, when did this happen, and what are the likely causes and remedies?

APPENDIX 18.A Minitab Instructions

To construct an $\bar{x}$ chart, type

> **XBARCHART C1 K**

where all the observations are stored in column 1 (in the order in which they occurred) and **K** is the sample size. The $\bar{x}$ chart will be created using the pooled standard deviation as the estimate of the process standard deviation. The subcommand **RBAR** instructs Minitab to estimate the process standard deviation using the mean of the sample ranges.

To perform the pattern tests, use the subcommand **TEST**. Simply type the test number(s) you want to apply. To perform all eight tests, type **TEST 1:8**. To draw the zones, add the subcommand **SLIMITS 1 2 3**. To illustrate, the $\bar{x}$ chart (using R instead of S), zones, and all eight tests for Example 18.3, would be created by typing the following.

> **XBARCHART C1 4;**
> **RBAR;**
> **TEST 1:8;**
> **SLIMITS 1 2 3.**

To create the S chart, type

> **SCHART C1 K**

The R chart is drawn using the command and subcommand

> **RCHART C1 K;**
> **RBAR.**

Finally we draw the p chart using the following command

> **PCHART C1 K**

where **K** is the sample size. Use the **TEST** subcommand to apply any of the four pattern tests. Use the **SLIMITS 1 2 3** subcommand to draw the zones.

19 Statistical Inference: Conclusion

19.1 Introduction

You now have been introduced to about 35 statistical techniques. If you are like most students, you probably understand statistical inference and are capable of interpreting computer output. However, at this point you may not be confident that you can apply statistical techniques in real life. The main problem is that it is difficult to ascertain which statistical procedure to apply. In this chapter, we attempt to calm your fears. We begin by displaying the flowchart that allows statisticians to determine the appropriate technique to apply. As we did in Chapter 13, we provide a guide detailing the parameters, test statistics (including the nonparametric techniques introduced in Appendixes 12.C, 14.B, and 16.C), confidence intervals, and required conditions. The flowchart is augmented by an Excel macro that performs the same function. It is described below.

The guide and flowchart apply to the procedures presented in Chapters 11 through 17. We have omitted statistical process control (Chapter 18) because the use of these techniques tends to be quite obvious and they represent a different kind of inference.

Use the flowchart and guide to determine how each of the exercises and cases is to be addressed. Because these exercises and cases were drawn from a wide variety of applications and require the use of many of the methods introduced in this book, they provide the same kind of challenge faced by real statisticians. By attempting to solve these problems, you will be getting a realistic exposure to statistical applications. Incidentally, this also provides practice in the approach required to succeed in a statistics course examination.

Figure 19.1

Flowchart of Techniques: Statistical Inference

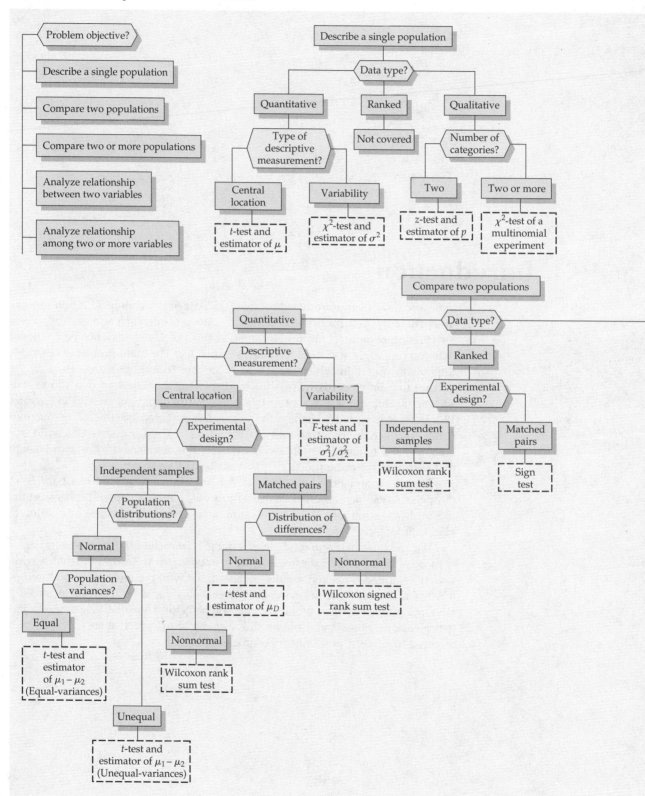

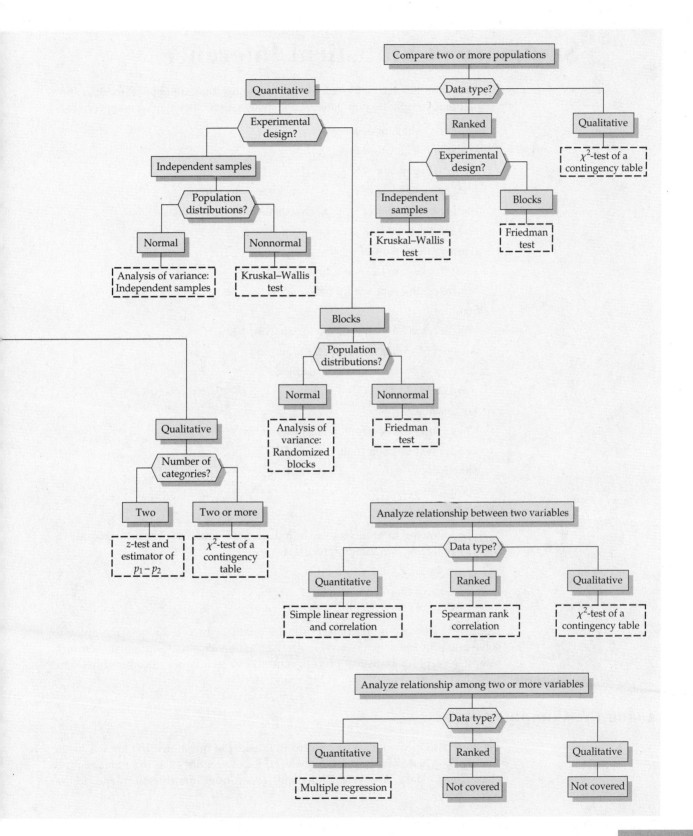

19.2 Identifying the Correct Technique: Summary of Statistical Inference

The following is a list of the inferential techniques that are applied in describing populations, comparing populations, and analyzing relationships among variables.

> t-test and estimator of μ
>
> χ^2-test and estimator of σ^2
>
> z-test and estimator of p
>
> t-test and estimator of $\mu_1 - \mu_2$ (equal-variances formulas)
>
> t-test and estimator of $\mu_1 - \mu_2$ (unequal-variances formulas)
>
> t-test and estimator of μ_D
>
> F-test and estimator of σ_1^2/σ_2^2
>
> z-test (Cases 1 and 2) and estimator of $p_1 - p_2$
>
> Wilcoxon rank sum test for independent samples
>
> Sign test
>
> Wilcoxon signed rank sum test for matched pairs
>
> Analysis of variance: independent samples
>
> Analysis of variance: randomized blocks
>
> Kruskal–Wallis test
>
> Friedman test
>
> Chi-squared test of a multinomial experiment
>
> Chi-squared test of a contingency table
>
> Simple linear regression and correlation
>
> Spearman rank correlation
>
> Multiple regression

The following techniques were introduced in Chapter 18. These techniques are used in analyzing production processes.

> Statistical process control
> > Control charts for variables
> >
> > Control charts for attributes

Figure 19.1 depicts the flowchart used to identify which technique to employ to solve any problem where we must draw an inference about a population from a sample (except for statistical process control). All techniques introduced in Chapters 11 to 17 are shown here and in the guide.

Using the Computer

We have also created an Excel macro that asks the questions that appear in the flowchart. When you supply the answers, Excel identifies the technique. Simply click **Tools**, **Data Analysis Plus**, and **Technique Identification** and follow instructions.

Table 19.1

Summary of Statistical Inference Techniques: Chapters 11 through 17

Problem objective: Describe a single population.

    Data type: Quantitative

        Descriptive measurement: Central location

            Parameter: μ

            Test statistic: $t = \dfrac{\bar{x} - \mu}{s/\sqrt{n}}$

            Interval estimator: $\bar{x} \pm t_{\alpha/2}\dfrac{s}{\sqrt{n}}$

            Required condition: Population is normal.

        Descriptive measurement: Variability

            Parameter: σ^2

            Test statistic: $\chi^2 = \dfrac{(n-1)s^2}{\sigma^2}$

            Interval estimator: $\text{LCL} = \dfrac{(n-1)s^2}{\chi^2_{\alpha/2}}$ $\text{UCL} = \dfrac{(n-1)s^2}{\chi^2_{1-\alpha/2}}$

            Required condition: Population is normal.

    Data type: Qualitative

        Number of categories: Two

            Parameter: p

            Test statistic: $z = \dfrac{\hat{p} - p}{\sqrt{pq/n}}$

            Interval estimator: $\hat{p} \pm z_{\alpha/2}\sqrt{\dfrac{\hat{p}\hat{q}}{n}}$

            Required condition: $np \geq 5$ and $nq \geq 5$ (for test)

                                    $n\hat{p} \geq 5$ and $n\hat{q} \geq 5$ (for estimate)

        Number of categories: Two or more

            Parameters: $p_1, p_2, \ldots, p_k$

            Test statistic: $\chi^2 = \displaystyle\sum_{i=1}^{k} \dfrac{(o_i - e_i)^2}{e_i}$

            Required condition: $e_i \geq 5$

Problem objective: Compare two populations.

    Data type: Quantitative

        Descriptive measurement: Central location

            Experimental design: Independent samples

                Population variances: $\sigma_1^2 = \sigma_2^2$

                Parameter: $\mu_1 - \mu_2$

                Test statistic: $t = \dfrac{(\bar{x}_1 - \bar{x}_2) - (\mu_1 - \mu_2)}{\sqrt{s_p^2\left(\dfrac{1}{n_1} + \dfrac{1}{n_2}\right)}}$

                Interval estimator: $(\bar{x}_1 - \bar{x}_2) \pm t_{\alpha/2}\sqrt{s_p^2\left(\dfrac{1}{n_1} + \dfrac{1}{n_2}\right)}$

                Required condition: Populations are normal.

                If populations are nonnormal, apply Wilcoxon rank sum test for independent samples.

                Population variances: $\sigma_1^2 \neq \sigma_2^2$

                Parameter: $\mu_1 - \mu_2$

(continued)

Test statistic: $t = \dfrac{(\bar{x}_1 - \bar{x}_2) - (\mu_1 - \mu_2)}{\sqrt{\dfrac{s_1^2}{n_1} + \dfrac{s_2^2}{n_2}}}$

d.f. $= \dfrac{(s_1^2/n_1 + s_2^2/n_2)^2}{\left(\dfrac{(s_1^2/n_1)^2}{n_1 - 1} + \dfrac{(s_2^2/n_2)^2}{n_2 - 1}\right)}$

Interval estimator: $(\bar{x}_1 - \bar{x}_2) \pm t_{\alpha/2}\sqrt{\dfrac{s_1^2}{n_1} + \dfrac{s_2^2}{n_2}}$

Required condition: Populations are normal.

Experimental design: Matched pairs

Parameter: μ_D

Test statistic: $t = \dfrac{\bar{x}_D - \mu_D}{s_D/\sqrt{n_D}}$

Interval estimator: $\bar{x}_D \pm t_{\alpha/2}\dfrac{s_D}{\sqrt{n_D}}$

Required condition: Differences are normal.

If differences are nonnormal, apply Wilcoxon signed rank sum test for matched pairs.

Nonparametric technique: Wilcoxon signed rank sum test for matched pairs

Test statistic: $z = \dfrac{T - E(T)}{\sigma_T}$

Required condition: Populations are identical in shape and spread.

Descriptive measurement: Variability

Parameter: σ_1^2/σ_2^2

Test statistic: $F = s_1^2/s_2^2$

Interval estimator: $\text{LCL} = \left(\dfrac{s_1^2}{s_2^2}\right)\dfrac{1}{F_{\alpha/2, \nu_1, \nu_2}}$ $\qquad$ $\text{UCL} = \left(\dfrac{s_1^2}{s_2^2}\right)F_{\alpha/2, \nu_2, \nu_1}$

Required condition: Populations are normal.

Data type: Ranked

Experimental design: Independent samples

Nonparametric technique: Wilcoxon rank sum test for independent samples

Test statistic: $z = \dfrac{T - E(T)}{\sigma_T}$

Required condition: Populations are identical in shape and spread.

Experimental design: Matched pairs

Nonparametric technique: Sign test

Test statistic: $z = \dfrac{x - .5n}{.5\sqrt{n}}$

Required condition: Populations are identical in shape and spread.

Data type: Qualitative

Number of categories: Two

Parameter: $p_1 - p_2$

Test statistic:

Case 1: $H_0: (p_1 - p_2) = 0$

$z = \dfrac{(\hat{p}_1 - \hat{p}_2)}{\sqrt{\hat{p}\hat{q}\left(\dfrac{1}{n_1} + \dfrac{1}{n_2}\right)}}$

Case 2: $H_0: (p_1 - p_2) = D \qquad (D \neq 0)$

$$z = \frac{(\hat{p}_1 - \hat{p}_2) - (p_1 - p_2)}{\sqrt{\dfrac{\hat{p}_1 \hat{q}_1}{n_1} + \dfrac{\hat{p}_2 \hat{q}_2}{n_2}}}$$

Interval estimator: $(\hat{p}_1 - \hat{p}_2) \pm z_{\alpha/2} \sqrt{\dfrac{\hat{p}_1 \hat{q}_1}{n_1} + \dfrac{\hat{p}_2 \hat{q}_2}{n_2}}$

Required conditions: $n_1 \hat{p}_1, n_1 \hat{q}_1, n_2 \hat{p}_2$, and $n_2 \hat{q}_2 \geq 5$

Number of categories: Two or more

Statistical technique: Chi-squared test of a contingency table

Test statistic: $\chi^2 = \sum_{i=1}^{k} \dfrac{(o_i - e_i)^2}{e_i}$

Required condition: $e_i \geq 5$

Problem objective: Compare two or more populations.

Data type: Quantitative

Experimental design: Independent samples

Parameters: $\mu_1, \mu_2, \ldots, \mu_k$

Test statistic: $F = \dfrac{\text{MST}}{\text{MSE}}$

Required conditions: Populations are normal with equal variances.

If populations are nonnormal, apply Kruskal–Wallis test.

Experimental design: Randomized blocks

Parameters: $\mu_1, \mu_2, \ldots, \mu_k$

Test statistic: $F = \dfrac{\text{MST}}{\text{MSE}}$

Required conditions: Populations are normal with equal variances.

If populations are nonnormal, apply Friedman test.

Data type: Ranked

Experimental design: Independent samples

Nonparametric technique: Kruskal–Wallis test

Test statistic: $H = \left[\dfrac{12}{n(n+1)} \sum_{j=1}^{k} \dfrac{T_j^2}{n_j} \right] - 3(n+1)$

Required condition: Populations are identical in shape and spread and $n_j \geq 5$.

Experimental design: Randomized blocks

Nonparametric technique: Friedman test

Test statistic: $F_r = \left[\dfrac{12}{b(k)(k+1)} \sum_{j=1}^{k} T_j^2 \right] - 3b(k+1)$

Required condition: Populations are identical in shape and spread and b or $k \geq 5$.

Data type: Qualitative

Statistical technique: Chi-squared test of a contingency table

Test statistic: $\chi^2 = \sum_{i=1}^{k} \dfrac{(o_i - e_i)^2}{e_i}$

Required condition: $e_i \geq 5$

Problem objective: Analyze the relationship between two variables.

Data type: Quantitative

Parameters: β_0, β_1, ρ (simple linear regression and correlation)

Test statistic: $t = \dfrac{\hat{\beta}_1 - \beta_1}{s_{\hat{\beta}_1}}$ and $t = r\sqrt{\dfrac{(n-2)}{1 - r^2}}$

(continued)

$$\text{Confidence interval: } \hat{y} \pm t_{\alpha/2} \, s_\epsilon \sqrt{\frac{1}{n} + \frac{(x_g - \bar{x})^2}{SS_x}}$$

$$\text{Prediction interval: } \hat{y} \pm t_{\alpha/2} \, s_\epsilon \sqrt{1 + \frac{1}{n} + \frac{(x_g - \bar{x})^2}{SS_x}}$$

Required conditions: ϵ is normally distributed with mean zero and standard deviation σ_ϵ; ϵ values are independent.

Data type: Ranked

Statistical technique: Spearman rank correlation coefficient test

Parameter: ρ_s

Test statistic: $z = r_s \sqrt{n - 1}$

Required condition: none

Data type: Qualitative

Statistical technique: Chi-squared test of a contingency table

Test statistic: $\chi^2 = \sum_{i=1}^{k} \frac{(o_i - e_i)^2}{e_i}$

Required condition: $e_i \geq 5$

Problem objective: Analyze the relationship among two or more variables.

Data type: Quantitative

$\beta_0, \beta_1, \beta_2, \ldots, \beta_k$ (multiple regression)

Test statistics: $t = \dfrac{\hat{\beta}_i - \beta_i}{s_{\hat{\beta}_i}}$ $(i = 1, 2, \ldots, k)$

$$F = \frac{MSR}{MSE}$$

Required conditions: ϵ is normally distributed with mean zero and standard deviation σ_ϵ; ϵ values are independent.

We illustrate the use of the guide and flowchart with the following cases.

CASE 19.1   DO BANKS DISCRIMINATE AGAINST WOMEN BUSINESS OWNERS?—I*

Increasingly, more women are becoming owners of small businesses. However, questions concerning how they are treated by banks and other financial institutions have been raised by women's groups. Banks are particularly important to small businesses, since studies show that bank financing represents about one-quarter of total debt, and that for medium-sized businesses the proportion rises to approximately one-half. If women's requests for loans are rejected more frequently than are men's requests, or if women must pay higher interest charges than men do, women have cause for complaint. Banks might then be subject to criminal as well as civil suits. To examine this issue, a research project was launched.

The researchers surveyed a total of 1,165 business owners, of which 115 were women. The percentage of women in the sample, 9.9%, compares favorably with

---

*Adapted from A. L. Riding and C. S. Swift, "Giving Credit Where It's Due: Women Business Owners and Canadian Financial Institutions," Carleton University Working Paper Series WPS 89-07, 1989.

other sources that indicate that women own about 10% of established small businesses. The survey asked a series of questions to men and women business owners who applied for loans during the previous month. It also determined the nature of the business, its size, and its age. Additionally, the owners were asked about their experiences in dealing with banks. The questions asked in the survey included the following.

1 What is the gender of the owner?

   1 female   2 male

2 Was the loan approved?

   0 no   1 yes

3 If it was approved, what interest rate did you get? (How much above the prime rate was your rate?)

Of the 115 women who asked for a loan, 14 were turned down. A total of 98 men who asked for a loan were rejected. The rates above prime for all loans that were granted were recorded. These data are stored in columns 1 (rates paid by women) and 2 (rates paid by men) in file C19-01.

What do these data disclose about possible gender bias by the banks?

SOLUTION

IDENTIFYING THE
TECHNIQUE

The problem objective is to compare two populations: small businesses owned by women and by men. We can compare them in two ways: whether their loan applications are denied; and for loans granted, how much above prime they pay in interest. Whether the loans are approved is a qualitative variable. Because there are only two possible categories, the appropriate technique is the z-test of $p_1 - p_2$. The interest rate is a quantitative variable, the descriptive measurement is central location, and the samples are independent. A preliminary analysis (shown below) reveals that the amount above prime rate is approximately normally distributed and that the F-test of the ratio of σ_1^2 / σ_2^2 (not shown) indicates that there is not sufficient reason to believe that the variances are unequal. Thus, we use the equal-variances t-test of $\mu_1 - \mu_2$. We will sove this problem using the computer except where manual calculations are necessary.

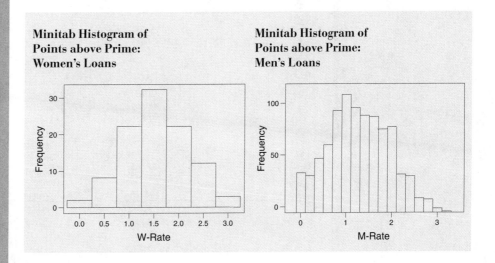

Minitab Histogram of
Points above Prime:
Women's Loans

Minitab Histogram of
Points above Prime:
Men's Loans

Minitab Output of Descriptive Statistics: Women's Loans

Descriptive Statistics

Variable	N	Mean	Median	TrMean	StDev	SEMean
W-Rate	101	1.5454	1.5600	1.5470	0.6367	0.0634

Variable	Min	Max	Q1	Q3
W-Rate	0.1000	2.9800	1.1200	2.0150

Minitab Output of Descriptive Statistics: Men's Loans

Descriptive Statistics

Variable	N	Mean	Median	TrMean	StDev	SEMean
M-Rate	952	1.2777	1.2600	1.2702	0.6676	0.0216

Variable	Min	Max	Q1	Q3
M-Rate	0.0000	3.2900	0.8025	1.7600

Excel Histogram of Points above Prime: Women's Loans

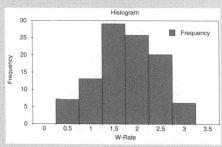

Excel Histogram of Points above Prime: Men's Loans

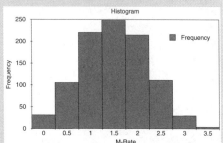

Excel Output of Descriptive Statistics: Women's Loans

	A	B
1	W-Rate	
2		
3	Mean	1.545445545
4	Standard Error	0.063356062
5	Median	1.56
6	Mode	1.44
7	Standard Deviation	0.636720543
8	Sample Variance	0.40541305
9	Kurtosis	-0.389027428
10	Skewness	-0.053613564
11	Range	2.88
12	Minimum	0.1
13	Maximum	2.98
14	Sum	156.09
15	Count	101
16	Confidence Level(95.000%)	0.124175416

Excel Output of Descriptive Statistics: Men's Loans

	A	B
1	M-Rate	
2		
3	Mean	1.277678571
4	Standard Error	0.021635759
5	Median	1.26
6	Mode	0
7	Standard Deviation	0.66756047
8	Sample Variance	0.445636982
9	Kurtosis	-0.465196293
10	Skewness	0.147472036
11	Range	3.29
12	Minimum	0
13	Maximum	3.29
14	Sum	1216.35
15	Count	952
16	Confidence Level(95.000%)	0.042405246

To determine if gender bias exists, we test to determine if the proportion of loans denied is greater for women (p_1) than for men (p_2).

$H_0: p_1 - p_2 = 0$

$H_A: p_1 - p_2 > 0$

This is an example of a Case 1 application. Thus, the test statistic is

$$z = \frac{(\hat{p}_1 - \hat{p}_2)}{\sqrt{\hat{p}\hat{q}\left(\dfrac{1}{n_1} + \dfrac{1}{n_2}\right)}}.$$

We compute the value of the test statistic manually.

$$\hat{p}_1 = \frac{14}{115} = .122$$

$$\hat{p}_2 = \frac{98}{1,050} = .093$$

$$\hat{p} = \frac{112}{1,165} = .096$$

$$z = \frac{(\hat{p}_1 - \hat{p}_2)}{\sqrt{\hat{p}\hat{q}\left(\dfrac{1}{n_1} + \dfrac{1}{n_2}\right)}} = \frac{(.122 - .093)}{\sqrt{(.096)(.904)\left(\dfrac{1}{115} + \dfrac{1}{1,050}\right)}} = 1.00$$

The *p*-value is $P(z > 1.00) = .1587$.

For loans granted, we wish to know whether there is evidence that women's rates (μ_1) are greater than men's (μ_2).

$H_0: \mu_1 - \mu_2 = 0$

$H_A: \mu_1 - \mu_2 > 0$

Minitab Output of Test of Difference between Two Means

Two Sample T-Test and Confidence Interval

```
Twosample T for W-Rate vs M-Rate
             N       Mean      StDev     SE Mean
W-Rate     101      1.545      0.637       0.063
M-Rate     952      1.278      0.668       0.022

95% C.I. for mu W-Rate - mu M-Rate: ( 0.131,  0.404)
T-Test mu W-Rate = mu M-Rate (vs >): T= 3.85  P=0.0001  DF=  1051
Both use Pooled StDev = 0.665
```

Excel Output of Test of Difference between Two Means

A	B	C
1 t-Test: Two-Sample Assuming Equal Variances		
2		
3	W-Rate	M-Rate
4 Mean	1.545445545	1.277678571
5 Variance	0.40541305	0.445636982
6 Observations	101	952
7 Pooled Variance	0.441809776	
8 Hypothesized Mean Difference	0	
9 df	1051	
10 t Stat	3.849500001	
11 P(T<=t) one-tail	6.27509E-05	
12 t Critical one-tail	1.646303645	
13 P(T<=t) two-tail	0.000125502	
14 t Critical two-tail	1.962225724	

INTERPRETING THE
RESULTS

There is not enough evidence to show that women's loan requests are denied more frequently than men's. However, there is overwhelming evidence to infer that the mean rate of women's loans is greater than that for men. There appears to be evidence of gender bias by banks.

DO BANKS DISCRIMINATE AGAINST WOMEN BUSINESS OWNERS?—II*

To help explain the apparent discrimination against women documented in Case 19.1, researchers performed further analyses. In the original study, the following pieces of information were gathered for each company.

1 form of business:

    a proprietorship

    b partnership

    c corporation

2 annual gross sales

3 age of the firm

These data, together with the data from Case 19.1, are stored in file C19-02 in the following way.

Column 1: rates above prime paid by women

Column 2: type of women's business (1 = proprietorship; 2 = partnership; 3 = corporation)

Column 3: annual gross sales of women's businesses (in thousands of dollars)

Column 4: age of women's businesses

Column 5: rates above prime paid by men

Column 6: type of men's business (1 = proprietorship; 2 = partnership; 3 = corporation)

Column 7: annual gross sales of men's businesses (in thousands of dollars)

Column 8: age of men's businesses

What do these data tell you about the alleged discrimination against women by banks?

We are looking for additional reasons to account for the results obtained from Case 19.1. Specifically, we would like to know whether there is a relationship between annual gross sales and interest rates and between age of firm and interest rates. If there are such relationships, we need to know whether men's businesses are older and have higher gross sales. If so, the apparent gender bias shown in Case 19.1 may be explained by banks' legitimate desire to grant favorable terms to more

---

*Adapted from A. L. Riding and C. S. Swift, "Giving Credit Where It's Due: Women Business Owners and Canadian Financial Institutions," Carleton University Working Paper Series WPS 89-07, 1989.

established businesses with higher sales. We can use the data about the type of business to determine whether banks view certain types of businesses more favorably than others, and if men's businesses tend to be of the types favored by banks. Before we can discuss the consequences of such findings, we need to conduct several tests. We will identify the technique to apply by asking specific questions.

1 Do banks grant lower interest rates to businesses with higher sales?

2 Do banks grant lower interest rates to older businesses?

IDENTIFYING THE
TECHNIQUE

For each question, we wish to analyze the relationship between two quantitative variables. Thus, the appropriate technique is simple linear regression and correlation. Because we want to discover whether a relationship exists (and not the mathematical form of the relationship), we will calculate and test the coefficient of correlation. For each pair of variables, we want to know whether the relationship is negative. We test

$H_0: \rho = 0$

$H_A: \rho < 0$

The test statistic is $t = r \sqrt{\dfrac{(n-2)}{1-r^2}}$

The rejection region is $t < -t_{.05,1051} = -1.645$

Minitab Output of Coefficients of Correlation between Interest Rates and Sales

Correlations (Pearson)

Correlation of Rate and Sales = -0.270

Minitab Output of Coefficients of Correlation between Interest Rates and Age

Correlations (Pearson)

Correlation of Rate and Age = -0.191

Excel Output of Coefficient of Correlation between Interest Rates and Sales

	A	B	C
1		Rate	Sales
2	Rates	1	
3	Sales	-0.26997	1

Excel Output of Coefficient of Correlation between Interest Rates and Age

	A	B	C
1		Rate	Age
2	Rates	1	
3	Age	-0.19147	1

The values of the test statistics are calculated below.

Interest rates and annual gross sales:

$$\text{Test statistic: } t = r\sqrt{\frac{(n-2)}{1-r^2}} = -.270\sqrt{\frac{(1,053-2)}{1-(-.270)^2}} = -9.09$$

Interest rates and age:

$$\text{Test statistic: } t = r\sqrt{\frac{(n-2)}{1-r^2}} = -.191\sqrt{\frac{(1,053-2)}{1-(-.191)^2}} = -6.31$$

INTERPRETING THE
RESULTS

There is overwhelming statistical evidence to infer that banks grant lower rates to older businesses and businesses with higher sales.

This result presents two additional questions.

3 Do women's businesses have lower gross sales than men's businesses?

4 Are women's businesses younger than men's businesses?

IDENTIFYING THE
TECHNIQUE

The problem objective is to compare two populations of quantitative data. Using a similar analysis to that employed in Case 19.1, we discover that the appropriate technique for each question is the t-test of $\mu_1 - \mu_2$. For both questions, we test the following hypotheses (where μ_1 equals the mean (annual gross sales and age) of women's businesses and μ_2 equals the mean (annual gross sales and age) of men's businesses).

$$H_0: \mu_1 - \mu_2 = 0$$
$$H_A: \mu_1 - \mu_2 < 0$$

Minitab Output of the Test of the Difference between Two Means: Sales

Two Sample T-Test and Confidence Interval

```
Twosample T for W-Sales vs M-Sales
             N      Mean     StDev    SE Mean
W-Sales    101       552       245         24
M-Sales    952      1183       359         12

95% C.I. for mu W-Sales - mu M-Sales: ( -703,  -560)
T-Test mu W-Sales = mu M-Sales (vs <): T= -17.27  P=0.0000  DF=  1051
Both use Pooled StDev =  349
```

Minitab Output of the Test of the Difference between Two Means: Age

Two Sample T-Test and Confidence Interval

```
Twosample T for W-Age vs M-Age
             N      Mean     StDev    SE Mean
W-Age      101      9.24      4.00       0.40
M-Age      952     12.58      5.20       0.17

95% C.I. for mu W-Age - mu M-Age: ( -4.39,  -2.29)
T-Test mu W-Age = mu M-Age (vs <): T= -6.26  P=0.0000  DF=  1051
Both use Pooled StDev = 5.10
```

Excel Output of the Test
of the Difference between
Two Means: Sales

	A	B ·	C
1	t-Test: Two-Sample Assuming Equal Variances		
2			
3		W-Sales	M-Sales
4	Mean	551.5544554	1183.109244
5	Variance	60133.2495	128618.4402
6	Observations	101	952
7	Pooled Variance	122102.247	
8	Hypothesized Mean Difference	0	
9	df	1051	
10	t Stat	-17.27086858	
11	P(T<=t) one-tail	2.50838E-59	
12	t Critical one-tail	1.646303645	
13	P(T<=t) two-tail	5.01676E-59	
14	t Critical two-tail	1.962225724	

Excel Output of the Test
of the Difference between
Two Means: Age

	A	B	C
1	t-Test: Two-Sample Assuming Equal Variances		
2			
3		W-Age	M-Age
4	Mean	9.237623762	12.57878151
5	Variance	15.9829703	27.05372386
6	Observations	101	952
7	Pooled Variance	26.00036957	
8	Hypothesized Mean Difference	0	
9	df	1051	
10	t Stat	-6.261410771	
11	P(T<=t) one-tail	2.77515E-10	
12	t Critical one-tail	1.646303645	
13	P(T<=t) two-tail	5.55031E-10	
14	t Critical two-tail	1.962225724	

There is very strong statistical evidence to infer that men own businesses that are older than women's and that men's businesses have larger gross sales than women's. This result is not surprising, since only in the last 20 years have women become involved in full-time work in large numbers. Up until about 1975 ownership of businesses had been a male domain. Moreover, more established businesses tend to have higher gross sales.

There is one more factor that may explain the outcome of Case 19.1. It is the type of business.

5 Do the data allow us to infer that certain types of businesses have different rates of interest?

There are three populations of quantitative data to compare: interest rates for proprietorships, for partnerships, and for corporations. The appropriate technique is the analysis of variance. (We can show that the required conditions are satisfied.)

H_0: $\mu_1 = \mu_2 = \mu_3$

H_A: At least two means differ.

Minitab Output of the
Analysis of Variance of
Interest Rates among the
Three Types of Businesses

One-Way Analysis of Variance

```
Analysis of Variance on Rate
Source      DF        SS        MS        F        p
Bus          2     3.455     1.728     3.88    0.021
Error     1050   467.434     0.445
Total     1052   470.889
                                    Individual 95% CIs For Mean
                                    Based on Pooled StDev
Level       N      Mean     StDev -+---------+---------+---------+-----
    1     193    1.4166    0.6415                      (-------*-------)
    2      86    1.2114    0.6830 (-----------*------------)
    3     774    1.2853    0.6717               (---*---)
                                  -+---------+---------+---------+-----
Pooled StDev =    0.6672
```

Excel Output of the
Analysis of Variance of
Interest Rates among the
Three Types of Businesses

	A	B	C	D	E	F	G
1	Anova: Single Factor						
2							
3	SUMMARY						
4	Groups	Count	Sum	Average	Variance		
5	Proprietorship	193	273.41	1.416632124	0.411483911		
6	Partnership	86	104.18	1.211395349	0.466553324		
7	Corporation	774	994.85	1.285335917	0.451192837		
8							
9							
10	ANOVA						
11	Source of Variation	SS	df	MS	F	P-value	F crit
12	Between Groups	3.455093045	2	1.727546522	3.880598812	0.02093512	3.004295479
13	Within Groups	467.4340061	1050	0.445175244			
14							
15	Total	470.8890991	1052				

The statistical analysis reveals that there are differences in rates among the three types of businesses.

Finally, we need to know whether men and women own different types of businesses.

6 Is there a relationship between gender and business type?

The problem objective is to analyze the relationship between two qualitative variables, gender and business type. The appropriate method is the chi-squared test of a contingency table.

H_0: The two variables are independent.

H_A: The two variables are dependent.

The test statistic is $\chi^2 = \sum_{i=1}^{k} \frac{(o_i - e_i)^2}{e_i}$

and the rejection region is $\chi^2 > \chi^2_{.05,2} = 5.99147$

Tabulated Statistics

```
ROWS: Gender      COLUMNS: Bus

              1        2        3       ALL

    1        31       10       60       101
    2       162       76      714       952
  ALL       193       86      774      1053
CHI-SQUARE =     12.750    WITH D.F.  =      2

    CELL CONTENTS --
              COUNT
```

	A	B	C	D	E
1	**Contingency Table**				
2					TOTAL
3		31	10	60	**101**
4		162	76	714	**952**
5	TOTAL	**193**	**86**	**774**	1053
6	Test Statistic CHI-Squared = 12.7504				
7	P-Value = 0.0017				

There is a relationship between gender and type of business. The proportion of women's businesses in this study is 9.6%. From the contingency table, you can see that the proportion of proprietorships owned by women is 31/193 = 16.1%. From the analysis of variance printout, we discover that, on average, proprietorships pay the highest interest rates. Apparently, women own businesses that banks view as riskier, resulting in higher rates of interest.

Interpreting the Results of Cases 19.1 and 19.2

Cases 19.1 and 19.2 present statisticians with real challenges. The results of the cases are contradictory. One case presents evidence of bias and the other provides evidence to suggest that the apparent bias is actually attributable to other factors. Results such as these have led less-than-competent observers to state that one can prove anything with statistics. Although there are often several different interpretations of data based on different analyses, we can perform further analyses to arrive at the truth. Consider how we can resolve the apparent contradictions in Cases 19.1 and 19.2. It is necessary to consider carefully which data and techniques we should use. You will encounter our answer eventually.

19.3 The Last Word

We have come to the end of the journey that began with the words "Statistics is a way to get information from data." You will shortly write the final examination in your statistics course. (We assume that readers of this book are taking a statistics course and not just reading it for fun.) If you believe that this event will be the point where you and statistics part company, you could not be more wrong. In the world into which you are about to graduate, the potential applications of statistical techniques are virtually limitless. However, if you are unable or unwilling to employ statistics, you cannot consider yourself to be competent. Can you imagine a marketing manager who does not fully understand marketing concepts and techniques? Can an accountant who knows little about accounting principles do his or her job? Similarly, you cannot be a competent decision maker without a comprehension of statistical concepts and techniques.

In our experience, we have come across far too many people who display an astonishing ignorance of probability and statistics. In some cases, this is displayed in the way they gamble. (Talk to people in a casino in Las Vegas or Atlantic City and discover how many believe in the law of averages; see how many of them lose money.) We have seen managers who regularly make decisions involving millions of dollars who don't understand the fundamental principles that should govern the way decisions are made. The worst may be the managers who have access to vast amounts of information no further away than the nearest computer but don't know how to get it or even that it is there.

This raises the question, "What statistical concepts and techniques will you need for your life after the final exam?" We don't expect students to remember the formulas (or computer commands) that calculate the interval estimates or test statistics. (Statistics reference books are available for that purpose.) However, you must know what you can and cannot do with statistical techniques. You must remember a number of important principles that were covered in this book. To assist you, we have selected the 12 most important concepts and listed them. They are drawn from the "Developing an Understanding of Statistical Concepts" subsections that are scattered throughout the book. We hope that they prove useful to you.

TWELVE STATISTICAL CONCEPTS YOU NEED FOR LIFE AFTER THE STATISTICS FINAL EXAM

1 Statistical techniques are methods that convert data into information. Descriptive techniques describe and summarize; inferential techniques allow us to make estimates and draw conclusions about populations from samples.

2 We need a large number of techniques because there are numerous objectives and types of data. There are three types of data: quantitative (real numbers), qualitative (categories), and ranked (ratings). Each combination of data type and objective requires specific techniques.

3 We gather data by various sampling plans. However, the validity of any statistical outcome is dependent on the validity of the sampling. "Garbage in–garbage out" very much applies in statistics.

4 The sampling distribution is the source of statistical inference. The interval estimator and the test statistic are derived directly from the sampling distribution. We can create the sampling distribution for any statistic either empirically or theoretically.

5 All inferences are actually probability statements based on the sampling distribution. Because the probability of an event is defined as the proportion of times the event occurs in the long run, we must interpret confidence

interval estimates in these terms. A 95% confidence interval estimator is an interval that will correctly estimate the parameter 95% of the time in the long run.

6 All tests of hypotheses are conducted similarly. We assume that the null hypothesis is true. We then compute the value of the test statistic. If the difference between what we have observed (and calculated) and what we expect to observe is too large, we reject the null hypothesis. The standard that decides what is "too large" is determined by the probability of a Type I error.

7 In any test of hypothesis (and in most decisions) there are two possible errors, Type I and Type II errors. The relationship between the probability of these errors helps us decide where to set the standard. If we set the standard so high that the probability of a Type I error is very small, we increase the probability of a Type II error. A procedure designed to decrease the probability of a Type II error must have a relatively large probability of a Type I error.

8 The sampling distributions that are used for quantitative data are the Student t and the F. These distributions are related so that the various techniques for quantitative data are themselves related. We can use the analysis of variance in place of the t-test of two means. We can use regression analysis with indicator variables in place of the analysis of variance. We often build a model to represent relationships among quantitative variables, including indicator variables.

9 In analyzing quantitative data, we attempt to explain as much of the variation as possible. By doing so, we can learn a great deal about whether populations differ and what variables affect the response (dependent) variable.

10 The techniques used on qualitative data require that we count the number of times each category occurs. The counts are then used to compute statistics. The sampling distributions we use for qualitative data are the z (standard normal) and the chi-squared distributions. These distributions are related, which also describes the relationship among the techniques.

11 The techniques used on ranked data are based on a ranking procedure. Statisticians call these techniques nonparametric. Because the requirements for the use of nonparametric techniques are less than those for a parametric procedure, we often use nonparametric techniques in place of parametric ones when the required conditions for the parametric test are not satisfied. To ensure the validity of a statistical technique, we must check the required conditions.

12 We can obtain data through experimentation or by observation. Observational data lend themselves to several conflicting interpretations. Data gathered by an experiment are more likely to lead to a definitive interpretation. In addition to designing experiments, statisticians can also select particular sample sizes to produce the accuracy and confidence they desire.

We believe that these concepts will serve you well in reading and understanding reports that use statistics. They will also allow you to exploit fully the sets of data that you will encounter in your professional life and apply the appropriate statistical technique that converts the data into information. In so doing, you will be a better decision-maker.

As in Chapter 13, the following exercises require the use of a computer and statistical software. All students should at least attempt to identify the techniques required to answer the questions. Students with the necessary resources should produce the answers and check the required conditions.

19.1 The widespread use of salt on roads in Canada and the northern United States during the winter and acid precipitation throughout the year combine to cause rust on cars. Car manufacturers and other companies offer rust-proofing services to help purchasers preserve the value of their cars. A consumer protection agency decides to determine whether there are any differences between the rust protection provided by automobile manufacturers and that provided by two competing types of rust-proofing services. As an experiment, 60 identical new cars are selected. Of these, 20 are rust-proofed by the manufacturer. Another 20 are rust-proofed using a method that applies a liquid to critical areas of the car. The liquid hardens, forming a (supposedly) lifetime bond with the metal. The last 20 are treated with oil and are retreated every 12 months. The cars are then driven under similar conditions in a Minnesota city. The number of months until the first rust appears is recorded and stored in columns 1 to 3, respectively, in file XR19-01.

Is there sufficient evidence to conclude that at least one rust-proofing method is different from the others?

19.2 Mutual funds minimize risks by diversifying the investments they make. There are mutual funds that specialize in particular types of investments. For example, the TD Precious Metal Mutual Fund buys shares in gold mining companies. The value of this mutual fund depends on a number of factors related to the companies in which the fund invests as well as on the price of gold. In order to investigate the relationship between the value of the fund and the price of gold, an M.B.A. student gathered the daily fund price and the daily price of gold for a 28-day period. These data are stored in columns 1 and 2, respectively, of file XR19-02. What conclusions can be drawn from these data? (The authors are grateful to Jim Wheat for writing this exercise.)

19.3 One of the ways in which advertisers measure the value of television commercials is by telephone surveys conducted shortly after commercials are aired. Respondents who watched a certain television station at a given time period, during which the commercial appeared are asked if they can recall the name of the product in the commercial. Suppose an advertiser wants to compare the recall proportions of two commercials. The first commercial is relatively inexpensive. A second commercial shown a week later is quite expensive to produce. The advertiser decides that the second commercial is viable only if its recall proportion is more than 15% higher than the recall proportion of the first commercial. Two surveys of 500 television viewers each were conducted after each commercial was aired. Each person was asked whether he or she remembererd the product name. The results are stored in columns 1 (commercial 1) and 2 (commercial 2) (1 = remembered the product name and 0 = did not remember the product name) in file XR19-03. Can we infer that the second commercial is viable?

19.4 A small but important part of a university library's budget is the amount collected in fines on overdue books. Last year, a library collected $75,652.75 in fine payments; however, the head librarian suspects that some employees are not bothering to collect the fines on overdue books. In an effort to learn more about the situation, she asked a sample of 400 students (out of a total student population of 50,000) how many books they had returned late to the library in the previous 12 months. They were also asked how many days overdue the books had been. The results indicated that the total number of days overdue ranged from 0 to 55 days. The number of days overdue was stored in file XR19-04.

  a Estimate with 95% confidence the average number of days overdue for all 50,000 students at the university.

b If the fine is 25 cents per day, estimate the amount that should be collected annually. Should the librarian conclude that not all the fines were collected?

19.5 There are two drugs used to treat heart attack victims. Streptokinase, which has been available since 1959, costs about $460. The second drug is t-PA, a genetically engineered product that sells for about $2,900. Both Streptokinase and t-PA work by opening the arteries and dissolving blood clots, which are the cause of heart attacks. Several previous studies have failed to reveal any differences between the effects of the two drugs. Consequently, in many countries where health care is funded by governments, physicians are required to use the less-expensive Streptokinase. However, t-PA's maker, Genentech Inc., contended that in the earlier studies showing no difference between the two drugs, their drug was not used in the right way. Genentech decided to sponsor a more thorough experiment. The experiment was organized in 15 countries, including the United States and Canada, and involved a total of 41,000 patients. In this study, t-PA was given to patients in 90 minutes instead of three hours as in previous trials. Half of the sample of 41,000 patients were treated by a rapid injection of t-PA with intravenous heparin, while the other half received Streptokinase along with heparin. The number of deaths in each sample was recorded. A total of 1,497 patients treated with Streptokinase died, while 1,292 patients who received t-PA died. Perform whatever statistical procedure you think is appropriate to help determine which drug is superior and whether the difference in cost should be ignored.

19.6 A large textile firm has been accused by the federal government of discrimination in hiring. In compliance with a court order, the firm produced the results of the last 1,000 job applications. These data are stored in file XR19-06 using the following format.

Column 1: code = 1 if person is hired
code = 0 if person is rejected

Column 2: code = 1 if person is male
code = 2 if person is female

Column 3: code = 1 if person is Caucasian
code = 2 if person is black
code = 3 if person is Hispanic

a On the basis of these data, can we conclude that the firm is guilty of discriminatory hiring practices on the basis of sex?

b Can we conclude that the firm is guilty of discrimination on the basis of race?

19.7 How consistent are professional athletes? Do they perform at about the same level year-in and year-out, or do they have great seasons interspersed with bad ones? To answer these questions for hockey players, an M.B.A. student randomly selected 50 National Hockey League players who played in the 1992–1993 and 1993–1994 seasons. For each player, he recorded the average points per game and their plus/minus scores. (Plus/minus scores measure the number of goals their teams score minus the number of goals the opposing team scores while that player is on the ice.) These data are stored in file XR19-07 in the following way.

Column 1: 1993–1994 points per game

Column 2: 1993–1994 plus/minus

Column 3: 1992–1993 points per game

Column 4: 1992–1993 plus/minus

What conclusions can you draw from these data? (The authors are grateful to Gordon Barnett for writing this exercise.)

19.8 Professional athletes in North America are paid very well for their ability to play games that amateurs play for fun. To determine the factors that influence a team to pay a hockey player's salary, an M.B.A. student randomly selected 50 hockey players who played in the 1992–1993 and 1993–1994 seasons. He recorded their salaries at the end of the 1993–1994 season as well as a number of performance measures in the previous two seasons. The following data were recorded in file XR19-08.

Columns 1 and 2: games played in 1992–1993 and 1993–1994

Columns 3 and 4: goals scored in 1992–1993 and 1993–1994

Columns 5 and 6: assists recorded in 1992–1993 and 1993–1994

Columns 7 and 8: plus/minus score in 1992–1993 and 1993–1994

Columns 9 and 10: penalty minutes served in 1992–1993 and 1993–1994

Column 11: salary in U.S. dollars

(Plus/minus is the number of goals scored by his team minus the number of goals scored by the opposing team while the player is on the ice.)

Develop a model that analyzes the relationship between salary and the performance measures. Describe your findings. (The authors wish to thank Gordon Barnett for writing this exercise.)

19.9 In the door-to-door selling of vacuum cleaners, various factors influence sales. The Birk Vacuum Cleaner Company considers its sales pitch and overall package to be extremely important. As a result, it often thinks of new ways to sell its product. Because the company's management dreams up so many new sales pitches each year, there is a two-stage testing process. In stage 1, a new plan is tested with a relatively small sample. If there is sufficient evidence that the plan increases sales, a second, considerably larger, test is undertaken. The statistical test is performed so that there is only a 1% chance of concluding that the new pitch is successful in increasing sales when it actually does not increase sales. In a stage 1 test to determine if the inclusion of a "free" 10-year service contract increases sales, 100 sales representatives were selected at random from the company's list of several thousand. The monthly sales of these representatives were recorded for one month prior to use of the new sales pitch and for one month after its introduction. The results are stored in file XR19-9.

Should the company proceed to stage 2?

19.10 Simco Inc. is a manufacturer that purchased a new piece of equipment designed to reduce costs. After several months of operation, the results were quite unsatisfactory. The operations manager believes that the problem lies with the machine's operators, who were unable to master the required skills. It was decided to establish a training program to upgrade the skills of those workers with the greatest likelihood of success. To do so, the company needed to know which skills are most needed to run the machine. Experts identified six such skills. They are dexterity, attention to detail, teamwork skills, mathematical ability, problem-solving skills, and technical knowledge. To examine the issue, a random sample of workers was drawn. Workers were measured on each of the six skills through a series of paper-and-pencil tests and through supervisor ratings. Additionally, each worker received a score on the quality of his or her actual work on the machine. These data are stored in columns 1 through 7 of file XR19-10. (Columns 1 to 6 are the scores on the skills tests and column 7 stores the quality-of-work scores.) Identify the skills that affect the quality of work. (We are grateful to Scott Bergen for writing this exercise.)

19.11 There are enormous differences between health care systems in the United States and Canada. In a study to examine one dimension of these differences, 300 heart attack victims in each country were randomly selected. (Results of the study conducted by Dr. Daniel Mark of Duke University Medical Center, Dr. David Naylor of Sunnybrook Hospital in Toronto, and Dr. Paul Armstrong of the University of

Alberta were published in the *Toronto Sun*, 27 October 1994.) Each patient was asked the following questions regarding the effect of his or her treatment.

1   How many days did it take you to return to work?

2   Do you still have chest pain? (This question was asked 1 month, 6 months, and 12 months after the patients' heart attacks.)

The responses are stored in file XR19-11 in the following way.

Column 1: code representing nationality: 1 = U.S.; 2 = Canada

Column 2: responses to question 1

Column 3: responses to question 2—1 month after heart attack: 1 = yes;
         0 = no

Column 4: responses to question 2—6 months after heart attack: 1 = yes;
         0 = no

Column 5: responses to question 2—12 months after heart attack: 1 = yes;
         0 = no

Can we conclude at the 5% significance level that recovery is faster in the United States?

19.12   Sales of a product may depend on its placement in a store. Cigarette manufacturers frequently offer discounts to retailers who display their products more prominently than competing brands. In order to examine this phenomenon more carefully, a cigarette manufacturer (with the assistance of a national chain of restaurants) planned the following experiment. In 20 restaurants, the manufacturer's brand was displayed behind the cashier's counter with all the other brands (this was called position 1). In another 20 restaurants, the brand was placed separately but close to the other brands (position 2). In a third group of 20 restaurants, the cigarettes were placed in a special display next to the cash register (position 3). The number of cartons sold during one week at each restaurant was recorded and is stored in file XR19-12 (column 1 contains all the sales and column 2 identifies the positions).

  a   Is there sufficient evidence to infer that sales of cigarettes differ according to placement?

  b   Comment on the policy of offering discounts to the retailer for displaying their product more prominently.

19.13   The Scholastic Aptitude Test (SAT), which is organized by the Educational Testing Service (ETS), is important to high school students seeking admission to colleges and universities throughout the United States. A number of companies offer courses to prepare students for the SAT. The Stanley H. Kaplan Educational Center claims that its students gain an average of 110–150 points by taking its course. ETS, however, insists that preparatory courses can improve a score by only 30–40 points. (The minimum and maximum scores of the SAT are 400 and 1,600, respectively.) Suppose a random sample of 40 students wrote the exam, then took the Kaplan preparatory course, and then wrote the exam again. The results of both tests are stored in columns 1 and 2, respectively, of file XR19-13. Do these data provide sufficient evidence to refute both the ETS and Kaplan claims?

19.14   After a recent study, researchers reported on the effects of folic acid on the occurrence of spina bifida—a birth defect in which there is incomplete formation of the spine. A sample of 2,000 women who gave birth to children with spina bifida was recruited. Prior to attempting to get pregnant again, half the sample were given regular doses of folic acid, and the other half were given a placebo. After 18 months, there were 1,209 births. The number of births and the number of children born with spina bifida are shown. Conduct any statistical procedure you think appropriate and comment on the effect of folic acid on the incidence of spina bifida.

	GROUP TAKING FOLIC ACID	GROUP TAKING PLACEBOS
Number of births	597	612
Number of children born with spina bifida	6	21

19.15 In recent years, North Americans have experienced flooding in various parts of the continent. In an effort to develop flood-forecasting tools, scientists wanted to determine the relationship between river flows and precipitation and evaporation. In one study, scientists gathered annual data for the total discharge of water on the Grand River at Galt, Ontario. They also recorded precipitation (snow and rain) and a measure of potential evaporation (which is a function of temperature, humidity, and wind) for each year between 1914 and 1980 around Galt. These data are stored in columns 1 (potential evaporation); 2 (precipitation in millimeters); and 3 (river flow in cubic decimeters) in file XR19-15. It is generally believed that flow and precipitation should be positively related and flow and potential evaporation should be negatively related. Do the data confirm the scientists' beliefs? (This exercise was prepared by Lynette Snelgrove. The data are from *The Impact of Climate Change on the Water in the Grand River Basin, Ontario*, Department of Geography Publication Series No. 40, University of Waterloo.)

19.16 The image of the U.S. Postal Service has suffered in recent years. One reason may be the perception that postal workers are rude in their dealings with the public. In an effort to improve its image, the Postal Service is contemplating the introduction of public relations seminars for all of its inside workers. Because of the substantial costs involved, the Postal Service decided to institute the seminars only if there is more than a 25% reduction in the number of written customer complaints about personnel who took the seminars. As a trial, the employees of 30 large postal centers attended the seminar. The monthly average number of complaints per center (for all centers) was 640 before the trial. The number of complaints in the 30 centers is stored in file XR19-16. Can we conclude that the seminars should be instituted?

19.17 Some psychologists believe that there are at least three different personality types: type A is the aggressive workaholic; type B is the relaxed underachiever; type C displays various characteristics of types A and B. The personnel manager of a large insurance company believes that, among life insurance salespersons, there are equal numbers of all three personality types and that their degree of satisfaction and sales ability are not influenced by personality type. In a survey of 150 randomly selected salespersons, he determined the type of personality, measured their job satisfaction on a seven-point scale (where 1 = very dissatisfied and 7 = very satisfied), and determined the total amount of life insurance sold by each during the previous year. The results are stored in file XR19-17 using the following format.

Column 1: personality type (A = 1; B = 2; C = 3)

Column 2: job satisfaction

Column 3: total amount of life insurance sold (in hundreds of thousands of
　　　　　dollars)

Test all three of the personnel manager's beliefs. That is, test to determine whether there is enough evidence to justify the following conclusions.
i The proportions of each personality type are different.
ii The job satisfaction measures for each personality type are different.
iii The life insurance sales for each personality type are different.

19.18 It is generally believed that salespeople who are paid on a commission basis out-perform salespeople who are paid a fixed salary. Some management consultants argue, however, that in certain industries the fixed-salary salesperson may sell more because the consumer will feel less sales pressure and respond to the salesperson less as an antagonist. In an experiment to study this, a random sample of 115 sales-people from a retail clothing chain was selected. Of these, 59 salespeople were paid a fixed salary, and the remaining 56 were paid a commission on each sale. The total dollar amount of one month's sales for each was recorded and stored in columns 1 (fixed salary) and 2 (commission) in file XR19-18.

    a   Can we conclude that the commission salesperson outperforms the fixed-salary salesperson?

    b   Estimate with 95% confidence the difference in average monthly sales between the two types of salespeople.

19.19 It is generally known that secondhand smoke can be detrimental to one's health. As a result, an insurance company that sells life insurance at group rates to large com-panies is considering offering discounts to companies that have no-smoking poli-cies. In order to help make the decision, the records of two companies are exam-ined. Company 1 has had a no-smoking policy for the past five years, while company 2 does not have such a policy. A total of 1,000 men between the ages of 50 and 60 are randomly selected from each company. Each man was categorized as suffering from lung disease, heart disease, heart and lung disease, or neither heart nor lung disease. These data are stored in file XR19-19 using the following format.

Column 1: 1 = company 1
             2 = company 2

Column 2: 1 = lung disease
             2 = heart disease
             3 = both lung and heart disease
             4 = neither lung nor heart disease

Do the data provide sufficient evidence to indicate that the no-smoking policy reduces the incidence of heart and lung disease?

19.20 Obesity among children in North America is said to be at near-epidemic propor-tions. Some experts blame television for the problem, citing the statistic that chil-dren watch on average about 26 hours per week. During this time, children are not engaged in any physical activity, which results in weight gains. However, the prob-lem may be compounded by a reduction in metabolic rate. In an experiment to address this issue (the study results were published in the February 1993 issue of the medical journal *Pediatrics*), scientists from Memphis State University and the University of Tennessee at Memphis took a random sample of 223 children aged 8 to 12, 41 of whom were obese. Each child's metabolic rate (the amount of calories burned per hour) was measured while at rest and also measured while the child watched a television program ("The Wonder Years"). The differences between the two rates were recorded and are stored in file XR19-20. (Column 1 contains the numbers representing the decrease in metabolic rate and column 2 codes the chil-dren: 1 = obese and 2 = nonobese.)

    a   Do these data allow us to conclude that there is a decrease in metabolism when children watch television?

    b   Can we conclude that the decrease in metabolism while watching television is greater among obese children?

19.21 Alcohol abuse is a serious problem in this country. To examine whether age is a factor in determining who drinks alcohol, the Gallup organization polled 1,054 adults and asked each, "Do you ever use alcoholic beverages such as liquor, wine, or beer?" Respondents were also asked to report their age category. The data are stored in file XR19-21. (Column 1 records age category: 1 = 18–29, 2 = 30–49, 3 = 50 and over; column 2 records whether the person uses alcohol: 1 = yes and 0 = no.) Can we infer that differences exist among the age categories with respect to alcohol use?

19.22 An insurance company that offers dental plans to large companies is reconsidering its premium structure. Currently, the premium paid by each individual is the same throughout the country. The insurance company's executives believe that the incidence of cavities differs from one part of the country to another. If that is the case, the premiums should vary according to locale. As part of a preliminary study, the company chose the records of randomly selected eight-year-old children who are covered by the dental plan in each of four different states scattered across the country. The number of cavities for which each child was treated during the previous two years was recorded and is stored in file XR19-22. (Column 1 contains the number of cavities per child and column 2 stores the state: 1 = New York; 2 = Florida; 3 = California; 4 = Washington.)

Do these data provide sufficient evidence to infer that children in different geographic regions differ in the number of cavities they have?

19.23 The game of Scrabble is one of the oldest and most popular board games. It is played all over the world and there is even an annual world championship competition. The game is played by forming words and placing them on the board to obtain the maximum number of points. It is generally believed that a large vocabulary is the only skill required to be successful. However, there is a strategic element to the game that suggests that mathematical skills are just as necessary. To determine which skills are most in demand, a statistician recruited a random sample of fourth-year university English and mathematics majors, and asked them to play the game. A total of 500 games were played by different pairs of English and mathematics majors. The scores in each game are stored in file XR19-23 (column 1: English major scores; column 2: mathematics major scores).

Do these data allow us to infer that the average score obtained by English majors is greater than that for mathematics majors?

19.24 Several years ago we heard about the "Mommy Track," the phenomenon of women being underpaid in the corporate world because of what is seen as their divided loyalties between home and office. There may also be a "Daddy Differential." The "Daddy Differential" refers to the situation where men whose wives stay at home earn more than men whose wives work. It is argued that the differential occurs because bosses reward their male employees if they come from "traditional families." Linda Stroh of Loyola University of Chicago studied a random sample of 348 male managers employed by 20 Fortune 500 companies. Each manager reported whether his wife stayed at home to care for their children or worked outside the home and his annual income. The incomes (in thousands of dollars) of all 348 managers are stored in column 1 of file XR19-24. Column 2 contains the code 1 if the manager's wife stays at home and the code 2 if she has a career outside the home.

a Can we conclude at the 5% significance level that men whose wives stay at home earn more than men whose wives work outside the home?

b If your answer in part (a) is affirmative, does this establish a case for discrimination? Can you think of another cause-and-effect scenario? Explain.

19.25 As all baseball fans know, first base is the only base that the base runner may overrun. At second and third base the runner may be tagged out if he runs past them. Consequently, on close plays at second and third base, the runner will slide, enabling him to stop at the base. In recent years, however, several players have chosen to slide headfirst when approaching first base, claiming that this is faster than simply running over the base. In an experiment to test this claim, the 25 players on one National League team were recruited. Each player ran to first base with and without sliding, and the times to reach the base were recorded. These data are stored in columns 1 (player), 2 (no slide), and 3 (slide) in file XR19-25.

Can we conclude at the 5% significance level that sliding is slower than not sliding?

19.26 Absenteeism is a serious employment problem in most countries. It is estimated that absenteeism reduces potential output by more than 10%. Two economists launched a research project to learn more about the problem. They randomly selected 100 organizations to participate in a one-year study. For each organization, they recorded the average number of days absent per employee and several variables thought to affect absenteeism. File XR19-26 contains the following information.

Column 1: average employee wage

Column 2: percentage of part-time employees

Column 3: percentage of unionized employees

Column 4: availability of shiftwork (1 = yes; 0 = no)

Column 5: union–management relationship (1 = good; 0 = not good)

Column 6: average number of days absent per employee

Develop a model that analyzes the relationship between absenteeism and the other variables. Describe your findings. (The authors are grateful to James Fong and Diana Mansour for developing this exercise. The data are based on M. Chadhury and I. Ng, "Absenteeism Predictors," *Canadian Journal of Economics,* August 1992.)

19.27 The high cost of medical care makes it imperative that hospitals operate efficiently and effectively. As part of a larger study, patients leaving a hospital were surveyed. They were asked how satisfied they were with the treatment they received. The responses were recorded with a measure of the degree of severity of their illness (as determined by the admitting physician) and the length of stay. These data are recorded in file XR19-27 in the following way.

Column 1: satisfaction level (1 = very unsatisfied and 5 = very satisfied)

Column 2: severity of illness (1 = least severe and 10 = most severe)

Column 3: number of days in hospital

a Is the satisfaction level affected by the severity of illness?

b Is the satisfaction level higher for patients who stay for shorter periods of time?

19.28 The state of the environment is an issue that affects all of us, which means that any environmental protection efforts must involve all the countries in the world. However, there does not appear to be universal agreement on the seriousness of the problem. To measure the amount of support for environmental action, the Gallup International Institute surveyed people in several countries and asked each of them the following questions.

1 Do you support actions that protect the environment, even at the risk of slowing economic growth?

2 Are you willing to pay higher prices so that industry can better protect the environment?

The results are stored in file XR19-28 in the following way.

Columns 1 and 2: responses to questions 1 and 2 in the United States (1 = yes; 0 = no)

Columns 3 and 4: responses to questions 1 and 2 in Canada

Columns 5 and 6: responses to questions 1 and 2 in Great Britain

Columns 7 and 8: responses to questions 1 and 2 in Japan

Columns 9 and 10: responses to questions 1 and 2 in Hungary

Columns 11 and 12: responses to questions 1 and 2 in Poland

Columns 13 and 14: responses to questions 1 and 2 in Russia

a   Estimate with 99% confidence the proportion of all Americans who would respond affirmatively to question 1.

b   Can we conclude at the 5% significance level that Americans and Japanese differ in their responses to question 1?

c   Can we infer at the 5% significance level that Canadians and Britons differ in their responses to question 2?

d   Do these results allow us to infer at the 1% significance level that differences exist among Hungarians, Poles, and Russians in their responses to question 1?

19.29   The use of sodium bicarbonate, more commonly known as baking soda, to clean teeth has been increasing in the last few years. However, many people fear that the substance is too abrasive and will eventually damage the enamel of teeth, resulting in teeth that are sensitive to heat and cold. To study the problem, two researchers, R. K. Lehne and A. E. Winston, conducted an experiment. (Study results were published in *Clinical Preventive Dentistry*, Vol. 5, No. 1, January–February 1993, pages 17–18.) Eight teeth were cleaned with a variety of dentifrices, including baking soda. Enamel abrasion for each product was measured by brushing eight freshly extracted human teeth. The quantity of enamel removed was determined by two processes: radioactive dentin abrasivity (RDA) and radioactive enamel abrasivity (REA). The results are stored in file XR19-29 using the following format.

Column 1: abrasivity value measured by RDA

Column 2: abrasivity value measured by REA

Column 3: dentifrice used: 1 = baking soda; 2 = Pepsodent; 3 = Crest; 4 = Colgate

a   Are there differences in abrasivity among the four products, using either measurement process?

b   Can we conclude that baking soda is less abrasive than other products?

19.30   The experiment to determine the effect of taking a preparatory course to improve SAT scores in Exercise 19.13 was criticized by other statisticians. They argued that the first test would provide a valuable learning experience that would produce a higher test score from the second exam even without the preparatory course. Consequently, another experiment was performed. Forty students wrote the SAT without taking any preparatory course. At the next scheduled exam (three months later), these same students took the exam again (again with no preparatory course). Another 40 students took a preparatory course and then wrote the SAT. The scores for all exams are stored in columns 1 (no preparatory course—first test scores), 2 (no preparatory course—second test scores), and 3 (preparatory course—test scores) in file XR19-30. What conclusions can be drawn from these data?

In July of 1990, a rock-and-roll museum opened in Atlanta, Georgia. The museum was located in a large city block containing a variety of stores. In late July 1992, a fire that started in one of these stores burned the entire block, including the museum. Fortunately, the museum had taken out insurance to cover the cost of rebuilding as well as lost revenue. As a general rule, insurance companies base their payment on how well the company performed in the past. Accordingly, they offered the museum owners $2,703,624. This sum is based on the average monthly revenues before the fire ($81,928) multiplied by 33 (the number of months the museum was closed). However, the owners of the museum argued that the revenues were increasing, and hence they are entitled to more money under their insurance plan. The argument was based on the revenues and attendance figures of an amusement park that was opened nearby, featuring rides and other similar attractions. The amusement park opened in December 1991. The two entertainment facilities were operating jointly during the last 4 weeks of 1991 and the first 28 weeks of 1992 (the point at which the fire destroyed the museum). In April 1995, the museum reopened with considerably more features than the original one.

The attendance for both facilities from December 1991 to October 1995 are listed in columns 1 (museum) and 2 (amusement park) in file C19-03. During the period when the museum was closed, the data show zero attendance.

The owners of the museum argue that the weekly attendance from the twenty-ninth week of 1992 to the sixteenth week of 1995 should be estimated using the most current data (seventeenth to forty-second week of 1995). The insurance company argues that the estimates should be based on the 4 weeks of 1991 and the 28 weeks of 1992, when both facilities were operating and before the museum reopened with more features than the original museum. For the purpose of estimating revenues, it is assumed that each attendee spends an average of $4.50 in entrance fees and other purchases.

    a Calculate how much the insurance company should pay, using the museum owners' argument.

    b Calculate how much should be paid to the museum, using the insurance company's argument.

    c How would a skilled statistician such as you resolve the impasse?

---

*The case and the data are real. The names have been changed to preserve anonymity. The authors wish to thank Dr. Kevin Leonard for supplying the problem and the data.

Every year, the graduates of Wilfrid Laurier University are surveyed to determine their employment status and annual income. The university offers undergraduate degrees in Arts and Music, Business Administration, and Science, as well as several master's degrees. The survey asked a random sample of 1994 graduates the following questions.

1 With which degree did you graduate?

    1 Arts and Music

    2 Business Administration—nonaccounting

    3 Business Administration—accounting

    4 Science

    5 master's

2 What is your current employment status?

    1 completing additional education

    2 employed

    3 other

    4 unemployed

3 If you are employed, what is your annual income?

The data are stored in columns 1 to 7 in file C19-04 in the following way.

Column 1: degree

Column 2: employment status

Columns 3–7: income for those employed with degrees in Arts and Music, Business (nonaccounting), Business (accounting), Science, and master's, respectively.

High school students who are about to choose a university program would like to know the following information.

Are there differences in the employment rates among the five groups of graduates? (Employment rate is defined as the percentage of graduates who are employed.)

Are there differences in income among the five groups of graduates?

Among Business Administration graduates, is there a difference in the employment rates and income between accounting and nonaccounting graduates?

*Source: "Wilfrid Laurier 1994 Graduate Survey Report" as printed in the *Atrium*, 8 November 1995.

AMBULANCE AND FIRE DEPARTMENT RESPONSE INTERVAL STUDY*

Every year, thousands of people die of heart attacks partly because of delays in waiting for emergency medical care to arrive. One form of heart attack is ventricular fibrillation rhythm, which is treated by a defibrillator. However, immediate medical attention is critical. In general, if a patient receives treatment within eight minutes, he or she is very likely to survive. It is estimated that the probability of survival is reduced by 7–10% for each minute thereafter that defibrillation is delayed.

The region in the Ambulance and Fire Department Response Interval Study is composed of the three cities of Cambridge, Waterloo, and Kitchener. Each city has a fire department, and the region has a 911 emergency telephone system. When a medical-related call is received by the Police Dispatch Center, it is relayed to the Central Ambulance Communication Center (CACC). The CACC dispatches both the ambulance and the fire department to certain calls that match one of several criteria indicating the need for fire department personnel. There are two ambulance services that cover the region: the Cambridge Memorial Hospital Ambulance Service and the Kitchener-Waterloo Regional Ambulance Service.

Currently, all defibrillation is performed by ambulance personnel sent to the patient after a 911 call. A city counselor recently suggested that, since the fire department has more centers, it is likely that fire department personnel could arrive at the scene more quickly than ambulance personnel. A study was undertaken to determine whether fire department personnel should be trained in the use of defibrillators and sent to treat ventricular fibrillation rhythm.

Between March 1, 1994, and August 31, 1994, all calls that involved both ambulance and fire department personnel were monitored. The times for each service to arrive at the scene were recorded and stored in file C19-05, using the format below.

Column 1: call number for Cambridge calls

Column 2: time in minutes for the ambulance to arrive

Column 3: time for fire truck to arrive

Column 4: call number for Kitchener calls

Column 5: time in minutes for the ambulance to arrive

Column 6: time for fire truck to arrive

Column 7: call number for Waterloo calls

Column 8: time in minutes for the ambulance to arrive

Column 9: time for fire truck to arrive

It has been decided that the training of fire department personnel is warranted only if it can be shown that a fire truck arrives at the scene on average more than

---

*The authors are grateful to Bruce Jermyn for supplying this case. The data are real. However, the sample size was reduced to ease disk-storage problems.

one minute sooner than an ambulance and that the frequency of arrival within eight minutes is greater for the fire department.

What conclusions can be drawn from the data?

NUTRITION EDUCATION PROGRAMS*

Nutrition education programs, which teach their clients how to lose weight or reduce cholesterol levels through better eating patterns, have been growing in popularity. The nurse in charge of one such program at a local hospital wanted to know whether the programs actually work. A random sample of 33 clients who attended a nutrition education program for those with elevated cholestrol levels was drawn. The study recorded the weight, cholesterol levels, total dietary fat intake per average day, total dietary cholesterol intake per average day, and percent of daily calories from fat. These data were gathered both before and three months after the program. The researchers also determined the sex, age, and height of the clients.

The data are stored in file C19-06 in the following way.

Column 1: sex (1 = female; 2 = male)

Column 2: age

Column 3: height (in meters)

Columns 4 and 5: weight, before and after (in kilograms)

Columns 6 and 7: cholesterol level, before and after

Columns 8 and 9: total dietary fat intake per average day, before and after (in grams).

Columns 10 and 11: dietary cholesterol intake per average day, before and after (in milligrams)

Columns 12 and 13: percent daily calories from fat, before and after

The nurse would like to know whether the program is successful and whether sex or age affects the reduction in weight, cholesterol level, fat intake, cholesterol intake, and percent fat.

---

*The authors would like to thank Karen Cavrag for writing this case.

DO BANKS DISCRIMINATE AGAINST WOMEN BUSINESS OWNERS?—III

A statistician made a final effort to determine whether banks discriminate against women business owners because of their gender. For each of the women business owners who had received a loan, he attempted to find a male business owner whose characteristics closely matched. The matching was done on the basis of type of business (proprietorship, partnership, or corporation), gross sales, and age of company. A match was made when the type of business was the same, the gross sales were within $10,000 of each other, and the ages were within one year of each other. The interest rates (points above prime) for each pair are recorded in columns 1 (women) and 2 (men) in file C19-07. What do these data tell you? Is this analysis definitive? Explain.

Answers to Selected
Even-Numbered Exercises

Chapter 1

1.4 a the complete production run
b 1,000 chips **c** proportion of the production run that is defective **d** proportion of sample chips that are defective (7.5%) **e** parameter **f** statistic **g** Because the sample proportion is less than 10%, we can conclude that the claim is true.
1.6 a Flip the coin 100 times and count the number of heads and tails. **b** outcomes of flips **c** outcomes of the 100 flips **d** proportion of heads **e** proportion of heads in the 100 flips

Chapter 2

2.2 a quantitative **b** qualitative **c** ranked **d** quantitative
2.4 a quantitative **b** qualitative **c** qualitative **d** ranked **e** quantitative
2.6 a quantitative **b** ranked **c** qualitative **d** quantitative **e** ranked
2.8 g .533; .467
2.16 a 48.67% **b** 61.34%
2.18 b 27.0% **c** 16.5%
2.22 b positive, linear **d** approx. $325
2.24 b no relationship **c** no
2.58 b no relationship **c** no

Chapter 4

4.2 1.417; 1; −3, 0, and 4
4.4 mode
4.8 a 5.85; 5; 5
4.10 $43.59; $26.91; $0.00
4.12 $28,015.50; $28,250
4.14 a 6.17; 5; 5
4.16 no
4.18 15; 19; 35.56; 5.96
4.20 −.14; 5.81; 2.41
4.22 a 9; 10; 3.16 **b** 0; 4; 2 **c** 6; 4; 2 **d** 5; 0; 0
4.24 a 46.5; 6.82 **b** 6.5; 2.55 **c** 174.5; 13.21
4.28 mean; standard deviation
4.30 a 10.2; −4.5; 13.65; 4.75; 30.7; 34.1; 21.3; 7.95; 9; 20.95 **b** 14% **c** 12.63% **d** Fund A, Portfolio, Fund B (lowest return and risk)
4.32 a 2.9571; 1.7196
4.34 a 47.83, 44; 52.7, 48; 65.355, 55.5 **b** 103, 176.25, 13.28; 128, 385.72, 19.64; 176, 890.68, 29.84
4.36 a (62, 76); (55, 83); (48, 90) **b** approx. 340; approx. 475; virtually all 500
4.38 a .04; .20 **b** approx. .20
4.40 a approx. 68%; virtually 100% **b** approx. 32% **c** approx. .975
4.42 a 6,473.68; 82.12 **b** approx. 59.5
4.44 −7.5; 8

4.46 c 60
4.48 largest; upper quartile; median; lower quartile; smallest
4.50 b A: higher avg. return and risk
4.52 b 64.25; 81; 90 **c** 11, 16, 18, 25
4.54 c common stocks; common stocks
4.56 a 215.45; .95
4.58 a .1215; .0055
4.60 a 14.38; .49
4.62 a 3.17; 4.5; 6.23 **b** 7.5; 0
4.64 b 100% **c** only very roughly **d** .64 vs. .68; 1.00 vs. .95
4.66 a 47.6 **b** 115.42 **c** 10.74
4.68 b .64 vs. .68
4.70 b $\bar{x}$ = 1.56 today, down from 3.36
4.72 a $(\bar{x}, s)$ = (7.28, 29.35), (9.44, 3.40), (8.52, 8.59), (8.8, 4.20), (13.42, 19.48)
4.74 a $\bar{x}$ = 3.316 hours
4.78 a −28.94; −0.91

Chapter 6

6.4 b S = {0, 1, 2, 3, 4} **c** 36/80; 28/80; 12/80; 2/80; 2/80 **d** relative frequency **e** .05
6.6 a 28/75; 7/25; 26/75; 43/75; 32/75 **b** 47/75
6.8 a 1/13 **b** 1/13 **c** yes
6.10 .20
6.12 a 67/125 **b** 41/125 **c** no **d** no
6.14 12/44
6.16 a .125 **b** .375 **c** .375 **d** .875
6.18 a .24 **b** .66 **c** .2
6.20 a 39% **b** 100%
6.22 a .16 **b** .84 **c** .36
6.24 42/90
6.26 a .7 **b** .18
6.28 a 3,600 **b** .41 **c** .34 **d** .805
6.30 .526
6.32 b yes **c** yes **d** discrete
6.34 b yes **c** yes **d** discrete
6.36 a 1 **b** .9 **c** .5 **d** .4 **e** 0
6.38

x	1	2	3	4	5	6
$p(x)$	$\frac{1}{6}$	$\frac{1}{6}$	$\frac{1}{6}$	$\frac{1}{6}$	$\frac{1}{6}$	$\frac{1}{6}$

6.40 a .89 **b** .03 **c** .48
6.42 a .870 **b** .020 **c** .999
6.44 a $p(x)$ = 1/11, where x = 0, 1, 2, . . . , 10 **b** 1/11 **c** 0 **d** 1/11
6.46 a −.2; 1.99 **b** no **c** 4; 14
6.48 a 2; 6.78 **b** 4; 13.56 **c** 9; 13.56
6.50 a 1.7; .9 **b** .6 **c** .6
6.52 a $4,838.50 **b** $11,666.60
6.54 a 1.85 **b** 1.0275 **c** 9,231
6.58 a 23.3; 2.8 **b** −18; 5.4
6.60 a $p(1)$ = .6 and $p(2)$ = .4, for both X and Y **b** 1.4; .24; .49; (for both X and Y) **c** $P(X = 1|Y = 1) = 5/6 = P(Y = 1|X = 1)$
$P(X = 2|Y = 1) = 1/6 = P(Y = 2|X = 1)$

$P(X = 1|Y = 2) = 1/4 = P(Y = 1|X = 2)$
$P(X = 2|Y = 2) = 3/4 = P(Y = 2|X = 2)$
d .140; 7/12 **e** no; $P(X = 1) \neq P(X = 1|Y = 1)$
6.62 d no
6.64 a 17%; 21.16% **b** portfolio
6.66 It depends on your desired level of risk. Portfolio: 14.5%; 29.95%
6.68 a 10 **b** 15 **c** 15 **d** 1 **e** 1
6.70 a .1488 **b** .2461 **c** .3151
6.72 a .0512 **b** .3241 **c** .3115
6.74 a .127 **b** .131 **c** .147 **d** .688 **e** 0 **f** .046
6.76 a .250 **b** .078; .014
6.78 a 0 **b** .058 **c** .665 **d** .328
6.80 a 0 **b** .434 **c** .319
6.82 a .015 **b** .558 **c** .594
6.84 a .758 **b** .028 **c** .713 **d** .456
6.86 a .778; .196; .024 **b** .779; .195; .024
6.88 a .992 **b** .715 **c** .185
6.90 a .050 **b** .577 **c** .101 **d** 156
6.92 a .968 **b** .027 **c** .006
6.94 .393
6.96 a subjective **b** classical **c** relative frequency **d** classical **e** relative frequency **f** subjective
6.98 yes
6.100 a .04 **b** .31
6.102 .3
6.104 a .19 **b** .61
6.106 a approx. 82 **b** .164
6.108 a S = {HH, HT, TH, TT} **b** P{HH} = 4/9; P{HT} = P{TH} = 2/9; P{TT} = 1/9
6.110 .73
6.112 2/3
6.114 a

x	0	1	2
$p(x)$	$\frac{2}{12}$	$\frac{8}{12}$	$\frac{2}{12}$

6.116 b 5 **c** $V(Y) < V(X) < V(W)$
6.118

y	1	2	3	4	5
$p(y)$	.41	.37	.16	.04	.02

6.120 a .377 **b** $2,400
6.124 a .018 **b** .986 **c** seven spare parts
6.126 .014
6.128 a .303 **b** .184 **c** .09
6.130 a .538 **b** .001

Chapter 7

7.2 c .8 **d** 0 **e** .5
7.4 a .25 **c** .58
7.6 a .0446 **b** .8289 **c** .025 **d** .9925 **e** .0823 **f** .8123
7.8 a 2.575 **b** 2.33 **c** 1.645
7.10 a .25 **b** −1.25 **c** −1.875 **d** 1.75 **e** −2.25 **f** −1.625

7.12 a .0918 **b** .9962 **c** .9082 **d** .0918
e .8854
7.14 a .0475 **b** .3830 **c** .9901
d $2,902,000
7.16 a .9544 **b** .1587
7.18 a 10 **b** 7796
7.20 a .0465 **b** approx. 1.0 **c** 36
7.22 a 20; 3.46 **b** .0968 **c** .9429
7.26 a .0025 **b** .999994 **c** .0497 **d** 0
7.28 .8892
7.30 b .865; .982 **c** .05 **d** .05
7.32 a .6703 **b** .3679 **c** .8647
7.34 a .0505 **b** .1059 **c** .6985 **d** .7439
7.36 6.082 ounces
7.38 .2912
7.40 .2703

Chapter 8

8.2 $\bar{x}$ is approximately normally distributed.
8.4 a .1587 **b** .2119 **c** .0228
8.6 a .2347 **b** .4435 **c** .5328
8.8 We can answer part (c) and possibly part (b). We cannot answer part (a).
8.10 .3085
8.12 a .2514 **b** .0681 **c** .0010
8.14 The professor needs to know the mean and standard deviation of the population of people who use the elevator and that the distribution is not extremely nonnormal.

Chapter 9

9.2 a widens **b** widens **c** widens
d no change
9.4 $22.50 \pm 6.98 = (15.52, 29.48)$
9.6 $1350 \pm 98 = (1252, 1448)$
9.8 $3.88 \pm .57 = (3.31, 4.45)$
9.10 $14.74 \pm .36 = (14.38, 15.10)$
9.12 385
9.14 55
9.16 a 1,037 **b** $18 \pm .5$
9.18 $15.00 \pm .59 = (14.41, 15.59)$
9.20 217

Chapter 10

10.2 $z = -1.5$; no
10.4 $z = 3.0$; yes
10.6 $z = 5.20$; yes
10.8 $z = 1.62$; no
10.10 $z = .80$; no
10.12 a $z = 1.66$; yes **b** σ (after campaign) = 3.87
10.14 .0076
10.16 .9599
10.18 .0526
10.20 $z = -2.26$; p-value = .0119
10.22 .1492
10.24 .6480
10.28 .2946; .6772; .9210; .9210; .6772; .2946

10.30 .0268
10.32 .5596
10.34 $z = 2.26$; p-value = .0119; yes
10.36 $z = -1.98$; p-value = .0239; yes
10.38 $z = -.78$; no

Chapter 11

11.2 a $22.6 \pm 1.41 = (21.19, 24.01)$ **b** $t = 3.81$; yes **c** Variable should be normally distributed.
11.4 $t = -1.45$; do not reject H_0
11.6 $5.125 \pm .462 = (4.663, 5.587)$
11.8 $t = 2.75$; yes
11.10 a $66.47 \pm 3.98 = (62.49, 70.45)$
b Prices are normally distributed.
11.12 $\chi^2 = 17.26$; reject H_0
11.14 $\chi^2 = 147.31$; yes
11.16 a $\chi^2 = 23.05$; no **b** (109.64, 441.10)
11.18 (171.46, 544.27)
11.20 $\chi^2 = 86.25$; replace bulbs as they burn out
11.22 $.84 \pm .025 = (.815, .865)$
11.24 $z = 1.4$; no
11.26 .0694
11.28 a $z = 1.4$; no **b** $z = 2.0$; yes
11.30 $.351 \pm .052 = (.299, .403)$
11.32 $.371 \pm .043 = (.328, .414)$
11.34 a $.193 \pm .026 = (.167, .219)$
b $z = 3.41$; yes
11.36 $\chi^2 = 32.61$; yes
11.38 a $71.88 \pm 2.85 = (69.03, 74.73)$
b $t = 2.74$; yes
11.40 $.632 \pm .050 = (.582, .682)$
11.42 a $5.79 \pm .68 = (5.11, 6.47)$
11.44 $.67 \pm .11 = (.56, .78)$
11.46 a $t = -2.64$; yes **b** $\chi^2 = 75.54$; yes
11.48 $.155 \pm .030 = (.125, .185)$

Chapter 12

12.2 $t = 3.38$; yes
12.4 $t = -1.58$; yes
12.6 $t = -1.71$; yes
12.8 $t = 1.07$ (p-value = .1440); no, switch to supplier B
12.10 a $t = 1.79$; no **b** $(-.6, 12.6)$
12.12 a $t = -11.61$; yes **b** $(-3.26, -2.31)$
12.18 $t = -1.90$; no
12.20 a $t = 1.16$; no **b** $(-7.5, 26.7)$
c $t = 7.25$; yes **d** (6.56, 12.28)
12.22 a $t = 2.10$; yes **b** (.1, 17.7)
c $t = 1.68$; no **d** $(-2.81, 20.97)$
12.24 a $t = -2.02$; yes **b** $(-4.36, .19)$
c The differences must be normally distributed. **e** experimental data **f** The samples should be independent.
12.26 a (11.59, 27.91) **b** $t = 4.08$; yes
12.28 $t = -2.44$ (p-value = .0091); yes
12.30 $F = .70$; no
12.32 (.335, 1.040)
12.34 $F = .298$; yes

12.36 a $z = -1.56$; do not reject H_0
b $z = 3.25$; reject H_0
12.38 $(-.18, .04)$
12.40 a $z = 2.75$; yes **b** $z = 1.80$; no
c (.025, .147)
12.42 a $z = 4.31$; yes **b** $z = 2.16$; yes
c $.10 \pm .045 = (.055, .145)$
12.44 a $z = 2.54$; yes **b** (.049, .28)
12.46 $z = -1.13$; no
12.48 $z = -1.00$, no
12.50 a $t = 26.92$; yes **b** (56.62, 66.71)
c The differences must be normally distributed.
12.52 a $t = -2.02$; yes
12.54 a $t = -1.13$; no
12.56 $t = 1.75$; purchase machine A
12.58 Dry cleaner: $t = .96$; Doughnut shop: $t = 3.24$; Convenience store: $t = 7.34$

Chapter 13

13.2 a $z = -2.83$ (p-value = .0023); yes
b $t = -1.58$ (p-value = .058); no **c** .434 $\pm .091 = (.343, .525)$ **d** (25.40, 58.72)
13.4 a $z = 1.54$ (p-value = .0619); no
b $z = 3.02$ (p-value = .0013); yes
13.6 PSI: (3.925, 4.465) Tire life: (392.5, 446.5) Gasoline consumption: (.3925, .4465)
13.8 $t = 3.36$ (p-value = .0005); yes
13.10 $t = .96$ (p-value = .17); no
13.12 $z = 1.02$ (p-value = .1548); no
13.14 a $t = -17.17$ (p-value = 0); yes
b $t = -4.56$ (p-value = 0); yes
13.16 Working memory: $t = 3.27$ (p-value = .0008) Reasoning: $t = 4.11$ (p-value = 0) Reaction time: $t = -.58$ (p-value = .56) Vocabulary: $t = 1.24$ (p-value = .22)
13.18 $t = -1.31$ (p-value = .097); no
13.20 $t = 1.88$ (p-value = .031); yes
13.22 Speeds: $t = 1.09$ (p-value = .28); no.

Chapter 14

14.4

Source	DF	SS	MS	F
Treatments	2	21.74	10.87	1.06
Error	120	1,229.77	10.25	
Total	122	1,251.51		

14.6 a $F = 4.75$ (p-value = .002); yes
14.8 a $F = 2.94$ (p-value = .036); there is a difference.
14.10 a $F = 1.73$ (p-value = .178); no
14.16 a $F = 9.73$ (p-value = .010); yes
b $F = 6.82$ (p-value = .029); yes
14.18 $F = 6.97$ (p-value = .006); yes
14.20 a $F = 21.16$ (p-value = 0); yes
b $F = 66.02$ (p-value = 0); the design is appropriate.

14.22 $F = 2.35$ (p-value = .106); no
14.24 $F = 13.79$ (p-value = 0); choose typeface 3.
14.26 a $F = 4.05$ (p-value = .029); yes
b Waiting times should be normally distributed with equal variances.
14.28 $F = 1.82$ (p-value = .166); no
14.30 $F = 5.12$ (p-value = .001); yes

Chapter 15

15.2 $\chi^2 = 4.98$ (p-value = .1734); do not reject H_0
15.4 $\chi^2 = 4.20$ (p-value = .3796); do not reject H_0
15.6 $\chi^2 = 11.40$ (p-value = .0439); yes
15.8 $\chi^2 = 14.88$ (p-value = .0006); the number of people hired is not proportional.
15.10 $\chi^2 = 16.567$ (p-value = 0); dependent
15.12 $\chi^2 = 2.266$ (p-value = .323); no
15.14 $\chi^2 = 1.724$ (p-value = .4223); no
15.16 a $\chi^2 = .643$ (p-value = .4226)
b Ignore opinions of investors.
15.18 $\chi^2 = .692$ (p-value = .4054); no
15.20 $\chi^2 = 1.282$ (p-value = .2575); no
15.22 $\chi^2 = 19.683$ (p-value = 0); there are differences among the questionnaires.
15.24 $\chi^2 = 5.424$ (p-value = .247); no
15.26 $\chi^2 = 6.515$ (p-value = .3679); the Coke-lover is wrong. (Rule of 5 applied.)

Chapter 16

16.4 b $\hat{y} = 8.24 - 1.07x$
16.6 b $\hat{y} = 3.64 + .267$ Length
16.10 $\hat{y} = 9.44 + .0949$ Degrees
16.12 a $s_\epsilon = 5.888$ **b** $t = 4.86$ (p-value = 0); yes **c** $R^2 = 28.9\%$
16.14 a $s_\epsilon = 3.225$ **b** $t = 12.03$ (p-value = 0); yes **c** $R^2 = 26.7\%$
16.16 $s_\epsilon = 12.98$; $R^2 = 6.5\%$; $t = 9.65$ (p-value = 0)
16.18 a $\hat{y} = 2.05 + .0909$ Exercise **c** $t = 7.06$ (p-value = 0) **d** $s_\epsilon = 10.53$; $R^2 = 51.0\%$
16.20 a (53.993, 83.051) **b** (67.002, 70.042)
16.22 a $(-16.767, 34.180) = (0, 34.180)$ **b** (7.899, 9.514)
16.24 $r = .937$, $t = 5.39$ (p-value = .006); yes
16.26 $r = .961$, $t = 11.53$, yes
16.28 $r = .343$, $t = 1.51$, no
16.38 a $\hat{y} = 115 + 2.47$ Age **c** $s_\epsilon = 43.32$ **d** $t = 4.84$ (p-value = 0); yes **e** $R^2 = 56.6\%$ **f** (318.10, 505.20)
16.40 a $\hat{y} = .828 - .080$ Team-ERA **b** $s_\epsilon = .05490$ **c** $t = -1.96$ (p-value = .0365); yes **d** $R^2 = 24.3\%$ **e** (.4061, .6092)
16.42 $r = .791$, $t = 18.19$, yes
16.44 a $\hat{y} = 13,836 + 323$ Height **b** $s_\epsilon =$

2734 **c** $t = 1.90$ (p-value = .034); yes
d $R^2 = 11.4\%$ **e (i)** (35,773, 38,417)
(ii) (30,754, 42,144)

Chapter 17

17.2 a $s_\epsilon = 3.752$; it is an estimate of the standard deviation of the error variable.
b $R^2 = 76.3\%$, which is the proportion of the variation in final marks that is explained by the model. **c** R^2 (adjusted) = 74.5%; the model fits well. **d** $F = 43.43$ (p-value = 0) **f** $t = .97$ (p-value = .342); no **g** $t = 9.12$ (p-value = 0); yes **h** The midterm mark is a better predictor.
17.4 a $s_\epsilon = 3.227$; it is an estimate of the standard deviation of the error variable.
b $R^2 = 26.7\%$, which is the proportion of the variation in heights of men that is explained by the model. **c** R^2 (adjusted) = 26.3%; the model does not fit well. **d** $F = 72.37$ (p-value = 0) **f** $t = 11.78$ (p-value = 0); yes **g** $t = -.58$ (p-value = .562); no
17.6 a $\hat{y} = .72 + .611$ HS_GPA $+ .00271$ SAT $+ .0463$ Activities **b** $S_\epsilon = 2.030$ **c** $R^2 = 28.8\%$ **d** R^2 (adjusted) = 26.6% **e** $F = 12.96$ (p-value = 0) **h** (4.445, 12.650) **i** (6.904, 8.216)
17.8 a $\hat{y} = 577 + 90.6$ Space $+ 9.66$ Water **b** $S_\epsilon = 213.7$ **c** $R^2 = 70.8\%$ **d** $F = 117.64$ (p-value = 0) **e** (7,747.8, 8,601.5) **f** (8,127.4, 8221.9)
17.10 a ($35,480, $172,260) **b** ($39,290, $90,310)
17.12 (16,710, 35,295)
17.14 a Macintosh **b** IBM **c** Other
17.16 a $F = 20.43$ (p-value = 0); yes **b** We cannot infer that weather is a factor. **c** $t = 3.30$ (p-value = .000); yes
17.18 b $\hat{y} = 4.65 + .00012$ Loon size $+ 4.08 I_1 + 10.2 T_2$ **c** $S_\epsilon = 4.203$, $R^2 = 53.3\%$ $F = 36.48$ (p-value = 0)
17.20 a $\hat{y} = .357 - .401$ BA $+ .0764$ ERA $- .0509$ Fired **d** $t = -8.61$ (p-value = 0); yes
17.36 a $\hat{y} = 3.719 - 46.8$ Price_A $+ 58.5$ Price_B **d** $S_\epsilon = 558.7$ $R^2 = 49.3\%$ $F = 23.85$ (p-value = 0)
17.38 a $\hat{y} = 75.52 + .77$ Trees $- .43$ Distance
17.40 a $\hat{y} = -2.556 + 4.84$ Permits
17.42 a Rns $-$ Scrd $= -703.7 + .5491$ Team_Wlk $+ .3898$ Team_BA $+ .8099$ Team_Hmr
17.48 a $\hat{y} = 303 + 14.9x_1 + 10.5x_2$ **f** $d = .77$
17.50 a $\hat{y} = 3,476 - 47.9x_1 + 22.5x_2 + 1.41x_3$ **f** $d = .70$ **g** $\hat{y} = 3,248 - 52.7x_1 + 17.1x_2 + 2.14x_3 + 10.4t$
17.54 $d = 2.20$
17.56 a $\hat{y} = 898 + 11.3$ Snowfall **b** $d =$

1.01 **d** $\hat{y} = 961 + 13.9$ Snowfall $- 7.69 t$ $d = 1.90$
17.58 a $\hat{y} = 195 + .123$ Fertilizer $+ .0248$ Water **b** $t = 1.66$ (p-value = 1.09; no **c** $t = 4.06$ (p-value = 0); yes **d** $S_\epsilon = 57.29$ $R^2 = 41.6\%$ **e** (10.47, 359.2)
17.60 a $\hat{y} = .447 - .00403$ L-size **b** $t = -3.37$ (p-value = .003); yes **c** $R^2 = 38.6\%$ **e** (.37293, .44041) **f** (.41464, .43096)
17.62 a $\hat{y} = 3.24 + .451$ Mother $+ .411$ Father $+ .0166$ Gmothers $+ .0869$ Gfathers **b** $F = 67.97$ (p-value = 0); yes **e** Only Mother and Father are linearly related to longevity. (Multicollinearity may affect this answer.) **f** (65.541, 77.310) **g** (68.748, 74.665)
17.64 a Lottery $= 11.9 - .430$ Eduction $+ .0292$ Age $+ .093$ Children $- .0745$ Income **b** $s_\epsilon = 2.910$, $R^2 = 43.3\%$, $F = 18.17$ (p-value = 0) **e 1** $t = -3.26$ (p-value = .001) **2** $t = 1.16$ (p-value = .125) **3** $t = .42$ (p-value = .339) **4** $t = -2.69$ (p-value = .0045) Beliefs 1 and 4 appear to be true.

Chapter 18

18.2 (170.1, 173.77, 177.43, 181.1, 184.77, 188.43, 192.1)
18.4 c no **d** level shift
18.6 c The process is under control.
18.8 The process went out of control at sample 19 ($\bar{x}$ chart).
18.10 a, b (25.25, 25.93, 26.62, 27.3, 27.99, 28.67, 29.36) **c** (1.12, 6.1, 11.08)
18.12 a (0, 11.68, 26.65) **b** (10.25, 18.76, 27.27) **c** The process went out of control at sample 13 ($\bar{x}$ chart).
18.14 The process is under control.
18.16 The process is under control.
18.18 The process went out of control at sample 19 ($\bar{x}$ chart).
18.20 The process went out of control at sample 25.
18.24 The process went out of control at sample 11 (S chart) and sample 21 ($\bar{x}$ chart).
18.26 The process went out of control at sample 23 (S chart) and sample 25 ($\bar{x}$ chart).
18.28 The process is under control.
18.30 The process went out of control at sample 24.
18.32 The process went out of control at sample 29 ($\bar{x}$ chart).

Chapter 19

19.2 $\hat{y} = -20.2 + .0851$ Gold $R^2 = 62.9\%$ $F = 44.02$ (p-value = 0)
19.4 a (6.402, 7.773) **b** ($80,025, 97,162.50)

19.6 a $\chi^2 = 7.808$ (p-value = .0052) **b** $\chi^2 = 84.507$ (p-value = 0)
19.8 $R^2 = 70.4\%$ $F = 9.28$ (p-value = 0)
19.10 Multiple regression model
Problem-solving: $t = 6.27$ (p-value = 0)
Technical knowledge: $t = 11.24$ (p-value = 0)
19.12 a $F = 3.35$ (p-value = .042)
19.14 $Z = -2.85$ (p-value = .0022)

19.16 $t = -1.31$ (p-value = .099)
19.18 a $t = -1.61$ (p-value = .055)
b $(-6,995, 722)$
19.20 a $t = 20.61$ (p-value = 0) **b** $t = 2.45$ (p-value = .0075)
19.22 $F = 3.53$ (p-value = .015)
19.24 a $t = 4.06$ (p-value = 0)
19.26 $R^2 = 53.2\%$; $F = 21.40$ (p-value = 0)

19.28 a $(.500, .680)$ **b** $Z = .21$ (p-value = .8329)
c $Z = -1.89$ (p-value = .0583) **d** $\chi^2 = 1.027$ (p-value = .5984)
19.30 t-test of μ_t: $t = -1.20$ (p-value = .12)
t-test of $\mu_1 - \mu_2$: $t = -1.42$ (p-value = .08)

Table 1

Binomial Probabilities

Tabulated values are $P(X \leq k) = \sum_{x=0}^{k} p(x)$. (Values are rounded to three decimal places.)

$n = 5$

k	.01	.05	.10	.20	.25	.30	.40	.50	.60	.70	.75	.80	.90	.95	.99
0	.951	.774	.590	.328	.237	.168	.078	.031	.010	.002	.001	.000	.000	.000	.000
1	.999	.977	.919	.737	.633	.528	.337	.187	.087	.031	.016	.007	.000	.000	.000
2	1.000	.999	.991	.942	.896	.837	.683	.500	.317	.163	.104	.058	.009	.001	.000
3	1.000	1.000	1.000	.993	.984	.969	.913	.812	.663	.472	.367	.263	.081	.023	.001
4	1.000	1.000	1.000	1.000	.999	.998	.990	.969	.922	.832	.763	.672	.410	.226	.049

$n = 6$

k	.01	.05	.10	.20	.25	.30	.40	.50	.60	.70	.75	.80	.90	.95	.99
0	.941	.735	.531	.262	.178	.118	.047	.016	.004	.001	.000	.000	.000	.000	.000
1	.999	.967	.886	.655	.534	.420	.233	.109	.041	.011	.005	.002	.000	.000	.000
2	1.000	.998	.984	.901	.831	.744	.544	.344	.179	.070	.038	.017	.001	.000	.000
3	1.000	1.000	.999	.983	.962	.930	.821	.656	.456	.256	.169	.099	.016	.002	.000
4	1.000	1.000	1.000	.998	.995	.989	.959	.891	.767	.580	.466	.345	.114	.033	.001
5	1.000	1.000	1.000	1.000	1.000	.999	.996	.984	.953	.882	.822	.738	.469	.265	.059

$n = 7$

k	.01	.05	.10	.20	.25	.30	.40	.50	.60	.70	.75	.80	.90	.95	.99
0	.932	.698	.478	.210	.133	.082	.028	.008	.002	.000	.000	.000	.000	.000	.000
1	.998	.956	.850	.577	.445	.329	.159	.063	.019	.004	.001	.000	.000	.000	.000
2	1.000	.996	.974	.852	.756	.647	.420	.227	.096	.029	.013	.005	.000	.000	.000
3	1.000	1.000	.997	.967	.929	.874	.710	.500	.290	.126	.071	.033	.003	.000	.000
4	1.000	1.000	1.000	.995	.987	.971	.904	.773	.580	.353	.244	.148	.026	.004	.000
5	1.000	1.000	1.000	1.000	.999	.996	.981	.937	.841	.671	.555	.423	.150	.044	.002
6	1.000	1.000	1.000	1.000	1.000	1.000	.998	.992	.972	.918	.867	.790	.522	.302	.068

Table 1

continued

n = 8

								p							
k	.01	.05	.10	.20	.25	.30	.40	.50	.60	.70	.75	.80	.90	.95	.99
0	.923	.663	.430	.168	.100	.058	.017	.004	.001	.000	.000	.000	.000	.000	.000
1	.997	.943	.813	.503	.367	.255	.106	.035	.009	.001	.000	.000	.000	.000	.000
2	1.000	.994	.962	.797	.679	.552	.315	.145	.050	.011	.004	.001	.000	.000	.000
3	1.000	1.000	.995	.944	.886	.806	.594	.363	.174	.058	.027	.010	.000	.000	.000
4	1.000	1.000	1.000	.990	.973	.942	.826	.637	.406	.194	.114	.056	.005	.000	.000
5	1.000	1.000	1.000	.999	.996	.989	.950	.855	.685	.448	.321	.203	.038	.006	.000
6	1.000	1.000	1.000	1.000	1.000	.999	.991	.965	.894	.745	.633	.497	.187	.057	.003
7	1.000	1.000	1.000	1.000	1.000	1.000	.999	.996	.983	.942	.900	.832	.570	.337	.077

n = 9

								p							
k	.01	.05	.10	.20	.25	.30	.40	.50	.60	.70	.75	.80	.90	.95	.99
0	.914	.630	.387	.134	.075	.040	.010	.002	.000	.000	.000	.000	.000	.000	.000
1	.997	.929	.775	.436	.300	.196	.071	.020	.004	.000	.000	.000	.000	.000	.000
2	1.000	.992	.947	.738	.601	.463	.232	.090	.025	.004	.001	.000	.000	.000	.000
3	1.000	.999	.992	.914	.834	.730	.483	.254	.099	.025	.010	.003	.000	.000	.000
4	1.000	1.000	.999	.980	.951	.901	.733	.500	.267	.099	.049	.020	.001	.000	.000
5	1.000	1.000	1.000	.997	.990	.975	.901	.746	.517	.270	.166	.086	.008	.001	.000
6	1.000	1.000	1.000	1.000	.999	.996	.975	.910	.768	.537	.399	.262	.053	.008	.000
7	1.000	1.000	1.000	1.000	1.000	1.000	.996	.980	.929	.804	.700	.564	.225	.071	.003
8	1.000	1.000	1.000	1.000	1.000	1.000	1.000	.998	.990	.960	.925	.866	.613	.370	.086

Table 1

continued

n = 10

k	.01	.05	.10	.20	.25	.30	.40	.50	.60	.70	.75	.80	.90	.95	.99
								p							
0	.904	.599	.349	.107	.056	.028	.006	.001	.000	.000	.000	.000	.000	.000	.000
1	.996	.914	.736	.376	.244	.149	.046	.011	.002	.000	.000	.000	.000	.000	.000
2	1.000	.988	.930	.678	.526	.383	.167	.055	.012	.002	.000	.000	.000	.000	.000
3	1.000	.999	.987	.879	.776	.650	.382	.172	.055	.011	.004	.001	.000	.000	.000
4	1.000	1.000	.998	.967	.922	.850	.633	.377	.166	.047	.020	.006	.000	.000	.000
5	1.000	1.000	1.000	.994	.980	.953	.834	.623	.367	.150	.078	.033	.002	.000	.000
6	1.000	1.000	1.000	.999	.996	.989	.945	.828	.618	.350	.224	.121	.013	.001	.000
7	1.000	1.000	1.000	1.000	1.000	.998	.988	.945	.833	.617	.474	.322	.070	.012	.000
8	1.000	1.000	1.000	1.000	1.000	1.000	.998	.989	.954	.851	.756	.624	.264	.086	.004
9	1.000	1.000	1.000	1.000	1.000	1.000	1.000	.999	.994	.972	.944	.893	.651	.401	.096

n = 15

k	.01	.05	.10	.20	.25	.30	.40	.50	.60	.70	.75	.80	.90	.95	.99
								p							
0	.860	.463	.206	.035	.013	.005	.000	.000	.000	.000	.000	.000	.000	.000	.000
1	.990	.829	.549	.167	.080	.035	.005	.000	.000	.000	.000	.000	.000	.000	.000
2	1.000	.964	.816	.398	.236	.127	.027	.004	.000	.000	.000	.000	.000	.000	.000
3	1.000	.995	.944	.648	.461	.297	.091	.018	.002	.000	.000	.000	.000	.000	.000
4	1.000	.999	.987	.836	.686	.515	.217	.059	.009	.001	.000	.000	.000	.000	.000
5	1.000	1.000	.998	.939	.852	.722	.403	.151	.034	.004	.001	.000	.000	.000	.000
6	1.000	1.000	1.000	.982	.943	.869	.610	.304	.095	.015	.004	.001	.000	.000	.000
7	1.000	1.000	1.000	.996	.983	.950	.787	.500	.213	.050	.017	.004	.000	.000	.000
8	1.000	1.000	1.000	.999	.996	.985	.905	.696	.390	.131	.057	.018	.000	.000	.000
9	1.000	1.000	1.000	1.000	.999	.996	.966	.849	.597	.278	.148	.061	.002	.000	.000
10	1.000	1.000	1.000	1.000	1.000	.999	.991	.941	.783	.485	.314	.164	.013	.001	.000
11	1.000	1.000	1.000	1.000	1.000	1.000	.998	.982	.909	.703	.539	.352	.056	.005	.000
12	1.000	1.000	1.000	1.000	1.000	1.000	1.000	.996	.973	.873	.764	.602	.184	.036	.000
13	1.000	1.000	1.000	1.000	1.000	1.000	1.000	1.000	.995	.965	.920	.833	.451	.171	.010
14	1.000	1.000	1.000	1.000	1.000	1.000	1.000	1.000	1.000	.995	.987	.965	.794	.537	.140

Table 1

continued

n = 20

k	|	.01	.05	.10	.20	.25	.30	.40	.50	.60	.70	.75	.80	.90	.95	.99
									p							
0	|	.818	.358	.122	.012	.003	.001	.000	.000	.000	.000	.000	.000	.000	.000	.000
1	|	.983	.736	.392	.069	.024	.008	.001	.000	.000	.000	.000	.000	.000	.000	.000
2	|	.999	.925	.677	.206	.091	.035	.004	.000	.000	.000	.000	.000	.000	.000	.000
3	|	1.000	.984	.867	.411	.225	.107	.016	.001	.000	.000	.000	.000	.000	.000	.000
4	|	1.000	.997	.957	.630	.415	.238	.051	.006	.000	.000	.000	.000	.000	.000	.000
5	|	1.000	1.000	.989	.804	.617	.416	.126	.021	.002	.000	.000	.000	.000	.000	.000
6	|	1.000	1.000	.998	.913	.786	.608	.250	.058	.006	.000	.000	.000	.000	.000	.000
7	|	1.000	1.000	1.000	.968	.898	.772	.416	.132	.021	.001	.000	.000	.000	.000	.000
8	|	1.000	1.000	1.000	.990	.959	.887	.596	.252	.057	.005	.001	.000	.000	.000	.000
9	|	1.000	1.000	1.000	.997	.986	.952	.755	.412	.128	.017	.004	.001	.000	.000	.000
10	|	1.000	1.000	1.000	.999	.996	.983	.872	.588	.245	.048	.014	.003	.000	.000	.000
11	|	1.000	1.000	1.000	1.000	.999	.995	.943	.748	.404	.113	.041	.010	.000	.000	.000
12	|	1.000	1.000	1.000	1.000	1.000	.999	.979	.868	.584	.228	.102	.032	.000	.000	.000
13	|	1.000	1.000	1.000	1.000	1.000	1.000	.994	.942	.750	.392	.214	.087	.002	.000	.000
14	|	1.000	1.000	1.000	1.000	1.000	1.000	.998	.979	.874	.584	.383	.196	.011	.000	.000
15	|	1.000	1.000	1.000	1.000	1.000	1.000	1.000	.994	.949	.762	.585	.370	.043	.003	.000
16	|	1.000	1.000	1.000	1.000	1.000	1.000	1.000	.999	.984	.893	.775	.589	.133	.016	.000
17	|	1.000	1.000	1.000	1.000	1.000	1.000	1.000	1.000	.996	.965	.909	.794	.323	.075	.001
18	|	1.000	1.000	1.000	1.000	1.000	1.000	1.000	1.000	.999	.992	.976	.931	.608	.264	.017
19	|	1.000	1.000	1.000	1.000	1.000	1.000	1.000	1.000	1.000	.999	.997	.988	.878	.642	.182

Table 1

continued

$n = 25$

k	.01	.05	.10	.20	.25	.30	.40	.50	.60	.70	.75	.80	.90	.95	.99
								p							
0	.778	.277	.072	.004	.001	.000	.000	.000	.000	.000	.000	.000	.000	.000	.000
1	.974	.642	.271	.027	.007	.002	.000	.000	.000	.000	.000	.000	.000	.000	.000
2	.998	.873	.537	.098	.032	.009	.000	.000	.000	.000	.000	.000	.000	.000	.000
3	1.000	.966	.764	.234	.096	.033	.002	.000	.000	.000	.000	.000	.000	.000	.000
4	1.000	.993	.902	.421	.214	.090	.009	.000	.000	.000	.000	.000	.000	.000	.000
5	1.000	.999	.967	.617	.378	.193	.029	.002	.000	.000	.000	.000	.000	.000	.000
6	1.000	1.000	.991	.780	.561	.341	.074	.007	.000	.000	.000	.000	.000	.000	.000
7	1.000	1.000	.998	.891	.727	.512	.154	.022	.001	.000	.000	.000	.000	.000	.000
8	1.000	1.000	1.000	.953	.851	.677	.274	.054	.004	.000	.000	.000	.000	.000	.000
9	1.000	1.000	1.000	.983	.929	.811	.425	.115	.013	.000	.000	.000	.000	.000	.000
10	1.000	1.000	1.000	.994	.970	.902	.586	.212	.034	.002	.000	.000	.000	.000	.000
11	1.000	1.000	1.000	.998	.989	.956	.732	.345	.078	.006	.001	.000	.000	.000	.000
12	1.000	1.000	1.000	1.000	.997	.983	.846	.500	.154	.017	.003	.000	.000	.000	.000
13	1.000	1.000	1.000	1.000	.999	.994	.922	.655	.268	.044	.011	.002	.000	.000	.000
14	1.000	1.000	1.000	1.000	1.000	.998	.966	.788	.414	.098	.030	.006	.000	.000	.000
15	1.000	1.000	1.000	1.000	1.000	1.000	.987	.885	.575	.189	.071	.017	.000	.000	.000
16	1.000	1.000	1.000	1.000	1.000	1.000	.996	.946	.726	.323	.149	.047	.000	.000	.000
17	1.000	1.000	1.000	1.000	1.000	1.000	.999	.978	.846	.488	.273	.109	.002	.000	.000
18	1.000	1.000	1.000	1.000	1.000	1.000	1.000	.993	.926	.659	.439	.220	.009	.000	.000
19	1.000	1.000	1.000	1.000	1.000	1.000	1.000	.998	.971	.807	.622	.383	.033	.001	.000
20	1.000	1.000	1.000	1.000	1.000	1.000	1.000	1.000	.991	.910	.786	.579	.098	.007	.000
21	1.000	1.000	1.000	1.000	1.000	1.000	1.000	1.000	.998	.967	.904	.766	.236	.034	.000
22	1.000	1.000	1.000	1.000	1.000	1.000	1.000	1.000	1.000	.991	.968	.902	.463	.127	.002
23	1.000	1.000	1.000	1.000	1.000	1.000	1.000	1.000	1.000	.998	.993	.973	.729	.358	.026
24	1.000	1.000	1.000	1.000	1.000	1.000	1.000	1.000	1.000	1.000	.999	.996	.928	.723	.222

Table 2

Poisson Probabilities

Tabulated values are $P(X \le k) = \sum_{x=0}^{k} p(x)$. (Values are rounded to three decimal places.)

k	.10	.20	.30	.40	.50	1.0	1.5	2.0	2.5	3.0	3.5	4.0	4.5	5.0	5.5	6.0
0	.905	.819	.741	.670	.607	.368	.223	.135	.082	.050	.030	.018	.011	.007	.004	.002
1	.995	.982	.963	.938	.910	.736	.558	.406	.287	.199	.136	.092	.061	.040	.027	.017
2	1.000	.999	.996	.992	.986	.920	.809	.677	.544	.423	.321	.238	.174	.125	.088	.062
3	1.000	1.000	1.000	.999	.998	.981	.934	.857	.758	.647	.537	.433	.342	.265	.202	.151
4	1.000	1.000	1.000	1.000	1.000	.996	.981	.947	.891	.815	.725	.629	.532	.440	.358	.285
5						.999	.996	.983	.958	.916	.858	.785	.703	.616	.529	.446
6						1.000	.999	.995	.986	.966	.935	.889	.831	.762	.686	.606
7							1.000	.999	.996	.988	.973	.949	.913	.867	.809	.744
8								1.000	.999	.996	.990	.979	.960	.932	.894	.847
9									1.000	.999	.997	.992	.983	.968	.946	.916
10										1.000	.999	.997	.993	.986	.975	.957
11											1.000	.999	.998	.995	.989	.980
12												1.000	.999	.998	.996	.991
13													1.000	.999	.998	.996
14														1.000	.999	.999
15															1.000	.999
16																1.000
17																
18																
19																
20																

Table 2

continued

k	6.5	7.0	7.5	8.0	8.5	9.0	μ 9.5	10	11	12	13	14	15
0	.002	.001	.001	.000	.000	.000	.000	.000	.000	.000	.000	.000	.000
1	.011	.007	.005	.003	.002	.001	.001	.000	.000	.000	.000	.000	.000
2	.043	.030	.020	.014	.009	.006	.004	.003	.001	.001	.000	.000	.000
3	.112	.082	.059	.042	.030	.021	.015	.010	.005	.002	.001	.000	.000
4	.224	.173	.132	.100	.074	.055	.040	.029	.015	.008	.004	.002	.001
5	.369	.301	.241	.191	.150	.116	.089	.067	.038	.020	.011	.006	.003
6	.527	.450	.378	.313	.256	.207	.165	.130	.079	.046	.026	.014	.008
7	.673	.599	.525	.453	.386	.324	.269	.220	.143	.090	.054	.032	.018
8	.792	.729	.662	.593	.523	.456	.392	.333	.232	.155	.100	.062	.037
9	.877	.830	.776	.717	.653	.587	.522	.458	.341	.242	.166	.109	.070
10	.933	.901	.862	.816	.763	.706	.645	.583	.460	.347	.252	.176	.118
11	.966	.947	.921	.888	.849	.803	.752	.697	.579	.462	.353	.260	.185
12	.984	.973	.957	.936	.909	.876	.836	.792	.689	.576	.463	.358	.268
13	.993	.987	.978	.966	.949	.926	.898	.864	.781	.682	.573	.464	.363
14	.997	.994	.990	.983	.973	.959	.940	.917	.854	.772	.675	.570	.466
15	.999	.998	.995	.992	.986	.978	.967	.951	.907	.844	.764	.669	.568
16	1.000	.999	.998	.996	.993	.989	.982	.973	.944	.899	.835	.756	.664
17		1.000	.999	.998	.997	.995	.991	.986	.968	.937	.890	.827	.749
18			1.000	.999	.999	.998	.996	.993	.982	.963	.930	.883	.819
19				1.000	.999	.999	.998	.997	.991	.979	.957	.923	.875
20					1.000	1.000	.999	.998	.995	.988	.975	.952	.917
21							1.000	.999	.998	.994	.986	.971	.947
22								1.000	.999	.997	.992	.983	.967
23									1.000	.999	.996	.991	.981
24										.999	.998	.995	.989
25										1.000	.999	.997	.994
26											1.000	.999	.997
27												.999	.998
28												1.000	.999
29													1.000

Table 3

Normal Curve Areas

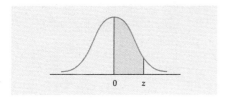

z	.00	.01	.02	.03	.04	.05	.06	.07	.08	.09
0.0	.0000	.0040	.0080	.0120	.0160	.0199	.0239	.0279	.0319	.0359
0.1	.0398	.0438	.0478	.0517	.0557	.0596	.0636	.0675	.0714	.0753
0.2	.0793	.0832	.0871	.0910	.0948	.0987	.1026	.1064	.1103	.1141
0.3	.1179	.1217	.1255	.1293	.1331	.1368	.1406	.1443	.1480	.1517
0.4	.1554	.1591	.1628	.1664	.1700	.1736	.1772	.1808	.1844	.1879
0.5	.1915	.1950	.1985	.2019	.2054	.2088	.2123	.2157	.2190	.2224
0.6	.2257	.2291	.2324	.2357	.2389	.2422	.2454	.2486	.2517	.2549
0.7	.2580	.2611	.2642	.2673	.2704	.2734	.2764	.2794	.2823	.2852
0.8	.2881	.2910	.2939	.2967	.2995	.3023	.3051	.3078	.3106	.3133
0.9	.3159	.3186	.3212	.3238	.3264	.3289	.3315	.3340	.3365	.3389
1.0	.3413	.3438	.3461	.3485	.3508	.3531	.3554	.3577	.3599	.3621
1.1	.3643	.3665	.3686	.3708	.3729	.3749	.3770	.3790	.3810	.3830
1.2	.3849	.3869	.3888	.3907	.3925	.3944	.3962	.3980	.3997	.4015
1.3	.4032	.4049	.4066	.4082	.4099	.4115	.4131	.4147	.4162	.4177
1.4	.4192	.4207	.4222	.4236	.4251	.4265	.4279	.4292	.4306	.4319
1.5	.4332	.4345	.4357	.4370	.4382	.4394	.4406	.4418	.4429	.4441
1.6	.4452	.4463	.4474	.4484	.4495	.4505	.4515	.4525	.4535	.4545
1.7	.4554	.4564	.4573	.4582	.4591	.4599	.4608	.4616	.4625	.4633
1.8	.4641	.4649	.4656	.4664	.4671	.4678	.4686	.4693	.4699	.4706
1.9	.4713	.4719	.4726	.4732	.4738	.4744	.4750	.4756	.4761	.4767
2.0	.4772	.4778	.4783	.4788	.4793	.4798	.4803	.4808	.4812	.4817
2.1	.4821	.4826	.4830	.4834	.4838	.4842	.4846	.4850	.4854	.4857
2.2	.4861	.4864	.4868	.4871	.4875	.4878	.4881	.4884	.4887	.4890
2.3	.4893	.4896	.4898	.4901	.4904	.4906	.4909	.4911	.4913	.4916
2.4	.4918	.4920	.4922	.4925	.4927	.4929	.4931	.4932	.4934	.4936
2.5	.4938	.4940	.4941	.4943	.4945	.4946	.4948	.4949	.4951	.4952
2.6	.4953	.4955	.4956	.4957	.4959	.4960	.4961	.4962	.4963	.4964
2.7	.4965	.4966	.4967	.4968	.4969	.4970	.4971	.4972	.4973	.4974
2.8	.4974	.4975	.4976	.4977	.4977	.4978	.4979	.4979	.4980	.4981
2.9	.4981	.4982	.4982	.4983	.4984	.4984	.4985	.4985	.4986	.4986
3.0	.4987	.4987	.4987	.4988	.4988	.4989	.4989	.4989	.4990	.4990

SOURCE: Abridged from Table 1 of A. Hald, *Statistical Tables and Formulas* (New York: Wiley & Sons, Inc.), 1952. Reproduced by permission of A. Hald and the publisher, John Wiley & Sons, Inc.

Table 4

Critical Values of *t*

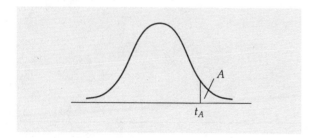

DEGREES OF FREEDOM	$t_{.100}$	$t_{.050}$	$t_{.025}$	$t_{.010}$	$t_{.005}$	DEGREES OF FREEDOM	$t_{.100}$	$t_{.050}$	$t_{.025}$	$t_{.010}$	$t_{.005}$
1	3.078	6.314	12.706	31.821	63.657	24	1.318	1.711	2.064	2.492	2.797
2	1.886	2.920	4.303	6.965	9.925	25	1.316	1.708	2.060	2.485	2.787
3	1.638	2.353	3.182	4.541	5.841	26	1.315	1.706	2.056	2.479	2.779
4	1.533	2.132	2.776	3.747	4.604	27	1.314	1.703	2.052	2.473	2.771
5	1.476	2.015	2.571	3.365	4.032	28	1.313	1.701	2.048	2.467	2.763
6	1.440	1.943	2.447	3.143	3.707	29	1.311	1.699	2.045	2.462	2.756
7	1.415	1.895	2.365	2.998	3.499	30	1.310	1.697	2.042	2.457	2.750
8	1.397	1.860	2.306	2.896	3.355	35	1.306	1.690	2.030	2.438	2.724
9	1.383	1.833	2.262	2.821	3.250	40	1.303	1.684	2.021	2.423	2.705
10	1.372	1.812	2.228	2.764	3.169	45	1.301	1.679	2.014	2.412	2.690
11	1.363	1.796	2.201	2.718	3.106	50	1.299	1.676	2.009	2.403	2.678
12	1.356	1.782	2.179	2.681	3.055	60	1.296	1.671	2.000	2.390	2.660
13	1.350	1.771	2.160	2.650	3.012	70	1.294	1.667	1.994	2.381	2.648
14	1.345	1.761	2.145	2.624	2.977	80	1.292	1.664	1.990	2.374	2.639
15	1.341	1.753	2.131	2.602	2.947	90	1.291	1.662	1.987	2.369	2.632
16	1.337	1.746	2.120	2.583	2.921	100	1.290	1.660	1.984	2.364	2.626
17	1.333	1.740	2.110	2.567	2.898	120	1.289	1.658	1.980	2.358	2.617
18	1.330	1.734	2.101	2.552	2.878	140	1.288	1.656	1.977	2.353	2.611
19	1.328	1.729	2.093	2.539	2.861	160	1.287	1.654	1.975	2.350	2.607
20	1.325	1.725	2.086	2.528	2.845	180	1.286	1.653	1.973	2.347	2.603
21	1.323	1.721	2.080	2.518	2.831	200	1.286	1.653	1.972	2.345	2.601
22	1.321	1.717	2.074	2.508	2.819	∞	1.282	1.645	1.960	2.326	2.576
23	1.319	1.714	2.069	2.500	2.807						

SOURCE: From M. Merrington, "Table of Percentage Points of the *t*-Distribution," *Biometrika* 32 (1941): 300. Reproduced by permission of the Biometrika Trustees.

Table 5

Critical Values of χ^2

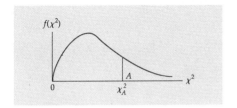

DEGREES OF FREEDOM	$\chi^2_{.995}$	$\chi^2_{.990}$	$\chi^2_{.975}$	$\chi^2_{.950}$	$\chi^2_{.900}$	$\chi^2_{.100}$	$\chi^2_{.050}$	$\chi^2_{.025}$	$\chi^2_{.010}$	$\chi^2_{.005}$
1	0.0000393	0.0001571	0.0009821	0.0039321	0.0157908	2.70554	3.84146	5.02389	6.63490	7.87944
2	0.0100251	0.0201007	0.0506356	0.102587	0.210720	4.60517	5.99147	7.37776	9.21034	10.5966
3	0.0717212	0.114832	0.215795	0.351846	0.584375	6.25139	7.81473	9.34840	11.3449	12.8381
4	0.206990	0.297110	0.484419	0.710721	1.063623	7.77944	9.48773	11.1433	13.2767	14.8602
5	0.411740	0.554300	0.831211	1.145476	1.61031	9.23635	11.0705	12.8325	15.0863	16.7496
6	0.675727	0.872085	1.237347	1.63539	2.20413	10.6446	12.5916	14.4494	16.8119	18.5476
7	0.989265	1.239043	1.68987	2.16735	2.83311	12.0170	14.0671	16.0128	18.4753	20.2777
8	1.344419	1.646482	2.17973	2.73264	3.48954	13.3616	15.5073	17.5346	20.0902	21.9550
9	1.734926	2.087912	2.70039	3.32511	4.16816	14.6837	16.9190	19.0228	21.6660	23.5893
10	2.15585	2.55821	3.24697	3.94030	4.86518	15.9871	18.3070	20.4831	23.2093	25.1882
11	2.60321	3.05347	3.81575	4.57481	5.57779	17.2750	19.6751	21.9200	24.7250	26.7569
12	3.07382	3.57056	4.40379	5.22603	6.30380	18.5494	21.0261	23.3367	26.2170	28.2995
13	3.56503	4.10691	5.00874	5.89186	7.04150	19.8119	22.3621	24.7356	27.6883	29.8194
14	4.07468	4.66043	5.62872	6.57063	7.78953	21.0642	23.6848	26.1190	29.1413	31.3193
15	4.60094	5.22935	6.26214	7.26094	8.54675	22.3072	24.9958	27.4884	30.5779	32.8013
16	5.14224	5.81221	6.90766	7.96164	9.31223	23.5418	26.2962	28.8454	31.9999	34.2672
17	5.69724	6.40776	7.56418	8.67176	10.0852	24.7690	27.5871	30.1910	33.4087	35.7185
18	6.26481	7.01491	8.23075	9.39046	10.8649	25.9894	28.8693	31.5264	34.8053	37.1564
19	6.84398	7.63273	8.90655	10.1170	11.6509	27.2036	30.1435	32.8523	36.1908	38.5822
20	7.43386	8.26040	9.59083	10.8508	12.4426	28.4120	31.4104	34.1696	37.5662	39.9968
21	8.03366	8.89720	10.28293	11.5913	13.2396	29.6151	32.6705	35.4789	38.9321	41.4010
22	8.64272	9.54249	10.9823	12.3380	14.0415	30.8133	33.9244	36.7807	40.2894	42.7956
23	9.26042	10.19567	11.6885	13.0905	14.8479	32.0069	35.1725	38.0757	41.6384	44.1813
24	9.88623	10.8564	12.4011	13.8484	15.6587	33.1963	36.4151	39.3641	42.9798	45.5585
25	10.5197	11.5240	13.1197	14.6114	16.4734	34.3816	37.6525	40.6465	44.3141	46.9278
26	11.1603	12.1981	13.8439	15.3791	17.2919	35.5631	38.8852	41.9232	45.6417	48.2899
27	11.8076	12.8786	14.5733	16.1513	18.1138	36.7412	40.1133	43.1944	46.9630	49.6449
28	12.4613	13.5648	15.3079	16.9279	18.9392	37.9159	41.3372	44.4607	48.2782	50.9933
29	13.1211	14.2565	16.0471	17.7083	19.7677	39.0875	42.5569	45.7222	49.5879	52.3356
30	13.7867	14.9535	16.7908	18.4926	20.5992	40.2560	43.7729	46.9792	50.8922	53.6720
40	20.7065	22.1643	24.4331	26.5093	29.0505	51.8050	55.7585	59.3417	63.6907	66.7659
50	27.9907	29.7067	32.3574	34.7642	37.6886	63.1671	67.5048	71.4202	76.1539	79.4900
60	35.5346	37.4848	40.4817	43.1879	46.4589	74.3970	79.0819	83.2976	88.3794	91.9517
70	43.2752	45.4418	48.7576	51.7393	55.3290	85.5271	90.5312	95.0231	100.425	104.215
80	51.1720	53.5400	57.1532	60.3915	64.2778	96.5782	101.879	106.629	112.329	116.321
90	59.1963	61.7541	65.6466	69.1260	73.2912	107.565	113.145	118.136	124.116	128.299
100	67.3276	70.0648	74.2219	77.9295	82.3581	118.498	124.342	129.561	135.807	140.169

SOURCE: From C. M. Thompson, "Tables of the Percentage Points of the χ^2-Distribution," *Biometrika* 32 (1941): 188–89. Reproduced by permission of the Biometrika Trustees.

Table 6(a)

Percentage Points of the *F* Distribution, *A* = .05

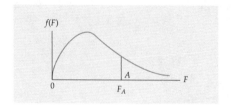

ν_2 \ ν_1	NUMERATOR DEGREES OF FREEDOM								
	1	2	3	4	5	6	7	8	9
1	161.4	199.5	215.7	224.6	230.2	234.0	236.8	238.9	240.5
2	18.51	19.00	19.16	19.25	19.30	19.33	19.35	19.37	19.38
3	10.13	9.55	9.28	9.12	9.01	8.94	8.89	8.85	8.81
4	7.71	6.94	6.59	6.39	6.26	6.16	6.09	6.04	6.00
5	6.61	5.79	5.41	5.19	5.05	4.95	4.88	4.82	4.77
6	5.99	5.14	4.76	4.53	4.39	4.28	4.21	4.15	4.10
7	5.59	4.74	4.35	4.12	3.97	3.87	3.79	3.73	3.68
8	5.32	4.46	4.07	3.84	3.69	3.58	3.50	3.44	3.39
9	5.12	4.26	3.86	3.63	3.48	3.37	3.29	3.23	3.18
10	4.96	4.10	3.71	3.48	3.33	3.22	3.14	3.07	3.02
11	4.84	3.98	3.59	3.36	3.20	3.09	3.01	2.95	2.90
12	4.75	3.89	3.49	3.26	3.11	3.00	2.91	2.85	2.80
13	4.67	3.81	3.41	3.18	3.03	2.92	2.83	2.77	2.71
14	4.60	3.74	3.34	3.11	2.96	2.85	2.76	2.70	2.65
15	4.54	3.68	3.29	3.06	2.90	2.79	2.71	2.64	2.59
16	4.49	3.63	3.24	3.01	2.85	2.74	2.66	2.59	2.54
17	4.45	3.59	3.20	2.96	2.81	2.70	2.61	2.55	2.49
18	4.41	3.55	3.16	2.93	2.77	2.66	2.58	2.51	2.46
19	4.38	3.52	3.13	2.90	2.74	2.63	2.54	2.48	2.42
20	4.35	3.49	3.10	2.87	2.71	2.60	2.51	2.45	2.39
21	4.32	3.47	3.07	2.84	2.68	2.57	2.49	2.42	2.37
22	4.30	3.44	3.05	2.82	2.66	2.55	2.46	2.40	2.34
23	4.28	3.42	3.03	2.80	2.64	2.53	2.44	2.37	2.32
24	4.26	3.40	3.01	2.78	2.62	2.51	2.42	2.36	2.30
25	4.24	3.39	2.99	2.76	2.60	2.49	2.40	2.34	2.28
26	4.23	3.37	2.98	2.74	2.59	2.47	2.39	2.32	2.27
27	4.21	3.35	2.96	2.73	2.57	2.46	2.37	2.31	2.25
28	4.20	3.34	2.95	2.71	2.56	2.45	2.36	2.29	2.24
29	4.18	3.33	2.93	2.70	2.55	2.43	2.35	2.28	2.22
30	4.17	3.32	2.92	2.69	2.53	2.42	2.33	2.27	2.21
40	4.08	3.23	2.84	2.61	2.45	2.34	2.25	2.18	2.12
60	4.00	3.15	2.76	2.53	2.37	2.25	2.17	2.10	2.04
120	3.92	3.07	2.68	2.45	2.29	2.17	2.09	2.02	1.96
∞	3.84	3.00	2.60	2.37	2.21	2.10	2.01	1.94	1.88

SOURCE: From M. Merrington and C. M. Thompson, "Tables of Percentage Points of the Inverted Beta (*F*)-Distribution," *Biometrika* 33 (1943): 73–88. Reproduced by permission of the Biometrika Trustees.

Table 6(a)

continued

Table 6(a)

ν_2 \ ν_1	NUMERATOR DEGREES OF FREEDOM									
	10	12	15	20	24	30	40	60	120	∞
1	241.9	243.9	245.9	248.0	249.1	250.1	251.1	252.2	253.3	254.3
2	19.40	19.41	19.43	19.45	19.45	19.46	19.47	19.48	19.49	19.50
3	8.79	8.74	8.70	8.66	8.64	8.62	8.59	8.57	8.55	8.53
4	5.96	5.91	5.86	5.80	5.77	5.75	5.72	5.69	5.66	5.63
5	4.74	4.68	4.62	4.56	4.53	4.50	4.46	4.43	4.40	4.36
6	4.06	4.00	3.94	3.87	3.84	3.81	3.77	3.74	3.70	3.67
7	3.64	3.57	3.51	3.44	3.41	3.38	3.34	3.30	3.27	3.23
8	3.35	3.28	3.22	3.15	3.12	3.08	3.04	3.01	2.97	2.93
9	3.14	3.07	3.01	2.94	2.90	2.86	2.83	2.79	2.75	2.71
10	2.98	2.91	2.85	2.77	2.74	2.70	2.66	2.62	2.58	2.54
11	2.85	2.79	2.72	2.65	2.61	2.57	2.53	2.49	2.45	2.40
12	2.75	2.69	2.62	2.54	2.51	2.47	2.43	2.38	2.34	2.30
13	2.67	2.60	2.53	2.46	2.42	2.38	2.34	2.30	2.25	2.21
14	2.60	2.53	2.46	2.39	2.35	2.31	2.27	2.22	2.18	2.13
15	2.54	2.48	2.40	2.33	2.29	2.25	2.20	2.16	2.11	2.07
16	2.49	2.42	2.35	2.28	2.24	2.19	2.15	2.11	2.06	2.01
17	2.45	2.38	2.31	2.23	2.19	2.15	2.10	2.06	2.01	1.96
18	2.41	2.34	2.27	2.19	2.15	2.11	2.06	2.02	1.97	1.92
19	2.38	2.31	2.23	2.16	2.11	2.07	2.03	1.98	1.93	1.88
20	2.35	2.28	2.20	2.12	2.08	2.04	1.99	1.95	1.90	1.84
21	2.32	2.25	2.18	2.10	2.05	2.01	1.96	1.92	1.87	1.81
22	2.30	2.23	2.15	2.07	2.03	1.98	1.94	1.89	1.84	1.78
23	2.27	2.20	2.13	2.05	2.01	1.96	1.91	1.86	1.81	1.76
24	2.25	2.18	2.11	2.03	1.98	1.94	1.89	1.84	1.79	1.73
25	2.24	2.16	2.09	2.01	1.96	1.92	1.87	1.82	1.77	1.71
26	2.22	2.15	2.07	1.99	1.95	1.90	1.85	1.80	1.75	1.69
27	2.20	2.13	2.06	1.97	1.93	1.88	1.84	1.79	1.73	1.67
28	2.19	2.12	2.04	1.96	1.91	1.87	1.82	1.77	1.71	1.65
29	2.18	2.10	2.03	1.94	1.90	1.85	1.81	1.75	1.70	1.64
30	2.16	2.09	2.01	1.93	1.89	1.84	1.79	1.74	1.68	1.62
40	2.08	2.00	1.92	1.84	1.79	1.74	1.69	1.64	1.58	1.51
60	1.99	1.92	1.84	1.75	1.70	1.65	1.59	1.53	1.47	1.39
120	1.91	1.83	1.75	1.66	1.61	1.55	1.50	1.43	1.35	1.25
∞	1.83	1.75	1.67	1.57	1.52	1.46	1.39	1.32	1.22	1.00

DENOMINATOR DEGREES OF FREEDOM

Table 6(b)

Percentage Points of the *F* Distribution, *A* = .025

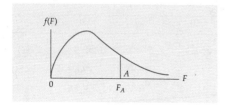

ν_2	NUMERATOR DEGREES OF FREEDOM								
ν_1	1	2	3	4	5	6	7	8	9
1	647.8	799.5	864.2	899.6	921.8	937.1	948.2	956.7	963.3
2	38.51	39.00	39.17	39.25	39.30	39.33	39.36	39.37	39.39
3	17.44	16.04	15.44	15.10	14.88	14.73	14.62	14.54	14.47
4	12.22	10.65	9.98	9.60	9.36	9.20	9.07	8.98	8.90
5	10.01	8.43	7.76	7.39	7.15	6.98	6.85	6.76	6.68
6	8.81	7.26	6.60	6.23	5.99	5.82	5.70	5.60	5.52
7	8.07	6.54	5.89	5.52	5.29	5.12	4.99	4.90	4.82
8	7.57	6.06	5.42	5.05	4.82	4.65	4.53	4.43	4.36
9	7.21	5.71	5.08	4.72	4.48	4.32	4.20	4.10	4.03
10	6.94	5.46	4.83	4.47	4.24	4.07	3.95	3.85	3.78
11	6.72	5.26	4.63	4.28	4.04	3.88	3.76	3.66	3.59
12	6.55	5.10	4.47	4.12	3.89	3.73	3.61	3.51	3.44
13	6.41	4.97	4.35	4.00	3.77	3.60	3.48	3.39	3.31
14	6.30	4.86	4.24	3.89	3.66	3.50	3.38	3.29	3.21
15	6.20	4.77	4.15	3.80	3.58	3.41	3.29	3.20	3.12
16	6.12	4.69	4.08	3.73	3.50	3.34	3.22	3.12	3.05
17	6.04	4.62	4.01	3.66	3.44	3.28	3.16	3.06	2.98
18	5.98	4.56	3.95	3.61	3.38	3.22	3.10	3.01	2.93
19	5.92	4.51	3.90	3.56	3.33	3.17	3.05	2.96	2.88
20	5.87	4.46	3.86	3.51	3.29	3.13	3.01	2.91	2.84
21	5.83	4.42	3.82	3.48	3.25	3.09	2.97	2.87	2.80
22	5.79	4.38	3.78	3.44	3.22	3.05	2.93	2.84	2.76
23	5.75	4.35	3.75	3.41	3.18	3.02	2.90	2.81	2.73
24	5.72	4.32	3.72	3.38	3.15	2.99	2.87	2.78	2.70
25	5.69	4.29	3.69	3.35	3.13	2.97	2.85	2.75	2.68
26	5.66	4.27	3.67	3.33	3.10	2.94	2.82	2.73	2.65
27	5.63	4.24	3.65	3.31	3.08	2.92	2.80	2.71	2.63
28	5.61	4.22	3.63	3.29	3.06	2.90	2.78	2.69	2.61
29	5.59	4.20	3.61	3.27	3.04	2.88	2.76	2.67	2.59
30	5.57	4.18	3.59	3.25	3.03	2.87	2.75	2.65	2.57
40	5.42	4.05	3.46	3.13	2.90	2.74	2.62	2.53	2.45
60	5.29	3.93	3.34	3.01	2.79	2.63	2.51	2.41	2.33
120	5.15	3.80	3.23	2.89	2.67	2.52	2.39	2.30	2.22
∞	5.02	3.69	3.12	2.79	2.57	2.41	2.29	2.19	2.11

DENOMINATOR DEGREES OF FREEDOM

SOURCE: From M. Merrington and C. M. Thompson, "Tables of Percentage Points of the Inverted Beta (*F*)-Distribution," *Biometrika* 33 (1943): 73–88. Reproduced by permission of the Biometrika Trustees.

Table 6(b)

continued

ν_2 \ ν_1	NUMERATOR DEGREES OF FREEDOM									
	10	**12**	**15**	**20**	**24**	**30**	**40**	**60**	**120**	**∞**
1	968.6	976.7	984.9	993.1	997.2	1,001	1,006	1,010	1,014	1,018
2	39.40	39.41	39.43	39.45	39.46	39.46	39.47	39.48	39.49	39.50
3	14.42	14.34	14.25	14.17	14.12	14.08	14.04	13.99	13.95	13.90
4	8.84	8.75	8.66	8.56	8.51	8.46	8.41	8.36	8.31	8.26
5	6.62	6.52	6.43	6.33	6.28	6.23	6.18	6.12	6.07	6.02
6	5.46	5.37	5.27	5.17	5.12	5.07	5.01	4.96	4.90	4.85
7	4.76	4.67	4.57	4.47	4.42	4.36	4.31	4.25	4.20	4.14
8	4.30	4.20	4.10	4.00	3.95	3.89	3.84	3.78	3.73	3.67
9	3.96	3.87	3.77	3.67	3.61	3.56	3.51	3.45	3.39	3.33
10	3.72	3.62	3.52	3.42	3.37	3.31	3.26	3.20	3.14	3.08
11	3.53	3.43	3.33	3.23	3.17	3.12	3.06	3.00	2.94	2.88
12	3.37	3.28	3.18	3.07	3.02	2.96	2.91	2.85	2.79	2.72
13	3.25	3.15	3.05	2.95	2.89	2.84	2.78	2.72	2.66	2.60
14	3.15	3.05	2.95	2.84	2.79	2.73	2.67	2.61	2.55	2.49
15	3.06	2.96	2.86	2.76	2.70	2.64	2.59	2.52	2.46	2.40
16	2.99	2.89	2.79	2.68	2.63	2.57	2.51	2.45	2.38	2.32
17	2.92	2.82	2.72	2.62	2.56	2.50	2.44	2.38	2.32	2.25
18	2.87	2.77	2.67	2.56	2.50	2.44	2.38	2.32	2.26	2.19
19	2.82	2.72	2.62	2.51	2.45	2.39	2.33	2.27	2.20	2.13
20	2.77	2.68	2.57	2.46	2.41	2.35	2.29	2.22	2.16	2.09
21	2.73	2.64	2.53	2.42	2.37	2.31	2.25	2.18	2.11	2.04
22	2.70	2.60	2.50	2.39	2.33	2.27	2.21	2.14	2.08	2.00
23	2.67	2.57	2.47	2.36	2.30	2.24	2.18	2.11	2.04	1.97
24	2.64	2.54	2.44	2.33	2.27	2.21	2.15	2.08	2.01	1.94
25	2.61	2.51	2.41	2.30	2.24	2.18	2.12	2.05	1.98	1.91
26	2.59	2.49	2.39	2.28	2.22	2.16	2.09	2.03	1.95	1.88
27	2.57	2.47	2.36	2.25	2.19	2.13	2.07	2.00	1.93	1.85
28	2.55	2.45	2.34	2.23	2.17	2.11	2.05	1.98	1.91	1.83
29	2.53	2.43	2.32	2.21	2.15	2.09	2.03	1.96	1.89	1.81
30	2.51	2.41	2.31	2.20	2.14	2.07	2.01	1.94	1.87	1.79
40	2.39	2.29	2.18	2.07	2.01	1.94	1.88	1.80	1.72	1.64
60	2.27	2.17	2.06	1.94	1.88	1.82	1.74	1.67	1.58	1.48
120	2.16	2.05	1.94	1.82	1.76	1.69	1.61	1.53	1.43	1.31
∞	2.05	1.94	1.83	1.71	1.64	1.57	1.48	1.39	1.27	1.00

DENOMINATOR DEGREES OF FREEDOM

Table 6(c)

Percentage Points of the F Distribution, $A = .01$

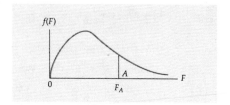

ν_2 \ ν_1	NUMERATOR DEGREES OF FREEDOM								
	1	**2**	**3**	**4**	**5**	**6**	**7**	**8**	**9**
1	4,052	4,999.5	5,403	5,625	5,764	5,859	5,928	5,982	6,022
2	98.50	99.00	99.17	99.25	99.30	99.33	99.36	99.37	99.39
3	34.12	30.82	29.46	28.71	28.24	27.91	27.67	27.49	27.35
4	21.20	18.00	16.69	15.98	15.52	15.21	14.98	14.80	14.66
5	16.26	13.27	12.06	11.39	10.97	10.67	10.46	10.29	10.16
6	13.75	10.92	9.78	9.15	8.75	8.47	8.26	8.10	7.98
7	12.25	9.55	8.45	7.85	7.46	7.19	6.99	6.84	6.72
8	11.26	8.65	7.59	7.01	6.63	6.37	6.18	6.03	5.91
9	10.56	8.02	6.99	6.42	6.06	5.80	5.61	5.47	5.35
10	10.04	7.56	6.55	5.99	5.64	5.39	5.20	5.06	4.94
11	9.65	7.21	6.22	5.67	5.32	5.07	4.89	4.74	4.63
12	9.33	6.93	5.95	5.41	5.06	4.82	4.64	4.50	4.39
13	9.07	6.70	5.74	5.21	4.86	4.62	4.44	4.30	4.19
14	8.86	6.51	5.56	5.04	4.69	4.46	4.28	4.14	4.03
15	8.68	6.36	5.42	4.89	4.56	4.32	4.14	4.00	3.89
16	8.53	6.23	5.29	4.77	4.44	4.20	4.03	3.89	3.78
17	8.40	6.11	5.18	4.67	4.34	4.10	3.93	3.79	3.68
18	8.29	6.01	5.09	4.58	4.25	4.01	3.84	3.71	3.60
19	8.18	5.93	5.01	4.50	4.17	3.94	3.77	3.63	3.52
20	8.10	5.85	4.94	4.43	4.10	3.87	3.70	3.56	3.46
21	8.02	5.78	4.87	4.37	4.04	3.81	3.64	3.51	3.40
22	7.95	5.72	4.82	4.31	3.99	3.76	3.59	3.45	3.35
23	7.88	5.66	4.76	4.26	3.94	3.71	3.54	3.41	3.30
24	7.82	5.61	4.72	4.22	3.90	3.67	3.50	3.36	3.26
25	7.77	5.57	4.68	4.18	3.85	3.63	3.46	3.32	3.22
26	7.72	5.53	4.64	4.14	3.82	3.59	3.42	3.29	3.18
27	7.68	5.49	4.60	4.11	3.78	3.56	3.39	3.26	3.15
28	7.64	5.45	4.57	4.07	3.75	3.53	3.36	3.23	3.12
29	7.60	5.42	4.54	4.04	3.73	3.50	3.33	3.20	3.09
30	7.56	5.39	4.51	4.02	3.70	3.47	3.30	3.17	3.07
40	7.31	5.18	4.31	3.83	3.51	3.29	3.12	2.99	2.89
60	7.08	4.98	4.13	3.65	3.34	3.12	2.95	2.82	2.72
120	6.85	4.79	3.95	3.48	3.17	2.96	2.79	2.66	2.56
∞	6.63	4.61	3.78	3.32	3.02	2.80	2.64	2.51	2.41

SOURCE: From M. Merrington and C. M. Thompson, "Tables of Percentage Points of the Inverted Beta (F)-Distribution," *Biometrika* 33 (1943): 73–88. Reproduced by permission of the Biometrika Trustees.

Table 6(c)

continued

ν_2 \ ν_1	NUMERATOR DEGREES OF FREEDOM									
	10	12	15	20	24	30	40	60	120	∞
1	6,056	6,106	6,157	6,209	6,235	6,261	6,287	6,313	6,339	6,366
2	99.40	99.42	99.43	99.45	99.46	99.47	99.47	99.48	99.49	99.50
3	27.23	27.05	26.87	26.69	26.60	26.50	26.41	26.32	26.22	26.13
4	14.55	14.37	14.20	14.02	13.93	13.84	13.75	13.65	13.56	13.46
5	10.05	9.89	9.72	9.55	9.47	9.38	9.29	9.20	9.11	9.02
6	7.87	7.72	7.56	7.40	7.31	7.23	7.14	7.06	6.97	6.88
7	6.62	6.47	6.31	6.16	6.07	5.99	5.91	5.82	5.74	5.65
8	5.81	5.67	5.52	5.36	5.28	5.20	5.12	5.03	4.95	4.86
9	5.26	5.11	4.96	4.81	4.73	4.65	4.57	4.48	4.40	4.31
10	4.85	4.71	4.56	4.41	4.33	4.25	4.17	4.08	4.00	3.91
11	4.54	4.40	4.25	4.10	4.02	3.94	3.86	3.78	3.69	3.60
12	4.30	4.16	4.01	3.86	3.78	3.70	3.62	3.54	3.45	3.36
13	4.10	3.96	3.82	3.66	3.59	3.51	3.43	3.34	3.25	3.17
14	3.94	3.80	3.66	3.51	3.43	3.35	3.27	3.18	3.09	3.00
15	3.80	3.67	3.52	3.37	3.29	3.21	3.13	3.05	2.96	2.87
16	3.69	3.55	3.41	3.26	3.18	3.10	3.02	2.93	2.84	2.75
17	3.59	3.46	3.31	3.16	3.08	3.00	2.92	2.83	2.75	2.65
18	3.51	3.37	3.23	3.08	3.00	2.92	2.84	2.75	2.66	2.57
19	3.43	3.30	3.15	3.00	2.92	2.84	2.76	2.67	2.58	2.49
20	3.37	3.23	3.09	2.94	2.86	2.78	2.69	2.61	2.52	2.42
21	3.31	3.17	3.03	2.88	2.80	2.72	2.64	2.55	2.46	2.36
22	3.26	3.12	2.98	2.83	2.75	2.67	2.58	2.50	2.40	2.31
23	3.21	3.07	2.93	2.78	2.70	2.62	2.54	2.45	2.35	2.26
24	3.17	3.03	2.89	2.74	2.66	2.58	2.49	2.40	2.31	2.21
25	3.13	2.99	2.85	2.70	2.62	2.54	2.45	2.36	2.27	2.17
26	3.09	2.96	2.81	2.66	2.58	2.50	2.42	2.33	2.23	2.13
27	3.06	2.93	2.78	2.63	2.55	2.47	2.38	2.29	2.20	2.10
28	3.03	2.90	2.75	2.60	2.52	2.44	2.35	2.26	2.17	2.06
29	3.00	2.87	2.73	2.57	2.49	2.41	2.33	2.23	2.14	2.03
30	2.98	2.84	2.70	2.55	2.47	2.39	2.30	2.21	2.11	2.01
40	2.80	2.66	2.52	2.37	2.29	2.20	2.11	2.02	1.92	1.80
60	2.63	2.50	2.35	2.20	2.12	2.03	1.94	1.84	1.73	1.60
120	2.47	2.34	2.19	2.03	1.95	1.86	1.76	1.66	1.53	1.38
∞	2.32	2.18	2.04	1.88	1.79	1.70	1.59	1.47	1.32	1.00

DENOMINATOR DEGREES OF FREEDOM

Table 7(a)

Critical Values for the Durbin–Watson d Statistic, $\alpha = .05$

n	$k = 1$ d_L	d_U	$k = 2$ d_L	d_U	$k = 3$ d_L	d_U	$k = 4$ d_L	d_U	$k = 5$ d_L	d_U
15	1.08	1.36	.95	1.54	.82	1.75	.69	1.97	.56	2.21
16	1.10	1.37	.98	1.54	.86	1.73	.74	1.93	.62	2.15
17	1.13	1.38	1.02	1.54	.90	1.71	.78	1.90	.67	2.10
18	1.16	1.39	1.05	1.53	.93	1.69	.82	1.87	.71	2.06
19	1.18	1.40	1.08	1.53	.97	1.68	.86	1.85	.75	2.02
20	1.20	1.41	1.10	1.54	1.00	1.68	.90	1.83	.79	1.99
21	1.22	1.42	1.13	1.54	1.03	1.67	.93	1.81	.83	1.96
22	1.24	1.43	1.15	1.54	1.05	1.66	.96	1.80	.86	1.94
23	1.26	1.44	1.17	1.54	1.08	1.66	.99	1.79	.90	1.92
24	1.27	1.45	1.19	1.55	1.10	1.66	1.01	1.78	.93	1.90
25	1.29	1.45	1.21	1.55	1.12	1.66	1.04	1.77	.95	1.89
26	1.30	1.46	1.22	1.55	1.14	1.65	1.06	1.76	.98	1.88
27	1.32	1.47	1.24	1.56	1.16	1.65	1.08	1.76	1.01	1.86
28	1.33	1.48	1.26	1.56	1.18	1.65	1.10	1.75	1.03	1.85
29	1.34	1.48	1.27	1.56	1.20	1.65	1.12	1.74	1.05	1.84
30	1.35	1.49	1.28	1.57	1.21	1.65	1.14	1.74	1.07	1.83
31	1.36	1.50	1.30	1.57	1.23	1.65	1.16	1.74	1.09	1.83
32	1.37	1.50	1.31	1.57	1.24	1.65	1.18	1.73	1.11	1.82
33	1.38	1.51	1.32	1.58	1.26	1.65	1.19	1.73	1.13	1.81
34	1.39	1.51	1.33	1.58	1.27	1.65	1.21	1.73	1.15	1.81
35	1.40	1.52	1.34	1.58	1.28	1.65	1.22	1.73	1.16	1.80
36	1.41	1.52	1.35	1.59	1.29	1.65	1.24	1.73	1.18	1.80
37	1.42	1.53	1.36	1.59	1.31	1.66	1.25	1.72	1.19	1.80
38	1.43	1.54	1.37	1.59	1.32	1.66	1.26	1.72	1.21	1.79
39	1.43	1.54	1.38	1.60	1.33	1.66	1.27	1.72	1.22	1.79
40	1.44	1.54	1.39	1.60	1.34	1.66	1.29	1.72	1.23	1.79
45	1.48	1.57	1.43	1.62	1.38	1.67	1.34	1.72	1.29	1.78
50	1.50	1.59	1.46	1.63	1.42	1.67	1.38	1.72	1.34	1.77
55	1.53	1.60	1.49	1.64	1.45	1.68	1.41	1.72	1.38	1.77
60	1.55	1.62	1.51	1.65	1.48	1.69	1.44	1.73	1.41	1.77
65	1.57	1.63	1.54	1.66	1.50	1.70	1.47	1.73	1.44	1.77
70	1.58	1.64	1.55	1.67	1.52	1.70	1.49	1.74	1.46	1.77
75	1.60	1.65	1.57	1.68	1.54	1.71	1.51	1.74	1.49	1.77
80	1.61	1.66	1.59	1.69	1.56	1.72	1.53	1.74	1.51	1.77
85	1.62	1.67	1.60	1.70	1.57	1.72	1.55	1.75	1.52	1.77
90	1.63	1.68	1.61	1.70	1.59	1.73	1.57	1.75	1.54	1.78
95	1.64	1.69	1.62	1.71	1.60	1.73	1.58	1.75	1.56	1.78
100	1.65	1.69	1.63	1.72	1.61	1.74	1.59	1.76	1.57	1.78

SOURCE: From J. Durbin and G. S. Watson, "Testing for Serial Correlation in Least Squares Regression, II," *Biometrika* 30 (1951): 159–78. Reproduced by permission of the Biometrika Trustees.

Table 7(b)

Critical Values for the Durbin–Watson d Statistic, $\alpha = 0.1$

n	$k = 1$ d_L	d_U	$k = 2$ d_L	d_U	$k = 3$ d_L	d_U	$k = 4$ d_L	d_U	$k = 5$ d_L	d_U
15	.81	1.07	.70	1.25	.59	1.46	.49	1.70	.39	1.96
16	.84	1.09	.74	1.25	.63	1.44	.53	1.66	.44	1.90
17	.87	1.10	.77	1.25	.67	1.43	.57	1.63	.48	1.85
18	.90	1.12	.80	1.26	.71	1.42	.61	1.60	.52	1.80
19	.93	1.13	.83	1.26	.74	1.41	.65	1.58	.56	1.77
20	.95	1.15	.86	1.27	.77	1.41	.68	1.57	.60	1.74
21	.97	1.16	.89	1.27	.80	1.41	.72	1.55	.63	1.71
22	1.00	1.17	.91	1.28	.83	1.40	.75	1.54	.66	1.69
23	1.02	1.19	.94	1.29	.86	1.40	.77	1.53	.70	1.67
24	1.04	1.20	.96	1.30	.88	1.41	.80	1.53	.72	1.66
25	1.05	1.21	.98	1.30	.90	1.41	.83	1.52	.75	1.65
26	1.07	1.22	1.00	1.31	.93	1.41	.85	1.52	.78	1.64
27	1.09	1.23	1.02	1.32	.95	1.41	.88	1.51	.81	1.63
28	1.10	1.24	1.04	1.32	.97	1.41	.90	1.51	.83	1.62
29	1.12	1.25	1.05	1.33	.99	1.42	.92	1.51	.85	1.61
30	1.13	1.26	1.07	1.34	1.01	1.42	.94	1.51	.88	1.61
31	1.15	1.27	1.08	1.34	1.02	1.42	.96	1.51	.90	1.60
32	1.16	1.28	1.10	1.35	1.04	1.43	.98	1.51	.92	1.60
33	1.17	1.29	1.11	1.36	1.05	1.43	1.00	1.51	.94	1.59
34	1.18	1.30	1.13	1.36	1.07	1.43	1.01	1.51	.95	1.59
35	1.19	1.31	1.14	1.37	1.08	1.44	1.03	1.51	.97	1.59
36	1.21	1.32	1.15	1.38	1.10	1.44	1.04	1.51	.99	1.59
37	1.22	1.32	1.16	1.38	1.11	1.45	1.06	1.51	1.00	1.59
38	1.23	1.33	1.18	1.39	1.12	1.45	1.07	1.52	1.02	1.58
39	1.24	1.34	1.19	1.39	1.14	1.45	1.09	1.52	1.03	1.58
40	1.25	1.34	1.20	1.40	1.15	1.46	1.10	1.52	1.05	1.58
45	1.29	1.38	1.24	1.42	1.20	1.48	1.16	1.53	1.11	1.58
50	1.32	1.40	1.28	1.45	1.24	1.49	1.20	1.54	1.16	1.59
55	1.36	1.43	1.32	1.47	1.28	1.51	1.25	1.55	1.21	1.59
60	1.38	1.45	1.35	1.48	1.32	1.52	1.28	1.56	1.25	1.60
65	1.41	1.47	1.38	1.50	1.35	1.53	1.31	1.57	1.28	1.61
70	1.43	1.49	1.40	1.52	1.37	1.55	1.34	1.58	1.31	1.61
75	1.45	1.50	1.42	1.53	1.39	1.56	1.37	1.59	1.34	1.62
80	1.47	1.52	1.44	1.54	1.42	1.57	1.39	1.60	1.36	1.62
85	1.48	1.53	1.46	1.55	1.43	1.58	1.41	1.60	1.39	1.63
90	1.50	1.54	1.47	1.56	1.45	1.59	1.43	1.61	1.41	1.64
95	1.51	1.55	1.49	1.57	1.47	1.60	1.45	1.62	1.42	1.64
100	1.52	1.56	1.50	1.58	1.48	1.60	1.46	1.63	1.44	1.65

SOURCE: From J. Durbin and G. S. Watson, "Testing for Serial Correlation in Least Squares Regression, II," *Biometrika* 30 (1951): 159–78. Reproduced by permission of the Biometrika Trustees.

Table 8

Control Chart Constants

SAMPLE SIZE n	A_2	d_2	d_3	D_3	D_4
2	1.880	1.128	.853	.000	3.267
3	1.023	1.693	.888	.000	2.575
4	.729	2.059	.880	.000	2.282
5	.577	2.326	.864	.000	2.115
6	.483	2.534	.848	.000	2.004
7	.419	2.704	.833	.076	1.924
8	.373	2.847	.820	.136	1.864
9	.337	2.970	.808	.184	1.816
10	.308	3.078	.797	.223	1.777
11	.285	3.173	.787	.256	1.744
12	.266	3.258	.778	.284	1.716
13	.249	3.336	.770	.308	1.692
14	.235	3.407	.762	.329	1.671
15	.223	3.472	.755	.348	1.652
16	.212	3.532	.749	.364	1.636
17	.203	3.588	.743	.379	1.621
18	.194	3.640	.738	.392	1.608
19	.187	3.689	.733	.404	1.596
20	.180	3.735	.729	.414	1.586
21	.173	3.778	.724	.425	1.575
22	.167	3.819	.720	.434	1.566
23	.162	3.858	.716	.443	1.557
24	.157	3.895	.712	.452	1.548
25	.153	3.931	.709	.459	1.541

SOURCE: From E. S. Pearson, "The Percentage Limits for the Distribution of Range in Samples from a Normal Population," *Biometrika* 24 (1932): 416. Reproduced by permission of the Biometrika Trustees.

Index

A

Acceptance sampling, 239
Addition rule, 190, 191
Alternative hypothesis, 328, 329
Analysis of variance, 534–578
   independent samples single-factor
      model, 536–550, 576
   randomized block design, 556–565,
      576
   repeated measures design, 557
   single-factor vs. multifactor
      models, 557
Analyzing sources of variation, 458
ANOVA table, 543, 544
Answers to questions, 823–827
Arithmetic mean, 106–108
Assignable variation, 750
Attribute sampling, 172
Audit Sampling Guide, 173
Auditing, 172, 173
Autocorrelation, 659
Automatic teller machines (ATMs),
   369, 370
Average, 106–108

B

Backward stepwise regression, 710,
   711
Bar charts, 55, 56
   line charts, compared, 62
   pie charts, compared, 56–61
Basic concepts, 806, 807
Bell-shaped, 34
Between-treatments variation, 539
Bias, 171
Billings, Josh, 411
Bimodal, 33
Binomial distributions, 225–234
   binomial tables, 230–234
   Excel, 254
   Minitab, 253
   Poisson distribution, and, 239
Binomial experiment, 225
Binomial probabilities, 830–834
Binomial probability distribution,
   226–228
Binomial random variable, 225, 226
Binomial tables, 230–234
Bivariate distributions
   bivariate frequency distributions,
      215–217

bivariate probability distributions,
      218, 219
   conditional probability, 219
   covariance, 220–222
   sum of two random variables, 220
Bivariate frequency distributions,
   215–217
Bivariate probability distributions,
   218, 219
Blocked experiments
   randomized block design, 556–565
   repeated measures design, 557
Bottlenecks, 370
Bound of the error of estimation, 320
Box-and-whisker plot, 135
Box plots, 39, 135–138
Bryson, Maurice C., 164n

C

Cases
   accounting course exemptions, 498
   ambulance and fire department re-
      sponse interval study, 819
   bank discrimination against
      women business owners, 796,
      800, 821
   Bombardier Inc., 73
   Bonanza International, 496
   Canadian federal budget, 103
   code of professional ethics, effect
      of, 608
   death of key executives, 528
   diversification strategy (multina-
      tional companies), 574
   Duxbury Press, 7, 671, 742
   financial planning and small busi-
      ness, 573
   graduate survey report, 818
   host selling and announcer com-
      mercials, 5, 529
   insurance compensation for lost
      revenues, 817
   Let's Make a Deal, 250
   market model of stock returns, 671
   market timing, 250
   National Patent Development Cor-
      poration, 3, 420
   North American Free Trade Agree-
      ment (NAFTA), 74
   nutrition education programs, 820
   Pacific Salmon catches, 73

Variance
  binomial random variables, of, 232
  laws of, 209, 210
  random variable, of, 207, 208
Variance of a sample, 122
Variation of a population, 121
Venn diagrams, 181, 182

W

Web page for book, 11
Whisker, 135
Wilcoxon rank sum test, 505

Wilcoxon signed rank sum test, 507
Within-treatments variation, 539

X

x-bar, 106
$\bar{x}$ charts, 756–764, 767, 770–773

Z

z-test of p, 398–408, 602
z-test of $p_1 - p_2$, 472–484, 602

Index of Computer Instructions

| Techniques | MINITAB | | EXCEL |
	Menu Commands Page	Session Commands Page	Commands Page
Histogram	27	82	28
Stem and leaf display	37	83	N/A
Dot plot	39	83	N/A
Scatter diagram	46	83	47
Pie chart	52	83	53
Bar chart	55	84	56
Data input and retrieval	N/A	76–81	85
Line chart	84	84	N/A
Descriptive statistics	111	152	112
Box plot	138	152	138*
Covariance	145	152	145
Correlation	145	152	145
Random-number generator	166	166	167
Binomial probability	253	253	254
Poisson probability	253	253	254
Normal probability	283	283	284
Exponential probability	283	283	284
z-estimator of μ	313	325	313*
z-test of μ	338	366	339*
t-test of μ	378	421	379*
t-estimator of μ	382	421	382*
z-test of p	N/A	401*	402*
z-estimator of p	N/A	404*	405*
Inference about $\mu_1-\mu_2$ (unequal variances)	433	501	434
Inference about $\mu_1-\mu_2$ (equal variances)	437	501	438
t-test of μ_D	454	502	455
F-test of σ_1^2/σ_2^2	N/A	N/A	469
z-test of p_1-p_2 (case 1)	N/A	477*	477*
z-test of p_1-p_2 (case 2)	N/A	480*	481*
z-estimator of p_1-p_2	N/A	483*	484*
Manipulating (stacking/unstacking) data	N/A	499–500	502–503
Descriptive techniques—stacked data	500–501	500–501	N/A
Wilcoxon rank sum test	506	N/A	506*
Sign test	507	N/A	507*
Wilcoxon signed rank sum test	509	N/A	509*
One-way analysis of variance	545	576	546
Analysis of variance: randomized blocks	561	576	562
Kruskal-Wallis test	577	N/A	577*
Friedman test	578	N/A	578*
χ^2-test of a contingency table	595	611	595–596*
Linear regression	623, 680	673, 743	674, 681
Prediction and confidence intervals	647, 688	673, 743	648
Spearman rank correlation coefficient	675	N/A	675*
Residual analysis	674	673	674
Durbin-Watson statistic	743	743	745*
Stepwise regression	722	744	723*, 745*
Forward selection method	N/A	744	N/A
Backward elimination method	N/A	744	N/A
$\bar{x}$ chart (using S)	759	786	760*
S chart	765	786	766*
$\bar{x}$ chart (using R)	772	786	773*
R chart	775	786	775*
p chart	780	786	781*

*Author-created macro